*Corporate Controller's
Handbook of
Financial Management*

CORPORATE CONTROLLER'S HANDBOOK OF FINANCIAL MANAGEMENT

by

JOEL G. SIEGEL, Ph.D., CPA
JAE K. SHIM, Ph.D.
NICKY A. DAUBER, MS, CPA

PRENTICE HALL
Englewood Cliffs, New Jersey 07632

Prentice-Hall International (UK) Limited, *London*
Prentice-Hall of Australia Pty. Limited, *Sydney*
Prentice-Hall Canada, Inc., *Toronto*
Prentice-Hall Hispanoamericana, S.A., *Mexico*
Prentice-Hall of India Private Limited, *New Delhi*
Prentice-Hall of Japan, Inc., *Tokyo*
Simon & Schuster Asia Pte. Ltd., *Singapore*
Editora Prentice-Hall do Brasil, Ltda., *Rio de Janeiro*

Library of Congress Cataloging-in-Publication Data

Siegel, Joel G.
   Corporate controller's handbook of financial management / by Joel
G. Siegel, Jae K. Shim, Nicky A. Dauber.
     p.   cm.
   Includes index.
   ISBN 0-13-174459-3
   1. Corporations—Finance. 2. Managerial accounting. I. Shim,
Jae K. II. Dauber, Nicky A. III. Title.
HG4026.S486 1991
658.15—dc20   91-26466
                                           CIP

ISBN 0-13-174459-3

Printed in the United States of America

DEDICATION
to
ROBERTA M. SIEGEL
Loving wife and colleague
and
CHUNG SHIM
Dedicated wife
and
KAREN J. DAUBER
Loving and devoted wife
KATIE DAUBER
Adorable and precious daughter
MARGIE, MARC, AND SUSAN DAUBER
Loving and wonderful mother, father, and sister

ABOUT THE AUTHORS

JOEL G. SIEGEL, Ph.D., CPA is a self-employed certified public accountant and Professor of Accounting and Finance at Queens College of the City University of New York.

He was previously employed by Coopers and Lybrand, CPAs, and Arthur Andersen, CPAs. Dr. Siegel has acted as a consultant in accounting and finance to many organizations including Citicorp, International Telephone and Telegraph, United Technologies, American Institute of CPAs, and Person-Wolinsky Associates.

Dr. Siegel is the author of 32 books and about 200 articles on accounting and financial topics. His books have been published by Prentice-Hall, McGraw-Hill, Harper and Row, John Wiley, International Publishing, Barron's, and the American Institute of CPAs.

His articles have been published in many accounting and financial journals including *Financial Executive, The Financial Analysts Journal, The CPA Journal, Practical Accountant*, and the *National Public Accountant*.

In 1972, he was the recipient of the Outstanding Educator of America Award. Dr. Siegel is listed in *Who's Where Among Writers* and *Who's Who in the World*.

JAE K. SHIM is a financial consultant to several companies and Professor of Accounting and Finance at California State University, Long Beach. He received his Ph.D. degree from the University of California at Berkeley.

Dr. Shim has 20 books to his credit and has published over 50 articles in accounting and financial journals including *Financial Management, Decision Sciences, Management Science, Long Range Planning*, and *Advances in Accounting*.

Dr. Shim is a recipient of the 1982 Credit Research Foundation Award for his article on financial management.

NICKY A. DAUBER, MS, CPA, is an accounting and financial practitioner with client responsibilities primarily in auditing and taxation. His prior experience includes service as an audit and tax manager.

He is also an Instructor of Auditing and Tax at Queens College of the City University of New York. Mr. Dauber has received many awards for his excellent teaching from the Foundation for Accounting Education of the New York State Society of CPAs.

Mr. Dauber is a coauthor of *The Vest-Pocket CPA* and has published many articles in accounting and financial journals including *The CPA Journal, National Public Accountant*, and *Massachusetts CPA*.

vii

What This Book Will Do for You

This handbook is directed toward: chief financial officers; corporate financial managers; controllers; treasurers; chief accountants and staff accountants; internal auditors; management accountants; and consultants. This book is a practical reference for all areas of corporate financial management and accounting. It applies to all size organizations whether they be small, medium, or large. It is comprehensive, authoritative, and practical. It is a working guide that will pinpoint what to look for, what to watch out for, what to do, how to do it, and how to apply it in performing the financial management and controllership functions.

The handbook is geared to the contemporary financial officer, who must follow some traditional elements common to controllership and financial management but must be cognizant of the ever-changing financial markets and technology of today. These factors make some of the traditional techniques of financial management obsolete—new strategies and techniques are necessary in order to do an effective job that ensures financial survival. This is a true handbook—a wealth of information, along with the tools that make it work for the professional. We look at the responsibilities of corporate financial managers and controllers who must meet present-day challenges in the business world. The corporate financial manager must help to maintain and even improve the company's competitive position. The handbook enlightens the corporate financial manager and controller by presenting the most current information, offering important directives, explaining technical procedures, and looking at emerging trends. The reference book will help you diagnose and evaluate accounting, financial, and operating situations faced daily. The controller is more than just the chief accountant. He or she must be able to provide upper management with financial information, evaluation, and advice.

Any topic of importance can be found in this book. We cover all the aspects of the controller's and financial manager's jobs including accounting and financial reporting activities, managerial analysis and planning, tax planning, implementation of corporate policies, and treasury functions. The book includes such "key" areas as management reports, managing assets, budgeting and variance analysis, accounting principles, sources of financing, capital structure analysis, measurement of divisional and departmental performance, financial analysis, break-even analysis, internal auditing, analysis and control of costs, mergers and acquisitions, management accounting, financial models and quantitative applications, computer applications, managing risk, optimizing return, investments, insurance protection, economic effects, divestiture, failure and reorganization, and international finance.

Illustrations and step-by-step instructions are provided on what to watch out for and how to do it. This enables you to see how the techniques and procedures are applied. "Real life" examples are given of the analytical points made so you may handle everyday problems. Checklists and summaries are also provided. The book is filled with facts, explanations, commentaries, sample documents and letters, agreements, reports, flowcharts, analysis, figures, and practices. Tables, statistical data, charts, exhibits, and diagrams are provided, as needed. You will find financial measures, ratios, formulas, and rules-of-thumb to help you analyze and evaluate any business-related situation. Sophisticated, up-to-date analytical techniques and managerial tools are presented.

The book provides detailed analysis of recurring problems as well as unusual situations that may crop up. It gives vital suggestions throughout! The latest developments, such as new tax laws, are also included. This reference book gives you all the information you need to do the financial management and controllership functions effectively and efficiently!

Guidelines are presented for evaluating proposals, whether they be short- or long-term, for profit potential, and risk-return comparison. Tips for preparing necessary reports are also provided.

You will be able to move quickly to take advantage of favorable situations or avoid unfavorable ones. Here is the guide that will help you make smart decisions in all areas of corporate financial management and controllership. It will be your daily problem-solver for financial and accounting situations.

The practical benefits of this guidebook are unlimited in that it:

- Shows you how to measure and appraise risk.
- Lists "red flags" for potential problem areas.
- Recommends proven ways to correct financial sickness and inefficiency.
- Shows you how to evaluate business proposals, operations, and activities.
- Offers tested techniques for analyzing the financial structure of the business.
- Provides interpretation of variances indicating inefficiencies in the organization.
- Gives you the tools for spotting financially strong or weak business segments.

Important questions facing the controller will be answered such as:

- What type of reports may be prepared to enhance the decision making process?
- How do I conform to the new pension laws?

- What should be done to achieve maximum benefit from the new income tax accounting rules?
- What should be known about recent laws and governmental regulations?
- How can inventory be managed to lower costs and better utilize production facilities?
- What factors should be taken into account when preparing financial forecasts?
- How can productivity and performance best be measured?

Part I (Chapters 1-4) looks at the responsibilities of the controller including the types of reports that must be prepared. The use of computers to incorporate the latest technology in performing controllership functions is also discussed. SEC filings are emphasized.

Part II (Chapters 5-10) covers generally accepted accounting principles. The financial reporting requirements that must be known to the controller include such important topics as leases, pensions, and accounting for income taxes.

Part III (Chapters 11-23) focuses on managerial accounting. The chapters cover what the controller should know about cost accounting including costing systems, joint costs, cost allocation, activity-based costing and just-in-time, capital budgeting, contribution margin, budgeting, variance analysis, relevant cost analysis, break-even analysis, and segmental performance. In addition, financial models and quantitative techniques are discussed.

Part IV (Chapters 24-26) deals with internal auditing and controls. This part covers the audit techniques involved in auditing assets, liabilities, equity, revenue, and expenses. The characteristics of a sound internal control structure are also indicated. Statistical sampling techniques useful in auditing are also presented.

Part V (Chapters 27-30) is directed toward financial analysis areas including risk/reward relationships and financial statement analysis for internal evaluation. Ways to analyze and control revenue and costs are addressed. Insurance and legal concerns are examined. Finally, economic factors are taken into account.

Part VI (Chapters 31-33) addresses the proper management of assets including cash, marketable securities, accounts receivable, and inventory.

Part VII (Chapter 34) informs the controller what should be known about investments in securities to earn a satisfactory return while controlling risk.

Part VIII (Chapters 35-41) covers how to adequately obtain financing for the business to meet its goals and requirements. Short-term, intermediate-term, and long-term financing instruments are explained and illustrated as well as indicating under what circumstances each would be appropriate. There is also a discussion of warrants and convertibles. Cost of capital determination and dividend policy are examined. For those involved in international finance this section will be of interest.

Part IX (Chapters 42-43) covers tax preparation and planning. There is a discussion of key tax topics such as tax saving alternatives, payroll taxes, tax aspects of business combinations and leveraged buyouts, and tax effects of stock option and incentive plans.

Part X (Chapters 44-47) provides what must be considered in the planning, financing, and accounting for mergers and acquisitions. Acquisition criteria and objectives to be accomplished are presented. The reasons and ways of divesting business segments are addressed. Failure and reorganization are also discussed. Consideration is given to shareholder value analysis.

The content of the handbook is clear, concise, and to the point. It is a valuable reference tool containing "how-to's" in controllership. The uses of this handbook are as varied as the topics presented. Keep it handy for easy, quick reference, and daily use.

In the index, a specific area of interest may easily be found.

Joel G. Siegel, Ph.D., CPA
Jae K. Shim, Ph.D.
Nicky A. Dauber, MS, CPA

ACKNOWLEDGMENTS

Our deepest appreciation and thanks to Ronald Cohen for his editorial advice and assistance on this book. We are grateful for his valuable contribution.

Thanks also goes to Gerald Galbo for his outstanding editorial input and advice. Special recognition is given to Tom Curtin who did a superb editorial job during the production process.

Thanks belong to Carol Klinger, MS, CPA, who coauthored Chapter 1. Stan Chu, MS, CPA, deserves recognition for coauthoring Chapter 27.

Thanks to Roberta M. Siegel and Karen J. Dauber, CPA for their invaluable input and editorial assistance.

Permission has been received from the Institute of Certified Management Accountants of the National Association of Accountants to use questions and/or unofficial answers from past CMA examinations.

Contents

What This Book Will Do for You ix

PART I INTRODUCTION (1)

1. The Responsibilities of the Controller 3
2. SEC Reporting 13
3. Controller's Reports 21
4. What the Controller Must Know About Computers 29

PART II GENERALLY ACCEPTED ACCOUNTING PRINCIPLES (55)

5. Financial Statement Reporting: The Income Statement 57
6. Financial Statement Reporting: The Balance Sheet 75
7. Financial Statement Reporting: The Statement of Cash Flows 115
8. Accounting and Disclosures 135
9. Key Financial Accounting Areas 153
10. Interim and Segmental Reporting 203

PART III MANAGEMENT ACCOUNTING (213)

11. Cost Concepts, Classifications, and Product Costing Systems 215
12. Joint Products and By-Products 247
13. Analysis of Cost Behavior 269
14. Cost-Volume-Profit Analysis and Leverage 285
15. Contribution Margin Analysis for Short-Term and Nonroutine
    Decisions 305
16. Cost Allocation 317
17. Budgeting and Financial Modeling 339
18. Using Variance Analysis as a Financial Tool 381
19. The Use of Capital Budgeting in Decision Making 449
20. Evaluation of Segmental Performance and Transfer Pricing 491
21. How to Analyze and Improve Management Performance 515
22. Activity-Based Costing and Just-in-Time Manufacturing 527
23. Quantitative Applications in Corporate Financial Management 551

PART IV   INTERNAL AUDITING AND CONTROL (587)

PART V   FINANCIAL ANALYSIS (699)

PART VI   MANAGEMENT OF ASSETS (777)

PART VII   INVESTMENTS (825)

PART VIII   FINANCING THE BUSINESS (849)

PART IX   TAX PREPARATION AND PLANNING (957)

PART X   MERGERS, DIVESTITURES, AND FAILURE (979)

I

INTRODUCTION

1

The Responsibilities of the Controller*

The responsibilities of the controller and the treasurer may overlap between different companies. However, controllership functions are basically similar between industries and companies.

The controller may provide financial information to diverse users including internal management, stockholders, creditors (including banks and suppliers), stock exchanges, employees, customers, the public at large, U.S. Government agencies (i.e., SEC, IRS, Department of Commerce, Department of Labor, and the Federal Trade Commission), and state and local tax and other agencies.

The role of the controller in the 1990s is changing. Since the turn of the century, businesses have grown in size and complexity. There has been more intervention by government and more diverse means of raising capital. This has increased the functions and responsibilities of the controller and these functions are continuing to change rapidly. Traditionally, one thought of the controller as the chief accounting officer and financial planner of a corporation. Indeed, *Webster's Dictionary* defines the word controller in just those terms. The typical controller was usually visualized as being the executive in charge of the record keeping for a company, the preparer of financial statements, and the person responsible for internal controls. The controller is still responsible for these functions but the controller's umbrella of responsibility has expanded. Today's controller is becoming more and more involved with strategic planning. Strategic planning means becoming involved with the decision-making pro-

---

*We express our appreciation to Carol Klinger, MS, CPA, for her assistance in the preparation of this chapter.

3

cesses of the organization. The controller is in the unique position of being able to do this as he or she has knowledge of the company plus the financial know-how that few others in the corporation possess. As more and more chief executive officers begin to depend on the controller's office as a source of information and for input into planning decisions, it is likely that the controller will become an even more valuable member of the management team. No longer is it sufficient for a controller to just add up the numbers. Most executives expect more of the controller. Besides being the individual who gathers the data of past performance and who pumps out reports, the controller can use the information that has been collected to become involved with the dynamics concerned with running the business. Controllers have already gathered much of the information required to improve profits and operations, reduce costs, and develop strategies for the company. Controllers have a "hands-on" feel of the operating environment, such as the interrelationships between management, production, and sales. The accounting function, by its very nature, provides a large percentage of the information needed by executives. The controller and his or her staff are in the unique position to impart this information to management, not just in the historical sense, but in a format useful for future planning.

Business is constantly being transformed by computers. Companies that take advantage of the information technology provided by the computer will have the advantage over their competitors. A controller that envisions this advantage and applies his or her knowledge of accounting and information technology toward planning for the future of the company will advance in his or her position as the company succeeds. Moving forward into decision making and strategic planning, with the computer as an aide, may not be an easy accomplishment for some controllers, however. While the controller may envision the scope of his or her functions as expanding, some chief executive officers may not always agree. Often the higher-level executive wants assistance in strategic planning but does not expect the controller to be able to provide it. The controller is thought of as having an historical role; i.e., as the reporter of financial information and the formulator of internal controls. It will be up to the individual who occupies the controllership position to reach out, offer suggestions, expand the useful functions, and become a member of the business team.

Becoming involved with strategic planning for the company may be a goal of the controller but rarely will the controller be relieved of the other duties that typically befall him or her. The controller is usually the head officer of the accounting department. This department can vary in size depending on the size of the company. The controller is responsible for the products of the accounting department as well as being responsible for running an efficient and effective department. Maintaining the company records for accounts payable, accounts receivable, inventory and other pertinent areas, has probably been considered the primary function of the controller. All transactions must be recorded properly and timely either manually or on a computerized basis. Along with record keeping, the controller is responsible for the preparation of financial statements, and if required, interpreting these statements for management. The controller may work closely with the independent auditors to ascertain that the statements are presented fairly in accordance with generally accepted accounting principles. The controller will also work hand-in-hand with the auditors as they perform the year-end independent audit. The controller's staff may be required to assist the auditors in certain tasks. Furthermore, the controller may play an important role in terms of involvement with the audit committee. In addition to assisting with the external audit, the controller will be involved with internal auditing on a year-round basis. The controller must evaluate the company's internal control structure in order to determine that it is operating effectively and efficiently. An added responsibility is to make improvements in the structure if it is determined that there are deficiencies and the controller may, on a regular basis, be called upon to report, to the audit committee or board of directors, the status of the internal control structure. Addressing the needs of management is another important aspect of the controller's role. It must not be overlooked that the goal of business is to realize a profit. Without information about the costs of production and distribution, management will not be able to determine how to proceed in regard to marketing decisions.

The controller must be able to construct reports relating to production costs and distribution costs. The controller should be acquainted with break-even analyses, cost-volume-profit relationships and standard cost methods in order to help management determine the most profitable course to follow. Adequate reporting to management to enable intelligent decision making requires not only the knowledge of cost accounting, but responsibility accounting and exception reporting, as well. Today's controller must be thoroughly conversant in these techniques. The controller must be able not only to report historical data but should be able to develop trends and relationships from existing data. The controller should know how to make use of financial relationships, determine the trend of ratios, present the ratios in suitable form and interpret the data in a comprehensive report. Here the knowledge of the computer is helpful, as the controller can make use of available graphic programs which will enable effective presentations.

Tax returns and other tax matters that pertain to the corporation will also be handled by the controller. While some companies refer tax matters to the public accountants, it is still the responsibility of the controller to avoid excess taxes. The controller must be fully informed about tax matters, particularly federal income taxes. Identifying and analyzing tax implications of a given transaction is an important function of the controller since the controller's role is not limited to verifying the validity of tax computations. Most importantly, to minimize the tax obligation, *tax planning* is crucial. The controller must recognize tax problems in the making; i.e., before the transactions are complete.

Any statistical reports that are needed by management will usually be prepared in the controller's department. The controller must be familiar with the operational flow of the company as well as the needs of its executives so that useful information can be developed and presented. The controller should be able to prepare a variety of reports to be distributed to different levels of management, depending on their needs. This will enable various managerial objectives to be attained. These reports can include sales reports on a weekly basis, perhaps segregated by territories or salesmen or products; labor reports based on actual and standard costs which can be presented by product, division, material usage, or other important variables. The annual budget, an important planning tool, is generally prepared by the controller's office. The construction of the budget and its basic guidelines will be determined by the controller. The controller will be expected to analyze the plan to ascertain that it is reasonable and reliable. In addition, proposing suggestions for improvements is crucial. The budget may be a flexible, fixed, or zero-based budget and the controller must be knowledgeable in these areas. The budget, once prepared, becomes a control device so the controller must be able to analyze variances and advise management to take corrective action, if necessary.

The controller may also be expected to determine whether the company is carrying adequate insurance on properties and other assets. It is important to maintain adequate records of all contracts and leases and it is the controller's function to determine that they are recorded properly. The controller will also be responsible for determining that the entity is satisfying all regulations prescribed by governmental agencies. If the Board of Directors sets any goals regarding financial transactions, these would be listed in the minutes of the Board and it will be the obligation of the controller's office to ensure that they are acted upon.

The passing of the Foreign Corrupt Practices Act in 1977 required corporations to maintain financial records and to establish and maintain an effective internal control structure. The controller must be aware of this Act and its requirements and realize that maintaining reasonable records and adequate controls are now a matter of law. The controller must be familiar with the mechanics of establishing a sound internal control structure as well as understand the cost-benefit relationships involved in establishing and monitoring the structure.

In many companies, the controller will also be responsible for data processing. This will require the controller to be familiar with and be able to direct the use of the computer. To do this will require a knowledge of current equipment and familiarity with computer software. The controller should keep abreast of important changes in the field such as the trend towards individual work stations. The controller must understand relevant internal controls for a computer system and continuously review the output of the system for reliability.

The reporting function of the controller's job is not just limited to internal uses. The controller will be called upon to assist in the formulation of the annual report to stockholders and to prepare other reports for government agencies such as the Securities and Exchange Commission. The information in the annual report must be easily understood, well written, and will frequently use graphical and other illustrative material. The financial information contained therein is typically prepared by the controller who will be responsible for its content.

There should always be adequate disclosure and the information must conform to generally accepted accounting principles and to SEC requirements.

To cope with all these various tasks, the controller must possess certain skills. It is important to possess a knowledge of current accounting principles and practices as well as an ability to effectively communicate to management the impact of recent promulgations. The controller must keep abreast of any significant changes to generally accepted accounting principles. This can usually be accomplished by receiving advice from the independent auditor or by referring to published sources. The controller must know how to communicate ideas both orally and through written representations. A forward-looking controller will understand that information should be presented in a useful and understandable format. He or she will always consider future consequences and directions.

The ability to motivate and organize subordinate staff members is essential. As the head of the accounting department, it is essential that the controller be able to direct the members of the department so that they are responsible for their own work. The controller should be a supervisor rather than being a clerical worker. It is important to be fair and reasonable when dealing with subordinates. In addition, the controller must be able to interact with people at all levels of the organization. Since the controller's position requires the providing of information to many levels of management, it is crucial that the controller possess a basic understanding of the problems faced by the business as a whole and the problems faced by individual departments within the company. While the controller is not expected to become an expert in engineering or production, it is important to be familiar with these areas so that one can anticipate the needs of all departments. To be effective, the controller needs to get involved to some extent with the day-to-day operations of the company. After formulating suggestions, the controller must be able to market them. Gaining respect from other executives will enable this. If others see that the controller wants to help, they will actually seek his or her advice.

It is a wise controller who knows the limits of his or her prescribed functions and knowledge base. The preparation of voluminous reports that are never read may make it appear that the controller is working to his or her utmost capacity, but in reality very little is being accomplished. The controller must realize that the business may prosper because of proposed suggestions but that one cannot replace the engineering or sales abilities of other people. Without the proper support staff, the controller cannot function at the level he or she would like to.

As in most corporate executive positions, the job of controller is ultimately defined by the person holding the position at a given time. Depending on personality, the controller may end up becoming a "pencil pusher" or a truly valuable member of the strategic planning team, and the "right-hand" to the president of the company.

Because of management information system technology, we are at the brink of a revolution in the business world. Most companies are uncertain how to get a handle on this information technology. Controllers have the opportunity, as they never have had before, to reach out and grab the advantage. People often view controllers as "passive" individuals, unwilling to take the lead. They wait for direction instead of being aggressive and assertive. It is now up to the individual to act in his or her own behalf and to the company's advantage by initiating actions and therefore widening the scope of his or her responsibilities. The head accounting officer should be considered the developer of intelligent information for the whole company. The controller's department should be the provider of financial information for all of phases of the business. The accounting department is already stocked with most of the information needed for business purposes. The trick is to put this information to use for the future and not just report on the past. Where is the company headed? While the controller must not turn his or her back on the traditionally assigned accounting tasks, the controller must, at the same time, apply a vast body of knowledge to the future prospects of the organization. It is in this regard that the controller will prove to be useful and valuable to any company.

CONTROLLER VS. TREASURER

Unlike the controller, the treasurer's responsibility is mostly custodial in nature and involves obtaining and managing the company's capital. He or she primarily deals with "money management" activities. The treasurer's activities are *external*, primarily involving financing matters and mix. He or she is involved with creditors (e.g., bank loan officers), stockholders, investors, underwriters for equity (stock) and bond issuances, and governmental regulatory bodies (e.g., SEC). The treasurer is responsible for managing corporate assets (e.g., accounts receivable and inventory), debt, credit appraisal and collection, planning the finances, planning capital expenditures, obtaining funds, dividend disbursement, managing the investment portfolio, and pension management.

In some organizations the duties between the controller and treasurer overlap, with the latter being in effect the controller's superior.

CONTROLLER'S REPORTS

As previously indicated, a successful controller will possess the ability to communicate ideas to various interested parties through the preparation of various types of reports. Prospective financial information is often needed to enable departments and segments to effectively plan the future. In this regard, planning reports are often issued by the controller. Information reports, analytical and control reports as well as exception reports prepared by the controller enable analysis of a diverse amount of information and situations. Reports prepared for the Board of Directors must address specific policy matters and general trends in revenue and profits. These reports must enable the Board to establish and attain specified goals. Reports prepared for other company employees must be useful and timely. Reports to stockholders and relevant stock exchanges must be informative and complete. The controller's role in reporting information therefore cannot be overstated.

COMPUTER KNOWLEDGE

A vast majority of businesses utilize computers in accumulating, assembling, and reporting financial information. The selection of essential software (i.e., programs) is a major concern. Electronic spreadsheets, data base management systems, integrated software, and accounting programs represent a few of the more vital computerized tools. To the extent possible, all corporate financial functions should be computerized.

GENERALLY ACCEPTED ACCOUNTING PRINCIPLES

Inasmuch as the controller is primarily responsible for the entity's accounting functions, he or she should be fully cognizant of recent promulgations in financial accounting. It is critical that the controller be able to prepare detailed and meaningful financial statements. There are a host of reporting mandates applicable to the income statement, balance sheet, and statement of cash flows. To properly inform readers, disclosures should be made of all important items not presented in the body of the financial statements.

MANAGEMENT ACCOUNTING

The controller truly serves as a financial advisor to management. He or she must be familiar with a wide variety of managerial accounting concepts and tools.

There are many basic cost concepts, classifications, and product costing systems. Knowledge of job order costing, process costing, direct costing, standard costing, and just-in-time manufacturing may be needed. Focus is also placed on cost analysis for planning, control, and decision making.

Regression analysis and mixed cost analysis may be required. The controller should be equipped with tools for sales mix analysis and "what-if" analysis.

In budgeting and financial modeling, the controller should use innovative and sophisticated techniques to maximize corporate objectives.

Knowledge of responsibility accounting and cost allocation is also needed. How has the performance of the responsibility centers been? Why? It is suggested that the controller be familiar with gross profit analysis, segment reporting, and contribution analysis. How may problems be identified and corrective action taken? Transfer pricing is also needed to determine divisional profit. Once such profit has been computed, the controller can calculate and analyze return on investment and residual income. In what ways may profit be improved? There must be efficient and effective analysis of company projects, proposals, and special situations. Consideration must therefore be given to time value concepts, capital rationing, capital budgeting, and mutually exclusive investments.

Quantitative applications in managerial accounting cannot be overlooked by the controller. The controller must understand decision theory and be able to make decisions under conditions involving uncertainty. Linear programming, shadow prices and the learning curve should not be ignored in fulfilling the role of controllership. A controller familiar with Program Evaluation and Review Techniques (PERT) and inventory planning models is in a position to further assist senior-level management. Multiple regression and correlation analysis depict previous relationships which will aid in making future predictions.

INTERNAL AUDITING AND CONTROL

The controller is often called upon to establish, monitor, and analyze the internal control structure of the company. In this regard, an internal control questionnaire may be useful. It is important to keep in mind that every company is different and therefore the internal control questionnaire should be tailored to the particular needs and peculiarities of your company. Internal controls should be done in conjunction with the outside auditors to facilitate their function and lessen audit costs.

In connection with the internal audit function, we must identify financial statement assertions, select appropriate audit procedures, and develop audit programs. Audit programs may be used for all accounts including cash, receivables, inventory, fixed assets, payables, equity accounts, income, and expenses.

FINANCIAL ANALYSIS

A truly effective controller is equipped with tools for financial analysis.

Risk and reward have to be considered. Techniques for analyzing and managing risk must be employed. Insurance policies must be scrutinized since proper financial management includes securing adequate insurance coverage in terms of insurance type and dollar amounts. Adequate insurance records must be kept for major assets.

Once financial statements are prepared, they must be analyzed for proper internal use. Attention should be given to horizontal and vertical analysis, evaluation of liquidity, examining corporate solvency, balance sheet analysis, and appraisal of income statement items.

Legal exposure of the firm must be monitored and means to minimize litigation undertaken. An example is product liability insurance.

The effect of the economy on business operations always has to be considered and protective measures taken. What exposure does the company have in a depression, recession, or an inflationary environment?

MANAGEMENT OF ASSETS

An organization's assets must be managed and used effectively to achieve the best possible return while controlling risk. Crucial assets to be managed include cash, marketable securities, accounts receivable, and inventory.

INVESTMENTS

The wealth of a service or sales organization can be strengthened by making sound investment and financing decisions. Investments in equity securities provide an excellent vehicle for achieving financial wealth. We must measure return and risk, value securities and make the best investment selections.

FINANCING

The optimal financing strategy has to be decided upon. Based on the particular facts, is it better to finance short-term, intermediate-term, or long-term? If long-term financing is chosen, should equity or debt be issued? Of course, there are a host of factors to be considered in selecting a financing vehicle including risk, maturity, liquidity, cost, and tax rate. The overall cost of capital must be minimized. Multinational companies have added international finance problems.

TAX PREPARATION AND PLANNING

Every business must consider the impact of payroll and income taxes. Proper corporate management involves selecting the proper form of business and minimizing the tax liability by judiciously applying relevant tax laws. Important business decisions are often based on tax factors, in addition to general business considerations. All businesses with employees must face the deposit and reporting requirements of various governmental agencies. Corporate financial managers should carefully review tax rules and use tax planning strategies to the fullest extent. Tax planning should be done in conjunction with the outside auditors.

MERGERS AND ACQUISITIONS

Proper planning is essential in executing business combinations. Objectives of a merger should be clearly defined, acquisition criteria should be definitively stipulated, and pitfalls should be avoided. Leveraged buyouts are very popular today but should be entered into with caution. Divestitures are also common in today's business world. Reasons for and objectives of divestitures must be established. Employee considerations should not be overlooked.

CONCLUSION

It is quite obvious that corporate financial management is predicated upon a strong controllership function. The role of the controller is diverse and includes not only reporting and accounting functions but decision making. The controller must consider the financial strengths and weaknesses of the business. Current and prospective problems must be considered along with ways to solve them. The objectives and policies of the business and its segments must be carried out.

The controller may deal with finance, accounting, production, marketing, personnel, and operations. Cost control is directed at manufacturing, administration, and distribution. Costs must be compiled, tracked, and analyzed.

2

SEC Reporting

The Securities and Exchange Commission (SEC) was established in order to protect investors by requiring full and fair disclosure in connection with the offering and sale of securities to the public. A major responsibility of the SEC is to ensure enforcement of the Securities Act of 1933 and the Securities Act of 1934.

SECURITIES ACT OF 1933

The Securities Act of 1933 (as amended) pertains to the initial offering and sale of securities through the mail, but does not apply to the subsequent trading of security investments. The Act requires that entities involved in a public offering file a registration statement with the SEC. Some of the more common exemptions under the registration provisions of the Act are (1) private offerings, (2) intrastate offerings, (3) governmental securities, (4) offerings of charitable institutions, and (5) bank offerings. The objective of this filing is to prevent misrepresentation, deceit, and other fraudulent activity in the sale of securities. Most of the information included in the registration statement must be provided to potential investors in a prospectus. Investor protection is provided by (1) the imposition of stiff penalties in the event of the filing of false and misleading information and (2) the ability of the investor to recover losses through litigation.

SECURITIES ACT OF 1934

The Securities Act of 1934 does not pertain to the initial offering and sale of securities to the public. Rather, the 1934 Act is designed to regulate the subsequent trading of securities on the various national stock exchanges. Under the

13

1934 Act, a scaled-down version of the 1933 Act registration statement must be filed by an entity if its securities are to be traded on a national exchange.

The 1934 Act requires the periodic filing of information reports with the SEC in order to maintain the full and fair disclosure objective of the 1933 Act. The annual Form 10-K and the quarterly Form 10-Q are the most common types of reports required by the 1934 Act. Most of the information included in these reports is available to the public.

INTEGRATED DISCLOSURE SYSTEM

The complexity of the reporting requirements under the 1933 and 1934 Acts were somewhat mitigated in 1980 when the SEC adopted the Integrated Disclosure System, which requires the Basic Information Package (BIP).

The BIP consists of the following:

- Audited balance sheets for the last two years and audited statements of income, retained earnings, and cash flows for the most recent three years.
- A five-year summary containing certain selected financial data.
- Management's discussion and analysis of the entity's financial condition and results of operations.

FORM S-1

Form S-1 is normally utilized by any entity that desires to issue a public offering and that has been subject to the SEC reporting requirements for less than three years. Some of the more common items required to be disclosed in Form S-1 include:

- A synopsis of the business including relevant industry and segment information
- A listing of properties
- Background and financial information pertaining to the entity's directors and officers, including pending litigation involving management
- A description of the securities being registered

Form S-1 also requires the disclosure of a five-year summary of selected financial data, which need not be audited by the independent certified public accountant. The data to be presented include the following items:

- Net sales or revenues
- Total income or loss from continuing operations
- Per share income or loss from continuing operations
- Total assets of the entity
- Long-term debt, including capital leases and redeemable preferred stock
- Declared cash dividends on a per common share basis
- Disagreements with the independent certified public accounting firm

FORM S-2

Form S-2 is a short form which is normally used by issuers that have been reporting to the SEC for at least three years, but have voting stock held by nonaffiliates of less than $150 million. If an entity elects to deliver to its shareholders its latest annual report along with its prospectus, information can be incorporated by reference from the annual report into the prospectus. Information which may be incorporated by reference includes (1) the most recent Form 10-K and (2) all reports submitted to the SEC after the end of the last year. If the annual report is not so delivered, incorporation of information is not allowed and the information must be included in the prospectus. In addition, the latest Form 10-Q financial information must also be submitted.

FORM S-3

Form S-3 may generally be used by a company that passes the "float test." In other words, at least $150 million of voting stock is owned by nonaffiliates. Form S-3 may also be used if the entity has a float of $100 million accompanied by an annual trading volume of 3 million shares. Annual trading volume is the number of shares traded during a recurring 12-month period culminating within 60 days before the filing.

Form S-3 is an abbreviated form since the public already has much of the information which would normally be required to be included. Accordingly, Form S-3 provides for incorporation by reference.

FORM S-4

Form S-4 is applicable in registrations of securities in connection with such business combinations as mergers, consolidations, and asset acquisitions. Form S-4 also provides for incorporation by reference to the 1934 Act reports.

FORM S-8

When registering securities to be offered to employees pursuant to an employee benefit plan, Form S-8 should be filed. Information presented in Form S-8 is normally limited to a description of the securities and the employee benefit plan. Disclosure is also made about the registrant, although this information is made available through other reports required by the 1934 Act.

FORM S-18

A company whose objective is to raise capital of $7.5 million or less may file a registration statement using Form S-18. Disclosures presented in Form S-18 are quite similar to those required in Form S-1. One difference between the two forms is that management's discussion and analysis is not required. Additionally, only one year's audited balance sheet and two years' audited statements of income and cash flows.

MANAGEMENT'S DISCUSSION AND ANALYSIS

Management's discussion and analysis is an integral part of the registration filing and pertains to (1) the three years covered in the audited financial statements which are submitted as part of the registration process and (2) any interim financial statements which are also submitted. Management's discussion and analysis should therefore specify the significant changes in financial condition and results of operations. To accomplish this, the following items must be disclosed:

- Liquidity
- Capital resources
- Results of operations
- Positive and negative trends
- Significant uncertainties
- Events of an unusual or infrequent nature
- Underlying causes of material changes in financial statement items
- A narrative discussion of the material effects of inflation

While not required, forecasted information may be presented.

REGULATION S-X

Regulation S-X stipulates the accounting requirements of the SEC. It encompasses the rules pertaining to the auditor's independence, the auditor's reports and the financial statements which must be submitted to the SEC. Regulation S-X is continually amended by the issuance of Financial Reporting Releases (FRRs). FRRs enable the SEC to present:

- New disclosure requirements
- The required treatment for certain transaction types
- The SEC's opinions on essential accounting issues
- Interpretations of current rules and regulations
- Amendments to financial statement reporting requirements

In general, the accounting rules under Regulation S-X parallel generally accepted accounting principles (GAAP). Occasionally, however, the disclosure rules under Regulation S-X are more expansive. For instance, financial statements filed with the SEC require the following disclosures which are not normally included in financial statements prepared in conformity with generally accepted accounting principles:

- Lines of credit
- Compensating balance arrangements
- Current liabilities if they represent in excess of 5% of the entity's total liabilities

Regulation S-X is divided into 12 Articles as follows:

- Article 1—Application of Regulation S-X
- Article 2—Qualifications and Reports of Accountants
- Article 3—General Instructions as to Financial Statements
- Article 3A—Consolidated and Combined Financial Statements
- Article 4—Rules of General Application
- Article 5—Commercial and Industrial Companies
- Article 6—Regulated Investment Companies
- Article 7—Insurance Companies
- Article 9—Bank Holding Companies
- Article 10—Interim Financial Statements
- Article 11—Pro Forma Information
- Article 12—Form and Content of Schedules

REGULATION S-K

Regulation S-K establishes the disclosure requirements for data and information which is not part of the financial statements and is divided into 9 major sections as follows:

General—Discusses the application of Regulation S-K, the SEC's policies on projections and security ratings

Business—Addresses the description of the business, its property, and the entity's involvement in legal proceedings

Securities of the Registrant—Pertains to the description of the entity's securities, the market price of such securities, as well as the dividends attributable thereto. Related stockholder matters are also addressed.

Financial Information—Coverage is afforded selected financial data, supplementary financial information, management's discussion and analysis, and changes in and disagreements with accountants involving accounting matters and financial disclosures.

Management and Certain Security Holders—Discusses disclosure requirements pertaining to (1) directors, executive officers, promoters and control persons, (2) executive compensation, (3) security ownership of certain beneficial owners and management, and (4) certain relationships and related transactions.

Registration Statement and Prospectus Provisions Exhibits

Miscellaneous—Covers recent sales of unregistered securities as well as indemnification of directors and officers.

List of Industry Guides—Lists the Securities Acts Industry Guides and Exchange Act Industry Guides which should be utilized by companies operating in specialized industries.

FORM 10-K

To comply with the Securities Act of 1934, most registrants will be required to file a Form 10-K on an annual basis. Form 10-K is due within 90 days subsequent to the closing of the registrant's fiscal year.

The contents of Form 10-K include general instructions, a cover page, signatures, supplemental information, and disclosures which are divided up into four parts as follows:

- Part I

  Item   1—Business

  Item   2—Properties

  Item   3—Legal Proceedings

  Item   4—Submission of Matters to a Vote of Security Holders

- Part II

  Item   5—Market for the Registrant's Common Equity and Related Stock-holder Matters

  Item   6—Selected Financial Data

  Item   7—Management's Discussion and Analysis of Financial Condition and Results of Operations

  Item   8—Financial Statements and Supplementary Data

  Item   9—Changes in and Disagreements with Accountants on Accounting and Financial Disclosure

- Part III

  Item 10—Directors and Executive Officers of the Registrant

  Item 11—Executive Compensation

  Item 12—Security Ownership of Certain Beneficial Owners and Management

  Item 13—Certain Relationships and Related Transactions

- Part IV

  Item 14—Exhibits, Financial Statement Schedules, and Reports of Form
    8-K

FORM 8-K

Form 8-K essentially must be filed immediately after the occurrence of a significant event that materially affects the company's financial position and/or operating results. Form 8-K lists these significant events as follows:

- Item 1—Change in control of registrant
- Item 2—Acquisition or disposition of assets
- Item 3—Bankruptcy or receivership
- Item 4—Changes in registrant's certifying accountant
- Item 5—Other events (for example, litigation)
- Item 6—Resignation of registrant's directors
- Item 7—Financial statements and exhibits

FORM 10-Q

Changes in operations and financial position since the filing of the most recent Form 10-K are disclosed in the quarterly Forms 10-Q. The quarterly Form 10-Q is due within 45 days after the end of each of the first three fiscal quarters. Form 10-Q specifically lists the items which must be disclosed as follows:

- Part I—Financial Information

  Item 1—Financial Statements

  Item 2—Management's Discussion and Analysis of Financial Condition
    and Results of Operations

- Part II—Other Information

  Item 1—Legal Proceedings

  Item 2—Changes in Securities

  Item 3—Defaults Upon Senior Securities

  Item 4—Submission of Matters to a Vote of Security Holders

  Item 5—Other Information

  Item 6—Exhibits and Reports on Form 8-K

CONCLUSION

It should be clear that regulation by the Securities and Exchange Commission imposes reporting and filing burdens. The controller has a vital role in ensuring that accurate data, for reporting purposes, is accumulated in a timely manner. The controller is also responsible for the timely filing of reports mandated by the SEC.

The controller of an entity regulated by the SEC should consider subscribing to a professional subscription service, such as Prentice-Hall's *SEC Compliance*, which is updated monthly. This service provides guidance by means of a comprehensive and current body of information. This reporter also provides complete illustrations of reports which must be filed with the SEC.

3
Controller's Reports

In addition to SEC reporting, discussed in Chapter 2, the controller is responsible for communicating useful and accurate information to senior-level management, the board of directors, divisional managers, employees, and interested third parties. It is crucial that reports be issued timely and that the reports be understood by a diverse audience.

The needs of management vary from one organization to another. Management reports should be sufficiently simplistic in order to enable the reader to center his or her attention on problems or predicaments that may or could arise. Consistency and uniformity in report format and issuance can only enhance the organization's operational effectiveness and efficiency. The data presented in reports issued to management, employees, and third parties should be based on facts which may be corroborated by underlying financial and accounting data.

PROSPECTIVE FINANCIAL STATEMENTS

Prospective financial statements encompass financial forecasts and financial projections. Pro forma financial statements and partial presentations are specifically excluded from this category.

Financial forecasts are prospective financial statements that present the entity's expected financial position, results of operations and cash flows, based on assumptions about conditions actually *expected* to exist and the course of action actually expected to be taken.

A financial forecast may be given in a single monetary amount based on the best estimate, or as a reasonable range. CAUTION: This range must *not* be chosen in a misleading manner.

21

Financial projections, on the other hand, are prospective statements that present the entity's financial position, results of operations and cash flows, based on assumptions about conditions expected to exist and the course of action expected to be taken, given one or more *hypothetical* (i.e., "what if") assumptions.

Financial projections may be most beneficial for limited users, since they may seek answers to questions involving hypothetical assumptions. These users may wish to alter their scenarios based on anticipated changing situations. A financial projection, like a financial forecast, may contain a range.

A financial projection may be presented to general users *only* when it *supplements* a financial forecast. Financial projections are not permitted in tax shelter offerings and other general-use documents.

Financial forecasts and financial projections may be in the form of either complete basic financial statements or financial statements containing the following minimum items:

- Sales or gross revenues
- Gross profit or cost of sales
- Unusual or infrequently occurring items
- Provision for income taxes
- Discontinued operations or extraordinary items
- Income from continuing operations
- Net income
- Primary and fully diluted earnings per share
- Significant changes in financial position
- Management's intent as to what the prospective statements present, a statement indicating that management's assumptions are predicated upon facts and circumstances in existence when the statements were prepared, and a warning that the prospective results may not materialize
- Summary of significant assumptions
- Summary of significant accounting policies

PLANNING REPORTS

The controller may prepare short-term company-wide or division-wide planning reports. This includes forecasted balance sheets, forecasted income statements, forecasted statements of cash flows, and projections of capital expenditures.

Special short-term planning studies of specific business segments may also be prepared. These reports may relate to the following:

- Product line expansion
- Plant location feasibility
- Product distribution by territory
- Warehouse handling
- Salesperson compensation

Long-range planning reports include five- to ten-year projections for the company and/or segments therein.

INFORMATIONAL REPORTS

Informational reports may be prepared by a controller for submission to management personnel. These reports are frequently used to depict trends over long periods of time. Accordingly, informational reports may be used to report trends in sales and purchase requirements over the last five years. The format of information reports is generally left to the preparer's judgment, although graphic depiction (including charts) is popular.

ANALYTICAL AND CONTROL REPORTS

Analytical and control reports contain data derived from analytical procedures. Analytical procedures involve comparisons of financial and nonfinancial information. As a result, analytical and control reports are often utilized to disclose current-period versus prior-period changes in financial statement accounts. For example, analytical and control reports might disclose the increases and decreases in selected expense accounts over the past two years. Analytical reports are also used to summarize and describe variances from forecasts and budgets. Analyses of variances may be by revenue, expense, profit, assets, territory, product, and division.

EXCEPTION REPORTS

Exception reports are used to present detailed listings of problems that have arisen during a specified period of time. Exception reports might encompass internal control deficiencies or questionable areas pertaining to the application of generally accepted accounting principles. This type of report may be used by or prepared by the controller. In an organization that utilizes electronic data processing, exception reports should be computer generated, and normally detail problems that may have arisen during the input, processing, and output stages of data processing.

FINANCIAL REPORTS

The controller is relied on to prepare complete and accurate financial statements which fairly present the financial position, results of operations, and cash flows of the company. Needless to say, the financial statements must include adequate and informative disclosures. The controller must keep in mind that the year-end financial statements must be audited by an independent certified public accountant. Accordingly, the year-end financial statements might have to include information which might not have been required had the controller prepared financial statements which were to be used solely by management.

Financial reports may also be prepared to describe operating results of individual divisions of the entity. These reports may not take the form of complete financial statements. As a result, these statements might include information that is not normally needed or used by individuals outside of the company.

REPORTS FOR THE BOARD OF DIRECTORS

The Board of Directors is typically interested in broad policy matters, general trends in revenue and profits, as well as competition. The Board of Directors is also concerned with short-term and long-term matters. Useful information in reports addressed to the Board of Directors includes company and divisional operating results, historical financial statements, prospective financial statements, status reports pertaining to capital expenditures, and special studies.

SPECIAL REPORTS TO SENIOR MANAGEMENT

Special situations and circumstances may arise which mandate separate analysis and study. For example, it may be necessary to identify the reason for a continual drop in the profitability of a particular product or territory. Another example is a feasibility study on the opening of a new plant facility. Narrative explanation of the analysis and the decision, along with proper statistical support, is crucial. Graphic presentations may also be enlightening.

REPORTS FOR DIVISIONAL MANAGERS

Reports prepared to aid divisional managers in gauging performance and improving operating results include:

- Sales and net income
- Return on investment
- Profitability by product line, project, or program
- Sales by geographic area
- Divisional contribution margin, segment margin, and short-term performance margin
- Divisional performance relative to other divisions in the same company and to competing divisions in other companies
- Expenses and labor performance by cost center
- Cash flow
- Production orders received and unfilled orders
- Idle time
- Comparison of operations with general indices of business conditions

REPORTS TO EMPLOYEES

Reports may be directed toward the interests and concerns of employees. These reports may contain the following information:

- Explanation of financial condition
- Profit per employee
- Profit per sales dollar, units sold, and amounts invested
- Taxes per employee relative to wages, per share of stock, dividends, and net income
- Salaries including comparison to other industries and cost of living
- Analytical profit and cost information
- Investment per employee
- Future outlook
- Industry trends
- Achievement in production, sales, or safety
- Nature and importance of break-even
- Explanation of changes in pension, welfare, and other benefit plans
- Need for stockholders
- Nature of properties
- Source of capital
- Dividends relative to wages, per employee and percent of investment

An illustrative report to employees follows:

X COMPANY
STATEMENT OF REVENUE AND EXPENSE FOR EMPLOYEES
FOR THE YEAR ENDED DECEMBER 31, 19X2

	Total Amount	Amount per Employee	Cents per Dollar of Receipts
The Company Received:			
From customers for goods and services rendered			
Dividends			
Interest			
Total amount received			
Corporate Expenses were:			
For materials, supplies, and other expenses			
Depreciation			
Taxes			
Total Expenses			
Balance remaining for salaries, dividends, and reinvestment in the business			
This was Divided as Follows:			
Paid to employees (excluding officers) as wages			
Paid for employee fringe benefits			
Total			
Compensation of officers			
Paid for officer fringe benefits			
Paid to shareholders as dividends			
Reinvested in the business for growth			
Total division			

REPORTS TO STOCKHOLDERS

An important role of the controller is to present useful information to stockholders. Reports to stockholders should be designed to communicate financial position, results of operations and cash flows for a specified period of time. The annual report to stockholders is required by companies regulated by the Securities and Exchange Commission (SEC). The SEC generally permits flexibility in the format and content of the annual report to stockholders, encouraging the use of graphs and charts. Although not required by any regulatory agency, a message from the company's president is usually included in the annual report to stockholders. The president's message is usually presented before the financial statements and the report of the independent certified public accountant. It should be remembered that the president's letter is the first item normally read by the user of the annual report. As such, it primes the reader, and should clearly present highlights of the company's operations and future expectations. Annual reports to shareholders also quite commonly include nonfinancial information in narrative and photographic form.

REPORTING TO THE NEW YORK STOCK EXCHANGE

The listing application to the New York Stock Exchange contains an agreement to furnish annual reports and periodic interim financial statements. Timely disclosure must be made of information that may impact security values or influence investment decisions.

CONCLUSION

The controller's role in reporting information cannot be understated. In addition to the ability to formulate useful financial and nonfinancial information, the controller must be able to effectively and efficiently communicate to management, employees, and outsiders. Reports containing data for decision-making purposes should be prepared in a timely manner.

4

What the Controller Must Know About Computers

Today's business world is so complex that the use of a computer is almost a certainty. The financial and accounting processes of businesses are so intricate that the pen, the pencil, and the ledger sheet are quickly becoming obsolete. Computerized tools available to the controller include spreadsheet programs (i.e., electronic worksheets), database software, and accounting packages.

The use of electronic data processing (EDP) can enhance an organization's operational efficiency and effectiveness. The use of EDP, however, may have an effect on the internal control structure of the organization.

ORGANIZATIONAL CHART OF A TYPICAL EDP DEPARTMENT

As discussed in Chapter 24, segregation of functions is essential. However, an organization that utilizes EDP has an inherent lack of segregation of functions, since computer systems often have built-in authorization of transactions which eliminates human intervention. To mitigate this situation, functions within the EDP department should be clearly separated.

The director of information services is the overall supervisor or manager of the department. His or her responsibilities include the delegation of responsibilities to others, the review of reports prepared by subordinate personnel, and the reconciliation of problems that arise within the department.

29

The systems analyst is responsible for evaluating management's objectives in computerizing their accounting and management applications. He or she will be responsible for

- Identifying management's objectives in computerizing their applications
- The creative design of the system
- Determining hardware requirements
- Recognizing system deficiencies
- Designing effective controls to be integrated into the system
- Linking human factors with technology

The programmer has the often difficult task of taking the analyst's blueprints and converting them into a language that the computer can understand. Programming involves incorporating all of management's wants and needs into a complete set of instructions which can be utilized by the computer. The programmer must be able to assure management that the necessary control procedures are embodied in the program. It is not uncommon for a newly written program to include "bugs" or problems. The programmer is the individual who is relied upon to eliminate such problems. Programmers must often be on call 24 hours a day in order to ensure that operations run smoothly.

Data entry operators are the individuals who actually enter the data into the system. These individuals must often be proficient in operating a variety of computer systems and computer programs. A skillful data entry operator can facilitate the generation of timely reports in addition to maximizing the cost/benefit relationship.

Computer operators generally are responsible for starting the computer system, loading programs and ensuring that proper maintenance of the system is achieved.

The librarian is essential for strong internal control. The librarian's function is custodial in nature. He or she is responsible for maintaining guardianship of computer programs, program and system documentation, as well as a log which tracks usage of programs and documentation.

The data base administrator is responsible for ensuring that data base functions are effective. A data base is a centralized accumulation of data which may be accessed by a variety of users for a variety of purposes. For example, within the organization many departments may need to access the names and addresses of thousands of customers. Rather than create many similar files containing identical information, a data base is created. This data base can then by accessed by means of a network.

A network administrator is responsible for ensuring that remote terminals are effectively linked to the central processing unit (i.e., the computer itself). Communication between computers is also a responsibility of the network administrator.

The data control group is responsible for reviewing output and ensuring that only authorized individuals have access to such output. This is normally based upon approved distribution lists. The data control group is also responsible for reviewing exception reports, which are detailed listings of problems that arose during the input, processing, and output phases of electronic data processing. It must be understood, though, that the data control group is normally not empowered to automatically rectify computer problems. The data control group must obtain authorization for changes from the departments responsible for the transactions involved in the problem situations.

CONTROLS AND PROCEDURES

In addition to segregating data processing functions, certain controls and procedures should be incorporated into the hardware (i.e., equipment) and the software (i.e., programs).

Input Controls

To reasonably ensure that the data entered is accurate and complete, input controls should be utilized by the electronic data processing department.

Batch totals represent the total dollars of input. In using batch totals, adding machine totals of input items are created. These totals are then compared to computer-generated totals. Differences indicate that data has been lost during input.

Record counts represent the total number of items entered into the system. These manually derived totals are then compared to computer-generated totals. The agreement of these totals, however, does not provide absolute assurance that data has been entered correctly. For instance, dollar amounts may have been entered incorrectly, while the number of items entered may have been correct.

Hash totals are totals which, while used for control purposes, are meaningless in terms of financial statement effects. For example, a manual total of check numbers is obtained and compared to a similar computer-generated total. The agreement of these totals provides reasonable assurance of the accuracy of input but does not relate a dollar amount affecting the books and financial statements.

A check digit is a single number that is used for identification purposes. The absence of the check digit results in the rejection of input. The check digit is algebraically determined by weighing the other numbers in the input sequence.

Passwords represent codes that are necessary for access to the computer room or the computer itself.

Logic tests involve comparisons of input items with software-incorporated criteria that determine the acceptability of input data. Examples of logic tests include sign tests, value tests, field size tests, and limit tests. A sign test is designed to accept only a positive number or only a negative number. A value test recognizes, for example, that only a "0" or a "1" is acceptable. A field size test will reject input data that includes more than a specified number of characters. A limit test, on the other hand, will reject input data above a prescribed limit. For example, when entering a number for a month, the limit test should reject the number "13."

Processing Controls

Processing controls are intended to provide reasonable assurance that the computer processing has been accomplished as intended. Accordingly, controls should prevent the (1) the loss, (2) the corruption, (3) the duplication, and (4) the addition of data.

To identify files, external and internal label checks may be used. External labels are affixed to disks to enable verification that the proper file is being utilized for processing. Internal file labels are read by the computer and are matched with specific commands before processing can commence.

Limit or reasonableness tests are similar to those used as input controls.

Processing controls may also be built into the hardware. Examples include parity checks and echo checks.

Output Controls

Output controls should be designed to provide reasonable assurance that processing product is accurate and distributed only to authorized users.

The accuracy of output may be verified by reconciling output totals with input and processing totals. Internal control is also enhanced by generating and reviewing exception reports, which represent detailed listings of problems that arose during input processing and output stages of data processing.

The utilization of approved distribution lists is the primary means of ensuring limited and authorized access to output data. Furthermore, logs should be maintained which detail the (1) the name of the individual receiving output and (2) the time of receipt.

File Controls

The objectives of file controls are to ensure that (1) files are protected, (2) copies of files are maintained, and (3) reconstruction of files is possible.

Computers and the files they generate should be protected from nature's elements. Accordingly, smoking, eating, and drinking should be prohibited by employees handling computer equipment and computer disks. If possible, rugs should not be used in computer rooms since they tend to create magnetic fields which could possibly erase data on disks. Air conditioning should be used in computer rooms in an effort to reduce humidity which can destroy computer components.

While the possibility of computer failure and file destruction are always concerns faced by electronic data processing personnel, proper backup of data and offsite storage of such backup files can greatly mitigate the potential of disaster. If files must be reconstructed due to computer failure and file destruction, either nondestructive or destructive EDP file update is possible. Nondestructive EDP file update is accomplished by means of maintaining three generations of data at all times, and is often referred to as the grandfather-father-son EDP file update method. This technique is most often used when data is batch processed (i.e., items of a similar nature are grouped together before being processed). Destructive EDP file update, on the other hand, involves the overwriting of new data on old data. Accordingly, new information automatically replaces old information. This technique is most often used in online-real time situations (i.e., situations in which input and output mechanisms have direct access to the central processing unit enabling update of files at the time data is entered, rather than on a delayed basis associated with batch processing. The dangers involved in destructive EDP file update may be ameliorated by employing (1) dumping, (2) adding, and (3) checking procedures. Dumping involves transferring information from one medium to another. For instance, personnel should perform periodic backup of data from hard disk drives to floppy disks or tape cartridges. Dumping is different from the grandfather-father-son EDP file update situation in that the former retains only one generation of data at a given point in time. In addition, before data is entered that replaces existing information, checks should be performed to ensure that the new data is authorized, accurate, and complete.

SPREADSHEET PROGRAMS

Spreadsheet programs permit values (numeric data or formulas) and text (words and labels) to be entered on an electronic columnar pad. Data is entered into cells identified by row and column location. The advantage of spreadsheets is that when one number is changed, every other number related to it is also altered. Spreadsheet programs can easily handle "what if" assumptions which can effortlessly be modified. A spreadsheet program is an invaluable tool to the controller, since it can be useful in budgeting, forecasting, tax planning, and preparation. Some of the more common spreadsheet applications include the following:

- Any imaginable type of "what-if" analysis involving alternative situations (e.g., what the company's tax liability will be assuming different tax options are taken)
- Preparing working papers (e.g., trial balances)
- Maintaining general and subsidiary ledgers
- Generating different types of financial reports the entity's management may require
- Preparing financial statements
- Planning budgets and forecasts

- Payroll preparation and analysis
- Revenue analysis by volume, price, and product-service mix
- Analyzing expenses
- Costs specified in terms of volume, price, and category
- Converting from cash to accrual basis and vice versa
- Aging accounts receivable
- Inventory management
- Inventory extensions and footings
- Determining inventory management figures, including estimated sales and carrying costs per unit
- Production forecasts
- Economic order quantity
- Liability valuation (such as aging accounts payable) and liability classification (such as breaking down notes payable into current and noncurrent portions)
- Expense calculations and reports such as for depreciation, amortization, leases, pensions, and accrued expenses
- Breakdown of expenses by category (e.g., selling expenses into promotion and entertainment, commissions, and travel)
- Cash flow analysis (e.g., debt levels, interest rates) and balancing the checkbook
- Formulating integrated business plans in which income statements, balance sheets, statements of cash flows, and other related schedules can be integrated into one model
- Financial statement analysis
    - Ratio computations
    - Earnings per share
    - Rate of return (i.e., assets, equity)
    - Cost-revenue relationship (i.e., advertising to sales)
    - Input-output relationship, such as effect of volume on costs
    - Horizontal and vertical trends over the years
- Financial aspects of the business
- Capital expenditure analysis
- Capital budgeting analysis
    - Present value
    - Payback
    - Discounted payback
    - Internal rate of return

- Ranking index
- Varying assumptions (i.e., interest rate) and determining the effect
- Future value analysis, such as with the future value table calculations
- Break-even analysis
- Managing assets (cash, accounts receivable, inventory, and securities)
  - Credit control management and analysis and means to improve credit management
- Lease versus buy
- Manufacture versus buy
- Determining the effects of inflation (i.e., the impact of price changes)
- Productivity measures
- Loan amortization tables
- Acquisition analyses of other companies
- Investment selection
- Preparing portfolio investment transactions and balances
- Optimal financing mix (i.e., debt-equity)
- Debt covenant compliance
- Cost and managerial accounting
  - Divisional and departmental performance evaluation (i.e., cost center)
  - Product line measures
  - Overhead calculations
  - Variance determination (standard to actual, budget to actual) in dollars and percentage terms
  - Job costing
- Tax preparation
- Tax planning
- Tax loss carry-forward and tax loss carry-back schedules
- Departmental control and analysis
  - Time sheets by employee for control and billing purposes
  - Entity statistics for evaluation and reporting purposes
  - Arriving at answers in seconds when meeting with other executives without the need to redo many calculations manually
- Generate data files compatible with certain statistical packages for conducting regression analysis and other statistical procedures. (Here, a single data file may be utilized for multiple applications.)
- Marketing aspects, such as product line evaluation by market share, revenue and costs by geographic area, and sales by customer

The selection of a spreadsheet package involves careful evaluation of both program attributes and hardware configurations. Features that are desirable in a spreadsheet program include:

- Ability to operate on existing hardware
- Available memory and capacity level
- Maximum number of rows and columns
- Ease of use and flexibility, such as ability to maneuver within the spreadsheet
- Availability of on-screen help
- Availability of compatible templates. A template is a preformatted setup that comes ready for use. You merely input data relevant to a specific application, since formulas have already been incorporated.
- Formulas involved and functions to be performed. Most spreadsheet packages include a variety of functions built into the system. Thus, the keypunching of extensive formulas is eliminated. For example, the @STD function in Lotus 1-2-3 permits the computation of the standard deviation of a group of values.
- Speed involved in loading the program and in processing or recalculating data
- Capability of handling:
  - Absolute values
  - Average values
  - Logarithms
  - Statistical calculations
- Recalculation order, such as row versus column
- Existence of data base commands within the spreadsheet. This eliminates the need to find a program that can import data from another database program.
- Alpha and numeric functions, which permit the entry of labels and mathematical calculations
- Logic functions which are useful when calculating conditional values
- Existence of minimum, maximum, and random functions
- Financial function abilities for planning purposes:
  - Present value
  - Future value
  - Internal rate of return
  - Rate of return
- Ability to title columns and add description columns to the rows
- Variable column widths

- Ability to add leading dollar signs
- Ability to change the format of negative numbers, in order to exercise a preference in presenting a negative number—such as ($300) or −$300.
- Ability to add or remove commas
- Ability to set the number of decimal places within numbers
- Display of numbers in scientific notation
- Display of numbers as percentages including the printing of the percent sign
- Ability to change the manner in which dates appear
- Justification of values. The capability to repeatedly center, right-justify, or left-justify cell contents is essential for presentation purposes
- Absolute, relative, and mixed cell addressing. This is a concern when formulas are copied from one range of cells to another. In absolute addressing, the formula and the original cell ranges are copied to new cell ranges. With relative addressing, the copied formula is automatically adjusted to include new cell ranges. Thus, while operations in the formula remain constant, the cells to be used relative to the formula are substituted. Mixed addressing is a combination of absolute and relative. Here, columns or rows can be kept absolute while the other becomes relative.
- Freezing titles
- Automatically filling cells. When a column or row of numbers is deleted, the deleted portion may remain as a blank, or the spreadsheet may automatically adjust to eliminate the gaps. Different keystrokes produce the desired alternative.
- Range intersections
- Transposition ability to interchange the presence of cells, columns, or rows
- Ability to perform "what-if" calculations. Formulas are the means by which mathematical and "what-if" calculations are performed. "What-if" analysis shows the effect of changes on another specific variable or on the whole picture (financial statements, budget, and financial analysis).
- Analytical formats—will accept the user's own mathematical formulations
- Ability to accept user-created simple accounting systems including the capability to generate financial statements
- Ability to type labels in cross-column boundaries
- Formatting abilities, such as placing dollar signs in the right columns
- Print formatting, including headers and footers
- Ability to put items in sequence alphabetically and numerically
- Sorting and searching capabilities, such as the ability to arrange and access data in alphabetical and numerical sequence

- Iteration, referring to changing a variable "what-if" situation. In changing a variable dependent upon another variable, which in turn is dependent on a third variable, it becomes apparent that an exact recalculation is often impossible. Iteration eliminates this problem by overcoming the circular reference structure.
- Inserting, editing, deleting, copying, retaining, and output functions. Included are column and row functions such as copying, moving, adding, or deleting multiple columns or rows
- Spreadsheet consolidation (linking) where columns from one spreadsheet can be moved to another
- A lock-up feature using the contents of one or two cells to find information in yet another cell
- Control functions such as true/false and error
- Locking (protecting) and unlocking (unprotecting) cells. This capability refers to the protection of cells so contents in rows and columns will not be accidentally destroyed by the operator entering data over them.
- Blank function for cell clearance
- Ability to make unlimited changes
- The number of different worksheets that can be displayed in the different windows
- Connection of windows for vertical and horizontal scrolling in one direction at a time. This allows the financial manager to access portions of a spreadsheet not initially visible because of monitor limitations.
- Ability to link parts of files created by one module with those created by another (i.e., a change in the value in the spreadsheet will automatically update the information in a letter produced by a word processing program).
- Integration ability with other packages, such as data base and graphics. Some spreadsheet programs such as *Symphony* have these features built-in.
- Management of lists of data

When utilizing spreadsheets, the controller should be concerned with the reliability of the input and output data, program support, verification methods, and the ability to detect operating bugs. Even the smallest error in a spreadsheet application can mushroom into a disastrous situation. Spreadsheet errors are often caused by keystroke errors involving the entering of a wrong number or formula into a particular cell. The more complicated the formula or data, the greater the likelihood of input error. Potential errors include the rounding of numbers, the incorrect order of arithmetic functions and the incorrect order of cell calculation and recalculation. Formula development can also result in errors as in the case when an absolute formula should have been entered as a relative formula. Macros, in which a single keystroke invokes a series of commands, if incorrectly structured, may also result in spreadsheet problems. Similarly, problems may arise when linking or consolidating financial spreadsheets as well as when data is transferred from one source to another.

In order to avoid errors or at least mitigate the effects of such errors, the controller should:

- Establish the objectives to be accomplished
- Rectify all problems immediately upon discovery, especially those involving circular reasoning
- Separate data from formulas
- When information is to be imported into a spreadsheet, specify it as text rather than as numbers
- Skillfully develop a template plan including purpose, required input, and desired output
- Place data in either a row or a column instead of both
- Construct a template as simply as possible, creating small sections of the model and testing them before combining them with other portions of the template
- Use parentheses in establishing the order or calculations
- Make commands as simple as possible in order to prevent misinterpretation errors and difficulty in revision
- Scan the entire spreadsheet, considering the formulas and the interrelationship of particular cells
- Watch for error messages in cell references
- Periodically test spreadsheet results by comparing with manual calculations
- Audit spreadsheets for mathematical errors as well as models containing judgmental errors
- Decompose long formulas and complex macros
- Evaluate the reasonableness of the assumptions and approach to the solution
- Calculate sample variables in order to ascertain their validity
- In a blank spreadsheet cell, test internally developed macros for reliability
- Provide for sufficient backup
- Avoid errors in entering data; in constructing formulas and macros, utilize pointing rather than typing. Accordingly, it is best to point to cells or ranges to indicate them in formulas and macros in lieu of typing cell addresses.
- Assure that only authorized individuals use the spreadsheet program and the files created with the program

- When creating or utilizing the spreadsheet, verify its validity section by section instead of checking the worksheet in its entirety at the end of its creation or use
- Verify that the correct version of the spreadsheet is being used
- Exercise caution with simultaneous equations and iterative calculations. The number of iterations must be accurately estimated in order to reliably calculate a simultaneous equation. Overestimation may result in wasted time; underestimation may result in an incorrect conclusion.
- When columns and rows are moved to different locations, define names for cell ranges in order to lower the probability of cell reference mistakes.
- To guard against cell destruction, consider cell protection
- Ensure that an environmental section of the spreadsheet contains information regarding the template's configuration, such as variable names, data values, and cell locations or ranges
- Provide for output documentation of cell locations of the report and printing guidelines
- Have assurance that templates conform to the independent accountant's policy on structure and documentation
- If a template uses data from other spreadsheets, provide for a proper interface between the cells of both spreadsheets
- Know the source of data in the spreadsheet

GRAPHICS SOFTWARE

An important attribute of a controller is the ability to communicate vital information to management, shareholders, and other interested third parties. Presentations are more impressive when graphics are incorporated. Graphic-based presentations are often more comprehensible, more powerful, and more convincing.

Graphic packages express numeric information in graphic form, including charts, diagrams, and signs. Graphs can be converted into photographic slides, overhead transparencies, and images on paper. Absolute amounts (e.g., totals and increases, percentages, dollars and units) can be illustrated. Rates of increase and trends can also be depicted. Presentation designed to impress the viewer may be multicolored. Software that allows free-style drawing is more useful for imaginative enhancements. Structured programs, on the other hand, are better in clarifying a simple chart.

Accounting graphics can capture complex data collections, portray relationships between different numbers, and present them immediately and dramatically. Graphics can be used to evaluate trends and make superior decisions.

Types of graphics include the following:

- Bar graphics—stacked, horizontal, and three-dimensional
- Line graphs
- Area graphs
- Pie shapes
- High-low-close charts
- Bubble charts, which depict the relative values of items by size and position of circles (bubbles) in a coordinate range
- Surface area charts
- Scatter diagrams
- Spherical diagrams

Graphics may be useful to controllers since they may be used to create displays in:

- Charting revenue and/or costs by product line, market share, and customer
- Analyzing trends in major expense categories
- Analyzing trends in capital expenditures
- Break-even analysis
- Depicting variance between budgeted and actual amounts
- Appraising backlog figures
- Reflecting personnel statistics, such as the number of employees and productivity measures

While the features included in graphics packages vary, selection of the appropriate package should be, in part, based on the following:

- Available memory
- Compatibility with other packages and applications
- User-friendliness, including menu options and "help" functions
- Maximum number of actions and symbols included
- Maximum number of columns and rows in charts, automatic overlapped column specifications, and three-dimensional columns
- Maximum number of bars
- Included and available image libraries, which allow the merging of pictures with a chart or other image
- Formatting aspects, such as screen resolution display and multiple size graphs
- Ability to modify predefined or drawn images
- Editing abilities pertaining to titles, labels, and graph types
- Ability to adjust plot orientation and page size

- Ability to rotate graph axes
- Types of graphs supported
- Printing features such as bold type, underlining, pattern handling, and multiple copies
- Existence of chart legends
- Extent of color choice
- Printers supported

DATA BASE MANAGEMENT SOFTWARE

A data base is an organized collection of readily accessible related information which may be used on a recurring basis by the corporate controller. Data base management software (DBMS) may be useful in numerous applications, including accounts receivable and inventory monitoring.

Data base software allows the controller to enter, manipulate, retrieve, display, extract, select, sort, edit, and index data. DBMS packages define the structure of collected data, design screen formats for data input, handle files, and generate reports. DBMS permits the creation of financial statement formats and the performance of arithmetic calculations. In essence, a data base is an electronic filing cabinet providing a common core of information accessible by the programs. Programs and applications may be customized by specifying the data to be entered and what should be done to it in order to generate the desired output.

While there are different types of DBMS, the relational data base manager software appears to be the most popular and useful. A relational data base manager has data sets of information in a table of rows and columns (i.e., matrix). Information is stored in two-dimensional data sets or tables similar to a traditional file processing system. The reports produced from this type of data base can have greater complexity and utility than those generated from other types of data base systems.

A relational data base allows for the access of data fields by enabling the user to ignore the traditional one-to-one relationship by permitting access to a particular grid or cell. For example, if a relational data base includes first and last names of customers as well as their street address, city, state, zip code, area code, and telephone number, data can be accessed by specifying any one of these parameters.

The basic operations possible with relational DBMS include:

- Creating or deleting tables and attributes
- Copying data from one table to another
- Retrieving or questioning a table or attribute
- Printing, reorganizing, or reading a table

- Combining tables based on a value included in a table
- Manipulating data in creative ways

Selection of DBMS is a difficult task because the market has been inundated with packages from a variety of publishers. To facilitate the purchase of DBMS, appraisal of individual packages should be made in terms of the following:

- Available memory
- Compatibility with other packages and applications in terms of ascertaining whether data formatted with other data base programs can be imported and translated into the format utilized by your program. In addition, the ability to exchange data with spreadsheet and word processing programs should be considered.
- "Help" functions, which are a must when the DBMS requires programming on the part of the user
- Commands that make sense in describing the operation to be performed
- Artificial intelligence features
- Search capabilities including query-by-example to retrieve records and generate reports
- Fields per record and field size
- The number of fields that can be simultaneously edited
- An enumerated field allowing for the specification of all of the field's possible values
- Flexibility in field type and record structure; i.e., adding or deleting fields even subsequent to entering information on records.
- Types and limitations of data fields
- Ability to hide selected data
- Ability to generate derived or computed fields. A derived field is a field that performs mathematical calculations on data sorted in other fields.
- Ability to simultaneously process multiple fields
- Available reporting formats
- Graphic capabilities
- Reformatting ease (allowing for changing a format at any time)
- New report formatting capability to modify the finished product for maximum presentability
- Inclusion of an integrated text editor
- Error-detection ability
- On-screen error messages, along with an indexed listing of all errors at the end of the program manual

- Number and size of records that can be contained in one file, including maximum records that may be accommodated. Always select DBMS that can accommodate more records than mandated by present needs.
- Linkage of files where a change in one automatically changes another
- Creation of a new data base representing a subset of a parent file
- Ability to peek into unopened files of the data base. For example, while viewing an inventory file, the user can pop up on the screen an unrelated file.
- Ability to modify data types on fields subsequent to data entry
- Supported key files
- Capability to sort data based on numeric, alphabetic, and conditional relationships
- Calculational ability including present value, future value, growth rate, logarithms, exponential notation, square root, and absolute values. If a derivation is modified, the program should automatically recompute the data throughout the data base.
- Capability to copy the data base to disk or tape, providing a backup in the event of hardware or software failure
- Ability to simultaneously work with multiple files
- Availability of compatible templates
- Support for windows, enabling the user to view and use different files and/or programs simultaneously
- Ability to incorporate color into input and output screens
- Availability of add-on modules
- Indexing ability
- Print capabilities
- Page characteristics
- Password security

DBMS may be used by the controller for a multitude of applications including the following:

- Retrieving information based on varied criteria. For instance, check information may be recalled based on date of issuance, payee, amount, or account posted to. This may assist in the internal audit function.
- Searching for accounting records possessing a key word or amount, such as listing accounts that are in excess of 90 days past due.
- Establishing upper and lower limits as in the case of customer credit limits. Internal auditor selection of accounts receivable and payable for confirmation may be enhanced.

- Calculating specified fields, as in the case of footing and extending inventory listings
- Developing statistical information, including variances
- Preparing forecasts and projections which are often based on hypothetical assumptions
- Performing analytical procedures when applying audit procedures
- Generating lists to control preparation and submission of reports
- Payroll preparation and reporting
- Inventory monitoring
- Preparation of general and subsidiary ledgers
- Analyzing potential investments since a data base can store information on thousands of companies which the company may want to track before making an investment
- Creating and updating mailing lists
- Tax planning and preparation

INTEGRATED PACKAGES

Integrated software consists of two or more modules that work in tandem. Integrated packages may combine functions like word processing, spreadsheets, data base management, graphics, and telecommunications. In essence, different processing tasks are applied to a single set of data. For example, spreadsheet data may be converted into graphs and then incorporated into a document which is word processed.

The decision to use an integrated package is complex. If identical source information is to be utilized for a variety of purposes and activities, an integrated package is ideal. It is superior to the situation wherein each program and data files must be loaded each time another program is needed. Integrated software is also perfect when canned software will not permit the interchange of data developed when using other programs.

When recurring specific applications are involved, an integrated package represents a poor choice. In this instance, an individual application package (e.g., a program dedicated to data base management) is a wise choice, since its performance and capabilities are generally greater than the module included in the integrated package. Furthermore, integrated packages typically require more memory and have a tendency to reduce processing speed.

ACCOUNTING SOFTWARE

Since the controller is responsible for the timely recording of accounting data as well as the preparation of reliable books, records, and financial statements, he or she should be concerned with the efficiency and effectiveness of the accounting system. The use of accounting software can greatly enhance the likelihood of accounting efficiency and effectiveness.

Today, a purchaser may acquire individual accounting modules or an integrated package. Smaller businesses may only need a single module, such as a general ledger package, while a larger business often needs several modules. Integrated accounting packages link a number of modules performing related tasks by enabling the transfer of data from one module to another, thereby eliminating the need to repetitively enter data. For example, the update of accounts payable automatically updates general ledger control accounts.

In determining the software that should be acquired, consideration should be given to the following:

- The ability to set up and integrate
- The maximum number of accounts
- The capability to account for separate departments, segments, and divisions
- The versatility, reliability, and ease of use
- The ability to produce a printed audit trail
- The interface abilities which include on-screen prompts
- The existence of security, including multi-level password protection
- The ability to identify and correct errors that arise during input, processing, and output
- The inclusion of recovery instructions
- The accommodation for standard and customized financial and accounting reports and schedules
- The ability to transfer files to hard disk
- The ability to convert files to a format which is compatible with spreadsheet and data base management programs
- The inclusion of a standardized and modifiable chart of accounts
- The ability to prepare bank reconciliations
- The ability to produce budgets
- The ability to retain transaction detail as required by the entity
- The provision for recurring monthly journal entries, thus eliminating the need to repetitively enter identical information
- The ability to provide account history analysis
- The recognition of out-of-balance entries, which should not be posted
- The support for nonfinancial data such as square footage and personnel statistics which might be used in cost allocations
- The handling of multiple open periods

- Extra features, including but not limited to, the preparation of mailing lists and multiple inventory pricing
- The preparation of exception reports
- The industries accommodated by the program

GENERAL LEDGER MODULE

Small organizations commonly require only the general ledger module. For large organizations, this module typically represents the nucleus of the entire accounting system. The general ledger module usually produces a chart of accounts, a variety of journals, a trial balance, a general ledger and, if report writing capabilities are incorporated, a complete set of financial statements, including the statement of cash flows. Flexibility is a key, since every company's accounting and reporting needs are different. Accordingly, it is crucial that the system and report formats be capable of being customized. As in all software, controls (as discussed in Chapter 24) should be incorporated.

The controller should keep in mind that, if other modules are to be integrated presently or possibly in the future, compatibility between software manufacturers might present a problem. In selecting a general ledger module the controller should specifically consider the following:

- General ledger balancing
- Number of accounts allowed
- Account number format which should provide for alpha and numeric conditions
- Number of journal entries accepted
- Number of clients, departments, and journals accommodated
- Maximum dollar amount accepted
- Ability to handle accrual and other comprehensive bases of accounting, including conversion between different bases
- Preparation and automatic posting of recurring and reversing entries
- Ability to keep old accounting periods open
- Validation of account numbers, zero balances, and input data
- Editing of journal entries and batch balancing
- Processing of entries temporarily terminated when specified edit criteria are not satisfied
- Preparation of exception reports
- The provision for multi-level subsidiary accounts
- Ability to open previously closed accounting periods

- On-line inquiry pertaining to user-designated accounts
- Ability to perform such analytical procedures as comparison of actual amounts to budgeted and prior-period amounts
- Generates reports on demand as well as at the end of an accounting period
- Provides for automatic backup of files
- Permits departmental reporting, multicompany reporting, as well as consolidation
- Allocates designated expenses
- Ability to interface with other programs, thereby eliminating unnecessary data entry. For example, it is important to have the ability to transfer account balances to a tax return preparation package. If this feature is not present, a bridge between the programs can often be purchased or developed.

ACCOUNTS RECEIVABLE MODULES

Larger organizations often have significant amounts of sales transactions. In these cases, tracking, reconciling, and aging receivables is crucial. An accounts receivable module can easily accomplish these tasks as well as assisting in cash flow planning and the granting of credit. In selecting an accounts receivable module, consideration should be given to the following:

- Types of receivables accommodated
- Number of customers and general ledger accounts permitted
- Customer number structure
- Maximum dollar amount for an individual transaction
- Number of invoices that may be generated
- Number of payments that may be accepted
- Number of lines per invoice and statement
- Ability to print invoices and statements with suppression for accounts with zero balances
- Capability to verify customer information before processing
- Determination of customer balances
- Application of cash payments to appropriate accounts and invoices
- Proper adjustment of customer accounts
- Summarizing and detailing journal entries
- Capability and number of recurring entries
- Generation of a subsidiary ledger
- Capability to generate aging analyses

- Assignment of statement cycle codes to customers having different credit attributes; for example, a company may mail statements to corporate customers monthly as opposed to bi-weekly mailings for noncorporate customers
- Comparison of individual accounts to credit limits
- Preparation of debit and credit memos
- Automatic calculation of finance charges, discounts, sales commissions and late payment penalties
- Flexible billing
- Batch balancing and control information
- Ability to interface with the existing general ledger module
- Ability to forecast cash flow
- Generation of sales analyses by salesperson, customer, and territory
- Automatic preparation of sales tax returns
- Capability of accepting credit card charge accounts
- Generating mailing labels

ACCOUNTS PAYABLE MODULES

An accounts payable module is essential when numerous checks are written. The accounts payable module should be flexible to permit daily, weekly, semi-monthly, or monthly check preparation. This provides assurance that all payments are made in time to secure vendor discounts.

The controller should carefully evaluate the features of an accounts payable module, which should:

- Accommodate a more than sufficient number of vendors, vouchers, checks, and invoices
- Alphabetically list vendors
- Generate a vendor log
- Provide supplier numbers
- Create and account for debit and credit memos
- Calculate discounts and finance charges
- Detail and summarize journal entries
- Accommodate recurring entries
- Identify duplicate vendor invoices
- Generate a check register
- Enable printing of checks
- List uncleared checks

- Pinpoint frequency and amounts of payments and payables
- Provide for entry of hand-drawn checks
- Permit partial and automatic payments
- Be capable of canceling an invoice approved for payment prior to payment
- List recurring checks
- List and account for voided checks
- Prepare a schedule of cash requirements due on a particular date
- Generate a due date register
- Analyze vendors
- Track lost discounts
- Compare receiving reports with supplier invoices
- Select items to be paid
- Permit entry of purchase orders
- Permit updating of purchase orders
- Generate a list of open purchase orders by vendor and item
- Require proper authorization for payments
- Offer multi-level password protection
- Provide a clear audit trail
- Restrict access to checks
- Provide a check log detailing ranges of check numbers and voided checks
- Interface with the general ledger module
- Satisfy tax reporting requirements
- Provide any required miscellaneous vendor information

PAYROLL MODULES

The decision to utilize a payroll module should be based on the cost/benefit relationship. Unless there are numerous employees, a payroll module is usually not justified. Manual processing of a small payroll is usually accomplished efficiently and effectively. When there are few employees, and manual processing is not desired, an inexpensive alternative is to utilize an outside payroll preparation service.

When payroll computation and accounting becomes complicated, such as when there are multiple user-defined pay types and voluntary deductions, the use of a payroll module is quite feasible. Fundamental considerations in selecting a payroll module include:

- Types of payroll information provided
- Personnel statistics

- Maximum payroll dollar amount
- Maximum number of employees supported
- Types of employee information stored on master files
- Hourly rate support
- Pay period(s) supported
- Payroll payment ceiling amount
- Number and types of payroll deductions accommodated
- Format of payroll register
- Ability to generate check register
- Ability to print checks and perform check reconciliation
- Handling of voided checks
- Treatment of payroll advances
- Ability to modify withholding tables upon enactment of new laws
- Detail and summary journals supported
- Ability to handle supplemental pay provisions, such as bonuses
- Support for overtime calculations
- Types of payroll reports and summaries
- Provision for sick and vacation pay
- Support for direct deposit arrangements
- Generation of mailing labels
- Interface with general ledger modules
- Ability to allocate payroll amounts to various income statement accounts
- Support for tax calculations and reports for federal, state, and city government agencies
- Multi-level password protection
- Ability to set up deposits to be made at company's bank

INVENTORY MODULES

Considerations pertaining to the selection of an inventory module relate to inventory management and reporting and include:

- Master files for inventory, related customers, and suppliers
- Number of inventory items handled
- Types of inventory records, including balances listed by item and category
- Inventory transactions for receipts, issuances, returns, and allowances
- Ability to interface with purchase and sales orders

- Ability to compare packing slips to purchase orders for quantity and part verification
- Interfacing with job cost accounting systems
- Reflection of in-transit inventory
- Bin location
- Reconciliation of promised date of delivery with actual delivery date
- Support for warehouse information
- Generation of printed receiving stubs
- Comparison of perpetual records to physical quantities
- Data entry error detection
- Variance analysis for inventory discrepancies
- Ability to keep multiple periods open
- Transferability of inventory items from one location to another
- Calculation of economic order quantity and economic order point
- Calculation of lead time in acquiring inventory items
- Determination of safety stock
- Preparation of shortage reports
- Variable lot sizes
- Calculation of inventory turnover and age of inventory items in order to identify slow-moving and obsolete inventory items
- Monitoring of shrinkage
- Cost accounting capabilities
- Preparation of back-order reports
- Reports identifying missing inventory tags

FIXED ASSET MODULES

A fixed asset module should be capable of the following:

- Describing and categorizing fixed assets
- Accepting a sufficient number and amount of fixed assets
- Providing information pertaining to:
  - Cost
  - Estimated life
  - Salvage value
- Utilizing different depreciation methods

- Calculate depreciation and accumulated depreciation for both financial and tax reporting purposes
- Calculating pro rata amounts

TAX RETURN PREPARATION AND PLANNING PACKAGES

If the entity's independent accountant does not prepare the required annual income tax returns, acquisition of tax preparation and planning software might be prudent. Criteria for selection of software in this area include:

- Reliability and responsiveness of the vendor in your time of need. Toll-free support is a definite advantage.
- Interactivity of computations between forms, elimination of duplicate entry of data
- Forms handled
- Storage capacity
- Ability to process multi-state returns
- Processing speed
- Annual update costs
- User-friendliness, including on-screen prompts
- Ability to recognize omitted items
- Ability to run on existing software
- Quality of utilities included
- Proforma capabilities; i.e., the ability to carry information from one year to the next
- Integration of tax software with accounting modules, thereby enabling transfer of data
- Print options, such as laser printing and use of overlays
- Collating abilities
- Output formats acceptable to governmental agencies
- Multi-level password protection
- Data validation and checking
- Ability to calculate interest and penalties
- Vendor background, such as number of packages in active use, reputation, and number of years in business
- Ability to calculate tax implications in buy-lease decisions
- Ability to determine whether it is better to invest an entire amount in the current period or to spread it over several years

- Determining the timing of security dispositions
- Determining the criteria which will trigger the imposition of the minimum tax

CONCLUSION

Today's controller cannot overlook the importance of computers in operational effectiveness and efficiency. The controller must not lose sight of the fact that internal controls in a computerized environment are germane to the attainment of entity objectives. The multitude of software packages compels the controller to carefully evaluate each acquisition possibility. The selection of software is the most crucial step in converting a manual system to a computerized one. Software should be selected first. Then, and only then, should hardware be selected. If hardware is selected first, the controller may find that suitable programs are unavailable. Unnecessary expenditures for customized programming may then result.

II

GENERALLY ACCEPTED ACCOUNTING PRINCIPLES

5

Financial Statement Reporting: The Income Statement

Income statement preparation involves proper revenue and expense recognition. There are many methods available to recognize revenue including specialized methods for particular industries. Extraordinary and nonrecurring items require separate presentation. The income statement format is highlighted along with the earnings per share computation.

INCOME STATEMENT FORMAT

The format of the income statement starting with income from continuing operations follows:

Income from continuing operations before tax

Less: Taxes

Income from continuing operations after tax

Discontinued operations:

    Income for discontinued operations (net of tax)

    Loss or gain on disposal of a division (net of tax)

Income before extraordinary items

Extraordinary items (net of tax)

Cumulative effect of a change in accounting principle (net of tax)

Net income

Note that earnings per share is shown on the above items as well.

Comprehensive Income

Comprehensive income is the change in equity occurring from transactions and other events with nonowners. It excludes investment (disinvestment) by owners. Items included in comprehensive income but excluded from net income are:

- Cumulative effect of a change in accounting principle
- Unrealized losses and gains on long-term investments
- Foreign currency translation gains and losses

Comprehensive income is subdivided into revenues and gains, as well as expenses and losses. These are further classified as either recurring or extraordinary.

Extraordinary Items

Extraordinary items are those that are *both* unusual in nature and infrequent in occurrence. Unusual in nature means the event is abnormal and not related to the typical operations of the entity. The environment of a company includes consideration of industry characteristics, geographic location of operations, and extent of government regulation. Infrequent in occurrence means the transaction is not anticipated to take place in the foreseeable future taking into account the corporate environment. Materiality is considered by judging the items individually and not in the aggregate. However, if arising from a single specific event or plan they should be aggregated. Extraordinary items are shown net of tax between income from discontinued operations and cumulative effect of a change in accounting principle. Extraordinary items include:

- Casualty losses
- Losses on expropriation of property by a foreign government
- Gain on life insurance proceeds
- Loss or gain on the early extinguishment of debt
- Gain on troubled debt restructuring
- Loss from prohibition under a newly enacted law or regulation
- Gain or loss on disposal of a major part of the assets of a previously separate company in a business combination when sale is made within two years subsequent to the combination date

Losses on receivables and inventory occur in the normal course of business and therefore are not extraordinary. There is an exception, however, that losses on receivables and inventory are extraordinary if they relate to a casualty loss (e.g., earthquake) or governmental expropriation (e.g., banning of product because of a health hazard).

Nonrecurring Items

Nonrecurring items are items that are *either* unusual in nature or infrequent in occurrence. They are shown as a separate line item before tax in arriving at income from continuing operations. An example is the gain or loss on the sale of a fixed asset.

Discontinued Operations

A business segment is a major line of business or customer class. A discontinued operation is an operation that has been discontinued during the year or will be discontinued shortly after year-end. A discontinued operation may be a segment that has been sold, abandoned, or spun off. Even though it may be operating, there exists a formal plan to dispose. Footnote disclosure regarding the discontinued operation should include an identification of the segment, disposal date, the manner of disposal, and description of remaining net assets of the segment at year-end.

The two components of discontinued operations are: (1) income or loss from operations and (2) loss or gain on disposal of division.

Income or Loss from Operations. In a year which includes the measurement date, it is the income from the beginning of the year to the measurement date. The measurement date is the date on which management commits itself to a formal plan of action. Applicable estimates may be required.

If comparative financial statements are presented including periods before the measurement date, discontinued operations should be separately shown from continuing operations.

Loss or Gain on Disposal of Division. Income or loss from activities subsequent to the measurement date and before the disposal date is an element of the gain or loss on disposal. The disposal date is the date of closing by sale or the date activities cease because of abandonment. The gain or loss is shown in the disposal year. However, if losses are expected such losses are recorded in the year of the measurement date even if disposal is not completed in that year. Loss or gain should include estimated net losses from operations between the measurement date and the disposal date. If the loss cannot be estimated, a footnote is required. Loss on disposal includes the costs directly associated with the disposal decision. On the other hand, if a gain is expected, it should be recognized at the disposal date. The estimated gain or loss is determined at the measurement date and includes consideration of the net realizable value of the segment's assets. Also, loss or gain on disposal includes costs and expenses *directly* applicable to the disposal decision. These costs include severance pay, additional pension costs, employment relocation, and future rentals on long-term leases where sub-rentals are not possible. Note: Normal business adjustments (e.g., routinely writing down accounts receivable) are not included in the loss on disposal. These ordinary adjustments apply to the discontinued segment's operation rather than to the disposal of the segment. Typically, disposal is expected within one year of the measurement date.

EXAMPLE 1

On 6/15/19X8, ABC Company set up a plan to dispose of segment X. It is expected that the sale will occur on 3/1/19X9 for a selling price of $800,000. In 19X8, disposal costs were $100,000. Segment X's actual and estimated operating losses were:

1/1/19X8 to 6/14/19X8	$85,000
6/15/19X8 to 12/31/19X8	40,000
1/1/19X9 to 3/1/19X9	12,000

The carrying value of the segment on 3/1/19X9 is expected to be $900,000. The loss on disposal of segment X in the 19X8 income statement is:

Selling price		$ 800,000
Less: Disposal costs	$100,000	
Actual and expected operating losses		
after the measurement date	52,000	
Carrying value	900,000	1,052,000
Loss on Disposal		$ 252,000

REVENUE RECOGNITION

Revenue, which is associated with a gross increase in assets or decrease in liabilities, may be recognized under different methods depending on the circumstances. (Special revenue recognition guidelines exist for franchisers and in sales involving a right of return. A product financing arrangement may also exist.) The basic methods of recognition include:

- Realization
- Completion of production
- During production
- Cash basis

Realization. Revenue is recognized when goods are sold or services are performed. It results in an increase in net assets. This method is used almost all of the time. At realization, the earnings process is complete. Further, realization is consistent with the accrual basis meaning that revenue is recognized when earned rather than when received. Realization should be used when the selling price is determinable, future costs can be estimated, and an exchange has taken place that can be objectively measured. There must exist a reasonable basis to determine anticipated bad debts. There are exceptional situations where another method of revenue recognition should be used. These are now discussed.

At the Completion of Production. Revenue is recognized prior to sale or exchange. There must exist a stable selling price, absence of material marketing costs to complete the final transfer, and interchangeability in units. This approach is used with agricultural products, by-products, and precious metals when the aforementioned criteria are met. It is also used in accounting for construction contracts under the completed contract method.

During Production. Revenue recognition is made in the case of long-term production situations where an assured price for the completed item exists by contractual agreement and a reliable measure is possible of the degree of completion at various stages of the production process. An example is the percentage of completion method used in accounting for long-term construction contracts.

Construction Contracts. Under the completed contract method, revenue should not be recognized until completion of a contract. The method should only be used when the use of the percentage of completion method is inappropriate.

Under the percentage of completion method, revenue is recognized as production activity is occurring. The gradual recognition of revenue levels out earnings over the years and is more realistic since revenue is recognized as performance takes place. This method is preferred over the completed contract method and should be used when reliable estimates of the extent of completion each period is possible. If not, the completed contract method should be used. Percentage of completion results in a matching of revenue against related expenses in the benefit period.

Using the cost-to-cost method, revenue recognized for the period equals:

$$\frac{\text{Actual Costs to Date}}{\text{Total Estimated Costs}} \times \text{Contract Price} = \text{Cumulative Revenue}$$

Revenue recognized in prior years is deducted from the cumulative revenue to determine the revenue in the current period. An example follows:

Cumulative Revenue (1-4 years)

Revenue Recognized (1-3 years)

Revenue (Year 4 - current year)

Revenue less expenses equals profit.

EXAMPLE 2

In year 4 of a contract, the actual costs to date were $50,000. Total estimated costs are $200,000. The contract price is $1,000,000. Revenue recognized in the prior years (years 1-3) were $185,000.

$$\frac{\$50,000}{\$200,000} \times \$1,000,000 = \$250,000 \text{ Cumulative Revenue}$$

Cumulative Revenue	$250,000
Prior Year Revenue	185,000
Current Year Revenue	$ 65,000

Regardless of whether the percentage of completion method or the completed contract method is used, conservatism dictates that an obvious loss on a contract should immediately be recognized even before contract completion.

Journal entries under the construction methods using assumed figures follow:

	Percentage of Completion	Completed Contract
Construction-in-Progress (CIP)	100,000	100,000
Cash	100,000	100,000
Construction costs		
Progress Billings Receivable	80,000	80,000
Progress Billings on CIP	80,000	80,000
Periodic billings		
Construction-in-Progress	25,000	No Entry
Profit	25,000	
Yearly profit recognition		

In the last year when the construction project is completed, the following additional entry is made to record the profit in the final year:

	Percentage of Completion	Completed Contract
Progress Billings on Construction-in-Progress	Total Billings	Total Billings
Construction-in-Progress	Cost & Profit	Cost
Profit	Incremental Profit for Last Year	Profit for All the Years

Construction-in-Progress less Progress Billings is shown net. Usually, a debit figure results which is shown as a current asset. Construction-in-Progress is an inventory account for a construction company. If a credit balance occurs, the net amount is shown as a current liability.

Cash Basis. In the case of a company selling inventory, the accrual basis is used. However, when certain circumstances exist, the cash basis of revenue recognition is used. Namely, revenue is recognized upon collection of the account. The cash basis instead of the accrual basis must be used when one or more of the following exist:

- Selling price is not objectively determinable at the time of sale
- Inability to estimate expenses at the time of sale
- Risk exists as to collections from customers
- Uncertain collection period.

Revenue recognition under the installment method equals the cash collected times the gross profit percent. Any gross profit not collected is deferred on the balance sheet until collection occurs. When collections are received, realized gross profit is recognized by debiting the deferred gross profit account. The balance sheet presentation is:

Accounts Receivable (Cost + Profit)

Less: Deferred Gross Profit

Net Accounts Receivable (Cost)

Note: A service business that does not deal in inventory has the option of either using the accrual basis or cash basis.

Revenue Recognition When A Right of Return Exists

In the situation when a buyer has a right of returning the merchandise bought, the seller can only recognize revenue at the time of sale in accordance with FASB 48 provided that *all* of the following conditions are satisfied:

- Selling price is known
- Buyer has to pay for the goods even if the buyer is unable to resell them. An example is a sale of a good from a manufacturer to wholesaler. No provision must exist that the wholesaler has to be able to sell the item to the retailer.
- If the buyer loses the item or it is damaged in some way, the buyer still has to pay for it
- Purchase by the buyer of the item has economic feasibility
- Seller does not have to render future performance in order that the buyer will be able to resell the goods
- Returns may be reasonably estimated

In the case that any one of the above criteria are not met, revenue must be deferred along with deferral of related expenses until the criteria have been satisfied or the right of return provision has expired. An alternative to deferring the revenue would be to record a memo entry as to the sale.

The ability of a company to predict future returns involves consideration of the following:

- Predictability is detracted from when there is technological obsolescence risk of the product, uncertain product demand changes, or other material external factors
- Predictability is lessened when there is a long-time period involved for returns
- Predictability is enhanced when there exists a large volume of similar transactions
- Seller's previous experience in estimating returns for similar products
- Nature of customer relationship and types of product involved

FASB 48 does not apply to dealer leases or real estate transactions, nor to service industries.

Product Financing Arrangements

As per FASB 49, the arrangement involving the sale and repurchase of inventory is in substance a financing arrangement. It mandates that the product financing arrangement be accounted for as a borrowing instead of a sale. In many cases, the product is stored on the company's (sponsor's) premises. Often the sponsor will guarantee the debt of the other entity.

Types of product financing arrangements include:

- Sponsor sells a product to another business and agrees to reacquire the product or one basically identical to it. The established price to be paid by the sponsor typically includes financing and holding costs.
- Sponsor has another company buy the product for it and agrees to repurchase the product from the other entity
- Sponsor controls the distribution of the product that has been bought by another company in accord with the aforementioned terms

In all situations, the company (sponsor) either agrees to repurchase the product at given prices over specified time periods, or guarantees resale prices to third parties.

When the sponsor sells the product to the other firm and in a related transaction agrees to repurchase it, the sponsor should record a liability when the proceeds are received to the degree the product applies to the financing arrangement. A sale should *not* be recorded and the product should be retained as inventory on the sponsor's book.

In the case where another firm buys the product for the sponsor, inventory is debited and liability credited at the time of purchase.

Costs of the product, except for processing costs, in excess of sponsor's original production cost or acquisition cost, or the other company's purchase cost constitute finance and holding costs. The sponsor accounts for these costs according to its typical accounting policies. Interest costs will also be incurred in connection with the financing arrangement. These should be separately shown and may be deferred.

EXAMPLE 3

On 1/1/19X1, a sponsor borrows $100,000 from another company and gives the inventory as collateral for the loan. The entry is:

Cash	100,000	
Liability		100,000

Note that a sale is *not* recorded and the inventory remains on the books of the sponsor. In effect, inventory serves as collateral for a loan.

On 12/31/19X1, the sponsor pays back the other company. The collateralized inventory item is returned. The interest rate on the loan was 8%. Storage costs were $2,000. The entry is:

Liability	100,000	
Deferred Interest	8,000	
Storage Expense	2,000	
Cash		110,000

Typically, most of the product in the financing arrangement is eventually used or sold by the sponsor. However, in some cases, small amounts of the product may be sold by the financing entity to other parties.

The entity that gives financing to the sponsor is usually an existing creditor, nonbusiness entity, or trust. It is also possible that the financier may have been established for the *only* purpose of providing financing for the sponsor.

Footnote disclosure should be made of the particulars of the product financing arrangement.

FRANCHISE FEE REVENUE

According to FASB 45, the franchiser can only record revenue from the initial sale of the franchise when all significant services and obligations applicable to the sale have been substantially performed. Substantial performance is indicated by:

- Absence of intent to give cash refunds or relieve the accounts receivable due from the franchisee

- Nothing material remains to be done by the franchiser
- Initial services have been rendered

The earliest date that substantial performance can occur is the franchisee's commencement of operations unless special circumstances can be shown to exist. In the case where it is probable that the franchiser will ultimately repurchase the franchise, the initial fee must be deferred and treated as a reduction of the repurchase price.

If revenue is deferred, the related expenses must be deferred for later matching in the year in which the revenue is recognized. This is illustrated below.

Year of initial fee:

Cash

    Deferred Revenue

Deferred Expenses

    Cash

Year when substantial performance takes place:

Deferred Revenue

    Revenue

Expenses

    Deferred Expenses

In the case where the initial fee includes both initial services and property (real or personal), there should be an appropriate allocation based on fair market values.

When part of the initial franchise fee applies to *tangible property* (e.g., equipment, signs, inventory), revenue recognition is based on the fair value of the assets. Revenue recognition may take place prior to or after recognizing the portion of the fee related to initial services. For instance, part of the fee for equipment may be recognized at the time title passes with the balance of the fee being recorded as revenue when future services are performed.

Recurring franchise fees are recognized as earned and receivable. Related costs are expensed. An exception does exist to this revenue recognition practice. If the price charged for the continuing services or goods to the franchisee is below the price charged to third parties, it indicates that the initial franchise fee was in essence a partial *prepayment* for the recurring franchise fee. In this situation, part of the initial fee has to be deferred and recognized as an adjustment of the revenue from the sale of goods and services at bargain prices.

When probability exists that continuing franchise fees will not cover the cost of the continuing services and provide for a reasonable profit to the franchiser, the part of the initial franchise fee should be deferred to satisfy the deficiency and amortized over the life of the franchise. The deferred amount should be adequate to meet future costs and generate an adequate profit on the recurring services. This situation may occur if the continuing fees are minimal relative to services provided or the franchisee has the privilege of making bargain purchases for a particular time period.

Unearned franchise fees are recorded at present value. Where a part of the initial fee constitutes a nonrefundable amount for services already performed, revenue should be accordingly recognized.

The initial franchise fee is *not* typically allocated to specific franchiser services before all services are performed. This practice can only be done if actual transaction prices are available for individual services.

If the franchiser sells equipment and inventory to the franchisee at no profit, a receivable and payable is recorded. *No* revenue or expense recognition is given.

In the case of a repossessed franchise, refunded amounts to the franchisee reduce current revenue. If there is no refund, the franchiser books additional revenue for the consideration retained which was not previously recorded. In either situation, *prospective* accounting treatment is given for the repossession. Warning: Do *not* adjust previously recorded revenue for the repossession.

Indirect costs of an operating and recurring nature are expensed immediately. Future costs to be incurred are accrued no later than the period in which related revenue is recognized. Bad debts applicable to expected uncollectibility of franchise fees should be recorded in the year of revenue recognition.

Installment or cost recovery accounting may be employed to account for franchise fee revenue *only* if a long collection period is involved and future uncollectibility of receivables cannot be accurately predicted.

Footnote disclosure is required of:

- Outstanding obligations under agreement
- Segregation of franchise fee revenue between initial and continuing

RESEARCH AND DEVELOPMENT COSTS

Research is the testing done in search for a new product, service, process, or technique. Research can also be aimed at deriving a material improvement to an existing product or process. Development is the translation of the research into a design for the new product or process. Development may also result in material improvement in an existing product or process. As per FASB 2, research and development (R&D) costs are expensed as incurred. However, R&D costs incurred under contract for others that is reimburseable are charged to a receivable account rather than expensed. Further, materials, equipment, and intangibles purchased from others that have alternative future benefit in R&D activities are capitalized. The depreciation or amortization on such assets are classified as R&D expense. If no alternative future use exists, the costs should be expensed.

R&D cost includes the salaries of personnel involved in R&D activities. R&D cost also includes a rational allocation of indirect (general and administrative) costs. If a group of assets are acquired, allocation should be made to those that relate to R&D efforts. When a business combination is accounted for as a purchase, R&D costs are assigned their fair market value.

Expenditures paid to others to conduct R&D activities for the company are expensed.

Examples of R&D activities include:

- Formulation and design of product alternatives and testing thereof
- Laboratory research
- Engineering functions until the point the product satisfies operational requirements for manufacture
- Design of tools, molds, and dies involving new technology
- Pre-production prototypes and models
- Pilot plant cost

Examples of activities that are not for R&D include:

- Quality control
- Seasonal design changes
- Legal costs of obtaining a patent
- Market research
- Identifying breakdowns during commercial production
- Engineering follow-up in the initial stages of commercial production
- Rearrangement and start-up activities including design and construction engineering
- Recurring and continuous efforts to improve the product
- Commercial use of the product

FASB 2 does not apply to regulated industries and to the extractive industries (e.g., mining).

According to FASB 86, costs incurred for computer software to be sold, leased, or otherwise marketed are expensed as R&D costs until technological feasibility exists as indicated by the development of a detailed program or working model. After technological feasibility exists, software production costs should be deferred and recorded at the lower of unamortized cost or net realizable value. Examples of such costs include debugging the software, improvements to subroutines, and adaptions for other uses. Amortization begins when the product is available for customer release. The amortization expense should be based on the higher of:

- The percent of current revenue to total revenue from the product
- The straight line amortization amount

As per FASB 68, if a business enters into an arrangement with other parties to fund the R&D efforts, the nature of the obligation must be determined. In the case where the entity has an obligation to repay the funds irrespective of the R&D results, a liability has to be recognized with the related R&D expense. The journal entries are:

Cash

    Liability

Research and Development Expense

    Cash

A liability does not exist when the transfer of financial risk involved to the other party is substantive and genuine. If the financial risk applicable with R&D is transferred because repayment depends only on the R&D possessing future economic benefit, the company accounts for its obligation as a contract to conduct R&D for others. In this case R&D costs are capitalized and revenue is recognized as earned and becomes billable under the contract. Footnote disclosure is made of the terms of the R&D agreement, the amount of compensation earned, and the costs incurred under the contract.

When repayment of loans or advances to the company depends only on R&D results, such amounts are deemed R&D costs incurred by the company and charged to expense.

If warrants or other financial instruments are issued in an R&D arrangement, the company records part of the proceeds to be provided by the other parties as paid-in-capital based on their fair market value on the arrangement date.

EARNINGS PER SHARE (EPS)

APB 15 requires that earnings per share must be computed by publicly held companies. It is not required for nonpublic companies. In a simple capital structure, no potentially dilutive securities exist. (Potentially dilutive means the security will be converted into common stock at a later date reducing EPS). Thus, only one EPS figure is necessary. In a complex capital structure, dilutive securities exist requiring dual presentation. The dual presentation of EPS for all periods presented is:

$$\text{Primary EPS} = \frac{\text{Net Income} - \text{Preferred Dividend}}{\text{Weighted-Average Common Stock Outstanding} + \text{Common Stock Equivalents}}$$

$$\text{Fully Diluted EPS} = \frac{\text{Net Income} - \text{Preferred Dividend}}{\text{Weighted-Average Common Stock Outstanding} + \text{Common Stock Equivalents} + \text{Other Fully Diluted Securities}}$$

Fully diluted EPS reflects the *maximum* potential dilution per share on a prospective basis.

Weighted-average common stock shares outstanding takes into account the number of months in which those shares were outstanding.

EXAMPLE 4

On 1/1/19X1, 10,000 shares were issued. On 4/1/19X1, 2,000 of those shares were bought back by the company. The weighted-average common stock outstanding is:

$$(10,000 \times 3/12) + (8,000 \times 9/12) = 8,500 \text{ shares}$$

The inclusion of common stock equivalents in determining EPS is an example of theoretical substance over legal form. Although the common stock equivalent (e.g., stock option) is not legally common stock, it is treated as such since in theoretical substance the common stock equivalent is common stock. Common stock equivalents are securities which can become common stock at a later date and are shown in both primary EPS and fully diluted EPS.

Common stock equivalents include:

- Stock options
- Stock warrants
- Subscribed stock
- Two-class common stock
- Contingent shares only related to the passage of time
- Convertible securities (convertible bonds, convertible preferred stock) when the yield at the time of issuance is less than $2/3$ of the average Aa bond yield at the time of issuance. Once a convertible security is defined as a common stock equivalent, it continues as such. Aa bonds are defined by Standard and Poor's and Moody's as of the highest quality. For zero-coupon bonds, the effective yield is the interest rate necessary to discount the maturity value of the bond to its present value. This rate is then used to determine common stock equivalent by company by comparing it to the $2/3$ average yield. In the situation where convertible securities are issued in a foreign country, we use the most comparable long-term yield in that country in performing the cash yield test.

Note: Although stock options are *always* deemed a common stock equivalent, they are only included in computing EPS if the market price of common stock is greater than the option price for substantially all of the last three months of the year. In this case, we assume the stock options were exercised at the beginning of the year (or at time of issuance, if later). While convertible securities are classified as common stock equivalents based on the circumstances at time of issue, warrants are classified according to the conditions at each period.

In computing EPS, common stock equivalents are included if they have a dilutive effect. Dilutive effect means that inclusion of a common stock equivalent reduced EPS by 3% or more in the aggregate and is applied by type of security. The 3% dilution also relates to presenting fully diluted EPS. Fully diluted EPS is also shown if it reduces primary EPS by 3% or more. Antidilutive securities that increase EPS are not shown in the EPS computation because they will increase EPS which violates conservatism.

When shares are issued because of a stock dividend or stock split, the computation of weighted-average common stock shares outstanding mandates retroactive adjustment as if the shares were outstanding at the beginning of the year.

The common stock equivalency of options and warrants is determined using the treasury stock method. Options and warrants are assumed exercised at the beginning of the year (or at time of issuances, if later). The proceeds received are assumed used to: (1) reacquire common stock at the average market price for the year as long as it does not exceed 20% of shares outstanding at year-end, (2) with the balance remaining reduce long or short-term debt, and (3) with any balance still remaining invest in U. S. government securities and commercial paper.

We assume the exercise of options only when the market price of stock exceeds the exercise price for three consecutive months ending with the year-end month.

In computing fully diluted EPS, the treasury stock method is modified in that the market price at the end of the accounting period is used if it is higher than the average market price for the period.

EXAMPLE 5

One hundred shares are under option at an option price of $10. The average market price of stock is $25. The common stock equivalent is 60 shares as calculated below:

Issued shares from option	100 shares × $10	=	$1,000
Less: Treasury shares	40 shares × $25	=	$1,000
Common Stock Equivalent	60 shares		

Convertible securities are accounted for using the "if converted method." The convertible securities are assumed converted at the beginning of the earliest year presented or date of security issuance. Interest or dividends on them are added back to net income since the securities are considered part of equity in the denominator of the EPS calculation.

Other fully diluted securities are defined as convertible securities that did not meet the 2/3 test. They are included only in the calculation of fully diluted EPS. Thus, fully diluted EPS will be a lower figure than primary EPS because of the greater shares in the denominator. Contingent issuance of shares in computing fully diluted EPS is assumed to have occurred at the beginning of the year, or at the time of issuance if later. Fully diluted EPS is a pro forma presentation showing what EPS would be if *all* potential contingencies of common stock issuances having a dilutive effect took place.

To accomplish the fullest dilution in arriving at fully diluted EPS, an assumption is made that all common stock issuances on exercise of options or warrants during the period were made at the start of the year. The higher of the closing price or the average price of common stock is used in determining the number of shares of treasury stock to be purchased from the proceeds received upon issuance of the options. If the ending market price exceeds the average market price, the assumed treasury shares acquired will be lessened resulting in higher assumed outstanding shares with the resulting decrease in EPS.

Net income less preferred dividends is in the numerator of the EPS fraction representing earnings available to common stockholders. On cumulative preferred stock, preferred dividends for the current year are subtracted out whether or not paid. Further, preferred dividends are only subtracted out for the current year. Thus, if preferred dividends in arrears were for five years all of which were paid plus the sixth year dividend, only the sixth year dividend (current year) is deducted. Note that preferred dividends for each of the prior years would have been deducted in those years.

In computing EPS, preferred dividends are only subtracted out on preferred stock that was not included as a common stock equivalent. If the preferred stock is a common stock equivalent, the preferred dividend would *not* be subtracted out since the equivalency of preferred shares into common shares are included in the denominator.

If convertible bonds are included in the denominator of EPS, they are considered as equivalent to common shares. Thus, interest expense (net of tax) has to be added back in the numerator.

Disclosure of EPS should include information on the capital structure, explanation of the computation of EPS, identification of common stock equivalents, assumptions made, and number of shares converted. Rights and privileges of the securities should also be disclosed. Such disclosure includes dividend and participation rights, call prices, conversation ratios, and sinking fund requirements.

A stock conversion occurring during the year, or between year-end and the audit report date may have materially affected EPS if it had taken place at the beginning of the year. Thus, supplementary footnote disclosure should be made reflecting on an "as if" basis what the effects of these conversions would have had on EPS if they were made at the start of the accounting period.

If a subsidiary has been acquired under the purchase accounting method during the year, the weighted-average shares outstanding for the year are used from the purchase date. However, if a pooling of interests occurred, the weighted-average shares outstanding for all the years are presented.

If common stock or a common stock equivalent are sold during the year and the monies obtained to buy back debt or retire preferred stock, there should be a presentation of supplemental EPS figures.

When comparative financial statements are presented, there is a retroactive adjustment for stock splits and stock dividends. Assume in 19X5 a 10% stock dividend occurs. The weighted-average shares used for previous years' computations have to be increased by 10% to make EPS data comparable.

When a prior period adjustment occurs that causes a restatement of previous years' earnings, EPS should also be restated.

EXAMPLE 6

The stockholders' equity section of ABC Company's balance sheet as of 12/31/19X3 appears below:

$1.20 cumulative preferred stock (par value of $10 per share, issued 1,200,000 shares, of which 500,000 were converted to common stock and 700,000 shares are outstanding)	$ 7,000,000
Common stock (par value of $2.50, issued and outstanding 6,000,000 shares)	15,000,000
Paid-in-capital	20,000,000
Retained earnings	32,000,000
Total stockholders' equity	$74,000,000

On 5/1/19X3, ABC Company acquired XYZ Company in a pooling-of-interest. For each of XYZ Company's 800,000 shares, ABC issued one of its own shares in the exchange.

On 4/1/19X3, ABC Company issued 500,000 shares of convertible preferred stock at $38 per share. The preferred stock is convertible to common stock at the rate of two shares of common for each share of preferred. On 9/1/19X3, 300,000 shares and on 11/1/19X3, 200,000 shares of preferred stock were converted into common stock. The market price of the convertible preferred stock is $38 per share.

During August, ABC Company granted stock options to executives to buy 100,000 shares of common stock at an option price of $15 per share. The market price of stock at year-end was $20.

ABC Company has 8%, $10,000,000 convertible bonds payable issued at fair value in 19X1. The conversion rate is four shares of common stock for each $100 bond. No conversions have occurred yet.

The Aa corporate bond yield is 10%. The tax rate is 34%. Net income for the year is $12,000,000.

The convertible bonds are not common stock equivalents because the interest rate is 8% is more than two thirds of the Aa bond yield of 10%.

The convertible preferred stock is a common stock equivalent because its yield of 3.16% ($1.20/$38.00) is less than two thirds of the Aa bond yield of 10%.

Note: Stock options are always considered common stock equivalents.

Shares outstanding from 1/1/19X3 (including
800,000 shares issued upon acquisition of
XYZ Company): 6,000,000 − 1,000,000   5,000,000

Shares issued upon conversion of 500,000
shares of preferred stock to common stock:

Issued 9/1/19X3 600,000 × 4/12	200,000	
Issued 11/1/19X3 400,000 × 2/12	66,667	266,667

Total shares of common stock   5,266,667

Common stock equivalents:

Convertible preferred stock:

500,000 shares of convertible preferred issued
on 4/1/19X3

    $500,000 \times 2 \times 9/12$ 750,000

Less: Common shares applicable to 500,000
preferred shares converted during the year   266,667

Common stock equivalents of convertible
preferred stock   483,333

Common stock equivalents of stock options:

Option	$100,000 \times \$15 =$	$\$1,500,000$	
Less: Treasury Stock	$75,000 \times \$20 =$	$1,500,000$	

Common stock
equivalent of
stock options   25,000   25,000

Weighted-average common stock outstanding
plus common stock equivalents for primary
EPS   5,775,000

Convertible bonds payable assumed converted
at 1/1/19X3 ($10,000,000/$100) = 100,000
bonds 100,000 bonds × 4 shares per bond   400,000

Weighted-average common stock outstanding
plus common stock equivalents plus other
fully diluted securities for fully diluted EPS   6,125,000

Primary EPS equals:

$$\frac{\$12,000,000}{5,775,000 \text{ shares}} = \underline{\$2.08}$$

Fully Diluted EPS equals:

$$\frac{\$12,000,000 + \$528,000^*}{6,175,000 \text{ shares}} = \underline{\$2.03}$$

$^*\$10,000,000 \times 8\% = \$800,000 \times 66\% = \underline{\$528,000}$

6

Financial Statement Reporting: The Balance Sheet

On the balance sheet, the financial officer is concerned with the accounting for and reporting of assets, liabilities, and stockholders' equity.

ASSETS

An asset is recorded at the price paid plus related costs of placing the asset in service (e.g., freight, insurance, installation). If an asset is bought in exchange for a liability, the asset is recorded at the present value of the payments.

EXAMPLE 1

A machine was acquired by taking out a loan requiring ten $10,000 payments. Each payment includes principal and interest. The interest rate is 10%. While the total payments (principal and interest) are $100,000, the present value will be less since the machine is recorded at the present value of the payments. The asset would be recorded at $61,450 ($10,000 × 6.145). The factor is obtained from the present value of annuity table for $n = 10$, $i = 10\%$.

Note: The asset is recorded at the principal amount excluding the interest payments. If an asset is acquired for stock, the asset is recorded at the fair value of the stock issued. If it is impossible to ascertain the fair market value of the stock (e.g., closely held company), the asset will be recorded at its appraised value.

75

Unearned discounts (except for quantity or cost), finance charges, and interest included in the face of receivables should be subtracted to obtain the net receivable.

Some of the major current and noncurrent assets include:

- Accounts receivable
- Inventory
- Fixed assets
- Intangibles

Accounts Receivable

When accounts receivable are assigned, the owner of the receivables borrows cash from a lender in the form of a note payable. The accounts receivable acts as collateral. New receivables substitute for receivables collected. The assignment of accounts receivable typically requires the incurrence of a financing charge as well as interest expense on the note.

At a particular date, the transferer's equity in the assigned receivables equals the difference between the accounts receivable assigned and the balance of the line ($5,000). When payments on the receivables are received, they are remitted by the company to the lending institution to reduce the liability. Assignment is on a non-notification basis to customers. It is made with recourse, where the company has to make good for uncollectible customer accounts.

EXAMPLE 2

On 4/1/19X1, X Company assigns accounts receivable totaling $600,000 to A Bank as collateral for a $400,000 note. X Company will continue to receive customer remissions since the customers are not notified of the assignment. There is a 2% finance charge of the accounts receivable assigned. Interest on the note is 13%. Monthly settlement of the cash received from assigned receivables is made. During the month of April there were collections of $360,000 of assigned receivables less cash discounts of $5,000. Sales returns were $10,000. On 5/1/19X1, April remissions were made plus accrued interest. In May, the balance of the assigned accounts receivable was collected less $4,000 that were uncollectible. On 6/1/19X1, the balance due was remitted to the bank plus interest for May. The journal entries follow:

4/1/19X1

Cash	388,000	
Finance Charge (2% × $600,000)	12,000	
Accounts Receivable Assigned	600,000	
Notes Payable		400,000
Accounts Receivable		600,000

During April:

Cash	355,000	
Sales Discount	5,000	
Sales Returns	10,000	
Accounts Receivable Assigned		370,000

5/1/19X1

Interest Expense	4,333*	
Notes Payable	355,000	
Cash		359,333

*$400,000 \times .13 \times 1/12 = \$4,333$

During May:

Cash	226,000	
Allowance for Bad Debts	4,000	
Accounts Receivable Assigned ($600,000 $- $370,000)		230,000

6/1/19X1

Interest Expense	488*	
Notes Payable ($400,000 $- $355,000)	45,000	
Cash		45,488

*$45,000 \times .13 \times 1/12 = \$488$

In a factoring of accounts receivable, the receivables are in effect sold to a finance company. The factor buys the accounts receivable at a discount from face value, usually at a discount of 6%. Customers are typically notified. Factoring is usually done without recourse, where the risk of uncollectibility of the customer's account rests with the financing institution. Billing and collection is typically done by the factor. On a factoring arrangement, the factor charges a commission of from ¾% to 1½% of the net receivables acquired. The entry is:

Cash (proceeds)

Loss on Sale of Receivables

Due from Factor (proceeds kept by factor to cover possible adjustments such as sales discounts, sales returns and allowances)

    Accounts Receivable (face amount of receivables)

Factoring is normally a continuous process. The seller of the goods receives orders and transmits the purchase orders to the factor for approval; on approval, the goods are shipped; the factor advances the money to the seller; the buyers pay the factor when payment is due, and the factor periodically remits any excess reserve to the seller of the goods. Once a routine is established, a continuous circular flow of goods and funds takes place among the seller, the buyers, and the factor. Once the agreement is in force, funds from this source are spontaneous.

EXAMPLE 3

T Company factors $200,000 of accounts receivable. There is a 4% finance charge. The factor retains 6% of the accounts receivable. Appropriate journal entries are:

Cash	180,000	
Loss on Sale of Receivables (4% $\times$ $200,000)	8,000	
Due from Factor (6% $\times$ $200,000)	12,000	
Accounts Receivable		200,000

Factors provide a needed and dependable source of income for small manufacturers and service businesses.

EXAMPLE 4

You need an additional $100,000. You are considering a factoring arrangement. The factor is willing to buy the accounts receivable and advance the invoice amount less a 4% factoring commission on the receivables purchased. Sales are on 30-day terms. A 14% interest rate will be charged on the total invoice price and deducted in advance. With the factoring arrangement, the credit department will be eliminated, reducing monthly credit expenses by $1,500. Also, bad debt losses of 8% on the factored amount will be avoided.

To net $100,000, the amount of accounts receivable to be factored would be:

$$\frac{\$100,000}{1 - (0.04 + 0.14)} = \frac{\$100,000}{0.82} = \underline{\$121,951}$$

The effective interest rate on the factoring arrangement is:

$$\frac{0.14}{0.82} = \underline{17.07\%}$$

The annual total dollar cost is

Interest (0.14 $\times$ $121,951)	$17,073
Factoring (0.04 $\times$ $121,951)	4,878
Total cost	$21,951

According to FASB 77, a sale is recorded for the transfer of receivables with recourse if *all* of the following criteria are satisfied:

1. The transferer gives up control of the future economic benefits applicable to the receivables (e.g., repurchase right).

2. The liability of the transferer under the recourse provisions is estimable.

3. The transferee cannot require the transferer to repurchase receivables unless there is a recourse provision in the contract.

When the transfer is treated as a sale, gain or loss is recognized for the difference between the selling price and the net receivables. The selling price includes normal servicing fees of the transferer and appropriate probable adjustments (e.g., debtor's failure to pay on time, effects of prepayment, and defects in the transferred receivable). Net receivables equals gross receivables plus finance and service charges minus unearned finance and service charges.

In the case when selling price varies during the term of the receivables due to a variable interest rate provision, the selling price is estimated with the use of an appropriate "going market interest rate" at the transfer date. Later changes in the rate causes a change in estimated selling price, not in interest income or interest expense.

If one of the aforementioned criteria is not satisfied, a liability is recognized for the proceeds received.

Footnote disclosure includes:

• Amount received by transferer

• Balance of the receivables at the balance sheet date

Inventory

Inventory may be valued at the lower of cost or market value. Specialized inventory methods may be used such as retail, retail lower of cost or market, retail LIFO, and dollar value LIFO. Losses on purchase commitments should be recognized in the accounts.

If ending inventory is overstated, cost of sales is understated, and net income is overstated. If beginning inventory is overstated, cost of sales is overstated, and net income is understated.

Lower of Cost or Market Value Method. Inventories are recorded at the lower of cost or market value for conservatism purposes applied on a total basis, category basis, or individual basis. The method used must be consistently applied.

If cost is below market value (replacement cost), cost is taken. If market value is below cost, we start with market value. However, market value cannot exceed the ceiling which is net realizable value (selling price less costs to complete and dispose). If it does, the ceiling is chosen. Further, market value cannot be less than the floor which is net realizable value less a normal profit margin. If market value is less than the floor, the floor value is used. Of course, market value is used when it lies between the ceiling and floor. The following diagram may be helpful:

EXAMPLE 5

The lower of cost or market value method is being applied on an item-by-item basis. The circled figure is the appropriate valuation.

Product	Cost	Market	Ceiling	Floor
A	(\$5)	\$7	\$9	\$6
B	14	12	(11)	7
C	18	(15)	16	12
D	20	12	18	(16)
E	(6)	5	12	7

Note that in case E, market value of \$5 was originally selected. The market value of \$5 exceeded the floor of \$7, so the floor value would be used. However, if after applying the lower cost or market value rule, the valuation derived (\$7) exceeds the cost (\$6), the cost figure is more conservative and thus is used.

Note that if market (replacement cost) is below the original cost but the selling price has not declined, no loss should be recognized. To do so would create an abnormal profit margin in the future period.

The lower of cost or market value method is not used with LIFO since under LIFO current revenue is matched against current costs.

Retail Method. The retail method is used by department stores and other large retail businesses. These businesses usually carry inventory items at retail selling price. The retail method is used to estimate the ending inventory at cost by employing a cost to retail (selling price) ratio. The ending inventory is first determined at selling price and then converted to cost. Markups and markdowns are both considered in arriving at the cost to retail ratio resulting in a higher ending inventory than the retail lower of cost or market value method.

Retail Lower of Cost or Market Value Method (Conventional Retail). This is a modification of the retail method and is preferable to it. In computing the cost to retail ratio, markups but not markdowns are considered resulting in a lower inventory figure.

The following example illustrates the accounting difference between the retail method and the retail lower of cost or market value method.

EXAMPLE 6

ILLUSTRATION

Retail Method vs. Retail Lower of Cost or Market Value Method

		Cost	Retail
Inventory. 1/1		16,000	30,000
Purchases		30,000	60,000
Purchase Returns		(5,000)	(10,000)
Purchase Discount		(2,000)	
Freight In		1,000	
Markups	25,000		
Markup Cancellations	5,000		20,000
Total		40,000	100,000 (40%)
Markdowns	22,000		
Markdown Cancellations	2,000		20,000
Cost of Goods Available		40,000	80,000 (50%)
Deduct :			
Sales	55,000		
Less: Sales Returns	5,000		50,000
Inventory- Retail			30,000
Retail Method:			
At Cost 50% x 30,000			15,000
Retail Lower of Cost or			
Market Method:			
40% x 30,000			12,000

Retail LIFO. In computing ending inventory, the mechanics of the retail method are basically followed. Beginning inventory is excluded and both markups and markdowns are included in computing the cost to retail ratio. A decrease in inventory during the period is deducted from the most recently added layer and then subtracted from layers in the inverse order of addition. A retail price index is used in restating inventory.

EXAMPLE 7

ILLUSTRATION

Retail LIFO

Retail price indices follow:

19X7	100
19X8	104
19X9	110

[Handwritten worksheet]

19x8   Cost   Retail
Inventory-Jan.1 (Base Inv.)   80,000   130,000
Purchases   240,000   410,000
Markups   10,000
Markdowns   (20,000)
Total (exclude Beg. Inv.)   240,000   400,000   60%
Total (include Beg. Inv.)   320,000   530,000
Sales   389,600
19x8 Inv.-End-Retail   140,400

Cost Basis
19x8 Inventory in terms of
19x7 Prices 140,400 ÷ 1.04   135,000
19x7 Base   80,000   130,000   130,000 x 1.04   135,200
19x8 Layer in 19x7 Prices   5,000
19x8 Layer in 19x8 Prices   5,200   5,000 x 1.04   5,200
                                                                                    140,400
19x8 LIFO Cost 60% x 5,200   3,120
                                     83,120   140,400

19x9   Cost   Retail
Inventory- Jan. 1   83,120   140,400
Purchases   260,400   430,000
Markups   20,000
Markdowns   (30,000)
Total (exclude Beg. Inv.)   260,400   420,000   62%
Total (include Beg. Inv.)   343,520   560,400
Sales   408,600
19x9 Inventory-End at Retail   151,800

Cost Basis
19x9 Inventory in 19x7 Prices
    151,800 ÷ 1.10   138,000
19x7 Base   80,000   130,000   130,000 x 1.10   143,000
Excess over Base Year   8,000
19x8 layer in 19x8 Prices   3,120   5,000   5,000 x 1.10   5,500
19x9 layer in 19x7 Prices   3,000
19x9 layer in 19x9 Prices   3,300   3,000 x 1.10   3,300

19x9 Increase in 19x9 Prices
    LIFO Cost 62% x 3,300   2,046
                                     85,166   151,800   151,800

Dollar Value LIFO. Dollar value LIFO is an extension of the historical cost principle. The method aggregates dollars instead of units into homogeneous groupings. The method assumes that an inventory decrease came from the last year.

The procedures under dollar value LIFO follow:

1. Restate ending inventory in the current year into base dollars by applying a price index.

2. Subtract the year 0 inventory in base dollars from the current year's inventory in base dollars.

3. Multiply the incremental inventory in the current year in base dollars by the price index to obtain the incremental inventory in current dollars.

4. Obtain the reportable inventory for the current year by adding to the year 0 inventory in base dollars the incremental inventory for the current year in current dollars.

EXAMPLE 8

At 12/31/19X1, the ending inventory is $130,000 and the price index is 1.30. The base inventory on 1/1/19X1 was $80,000. The 12/31/19X1 inventory is computed below:

12/31/19X1 inventory in base dollars $130,000/1.30	$100,000
1/1/19X1 beginning base inventory	80,000
19X1 Increment in base dollars	$20,000
19X1 Increment in current year dollars	× 1.3
	$26,000
Inventory in base dollars	$80,000
Increment in current year dollars	26,000
Reportable inventory	$106,000

Losses on Purchase Commitments. Significant net losses on purchase commitments should be recognized at the end of the reporting period.

EXAMPLE 9

In 19X8, ABC Company committed itself to buy raw materials at $1.20 per pound. At the end of the year, before fulfilling the purchase commitment, the price of the materials dropped to $1.00 per pound. Conservatism dictates that a loss on purchase commitment of $.20 per pound be recognized in 19X8. Loss on Purchase Commitment is debited and Allowance for Purchase Commitment Loss is credited.

Inventory Valuation Difficulties. While the basics of inventory cost measurement is easily stated, difficulties arise because of cost allocation problems. For example, idle capacity costs and abnormal spoilage costs may have to be written-off immediately in the current year instead of being allocated as an element of inventory valuation. Furthermore, general and administrative expenses are inventoried when they specifically relate to production activity.

Inventory Stated at Market Value in Excess of Cost. In unusual circumstances, inventories may be stated in excess of cost. This may occur when there is no basis for cost apportionment (e.g., meat packing industry). Market value may also be used when immediate marketability exists at quoted prices (e.g., certain precious metals or agricultural products). Disclosure is necessary when inventory is stated above cost.

Fixed Assets

A fixed asset is recorded at its fair market value or the fair market value of the consideration given, whichever is more clearly evident.

The cost of buying an asset includes all costs necessary to put that asset into existing use and location, including insurance, taxes, installation, freight, and breaking-in costs (e.g., instruction).

Additions to an existing building (such as constructing a new garage for the building) are capitalized and depreciated over the shorter of the life of the addition or the life of the building. Rearrangement and reinstallation costs are capitalized when future benefit is created. If not, they should be expensed. Obsolete fixed assets should be reclassified from property, plant and equipment to other assets and shown at salvage value reflecting a loss.

When two or more assets are bought for one price, cost is allocated to the assets based on their relative fair market values. If an old building is demolished to make way for the construction of a new building, the costs of demolishing the old building are charged to the land account.

Self-constructed assets are recorded at the incremental costs to build assuming idle capacity. However, they should not be recorded at more than the outside price.

EXAMPLE 10

Incremental costs to self-construct equipment is $12,000. The equipment could have been bought outside for $9,000. The journal entry is:

Equipment	9,000	
Loss	3,000	
Cash		12,000

A donated fixed asset to the company should be reflected at fair market value. The entry is to charge fixed assets and credit paid-in-capital (donation).

Note: Fixed assets cannot be written-up except in the case of a discovery on a natural resource or in a purchase combination. In a discovery of a natural resource (e.g., oil), the land account is debited at appraised value and then depleted by the units of production method.

Land improvements (e.g., driveways, sidewalks, fencing) are capitalized and depreciated over useful life. Land held for investment purposes or for a future plant site should be classified under investments and not fixed assets.

Ordinary repairs to an asset (e.g., tune-up for a car) are expensed because they have a life of less than one year.

Extraordinary repairs are capitalized since they benefit a period of one year or more (e.g., new motor for a car). Extraordinary repairs add to an asset's life or make the asset more useful. Capital expenditures improve the quality or quantity of services to be derived from the asset.

Depreciation is the allocation of the historical cost of a fixed asset into expense over the period benefited to result in matching expense against revenue.

Fractional year depreciation is computing depreciation when the asset is acquired during the year. A proration is required.

EXAMPLE 11

On 10/1/19X7, a fixed asset costing $10,000 with a salvage value of $1,000 and a life of 5 years is acquired.

Depreciation expense for 19X8 using the sum-of-the-years' digits method is:

1/1/19X8 − 9/30/19X8 5/15 × $9,000 × 9/12	$2,250
10/1/19X8 − 12/31/19X8 4/15 × $9,000 × 3/12	600
	$2,850

Depreciation expense for 19X8 using double declining balance is:

Year	Computation	Depreciation	Book Value
0			$10,000
10/1/19X7 - 12/31/19X7	3/12 × $10,000 × 40%	$1,000	9,000
1/1/19X8 - 12/31/19X8	$9,000 × 40%	3,600	5,400

Group and composite depreciation methods involve similar accounting. The group method is used for similar assets while the composite method is used for dissimilar assets. Both methods are generally accepted. There is one accumulated depreciation account for the entire group. The depreciation rate equals:

Depreciation

Gross Cost

Depreciation expense for a period equals:

Depreciation Rate × Gross Cost

The depreciable life equals:

Depreciable Cost

Depreciation

When an asset is sold in the group, the entry is:

Cash (proceeds received)

Accumulated Depreciation (plug figure)

Fixed Asset (cost)

Note that upon sale of a fixed asset in the group the difference between the proceeds received and the cost of the fixed asset is plugged to accumulated depreciation. No gain or loss is recognized upon the sale. The only time a gain or loss would be recognized is if the entire assets were sold.

EXAMPLE 12

Calculations for composite depreciation follow:

Asset	Cost	Salvage	Depreciable Cost	Life	Depreciation
A	$ 25,000	$ 5,000	$ 20,000	10	$ 2,000
B	40,000	2,000	38,000	5	7,600
C	52,000	4,000	48,000	6	8,000
	$117,000	$11,000	$106,000		$17,600

Composite Rate:

$$\frac{\$17,600}{\$117,000} = 15.04\%$$

Composite Life:

$$\frac{\$106,000}{\$17,600} = 6.02 \text{ years}$$

The entry to record depreciation is:

Depreciation	17,600	
Accumulated Depreciation		17,600

The entry to sell asset B for $36,000 is:

Cash	36,000	
Accumulated Depreciation	4,000	
Fixed Asset		40,000

Capitalized interest: Disclosure should be given of the interest capitalized and expensed. Interest incurred on borrowed funds is expensed.

However, interest on borrowed funds is capitalized to the asset account and then amortized in the following cases:

- Self-constructed assets for the company's own use. To justify interest capitalization, a time period must exist for assets to be prepared for use.

- Assets for sale or lease constructed as discrete, individual projects (e.g., real estate development)

- Assets purchased for the entity's own use by arrangements requiring a down payment and/or progress payments.

Interest is *not* capitalized for:

- Assets in use or ready for use
- Assets not in use and not being prepared for use
- Assets produced in large volume or on a recurring basis

Interest capitalized is based on the average accumulated expenditures for that asset. The interest rate used is either:

- Interest rate on the specific borrowing
- Weighted-average interest rate of corporate debt

EXAMPLE 13

In the purchase of a qualifying asset, a company expends $100,000 on January 1, 19X1 and $150,000 on March 1, 19X1. The average accumulated expenditures for 19X1 are computed as follows:

Expenditure	Number of Months	Average Expenditure
$100,000	12	$100,000
150,000	10	125,000
$250,000		$225,000

The interest capitalization period begins when the following exist:

- Interest is being incurred
- Expenditures have been incurred
- Work is taking place to make the asset ready for intended use. These activities are not restricted to actual construction but may also include administrative and technical activities prior to the time of construction. Included are costs of unforeseen events occurring during construction. Examples: Labor unrest and litigation.

The capitalization period ends when the asset is substantially complete and usable. When an asset consists of individual elements (e.g., condominium units), the capitalization period of interest costs applicable to one of the separate units ends when the particular unit is materially finished and usable. Capitalization of interest is not continued when construction ends, except for brief or unanticipated delays.

When the total asset must be finished to be useful, interest capitalization continues until the total asset is substantially finished. Example: A manufacturing plant where sequential production activities must take place.

Nonmonetary exchange of assets: Nonmonetary transactions covered under APB Opinion 29 primarily deal with exchanges or distributions of fixed assets.

In an exchange of similar assets (e.g., truck for truck), the new asset received is recorded at the book value of the old asset plus the cash paid. Since book value of the old asset is the basis to charge the new asset, no gain is possible. However, a loss is possible because in no case can the new asset exceed the fair market value of the new asset.

In an exchange of dissimilar assets (e.g., truck for machine), the new asset is recorded at the fair market value of the old asset plus the cash paid. Thus, a gain or loss may arise because the fair market value of the old asset will be different than the book value of the old asset. However, the new asset cannot be shown at more than its fair market value. Fair market value in a nonmonetary exchange may be based upon:

- Quoted market price
- Appraisal
- Cash transaction for similar items

EXAMPLE 14

An old fixed asset which cost $10,000 with accumulated depreciation of $2,000 is traded in for a similar, new fixed asset having a fair market value of $22,000. Cash paid on the exchange is $4,000. The fair market value of the old asset is $5,000.

If a similar exchange is involved the entry is:

Fixed Asset (8,000 + 4,000)	12,000	
Accumulated Depreciation	2,000	
Fixed Asset		10,000
Cash		4,000

Assume instead that the fair market value of the new asset was $11,000, resulting in the exception where the new fixed asset must be recorded at $11,000. **Note:** The new fixed asset cannot be shown at more than its fair market value. In this case, the entry is:

Fixed Asset	11,000	
Accumulated Depreciation	2,000	
Loss	1,000	
Fixed Asset		10,000
Cash		4,000

Assume the original facts except that a dissimilar exchange is involved. The entry is:

Fixed Asset (5,000 + 4,000)	9,000	
Accumulated Depreciation	2,000	
Loss	3,000	
Fixed Asset		10,000
Cash		4,000

In a nonmonetary exchange, the entity receiving the monetary payment (boot) recognizes a gain to the degree the monetary receipt is greater than the proportionate share of the book value of the asset given up.

$$\text{Gain} = \text{Monetary Receipt} - \left(\frac{\text{Monetary Receipt}}{\substack{\text{Fair Market Value of} \\ \text{Total Consideration} \\ \text{Received}}} \right) \times \left(\substack{\text{Book Value} \\ \text{of Asset} \\ \text{Given Up}} \right)$$

The company receiving the "boot" records the asset acquired at the carrying value of the asset surrendered minus the portion considered sold.

The company paying the "boot" records the asset purchased at the carrying value of the asset surrendered plus the "boot" paid.

Involuntary conversion: There may arise an involuntary conversion of nonmonetary assets into monetary assets, followed by replacement of the involuntarily converted assets. Example: A warehouse is destroyed by a fire, and the insurance proceeds received are used to purchase a similar warehouse.

According to Interpretation 30, gain or loss is recognized for the difference between the insurance recovery and the book value of the destroyed asset. Example: The new warehouse (replacing the destroyed one) is recorded at its purchase price.

Caution: A contingency arises if the old fixed asset is damaged in one period, but the insurance recovery is not received until a later period. A contingent gain or loss is reported in the period the old fixed asset was damaged. The gain or loss may be recognized for book and tax purposes in different years resulting in a temporary difference for income tax allocation purposes.

Intangibles

Intangible assets are assets having a life of one year or more and lack physical substance (e.g., goodwill), or represent a right granted by the government (e.g., patent) or another company (e.g., franchise fee). APB 17 covers accounting for intangible assets whether purchased or internally developed. The costs of intangibles acquired from others should be reported as assets. The cost equals the cash or fair market value of the consideration given. The individual intangibles that can be separately identified must be costed separately. If not separately identified, the intangibles are assigned a cost equal to the difference between the total purchase price and the cost of identifiable tangible and intangible assets. Note "goodwill" does not include identifiable assets.

The cost of developing and maintaining intangibles should be charged against earnings if the assets are not specifically identifiable, have indeterminate lives, or are inherent in the continuing business (e.g., goodwill). An example of internally developed goodwill that is expensed are the costs incurred in developing a name (e.g., Burger King).

All intangible assets are amortized over the period benefitted using the straight-line method not exceeding a 40-year life. Factors in estimating useful lives include:

- Legal, contractual, and regulatory provisions
- Renewal or extension provisions. If a renewal occurs, the life of the intangible may be increased.
- Obsolescence and competitive factors
- Product demand
- Service lives of essential employees within the organization

For example, an intangible may be enhanced because of good public relations staff.

Intangibles on the books before 1970 need *not* be amortized.

Footnote disclosure is made of the amortization period and method.

If a firm buys, on a step-by-step basis, an investment using the equity method, the fair value of the acquired assets and the goodwill for each step purchased must be separately identified.

When the purchase of assets results in goodwill, later sale of a separable portion of the entity acquired mandate a proportionate reduction of the goodwill account. A portion of the unamortized goodwill is included in the cost of assets sold.

Goodwill is only recorded in a business combination accounted for under the purchase method when the cost to the acquirer exceeds the fair market value of the net assets acquired. Goodwill may be determined by an individual appraiser, a purchase audit done by the acquiring company's public accounting firm, and so on. Goodwill is then amortized using the straight line method over the period benefitted not exceeding 40 years. If the cost to the acquirer is less than the fair market value of the net assets acquired, a credit arises which reduces the noncurrent assets acquired on a proportionate basis (excluding long-term investments). If a credit still remains, it is treated as a deferred credit not to be amortized over more than 40 years under the straight line method.

Goodwill is theoretically equal to the present value of future excess earnings of a company over other companies in the industry. However, it is difficult to predict the length of time superior earnings will occur. Some factors involved in the makeup of goodwill are superior salesforce, outstanding management talent, effective advertising, strategic location, and dependable suppliers.

In buying a new business, a determination must often be made as to the estimated value of the goodwill. Two possible methods that can be used are (1) capitalization of earnings, and (2) capitalization of excess earnings.

EXAMPLE 15

The following information is available for a business that we are contemplating acquiring:

Expected average annual earnings	$10,000
Expected future value of net assets exclusive of goodwill	$45,000
Normal rate of return	20%

Using the capitalization of earnings approach, goodwill is estimated at:

Total asset value implied ($10,000/20%)	$50,000
Estimated fair value of assets	45,000
Estimated goodwill	$ 5,000

Assuming the same facts as above except a capitalization rate of excess earnings of 22% and using the capitalization of excess earnings method, goodwill is estimated at:

Expected average annual earnings	$10,000
Return on expected average assets ($45,000 $\times$ 20%)	9,000
Excess earnings	$ 1,000

Goodwill ($1,000/.22) = $4,545

EXAMPLE 16

The net worth of ABC Company excluding goodwill is $800,000 and profits for the last four years were $750,000. Included in the latter figure are extraordinary gains of $50,000 and nonrecurring losses of $30,000. It is desired to determine a selling price of the business. A 12% return on net worth is deemed typical for the industry. The capitalization of excess earnings is 45% in determining goodwill.

Net Income or 4 years	$750,000
Less: Extraordinary gains	50,000
Add: Nonrecurring losses	30,000
Adjusted 4-year earnings	$730,000
Average earnings ($730,000/4)	$182,500
Normal earnings ($800,000 $\times$ .12)	96,000
Excess annual earnings	$ 86,500

Excess earnings capitalized at 45%:

$$\frac{\$86,500}{.45} = \$192,222$$

The determination of goodwill and its amortization can have a large impact on the balance sheet and financial position of a company. A good example of this is when Turner Broadcasting attempted to take over CBS. Turner assigned the difference of what he would pay for CBS and its book value entirely to goodwill and amortized this amount over 40 years. CBS claimed a smaller amount should be assigned to goodwill and their assets revalued which would have lowered the net income of the combined Turner-CBS Company. Here, the valuation of goodwill was extremely important in this takeover battle.

Internally generated costs to derive a patented product are expensed such as R&D incurred in developing a new product. The patent is recorded at the registration fees to secure and register it, legal fees in successfully defending it in court, and the cost of acquiring competing patents from outsiders. The patent account is amortized over its useful life not exceeding 17 years. If an intangible asset is deemed worthless, it should be written-off recognizing an extraordinary item.

Organization costs are the costs incurred to incorporate a business (e.g., legal fees). They are deferred and amortized.

Leaseholds are rent paid in advance and are amortized over the life of the lease.

If the amortization expense of an intangible is not tax deductible (e.g., amortization of goodwill), a permanent difference arises. Thus, no interperiod tax allocation is involved.

LIABILITIES

In accounting for liabilities, the corporate financial officer must take into account many reporting and disclosure responsibilities:

- Bonds payable may be issued between interest dates at a premium or discount
- Bonds may be amortized using the straight-line method or effective interest method
- Debt may be extinguished prior to the maturity date when the company can issue new debt at a lower interest rate
- Estimated liabilities must be recognized when it is *probable* that an asset has been impaired or liability has been incurred by year-end, and the amount of loss is subject to reasonable estimation
- An accrued liability may also be made for future absences, for example sick leave or vacation time
- Special termination benefits such as early retirement may also be offered to and accepted by employees
- Short-term debt may be rolled over to long-term debt, requiring special reporting
- A callable obligation by the creditor may also exist
- Long-term purchase obligations have to be disclosed

Bonds Payable

The cost of a corporate bond is expressed in terms of yield. Two types of yield calculations are:

1. *Simple Yield.*

$$\frac{\text{Nominal Interest}}{\text{Present Value of Bond}}$$

It is not as accurate as yield to maturity.

2. *Yield to Maturity* (Effective Interest Rate).

$$\frac{\text{Nominal Interest} + \dfrac{\text{Discount}}{\text{Years}} - \dfrac{\text{Premium}}{\text{Years}}}{\dfrac{\text{Present Value} + \text{Maturity Value}}{2}}$$

EXAMPLE 17

A $100,000, 10%, 5-year bond is issued at 96. The simple yield is:

$$\frac{\text{Nominal Interest}}{\text{Present Value of Bond}} = \frac{\$10,000}{\$96,000} = 10.42\%$$

The yield to maturity is:

$$\frac{\text{Nominal Interest} + \dfrac{\text{Discount}}{\text{Years}}}{\dfrac{\text{Present Value} + \text{Maturity Value}}{2}} = \frac{\$10,000 + \dfrac{\$4,000}{5}}{\dfrac{\$96,000 + \$100,000}{2}}$$

$$\frac{\$10,800}{\$98,000} = \underline{11.02\%}$$

When a bond is issued at a discount, the yield (effective interest rate) is greater than the nominal (face, coupon) interest rate.

When a bond is issued at a premium, the yield is less than the nominal interest rate.

The two methods of amortizing bond discount or bond premium are:

- *Straight Line Method* results in a constant dollar amount of amortization but a different effective rate each period.

- *Effective Interest Method* results in a constant rate of interest but different dollar amounts each period. This method is preferred over the straight line method. The amortization entry is:

Interest Expense (Yield $\times$ Carrying Value of Bond at the Beginning of the Year)
Discount
Cash (Nominal Interest $\times$ Face Value of Bond)

In the early years, the amortization amount under the effective interest method is lower, relative to the straight line method (either for discount or premium).

EXAMPLE 18

On 1/1/19X1, a $100,000 bond is issued at $95,624. The yield rate is 7% and the nominal interest rate is 6%. The following schedule is the basis for the journal entries to be made:

Date	Debit Interest Expense	Credit Cash	Credit Discount	Carrying Value
1/1/19X1				$95,624
12/31/19X1	$6,694	$6,000	$694	96,318
12/31/19X2	6,742	6,000	742	97,060

The entry on 12/31/19X1 is:

Interest Expense	6694	
Cash		6000
Discount		694

At maturity, the bond will be worth its face value of $100,000. When bonds are issued between interest dates, the entry is:
Cash
    Bonds Payable
    Premium (or debit discount)
    Interest Expense

EXAMPLE 19

A $100,000, 5% bond having a life of 5 years is issued at 110 on 4/1/19X0. The bonds are dated 1/1/19X0. Interest is payable on 1/1 and 7/1. Straight line amortization is used. The journal entries are:

4/1/19X0 Cash (110,000 + 1,250)	111,250	
Bonds Payable		100,000
Premium on Bonds Payable		10,000
Bond Interest Expense (100,000 $\times$ 5% $\times$ 3/12)		1,250

7/1/19X0 Bond Interest Expense	2,500	
Cash		2,500
$100,000 \times 5\% \times 6/12$		
Premium on Bonds Payable	526.50	
Bond Interest Expense		526.50

$4/1/19X0 - 1/1/19X5$ 4 years, 9 months $= 57$ months

$$\frac{\$10,000}{57} = \$175.50 \text{ per month}$$

$\$175.50 \times 3$ months $= \$526.50$

12/31/19X0 Bond Interest Expense	2,500	
Interest Payable		2,500
Premium on Bonds Payable	1,053	
Bond Interest Expense		1,053
1/1/19X1 Interest Payable	2,500	
Cash		2,500

Bonds Payable is shown on the balance sheet at its present value in the following manner:

Bonds Payable

Add: Premium

Less: Discount

Carrying Value

Bond issue costs are the expenditures incurred in issuing the bonds such as legal, registration, and printing fees. Preferably, bond issue costs are deferred and amortized over the life of the bond. They are shown as a Deferred Charge.

In determining the price of a bond, the face amount is discounted using the present value of $1 table. The interest payments are discounted using the present value of annuity of $1 table. The yield rate is used as the discount rate.

EXAMPLE 20

A $50,000, 10-year bond is issued with interest payable semiannually at an 8% nominal interest rate. The yield rate is 10%. The present value of $1 table factor for $n = 20$, $i = 5\%$ is .37689. The present value of annuity of $1 table factor for $n = 20$, $i = 5\%$ is 12.46221. The price of the bond should be:

Present Value of Principal $50,000 $\times$ .37689	$18,844.50
Present Value of Interest Payments $20,000 $\times$ 12.46221	24,924.42
	$43,768.92

There are three alternative methods that can be used in converting a bond into stock: book value of bond, market value of bond, and market value of stock.

Under the book value of bond method, no gain or loss on bond conversion will result because the book value of the bond is the basis to credit equity. Under the market value methods, gain or loss will result because the book value of the bond will be different from the market value of bond or market value of stock which is the basis to credit the equity accounts.

EXAMPLE 21

A $100,000 bond with unamortized premium of $8,420.50 is converted to common stock. There are 100 bonds ($100,000/$1,000). Each bond is converted into 50 shares of stock. Thus, 5,000 shares of common stock are involved. Par value is $15 per share. The market value of the stock is $25 per share. The market value of the bond is 120. Using the book value method, the entry for the conversion is:

Bonds Payable	100,000	
Premium on Bonds Payable	8,420.50	
Common Stock (5,000 × 15)		75,000
Premium on Common Stock		33,420.50

Using the market value of stock method, the entry is:

Bonds Payable	100,000	
Premium on Bonds Payable	8,420.50	
Loss on Conversion	16,579.50	
Common Stock		75,000
Premium on Common Stock		50,000
5,000 × $25 = $125,000		

Using the market value of the bond method, the entry is:

Bonds Payable	100,000	
Premium on Bonds Payable	8,420.50	
Loss on Conversion	11,579.50	
Common Stock		75,000
Premium on Common Stock		45,000
$100,000 × 120% = $120,000		

Early Extinguishment of Debt

Long-term debt may be called back early when new debt can be issued at a lower interest rate. It can also occur when the company has excess cash and wants to avoid paying interest charges and having the debt on its balance sheet. The gain or loss on the early extinguishment of debt is an extraordinary item shown net of tax. Extraordinary classification occurs whether the extinguishment is early, at scheduled maturity, or later. An exception exists in that the gain or loss on extinguishment is an ordinary item if it satisfies a sinking fund requirement that has to be met within one year of the date of extinguishment. However, serial bonds do not have characteristics of sinking fund requirements.

Debt may be construed as being extinguished in the case where the debtor is relieved of the principal liability and it is probable the debtor will not have to make future payments.

EXAMPLE 22

A $100,000 bond payable with an unamortized premium of $10,000 is called at 85. The entry is:

Bonds Payable	100,000	
Premium on Bonds Payable	10,000	
Cash (85% × 100,000)		85,000
Extraordinary Gain		25,000

Footnote disclosures regarding extinguishment of debt follow:

- Description of extinguishment transaction including the source of funds used

- Per share gain or loss net of tax

If convertible debt is converted to stock in connection with an "inducement offer" where the debtor alters conversion privileges, the debtor recognizes an expense rather than an extraordinary item. The amount is the fair value of the securities transferred in excess of the fair value of securities issuable according to the original conversion terms. This fair market value is measured at the earlier of the conversion date or date of the agreement. An inducement offer may be accomplished by giving debt holders a higher conversion ratio, payment of additional consideration, or other favorable changes in terms.

According to FASB 76, if the debtor puts cash or other assets in a trust to be only utilized for paying interest and principal on debt on an irrevocable basis, disclosure should be made of the particulars including a description of the transaction and the amount of debt considered to be extinguished.

Estimated Liabilities (Contingencies)

A loss contingency should be accrued if *both* of the following criteria exist:

- At year-end, it is probable (likely to occur) that an asset was impaired or a liability was incurred

- The amount of loss is subject to reasonable estimation

The loss contingency is booked because of the principle of conservatism. The entry for a probable loss is:

Expense (Loss)

    Estimated Liability

A probable loss that cannot be estimated should be footnoted.

EXAMPLE 23

On 12/31/19X6, warranty expenses are estimated at $20,000. On 3/15/19X7, actual warrant costs paid for were $16,000. The journal entries are:

12/31/19X6 Warranty Expense	20,000	
Estimated Liability		20,000
3/15/19X7 Estimated Liability	16,000	
Cash		16,000

If a loss contingency exists at year-end but no asset impairment or liability incurrence exists (e.g., uninsured equipment), footnote disclosure may be made.

A probable loss occurring after year-end but before the audit report date only requires subsequent event disclosure.

Examples of probable loss contingencies may be:

- Warranties
- Lawsuits
- Claims and assessments
- Expropriation of property by a foreign government
- Casualties and catastrophes (e.g., fire)

If the amount of loss is within a range, the accrual is based on the best estimate within that range. However, if no amount within the range is better than any other amount, the minimum amount (not maximum amount) of the range is booked. The exposure to additional losses should be disclosed.

In the case of a reasonably possible loss (more than remote but less than likely), no accrual is made but rather footnote disclosure is required. The disclosure includes the nature of the contingency and the estimate of probable loss or range of loss. If an estimate of loss is not possible, that fact should be stated.

A remote contingency (slight chance of occurring) is usually ignored and no disclosure is made. There are exceptions when a remote contingency would be disclosed in the case of guarantees of indebtedness, standby letters of credit, and agreements to repurchase receivables or properties.

General (unspecified) contingencies are not accrued. Examples are self-insurance and possible hurricane losses. Disclosure and/or an appropriation of retained earnings can be made for general contingencies. To be booked as an estimated liability, the future loan must be specific and measurable such as parcel post and freight losses.

Gain contingencies cannot be booked because it violates conservatism. However, footnote disclosure can be made.

Accounting for Compensated Absences

Compensated absences include sick leave, holiday, and vacation time. FASB 43 is *not* applicable to severance or termination pay, post retirement benefits, deferred compensation, stock option plans, and other long-term fringe benefits (e.g., disability, insurance).

The employer shall accrue a liability for employee's compensation for future absences when *all* of these criteria are met:

- Employee rights have vested
- Employee services have already been performed
- Probable payment exists
- Amount of estimated liability can reasonably be determined. **Note:** If the criteria are met except that the amount is not determinable, only a footnote can be made because an accrual is not possible.

Accrual for sick leave is required only when the employer allows employees to take accumulated sick leave days off regardless of actual illness. No accrual is required if employees may only take accumulated days off for actual illness, since losses for these are usually immaterial.

EXAMPLE 24

Estimated compensation for future absences is $30,000. The entry is:

Expense	30,000	
Estimated Liability		30,000

If at a later date a payment of $28,000 is made, the entry is:

Estimated Liability	28,000	
Cash		28,000

Accounting for Special Termination Benefits to Employees

An expense should be accrued when an employer offers special termination benefits to an employee, he accepts the offer, and the amount is subject to reasonable estimation. The amount equals the current payment plus the discounted value of future payments.

When it can be objectively measured, the effect of changes on the employer's previously accrued expenses applicable to other employee benefits directly associated with employee termination should be included in measuring termination expense.

EXAMPLE 25

On 1/1/19X1, as an incentive for early retirement, the employee receives a lump sum payment today of \$50,000 plus payments of \$10,000 for each of the next 10 years. The discount rate is 10%. The journal entry is:

Expense	111,450	
Estimated Liability		111,450
Present value \$10,000 $\times$ 6.145* =	\$ 61,450	
Current payment	50,000	
Total	\$111,450	

*Present value factor for $n = 10$, $i = 10\%$ is 6.145

Refinancing of Short-Term Debt to Long-Term Debt

A short-term obligation shall be reclassified as a long-term obligation in the following cases:

1. After the year-end of the financial statements but before the audit report is issued, the short-term debt is rolled over into a long-term obligation or an equity security is issued in substitution.

     OR

2. Prior to the audit report date, the company enters into a contract for refinancing of the current obligation on a long-term basis and *all* of the following are met:
   - Agreement does not expire within one year
   - No violation of the agreement exists
   - The parties are financially capable of meeting the requirements of the agreement

The proper classification of the refinanced item is under long-term debt and not stockholders' equity even if equity securities were issued in substitution of the debt. When short-term debt is excluded from current liabilities, a footnote should describe the financing agreement and the terms of any new obligation to be incurred.

If the amounts under the agreement for refinancing vary, the amount of short-term debt excluded from current liabilities will be the minimum amount expected to be refinanced based on conservatism. The exclusion from current liabilities cannot be greater than the net proceeds of debt or security issuances, or amounts available under the refinancing agreement.

Once cash is paid for the short-term debt even though the next day long-term debt of a similar amount is issued, the short-term debt shall be shown under current liabilities since cash was disbursed.

Callable Obligations by the Creditor

Included as a current liability is a long-term debt callable by the creditor because of the debtor's violation of the debt agreement except if one of the following conditions exist:

- The creditor waives or lost his right to require repayment for a period in excess of one year from the balance sheet date
- There is a grace period in the terms of the long-term debt issue that the debtor may cure the violation which makes it callable, and it is probable that the violation will be rectified within the grace period

Disclosure of Long-term Purchase Obligations

An unconditional purchase obligation is an obligation to provide funds for goods or services at a determinable future date. An example is a take-or-pay contract making the buyer obligated to pay specified periodic amounts for products or services. Even in the case where the buyer does not take delivery of the goods, periodic payments must still be made.

When unconditional purchase obligations are recorded in the balance sheet, disclosure is still made of the following:

- Payments made for recorded unconditional purchase obligations
- Maturities and sinking fund requirements for long-term borrowings

Unconditional purchase obligations that are not reflected in the balance sheet should usually be disclosed if they meet the following criteria:

- Noncancellation. However, it may be canceled upon a remote contingency.
- Negotiated to arrange financing to provide contracted goods or services
- A term in excess of one year

The disclosure needed for unconditional purchase obligations when not recorded in the accounts are:

- Nature and term
- Fixed and variable amounts
- Total amount for the current year and for the next five years
- Purchases made under the obligation for each year presented

Optional disclosure exists of the amount of imputed interest required to reduce the unconditional purchase obligation to present value.

STOCKHOLDERS' EQUITY

In accounting for stockholders' equity, consideration is given to preferred stock characteristics, conversion of preferred stock to common stock, stock retirement, appropriation of retained earnings, treasury stock, quasi-reorganization, dividends, fractional share warrants, stock options, stock warrants, and stock splits.

The stockholders' equity section of the balance sheet includes major categories for:

- Capital stock (stock issued and stock to be issued)
- Paid-in capital
- Retained earnings
- Unrealized loss on long-term investments
- Gains or losses on foreign currency translation
- Treasury stock

Note: Disclosure should be made for required redemptions of capital stock redeemable at given prices on specific dates.

Preferred Stock

Although participating preferred stock rarely exists, if it does, it may be partially or fully participating. In the case of partially participating, preferred stockholders participate in excess dividends over the preferred dividend rate proportionately with common stockholders but there is a maximum additional rate. For example, an 8% preferred stock issue may permit participating up to 12%, so that an extra 4% dividend may be tacked on. In the case of fully participating preferred stock, there is a distribution for the current year at the preference rate plus any cumulative preference. Further, the preferred stockholders share in dividend distributions in excess of the preferred stock rate on a proportionate basis using the total par value of the preferred stock and common stock. For instance, a 10% fully participating preferred stock will get the 10% preference rate plus a proportionate share based on the total par value of the common and preferred stock of excess dividends once common stockholders have obtained their matching 10% of par of the common stock.

EXAMPLE 26

Assume 5% preferred stock, $20 par, 5,000 shares. The preferred stock is partially participating up to an additional 2%. Common stock is $10 par, 30,000 shares. A $40,000 dividend is declared. Dividends are distributed as follows:

	Preferred	Common
Preferred stock, current year ($100,000 × 5%)	$5,000	
Common stock, current year ($300,000 × 5%)		$15,000

	Preferred	Common
Preferred stock, partial ($100,000 × 2%)	2,000	
Common stock, matching ($300,000 × 2%)		6,000
Balance to common stock		12,000
Total	$7,000	$33,000

Cumulative preferred stock means that if no dividends are paid in a given year, the dividends accumulate and must be paid before any dividends can be paid to noncumulative stock.

The liquidation value of preferred stock means that in corporate liquidation, preferred stockholders will receive the liquidation value (sometimes stated as par value) before any funds may be distributed to common stockholders.

Disclosure for preferred stock includes liquidation preferences, call prices, and cumulative dividends in arrears.

When preferred stock is converted to common stock, the preferred stock and paid-in-capital account are eliminated and the common stock and paid-in-capital account are credited. If a deficit results, retained earnings would be charged.

EXAMPLE 27

Preferred stock having a par value of $300,000 and paid-in-capital (preferred stock) of $20,000 are converted into common stock. There are 30,000 preferred shares having a $10 par value per share. Common stock issued are 10,000 shares having a par value of $25. The journal entry is:

Preferred Stock	300,000	
Paid-in-Capital (Preferred Stock)	20,000	
Common Stock (10,000 × $25)		250,000
Paid-in-Capital (Common Stock)		70,000

Stock Retirement

A company may elect to retire its stock. If common stock is retired at par value, the entry is:

Common Stock } Par Value
Cash

If common stock is retired for less than par value, the entry is:

Common Stock
Cash
Paid-in-Capital

If common stock is retired for more than par value, the entry is:

Common Stock

Paid-in-Capital (original premium per share)

Retained Earnings (excess over original premium per share)

   Cash

Note: In retirement of stock, retained earnings can only be debited, not credited.

Appropriation of Retained Earnings (Reserve)

Appropriation of retained earnings means setting aside retained earnings and making them unavailable for dividends. It indicates the need to stockholders to restrict asset disbursements due to expected major uses or contingencies. Examples: Appropriations for sinking fund, plant expansion, debt retirement, and general contingencies (e.g., self-insurance).

The entry to record an appropriation is:

Retained Earnings

   Appropriation of Retained Earnings

When the contingency actually takes place, the above entry is reversed.

Treasury Stock

Treasury stock is issued shares that have been bought back by the company. The two methods to account for treasury stock are:

1. *Cost Method.* Treasury stock is recorded at the cost to purchase it. If treasury stock is later sold above cost, the entry is:
   Cash
      Treasury Stock
      Paid-in-Capital

If treasury stock was sold instead at below cost, the entry is:

   Cash
   Paid-in-Capital—Treasury Stock (up to amount available)
   Retained Earnings (if paid-in-capital is unavailable)
      Treasury Stock

If treasury stock is donated only a memo entry is required. When the treasury shares are subsequently sold the entry based on the market price at that time is:

   Cash
      Paid-in-Capital—Donation

An appropriation of retained earnings equal to the cost of treasury stock on hand is required.

Treasury stock is shown as a reduction from total stockholders' equity.

2. *Par Value Method.* Treasury stock is recorded at its par value when bought. If treasury stock is purchased at more than par value, the entry is:

> Treasury Stock—Par Value
> Paid-in-Capital—original premium per share
> Retained Earnings—if necessary
> > Cash

If treasury stock is purchased at less than par value, the entry is:

> Treasury Stock—Par Value
> > Cash
> > Paid-in-Capital

Upon sale of the treasury stock above par value, the entry is:

> Cash
> > Treasury Stock
> > Paid-in-Capital

Upon sale of the treasury stock at less than par value, the entry is:

> Cash
> Paid-in-Capital (amount available)
> Retained Earnings (if Paid-in-Capital is insufficient)
> > Treasury Stock

An appropriation of retained earnings equal to the cost of the treasury stock on hand is required. Treasury stock is shown as a contra account to the common stock it applies to under the capital stock section of stockholders' equity.

Quasi-Reorganization

A quasi-reorganization provides a financially troubled company with a deficit in retained earnings a "fresh start." A quasi-reorganization occurs to avoid bankruptcy. There is a revaluation of assets and an elimination of the deficit by reducing paid-in-capital.

- Stockholders and creditors must agree to the quasi-reorganization
- Net assets are reduced to fair market value. If fair value is not readily determinable, then conservative estimates of such value may be made.
- Paid-in-capital is reduced to eliminate the deficit in retained earnings. If paid-in-capital is insufficient, then capital stock is charged.
- Retained earnings becomes a zero balance. Retained earnings will bear the quasi-reorganization date for 10 years after the reorganization.

The retained earnings account consists of the following components:

Retained Earnings—Unappropriated

Dividends	Net Income
Appropriations	
Prior Period Adjustments	
Quasi-reorganization	

The entry for the quasi-reorganization is:

Paid-in-Capital

Capital Stock (if necessary)

    Assets

    Retained Earnings

Caution: If potential losses exist at the readjustment date but the amounts of losses cannot be determined, there should be a provision for the maximum probable loss. If estimates used are later shown to be incorrect, the difference goes to the paid-in-capital account.

Note: New or additional common stock or preferred stock may be issued in exchange for existing indebtedness. Thus, the current liability account would be charged for the indebtedness and the capital account credited.

EXAMPLE 28

A business having a $3,500,000 deficit undertakes a quasi-reorganization. There is an overstatement in assets of $800,000 compared to fair market value. The balances in capital stock and paid-in-capital are $5,000,000 and $1,500,000 respectively. The following entry is made to effect the quasi-reorganization:

Paid-in-Capital	1,500,000	
Capital Stock	2,800,000	
Assets		800,000
Retained Earnings		3,500,000

Note that the paid-in-capital account has been fully wiped out, so the residual debit goes to capital stock.

Dividends

Dividends represent distributions paid out by the company to stockholders. After the date of declaration of a dividend is the date of record. In order to qualify to receive a dividend a person must be registered as the owner of the stock on the date of record. Several days prior to the date of record, the stock will be selling "ex-dividend." This is done to alert investors that those owning the stock before the record date are eligible to receive the dividend, and that those selling the stock before the record date will lose their rights to the dividend.

A dividend is usually in the form of cash or stock. A dividend is based on the outstanding shares (issued shares less treasury shares).

EXAMPLE 29

Issued shares are 5,000, treasury shares are 1,000, and outstanding shares are therefore 4,000. The par value of the stock is $10 per share. If a $.30 dividend per share is declared, the dividend is:

$$4,000 \times \$.30 = \underline{\$1,200}$$

If the dividend rate is 6%, the dividend is:

4,000 shares × $10 par value =	$40,000
	× .06
	$ 2,400

Assuming a cash dividend of $2,400 is declared, the entry is:

Retained Earnings	2,400	
Cash Dividend Payable		2,400

No entry is made at the record date.
The entry at the payment date is:

Cash Dividend Payable	2,400	
Cash		2,400

A property dividend is a dividend payable in assets of the company other than cash. When the property dividend is declared, the company restates the distributed asset to fair market value, recognizing any gain or loss as the difference between the fair market value and carrying value of the property at the declaration date.

EXAMPLE 30

A company transfers investments in marketable securities costing $10,000 to stockholders by declaring a property dividend on December 16, 19X8, to be distributed on 1/15/19X9. At the declaration date, the securities have a market value of $14,000. The entries are

Declaration:

12/16/19X8 Investment in Securities	4,000	
Gain on Appreciation of Securities		4,000
Retained Earnings	14,000	
Property Dividend Payable		14,000

Note that the net reduction is still the $10,000 cost of the asset.

Distribution:

1/15/19X9 Property Dividend Payable	14,000	
Investment in Securities		14,000

A stock dividend is issued in the form of stock. Stock dividend distributable is shown in the capital stock section of stockholders' equity. It is not a liability. If the stock dividend is less than 20%–25% of outstanding shares at the declaration date, retained earnings is reduced at the market price of the shares. If the stock dividend is in excess of 20%–25% of outstanding shares, retained earnings is charged at par value. Between 20%–25% is a gray area.

EXAMPLE 31

A stock dividend of 10% is declared on 5,000 shares of $10 par value common stock having a market price of $12. The entry at the declaration and issuance dates follow:

Retained Earnings (500 shares $\times$ $12)	6,000	
Stock Dividend Distributable (500 shares $\times$ $10)		5,000
Paid-in-Capital		1,000
Stock Dividend Distributable	5,000	
Common Stock		5,000

Assume instead that the stock dividend was 30%. The entries would be:

Retained Earnings (5000 $\times$ $10)	5,000	
Stock Dividend Distributable		5,000
Stock Dividend Distributable	5,000	
Common Stock		5,000

A liability dividend (scrip dividend) is payable in the form of a liability (e.g., notes payable). A liability dividend sometimes occurs when a company has financial problems.

EXAMPLE 32

On 1/1/19X2, a liability dividend of $20,000 is declared in the form of a one year, 8% note. The entry at the declaration date is:

Retained Earnings	20,000	
Scrip Dividend Payable		20,000

When the scrip dividend is paid, the entry is:

Scrip Dividend Payable	20,000	
Interest Expense	1,600	
Cash		21,600

A liquidating dividend can be deceptive as it is not actually a dividend. It is a return of capital and not a distribution of earnings. The entry is to debit paid-in-capital and credit dividends payable. The recipient of a liquidating dividend pays no tax on it.

Stock Split

In a stock split, the shares are increased and the par value per share is decreased. However, total par value is the same.

Only a memo entry is needed.

EXAMPLE 33

Before: 1,000 shares, $10 par value = $10,000 total par value
       2 for 1 stock split declared
After: 2,000 shares, $5 par value = $10,000 total par value
If there was a reverse split, it would have the opposite effect.

Stock Options

A contractual privilege provided to a company's officers and other employees giving them the right to buy a given number of shares of the company's stock, at a stated price, within a specified time period. Usually, such rights are given to corporate employees as compensation for services or as incentives.

Non-compensatory plans are not primarily designed to provide employees compensation for services rendered. No compensation expense is recognized. A non-compensatory plan has all of the following characteristics:

- All employees are offered stock on some basis (e.g., equally, percent of salary)
- Most full-time employees may participate
- A reasonable period of time exists to exercise the options
- The price discount for employees on the stock is not better than that afforded to corporate stockholders if there was an additional issuance to the stockholders

The purpose of a non-compensatory plan is to obtain funds and to reduce greater widespread ownership in the company among employees.

Accounting for a non-compensatory stock plan is one of simple sale. The option price is the same as the issue price.

A compensatory plan exists if any one of the above four criteria are not met. Consideration received by the firm for the stock equals the cash, assets, or employee services obtained.

In a compensatory stock option plan for executives, compensation expense should be recognized in the year in which the services are performed. The deferred compensation is determined at the measurement date as the difference between the market price of the stock at that date and the option price. When there exists more than one option plan, compensation cost should be computed separately for each. If treasury stock is used in the stock option plan, its market value and not cost is to be used in measuring the compensation.

The measurement date is the date upon which the number of shares to be issued and the option price are known. The measurement date cannot be changed by provisions that reduce the number of shares under option in the case of employee termination. A new measurement date occurs when an option renewal takes place. The measurement date is not altered when stock is transferred to a trustee or agent. In the case of convertible stock being awarded to employees, the measurement date is the one upon which the conversion rate is known. Compensation is measured by the higher of the market price of the convertible stock or the market price of the securities to which the convertible stock is to be converted into.

There may be a postponement in the measurement date to the end of the reporting year if all of the below conditions exist:

- A formal plan exists for the award
- The factors determining the total dollar award is designated
- The award relates to services performed by employees in the current year

EXAMPLE 34

On 1/1/19X1, 1,000 shares are granted under a stock option plan. At the measurement date, the market price of the stock is $10 and the option price is $6. The amount of the deferred compensation is:

Market price	$10
Option price	6
Deferred compensation	$ 4

Deferred compensation equals:
1,000 shares $\times$ $4 = $4,000

Assume the employees must perform services for four years before they can exercise the option.

On 1/1/19X1, the journal entry to record total deferred compensation cost is:

Deferred Compensation Cost	4,000	
Paid-in-Capital—Stock Options		4,000

Deferred compensation is a contra account against stock options to derive the net amount under the capital stock section of the balance sheet.

On 12/31/19X1, the entry to record the expense is:

Compensation Expense	1,000	
Deferred Compensation		1,000

$4,000/4 years = $1,000

The capital stock section on 12/31/19X1 would show stock options as follows:

Stock options	$4,000
Less: Deferred compensation	1,000
Balance	$3,000

Compensation expense of $1,000 would be reflected for each of the next three years as well.

At the time the options are exercised when the market price of the stock at the exercise date exceeds the option price, an entry must be made for stock issuance.

Assuming a par value of $5 and a market price of $22, the journal entry for the exercise is:

Cash ($6 $\times$ 1,000)	6,000	
Paid-in Capital—Stock Options	4,000	
Common Stock ($5 $\times$ 1,000)		5,000
Paid-in Capital		5,000

If the market price of the stock was below the option price, the options would lapse requiring the following entry:

Paid-in Capital—Stock Options	4,000	
Paid-in Capital		4,000

Note: In the case where an employee leaves after finishing the required service years, no effect is given to recorded compensation and the nonexercised options are transferred to paid-in capital. In the situation where the employee leaves before the exercise period, previously recognized compensation is adjusted currently.

If the grant date is prior to the measurement date, we have to estimate the deferred compensation costs until the measurement date so that compensation expense is recognized when services are performed. The difference between the actual figures and estimates are treated as a change in estimate during the year in which the actual cost is determined.

When the measurement date comes after the grant date, compensation expense for each period from the date of award to the measurement date should be based on the market price of the stock at the close of the accounting period.

In a variable plan granted for previous services, compensation should be expensed in the period the award is granted.

When the employee performs services for several years prior to the stock being issued, an accrual should be made during these periods for compensation expense applicable to the stock issuance related thereto.

When employees receive cash in settlement of a previous option, the cash paid is used to measure the compensation. If the ultimate compensation differs from the amount initially recorded, an adjustment should be made to the original compensation. It is accounted for as a change in estimate.

The accrual of compensation expense may necessitate estimates which have to later be revised. An example is when an employee resigns from the company and hence does not exercise his stock option. Compensation expense should be reduced when employee termination occurs. The adjustment is accounted for as a change in estimate.

Footnote disclosure for a stock option plan includes the status of the plan, number of shares under option, option price, number of shares exercisable, and the number of shares issued under the option during the year.

Compensation expense is deductible for tax purposes when paid but deducted for book purposes when accrued. This results in interperiod income tax allocation involving a deferred income tax credit. If for some reason reversal of the temporary difference will not occur, a permanent difference exists which does not affect profit. The difference should adjust paid-in capital in the period the accrual takes place.

Debt Issued with Stock Warrants

If bonds are issued along with detachable stock warrants, the portion of the proceeds applicable to the warrants is credited to paid-in-capital. The basis for allocation is the relative values of the securities at the time of issuance. In the event that the warrants are not detachable, the bonds are accounted for solely as convertible debt. There is no allocation of the proceeds to the conversion feature.

EXAMPLE 35

A $20,000 convertible bond is issued at $21,000 with $1,000 applicable to stock warrants. If the warrants are not detachable, the entry is:

Cash	21,000	
Bonds Payable		20,000
Premium on Bonds Payable		1,000

If the warrants are detachable, the entry is:

Cash	21,000	
Bonds Payable		20,000
Paid-in-Capital—Stock Warrants		1,000

In the event that the proceeds of the bond issue were only $20,000 instead of $21,000 and $1,000 could be attributable to the warrants, the entry is:

Cash	20,000	
Discount	1,000	
Bonds Payable		20,000
Paid-in-Capital—Stock Warrants		1,000

Fractional Share Warrants

Fractional share warrants may be issued.

EXAMPLE 36

There are 1,000 shares of $10 par value common stock. The common stock has a market price of $15. A 20% dividend is declared resulting is 200 shares (20% $\times$ 1,000). Included in the 200 shares are fractional share warrants. Each warrant equals one fifth of a share of stock. There are 100 warrants resulting in 20 shares of stock (100/5). Thus, 180 regular shares and 20 fractional shares are involved.

The journal entries follow:

At the declaration date:

Retained Earnings (200 shares $\times$ 15)	3,000	
Stock Dividends Distributable (180 shares $\times$ 10)		1,800
Fractional Share Warrants (20 shares $\times$ 10)		200
Paid-in-Capital		1,000

At time of issuance:

Stock Dividend Distributable	1,800	
Common Stock		1,800
Fractional Share Warrants	200	
Common Stock		200

If instead of all the fractional share warrants being turned in, only 80% were turned in the entry is:

Fractional Share Warrants	200	
Common Stock		160
Paid-in-Capital		40

7

Financial Statement Reporting: The Statement of Cash Flows

As per FASB 95, a Statement of Cash Flows is required in the annual report. This chapter discusses how the Statement may be prepared as well as the analytical implications for the financial manager. The objective of the Statement is to furnish useful data regarding a company's cash receipts and cash payments for a period. There should exist a reconciliation between net income and net cash flow from operations. In addition, separate reporting is mandated for certain information applicable to noncash investments and financing transactions.

PREPARATION OF THE STATEMENT

The Statement of Cash Flows explains the change in cash and cash equivalents for the period. A cash equivalent is a short-term very liquid investment satisfying the following criteria: (1) easily convertible into cash, and (2) very near the maturity date so there is hardly any chance of change in market value due to interest rate changes. Typically, this criterion is solely applicable to investments having original maturities of three months or less. Examples of cash equivalents are commercial paper, money market fund, and Treasury bills. Disclosure should be made of the company's policy for determining which items represent cash equivalents. A change in such policy is accounted for as a change in accounting principle requiring the restatement of previous years' financial statements for comparative purposes.

The Statement of Cash Flows classifies cash receipts and cash payments as arising from investing, financing, and operating activities.

Investing Section

Investing activities involve cash flows generally applicable to changes in long-term asset items. Investing activities include purchasing debt and equity securities in other entities, buying and selling fixed assets, and making and collecting loans. Cash inflows from investing are comprised of: (1) receipts from sales of equity or debt securities of other companies, (2) amount received from disposing of fixed assets, and (3) collections or sales of loans made by the company. Cash outflows for investing activities include: (1) disbursements to buy equity or debt securities of other companies, (2) payments to buy fixed assets, and (3) disbursements for loans made by the company.

Note: Activities related to acquisition or sale of a business or part thereof are investing items.

Caution: Gains or losses on sales of noncurrent assets are included as investing activities along with the assets they relate to. These gains or losses are not included in net cash flow from operating items. Thus, they are an adjustment to net income in obtaining cash flow from operations.

Financing Section

Financing activities include cash flows generally resulting from changes in long-term liabilities and stockholders' equity items. Included in financing activities are receiving equity funds and furnishing owners with a return on their investment. Also included is debt financing and repayment or settlement of debt. Another element is obtaining and paying for other resources derived from creditors on noncurrent credit. Cash inflows from financing activities are comprised of (1) funds received from the sale of stock, and (2) funds obtained from the incurrence of debt. Cash outflows for financing activities include (1) paying-off debt, (2) repurchase of stock, (3) dividend payments, and (4) other principal payments to long-term creditors.

Note: Stock dividends, stock splits, and appropriations of retained earnings are not included as financing activities because they do not use cash. They are intrastockholder equity transactions.

Caution: Gains or losses from the early extinguishment of debt are part of the cash flow related to the repayment of the amount borrowed as a financing activity. Such gains or losses are not an element of net cash flow from operating activities.

Operating Section

Operating activities relate to manufacturing and selling goods or the rendering of services. They do not apply to investing or financing functions. Cash flow derived from operating activities typically applies to the cash effects of transactions entering into profit computations. Cash inflows from operating activities include: (1) cash sales or collections on receivables arising from the initial sale of merchandise or rendering of service; (2) cash receipts from returns on loans, debt securities (e.g., interest income), or equity securities (e.g., dividend income) of other entities; (3) cash received from licensees and lessees; (4) receipt of a litigation settlement; and (5) reimbursement under an insurance policy. Cash outflows for operating activities include: (1) cash paid for raw material or merchandise for resale, (2) principal payments on accounts payable arising from the initial purchase of goods, (3) payments to suppliers of operating expense items (e.g., office supplies, advertising, insurance), (4) wages, (5) payments to governmental agencies (e.g., taxes, penalties), (6) interest expense, (7) lawsuit payment, (8) charitable contributions, and (9) cash refund to customers for defective merchandise.

Additional breakdowns of operating cash receipts and disbursements may be made to enhance financial reporting. For example, a manufacturing company may divide cash paid to suppliers into payments applicable to inventory acquisition and payments for selling expenses.

Other Considerations

There should be a separate presentation within the Statement of Cash Flows of cash inflows and cash outflows from investing and financing activities. For example, the purchase of fixed assets is an application of cash while the sale of a fixed asset is a source of cash. Both are shown separately to aid analysis by readers of the financial statements. Debt incurrence would be a source of cash while debt payment would be an application of cash. Thus, cash received of $800,000 from debt incurrence would be shown as a source while the payment of debt of $250,000 would be presented as an application. The net effect is $550,000.

Separate disclosure shall be made of investing and financing activities impacting upon assets or liabilities that do not affect cash flow. Examples of noncash activities of an investing and financing nature are bond conversion, purchase of a fixed asset by the incurrence of a mortgage payable, capital lease, and nonmonetary exchange of assets. This disclosure may be footnoted or shown in a schedule. Illustrative presentation follows:

Net increase in cash	$980,000
Noncash investing and financing activities:	
Purchase of land by the issuance of common stock	$400,000
Conversion of bonds payable to common stock	200,000
	$600,000

If a cash receipt or cash payment applies to more than one classification (investing, financing, operating), classification is made as to the activity which is the main source of that cash flow. For instance, the purchase and sale of equipment to be used by the company is typically construed as an investing activity.

In the case of foreign currency cash flows, use the exchange rate at the time of the cash flow in reporting the currency equivalent of foreign currency cash flows. The effect of changes in the exchange rate on cash balances held in foreign currencies should be reported as a separate element of the reconciliation of the change in cash and cash equivalents for the period.

Cash flow per share shall not be shown in the financial statements since it will detract from the importance of the earnings per share statistic.

Direct Method vs. Indirect Method

The direct method is preferred in that companies should report cash flows from operating activities by major classes of gross cash receipts and gross cash payments and the resulting net amount in the operating section. A reconciliation of net income to cash flow from operating activities should be shown in a separate schedule after the body of the statement. **Note:** This schedule has the same net result as gross cash receipts and cash payments from operating activities.

Although the direct method is preferred, a company has the option of using the indirect (reconciliation) method. In practice, most companies are using the indirect method because of its easier preparation. Under the indirect method, the company reports net cash flow from operating activities indirectly by adjusting profit to reconcile it to net cash flow from operating activities. This is shown in the operating section within the body of the Statement of Cash Flows or in a separate schedule. If presented in a separate schedule, the net cash flow from operating activities is presented as a single line item. The adjustment to reported earnings for noncash revenues and expenses involves:

- Effects of deferrals of past operating cash receipts and cash payments (e.g., changes in inventory and deferred revenue), and accumulations of expected future operating cash receipts and cash payments (e.g., changes in receivables and payables)
- Effects of items whose cash impact apply to investing or financing cash flows (e.g., depreciation, amortization expense, gain or loss on the retirement of debt, and gain or loss on the sale of fixed assets)

From the above discussion, we can see that there is basically one difference in statement presentation between the direct and indirect method. It solely relates to the operating section. Under the direct method, the operating section presents gross cash receipts and gross cash payments from operating activities with a reconciliation of net income to cash flow from operations in a separate schedule. Under the indirect method, gross cash receipts and gross cash payments from operating activities are not shown. Instead, only the reconciliation of net income to cash flow from operations is shown in the operating section or in a separate schedule with the final figure of cash flow from operations presented as a single line item in the operating section.

Since the indirect method is the one commonly used in practice, we will concentrate on it.

We show in Exhibit 1 the reconciliation process of net income to cash flow from operating activities.

Exhibit 1

INDIRECT METHOD OF COMPUTING CASH PROVIDED BY OPERATIONS

	Add (+) or deduct (−) to adjust net income
Net income	$XXX
Adjustments required to convert net income to cash basis:	
Depreciation, depletion, amortization expense, and loss on sale of noncurrent assets	+
Amortization of deferred revenue, amortization of bond premium, and gain on sale of noncurrent assets	−
Add (deduct) changes in current asset accounts affecting revenue or expenses (a)	
Increase in the account	−
Decrease in the account	+
Add (deduct) changes in current liability accounts affecting revenue or expense (b)	
Increase in the account	+
Decrease in the account	−
Add (deduct) changes in the Deferred Income Taxes account	
Increase in the account	+
Decrease in the account	−
Cash provided by operations	$XXX

(a) Examples include accounts receivable, accrued receivables, inventory, and prepaid expenses.

(b) Examples include accounts payable, accrued liabilities, and deferred revenue.

Exhibit 2 shows a skeleton outline of the indirect method.

Exhibit 2

FORMAT OF THE STATEMENT OF CASH FLOWS
(INDIRECT METHOD)

Net cash flow from operating activities:

Net income	x	
Adjustments for noncash expenses, revenues, losses		
and gains included in income:	x	
	(x)	
Net cash flow from operating activities		x
Cash flows from investing activities:		
	x	
	(x)	
Net cash flows provided (used) by investing activities		x
Cash flows from financing activities:		
	x	
	(x)	
Net cash provided (used) by financing activities		x
Net increase (decrease) in cash		xx
Schedule of Noncash Investing and Financing Activities:		
	x	
	x	

FINANCIAL ANALYSIS OF THE STATEMENT

An analysis of the Statement of Cash Flows will provide financial managers with essential information about the company's cash receipts and cash payments for a period as they apply to operating, investing, and financing activities. The statement assists in the appraisal of the effect on the firm's financial position of cash and noncash investing and financing transactions.

Comparative Statements of Cash Flows must be analyzed in detail because they hold clues to a company's earnings quality, risk, and liquidity. Comparative Statements show the degree of repeatability of the company's sources of funds, their costs, and whether such sources may be relied upon in future years. Uses of funds for growth as well as for maintaining competitive share are revealed. An analysis of Comparative Statements of Cash Flows holds the key to a full and reliable analysis of corporate financial health in the present and future. It aids in planning future ventures and financing needs. Comparative data help managerial accountants identify abnormal or cyclical factors as well as changes in the relationship among each flow component.

The statement serves as a basis to forecast earnings based on plant, property, and equipment posture. It assists in evaluating growth potential and incorporates cash flow requirements, highlighting specific fund sources and future means of payment. Will the company be able to meet its obligations and pay cash dividends?

The statement reveals the type and degree of financing required to expand long-term assets and to bolster operations.

The financial executive should calculate for analytical purposes cash flow per share equal to net cash flow divided by the number of shares. A high ratio is desirable because it indicates the company is in a very liquid position.

We now discuss the analysis of the operating, investing, and financing sections of the Statement of Cash Flows.

Operating Section

An analysis of the operating section of the Statement of Cash Flows enables the financial manager to determine the adequacy of cash flow from operating activities to satisfy company requirements. Can the firm obtain positive future net cash flows? The reconciliation tracing net income to net cash flow from operating activities should be examined to see the effect of noncash revenue and noncash expense items.

An award under a lawsuit is a cash inflow from operating activities which results in a nonrecurring source of revenue.

An operating cash outlay for refunds given to customers for deficient goods indicates a quality problem with the firm's merchandise.

Payments of penalties, fines, and lawsuit damages are operating cash outflows which show poor management in that a problem arose which required a nonbeneficial expenditure to the organization.

Investing Section

An analysis of the Investing Section of the Statement of Cash Flows enables identifying an investment in another company which may point to an attempt for eventual control for diversification purposes. It may also indicate a change in future direction or change in business philosophy.

An increase in fixed assets indicates capital expansion and growth. Determine which assets have been bought. Are they assets for risky (specialized) ventures or are they stable (multipurpose) ones? This provides a clue as to risk potential and expected return. The nature of the assets gives signals of future direction and earning potential of product lines, business segments, and so on. Are these directions sound and viable?

The financial manager should ascertain whether there is a contraction in the business arising from the sale of fixed assets without adequate replacement. Is the problem corporate (e.g., product line is weakening) or industry wide (e.g., industry is on the downturn)? If corporate, management is not optimistic regarding the future. Nonrecurring gains may occur because of the sale of low-cost basis fixed assets (e.g., land). Such gains cause temporary increases in profits above normal levels and represent low quality of earnings sources. They should be discounted by the analyst.

Financing Section

An appraisal of the Financing Section will help the financial manager form an opinion of the company's ability to obtain financing in the money and capital markets as well as its ability to satisfy its obligations. The financial mixture of equity, bonds, and long-term bank loans impact the cost of financing. A major advantage of debt is the tax deductibility of interest. However, dividends on stock are not tax deductible. In inflation, paying debt back in cheaper dollars will result in purchasing power gains. The risk of debt financing is the required repayment of principal and interest. Will the company have the needed funds at maturity? You must evaluate the stability of the fund source to ascertain whether it may be relied upon in the future, even in a tight money market. Otherwise, there may be problems in maintaining corporate operations in a recession. The question is: Where can the company go for funds during times of cash squeeze?

By appraising the financing sources, the financing preferences of management are revealed. Is there an inclination toward risk or safety? Creditors favor equity issuances because they protect their loans. Excessive debt may be a problem during economic downturn.

The ability of a company to finance with the issuance of common stock on attractive terms (high stock price) indicates that investors are positive about the financial health of the entity.

The issuance of preferred stock may be a negative indicator because it may mean the company has a problem issuing common stock.

An appraisal should be made of the company's ability to meet debt. Excessive debt means greater corporate risk. The problem is acute if earnings are unstable or dropping. On the contrary, the reduction in long-term debt is favorable because it lessens corporate risk.

A financing cash outflow for the early extinguishment of debt will result in an extraordinary gain or loss resulting in a one-time earnings impact.

The financial manager should appraise the firm's dividend paying ability. Stockholders favor a company with a high dividend payout.

Is there a purchase of treasury stock resulting in an artificial increase in earnings per share?

Schedule of Noncash Financing and Investing Activities

A bond conversion is a positive signal about the entity's financial health since it indicates that bondholders are optimistic about the firm's financial well-being and/or the market price of stock has increased. A conversion of preferred stock to common stock is also favorable because it shows preferred stockholders are impressed with the company's future and are willing to have a lower priority in liquidation.

Note that bond and preferred stock conversions affect the existing position of long-term creditors and stockholders. For example, a reduction in debt by conversion to stock protects to a greater degree the loans of the remaining bond holders and banks.

CONCLUSION

Current profitability is only one important factor for corporate success. Also essential are the current and future cash flows. In fact, a profitable company may have a cash crisis.

Management is responsible for planning how and when cash will be used and obtained. When planned expenditures necessitate more cash than planned activities are likely to produce, managers must decide what to do. They may decide to obtain debt or equity financing or to dispose of some fixed assets or a whole business segment. Alternatively, they may decide to cut back on planned activities by modifying operational plans such as ending a special advertising campaign or delaying new acquisitions. Or, they may decide to revise planned payments to financing sources such as delaying bond repayment or reducing dividends. Whatever is decided, the managers' goal is to balance, over both the short and the long term, the cash available and the needs for cash.

Managerial planning is aided when evaluating the Statement of Cash Flows in terms of coordinating dividend policy with other corporate activities, financial planning for new products and types of assets needed, strengthening a weak cash posture and credit availability, and ascertaining the feasibility and implementation of existing top management plans.

The analysis and evaluation of the Statement of Cash Flows is essential if the analyst is to properly appraise an entity's cash flows from operating, investing, and financing activities. The company's liquidity and solvency positions as well as future directions are revealed. Inadequacy in cash flow has possible serious implications since it may lead to declining profitability, greater financial risk, and even bankruptcy.

EXAMPLE 1

X Company provides the following financial statements:

X Company
Comparative Balance Sheets
December 31
(In Millions)

	19X9	19X8
ASSETS		
Cash	$ 40	$ 47
Accounts receivable	30	35
Prepaid expenses	4	2
Land	50	35
Building	100	80
Accumulated depreciation	(9)	(6)
Equipment	50	42
Accumulated depreciation	(11)	(7)
Total assets	$254	$228
LIABILITIES AND STOCKHOLDERS' EQUITY		
Accounts payable	$ 20	$ 16
Long-term notes payable	30	20
Common stock	100	100
Retained earnings	104	92
Total liabilities and stockholders' equity	$254	$228

X Company
Income Statement
for the Year Ended December 31, 19X9
(In Millions)

Revenue		$300
Operating expenses (excluding depreciation)	$200	
Depreciation	7	207
Income from operations		$ 93
Income tax expense		32
Net income		$ 61

Additional information:

1. Cash dividends paid $49.

2. The company issued long-term notes payable for cash.

3. Land, building, and equipment were acquired for cash.

We can now prepare the Statement of Cash Flows under the indirect method as follows:

X Company
Statement of Cash Flows
for the Year Ended December 31, 19X9
(In Millions)

Cash flow from operating activities		
Net income		$ 61
Add (deduct) items not affecting cash		
Depreciation expense	$ 7	
Decrease in accounts receivable	5	
Increase in prepaid expenses	(2)	
Increase in accounts payable	4	14
Net cash flow from operating activities		$ 75
Cash flow from investing activities		
Purchase of land	($15)	
Purchase of building	(20)	
Purchase of equipment	(8)	(43)
Cash flow from financing activities		
Issuance of long-term notes payable	$ 10	
Payment of cash dividends	(49)	(39)
Net decrease in cash		$ 7

A financial analysis of the Statement of Cash Flows reveals that the profitability and operating cash flow of X Company improved. This indicates good earnings performance as well as the fact that earnings are backed up by cash. The decrease in accounts receivable may reveal better collection efforts. The increase in accounts payable is a sign that suppliers are confident in the company and willing to give interest-free financing. The acquisition of land, building, and equipment points to a growing business undertaking capital expansion. The issuance of long-term notes payable indicates that part of the financing of assets is through debt. Stockholders will be happy with the significant dividend payout of 80.3% (dividends divided by net income, or $49/$61). Overall, there was a decrease in cash of $7 but this should *not* cause alarm because of the company's profitability and the fact that cash was used for capital expansion and dividend payments. We recommend that the dividend payout be reduced from its high level and the funds be reinvested in the profitable business. Also, the curtailment of dividends by more than $7 would result in a positive net cash flow for the year. Cash flow is needed for immediate liquidity needs.

EXAMPLE 2

Y Company presents the following statement of cash flows:

Y Company
Statement of Cash Flows
for the Year Ended December 31, 19X8

Cash flows from operating activities		
Net income		$134,000
Add (deduct) items not affecting cash		
Depreciation expense	$ 21,000	
Decrease in accounts receivable	10,000	
Increase in prepaid expenses	(6,000)	
Increase in accounts payable	35,000	60,000
Net cash flow from operating activities		$194,000
Cash flows from investing activities		
Purchase of land	$(70,000)	
Purchase of building	(200,000)	
Purchase of equipment	(68,000)	
Cash used by investing activities		(338,000)
Cash flows from financing activities		
Issuance of bonds	150,000	
Payment of cash dividends	(18,000)	
Cash provided by financing activities		132,000
Net decrease in cash		$(12,000)

An analysis of the Statement of Cash Flows reveals that the company is profitable. Also, cash flow from operating activities exceeds net income, which indicates good internal cash generation. The ratio of cash flow from operating activities to net income is a solid 1.45 ($194,000/$134,000). A high ratio is desirable because it shows that earnings are backed up by cash. The decline in accounts receivable could indicate better collection efforts. The increase in accounts payable shows the company can obtain interest-free financing. The company is definitely in the process of expanding for future growth as evidenced by the purchase of land, building, and equipment. The debt position of the company has increased indicating greater risk. The dividend payout was 13.4% ($18,000/$134,000). Stockholders look positively on a firm which pays dividends. The decrease in cash flow for the year of $12,000 is a negative sign.

EXAMPLE 3

Summarized below is financial information for the current year for Company M, which provides the basis for the statements of cash flows:

COMPANY M
CONSOLIDATED STATEMENT OF FINANCIAL POSITION

	1/1/X1	12/31/X1	Change
Assets:			
Cash and cash equivalents	$ 600	$ 1,665	$ 1,065
Accounts receivable (net of allowance for losses of $600 and $450)	1,770	1,940	170
Notes receivable	400	150	(250)
Inventory	1,230	1,375	145
Prepaid expenses	110	135	25
Investments	250	275	25
Property, plant, and equipment, at cost	6,460	8,460	2,000
Accumulated depreciation	(2,100)	(2,300)	(200)
Property, plant, and equipment, net	4,360	6,160	1,800
Intangible assets	40	175	135
Total assets	$ 8,760	$ 11,875	$ 3,115
Liabilities:			
Accounts payable and accrued expenses	$ 1,085	1,090	$ 5
Interest payable	30	45	15
Income taxes payable	50	85	35
Short-term debt	450	750	300
Lease obligation	—	725	725
Long-term debt	2,150	2,425	275
Deferred taxes	375	525	150
Other liabilities	225	275	50
Total liabilities	4,365	5,920	1,555
Stockholders' equity:			
Capital stock	2,000	3,000	1,000
Retained earnings	2,395	2,955	560
Total stockholders' equity	4,395	5,955	1,560
Total liabilities and stockholders' equity	$ 8,760	$ 11,875	$ 3,115

Source: Statement of Financial Accounting Standards No. 95, *Statement of Cash Flows*, 1987, Appendix C, Example 1, pp. 44–51. Reprinted with permission of the Financial Accounting Standards Board.

COMPANY M
CONSOLIDATED STATEMENT OF INCOME
FOR THE YEAR ENDED DECEMBER 31, 19X1

Sales	$ 13,965
Cost of sales	(10,290)
Depreciation and amortization	(445)
Selling, general, and administrative expenses	(1,890)
Interest expense	(235)
Equity in earnings of affiliate	45
Gain on sale of facility	80
Interest income	55
Insurance proceeds	15
Loss from patent infringement lawsuit	(30)
Income before income taxes	1,270
Provision for income taxes	(510)
Net income	$ 760

The following transactions were entered into by Company M during 19X1 and are reflected in the above financial statements:

a. Company M wrote off $350 of accounts receivable when a customer filed for bankruptcy. A provision for losses on accounts receivable of $200 was included in Company M's selling, general, and administrative expenses.

b. Company M collected the third and final annual installment payment of $100 on a note receivable for the sale of inventory and collected the third of four annual installment payments of $150 each on a note receivable for the sale of a plant. Interest on these notes through December 31 totaling $55 was also collected.

c. Company M received a dividend of $20 from an affiliate accounted for under the equity method of accounting.

d. Company M sold a facility with a book value of $520 and an original cost of $750 for $600 cash.

e. Company M constructed a new facility for its own use and placed it in service. Accumulated expenditures during the year of $1,000 included capitalized interest of $10.

f. Company M entered into a capital lease for new equipment with a fair value of $850. Principal payments under the lease obligation totaled $125.

g. Company M purchased all of the capital stock of Company S for $950. The acquisition was recorded under the purchase method of accounting. The fair values of Company S's assets and liabilities at the date of acquisition are presented below:

Cash	$ 25
Accounts receivable	155
Inventory	350
Property, plant, and equipment	900
Patents	80
Goodwill	70
Accounts payable and accrued expenses	(255)
Long-term note payable	(375)
Net assets acquired	$ 950

h. Company M borrowed and repaid various amounts under a line-of-credit agreement in which borrowings are payable 30 days after demand. The net increase during the year in the amount borrowed against the line-of-credit totaled $300.

i. Company M issued $400 of long-term debt securities.

j. Company M's provision for income taxes included a deferred provision of $150.

k. Company M's depreciation totaled $430, and amortization of intangible assets totaled $15.

l. Company M's selling, general, and administrative expenses included an accrual for incentive compensation of $50 that has been deferred by executives until their retirement. The related obligation was included in other liabilities.

m. Company M collected insurance proceeds of $15 from a business interruption claim that resulted when a storm precluded shipment of inventory for one week.

n. Company M paid $30 to settle a lawsuit for patent infringement.

o. Company M issued $1,000 of additional common stock of which $500 was issued for cash and $500 was issued upon conversion of long-term debt.

p. Company M paid dividends of $200.

Based on the financial data from the preceding example, the following computations illustrate a method of indirectly determining cash received from customers and cash paid to suppliers and employees for use in a statement of cash flows under the direct method:

Cash received from customers during the year:

Customer sales		$13,965
Collection of installment payment for sale of inventory		100
Gross accounts receivable at beginning of year	$ 2,370	
Accounts receivable acquired in purchase of Company S	155	
Accounts receivable written off	(350)	
Gross accounts receivable at end of year	(2,390)	
Excess of new accounts receivable over collections from customers	(215)	
Cash received from customers during the year		$13,850

Cash paid to suppliers and employees during the year:

Cost of sales		$10,290
General and administrative expenses	$ 1,890	
Expenses not requiring cash outlay (provision for uncollectible accounts receivable)	(200)	
Net expenses requiring cash payments	1,690	
Inventory at beginning of year	(1,230)	
Inventory acquired in purchase of Company S	(350)	
Inventory at end of year	1,375	
Net decrease in inventory from Company M's operations		(205)
Adjustments for changes in related accruals:		
Account balances at beginning of year		
Accounts payable and accrued expenses	$ 1,085	
Other liabilities	225	
Prepaid expenses	(110)	
Total	1,200	
Accounts payable and accrued expenses acquired in purchase of Company S	255	

Account balances at end of year
  Accounts payable and accrued
    expenses ... 1,090
  Other liabilities ... 275
  Prepaid expenses ... (135)
    Total ... (1,230)

Additional cash payments not included
  in expense ... 225

Cash paid to suppliers and employees
  during the year ... $12,000

Presented below is a statement of cash flows for the year ended December 31, 19X1 for Company M. This statement of cash flows illustrates the direct method of presenting cash flows from operating activities.

COMPANY M
CONSOLIDATED STATEMENT OF CASH FLOWS
FOR THE YEAR ENDED DECEMBER 31, 19X1
Increase (Decrease) in Cash and Cash Equivalents

Cash flows from operating activities:

Cash received from customers	$13,850
Cash paid to suppliers and employees	(12,000)
Dividend received from affiliate	20
Interest received	55
Interest paid (net of amount capitalized)	(220)
Income taxes paid	(325)
Insurance proceeds received	15
Cash paid to settle lawsuit for patent infringement	(30)
Net cash provided by operating activities	$1,365

Cash flows from investing activities:

Proceeds from sale of facility	600
Payment received on note for sale of plant	150
Capital expenditures	(1,000)
Payment for purchase of Company S, net of cash acquired	(925)
Net cash used in investing activities	(1,175)

Cash flows from financing activities:

Net borrowings under line-of-credit agreement	300
Principal payments under capital lease obligation	(125)
Proceeds from issuance of long-term debt	400
Proceeds from issuance of common stock	500
Dividends paid	(200)
Net cash provided by financing activities	875
Net increase in cash and cash equivalents	1,065
Cash and cash equivalents at beginning of year	600
Cash and cash equivalents at end of year	$1,665

Reconciliation of net income to net cash provided by operating activities:

Net income		$ 760
Adjustments to reconcile net income to net cash provided by operating activities:		
Depreciation and amortization	$ 445	
Provision for losses on accounts receivable	200	
Gain on sale of facility	(80)	
Undistributed earnings of affiliate	(25)	
Payment received on installment note receivable for sale of inventory	100	
Change in assets and liabilities net of effects from purchase of Company S:		
Increase in accounts receivable	(215)	
Decrease in inventory	205	
Increase in prepaid expenses	(25)	
Decrease in accounts payable and accrued expenses	(250)	
Increase in interest and income taxes payable	50	
Increase in deferred taxes	150	
Increase in other liabilities	50	
Total adjustments		605
Net cash provided by operating activities		$1,365

Supplemental schedule of noncash investing and financing activities:

The Company purchased all of the capital stock of Company S for $950. In conjunction with the acquisition, liabilities were assumed as follows:

Fair value of assets acquired	$ 1,580
Cash paid for the capital stock	(950)
Liabilities assumed	$ 630

A capital lease obligation of $850 was incurred when the Company entered into a lease for new equipment.

Additional common stock was issued upon the conversion of $500 of long-term debt.

Disclosure of accounting policy:

For purposes of the statement of cash flows, the Company considers all highly liquid debt instruments purchased with a maturity of three months or less to be cash equivalents.

Presented below is Company M's statement of cash flows for the year ended December 31, 19X1 prepared using the indirect method.

COMPANY M
CONSOLIDATED STATEMENT OF CASH FLOWS
FOR THE YEAR ENDED DECEMBER 31, 19X1
Increase (Decrease) in Cash and Cash Equivalents

Cash flows from operating activities:

Net income		$ 760
Adjustments to reconcile net income to net cash provided by operating activities:		
Depreciation and amortization	$ 445	
Provision for losses on accounts receivable	200	
Gain on sale of facility	(80)	
Undistributed earnings of affiliate	(25)	
Payment received on installment note receivable for sale of inventory	100	
Change in assets and liabilities net of effects from purchase of Company S:		
Increase in accounts receivable	(215)	
Decrease in inventory	205	
Increase in prepaid expenses	(25)	
Decrease in accounts payable and accrued expenses	(250)	
Increase in interest and income taxes payable	50	
Increase in deferred taxes	150	
Increase in other liabilities	50	
Total adjustments		605
Net cash provided by operating activities		$1,365

Cash flows from investing activities:

Proceeds from sale of facility	600	
Payment received on note for sale of plant	150	
Capital expenditures	(1,000)	
Payment for purchase of Company S, net of cash acquired	(925)	
Net cash used in investing activities		(1,175)

Cash flows from financing activities:

Net borrowings under line-of-credit agreement	300
Principal payments under capital lease obligation	(125)
Proceeds from issuance of long-term debt	400
Proceeds from issuance of common stock	500
Dividends paid	(200)
Net cash provided by financing activities	875

Net increase in cash and cash equivalents	1,065
Cash and cash equivalents at beginning of year	600
Cash and cash equivalents at end of year	$1,665

Supplemental disclosures of cash flow information:

Cash paid during the year for:

Interest (net of amount capitalized)	$ 220
Income taxes	325

Supplemental schedule of noncash investing and financing activities:

The Company purchased all of the capital stock of Company S for $950. In conjunction with the acquisition, liabilities were assumed as follows:

Fair value of assets acquired	$ 1,580
Cash paid for the capital stock	(950)
Liabilities assumed	$ 630

A capital lease obligation of $850 was incurred when the Company entered into a lease for new equipment.

Additional common stock was issued upon the conversion of $500 of long-term debt.

Disclosure of accounting policy:

For purposes of the statement of cash flows, the Company considers all highly liquid debt instruments purchased with a maturity of three months or less to be cash equivalents.

8

Accounting and Disclosures

This chapter discusses the accounting for changes in principle, estimate, and reporting entity. Corrections of errors are also delved into. The accounting requirements for development stage companies are mentioned. In a troubled debt situation, the debtor wants relief from the creditor. Noninterest bearing notes and futures contracts are presented. Disclosure about financial instruments with off-balance-sheet risk are discussed.

ACCOUNTING CHANGES

The types of accounting changes provided for in APB 20 are principle, estimate, and reporting entity. Proper disclosure of accounting changes is necessary.

Change in Accounting Principle

Once adopted, it is presumed that an accounting principle should not be changed for events or transactions of a similar nature. A method used for a transaction which is being terminated or was a single, nonrecurring event in the past should not be changed. Only where necessary should a change in principle be made.

A change in accounting principle is accounted for in the current year's income statement in an account called "cumulative effect of a change in accounting principle." The amount equals the difference between retained earnings at the beginning of the year with the old method versus what retained earnings would have been at the beginning of the year if we used the new method in prior years. The account is shown net of tax with EPS on it. The new principle is used in the current and future years. Consistency is needed to make proper user comparisons. The cumulative effect account is shown after extraordinary items and before net income in the income statement. Note that a change in depreciation method for a new fixed asset is not a change in principle. Footnote disclosure should be made of the nature and justification of a change in principle including an explanation of why the new principle is preferred. Proper justification may take the form of a new FASB pronouncement, new tax law, new AICPA recommended practice, a change in circumstances, and to more readily conform to industry practice. According to FASB 32, specialized accounting practices and principles included in the AICPA Statements of Position (SOPs) and Guides are "preferable accounting principles" for the application of APB 20.

In the case where summaries of financial data for several years are presented in financial reports, APB 20 applies to them.

Indirect effects are included in the cumulative effect only if they are to be recorded on the books as a result of a change in accounting principle. The cumulative effect does *not* include nondiscretionary adjustments based on earnings (e.g., employee bonuses) which would have been recognized if the new principle had been used in prior years.

If comparative financial statements are now shown, pro forma disclosures (recalculated figures) should be made between the body of the financial statements and the footnotes of what earnings would have been in prior years if the new principle was used in those prior years along with showing the actual amounts for those years. If income statements are presented for comparative purposes, they should reflect the change on a pro forma basis as if the change had been in effect in each of such years. Financial statements of prior years, presented for comparative purposes, are presented as previously reported. However, income before extraordinary items, net income, and earnings per share for previous years presented are recalculated and disclosed on the face of the prior periods' income statements as if the new principle had been in use in those periods. If space does not allow, this information may be presented in separate schedules showing both the original and recalculated figures. If only the current period's income statement is presented, the actual and pro forma (recalculated) figures for the immediate preceding period should be disclosed.

In exceptional cases, pro forma amounts are not determinable for prior years even though the cumulative effect on the opening retained earnings balance can be computed. The cumulative effect of a change in principle is presented in the usual fashion with reasons given for omitting pro forma figures. In a similar vein, when the cumulative effect of a change in principle is impossible to calculate, disclosure is given for the effect of the change on income data of the current period and explaining the reason for omitting the cumulative effect and pro forma amounts for prior periods. An example of a situation where the cumulative effect is not determinable is a switch from the FIFO to LIFO inventory pricing method.

If an accounting change in principle is deemed immaterial in the current year but it is anticipated to be material in later years, disclosure is necessary.

Certain types of changes in accounting principle instead of being shown in a cumulative effect account require the restatement of prior years as if the new principle was used in those years. These changes are:

- Change from LIFO to another inventory method
- Change in accounting for long-term construction contracts (e.g., changing from the completed contract method to the percentage of completion method)
- Change to or from the full cost method used in the extractive industry. The full cost method is where both successful and unsuccessful exploration costs are deferred to the asset account and amortized. An alternative method is successful efforts where only successful costs are deferred while unsuccessful ones are expensed.

Exempt from the requirements of this opinion is a closely held business which for the first time registers securities, obtains equity capital, or effects a business combination. Such company may restate prior year financial statements.

Not considered a change in accounting principle are:

- A principle adopted for the first time on new or previously immaterial events or transactions
- A principle adopted or changed due to events or transactions clearly different in substance

As per Interpretation 1, an accounting principle is not only an accounting principle or practice, but also includes the methods used to apply such principles and practices. Changing the composition of the cost elements (e.g., material, labor, and overhead) of inventory qualifies as an accounting change. Changing the composition must be reported and justified as preferable. The basis of preferability among the different accounting principles is established in terms of whether the new principle improves the financial reporting function. Preferability is not determinable considering income tax effect alone.

EXAMPLE 1

X Company changed from double declining balance to straight-line depreciation in 19X7. It uses ACRS depreciation for tax purposes which results in depreciation higher than the double declining balance method for each of the three years. The tax rate is 34%. Relevant data follow:

Year	Double Declining Balance Depreciation	Straight-Line Depreciation	Difference
19X5	$250,000	$150,000	$100,000
19X6	200,000	150,000	50,000
19X7	185,000	150,000	35,000

The entries to reflect the change in depreciation in 19X7 follow:

Depreciation   150,000
   Accumulated Depreciation   150,000

For current year depreciation under the straight line method.

Accumulated Depreciation (100,000 + 50,000)   150,000
   Deferred Income Tax Credit (150,000 × .34)   51,000
   Cumulative Effect of a Change in Accounting Principle   99,000

Change in Accounting Estimate

A change in accounting estimate is caused by new circumstances or events requiring a revision in the estimates, such as a change in salvage value or life of an asset. A change in accounting estimate is accounted for prospectively over current and future years. There is *no* restatement of prior years. A footnote should describe the nature of the change. Disclosure is required in the period of the change for the effect on income before extraordinary items, net income, and earnings per share. However, such disclosure is not required for estimate changes in the ordinary course of business when immaterial. Examples are revising estimates of uncollectible accounts or inventory obsolescence. If a change in estimate is coupled with a change in principle and the effects cannot be distinguished, it is accounted for as a change in estimate. For instance, a change may be made from deferring and amortizing a cost to expensing it as incurred because future benefits may be doubtful. This should be accounted for as a change in estimate.

EXAMPLE 2

Equipment was bought on 1/1/19X2 for $40,000 having an original estimated life of 10 years with a salvage value of $4,000. On 1/1/19X6, the estimated life was revised to eight more years remaining with a new salvage value of $3,200. The journal entry on 12/31/19X6 for depreciation expense is:

Depreciation   2,800
   Accumulated Depreciation   2,800

Computations follow:

Book value on 1/1/19X6:

Original cost $40,000
Less: Accumulated Depreciation

$$\frac{\$40,000 - \$4,000}{10} = \$3,600 \times 4 \qquad \underline{14,400}$$

Book value $\underline{\underline{\$25,600}}$

Depreciation for 19X6:

Book value			$25,600
Less: New Salvage value			3,200
Depreciable cost			$22,400
$\dfrac{\text{Depreciable cost}}{\text{New life}}$	$\dfrac{\$22,400}{8}$	=	$2,800

Change in Reporting Entity

A change in reporting entity (e.g., two previously separate companies combine) is accounted for by restating prior years' financial statements as if both companies were always combined. Restatement for a change in reporting entity is necessary to show proper trends in comparative financial statements and historical summaries. The effect of the change on income before extraordinary items, net income, and per share amounts is reported for all periods presented. The restatement process does not have to go back more than five years. Footnote disclosure should be made of the nature of and reason for the change in reporting entity only in the year of change. Examples of changes in reporting entity are:

- Presenting consolidated statements instead of statements of individual companies
- Change in subsidiaries included in consolidated statements or those included in combined statements
- A business combination accounted for under the pooling-of-interests method

PRIOR PERIOD ADJUSTMENTS

The two types of prior period adjustments are:

- Correction of an error that was made in a prior year
- Recognition of a tax loss carryforward benefit arising from a purchased subsidiary (curtailed by the 1986 Tax Reform Act)

When a single year is presented, prior period adjustments adjust the beginning balance of retained earnings. The presentation follows:

Retained Earnings—1/1 Unadjusted

Prior Period Adjustments (net of tax)

Retained Earnings—1/1 Adjusted

Add: Net Income

Less: Dividends

Retained Earnings—12/31

Errors may be due to mathematical mistakes, errors in applying accounting principles, or misuse of facts existing when the financial statements were prepared. Further, a change in principle from one that is not GAAP to one that is GAAP is an error correction. Disclosure should be made of the nature of the error and the effect of correction on earnings.

When comparative statements are prepared, a retroactive adjustment for the error is made as it effects the prior years. The retroactive adjustment is disclosed by showing the effects of the adjustment on previous years' earnings and component items of net income.

EXAMPLE 3

In 19X1, a company incorrectly charged furniture for promotion expense amounting to $30,000. The error was discovered in 19X2. The correcting journal entry is:

Retained Earnings	30,000	
Furniture		30,000

EXAMPLE 4

X Company acquired Y Company on 1/1/19X3 recording goodwill of $60,000. Goodwill was not amortized. The correcting entry on 12/31/19X5 follows:

Amortization Expense (1500 × 1 for 19X5)	1,500	
Retained Earnings (1500 × 2 for 19X3 and 19X4)	3,000	
Goodwill		4,500

EXAMPLE 5

At the end of 19X2, a company failed to accrue telephone expense which was paid at the beginning of 19X3. The correcting entry on 12/31/19X3 is:

Retained Earnings	16,000	
Telephone Expense		16,000

EXAMPLE 6

On 1/1/19X2, an advance retainer fee of $50,000 was received covering a 5-year period. In error, revenue was credited for the full amount. The error was discovered on 12/31/19X4 before closing the books. The correcting entry is:

12/31/19X4 Retained Earnings	30,000	
Revenue		10,000
Deferred Revenue		20,000

EXAMPLE 7

A company bought a machine on January 1, 19X4 for $32,000 with a $2,000 salvage value and a 5-year life. By mistake, repairs expense was charged. The error was discovered on December 31, 19X7 before closing the books. The correcting entry follows:

Depreciation Expense	6,000	
Machine	32,000	
Accumulated Depreciation		24,000
Retained Earnings		14,000

Accumulated Depreciation of $24,000 is calculated below:

$$\frac{\$32,000 - \$2,000}{5} = \$6,000 \text{ per year} \times 4 \text{ years} = \$24,000$$

The credit to retained earnings reflects the difference between the erroneous repairs expense of $32,000 in 19X4 versus showing depreciation expense of $18,000 for three years (19X4-19X6).

EXAMPLE 8

At the beginning of 19X5, a company bought equipment for $300,000 with a salvage value of $20,000 and an expected life of 10 years. Straight line depreciation is used. In error, salvage value was not deducted in computing depreciation. The correcting journal entries on 12/31/19X7 follow:

		19X5 and 19X6
Depreciation taken $300,000/10 × 2 years		$60,000
Depreciation correctly stated $280,000/10 × 2 years		$56,000
		$ 4,000

Depreciation	28,000	
Accumulated Depreciation		28,000
Depreciation for current year		
Accumulated Depreciation	4,000	
Retained Earnings		4,000
Correct prior year depreciation misstatement		

DISCLOSURE OF ACCOUNTING POLICIES

Accounting policies of a business entity are the specific accounting principles and methods of applying them that are selected by management. Accounting policies used should be those that are most appropriate in the circumstances to fairly present financial position and results of operations for the period.

Accounting policies can relate to reporting and measurement methods as well as disclosures. They include:

- A selection from generally accepted accounting principles
- Practices unique to the given industry
- Unusual applications of generally accepted accounting principles

The first footnote or section preceding the notes to the financial statements should be a description of the accounting policies followed by the company.

The application of GAAP requires the use of judgement where alternative acceptable principles exist and where varying methods of applying a principle to a given set of facts exist. Disclosure of these principles and methods is vital to the full presentation of financial position and operations so that rational economic decisions can be made.

Examples of accounting policy disclosures are the depreciation method used, consolidation bases, amortization period for goodwill, construction contract method, and inventory pricing method.

Notes: Financial statement classification methods and qualitative data (e.g., litigation) are not accounting policies.

Some types of financial statements need not describe the accounting policies followed. Examples are quarterly unaudited statements when there has not been a policy change since the last year-end, and statements solely for internal use.

DEVELOPMENT STAGE COMPANIES

A development stage entity is one concentrating on establishing a new business and either major operations have not begun or principal operations have started but no significant revenue has been derived. Some types of activities of a development stage enterprise are establishing sources of supply, developing markets, obtaining financing, financial and production planning, research and development, buying capital assets, and recruiting staff. The same generally accepted accounting principles for an established company must be followed by a development stage enterprise. A balance sheet, income statement, and statement of cash flows are prepared. The balance sheet shows the accumulated net losses as a deficit. The income statement presents cumulative amounts of revenues and expenses since inception of the business. Similarly, the Statement of Cash Flows presents the operating, investing, and financing cash receipts and cash payments. The stockholders' equity statement shows for each equity security from inception: (1) date and number of shares issued, and (2) dollar figures per share applicable to cash and noncash consideration. The nature and basis to determine amounts for noncash consideration must also be provided.

Financial statements must be headed "development stage enterprise." A footnote should describe the development stage activities. In the first year the entity is no longer in the development stage, it should disclose that in previous years it was.

TROUBLED DEBT RESTRUCTURING

When a troubled debt restructuring occurs, the debtor, because of his or her financial problems, is relieved of part or all of the amount owed the creditor. The concession arises from the debtor-creditor agreement, law, or applies to foreclosure and repossession. The types of troubled debt restructurings follow:

- Debtor transfers to creditor receivables from third parties or other assets
- Debtor gives creditor equity securities to satisfy the debt
- Modification of the debt terms including reducing the interest rate, extending the maturity date, or reducing the principal of the obligation.

The debtor books an extraordinary gain (net of tax) on the restructuring, while the creditor recognizes a loss. The loss may be ordinary or extraordinary, depending on whether the arrangement by the creditor is unusual and infrequent. Typically, the loss is ordinary.

Debtor

The gain to the debtor equals the difference between the fair value of assets exchanged and the book value of the debt including accrued interest. Further, there may arise a gain on disposal of assets exchanged equal to the difference between the fair market value and the book value of the transferred assets. The latter gain or loss is not a gain or loss on restructuring, but instead an ordinary gain or loss in connection with asset disposal.

EXAMPLE 9

A debtor transfers assets having a fair market value of $70 and a book value of $50 to settle a payable having a carrying value of $85. The gain on restructuring is $15 ($85 − $70). The ordinary gain is $20 ($70 − $50).

A debtor may provide the creditor with an equity interest. The debtor records the equity securities issued based on fair market value and not the recorded value of the debt extinguished. The excess of the recorded payable satisfied over the fair value of the issued securities represents an extraordinary item.

A modification in terms of an initial debt contract is accounted for prospectively. A new interest rate may be determined based on the new terms. This interest rate is then used to allocate future payments to lower principal and interest. When the new terms of the agreement results in the sum of all the future payments to be *less* than the carrying value of the payable, the payable is reduced and a restructuring gain recorded for the difference. Future payments are deemed a reduction of principal only. Interest expense is not recorded.

A troubled debt restructuring may result in a combination of concessions to the debtor. This may take place when assets or an equity interest are given in partial satisfaction of the obligation and the balance is subject to a modification of terms. Two steps are involved. First, the payable is reduced by the fair value of the assets or equity transferred. Second, the balance of the debt is accounted for as a "modification of terms" type restructuring.

Direct costs, such a legal fees, incurred by the debtor in an equity transfer reduce the fair value of the equity interest. All other costs reduce the gain on restructuring. If there is no gain involved, they are expensed.

EXAMPLE 10

The debtor owes the creditor $200,000 and has expressed that due to financial problems there may be difficulty in making future payments. Footnote disclosure of the problem should be made by both debtor and creditor.

EXAMPLE 11

The debtor owes the creditor $80,000. The creditor relieves the debtor of $10,000. The balance of the debt will be paid at a subsequent time.

The journal entry for the debtor is:

Accounts Payable	10,000	
Extraordinary Gain		10,000

The journal entry for the creditor is:

Ordinary Loss	10,000	
Accounts Receivable		10,000

EXAMPLE 12

The debtor owed the creditor $90,000. The creditor agrees to accept $70,000 in full satisfaction of the obligation.

The journal entry for the debtor is:

Accounts Payable	20,000	
Extraordinary Gain		20,000

The journal entry for the creditor is:

Ordinary Loss	20,000	
Accounts Receivable		20,000

The debtor should disclose the following in the footnotes:

- Particulars of the restructuring agreement
- The aggregate and per share amounts of the gain on restructuring
- Amounts that are contingently payable including the contingency terms

Creditor

The creditor's loss is the difference between the fair value of assets received and the book value of the investment. When terms are modified, the creditor recognizes interest income to the degree that total future payments are greater than the carrying value of the investment. Interest income is recognized using the effective interest method. Assets received are reflected at fair market value. When the book value of the receivable is in excess of the aggregate payments, an ordinary loss is recognized for the difference. All cash received in the future is accounted for as a recovery of the investment. Direct costs of the creditor are expensed.

The creditor does not recognize contingent interest until the contingency is removed and interest has been earned. Further, future changes in the interest rate are accounted for as a change in estimate.

The creditor discloses the following in the footnotes:

- Loan commitments of additional funds to financially troubled companies
- Loans and/or receivables by major type
- Debt agreements in which the interest rate has been downwardly adjusted, including an explanation of the circumstances
- Description of the restructuring terms

IMPUTING INTEREST ON NOTES

In the case where the face amount of a note does not represent the present value of the consideration given or received in the exchange, imputation of interest is needed to avoid the misstatement of profit. Interest is imputed on noninterest bearing notes, notes that provide for an unrealistically low interest rate, and when the face value of the note is significantly different from the "going" selling price of the property or market value of the note.

If a note is issued only for cash, the note should be recorded at the cash exchanged irrespective of whether the interest rate is reasonable. The note has a present value at issuance equal to the cash transacted. When a note is exchanged for property, goods, or services a presumption exists that the interest rate is fair and reasonable. Where the stipulated interest rate is not fair and adequate, the note has to be recorded at the fair value of the merchandise or services or at an amount that approximates fair value. If fair value is not determinable for the goods or services, the discounted present value of the note has to be used.

The imputed interest rate is the one that would have resulted if an independent borrower or lender had negotiated a similar transaction. For example, it is the prevailing interest rate the borrower would have paid for financing. The interest rate is based on economic circumstances and events.

Factors to be considered in deriving an appropriate discount rate include:

- Prime interest rate
- "Going" market rate for similar quality instruments
- Issuer's credit standing
- Collateral
- Restrictive covenants and other terms in the note agreement
- Tax effects of the arrangement

APB 21 applies to long-term payables and receivables. Short-term payables and receivables are typically recorded at face value since the extra work of amortizing a discount or premium on a short-term note is not worth the information benefit obtained. APB 21 is not applicable to:

- Security deposits
- Usual lending activities of banks
- Amounts that do not mandate repayment
- Receivables or payables occurring within the ordinary course of business
- Transactions between parent and subsidiary

The difference between the face value of the note and the present value of the note represents discount or premium which has to be accounted for as an element of interest over the life of the note. Present value of the payments of the note is based on an imputed interest rate.

The interest method is used to amortize the discount or premium on the note. The interest method results in a constant rate of interest. Under the method, amortization equals:

Interest Rate × Present Value of the Liability/Receivable at the beginning of the year

Interest expense is recorded for the borrower while interest revenue is recorded for the lender. Issuance costs are treated as a deferred charge.

The note payable and note receivable are presented in the balance sheet as follows:

Notes Payable (principal plus interest)

Less: Discount (interest)

Present Value (principal)

Notes Receivable (principal plus interest)

Less: Premium (interest)

Present Value (principal)

EXAMPLE 13

On 1/1/19X1 equipment is acquired in exchange for a one year note payable of $1,000 maturing on 12/31/19X1. The imputed interest rate is 10% resulting in the present value factor for $n = 1$, $i = 10\%$ of .91. Relevant journal entries follow:

1/1/19X1 Equipment	910	
Discount	90	
Notes Payable		1,000
12/31/19X1		
Interest Expense	90	
Discount		90
Notes Payable	1,000	
Cash		1,000

EXAMPLE 14

On 1/1/19X1, a machine is bought for cash of $10,000 and the incurrence of a $30,000, 5-year, noninterest bearing note payable. The imputed interest rate is 10%. The present value factor for $n = 5$, $i = 10\%$ is .62. Appropriate journal entries follow:

1/1/19X1		
Machine (10,000 + 18,600)	28,600	
Discount	11,400	
Notes Payable		30,000
Cash		10,000

Present value of note equals $30,000 \times .62 = \$18,600$

On 1/1/19X1, the balance sheet shows:

Notes Payable	$30,000
Less: Discount	11,400
Present Value	$18,600

12/31/19X1		
Interest Expense	1,860	
Discount		1,860
$10\% \times \$18,600 = \$1,860$		

1/1/19X2	
Notes Payable	$30,000
Less: Discount (11,400 − 1,860)	9,540
Present Value	$20,460

12/31/19X2		
Interest Expense	2,046	
Discount		2,046
$10\% \times \$20,460 = \$2,046$		

FUTURES CONTRACTS

A futures contract is a legal arrangement entered into by the purchaser or seller and a regulated futures exchange in the United Stages or overseas. However, FASB 80 does not apply to foreign currencies futures which are dealt with in FASB 82. Futures contracts involve:

- A buyer or seller receiving or making a delivery of a commodity or financial instrument (e.g., stocks, bonds, commercial paper, mortgages) at a given date. Cash settlement rather than delivery often exists (e.g., stock index future).

- A futures contract may be eliminated prior to the delivery date by engaging in an offsetting contract for the particular commodity or financial instrument involved. For instance, a futures contract to buy 100,000 pounds of a commodity by December 31, 19X1 may be canceled by entering into another contract to sell 100,000 pounds of that same commodity on December 31, 19X1.

- Changes in value of open contracts are settled regularly (e.g., daily). The usual contract provides that when a decrease in the contract value occurs, the contract holder has to make a cash deposit for such decline with the clearinghouse. If the contract increases in value, the holder may withdraw the increased value.

The change in market value of a futures contract involves a gain or loss that should be recognized in earnings. An exception exists that for certain contracts the timing of income statement recognition relates to the accounting for the applicable asset, liability, commitment, or transaction. This accounting exception applies when the contract is designed as a hedge against price and interest rate fluctuation. When the criteria below are satisfied, the accounting for the contract relates to the accounting for the hedged item. Thus, a change in market value is recognized in the same accounting period that the effects of the related changes in price or interest rate of the hedged item is reflected in income.

A hedge exists when both of the following criteria are met:

- The hedged item places price and interest rate risk on the firm. Risk means the sensitivity of corporate earnings to market price changes or rates of return of existing assets, liabilities, commitments, and expected transactions. This criteria is *not* met in the case where other assets, liabilities, commitments, and anticipated transactions already offset the risk.

- The contract lowers risk exposure and is entered into as a hedge. High correlation exists between the change in market value of the contract and the fair value of the hedged item. In effect, the market price change of the contract offsets the price and interest rate changes on the exposed item. An example is when there exists a futures contract to sell silver that offsets the changes in the price of silver.

A change in market value of a futures contract that meets the hedging criteria of the related asset or liability should adjust the carrying value of the hedged item. For instance, a company has an investment in a government bond that it anticipates to sell at a later date. The company can reduce its susceptibility to changes in fair value of the bonds by engaging in a futures contract. The changes in the market value of the futures contract adjusts the book value of the bonds.

A change in market value of a futures contract that is for the purpose of hedging a firm commitment is included in measuring the transaction satisfying the commitment. An example is when the company hedges a firm purchase commitment by using a futures contract. When the acquisition takes place thus satisfying the purchase commitment, the gain or loss on the futures contract is an element of the cost of the acquired item. Assume ABC Company has a purchase commitment for 30,000 pounds of a commodity at $2 per pound, totaling $60,000. At the time of the consummation of the transaction, the $60,000 cost is *decreased* by any gain (e.g., $5,000) arising from the "hedged" futures contract. The net cost is shown as the carrying value (e.g., $55,000).

A futures contract may apply to transactions the company expects to conduct in the ordinary course of business. It is not obligated to do so. These expected transactions do not involve existing assets or liabilities, or transactions applicable to existing firm commitments. For instance, a company may anticipate buying a certain commodity in the future but has not made a formal purchase commitment. The company may minimize risk exposure to price changes by entering into a futures contract. The change in market value of this "anticipatory hedge contract" is included in measuring the subsequent transaction. The change in market value of the futures contract adjusts the cost of the acquired item. The following criteria must be met for "anticipatory hedge accounting":

1. and 2. are the same as the criteria for regular hedge contracts related to existing assets, liabilities, or firm commitments.

3. Identification exists of the major terms of the contemplated transaction. Included are the type of commodity or financial instrument, quantity, and expected transaction date. If the financial instrument carries interest, the maturity date should be given.

4. It is probable that the expected transaction will take place. Probability of occurrence depends on the following:

   • Time period involved

   • Monetary commitment for the activity

   • Financial capability to conduct the transaction

   • Frequency of previous transactions of a similar nature

   • Possibility that other types of transactions may be undertaken to accomplish the desired goal

   • Adverse operational effects of not engaging in the transaction

The accounting applicable for a hedge type futures contract related to an expected asset acquisition or liability incurrence should be consistent with the company's accounting method employed for those assets and liabilities. For instance, the firm should book a loss for a futures contract that is a hedge of an expected inventory acquisition if the amount will not be recovered from the sale of inventory.

If a hedged futures contract is closed prior to the expected transaction, the accumulated value change in the contract should be carried forward to be included in measuring the related transaction. If it is probable that the quantity of an expected transaction will be less than the amount initially hedged, recognize a gain or loss for a pro rata portion of futures results that would have been included in the measurement of the subsequent transaction.

A hedged futures contract requires disclosure of:

- Firm commitments
- Nature of assets and liabilities
- Accounting method used for the contract including a description of events or transactions resulting in recognizing changes in contract values
- Expected transactions that are hedged with futures contracts

DISCLOSURE OF FINANCIAL INSTRUMENTS

FASB No. 105 requires disclosure of information about financial instruments with off-balance sheet risk and financial instruments with concentrations of credit risk. A financial instrument is defined as cash, evidence of an ownership interest in another entity, or a contract that *both*: (1) imposes on one entity a contractual obligation to deliver cash or another financial instrument to a second entity, or exchange financial instruments on unfavorable terms, and (2) conveys to the second entity a contractual right to receive cash, another financial instrument, or exchange financial instruments on favorable terms with the first entity. Examples of financial instruments include letters of credit or loan commitments written, foreign currency or interest rate swaps, financial guarantees written, forward or futures contracts, call and put options written, and interest rate caps or floors written.

An entity must disclose information about financial instruments that may result in future loss but have *not* been recognized in the accounts as liabilities and are thus not reported in the income statement or balance sheet. A financial instrument has an off-balance sheet risk of accounting loss if the risk of loss to the company exceeds the amount recognized as an asset (if any), or if the ultimate obligation may exceed the amount recognized as a liability.

The following must be footnoted:

- The entity's policy for requiring collateral or other security on financial instruments it accepts
- Identification and description of collateral held

- The face or principal amounts of the financial instruments
- The extent, nature, and terms of the financial instruments, including any cash requirements
- A discussion of credit risks associated with financial instruments because of the failure of another party to perform
- A discussion of market risk that will make a financial instrument less valuable including future changes in market prices caused by foreign exchange and interest rate fluctuations
- The entity's accounting policies regarding financial instruments
- The potential loss arising from the financial instrument if a party fails to carry out the contractual terms
- Information about a region, activity, or economic factor that may result in a concentration of credit risk

9
Key Financial Accounting Areas

This chapter discusses the accounting requirements for major financial areas including consolidation, investing in stocks and bonds, leases, pensions, post retirement benefits excluding pensions, tax allocation, and foreign currency translation and transactions.

CONSOLIDATION

Consolidation occurs when the parent owns in excess of 50% of the voting common stock of the subsidiary. The major objective of consolidation is to present as one economic unit the financial position and operating results of a parent and subsidiaries. It shows the group as a single company (with one or more branches or divisions) rather than separate companies. It is an example of theoretical substance over legal form. The companies making up the consolidated group keep their individual legal identity. Adjustments and eliminations are for the sole purpose of financial statement reporting. Consolidation is still appropriate even if the subsidiary has a material amount of debt. Disclosure should be made of the firm's consolidation policy in footnotes or by explanatory headings.

A consolidation is negated, even if more than 50% of voting common stock is owned by the parent, in the following cases:

- Parent is not in actual control of subsidiary (e.g., subsidiary is in receivership, subsidiary is in a politically unstable foreign country)
- Parent has sold or contracted to sell subsidiary shortly after year-end. The subsidiary is a temporary investment.
- Minority interest is very large in comparison to the parent's interest, thus individual financial statements are more meaningful.

153

Intercompany eliminations include that for intercompany payables and receivables, advances, and profits. However, for certain regulated companies, intercompany profit does not have to be eliminated to the extent the profit represents a reasonable return on investment. Subsidiary investment in the parent's shares is not consolidated outstanding stock in the consolidated balance sheet. Consolidated statements do not reflect capitalized earnings in the form of stock dividends by subsidiaries subsequent to acquisition.

Minority interest in a subsidiary is the stockholders' equity of those outside to the parent's controlling interest in the partially owned subsidiaries. Minority interest should be shown as a separate component of stockholders' equity. When losses applicable to the minority interest in a subsidiary exceed the minority interest's equity capital, the excess and any subsequent losses related to the minority interest are charged to the parent. If profit subsequently occurs, the parent's interest is credited to the degree of prior losses absorbed.

If a parent acquires a subsidiary in more than one block of stock, each purchase is on a step-by-step basis and consolidation does not occur until control exists.

In the case the subsidiary is acquired within the year, the subsidiary should be included in consolidation as if it had been bought at the beginning of the year with a subtraction for the preacquisition part of earnings applicable to each block of stock. An alternative, but less preferable approach, is to include in consolidation the subsidiary's earnings subsequent to the acquisition date.

The retained earnings of a subsidiary at the acquisition date is not included in the consolidated financial statements.

When the subsidiary is disposed of during the year, the parent should present its equity in the subsidiary's earnings prior to the sale date as a separate line item consistent with the equity method.

A subsidiary whose major business activity is leasing to a parent should always be consolidated.

Consolidation is still permissible without adjustments when the fiscal year-ends of the parent and subsidiary are three months or less apart. Footnote disclosure is needed of material events occurring during the intervening period.

The equity method of accounting is used for unconsolidated subsidiaries unless there is a foreign investment or a temporary investment. In a case where the equity method is not used, the cost method is followed. The cost method recognizes the difference between the cost of the subsidiary and the equity in net assets at the acquisition date. Depreciation is adjusted for the difference as if consolidation of the subsidiary was made. There is an elimination of intercompany gain or loss for unconsolidated subsidiaries to the extent the gain or loss exceeds the unrecorded equity in undistributed earnings. Unconsolidated subsidiaries accounted for with the cost method should have adequate disclosure of assets, liabilities, and earnings. Such disclosure may be in footnote or supplementary schedule form.

There may be instances when combined rather than consolidated financial statements are more meaningful, such as where a person owns a controlling interest in several related operating companies (brother-sister corporation).

There are cases where parent company statements are required to properly provide information to creditors and preferred stockholders. In this event, *dual columns* are needed—one column for the parent and other columns for subsidiaries.

The accounting for business combinations is discussed in Chapter 44.

INVESTMENTS IN STOCKS AND BONDS

Investments in stock may be accounted for under the cost or equity method depending on the percentage of ownership in the voting common stock.

Notes: Nonvoting stock (e.g., preferred stock) is always accounted for under the cost method.

FASB 12 does *not* apply to not-for-profit organizations, mutual life insurance companies, or employee benefit plans.

Cost Method

A security is usually classified as current if it is liquid and used for temporary excess cash. A security is usually classified as long-term if the intent is to hold for one year or more, it is for capital appreciation purposes, dividend income is desired, possible eventual control is involved, there is a lack of market price quotations, and restricted marketability exists. "Restricted" stock is noncurrent except if it qualifies for sale within one year of the balance sheet date and there are readily available price quotations.

The cost method of accounting for investments is used when the holder owns less than 20% of the voting common stock of the company. However, the cost method could be used instead of the equity method when the holder owns between 20%-50% of the voting common stock but lacks significant influence (effective control).

Significant influence may be indicated by one or more of the following:

- Involvement in decision making of owned company
- Material intercompany transactions
- Representation on the Board of Directors of the investee company
- Investor owns a high percentage of investee's shares relative to other stockholders
- Managerial personnel are interchanged between the investor and investee
- Investor provides investee with technological expertise

Indicators of a lack of significant influence follow:

- Concentration of majority ownership of investee among a limited number of stockholders, especially when the group operates the investee in disregard of the investor's viewpoints
- Investor is unable to obtain the financial data needed from the investee to use the equity method

- Investor and investee sign an agreement (called "standstill") in which the investor surrenders material shareholder rights. The standstill agreement is typically employed to settle disputes between the investor and investee.
- Investee opposes the investment (e.g., a lawsuit or complaint is filed)

The cost method must be used for equity securities. While it is not required for debt securities, debt securities in practice are usually reflected in the entire investment portfolio at the lower of cost or market value.

The investment portfolio is broken down into current and noncurrent. Current securities are shown as marketable securities under current assets. Noncurrent securities are shown as noncurrent assets. The lower of cost or market value is applied to each portfolio separately.

If market value is in excess of cost, the securities are shown at cost with market value either disclosed in parentheses or in a footnote. If market value is less than cost, the securities portfolio is written down to market value reflecting an unrealized loss due to conservatism. Thus, a temporary decline in value of the portfolio is reflected. The portfolio is shown on the balance sheet at the lower of total cost or total market value. The following entry is made at the end of the year:

Unrealized Loss

     Allowance to Reduce Securities from Cost to Market Value

For short-term securities, the unrealized loss is shown in the income statement. For long-term securities, the unrealized loss is shown as a separate item in the stockholders' equity section. The allowance account is a contra account to Investments to derive the net amount. The only time the allowance account is entered into is at the end of the year.

In the following year, if there is a partial or full recovery from cost to market value, the entry is:

Allowance to Reduce Securities from Cost to Market Value

     Unrealized Gain

However, in recording the recovery from cost to market value, the portfolio can never be written up at an amount in excess of the original cost.

If securities are sold during the year, a realized loss or realized gain will occur. The realized loss or gain is shown in the income statement irrespective of whether the portfolio is current or noncurrent. The same realized loss or gain on sale is reflected for tax return preparation purposes.

The entry to record the sale of securities is:

Cash (proceeds received)

Loss

     Securities (at cost)

     Gain

A loss or gain will either be involved in the above entry.

A security cannot be recorded at more than cost since that will lack conservatism. The only time market value can be used for valuation is the case of a permanent increase in value. However, accountants are very reluctant to state that a permanent increase has occurred because of legal liability exposure.

If a balance sheet is unclassified, the investment security portfolio is considered to be noncurrent.

A permanent decline in value of a particular security is immediately recognized with a realized loss being booked shown in the income statement even if it is a noncurrent portfolio. The investment account is credited directly. The new market value becomes the new cost basis which means it cannot later be written up.

A permanent decline in market price of stock may be indicated when the company has several years of losses, a very weak financial condition, and has issued a liquidating dividend. For example, if the company sells some of its major divisions and distributes the proceeds to stockholders, a writedown of the investment may be appropriate.

EXAMPLE 1

In a long-term investment portfolio, one stock in ABC Company has suffered a permanent decline in value from cost of $6,000 to market value of $5,000. The entry is:

Realized Loss	1,000	
Long-term Investment		1,000

The new cost now becomes $5,000 (the market value). If in a later period the market value increased above $5,000, the stock would not be written up above $5,000.

If a particular stock is reclassified from noncurrent to current, or vice versa, it is transferred at the lower of cost or market value at the transfer date. If market value exceeds cost, it is transferred at cost intact with no unrealized gain being recorded. If market value is below cost, a realized loss in the income statement is booked and the investment account is credited. The new cost basis becomes the market value which means the portfolio cannot be written up above cost.

EXAMPLE 2

XYZ stock is reclassified from noncurrent to current. If cost is $3,000 and market value is $2,700, the entry for the reclassification is:

Short-term Securities	2,700	
Realized Loss	300	
Long-term Investment		3,000

If a later recovery occurs and market value becomes $2,900, no entry will be made.

If market value of a portfolio substantially drops below cost between year-end and the audit report date, subsequent event footnote disclosure is required.

Income tax allocation occurs with investments due to resulting temporary differences. A deferred tax credit will arise because unrealized losses and gains on securities are not reflected for tax return preparation purposes.

EXAMPLE 3

On 1/1/19X1, Company X purchases long-term securities of $480,000 plus brokerage commissions of $20,000. On 5/12/19X1, a cash dividend of $15,000 is received. On 12/31/19X1, the market value of the portfolio is $490,000. On 2/6/19X2 securities costing $50,000 are sold for $54,000. On 12/31/19X2, the market value of the portfolio is $447,000. The journal entries follow:

1/1/19X1 Long-term Investments	500,000	
Cash		500,000
5/12/19X1 Cash	15,000	
Dividend Revenue		15,000
12/31/19X1		
Unrealized Loss	10,000	
Allowance		10,000

The balance sheet presentation of the long-term investments is:

Long-term Investments	$500,000
Less: Allowance	10,000
Net Balance	$490,000

If market value were $510,000 instead of $490,000, the securities portfolio would remain intact at $500,000 with the market value of $510,000 being disclosed.

2/6/19X2 Cash	54,000	
Long-term Investments		50,000
Gain		4,000
12/31/19X2		
Allowance	7,000	
Unrealized Loss		7,000

The balance sheet presentation of the long-term securities is:

Long-term Investments	$450,000
Less: Allowance	3,000
Net Balance	$447,000

If instead market value was $435,000, the entry would have been:

Unrealized Loss	5,000	
Allowance		5,000

If instead market value was $452,000, the entry would have been:

```
Allowance                                    10,000
    Unrealized Loss                                    10,000
```

If two or more securities are purchased at one price, the cost is allocated among the securities based on their relative fair market value. In the exchange of one security for another, the new security received in the exchange is valued at its fair market value.

EXAMPLE 4

Preferred stock costing $10,000 is exchanged for 1,000 shares of common stock having a market value of $15,000. The entry is:

```
Investment in Common Stock                   15,000
    Investment in Preferred Stock                      10,000
    Gain                                                5,000
```

A stock dividend involves a memo entry reflecting more shares at no additional cost. As a result, the cost per share decreases.

EXAMPLE 5

Fifty shares at $12 per share for a total cost of $600 is owned. A 20% stock dividend is declared amounting to 10 shares. A memo entry is made reflecting the additional shares as follows:

		Investment	
50	$12	$600	
10		0	
60	$10	$600	

If shares are later sold at $15, the entry is:

```
Cash                                         150
    Long-term Investment                              100
    Gain                                               50
```

A stock split has the effect of increasing the shares and reducing the cost basis on a proportionate basis. A memo entry is made. Assume 100 shares costing $20 per share were owned. A two for one split would result in 200 shares at a cost per share of $10. Total par value remains at $2,000.

Equity Method

The investor company is the owner and the investee company is being owned. If an investor owns between 20% to 50% of the voting common stock of an investee, the equity method is used. The equity method would also be employed if the holder owned less than 20% of the voting common stock but possessed significant influence (effective control). The equity method is also used if more than 50% of the voting common stock was owned but one of the negating factors for consolidation existed. Further, investments in joint ventures have to be accounted for under the equity method.

The accounting under the equity method can be illustrated by examining the following "T-accounts" which will be described in more detail shortly:

Investment in Investee

Cost	Dividends
Ordinary Profit	Amortization Expense on
	Goodwill
Extraordinary Gain	Depreciation on Excess of Fair
	Market Value Less Book
	Value of Specific Assets
	Permanent Decline

Equity in Earnings of Investee

| Amortization Expense | Ordinary Profit |
| Depreciation | |

Loss

| Permanent Decline | |

Extraordinary Gain

| | Extraordinary Gain |

The cost of the investment includes brokerage fees. The investor recognizes his percentage ownership interest in the ordinary profit of the investee by debiting investment in investee and crediting equity in earnings of investee. The investor's share in investee's earnings is computed after deducting cumulative preferred dividends, whether or not declared. Investor's share of investee's profit should be based on the investee's most recent income statement applied on a consistent basis. Extraordinary gains or losses as well as prior period adjustments are also picked up as shown on the investee's books. Dividends reduce the carrying value of the investment account.

The excess paid by the investor for the investee's net assets is first assigned to the specific assets and liabilities and depreciated. The unidentifiable portion of excess is considered goodwill which is amortized over the period benefited not exceeding 40 years. The amortization expense on goodwill and depreciation on excess value of assets reduce the investment account and are charged to equity in earnings. Temporary decline in price of the investment in the investee is ignored. Permanent decline in value of the investment is reflected by debiting loss and crediting investment in investee.

When the investor's share of the investee's losses is greater than the balance in the investment account, the equity method should be discontinued at the zero amount unless the investor has guaranteed the investee's obligations or where immediate profitability is assured. A return to the equity method is made only after offsetting subsequent profits against losses not recorded.

When the investee's stock is sold, a realized gain or loss will arise for the difference between selling price and the cost of the investment account.

The mechanics of consolidation essentially apply with the equity method. For example, intercompany profits and losses are eliminated. Investee capital transactions impacting the investor's share of equity should be accounted for as in a consolidation. Investee's capital transactions should be accounted for as if the investee was a consolidated subsidiary. For example, when the investee issues its common stock to third parties at a price in excess of book value, there will be an increase in the value of the investment and a related increase in the investor's paid-in-capital.

Interperiod income tax allocation will occur because the investor shows the investee's profits for book reporting but dividends for tax reporting. This results in a deferred income tax credit account.

If the ownership goes below 20% or the investor for some reason is unable to control the investee, the investor should cease recognizing the investee's earnings. The equity method is discontinued but the balance in the investment account is maintained. The cost method should then be applied.

If the investor increases his ownership in the investee to 20% or more, the equity method should be used for current and future years. Further, the effect of using the equity method rather than the cost method on prior years at the old percentage (e.g., 15%) should be recognized as an adjustment to retained earnings and other accounts so affected such as investment in investee. The retroactive adjustment on the investment, earnings, and retained earnings should be applied in the same manner as a step-by-step acquisition of a subsidiary.

Disclosures should be made by the investor in footnotes, separate schedules, or parenthetically of the following: percent owned, name of investee, investor's accounting policies employed, material effects of possible conversions and exercises of investee common stock, and quoted market price (for investees not qualifying as subsidiaries). Further, summarized financial data as to assets, liabilities, and earnings should be given in footnotes or separate schedules for material investments in unconsolidated subsidiaries. Material realized and unrealized gains and losses relating to the subsidiary's portfolio occurring between the dates of the financial statements of the subsidiary and parent must also be disclosed.

EXAMPLE 6

On 1/1/19X5, X Company bought 30,000 shares for a 40% interest in the common stock of AB Company at $25 per share. Brokerage commissions were $10,000. During 19X5, AB's net income was $140,000 and dividends received were $30,000. On 1/1/19X6, X Company received 15,000 shares of common stock as a result of a stock split by AB Company. On 1/4/19X6, X Company sold 2,000 shares at $16 per share of AB stock. The journal entries follow:

1/1/19X5 Investment in Investee	760,000	
Cash		760,000
12/31/19X5 Investment in Investee	56,000	
Equity in Earnings of Investee		56,000
40% × $140,000 = $56,000		
Cash	30,000	
Investment in Investee		30,000
1/1/19X6 Memo entry for stock split		
1/4/19X6 Cash (2,000 × $16)	32,000	
Loss on Sale of Investment	2,940	
Investment in Investee (2,000 × $17.47)		34,940

$$\frac{\$786,000}{45,000} = \$17.47 \text{ per share}$$

Investment in Investee

1/1/19X5	760,000	12/31/19X5	30,000
12/31/19X5	56,000		
	816,000		
	786,000		

EXAMPLE 7

On 1/1/19X6, an investor purchased 100,000 shares of the investee's 400,000 shares outstanding for $3,000,000. The book value of net assets acquired was $2,500,000. Of the $500,000 excess paid over book value, $300,000 is attributable to undervalued tangible assets and the remainder is attributable to unidentifiable assets. The depreciation period is 20 years and the maximum period is used to amortize goodwill. In 19X6, the investee's net income was $800,000 including an extraordinary loss of $200,000. Dividends of $75,000 were paid of June 1, 19X6. The following journal entries are necessary for the acquisition of the investee by the investor accounted for under the equity method.

1/1/19X6 Investment in Investee	3,000,000	
Cash		3,000,000
6/1/19X6 Cash	18,750	
Investment in Investee		18,750
25% × $75,000		
12/31/19X6		
Investment in Investee	250,000	
Equity in Earnings of Investee		250,000
$1,000,000 × 25% = $250,000		
Extraordinary Loss from Investment	50,000	
Investment in Investee		50,000
$200,000 × 25% = $50,000		
Equity in Earnings of Investee	20,000	
Investment in Investee		20,000

Computation follows:

Undervalued depreciable assets $300,000/20 years	$ 15,000
Unrecorded goodwill $200,000/40 years	5,000
	$ 20,000

Bond Investments

The rules of FASB 12 do *not* require debt securities to be written down from cost to market value for a temporary change. A company has the option, which is typically practiced, of retaining investments in debt securities (e.g., bonds) at cost. However, a permanent decline in the price of bonds requires loss recognition.

The difference between the cost of a bond and its face value is discount or premium. Discount or premium is amortized over the life of the bond from the acquisition date.

The bond investment account is usually recorded net of the discount or premium. If bonds are acquired between interest dates, accrued interest should be recorded separately.

The market price of the bond takes into account:

- The financial health of the issuer
- "Going" interest rates in the market
- The maturity period

The market price is computed by discounting the principal and interest payments using the yield rate.

EXAMPLE 8

An investor buys $100,000, 6%, 20-year bonds on 3/1/19X5. Interest is payable on 1/1 and 6/30. The bonds are bought at face value.

3/1/19X5
Investment in Bonds	100,000	
Accrued Bond Interest Receivable	1,000	
Cash		101,000

$100,000 \times 6\% = \$6,000$ per year
$\$6,000 \times 2/12 = \$1,000$

6/30/19X5
Cash	3,000	
Accrued Bond Interest Receivable (2 months)		1,000
Interest Income (4 months)		2,000

$\$6,000 \times 6/12 = \$3,000$

12/31/19X5
Accrued Bond Interest Receivable	3,000	
Interest Income		3,000

1/1/19X6
Cash	3,000	
Accrued Bond Interest Receivable		3,000

6/30/19X6
Cash	3,000	
Interest Income		3,000

EXAMPLE 9

On 1/1/19X5, $10,000 of ABC Company 6%, 10-year bonds are bought for $12,000. Interest is payable 1/1 and 6/30. On 4/1/19X6, the bonds are sold for $11,000. There is a commission charge on the bonds of $100. Applicable journal entries follow:

1/1/19X5
Investment in Bonds	12,000	
Cash		12,000

6/30/19X5
Interest Income	100	
Investment in Bonds		100

Amortization of premium computed as follows:
    $\$2,000/10$ years $= \$200$ per year $\times 6/12 = \$100$

Cash	300	
Interest Income		300

$6\% \times \$10,000 \times 6/12 = \$300$

12/31/19X5

Accrued Bond Interest Receivable	300	
Interest Income		300
Interest Income	100	
Investment in Bonds		100
4/1/19X6		
Accrued Bond Interest Receivable	150	
Interest Income		150
$6\% \times \$10,000 \times 3/12 = 150$		
Interest Income	50	
Investment in Bonds		50
Amortization of premium computed as follows:		
$\$200$ per year $\times 3/12 = \$50$		
Cash $(11,000 + 150 - 100)$	11,050	
Loss on Sale of Investments	850	
Investment in Bonds $(12,000 - 100 - 100 - 50)$		11,750
Accrued Bond Interest Receivable		150

LEASES

Leases are typically long-term noncancelable commitments. In a lease, the lessee acquires the right to use property owned by the lessor. Even though no legal transfer of title occurs, many leases transfer substantially all the risks and ownership benefits. Theoretical substance governs over legal form in accounting resulting in the lessee recording an asset and liability for a capital lease.

A lease may be between related parties. This occurs when an entity has significant influence over operating and financial policies of another entity.

The date of inception of a lease is the time of lease agreement or commitment, if earlier. A commitment has to be in writing, signed, and provide principal provisions. If any major provisions are to be negotiated later there is no committed agreement.

Lessee

The two methods to account for a lease by the lessee are the operating method and capital method.

Operating Lease. An operating lease is a regular rental of property. As rental payments become payable, rent expense is debited and cash and/or payables credited. The lessee does not show anything on his balance sheet. Rent expense is reflected on a straight-line basis unless another method is more appropriate under the circumstances. Accrual basis accounting is followed.

Capital Lease. The lessee uses the capital lease method if any one of the following four criteria are met:

- The lessee obtains ownership to the property at the end of the lease term
- There is a bargain purchase option where either the lessee can acquire the property at a nominal amount or renew the lease at nominal rental payments
- The life of the lease is 75% or more of the life of the property
- The present value of minimum lease payments at the inception of the lease equals or is greater than 90% of the fair market value of the property. Minimum lease payments exclude executory costs to be paid by the lessor such as maintenance, insurance, and property taxes.

If criteria 1 or 2 are met, the depreciation period is the life of the property. If criteria 3 or 4 are satisfied, the depreciation period is the life of the lease.

It should be noted that the third and fourth criteria do not apply where the beginning of the lease term falls within the last 25% of the total economic life of the property, including earlier years of use.

The asset and liability are recorded at the present value of the minimum lease payments plus the present value of the bargain purchase option. The expectation is that the lessee will take advantage of the nominal purchase price. If the present value of the minimum lease payments plus the bargain purchase option is greater than the fair value of the leased property at the time of lease inception, the asset should be capitalized at the fair market value of the property. The discount rate used by the lessee is the lower of the lessee's incremental borrowing rate (the rate the lessee would have to borrow at to be able to buy the asset) or the lessor's implicit interest rate. The lessor's implicit interest rate is the one implicit in the recovery of the fair value of the property at lease inception through the present value of minimum lease payments including the lessee's guarantee of salvage value. The liability is broken down between current and noncurrent.

The lessee's minimum lease payments (MLP) usually includes MLP over the lease term plus any residual value guaranteed by the lessee. The guarantee is the determinable amount for which the lessor has the right to require the lessee to buy the property at the lease termination. It is the stated amount when the lessee agrees to satisfy any dollar deficiency below a stated amount in the lessor's realization of the residual value. MLP also includes any payment the lessee must pay due to failure to extend or renew the lease at expiration. If there exists a bargain purchase option, MLP includes only MLP over the lease term and exercise option payment. MLP does not include contingent rentals, the lessee's guarantee of the lessor's debt, and the lessee's obligation for executory costs.

Each minimum lease payment is allocated as a reduction of principal (debiting the liability) and as interest (debiting interest expense). The interest method is used to result in a constant periodic rate of interest. Interest expense equals the interest rate times the carrying value of the liability at the beginning of the year.

The balance sheet shows the "Asset Under Lease" less "Accumulated Depreciation." The income statement shows interest expense and depreciation expense. In the first year, the expenses under a capital lease (interest expense and depreciation) are greater than the expenses under an operating lease (rent expense).

As per Interpretation 26, when a lessee buys a leased asset during the lease term which has been originally capitalized, the transaction is considered an extension of a capital lease rather than a termination. Thus, the difference between the purchase price and the carrying amount of the lease obligation recorded is an adjustment of the carrying amount of the asset. No loss recognition is required on an extension of a capital lease.

EXAMPLE 10

On 1/1/19X1, the lessee enters into a capital lease for property. The minimum rental payment is $20,000 a year for six years to be made at the end of the year. The interest rate is 5%. The present value of an ordinary annuity factor for $n = 6$, $i = 5\%$ is 5.0757. The journal entries for the first two years follow:

```
1/1/19X1  Asset                          101,514
              Liability                                101,514
12/31/19X1
          Interest Expense                 5,076
          Liability                       14,924
            Cash                                     20,000
          5% × $101,514 = $5,076
          Depreciation                    16,919
            Accumulated Depreciation                 16,919
```

$$\frac{\$101,514}{6} = \$16,919$$

The liability as of 12/31/19X1 appears below:

	Liability		
12/31/19X1	14,924	1/1/19X1	101,514
		12/31/19X1	86,590

```
12/31/19X2
          Interest Expense                 4,330
          Liability                       15,670
            Cash                                     20,000
          5% × $86,590 = $4,330
          Depreciation                    16,919
            Accumulated Depreciation                 16,919
```

Footnote disclosures under a capital lease include:

- Assets under lease by class
- Future minimum lease payments in total and for each of the next five years
- Contingent rentals (rentals based on other than time such as based on sales)
- Total future sublease rentals
- Description of leasing arrangement including renewal terms, purchase options, escalation options, and restrictions in the lease agreement.

Lessor

The three methods of accounting for leases by the lessor are the operating, direct-financing, and sales-type methods.

Operating Method. The operating method is a regular rental by the lessor. An example is Avis renting automobiles. Under the operating method, the lessor records rental revenue less related expenses including depreciation and maintenance expense. The income statement shows rental revenue less expenses to obtain profit. The balance sheet presents the asset under lease less accumulated depreciation to derive book value.

Rental income is recognized as earned using the straight-line basis over the lease term except if there is another preferable method. Initial direct costs are deferred and amortized over the lease term on a prorata basis based on rental income recognized. However, if immaterial relative to the allocation amount, the initial direct costs may be expensed.

EXAMPLE 11

Hall Corporation produced machinery costing $5,000,000 which it held for resale from January 1, 19X1 to June 30, 19X1 at a price to Travis Company under an operating lease. The lease is for four years with equal monthly payments of $85,000 due on the first of the month. The initial payment was made on July 1, 19X1. The depreciation period is 10 years with no salvage value.

Lessee's rental expense for 19X1: $85,000 × 6	$510,000
Lessor's income before taxes for 19X1:	
Rental income	$510,000
Less: Depreciation $\dfrac{\$5,000,000}{10} \times \dfrac{6}{12}$	250,000
Income before taxes	$260,000

Direct Financing Method. The direct financing method satisfies one of the four criteria for a capital lease by the lessee plus both of the following two criteria for the lessor:

- Collectibility of lease payments is assured
- No important uncertainties exist regarding future costs to be incurred

The lessor is not a manufacturer or dealer. The lessor acquires the property for the sole purpose of leasing it out. An example is a bank leasing computers. The carrying value and fair value of the leased property are the same at the inception of the lease.

The lessor uses as the discount rate the interest rate implicit in the lease.

Interest income is only recognized in the financial statements over the life of the lease using the interest method. Unearned interest income is amortized as income over the lease term to result in a constant rate of interest. Interest revenue equals the interest rate times the carrying value of the receivable at the beginning of the year.

Contingent rentals are recognized in earnings as earned.

The lessor's MLP includes the (1) MLP made by the lessee (net of any executory costs together with any profit thereon) and (2) any guarantee of the salvage value of the leased property, or of rental payments after the lease term, made by a third party unrelated to either party in the lease provided the third party is financially able to satisfy the commitment. A guarantee by a third party related to the lessor makes the residual value unguaranteed. A guarantee by a third party related to the lessee infers a guaranteed residual value by the lessee.

Changes in lease provisions, that would have resulted in a different classification had they taken place at the beginning of the lease, mandate that the lease be considered a new agreement and classified under the new terms. However, exercise of existing renewal options are not deemed lease changes. A change in estimate does not result in a new lease.

A provision for escalation of the MLP during a construction or preacquisition period may exist. The resulting increase in MLP is considered in determining the fair value of the leased property at the lease inception. There may also exist a salvage value increase that takes place from an escalation clause.

Initial direct costs are incurred by the lessor directly applicable with negotiating and consummating completed leasing transactions such as legal fees, commissions, document preparation and processing for new leases, credit investigation, and the relevant portion of salespersons' and other employees' compensation. It does not include costs for leases not consummated nor supervisory, administrative, or other indirect expenses. Initial direct costs of the lease are expensed as incurred. A portion of the unearned income equal to the initial direct costs shall be recognized as income in the same accounting period.

If the lease agreement contains a penalty for failure to renew and becomes inoperative due to lease renewal or other extension of time, the unearned interest income account must be adjusted for the difference between the present values of the old and revised agreements. The present value of the future minimum lease payments under the new agreement should be computed employing the original rate used for the initial lease.

Lease termination is accounted for by the lessor through eliminating the net investment, recording the leased property at the lower of cost or fair value, and the net adjustment is charged against earnings.

The lessor shows on his balance sheet, as the gross investment in the lease, the total minimum lease payments plus salvage value of the property accruing to the lessor. This represents lease payments receivable. Deducted from lease payments receivable is unearned interest revenue. The balance sheet presentation follows:

Lease Payments Receivable (Principal + Interest)

Less: Unearned Interest Revenue (Interest)

Net Receivable Balance (Principal)

The income statement shows:

Interest Revenue

Less: Initial Direct Costs

Less: Executory Costs

Net Income

Footnote disclosure should include assets leased out by category, future lease payments in total and for each of the next five years, contingent rentals, and the terms of the lease.

Sales-Type Method. The sales-type method must satisfy the same criteria as the direct financing method. The only difference is that the sales-type method involves a lessor who is a manufacturer or dealer in the leased item. Thus, a manufacturer or dealer profit results. Although legally there is no sale of the item, theoretical substance governs over legal form and a sale is assumed to have taken place.

Note: The distinction between a sales-type lease and a direct financing lease affects only the lessor; as to the lessee, either type would be a capital lease.

If there is a renewal or extension of an existing sales-type or financing lease, it shall not be classified as a sales-type lease. There is an exception which may exist when the renewal occurs toward the end of the lease term.

In a sales-type lease, profit on the assumed sale of the item is recognized in the year of lease as well as interest income over the life of the lease. The cost and fair value of the leased property are different at the inception of the lease.

An annual appraisal should be made of the salvage value, and where necessary, reduce the net investment and recognize a loss but do not adjust the salvage value.

The cost of the leased property is matched against the selling price in determining the assumed profit in the year of lease. Initial direct costs of the lease are expensed.

Except for the initial entry to record the lease, the entries are the same for the direct financing and sales-type methods.

EXAMPLE 12

Assume the same facts as in the capital lease example. The accounting by the lessor assuming a direct financing lease and a sales-type lease follow:

Direct Financing			Sales-Type		
1/1/19X1					
Receivable	120,000		Receivable	120,000	
Asset		101,514	Cost of Sales	85,000	
Unearned Interest					
Revenue		18,486	Inventory		85,000
			Sales		101,514
			Unearned		
			Interest		
			Revenue		18,486
12/31/19X1					
Cash	20,000				
Receivable		20,000			
Unearned					
Interest					
Revenue	5,076				
Interest					
Revenue		5,076			
12/31/19X2				**Same Entries**	
Cash	20,000				
Receivable		20,000			
Unearned					
Interest					
Revenue	4,330				
Interest					
Revenue		4,330			

The income statement for 19X1 presents:

Interest Revenue	$5,076	Sales	$101,514
		Less: Cost of Sales	85,000
		Gross Profit	$ 16,514
		Interest Revenue	5,076

EXAMPLE 13

Jones leased equipment to Tape Company on October 1, 19X1. It is a capital lease to the lessee and a sales type lease to the lessor. The lease is for eight years with equal annual payments of $500,000 due on October 1 each period. The first payment was made on October 1, 19X1. The cost of the equipment to Tape Company is $2,500,000. The equipment has a life of 10 years with no salvage value. The appropriate interest rate is 10%.

Tape reports the following in its income statement for 19X1.

Asset Cost ($500,000 $\times$ 5.868 = $2,934,000)

$$\text{Depreciation} \left(\frac{\$2,934,000}{10} \times \frac{3}{12} \right) \qquad\qquad \$73,350$$

Interest Expense:
Present value of lease payments	$2,934,000	
Less: Initial payment	500,000	
Balance	$2,434,000	

Interest Expense $2,434,000 $\times$ 10% $\times$ $\frac{3}{12}$		60,850
Total Expenses		$134,200
Jones' income before tax is:		
Interest revenue		$60,850
Gross profit on assumed sale of property:		
Selling price	$2,934,000	
Less: Cost	2,500,000	
Gross Profit		434,000
Income before tax		$494,850

Sales-Leaseback Arrangement

A sales-leaseback is when the lessor sells the property and then leases it back. The lessor may do this when he is in need of funds.

The profit or loss on the sale is deferred and amortized as an adjustment on a proportionate basis to depreciation expense in the case of a capital lease or in proportion to rental expense in the case of an operating lease. However, if the fair value of the property at the time of the sales-leaseback is below its book value, a loss is immediately recognized for the difference between book value and fair value.

EXAMPLE 14

The deferred profit on a sales-leaseback is $50,000. An operating lease is involved where rental expense in the current year is $10,000 and total rental expense is $150,000. Rental expense is adjusted as follows:

Rental Expense $10,000
Less: Amortization of deferred gross profit

$$50,000 \times \frac{\$10,000}{\$150,000} \qquad\qquad \underline{3,333}$$

$$\underline{\underline{\$6,667}}$$

Subleases and Similar Transactions

There are three types of transactions. In a *sublease,* the original lessee leases the property to a third party. The lease agreement of the original parties remains intact. Another possibility is where a new lessee is substituted under the original agreement. The original lessee may still be secondarily liable. Finally, the new lessee is substituted in a new agreement. There is a cancellation of the original lease.

In accounting by the original lessor, he continues his present accounting method if the original lessee subleases or sells to a third party. If the original lease is replaced by a new agreement with a new lessee, the lessor terminates the initial lease and accounts for the new lease in a separate transaction.

In accounting by the original lessee, if the original lessee is relieved of primary obligation by a transaction other than a sublease, terminate the original lease:

- If original lease was a capital lease remove the asset and liability, recognize a gain or loss for the difference including any additional consideration paid or received, and accrue a loss contingency where secondary liability exists

- If the original lease was an operating one and the initial lessee is secondarily liable, recognize a loss contingency accrual

If the original lessee is not relieved of primary obligation under a sublease, the original lessee (now sublessor) accounts in the following manner:

- If original lease met lessee criteria 1 or 2, classify the new lease per normal classification criteria by lessor. If sublease is sales-type or direct financing lease, the unamortized asset balance becomes the cost of the leased property. Otherwise, it is an operating lease. Continue to account for the original lease obligation as before.

- If original lease met only lessee criteria 3 or 4, classify the new lease using lessee criteria 3 and lessor criteria 1 and 2. Classify as a direct financing lease. The unamortized balance of the asset becomes the cost of the leased property. Otherwise, it is an operating lease. Continue to account for original lease obligation as before.

If the original lease was an operating lease, account for old and new leases as operating leases.

Leveraged Leases

A leveraged lease occurs when the lessor (equity participant) finances a small part of the acquisition (retaining total equity ownership) while a third party (debt participant) finances the balance. The lessor maximizes his leveraged return by recognizing lease revenue and income tax shelter (e.g., interest deduction, rapid depreciation).

A leveraged lease meets all of the following:

- It satisfies the tests for a direct financing lease. Sales-type leases are not leveraged leases.
- It involves at least three parties: lessee, long-term creditor (debt participant), and lessor (equity participant).
- The long-term creditor provides nonrecourse financing as to the general credit of the lessor. The financing is adequate to give the lessor significant leverage.
- The lessor's net investment (see below) decreases during the initial lease years, then increases in the subsequent years just before its liquidation by sale. These increases and decreases in the net investment balance may take place more than once during the lease life.

The lessee classifies and accounts for leveraged leases in the same way as non-leveraged leases. The lessor records investment in the leveraged lease net of the nonrecourse debt. The net of the following balances represents the initial and continuing investment: rentals receivable (net of the amount applicable to principal and interest on the nonrecourse debt), estimated residual value, and unearned and deferred income. The initial entry to record the leveraged lease is:

Lease receivable

Residual value of asset

    Cash investment in asset

    Unearned income

The lessor's net investment in the leveraged lease for computing net income is the investment in the leveraged lease less deferred income taxes. Periodic net income is determined in the following manner employing the net investment in the leveraged lease:

- Determine annual cash flow equal to the following:

  Gross lease rental (plus residual value of asset in last year of lease term)

  Less: Loan interest payments

  Less: Income tax charges (or add income tax credits)

  Less: Loan principal payments

  Annual Cash Flow

- Determine the return rate on the net investment in the leveraged lease. The rate of return is the one when applied to the net investment in the years when it is positive will distribute the net income (cash flow) to those positive years. The net investment will be positive (but declining rapidly due to accelerated depreciation and interest expense) in early years; it will be negative during the middle years; and it will again be positive in the later years (because of the declining tax shelter).

PENSION PLANS

A company does not have to have a pension plan. If it does, the firm must conform to FASB and governmental rules regarding the accounting and reporting for the pension plan. FASB 87 requires accounting for pension costs on the accrual basis. Pension expense is reflected in the service periods using a method that considers the benefit formula of the plan. On the income statement, pension expense is presented as a single amount. The pension plan relationship between the employer, trustee, and employee is depicted below.

Figure 1

PENSION PLAN RELATIONSHIP

The two types of pension plans are:

- *Defined Contribution.* In a defined contribution plan, the annual contribution amount by the employer is specified instead of the benefits to be paid.

- *Defined Benefit.* In a defined benefit plan, the determinable pension benefit to be received by participants upon retirement is specified. In determining amounts, consideration is given to such factors as age, salary, and service years. The employer has to provide plan contributions so that sufficient assets are accumulated to pay for the benefits when due. Typically, an annuity of payments is made. Pension expense applicable to administrative staff is expensed. Pension expense related to factory personnel is inventoriable.

The following pension plan terminology should be understood:

- *Actuarial Assumptions.* Actuaries make assumptions as to variables in determining pension expense and related funding. Examples of estimates are mortality rate, employee turnover, compensation levels, and rate of return.
- *Actuarial Cost (Funding) Method.* The method used by actuaries in determining the employer contribution to assure sufficient funds will be available at employee retirement. The method used determines the pension expense and related liability.
- *Actuarial Present Value of Accumulated Plan Benefits.* The discounted amount of money that would be required to satisfy retirement obligations for active and retired employees.
- *Benefit Information Date.* The date the actuarial present value of accumulated benefits is presented.
- *Vested Benefits.* Employee vests when he has accumulated pension rights to receive benefits upon retirement. The employee no longer has to remain in the company to receive pension benefits.
- *Projected Benefit Obligation.* The projected benefit obligation is the year-end pension obligation based on future salaries. It is the actuarial present value of vested and nonvested benefits for services performed before a particular actuarial valuation date based on expected future salaries.
- *Accumulated Benefit Obligation.* The accumulated benefit obligation is the year-end obligation based on current salaries. It is the actuarial present value of benefits (vested and nonvested) attributable to the pension plan based on services performed before a specified date based on current salary levels. The accumulated and projected benefit obligation figures will be the same in the case of plans having flat-benefit or nonpay-related pension benefit formulas.
- *Net Assets Available for Pension Benefits.* Net assets represents plan assets less plan liabilities. The plan's liabilities exclude participants' accumulated benefits.

Defined Contribution Pension Plan

Pension expense equals the employer's cash contribution for the year. There is no deferred charge or deferred credit arising. If the defined contribution plan stipulates contributions are to be made for years subsequent to an employee's rendering of services (e.g., after retirement), there should be an accrual of costs during the employee's service period.

Footnote disclosure includes:

- Description of plan including employee groups covered
- Basis of determining contributions
- Nature and effect of items affecting interperiod comparability
- Cost recognized for the period

Defined Benefit Pension Plan

The components of pension expense in a defined benefit pension plan follow:

- Service Cost
- Prior Service Cost
- Expected Return on Plan Assets (reduces pension expense)
- Interest on Projected Benefit Obligation
- Actuarial Gain or Loss

Service cost is based on the present value of future payments under the benefit formula for employee services of the current period. It is recognized in full in the current year. The calculation involves actuarial assumptions.

Prior service cost is the pension expense applicable to services rendered before the adoption or amendment date of a pension plan. The cost of the retroactive benefits is the increase in the projected benefit obligation at the date of amendment. It involves the allocation of amounts of cost to future service years. Prior service cost determination involves actuarial considerations. The total pension cost is not booked but rather there are periodic charges based on actuarial determinations. Amortization is accomplished by assigning an equal amount to each service year of active employees at the amendment date who are expected to receive plan benefits. The amortization of prior service cost may take into account future service years, change in the projected benefit obligation, period employees will receive benefits, and decrement in employees receiving benefits each year.

EXAMPLE 15

X Company changes its pension formula from 2% to 5% of the last three years of pay multiplied by the service years on January 1, 19X1. This results in the projected benefit obligation being increased by $500,000. Employees are anticipated to receive benefits over the next 10 years.

Total Future Service Years Equals: $\dfrac{n\,(n\,+\,1)}{2} \times P$

n is the number of years services are to be made
P is the population decrement each year

$$\frac{10\,(10\,+\,1)}{2} \times 9 = 495$$

Amortization of prior service cost in 19X1 equals:

$$\$500,000 \times \frac{10 \times 9}{495} = \$90,909$$

The expected return on plan assets (e.g., stocks, bonds) reduces pension expense. Plan assets are valued at the moving average of asset values for the accounting period.

Interest is on the projected benefit obligation at the beginning of the year. The settlement rate is employed representing the rate that pension benefits could be settled for. Interest equals:

Interest Rate $\times$ Projected Benefit Obligation at the Beginning of the Year

Actuarial gains and losses are the differences between estimates and actual experience. For example, if the assumed interest rate is 10% and the actual interest rate is 12%, an actuarial gain results. There may also be a change in actuarial assumptions regarding the future. Actuarial gains and losses are deferred and amortized as an adjustment to pension expense over future years. Actuarial gains and losses related to a single event *not* related to the pension plan and not in the ordinary course of business are immediately recognized in the current year's income statement. Examples are plant closing and segment disposal.

Pension expense will not usually equal the employer's funding amount. Pension expense is typically based on the unit credit method. Under this approach, pension expense and related liability is based on estimating future salaries for total benefits to be paid.

If Pension Expense $>$ Cash Paid $=$ Deferred Pension Liability

If Pension Expense $<$ Cash Paid $=$ Deferred Pension Charge

Interest on the deferred pension liability reduces future pension expense. On the other hand, interest on the deferred pension charge increases pension expense.

Note: The "unit credit" method is used for flat-benefit plans (benefits are stated as a constant amount per year of service). In the case of final-pay plans, the projected unit credit method is used.

Minimum Pension Liability. A minimum pension liability must be recognized when the accumulated benefit obligation exceeds the fair value of pension plan assets. However, no minimum pension assets are recognized because it violates conservatism. When there is an accrued pension liability, an additional liability is booked up to the minimum pension liability.

When an additional liability is recorded, the debit is to an intangible asset under the pension plan. However, the intangible asset cannot exceed the unamortized prior service cost. If it does, the excess is reported as a separate component of stockholders' equity shown net of tax. While these items may be adjusted periodically, they are not amortized.

EXAMPLE 16

Accumulated Benefit Obligation	$500,000
Less: Fair Value of Pension Plan Assets	200,000
Minimum Pension Liability	$300,000
Less: Accrued Pension Liability	120,000
Additional Liability	$180,000

Note: If there was an accrued pension asset of $120,000, the additional liability would have been $420,000.

Assume unamortized prior service cost is $100,000. The entry is:

New Intangible Asset Under Pension Plan	100,000	
Stockholders' Equity	80,000	
Additional Liability		180,000

EXAMPLE 17

Mr. A has six years of service prior to retirement. The estimated salary at retirement is $50,000. The pension benefit is 3% of final salary for each service year payable at retirement. The retirement benefit is computed below:

Final Annual Salary	$50,000
Formula Rate	$\times$ 3%
	$ 1,500
Years of Service	$\times$ 6
Retirement Benefit	$ 9,000

EXAMPLE 18

On 1/1/19X1, a company adopts a defined benefit pension plan. Expected return and interest rate are both 10%. Service cost for 19X1 and 19X2 are $100,000 and $120,000, respectively. The funding amount for 19X1 and 19X2 are $80,000 and $110,000, respectively.

The entry for 19X1 is:

Pension Expense	100,000	
Cash		80,000
Pension Liability		20,000

The entry in 19X2 is:

Pension Expense	122,000	
Cash		110,000
Pension Liability		12,000

Computation:

Service Cost	$120,000
Interest on Projected Benefit Obligation	
10% × $100,000	10,000
Expected Return on Plan Assets 10% ×	
$80,000	(8,000)
	$122,000

At 12/31/19X2:

Projected Benefit Obligation $230,000 ($100,000 + $120,000 + $10,000).

Pension Plan Assets $198,000 ($80,000 + $110,000 + 8,000).

EXAMPLE 19

Company X has a defined benefit pension plan for its 100 employees. On 1/1/19X1, pension plan assets have a fair value of $230,000, accumulated benefit obligation is $285,000, and the projected benefit obligation is $420,000. Ten employees are expected to resign each year for the next 10 years. They will be eligible to receive benefits. Service cost for 19X1 is $40,000. On 12/31/19X1, the projected benefit obligation is $490,000, fair value of plan assets is $265,000, and accumulated benefit obligation is $340,000. The expected return on plan assets and the interest rate are both 8%. No actuarial gains or losses occurred during the year. Cash funded for the year is $75,000.

Pension expense equals:

Service Cost	$ 40,000
Interest on Projected Benefit Obligation 8% × $420,000	33,600
Expected Return on Plan Assets 8% × $230,000	(18,400)
Amortization of Actuarial Gains and Losses	—
Amortization of Unrecognized Transition Amount	34,545*
Pension Expense	$ 89,745

*Projected Benefit Obligation	$420,000
Fair Value of Pension Plan Assets	230,000
Initial Net Obligation	$190,000

$$\text{Amortization } \frac{\$190,000}{5.5 \text{ years}^{**}} = \underline{\$34,545}$$

$$^{**}\frac{n\,(n\,+\,1)}{2} \times P = \frac{10\,(10\,+\,1)}{2} \times 10 = 550$$

$$\frac{550}{100} = 5.5 \text{ years (average remaining service period)}$$

The journal entries at 12/31/19X1 follow:

Pension Expense	89,745	
Cash		75,000
Deferred Pension Liability		14,745
Intangible Asset—Pension Plan	60,255	
Additional Pension Liability		60,255
Computation follows:		
Accumulated Benefit Obligation—12/31/19X1		$340,000
Fair Value of Plan Assets—12/31/19X1		265,000
Minimum Liability		$75,000
Deferred Pension Liability		14,745
Additional Pension Liability		$60,255

Disclosures. Footnote disclosures for a pension plan follow:

- Describing the plan including benefit formula, funding policy, employee groups covered, and retirement age
- Components of pension expense
- Pension assumptions (e.g., interest rate, mortality rate, employee turnover)

- Reconciling funded status of plan with employer amounts recognized on the balance sheet including fair value of plan assets, projected benefit obligation, and unrecognized prior service cost
- Present value of vested and nonvested benefits
- Weighted-average assumed discount rate involved in measuring the projected benefit obligation
- Weighted-average expected return rate on pension plan assets
- Amounts and types of securities included in pension plan assets
- Amount of approximate annuity benefits to employees

Settlement in a Pension Plan

As per FASB 88, a settlement is discharging some or all of the employer's pension benefit obligation. Excess plan assets can revert back to the employer. A settlement must satisfy *all* of the following criteria:

- Irrevocable
- Relieves pension benefit responsibility
- Materially curtails risk related to the pension obligation

The amount of gain or loss recognized in the income statement when a pension obligation is settled is limited to the unrecognized net gain or loss from realized or unrealized changes in either the pension benefit obligation or plan assets caused from actual experiences being different than original assumptions. All or a prorata share of the unrecognized gain or loss is recognized when a plan is settled. If full settlement occurs, all unrecognized gains or losses are recognized. If only a part of the plan is settled, a prorata share of the unrecognized net gain or loss is recognized.

An example of a settlement is when the employer furnishes employees with a lump-sum amount to give up pension rights. The gain or loss resulting is included in the current year's income statement.

Curtailment in a Pension Plan

As per FASB 88, a curtailment occurs when an event significantly reduces future service years of present employees or eliminates for most employees the accumulation of defined benefits for future services. An example is a plant closing ending employee services prior to pension plan expectations. The gain or loss is recognized in the current year's income statement and contains the following elements:

- Unamortized prior service cost attributable to employee services no longer needed
- Change in pension benefit obligation due to the curtailment

Termination in a Pension Plan

When termination benefits are offered by the employer, accepted by employees, and the amount can reasonably be determined, an expense and liability are recognized. The amount of the accrual equals the down payment plus the present value of future payments to be made by the employer. The entry is to debit loss and credit cash (down payment) and liability (future payments). Footnote disclosure should be given of the arrangement.

Trustee Reporting for a Defined Benefit Pension Plan

FASB 35 deals with the reporting and disclosures of the trustee of a defined benefit pension plan. Generally accepted accounting principles must be followed. Financial statements are not required to be issued by the plan. If they are issued, reporting guidelines have to be followed. The prime objective is to assess the plan's capability to meet retirement benefits.

The balance sheet presents pension assets and liabilities as an offset. Operating assets are at book value. In determining net assets available, accrual accounting is followed. An example is accruing for interest earned but not received. Investments are shown at fair market value. An asset shown is "contributions receivable due from employer." In computing pension plan liability, participants' accumulated benefits are excluded. In effect, plan participants are equity holders rather than creditors of the plan.

Disclosure is required of:

- Net assets available for benefits
- Changes in net assets available for benefits including net appreciation in fair value of each major class of investments
- Actuarial present value of accumulated plan benefits. Accumulated plan benefits include benefits anticipated to be paid to retired employees, beneficiaries, and present employees
- Changes in actuarial present value of accumulated plan benefits
- Description of the plan including amendments
- Accounting and funding policies

There may exist an annuity contract where an insurance company agrees to give specified pension benefits in return for receiving a premium.

POST RETIREMENT BENEFITS EXCLUDING PENSIONS

FASB No. 106 titled "Employers' Accounting for Postretirement Benefits Other Than Pensions" is effective for fiscal years beginning after December 15, 1992. Although the pronouncement deals with all types of postretirement benefits, it *concentrates* on postretirement health care benefits. However, brief references are made to long-term care, tuition assistance, legal advisory services, and housing subsidies.

The pronouncement drastically changes the prevalent current practice of accounting for postretirement benefits on the pay-as-you-go (cash) basis by requiring *accrual* of the expected cost of postretirement benefits during the years in which active employee services are rendered. These expected postretirement benefits may be paid to employees, employees' beneficiaries, and covered dependents.

Companies must also charge-off the cost of benefits earned previously, either all at one time or in installments over a period of up to 20 years. For example, in 1990, the Aluminum Company of America deducted about $1 billion from its earnings because of this immediate charge-off. In 1990, International Business Machines charged off $2.3 billion against earnings to pay for retirement costs of current employees.

The employer's obligation for postretirement benefits expected to be provided must be *fully accrued* by the date that the employee attains full eligibility for all of the benefits expected to be received (the full eligibility date), even if the employee is expected to perform additional services beyond that date.

The beginning of the accrual (attribution) period is the *date of employment* unless the plan only grants credit for service from a later date, in which instance benefits are generally attributed from the beginning of that credited service period. An equal amount of the anticipated postretirement benefit is attributed to each year of service unless the plan provides a disproportionate share of the expected benefits to early years of service.

The pronouncement requires a single measurement approach to spread costs from the date of hire to the date the employee is *fully* eligible to receive benefits. If information on gross charges is not available, there is a measurement approach based on net claims cost (e.g., gross changes less deductibles, copayments, Medicare). There is a projection of future retiree health care costs based on a health care cost trend assumption to current costs.

The transition obligation is the unfunded and unrecognized accumulated postretirement benefit obligation for all plan participants. There are two acceptable methods of recognizing the transition obligation. An employer may *immediately recognize* the transition obligation as the effect of an accounting change, subject to certain limits. Alternatively, the employer may recognize the transition obligation on a delayed basis over future years of service, with disclosure of the unrecognized amount. However, this delayed recognition cannot result in less rapid recognition than using the cash basis for the transition obligation. The *amortization* of the transition obligation to expense would be over the *greater of the average remaining service period of active plan participants or 20 years*.

The *expected postretirement benefit obligation* is the *actuarial present value* as of a given date of the *postretirement benefits expected to be paid* to the employees, their beneficiaries, or covered dependents.

Net periodic postretirement benefit cost is comprised of the following components:

- *Service cost*—actuarial present value of benefits applicable to services performed during the *current year.*
- *Interest cost*—interest on the accumulated postretirement benefit obligation at the beginning of the period.
- *Actual return on plan assets*—return based on the fair value of plan assets at the beginning and end of the period, adjusted for contributions and benefit payments.
- *Amortization expense on prior service cost*—expense provision for the current year due to amortization of the prior service cost arising from adoption or amendment to the plan. Prior service cost applies to credited services *before* adoption or amendment, and is accounted for over current and future years.
- *Amortization of the transition obligation or transition assets*—applies to the effect of switching from the pay-as-you-go basis to the accrual basis of accounting for postretirement benefits.
- *Gain or loss component*—gains and losses apply to changes in the amount of either the accumulated postretirement benefit obligation or plan assets resulting from actual experience being different from the actuarial assumptions. Gains and losses may be realized (i.e., sale of securities) or unrealized.

Footnote disclosure includes:

- A description of the postretirement plan including employee groups covered, type of benefits provided, funding policy, types of assets held and liabilities assumed.
- The components of net periodic postretirement cost.
- The fair value of plan assets.
- Accumulated postretirement benefit obligation showing separately the amount applicable to retirees, other fully eligible participants, and other active plan participants.
- Unamortized prior service cost.
- Unrecognized net gain or loss.
- Unrecognized transition obligation or transition asset.
- The amount of net postretirement benefit asset or liability recognized in the balance sheet.
- The assumed health care cost trends used to measure the expected postretirement benefit cost for the next year.
- The discount rate used to determine the accumulated postretirement benefit obligation.

• The return rate used on the fair value of plan assets.

• The cost of providing termination benefits recognized during the period.

Individual deferred compensation contracts must be fully *accrued* by the date the employee is fully eligible to receive benefits.

For further reference, see J. Siegel, *The Sourcebook on Postretirement Health Care Benefits*, 1990 Supplement, Panel Publishers, pp. 165-184.

INCOME TAX ACCOUNTING

FASB No. 96 provides that income taxes should be allocated to financial periods using the *liability method*. Tax allocation is required when temporary differences rather than permanent differences exist.

The deferred tax liability or asset is measured at the tax rate under existing law which will be in effect when the temporary difference reverses itself. Further, the deferred tax liability or asset must be adjusted for changes in tax law or in tax rate. The liability method is balance sheet oriented since emphasis is placed on asset and liability recognition.

Comprehensive deferred tax accounting is followed where tax expense equals taxes payable plus the tax effects of all temporary differences.

Income taxes are accounted for on the accrual basis.

Interperiod tax allocation is employed to recognize current (or deferred) tax liability or asset for the current (or deferred) tax effect of events that have taken place at year-end. Tax effects of future events should be reflected in the year they take place. It is improper to anticipate them for recognizing a deferred tax liability or asset in the current year.

Temporary Differences

Temporary differences are differences between periods in which transactions affect taxable income and accounting income. They originate in one period and subsequently reverse in another. Temporary differences are created by four types of transactions, the nature of which (and examples) are as follows:

1. Income included in taxable income after being included in accounting income (e.g., installment sales).

2. Expenses deducted for taxable income after being deducted for accounting income (e.g., warranty provision).

3. Income included in taxable income before being included in accounting income (e.g., rents received in advance).

4. Expenses deducted for taxable income before being deducted for accounting income (e.g., accelerated depreciation).

A temporary difference may result from increases in the tax basis of assets because of indexing for inflation.

If tax rates are graduated based on taxable income, aggregate calculations may be made using an estimated average rate.

Permanent Differences

Permanent differences do not reverse (turn around), and as such do not require tax allocation. Examples of non-taxdeductible expenses are goodwill amortization, premiums on officers' life insurance, and fines. An example of income that is not taxable is interest on municipal bonds.

Financial Statement Presentation

In the balance sheet, deferred charges and credits are netted against each other and shown (a) net current and (b) net noncurrent. However, offset is not permitted for deferred tax liabilities or assets that apply to different tax jurisdictions.

Deferred taxes are classified as current or noncurrent based on the expected reversal dates of the temporary differences. Temporary differences reversing within one year are current while those reversing in greater than one year are noncurrent.

In the income statement, disclosure is made of (a) income tax expense currently payable (the liability) and (b) the deferred portion of the expense (this is the portion of the expense based on temporary differences). (The total expense provision is based on financial reporting income excluding permanent differences.)

Presentation of these two expense portions (with numbers and a 40% tax rate assumed) would be as follows:

Income before income taxes		$200
Income tax expense:		
Amount currently payable	$400	
Deferred portion	(320)	80
Net income		$120

Intraperiod tax allocation is when tax expense is shown in different parts of the financial statements for the current year. The income statement shows the tax allocated to (a) income from continuing operations, (b) income from discontinued operations, (c) extraordinary items, and (d) cumulative effect of a change in accounting principle. Note that in the retained earnings statement, prior period adjustments are shown net of tax.

Loss Carrybacks and Loss Carryforwards

The tax effects of net operating loss carrybacks should be allocated to the loss period. An entity may carryback a net operating loss three years and obtain a refund for taxes paid in those years. The loss is first applied to the earliest year. Any residual loss is carried forward up to 15 years.

Presentation of loss carryback with recognition of refund during loss year:

Loss before refundable income taxes	$1,000
Refund of prior years' income taxes arising from carryback of operating loss	485
Net loss	$ 515

Note: The refund should be computed at the amount actually refunded regardless of current tax rates.

The tax effects of net operating loss carryforwards and tax credits (e.g., alternative minimum tax credit) generally cannot be recognized until the year realized (the year in which the tax liability is reduced). A journal entry typically cannot be made in the loss year for any possible tax benefits because of the uncertainty of future earnings.

When the tax benefit of a loss carryforward is recognized when realized in a later year, it is classified in the same way as the income enabling recognition (typically reducing tax expense).

Presentation of the loss carryforward with recognition of benefit in year realized (numbers and 50% rate assumed):

Income before income taxes		$1,000
Income tax expense:		
Without carryforward	$ 500	
Reduction of income taxes arising from carryforward of prior years' operating losses	(300)	200
Net Income		$ 800

An exception exists to the general rule of not permitting the recognition of a net operating loss carryforward in the current year. The net operating loss carryforward may be recognized to the extent of net taxable amounts in the carryforward period (deferred tax liabilities now exist to absorb them).

Disclosure should be made of the amounts and expiration dates of operating loss carryforwards.

Deferred Tax Liability Versus Deferred Tax Asset

Deferred Tax Liability

If book income exceeds taxable income, tax expense exceeds tax payable so a deferred tax liability results. If book income is less than taxable income, tax expense is less than tax payable so a deferred tax asset results.

EXAMPLE 20

Assume book income and taxable income are $1,000. Depreciation for book purposes is $50 based on the straight line method and $100 for tax purposes based on the accelerated cost recovery system. Assuming a tax rate of 34%, the entry is:

Income Tax Expense (950 × 34%)	323	
Income Tax Payable (900 × 34%)		306
Deferred Tax Liability		17

At the end of the asset's life, the deferred tax liability of $17 will be fully reversed.

EXAMPLE 21

At the end of year 1, future recovery of the reported amount of an enterprise's installment receivables will result in taxable amounts totaling $240,000 in years 2-4. Also, a $20,000 liability for estimated expenses has been recognized in the financial statements in year 1, and those expenses will be deductible for tax purposes in year 4 when the liability is expected to be paid. Those temporary differences are estimated to result in net taxable amounts in future years as presented below.

	Year 2	Year 3	Year 4
Taxable amounts	$70,000	$110,000	$60,000
Deductible amount	—	—	(20,000)
Net taxable amounts	$70,000	$110,000	$40,000

This example assumes that the enacted tax rates for years 2-4 are 20% for the first $50,000 of taxable income, 30% for the next $50,000, and 40% for taxable income over $100,000. The liability for deferred tax consequences is measured as follows:

	Year 2	Year 3	Year 4
20% tax on first $50,000	$10,000	$ 10,000	$ 8,000
30% tax on next $50,000	6,000	15,000	—
40% tax on over $100,000	—	4,000	—
	$16,000	$ 29,000	$ 8,000

A deferred tax liability is recognized for $53,000 (the total of the taxes payable for years 2-4) at the end of year 1.

Source: Financial Accounting Standards Board, FASB No. 96, "Accounting for Income Taxes," Stamford, Connecticut, December 1987, p. 32.

Deferred Tax Asset. A deferred tax asset results in a future deductible amount (for tax purposes) which can only be recognized as an asset in the current year if the entity is certain to have taxable income in the future. Thus, a deferred tax asset can only be booked for the amount of the certain future deductibility of the item for tax purposes (e.g., resulting from temporary differences due to deferred tax liabilities already existing).

EXAMPLE 22

In 19X8, a company sold a fixed asset reporting a gain of $70,000 for book purposes which was deferred for tax purposes (installment method) until 19X9. In addition, in 19X8, $40,000 of subscription income was received in advance. The income was recognized for tax purposes in 19X8 but was deferred for book purposes until 19X9.

The deferred tax asset may be recorded since the deductible amount in the future ($40,000) offsets the taxable amount ($70,000). Assuming a 34% tax rate and income taxes payable of $100,000, the entry in 19X8 is:

Income Tax Expense	110,200	
Deferred Tax Asset ($40,000 $\times$ 34%)	13,600	
Deferred Tax Liability ($70,000 $\times$ 34%)		23,800
Income Taxes Payable		100,000

Note: The deferred tax asset can only be recognized up to the later years' deferred tax liabilities caused from temporary differences. Thus, if the gain on the sale of fixed assets was $25,000, the maximum amount of deferred revenue that could be recognized as a deferred tax asset would be $25,000. In this case, the entry is:

Income Tax Expense	100,000	
Deferred Tax Asset (maximum up to deferred liability)	8,500	
Deferred Tax Liability (25,000 $\times$ 34%)		8,500
Income Taxes Payable		100,000

A deferred tax asset can also be recognized for the tax benefit of deductible amounts realizable by carrying back a loss from future years to reduce taxes paid in the current or a prior year.

The restrictions on the recording of the deferred tax asset is based on *conservatism.*

Tax Rates

Tax rates in later years may be different. Further, a change in tax law may occur.

Different Tax Rates in the Future. Deferred taxes are reflected at the amounts of settlement when the temporary differences reverse.

EXAMPLE 23

Assume in 19X3 a cumulative temporary difference of $200,000 which will reverse in the future generating the following taxable amounts and tax rate:

	19X4	19X5	19X6	Total
Reversals	$60,000	$90,000	$50,000	$200,000
Tax Rate	× .34	× .30	× .25	
Deferred tax liability	$20,400	$27,000	$12,500	$59,900

On Dec. 31, 19X3, the deferred tax liability is recorded at $59,900.

A future tax rate can only be used if it has been enacted by law.

While there may be graduated tax rates, the highest tax rate may be used when the difference is not material.

Change in Tax Rate. Immediately reflect the impact of a change in tax rate on the accounts. Tax expense and deferred tax are appropriately adjusted in the year of change.

EXAMPLE 24

Assume at the end of 19X2, a law is passed reducing the tax rate from 34% to 30% starting in 19X4. In 19X2, there was deferred profit of $100,000 showing a deferred tax liability of $34,000 as of 19X2. The gross profit is to be reflected equally in 19X3, 19X4, 19X5, and 19X6. Thus, the deferred tax liability at the end of 19X2 is $31,000 as shown below:

	19X3	19X4	19X5	19X6	Total
Reversals	$25,000	$25,000	$25,000	$25,000	
Tax Rate	× .34	× .30	× .30	× .30	
Deferred Tax Liability	$8,500	$7,500	$7,500	$7,500	$31,000

The appropriate entry in 19X2 is:

Deferred Tax Liability	3,000	
Income Tax Expense		3,000

Purchase Combination

In a purchase combination, the net assets acquired are reflected at their gross fair values with a separate deferred tax balance for the applicable tax effects. Further, a temporary difference will occur for the difference between the financial reporting and tax basis of assets and liabilities acquired. If the acquired company has an operating loss or tax credit carryforward, it may be used to reduce the deferred tax liability of the acquired company.

Disclosures

Disclosure should be made of the types of temporary differences that have occurred causing a material deferred tax liability or asset. An example is the disclosure that ACRS is used for tax and straight line depreciation is used for books.

If a deferred tax liability is not recognized, disclosure should be made of the following:

- Description of the kinds of temporary differences for which no recognition has been given to a deferred tax liability and the types of events that would result in tax recognition of the temporary differences
- Cumulative amount of each kind of temporary difference

A reconciliation should exist between the reported amount of tax expense and the tax expense that would have occurred using federal statutory tax rates. The reconciliation should be in terms of percentages or dollar amounts. If statutory tax rates do not exist, use the regular tax rates for alternative tax systems. Disclosure should be given of the estimated amount and the nature of each material reconciling item.

Disclosure should be made of the provisions of intercorporate tax sharing arrangements and tax-related balances due to or from affiliates.

Extensions of Tax Allocations

In accordance with APB Opinions No. 23 and 24, undistributed earnings (parent/investor share of subsidiary/investee income less dividends received) are considered to be temporary differences.

The rationale for this treatment is based on the basic presumption that such earnings will eventually be transferred.

Temporary Difference. Income taxes related to temporary differences should be accounted for in accordance with FASB No. 96. In the case of investee income arising from the application of APB No. 18, if evidence indicates eventual realization by disposition of investment, income taxes should be determined at capital gains or other appropriate rates.

Indefinite Reversal. There is no interperiod tax allocation in the case of indefinite reversal. Indefinite reversal is when undistributed earnings in a foreign subsidiary will indefinitely be postponed or when earnings will be remitted in a tax-free liquidation.

If there is a change in circumstances and the presumption of indefinite reversal no longer holds, there should be an adjustment to tax expense.

Disclosure should be made of the declaration to reinvest indefinitely or to remit tax free, and the cumulative amount of undistributed earnings.

Amount of Temporary Difference. Eighty percent of the dividends received from affiliated corporations are generally exempt from tax. Consequently, the temporary difference is equal to 20% of the undistributed earnings (parent/investor interest less dividends received).

FOREIGN CURRENCY TRANSLATION AND TRANSACTIONS

FASB 52 applies to foreign currency transactions such as exports and imports denominated in other than a company's functional currency. It also relates to foreign currency financial statements of branches, divisions, and other investees incorporated in the financial statements of a U.S. company by combination, consolidation, or the equity method.

A purpose of translation is to furnish data of expected impacts of rate changes on cash flow and equity. Also, it provides data in consolidated financial statements relative to the financial results of each individual foreign consolidated entity.

Covered in FASB 52 are the translation of foreign currency statements and gains and losses on foreign currency transactions. Translation of foreign currency statements is typically needed when the statements of a foreign subsidiary or equity-method investee having a functional currency other than the U.S. dollar are to be included in the financial statements of a domestic enterprise (e.g., through consolidation or using the equity method). Generally, the foreign currency statements should be translated using the exchange rate at the end of the reporting year. Resulting translation gains and losses are shown as a separate item in the stockholders' equity section.

Also important is the accounting treatment of gains and losses emanating from transactions denominated in a foreign currency. These are presented in the current year's income statement.

Foreign Currency Terminology

Key definitions to be understood by the practitioner follow:

- *Conversion*—An exchange of one currency for another
- *Currency Swap*—An exchange between two companies of the currencies of two different countries as per an agreement to re-exchange the two currencies at the same rate of exchange at a specified future date
- *Denominate*—Pay or receive in that same foreign currency. It can only be denominated in one currency (e.g., pounds). It is a real account (asset or liability) fixed in terms of a foreign currency irrespective of exchange rate.
- *Exchange Rate*—Ratio between a unit of one currency and that of another at a particular time. If there is a *temporary lack of exchangeability* between two currencies at the transaction date or balance sheet date, the first rate available thereafter at which exchanges could be made is used.

- *Foreign Currency*—A currency other than the functional currency of the business. (For instance, the dollar could be a foreign currency for a foreign entity).
- *Foreign Currency Statements*—Financial statements using a functional currency that is not the reporting currency of the business
- *Foreign Currency Transactions*—Transactions whose terms are denominated in a currency other than the entity's functional currency. Foreign currency transactions take place when a business (a) buys or sells on credit goods or services whose prices are denominated in foreign currency, (b) borrows or lends funds and the amounts payable or receivable are denominated in foreign currency, (c) is a party to an unperformed forward exchange contract or (d) acquires or disposes of assets, or incurs or settles liabilities denominated in foreign currency.
- *Foreign Currency Translation*—Expressing in the reporting currency of the company those amounts that are denominated or measured in a different currency
- *Foreign Entity*—An operation (e.g., subsidiary, division, branch, joint venture) whose financial statements are prepared in a currency other than the reporting currency of the reporting entity
- *Functional Currency*—An entity's functional currency is the currency of the primary economic environment in which the business operates. It is typically the currency of the environment that the business primarily obtains and uses cash. This is usually the foreign country. The functional currency of a foreign operation may be the same as a related affiliate in the case where the foreign activity is an essential component or extension of the related affiliate.

Prior to translation, the foreign country figures are remeasured in the functional currency. For instance, if a company in Italy is an independent entity and received cash and incurred expenses in Italy, the Italian currency is the functional currency. However, in the event the Italian company was an extension of a Canadian parent, the functional currency is the Canadian currency. The functional currency should be used consistently except if material economic changes necessitate a change. However, previously issued financial statements are not restated for an alteration in the functional currency.

If a company's books are not kept in its functional currency, remeasurement into the functional currency is mandated. The remeasurement process occurs before translation into the reporting currency takes place. When a foreign entity's functional currency is the reporting currency, remeasurement into the reporting currency obviates translation. The remeasurement process is intended to generate the same result as if the entity's books had been kept in the functional currency.

Guidelines are referred to in determining the functional currency of a foreign operation. The "benchmarks" apply to selling price, market, cash flow, financing, expense, and intercompany transactions. A detailed discussion follows:

1. *Selling price.* The functional currency is the foreign currency when the foreign operation's selling price of products or services are primarily because of local factors such as government law and competition. It is not due to changes in exchange rate. The functional currency is the parent's currency when the foreign operation's sales prices mostly apply in the short-run to fluctuation in the exchange rate resulting from international factors (e.g., worldwide competition).

2. *Market.* The functional currency is the foreign currency when the foreign activity has a strong local sales market for products or services even though a significant amount of exports may exist. The functional currency is the parent's currency when the foreign operation's sales market is mostly in the parent's country.

3. *Cash flow.* The functional currency is the foreign currency when the foreign operation's cash flows are primarily in foreign currency not directly affecting the parent's cash flow. The functional currency is the parent's currency when the foreign operation's cash flows directly impact the parent's cash flows. They are usually available for remittance via intercompany accounting settlement.

4. *Financing.* The functional currency is the foreign currency if financing the foreign activity is in foreign currency and funds obtained by the foreign activity are sufficient to meet debt obligations. The functional currency is the parent's currency when financing foreign activity is provided by the parent or occurs in U.S. dollars. Funds obtained by the foreign activity are insufficient to satisfy debt requirements.

5. *Expenses.* The functional currency is the foreign currency when foreign operation's production costs or services are usually incurred locally. However, some foreign imports may exist. The functional currency is the parent's currency when foreign operation's production and service costs are primarily component costs obtained from the parent's country.

6. *Intercompany transactions.* The functional currency is the foreign currency when minor interrelationship occurs between the activities of the foreign entity and parent except for competitive advantages (e.g., patents). There is a restricted number of intercompany transactions. The functional currency is the parent's currency when material interrelationship exists between the foreign entity and parent. Many intercompany transactions exist.

Consistent use of the functional currency of the foreign entity must exist over the years except if there are changes in circumstances warranting a change. If a change in the functional currency takes place, it is accounted for as a change in estimate.

- *Local Currency*—The currency of the particular foreign country
- *Measure*—Translation into a currency other than the original reporting currency. Foreign financial statements are measured in U.S. dollars by using the applicable exchange rate.
- *Reporting Currency*—The currency in which the business prepares its financial statements. It is usually U.S. dollars.
- *Spot Rate*—Exchange rate for immediate delivery of currencies exchanged
- *Transaction Gain or Loss*—Transaction gains or losses occur due to a change in exchange rates between the functional currency and the currency in which a foreign currency transaction is denominated. They represent an increase or decrease in (a) the actual functional currency cash flows realized upon settlement of foreign currency transactions and (b) the expected functional currency cash flows on unsettled foreign currency transactions.
- *Translation Adjustments*—Translation adjustments arise from translating financial statements from the entity's functional currency into the reporting one

Translation Process

Translation of Foreign Currency Statements When the U.S. Dollar is the Functional Currency. The foreign entity's financial statements in a highly inflationary economy is not stable enough and should be remeasured as if the functional currency were the reporting currency. Thus, the financial statements of those entities should be remeasured into the reporting currency (the U.S. dollar becomes the functional currency). In effect, the reporting currency is used directly.

A highly inflationary environment is one that has cumulative inflation of about 100% or more over a 3 year period. In other words, the inflation rate must be increasing at a rate of about 35% a year for three consecutive years. **Tip:** The International Monetary Fund of Washington, D.C. publishes monthly figures on international inflation rates.

Translation of Foreign Currency Statements When the Foreign Currency is the Functional Currency. Balance sheet items are translated via the current exchange rate. For assets and liabilities, use the rate at the balance sheet date. If a current exchange rate is not available at the balance sheet date, use the first exchange rate available after that date. The current exchange rate is also used to translate the Statement of Cash Flows, except for those items found in the Income Statement which are translated using the weighted-average rate. For income statement items (revenues, expenses, gains, and losses), use the exchange rate at the dates those items are recognized. Since translation at the exchange rates at the dates the many revenues, expenses, gains, and losses are recognized is almost always impractical, use a weighted-average exchange rate for the period in translating income statement items.

A material change occurring between the date of the financial statements and the audit report date should be disclosed as a subsequent event. Disclosure should also be made of the effects on unsettled balances pertaining to foreign currency transactions.

Translation Adjustments. There are several steps in translating the foreign country's financial statements into U.S. reporting requirements. They are:

1. Conform the foreign country's financial statements to U.S. GAAP

2. Determine the functional currency of the foreign entity

3. Remeasure the financial statements in the functional currency, if necessary. Gains or losses from remeasurement are includable in remeasured current net income.

4. Convert from the foreign currency into U.S. dollars (reporting currency).

If a company's functional currency is a foreign currency, translation adjustments arise from translating that company's financial statements into the reporting currency. Translation adjustments are unrealized and should not be included in the income statement but should be reported separately and accumulated in a separate component of equity. However, if remeasurement from the recording currency to the functional currency is required before translation, the gain or loss is reflected in the income statement.

Upon sale or liquidation of an investment in a foreign entity, the amount attributable to that entity and accumulated in the translation adjustment component of equity is removed from the stockholders' equity section and considered a part of the gain or loss on sale or liquidation of the investment in the income statement for the period during which the sale or liquidation occurs.

As per Interpretation 37, a sale of an investment in a foreign entity may include a partial sale of an ownership interest. In that case, a pro rata amount of the cumulative translation adjustment reflected as a stockholders' equity component is includable in arriving at the gain or loss on sale. For example, if a business sells a 40% ownership interest in a foreign investment, 40% of the translation adjustment applicable to it is included in calculating gain or loss on sale of that ownership interest.

Foreign Currency Transactions

Foreign currency transactions are those denominated in a currency other than the company's functional currency. Foreign currency transactions may result in receivables or payables fixed in terms of the amount of foreign currency to be received or paid.

A foreign currency transaction requires settlement in a currency other than the functional currency. A change in exchange rates between the functional currency and the currency in which a transaction is denominated increases or decreases the expected amount of functional currency cash flows upon settlement of the transaction. This change in expected functional currency cash flows is a foreign currency transaction gain or loss that typically is included in arriving at earnings in the income statement for the period in which the exchange rate is altered. An example of a transaction gain or loss is when a British subsidiary has a receivable denominated in pounds from a French customer.

Similarly, a transaction gain or loss (measured from the transaction date or the most recent intervening balance sheet date, whichever is later) realized upon settlement of a foreign currency transaction usually should be included in determining net income for the period in which the transaction is settled.

EXAMPLE 25

An exchange gain or loss occurs when the exchange rate changes between the purchase date and sale date.

Merchandise is bought for 100,000 pounds. The exchange rate is four pounds to one dollar. The journal entry is:

Purchases	$25,000	
Accounts Payable		$25,000
100,000/4 = $25,000		

When the merchandise is paid for, the exchange rate is five to one. The journal entry is:

Accounts Payable	$25,000	
Cash		$20,000
Foreign exchange gain		5,000
100,000/5 = $20,000		

The $20,000, using an exchange rate of five to one can buy 100,000 pounds. The transaction gain is the difference between the cash required of $20,000 and the initial liability of $25,000.

Note that a foreign transaction gain or loss has to be determined at each balance sheet date on all recorded foreign transactions that have not been settled.

EXAMPLE 26

A U.S. company sells goods to a customer in England on 11/15/X7 for 10,000 pounds. The exchange rate for one pound is $.75. Thus, the transaction is worth $7,500 (10,000 pounds × .75). Payment is due two months later. The entry on 11/15/X7 is:

Accounts Receivable—England	$7,500	
Sales		$7,500

Accounts receivable and sales are measured in U.S. dollars at the transaction date employing the spot rate. Even though the accounts receivable is measured and reported in U.S. dollars, the receivable is fixed in pounds. Thus, there can occur a transaction gain or loss if the exchange rate changes between the transaction date (11/15/X7) and the settlement date (1/15/X8).

Since the financial statements are prepared between the transaction date and settlement date, receivables which are denominated in a currency other than the functional currency (U.S. dollar) have to be restated to reflect the spot rate on the balance sheet date. On December 31, 19X7 the exchange rate is one pound equals $.80. Hence the 10,000 pounds are now valued at $8,000 (10,000 × $.80). Therefore, the accounts receivable denominated in pounds should be upwardly adjusted by $500. The required journal entry on 12/31/X7 is:

Accounts Receivable—England	$500	
Foreign Exchange Gain		$500

The income statement for the year-ended 12/31/X7 shows an exchange gain of $500. Note that sales is not affected by the exchange gain since sales relates to operational activity.

On 1/15/X8, the spot rate is one pound = $.78. The journal entry is:

Cash	$7,800	
Foreign Exchange Loss	200	
Accounts Receivable—England		$8,000

The 19X8 income statement shows an exchange loss of $200.

Transaction Gains and Losses to Be Excluded from Determination of Net Income. Gains and losses on the following foreign currency transactions are not included in earnings but rather reported as translation adjustments:

- Foreign currency transactions designated as *economic hedges* of a net investment in a foreign entity, beginning as of the designation date

- Intercompany foreign currency transactions of a long-term investment nature (settlement is not planned or expected in the foreseeable future), when the entities to the transaction are consolidated, combined, or accounted for by the equity method in the reporting company's financial statements

A gain or loss on a forward contract or other foreign currency transaction that is intended to *hedge* an identifiable foreign currency commitment (e.g., an agreement to buy or sell machinery) should be deferred and included in the measurement of the related foreign currency transaction. Losses should not be deferred if it is anticipated that deferral would cause recognizing losses in subsequent periods. A foreign currency transaction is considered a hedge of an identifiable foreign currency commitment provided both of the following criteria are satisfied:

- The foreign currency transaction is designated as a hedge of a foreign currency commitment
- The foreign currency commitment is firm

Forward Exchange Contracts

A forward exchange contract is an agreement to exchange different currencies at a given future date and at a specified rate (forward rate). A forward contract is a foreign currency transaction. A gain or loss on a forward contract that does not meet the conditions described below are includable in net income. **Note:** Currency swaps are accounted for in a similar fashion.

A gain or loss (whether or not deferred) on a forward contract, except a speculative forward contract, should be computed by multiplying the foreign currency amount of the forward contract by the difference between the *spot rate* at the Balance Sheet date and the spot rate at the date of inception of the forward contract.

The *discount or premium on a forward contract* (that is, the foreign currency amount of the contract multiplied by the difference between the contracted forward rate and the spot rate at the date of inception of the contract) should be accounted for separately from the gain or loss on the contract and typically should be included in computing net income over the life of the forward contract.

A gain or loss on a *speculative forward contract* (a contract that does not hedge an exposure) should be computed by multiplying the foreign currency amount of the forward contract by the difference between the forward rate available from the remaining maturity of the contract and the contracted forward rate (or the forward rate last used to measure a gain or loss on that contract for an earlier period). No separate accounting recognition is given to the discount or premium on a speculative forward contract.

Hedging. Foreign currency transactions, gains and losses on assets, and liabilities, denominated in a currency other than the functional currency, can be hedged if the U.S. company engages into a forward exchange contract.

A hedge can occur even if there does not exist a forward exchange contract. For instance, a foreign currency transaction can serve as an economic hedge offsetting a parent's net investment in a foreign entity when the transaction is entered into for hedging purposes and is effective.

EXAMPLE 27

A U.S. parent completely owns a French subsidiary having net assets of $3 million in francs. The U.S. parent can borrow $3 million francs to hedge its net investment in the French subsidiary. Also assume the French franc is the functional currency and the $3 million obligation is denominated in francs. Variability in the exchange rate for francs does *not* have a net impact on the parent's consolidated balance sheet since increases in the translation adjustments balance arising from translation of the net investment will be netted against decreases in this balance emanating from the adjustment of the liability denominated in francs.

10
Interim and Segmental Reporting

This chapter discusses the requirements for the preparation of interim financial statements and segmental disclosures included in the annual report.

INTERIM REPORTS

Interim reports may be issued at periodic reporting intervals, for example quarterly or monthly. Complete financial statements or summarized data may be provided, but interim financial statements do not have to be certified by the outside auditors.

Interim balance sheets and cash flow information should be given. If these statements are not presented, significant changes in liquid assets, cash, long-term debt, and stockholders' equity should be disclosed.

Usually, interim reports include results of the current interim period and the cumulative year-to-date figures. Typically, comparisons are made to results of comparable interim periods for the prior years.

Interim results should be based on the accounting principles used in the last year's annual report unless a change has been made in the current year.

A gain or loss cannot be deferred to a later interim period except if such deferral would have been permissible for annual reporting.

Revenue from merchandise sold and services performed should be accounted for as earned in the interim period in the same way as accounted for in annual reporting. If an advance is received in the first quarter and benefits the entire year, it should be allocated ratably to the interim periods affected.

Costs and expenses should be matched to related revenue in the interim period. If a cost cannot be associated with revenue in a future interim period, it should be expensed in the current period. Yearly expenses such as administrative salaries, insurance, pension plan expense, and year-end bonuses should be allocated to the quarters. The allocation basis may be based on such factors as the time expired, benefit obtained, and activity.

The gross profit method can be used to estimate interim inventory and cost of sales. Disclosure should be made of the method, assumptions made, and material adjustments by reconciliations with the annual physical inventory.

A permanent inventory loss should be reflected in the interim period it occurs. A subsequent recovery is treated as a gain in the later interim period. However, if the change in inventory value is temporary, no recognition is given in the accounts.

When there is a temporary liquidation of the LIFO base with replacement expected by year-end, cost of sales should be based on replacement cost.

EXAMPLE 1

The historical cost of an inventory item is $10,000 with replacement cost expected at $15,000. The entry is:

Cost of Sales	15,000	
Inventory		10,000
Reserve for Liquidation of LIFO Base		5,000

Note the Reserve for Liquidation of LIFO Base account is shown as a current liability.

When replenishment is made at year-end the entry is:

Reserve for Liquidation of LIFO Base	5,000	
Inventory	10,000	
Cash		15,000

Volume discounts given to customers tied into annual purchases should be apportioned to the interim period based on the ratio of:

$$\frac{\text{Purchases for the interim period}}{\text{Total estimated purchases for the year}}$$

When a standard cost system is used, variances expected to be reversed by year-end may be deferred to an asset or liability account.

With regard to income taxes, the income tax provision includes current and deferred taxes. Federal and local taxes are provided for. The tax provision for an interim period should be cumulative (e.g., total tax expense for a 9-month period is shown in the third quarter based on nine months income). The tax expense for the 3-month period based on three months revenue may also be presented (e.g., third quarter tax expense based on only the third quarter). In computing tax expense, the estimated annual effective tax rate should be used. The effective tax rate should be based on income from continuing operations. If a reliable estimate is not practical, the actual year-to-date effective tax rate should be used.

At the end of each interim period, a revision to the effective tax rate may be necessary employing the best current estimates of the annual effective tax rate. The projected tax rate includes adjustment for net deferred credits. Adjustments should be contained in deriving the maximum tax benefit for year-to-date figures.

The estimated effective tax rate should incorporate all available tax credits (e.g., foreign tax credit) and available alternative tax methods in determining ordinary earnings. A change in tax legislation is only reflected in the interim period affected.

Income statement items after income from continuing operations (e.g., income from discontinued operations, extraordinary items, cumulative effect of a change in accounting principle) should be presented net of the tax effect. The tax effect on these unusual line items should be reflected only in the interim period they actually occur. For example, we should not predict items before they occur. Prior period adjustments in the retained earnings statement are also shown net of tax when they take place.

The tax implication of an interim loss is recognized *only* when realization of the tax benefit is assured beyond reasonable doubt. If a loss is expected for the remainder of the year, and carryback is not possible, the tax benefits typically should not be recognized.

The tax benefit of a previous year operating loss carryforward is recognized as an extraordinary item in each interim period to the extent that income is available to offset the loss carryforward.

When a change in principle is made in the first interim period, the cumulative effect of a change in principle account should be shown net of tax in the first interim period. If a change in principle is made in a quarter other than the first (e.g., third quarter), we assume the change was made at the beginning of the first quarter showing the cumulative effect in the first quarter. The interim periods will have to be restated using the new principle (e.g., first, second, and third quarters).

When interim data for previous years is presented for comparative purposes, data should be restated to conform with newly adopted policies. Alternatively, disclosure can be made of the effect on prior data had the new practice been applied to that period.

For a change in principle, disclosure should be made of the nature and justification in the interim period of change. The effect of the change on per share amounts should be given.

Disclosure should be made of seasonality aspects affecting interim results and contingencies. When a change in the estimated effective tax rate occurs it should be disclosed. Further, if a fourth quarter is not presented, any material adjustments to that quarter must be commented upon in the footnotes to the annual report. If an event is immaterial on an annual basis but material in the interim period, it should be disclosed. Purchase or pooling transactions should be noted.

The financial statement presentation for prior period adjustments follow:

- Include in net income for the current period, the portion of the effect related to current operations
- Restate earnings of impacted prior interim periods of the current year to include the portion related thereto
- If the prior period adjustment affects prior years, include it in the earnings of the first interim period of the current year

The criteria to be met for prior period adjustments in interim periods follow:

- Materiality
- Estimable
- Identified to a prior interim period

Examples of prior period adjustments for interim reporting are:

- Error corrections
- Settlement of litigation or claims
- Adjustment of income taxes
- Renegotiation proceedings
- Utility revenue under rate making processes

Earnings per share is computed for interim purposes the same way as for annual purposes.

Segmental disposal is separately shown in the interim period in which it occurs.

SEGMENTAL REPORTING

Financial reporting for business segments is useful in evaluating segmental performance, earning potential, and risk. Segmental reporting may be by industry, foreign geographic area, export sales, major customers, and governmental contracts. The financial statement presentation for segments may appear in the body, footnotes, or separate schedule to the financial statements. Segmental information is not required for nonpublic companies or in interim reports. An industry segment sells merchandise or renders services to outside customers. Segmental information assists financial statement users in analyzing financial statements by allowing improved assessment of an enterprise's past performance and future prospects.

Segmental data occurs when a company prepares a full set of financial statements (balance sheet, income statement, statement of cash flows, and related footnotes). Segmental data is shown for each year presented. Information reported is a disaggregation of consolidated financial information.

Accounting principles employed in preparing financial statements should be used for segment information, except that numerous intercompany transaction eliminated in consolidation are included in segmental reporting on a gross basis.

Reporting Requirements

A segment must be reported if one or more of the following criteria are met:

- Revenue is 10% or more of total revenue
- Operating income or loss is 10% or more of the combined operating profit
- Identifiable assets are 10% or more of the total identifiable assets

Factors to be considered when determining industry segments are:

- Nature of the product. Related products or services have similar purposes or end uses (e.g., similarity in profit margins, risk, and growth).
- Nature of the production process. Homogeneity may be indicated when there is interchangeable production or sales facilities, equipment, service groups, or labor force.
- Nature of the market. Similarity exists in geographic markets serviced or types of customers serviced.

Reportable segments are determined by:

- Identifying specific products and services
- Grouping those products and services by industry line into segments
- Selecting material segments to the company as a whole

A grouping of products and services by industry lines should take place. A number of approaches are possible. However, not one method is appropriate in determining industry segments in every case. In many cases, management judgment is necessary to determine the industry segment. A starting point in deriving an industry segment is by *profit center*. A profit center is a component that sells mostly to outsiders for a profit.

When the profit center goes across industry lines, it should be broken down into smaller groups. A company in many industries not accumulating financial information on a segregated basis must disaggregate its operations by industry line.

Although worldwide industry segmentation is recommended, it may not be practical to gather. If foreign operations cannot be disaggregated, the firm should disaggregate domestic activities. Foreign operations should be disaggregated where possible and treat the remaining foreign operations as a single segment.

As per FASB 14, a segment that was significant in the past, even though not meeting the 10% test in the current year, should still be reported upon if it is expected that the segment will be significant in the future.

Segments should constitute a substantial portion, meaning 75% or more, of the company's total revenue to outside customers. The 75% test is applied separately each year. However, in order to derive 75%, as a matter of practicality not more than 10 segments should be shown. If more than 10 are identified, it is possible to combine similar segments.

Note that even though intersegment transfers are eliminated in the preparation of consolidated financial statements, they are includable for segmental disclosure in determining the 10% and the 75% rules.

In applying the 10% criteria, the accountant should note the following:

- *Revenue.* A separation should exist between revenue to unaffiliated customers and revenue to other business segments. Transfer prices are used for intersegmental transfers. Accounting bases followed should be disclosed.

- *Operating Profit or Loss.* Operating earnings of a segment excludes general corporate revenue and expenses that are not allocable, interest expense (unless the segment is a financial type, such as one involved in banking), domestic and foreign income taxes, income from unconsolidated subsidiaries or investees, income from discontinued operations, extraordinary items, cumulative effect of a change in accounting principles, and minority interest. Note that directly traceable and allocated costs should be charged to segments when applicable thereto.

- *Identifiable Assets.* Assets of a segment include those directly in it and general corporate assets that can rationally be allocated to it. Allocation methods should be consistently applied. Identifiable assets include those consisting of a part of the company's investment in the segment (e.g., goodwill). Identifiable assets do not include advances or loans to other segments except for income that is used to compute the results of operations (e.g., a segment of a financial nature).

EXAMPLE 2

A company provides the following data regarding its business segments and overall operations:

	Segment A	Segment B	Company*
Revenue	$2,000	$1,000	$12,000
Direct costs	500	300	5,000
Company-wide costs (allocated)			800
General company costs (not allocated)			1,700

*Excludes segment amounts

Company-wide costs are allocated based on the ratios of direct costs. The tax rate is 34%.

The profits to be reported by segment and for the company as a whole are as follows:

	Segment A	Segment B	Company
Revenues	$2,000	$1,000	$15,000
Less:			
Direct costs	(500)	(300)	(5,800)
Indirect costs (allocated)			
$800 x $500/$5,800	(69)		
$800 x $300/$5,800		(41)	
			(800)
Segment margin	$1,431	$659	
General company costs			(1,700)
Income before tax			$6,700
Income tax (34%)			2,278
Net income			$4,422

Disclosures

Disclosures are not required for 90% enterprises (e.g., a company that derives 90% or more of its revenue, operating profit, and total assets from one segment). In effect, that segment is the business. The dominant industry segment should be identified.

Disclosures to be made by segments include:

- Aggregate depreciation, depletion, and amortization expense
- Capital expenditures
- Company's equity in vertically integrated unconsolidated subsidiaries and equity method investees. Note the geographic location of equity method investees.
- Effect of an accounting principle change on the operating profit of the reportable segment. Also include its effect on the company.
- Material segmental accounting policies not already disclosed in the regular financial statements
- Transfer price used
- Allocation method for costs
- Unusual items affecting segmental profit
- Type of products

Consolidation Aspects

If a segment includes a purchase method consolidated subsidiary, the required segmental information is based upon the consolidated value of the subsidiary (e.g., fair market value and goodwill recognized) and not on the values recorded in the subsidiary's own financial statements. However, transactions between the segment and other segments, which are eliminated in consolidation, are included in reportable segmental information.

Segmental data is not required for unconsolidated subsidiaries or other unconsolidated investees. Note that each subsidiary or investee is subject to the rules of FASB 14 that segment information be reported.

Some types of typical consolidation eliminations are not eliminated when reporting for segments. For instance, revenues of a segment includes intersegmental sales and sales to unrelated customers.

A full set of financial statements for a foreign investee that is *not* a subsidiary does not have to disclose segmental information when presented in the same financial report of a primary reporting entity except if the foreign investee's separately issued statements already disclose the required segmental data.

Other Requirements

Segmental disclosure is also required when:

- 10% or more of revenue or assets is associated with a foreign area. Presentation must be made of revenue, operating profit or loss, and assets for foreign operations in the aggregate or by geographic locality. A foreign geographical area is a foreign country or group or homogeneous countries. Factors considered in deriving this grouping decision are proximity, economic affinity, and similar business environments.

- 10% or more of sales is to one customer. A group of customers under common control is construed as one customer.

- 10% or more of revenue is obtained from domestic government contracts or a foreign government.

In the above cases, the source of the segmental revenue should be disclosed along with the percent so derived.

In some instances, restatement of prior period information is required for comparative reasons. The nature and effect of restatement should be disclosed. Restatement is needed when financial statements of the company as a whole have been restated. Also, restatement occurs when there is a pooling-of-interest. Restatement is also needed when a change has occurred in grouping products or services for segment determination or change in grouping of foreign activities into geographic segments.

As per FASB 24, segmental data are not required in financial statements that are presented in another company's financial report if those statements are:

- Combined in a complete set of statements and both sets are presented in the same report

- Presented for a foreign investee (not a subsidiary of the primary enterprise) unless the financial statements disclose segment information (e.g., those foreign investees for which such information is already required by the SEC)

- Presented in the report of a nonpublic company

If an investee uses the cost or equity method and is not exempted by one of the above provisions, its full set of financial statements presented in another enterprise's report must present segment information if such data are significant to statements of the primary enterprise. Significance is determined by applying the percentage tests of FASB 14 (e.g., 10% tests) in relation to financial statements of the primary enterprise without adjustment for the investee's revenue, operating results, or identifiable assets.

III

MANAGEMENT ACCOUNTING

11

Cost Concepts, Classifications, and Product Costing Systems

Management accounting as defined by the National Association of Accountants (NAA) is the process of identification, measurement, accumulation, analysis, preparation, interpretation, and communication of financial information, which is used by management to plan, evaluate, and control within an organization. It ensures the appropriate use of and accountability for an organization's resources. Management accounting also relates to the preparation of financial reports for nonmanagement groups such as regulatory agencies and tax authorities. Simply stated, management accounting is the accounting for the planning, control, and decision-making activities of an organization.

COST ACCOUNTING VERSUS MANAGEMENT ACCOUNTING

The difference between cost accounting and management accounting is a subtle one. The NAA defines cost accounting as "a systematic set of procedures for recording and reporting measurements of the cost of manufacturing goods and performing services in the aggregate and in detail. It includes methods for recognizing, classifying, allocating, aggregating and reporting such costs and comparing them with standard costs." From this definition of cost accounting and the NAA's definition of management accounting, one thing is clear: the major function of cost accounting is cost accumulation for inventory valuation and income determination. Management accounting, however, emphasizes the use of the cost data for planning, control, and decision-making purposes.

COST CONCEPTS, TERMS, AND CLASSIFICATIONS

In financial accounting, the term cost is defined as a measurement, in monetary terms, of the amount of resources used for some purposes. In managerial accounting, the term cost is used in many different ways. That is, there are different types of costs used for different purposes. Some costs are useful and required for inventory valuation and income determination. Some costs are useful for planning, budgeting, and cost control. Still others are useful for making short-term and long-term decisions.

Cost Classifications

Costs can be classified into various categories, according to:

1. Their management function
   a. Manufacturing costs
   b. Nonmanufacturing (operating) costs

2. Their ease of traceability
   a. Direct costs
   b. Indirect costs

3. Their timing of charges against sales revenue
   a. Product costs
   b. Period costs

4. Their behavior in accordance with changes in activity
   a. Variable costs
   b. Fixed costs
   c. Mixed (semivariable) costs

5. Their degree of averaging
   a. Total costs
   b. Unit (average) costs

6. Their relevance to planning, control and decision making
   a. Controllable and noncontrollable costs
   b. Standard costs
   c. Incremental costs
   d. Sunk costs
   e. Out-of-pocket costs
   f. Relevant costs
   g. Opportunity costs

We will discuss each of the cost categories in the remainder of this chapter.

Costs by Management Function

In a manufacturing firm, costs are divided into two major categories, by the functional activities they are associated with: (1) manufacturing costs, and (2) nonmanufacturing costs, also called operating expenses.

Manufacturing Costs. Manufacturing costs are those costs associated with the manufacturing activities of the company. Manufacturing costs are subdivided into three categories: direct materials, direct labor, and factory overhead. Direct materials are all materials that become an integral part of the finished product. Examples are the steel used to make an automobile and the wood to make furniture. Glues, nails, and other minor items are called indirect materials (or supplies) and are classified as part of factory overhead, which is explained below.

Direct labor is the labor directly involved in making the product. Examples of direct labor costs are the wages of assembly workers on an assembly line and the wages of machine tool operators in a machine shop. Indirect labor, such as wages of supervisory personnel and janitors, is classified as part of factory overhead. Factory overhead can be defined as including all costs of manufacturing except direct materials and direct labor. Some of the many examples include depreciation, rent, taxes, insurance, fringe benefits, payroll taxes, and cost of idle time. Factory overhead is also called manufacturing overhead, indirect manufacturing expenses, and factory burden. Many costs overlap within their categories. For example, direct materials and direct labor when combined are called prime costs. Direct labor and factory overhead when combined are termed conversion costs (or processing costs).

Nonmanufacturing Costs. Nonmanufacturing costs (or operating expenses) are subdivided into selling expenses and general and administrative expenses. Selling expenses are all the expenses associated with obtaining sales and the delivery of the product. Examples are advertising and sales commissions. General and administrative expenses (G & A) include all the expenses that are incurred in connection with performing general and administrative activities. Examples are executives' salaries and legal expenses. Many other examples of costs by management function and their relationships are found in Figure 1.

Direct Costs and Indirect Costs

Costs may be viewed as either direct or indirect in terms of the extent they are traceable to a particular object of costing such as products, jobs, departments, and sales territories. Direct costs are those costs that can be directly traceable to the costing object. Factory overhead items are all indirect costs. Costs shared by different departments, products, or jobs, called common costs or joint costs, are also indirect costs. National advertising that benefits more than one product and sales territory is an example of an indirect cost.

Figure 1 Costs by Management Function

Direct Materials

plus

Direct Labor

plus

Factory Overhead

equals

Indirect Materials

Factory supplies
Glues and nails
Small tools

plus

Indirect Labor

Supervision
Inspection
Security guards
Factory clerks
Janitors

plus

Other overhead Costs

Rent
Insurance
Property tax
Depreciation—factory
Maintenance and repair
Utilities
Employer payroll
    taxes—factory labor
Overtime premium
Cost of idle time

equals

Manufacturing Cost

plus

Non-manufacturing Expenses
(or operating expenses)

equals

Total Cost

Selling Expenses

plus

General & Administrative
Expenses

equals

Selling Expenses

Sales salaries and
  commissions
Employer payroll taxes—sales
Advertising
Samples
Entertainment and travel
Rent
Depreciation—sales
Property tax on sales office
Freight out

General & Administrative Expenses

Administrative and office salaries
Employer payroll taxes—office
Rent
Depreciation—office
Property tax—office
Auditing expense
Legal expense
Bad debts
Travel and entertainment

219

Figure 2 Various Classifications of Costs

Product Costs (Inventoriable Costs)

Period Costs (Non-inventoriable costs)

Direct Material

Direct Labor

Factory Overhead

Selling and General and Administrative Expenses

Prime Costs

Conversion Costs

Direct Cost

Indirect Cost

Direct or Indirect Cost

Product Costs and Period Costs

By their timing of charges against revenue or by whether they are inventoriable, costs are classified into product costs and period costs.

Product costs are inventoriable costs, identified as part of inventory on hand. They are therefore assets until they are sold. Once they are sold, they become expenses (i.e., cost of goods sold). All manufacturing costs are product costs.

Period costs are not inventoriable and hence are charged against sales revenues in the period in which the revenue is earned. Selling and general and administrative expenses are period costs.

Figure 2 shows the relationship of product and period costs and other cost classifications presented thus far.

Variable Costs, Fixed Costs, and Mixed Costs

From a planning and control standpoint, perhaps the most important way to classify costs is by how they behave in accordance with changes in volume or some measure of activity. By behavior, costs can be classified into three basic categories—variable, fixed, or mixed.

Variable costs are costs that vary in total in direct proportion to changes in activity. Examples are direct materials and gasoline expense based on mileage driven. Fixed costs are costs that remain constant in total regardless of changes in activity. Examples are rent, insurance, and taxes. Mixed (or semivariable) costs are costs that vary with changes in volume but, unlike variable costs, do not vary in direct proportion. In other words, these costs contain both a variable component and a fixed component. Examples are the rental of a delivery truck, where a fixed rental fee plus a variable charge based on mileage is made; and power costs, where the expense consists of a fixed amount plus a variable charge based on consumption. Costs by behavior will be examined further in a later chapter. The breakdown of costs into their variable components and their fixed components is very important in many areas of management accounting, such as flexible budgeting, break-even analysis, and short-term decision making.

Unit Costs and Total Costs

For external reporting and pricing purposes, accountants are frequently interested in determining the unit (average) cost per unit of product or service. The unit cost is simply the average cost, which is the total cost divided by the volume in units. Alternatively, the unit cost is the sum of (a) the variable cost per unit, and (b) the fixed cost per unit. It is important to realize that the unit cost declines as volume increases since the total fixed costs that are constant over a range of activity are being spread over a larger number of units.

EXAMPLE 1

Fixed costs are $1,000 per period and variable costs are $.10 per unit. The total and unit (average) costs at various production levels are as follows:

Volume in units (a)	Total Fixed Costs (b)	Total Variable Costs (c)	Total Costs (b) + (c) = (d)	Variable Cost per unit (c)/(a) = (e)	Fixed Cost per unit (b)/(a) = (f)	Unit (Average Cost (d)/(a) c (e) + (f
1,000	$1,000	$100	$1,100	$.10	$1.00	$1.10
5,000	1,000	500	1,500	.10	.20	.30
10,000	1,000	1000	2,000	.10	.10	.20

The increase in total costs and the decline in unit costs are illustrated in Figure 3. Also note the relationships for variable and fixed costs per unit:

Behavior as Volume Changes from 5,000 to 10,000

	Total Cost	Unit Cost
Variable Cost	Change ($500 to $1,000)	No change ($.10)
Fixed cost	No change ($1,000)	Change ($.20 to $.10)

Figure 3   Total and Unit (Average) Costs

Costs for Planning, Control, and Decision Making

Controllable and Noncontrollable Costs. A cost is said to be controllable when the amount of the cost is assigned to the head of a department and the level of the cost is significantly under the manager's influence. Noncontrollable costs are those costs not subject to influence at a given level of managerial supervision.

EXAMPLE 2

All variable costs such as direct materials, direct labor, and variable overhead are usually considered controllable by the department head. Further, a certain portion of fixed costs can also be controllable. For example, depreciation on the equipment used specifically for a given department would be an expense controllable by the head of the department.

Standard Costs. Standard costs are the costs established in advance to serve as goals, norms or yardsticks to be achieved and, after the fact, to determine how well those goals were met. They are based on the quantities and prices of the various inputs (e.g., direct materials, direct labor, and factory overhead) needed to produce output efficiently. Standard costs can also be set for service businesses.

EXAMPLE 3

The standard cost of materials per pound is obtained by multiplying standard price per pound by standard quantity per unit of output in pounds as follows:

Purchase price	$3.00
Freight	0.12
Receiving and handling	0.02
Less: Purchase discounts	(0.04)
Standard price per pound	$3.10
Per bill of materials in pounds	1.2
Allowance for waste and spoilage in lbs.	0.1
Allowance for rejects in lbs.	0.1
Standard quantity per unit of output	1.4 lbs.

The standard cost of material is 1.4 pounds $\times$ \$3.10 = \$4.34 per unit.

Incremental (or Differential) Costs. The incremental cost is the difference in costs between two or more alternatives.

EXAMPLE 4

Consider the two alternatives A and B whose costs are as follows:

	A	B	Difference (B − A)
Direct materials	$10,000	$10,000	$ 0
Direct labor	10,000	15,000	5,000

The incremental costs are simply B − A (or A − B) as shown in the last column. The incremental costs are relevant to future decisions.

Sunk Costs. Sunk costs are the cost of resources that have already been incurred whose total will not be affected by any decision made now or in the future. Sunk costs are considered irrelevant to future decisions since they are past or historical costs.

EXAMPLE 5

Suppose you acquired an asset for $50,000 three years ago which is now listed at a book value of $20,000. The $20,000 book value is a sunk cost which does not affect a future decision.

Out-of-Pocket Costs. Out-of-pocket costs, also known as outlay costs, are costs that require future expenditures of cash or other resources. Out-of-pocket costs are usually relevant to a particular decision.

EXAMPLE 6

A capital investment project requires $120,000 in cash outlays. $120,000 is an out-of-pocket cost.

Relevant Costs. Relevant costs are expected future costs that will differ between alternatives.

EXAMPLE 7

The incremental cost is said to be relevant to the future decision. The sunk cost is considered irrelevant.

Opportunity Costs. An opportunity cost is the net benefit foregone by rejecting an alternative. There is always an opportunity cost involved in making a choice decision. It is a cost incurred relative to the alternative given up and does not appear on the formal accounting records.

EXAMPLE 8

Suppose a company has a choice of using its capacity to produce an extra 10,000 units or renting it out for $20,000. The opportunity cost of using the capacity is $20,000.

Income Statements and Balance Sheets—Manufacturer

Figure 4 illustrates the income statement of a manufacturer. The important characteristics of the income statement is that it is supported by a schedule of cost of goods manufactured (see Figure 5). This schedule shows the specific costs (i.e., direct materials, direct labor, and factory overhead) that have gone into the goods completed during the period. Since the manufacturer carries three types of inventory (raw materials, work-in-process, and finished goods) all three items must be incorporated into the computation of the cost of goods sold. These inventory accounts also appear on the balance sheet for a manufacturer, as shown in Figure 6.

COST ACCUMULATION SYSTEMS

A cost accumulation system is a product costing system, which is the process of accumulating manufacturing costs such as materials, labor, and factory overhead and assigning them to cost objectives, such as finished goods and work-in-process. Product costing is necessary not only for inventory valuation and income determination but also for establishing the unit selling price. We will discuss the essentials of the cost accumulation system that is used to measure the manufacturing costs of products. This is essentially a two-step process: (1) the measurement of costs that are applicable to manufacturing operations during a given accounting period, and (2) the assignment of these costs to products.

There are two basic approaches to cost accounting and accumulation:

(1) Job order costing

(2) Process costing

Figure 4   Manufacturer's Income Statements
For the Year Ended December 31, 19x1

Sales		$320,000
Less: Cost of Goods Sold		
Finished Goods, Dec. 31		
19x0	$ 18,000	
Cost of Goods Manufactured (see Schedule,		
Figure 5)	121,000	
Cost of Goods Available for Sale	$139,000	
Finished Goods, Dec. 31		
19x1	21,000	
Cost of Goods Sold		$118,000
Gross Margin		$202,000
Less: Selling and Administrative Expenses		60,000
Net Income		$142,000

Figure 5 Manufacturer's Schedule of Cost Goods Manufactured

Direct Materials:

Inventory, Dec. 31, 19x0	$23,000	
Purchases	64,000	
Cost of Direct Materials Available for Use	$87,000	
Inventory, Dec. 31, 19x1	7,800	
Direct Materials Used		$ 79,200
Direct Labor		25,000
Factory Overhead		
Indirect Labor	$ 3,000	
Indirect Material	2,000	
Factory Utilities	500	
Factory Depreciation	800	
Factory Rent	2,000	
Miscellaneous	1,500	9,800
Total Manufacturing Costs Incurred During 19x1		$114,000
Add: Work-in-Process Inventory, Dec. 31, 19x0		9,000
Manufacturing Costs to Account for		$123,000
Less: Work-in-Process Inventory, Dec. 31, 19x1		2,000
Cost of Goods Manufactured (to Income Statement, Figure 4)		$121,000

Job Order Costing

Job order cost accounting is the cost accumulation system under which costs are accumulated by specific jobs, contracts, or orders. This costing method is appropriate when the products are manufactured in identifiable lots or batches or when the products are manufactured to customer specifications. Job order costing is widely used by custom manufacturers such as printing, aircraft, construction, auto repair, and professional services. Job order costing keeps

Figure 6 Manufacturer's Current Asset Section of Balance Sheet
December 31, 19x1

Current Assets:

Cash		$ 25,000
Accounts Receivable		78,000
Inventories:		
Raw Materials	$ 7,800	
Work-in-Process	2,000	
Finished Goods	21,000	30,800
Total		$133,800

track of costs as follows: direct material and direct labor are traced to a particular job. Costs not directly traceable—factory overhead—are applied to individual jobs using a predetermined overhead (application) rate. The overhead rate is determined as follows:

$$\text{Overhead rate} = \frac{\text{Budgeted annual overhead}}{\substack{\text{Budgeted annual activity units} \\ \text{(direct labor hours, machine} \\ \text{hours, and so on)}}}$$

At the end of the year, the difference between actual overhead and overhead applied is closed to cost of goods sold, if an immaterial difference. If a material difference exists, work-in-process, finished goods, and cost of goods sold are adjusted on a proportionate basis based on units or dollars at year-end for the deviation between actual and applied overhead.

A job cost sheet is used to record various production costs for work-in-process inventory. A separate cost sheet is kept for each identifiable job, accumulating the direct materials, direct labor, and factory overhead assigned to that job as it moves through production. The form varies according to the needs of the company. A sample job cost sheet and a system flow chart for job costing are presented in Figure 7 and Figure 8, respectively.

Typical journal entries required to account for job order costing transactions are as follows:

1. To apply direct material and direct labor to, say, Job X.
   Work-in-process (WIP)—Job X   xx
       Stores Control   xx
       Accrued payroll   xx

Figure 7 Job Cost Sheet

PRODUCT _____   JOB NO. _____
DATE STARTED _____
DATE COMPLETED _____

Direct Material			Direct Labor			Overhead	
Date	Reference	Amount	Date	Reference	Amount	Date	Amount
	(Store Requisition No.)			(Work Ticket No.)			(Based on Predetermined Overhead rate)

Figure 8 Job Cost System—Flow Chart of Ledger Relationships

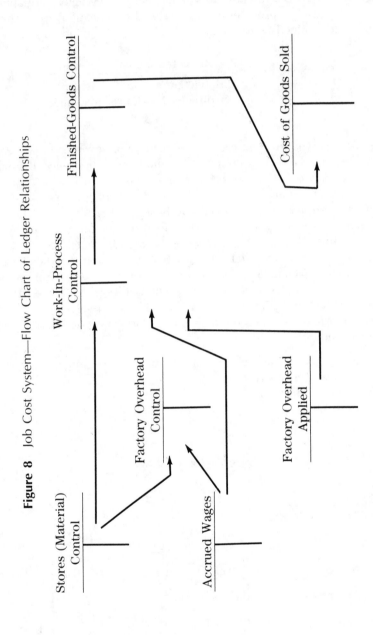

2. To apply overhead to the job in process
   WIP—Job X   xx
      Overhead applied   xx
3. To record actual overhead
   Overhead control   xx
      Stores control, accrued payroll, other sundries   xx
4. To transfer completed goods
   Finished goods—Job X   xx
      WIP—Job X   xx
5. To record the sale of finished goods
   Cost of goods sold   xx
      Finished goods   xx
   Accounts receivable   xx
      Sales   xx

PROCESS COSTING

Process costing is a cost accumulation system that aggregates manufacturing costs by departments or by production processes. Total manufacturing costs are accumulated by two major categories, direct materials and conversion costs (the sum of direct labor and factory overhead applied). Unit cost is determined by dividing the total costs charged to a cost center by the output of that cost center. In that sense, the unit costs are averages. Process costing is appropriate for companies that produce a continuous mass of like units through a series of operations or processes. Process costing is generally used in such industries as petroleum, chemicals, oil refinery, textiles, and food processing.

Identification of System and Problems and Choice of a System

Since the unit costs under process costing are more of averages, the process costing system requires less bookkeeping than a job order costing system. A lot of companies prefer to use a process costing system for this reason. However, before any particular system is chosen, the principal system problem(s) must be identified in a broader perspective. Typically, which method of costing to use depends more upon the characteristics of the production process and the types of products manufactured. If the products are alike and move from one processing department to another in a continuous chain, a process costing method is desirable. If, however, there are significant differences among the costs of the various products, a process costing system would not provide adequate product cost information and thus a job order costing method is more appropriate. For example, a job order costing system would invariably be used if the customer paid for the specific item, production order, or service on the basis of its cost, which is often the case in repair shops and custom work.

Of course, some companies might find it necessary to use some kind of hybrid of these two systems, depending on how a product flows through the factory. For example, in a parallel processing situation, which is discussed later, some form of hybrid of the two systems has proven to be the optimal system choice.

Those industries that are most suitable for process costing have the following characteristics:

1. Production quantity is uniform.
2. A given order does not affect the production process.
3. Customer orders are filled from the manufacturer's stock.
4. There is continuous mass production through an assembly line approach.
5. There exists a standardization of the process and product.
6. There is a desire to implement cost control on a departmental basis rather than on a customer or product basis.
7. There is continuity of demand for the output.
8. Quality standards can be implemented on a departmental basis such as on-line inspection as processing proceeds.

Product Flow

There are essentially three different types of product (processing) flow in processing. They are sequential, parallel, and selective, as shown in Figure 9. In a sequential flow, each product item manufactured goes through the same set of operations. For example, in a textile industry, a typical plant operates a dyeing department as well as a spinning department. The dyeing department receives yarn from the spinning department and dyes it, then transfers it to finished goods. Thus, the product flow in textile operations is sequential.

In a parallel flow, certain portions of work are done simultaneously and then brought together in a particular process in chain form. The portions of work done simultaneously may require a job order type of costing, since they may be needed to keep track of the differences in costs between the portions of work done simultaneously. Canned food processing industries employ this type of system. In manufacturing fruit cocktail products, different kinds of fruits are peeled and processed simultaneously in different locations in a factory. They are then brought together in a final process or processes for canning and transfer to finished goods inventory.

Finally, in a selective flow, the product goes through a selected set of processing departments within a factory, depending on the desired final product. Meat processing and petroleum refining falls in this category. Take meat processing, for example. After initial butchering, some of the meat product goes to grinding, then to packing, and then to finished goods; and some goes to smoking, packaging, and finished goods in that order. The selected flows may take a wide variety of forms.

Figure 9 Types of Processing Flow

Sequential

Dept. 1 ⟶ Dept. 2 ⟶ ... ⟶ Finished Goods

Parallel

Dept. 1 ⟶ Dept. 2 ⟶ Dept. X ⟶ ... Finished Goods

Dept. A ⟶ Dept. B ⟶

Selective

Dept. 1 ⟶ Dept. 4 ⟶ ... Finished Goods

Dept. 2

Dept. 3

Steps in Process Costing Calculations

There are basically four steps to be followed in accounting for process costs. They are summarized below.

(1) Summarize the flow of physical units.

The first step of the accounting provides a summary of all units on which some work was done in the department during the period. Input must equal output. This step helps to detect lost units during the process. The basic relationship may be expressed in the following equation:

Beginning inventory + Units started for the period = Units completed and transferred out + Ending inventory

(2) Compute output in terms of equivalent units

In order to determine the unit costs of the product in a processing environment, it is important to measure the total amount of work done during an accounting period. A special problem arises in processing industries in connection with how to deal with work still in process, that is, the work partially completed at the end of the period. The partially completed units are measured on an equivalent whole unit basis for process costing purposes.

Equivalent units are a measure of how many whole units of production are represented by the units completed plus the units partially completed. For example, 100 units that are 60% completed are the equivalent of 60 completed units in terms of processing costs.

(3) Summarize the total costs to be accounted for and compute the unit costs per equivalent unit.

This step summarizes the total costs assigned to the department during the period. Then the unit costs per equivalent is computed as follows:

$$\text{Unit cost} = \frac{\text{Total costs incurred during the period}}{\text{Equivalent units of production during the period}}$$

(4) Apply total costs to units completed and transferred out and to units in ending work-in-process.

The process costing method uses what is called the cost of production report. It summarizes both total and unit costs charged to a department and indicates the allocation of total costs between work-in-process inventory and the units completed and transferred out to the next department or the finished goods inventory. The cost of production report covers all four steps described above. It is also the source for monthly journal entries and is also a convenient compilation from which cost data may be presented to management.

Weighted-Average versus First-In First-Out (FIFO)

When there is a beginning inventory of work in process, the production completed during the period comes from different batches, some from work partially completed in a prior period and some from new units started in the current period. Since costs tend to vary from period to period, each batch may carry different unit costs. There are two ways to treat the costs of the beginning inventory. One is weighted-average costing and the other is first-in-first-out (FIFO).

Under the weighted-average method of costing, both units costs of work in process at the beginning of the period are combined with current production units started in the current period and their costs and an average cost is computed. In determining equivalent production units, no distinction is made between work partially completed in the prior period and the units started and completed in the current period. Thus, there is only one average cost for goods completed.

Equivalent units under weighted-average costing may be computed as follows:

Units completed + [Ending work in process × Degree of completion (%)].

Under FIFO, on the other hand, beginning work in process inventory costs are separated from added costs applied in the current period. Thus, there are two unit costs for the period: (1) beginning work in process units completed and

(2) units started and completed in the same period. Under FIFO, the beginning work in process is assumed to be completed and transferred first. Equivalent units under FIFO costing may be computed as follows:

Units completed + [Ending work in process $\times$ Degree of completion (%)]
$\quad$ − [Beginning work in process $\times$ Degree of completion (%)]

EXAMPLE 9

To illustrate, the following data relate to the activities of Department A during the month of January:

	Units
Beginning work in process (100% complete as to materials; 2/3 complete as to conversion)	1,500
Started this period	5,000
Completed and transferred	5,500
Ending work in process (100% complete as to materials; 6/10 complete as to conversion)	1,000

Equivalent production in Department A for the month is computed, using weighted-average costing, as follows:

	Materials	Conversion costs
Units completed and transferred	5,500	5,500
Ending work in process		
$\quad$ Materials (100%)	1,000	
$\quad$ Conversion costs (60%)		600
Equivalent production	6,500	6,100

Equivalent production in Department A for the month is computed, using FIFO costing, as follows:

	Materials	Conversion costs
Units completed and transferred	5,500	5,500
Ending work in process		
$\quad$ Materials (100%)	1,000	
$\quad$ Conversion costs (60%)		600
Equivalent production	6,500	6,100
Minus: Beginning work in process		
$\quad$ Materials (100%)	1,500	
$\quad$ Conversion costs (2/3)		1,000
	5,000	5,100

In the following example, we will illustrate, step-by-step, the weighted-average and FIFO methods.

EXAMPLE 10

The Portland Cement Manufacturing Company, Inc. manufactures cement. Its processing operations involve quarrying, grinding, blending, packing, and sacking. For cost accounting and control purposes, there are four processing centers: Raw Material No. 1, Raw Material No. 2, Clinker, and Cement. Separate cost of production reports are prepared in detail with respect to the foregoing cost centers. The following information pertains to the operation of Raw Material No. 2 Department for July 19A:

	Materials	Conversion
Units in process July 1		
800 bags	complete	60% complete
Costs	$12,000	$ 56,000
Units transferred out		
40,000 bags		
Current costs	$41,500	$521,500
Units in process July 31		
5,000 bags	complete	30% complete

Using weighted average costing and FIFO costing, we will compute the following:

(a) Equivalent production units and unit costs by elements
(b) Cost of work in process for July
(c) Cost of units completed and transferred

Computation of Output in Equivalent Units

	Physical Flow	Materials	Conversion
WIP, beginning	800 (60%)		
Units transferred-in	44,200		
Units to account for	45,000		
Units completed and transferred out	40,000	40,000	40,000
WIP, end	5,000 (30%)	5,000	1,500
Units accounted for	45,000		
Equivalent units used for weighted average		45,000	41,500

Less: Old equivalent units for
work done on beginning
inventory in prior period 800 480
Equivalent units used for FIFO 44,200 41,020

Cost of Production Report—Weighted Average
Raw Material No. 2 Department
For the Month Ended July 31, 19A

	WIP beginning	Current costs	Total costs	Equivalent units	Average unit cost
Materials	$12,000	$ 41,500	$ 53,500	45,000	$ 1.1889
Conversion costs	56,000	521,500	577,500	41,500	13.9156
	$68,000	563,000	631,000		$15.1045

Cost of goods
completed
40,000 × $15.1045 $604,180
WIP, end:
   Materials 5,000 × $1.1889 $ 5,944.50
   Conversion 1,500 × 13.9156   20,873.40 $ 26,817.90
Total costs accounted for $631,000 (rounded)

Cost of Production Report—FIFO
Raw Material No. 2 Department
For the Month Ended July 31, 19A

	Total costs	Equivalent units	Unit costs
WIP, beginning	$ 68,000		
Current costs:			
Materials	41,500	44,200	$ .9389
Conversion costs	521,500	41,020	12.7133
Total costs to account for	$631,000		$13.6522

WIP, end:
  Materials
    5,000 × $.9389 $ 4,694.50
  Conversion
    1,500 × 12.7133   19,069.95   23,764.45

Cost of goods
completed,
40,000 units:
- WIP, beginning to
be transferred
out first   68,000
- Additional costs
to complete
$800 \times (1 - .6)$
$\times \$12.7133$ 4,068.26
- Cost of goods
started and
completed this
month
$39,200 \times$
$\$13.6522$ 535,166.24   \$607,234.50

Total costs accounted for   \$631,000 (rounded)

Answers are summarized as follows:

	Weighted Average		FIFO	
	Materials	Conversion	Materials	Conversion
(a) Equivalent units	45,000	41,500	44,200	41,020
Unit costs	\$1.1889	\$13.9156	\$.9389	\$12.7133
(b) Cost of WIP	\$ 26,817.90		\$ 23,764.45	
(c) Cost of units completed and transferred	\$604,180		\$607,234.50	

Estimating Degree of Completion

Estimating the degree of completion for work in process is critical. Inaccurate estimates will undoubtedly lead to inaccurate computation of unit costs especially for conversion. Estimating the degree of completion is usually easier for materials than for processing or conversion costs. The degree of completion for materials is normally 100% unless the material is added during or at the end of any given process. On the other hand, the stage of completion for conversion costs requires specific knowledge about the conversion sequence. The sequence consists of a standard number of processing operations or a standard number of days, weeks, or months for mixing, refining, aging, and finishing.

Thus, in order to estimate the degree of completion for conversion, one has to determine what proportions of the total effort (in terms of direct labor and overhead) is needed to complete one unit or one batch of production. Industrial engineers should be able to measure the proportion of conversion needed with reasonable accuracy. In practice, instead of putting effort into estimating the actual stage of completion, the assumption is often made that work still in process at the end of the accounting period is 50% complete. At the other extreme, some firms ignore the work in process completely and show no work in process inventory account. This approach is acceptable only if the work in process inventory is insignificant in amount or if it remains relatively constant in size.

Application of Factory Overhead Using Predetermined Rates

As discussed previously, it is common to charge factory overhead to work in process using a predetermined overhead application rate, since the actual overhead is not available until the end of the period. In process costing, the overhead is usually applied only at the end of the period; however, in many cases the duration of the time period desired for product costing and control information is not the same as the time period satisfactory for financial reporting. When the time periods are equal and actual overhead costs can be obtained on a timely basis, the application of overhead to each processing unit's production is not necessary, and using actual overhead is preferable. When production and overhead costs vary significantly from period to period however, it is desirable to apply overhead using predetermined application rates. This provides representative unit costs especially if dealing with a seasonal business. The rates may be based on direct labor hours, machine hours, direct labor costs, direct material costs, production volume, and so on. The use of departmental rates reflecting the different characteristics of different processing departments are certainly desirable. For example, it may be most realistic to apply overhead on a direct labor basis in one department and machine hours in another department.

Managerial Use of Process Cost Data

A process costing system, just like a job order costing system, is essentially a cost accumulation system which produces the unit manufacturing cost for a given process. Per unit manufacturing costs are used primarily for product costing, inventory valuation, and income determination. Equally important, however, are the per unit cost data vital for pricing purposes. They are used not only for pricing finished products but also for product mix strategies to maximize profits, and determining optimal production methods. Perhaps the most effective way to fully utilize process cost data is to integrate the output into the standard costing system of the firm. Blended with standard costing, the process cost data provides the basis for which management can judge the cost performance of a processing department as a cost center in all categories of costs such as direct material, direct labor, and overhead. An increase in any one of these cost components is a "red light" to management as to a possible inefficient operation in a given department. This topic will be explored in further detail in Chapter 18.

The process cost data also aids management in many processing decisions. In a multi-product and joint product situation, management is often faced with the decision as to whether to sell the product at what is called the split-off point or process it further in the hope of increased revenues. In addition, for external reporting purposes, process cost data, whether in total or in units, will help management allocate joint manufacturing costs to different joint products so that they can produce income statements by products.

In designing the system to meet the needs of both product costing and cost control, management should identify the cost centers. Cost centers may be assigned to each division, department, or section. The number of processing departments as cost centers will depend on the detail desired by management. Cost centers should typically be set up along organizational lines for control purposes. Management must weigh the cost/benefit relationship in deciding on the number of cost centers desired.

Process Costing and Decision Making

Process costing has many advantages for management decision making, including:

1. It monitors production of component parts and subassemblies.
2. It provides good inventory management by retaining accurate records of the amount of materials, labor, and overhead on an equivalent unit basis.
3. It assists management in the evaluation of the performance of processing departments and product managers.
4. It helps to determine the most efficient or least costly alternative production methods or processes. The information may assist management in deciding to invest in a new plant, new machinery, or repair existing machinery.
5. It reveals to management the number of unfinished period-end units so management can anticipate how quickly those units will be completed the next period.

While process costing requires less paperwork and detail, it has certain drawbacks. Under a process costing system, management is unable to explicitly identify actual costs with individual items. Therefore, if a particular product incurs any unusual costs, such as excessive spoilage or rework, its costs would be averaged with the other products' costs. Averaging simplifies but makes cost less specific and less informative.

More on Factory Overhead Application

Regardless of the cost accumulation system used (i.e., job order, process, or standard costing), factory overhead is applied to a job or process, using a predetermined overhead rate, which is determined, based on budgeted factory overhead cost and budgeted activity. The rate is calculated as follows:

$$\text{Predetermined overhead rate} = \frac{\text{Budgeted yearly total factory overhead costs}}{\text{Budgeted yearly activity (direct labor hours, and so on)}}$$

Budgeted activity units (capacity) used in the denominator of the formula, more often called the denominator level, are measured in direct labor hours, machine hours, direct labor costs, production units, or any other surrogate of production activity.

EXAMPLE 11

Assume that two companies have prepared the following budgeted data for the year 19A:

	Company X	Company Y
Predetermined rate based on	Machine hours	Direct labor cost
Budgeted overhead	$200,000 (1)	$240,000 (1)
Budgeted machine-hours	100,000 (2)	
Budgeted direct labor cost		$160,000 (2)
Predetermined overhead rate (1)/(2)	$2 per machine-hour	150% of direct labor cost

Now assume that actual overhead costs and the actual level of activity for 19A for each firm are shown as follows:

	Company X	Company Y
Actual overhead costs	$198,000	$256,000
Actual machine hours	96,000	
Actual direct labor cost		$176,000

Note that for each company the actual cost and activity data differ from the budgeted figures used in calculating the predetermined overhead rate. The computation of the resulting underapplied and overapplied overhead for each company is provided below:

	Company X	Company Y
Actual overhead costs	$198,000	$256,000
Factory overhead applied to Work-in-Process during 19A:		
96,000 actual machine-hours × $2	192,000	
$176,000 actual direct labor cost × 150%		264,000
Underapplied (overapplied) factory overhead	$6,000	($ 8,000)

Selecting the Denominator (Capacity) Measures

It is important to define different denominator (capacity) measures since they affect underapplied or overapplied factory overhead. Capacity is the ability to produce during a given time period, with an upper limit imposed by the availability of space, machinery, labor, materials, or capital. It may be expressed in units, weights, size, dollars, man hours, labor cost, and so on. There are typically four concepts of capacity.

1. Theoretical capacity—the volume of activity that could be attained under ideal operating conditions, with minimum allowance for inefficiency. It is the largest volume of output possible, also called ideal capacity, engineered capacity, or maximum capacity.

2. Practical capacity—the highest activity level at which the factory can operate with an acceptable degree of efficiency, taking into consideration unavoidable losses of productive time (i.e., vacations, holidays, repairs to equipment), also called maximum practical capacity.
Two variations of the practical capacity concept are widely used as the denominator volume. They are: normal capacity and expected annual activity.

3. Normal capacity—the average level of operating activity that is sufficient to fill the demand for the company's products or services for a span of several years, taking into consideration seasonal and cyclical demands and increasing or decreasing trends in demand.

4. Expected annual activity—similar to normal capacity except it is projected for a particular year, also called planned capacity.

The choice of activity level used in determining the overhead application rate potentially will have a large effect on overapplied or underapplied overhead. The four capacity measures above may be 100,000, 95,000, 70,000, and 80,000 units of activity, respectively. If the actual level of activity were 85,000 units, over or under application will result.

ALLOCATION OF SERVICE DEPARTMENT COSTS TO PRODUCTION DEPARTMENTS

There are two basic types of departments in a manufacturing company: production departments and service departments. A production department (such as assembly or machining) is where the production or conversion occurs. A service department (such as engineering or maintenance) provides support to production departments. Before departmental factory overhead rates are developed for product costing, the costs of a service department should be allocated to the appropriate production departments (as part of factory overhead).

Basis of Assigning Service Department Costs

Some service department costs are direct. Examples are the salaries of the workers in the department. Other service department costs are indirect—that is, they are incurred jointly with some other department. An example is depreciation of building. These indirect costs must be allocated on some arbitrary basis.

The problem is that of selecting appropriate bases for assigning the indirect costs of service departments to other departments. Service department costs should be allocated on a basis that reflects the type of activity in which the service department is engaged. The ideal basis should be logical, have a high cause-and-effect relationship between the service provided and the costs of providing it, and be easy to implement. The basis selected may be supported by physical observation, by correlation analysis, or logical analysis of the relationships between the departments. A list of some service departments and possible bases for allocation is given below.

Service Departments	Allocation Basis
• Supplies	Number of requisitions
• Power	Kilowatt-hours used
• Buildings and grounds	Number of square or cubic feet
• Maintenance and repairs	Machine hours or number of calls
• Personnel	Number of employees
• Cafeteria	Number of employees
• Purchasing	Number of orders

Procedure for Service Department Cost Allocation

Once the service department costs are known, the next step is to allocate the service department costs to the production departments. This may be accomplished by one of the following procedures:

(1) Direct method

(2) Step method

(3) Reciprocal method

Direct Method

Direct method is a method of allocating the costs of each service department directly to production departments, with no intermediate allocation to other service departments. That is, no consideration is given to services performed by one service department for another. This is perhaps the most widely used method because of its simplicity and ease of use.

EXAMPLE 12

Assume the following data:

	Service Departments		Production Departments	
	General Plant (GP)	Engineering (E)	A Machining	B Assembly
Overhead costs before allocation	$ 20,000	$ 10,000	$30,000	$40,000
Direct labor hours by General Plant (GP)	15,000	20,000	60,000	40,000
Engineering hours by Engineering (E)	5,000	4,000	50,000	30,000

Using the direct method yields:

	Service Departments		Production Departments	
	GP	E	A	B
Overhead costs	$ 20,000	$ 10,000	$30,000	$40,000
Reallocation:				
GP(0, 0, 60%, 40%)*	($20,000)		12,000	8,000
E(0, 0, 5/8, 3/8)#		($10,000)	6,250	3,750
			$48,250	$51,750

*Base is (60,000 + 40,000 = 100,000); 60,000/100,000 = .6; 40,000/100,000 = .4
#Base is (50,000 + 30,000 = 80,000); 50,000/80,000 = 5/8; 30,000/80,000 = 3/8

Step Method

This is a method of allocating services rendered by service departments to other service departments using a sequence of allocation; also called the step-down method, and the sequential method. The sequence normally begins with the department that renders service to the greatest number of other service departments; the sequence continues in a step-by-step fashion and ends with the allocation of costs of service departments that provide the least amount of service. After a given service department's costs have been allocated, it will not receive any charges from the other service departments.

Using the same data, the step allocation method yields:

	Service Departments		Production Departments	
	GP	E	A	B
Overhead costs	$ 20,000	$ 10,000	$30,000	$40,000
Reallocation:				
$GP(0, 1/6, 1/2, 1/3)^*$	($20,000)	3,333	10,000	6,667
$E(0, 0, 5/8, 3/8)^\#$		($13,333)	8,333	5,000
			$48,333	$51,667

*Base is $(20,000 + 60,000 + 40,000 = 120,000)$; $20,000/120,000 = 1/6$; $60,000/120,000 = 1/2$; $40,000/120,000 = 1/3$

#Base is $(50,000 + 30,000 = 80,000)$; $50,000/80,000 = 5/8$; $30,000/80,000 = 3/8$

Reciprocal Method

Reciprocal allocation method, also known as the reciprocal service method, the matrix method, and the simultaneous allocation method, is a method of allocating service department costs to production departments, where reciprocal services are allowed between service departments. The method sets up simultaneous equations to determine the allocable cost of each service department.

Using the same data, we set up the following equations:

$$GP = \$20,000 + 50/85 \; E$$
$$E \;\; = \$10,000 + 1/6 \; GP$$

Substituting E from the second equation into the first:

$$GP = \$20,000 + 50/85 \; (\$10,000 + 1/6 \; GP)$$

Solving for GP gives $GP = \$28,695$. Substituting $GP = \$28,695$ into the second equation and solving for E gives $E = \$14,782$.

Using these solved values, the reciprocal method yields:

	Service Departments		Production Departments	
	GP	E	A	B
Overhead costs	$ 20,000	$ 10,000	$30,000	$40,000
Reallocation:				
$GP(0, 1/6, 1/2, 1/3)$	($28,695)	4,782	14,348	9,565
$E(50/85, 0, 30/85, 5/85)$	8,695	($14,782)	5,217	870
	0	0	$49,565	$50,435

Solving Simultaneous Equations with Lotus 1-2-3

Solving simultaneous equations with more than three unknowns is a time-consuming and difficult task. It uses typically the matrix operation procedure. Using algebra, the solution for simultaneous equations $Ax = b$ is $x^* = A^{-1} b$. Matrix inversion and multiplication can be done quickly, utilizing a spreadsheet program such as Lotus 1-2-3.

More specifically, solving simultaneous equations involve three steps.

Step 1: Rearrange the equations in the form of $Ax = b$

Given: $GP = \$20,000 + 50/85\ E$

$E = \$10,000 + 1/6\ GP$

Transforming them into the form of $Ax = b$ yields:

$$GP - 50/85E = 20000$$
$$-1/6GP + E = 10000$$

or

$$\begin{pmatrix} 1 & -0.58823 \\ -0.16666 & 1 \end{pmatrix} \begin{pmatrix} GP \\ E \end{pmatrix} = \begin{pmatrix} 20000 \\ 10000 \end{pmatrix}$$

which is in the form of $Ax = b$

Step 2: Invoke /Data Matrix Invert to find the inverse of matrix A to obtain the following:

$$A^{-1} = \begin{pmatrix} 1.108695 & 0.652173 \\ 0.184782 & 1.108695 \end{pmatrix}$$

Step 3: Multiply A^{-1} by b, invoke /Data Matrix Multiply to obtain the following solution x^*:

$$x^* = \begin{pmatrix} GP \\ E \end{pmatrix} = \begin{pmatrix} 28695.65 \\ 14782.60 \end{pmatrix}$$

Note that Lotus 1-2-3 is capable to invert a matrix of (80×80). It is strongly recommended that managerial accountants should take advantage of the reciprocal service method for their cost allocation.

CONCLUSION

Management accounting is the accumulation and analysis of cost data to provide information for external reporting, for internal planning and control of an organization's operations, and for short-term and long-term decisions. It is important to realize that there are different costs used for different purposes. The management accountant must determine the use to be made of cost data in order to supply the most appropriate cost information.

Job order costing and process costing are two primary approaches to assigning manufacturing costs to units produced. Job order costing is used when many different products are produced in batches that receive uneven degrees of attention in each production operation. Process costing is used by manufacturers whose products are produced on a continuous basis with units receiving equal attention in each processing center. The chapter discussed the basic procedures that are pertinent to each of these costing methods. Also covered is an important topic faced by managerial accountants, that is, the identification of system problems and choice of a cost accumulation system. How to allocate service department costs to production department costs are also covered.

12

Joint Products and By-Products

Joint products are two or more products produced simultaneously by a common manufacturing process. The common manufacturing costs are called joint costs which have to be allocated on some basis to these products. Each joint product is relatively significant to total revenue. By-products are two or more products produced from a common source that are not significant to the makeup of total revenue. By-products have a relatively low sales value in relation to the firm's other products.

ALLOCATION OF COSTS TO JOINT PRODUCTS

A joint product, unlike a by-product, has a high sales value and is marketable. For example, gasoline, heating oil, and kerosene are joint products in oil refining. **Note:** An item can go from a joint product classification to a by-product one as technology and market conditions change.

Joint cost allocations may be necessary for inventory valuation, determination of cost of goods sold, deriving selling prices, meeting regulatory agency requirements, and taxation.

Some ways to allocate costs among joint products are

- Market value at the split-off point
- Net realizable value (final sales price less separable costs)
- Final sales price
- Physical measure (Example: units, feet, pounds)

247

- Unit cost
- Gross margin
- Chemical property
- Energy potential
- Weighted-average
- Opportunity cost
- Arbitrary mathematical techniques
- Judgmental allocation

The most commonly used allocation methods are net realizable value and physical measure. The net realizable value method is widely used because of the desire to value inventory based on the relative income-generating ability of the inventory items. Joint cost allocation using a physical measure is feasible when there is homogeneity of units in physical terms, the market potential of the products is similar, and there are new products. A major limitation of the physical measure method is that it bears no relationship to the revenue-producing ability of the products. Also, there is a distortion in the gross profit computation any time the sales price per unit of quantity is not the same for the joint products.

The market value at split-off point method is recommended when market values are available for raw materials at the separation point. The market value allocation ratio equals:

$$\frac{\text{Market value of each item}}{\text{Market value of all items}} \times \text{Joint cost}$$

The use of final selling price as a basis for joint cost allocation is feasible when a close relationship exists between cost and selling price. It may be advisable when the company must justify its selling prices, based on price-cost relationships, to governmental agencies. It may also be used when there is a rapid inventory turnover or a low normal profit percentage.

Note: When there is wide vacillation in selling price, average anticipated prices for the period may be used.

The amount of each joint product to be produced depends on manufacturing technology, product salability, and the expected future market. Short-term factors like inventory levels also need to be considered.

Joint cost information assists you in looking at the effect of altering the output mix on costs and profitability, establishing a selling price for the product, determining the relative profitability between products, and controlling and evaluating the production and distribution processes.

Processing efficiency may be appraised by determining the physical yield for each product. In this regard, an index of production (i.e., weighted-average index) may be computed to evaluate output efficiency.

COMPARING THE METHODS OF JOINT COST ALLOCATION

The allocation of joint costs by physical units results in an equal price per unit for each product.

EXAMPLE 1

Assume a refining process results in two products, A and B, in quantities of 2,000 gallons of product A and 4,000 gallons of product B. Since product A contains 2,000 gallons out of the total 6,000 gallons, product A would be assigned one-third of the joint costs of the process of refining. Product B would be assigned the other two-thirds. If the process costs $36,000, product A would be charged one-third of these joint costs, or $12,000. Product B would be assigned the remaining $24,000, or two-thirds of the joint costs. Since 2,000 gallons of product A were produced at a cost of $12,000, the unit cost is $6 per gallon. The 4,000 gallons of product B were produced at a cost of $24,000, giving the same unit cost of $6 per gallon.

EXAMPLE 2

Now assume that product A could be sold at $14 per gallon while product B could be sold at $5 per gallon at the split-off point. Since the costs of products A and B were $6 per gallon each, product A shows a profit of $8 per gallon while product B shows a loss of $1 per gallon. It seems less than desirable to sell a product for consistently less than its cost.

The allocation of joint costs by the physical units method is appropriate if the net realizable value of the products are approximately the same. In many cases in which the net realizable value of the products are not close, one could use the method of allocating joint costs according to the ability of a product to absorb these joint costs.

EXAMPLE 3

Once again, assume that product A could be sold for $14 per gallon and product B for $5 per gallon after the joint refining process. Therefore, the 2,000 gallons of product A could be sold for $28,000 while the 4,000 gallons of product B could be sold for $20,000. Product A would absorb $28,000 divided by the $48,000 total sales value, or seven-twelfths of the joint costs. Product B would absorb $20,000 divided by the cost of the $48,000 total sales value, or five-twelfths of the joint costs. The total joint cost was $36,000. Product A would absorb seven-twelfths of $36,000, or $21,000. Product B would absorb five-twelfths of $36,000, or $15,000. This results in product A selling for $28,000 and costing $21,000, for a profit of $7,000. This is 25% of the sales price. Product B sells for $20,000 and costs $15,000 for a profit of $5,000. This is also 25% of its sales price.

The method of allocation of joint costs according to the ability of each product to absorb these costs will result in the same gross profit margin for each product when there are no separable costs. This is generally called the relative sales value method.

It is very possible that a market for the joint products at the split-off point does not exist. The joint products must then be operated on further before there is a market for them. The net realizable value at the split-off point is determined by subtracting the separable costs from the sales value.

EXAMPLE 4

As in the previous example, assume that the 2,000 gallons of product A could be sold for $14 per gallon and the 4,000 gallons of product B could be sold for $5 per gallon. However, after the split-off point, product A undergoes further processing and incurs $4 per gallon of separable costs. Product B undergoes no further processing and therefore incurs no separable costs. To determine the net realizable value of product A at the split-off point, the $4-per gallon separable cost is subtracted from the $14-per-gallon sale price. Therefore, the net realizable value of product A at the split-off point is $10 per gallon for the 2,000 gallons. Product A has a total net realizable value of $20,000 at the split-off point. The 4,000 gallons of product B selling for $5 per gallon at the split-off point also has a total net realizable value of $20,000. Since products A and B have the same net realizable value at the split-off point, they will share equally in the $36,000 of joint costs. Products A and B are each allocated $18,000 of the joint costs.

The profit margin would no longer be the same for the two products. Product A has separable costs of $4 per gallon, or $8,000, and joint costs of $18,000. The total cost is $26,000 with a sales value of $28,000, giving a profit of $2,000. This is only a 7% gross profit margin. Product B has only the joint costs of $18,000 and sells for $20,000. The profit of the same $2,000 is just a coincidence. The gross profit margin of product B is 10% larger than the 7% gross profit margin of product A. The reasons for the profit margin of product B being less than it was in the previous example is that product B is absorbing a larger share of the joint costs than before.

ILLUSTRATION OF UNIT COST AND WEIGHTED-AVERAGE UNIT COST METHODS

The unit cost of a joint product will have to be determined based upon a simple unit cost or weighted-average unit cost.

EXAMPLE 5

The joint cost of manufacturing products X, Y, and Z is $150,000. The units produced are product X, 20,000; product Y, 25,000; and product Z, 30,000.

The cost per unit is

$$\frac{\$150,000}{75,000} = \$2$$

Using the unit cost method, the joint cost is allocated in the following manner:

$$
\begin{array}{lll}
\text{Product X} & = \$2 \times 20,000 = & \$40,000 \\
\text{Product Y} & = \$2 \times 25,000 = & 50,000 \\
\text{Product Z} & = \$2 \times 30,000 = & \underline{60,000} \\
\text{Total} & & \underline{\underline{\$150,000}}
\end{array}
$$

The weighted-average unit cost method should be used when complexities exist regarding the joint products, complexities such as production problems, time required to produce, and the quality of materials or labor. Taking these complexities into account requires us to weigh the factors in order to arrive at a reasonable allocation basis.

Assume products X, Y, and Z are weighted per unit as follows: 2.8, 2.3, and 3.5.

Using the weighted-average method, the allocation of the joint cost follows:

$$\text{Product X} = 20,000 \times 2.8 = \frac{56,000}{218,500} \times \$150,000 = \$\ 38,444$$

$$\text{Product Y} = 25,000 \times 2.3 = \frac{57,500}{218,500} \times \$150,000 = \ \ 39,474$$

$$\text{Product Z} = 30,000 \times 3.5 = \frac{105,000}{218,500} \times \$150,000 = \underline{\ \ 72,082}$$

$$\text{Total} \qquad\qquad\qquad\qquad\qquad\qquad\qquad\qquad\qquad \underline{\underline{\$150,000}}$$

ILLUSTRATION OF JOINT COST ALLOCATION BASED ON BOTH PHYSICAL AND NET REALIZABLE VALUE

We now show the allocation of joint costs using both physical measure and net realizable value.

EXAMPLE 6

The Audio Processing Company refines two products by a joint process, product A and product B, in quantities of 2,000 gallons and 4,000 gallons, respectively. The joint costs are $36,000.

1. Use the allocation by physical units to determine the portion each product will absorb.

2. Assume that product A sells for $14 per gallon and product B for $5 per gallon at the split-off point. Find the gross profit for each product.

3. Assuming the same information in 2, use the net realizable value at split-off method to determine the allocated costs and gross profit for each product.

4. Assume the same information as in 2 except that product A must undergo $4 per gallon in separable costs before it can be sold for $14 per gallon. Use the net realizable value at the split-off point method to allocate the joint costs and find the gross profit.

1.

	Number of Units	Fractional Part of Total Units	Joint Costs to be Allocated	Allocated Joint Costs
Product A	2,000 gal	1/3	36,000	$12,000
Product B	4,000 gal	2/3	36,000	24,000
Total	6,000 gal			$36,000

The allocated joint costs for Products A and B are $6 per gallon.

2.

	Number of Units	Sale Price Per Gallon	Total Sale Price	Allocated Joint Costs	Gross Margin
Product A	2,000 gal	$14	$28,000	12,000	$16,000
Product B	4,000 gal	5	20,000	24,000	(4,000)

The gross margin of Product A is $8 per gallon.
The gross margin of Product B is a loss of $1 per gallon.

3.

	Net Realizable Value	Fractional Part of Total Net Realizable Value	Joint Costs to be Allocated	Allocated Joint Costs
Product A	$28,000	7/12	$36,000	$21,000
Product B	20,000	5/12	36,000	15,000
	$48,000			$36,000

	Sales Price	Allocated Joint Costs	Gross Margin	Gross Margin Percentage
Product A	$28,000	$21,000	$7,000	25%
Product B	20,000	15,000	5,000	25%

4.

	Sales Price	Separable Costs	Net Realizable Value	Fractional Part of Total Net Realizable Value	Joint Costs to be Allocated	Allocated Joint Costs
Product A	$28,000	$8,000	$20,000	1/2	$36,000	$18,000
Product B	20,000	-0-	20,000	1/2	36,000	18,000
			$40,000			$36,000

	Sales Price	Separable Costs	Allocated Joint Costs	Total Costs	Gross Margin
Product A	$28,000	$8,000	$18,000	$26,000	$2,000
Product B	20,000	-0-	18,000	18,000	2,000

The gross margin of product A is $1 per gallon.
The gross margin of product B is $.50 per gallon.

EXAMPLE 7

A machine of the Berry Machine Shop cuts nails of two different sizes, small and large, and then packages them. A box of large nails sells for $1.75 and a box of small nails sells for $1.30. During the month of June, the machine cut and boxed 10,000 boxes of small nails and 8,000 boxes of large nails. The cost of running the machine for the month was $9,000.

We find the allocated joint costs to each type of box of nails using

1. The number of units

2. The net realizable value method of costing for joint products

1. Number of Units

BERRY MACHINE SHOP
ALLOCATION OF JOINT COSTS
PHYSICAL UNITS METHOD
For the Month of June

Type	Number of Units	Fractional Part of Joint Cost	Total Joint Cost	Allocated Joint Cost
Small nails	10,000	5/9	$9,000	$5,000
Large nails	8,000	4/9	9,000	4,000
Total	18,000			$9,000

Divide the number of units of each type by the total number of units.

Multiply the fractional part of joint costs times the total joint cost to be allocated.

Answer: $5,000 allocated to the boxes of small nails or $.50 per box, and $4,000 allocated to the boxes of large nails, or also $.50 per box.

2.

BERRY MACHINE SHOP
ALLOCATION OF JOINT COSTS
NET REALIZABLE VALUE METHOD

Type	Sales Value or Net Realizable Value	Fractional Part of Joint Costs	Total Joint Costs	Allocated Joint Costs
Large nails	$14,000	14/27	$9,000	$4,667
Small nails	13,000	13/27	9,000	4,333
Total	$27,000			$9,000

$1.75 \times 8,000 = \$14,000$
$1.30 \times 10,000 = \$13,000$

Divide the net realizable value of each product by the total net realizable value.

Multiply the fractional part of joint costs times the total joint costs.

Answer: $4,667 for the boxes of large nails, or $.58 each box, and $4,333 for the boxes of small nails, or $.43 per box.

EXAMPLE 8

The M.J.H. Company manufactures three products, M, J, and H, using the same machinery. Product J is sold at the split-off point while M and H are processed further. For the month of November, the joint costs for the three products are $48,000, and the costs after the split-off for M are $6,000 and for H are $10,000. Product M sells for $36,000, product J for $20,000, and product H for $20,000.

1. Use the net realizable value at split-off to allocate the joint costs.

2. Find the gross margin for each product.

1.

M.J.H. COMPANY
ALLOCATION OF JOINT COSTS
NET REALIZABLE VALUE METHOD
For the Month of November

Product	Sales Value	Separable Costs	Net Realizable Value	Fractional Part of Joint Cost	Total Joint Cost	Allocated Joint Cost
M	$36,000	$ 6,000	$30,000	1/2	$48,000	$24,000
J	20,000	—	20,000	1/3	48,000	16,000
H	20,000	10,000	10,000	1/6	48,000	8,000
Total			$60,000			$48,000

2.

		M		J		H
Sales Value		$36,000		$20,000		$20,000
Costs:						
Joint	$24,000		$16,000		$8,000	
Separable	6,000	30,000	—	16,000	10,000	18,000
Gross Margin		$ 6,000		$ 4,000		$ 2,000

ILLUSTRATION OF MULTIPLE SPLIT-OFF POINTS

When more than one split-off point exists, management should

1. Diagram the physical flow and cost incurrence of products
2. Determine the net realizable values at each split-off point
3. Allocate joint costs based on relative net realizable value

EXAMPLE 9

The following data are given for a manufacturer for the month of December:

In Department 1, 5,000 feet of A are converted into 4,000 feet of B and 1,000 feet of C. In Department 2, 3,000 feet of X were added to the 1,000 feet of C to manufacture 1,000 feet of D, 2,000 feet of E, and 1,000 feet of waste. Before sale, D had to be further processed in Department 3.

Production costs were

	Department		
	1	2	3
Material	$50,000	$10,000	—
Labor	20,000	8,000	$ 5,000
Overhead	20,000	3,000	6,000
	$90,000	$21,000	$11,000

Unit selling prices per foot are

B	$20
D	45
E	15

The diagramming of the process follows:

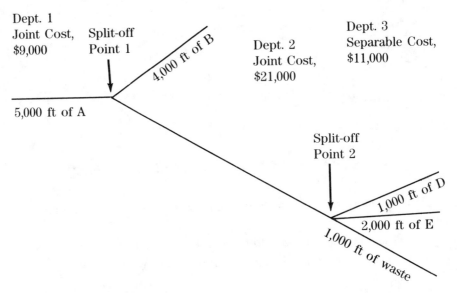

The relative net realizable values are

	Sales Value		Separable Cost		Net Realizable Value	Relative Net Realizable Value
Split-Off Point 2						
D	(1,000 × $45)	−	$11,000	=	$ 34,000	53.1%
E	(2,000 × $15)	−	0		30,000	46.9%
					$ 64,000	100.0%

Split-Off
Point 1

B	$(4,000 \times \$20)$	$-$	0	$=$	\$ 80,000	65.0%
C	64,000	$-$	\$21,000		\$ 43,000	35.0%
					\$123,000	100.0%

The allocation of joint costs follow:

	Allocated Joint Cost	+	Additional Joint Cost	=	Total	Relative Net Realizable Value	Allocation of Joint Cost
Split-Off Point 1:							
B	0	+	\$90,000	=	\$90,000	65.0%	\$58,500
C						35.0%	31,500
							\$90,000
Split-Off Point 2:							
D	\$31,500	+	\$21,000	=	\$52,500	53.1%	\$27,878
E						46.9%	24,622
							\$52,500

The final total and per foot product costs are:

		Total Cost	Feet	Cost per Foot
B		\$ 58,500	4,000	\$14.63
D	27,878 + \$11,000	38,878	1,000	38.88
E		24,622	2,000	12.31
		\$122,000		

ILLUSTRATION OF MANUFACTURING JOINT PRODUCTS IN DIFFERENT PROPORTIONS

In the case where two or more joint products can be manufactured in different proportions, you may determine the differential cost of each by varying the output of these products. An example involving alternative products follows.

EXAMPLE 10

The total cost of manufacturing joint products A and B is $10,000 in the proportions of 40 to 60, respectively. A change in the proportion of 50 to 50 will increase the joint cost by $2,000. The total $12,000 cost assigned to A and B will now be:

Differential cost of 10 more As = $2,000 + 10Bs

Total cost is

50 As + Bs = $12,000

Therefore,

50 As = 5 (10As) = 5 ($2,000 + 10Bs)

Therefore,

$$5 (\$2,000 + 10 \text{ Bs}) + 50 \text{ Bs} = \$12,000$$

$$\$10,000 + 50 \text{ Bs} + 50 \text{ Bs} = \$12,000$$
$$100 \text{ Bs} = \$2,000$$
$$50 \text{ Bs cost} = \$1,000$$
$$50 \text{ As cost} = \$11,000$$

DECIDING WHETHER A JOINT PRODUCT SHOULD BE PROCESSED FURTHER OR SOLD AT SPLIT-OFF POINT

A joint product should be processed further when the incremental revenue exceeds the incremental costs. Some considerations regarding the decision to sell or process further are the impact on profitability, the market for the intermediate product versus the final product, sales volume, the advertising effort needed, time required and risk involved of additional processing, and the ability to obtain materials or labor for further processing.

EXAMPLE 11

Production of joint product A is 200 units having a selling price of $.90 per unit. Product A may be further processed into 200 units of product AB having a selling price of $1.05. The additional processing cost is $35.

Should product A be sold at the split-off point or processed further?

Answer:

Additional revenue 200 × $.15	$30
Additional cost	35
Loss	$ 5

Product A should be sold at the split-off point.

EXAMPLE 12

Company T has five products produced from a joint process. The joint cost is allocated based on the sales value of each product at the split-off point. Waste arises from the joint process, which is discarded. However, the company's research division has now found that the waste could be salable as fertilizer with additional processing at a cost of $200,000. The sales value of fertilizer is $280,000. Management has decided to allocate the joint cost based on relative sales value at split-off of the five products and the waste. As a result of this allocation, the waste product was assigned a joint cost of $110,000. The fertilizer thus showed a net loss of

Sales value	$280,000
Assignable	310,000
Loss	$ 30,000

Because of the loss, management decided not to process the waste further.

Management has made the wrong decision. The joint cost is the same whether or not the waste product is further processed. In other words, the joint process involves the same total cost for the five products. It is, in fact, financially advantageous to process the waste further as fertilizer since there exists an incremental profit of $80,000 ($280,000 − $200,000).

Management must recognize that joint product costs incurred up to the point of split-off are sunk costs and, thus, are irrelevant in decisions regarding what should be done subsequent to the split-off point.

EXAMPLE 13

A manufacturer produces three products from a process involving a vat and a furnace. A diagram of the flow process follows:

Before going into the furnace, part 1 has a separable cost of $400. Parts 2 and 3 go through a vat prior to being put in the furnace. In addition to the $3,000 vat costs, parts 2 and 3 require "dipping" in the vat at $.30 per cubic foot. The volume of cubic feet per unit of parts 2 and 3 are .6 and .8, respectively. Information regarding selling price per unit and production follows:

Part	Selling Price	Production
1	$4	800
2	5	1,000
3	7	1,200

Management decides to allocate the vat cost based on cubic feet and the furnace cost based on the relative sales value before the parts are placed in the furnace.

1. Determine the profitability of parts 1, 2, and 3

2. Management has an opportunity to sell part 2 undipped at $4.60.

Should management sell part 2 undipped or fully processed?

1.

Part	Sales Value	−	Separable Costs and Allocated Vat Costs	=	Sales Value before Furnace	−	Allocated Furnace Cost	=	Profit
1 ($4 × 800) =	$ 3,200	−	$400	=	$ 2,800	−	$2,090	=	$ 710
			(*DIP + **VAT)						
2 ($5 × 1,000) =	5,000	−	($180 + $1154)	=	3,666	−	2,735	=	931
3 ($7 × 1,200) =	8,400	−	(288 + 1846/2)	=	6,266	−	4,675	=	1,591
	$16,600		3,868	=	$12,732	−	$9,500	=	3,232

Dip and Vat Costs

Part		Cubic Volume	*Dip Cost at $.30ᵃ	**Allocated Vat Costᵇ
2	1,000 × .6	600	$180	$1,154
3	1,200 × .8	960	288	1,846
Total		1,560	$468	$3,000

a) $600 \times \$.30 = \$180$

b) $\dfrac{600}{1560} \times \$3,000 = \$1,154$

2.

Reduction in selling price if Part 2 is sold undipped	$.40
Savings in dip cuts if Part 2 is sold undipped ($180/1000)	.18
Decline in profitability	$.22

Part 2 should be processed further since profitability per unit will decline by $.22 if it is sold undipped. Note that the vat and furnace costs are still the same even if Part 2 is sold undipped.

COSTS ASSIGNED TO BY-PRODUCTS

Generally speaking, if a product's value is too small to affect the decision to produce, it is a by-product. By-products are produced in limited quantity, and result from the manufacture of main products. Examples of by-products are sawdust in lumber mills and bone in meat-packing plants.

The method used for by-product valuation depends on whether

- The by-product's value is uncertain when produced
- There is an established market for the by-product. Market stability and the reliability of market values determine whether a value should be placed on the by-product before sale. If there is a very unstable market, the sale of the by-product should be reflected in income with no value assigned to the by-product inventory.
- The by-product can be used as a substitute for other raw materials
- The by-product is a possible alternative to the main product
- The by-product can be used as an energy source for the firm
- The external outlet for by-products cannot be used internally
- The market is characterized as a long-term rather than a temporary short-term situation

Note: If there is an abnormal increase in by-products, one may infer that production inefficiencies may exist.

When there is an internal transfer of a by-product, the transfer price should preferably be its market value at the separation point.

By-products may be accounted for in the following ways:

- Income from by-products may be reported as "other income"
- Income from by-products may reduce cost of sales or the manufacturing cost of the main product
- Income from by-products is reflected as in the foregoing methods above except that the by-product income is reduced by appropriate expenses, such as marketing and administrative costs

The replacement method is suggested for a by-product when it is used in the production process rather than being sold. Under this method, the production cost of the principal product is reduced by the replacement cost of the by-product materials.

When a by-product is both sold and used as a raw material for other products, it should be valued at the market price, less costs and less a profit provision.

When a by-product is used internally (e.g., for fuel or as a new raw material for the main product), it may be valued at net realizable value or replacement cost.

ILLUSTRATION OF THE ACCOUNTING FOR BY-PRODUCTS

Since by-products are incidental to the manufacturing process, they usually do not share in the joint costs. The net realizable value of a by-product is the sales value, less any separable or disposal costs. This value is either accounted for as "other income" on the income statement, or subtracted from the joint costs of the production process before these joint costs are allocated among the joint products. If one is to recognize a profit on by-product sales, the net realizable value could be reduced by an allowance for the profit. The result would be subtracted from the joint costs.

EXAMPLE 14

Assume that 6,500 gallons of a product are refined to produce 2,000 gallons of product A, 4,000 gallons of product B, and 500 gallons of product C. Also assume that the revenue produced by product C is insignificant relative to the revenue produced by products A and B, and therefore, product C is a by-product. Product C could be sold for $1.50 per gallon at the split-off point. The net realizable value of the 500 gallons of product C at $1.50 per gallon is $750. The refining process costs $36,000.

Under the first method, the entire $36,000 joint costs would be allocated between products A and B. The $750 would be recorded as "other income" on the income statement.

Under the second method, the $750 would be subtracted from the $36,000 joint costs, and the remaining $35,250 would be allocated between products A and B. The method used to allocate the joint costs between A and B does not affect, and is not affected by, the method chosen to account for by-product revenue.

Under the third method, assume a normal profit margin of 30% in sales. Thirty percent of the sales value of $750 is $225. The $225 would be recognized as profit from the sales of the by-product. The remaining $525 would be deducted from the $36,000 joint costs. The difference of $35,475 would be allocated between products A and B. This assumes no identifiable separable costs for the by-products.

If a by-product has separable or disposal costs, these are subtracted from the sales revenue to reach the net realizable value. Assume the 500 gallons of product C could be sold for $4 per gallon after separable costs of one dollar are incurred. The net realizable value would be $3 per gallon, giving a total net revenue of the by-product as $1,500. This $1,500 net revenue could be shown as other income or subtracted from the $36,000 joint costs. If subtracted, the sum of $36,000 less the $1,500 revenue from the by-product gives $34,500 to be allocated between the joint products. The net realizable value of $1,500 could be further reduced by a profit margin. Taking the same 30% of the sales price as before, the profit margin is $600, 30% of $2,000. The separable costs were $500. The sum of the two, $1,100, would be subtracted from the sales value of $2,000 to get a remainder of $900. This $900 would be subtracted from the joint costs. The $36,000 minus $900, or $35,100, would be allocated between the joint products A and B.

The net revenue of the by-product could be recognized when produced or when sold. If the net revenue is recognized when the by-product is produced, an estimated sales value is used as the sales price. If the actual price is different, an account called gain or loss on sales of by-product could be used to record the difference. If the net revenue is recognized as sold, the actual sales price would be used. When the salability of the by-product is uncertain, or price is unstable, it would be better to defer revenue recognition until sold.

The value of the inventory of the by-product could be found by calculating the cost per unit, using any of the foregoing methods, and assigning this amount times the number of units in inventory to get the inventory value. Also, if the value of the inventory is so small as to be immaterial, it could be simply ignored.

Certain, by-products are not sold, but are used in the manufacturing process within the plant. In these cases, the value assigned to the by-product would be its replacement value. This value would be equal to the price the company would have to pay to purchase the by-product in the open market.

The most popular accounting method is to subtract the net realizable value of the by-product from the joint costs. A variation would be to subtract this amount from the cost of sales. The inventory of the joint products would then be unaffected by this reduction. It is possible that the costs of production are used as a control device, and it may be advised to consider by-product revenue as "other income." In this way, by-product yields and revenue do not effect costs. However, in most cases, the revenue should be inconsequential.

Scrap metal is actually a by-product that is disposed of at the split-off point. It usually has a very minor sales value and would follow one of the previous accounting methods described for the by-product.

Recommendation. Choose the method that is most feasible and logical, but that would also enhance the profits of the company. Since in most cases, by-products are relatively insignificant, the most convenient method may be used. If the values associated with the by-product are significant, it is possible that the by-product has moved into a position where it should be considered a joint product.

EXAMPLE 15

Dart Refinery produces 2,000 gallons of product A, 4,000 gallons of product B, and 500 gallons of product C. The revenue produced by product C is insignificant relative to the revenue produced by products A and B. Therefore, product C is a by-product. Product C sells for $1.50 per gallon at the split-off point, while products A and B sell for $14 per gallon and $5 per gallon, respectively. The refining process costs $36,000.

1. Allocate the joint costs if the revenue from product C is listed in "other income." The net realizable value of the split-off point method is used to allocate joint costs.

2. Allocate the joint costs if the revenue from product C is used to reduce the costs of the joint process. The net realizable value at the split-off point method is used to allocate the joint costs.

3. Assume a 30% profit on the sale of by-products. Allocate the joint costs using the net realizable value at the split-off point method. The remainder of the sales price of the by-product is subtracted from the joint costs.

4. Assume product C undergoes $1 per gallon of separable costs and can then be sold for $4 per gallon. Also, product A undergoes $4 per gallon of separable costs before it can be sold for $14 per gallon. Allocate the joint costs and find the gross profit when the joint costs are allocated using the net realizable value at the split-off point and the revenue from the by-product is:

   a. Subtracted from the joint costs

   b. Considered as other income

   c. Subtracted from the joint costs after a 30% profit is recognized for the by-product

1.

Joint Products	Number of Gallons	Net Realizable Value	Fractional Part of Total Net Realizable Value	Joint Costs to be Allocated	Allocated Joint Costs
A	2,000	$28,000	7/12	$36,000	$21,000
B	4,000	20,000	5/12	36,000	$15,000
		$48,000			$36,000
C	500	$ 750			

$750 listed as Other Income.

2. Product C − 500 gallons at $1.50 per gallon, total revenue $750. Subtract $750 from the joint costs of $36,000, leaving $35,250 to be allocated.

Joint Products	Net Realizable Value	Fractional Part of Total Net Realizable Value	Joint Costs to be Allocated	Allocated Joint Costs
A	$28,000	7/12	$35,250	$20,562.50
B	20,000	5/12	35,250	14,687.50
	$48,000			$35,250.00

3.
$750	sales price for the by-product
30%	profit on by-product
$225	profit recognized as Other Income on sale of by-products
$525	is subtracted from $36,000 joint costs
$35,475	joint costs must be allocated between Products A and B

Product	Net Realizable Value	Fractional Part of Total Net Realizable Value	Joint Costs to be Allocated	Allocated Joint Costs
A	$28,000	7/12	$35,475	$20,693.75
B	20,000	5/12	35,475	14,781.25
	$48,000			$35,475.00

4. The total sales price for Product C is $4 per gallon times 500 gallons, or $2,000. The only costs to consider are the separable costs of $1 per gallon, or $500. The net realizable value of the by-product is $1,500.

a. The $1,500 would be subtracted from the 36,000 joint costs leaving $34,500 to be allocated as follows:

Product	Sales Value	Separable Costs	Net Realizable Value	Fractional Part of Total Net Realizable Value	Joint Costs to be Allocated	Allocated Joint Costs	Gross Profit
A	$28,000	$8,000	$20,000	1/2	$34,500	$17,250	10,750
B	20,000	-0-	20,000	1/2	34,500	17,250	2,750
			$40,000			$34,500	

b. The $1,500 is recognized as Other Income. The joint costs are allocated as in (4a) above, except that $36,000 is split 50/50 over products A and B, i.e., $18,000 each yielding a gross profit of $11,500 and $3,500 respectively.

c. $ 1,500   net realizable value for the by-product
$\underline{\quad 30\%}$ profit on by-product

$ 450   profit recognized as Other Income
$ 1,050   is subtracted from the $36,000 joint costs
$34,950   joint costs must be allocated between Products A and
B yielding a gross profit of $10,525 and $2,525 respectively.

Product	Sales Value	Separable Costs	Net Realizable Value	Fractional Part of Total Net Realizable Value	Joint Costs to be Allocated	Allocated Joint Costs
A	$28,000	$8,000	$20,000	1/2	$34,950	$17,475
B	20,000	-0-	20,000	1/2	34,950	17,475
			$40,000			$34,950

EXAMPLE 16

The L. J. Company manufactures ice cream pop sticks and tongue depressors by a joint process. The scrap wood is turned into toothpicks and is classified as a by-product. The policy of the company is to reduce the joint costs by the expected revenue of the toothpicks manufactured.

During the second quarter of 19X1, the company incurred $37,000 of joint costs to manufacture 40,000 boxes of ice cream pop sticks and 80,000 boxes of tongue depressors. Five thousand boxes of toothpicks were also produced. A box of toothpicks sells for $.20. The ice cream pop stick boxes sell for $.50 per box after $2,000 of additional costs for packaging and selling. The tongue depressors sell for $.75 per box after the additional cost of $3,000 for packaging and selling. The toothpick boxes do not require any additional costs.

There was no beginning inventory, and the inventory is valued at allocated costs with the exception of the toothpicks. These are valued at the sales price. The company uses the net realizable value method to allocate costs.

We find the value of the inventory on hand if 38,000 boxes of ice cream pop sticks, 75,000 boxes of tongue depressors, and 4,500 boxes of the toothpicks were sold.

The company reduces its joint costs by the expected sales revenue of the by-product, toothpicks:

Joint costs $37,000
Expected sales value of by-product (5,000 $\times$ .20)   1,000
Joint costs to be allocated $36,000

L.J. COMPANY
ALLOCATION OF JOINT COSTS
NET REALIZABLE VALUE METHOD
For the 2nd Quarter, 19X1

Product	Sales Value	Separable Costs	Net Realizable Value	Fractional Part of Joint Cost	Total Joint Cost	Allocated Joint Cost
Tongue depressors	$60,000	$3,000	$57,000	19/25	$36,000	$27,360
Ice cream pop sticks	20,000	2,000	18,000	6/25	36,000	8,640
			$75,000			$36,000

TOTAL COSTS

	Tongue Depressors	Ice Cream Pop Sticks
Separate costs	3,000	2,000
Joint costs	27,360	8,640
Total costs	30,360	10,640
Total number of boxes produced	80,000	40,000
Cost per box	$.3795	$.266

INVENTORY

	Number of Boxes	Cost per Box	Total Value in Inventory
Tongue Depressors	5,000	$.3795	$1,897.50
Ice cream pop sticks	2,000	.266	532.00
Toothpicks			-0-

Note: The by-product (toothpicks) should have no inventory value because the expected sales value ($1,000) is treated as a reduction of the manufacturing joint costs. There are two cost accounting alternatives here: The company should either credit the cost of goods sold account or adjust the inventory value of the principal product(s).

CONCLUSION

Joint products are two or more products produced from the same manufacturing process. Joint costs may be allocated to joint products under different methods including relative sales value and volume. By-products have little value relative to the main product. There are various ways to handle the value of the by-product including reducing the cost of the main product or treating it as "other revenue." The methods selected to determine the cost of a joint product and by-product should be logical and realistic given the particular circumstances of a given company's manufacturing process.

13

Analysis of Cost Behavior

Not all costs behave in the same way. There are certain costs that vary in proportion to changes in volume or activity, such as labor hours and machine hours. There are other costs that do not change even though volume changes. An understanding of cost behavior is helpful:

1. For break-even and cost-volume-profit analysis
2. To appraise divisional performance
3. For flexible budgeting
4. To make short-term choice decisions
5. To make transfer decisions

A Further Look at Costs by Behavior

As was discussed in Chapter 11, depending on how a cost will react or respond to changes in the level of activity, costs may be viewed as variable, fixed, or mixed (semivariable). This classification is made within a specified range of activity, called the relevant range. The relevant range is the volume zone within which the behavior of variable costs, fixed costs, and selling prices can be predicted with reasonable accuracy.

Variable Costs. As previously discussed, variable costs are those costs that vary in total with change in volume or level of activity. Examples of variable costs include the costs of direct materials, direct labor, and sales commissions. The following factory overhead items fall in the variable cost category:

269

Variable Factory Overhead

Supplies	Receiving costs
Fuel and power	Overtime premium
Spoilage and defective work	

Fixed Costs. As previously discussed, fixed costs are costs that do not change in total regardless of the volume or level of activity. Examples include advertising expense, salaries, and depreciation. The following factory overhead items fall in the fixed cost category:

Fixed Factory Overhead

Property taxes	Rent on factory building
Depreciation	Indirect Labor
Insurance	Patent amortization

Mixed (Semivariable) Costs. Mixed costs that contain both a fixed element and a variable one. Salespersons' compensation including salary and commission is an example. The following factory overhead items may be considered mixed costs:

Mixed Factory Overhead

Supervision	Maintenance and repairs
Inspection	Compensation insurance
Service department costs	Employer's payroll taxes
Utilities	Rental of delivery truck
Fringe benefits	

Note that factory overhead, taken as a whole, would be a perfect example of mixed costs. Figure 1 displays how each of these three types of costs varies with changes in volume.

Types of Fixed Costs—Committed or Discretionary

Strictly speaking, there is no such thing as a fixed cost. In the long run, all costs are variable. In the short run, however, some fixed costs, called discretionary (or managed or programmed) fixed costs, will change. It is important to note that these costs change because of managerial decisions, not because of changes in volume. Examples of discretionary types of fixed costs are advertising, training, and research and development. Another type of fixed costs, called committed fixed costs, are those costs that do not change and are the results of commitments previously made. Fixed costs such as rent, depreciation, insurance, and executive salaries are committed types of fixed costs since management has committed itself for a long period of time regarding the company's production facilities and manpower requirements.

ANALYSIS OF MIXED (SEMIVARIABLE) COSTS

For planning, control, and decision-making purposes, mixed costs need to be separated into their variable and fixed components. Since the mixed costs contain both fixed and variable elements, the analysis takes the following mathematical form, which is called a cost-volume formula (flexible budget formula or cost function):

$$y = a + bx$$

where y = the mixed cost to be broken up

x = any given measure of activity such as direct labor hours, machine hours, or production volume

a = the fixed cost component

b = the variable rate per unit of x

Separating the mixed cost into its fixed and variable components is the same thing as estimating the parameter values a and b in the cost-volume formula. There are several methods available to be used for this purpose

Figure 1   Cost Behavior Patterns

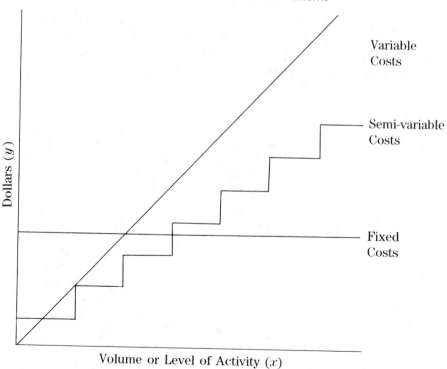

Volume or Level of Activity (x)

including the high-low method and the least-squares method (regression analysis). They are discussed below.

The High-Low Method

The high-low method, as the name indicates, uses two extreme data points to determine the values of a (the fixed cost portion) and b (the variable rate) in the equation $y = a + bx$. The extreme data points are the highest representative $x - y$ pair and the lowest representative $x - y$ pair. The activity level x, rather than the mixed cost item y, governs their selection.

The high-low method is explained, step by step, as follows:

Step 1   Select the highest pair and the lowest pair

Step 2   Compute the variable rate b, using the formula:

$$\text{Variable rate} = \frac{\text{Difference in cost } y}{\text{Difference in activity } x}$$

Step 3   Compute the fixed cost portion as:
Fixed cost portion = Total mixed cost − Variable cost

EXAMPLE 1

Flexible Manufacturing Company decided to relate total factory overhead costs to direct labor hours (DLH) to develop a cost-volume formula in the form of $y = a + bx$. Twelve monthly observations are collected. They are given in Table 1 and plotted as shown in Figure 2.

Table 1

Month	Direct Labor Hours (x) (000 omitted)	Factory Overhead (y) (000 omitted)
January	9 hours	$ 15
February	19	20
March	11	14
April	14	16
May	23	25
June	12	20
July	12	20
August	22	23
September	7	14
October	13	22
November	15	18
December	17	18
Total	174 hours	$225

Figure 2 Scatter Diagram

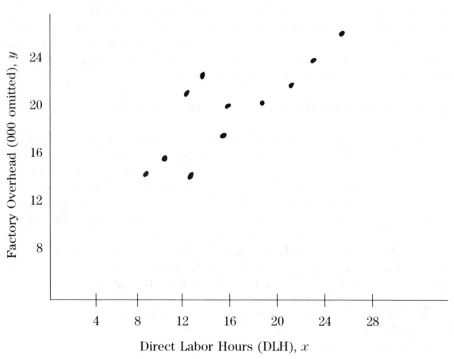

The high-low points selected from the monthly observations are

	x		y	
High	23	hours	$25	(May pair)
Low	7		14	(September pair)
Difference	16	hours	$11	

Thus

$$\text{Variable rate } b = \frac{\text{Difference in } y}{\text{Difference in } x} = \frac{\$11}{16 \text{ hours}} = \$0.6875 \text{ per DLH}$$

The fixed cost portion is computed as

	High	*Low*
Factory overhead (y)	$25	$14
Variable expense ($0.6875/DLH)	(15.8125)	(4.8125)
	$9.1875	$9.1875

Therefore, the cost-volume formula for factory overhead is $9.1875 fixed plus $0.6875 per DLH.

The high-low method is simple and easy to use. It has the disadvantage, however, of using two extreme data points, which may not be representative of normal conditions. The method may yield unreliable estimates of a and b in our formula. In such a case, it would be wise to drop them and choose two other points that are more representative of normal situations. Be sure to check the scatter diagram in Figure 2 for this possibility.

The Least-Squares Method (Regression Analysis)

One popular method for estimating the cost-volume formula is regression analysis. Regression analysis is a statistical procedure for estimating mathematically the average relationship between the dependent variable and the independent variable(s). Simple regression involves one independent variable, e.g., DLH or machine hours alone, whereas multiple regression involves two or more activity variables. We will assume a simple linear regression, which means that we will maintain the $y = a + bx$ relationship.

Unlike the high-low method, in an effort to estimate the variable rate and the fixed cost portion, the regression method includes all the observed data and attempts to find a line of best fit. To find this line, a technique called the least-squares method is used.

To explain the least-squares method, we define the error as the difference between the observed value and the estimated one of some mixed cost and denote it with u.

Symbolically, $\quad u = y - y'$

where y = observed value of a semivariable expense

$\quad y'$ = estimated value based on $y' = a + bx$

The least-squares criterion requires that the line of best fit be such that the sum of the squares of the errors (or the vertical distance in Figure 3 from the observed data points to the line) is a minimum, i.e.,

$$\text{minimum: } \Sigma u^2 = \Sigma (y - y')^2$$

Using differential calculus we obtain the following equations, called normal equations:

$$\Sigma y = na + b\Sigma x$$
$$\Sigma xy = a\Sigma x + b\Sigma x^2$$

solving the equations for b and a yields

$$b = \frac{n\Sigma xy - (\Sigma x)(\Sigma y)}{n\Sigma x^2 - (\Sigma x)^2}$$
$$a = \bar{y} - b\bar{x}$$

where $\bar{y} = \Sigma y/n$ and $\bar{x} = \Sigma x/n$.

Figure 3. Y and Y'

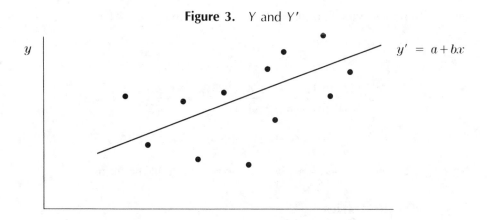

EXAMPLE 2

To illustrate the computations of b and a, we will once again refer to the data in Table 1. All the sums required are computed and shown below.

DLH (x)	Factory Overhead (y)	xy	x^2	y^2
9 hours	$ 15	135	81	225
19	20	380	361	400
11	14	154	121	196
14	16	224	196	256
23	25	575	529	625
12	20	240	144	400
12	20	240	144	400
22	23	506	484	529
7	14	98	49	196
13	22	286	169	484
15	18	270	225	324
17	18	306	289	324
174 hours	$225	3,414	2,792	4,359

From the table above:

$$\Sigma x = 174 \quad \Sigma y = 225 \quad \Sigma xy = 3,414 \quad \Sigma x^2 = 2,792$$

$$\bar{x} = \Sigma x/n = 174/12 = 14.5 \quad \bar{y} = \Sigma y/n = 225/12 = 18.75$$

Substituting these values into the formula for b first:

$$b = \frac{n\Sigma xy - (\Sigma x)(\Sigma y)}{n\Sigma x^2 - (\Sigma x)^2}$$

$$= \frac{(12)(3,414) - (174)(225)}{(12)(2,792) - (174)^2} = \frac{1,818}{3,228} = 0.5632$$

$$a = \bar{y} - b\bar{x} = 18.75 - (0.5632)(14.5) = 18.75 - 8.1664 = 10.5836$$

Note that Σy^2 is not used here but rather is computed for future use.

Regression Statistics

Unlike the high-low method, regression analysis is a statistical method. It uses a variety of statistics to tell about the accuracy and reliability of the regression results. They include:

1. Correlation coefficient (r) and coefficient of determination (r^2)
2. Standard error of the estimate (S_e)
3. Standard error of the regression coefficient (S_b) and t-statistic

Correlation coefficient (r) and coefficient of determination (r^2). The correlation coefficient r measures the degree of correlation between y and x. The range of values it takes on is between -1 and $+1$. More widely used, however, is the coefficient of determination, designated r^2 (read as r-squared). Simply put, r^2 tells us how good the estimated regression equation is. In other words, it is a measure of "goodness of fit" in the regression. Therefore, the higher the r^2, the more confidence we have in our estimated cost formula.

More specifically, the coefficient of determination represents the proportion of the total variation in y that is explained by the regression equation. It has the range of values between 0 and 1.

EXAMPLE 3

The statement "Factory overhead is a function of machine hours with r^2 of 70%," can be interpreted as "70% of the total variation of factory overhead is explained by the regression equation or the change in machine hours and the remaining 30% is accounted for by something other than machine hours."

The coefficient of determination is computed as

$$r^2 = 1 - \frac{\Sigma(y - y')^2}{\Sigma(y - \bar{y})^2}$$

In a simple regression situation, however, there is a shortcut method available:

$$r^2 = \frac{[n\Sigma xy - (\Sigma x)(\Sigma y)]^2}{[n\Sigma x^2 - (\Sigma x)^2][n\Sigma y^2 - (\Sigma y)^2]}$$

Comparing this formula with the one for b, we see that the only additional information we need to compute r^2 is Σy^2.

EXAMPLE 4

From the table prepared in Example 2, $\Sigma y^2 = 4,359$.
Using the shortcut method for r^2,

$$r^2 = \frac{(1,818)^2}{(3,228)[(12)(4,359) - (225)^2]} = \frac{3,305,124}{(3,228)(52,308 - 50,625)}$$

$$= \frac{3,305,124}{(3,228)(1,683)} = \frac{3,305,124}{5,432,724} = 0.6084 = 60.84\%$$

This means that about 60.84% of the total variation in total factory overhead is explained by DLH and the remaining 39.16% is still unexplained. A relatively low r^2 indicates that there is a lot of room for improvement in our estimated cost-volume formula ($y' = \$10.5836 + \$0.5632x$). Machine hours or a combination of DLH and machine hours might improve r^2.

Standard error of the estimate (S_e). The standard error of the estimate, designated S_e, is defined as the standard deviation of the regression. It is computed as

$$S_e = \sqrt{\frac{\Sigma(y - y')^2}{n - 2}} = \sqrt{\frac{\Sigma y^2 - a\Sigma y - b\Sigma xy}{n - 2}}$$

The statistics can be used to gain some idea of the accuracy of our predications.

EXAMPLE 5

Going back to our example data, S_e is calculated as

$$S_e = \sqrt{\frac{4,359 - (10.5836)(225) - (0.5632)(3,414)}{12 - 2}}$$

$$= \sqrt{\frac{54.9252}{10}} = 2.3436$$

If the managerial accountant wants to be 95% confident in his prediction, the confidence interval would be the estimated cost $+ - 2(2.3436)$.

Standard error of the regression coefficient (S_b) and the t-statistic.
The standard error of the regression coefficient, designated, S_b, and the t-statistic are closely related. S_b is calculated as:

$$S_b = \frac{S_e}{\sqrt{\Sigma (x - x)^2}}$$

or in short-cut form

$$S_b = \frac{S_e}{\sqrt{\Sigma x^2 - \bar{x} \Sigma x}}$$

S_b gives an estimate of the range where the true coefficient will "actually" fall. The t-statistic shows the statistical significance of an independent variable x in explaining the dependent variable y. It is determined by dividing the estimated regression coefficient b by its standard error S_b. Thus, the t-statistic measures how many standard errors the coefficient is away from zero. Generally, any t value greater than $+2$ or less than -2 is acceptable. The higher the t value, the greater is the confidence in the coefficient as the predictor.

EXAMPLE 6

The S_b for our example is:

$$S_b = \frac{2.3436}{\sqrt{2,792 - (14.5)\,(174)}}$$

$$= \frac{2.3436}{\sqrt{2,792 - 2,523}} = \frac{2.3436}{\sqrt{269}} = .143$$

Thus, t-statistic $= b/S_b = .5632 = 3.94$
Since, $t = 3.94 > 2$, we conclude that the b coefficient is statistically significant.

Use of a Spreadsheet Program for Regression

We can use a spreadsheet program such as Lotus 1-2-3 in order to develop a model and estimate most of the statistics we discussed thus far. This involves the following steps. (Figure 4 illustrates the Lotus 1-2-3 regression output):

Multiple Regression

The least-squares method provides the opportunity for the managerial accountant to consider more than one independent variable. In case a simple regression is not good enough to provide a satisfactory cost-volume formula (as

Figure 4 Spreadsheet Regression Result

Step 1 Enter the data on y and x as shown below

y Factory Overhead (00)	x Direct Labor Hr. (00)
15	9
20	19
14	11
16	14
25	23
20	12
20	12
23	22
14	7
22	13
18	15
18	17

Step 2 Press "/Data Regression"
Step 3 Define y and x range
Step 4 Define output range
Step 5 Hit Go

This will produce the following regression output:

Regression Output

Constant	10.58364
Std Err of Y Est	2.343622
R Squared	0.608373
No. of Observations	12
Degrees of Freedom	10

X Coefficient(s) 0.563197
Std Err of Coef. 0.142893

The result shows:

$y' = 10.58364 + 0.563197x$
r-squared $(r^2) = .608373 = 60.84\%$
Standard error of the estimate $(S_e) = 2.343622$
Standard error of the coefficient $(S_b) = 0.142893$

All of the above are the same as the ones manually obtained.

indicated typically by a low r-squared), the managerial accountant should use multiple regression. Presented below is an example of multiple regression and a spreadsheet printout.

EXAMPLE 7

Assume the following data:

Factory overhead costs (y)	Direct labor hours (x_1)	Machine hours (x_2)
$3,200	26	50
2,001	15	35
2,700	18	40
3,135	21	45
2,964	20	40

First, we present two simple regression results (one variable at a time):

Simple regression 1
$$y = a + b\,x_1$$

Simple regression 2
$$y = a + b\,x_2$$

The Contribution Income Statement

The traditional (absorption) income statement for external reporting shows the functional classification of costs, that is, manufacturing costs versus non-manufacturing expenses (or operating expenses). An alternative format of income statement, known as the contribution income statement organizes the costs by behavior rather than by function. It shows the relationship of variable costs and fixed costs, regardless of the functions a given cost item is associated with.

Figure 5. Simple and Multiple Regression Results for Cost-Volume Formula

Factory Overhead Cost (y)	Direct Labor Hours (x_1)	Machine Hours (x_2)
3200	26	50
2001	15	35
2700	18	40
3135	21	45
2964	20	40

Simple regression 1: $y = a + bx_1$

Figure 5. (*Continued*).

Regression Output:

Constant	700
Std Err of Y Est	270.7224
R-Squared	0.767950
No. of Observations	5
Degrees of Freedom	3

X-Coefficient(s)	105	
Std Err of Coef.	33.32363	
T-value	3.150916	(calculated independently)

$$y' = 700 + 105\, x_1 \text{ with } r^2 = 0.767950 = 76.80\%$$

Simple regression 2: $y = a + b\, x_2$

Regression Output:

Constant	-324.153
Std Err of Y Est	275.8156
R-Squared	0.759137
No. of Observations	5
Degrees of Freedom	3

X-Coefficient(s)	74.38461	
Std Err of Coef.	24.19063	
T-value	3.074935	(calculated independently)

$$y' = -324.153 + 74.38461\, x_2 \text{ with } r^2 = 0.759137 = 75.91\%$$

Multiple regression: $y = a + b\, x_1 + c\, x_2$

Regression Ouput:

Constant	254.5
Std Err of Y Est	326.5095
R-Squared	0.774974
No. of Observations	5
Degrees of Freedom	2

X-Coefficient(s)	63.75	30.25	
Std Err of Coef.	169.9209	121.0729	
T-value	0.375174	0.249849	(calculated independently)

$$y' = 254.5 + 63.75\, x_1 + 30.25\, x_2 \text{ with } r^2 = 0.774974 = 77.50\%$$

281

Summary and Conclusion

As can be seen, there was only a slight increase in r^2, from 76.8% in simple regression 1 and 75.91% in simple regression 2 to 77.50%. Apparently, the extra independent variable added little new explanatory power. Futhermore, t-values for both independent variables came out to be much less than 2 (approximately 0.38 and 0.25, respectively), which means both variables together in the same regression equation were not statistically significant. All this indicates that either simple regression was good enough for the purpose of developing the cost-volume formula.

The contribution approach to income determination provides data that are useful for managerial planning and decision making. For example, the contribution approach is useful:

(1) For breakeven and cost-volume-profit analysis,

(2) In evaluating the performance of the division and its manager, and

(3) For short-term and nonroutine decisions.

The contribution income statement is not acceptable, however, for income tax or external reporting purposes because it ignores fixed overhead as a product cost.

The statement highlights the concept of contribution margin, which is the difference between sales and variable costs. The traditional format, on the other hand, emphasizes the concept of gross margin, which is the difference between sales and cost of goods sold. These two concepts are independent and have nothing to do with each other. Gross margin is available to cover nonmanufacturing expenses, whereas contribution margin is available to cover fixed costs. The concept of contribution margin has numerous applications for internal management, which will be taken up in later chapters.

A comparison is made between the traditional format and the contribution format below.

Traditional Format

Sales		$15,000
Less: Cost of Goods Sold		7,000
Gross Margin		$ 8,000
Less: Operating Expenses		
Selling	$2,100	
Administrative	1,500	3,600
Net Income		$ 4,400

Contribution Format

Sales		$15,000
Less: Variable Expenses		
Manufacturing	$4,000	
Selling	1,600	
Administrative	500	6,100
Contribution Margin		$ 8,900
Less: Fixed Expenses		
Manufacturing	$3,000	
Selling	500	
Administrative	1,000	4,500
Net Income		$ 4,400

CONCLUSION

Accountants and financial managers analyze cost behavior for cost-volume-profit analysis, for appraisal of managerial performance, for flexible budgeting, and to make short-term choice decisions. We have looked at three types of cost behavior—variable, fixed, and mixed. We have discussed two basic methods of separating a mixed cost into its variable and fixed components. Heavy emphasis was placed on the use of simple and multiple regression.

Managerial accountants prepare the income statement in a contribution format which organizes costs by behavior rather than by the functions of manufacturing, sales, and administration. The contribution income statement is widely used as an internal planning and decision-making tool.

14

Cost-Volume-Profit Analysis and Leverage

Cost-volume-profit (CVP) analysis, together with cost behavior information, helps managerial accountants perform many useful analyses. CVP analysis deals with how profit and costs change with a change in volume. More specifically, it looks at the effects on profits of changes in such factors as variable costs, fixed costs, selling prices, volume, and mix of products sold. By studying the relationships of costs, sales, and net income, management is better able to cope with many planning decisions. Break-even analysis, a branch of CVP analysis, determines the break-even sales. Break-even point—the financial crossover point when revenues exactly match costs—does not show up in corporate earnings reports, but financial officers find it an extremely useful measurement in a variety of ways.

Questions Answered by CVP Analysis

CVP analysis tries to answer the following questions:

(a) What sales volume is required to break even?

(b) What sales volume is necessary to earn a desired profit?

(c) What profit can be expected on a given sales volume?

(d) How would changes in selling price, variable costs, fixed costs, and output affect profits?

(e) How would a change in the mix of products sold affect the break-even and target income volume and profit potential?

285

Contribution Margin (CM)

For accurate CVP analysis, a distinction must be made between costs as being either variable or fixed. Mixed costs must be separated into their variable and fixed components.

In order to compute the break-even point and perform various CVP analyses, note the following important concepts.

Contribution Margin (CM). The contribution margin is the excess of sales (S) over the variable costs (VC) of the product. It is the amount of money available to cover fixed costs (FC) and to generate profits. Symbolically, $CM = S - VC$.

Unit CM. The unit CM is the excess of the unit selling price (p) over the unit variable cost (v). Symbolically, unit $CM = p - v$.

CM Ratio. The CM ratio is the contribution margin as a percentage of sales, i.e.,

$$CM \text{ ratio} = \frac{CM}{S} = \frac{S - VC}{S} = 1 - \frac{VC}{S}$$

The CM ratio can also be computed using per-unit data as follows:

$$CM \text{ ratio} = \frac{\text{Unit } CM}{p} = \frac{p - v}{p} = 1 - \frac{v}{p}$$

Note that the CM ratio is 1 minus the variable cost ratio. For example, if variable costs account for 70% of the price, the CM ratio is 30%.

EXAMPLE 1

To illustrate the various concepts of CM, consider the following data for company Z:

	Total	Per Unit	Percentage
Sales (1,500 units)	$37,500	$25	100%
Less: Variable costs	15,000	10	40
Contribution margin	$22,500	$15	60%
Less: Fixed costs	15,000		
Net income	$ 7,500		

From the data listed above, CM, unit CM, and the CM ratio are computed as:

$$CM = S - VC = \$37,500 - \$15,000 = \$22,500$$
$$\text{Unit } CM = p - v = \$25 - \$10 = \$15$$
$$CM \text{ ratio} = \frac{CM}{S} = \frac{\$22,500}{\$37,500} = 60\%$$
$$\text{or } \frac{\text{Unit } CM}{p} = \frac{\$15}{\$25} = 0.6 = 60\%$$

Break-Even Analysis

The break-even point represents the level of sales revenue that equals the total of the variable and fixed costs for a given volume of output at a particular capacity use rate. For example, you might want to ask the break-even occupancy rate (or vacancy rate) for a hotel or the break-even load rate for an airliner. Generally, the lower the break-even point, the higher the profits and the less the operating risk, other things being equal. The break-even point also provides managerial accountants with insights into profit planning. It can be computed using the following formulas:

$$\text{Break-even point in units} = \frac{\text{Fixed costs}}{\text{Unit CM}}$$

$$\text{Break-even point in dollars} = \frac{\text{Fixed costs}}{\text{CM ratio}}$$

EXAMPLE 2

Using the same data given in Example 1, where unit CM = \$25 − \$10 = \$15 and CM ratio = 60%, we get:

Break-even point in units = \$15,000/\$15 = 1,000 units
Break-even point in dollars = 1,000 units × \$25 = \$25,000 or, alternatively,

$$\$15,000/0.6 = \$25,000$$

Graphical Approach in a Spreadsheet Format

The graphical approach to obtaining the break-even point is based on the so-called break-even chart as shown in Figure 1. Sales revenue, variables costs, and fixed costs are plotted on the vertical axis while volume x, is plotted on the horizontal axis. The chart can be easily produced in a spreadsheet format. The break-even point is the point where the total sales revenue line intersects the total cost line. The chart can also effectively report profit potentials over a wide range of activity and therefore be used as a tool for discussion and presentation.

Figure 1　Break-Even Chart

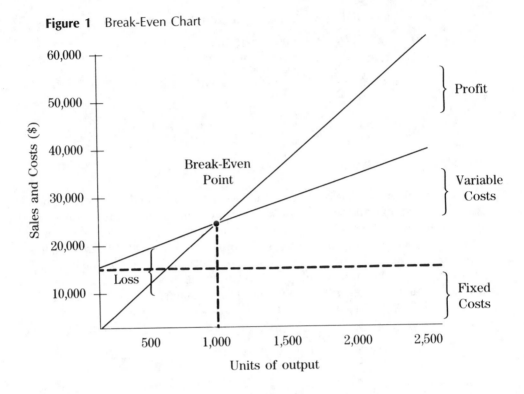

The profit-volume (P-V) chart as shown in Figure 2, focuses directly on how profits vary with changes in volume. Profits are plotted on the vertical axis while units of output are shown on the horizontal axis. The P-V chart provides a quick condensed comparison of how alternatives on pricing, variable costs, or fixed costs may affect net income as volume changes. Note that the slope of the chart is the unit CM.

Determination of Target Income Volume

Besides determining the break-even point, CVP analysis determines the sales required to attain a particular income level or target net income. The formula is:

$$\text{Target income sales volume} = \frac{\text{Fixed costs plus Target income}}{\text{Unit CM}}$$

EXAMPLE 3

Using the same data given in Example 1, assume that company Z wishes to attain a target income of $15,000 before tax.

Then, the target income volume required would be:

Figure 2   Profit-Volume (P-V) Chart

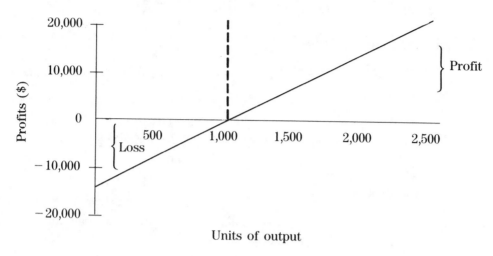

Units of output

$$\frac{\$15,000 + \$15,000}{\$25 - \$10} = \frac{\$30,000}{\$15} = 2,000 \text{ units}$$

Cash Break-Even Point

If a company has a minimum of available cash or the opportunity cost of holding excess cash is too high, management may want to know the volume of sales that will cover all cash expenses during a period. This is known as the cash break-even point. Not all fixed operating costs involve cash payments. For example, depreciation expenses are noncash fixed charges. To find the cash break-even point, the noncash charges must be subtracted from fixed costs. Therefore, the cash break-even point is lower than the usual break-even point. The formula is:

$$\text{Cash break-even point} = \frac{\text{Fixed costs} - \text{depreciation}}{\text{Unit CM}}$$

EXAMPLE 4

Assume from Example 1 that the total fixed costs of $15,000 include depreciation of $1,500. Then the cash break-even point is:

$$\frac{\$15,000 - \$1,500}{\$25 - \$10} = \frac{\$13,500}{\$15} = 900$$

Company Z has to sell 900 units to cover only the fixed costs involving cash payments of $13,500 and to break even.

Impact of Income Taxes

If target income is given on an after-tax basis, the target income volume formula becomes:

$$\text{Target income volume} = \frac{\text{Fixed costs} + [\text{Target after-tax income}/(1\text{-tax rate})]}{\text{Unit CM}}$$

EXAMPLE 5

Assume in Example 1 that company Z wants to achieve an after-tax income of $6,000. The tax rate is 40%. Then,

$$\text{Target income volume} = \frac{\$15,000 + [\$6,000/(1 - 0.4)]}{\$15}$$

$$= \frac{\$15,000 + \$10,000}{\$15} = 1,667 \text{ units}$$

Margin of Safety

The margin of safety is a measure of difference between the actual sales level and the break-even sales. It is the amount by which sales revenue may drop before losses begin, and is expressed as a percentage of expected sales:

$$\text{Margin of safety} = \frac{\text{Expected sales} - \text{Break-even sales}}{\text{Expected sales}}$$

The margin of safety is often used as a measure of operating risk. The larger the ratio, the safer the situation since there is less risk of reaching the break-even point.

EXAMPLE 6

Assume company Z projects sales of $35,000, with a break-even sales level of $25,000. The projected margin of safety is

$$\frac{\$35,000 - \$25,000}{\$35,000} = 28.57\%$$

Some Applications of CVP Analysis and What-If Analysis

The concepts of contribution margin and the contribution income statement have many applications in profit planning and short-term decision making. Many "what-if" scenarios can be evaluated using them as planning tools, especially utilizing a spreadsheet program such as Lotus 1-2-3. Some applications are illustrated in Examples 7 to 10 using the same data as in Example 1.

EXAMPLE 7

Recall from Example 1 that company Z has a CM of 60% and fixed costs of $15,000 per period. Assume that the company expects sales to go up by $10,000 for the next period. How much will income increase?

Using the CM concepts, we can quickly compute the impact of a change in sales on profits. The formula for computing the impact is:

$$\text{Change in net income} = \text{Dollar change in sales} \times \text{CM ratio}$$

Thus:

$$\text{Increase in net income} = \$10,000 \times 60\% = \$6,000$$

Therefore, the income will go up by $6,000, assuming there is no change in fixed costs.

If we are given a change in unit sales instead of dollars, then the formula becomes:

$$\text{Change in net income} = \text{Change in unit sales} \times \text{Unit CM}$$

EXAMPLE 8

What net income is expected on sales of $47,500?
The answer is the difference between the CM and the fixed costs:

CM: $47,500 × 60% $28,500
Less: Fixed costs   15,000
Net income $13,500

EXAMPLE 9

Company Z is considering increasing the advertising budget by $5,000, which would increase sales revenue by $8,000. Should the advertising budget be increased?

The answer is no, since the increase in the CM is less than the increased cost:

Increase in CM: $8,000 × 60% $4,800
Increase in advertising   5,000
Decrease in net income $(200)

EXAMPLE 10

Consider the original data. Assume again that company Z is currently selling 1,500 units per period. In an effort to increase sales, management is considering cutting its unit price by $5 and increasing the advertising budget by $1,000. If these two steps are taken, management feels that unit sales will go up by 60%. Should the two steps be taken?

A $5 reduction in the selling price will cause the unit CM to decrease from $15 to $10. Thus,

Proposed CM: 2,400 units × $10 $24,000
Present CM: 1,500 units × $15   22,500
Increase in CM $ 1,500
Increase in advertising outlay   1,000
Increase in net income $ 500

The answer, therefore, is yes. Alternatively, the same answer can be obtained by developing comparative income statements in a contribution format:

	Present (1,500 units)	Proposed (2,400 units)	Difference
Sales	$37,500 (@$25)	$48,000 (@$20)	$10,500
Less: Variable cost	15,000	24,000	9,000
CM	$22,500	$24,000	$ 1,500
Less: Fixed costs	15,000	16,000	1,000
Net income	$ 7,500	$ 8,000	$ 500

Sales Mix Analysis

Break-even and cost-volume-profit analysis requires some additional computations and assumptions when a company produces and sells more than one product. In multiproduct firms, sales mix is an important factor in calculating an overall company break-even point.

Different selling prices and different variable costs result in different unit CM and CM ratios. As a result, the break-even points and cost-volume-profit relationships vary with the relative proportions of the products sold, called the sales mix. In break-even and CVP analysis, it is necessary to predetermine the sales mix and then compute a weighted average unit CM. It is also necessary to assume that the sales mix does not change for a specified period. The break-even formula for the company as a whole is:

$$\text{Break-even sales in units (or in dollars)} = \frac{\text{Fixed costs}}{\text{Weighted average unit CM (or CM ratio)}}$$

EXAMPLE 11

Assume that company X has two products with the following unit CM data:

	A	B
Selling price	$15	$10
Variable cost per unit	12	5
Unit CM	$ 3	$ 5
Sales mix	60%	40%
Fixed costs	$76,000	

The weighted average unit CM = ($3) (0.6) + ($5) (0.4) = $3.80. Therefore the company's break-even point in units is

$$\$76,000/\$3.80 = 20,000 \text{ units}$$

which is divided as follows:

A: 20,000 units × 60% = 12,000 units
B: 20,000 units × 40% = 8,000
                        20,000 units

EXAMPLE 12

Assume that company Y produces and sells three products with the following data:

	A	B	C	Total
Sales	$30,000	$60,000	$10,000	$100,000
Sales mix	30%	60%	10%	100%
Less: VC	24,000	40,000	5,000	69,000

CM	$ 6,000	$20,000	$ 5,000	$ 31,000
CM ratio	20%	33⅓%	50%	31%
Fixed costs				$ 18,600
Net income				$ 12,400

The CM ratio for company Y is $31,000/$100,000 = 31%. Therefore, the break-even point in dollars is

$$\$18,600/0.31 = \$60,000$$

which will be split in the mix ratio of $3:6:1$ to give us the following break-even points for the individual products A, B, and C:

A: $60,000 × 30% = $18,000
B: $60,000 × 60% = 36,000
C: $60,000 × 10% = 6,000
$60,000

One of the most important assumptions underlying CVP analysis in a multiproduct firm is that the sales mix will not change during the planning period. However, if the sales mix changes, the break-even point will also change.

EXAMPLE 13

Assume that total sales from Example 11 remain unchanged at $100,000 but that a shift is expected in mix from product B to product C, as follows:

	A	B	C	Total
Sales	$30,000	$30,000	$40,000	$100,000
Sales mix	30%	30%	40%	100%
Less: VC	24,000	20,000*	20,000	64,000
CM	$ 6,000	$10,000	$20,000	$ 36,000
CM ratio	20%	33⅓%	50%	36%
Fixed costs				$ 18,600
Net income				$ 17,400

*$20,000 = $30,000 × 66⅔%

Note that the shift in sales mix toward the more profitable line C has caused the CM ratio for the company as a whole to go up from 31% to 36%. The new break-even point will be $18,600/0.36 = $51,667. The break-even dollar volume has decreased from $60,000 to $51,667. The improvement in the mix caused net income to go up. Generally, the shift of emphasis from low-margin products to high-margin ones will increase the overall profits of the company.

COST-VOLUME-REVENUE ANALYSIS AND NON-PROFIT ORGANIZATIONS

Cost-volume-profit (CVP) analysis and Break-Even Analysis is not limited to profit firms. CVP is appropriately called cost-volume-revenue (CVR) analysis, as it pertains to non-profit organizations. The CVR model not only calculates the break-even service level, but helps answer a variety of "what-if" decision questions.

EXAMPLE 14

A county has a $1,200,000 lump-sum annual budget appropriation for an agency to help rehabilitate mentally ill patients. On top of this, the agency charges each patient $600 a month for board and care. All of the appropriation and revenue must be spent. The variable costs for rehabilitation activity averge $700 per patient per month. The agency's annual fixed costs are $800,000. The agency manager wishes to know how many patients can be served. Let x = number of patients to be served.

$$\text{Revenue} = \text{Total expenses}$$

$$\text{Revenue} = \text{Variable expenses} + \text{Fixed costs}$$

$$\begin{aligned}
\$1{,}200{,}000 + \$7{,}200x &= \$8{,}400\ x + \$800{,}000 \\
(\$7{,}200 - \$8{,}400)x &= \$800{,}000 - \$1{,}200{,}000 \\
- \$1{,}200x &= -\$400{,}000 \\
x &= \$400{,}000/\$1{,}200 \\
x &= 333 \text{ patients}
\end{aligned}$$

We will investigate the following two "what-if" scenarios:

(1) Suppose the manager is concerned that the total budget for the coming year will be cut by 10% to a new amount of $1,080,000. All other things remain unchanged. The manager wants to know how this budget cut affects the next year's service level.

$$\begin{aligned}
\$1{,}080{,}000 + \$7{,}200x &= \$8{,}400x + \$800{,}000 \\
(\$7{,}200 - \$8{,}400)x &= \$800{,}000 - \$1{,}080{,}000 \\
- \$1{,}200x &= -\$280{,}000 \\
x &= \$280{,}000/\$1{,}200 \\
x &= 233 \text{ patients}
\end{aligned}$$

(2) The manager does not reduce the number of patients served despite a budget cut of 10%. All other things remain unchanged. How much more does he/she have to charge his/her patients for board and care? In this case, x = board and care charge per year

$$\$1,080,000 + 333x = \$8,400 \ (333) + \$800,000$$
$$333x = \$2,797,200 + \$800,000 - \$1,080,000$$
$$333x = \$2,517,200$$
$$x = \$2,517,200/333 \text{ patients}$$
$$x = \$7,559$$

Thus, the monthly board and care charge must be increased to $630 ($7,559/12 months).

ASSUMPTIONS UNDERLYING BREAK-EVEN AND CVP ANALYSIS

The basic break-even and CVP models are subject to a number of limiting assumptions. They are:

(a) The behavior of both sales revenue and expenses is linear throughout the entire relevant range of activity.

(b) All costs are classified as fixed or variable.

(c) There is only one product or a constant sales mix.

(d) Inventories do not change significantly from period to period.

(e) Volume is the only factor affecting variable costs.

COST-VOLUME-PROFIT ANALYSIS UNDER CONDITIONS OF UNCERTAINTY

The CVP analysis, discussed so far, assumed that all variables determining profit or contribution margin—the selling price, variable costs, sales volume, and fixed costs—are known with certainty. This is not a realistic assumption. If one or more of these variables are subject to uncertainty, management should analyze the potential impact of this uncertainty. This additional analysis is required in evaluating alternative courses of action and in developing contingency plans. If management must choose between two products, expected profitability and risk should be considered before a choice is made. For example, if both products have the same expected profits, management might want to select the less risky product (less variation in profits).

One way of handling the conditions of uncertainty is to use sensitivity analysis (what-if analysis), which was already discussed.

Statistical Method

Another approach to dealing with uncertainty is to use a statistical (probability) model. Let us suppose that sales volume is subject to uncertainty and, in fact, normally distributed. Then we can utilize the standard statistical method to summarize the effect of this uncertainty on a dependent variable such as profit or contribution margin. Also, we can answer the following planning questions:

1. What is the probability of breaking even?
2. What is the chance that profits from the proposal would be at least a certain amount?
3. What are the chances that the proposal would cause the company to lose as much as a specified amount?

Any uncertainty in sales volume affects the total contribution margin (CM) and profits (P). The expected contribution margin $E(CM)$, is the unit CM times the expected volume, $E(x)$:

$$E(CM) = \text{unit } CM \times E(x)$$
$$= (p - v) \, E(x)$$

The expected profit $E(\pi)$, is the expected contribution minus the fixed costs (FC):

$$E(\pi) = E(CM) - FC = (p - v) \, E(x) - FC$$

Because of the uncertainty in sales volume, the expected contribution margin and profits are also uncertain. The standard deviation of the expected contribution margin and profits is equal to the unit CM times the standard deviation of the sales volume. In equation form,

$$\sigma_\pi = (p - v) \, \sigma_x$$

where σ_π = standard deviation of expected profits
σ_x = standard deviation of sales volume

EXAMPLE 15

ABC Corporation has annual fixed costs of $1,500,000 and variable costs of $4.50 per unit. The selling price per unit is stable at $7.50, but the annual sales volume is uncertain and normally distributed with mean expected sales of 600,000 units and a standard deviation of 309,278 units. Management expects this pattern to continue in the future. The normal distribution of profits is illustrated in Figure 3. Then

The expected contribution is $1,800,000:

Figure 3 Probability Distribution of Profits

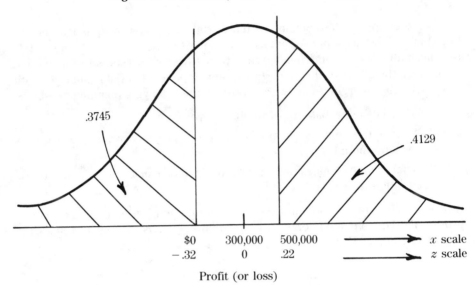

	$0	300,000	500,000		x scale
	−.32	0	.22		z scale

Profit (or loss)

$$E(CM) = (\$7.50 - \$4.50) \times 600,000 \text{ units}$$
$$= \$3 \times 600,000 = \$1,800,000$$

The expected profits are $300,000:

$$E(\pi) = \$1,800,000 - \$1,500,000 = \$300,000$$

The standard deviation of the expected profits is $927,834:

$$\sigma_\pi = \$3 \times 309,278 = \$927,834$$

EXAMPLE 16

From the results obtained in Example 15, we will answer the following questions:

1. What is the probability of breaking even?
2. What is the probability of obtaining a profit of $500,000 or more?
3. What is the probability of losing as much as $250,000?

In each case, we must determine the standard normal variate, better known as z, which is the number of standard deviations from any profit to the expected (mean) profit.

To determine the probability of at least breaking even, we first determine z as follows:

$$z = \frac{0 - E(\pi)}{\sigma_\pi} = \frac{\$0 - \$300,000}{\$927,834} = -.32$$

In Table 1 of the Appendix (Normal Distribution), the probability of obtaining a z value of $-.32$ or less is .3745 $(1 - .6255 = .3745)$, which means there is only a 37.45% chance that the company would lose money or about a 62.55% chance the company will at least break even.

To find the probability of obtaining at least a profit of \$500,000 we first determine the number of standard deviations \$500,000 is from the expected profit:

$$z = \frac{\$500,000 - \$300,000}{\$927,834} = \frac{\$200,000}{\$927,834} = .22$$

From Table 1 we can calculate that the chances are only .5871 of earning less than \$500,000; thus we conclude that the chances of bettering a \$500,000 profit are .4129 or 41.29% $(1 - .5871 = .4129)$.

To find the probability of losing as much as \$250,000, again we calculate the value for z:

$$z = \frac{-\$250,000 - \$300,000}{\$927,834} = \frac{-\$550,000}{\$927,834} = -.59$$

Table 1 indicates that there is only a 2.776 $(1 - .7224 = .2776)$ chance of losing \$250,000 or more.

To summarize,

1. The chance of breaking even is better than 62.55%.
2. The chance of making at least \$500,000 is 41.29%.
3. The chance of losing \$250,000 or more is only about 27.76%.

Figure 3 depicts the probability distribution of profits for this example.

Caution

In the previous example, we have considered sales volume to be subject to uncertainty—random variable. It is also possible to consider fixed costs, variable costs, and selling price as random variables to test the effect of their uncertainty on profits. When one of these four variables—sales volume, price,

Table 1

NORMAL DISTRIBUTION TABLE

AREAS UNDER THE NORMAL CURVE

Z	0	1	2	3	4	5	6	7	8	9
.0	.5000	.5040	.5080	.5120	.5160	.5199	.5239	.5279	.5319	.5359
.1	.5398	.5438	.5478	.5517	.5557	.5596	.5636	.5675	.5714	.5753
.2	.5793	.5832	.5871	.5910	.5948	.5987	.6026	.6064	.6103	.6141
.3	.6179	.6217	.6255	.6293	.6331	.6368	.6406	.6443	.6480	.6517
.4	.6554	.6591	.6628	.6664	.6700	.6736	.6772	.6808	.6844	.6879
.5	.6915	.6950	.6985	.7019	.7054	.7088	.7123	.7157	.7190	.7224
.6	.7257	.7291	.7324	.7357	.7389	.7422	.7454	.7486	.7517	.7549
.7	.7580	.7611	.7642	.7673	.7703	.7734	.7764	.7794	.7823	.7852
.8	.7881	.7910	.7939	.7967	.7995	.8023	.8051	.8078	.8106	.8133
.9	.8159	.8186	.8212	.8238	.8264	.8289	.8315	.8340	.8365	.8389
1.0	.8413	.8438	.8461	.8485	.8508	.8531	.8554	.8577	.8599	.8621
1.1	.8643	.8665	.8686	.8708	.8729	.8749	.8770	.8790	.8810	.8830
1.2	.8849	.8869	.8888	.8907	.8925	.8944	.8962	.8980	.8997	.9015
1.3	.9032	.9049	.9066	.9082	.9099	.9115	.9131	.9147	.9162	.9177
1.4	.9192	.9207	.9222	.9236	.9251	.9265	.9278	.9292	.9306	.9319
1.5	.9332	.9345	.9357	.9370	.9382	.9394	.9406	.9418	.9430	.9441
1.6	.9452	.9463	.9474	.9484	.9495	.9505	.9515	.9525	.9535	.9545
1.7	.9554	.9564	.9573	.9582	.9591	.9599	.9608	.9616	.9625	.9633
1.8	.9641	.9648	.9656	.9664	.9671	.9678	.9686	.9693	.9700	.9706
1.9	.9713	.9719	.9726	.9732	.9738	.9744	.9750	.9756	.9762	.9767
2.0	.9772	.9778	.9783	.9788	.9793	.9798	.9803	.9808	.9812	.9817
2.1	.9821	.9826	.9830	.9834	.9838	.9842	.9846	.9850	.9854	.9857
2.2	.9861	.9864	.9868	.9871	.9874	.9878	.9881	.9884	.9887	.9890
2.3	.9893	.9896	.9898	.9901	.9904	.9906	.9909	.9911	.9913	.9916
2.4	.9918	.9920	.9922	.9925	.9927	.9929	.9931	.9932	.9934	.9936
2.5	.9938	.9940	.9941	.9943	.9945	.9946	.9948	.9949	.9951	.9952
2.6	.9953	.9955	.9956	.9957	.9959	.9960	.9961	.9962	.9963	.9964
2.7	.9965	.9966	.9967	.9968	.9969	.9970	.9971	.9972	.9973	.9974
2.8	.9974	.9975	.9976	.9977	.9977	.9978	.9979	.9979	.9980	.9981
2.9	.9981	.9982	.9982	.9983	.9984	.9984	.9985	.9985	.9986	.9986
3.	.9987	.9990	.9993	.9995	.9997	.9998	.9998	.9999	.9999	1.0000

variable cost, and fixed cost—is allowed to be uncertain, the analysis is accomplished exactly as we illustrated it above. However, if they become random variables simultaneously, the analysis is complicated and reserved for a more advanced statistical text.

LEVERAGE

Leverage is that portion of the fixed costs which represents a risk to the firm. Operating leverage, a measure of operating risk, refers to the fixed operating costs found in the firm's income statement. Financial leverage, a measure of financial risk, refers to financing a portion of the firm's assets, bearing fixed financing charges in hopes of increasing the return to the common stockholders. The higher the financial leverage, the higher the financial risk, and the higher the cost of capital. Cost of capital rises because it costs more to raise funds for a risky business. Total leverage is a measure of total risk.

Operating Leverage

Operating leverage is a measure of operating risk and arises from fixed operating costs. A simple indication of operating leverage is the effect that a change in sales has on earnings. The formula is:

Operating leverage at a given level of sales (x)

$$= \frac{\text{Percentage change in EBIT}}{\text{Percentage change in sales}} = \frac{(p - v)x}{(p - v)x - FC}$$

where EBIT = earnings before interest and taxes
$$= (p - v)x - FC$$

EXAMPLE 17

The Wayne Company manufactures and sells doors to home builders. The doors are sold for $25 each. Variable costs are $15 per door, and fixed operating costs total $50,000. Assume further that the Wayne Company is currently selling 6,000 doors per year. Its operating leverage is:

$$\frac{(p - v)x}{(p - v)x - FC} = \frac{(\$25 - \$15)\,(6,000)}{(\$25 - \$15)\,(6,000) - \$50,000} = \frac{\$60,000}{10,000} = 6$$

which means if sales increase by 1%, the company can expect its net income to increase by six times that amount, or 6%.

Financial Leverage

Financial leverage is a measure of financial risk and arises from fixed financial costs. One way to measure financial leverage is to determine how earnings per share are affected by a change in EBIT (or operating income).

Financial leverage at a given level of sales (x)

$$= \frac{\text{Percentage in change in EPS}}{\text{Percentage in change in EBIT}} = \frac{(p - v)x - FC}{(p - v)x - FC - IC}$$

where EPS is earnings per share, and IC is fixed finance charges, i.e., interest expense or preferred stock dividends. [Preferred stock dividend must be adjusted for taxes, i.e., preferred stock dividend/ $(1-t)$.]

EXAMPLE 18

Using the data in Example 17, the Wayne Company has total financial charges of $2,000, half in interest expense and half in preferred stock dividend. The corporate tax rate is 40%. First, the fixed financial charges are:

$$IC = \$1,000 + \frac{\$1,000}{(1 - 0.4)} = \$1,000 + \$1,667 = \$2,667$$

Therefore, Wayne's financial leverage is computed as follows:

$$\frac{(p - v)\,x - FC}{(p - v)\,x - FC - IC} = \frac{(\$25 - \$15)\,(6,000) - \$50,000}{(\$25 - \$15)\,(6,000) - \$50,000 - \$2,667}$$

$$= \frac{\$10,000}{\$7,333} = 1.36$$

which means that if EBIT increases by 1%, Wayne can expect its EPS to increase by 1.36 times, or by 1.36%.

Total Leverage

Total leverage is a measure of total risk. The way to measure total leverage is to determine how EPS is affected by a change in sales.

$$\begin{aligned}
\text{Total leverage at a given level of sales } (X) &= \frac{\text{Percentage in change in EPS}}{\text{Percentage in change in sales}} \\
&= \text{operating leverage} \times \text{financial leverage} \\
&= \frac{(p - v)x}{(p - v)x - FC} \cdot \frac{(p - v)x - FC}{(p - v)x - FC - IC} \\
&= \frac{(p - v)x}{(p - v)x - FC - IC}
\end{aligned}$$

EXAMPLE 19

From Examples 17 and 18, the total leverage for Wayne company is:

Operating leverage x financial leverage $= 6 \times 1.36 = 8.16$

or

$$\frac{(p - v)x}{(p - v)x - FC - IC} = \frac{(\$25 - \$15)\ (6,000)}{(\$25 - \$15)\ (6,000) - \$50,000 - \$2,667}$$

$$= \frac{\$60,000}{\$7,333} = 8.18 \text{ (due to rounding error)}$$

CONCLUSION

The cost-volume-profit analysis is useful as a frame of reference for analysis, as a vehicle for expressing overall managerial performance, and as a planning device via break-even techniques and "what-if" experiments. We note the following points that highlight the analytical usefulness of CVP analysis as a tool for profit planning:

1. A change in either the selling price or the variable cost per unit alters CM or the CM Ratio and thus the break-even point.

2. As sales exceed the break-even point, a higher unit CM or CM ratio will result in greater profits than a small unit CM or CM ratio.

3. The lower the break-even sales, the less risky the business and the safer the investment, other things being equal.

4. A large margin of safety means lower operating risk since a large decrease in sales can occur before losses are suffered.

5. Using the contribution income statement model and a spreadsheet program such as Lotus 1-2-3, a variety of "what-if" planning and decision scenarios can be evaluated.

6. In a multiproduct firm, sales mix is often more important than overall market share. The emphasis on high-margin products tend to maximize overall profits of the firm.

7. If one of the variables that enter into the determination of profit is a random variable and normally distributed, we can introduce the standard statistical procedure to summarize the effect of this uncertainty on contribution margin or profit.

8. Leverage is that portion of the fixed costs which represents a risk to the firm. Operating leverage, a measure of operating risk, refers to the fixed operating costs found in the firm's income statement. CVP analysis and operating leverage are closely related. This chapter also discussed how CVP analysis can be applied to non-profit organizations with an illustrative example.

15

Contribution Margin Analysis for Short-Term and Nonroutine Decisions

Contribution margin analysis is an important tool the financial manager can use for decision making. It can be used to appraise the performance of department managers, their departments, and particular programs. When performing the manufacturing and selling functions, financial management is constantly faced with the problem of choosing between alternative courses of action. Typical questions to be answered include: What to make? How to make it? Where to sell the product? What price should be charged? In the short run, financial management is faced with many nonroutine, nonrecurring types of decisions.

CONTRIBUTION MARGIN INCOME STATEMENT

In the contribution margin approach, expenses are categorized as either fixed or variable. The variable costs are deducted from sales to obtain the contribution margin. Fixed costs are then subtracted from contribution margin to obtain net income. The contribution margin income statement looks at cost behavior. It shows the relationship between variable and fixed cost, irrespective of the functions a given cost item is associated with. This information helps the manager to (1) decide whether to drop or push a product line, (2) evaluate alternatives arising from production, special advertising, and so on, and (3) appraise performance. For instance, contribution margin analysis tells you how

305

to optimize capacity utilization, how to formulate a bid price on a contract, and whether to accept an order even if it is below the normal selling price.

The format of the contribution margin income statement appears below:

Sales

Less variable cost of sales

Manufacturing contribution margin

Less variable selling and administrative expenses

Contribution margin

Less fixed cost

Net income

The advantages of contribution margin income statement are:

- Aids in decision making, such as whether to drop or push a product line
- Aids in deciding whether to ask a selling price that is below the normal price

Tip: When idle capacity exists, an order should be accepted at below the normal selling price as long as a contribution margin is earned, since fixed cost will not change.

The disadvantages of contribution margin income statement are:

- Not accepted for financial reporting or tax purposes
- Ignores fixed overhead as a product cost
- Difficult to segregate fixed cost and variable cost

EXAMPLE 1

Assume the following information:

Selling price	$ 15
Variable manufacturing cost per unit	$ 7
Variable selling cost per unit	$ 2
Fixed manufacturing overhead	$150,000
Fixed selling and administrative expenses	$ 60,000
Sales volume	600,000
Beginning inventory	50,000 units
Ending inventory	70,000 units

Production is:

Sales	600,000
Add ending inventory	70,000
Need	670,000
Less beginning inventory	50,000
Production	620,000

Contribution margin income statement follows:

Sales (600,000 × $15)		$9,000,000
Less variable cost of sales		
Beginning inventory (50,000 × $7)	$ 350,000	
Variable cost of goods manufactured (620,000 × $7)	4,340,000	
Variable cost of goods available	$4,690,000	
Less ending inventory (70,000 × $7)	490,000	
Total variable cost of sales		4,200,000
Manufacturing contribution margin		$4,800,000
Less variable selling and administrative expenses (600,000 × $2)		1,200,000
Contribution margin		$3,600,000
Less fixed costs		
Fixed overhead	$ 150,000	
Fixed selling and administrative	60,000	
Total fixed costs		210,000
Net income		$3,390,000

RELEVANT COSTS

Not all costs are of equal importance in decision making, and managers must identify the costs that are relevant to a decision. Such costs are called relevant costs. The relevant costs are the expected future costs (and also revenues) which differ between the decision alternatives. Therefore, the sunk costs (past and historical costs) are not considered relevant in the decision at hand. What is relevant are the incremental or differential costs. The decision involves the following steps:

1. Gather all costs associated with each alternative.
2. Drop the sunk costs.
3. Drop those costs which do not differ between alternatives.
4. Select the best alternative based on the remaining cost data.

SHOULD FURTHER PROCESSING OF A PRODUCT OCCUR?

You are sometimes faced with a decision whether to process an item further. This will be done when incremental profitability occurs.

EXAMPLE 2

Product X may be sold at split-off or processed further. Relevant data follow:

Production	Sales value at Split-off	Additional Cost and Sales Value for Further Processing	
		Sales	Cost
5,000	$95,000	$120,000	$18,000
Incremental revenue ($120,000 − $95,000)			$25,000
Incremental cost			18,000
Incremental gain			$ 7,000

You should process this product further because it results in incremental earnings.

UTILIZATION OF CAPACITY

Contribution margin analysis can be used to ascertain the best way of utilizing capacity. In general, the emphasis on products with higher contribution margin maximizes the company's total net income, even though total sales may decrease. This is not true, however, where there are constraining factors and scarce resources. The constraining factor is the factor that restricts or limits the production or sale of a given product. The constraining factor may be machine hours, labor hours, or cubic feet of warehouse space. In the presence of these constraining factors, maximizing total profits depends on getting the highest contribution margin per unit of the factor (rather than the highest contribution margin per unit of product output).

EXAMPLE 3

You can make a raw metal that can either be sold at this stage or worked on further and sold as an alloy. Relevant data follow.

	Raw Metal	Alloy
Selling price	$200	$315
Variable cost	90	120

Total fixed cost is $400,000 and 100,000 hours of capacity are interchangeable between the products. There is unlimited demand for both products. Three hours are required to produce the raw metal, and five hours are needed to make the alloy.

Contribution margin per hour follows.

	Raw Metal	Alloy
Selling price	$200	$315
Less variable cost	90	120
Contribution margin	$110	$195
Hours per ton	3	5
Contribution margin per hour	$36.67	$ 39

You should sell only the alloy because it results in the highest contribution margin per hour. Fixed costs are not considered because they are constant and are incurred irrespective of which product is manufactured.

SHOULD AN ORDER BE ACCEPTED BELOW THE NORMAL SELLING PRICE?

You often receive a short-term, special order for products at lower prices than usual. In normal times, you may refuse such an order since it will not yield a satisfactory profit. If times are bad, however, such an order should be accepted if the incremental revenue obtained from it exceeds the incremental costs involved. Fixed costs are constant at idle capacity. The company is better off to receive some revenue, above its variable costs than to receive nothing at all. Such a price, one lower than the regular price, is called a *contribution price*. This approach is more appropriate under the following conditions:

- When operating in a distress situation
- When there is idle capacity
- When faced with sharp competition or in a competitive bidding situation

EXAMPLE 4

You currently sell 8,000 units at $30 per unit. Variable cost per unit is $15. Fixed costs are $60,000 (fixed cost per unit is thus $7.50; $60,000/8,000). Idle capacity exists. A potential customer is willing to purchase 500 units at $21 per unit.

You should accept this order because it increases your profitability.

Sales (500 × $21)	$10,500
Less variable costs (500 × $15)	7,500
Contribution margin	$ 3,000
Less fixed costs	0
Net income	$ 3,000

Note: If idle capacity exists, the acceptance of an additional order does not increase fixed cost. If fixed cost were to increase, say by $1,200 to buy a special tool for this job, it still is financially attractive to accept this order because a positive profit of $1,800 ($3,000 − $1,200) would arise.

EXAMPLE 5

You manufacture a product. You can produce 200,000 units per year at a total variable cost of $800,000 and a total fixed cost of $500,000. You estimate that you can sell 150,000 units at a normal selling price of $4 each. Further, a special order has been placed by a customer for 50,000 units at a 25% discount.

Your profit will rise by $50,000 due to this special order.

Variable cost per unit $= \dfrac{\$800,000}{200,000} =$ $4

Special order price 0.75 × $4 $\underline{3}$

Incremental profit per unit $\underline{\$1}$

Incremental earnings $1 × 50,000 units = $\underline{\$50,000}$

EXAMPLE 6

Financial data for your department follows:

Selling price	$15
Direct material	$ 2
Direct labor	$ 1.90
Variable overhead	$ 0.50
Fixed overhead ($100,000/20,000 units)	$ 5

Selling and administrative expenses are fixed except for sales commissions, which are 14% of the selling price. Idle capacity exists.

You receive an additional order for 1,000 units from a potential customer at a selling price of $9.

Even though the offered selling price of $9 is much less than the current selling price of $15, the order should be accepted.

Sales (1,000 × $9)	$9,000
Less variable manufacturing costs (1,000 × $4.40)*	4,400
Manufacturing contribution margin	$4,600
Less variable selling and administrative expenses (14% × $9,000)	1,260
Contribution margin	$3,340
Less fixed cost	0
Net income	$3,340

*Variable manufacturing cost = $2 + $1.90 + $0.50 = $\underline{\$4.40}$

EXAMPLE 7

You want a markup of 40% over cost on a product. Relevant data regarding the product appears below.

Direct material	$ 5,000
Direct labor	12,000
Overhead	4,000
Total cost	$21,000
Markup on cost (40%)	8,400
Selling price	$29,400

Total direct labor for the year is $1,800,000. Total overhead for the year is 30% of direct labor. The overhead consists of 25% fixed and 75% variable. A customer offers to buy the item for $23,000. There is idle capacity. You should accept the incremental order since additional profitability arises.

Selling price		$23,000
Less variable costs		
Direct material	$ 5,000	
Direct labor	12,000	
Variable overhead ($12,000 × 22.5%)*	2,700	19,700
Contribution margin		$ 3,300
Less fixed cost		0
Net income		$ 3,300

*Total overhead 0.30 × $1,800,000 = $540,000

Variable overhead = 22.5% of direct labor, computed as follows:

$$\frac{\text{Variable overhead}}{\text{Direct labor}} = \frac{0.75 \times \$540,000}{\$1,800,000} = \frac{\$405,000}{\$1,800,000} = 22.5\%$$

BID PRICE DETERMINATION

Pricing policies using contribution margin analysis may be helpful in contract negotiations for a product or service. Often such business is sought during the slack season, when it may be financially beneficial to bid on extra business at a competitive price that covers all variable costs and makes some contributions to fixed costs plus profits. A knowledge of your variable and fixed costs is necessary to make an accurate bid price determination.

EXAMPLE 8

You receive an order for 10,000 units. You wish to know the minimum bid price that will result in a $20,000 increase in profits. The current income statement follows.

Sales (50,000 units × $25)		$1,250,000
Less cost of sales		
Direct material	$120,000	
Direct labor	200,000	
Variable overhead ($200,000 × 0.30)	60,000	
Fixed overhead	100,000	480,000
Gross margin		$ 770,000
Less selling and administrative expenses		

Variable (includes freight costs of $0.40 per unit)	$ 60,000	
Fixed	30,000	90,000
Net income		$ 680,000

In the event the contract is awarded, cost patterns for the incremental order are the same except that:

- Freight costs will be borne by the customer
- Special tools of $8,000 will be required for this order and will not be reused again
- Direct labor time for each unit under the order will be 20% longer

Preliminary computations:

	Per Unit Cost
Direct material ($120,000/50,000)	$2.40
Direct labor ($200,000/50,000)	4.00
Variable selling and administrative expense ($60,000/50,000)	1.20

A forecasted income statement follows:

FORECASTED INCOME STATEMENT

	Current	Forecasted	Explanation
Units	50,000	60,000	
Sales	$1,250,000	$1,372,400	a Computed Last
Cost of Sales			
Direct material	$120,000	$144,000	($2.40 x 60,000)
Direct labor	200,000	248,000	($200,000 + [10,000 x $4.80 b])
Variable overhead	60,000	74,400	($248,000 x .30)
Fixed overhead	100,000	108,000	
Total	$480,000	$574,400	
Selling and Administrative Expenses			
Variable	$60,000	$68,000	($60,000 + [10,000 x $.80 c])
Fixed	30,000	30,000	
Total	$90,000	$98,000	
Net income	$680,000	$700,000	d

a Net income + Selling and administrative expenses + cost of sales = Sales
$700,000 + $98,000 + $574,400 = $1,372,400

b $4 x 1.2 = $4.80

c $1.20 – $.40 = $.80

d $680,000 + $20,000 = $700,000

The contract price for the 10,000 units should be $122,400 ($1,372,400 – $1,250,000), or $12.24 per unit ($122,400/10,000).

The contract price per unit of $12.24 is below the $25 current selling price per unit. Keep in mind that total fixed cost is the same except for the $8,000 expenditure on the special tool.

ADDING OR DROPPING A PRODUCT LINE

The decision whether to drop an old product line or add a new one must take into account both qualitative and quantitative factors. However, any final decision should be based primarily on the impact the decision will have on contribution margin or net income.

EXAMPLE 9

The ABC Company has three major product lines: P, M, and C. The company is considering the decision to drop the M line because the income statement shows it is being sold at a loss. Note the income statement for these product lines below:

	P	M	C	Total
Sales	$10,000	$15,000	$25,000	$50,000
Less: Variable costs	6,000	8,000	12,000	26,000
Contribution margin	$4,000	$7,000	$13,000	$24,000
Less: Fixed costs				
Direct	$2,000	$6,500	$4,000	$12,500
Allocated	1,000	1,500	2,500	5,000
Total	$3,000	$8,000	$6,500	$17,500
Net income	$1,000	($1,000)	$6,500	$6,500

Direct fixed costs are those costs that are identified directly with each of the product lines, whereas allocated fixed costs are the amount of common fixed costs allocated to the product lines using some base such as space occupied. The amount of common fixed costs typically continues regardless of the decision and thus cannot be saved by dropping the product line to which it is distributed.

If product M is dropped, we have the following:

Sales revenue lost		$15,000
Gains:		
Variable cost avoided	$8,000	
Direct fixed costs avoided	6,500	14,500
Increase (decrease) in net income		$ (500)

By dropping product M the company will lose an additional $500. Therefore, the M product line should be kept. One of the great dangers in allocating common fixed costs is that such allocations can make a product line look less profitable than it really is. Because of such an allocation, the

M product line showed a loss of $1,000, but in effect contributes $500 ($7,000 - $6,500) to the recovery of the company's common fixed costs.

THE MAKE-OR-BUY DECISION

The decision whether to produce a component part internally or to buy it externally from an outside supplier may have to be made. This decision involves both quantitative and qualitative factors. The qualitative factors include ensuring product quality and the necessity for long-run business relationships with the supplier. The quantitative factors deal with cost. The quantitative effects of the make-or-buy decision are best seen through the relevant cost approach.

EXAMPLE 10

Assume that your company has prepared the following cost estimates for the manufacture of a subassembly component based on an annual production of 8,000 units:

	Per Unit	Total
Direct materials	$ 5	$ 40,000
Direct labor	4	32,000
Variable factory overhead applied	4	32,000
Fixed factory overhead applied (150% of direct labor cost)	6	48,000
Total cost	$19	$152,000

The supplier has offered to provide the subassembly at a price of $16 each. Two thirds of fixed factory overhead which represents executive salaries, rent, depreciation, and taxes, continue regardless of the decision. Should your company buy or make the product?

The key to the decision lies in the investigation of those relevant costs that change between the make-or-buy alternatives. Assuming that the productive capacity will be idle if not used to produce the subassembly, the analysis takes the following form:

Schedule of Make-or-Buy

	Per Unit		Total of 8,000 Units	
	Make	Buy	Make	Buy
Purchase price		$16		$128,000
Direct materials	$5		$40,000	
Direct labor	4		32,000	
Variable overhead	4		32,000	
Fixed overhead that can be avoided by not making	2		16,000	
	$15	$16	$120,000	$128,000
Difference in favor of making	$1		$8,000	

The make-or-buy decision must be investigated, along with the broader perspective of considering how best to utilize available facilities. The alternatives are:

- Leaving facilities idle
- Buying the parts and renting out idle facilities
- Buying the parts and using idle facilities for other products

DESIRE TO MAINTAIN SOME PROFIT WITH LOWER SALES BASE

Contribution margin analysis assists in determining how to derive the same profit as last year even though there is a drop in sales volume.

EXAMPLE 11

In 19X1, sales volume was 200,000 units, selling price was $25, variable cost per unit was $15, and fixed cost was $500,000.

In 19X2, sales volume is expected to total 150,000 units. As a result, fixed costs have been slashed by $80,000. On 4/1/X2, 40,000 units have already been sold. You wish to compute the contribution margin that has to be earned on the remaining units for 19X2.

Net income computation for 19X1:

$$S = FC + VC + P$$
$$\$25 \times 200,000 = \$500,000 + (\$15 \times 200,000) + P$$
$$\$1,500,000 = P$$

Contribution margin to be earned in 19X2:

Total fixed cost ($500,000 − $80,000)	$ 420,000
Net income	1,500,000
Contribution margin needed for year	$1,920,000
Contribution margin already earned: (Selling price − variable cost) × units ($25 − $15) = $10 × 40,000 units	400,000
Contribution margin remaining	$1,520,000

$$\frac{\text{Contribution margin}}{\text{per unit needed}} = \frac{\text{Contribution margin remaining}}{\text{Units remaining}}$$

$$= \frac{\$1,520,000}{110,000} = \$13.82$$

CONCLUSION

Contribution margin analysis aids you in making sound departmental decisions. Is an order worth accepting even though it is below the normal selling price? Which products should be emphasized? What should the price of your product or service be? What should the bid price be on a contract? Is a proposed agreement advantageous? What is your incremental profitability? What is the best way of using departmental capacity and resources?

In some cases, your bonus may be based on the contribution margin you earn for your department. Thus, an understanding of the computation of contribution margin is necessary.

16

Cost Allocation

One important aspect of controllership and financial management deals with the problem of allocating costs to various parts (segments) of an organization. The segment can be products, divisions, departments, or sales territories. Cost allocation (assignment) is necessary to provide useful data for the following purposes: (1) product costing and establishment of selling price; (2) evaluation of managerial performance and control; and (3) making special decisions.

ASPECTS OF COST ALLOCATION

There are basically three aspects of cost allocation: (1) choosing the object of costing. A cost objective is an activity for which a separate measure of cost is needed. Examples are departments, products, processes, jobs, contracts, customers, and sales territories; (2) choosing and accumulating the costs that relate to the object of costing. Examples are manufacturing expenses, selling and administrative expenses, joint costs, common costs, service department costs, and fixed costs; and (3) choosing a method of identifying (2) with (1). For example, a cost allocation base for allocating manufacturing costs would typically be labor hours, machine hours, or production units.

The allocation of revenues and variable costs are typically straightforward because they are directly traceable to a specific segment of activity. Direct costs are directly chargeable to the product or territory. Semidirect costs (e.g., advertising) cover several products. Indirect costs are not directly identified and thus must be allocated to the cost objective on a logical basis, such as allocating rent based on square footage in a department.

COST ALLOCATION GUIDELINES

Cost accumulation determines actual cost by program, cost center, or account number for accounting and planning purposes.

Cost allocation assigns a common cost to two or more departments or products. The costs are allocated in proportion to the relative responsibility for their incurrence. While allocation methods are arbitrary, some allocation plans make more sense than others. Possible allocation bases include units produced, direct labor cost, direct labor hours, machine hours, number of employees, floor space, and replacement cost of equipment.

The guiding criteria in choosing proper allocation bases follow:

- *Benefits Obtained.* Costs are allocated based on benefits received. Corporate advertising may be allocated, for example, based on divisional sales. The higher the sales, the more the benefit received from the advertising. Heating can be allocated to user departments based on space occupied. Although the management of the user department does not control heating cost, his or her department must have heat to operate.

- *Equity.* Costs are allocated based on fairness. The "equity basis" is often used in government contracting to come up with a mutually agreeable price.

- *Cause-Effect Relationship.* Costs are allocated based on services provided. It is easy to formulate this relationship when dealing with direct manufacturing costs (e.g., direct material, direct labor). Relationships aid in relating the cost objective to the cost incurred. A preferable relationship assists in predicting changes in total costs.

- *Ability to Bear.* Costs are allocated based on the cost objective's ability to bear. An example is allocating corporate executive salaries based on divisional profitability. It is assumed that a more profitable division can absorb more costs.

The National Association of Accountants favors the allocation of centralized costs only if they satisfy one or more of the following four criteria:[1]

1. The costs can be influenced by a division manager's actions, even if just indirectly;

2. The costs reflect the amount of resources that headquarters gives as divisional support;

3. The allocated costs enhance comparabiity of the division's performance with that of an independent firm that incurs such costs directly; or

4. The costs are the basis for pricing decisions.

---

[1]National Association of Accountants, *Statement of Management Accounting No. 4B*, "Allocation of Service and Administrative Costs" June 13, 1985, paragraph 20.

Besides using the most representative basis, other considerations in selecting a basis are cost-benefit, ease of use, and what is commonly done in the industry.

An equitable basis should be selected to allocate common costs among divisions, products, territories, and so on. If no demonstrable relationship exists between a cost and benefit, guidelines for allocation may include:

- Cost Accounting Standards Board guidelines of allocating costs to cost objectives
- Scatter charts may be used to measure an activity and related costs

Tip: A factor that acts as a sound measure of activity in controlling cost is often a good basis to allocate that cost.

- Time studies and job analyses of specific employee activities may give insight into the factors affecting costs and the relationship to individual segment activities
- Searching inquiries as to the factors bearing upon the costs of the function

Allocation techniques favored by the Cost Accounting Standards Board (CASB) are:

1. Activity measure of the cause of the pool of cost, such as labor hours, machine hours, or space occupied
2. Measure of the functions output, such as number of purchase orders processed
3. Measure of activity based on service received, such as number of employees served by personnel

Beware: Sales dollars is typically a poor allocation base because sales vary each period while allocated costs are usually fixed in nature. The use of a variable base to allocate costs may result in inequity between departments because the costs being allocated to one department depends largely on what occurs in another department. For instance, less selling effort in one department will move more allocated costs into another more productive department. **Recommendation**: Sales dollars should only be used as a basis of allocation when a direct causal relationship exists between sales dollars and the allocated service department costs.

Cost Accounting Standard (CAS) No. 418 applies to cost allocation methods used by government contractors. It states that indirect costs should be allocated to cost objectives in a "reasonable proportion to the beneficial or causal relationship of the pooled costs to cost objective."

A segment should be allocated the fixed costs that the company could save if it were to withdraw from that segment.

Material should be used as an allocation basis when overhead is closely related to the value of that material.

Because most administrative expenses are budgeted as fixed for a budget period, adequate accuracy is accomplished in reporting when budgeted rather than actual costs are allocated to product lines. Some administrative expenses may be allocated directly to products, others to factories, and others to sales divisions.

Fringe benefits should be allocated based on the percentage of related total salary. A refinement may be to allocate some fringe-related costs (e.g., pension plan, payroll taxes) based on salaries with the other (e.g., dental insurance) based on number of employees.

Divisions would require financing if they were separate entities so the company may charge them an allocable fee for that service. The fee may be a percentage of revenue, total divisional assets, or other reasonable basis.

CAUTIONS WITH COST ALLOCATION

Arbitrary cost allocations should not be made because they may lead to wrong decisions. However, such allocations may be used with care under certain circumstances as follows:

- The arbitrary allocation is done so that employees will act in a certain desired way according to upper management preferences. For example, central R&D costs may be charged to a division so the manager becomes interested in helping central research efforts.

- A retainer-fee should be charged for essential services such as legal or internal auditing so the user department is motivated to use the important service even though it may not feel it necessary. If the manager is being charged for the service, why not use it?

ALLOCATION OF SERVICE DEPARTMENT COSTS
TO PRODUCTION DEPARTMENTS

There are two basic types of departments in a manufacturing company: production departments and service departments. A production department (such as assembly and machining) is where the production or conversion occurs. A service department (such as engineering and maintenance) provides support to production departments.

Before developing departmental overhead rates for product costing, service department costs must first be assigned to production departments.

In allocating service department costs, there are two general approaches that may be followed comprising of:

1. *Single-Rate Method.* Departmental costs are accumulated into a single-cost pool. There is no distinction between variable costs and fixed costs.

2. *Dual-Rate Method.* Departmental costs are accumulated into two or more cost pools. One pool may be the fixed costs while the other pool may be the variable costs.

Service costs (e.g., computer services, accounting and legal, printing, management consulting) should preferably be allocated based on usage, such as through a competitive hourly rate charged by outsiders.

An allocation base, once chosen, typically remains unchanged for a long time period because it represents a major policy. It is usually only reviewed infrequently or when an inequity is evident.

The allocation base should be straight-forward because complexity may result in the computational cost and time exceeding the benefits to be derived. Further, clearness is needed so that managers can easily understand the allocation formulas and rationale.

Other than product costing, the reasons to allocate service department costs include:

- Accomplish control and aid in efficiency evaluation

- Result in superior income and asset measurement for external parties

- Remind production department managers of the existence of indirect costs they have to absorb. Users benefit from service department costs and should have to pay for them! Without allocation, there is an understatement in the full costs of the operating center. Managers being charged for service department costs will make sure that managers in the service departments are properly controlling those costs.

- Have department managers use services wisely. If the service department costs were not allocated, production managers would perhaps overuse what they consider to be as "free" services. For instance, without allocating computer service time, user managers would inefficiently use computer time because they are not paying for it. If a service is underused, allocating the costs for such services would prompt managers to utilize the service to a greater extent.

- Accomplish a basis for cost justification or reimbursement. An example of cost justification is to derive an "equitable" price, such as when a defense contractor wants to obtain cost reimbursement.

Note: Although most service departments are cost centers generating no revenue, a few may in fact obtain some revenues (e.g., cafeteria). In such a case, the revenues should be netted against the costs, and the net cost should be allocated to other departments. In this way, the other departments do not have to absorb costs that the service department has already been reimbursed for.

There are three basic methods of allocating service department costs to production departments. They are:

(1) Direct allocation method

(2) Step down method

(3) Reciprocal service method

These methods are discussed in Chapter 11.

Variable Costs Versus Fixed Costs

Generally, variable costs should be charged to user departments using the activity base for the incurrence of the cost involved. For example, variable costs of the maintenance department should be charged to production departments based on machine hours. Thus, departments responsible for the incurrence of service costs must bear them in proportion to actual usage of services.

The fixed costs of service departments constitute the cost of having long-run service capacity available. An equitable allocation basis for the consuming departments is predetermined lump-sum amounts. Predetermined lump-sums represent amounts to be charged to consuming departments that have been determined in advance and will be the same each period. Usually, the lump-sum amount charged to a department is based either on the department's peak-period or long-term average servicing needs. Budgeted fixed costs, not actual fixed costs, should be allocated.

Budgeted service department costs are allocated to production departments at the beginning of the period in order to derive the production department's predetermined overhead application rate.

During the accounting period, actual service department costs are allocated to production departments. Thus, a comparison can be made at the end of the reporting period between budgeted costs and actual costs. The allocation of service department costs to production departments is essentially an imposed form of transfer pricing.

Often, we have multistage allocations where service departments serve each other and production departments. Complex interrelationships may therefore arise. In a simple relationship, management is costing a product requiring two hours of machine time in product department C. Department C utilizes Department A's services, which in turn need the services of Department B. Hence, we may allocate part of B's cost to A and a part of A's cost to C so that A and B costs are proportionately included in the cost of product Z. This relationship may be depicted in Exhibit 1. With this approach, the unit cost of a department's output includes direct labor of that department, part of the costs of departments furnishing the services, and part of the untraceable costs of the entire factory. Of course, the output may either be in volume of the product or service.

Exhibit 1

COST ALLOCATION SEQUENCE

When it is impractical to distinguish between variable costs and fixed costs of a service department, departmental costs should be allocated to consuming departments according to the base reflecting the optimal measure of benefits received. In general, all service department costs incurred to perform specific services to operating departments should be allocated. The allocated costs are used in determining overhead rates and measuring profitability.

Exhibit 1

COST ALLOCATION SEQUENCE

Initial Cost Allocation — Untraceable Costs → Service Department B, Other Departments

Second Cost Allocation — Service Department B → Service Department A, Other Departments

Third Cost Allocation — Service Department A → Production Department C, Other Departments

Cost Application — Production Department C → Product Z, Other Departments

Cost Pools and Allocation Bases

A cost pool is homogeneous when the activity whose costs are included have a similar cause-effect relationship to the cost objective as other activities whose costs are included in the cost pool. Exhibit 2 presents corporate head-quarter cost pools.

Exhibit 2

CORPORATE HEADQUARTER COST POOLS

Department	Allocation Basis
Payroll	Number of employees or dollar salaries
Personnel	Number of employees
Purchasing	Dollar amount of purchases
Accounts Payable	Number of vendor invoices paid
Internal Audit	Audit time reports
Central Cost and Budget	Dollar of factory cost and selling expenses
Traffic	Number of freight bills
Central Stenographic	Hours spent or number of pages typed
Marketing	Sales
Laundry	Pounds of laundry or number of items processed
Cafeteria	Number of employees
Medical Facilities	Number of employees or hours spent
Custodial Services (building and grounds)	Square footage occupied
Engineering	Periodic evaluation of services rendered or direct labor hours
Production Planning and Control	Periodic evaluation of services performed or direct labor hours
Receiving and Shipping	Volume handled, number of requisition and issue slips, or square footage occupied
Factory Administration	Labor hours
Bookkeeping	Number of sales invoices or lines per invoice for each product
Accounting	Volume of transactions or labor hours
Tax	Dollar of tax paid
Legal	Research hours for particular case
Tabulating	Number of punched cards processed
Property	Cost of fixed assets
Credit	Number of accounts in division
Billing	Number of invoices

Accounts Receivable	Number of customer accounts or number of postings to customer accounts
Treasury	Identifiable assets

Exhibit 3 presents cost items and the basis for their allocation.

Exhibit 3

COMMON BASES OF COST ALLOCATION

Cost	Allocation Basis
Plant management (including area management and general supervisor)	Number of plants or number of hourly employees
Heat and light (energy)	Square footage
Depreciation on building	Square footage
Maintenance and repairs in building	Square footage
Rent	Square footage
Property taxes	Square footage
Insurance	Square footage
Taxes and insurance on equipment	Book value of equipment
Laboratory	Number of jobs performed or time spent on jobs
Power	Horsepower of equipment
Inspection	Number of units inspected
Maintenance and repairs for machinery and equipment	Machine hours or value of equipment
Plant superintendent	Direct labor dollars
Credit and collection	Sales value of products
Administrative expenses	Sales value of products or the number of orders received for each product
Corporate executive salaries	Sales
Office space	Square footage
Corporate income taxes	Determinants of taxable income

EXAMPLE 1

ABC Company produces inexpensive merchandise. The three production departments are molding, filing, and packing. There are two service departments—administration and maintenance. The direct factory costs of these cost centers follow:

| | ← Service Departments → | | ← Production Departments → | | |
	Administration	Maintenance	Molding	Filing	Packing
Materials		$500	$4,000	$10,000	$6,000
Salaries	$8,000	4,000	7,000	6,000	9,000
Depreciation	200	800	3,000	2,000	200
Rent	14,000				
Power	1,500				
Other	4,000	700	2,000	3,000	1,000
Total	$27,700	$6,000	$16,000	$21,000	$16,200

Material costs in a cost center are proportional to volume. Salaries are 10% fixed and 90% variable with volume in the production centers, and 100% fixed in the service centers. Depreciation is fixed. Power is 70% fixed and 30% variable. Other costs are 75% fixed and 25% variable in factory administration, and 50% fixed and 50% variable in the other cost centers. Six thousand units were manufactured.

The variable cost per unit is computed below:

	Administration	Maintenance	Molding	Filing	Packing
Materials		$500	$4,000	$10,000	$6,000
Salaries			6,300	5,400	8,100
Power	$450				
Other	1,000	350	1,000	1,500	500
Total	$1,450	$850	$11,300	$16,900	$14,600
Variable cost per unit	$.24 @	$.14	$1.88	$2.82	$2.43

@ $1,450/6,000 = $.24

EXAMPLE 2

XYZ Company has three divisions operating as profit centers and three central administrative departments operating as service centers. Data for the three profit centers follow:

	Western Division	Central Division	Eastern Division	Total
Sales	$3,000,000	$6,000,000	$4,000,000	$13,000,000
Profit Contribution	400,000	1,800,000	1,000,000	3,200,000
Investment	2,000,000	3,000,000	1,000,000	6,000,000
Number of employees	1,000	2,000	1,500	4,500

The operating costs of the administrative departments follow:

Accounting	$400,000
Marketing	200,000
Executive offices	300,000

The allocation bases are:

Accounting—number of employees
Marketing—Sales
Executive offices—investment

The income before tax for each division follows:

	Western Division	Central Division	Eastern Division
Profit contribution	$400,000	$1,800,000	$1,000,000
Allocations:			
Accounting $400,000	$ 88,888 [a]	$ 177,778	$ 133,333
Marketing $200,000	46,154 [b]	92,308	61,538
Executive offices $300,000	100,000 [c]	150,000	50,000
Total	$235,042	$420,086	$ 244,871
Income before tax	$164,958	$1,379,914	$ 755,129

[a] $400,000 × $\dfrac{1,000}{4,500}$ = $88,888

[b] $200,000 × $\dfrac{\$3,000,000}{\$13,000,000}$ = $46,154

[c] $300,000 × $\dfrac{\$2,000,000}{\$6,000,000}$ = $100,000

SEGMENTAL REPORTING AND THE CONTRIBUTION APPROACH TO COST ALLOCATION

A segment is any part or activity of the entity that the managerial accountant seeks to obtain cost data about.

Cost allocation is an important issue in managerial accounting for segmental reporting purposes. Segmental reporting is the process of reporting activities of various segments of an organization such as divisions, product lines, or sales territories. Segmental information is useful for many purposes. Some product lines may be profitable while others are not. Some sales territories may have a poor sales mix and not taking advantage of opportunities. Some salespersons may be doing a good job while others are not. Some production divisions may not be properly utilizing their resources. These are just some examples of the usefulness of segmental reporting. Segmental reports may be prepared for activity at different levels of the business and in varying formats depending on the needs of the managerial accountant.

The contribution approach is valuable for segmental reporting because it emphasizes the cost behavior patterns and the controllability of costs that are generally useful for evaluating performance and making decisions. To be specific, the contribution approach to cost allocation is based on the following:

1. Fixed costs are much less controllable than variable costs.

2. Direct fixed costs and common fixed costs must be clearly distinguished. Direct fixed costs are those fixed costs which can be identified directly with a particular segment of an organization, whereas common fixed costs are those costs which cannot be identified directly with a particular segment.

3. Common fixed costs should be clearly identified as unallocated in the contribution income statement by segments. Any attempt to allocate these types of costs, on some arbitrary basis, to the segments of the organization would simply destroy the value of responsibility accounting. It would lead to unfair evaluation of performance and misleading managerial decisions.

Figure 1 presents a contribution margin income statement by division with a further breakdown into product lines.

DISTRIBUTION COSTS

Distribution cost analysis aids in planning sales effort. Distribution costs relate to the distribution of the product to the customer. They include the costs of storing, handling, packaging, advertising and promotion, selling, transportation (shipping costs to the customer and paying for the delivery of returned goods), and market research. Some companies include credit and administrative costs. Distribution costs may be analyzed by product, department, branch, territory, class of customer, distribution outlet, and method of sale. Distribution costs are typically controllable by the marketing and sales department.

Distribution cost standards may be set jointly by the sales executives and the controller. Distribution cost standards may be either (1) general applicable to overall distribution functions as a whole or by major division, or (2) units that measure individual performance. Some illustrative standards that may be used for distribution costs include cost per sales order, cost per customer account, cost per call, cost per mile traveled, cost per day, cost per dollar of gross profit, selling expense as a percent of net sales, and selling expense per unit sold.

Distribution cost data may be analyzed in terms of number of new customers obtained, number of miles or days a salesperson travels, number of sales demonstrations, number of trucking miles, volume of goods handled in warehouse, and number of shipments handled.

Unlike manufacturing where there is typically only one standard cost for a

FIGURE 1
Contribution Margin Income Statement By Segments

	Entire Company	Divisional Breakdown Division X	Divisional Breakdown Division Y	Breakdown of Division Y Unallocable	Breakdown of Division Y Product 1	Breakdown of Division Y Product 2	Product 3	Product 4
Sales	$1,200	$300	$900		$300	$100	$200	$300
Variable Manufacturing cost of Sales	700	200	500		100	50	100	250
Manufacturing contribution margin	$500	$100	$400		$200	$50	$100	$50
Variable selling and administrative costs	200	50	150		40	40	40	30
Contribution margin	$300	$50	$250		$160	$10	$60	$20
Controllable fixed costs by segment managers	180	40	140	$40	30	5	50	15
Contribution controllable by segment managers	$120	$10	$110	$(40)	$130	$5	$10	$5
Fixed costs controllable by others	70	6	64	20	20	15	5	4
Segmental contribution	$50	$4	$46	$(60)	$110	$(10)	$5	$1
Unallocated costs	23							
Net income	$27							

*only those costs logically traceable to a product line should be allocated.

329

product, many standard costs exist for distribution of the same item. For example, the cost per call may vary by territory. Further, even in one territory the standard cost to sell may vary depending on the class of customers. Standards will vary because of different distribution channels, products, departments, territories, and customer classes. The conditions in each are not the same.

Distribution costs may be analyzed by size of order. Costs are segregated by factor of variability. Some costs will be recognized as fixed for all order sizes while other costs may vary depending on volume (e.g., money volume, physical volume).

While many distribution costs may be allocated based on sales, some distribution costs vary with factors other than sales volume itself, such as weight.

When distribution costs are to be prorated and determined based on products or territories, the predetermined distribution cost rate should be based on estimated sales by products or territories. The manager must establish standards for the activities of order getting and order filling.

When distribution costs are determined based on customers, costs should be allocated based on the amount of services received by each customer. This information will also help in determining which customers are entitled to price concessions and discounts.

The allocation of distribution expenses may be based on the credit terms associated with sales such as based on cash sales, credit sales, and installment sales.

Marketing costs may be evaluated based on distribution methods such as direct selling to retailers and wholesalers as well as mail order sales.

Allocation of Costs to Products

In allocating distribution costs to products, some guidelines that may be used are:

- Actual costs may be allocted based on actual activity.
- Budgeted costs may be allocated based on budgeted activity.
- Budgeted costs may be used because distribution costs for product lines are typically fixed and do not significantly change from actual costs. At the end of the year, the variance between budgeted and actual may be allocated to the product lines.
- Sales-effort costs (e.g., advertising samples) may be allocated on planned activity while sales-service costs may be allocated based on actual activity. For example, when salespeople are required to report their time by product line their salaries and related expenses should be allocated on this basis.

Recommendation: The above approaches will typically provide better product line costs than the generally used method of allocating total distribution costs on actual sales dollars or units.

Exhibit 4 presents different distribution costs and how they may be allocated to product lines.

Exhibit 4

DISTRIBUTION COSTS AND ALLOCATION BASES TO PRODUCTS

Distribution Cost	Allocation Basis
Warehousing	Units or tonnage handled
Sales-service costs	Orders and invoices for each product
Direct selling costs (salespersons' salaries, commissions, and bonuses as well as sales or branch office expenses)	Sales value of product
Samples	Specific cost of each product sample
General corporate advertising	Sales value of products
Direct product advertising, newspaper, magazine, and direct mail	Directly to product being advertised
Shipping department sales and supplies	Sales value of each product or relative weight of product sales
Delivery expenses	Size of product weighted by quantity sold

In determining the amount of sales office expense assigned by dollar of sale groupings (e.g., sales less than $10,000, sales between $10,000 and $20,000, and so on), the managerial accountant should consider the cost of taking an order, entering the order, billings, and accounting for the sale.

In evaluating a product line, consideration should be given to profitabiity, growth, competition, and capital employed. Accurate cost information aids in determining whether to drop unprofitable products or substantially raising prices.

The purpose of allocating departmental overhead costs to products is similar to the purpose of allocating service department costs to production departments. We want a "fair share" of departmental overhead assigned to each product manufactured in the department.

An economic decision to allocate resources may have to be made, such as the allocation of capacity among products. This is especially important in the case of introducing a new product line.

When specific products have associated with them a greater portion of indirect costs, it may be preferable to allocate indirect costs to product lines. This approach may be feasible in pricing, and decisions whether to continue producing a product based on profit margins.

Caution: Be careful in allocating a cost to a specific product because an inappropriate allocation may make a profitable product look bad, and vice versa.

Exhibit 5 shows the contribution of a company's product lines to the total.

EXHIBIT 5

CONTRIBUTION BY PRODUCTS

	Entire Company	Product A	Product B
Projected sales	$100,000	$60,000	$40,000
Variable costs			
Goods sold	$30,000	$10,000	$20,000
Marketing	5,000	4,000	1,000
Total variable costs	$35,000	$14,000	$21,000
Contribution margin	$65,000	$46,000	$19,000
Direct fixed costs			
Production	$4,000	$2,000	$2,000
Marketing	3,000	2,000	1,000
Total direct fixed costs	$7,000	$4,000	$3,000
Profit contribution	$58,000	$42,000	$16,000
Common fixed costs			
Production	$10,000		
Marketing	8,000		
Administrative and general	5,000		
Total common costs	$23,000		
Income before tax	$35,000		

You should determine if the company is making money on a particular account. Customer classes may be analyzed in terms of geographic location, type of agent (i.e., wholesaler, retailer), call frequency, annual volume of business, order size, and credit rating.

An illustrative profit and loss statement by customer class is presented in Exhibit 6.

EXAMPLE 3

The Justa Corporation produces and sells three products. The three products, A, B, and C, are sold in a local market and in a regional market. At

EXHIBIT 6

PROFIT AND LOSS STATEMENT BY CUSTOMER CLASS

	Total Sales		Retail Sales		Mail Order Sales	
	Amount	Percent of Sales	Amount	Percent of Sales	Amount	Percent of Sales

Gross sales

Less: Sales discount and returns

Net sales

Less: Cost of sales

Gross profit

Less: Direct customer distribution
   costs

Profit after direct distribution
   costs

Indirect customer distribution
   costs

Net profit after distribution
   costs

the end of the first quarter of the current year, the following income statement has been prepared:

	Total	Local	Regional
Sales	$1,300,000	$1,000,000	$300,000
Cost of goods sold	1,010,000	775,000	235,000
Gross margin	$ 290,000	$ 225,000	$ 65,000
Selling expenses	$ 105,000	$ 60,000	$ 45,000
Administrative expenses	52,000	40,000	12,000
Total	$ 157,000	$ 100,000	$ 57,000
Net Income	$ 133,000	$ 125,000	$ 8,000

Management has expressed special concern with the regional market because of the extremely poor return on sales. This market was entered a year ago because of excess capacity. It was originally believed that the return on sales would improve with time, but after a year no noticeable improvement can be seen from the results as reported in the above quarterly statement.

In attempting to decide whether to eliminate the regional market, the following information has been gathered:

Products

	A	B	C
Sales	$500,000	$400,000	$400,000
Variable manufacturing expenses as a percentage of sales	60%	70%	60%
Variable selling expenses as a percentage of sales	3%	2%	2%

Sales by Markets

Product	Local	Regional
A	$400,000	$100,000
B	300,000	100,000
C	300,000	100,000

All administrative expenses and fixed manufacturing expenses are common to the three products and the two markets and are fixed for the period. Remaining selling expenses are fixed for the period and separable by market. All fixed expenses are based upon a prorated yearly amount.

1. Prepare the quarterly income statement showing contribution margins by markets.

2. Assuming there are no alternative uses for the Justa Corporation's present capacity, would you recommend dropping the regional market? Why or why not?

3. Prepare the quarterly income statement showing contribution margins by products.

4. It is believed that a new product can be ready for sale next year if the Justa Corporation decides to go ahead with continued research. The new product can be produced by simply converting equipment presently used in producing product C. This conversion will increase fixed costs by $10,000 per quarter. What must be the minimum contribution margin per quarter for the new product to make the change-over financially feasible?

(CMA, adapted)

1.

JUSTA CORPORATION
Quarterly Income Statement

	Total	Local	Regional
Sales	$1,300,000	$1,000,000	$300,000
Variable Expenses:			
Manufacturing (Schedule A)	$ 820,000	$ 630,000	$190,000
Selling (Schedule B)	31,000	24,000	7,000
Total Variable Expenses	$ 851,000	$ 654,000	$197,000
Contribution Margin	$ 449,000	$ 346,000	$103,000
Separable Fixed Selling Expenses	74,000	36,000	38,000
Net Market Contributions	$ 375,000	$ 310,000	$ 65,000
Common Fixed Expenses:			
Manufacturing	$ 190,000		
Administrative	52,000		
Total Common Fixed Expenses	$ 242,000		
Net Income	$ 133,000		

Schedule A—Variable Manufacturing Expenses

(1)	(2)	(3)	(4) Local— Variable Expenses $(2) \times (3)$	(5)	(6) Regional Variable Expenses $(2) \times (5)$	(7) Total Variable Expenses $(4) + (6)$
Product	%	Local Sales		Regional Sales		
A	60	$400,000	$240,000	$100,000	$ 60,000	$300,000
B	70	300,000	210,000	100,000	70,000	280,000
C	60	300,000	180,000	100,000	60,000	240,000
Totals			$630,000		$190,000	$820,000

Schedule B—Variable Selling Expenses

A	3	$400,000	$ 12,000	$100,000	$ 3,000	$ 15,000
B	2	300,000	6,000	100,000	2,000	8,000
C	2	300,000	6,000	100,000	2,000	8,000
Totals			$ 24,000		$ 7,000	$ 31,000

Separable fixed selling expense computation:

	Local	Regional
Total selling expense	$60,000	$45,000
Less: Variable (Schedule B)	24,000	7,000
Fixed selling expense	$36,000	$38,000

2. The answer is no; The regional market should not be dropped. The regional market sales are adequate to cover variable expenses and separable fixed expenses of the regional market and contribute $65,000 toward the recovery of the $242,000 common fixed expenses and net income.

If the regional market is dropped, the local market contribution margin must absorb its separable fixed selling expenses plus all common fixed expenses, as shown below:

Contribution margin	$346,000
Separable fixed selling expenses	36,000
Net market contribution	$310,000
Total common fixed expenses	242,000
Net income	$ 68,000

The corporation net income thus declines from $133,000 to $68,000. This $65,000 is the amount of the contribution loss from the regional market.

3.

JUSTA CORPORATION

Quarterly Income Statement

	Total	Product A	Product B	Product C
Sales	$1,300,000	$500,000	$400,000	$400,000
Variable Expenses:				
Manufacturing (Schedule A)	$ 820,000	$300,000	$280,000	$240,000
Selling (Schedule B)	31,000	15,000	8,000	8,000
Total Variable Expenses	$ 851,000	$315,000	$288,000	$248,000
Contribution Margin	$ 449,000	$185,000	$112,000	$152,000
Fixed Expenses:				
Manufacturing	$ 190,000			
Selling	74,000			
Administrative	52,000			
Total Fixed Expenses	$ 316,000			
Net Income	$ 133,000			

4. When the new product replaces product C, the minimum contribution margin per quarter must be at least $162,000 (the present contribution margin of product C + $10,000 of new fixed expenses) in order for Justa Corporation to be no worse off financially than it is currently. This contribution margin will still provide a net income of $133,000.

EXHIBIT 7

CONTRIBUTION BY SALES TERRITORY
(000 omitted)

	Company		Sales Territories					
			Eastern		Central		Western	
	Amount	Percent	Amount	Percent	Amount	Percent	Amount	Percent
Net sales	$6,000	100	$3,000	100	$2,000	100	$1,000	100
Variable cost of sales								
Production	$1,000	17	$ 300	10	$ 500	25	$ 200	20
Marketing	500	8	400	13	50	3	50	5
Total Variable cost of sales	$1,500	25	700	23	$ 550	27	$ 250	25
Contribution margin	$4,500	75	$2,300	77	$1,450	72	$ 750	75
District territory costs								
Advertising and promotion	$ 600	10	$ 300	10	$ 200	10	$ 100	10
District sales office	400	7	200	7	100	5	100	10
Travel and entertainment	800	13	400	13	350	18	50	5
Total direct territory costs	$ 1,800	30	$ 900	30	$ 650	33	$ 250	25
Territory Contribution	$2,700	45	$1,400	47	$ 800	39	$ 750	75
Common fixed costs								
Production	$ 600	10						
Marketing	400	7						
General and administrative	200	3						
Total common fixed costs	$ 1,200	20						
Net income	$ 1,500	25						

Allocation of Costs to Territories

Distribution costs should be analyzed by territories since each territory may have its own particular characteristics. For example, the cost to sell in a populated area such as California is different than to sell in a densely populated area such as Texas.

In allocating costs by territory, the following guidelines exist:

Cost	Allocation Base
Salesperson's wages and expenses	Hours spent in each territory
Billing and office expenses	Number of billing items or direct charge
Advertising	Territory covered by media
Transportation	Direct or based on mileage
Credit and collection	Number of customer accounts or sales dollars in territory

Exhibit 7 reveals the contribution of a company's sales territories to overall profits.

CONCLUSION

Costs may be allocated to divisions, products, contracts, customers, territories, or any other logical cost objective. Many allocation methods may be used such as by benefits received, equity, and cause-effect. Proper allocation is needed to derive accurate cost figures for product costing, pricing, control, and decision making purposes.

In appraising the distribution effort, consideration should be given to number of calls on existing and new customers, number of deliveries, and number of samples distributed.

17

Budgeting and Financial Modeling

A comprehensive (master) budget is a formal statement of management's expectation regarding sales, expenses, volume, and other financial transactions of an organization for the coming period. Simply put, a budget is a set of pro forma (projected or planned) financial statements. It consists basically of a pro forma income statement, pro forma balance sheet, and cash budget.

A budget is a tool for both planning and control. At the beginning of the period, the budget is a plan or standard; at the end of the period it serves as a control device to help management measure its performance against the plan so that future performance may be improved.

It is important to realize that with the aid of computer technology, budgeting can be used as an effective device for evaluation of "what-if" scenarios. This way management should be able to move toward finding the best course of action among various alternatives through simulation. If management does not like what they see on the budgeted financial statements in terms of various financial ratios such as liquidity, activity (turnover), leverage, profit margin, and market value ratios, they can always alter their contemplated decision and planning set.

The budget is classified broadly into two categories:

1. Operating budget, reflecting the results of operating decisions
2. Financial budget, reflecting the financial decisions of the firm

The operating budget consists of:

- Sales budget
- Production budget
- Direct materials budget
- Direct labor budget
- Factory overhead budget

- Selling and administrative expense budget
- Pro forma income statement

The financial budget consists of:

- Cash budget
- Pro forma balance sheet

The major steps in preparing the budget are:

1. Prepare a sales forecast
2. Determine expected production volume
3. Estimate manufacturing costs and operating expenses
4. Determine cash flow and other financial effects
5. Formulate projected financial statements

Figure 1 shows a simplified diagram of the various parts of the comprehensive (master) budget, the master plan of the company.

To illustrate how all these budgets are put together, we will focus on a manufacturing company called the Johnson Company, which produces and markets a single product. We will assume that the company develops the master budget in contribution format for 19B on a quarterly basis. We will highlight the variable cost-fixed cost breakdown throughout the illustration.

THE SALES BUDGET

The sales budget is the starting point in preparing the master budget, since estimated sales volume influences nearly all other items appearing throughout the master budget. The sales budget ordinarily indicates the quantity of each product expected to be sold. After sales volume has been estimated, the sales budget is constructed by multiplying the expected sales in units by the expected unit selling price. Generally, the sales budget includes a computation of expected cash collections from credit sales, which will be used later for cash budgeting.

EXAMPLE 1

THE JOHNSON COMPANY
Sales Budget
For the Year Ending December 31, 19B

	Quarter				Total
	1	2	3	4	
Expected sales in units	800	700	900	800	3,200
Unit sales price	× $80	× $80	× $80	× $80	× $80
Total sales	$64,000	$56,000	$72,000	$64,000	$256,000

Figure 1 Comprehensive (Master) Budget

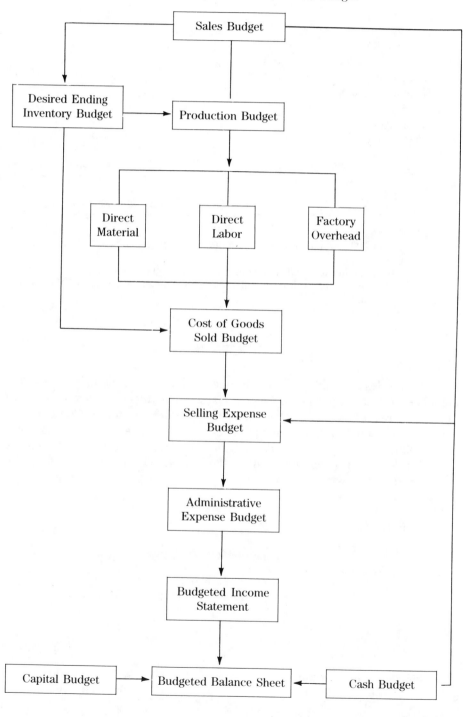

SCHEDULE OF EXPECTED CASH COLLECTIONS

Accounts receivable, 12/31/19A	$ 9,500*				$ 9,500
1st quarter sales ($64,000)	44,800[†]	$17,920[‡]			62,720
2d quarter sales ($56,000)		39,200	$15,680		54,880
3d quarter sales ($72,000)			50,400	$20,160	70,560
4th quarter sales ($64,000)				44,800	44,800
Total cash collections	$54,300	$57,120	$66,080	$64,960	$242,460

*All $9,500 accounts receivable balance is assumed to be collectible in the first quarter

[†]70% of a quarter's sales are collected in the quarter of sale

[‡]28% of a quarter's sales are collected in the quarter following, and the remaining 2% are uncollectible

THE PRODUCTION BUDGET

After sales are budgeted, the production budget can be determined. The number of units expected to be manufactured to meet budgeted sales and inventory requirements is set forth in the production budget. The expected volume of production is determined by subtracting the estimated inventory at the beginning of the period from the sum of the units expected to be sold and the desired inventory at the end of the period. The production budget is illustrated as follows:

EXAMPLE 2

THE JOHNSON COMPANY

Production Budget
For the Year Ending December 31, 19B

	Quarter				
	1	2	3	4	Total
Planned sales (Example 1)	800	700	900	800	3,200
Desired ending inventory*	70	90	80	100[†]	100
Total Needs	870	790	980	900	3,300

	Quarter				
	1	2	3	4	Total
Less: Beginning inventory[‡]	80	70	90	80	80
Units to be produced	790	720	890	820	3,220

[*]10% of the next quarter's sales
[†]Estimated
[‡]The same as the previous quarter's ending inventory

THE DIRECT MATERIAL BUDGET

When the level of production has been computed, a direct material budget should be constructed to show how much material will be required for production and how much material must be purchased to meet this production requirement. The purchase will depend on both expected usage of materials and inventory levels. The formula for computation of the purchase is:

Purchase in units = Usage + Desired ending material inventory units
  − Beginning inventory units

The direct material budget is usually accompanied by a computation of expected cash payments for materials.

EXAMPLE 3

THE JOHNSON COMPANY

Direct Material Budget
For the Year Ending December 31, 19B

	Quarter				
	1	2	3	4	Total
Units to be produced (Ex 2)	790	720	890	820	3,220
Material needs per unit (lbs)	× 3	× 3	× 3	× 3	× 3
Material needs for production	2,370	2,160	2,670	2,460	9,660
Desired ending inventory of materials*	216	267	246	250[†]	250
Toal needs	2,586	2,427	2,916	2,710	9,910
Less: Beginning inventory of materials[‡]	237	216	267	246	237
Materials to be purchased	2,349	2,211	2,649	2,464	9,673
Unit price	× $2	× $2	× $2	× $2	× $2
Purchase cost	$4,698	$4,422	$5,298	$4,928	$19,346

SCHEDULE OF EXPECTED CASH DISBURSEMENTS

Accounts payable, 12/31/19A	$2,200				$ 2,200
1st quarter purchases ($4,698)	2,349	$2,349**			4,698
2d quarter purchases ($4,422)		2,211	$2,211		4,422
3d quarter purchases ($5,298)			2,649	2,649	5,298
4th quarter purchases ($4,928)				2,464	2,464
Total disbursements	$4,549	$4,560	$4,860	$5,113	$19,082

*10% of the next quarter's units needed for production
†Estimated
‡The same as the prior quarter's ending inventory
**50% of a quarter's purchases are paid for in the quarter of purchase; the remainder are paid for in the following quarter

THE DIRECT LABOR BUDGET

The production requirements as set forth in the production budget also provide the starting point for the preparation of the direct labor budget. To compute direct labor requirements, expected production volume for each period is multiplied by the number of direct labor hours required to produce a single unit. The direct labor hours to meet production requirements is then multiplied by the direct labor cost per hour to obtain budgeted total direct labor costs.

EXAMPLE 4

THE JOHNSON COMPANY

Direct Labor Budget
For the Year Ending December 31, 19B

	Quarter				
	1	2	3	4	Total
Units to be produced (Example 2)	790	720	890	820	3,220
Direct labor hours per unit	× 5	× 5	× 5	× 5	× 5
Total hours	3,950	3,600	4,450	4,100	16,100
Direct labor cost per hour	× $5	× $5	× $5	× $5	× $5
Total direct labor cost	$19,750	$18,000	$22,250	$20,500	$80,500

THE FACTORY OVERHEAD BUDGET

The factory overhead budget should provide a schedule of all manufacturing costs other than direct materials and direct labor. Using the contribution approach to budgeting requires the development of a predetermined overhead rate for the variable portion of the factory overhead. In developing the cash budget, we must remember that depreciation does not entail a cash outlay and therefore must be deducted from the total factory overhead in computing cash disbursement for factory overhead.

EXAMPLE 5

To illustrate the factory overhead budget, we will assume that

- Total factory overhead budgeted = $6,000 fixed (per quarter), plus $2 per hour of direct labor
- Depreciation expenses are $3,250 each quarter
- All overhead costs involving cash outlays are paid for in the quarter incurred

THE JOHNSON COMPANY

Factory Overhead Budget
For the Year Ending December 31, 19B

	Quarter				
	1	2	3	4	Total
Budgeted direct labor hours (Example 4)	3,950	3,600	4,450	4,100	16,100
Variable overhead rate	× $2	× $2	× $2	× $2	× $2
Variable overhead budgeted	$ 7,900	$ 7,200	$ 8,900	$ 8,200	$32,200
Fixed overhead budgeted	6,000	6,000	6,000	6,000	24,000
Total budgeted overhead	$13,900	$13,200	$14,900	$14,200	$56,200
Less: Depreciation	3,250	3,250	3,250	3,250	13,000
Cash disbursement for overhead	$10,650	$ 9,950	$11,650	$10,950	$43,200

THE ENDING INVENTORY BUDGET

The desired ending inventory budget provides us with the information required for the construction of budgeted financial statements. Specifically, it will help compute the cost of goods sold on the budgeted income statement. Secondly, it will give the dollar value of the ending materials and finished goods inventory to appear on the budgeted balance sheet.

EXAMPLE 6

THE JOHNSON COMPANY

Ending Inventory Budget
For the Year Ending December 31, 19B
Ending Inventory

	Units	Unit Cost	Total
Direct materials	250 pounds (Example 3)	$2	$ 500
Finished goods	100 units (Example 2)	$41*	$4,100

*The unit variable cost of $41 is computed as follows:

	Unit Cost	Units	Total
Direct materials	$2	3 pounds	$ 6
Direct labor	5	5 hours	25
Variable overhead	2	5 hours	10
Total variable manufacturing cost			$41

THE SELLING AND ADMINISTRATIVE EXPENSE BUDGET

The selling and administrative expense budget lists the operating expenses involved in selling the products and in managing the business. In order to complete the budgeted income statement in contribution format, variable selling and administrative expense per unit must be computed.

EXAMPLE 7

THE JOHNSON COMPANY

Selling and Administrative Expense Budget
For the Year Ending December 31, 19B

	Quarter				
	1	2	3	4	Total
Expected sales in units	800	700	900	800	3,200
Variable selling and admin. exp. per unit*	× $4	× $4	× $4	× $4	× $4
Budgeted variable expense	$ 3,200	$ 2,800	$ 3,600	$ 3,200	$12,800

	Quarter				
	1	2	3	4	Total
Fixed selling and administrative expenses:					
Advertising	1,100	1,100	1,100	1,100	4,400
Insurance	2,800				2,800
Office salaries	8,500	8,500	8,500	8,500	34,000
Rent	350	350	350	350	1,400
Taxes			1,200		1,200
Total budgeted selling and administrative expenses[†]	$15,950	$12,750	$14,750	$13,150	$56,600

*Includes sales agents' commissions, shipping, and supplies
†Paid for in the quarter incurred

THE CASH BUDGET

The cash budget is prepared for the purpose of cash planning and control. It presents the expected cash inflow and outflow for a designated time period. The cash budget helps management keep cash balances in reasonable relationship to its needs. It aids in avoiding unnecessary idle cash and possible cash shortages. The cash budget consists typically of four major sections:

1. The receipts section, which is the beginning cash balance, cash collections from customers, and other receipts

2. The disbursements section, which comprises all cash payments made by purpose

3. The cash surplus or deficit section, which simply shows the difference between the cash receipts section and the cash disbursements section

4. The financing section, which provides a detailed account of the borrowings and repayments expected during the budgeting period

EXAMPLE 8

To illustrate, we will make the following assumptions:

- The company desires to maintain a $5,000 minimum cash balance at the end of each quarter

• All borrowing and repayment must be in multiples of $500 at an interest rate of 10% per annum. Interest is computed and paid as the principal is repaid. Borrowing takes place at the beginning of each quarter and repayment at the end of each quarter.

THE JOHNSON COMPANY

Cash Budget
For the Year Ending December 31, 19B

	Example	Quarter				Total
		1	2	3	4	
Cash balance, beginning	Given	$10,000	$ 9,401	$ 5,461	$ 9,106	$ 10,000
Add: Receipts:						
Collection from customers	1	54,300	57,120	66,080	64,960	242,460
Total cash available		$64,300	$66,521	$71,541	$74,066	$252,460
Less: Disbursements:						
Direct materials	3	$ 4,549	$ 4,560	$ 4,860	$ 5,113	$ 19,082
Direct labor	4	19,750	18,000	22,250	20,500	80,500
Factory overhead	5	10,650	9,950	11,650	10,950	43,200
Selling and Admin.	7	15,950	12,750	14,750	13,150	56,600
Machinery purchase	Given	—	24,300	—	—	24,300
Income tax	Given	4,000	—	—	—	4,000
Total disbursements		$54,899	$69,560	$53,510	$49,713	$227,682
Cash surplus (deficit)		$ 9,401	$(3,039)	$18,031	$24,353	$ 24,778
Financing:						
Borrowing		—	$ 8,500	—	—	$ 8,500
Repayment		—	—	$ (8,500)	—	(8,500)
Interest		—	—	(425)	—	(425)
Total financing		—	$ 8,500	$ (8,925)	—	$ (425)
Cash balance, ending		$ 9,401	$ 5,461	$ 9,106	$24,353	$ 24,353

THE BUDGETED INCOME STATEMENT

The budgeted income statement summarizes the various component projections of revenue and expenses for the budgeting period. However, for control purposes the budget can be divided into quarters or even months depending on the need.

EXAMPLE 9

THE JOHNSON COMPANY

Budgeted Income Statement
For the Year Ending December 31, 19B

	Example No.		
Sales (3,200 units @ $80)	1		$256,000
Less: Variable expenses			
Variable cost of goods sold			
(3,200 units @ $41)	6	$131,200	
Variable selling & Admin.	7	12,800	144,000
Contribution margin			112,000
Less: Fixed expenses			
Factory overhead	5	24,000	
Selling and Admin.	7	$ 43,800	67,800
Net operating income			44,200
Less: Interest expense	8		425
Net income before taxes			43,775
Less: Income taxes	20%		8,755
Net income			$ 35,020

THE BUDGETED BALANCE SHEET

The budgeted balance sheet is developed by beginning with the balance sheet for the year just ended and adjusting it, using all the activities that are expected to take place during the budgeting period. Some of the reasons why the budgeted balance sheet must be prepared are:

- It could disclose some unfavorable financial conditions that management might want to avoid.
- It serves as a final check on the mathematical accuracy of all the other schedules.
- It helps management perform a variety of ratio calculations.
- It highlights future resources and obligations.

EXAMPLE 10

To illustrate, we will use the following balance sheet for the year 19A.

THE JOHNSON COMPANY

Balance Sheet
December 31, 19A

ASSETS			LIABILITIES AND STK EQUITY		
Current Assets:			Current Liabilities:		
Cash	10,000		Accounts Payable	2,200	
Accounts Rec.	9,500		Income Tax Payable	4,000	
Material Inv.	474		Total Cur. Liab.	6,200	
Finished Gd Inv.	3,280		Total Equity		
Total Cur. Assets	$ 23,254				
Fixed Assets:			Stockholders' Equity:		
Land	50,000		Common Stock, No-Par	70,000	
Build and Eqpt	100,000		Retained Earnings	37,054	
Accumtd Depr	(60,000)			$107,054	
Total Fixed Assets	$ 90,000				
Total Assets	$113,254		Total Liab and Stk Eq	$113,254	

THE JOHNSON COMPANY

Budgeted Balance Sheet
December 31, 19B

ASSETS			LIABILITIES AND STK EQUITY		
Current Assets:			Current Liabilities:		
Cash	$ 24,353	(a)	Accounts Payable	$ 2,464	(h)
Accounts Rec	23,040	(b)	Income Tax		
Material Inv	500	(c)	Payable	8,755	(i)
			Total Cur.		
Finished Gd Inv	4,100	(d)	Liab.	$11,219	
Total Cur. Assets	$ 51,993				
			Stockholders'		
Fixed Assets:			Equity:		
			Common Stock,		
Land	$ 50,000	(e)	No-Par	$ 70,000	(j)
Build and Eqpt	124,300	(f)	Retained Earnings	72,074	(k)
Accumtd Depr	(73,000)	(g)	Total Equity	$142,074	
Total Fixed Assets	$101,300				
Total Assets	$153,293		Total Liab & Stk Eq	$153,293	

Computations:

(a) From Example 8 (cash budget)

(b) $9,500 + $256,000 sales − $242,460 receipts = $23,040

(c) and (d) From Example 6 (ending inventory budget)

(e) No change

(f) $100,000 + $24,300 (from Example 8) = $124,300

(g) $60,000 + $13,000 (from Example 5) = $73,000

(h) $2,200 + $19,346 − $19,082 = $2,464 (all accounts payable relate to material purchases), or 50% of 4th quarter purchase = 50% ($4,928) = $2,464

(i) From Example 9 (budgeted income statement)

(j) No change

(k) $37,054 + $35,020 net income = $72,074

Some Financial Calculations

To see what kind of financial condition the Johnson Company is expected to be in for the budgeting year, a sample of financial ratio calculations are in order: (Assume $19 \times A$ after-tax net income was $15,000).

	19xA	19xB
Current ratio		
(Current assets/	$23,254/$6,200	$51,993/$11,219
current liabilities)	= 3.75	= 4.63
Return on total assets		
(Net income after taxes/	$15,000/$113,254	$35,020/$153,293
total assets)	= 13.24%	= 22.85%

Sample calculations indicate that the Johnson Company is expected to have better liquidity as measured by the current ratio. Overall performance will be improved as measured by return on total assets. This could be an indication that the contemplated plan may work out well.

BUDGETING THROUGH FINANCIAL MODELING

Many companies are increasingly using financial modeling to develop their budgets. We discuss:

• What is a financial model?

• What are some typical uses of financial models?

• What are the types of financial modeling?

• How widespread is the use of financial modeling in practice?

• How do we go about building a financial model?

We also discuss use of spreadsheets and financial modeling languages for financial modeling.

A FINANCIAL MODEL

A financial model, narrowly called a budgeting model, is a system of mathematical equations, logic, and data which describes the relationships among financial and operating variables. A financial model can be viewed as a subset of broadly defined corporate planning models or a stand-alone functional system that attempts to answer a certain financial planning problem. A financial model is one in which:

(1) one or more financial variables appear (expenses, revenues, investment, cash flow, taxes, earnings, etc.);

(2) the model user can manipulate (set and alter) the value of one or more financial variables; and

(3) the purpose of the model is to influence strategic decisions by revealing to the decision-maker the implications of alternative values of these financial variables.

Financial models fall into two types: simulation better known as "what-if" models and optimization models. What-if models attempt to simulate the effects of alternative management policies and assumptions about the firm's external environment. They are basically a tool for management's laboratory. Optimization models are the ones in which the goal is to maximize or minimize an objective such as present value of profit or cost. Multi-objective techniques such as goal programming are being experimented. Models can be deterministic or probabilistic. Deterministic models do not include any random or probabilistic variables whereas probabilistic models incorporate random numbers and/or one or more probability distributions for variables such as sales, costs, and so on. Financial models can be solved and manipulated computationally to derive from it the current and projected future implications and consequences. Due to technological advances in computers (such as spreadsheets, financial modeling languages, graphics, data base management systems, and networking), more companies are using modeling.

BUDGETING AND FINANCIAL MODELING

Basically, a financial model is used to build a comprehensive budget (that is, projected financial statements such as the income statement, balance sheet, and cash flow statement). Such a model can be called a budgeting model, since we are essentially developing a master budget with such a model. Applications and uses of the model, however, go beyond developing a budget. They include:

- Financial forecasting and analysis
- Capital expenditure analysis
- Tax planning
- Exchange rate analysis
- Analysis for mergers and acquisitions
- Labor contract negotiations
- Capacity planning
- Cost-volume-profit analysis
- New venture analysis
- Lease/purchase evaluation
- Appraisal of performance by segments
- Market analysis
- New product analysis
- Development of long-term strategy
- Planning financial requirements
- Risk analysis
- Cash flow analysis
- Cost and price projections

USE OF FINANCIAL MODELING IN PRACTICE

The use of financial modeling, especially a computer-based financial modeling system, is rapidly growing. The reason is quite simple: the growing need for improved and quicker support for management decisions as a decision support system (DSS) and wide and easy availability of computer hardware and software.

Some of the functions currently served by financial models, as described by the users, are:

- Projecting financial results under any given set of assumptions; to evaluate the financial impact of various assumptions and alternative strategies; and to prepare long range financial forecasts
- Computing income, cash flow, and ratios for five years by months; also energy sales, revenue, power generation requirements, operating and manufacturing expenses, manual or automatic financing, and rate structure analysis

- Providing answers and insights into financial "what-if" questions, and to produce financial scheduling information
- Forecast the balance sheet and income statement with emphasis on alternatives for the investment securities portfolio
- Projecting operating results and various financing needs, such as plant and property levels and financing requirements
- Computing manufacturing profit, given sales forecasts, and any desired processing sequence through the manufacturing facilities; simulate effect on profits of inventory policies
- Generating profitability reports of various cost centers
- Projecting financial implications of capital investment programs
- Showing the effect of various volume and activity levels on budget and cash flow
- Forecasting corporate sales, costs, and income by division, by month
- Providing sales revenue for budget; a basis for evaluating actual sales department performance, and other statistical comparisons
- Determine pro forma cash flow for alternative development plans for real estate projects
- Analyzing the impact of acquisition on company earnings
- Determining economic attractiveness of new ventures, i.e., products, facilities, acquisitions, and so on
- Evaluate alternatives of leasing or buying computer equipment
- Determining corporate taxes as a function of changes in price
- Evaluate investments in additional capacity at each major refinery
- Generating income statements, cash flow, present value, and discounted rate of return for potential mining ventures, based on production and sales forecasts

Supported by the expanded capabilities provided by models, many companies are increasingly successful in including long-term strategic considerations in their business plans, thus enabling them to investigate the possible impact of their current decisions on the long term welfare of the organization.

WHAT QUANTITATIVE METHODS ARE USED IN FINANCIAL MODELS?

In view of the development of sophisticated quantitative models for analysis in business planning and decision making, there is a rapid growing trend for their use, certainly with the aid of computer technology. Here is a list of these techniques used by the model builders:

- Econometric and statistical methods
    Simple and multiple regressions
    Econometric modeling
    Time series models
    Exponential smoothing
    Risk analysis
    Simulation
- Optimization models
    Linear programming
    Goal programming
    Integer programming
    Dynamic programming

DEVELOPING FINANCIAL MODELS

Develpment of financial models essentially involves three steps: (1) definition of variables, (2) input parameter values, and (3) model specification. As far as model specification goes, we will concentrate only on the simulation-type model in this section. Generally speaking, the model consists of three important ingredients:

- Variables
- Input parameter values
- Definitional and/or functional relationships

DEFINITION OF VARIABLES

Fundamental to the specification of a financial model is the definition of the variables to be included in the model. There are basically three types of variables: policy variables (Z), external variables (X), and performance variables (Y).

- *Policy variables.* The policy variables (often called control variables) are those management can exert some degree of control over. Examples of financial variables are cash management, working capital, debt management, depreciation, tax, merger-acquisition decisions, the rate and direction of the firm's capital investment programs, the extent of its equity and external debt financing and the financial leverage represented thereby, and the size of its cash balances and liquid asset position. Policy variables are denoted by the symbol Z in Figure 2.

Figure 2   Financial Model Variables

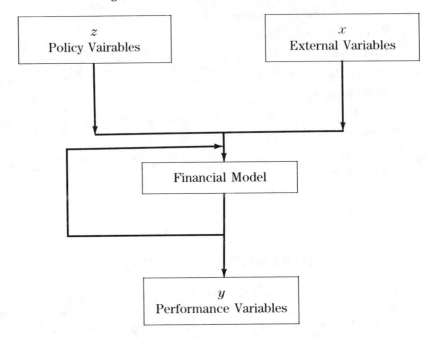

- *External variables.* The external variables are the environmental variables that are external to the company and which influence the firm's decisions from outside of the firm, generally exogenous in nature. Generally speaking, the firm is embedded in an industry environment. This industry environment, in turn, is influenced by overall general business conditions. General business conditions exert influences upon particular industries in several ways. Total volume of demand, product prices, labor costs, material costs, money rates, and general expectations are among the industry variables affected by the general business conditions. The symbol X represents the external variables in Figure 2.

- *Performance variables.* The performance variables measure the firm's economic and financial performance, which are usually endogenous. We use the symbol Y in the diagram. The Ys are often called output variables. The output variables of a financial model would be the line items of the balance sheet, cash budget, income statement, or statement of cash flows. How to define the output variables of the firm will depend on the goals and objectives of management. They basically indicate how management measures the performance of the organization or some segments of it. Management is likely to be concerned with: (1) the firm's level of earnings; (2) growth in earnings; (3) projected earnings; (4) growth in sales; and (5) cash flow.

Frequently when we attempt to set up a financial model we face risk or uncertainty associated with particular projections. In a case such as this, we treat some of these variables such as sales as random variables with given probability distributions. The inclusion of random variables in the model transforms it from a deterministic model to a risk analysis model. However, the use of the risk analysis model in practice is rare because of the difficulty involved in modeling and computation.

Input Parameter Values

The model includes various input parameter values. For example, in order to generate the balance sheet, the model needs to input beginning balances of various asset, liability, and equity accounts. These input and parameter values are supplied by management. The ratio between accounts receivable and financial decision variables such as the maximum desired debt-equity ratio would be good examples of parameters.

Model Specification

Once we define various variables and input parameters for our financial model, we must then specify a set of mathematical and logical relationships linking the input variables to the performance variables. The relationships usually fall into two types of equations: definition equations and behavioral equations. Definitional equations take the form of accounting identities. Behavioral equations involve theories or hypotheses about the behavior of certain economic and financial events. They must be empirically tested and validated before they are incorporated into the financial model.

Definitional Equations. Definitional equations are exactly what the term refers to—mathematical or accounting definitions. For example,

$$Assets = Liabilities + Equity$$
$$Net\ Income = Revenues - Expenses$$

These definitional equations are fundamental definitions in accounting for the balance sheet and income statement, respectively. Two more examples are given below:

$$CASH = CASH(-1) + CC + OCR + DEBT - CD - LP$$

This equation is a typical cash equation in a financial model. It states that ending cash balance (CASH) is equal to the beginning cash balance (CASH(-1)) plus cash collections from customers (CC) plus other cash receipts (OCR) plus borrowings (DEBT) minus cash disbursements (CD) minus loan payments (LP).

$$INV = INV(-1) + MAT + DL + MO - CGS$$

This equation states that ending inventory (INV) is equal to the beginning inventory (INV(-1)) plus cost of materials used (MAT) plus cost of direct labor (DL) plus manufacturing overhead (MO) minus the cost of goods sold (CGS).

Behavioral Equations. Behavior equations describe the behavior of the firm regarding the specific activities that are subject to empirical testing and validation. The classical demand function in economics is:

$$Q = f(P) \text{ or more specifically } Q = a - bP$$

It simply says that the quantity demanded is negatively related to the price. That is to say, the higher the price the lower the demand.

However, the firm's sales is more realistically described as follows:

$$SALES = f(P, ADV., I, GNP, Pc, \text{ and so on) or}$$

assuming linear relationship among these variables, we can specify the model as follows:

$$SALES = a + bP + cADV + dI + eGNP + fPc$$

which says that the sales are affected by such factors as price (P), advertising expenditures (ADV), consumer income (I), gross national product (GNP), prices of competitive goods (Pc), and so on.

With the data on SALES, P, ADV, I, GNP, and Pc, we will be able to estimate parameter values a, b, c, d, e, and f, using linear regression. We can test the statistical significance of each of the parameter estimates and evaluate the overall explanatory power of the model, measured by the t-statistic and r-squared, respectively. This way we will be able to identify the most influential factors that affect the sales of a particular product. With the best model chosen, management can simulate the effects on sales of alternative pricing and advertising strategies. We can also experiment with alternative assumptions regarding the external economic factors such as GNP, consumer income, and prices of competitive goods.

Model Structure. A majority of financial models that have been in use are recursive and/or simultaneous models. Recursive models are the ones in which each equation can be solved one at a time by substituting the solution values of the preceding equations into the right hand side of each equation. An example of a financial model of the recursive type is given below:

```
(1) SALES    = A - B*PRICE + C*ADV
(2) REVENUE  = SALES*PRICE
(3) CGS      = .70*REVENUE
(4) GM       = SALES - CGS
(5) OE       = $10,000 + .2*SALES
(6) EBT      = GM - OE
(7) TAX      = .46*EBT
(8) EAT      = EBT - TAX
```

In this example, the selling price (PRICE) and advertising expenses (ADV) are given. A, B, and C are parameters to be estimated and

SALES	=	sales volume in units
REVENUE	=	sales revenue
CGS	=	cost of goods sold
GM	=	gross margin
OE	=	operating expenses
EBT	=	earnings before taxes
TAX	=	income taxes
EAT	=	earnings after taxes

Simultaneous models are frequently found in econometric models which require a higher level of computational methods such as matrix inversion. An example of a financial model of this type is presented below:

(1) INT   = .10*DEBT
(2) EARN = REVENUE − CGS − OE − INT − TAX − DIV
(3) DEBT = DEBT(−1) + BOW
(4) CASH = CASH(−1) + CC + BOW + EARN − CD − LP
(5) BOW = MBAL − CASH

Note that earnings (EARN) in equation (2) is defined as sales revenue minus CGS, OE, interest expense (INT), TAX, and dividend payment (DIV). However, INT is a percentage interest rate on total debt in equation (1). Total debt in equation (3) is equal to the previous period's debt (DEBT(−1)) plus new borrowings (BOW). New debt is the difference between a minimum cash balance (MBAL) minus cash. Finally, the ending cash balance in equation (5) is defined as the sum of the beginning balance (CASH(−1)), cash collections, new borrowings and earnings minus cash disbursements and loan payments of the existing debt (LP). Even though the model presented here is a simple variety, it is still simultaneous in nature, which requires the use of a method capable of solving simultaneous equations. Very few of the financial modeling languages have the capability to solve this kind of system.

Decision Rules. The financial model may, in addition to the ones previously discussed, that is definitional equations and behavioral equations, include basic decision rules specified in a very general form. The decision rules are not written in the form of conventional equations. They are described algebraically using conditional operators, consisting of statements of the type: "IF . . . THEN . . . ELSE." For example, suppose that we wish to express the following decision rule: "If X is greater than 0, then Y is set equal to X multiplied by 5. Otherwise, Y is set equal to 0." Then we can express the rule as follows:

$$Y = \text{IF } X \text{ GT } 0 \text{ THEN } X^*5 \text{ ELSE } 0$$

Suppose the company wishes to develop a financing decision problem based upon alternative sales scenarios. To determine an optimal financing alternative, managers might want to incorporate some decision rules into the model for a "what-if" or sensitivity analysis. Some examples of these decision rules are as follows:

- The amount of dividends paid are determined on the basis of targeted earnings available to common stockholders and a maximum dividend payout ratio specified by management.
- After calculating the external funds needed to meet changes in assets as a result of increased sales, dividends, and maturing debt, the amount of long-term debt to be floated is selected on the basis of a prespecified leverage ratio.
- The amount of equity financing to be raised is chosen on the basis of funds needed which are not financed by new long-term debt, but is constrained by the responsibility to meet minimum dividend payments.

In the model we have just described, simultaneity is quite evident. A sales figure is used to generate earnings and this in turn leads to, among other items, the level of long-term debt required. Yet the level of debt affects the interest expense incurred within the current period and therefore earnings. Furthermore, as earnings are affected, so is the price at which new shares are issued, the number of shares to be sold, and thus earnings per share. Earnings per share then "feeds back" into the stock price calculation.

Lagged Model Structure. Lagged model structure is common in financial modeling. Virtually all balance sheet equations or identities are of this type. For example,

Capital $=$ capital (-1) + net income + contributions $-$ cash dividends

More interestingly,

$$CC = a^*SALES + b^*SALES(-1) + c^*SALES(-2)$$

where CC = cash collections from customers

a = percent received in the month of sale

b = percent received in the month following sale

c = percent received in the second month following sale

This indicates that the realization of cash lags behind credit sales. Figure 3 illustrates a sample financial (budgeting) model.

USE OF COMPUTER SOFTWARE FOR FINANCIAL MODELING AND BUDGETING

Financial modeling for profit planning and budgeting can be done using a microcomputer with a powerful spreadsheet program such as Lotus 1-2-3, VP

Figure 3. A Corporate Financial Model

BALANCE SHEET EQUATIONS

$Cash_t = Cash_{t-1} + Cash\ Receipts_t - Cash\ Disbursements_t$

$Accounts\ Receivable_t = (1-a)\ Sales + (1-b-a)\ Sales_{t-1}$
$+ (1-c-b-a)\ Sales_{t-2}$

$Inventory_t = Inventory_{t-1} + Inventory\ Purchase_t$

$- Variable\ Cost\ Per\ Unit \left(\dfrac{Sales_t}{Selling\ Price\ Per\ Unit} \right)$

$Plant = Initial\ Value$

$Accounts\ Payable_t = (m)\ Variable\ Selling/Administrative\ Expenses_{t-1}$
$+ (n)\ Variable\ Selling/Administrative\ Expenses_t + Inventory\ Purchase_t$
$+ Fixed\ Expenses_t$

$Bank\ Loan_t = Bank\ Loan_{t-1} + Loan_t - Loan\ Repayment_t$

$Common\ Stock = Initial\ Value$

$Retained\ Earnings_t = Retained\ Earnings_{t-1} + Net\ Income_t$

INCOME STATEMENT AND CASH FLOW EQUATIONS

$Cash\ Receipts_t = (a)\ Sales_t + (b)\ Sales_{t-1} + (c)\ Sales_{t-2} + Loan_t$

$Cash\ Disbursements_t = Accounts\ Payable_{t-1} + Interest_t + Loan\ Repayments_t$

$Inventory\ Purchase_t\ [\geq 0] = Variable\ Cost\ Per\ Unit$

$\left(\dfrac{Sales_t + Sales_{t-1} + Sales_{t-2} + Sales_{t-3}}{Selling\ Price\ Per\ Unit} \right) - Inventory_{t-1}$

$Interest_t = (i)\ Bank\ Loan_t$

$Variable\ Cost\ of\ Sales_t = Sales_t \left(\dfrac{Variable\ Cost\ Per\ Unit}{Selling\ Price\ Per\ Unit} \right)$

$Variable\ Selling/Administrative\ Expenses_t = (v)\ Sales_t$

$Net\ Income\ Before\ Taxes_t = Sales_t - Interest_t + Variable\ Cost\ of\ Sales_t$
$+ Variable\ Selling/Administrative\ Expenses_t - Fixed\ Expenses_t$
$- Depreciation_t$

$Tax\ Expense_t\ [\geq 0] = (t)\ Net\ Income\ Before\ Taxes_t$

$Net\ Income_t = Net\ Income\ Before\ Taxes_t - Tax\ Expense_t$

Input Variables (Dollars)

Figure 3. *Continued*

$Sales_{t-1, t-2, t-3}$

$Loan_t$

$Loan\ Repayment_t$

$Fixed\ Expense_t$

$Depreciation_t$

Selling Price Per Unit

Variable Cost Per Unit

INPUT PARAMETERS

Accounts Receivable Collection Patterns
a—Percent Received within Current Period
b—Percent Received with One Period Lag
c—Percent Received with Two Period Lag
$a+b+c<1$

Lag in Accounts Payable Cash Flow
m—Percent Paid from Previous Period
n—Percent Paid from Current Period
$m+n=1$

$t=$ Tax Rate

$i=$ Interest Rate

$v=$ Variable Selling/Administrative Expense Ratio to Sales

Initial Values (Dollars)

Plant

Common Stock

$Cash_{t-1}$

$Sales_{t-1, t-2}$

$Inventory_{t-1}$

$Retained\ Earnings_{t-1}$

$Bank\ Loan_{t-1}$

$Variable\ Selling/Administrative\ Expenses_{t-1}$

$Accounts\ Payable_{t-1}$

Assumptions; time interval equals one month; accounts payable paid in full in next period; no lag between inventory purchase and receipt of goods; and no dividends paid.

362

Planner, SuperCalc, Excel, and Quattro, while integrated software containing spreadsheets include Enable, Symphony, Multiplan, and Framework.

There are also many user-oriented financial modeling languages specifically designed for corporate planners, financial officers, controllers, treasurers, budget preparers, and managerial accountants. These languages do not require any knowledge of computer prgramming (such as BASIC, FORTRAN, PASCAL, and COBOL). They are all English-like languages. Among the well-known system packages are: IFPS (Interactive Financial Planning System), SIMPLAN, EXPRESS, XSIM, FSC-EPS, EDUCOM Financial Planning Model (EFPM), EMPIRE, FORESIGHT, and ORION.

In this section, we will illustrate how to use, for financial planning and modeling, two more popular programs: (1) Lotus 1-2-3 spreadsheet program and (2) IFPS, a financial modeling package.

Use of Lotus 1-2-3 Spreadsheet Program

For an illustration of financial modeling, we will show how to develop a projected income statement.

Financial Modeling Languages

In what follows, we will discuss one of the most popular modeling language—IFPS—with illustrations.

IFPS (Interactive Financial Planning System). IFPS is a multipurpose, interactive financial modeling system which supports and facilitates the building, solving, and asking of "what-if" questions of financial models. The output from an IFPS model is in the format of a spreadsheet, that is a matrix or table in which:

- The rows representing user-specified variables such as market share, sales, growth in sales, unit price, gross margin, variable cost, contribution margin, fixed cost, net income, net present value, internal rate of return, and earnings per share.

- The column designates a sequence of user-specified time periods such as month, quarter, year, total, percentages, or divisions.

- The entries in the body of the table display the values taken by the model variable over time or by segments of the firm such as divisions, product lines, sales territories, and departments. IFPS offers the following key features:

- Like other special purpose modeling languages, IFPS provides an English-like modeling language. That means without an extensive knowledge of computer programming, the financial officer can build financial models of

Given   Sales for 1st month = $60,000

Cost of Sales = 42% of sales, all variable

Operating Expenses = $10,000 fixed plus 5% of sales

Taxes = 25% net income

Sales increase by 5% each month

Based on this information, we will create a spreadsheet for the contribution income statement for the next 12 months and in total.

The formulas are shown in Exhibit 1.

Exhibit 1

	JANUARY	FEBRUARY	MARCH	APRIL	MAY	JUNE
Sales	60000	(B23*1.05)	(C23*1.05)	(D23*1.05)	(E23*1.05)	(F23*1.05)
Variable Costs						
Cost of Sales	(0.42*B23)	(0.42*C23)	(0.42*D23)	(0.42*E23)	(0.42*F23)	(0.42*G23)
Operating Expense	(0.05*B23)	(0.05*C23)	(0.05*D23)	(0.05*E23)	(0.05*F23)	(0.05*G23)
Total variable costs	(B25+B26)	(C25+C26)	(D25+D26)	(E25+E26)	(F25+F26)	(G25+G26)
Contribution Margin	(B23−B28)	(C23−C28)	(D23−D28)	(E23−E28)	(F23−F28)	(G23−G28)
Fixed Costs	10000	10000	10000	10000	10000	10000
Net Income Before Tax	(B30−B31)	(C30−C31)	(D30−D31)	(E30−E31)	(F30−F31)	(G30−G31)
Tax	(0.25*B33)	(0.25*C33)	(0.25*D33)	(0.25*E33)	(0.25*F33)	(0.25*G33)
Net Income	(B33−B34)	(C33−C34)	(D33−D34)	(E33−E34)	(F33−F34)	(G33−G34)

Based on the formulas above, the complete Lotus 1-2-3 spreadsheet solution is produced as shown in Exhibit 2.

Exhibit 2

	JANUARY	FEBRUARY	MARCH	APRIL	MAY	JUNE
Sales	$60,000.00	$63,000.00	$66,150.00	$69,457.50	$72,930.38	$76,576.89
Variable Costs						
Cost of Sales	25,200.00	26,460.00	27,783.00	29,172.15	30,630.76	32,162.30
Operating Expense	3,000.00	3,150.00	3,307.50	3,472.88	3,646.52	3,828.84
Total variable costs	28,200.00	29,610.00	31,090.50	32,645.03	34,277.28	35,991.14
Contribution Margin	31,800.00	33,390.00	35,059.50	36,812.48	38,653.10	40,585.75
Fixed Costs	10,000.00	10,000.00	10,000.00	10,000.00	10,000.00	10,000.00
Net Income Before Tax	21,800.00	23,390.00	25,059.50	26,812.48	28,653.10	30,585.75
Tax	5,450.00	5,847.50	6,264.88	6,703.12	7,163.27	7,646.44
Net Income	$16,350.00	$17,542.50	$18,794.63	$20,109.36	$21,489.82	$22,939.32

his/her own, and use them for "what-if" scenarios and managerial decisions.

- IFPS has a collection of built-in financial functions that perform calculations such as net present value (NPV), internal rate of return (IRR), loan amortization schedules, and depreciation alternatives.

- IFPS also has a collection of built-in mathematical and statistical functions such as linear regression, linear interpolation, polynomial autocorrelation, and moving average functions.

- IFPS supports use of leading and/or lagged variables which are commonly used in financial modeling. For example, cash collections lag behind credit sales of prior periods.
- IFPS also supports deterministic and probabilistic modeling. It offers a variety of functions for sampling from probability distributions such as uniform, normal, bivariate normal, and user-described empirical distributions.

Exhibit 1 (*Continued*)

JULY	AUGUST	SEPTEMBER	OCTOBER	NOVEMBER	DECEMBER	TOTAL
(G23*1.05)	(H23*1.05)	(I23*1.05)	(J23*1.05)	(K23*1.05)	(L23*1.05)	(@ SUM(B23..M23)
(0.42*H23)	(0.42*I23)	(0.42*J23)	(0.42*K23)	(0.42*L23)	(0.42*M23)	(@ SUM(B25..M25)
(0.05*H23)	(0.05*I23)	(0.05*J23)	(0.05*K23)	(0.05*L23)	(0.05*M23)	(@ SUM(B26..M26)
(H25 + H26)	(I25 + I26)	(J25 + J26)	(K25 + K26)	(L25 + L26)	(M25 + M26)	(@ SUM(B28..M28)
(H23 − H28)	(I23 − I28)	(J23 − J28)	(K23 − K28)	(L23 − L28)	(M23 − M28)	(@ SUM(B30..M30)
10000	10000	10000	10000	10000	10000	(@ SUM(B31..M31)
(H30 − H31)	(I30 − I31)	(J30 − J31)	(K30 − K31)	(L30 − L31)	(M30 − M31)	(@ SUM(B33..M33)
(0.25*H33)	(0.25*I33)	(0.25*J33)	(0.25*K33)	(0.25*L33)	(0.25*M33)	(@ SUM(B34..M34)
(H33 − H34)	(I33 − I34)	(J33 − J34)	(K33 − K34)	(L33 − L34)	(M33 − M34)	(@ SUM(B36..M36)

Exhibit 2 (*Continued*)

JULY	AUGUST	SEPTEMBER	OCTOBER	NOVEMBER	DECEMBER	TOTAL
$80,405.74	$84,426.03	$88,647.33	$93,079.69	$97,733.68	$102,620.36	$955,027.59
33,770.41	35,458.93	37,231.88	39,093.47	41,048.14	43,100.55	$401,111.59
4,020.29	4,221.30	4,432.37	4,653.98	4,886.68	5,131.02	$ 47,751.38
37,790.70	39,680.23	41,664.24	43,747.46	45,934.83	48,231.57	$448,862.97
42,615.04	44,745.79	46,983.08	49,332.24	51,798.85	54,388.79	$506,164.62
10,000.00	10,000.00	10,000.00	10,000.00	10,000.00	10,000.00	$120,000.00
32,615.04	34,745.79	36,983.08	39,332.24	41,798.85	44,388.79	$386,164.62
8,153.76	8,686.45	9,245.77	9,833.06	10,449.71	11,097.20	$ 96,541.16
$24,461.28	$26,059.35	$27,737.31	$29,499.18	$31,349.14	$33,291.59	$289,623.47

- IFPS is non-procedural in nature. This means that the relationships, logic, and data used to calculate the various values in the output do not have to be arranged in any particular top-to-bottom order in an IFPS model. IFPS automatically detects and solves a system of two or more linear or nonlinear equations.

- IFPS has extensive editing capabilities that include adding statements to and deleting statements from a model, making changes in existing statements, and making copies of parts or all of a model.

- IFPS supports sensitivity analysis by providing the following solution options:

(a) WHAT-IF. The IFPS lets you specify one or more changes in the relationships, logic, data, and/or parameter values, in the existing model and recalculates the model to show the impact of these changes on the performance measures.

(b) GOAL-SEEKING. In the GOAL SEEKING mode, IFPS can determine what change would have to take place in the value of a specified variable in a particular time period to achieve a specified value for another variable. For example, the financial officer can ask the system to answer the question "What would the unit sales price have to be for the project to achieve a target return on investment of 20%?"

(c) SENSITIVITY. This particular command is employed to determine the effect of a specified variable on one or more other variables. The SENSITIVITY command is similar to the WHAT-IF command but it produces a convenient, model-produced tabular summary for each new alternative value of the specified variable.

(d) ANALYZE. The ANALYZE command examines in detail those variables and their values that have contributed to the value of a specified variable.

(e) IMPACT. The IMPACT command is used to determine the effect on a specified variable of a series of percentage changes in one or more variables.

(f) IFPS/OPTIMUM. The IFPS/OPTIMUM routine is employed to answer questions of "What is the best?" type rather than "What-if."

(g) Other features of IFPS include:

- Routine graphic output
- Interactive color graphics
- Data files that contain both data and relationships
- A consolidation capability that lets the financial officer produce composite reports from two or more models
- Extraction of data from existing non-IFPS data files and placing them in IFPS-compatible data files
- Operating on all major computer mainframes and microcomputers

Prospective users of IFPS are encouraged to refer to the following sources:

- Execucom, IFPS Cases and Models, Austin, TX, 1979
- Execucom, IFPS Tutorial, Austin, TX, 1980
- Execucom, IFPS User's Manual, Austin, TX, 1984
- Execucom, IFPS/Personal User's Manual, Austin, TX 1984
- Execucom, *IFPS Fundamentals Seminar Book*, Austin, TX, 1987

- Execucom, Papers Available from the Execucom University Support Programs, Austin, TX, 1986
- Execucom, *Planners*, various quarterly issues

In the following section, we show how to build a model using IFPS.

EXAMPLE 11*

The following case illustrates how to use IFPS.

The MCL Corporation is considering diversifying and wishes to evaluate the profitability of the new venture over the next two years. A quarterly profit picture is desired. Marketing research has provided the following information: (1) The total market for the product will be 7,000 units at the start of production and will grow at the rate of 1% per quarter; (2) MCL's initial share of the market is 11%, and this is expected to grow at the rate of ½% per quarter if intense marketing efforts are maintained; (3) The selling price is expected to be $2.50 per unit the first year and $2.65 the following year; (4) The standard cost system has produced the following estimates: (a) selling expenses, $0.233 per unit; (b) labor cost, $0.61 per unit; and (c) raw materials, $0.42 per unit; (5) General and administrative expenses are estimated to be $450 in the first quarter with a quarterly growth rate of 1%; and (6) set-up costs for the line are $3,500.

First, "log in" to your computer and access IFPS.

(1) *To establish the model*

INTERACTIVE FINANCIAL PLANNING SYSTEM

ENTER NAME OF FILE CONTAINING MODELS AND REPORTS
? PROFIT

FILE PROFIT NOT FOUND - NEW FILE WILL BE CREATED
READY FOR EXECUTIVE COMMAND
? MODEL EXAMPLE

BEGIN ENTERING NEW MODEL
? AUTO 10, 5

10? (Model on the next page is entered)

(2) *The model is entered as listed below* (from 10 on down)

10 COLUMNS 1–8, 1991, 1992, GROWTH
15 *EXAMPLE OF IFPS
20 *

---

*This example was adapted from EXECUCOM, *IFPS Fundamentals Seminar Book*, 1989, pp. 6–20 with permission.

EXAMPLE 11 (*Continued*)

```
25 **
30 PERIODS 4
35 * SALES DATA AND PROJECTIONS
40 PRICE = 2.5 FOR 4, 2.65
45 MARKET SHARE = .11, PREVIOUS MARKET SHARE + .005
50 TOTAL MARKET = 7000, PREVIOUS TOTAL MARKET*1.01
55 SALES VOLUME = L45*L50
60 * PREVIOUS CALCULATIONS
65 SALES REVENUE = SALES VOLUME*PRICE
70 NET INCOME = SALES REVENUE - TOTAL EXPENSES
75 * COSTS
80 UNIT SELLING COST = .233
85 UNIT LABOR COST = .61
90 UNIT MATERIAL COST = .42
95 UNIT COST = SUM(UNIT SELLING COST THRU UNIT MATERIAL COST)
100
65 SALES REVENUE = SALES VOLUME*PRICE
70 NET INCOME = SALES REVENUE - TOTAL EXPENSES
75 * COSTS
80 UNIT SELLING COST = .233
85 UNIT LABOR COST = .61
90 UNIT MATERIAL COST = .42
95 UNIT COST = SUM(UNIT SELLING COST THRU UNIT MATERIAL COST)
100 VARIABLE COST = UNIT COST*SALES VOLUME
105 ADMIN EXPENSES = 450, PREVIOUS ADMIN EXPENSES*1.01
110 TOTAL EXPENSES = VARIABLE COST + ADMIN EXPENSES
115 *PERFORMANCE MEASURES
120 INITIAL INVESTMENT = 3500,0
125 DISCOUNT RATE = .12
130 PRESENT VALUE = NPVC(NET INCOME,DISCOUNT RATE,INITIAL INVEST-
MENT)
140 RATE OF RETURN = IRR(NET INCOME, INITIAL INVESTMENT)
145 *
150 COLUMN 1991 FOR L55,L65,L70,L100,L105,L110,L120 = '
155              SUM(C1 THRU C4)
160 COLUMN 1992 FOR L55,L65,L70,L100,L105,L110,L120 = '
165              SUM(C5 THRU C8)
170 COLUMN GROWTH FOR L55,L65,L70,L100,L105,L110,L120 = '
175              100*(C10-C9)/C9
END OF MODEL
?
```

(3) *The model is displayed*:

Once the model is complete, the solution can be displayed by using a sequence of commands like the ones below. A brief discussion of each command follows the illustration.

EXAMPLE 11 (*Continued*)

180? SOLVE
MODEL NEWPROD VERSION OF 12/20/90 16:38 -- 11 COLUMNS 17 VARI-
    ABLES
ENTER SOLVE OPTIONS
? COLUMNS 1991,5-8,1992,GROWTH
? WIDTH 72, 16, 8
? ALL

ALL instructs IFPS to print the values of all variables.

IFPS OUTPUT

	1991	5	6	7	8	1992	GROWTH
EXAMPLE OF IFPS							
*SALES DATA AND PROJECTIONS:							
PRICE		2.650	2.650	2.650	2.650		
MARKET SHARE		.1300	.1350	.1400	.1450		
TOTAL MARKET		7284	7357	7431	7505		
SALES VOLUME	3341	946.9	993.2	1040	1088	4069	21.76
*PREVIOUS CALCULATIONS:							
SALES REVENUE	8354	2509	2632	2757	2884	10782	29.07
NET INCOME	2306	845.1	904.6	965.2	1027	3742	62.25
*COSTS:							
UNIT SELLING COST		.2330	.2330	.2330	.2330		
UNIT LABOR COST		.6100	.6100	.6100	.6100		
UNIT MATERIAL COST		.4200	.4200	.4200	.4200		
UNIT COST		1.263	1.263	1.263	1.263		
VARIABLE COST	4220	1196	1254	1314	1374	5139	21.76
ADMIN. EXPENSES	1827	468.3	473.0	477.7	482.5	1901	4.060
TOTAL EXPENSES	6047	1664	1727	1792	1857	7040	16.41
*PERFORMANCE MEASURES							
INITIAL INVESTMENT	3500	0	0	0	0	0	-100
DISCOUNT RATE		.1200	.1200	.1200	.1200		
PRESENT VALUE		-623.5	139.7	931.3	1750		
RATE OF RETURN			.1676	.3988	.5812		

(4) *"What if" Analysis*

Instead of merely solving a model as it is, the WHAT IF command can be
used to determine the effect of changes in the definitions of variables in the
model. The examples which follow show how these questions can be
answered:

369

EXAMPLE 11 (*Continued*)

Case	Question
1	What if the total market size starts out at 6,000 units instead of 7,000, but grows by 5% per quarter, instead of 1%?
2	What if the selling price is $2.70 in the second year instead of $2.65 (and total market follows the original assumptions)?
3	What if, in addition to price being $2.70 in 1991, unit material cost is three cents higher than expected in both years?

Note that Cases 1 and 2 are independent while Case 3 builds on the changes made in Case 2. To handle both kinds of situations, two different WHAT IF commands are available:

WHAT IF	Enables the user to modify temporarily as many individual model statements as desired to determine the effect on the solution. Each WHAT IF erases the assumptions made by the previous one.
WHAT IF CONTINUE	Since each WHAT IF normally starts from the base case, this command makes possible successive, cumulative WHAT IF statements.

In the print-out which follows, the user has asked to see only selected variables. In Case 1, individual variable names, separated by commas, are used. In Case 2, model line numbers have been used instead. Case 3 illustrates the use of THRU to print an inclusive list of variables.

The SOLVE OPTIONS entered earlier to specify columns and page layout remain in effect through the modeling session.

? WHAT IF

WHAT IF CASE 1
ENTER STATEMENTS

? TOTAL MARKET = 6000, PREVIOUS TOTAL MARKET * 1.05
? SOLVE

ENTER SOLVE OPTIONS

? NET INCOME, PRESENT WORTH, RATE OF RETURN

EXAMPLE 11 (*Continued*)

```
***** WHAT IF CASE 1 *****
1 WHAT IF STATEMENT PROCESSED
```

	1991	5	6	7	8	1992	GROWTH
NET INCOME	1941	846.7	960.9	1084	1215	4107	111.5
PRESENT WORTH		−966.3	−155.6	733.1	1702		
RATE OF RETURN			.0703	.3240	.5318		

```
ENTER SOLVE OPTIONS

? WHAT IF

WHAT IF CASE 2
ENTER STATEMENTS

? PRICE  = 2.5 FOR 4, 2.70
? SOLVE

ENTER SOLVE OPTIONS

? L70, L130, L140

***** WHAT IF CASE 2 *****
1 WHAT IF STATEMENT PROCESSED
```

	1991	5	6	7	8	1992	GROWTH
NET INCOME	2306	892.5	954.3	1017	1081	3945	71.07
PRESENT WORTH		−582.4	222.7	1057	1919		
RATE OF RETURN			.1952	.4333	.6198		

```
ENTER SOLVE OPTIONS

? WHAT IF CONTINUE

WHAT IF CASE 3
ENTER STATEMENTS

? UNIT MATERIAL COST = UNIT MATERIAL COST + .03
? SOLVE

ENTER SOLVE OPTIONS
? UNIT MATERIAL COST THRU VARIABLE COST
```

EXAMPLE 11 (*Continued*)

***** WHAT IF CASE 3 ******
2 WHAT IF STATEMENTS PROCESSED

	1991	5	6	7	8	1992	GROWTH
UNIT MATERIAL CO		.4500	.4500	.4500	.4500		
UNIT COST		1.293	1.293	1.293	1.293		
VARIABLE COST	4320	1224	1284	1345	1407	5261	21.76

Summary of "What-If" Analysis

Case 1 If the total market size starts out at 6,000 units and grows by 5% per quarter, then net income will go up by 111.5%.

Case 2 If the selling price is $2.70 in the second year, then the net income will go up by 71.07%.

Case 3 If, in addition to price being $2.70 in 1991, unit material cost is three cents higher than expected in both years, then the variable cost will go up by 21.76%.

(5) *"Goal Seeking" Analysis*

The GOAL SEEKING command allows the user to work backwards. That is, the user tells IFPS what assumption can be adjusted and what objective is to be sought. IFPS then solves the model repetitively until it finds the value that yields the desired objective. To illustrate the use of this command, consider the following two situations:

Case	Question
1	Market share estimates could be less than originally expected. How low could it be and still provide first quarter net income of $700 and 3% more in each subsequent quarter?
2	The required initial investment might be larger than originally expected. How much larger could it be and still permit a 25% return over the eight-quarter horizon?

The first question is really asking what market share would have to be in *each column* in order to achieve a certain net income in the same column. The second question asks what investment has to be in column 1 to produce a certain rate of return in column 8.

As shown in the example below, the second question is handled by enclosing the column number in parentheses after the variable name. The variable is then said to be "subscripted."

EXAMPLE 11 (*Continued*)

The command BASE MODEL is issued before GOAL SEEKING. Without this command, modifications made by the last WHAT IF command would still be in effect.

ENTER SOLVE OPTIONS

? BASE MODEL
? GOAL SEEKING

GOAL SEEKING CASE 1
ENTER NAME OF VARIABLE TO BE ADJUSTED TO ACHIEVE PERFORMANCE

? MARKET SHARE

ENTER COMPUTATIONAL STATEMENT FOR PERFORMANCE

? NET INCOME = 700, PREVIOUS NET INCOME * 1.03

***** GOAL SEEKING CASE 1 *****

	1991	5	6	7	8	1992	GROWTH
MARKET SHARE		.1243	.1259	.1274	.1291		

ENTER SOLVE OPTIONS

? NET INCOME, PRESENT WORTH, RATE OF RETURN

	1991	5	6	7	8	1992	GROWTH
NET INCOME	2929	787.9	811.5	835.8	860.9	3296	12.55
PRESENT WORTH		−89.41	595.2	1281	1967		
RATE OF RETURN		.0822	.3446	.5494	.7073		

ENTER SOLVE OPTIONS

? GOAL SEEKING

GOAL SEEKING CASE 2
ENTER NAME OF VARIABLE TO BE ADJUSTED TO ACHIEVE PERFORMANCE

? INITIAL INVESTMENT(1)

ENTER COMPUTATIONAL STATEMENT FOR PERFORMANCE

? RATE OF RETURN(8) = 25%

***** GOAL SEEKING CASE 2 *****

	1991	5	6	7	8	1992	GROWTH
INITIAL INVESTMENT	4595	0	0	0	0	0	−100

ENTER SOLVE OPTIONS

EXAMPLE 11 (*Continued*)

? RATE OF RETURN

	1991	5	6	7	8	1992	GROWTH
RATE OF RETURN				.0835	.2500		

ENTER SOLVE OPTIONS
?

Summary of "Goal-Seeking" Analysis

Case 1 The market share could be as low as .1243 in the first quarter and still provide first quarter net income of $700 and 3% more in each subsequent quarter.

Case 2 The initial investment would have to be $4,595 in order to permit a 25% return over the eight-quarter horizon.

ZERO BASE BUDGETING

The traditional budgeting techniques involve adding or subtracting a given percentage increase or decrease to the preceding period's budget and arriving at a new budget. The prior period's costs are considered to be basic and the emphasis is usually placed on what upward revisions are to be made for the upcoming year. The traditional method focuses on inputs rather than outputs related to goal achievement and as such never calls for the evaluation of corporate activities from a cost/benefit perspective.

Zero-Base Budgeting (ZBB) can generally be described as a technique which requires each manager to justify his entire budget request in detail from a base of zero and as such asks for an analysis of the output values of each activity of a particular cost/responsibility center. This approach requires that all activities under scrutiny be defined in decision packages which are to be evaluated and ranked in order of importance at various levels. As an end product, a body of structured data is obtained that enables management to allocate funds confidently to the areas of greatest potential gain.

ZBB is most applicable in planning service and support expenses rather than direct manufacturing expenses. This technique is best suited to operations and programs over which management has some discretion. For example, it can be used to develop:

— Administrative and general support
— Marketing
— Research
— Engineering
— Manufacturing support
— Capital budgets

Figure 4. Differences Between Traditional and Zero Base Budgeting

Traditional	Zero Base
Starts from existing base	Starts with base zero
Examines cost/benefit for new activities	Examines cost/benefit for all activities
Starts with dollars	Starts with purposes and activities
Does not examine new ways of operating as integral part of process	Explicitly examines new approaches
Results in a non-alternative budget	Results in a choice of several levels of service and cost

It should not be used for:

— Direct labor

— Direct material

— Factory overhead

which are usually budgeted through various methods discussed in the previous section. Figure 4 helps our understanding of ZBB by indicating the key differences between ZBB and traditional (incremental) budgeting systems.

Methodology

ZBB is designed to result in a more rational and efficient allocation of firm resources and replanning support functions by requiring the evaluation of segment overhead activity relative to desired output (company goals). The various actions one would have to take in implementing ZBB are outlined below.

A. Setting Objectives and Assumptions

The business objectives and plan assumptions begin the zero-base budgeting process. Plan assumptions serve as input to the various operating departments in preparing their individual budgets. To effectively analyze the operation, lower management will need planning assumptions about inflation rates, salary increases, and so on. It is possible that in beginning phases, a company would want to test ZBB in a specific division before widespread organizational application.

B. Defining Identifiable Segments

An Activity Unit is the basic cost element which is the subject of ZBB. An Activity Unit is usually made up of a group of employees who work toward a common goal. Such Activity Units are normally broken down into the traditional boundaries of a business although ZBB allows further definition. Activity Units or Division Units can be analyzed for discretionary activity. Activities fixed by law, industry practice, or other constraints are distinguished from those where action can be effected.

These decision units need to be established at an organizational level high enough so that the person responsible for the unit has effective control over the activities. Furthermore, it is desirable for decision units to be roughly similar in size (in terms of personnel and dollars) to allow effective comparison and the definition of the activity units should be specific enough to avoid complications arising from including a multiplicity of activities in a decision unit.

C. Decision Unit Analysis

1. Description of Current Practice

Following the listing of activity objectives, the decision manager describes how his/her department currently operates and the resources used (people/dollars). The description of the operation cannot become overly detailed but should contain the essentials of activities performed and are usually organized to define the flow of work.

2. Work Load and Performance Measurement

Performance measurements are next developed to examine the productivity and effectiveness of the manager's current approach. Some sample performance measurements might include:

- Production Control   — On time delivery performance
- Regional Sales Manager — Number of customer requests for cancellations
- Internal Audit   — Cycle for audit coverage of reporting units
- Quality Control   — Number of shipment deficiencies

3. Alternatives

ZBB next requires that the manager consider alternative ways of operating. After reviewing both the current and alternative operation methods, the manager and superiors will attempt to select the best method of operation on the basis of this analysis which will define the advantages and disadvantages of each method.

Examples of different operating modes would be:

- Centralizing the function
- Decentralizing the function
- Contracting for the function
- Combining the function with other activities
- Eliminating the function

4. Ranking Analysis

In this step, the manager determines which is the most important service provided by his/her unit. The highest priority is given to the minimum increment of service; the amount of service that the organization must undertake to provide any meaningful service. Additional increments are developed with each successive increment containing those services which are next in order of priority. Workload and performance measurements are included in each analysis since they identify meaningful quantitative measurements to assist in the activity unit decision process.

5. Review and Reallocate Resources

The increments developed by unit managers provide top-level management with the basic information for resource allocation decisions. The prioritization of service levels is the key factor in this process. Ranking takes place when the manager meets with all of the decision unit managers to prioritize the unit activities, based on group objectives. Ranking is based on discussions between the decision unit managers and the ranking manager and written cost-benefit analyses provided by each decision unit. Once ranking has been performed at various levels, a ranking table is prepared as a record of all the decisions that have been made in ZBB. This ranking table will indicate what will and will not be funded and rank activities in priorities to allow for easy adjustments to be made during the year.

6. Detailed Budgets Prepared

Once allocation decisions are made, detail budgets are prepared. These budgets usually are prepared on the basis of incremental activities indicated on management's ranking table.

7. Evaluate Performance

ZBB provides financial data as well as work load and performance measurements that can be monitored periodically. To be effective, ZBB needs to be measured and controlled. Some control measures include the following:

• Monthly financial review of each unit—based on costs expended—actual versus budget
• Quarterly output review—based on pre-established performance measurements
• Quarterly plan and budget revisions for company and decision units— based on to-date performance—changed environment factors.

Figure 5 offers a graphic illustration of the steps a company would take in developing and implementing Zero Based Budgeting.

Figure 5. Zero Base Budgeting Process

SENIOR
MANAGEMENT

PLANNING   RANKING   EVALUATION
ASSUMPTIONS   ALLOCATION   AND CONTROL

                                    BUDGET
- PREPARATION- - - - - - - -

IDENTIFY   DECISION
DECISION   UNIT
UNITS   ANALYSIS

MIDDLE

Advantages and Disadvantages

The advantages and disadvantages of ZBB are as follows:

A. Advantages

1. ZBB creates an analytical atmosphere which promotes the reorganization of activities to a more efficient mode and causes the evaluation of tasks from an output perspective.

2. ZBB involves line managers in the budgeting process and as such fosters support for implementation down the company levels.

3. ZBB allows top management to define those service levels required from each business segment.

4. ZBB matches service levels to available resources and ensures overheads are appropriate to the market place.

B. Disadvantages

1. ZBB is perceived as an implied threat to existing programs.

2. ZBB requires a good data system to support analysis and in many cases no such system exists.

3. ZBB increases the demand of time placed on line managers.

4. Managers tend to overlook the goal of ZBB in evaluating Activity Units and focus on personnel security and interests.

5. Thrust usually comes from top to bottom and subordinates see little benefit for themselves.

6. The thought of creating a budget from scratch usually causes considerable resistance given the lack of support groups and training programs.

CONCLUSION

A budget is a detailed quantitative plan outlining the acquisition and use of financial and other resources of an organization over some given time period. It is a tool for planning. If properly constructed, it is used as a control device. This chapter showed, step-by-step, how to formulate a master budget. The process begins with the development of a sales budget and proceeds through a number of steps that ultimately lead to the cash budget, the budgeted income statement, and the budgeted balance sheet.

In recent years, computer-based models and spreadsheet software have been utilized for budgeting in an effort to speed up the budgeting process and allow budget analysts to investigate the effects of changes in budget assumptions. Financial models comprise a functional branch of a general corporate planning model. They are essentially used to generate pro-forma financial statements and financial ratios. These are the basic tools for budgeting and profit planning. Also, the financial model is a technique for risk analysis and "what-if" experiments. The financial model is also needed for day-to-day operational and tactical decisions for immediate planning problems.

Zero-base budgeting (ZBB) has received considerable attention recently as a new approach to budgeting, particularly for use in nonprofit, governmental, and service-type organizations. This chapter discussed the pros and cons of ZBB.

18

Using Variance Analysis as a Financial Tool

A standard cost is a predetermined cost of manufacturing, servicing, or marketing an item during a given future period. It is based on current and projected future conditions. The norm is also dependent upon quantitative and qualitative measurements. Standards may be based on engineering studies looking at time and motion. While the development of standards is primarily the responsibility of the industrial engineer, the managerial accountant should work closely with the engineer to assure that the formulated standard is accurate and useful for control purposes.

Standards are set at the beginning of the period. They may be in physical and dollar terms. Standards assist in the measurement of both effectiveness and efficiency. Examples are sales quotas, standard costs (e.g. material price, wage rate), and standard volume. Variances are not independent, so a favorable variance in one responsibility area may result in an unfavorable one in other segments of the business.

Variance analysis compares standard to actual performance. It could be done by department, program, or cost center. When more than one department is used in a production process, individual standards should be developed for each department in order to assign accountability to department managers. Variances may be as detailed as necessary considering the cost-benefit relationship. Evaluation of variances may be done yearly, quarterly, monthly, daily, or hourly, depending on the importance of identifying a problem quickly. Since you do not know actual figures (e.g., hours spent) until the end of the period, variances can only be arrived at this time. A material variance requires highlighting who is responsible and taking corrective action. Insignificant variances need not be looked into further unless they recur repeatedly and/or reflect potential difficulty. Generally, a variance should be investigated when the inquiry is anticipated to result in corrective action that will reduce costs by an amount exceeding the cost of the inquiry.

When the production cycle is long, variances that are computed at the time of product completion may be too late for prompt corrective action to be taken. In such a case, inspection may be undertaken at "key" points during the processing stage. This allows for spoilage, labor inefficiency, and other costs associated with problems to be recognized before product completion.

One measure to materiality is to divide the variance by the standard cost. A variance of less that 5% may be deemed immaterial. A 10% variation may be more acceptable to a company using tight standards compared to a 5% variation to a company employing loose standards. In some cases, materiality is looked at in terms of dollar amount or volume level. For example, you may set a policy looking into any variance that exceeds $10,000 or 20,000 units, whichever is less. Guidelines for materiality also depend upon the nature of the particular element as it affects performance and decision making. For example, where the item is critical to the future functioning of the business (e.g., critical part, promotion, repairs), limits for materiality should be such that reporting is encouraged. Further, statistical techniques can be used to ascertain the significance of cost and revenue variances. The managerial accountant must establish an acceptable range of tolerance for management (e.g., percent). Even if a variance never exceeds a minimum allowable percentage or minimum dollar amount, the managerial accountant may want to bring it to management's attention if the variance is consistently close to the prescribed limit each year. Perhaps this may indicate the standard is out-of-date and proper adjustment to current levels is mandated so as to improve overall profit planning. It could also indicate lax cost control requiring a check by the supervisor as to operations.

Because of the critical nature of costs, such as advertising and mainte-nance, materiality guidelines are more stringent.

Often the reason for the variance is out-of-date standards or a poor bud-getary process. Thus, it may not be due to actual performance.

By questioning the variances and trying to find answers, the managerial accountant can make the operation more efficient and less costly. It must be understood, however, that quality should be maintained.

If a variance is out of management's control, follow-up action by manage-ment is not called for. For instance, utility rates are not controllable internally.

Standards may change at different operational volume levels. Further, standards should be periodically appraised, and when they no longer real-istically reflect conditions they should be modified. Standards may not be realistic any longer because of internal events (e.g., product design) or external conditions such as management and competitive changes. For instance, stan-dards should be revised when prices, material specifications, product designs, labor rates, labor efficiency, and production methods change to such a degree that present standards no longer provide a useful measure of performance.

Changes in the methods or channels of distribution, or basic organizational or functional changes, would require changes in selling and administrative activities.

Note: Significant favorable variances should also be investigated and should be further taken advantage of. Those responsible for good performance should be rewarded.

For variable and semi-variable costs, the accuracy of standards developed depends on the ability of the method to measure the correlation between cost incurrence and output bases. Regression analysis may provide reliable association.

Variances are interrelated and hence the net effect has to be examined. For example, a favorable price variance may arise when lower quality materials are bought at a cheaper price but the quantity variance will be unfavorable because of more production time to manufacture the goods due to poor material quality.

In the case of automated manufacturing facilities, standard cost information can be integrated with the computer that directs operations. Variances can then be identified and reported by the computer system and necessary adjustments made as the operation proceeds.

In appraising variances, consideration should be given to information that may have been for whatever reason, omitted from the reports. Have there been changes in the production processes which have not been reflected in the reports? Have new product lines increased set-up times that necessitate changes in the standards?

USEFULNESS OF VARIANCE ANALYSIS

Standards and variance analyses resulting therefrom are essential in financial analysis and decision making.

Advantages of Standards and Variances

- Aid in inventory costing
- Assist in decision making
- Sell price formulation based on what costs should be
- Aid in coordinating by having all departments focus on common goals
- Set and evaluate corporate objectives
- Cost control and performance evaluation by comparing actual to budgeted figures. The objective of cost control is to produce an item at the lowest possible cost according to predetermined quality standards.
- Highlight problem areas through the "management by exception" principle
- Pinpoint responsibility for undesirable performance so that corrective action may be taken. Variances in product activity (cost, quality, quantity)

are typically the foreman's responsibility. Variances in sales orders and market share are often the responsibility of the marketing manager. Variances in prices and methods of deliveries are the responsibility of purchasing personnel. Variances in profit usually relate to overall operations. Variances in return on investment relate to asset utilization.

- Act in motivating employees to accomplish predetermined goals
- Facilitate communication within the organization such as between top management and supervisors
- Assist in planning by forecasting needs (e.g., cash requirements)
- Establish bid prices on contracts
- Simplify bookkeeping procedures by keeping the records at standard cost

Standard costing is not without some drawbacks. Examples: The possible biases in deriving standards and the dysfunctional effects of establishing improper norms and standards.

When a variance has multiple causes, each cause should be cited.

STANDARD SETTING

Standards may be set by engineers, production managers, purchasing managers, personnel administrators, managerial accountants, and so on. Depending on the nature of the cost item, computerized models can be used to corroborate what the standard costs should be. Standards may be established through test runs or mathematical and technological analysis.

Standards are based on the particular situation being appraised. Some examples follow:

Situation	Standard
Cost reduction	Tight
Pricing policy	Realistic
High-quality goods	Perfection

Capacity may be expressed in units, weight, size, dollars, selling price, direct labor hours, and so on. It may be expressed in different time periods (e.g., weekly, monthly, yearly).

Types of Standards

- *Basic.* These are not changed from period to period and are used in the same way as an index number. They form the basis to which later period performance is compared. What is unrealistic about it is that no consideration is given to a change in the environment.
- *Maximum efficiency.* These are perfect standards assuming ideal, optimal conditions, allowing for no losses of any kind even those considered

unavoidable. They will always result in unfavorable variances. Realistically, certain inefficiencies will occur such as materials will not always arrive at work stations on time and tools will break. Ideal standards can not be used in forecasting and planning because they do not provide for normal inefficiencies.

- *Currently attainable (practical)*. These refer to the volume of output possible if a facility operated continuously, but after allowing for normal and unavoidable losses such as vacations, holidays, and repairs. Currently attainable standards are based on efficient activity. They are possible but difficult to achieve. Considered are normal occurrences such as anticipated machinery failure and normal materials shortage. Practical standards should be set high enough to motivate employees and low enough to permit normal interruptions. Besides pointing to abnormal deviations in costs, practical standards may be used in forecasting cash flows and in planning inventory. Attainable standards are typically used in practice.
- *Expected*. These are expected figures based on foreseeable operating conditions and costs. They come very close to actual figures.

Standards should be set at a level that is realistic to accomplish. Those affected by the standards should participate in formalizing them so there will be internalization of goals. When reasonable standards exist employees typically become cost conscious and try to accomplish the best results at the least cost. If standards are too tight, they will discourage employee performance. If they are too loose, they will result in inefficient operations. If employees receive bonuses for exceeding normal standards, the standards may be even more effective as motivation tools.

A standard is not an absolute and precise figure. Realistically, a standard constitutes a range of possible acceptable results. Thus, variances can and do occur within a normal upper-lower limit. In determining tolerance limits, relative magnitudes are more important than absolute values. For instance, if the standard cost for an activity is $100,000 a plus or minus range of $4,000 may be tolerable.

Variance analysis is usually complicated by the problem of computing the number equivalent units of production.

Variances may be controllable, partly controllable, or uncontrollable. It is not always easy to assign responsibility even in the case of controllable variances. The extent to which a variance is controllable depends on the nature of the standard, the cost involved, and the particular factors causing the variance.

EXAMPLE 1

Manufacturing, service, food, and not-for-profit entities use standards (costs or quantities) to some degree. For instance, auto service centers establish labor time standards for the completion of certain tasks, such as for a tuneup, and then measure actual results against the standards. Fast-food stores (e.g., Burger King) have standards as to the amount of meat for a sandwich, as well as standards for the cost of the meat. Hospitals have standards (e.g., food, laundry) for each patient per day, as well as standard times to perform certain typical activities, such as laboratory testing.

PLANNING VARIANCE

The planning variance arises when expected industry or other environmental factors do not materialize. For example, at the beginning of the period, the sales projection may be based on reviewing supply and demand. However, because of actual conditions in the industry, the actual sales may be much less. This sales unit variance may then be deemed a planning error, and not a performance problem. Industry sales are typically considered beyond management control.

SALES VARIANCES

Sales standards may be established to control and measure the effectiveness of the marketing operations as well as for other relevant purposes such as stimulating sales, reallocating sales resources, and providing incentive awards. The usual standard set for a salesperson, branch, or territory is a sales quota. While the sales quota is typically expressed in dollars it may also be expressed in volume. Other types of standards that may be set to evaluate sales efforts are number of calls, order size, gross profit obtained, new customers obtained, and number of regular customers retained.

Sales variances are computed to gauge the performance of the marketing function.

EXAMPLE 2

Western Corporation's budgeted sales for 19X1 were

Product A 10,000 units at $6.00 per unit	$ 60,000
Product B 30,000 units at $8.00 per unit	240,000
Expected sales revenue	$300,000

Actual sales for the year were

Product A 8,000 units at $6.20 per unit	$ 49,600
Product B 33,000 units at $7.70 per unit	254,100
Actual sales revenue	$303,700

There is a favorable sales variance of $3,700, consisting of the sales price variance and the sales volume variance.

The sales price variance equals
(Actual Selling Price versus Budgeted Selling Price) $\times$
Actual Units Sold

Product A ($6.20 versus $6.00 $\times$ 8,000)	$ 1,600 Favorable
Product B ($7.70 versus $8.00 $\times$ 33,000)	9,900 Unfavorable
Sales price variance	$ 8,300 Unfavorable

The sales volume variance equals
(Actual Quantity versus Budgeted Quantity) $\times$ Budgeted Selling Price

Product A (8,000 versus 10,000 $\times$ $6.00)	$12,000 Unfavorable
Product B (33,000 versus 30,000 $\times$ $8.00)	24,000 Favorable
Sales volume variance	$12,000 Favorable

The sales price variance indicates if the product is being sold at a discount or premium. Sales price variances may be due to uncontrollable market conditions or managerial decisions. However, a sales price variance is not recorded in the books.

The analysis of sales volume includes consideration of budgets, standards, sales plans, industry comparisons, and manufacturing costs. Note that high sales volume does not automatically mean high profits. There may be high costs associated with the products.

An unfavorable sales volume variance may arise from poor marketing or to price cuts by competing companies. If the unfavorable volume variance is coupled with a favorable price variance, your company may have lost sales by raising its prices.

The sales volume variance reflects the effect on the total budgeted contribution margin that is caused by changes in the total number of units sold. The variance can be caused by unpredictable product demand, lack of product demand, or from poor sales forecasting. The sales volume variance is not recorded in the accounts.

An unfavorable total sales variance may signal a problem with the marketing manager because he or she has control over sales, advertising, and often pricing. Another possible cause of the unfavorable sales situation may be due to a lack in quality control, substitution of poorer quality components due to deficient purchasing, or deficient product design emanating from poor engineering.

The sales variances (price and volume) are prepared only for the product sales report and the sales district report.

The sales vice-president is responsible for sales variances and must explain deviations to the president.

An electronic worksheet can be used to compute sales variances (refer to the July, 1985 issue of LOTUS, pp. 46–48).

COST VARIANCES

When a product is made or a service is performed, you have to determine these three measures:

- Actual cost equals actual price times actual quantity, where actual quantity equals actual quantity per unit of work times actual units of work produced
- Standard cost equals standard price times standard quantity, where standard quantity equals standard quantity per unit of work times actual units of work produced.
- Total (control) variance equals actual cost less standard cost
  Total (control) variance has the following elements:
- Price (rate, cost) variance:
  (Standard Price versus Actual Price) × Actual Quantity
- Quantity (usage, efficiency) variance:
  (Standard Quantity versus Actual Quantity) × Standard Price
    These are computed for both material and labor.
    Figure 1 depicts the variance analysis.

A variance is unfavorable when actual cost is higher than standard cost.

MATERIAL VARIANCES

Quantity and delivery standards have to be established before a standard price per unit can be determined. Material price standards are set by the cost accounting department and/or purchasing department because they have

Figure 1. Variance Analysis

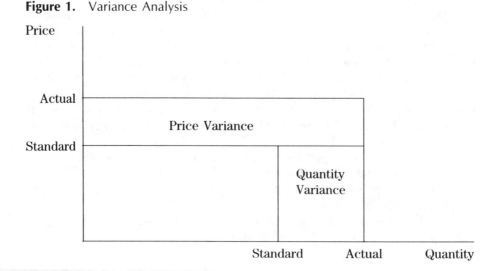

knowledge of price data and market conditions. The company should increase the initial standard price per unit to a standard weighted-average price per unit to incorporate expected price increases for the period. The standard price should reflect the total cost of buying the material which includes the basic price less discounts plus freight, receiving, and handling. The standard price must coincide with the specific quality material. In setting the material price standard, the price should be in accord with the firm's inventory policies regarding the most economical order size and/or frequency of ordering. It is further assumed that buying, shipping, and warehousing will occur on favorable terms. Special bargain prices are ignored unless they are readily available. The material price standard should include normal or unavoidable spoilage allocations.

You can use the material price variance to evaluate the activity of the purchasing department and to see the impact of raw material cost changes on profitability. A material price variance may be isolated at the time of purchase or usage.

The material quantity variance is the responsibility of the production supervisor. Material quantity standards should not only include the raw materials but also purchased parts, cartons, and packing materials which are visible in, or can be directly related to the product. Material quantity standards are basically determined from material specifications prepared by engineers based on product design and production flow. The standard quantity should be based on the most economical size and quality of product. It should be increased to take into account normal waste, rejections, and spoilage. The standard should consider prior experience for the same or similar operation. Test runs may be made under controlled conditions. Material standards may be aided by analyzing previous experiences using descriptive statistics and/or test runs under controlled conditions. Physical standards for materials are based on determination of kind and quality specifications, quantity specifications, and assembly specifications.

When many different types of raw materials are needed for a product, the types and standard quantities of each raw material is itemized on the *standard bill of materials*.

EXAMPLE 3

The standard cost of one unit of output (product or service) was $15: three pieces at $5 per piece. During the period, 8,000 units were made. Actual cost was $14 per unit; two pieces at $7 per piece.

Total Material Variance

Standard quantity times standard price (24,000 × $5)	$120,000
Actual quantity times actual price (16,000 × $7)	112,000
	$ 8,000 F

Material Price Variance

(Standard price versus actual price) times actual quantity
   ($5 versus $7 $\times$ 16,000) $ 32,000 U

Material Quantity Variance

(Standard quantity versus actual quantity) times standard
   price (24,000 versus 16,000 $\times$ $5) $ 40,000 F

When the amount of material purchased is different from the amount issued to production, the stores account should be carried at standard cost and a price variance determined at the time of purchase. When material is issued, a quantity (usage) variance is determined. In this case, the variances are determined as follows:

Material Price Variance

(Actual price versus standard price) times actual quantity bought

Material Quantity Variance

(Actual quantity issued versus standard quantity issued) times standard price

EXAMPLE 4

Material purchased was 20,000 pounds. Material issued to production was 15,000 pounds. Material budgeted per unit is one pound. Budgeted price is $2.50 per pound while actual price is $3.00 per pound. Production was 10,000 units.

Material Price Variance

(Actual price versus standard price) times quantity
   purchased

($3.00 versus $2.50) $\times$ 20,000 $10,000 U

Material Quantity Variance

(Actual quantity issued versus standard quantity) $\times$
   standard price

(15,000 versus 10,000) $\times$ $2.50 $12,500 U

You cannot control material price variances when higher prices are due to inflation or shortage situations, or when rush orders are required by the customer who will bear the ultimate cost increase.

If the material price variance is favorable, one would expect higher quality material being acquired. Thus, a favorable usage variance should be forthcoming. If it is not, there is an inconsistency. A favorable material price variance may occur from other causes such as when actual price is less than expected because of excess supply of the raw material in the industry.

The controllable portion of a price variance should be segregated from the uncontrollable in management reports. Exhibit 1 presents a Daily Material Price Variance Report.

Generally, the material quantity variance is the responsibility of the production department. However, the purchasing department will be responsible for inferior goods to economize on cost.

The reason and responsible party for an unfavorable material variance follows:

Reason

Overstated price paid, failure to take discounts, improper specifications, insufficient quantities, use of a lower grade material purchased to economize on price, uneconomical size of purchase orders, failure to obtain an adequate supply of a needed variety, purchase at an irregular time, or sudden and unexpected purchase required	Responsible Party Purchasing
Poor mix of materials, poorly trained workers, improperly adjusted machines, substitution of nonstandard materials, poor production scheduling, poor product design or production technique, lack of proper tools or machines, carelessness in not returning excess materials to storeroom, or unexpected volume changes	Production Manager
Failure to detect defective goods	Receiving
Inefficient labor, poor supervision, or waste on the production line	Foreman
Inaccurate standard price	Budgeting
Excessive transportation charges or too small a quantity purchased	Traffic management
Insufficient quantity bought because of a lack of funds	Financial

To correct an unfavorable material price variance, you can increase selling price, substitute cheaper materials, change a production method or specification, or engage in a cost-reduction program.

An unfavorable price variance does not automatically mean the purchasing department is not performing well. It may point to a need for new pricing, product, or buying decisions. For these purposes, price variances may be

Exhibit 1

DETAIL OF MATERIAL PRICE VARIANCE

Date _____ Prepared by _____ Approved by _____

Voucher No.	Item No.	Item Name	Vendor No.	Quantity Purchased	Standard Cost		Actual Cost		Variance		Percent from Standard	Explanation
					Per Unit	Total	Per Unit	Total	Per Unit	Total		

broken down by product, vendor class, or other appropriate distinction. When several types of raw materials are used, it might be better to break down the price variance by major category of material used (e.g., steel, paint).

Tip: You should examine the variability in raw material costs. Look at price instability in trade publications. Emphasize vertical integration to reduce the price and supply risk of raw materials.

To aid in identifying material usage variances, if additional material is required to complete the job, additional materials requisitions could be issued in a different color with a distinctive code number to show that the quantity of material is above standard. This approach brings attention to the excessive usage of materials while production is in process and allows for the early control of a developing problem. When material usage is recorded by flow meters, such as in chemical operations, usage variances can be identified on materials usage forms in a similar manner as excess labor hours identified on labor time tickets.

Managers should have the option to acquire cheaper raw materials or to combine available resources so that overall corporate costs are minimized. For instance, slightly inferior raw materials (i.e., lower grade of metals) may intentionally be purchased at a bargain price. The material price variance may thus be quite favorable. However, such raw material component may cause above average defective finished items and/or excessive productive labor hours resulting in an unfavorable efficiency variance. The manager may have permission to engage in this tradeoff if it results in a significant net reduction in total manufacturing costs. A standard cost system should not be rigid in the sense that an unfavorable variance is regarded as always being bad. One should look to see if overall corporate objectives have been accomplished. Since many interdependencies exist, one should look at the entire picture rather than at just the fact that a given variance is unfavorable.

When computing material price variances, it may be good to eliminate increasing costs due to inflation, which are not controllable by management.

Illustration of How Inflationary Cost Increases May Be Isolated from the Material Price Variance

Assume the following data for Charles Company for 19X1.

Standard price of material per foot	$3.00
Actual price of material per foot	3.80
Actual material used	10,000 ft.
The inflation rate for the year is 16%.	

The direct material price variance can be broken down into the inflation aspect and the controllable element.

Price variance due to inflation

(Standard price versus Inflation adjusted price) × actual quantity

$3.00 versus $3.48 $\times$ 10,000 ft $4,800

Controllable price variance

(Inflation adjusted price versus actual price) $\times$ actual quantity

$3.48 versus $3.80 $\times$ 10,000 ft $3,200

Proof—Material Price Variance

(Standard price versus actual price) $\times$ actual quantity

$3.00 versus $3.80 $\times$ 10,000 ft $8,000

It is important to have prompt reporting to lower managerial levels. Production managers should immediately be informed of variances so problems are identified and corrections made at the production level.

Exhibit 2 presents a daily material usage report. Exhibit 3 presents a monthly material variance report.

LABOR VARIANCES

Standard labor rates may be computed based on the current rates adjusted for future changes in such variables as:

- Union contracts
- Changes in operating conditions
- Changes in the mix of skilled versus unskilled labor
- The average experience of workers

Exhibit 2

DAILY MATERIAL USAGE REPORT

Cost Center   Unit
Material Type   Date

		Daily			Month		Year	
Date	Variance	Variance Percent	Explanation	Variance	Variance Percent	Variance	Variance Percent

Exhibit 3

MONTHLY MATERIAL VARIANCE REPORT

| Department | Month | | Year to Date | |
	Variance	Percent	Variance	Percent

The wage system affects the standard cost rates. The basic rates are (1) day or hourly, (2) straight piece rate, and (3) multiple piece rates or bonus systems. Wage incentive systems can be tied to a standard cost system once standards have been formulated.

While direct labor quantities may be obtained from engineering estimates, line supervisors can corroborate the estimates by observing and timing employees.

When salary rates are set by union contract, the labor rate variance will usually be minimal. For planning purposes, the rate standard should be the average rate expected to prevail during the planning period. **Note:** Labor rates for the same operation may vary due to seniority or union agreement.

Labor time standards should include only the elements controllable by the worker or work center. If the major purpose of a cost system is control, there should be a tight labor time standard. If costing or pricing is the major purpose of the cost system, looser labor standards are needed. Labor efficiency standards are typically estimated by engineers on the basis of an analysis of the production operation. The standard time may include allowances for normal breaks, personal needs, and machine downtime.

Labor variances are determined in a manner similar to that in which material variances are determined. Labor variances are isolated when labor is used for production.

EXAMPLE 5

The standard cost of labor is four hours times $9 per hour, or $36 per unit. During the period, 7,000 units were produced. The actual cost is six hours times $8 per hour, or $48 per unit.

Total Labor Variance

Standard quantity times standard price ($28,000 \times \$9$)	$252,000
Actual quantity times actual price ($42,000 \times \$8$)	336,000
	$ 84,000 U

Labor Price Variance

(Standard price versus actual price) times actual quantity
($9 versus $8 $\times$ 42,000) $ 42,000 F

Labor Quantity Variance

(Standard quantity versus actual quantity) $\times$ standard price
(28,000 versus 42,000 $\times$ $9) $126,000 U

Possible causes of *unfavorable* labor variances are:
For a labor price (rate) variance:

- Increase in wages
- Poor scheduling of production resulting in overtime work
- Use of workers commanding higher hourly rates than expected

For a labor efficiency variance:

- Poor supervision
- Use of unskilled workers paid lower rates or the wrong mixture of labor for a given job
- Use of poor quality machinery
- Improperly trained workers
- Poor quality of materials requiring more labor time in processing
- Machine breakdowns
- Employee unrest
- Production delays due to power failure

Possible reasons for a labor price variance and the one responsible follow.

Reason	Responsible Party
Use of overpaid or excessive number of workers	Production manager or union contract
Poor job descriptions or excessive wages	Personnel
Overtime and poor scheduling of production	Production Planning

In the case of a shortage of skilled workers, it may be impossible to avoid an unfavorable labor price variance.

Price variances due to external factors are beyond management control (e.g., a new minimum wage established by the government).

The cause and responsible party for an unfavorable labor efficiency variance follows:

Cause	Responsible Entity
Poor quality workers or poor training	Personnel or Training
Inadequate supervision, inefficient flow of materials, wrong mixture of labor for a given job, inferior tools or idle time from production delays	Foreman
Employee unrest	Personnel or Foreman
Improper functioning of equipment	Maintenance
Insufficient material supply or poor quality	Purchasing

To control against an unfavorable labor efficiency variance due to inadequate materials or sales orders, a daily direct labor report should be prepared.

An unfavorable labor efficiency variance may indicate that better machinery is needed, plant layout should be revised, improved operating methods are needed, and better employee training and development are required.

If a permanent change occurs in the amount of labor required or the labor wage rate for the various types of employee help, the company may wish to switch to more capital assets than labor.

Variances interrelate. A favorable labor efficiency variance coupled with an unfavorable labor rate variance may mean that higher skilled labor was employed than was necessary. However, the supervisor would be justified in doing this if a rush order arose in which the selling price was going to be upwardly adjusted.

Exhibit 4 presents a daily labor mix report. Exhibit 5 presents a labor performance report. Looking at this report aids in evaluating labor effectiveness and coming up with a revision in labor policies. A graph of weekly labor efficiency is presented in Figure 2.

Exhibit 4

DAILY LABOR MIX REPORT

Department Skill level	Actual Hours	Actual Hours in Standard Proportions	Output Variance
I			
II			
III			

Exhibit 5

LABOR PERFORMANCE REPORT

Department

	Day		Date	
Machine Operator	Achieved in Percent	Explanation	Month to Date in Percent	Year to Date in Percent

OVERHEAD VARIANCES

Management is concerned with the tradeoff between fixed and variable costs. As the output level increases, the capital intensive business will be more efficient. The cost associated with a wrong decision is the variance between the total costs of operating the given plant and the total costs of operating the most efficient one based on the actual output level.

Overhead variances may be determined by department and by cost center. Fixed and variable overhead variances should be analyzed independently. In many firms, variances are expressed in both dollars and physical measures.

Figure 2. Labor Efficiency by Week

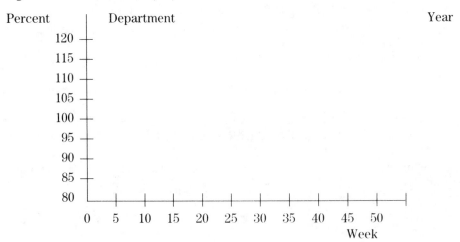

Variable Overhead Variances

The two variances associated with variable overhead are price (spending) and efficiency.

Variable Overhead Price (Spending) Variance

Actual variable overhead versus Budget adjusted to actual hours (actual hours $\times$ standard variable overhead rate)

Variable Overhead Efficiency Variance

Budget adjusted to actual hours versus budget adjusted to standard hours (standard hours $\times$ standard variable overhead rate)

Variable overhead variance information is helpful in arriving at the output level and output mix decisions. The production department is usually responsible for any variable overhead variance that might occur. It also assists in appraising decisions regarding variable inputs.

EXAMPLE 6

The standard hours is three hours per unit. The standard variable overhead rate is $12 per hour. Actual variable overhead is $13,000. There are 2,500 actual hours. Production is 1,000 units. The variable overhead variances are:

Variable Overhead Price Variance

Actual variable overhead	$13,000
Budget adjusted to actual hours (2,500 $\times$ $4)	10,000
Price Variance	$ 3,000 U

Variable Overhead Efficiency Variance

Budget adjusted to actual hours	$10,000
Budget adjusted to standard hours (3,000 $\times$ $4)	12,000
Efficiency Variance	$ 2,000 F

Fixed Overhead Variances

Fixed overhead may be analyzed in terms of the budget (flexible-budget, spending) variance and volume (production volume) variances. The volume variance may be further broken down into the efficiency and pure volume variances.

Fixed Overhead Budget Variance

Actual fixed overhead versus budgeted fixed overhead (denominator or budget hours $\times$ standard fixed overhead rate).

Note: Budgeted fixed overhead may also be referred to as lump-sum amount.

Fixed Overhead Volume Variance

Budgeted fixed overhead versus standard overhead (standard hours $\times$ standard fixed overhead rate)

The breakdown of the volume variance follows:

Fixed Overhead Efficiency Variance
(Actual hours versus standard hours) $\times$ standard fixed overhead rate

Fixed Overhead Pure Volume Variance

(Actual hours versus budgeted hours) $\times$ standard fixed overhead rate

Fixed overhead variance data provide information about decision-making astuteness when buying some combination of fixed plant size variable production inputs. However, variances for fixed overhead are of questionable usefulness for control purposes, since these variances are usually beyond the control of the production department.

The volume variance is a measure of the cost of deviating from denominator (budgeted) volume used to set the fixed overhead rate. When actual volume is less than budgeted volume, the volume variance will be unfavorable. In the opposite case, the volume variance is favorable because it is considered as a benefit of better than anticipated utilization of facilities.

EXAMPLE 7

Standard hours are two hours per unit. Standard fixed overhead rate is $20 per hour. Actual hours per unit are two. Total production is 9,500 units. Actual hours are 20,200. Actual fixed overhead is $420,000. The denominator activity is 10,000 units. The fixed overhead variances are:

Fixed Overhead Budget Variance

Actual fixed overhead	$420,000
Budgeted fixed overhead (10,000 $\times$ 2 = 20,000 $\times$ $20)	400,000
Budget Variance	$ 20,000 U

Volume Variance

Budgeted fixed overhead	$400,000
Standard fixed overhead (9,500 $\times$ 2 = 19,000 $\times$ $20)	380,000
Volume Variance	$ 20,000 U

The production volume variance of $20,000 is now broken down into the efficiency and pure volume variances.

Fixed Overhead Efficiency Variance

(Actual hours versus standard hours) $\times$ standard fixed overhead rate

(20,200 versus 19,000) $\times$ $20 $ 24,000 U

Fixed Overhead Pure Volume Variance

(Actual hours versus budget hours) $\times$ standard fixed overhead rate

(20,200 versus 20,000) $\times$ $20 $ 4,000 F

Variances for Total Overhead

One way, two-way, and three-way analysis may be used for total overhead.

One-Way Method

The total (control, net) variance is:

Total Overhead Variance

Actual overhead

Standard overhead (standard hours $\times$ standard overhead rate)

Two-Way Method

Under the two-variance method, the overhead variance comprises the controllable (budget, flexible budget, spending) and volume (capacity, idle capacity, activity, denominator) variances.

Controllable Variance

Actual overhead

Budget adjusted to standard hours

     Fixed overhead (denominator hours $\times$ standard fixed overhead rate)

     Variable overhead (standard hours $\times$ standard variable overhead rate)

Volume (Production) Variance

Standard overhead

Budget adjusted to standard hours

The controllable (budget) variance may indicate changes in the amount charged for overhead services or in the correlation between overhead items and the variable used to measure output. If such changes are of a permanent nature, output levels may have to be revised.

Management uses the overhead budget variance as a basis for determining the extent to which the cost centers were within their budgeted cost levels. Such variances are useful in formulating decisions regarding cost center operations.

The controllable variance is the responsibility of the foreman, since he influences actual overhead incurred. An unfavorable variance may be due to price increases, a lack of control over costs, and to waste.

The volume variance is the responsibility of management executives and production managers, since they are involved with plant utilization. **Note:** A consistently unfavorable volume variance may be due to having purchased the incorrect size plant. An unfavorable volume variance may arise from controllable factors such as poor scheduling, lack of orders, shortages or defectiveness in raw materials, inadequate tooling, lack of employees, machine breakdowns, long operating times, and incompetent workers. Uncontrollable factors for the overhead volume variance are decrease in customer demand, excess plant capacity, and calendar fluctuations (e.g., differences in number of working days in a month).

Overhead capacity variances can bring to a manager's attention the existence of slack resources. Idle capacity may imply long-run operating planning deficiencies.

The volume of activity is often determined outside the factory based on customer orders. If this is the case, volume variances may not be controllable by the department head or even by the plant manager. They should still be reported to plant managers to help in explaining the total overhead variance to higher management.

Responsibility for the factory overhead volume variance rests with those responsible in generating volume. In some cases, marketing managers, rather than manufacturing managers, bear this responsibility.

Possible Reasons for a Recurring Unfavorable Overhead Volume Variance

- Buying the wrong size plant
- Improper scheduling
- Insufficient orders
- Shortages in material
- Machinery failure
- Long operating time
- Inadequately trained workers

When idle capacity exists, this may indicate long-term operating planning problems.

A deficiency of controllable overhead variance analysis is the failure to segregate the responsibility for increased costs due to inflation from those due to inefficient spending. This deficiency can be corrected through a revised method of overhead analysis taking into account inflation [see A. Adelberg and R. Polimeni, "The Analysis of Factory Overhead Variances (Under Conditions of General and Specific Price-Level Changes)," *Cost and Management*, December 1987, pp. 28–31].

Note: A favorable variance may be causing an unfavorable one. For example, lower maintenance expenditures for equipment may lower the overhead budget variance, but lead to machinery breakdowns causing an unfavorable volume variance.

Three-Way Method

The three-variance method involves further analysis of the two-variance method. The three-way approach consists of the spending, efficiency, and volume variances. **Note:** The volume variance is identical under the three-way and two-way approaches. The controllable variance under the two-way method is broken down into the spending and efficiency variances under the three-way method.

Spending Variance

Actual overhead

Budget adjusted to actual hours

Fixed overhead (denominator hours × standard fixed overhead rate)

Variable overhead (Actual hours × standard variable overhead rate)

Efficiency Variance

Budget adjusted to actual hours

Budget adjusted to standard hours

Volume (Production) Variance

Budget adjusted to standard hours

Standard overhead

The efficiency variance is the responsibility of the foreman and arises from inefficiencies or efficiencies in the production process. The variance is unfavorable when actual hours exceed standard hours charged to production. Inefficiencies may arise from such factors as unskilled labor, modification of operations, deficient machinery, and inferior quality materials.

Spending and efficiency variances are under the responsibility of the department supervisor. The volume variance is attributable to executive management since the decision as to the degree of plant utilization rests with them. Idle capacity may be due to the lack of a proper balance between production facilities and sales. It may also arise from a favorable selling price that recover fixed overhead at an exceptionally low production level.

EXAMPLE 8

The standards for total overhead are:
Variable overhead 2 hrs. @ \$6 = \$12 per unit
Fixed overhead   2 hrs. @ \$20 = \$40 per unit
The actual figures are:
Production 9,500 units
Denominator activity 10,000 units
Variable overhead \$115,000
Fixed overhead \$420,000
Actual hours 20,200

Part 1: *One-Way Analysis*

Control Variance

Actual overhead (\$115,000 + \$420,000)	\$535,000	
Standard overhead (9,500 × 2 = 19,000 × \$26)	494,000	
Control Variance	\$ 41,000	U

Part 2: *Two-Way Analysis*

Controllable Variance

Actual overhead		\$535,000	
Budget adjusted to standard hours			
Fixed overhead (10,000 × 2 = 20,000 × \$20)	\$400,000		
Variable overhead (19,000 × \$6)	114,000		
		514,000	
Controllable Variance		\$ 21,000	U

Volume (Production) Variance

Budget adjusted to standard hours	\$514,000	
Standard overhead	494,000	
Volume Variance	\$ 20,000	U

OR

Budgeted hours	20,000	
Standard hours	19,000	
Difference in hours	1,000	
× Fixed overhead rate	× \$20	
Volume Variance	\$ 20,000	U

Part 3: *Three-Way Analysis*

Spending Variance

Actual overhead	\$535,000
Budget adjusted to actual hours	

Fixed overhead ($10,000 \times 2 = 20,000 \times \$20$)   \$400,000
Variable overhead ($20,200 \times \$6$)   121,200

     521,200

Spending Variance   \$ 13,800 U

Efficiency Variance

Budget adjusted to actual hours   \$521,200
Budget adjusted to standard hours   514,000
Efficiency Variance   \$ 7,200 U

OR

Actual hours   20,200
Standard hours   19,000
Difference in hours   1,200
$\times$ Standard variable overhead rate $\times$ \$6
Efficiency Variance   \$ 7,200 U

Volume Variance

Budget adjusted to standard hours   \$514,000
Standard overhead   494,000
Volume Variance   \$ 20,000 U

Comprehensive Illustration

A comprehensive illustration showing *all* the variances for material, labor, and overhead follows:

EXAMPLE 9

The following standards are given:

                   Per Unit

Direct Material   5 lbs. @ \$ 4 per lb.   \$ 20
Direct Labor   3 hrs. @ \$12 per hr.   36
Variable overhead   3 hrs. @ \$ 7 per hr.   21
Fixed overhead   3 hrs. @ \$20 per hr.   60

     \$137

Actual data follow:

Production 9,800 units
Denominator (budget) activity 11,000 units
Purchases 50,000 lbs. @ \$150,000
Direct material used 44,000 lbs.
Direct labor 22,000 hrs. @ \$220,000
Variable overhead \$125,000
Fixed overhead \$450,000

EXAMPLE 9 (*Continued*)

Part 1: *Material*

Material Price Variance

(Actual price versus standard price) $\times$ actual quantity bought
($3 versus $4) $\times$ 50,000 $ 50,000 F

Material Quantity Variance

(Actual quantity issued versus standard quantity) $\times$ standard price
(44,000 versus 49,000) $\times$ $4 $ 20,000 F

Part 2: *Labor*

Control Variance

Standard quantity $\times$ standard price (29,400 $\times$ $12)	$352,800
Actual quantity $\times$ actual price (22,000 $\times$ $10)	220,000
Control Variance	$132,800 F

Labor Price Variance

(Actual price versus standard price) $\times$ actual quantity
   ($10 versus $12) $\times$ 22,000 $ 44,000 F

Labor Quantity Variance

(Actual quantity versus standard quantity) $\times$ standard price
(22,000 versus 29,400*) $\times$ $12 $ 88,800 F

*9,800 $\times$ 3 = 29,400

Part 3: *Variable Overhead*

Variable Overhead Price Variance

Actual variable overhead	$125,000
Budget adjusted to actual hours (22,000 $\times$ $7)	154,000
Price Variance	$ 29,000 F

Variable Overhead Efficiency Variance

Budget adjusted to actual hours	$154,000
Budget adjusted to standard hours (9,800 $\times$ 3 = 29,400 $\times$ $7)	205,800
Efficiency Variance	$ 51,800 F

Part 4: *Fixed Overhead*

Fixed Overhead Budget Variance

Actual fixed overhead	$450,000
Budgeted fixed overhead (11,000 $\times$ 3 = 33,000 $\times$ $20)	660,000
Budget Variance	$210,000 F

EXAMPLE 9 (*Continued*)

Fixed Overhead Volume Variance

Budgeted fixed overhead	$660,000
Standard overhead ($9,800 \times 3 = 29,400 \times \$20$)	588,000
Volume Variance	$ 72,000 U

The fixed overhead volume variance is broken down into the fixed overhead efficiency variance and fixed overhead pure volume variance.

Fixed Overhead Efficiency Variance
(Actual hours versus standard hours) $\times$ standard fixed overhead rate
(22,000 versus 29,400) $\times$ \$20 $148,000 F

Fixed Overhead Pure Volume Variance
(Actual hours versus budgeted hours) $\times$ standard fixed overhead rate
(22,000 versus 33,000) $\times$ \$20 $220,000 U

Part 5: *One-Way Analysis*

Total Overhead Variance

Actual overhead	$575,000
Standard overhead ($29,400 \times \$27$)	793,800
Total Overhead Variance	$218,800 F

Part 6: *Two-Way Analysis*

Controllable Variance

Actual overhead		$575,000
Budget adjusted to standard hours		
Fixed overhead ($11,000 \times 3 =$		
$33,000 \times \$20$)	$660,000	
Variable overhead ($9,800 \times 3 =$		
$29,400 \times \$7$)	205,800	865,800
Controllable Variance		$290,800 F

Volume Variance

Budget adjusted to standard hours	$865,800
Standard overhead	793,800
Volume Variance	72,000 U

Part 7: *Three-Way Analysis*

Spending Variance

Actual overhead		$575,000
Budget adjusted to actual hours		
Fixed overhead ($11,000 \times 3 =$		
$33,000 \times \$20$)	$660,000	
Variable overhead ($22,000 \times \$7$)	154,000	814,000

EXAMPLE 9 (*Continued*)

Spending Variance $239,000 F

Efficiency Variance

Budget adjusted to actual hours $814,000
Budget adjusted to standard hours   865,800
Efficiency Variance $ 51,800 F

Volume Variance

Budget adjusted to standard hours $865,800
Standard overhead   793,800
Volume Variance $ 72,000 U

DISPOSITION OF VARIANCES

Variance accounts are closed out at the end of the reporting period so that the financial statements are reflected at actual cost. Cost Accounting Standards Board requirements, applicable to defense contractors dealing with governmental units, specify that significant cost variances should be adjusted to work-in-process, finished goods, and cost of sales on a pro-rata basis according to the number of units or dollars associated with these accounts. Where immaterial variances exist, cost of sales may be adjusted for the net effect of the variances. In cases where a variance is considered a managerial cost rather than a manufacturing one, a loss account may be charged.

With regard to Internal Revenue Service requirements, inventories must include an allocated portion of significant variances. If immaterial, such a method is not required unless the allocation approach has been used for book reporting. However, idle capacity variances may be expensed for tax purposes.

Variances that exist at the end of each quarter may be deferred if they are expected to reverse at year-end. If they are not, they should be disposed of immediately as described in APB Opinion 28.

INTERRELATIONSHIP OF VARIANCES

With regard to variance analysis for all production costs (direct material, direct labor, and overhead), it is important to note that each variance does *not* represent a separate and distinct problem to be handled in isolation. All variances in one way or another are interdependent. For example, the labor rate variance may be favorable because lower paid workers are being used. This could lead to: (1) an unfavorable material usage variance because of a higher incidence of waste, (2) an unfavorable labor efficiency variance because it takes longer hours to make the equivalent number of products, (3) an unfavorable overhead efficiency variance because the substandard work causes more hours to be spent for a specified output, and (4) an unfavorable overhead volume variance arising from abnormally high machine break downs because of lower-skilled operators.

A tradeoff between variances may be a managerial objective. For example, a material price variance may be favorable because of a bargain purchase opportunity or because of a combination of available resources designed to save overall corporate costs. However, the raw material acquired may be somewhat inferior in quality to that which is usually purchased. In processing, use of this material may lead to greater waste or more labor hours in producing a finished item that will satisfy product quality guidelines. The company goal here may be to minimize total production costs through the tradeoff of a favorable price variance and an unfavorable quantity variance. The net effect of the variances, in this case, is what counts.

MIX AND YIELD VARIANCES FOR MATERIAL AND LABOR

Mix refers to the relative proportion of various ingredients of input factors such as materials and labor. *Yield* is a measure to productivity.

Material and Labor Mix Variances

The material mix variance indicates the impact on material costs of the deviation from the standard mix. The labor mix variance measures the impact of changes in the labor mix on labor costs.

Formulas

$$\text{Material Mix Variance} = \left(\begin{array}{l} \text{Actual Units} \\ \text{Used at} \\ \text{Standard Mix} \end{array} - \begin{array}{l} \text{Actual Units} \\ \text{Used at} \\ \text{Actual Mix)} \end{array} \right) \times \begin{array}{l} \text{Standard} \\ \text{Unit} \\ \text{Price} \end{array}$$

$$\text{Labor Mix Variance} = \left(\begin{array}{l} \text{Actual Hrs.} \\ \text{Used at} \\ \text{Standard Mix} \end{array} - \begin{array}{l} \text{Actual Hrs.} \\ \text{Used at} \\ \text{Actual Mix} \end{array} \right) \times \begin{array}{l} \text{Standard} \\ \text{Hourly} \\ \text{Rate} \end{array}$$

Recording Mix Variances

The material and labor mix variances are isolated and recorded when materials and labor are used for production. They are debited if they are unfavorable, credited if they are favorable.

Mix and Yield Variances

The material quantity variance is divided into a material mix variance and a material yield variance. The material mix variance measures the impact of the deviation from the standard mix on material costs, while the material yield variance reflects the impact on material costs of the deviation from the standard input material allowed for actual production. We compute the material mix variance by holding the total input units constant at their actual amount.

We compute the material yield variance by holding the mix constant at the standard amount. The computations for labor mix and yield variances are the same as those for materials. If there is no mix, the yield variance is the same as the quantity (or usage) variance.

Formulas

$$\text{Material Yield Variance} = \left(\begin{array}{ccc} \text{Actual Units Used at Standard Mix} & - & \text{Actual Output at Standard Mix} \end{array} \right) \times \begin{array}{c} \text{Standard Unit Price} \end{array}$$

$$\text{Labor Yield Variance} = \left(\begin{array}{ccc} \text{Actual Hrs. Used at Standard Mix} & - & \text{Actual Output Hrs. at Standard Mix} \end{array} \right) \times \begin{array}{c} \text{Standard Hourly Rate} \end{array}$$

Probable Causes of Unfavorable Mix Variances

(a) When capacity restraints force substitution

(b) Poor production scheduling

(c) Lack of certain types of labor

(d) Certain materials are in short supply

Probable Causes of Unfavorable Yield Variances

(a) The use of low quality materials and/or labor

(b) The existence of faulty equipment

(c) The use of improper production methods

(d) An improper or costly mix of materials and/or labor

EXAMPLE 10 (Mix Variances)

J Company produces a compound composed of Materials Alpha and Beta which is marketed in 20 lb. bags. Material Alpha can be substituted for Material Beta. Standard cost and mix data have been determined as follows:

	Unit Price	Standard Unit	Standard Mix Proportions
Material Alpha	$3	5 lbs.	25%
Material Beta	4	15	75
		20 lbs.	100%

Processing each 20 lbs. of material requires 10 hrs. of labor. The company employs two types of labor, "skilled" and "unskilled," working on two processes, assembly and finishing. The following standard labor cost has been set for a 20 lb. bag.

	Standard Hrs.	Standard Wage Rate	Total	Standard Mix Proportions
Unskilled	4 hrs.	$2	$ 8	40%
Skilled	6	3	18	60
	10	2.60	26	100%

At standard cost, labor averages $2.60 per unit. During the month of December, 100 20-lb. bags were produced with the following labor costs:

	Actual Hrs.	Actual Rate	Actual Wages
Unskilled	380 hrs.	$2.50	$ 950
Skilled	600	3.25	1,950
	980		$2,900

Material records show:

	Beginning Inventory	Purchase	Ending Inventory
Material Alpha	100 lbs.	800 @ $3.10	200 lbs.
Material Beta	225	1,350 @ $3.90	175

We now want to determine the following variances from standard costs.

(a) Material purchase price
(b) Material mix
(c) Material quantity
(d) Labor rate
(e) Labor mix
(f) Labor efficiency

We will show how to compute these variances in a tabular form as follows:

(a) *Material Purchase Price Variance*

	Material Price per Unit			Actual Quantity Purchased	Variance ($)
	Standard	Actual	Difference		
Material Alpha	$3	$3.10	$.10 U	800 lbs.	$ 80 U
Material Beta	4	3.90	.10 F	1,350	135 F
					$ 55 F

(b) *Material Mix Variance*

	Units Which Should Have Been Used at Standard Mix*	Actual Units at Actual Mix**	Diff.	Standard Unit Price	Variance ($)
Material Alpha	525 lbs.	700 lbs.	175 U	$3	$525 U
Material Beta	1,575	1,400	175 F	4	700 F
	2,100	2,100			$175 F

The material mix variance measures the impact on material costs of the deviation from the standard mix. Therefore, it is computed holding the total quantity used constant at its actual amount and allowing the material mix to vary between actual and standard. As shown above, due to a favorable change in mix, we ended up with a favorable material mix variance of $175.

*This is the standard mix proportions of 25% and 75% applied to the actual material units used of 2,100 lbs.
**Actual units used = Beginning inventory + purchases − Ending inventory. Therefore,
Material Alpha: 700 lbs. = 100 + 800 − 200
Material Beta: 1,400 lbs. = 225 + 1,350 − 175

(c) *Material Quantity Variance*

	Units Which Should Have Been Used at Standard Mix	Standard Units at Standard Mix	Diff.	Standard Unit Price	Variance ($)
Material Alpha	525 lbs.	500 lbs.	25 U	$3	$ 75 U
Material Beta	1,575	1,500	75 U	4	300 U
	2,100	2,000			$375 U

The total material variance is the sum of the three variances:

Purchase price variance	$ 55 F
Mix variance	175 F
Quantity variance	375 U
	$145 U

The increase of $145 in material costs was due solely to an unfavorable quantity variance of 100 pounds of material Alpha and Beta. The unfavorable quantity variance, however, was compensated largely by favorable mix and price variances. J Company must look for ways to cut down waste and spoilage.

The labor cost increase of $300 ($2,900–$2,600) is attributable to three causes:

1. An increase of $.50 per hour in the rate paid to skilled labor and $.25 per hour in the rate paid to unskilled labor

2. An unfavorable mix of skilled and unskilled labor

3. A favorable labor efficiency variance of 20 hours

Three labor variances are computed below.

(d) *Labor Rate Variance*

	Labor Rate per Hr.			Actual Hrs.	Variance
	Standard	Actual	Diff.	Used	($)
Unskilled	$2	$2.50	$. 5 U	380 hrs.	$190 U
Skilled	3	3.25	.25 U	600	150 U
					$340 U

(e) *Labor Mix Variance*

	Actual Hrs. at Standard Mix*	Actual Hrs. at Actual Mix	Diff.	Standard Rate	Variance ($)
Unskilled	392 hrs.	380 hrs.	12 F	$2	$24 F
Skilled	588	600	12 U	3	36 U
	980	980			$12 U

*This is the standard proportions of 40% and 60% applied to the actual total labor hrs. used of 980.

(f) *Labor Efficiency Variance*

	Actual Hrs. at Standard Mix	Standard Hrs. at Standard Mix	Diff.	Standard Rate	Variance ($)
Unskilled	392 hrs.	400 hrs.	8 F	$2	$16 F
Skilled	588	600	12 F	3	36 F
	980	1,000			$52 F

The total labor variance is the sum of these three variances:

Rate variance	$340 U
Mix variance	12 U
Efficiency variance	52 F
	$300 U

which is proved to be:

Total Labor Variance

	Actual Hrs. Used	Actual Rate	Total Actual Cost	Standard Hrs. Allowed	Standard Rate	Total Standard Cost	Variance ($)
Unskilled	380 hrs.	$2.50	$ 950	400	$2	$ 800	$150 U
Skilled	600	3.25	1,950	600	3	1,800	150 U
			$2,900			$2,600	$300 U

The unfavorable labor variance, as evidenced by the cost increase of $300, may be due to:

1. Overtime necessary because of poor production scheduling resulting in a higher average labor cost per hour; and/or

2. Unnecessary use of more expensive skilled labor. J Company should put more effort into better production scheduling.

EXAMPLE 11 (Yield Variances)

The Giffen Manufacturing Company uses a standard cost system for its production of a chemical product. This chemical is produced by mixing three major raw materials, A, B, and C. The company has the following standards.

36	lbs. of Material A	@	$1.00	=	$ 36.00
48	lbs. of Material B	@	2.00	=	96.00
36	lbs. of Material C	@	1.75	=	63.00
120	lbs. of standard mix	@	$1.625	=	$195.00

The company should produce 100 lbs. of finished product at a standard cost of $1.625 per lb. ($195.00/120 lbs.)

To convert 120 pounds of materials into 100 pounds of finished chemical requires 400 DLH at $3.50 per DLH, or $14.00 per pound. During the month of December, the company produced 4,250 pounds of output with the following direct labor: 15,250 hrs. @ $3.50

	Materials Purchased During the month	Materials used During the month
Material A	1,200 @ $1.10	1,160 lbs.
Material B	1,800 @ 1.95	1,820
Material C	1,500 @ 1.80	1,480

The material *price variance is isolated at the time of purchase.* We want to compute the material purchase price, quantity, mix, and yield variances.

We will show the computations of variances in a tabular form as follows:

(a) *Material Variances*

Material Purchase Price Variance

| | Material Price per unit | | | Actual Quantity | Variance |
	Standard	Actual	Diff.	Purchased	($)
Material A	$1.00	$1.10	$.10 U	1,200 lbs.	$120 U
Material B	2.00	1.95	.05 F	1,800	90 F
Material C	1.75	1.80	.05 U	1,500	75 U
					$105 U

The material quantity variance computed below results from changes in the mix of materials as well as from changes in the total quantity of materials. The standard input allowed for actual production consists of 1,275 pounds of Material A, 1,700 pounds of Material B and 1,275 pounds of Material C, a total of 4,250 pounds. The actual input consisted of 1,160 pounds of Material A, 1,820 pounds of Material B and 1,480 pounds of Material C, a total of 4,460 pounds. To separate these two changes, the material quantity variance is subdivided into a material mix variance and a material yield variance, as shown below.

Material Quantity Variance

	Actual Units Used at Actual Mix	"Shouid have been" inputs based upon actual output	Diff.	Standard Unit Price	Variance ($)
Material A	1,160 lbs.	1,275 lbs.	115 F	$1.00	$115 F
Material B	1,820	1,700	120 U	2.00	240 U
Material C	1,480	1,275	205 U	1.75	358.75 U
	4,460	4,250			$483.75 U

The computation of the material mix variance and the material yield variance for the Giffen Manufacturing Company is given below.

Material Mix Variance

	"Should have been" individual inputs based upon total actual throughput*	Actual Units Used at Actual Mix	Diff.	Standard Unit Price	Variance ($)
Material A	1,338 lbs.	1,160 lbs.	178 F	$1.00	$178 F
Material B	1,784	1,820	36 U	2.00	72 U
Material C	1,338	1,480	142 U	1.75	248.5 U
	4,460	4,460			$142.5 U

*This is the standard mix proportions of 30%, 40%, and 30% applied to the actual material units used of 4,460 pounds.

Material Yield Variance

	Expected Input Units at Standard Mix	"Should have been" inputs based upon actual output*	Diff.	Standard Unit Price	Variance ($)
Material A	1,338 lbs.	1,275 lbs.	63 U	$1.00	$ 63 U
Material B	1,784	1,700	84 U	2.00	168 U
Material C	1,338	1,275	63 U	1.75	110.25 U
	4,460	4,250			$341.25 U**

*This is the standard mix proportions of 30%, 40%, and 30% applied to the actual throughput of 4,460 pounds or *output* of 4,250 pounds.
**The material yield variance of $341.25 U can be computed alternatively as follows.

Actual input quantity at standard prices
Material A 1,338 lbs. @ $1.00 = $1,338
Material B 1,784 lbs. @ 2.00 = 3,568
Material C 1,338 lbs. @ 1.75 = 2,341.5 $7,247.50

Actual output quantity at standard price
4,250 lbs. @ 1.625 $6,906.25

Hence, $7,247.5 - $6,906.25 = $341.25 U

The material mix and material yield variances are unfavorable indicating that a shift was made to a more expensive (at standard) input mix and that an excessive quantity of material was used. Poor production scheduling requiring an unnecessarily excessive use of input materials and an undesirable mix of Materials A, B, and C was responsible for this result. To remedy the situation, the company must ensure that:

(a) The material mix is adhered to in terms of the least cost combination without affecting product quality;

(b) The proper production methods are being implemented;

(c) Inefficiencies, waste, and spoilage are within the standard allowance; and

(d) Quality materials, consistent with established standards are being used.

Employees seldom complete their operations according to standard times. Two factors should be brought out in computing labor variances if the analysis and computation will be used to fix responsibility:

1. The change in labor cost resulting from the efficiency of the workers, measured by a labor efficiency variance. (In finding the change, allowed hours are determined through the material input.)

2. The change in labor cost due to a difference in the yield, measured by a labor yield variance. (In computing the change, actual output is converted to allowed input hours.)

For the Giffen Manufacturing Company, more efficient workers resulted in a savings of 383.33 hours (15,250 hrs. − 14,866.67 hrs.). Priced at the standard rate per hour, this produced an unfavorable labor efficiency variance of $1,341.66 as shown below:

Labor Efficiency Variance

Actual hrs. at standard rate	$53,375
Actual hrs. at expected output	
(4,460 hrs. × 400/120 = 14,866.67 hrs @ $3.5)	52,033.34
	$ 1,341.66 U

With a standard yield of 83 1/3% (= 100/120), 4,250 pounds of finished material should have required 17,000 hours of direct labor (4,250 lbs. × 400 DLH/100). Comparing the hours allowed for the actual input, 14,866.67 hours with the hours allowed for actual output, 17,000 hours, we find a favorable labor yield variance of $7,466.66, as show below.

Labor Yield Variance

Actual hrs. at expected output	$52,033.34
Actual output (4,250 lbs. × 400/100 =	
17,000 hrs. @ $3.5 or 4,250 lbs. @ $14.00)	59,500
	$ 7,466.66 F

The labor efficiency variance can be combined with the yield variance to give us the *traditional* labor efficiency variance, which turns out to be favorable as follows.

Labor efficiency variance	$ 1,341.66 U
Labor yield variance	7,466.66 F
	$ 6,125 F

This division is necessary when there is a difference between the actual yield and standard yield, if responsibility is to be fixed. The producing department can not be rightfully credited with a favorable efficiency variance of $6,125. Note, however, that a favorable yield variance, which is a factor most likely outside the control of the producing department, more than offsets the *unfavorable* labor efficiency variance of $1,341.66, which the producing department rightfully should have been responsible for.

PROFIT VARIANCE ANALYSIS

Gross profit analysis is determining the causes for the change in gross profit. Any variances that impact upon gross profit are reported to management so corrective steps may be taken.

Causes of Profit Variance:

- Changes in unit sales price and cost
- Changes in the volume of products sold
- Changes in sales mix

Analysis of the changes furnishes data needed to bring actual operations in line with budgeted expectations. Comparisons should be made between budgeted and actual operations for the current year or between actual operations for the previous year and those for the current year. Changes in gross profit may be looked at in terms of the entire company or by product line.

In an effort to improve profitability, the change in character of sales or mix of sales is just as important as the increase in total volume. For example, if the total volume in the budget is constant, but a larger proportion of high-margin products are sold than were budgeted, then higher profits will result. For instance, in the furniture business, there is an increasing trend toward more expensive and durable pieces carrying a higher margin per unit, although volume may not be all that great. Computations and analysis of sales mix variances are a very important part of profit analysis. It provides an additional insight into (a) what caused the increase or decrease in profit over the previous year and (b) why the actual profit differed from the original expectation.

Gross profit (or contribution margin) is usually the joint responsibility of the managers of the sales department and the production department; the sales department manager is responsible for the sales revenue component, and the production department manager is accountable for the cost-of-goods-sold component. However, it is the task of top management to ensure that the target profit is met. The sales department manager must hold fast to prices, volume and mix; the production department supervisor must control the costs of materials, labor and factory overhead, and quantities; the purchasing manager must purchase materials at budgeted prices; and the personnel manager must employ the right people at the right wage rates. The internal audit department must ensure that the budgetary figures for sales and costs are being adhered to by all the departments which are, directly or indirectly, involved in contributing to making profit.

The computation of the production mix variance is very similar to that of the sales mix variance. While the sales mix variance is part of profit analysis, the production mix variance for materials and labor is an important part of cost variance analysis. We must realize, however, that the analysis of standard cost variances should be understood as part of what is broadly known as profit analysis. In industries where each cost element is substituted for each other and production is at or near full capacity, how we combine different types of materials and different classes of labor will affect the extent to which the costs are controlled and gross profit maximized. The production volume variance must be further analyzed to separate the effect on costs of a change in mix of the production inputs such as materials and labor.

The yield variances for materials, labor, and overhead are useful in managerial control of material consumption. In some cases, the newly found mix is accompanied by either a favorable or unfavorable yield of the finished product. Usually, the favorable mix variance may be offset by an unfavorable yield variance, or vice versa. It is the responsibility of the laboratory or the engineering department to make sure that no apparent advantage created by one type of variance is canceled out by another.

Taken as a whole, the analysis of profit involves careful evaluation of all facets of variance analysis, that is, sales variances and cost variances. Especially, the effect of changes in mix, volume, and yield on profits must be separated and analyzed. The analysis of these variances provide management with added dimensions to responsibility accounting since it provides additional insight into what caused the increase or decrease in profits or why the actual profit deviated from the target profit. Analyzing the change in gross profit via an effective responsibility accounting system based on the control of costs and sales variances is a step toward maximization of profits.

We now discuss the computation of the profit variances.

Profit Variance Analysis for a Single Product:

(a) Sales price variance
= (Actual price − Budget or standard price) × Actual sales

(b) Cost price variance
= (Actual cost − Budget or standard cost) × Actual sales

(c) Sales volume variance
= (Actual sales − Budget or standard sales) × Budget or standard price

(d) Cost volume variance
= (Actual sales − Budget or standard sales) × Budget or standard cost per unit

(e) Total volume variance
= Sales volume variance − Cost volume variance

Profit Variance Analysis for Multiple Products:

The total volume variance in a single product situation is comprised of (a) sales mix variance and (b) sales quantity variance.

(a) Sales mix variance

$$= \left(\begin{array}{l} \text{Actual sales at budget} \\ \text{or standard mix} \end{array} - \begin{array}{l} \text{Budget or standard sales} \\ \text{at budget or standard mix} \end{array} \right) \times \begin{array}{l} \text{Budget or} \\ \text{standard CM} \\ \text{(or GM) per} \\ \text{unit} \end{array}$$

CM = contribution margin and GM = gross margin.

(b) Sales quantity variance

$$= \left(\begin{array}{l} \text{Actual sales at} \\ \text{budgeted or standard} \\ \text{mix} \end{array} - \begin{array}{l} \text{Actual sales at budgeted or} \\ \text{standard mix} \end{array} \right) \times \begin{array}{l} \text{Budgeted or} \\ \text{standard CM} \\ \text{(or GM) per} \\ \text{unit} \end{array}$$

(c) Total volume variance
= Sales mix variance + sales quantity variance

$$\text{or} = \left(\begin{array}{l} \text{Actual sales} \\ \text{at actual mix} \end{array} - \begin{array}{l} \text{Budgeted or standard sales} \\ \text{at budgeted or standard} \\ \text{mix} \end{array} \right) \times \begin{array}{l} \text{Budgeted or} \\ \text{standard CM} \\ \text{(or GM) per} \\ \text{unit} \end{array}$$

The sales price variance and the cost price variance are calculated the same way as for a single product.

Frequently, a contribution margin approach is superior to the gross profit approach. That is because "gross profit" has as a deduction for fixed costs which may be beyond the control of a particular level of management. A simple example follows:

	Budget (00) omitted		Actual (00) omitted		Variance	
	Unit A	Unit B	Unit A	Unit B	Unit A	Unit B
Sales Price	$10	$5	$11	$6	$1 F	$1
Units	10	8	10	8	–0–	–0–
Variable Manufacturing Costs	$ 4	$3	$ 6	$4	$2 U	$1
Fixed Manufacturing Costs	$ 3	$1	$ 4	$2	$1 U	$1
Manufacturing Contribution Margin per Unit	$ 6	$2	$ 5	$2	$1 U	$–0–
Gross Profit per Unit	$ 3	$1	$ 1	$0	$2 U	$1

Using the above data, an unfavorable manufacturing contribution margin variance of $10 for Unit A and $0 for Unit B is more meaningful than the $20 and $8 unfavorable gross profit variance if local management had no control over fixed costs.

EXAMPLE 12 (Profit Variance Analysis)

The Lake Tahoe Ski Store sells two ski models, Model X and Model Y. For the years 19X1 and 19X2, the store realized a gross profit of $246,640 and only $211,650, respectively. The owner of the store was astounded since the total sales volume in dollars and in units was higher for 19X2 than for 19X1 yet the gross profit achieved actually declined. Given below are the store's unaudited operating results for 19X1 and 19X2. No fixed costs were included in the cost of goods sold per unit.

	Model X				Model Y			
Year	Selling Price	Cost of Goods Sold per Unit	Sales (in units)	Sales Revenue	Selling Price	Cost of Goods Sold per Unit	Sales (in units)	Sales Revenue
1	$150	$110	2,800	$420,000	$172	$121	2,640	$454,080
2	160	125	2,650	424,000	176	135	2,900	510,400

We explain why the gross profit declined by $34,990. We include a detailed variance analysis of price changes and changes in volume both for sales and cost. Also we subdivide the total volume variance into changes in price and changes in quantity.

Sales price and sales volume variances measure the impact on the firm's CM (or GM) of changes in the unit selling price and sales volume. In computing these variances, all costs are held constant in order to stress changes in price and volume. Cost price and cost volume variances are computed in the same manner, holding price and volume constant. All these variances for the Lake Tahoe Ski Store are computed below.

Sales Price Variance

Actual Sales for 19X2:
  Model X 2,650 $\times$ $160 = $424,000
  Model Y 2,900 $\times$ 176 =   510,400 $934,400

Actual 19X2 sales at 19X1 prices:
  Model X 2,650 $\times$ $150 = $397,500
  Model Y 2,900 $\times$ 172 =   498,800   896,300
                                                             $ 38,100 F

Sales Volume Variance

Actual 19X2 sales at 19X1 prices: $896,300

Actual 19X1 sales (at 19X1 prices):
  Model X 2,800 $\times$ $150 = $420,000
  Model Y 2,640 $\times$ 172 =   454,080   874,080
                                                             $ 22,220 F

Cost Price Variance

Actual cost of goods sold for 19X2:
  Model X 2,650 $\times$ $125 = $331,250
  Model Y 2,900 $\times$ 135 =   391,500 $722,750

Actual 19X2 sales at 19X1 costs:
  Model X 2,650 $\times$ $110 = $291,500
  Model Y 2,900 $\times$ 121 =   350,900   642,400
                                                             $ 80,350 U

Cost Volume Variance

Actual 19X2 sales at 19X1 costs: $642,400

Actual 19X1 sales (at 19X1 costs):
  Model X 2,800 $\times$ $110 = $308,000
  Model Y 2,640 $\times$ 121 =   319,440   627,440
                                                             $ 14,960 U

Total volume variance = sales volume variance − cost volume variance
$$= \$22,250 \text{ F} - \$14,960 \text{ U} = \underline{\underline{\$7,260 \text{ F}}}$$

The total volume variance is computed as the sum of a sales mix variance and a sales quantity variance as follows:

Sales Mix Variance

	19X2 Actual Sales at 19X1 Mix*	19X2 Actual Sales at 19X2 Mix	Diff.	19X1 Gross Profit per Unit	Variance ($)
Model X	2,857	2,650	207 U	$40	$ 8,280 U
Model Y	2,693	2,900	207 F	51	10,557 F
	5,550	5,550			$ 2,277 F

*This is the 19X1 mix (used as standard or budget) proportions of 51.47% (or 2,800/5,440 = 51.47%) and 48.53% (or 2,640/5,440 = 48.53%) applied to the actual 19X2 sales figure of 5,550 units.

Sales Quantity Variance

	19X2 Actual Sales at 19X1 Mix*	19X1 Actual Sales at 19X1 Mix	Diff.	19X1 Gross Profit per Unit	Variance ($)
Model X	2,857	2,800	57 F	$40	$2,280 F
Model Y	2,693	2,640	53 F	51	2,703 F
	5,550	5,440			$4,983 F

A favorable total volume variance is due to a favorable shift in the sales mix (that is, from Model X to Model Y) and also to a favorable increase in sales volume (by 110 units) which is shown as follows.

Sales mix variance	$2,277 F
Sales quantity variance	4,983 F
	$7,260 F

However, there remains the decrease in gross profit. The decrease in gross profit of $34,990 can be explained as follows.

	Gains	Losses
Gain due to increased sales price	$38,100 F	
Loss due to increased cost		80,350 U
Gain due to increase in units sold	4,983 F	
Gain due to shift in sales mix	2,277 F	
	$45,360 F	$80,350 U

Hence, net decrease in gross profit = $80,350 − $45,360 = $34,990 U

Despite the increase in sales price and volume and the favorable shift in sales mix, the Lake Tahoe Ski Store ended up losing $34,990 compared to 19X1. The major reason for this comparative loss was the tremendous increase in cost of goods sold, as indicated by an unfavorable cost price variance of $80,350. The costs for both Model X and Model Y went up quite significantly over 19X1. The Store has to take a close look at the cost picture. Even though only variable costs were included in cost of goods sold per unit, both variable and fixed costs should be analyzed in an effort to cut down on controllable costs. In doing that, it is essential that responsibility be clearly fixed to given individuals. In a retail business like the Lake Tahoe Ski Store, operating expenses such as advertising and payroll of store employees must also be closely scrutinized.

EXAMPLE 13 (Sales Mix and Quantity Variances)

Shim and Siegel, Inc. sells two products, C and D. Product C has a budgeted unit CM (contribution margin) of $3 and Product D has a budgeted unit CM of $6. The budget for a recent month called for sales of 3,000 units of C and 9,000 units of D, for a total of 12,000 units. Actual sales totaled 12,200 units, 4,700 of C, and 7,500 of D. We compute the sales volume variance and break this variance down into the (a) sales quantity variance and (b) sales mix variance.

Shim and Siegel's sales volume variance is computed below. As we can see, while total unit sales increased by 200 units, the shift in sales mix resulted in a $3,900 unfavorable sales volume variance.

Sales Volume Variance

	Actual Sales at Actual Mix	Standard Sales at Budget Mix	Difference	Budgeted CM per Unit	Variance ($)
Product C	4,700	3,000	1,700 F	$3	$5,100 F
Product D	7,500	9,000	1,500 U	6	9,000 U
	12,200	12,000			$3,900 U

In multiproduct firms, the sales volume variance is further divided into a sales quantity variance and a sales mix variance. The computations of these variances are shown below.

Sales Quantity Variance

	Actual Sales at Budgeted Mix	Standard Sales at Budgeted Mix	Difference	Standard CM per Unit	Variance ($)
Product C	3,050	3,000	50 F	$3	$ 150 F
Product D	9,150	9,000	150 F	6	900 F
	12,200	12,000			$1,050 F

Sales Mix Variance

	Actual Sales at Budgeted Mix	Actual Sales at Actual Mix	Difference	Standard CM per Unit	Variance ($)
Product C	3,050	4,700	1,650 F	$3	$4,950 F
Product D	9,150	7,500	1,650 U	6	9,900 U
	12,200	12,200			$4,950 U

The sales quantity variance reflects the impact on the CM or GM (gross margin) of deviations from the standard sales volume, whereas the sales mix variance measures the impact on the CM of deviations from the budgeted mix. In the case of Shim and Siegel, Inc., the sales quantity variance came out to be favorable, i.e., $1,050 F and the sales mix variance came out to be unfavorable, i.e., $4,950 U. These variances indicate that while there was favorable increase in sales volume by 200 units, it was obtained by an unfavorable shift in the sales mix, that is, a shift from Product D, with a high margin, to product C, with a low margin.

Note that the sales volume variance of $3,900 U is the algebraic sum of the following two variances.

Sales quantity variance	$1,050 F
Sales mix variance	4,950 U
	$3,900 U

In conclusion, the product emphasis on high margin sales is often a key to success for multiproduct firms. Increasing sales volume is one side of the story; selling the more profitable products is another.

In view of the fact that Shim and Siegel, Inc. experienced an unfavorable sales volume variance of $3,900 due to an unfavorable (or less profitable) mix in the sales volume, the company is advised to put more emphasis on increasing the sale of Product D.

In doing that the company might wish to:

(a) Increase the advertising budget for succeeding periods to boost Product D sales;

(b) Set up a bonus plan in such a way that the commission is based on quantities sold rather than higher rates for higher margin item such as Product D or revise the bonus plan to consider the sale of Product D;

(c) Offer a more lenient credit term for Product D to encourage its sale;

(d) Reduce the price of Product D enough to maintain the present profitable mix while increasing the sale of product. This strategy must take into account the price elasticity of demand for Product D.

STANDARD COSTING INTEGRATED WITH OTHER COST SYSTEMS

Standard costing is an "accessory" that may be added to either job order costing or process costing to aid these basic cost systems.

Job Order Costing and Standard Costing

With job order costing, individual jobs consist of a single complex unit or a small batch of complex units. The units are customized to meet particular specifications. Thus, standard setting may be used in formulating "custom made" direct material, direct labor, and factory overhead standards prior to starting each unique job.

Process Costing and Standard Costing

Process costing can be combined with standard costing and variances determined. Certain requirements exist issued by the Cost Accounting Standards Board.

EXAMPLE 14

The Curry Quality Products, Inc. manufactures fabrics for a variety of uses including automotive, furniture, belts, shoe, garter, suspenders, and industrial applications. A substantial percentage of the company's operations embrace the manufacture of a variety of webbings for the foregoing purposes. The company has the following standard cost at a normal monthly volume of 10,000 units for the Weaving Department:

Direct materials – yarn (2 lbs. @ $15)	$30.00
Direct labor (1 DLH @ $9)	9.00
Factory overhead:	
Variable (1DLH @ $6)	6.00
Fixed (1 DLH @ $5)	5.00
Total Standard Cost	$50.00

Budgeted fixed factory overhead is $50,000. Material is introduced at the beginning of the process. Data for the month of September 19X8 include the following:

Work in process, beginning	3,000 units, 1/3 complete as to conversion
Units started during September	10,000 units
Units completed and transferred to Finished Goods inventory	12,000 units
Materials purchased	20,000 lbs. @ $14.00/lb. 25,000/lb. placed into production.
Work in process, end	1,000 units, 1/2 complete
Actual September conversion costs were:	
Direct labor (12,000 hours @ $9)	$108,000
Variable overhead	78,000
Fixed overhead	51,000
	$237,000

The Curry Company uses a standard cost system. Raw materials are inventoried at standard. Costs in process on September 1 were recorded at standard. A separate variance account is maintained for record keeping purposes. Especially, separate control and applied accounts for variable overhead and fixed overhead are maintained for control purposes.

1. The equivalent units used for standard costing purposes are:

	Physical Flow	Materials	Conversion
WIP, beginning	3,000 (1/3)		
Units started	10,000		
Units to account for	13,000		
Units completed and transferred	12,000	12,000	12,000
WIP, end	1,000 (1/2)	1,000	500
Units accounted for	13,000		
Total work done		13,000	12,500
Less: old equivalent units on beginning WIP		3,000*	1,000**
Equivalent units produced		10,000	11,500

*3,000 units, 100% complete as to materials
**3,000 units, 2/3 complete as to conversion are equivalent to 1,000 fully completed units

2. To compute all the variances, we will use a 3-column worksheet for

direct materials and direct labor and a 4-column worksheet for factory overhead.

Variance Analysis for Direct Materials

(1)	(2)	(3)
Actual Quantity × Actual Price	Actual Quantity × Standard Price	Standard Quantity Allowed × Standard Price
(purchase)	(purchase)　　　(usage)	
20,000 × $14 = $280,000	20,000 × $15 = $300,000　　25,000 × $15 = $375,000	20,000 × $15 = $300,000

Material Purchase Price Variance = $20,000 (F)　　　Material Quantity Variance = $75,000 (U)

In the above, F and U stand for "favorable" and "unfavorable," respectively. The standard material quantity allowed was computed on the basis of equivalent units produced for materials (i.e., 1,000 units), multiplied by 2 lbs. = 20,000 units.

Since the responsibility for the material purchase price variance does not rest with the Weaving Dept., it does not appear on its cost of production report and also on its performance report. It would appear on the performance report of the purchasing department.

Variance Analysis for Direct Labor

(1)	(2)	(3)
Actual Hours × Actual Rate	Actual Hours × Standard Rate	Standard Hours Allowed × Standard Rate
12,000 hrs. × $9 = $108,000	12,000 × $9 = $108,000	11,500 × $9 = $103,500

Labor Rate Var. = $0　　　Labor Efficiency Variance = $4,500 (U)

The standard hours allowed for actual equivalent units produced were computed on the basis of equivalent units manufactured for direct labor—that is, 11,500 units of equivalent production for direct labor, multiplied by 1 DLH = 11,500 hours.

Variance Analysis for Variable Overhead and Fixed Overhead

Before we perform variance analysis for factory overhead, it is necessary to develop (1) a flexible budget formula used for *cost control* purposes and (2) applied rates for variable overhead and fixed overhead used for product costing. In this illustrative case, they are

(1) Flexible budget formula

Variable overhead rate : $6 per DLH
Budgeted fixed overhead: $50,000, which is 10,000
units of normal volume × 1 DLH × $5 = 50,000

(2) Applied rates:

Variable overhead rate: $6 per DLH
Fixed overhead rate: $5 per DLH

Now we are in a position to isolate spending, efficiency, and volume variances for factory overhead. We will use a 4-column worksheet approach.

	(1) Actual Hours × Actual Price = Actual Overhead Incurred (12,000 hrs.)	(2) Actual Hours × Standard Price = Flexible Budget Based on Actual Hours Worked (12,000 hrs.)	(3) Standard Hours Allowed × Standard Price = Flexible Budget Based on Standard Hours Allowed (11,500 hrs.)	(4) Applied (11,500 hrs.)
Variable	$78,000	$72,000 (12,000 hrs. × $6)	$69,000 (11,500 hrs. × $6)	$69,000 (11,500 hrs. × $6)
Fixed	51,000	50,000	50,000	57,500 (11,500 hrs. × $5)
	$129,000	$122,000	$119,000	$126,500

	Spending Variance:		Efficiency Variance:		Volume Variance:	
	Variable	$6,000 (U)	Variable	$3,000 (U)	Variable	not applicable
	Fixed	1,000 (U)	Fixed	not applicable	Fixed	$7,500 (F)
		$7,000 (U)		$3,000 (U)		$7,500 (F)

In summary,

Variable overhead spending variance	$6,000 (U)
Fixed overhead spending variance	1,000 (U)
Variable overhead efficiency variance	3,000 (U)
Fixed overhead volume variance	7,500 (F)
	$2,500 (U)

3. The *favorable* material purchase price variance of $20,000 may be due to taking advantage of the $1 cash discount on the quantity purchase (@ $14 vs. @ $15). The *unfavorable* material quantity variance results from the fact that Weaving Department used 5,000 pounds more of materials than the standard quantity, which may be explained by controllable factors such as use of inefficient workers, poor equipment, changes in production methods, or faulty blueprints. Controllable causes must be detected before any corrective action can be taken. There may also exist uncontrollable factors such as the use of faulty

materials whose responsibility rests with the purchasing department rather than with the Weaving Department.

There was no labor rate variance. The unfavorable labor efficiency variance of $4,500 could be due to a variety of reasons including materials being in short supply, the use of poor equipment or inefficient workers, and poor production scheduling resulting in overtime work. The undesirable efficiency variance could be explained by such factors as machine breakdown which is usually outside the responsibility of the Weaving Department. In the Curry Company, the unfavorable variable overhead spending variance may be explained in the same way as the unfavorable labor efficiency variance. An unfavorable spending variance for both variable overhead and fixed overhead must be studied carefully on a cost-by-cost basis. The difference between actual spending and budgeted amounts are usually caused by higher prices paid for supplies, indirect labor, maintenance and repair, and unexpected increases in such committed types of fixed overhead expenses as rent, insurance, and taxes, which are not controllable by the department head. The Weaving Department's performance report should distinguish between controllable items and uncontrollable items so that the entire system of responsibility accounting functions properly and efficiently. Perhaps a certain uncontrollable item might safely be dropped from the report of the department. For example, the material purchase price variance should not appear on the performance report of the Weaving Department; it should be charged to the purchasing manager.

A favorable overhead volume income variance indicates that the Weaving Department operated at more than average capacity and the fixed costs "attached" to better-than-average utilization of capacity amounted to $7,500 (F). However, this factor may be beyond the control of the manager of the Weaving Department. Whether or not the favorable variance should appear on his performance report will require further investigation.

4. Here is the cost of production report.

Cost of Production Report
Weaving Department
For the Month Ended September 30, 19A

WIP, beginning *at standard:*		
Materials (3,000 × $30)	$ 90,000	
Conversion (1,000 × $20)	20,000	$110,000
Current costs assigned to Weaving Department:		
Materials (25,000 × $15)	$375,000 *	

Direct Labor ($12,000 \times \$9$)	108,000	
Factory Overhead	129,000	612,000
Total costs to account for		$722,000

WIP, end *at standard:*

Materials ($1,000 \times \$30$)	$ 30,000	
Conversion ($500 \times \$20$)	10,000	40,000

Goods completed and transferred *at standard:*

$12,000 \times \$50$	600,000

Variances:

Material quantity	75,000	(U)
Labor efficiency	4,500	(U)
Variable overhead spending	6,000	(U)
Fixed overhead spending	1,000	(U)
Variable overhead efficiency	3,000	(U)
Fixed overhead volume	(7,500)	(F) 82,000
Total costs accounted for		$722,000

*Note that the costs assigned to Weaving Department include the standard cost of materials used ($375,000 = 25,000 units \times \$15$ standard cost) and the actual costs of direct labor and factory overhead. Also note that material purchase price variance is assumed to be assigned to the purchasing department.

5. The CASB requirement for the use of standard costs would not greatly affect the company's present standard costing system. Some of the things that are affected are the following.

- Since material purchase price variances are recognized at the time the materials are purchased, and valued at standard costs, they must be accumulated separately by homogeneous groupings and may be included in appropriate indirect cost pools.

- Labor rate variances and labor efficiency variances may be combined to form a single labor cost variance account.

- These variances (presumably including various overhead variances) must be allocated at least annually between inventory and production units based on various criteria described in the Standard. For example, they may be allocated in proportion to the related standard costs in each account.

EXAMPLE 15

CPA Manufacturing Company produces a product in two processing departments: Finishing Department and Cutting Department. The Finishing

Department assembles and puts a finishing touch on the product it receives from the Cutting Department. Materials are introduced at the start of the Cutting Department, while conversion costs are applied uniformly throughout the department. The company has the following standard cost at a normal monthly production volume of 1,300 direct labor hours:

Raw materials (2 units @ $5)	$10
Direct labor (1 hour @ $6)	6
Factor overhead:	
Variable (1 hour @ $2)	2
Fixed (1 hour @ $5)	5
	$23

Fixed overhead budgeted is $6,500 per month. The Finishing Department has work in process at the beginning and end of March as follows:

	Units	Percentage of completion as to conversion
Beginning	400	1/2
End	200	3/4

In addition to the work-in-process inventory at the beginning, the Finishing Department also received 1,100 units from the Cutting Department and processed them during the month of March. During the process, no units were lost. During the month of March, the following events occurred:

Actual overhead costs:	
Variable	$2,853
Fixed	6,725
Materials (@ $5.20 per unit):	
Purchased	2,600 units
Used	2,500 units
Direct labor hours used @ $6.50/hr.	1,350 hours

1. Equivalent units produced for the month of March are:

	Physical flow	Materials	Conversion
WIP, beginning	400 (1/2)		
Units started	1,100		
Units to account for	1,500		
Units completed	1,300	1,300	1,300
WIP, end	200 (3/4)	200	150
Units accounted for	1,500		

Total work done	1,500	1,450
Less: old equivalent units		
on beginning WIP	400	200
Equivalent units produced	1,100	1,250

2. *Variance analysis for materials*

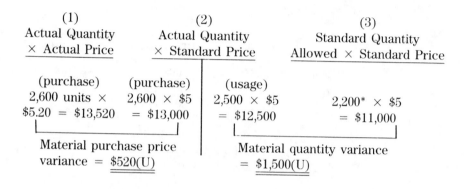

(1)	(2)	(3)
Actual Quantity × Actual Price	Actual Quantity × Standard Price	Standard Quantity Allowed × Standard Price

|(purchase)|(purchase)|(usage)| |
|2,600 units × $5.20 = $13,520|2,600 × $5 = $13,000|2,500 × $5 = $12,500|2,200* × $5 = $11,000|

Material purchase price variance = $520(U)

Material quantity variance = $1,500(U)

*The standard input quantity allowed, 2,200 units = 1,100 × 2

Variance analysis for direct labor:

(1)	(2)	(3)
Actual Hours × Actual Price 1,350 hrs. × $6.50 = $8,775	Actual Hours × Standard Price 1,350 × $6 = $8,100	Standard Hours Allowed × Standard Price 1,250* × $6 = $7,500

Labor rate variance = $675 (U)

Labor efficiency variance = $600 (U)

*Standard hours allowed, 1,250 hours = 1,250 equivalent units for conversion × 1 hour.

Variance analysis for variable overhead and fixed overhead combined:

(1) Flexible budget formula: variable overhead rate, $2 per DLH
fixed overhead budgeted, $6,500
(2) Applied rates: variable, $2 per DLH
fixed, $5 per DLH

	(1) Actual Overhead Incurred (1,350 hrs.)	(2) Flexible Budget Based on Actual Hours Worked (1,350 hrs.)	(3) Flexible Budget Based on Standard Hours Allowed (1,250 hrs.)	(4) Applied (1,250 hrs.)
Variable	$2,853	$2,700 (1,350 × $2)	$2,500 (1,250 × $2)	$2,500
Fixed	6,725	6,500	6,500	6,250
	$9,578	$9,200	$9,000	$8,750

	Spending Var.	Efficiency Var.	Volume Var.
Variable	$153 (U)	$200 (U)	not applicable
Fixed	225 (U)	not applicable	$250 (U)
	$378 (U)	$200 (U)	$250 (U)

3.

Cost of Production Report
Finishing Department
For the Month of March

WIP, beginning *at standard*:		
Materials (400 × $10)	$ 4,000	
Conversion (200 × $13)	2,600	$ 6,600
Current costs charged to Finishing Dept.:		
Materials (2,500 × $5)	12,500	
Direct Labor (1,350 hrs. × $6.50)	8,775	
Factory overhead:		
Variable $2,853		
Fixed 6,725	9,578	30,853
Total costs to account for		$37,453
WIP, end *at standard*:		
Materials (200 × $10)	$ 2,000	
Conversion (150 × $13)	1,950	3,950
Goods completed and transferred *at standard*: 1,300 × $23		29,900
Variances:		
Material quantity	$ 1,500 (U)	
Labor rate	675 (U)	
Labor efficiency	600 (U)	
Variable overhead spending	153 (U)	
Fixed overhead spending	225 (U)	
Variable overhead efficiency	200 (U)	
Fixed overhead volume	250 (U)	3,603
		$37,453

Note that the materials are valued at standard, that is, $12,500 = 2,500$ units used x \$5 standard price per unit. The material purchase price variance does not appear on the cost of production report.

EXAMPLE 16

The Fernandez Company uses a standard process costing system. The following are the March performance reports for the purchasing department and the Production Department B:

Schedule 1 Performance Report—Purchasing Dept.

	Actual		Standard		Variance
Units		Amount	Units	Amount	(F or U)
Purchased Materials	5,400	\$36,720	5,400	\$37,800	\$1,080 (F)

Variance
Analysis $37,800 - $36,720 = $1,080$ (F)

Evaluation: The purchasing department purchased materials for \$6.80, which is \$.20 lower than the standard price. It was due to the quantity purchase which resulted in a \$.20 per unit discount.

Schedule 2 Performance Report—Department B

	Actual	Budget (or standard) Adjusted for Actual Output	Variance (F or U)
Production volume	2,400 units		
Actual direct labor hours worked	2,800 hrs.		
Standard DLH		2,400 hrs.	
Direct materials	5,200 units	5,000 units	
	\$36,400	\$35,000	1,400 (U)*
Direct labor	\$23,800	\$21,600	2,200 (U)**

$$
\begin{aligned}
&\text{* 200 units} \times \$7.00 \\
&\text{** Labor Efficiency} = (2800 - 2400)\,(\$9) = \$3600 \text{ (U)} \\
&\phantom{\text{** }} \text{Labor Rate} = (9.00 - 8.50)\,(2800) = \underline{1400 \text{ (F)}} \\
&\phantom{\text{** Labor Rate} = (9.00 - 8.50)\,(2800) = } 2200 \text{ (U)}
\end{aligned}
$$

Departmental overhead:			
Variable:			
Indirect materials		\$4,200	\$3,900	\$300 (U)
Indirect labor		5,500	4,950	550 (U)

Utilities	800	750	50 (U)
Fixed:			
Depreciation	3,300	3,300	—
Insurance and taxes	700	700	—
Utilities	500	500	—
Total Overhead	$15,000	$14,100	$900

Budgeted annual output in hours: 30,000
Budgeted annual overhead: Variable, $120,000
                                        Fixed,   54,000

We now calculate and evaluate the variances for each cost item.

Direct materials:

Material quantity variance: $36,400 − $35,000 = $1,400 (U)
        or (5,200 units − 5,000) × $7 = $1,400 (U)

Evaluation: The $1,400 unfavorable overall variance is due solely to excess usage. Department B used 200 units more than it should have in producing 2,400 units of output. Note that the material price variance, based on units purchased, is reflected on the performance report of the purchasing department.

Direct labor:

Wage rates: Actual, $23,800/2,800 hrs. = $8.50
                    Standard, $21,600/2,400 hrs. = $9

Actual Hours × Actual Rate (1)	Actual Hours × Standard Rate (2)	Standard Hours Allowed × Standard Rate (3)
2,800 hrs. × $8.5 = $23,800	2,800 × $9 = $25,200	2,400 × $9 = $21,600

Labor rate var. = $1,400 (F)

Labor efficiency variance = $3,600 (U)

Evaluation: The labor efficiency variance should be investigated further to determine the cause. It may be due to such factors as use of faulty equipment and improper production methods. Since there is a favorable rate variance of $1,400, however, it may be that the foreman used low quality, lower wage workers with a consequent drop in efficiency.

Factory overhead:
Flexible budget formula: variable $120,000/30,000 units = $4/hr.
                                    fixed $54,000/12 = $4,500
        Applied rates: variable $4/hr.
                                fixed $54,000/30,000 units = $1.8/hr.

	Actual Overhead (2,800 hrs.) (1)	Budget Based on Actual Hrs. (2,800 hrs.) (2)	Budget Based on Standard Hrs. (2,400 hrs.) (3)	Applied (2,400 hrs.) (4)
Variable	$10,500	11,200 (2,800 hrs. × $4)	9,500 (2,400 hrs. × $4)	9,600
Fixed	4,500	4,500	4,500	4,320
				(2,400 hrs. × $1)
	$15,000	$15,700	$14,100	$13,920

	Spending Var.	Efficiency Var.	Volume Var.
Variable:	$700 (F)	$1,600 (U)	not applicable
Fixed:	0	not applicable	$180 (U)
	$700 (F)	$1,600 (U)	$180 (U)

Evaluation: The $900 unfavorable variance is explained as follows:

Favorable spending variance	$ 700 (F)
Unfavorable efficiency variance	1,600 (U)
	$ 900 (U)

This may be the result of the use of low quality labor and materials coupled with a consequent drop in efficiency. It appears that indirect materials and indirect labor should be investigated further. The $180 unfavorable fixed overhead volume variance is an indication of below-average utilization of capacity. The department operated 100 hours below its normal capacity of 2,500 hours (30,000 hrs./12). If below-capacity operations is demand-related, this variance is not controllable by the department supervisor and therefore should not appear on his performance report. However, it could also be the result of inefficient operations, in which case, the supervisor should be held accountable.

NONMANUFACTURING ACTIVITIES

When nonmanufacturing activities repeat and result in a homogeneous product, standards may be used. The manner of estimating and employing standards can be similar to that applicable with a manufactured product. For instance, standards may be used for office personnel involved in processing sales orders, and a standard unit expense for processing a sales order may be derived. The variance between the actual cost of processing a sales order with the standard cost can be appraised by management and corrective steps taken. The number of payroll checks prepared should be a reliable measure of the activity of the payroll department. The number of invoices or vouchers prepared apply to billing and accounts payable. In these two cases, a standard cost per unit could be based on the variable expenses involved.

Variance analysis is used in non-production-oriented companies such as service businesses. Since we are not dealing with a product, a measure of volume other than units is necessary, for example, time spent. The measure of revenue is fee income.

The cost variances are still the same as in a manufacturing concern, namely budgeted costs versus actual costs. We also can derive the gross margin or contribution margin variance as the difference between that budgeted and that actually obtained. The profitability measures are expressed as a percent of sales rather than as dollars per unit. The relationship between costs and sales is often highlighted.

Service firms typically have numerous variances expressed in physical, rather than dollar, measures. Examples of physical measures are number of customers serviced and turnover rate in customers.

AN ILLUSTRATIVE VARIANCE ANALYSIS REPORT FOR A SERVICE BUSINESS

For a service business, cost variances may be reported to management in special reports. For example, the variance in time and cost spent for processing payments to creditors may be analyzed. An illustrative format follows.

	Variance in Time	Variance in Cost
Function		
Processing purchase orders		
Processing receiving reports		
Processing vendors' invoices		
Preparing checks		
Filing paid vouchers and supporting documents		

Variances for these functions are useful only for large companies where the volume of activity allows for the arrangement and analysis of such repetitive tasks.

VARIANCES TO EVALUATE MARKETING EFFORT

Prior to setting a marketing standard in a given trade territory, you should examine prior, current, and forecasted conditions for the company itself and that given geographical area. Standards will vary depending upon geographical location. In formulating standard costs for the transportation function, minimum cost traffic routes should be selected on the basis of the given distribution pattern.

Standards for advertising cost in particular territories will vary depending upon the types of advertising media needed, which are in turn based on the type of customers the advertising is intended to reach, as well as the nature of the competition.

Some direct selling costs can be standardized, such as product presentations for which a standard time per sales call can be established. Direct selling expenses should be related to distance traveled, frequency of calls made, and so on. If sales commissions are based on sales generated, standards can be based on a percentage of net sales.

Time and motion studies are usually a better way of establishing standards than prior performance, since the past may include inefficiencies.

Cost variances for the selling function may pertain to the territory, product, or personnel.

Variances in Selling Expenses

The control of selling expenses is not as significant for a company manufacturing a standard line of products with a limited number of established customers as for a manufacturer of custom products in a very competitive market. For the latter, significant advertising and salesmen costs are mandated. The variance in selling costs is equal to the actual cost versus the flexible budgeted cost.

Assume actual cost is $88,000 and the flexible budget is:

$40,000 + (5% × sales revenue) + ($.03 per unit shipped)

If sales revenue is $500,000 and 100,000 units are shipped, the flexible budgeted cost is:

$40,000 + (5% × $500,000) + ($.03 × 100,000 units) = $\underline{\$68,000}$

The variance is unfavorable by $20,000. Perhaps advertising and travel should be further investigated. These costs are highly discretionary in that they may easily be altered by management.

Further refinement of the selling expense variance is possible. Each element of selling expense (i.e., advertising, travel, commissions, shipping costs) could be looked at in terms of the difference between budgeted cost and actual cost.

Sales Personnel Performance

Actual sales may not be the best measure of sales personnel performance. It does not take into account differing territory potentials. Also, a high volume salesperson may have to absorb high selling cost making the profit generated by him low. Profit is what counts, not sales!

The evaluation of sales personnel based on the trend in their sales generated over the years shows signs of improvement. However, not considered here are customer's market demand, potential markets as defined by the company, product mix, and cost incurrence.

Travel expense standards are often formulated based on distance traveled and the frequency of customer calls. Standards for salesperson automobile expense may be in terms of cost per mile traveled and cost per day. Entertainment and gift expenditures can be based on the amount, size, and potential for customers. The standard might relate to cost per customer or cost per dollar of net sales. Selling expense standards are frowned upon by sales managers because they may create ill-will among sales personnel. The standards also do not take into account sales volume or product mix.

Profitability per salesperson may be a good measurement yardstick. Sales, less variable product costs, less selling expenses, per salesperson will give us the relevant profitability. Not considered here, however, are territory expectations or territory demand.

Standard costing procedures and performance measures should be used to control sales personnel costs and compute earnings generated by salesperson category. Further, revenue, cost, and profit by type of sales solicitation (i.e., personal visit, telephone call, mail) should be determined.

A break-even analysis for individual salesmen may also be performed.

Sales commissions should be higher for higher profit merchandise. Any quotas established should be based on a desired sales mix.

Consideration of fixed versus variable costs for a function is critical in marketing cost control and in deciding whether to add or drop sales regions and product lines.

Fixed marketing costs include administrative salaries, wages of warehousing and shipping personnel, rent, and insurance. Variable marketing costs are comprised of processing, storing, and shipping goods, which tend to fluctuate with sales volume. Also of a variable nature, are sales personnel salaries and commissions as well as travel and entertainment.

It is difficult to project marketing costs because they may materially change as market conditions are altered. An example is a modification in the channels of distribution. Also, customer brand loyalty is difficult to predict. The point here is that it is more difficult to forecast and analyze marketing costs than manufacturing costs. Thus, standards established in this area are quite tentative and very difficult to manage.

ILLUSTRATIVE MARKETING PERFORMANCE REPORT

An illustrative format for a marketing performance report designed for the vice-president of marketing follows.

	Budget	Percent	Actual	Percent	Variance
Sales					
Less: Standard variable cost of sales					
Manufacturing margin					

	Budget	Percent	Actual	Percent	Variance
Less: Variable distribution costs					
Contribution margin					
Less: Regional fixed charges					
Controllable regional contribution margin					
Less: Marketing fixed charges (i.e., central marketing administration costs, national advertising)					
Marketing contribution margin					

An illustrative format for a marketing performance report designed for the regional sales manager is presented below.

	Budget	Percent	Actual	Percent	Variance
Sales					
Less: Standard variable cost of sales					
Manufacturing margin					
Less: Variable distribution costs (i.e., sales personnel commissions, freight out)					
Contribution margin					
Less: Regional fixed charges (i.e., salesmen salaries, travel and entertainment, local advertising)					
Controllable regional contribution margin					

The marketing manager should be responsible for standard variable cost of sales, distribution costs (i.e., packing, freight out, marketing administration), and sales. The reason standard variable cost of sales is used is not to have the marketing area absorb manufacturing efficiencies and inefficiencies. An illustrative format follows.

Sales
Less: Standard variable cost of sales
Less: Distribution costs
Profitability

The profit figure constitutes the marketing efforts contribution to fixed manufacturing costs and administration costs.

How to Analyze Salesperson Variances

You should appraise sales force effectiveness within a territory, including time spent and expenses incurred.

EXAMPLE 17

Sales data for your company follow.

Standard cost	$240,000
Standard salesperson days	2,000
Standard rate per salesperson day	$ 120
Actual cost	$238,000
Actual salesperson days	1,700
Actual rate per salesperson day	$ 140

Total Cost Variance

Actual cost	$238,000
Standard cost	240,000
	$ 2,000 F

The control variance is broken down into salesperson days and salesperson costs.

Variance in Salesperson Days

Actual days versus standard days times standard rate per day
(1,700 versus 2,000 $\times$ $120) $ 36,000 F

The variance is favorable because the territory was handled in fewer days than expected.

Variance in Salesperson Costs

Actual rate versus standard rate times actual days
($140 versus $120 $\times$ 1,700) $ 34,000 U

An unfavorable variance results because the actual rate per day is greater than the expected rate per day.

EXAMPLE 18

A salesperson called on 55 customers and sold each an average of $2,800 worth of merchandise. The standard number of calls is 50, and the standard sales is $2,400. Variance analysis looking at calls and sales follows.

Total Variance

Actual calls × actual sale 55 × $2,800	$154,000
Standard calls × standard sale 50 × $2,400	120,000
	$ 34,000

The elements of the $34,000 variance are

Variance in Calls

Actual calls versus standard calls × standard sale	
(55 versus 50 × $2,400)	$ 12,000

Variance in Sales

Actual sale versus standard sale × standard calls	
($2,800 versus $2,400 × 50)	$ 20,000

Joint Variance

(Actual calls versus standard calls) × (Actual sale versus standard sale)	
(55 versus 50) × ($2,800 versus $2,400)	$ 2,000

Additional performance measures of sales force effectiveness include meeting sales quotas, number of orders from existing and new customers, profitability per order, and the relationship between salesperson costs and revenue obtained.

The trend in the ratios of (1) selling expense to sales, (2) selling expense to sales volume, and (3) selling expense to net income should be computed. Are selling expenses realistic in light of revenue generated? Are selling expenses beyond limitations pointing to possible mismanagement and violation of controls?

Variances in Warehousing Costs

In warehousing, standards for direct labor may be in terms of cost per item handled, cost per pound handled, cost per order filled, and cost per shipment.

Variances in warehousing costs can be calculated by looking at the cost per unit to store the merchandise and the number of orders anticipated.

EXAMPLE 19

The following information applies to a product:

Standard cost	$12,100
Standard orders	5,500
Standard unit cost	$ 2.20
Actual cost	$14,030
Actual orders	6,100
Actual unit cost	$ 2.30

Total Warehousing Cost Variance

Actual cost	$14,030
Standard cost	12,100
	$ 1,930 U

The total variance is segregated into the variance in orders and variance in cost.

Variance in Orders

Actual orders versus standard orders $\times$ standard unit cost
6,100 versus 5,500 $\times$ $2.20 $ 1,320 U

Variance in Cost

Actual cost per unit versus standard cost per unit $\times$ actual orders
$2.30 versus $2.20 $\times$ 6,100 $ 610 U

VARIANCES IN ADMINISTRATIVE EXPENSES

As business expands, there is a tendency for administrative expenses to increase proportionately and get out of line. However, central general and administrative expenses typically are of a fixed cost nature and hence there is less need to monitor these types of costs. Here, comparison of budgeted to actual costs can be made quarterly or even yearly! These comparisons should be done by department or unit of responsibility. Suggested standards for administrative expenses appear below.

Administrative Function	Unit of Standard Measurement
Handling orders	Number of orders handled
Billing	Number of invoices
Check writing	Number of checks written
Clerical	Number of items handled

Administrative Function	Unit of Standard Measurement
Customer statements	Number of statements
Order writing	Number of orders
Personnel	Number of employees hired
Payroll	Number of employees

Selling and administrative variances for nonoperating items are the responsibility of top management and staff. Such items include taxes and insurance. Performance reports may be prepared for the administrative function such as the salaries of top executives and general department service costs such as data processing. Performance measures may also be of a non-monetary nature such as the number of files processed, the number of phone calls taken, and the number of invoices written. Variances between the dollar and non-dollar factors can be determined and analyzed.

CAPITAL EXPENDITURES

Variance reports are useful in controlling capital expenditures by looking at the actual versus budgeted costs as well as actual versus budgeted times for proposals at each stage of activity. Such reports enable management to take corrective cost-saving action such as changing the construction schedule. The director of the project is held accountable for the construction cost and time budget. Component elements within the project should also be analyzed. We can also compare the expected payback period and actual payback period. This assists in measuring operational results and budgeting efficiency. Also, estimated cash flows of the project can be compared with actual cash flows.

VARIANCE ANALYSIS REPORTS

Performance reports may be prepared looking at the difference between budgeted and actual figures for (1) production in terms of cost, quantity, and quality; (2) sales; (3) profit; (4) return on investment; (5) turnover of assets; (6) income per sales dollar; (7) market share; and (8) growth rate. Variance reports raise questions rather than answering them. For example, is sales volume down because of deficiencies in sales effort or the manufacturer's inability to produce?

Variance analysis reports may be expressed not only in dollars, but also in percentages, ratios, graphs, and narrative.

Performance reports are designed to motivate managers and employees to change their activities and plans when variances exist. They should be terse and should concentrate on potential difficulties and opportunities. A section for comments should be provided so that explanations may be given for variances.

The timeliness of performance reports and detail supplied depends upon the management level the report is addressed to and the nature of the costs whose performance is being measured. A production supervisor may need daily information on the manufacturing operations, the plant superintendent may need only weekly data from his supervisor, and the vice-president for manufacturing may be satisfied with monthly performance figures for each plant. As we become more distant from the actual operation, the time interval for performance evaluation lengthens. Also, as we go up the ladder in the organization, performance reports contain data in increasingly summarized form.

Since performance reports depend upon the organizational structure, they should be designed based on the company's organization chart. Performance reports designed for a senior vice president might deal with the entire business operations of the firm and the earnings derived from it; the vice president of manufacturing would look at the efficiency of the production activity; the vice president of marketing would evaluate the selling and distribution function; a plant head would be concerned with the output and earnings generated from his plant; a department head within the plant would be concerned with cost control.

Performance reports should contain analytical information. To obtain it we should evaluate source data such as work orders, material requisitions, and labor cards. Reasons for inefficiency and excessive costs should be noted such as those due to equipment malfunction and low quality raw materials.

For labor, the productivity measurement ratio of volume output per direct labor hour should be computed. Further, the output of the individual or machine should be compared to the "normal" output established at the beginning of the reporting period. Operating efficiency can thus be measured. A labor efficiency ratio can also be computed which is the variation between actual hours incurred and standard hours.

With regard to the evaluation of the divisional manager, fixed costs are generally not controllable by him, but variable costs are. There are instances, however, where variable costs are controllable by those above the division manager's level. An example is fringe benefits. These items should be evaluated independently since the division manager has no responsibility for them. The opposite may also be true, that is, the department manager may have control over certain fixed expenses such as lease costs. In such cases he should similarly be assigned responsibility, although a successor not involved in the lease negotiation may not be assigned responsibility.

Appraisal of Marketing Department

Revenue, cost, and profitability information should be provided by product line, customer, industry segment, geographic area, channel of distribution, type of marketing effort, and average order size. New product evaluations should also be undertaken balancing risk with profitability. Analysis of competition in terms of strengths and weaknesses should be made. Sales force effectiveness measures should also be employed for income generated by salesmen, call frequency, sales incentives, sales personnel costs and dollar value of orders generated per hours spent. Promotional effectiveness measures should be employed for revenue, marketing costs, and profits prior to, during, and subsequent to promotional efforts, including a discussion of competitive reactions. Advertising effectiveness measures, such as sales generated based on dollar expenditure per media and media measures (i.e., audience share) are also useful. Reports discussing product warranty complaints and disposition should also be provided.

Marketing costs may be broken down into the following areas: selling, promotion, credit evaluation, accounting, and administration (i.e., product development, market research). Another element is physical distribution—inventory management, order processing, packaging, warehousing, shipping outbound transportation, field warehousing, and customer services.

Control of marketing cost is initiated when such costs are assigned to functional groups such as geographic area, product line, and industry segment. Budgeted costs and rates should be provided and comparisons made between standard costs and actual costs at the end of the reporting period.

CONCLUSION

Variance analysis is essential in the organization for the appraisal of all aspects of the business, including manufacturing, marketing, and service. Variances should be investigated if the benefits outweigh the costs of analyzing and correcting the source of the variance. Variance analysis reports should be in dollars and percentages.

Significant unfavorable variances must be examined to ascertain whether they are controllable by management or uncontrollable because they relate solely to external factors. When controllable, immediate corrective action must be undertaken to handle the problem. The managerial accountant should provide his recommendations. If a variance is favorable, an examination should be made of the reasons for it so that corporate policy may include the positive aspects found. Further, the responsible entity for a favorable variance should be recognized and rewarded.

Different degrees of significance of variances may be present including:

- The variance is within tolerable and normal range and thus no remedial steps are necessary.
- The variance is intolerable and thus either performance must be improved or new standards formulated in light of the current environment.
- The decision model was inappropriate, considering the goal to be achieved and thus a more relevant model should be developed.

Reports on operating performance should show where performance varies from standard, the trend of performance, and the reasons for the variances, including the manager's explanation.

Reporting systems differ among companies regarding the frequency and timeliness of reports, details presented, arrangement of data, employee distribution, and size of variances necessitating follow-up. Variances can be evaluated by divisions, subdivisions, departments, and cost centers. Variance analysis should be made to the point that additional savings from cost control justify the additional cost of appraisal and reporting.

If responsibility for a variance is joint, corrective action should also be joint. If correction of an unfavorable variance involves a conflict with a corporate policy, the policy should be reevaluated and perhaps changed. If the policy is not changed, the variance should be considered uncontrollable.

Even if a variance is below a cut-off percent or dollar figure, management may still want to investigate it if the variance is consistently unfavorable because it may reveal a problem (e.g., poor supervision, wasteful practice). The cumulative impact of a repeated small unfavorable variance may be just as damaging as an occasional one.

19

The Use of Capital Budgeting in Decision Making

Capital budgeting relates to planning for the best selection and financing of long-term investment proposals. Capital budgeting decisions are not equally essential to all companies; the relative importance of this essential function varies with company size, the nature of the industry, and the growth rate of the firm. As a business expands, problems regarding long-range investment proposals become more important. Strategic capital budgeting decisions can turn the tide for a company.

The types of scarce resources that may be committed to a project include cash, time of key personnel, machine hours, and floor space in a factory. When estimating costs for a proposed project, the allocation of the company's scarce resources must be converted in terms of money.

There are two broad categories of capital budgeting decisions, namely *screening decisions* and *preference decisions*. Screening decisions relate to whether a proposed project satisfies some present acceptance standard. For instance, your company may have a policy of accepting cost reduction projects only if they provide a return of 15%. On the other hand, preference decisions apply to selecting from *competing* courses of action. For example, your company may be looking at four different machines to replace an existing one in the manufacture of a product. The selection of which of the four machines is best is referred to as a preference decision.

The basic types of investment decisions are selecting between proposed projects and replacement decisions. Selection requires judgments concerning future events over which you have no direct knowledge. You have to consider timing and risk. Your task is to minimize your chances of being wrong. To help

449

you deal with uncertainty, you may use the risk-return tradeoff method. Discounted cash flow methods are more realistic than methods not taking into account the time value of money in appraising investments. Consideration of the time value of money becomes more essential in inflationary periods. Capital budgeting can be used in profit and nonprofit settings.

Planning for capital expenditures requires you to determine the "optimal" proposal, the number of dollars to be spent, and the amount of time required for completion. An appraisal is needed of current programs evaluating new proposals, and coordinating interrelated proposals within the company. In planning a project, consideration should be given to time, cost, and quality, which all interact. For control, a comparison should be made between budgeted cost and time compared to actual cost and time.

Capital budgeting decisions must conform to your cash position, financing strategy, and growth rate. Will the project provide a return exceeding the long-range expected return of the business? Projects must be tied into the company's long-range planning, taking into account corporate strengths and weaknesses. The objectives of the business and the degree to which they depend on economic variables (e.g., interest rate, inflation), production (e.g., technological changes), and market factors must be established. Also, the capital budget may have to be adjusted after considering financial, economic, and political concerns. However, consideration should be given to "sunk" and "fixed" costs that are difficult to revise once the initial decision is made.

Recommendation: Use cost-benefit analysis. Is there excessive effort for the proposal? Can it be performed internally or must it be done externally (e.g., make or buy)? Is there a more efficient means and less costly way of accomplishing the end result? Further, problem areas must be identified. An example is when long-term borrowed funds are used to finance a project where sufficient cash inflows will not be able to meet debt at maturity.

Suggestion: Measure cash flows of a project using different possible assumed variations (e.g., change in selling price of a new product). By modifying the assumptions and appraising the results you can see the sensitivity of cash flows to applicable variables. An advantage is the appraisal of risk in proposals based on varying assumptions. An increase in risk should result in a higher return rate.

Taxes have to be considered in making capital budgeting decisions because a project that looks good on a before-tax basis may not be acceptable on an after-tax basis. Taxes have an effect on the amount and timing of cash flows.

What-if questions are often the most crucial and difficult with regard to the capital expenditure budget and informed estimates are needed of the major assumptions. Spreadsheets can be used to analyze the cash flow implications of acquiring fixed assets.

Once an investment proposal is approved, there has to be an implementation of controls over expenditures and a reporting system regarding the project's status. Expenditures should be traced to the project and controls in place assuring the expenditures are in conformity with the approved investment proposal. Continuous monitoring should be made of how well the project is doing relative to the original plan.

FACTORS TO CONSIDER IN DETERMINING CAPITAL EXPENDITURES

- Rate of return
- Budget ceiling
- Probability of success
- Competition
- Tax rate
- Dollar amounts
- Time value of money
- Risk
- Liquidity
- Tax credits
- Long-term business strategy
- Forecasting errors

TYPES OF CAPITAL BUDGETING DECISIONS TO BE MADE

- Cost reduction program
- Undertaking an advertising campaign
- Replacement of assets
- Obtaining new facilities or expanding existing ones
- Merger analysis
- Refinancing an outstanding debt issue
- New and existing product evaluation
- No profit investments (e.g., health and safety)

Exhibit 1 shows a typical project application form while Exhibit 2 presents an advice of project change. In Exhibit 3, we see an appropriation request.

This chapter discusses the various capital budgeting methods including accounting rate of return, payback, discounted payback, net present value, profitability index, and internal rate of return. Consideration is also given to contingent proposals, capital rationing, and nondiscretionary projects. The incorporation of risk into the analysis is also dealt with.

Exhibit 1

POWERS CHEMCO, INC.
Capital Planning and Control System

PROJECT APPLICATION

DEPARMENT NAME				APPLICATION NO.	
DEPARTMENT CODE _____				OFFENSIVE ☐	
FUNCTION CODE _____				DEFENSIVE ☐	
PROJECT TITLE					
DESCRIPTION/OBJECTIVES					

EXPENDITURE AMOUNTS

FISCAL YEAR	1st Qtr.	2nd Qtr.	3rd Qtr.	4th Qtr.	TOTAL
19					
19					
19					
19					
19					
TOTAL					

DATE	SUBMITTED BY
COMMENTS	

_____
For The Division

452

Exhibit 2

POWERS CHEMCO, INC.
Capital Planning and Control System

ADVICE OF PROJECT CHANGE

DEPARMENT NAME	DATE
DEPARTMENT CODE	APPROPRIATION REQUEST NO.
PROJECT TITLE	

EXPENDITURE AMOUNTS

	ORIGINAL AUTHORIZED	LATEST ESTIMATE	INCREASE (DECREASE)
CAPITAL			
EXPENSE			
TOTAL			

AMOUNT SPENT TO DATE $_____   AMOUNT COMMITTED TO DATE $_____

WHY IS THIS NEW AMOUNT BEING REQUESTED?

_____   _____
PROJECT SPONSOR   DEPARTMENT/AREA SUPERVISOR

PROJECT TO BE CONTINUED ☐
REVISED REQUEST REQUIRED ☐
SEE COMMENT ON REVERSE SIDE ☐ FINAL APPROVER _____
                                DATE _____

ACCOUNTING (SIMPLE) RATE OF RETURN

Accounting rate of return (ARR) measures profitability from the conventional accounting standpoint by comparing the required investment (sometimes average investment) to future annual earnings. *Rule of Thumb:* Select the proposal with the highest ARR.

Exhibit 3

POWERS CHEMCO, INC.
APPROPRIATION REQUEST

(See Reverse Side for Instructions)

ORIG. DEPT. NAME		DEPT. CODE	APPROPRIATION NO.
BUDGET CAPITALIZED ☐ EXPENSED ☐		PROJECT APPLIC. NO.	
ACCOUNTING CODE		PROJECT APPL. TOT. EXP. $	APPROPRIATION TOTAL $
DESCRIPTION			
PURPOSE			
CURRENT FACILITIES			
PROPOSED FACILITIES			
COST JUSTIFICATION (SAVINGS/BENEFITS)			

PROPOSED EXPENDITURES		APPROVALS		DATE
Equipment Cost	_____	Originator	_____	___
Material Cost	_____		_____	___
Installation Costs:			_____	___
External Services	_____	Dept/Area Suprv.	_____	___
Internal Services	_____	V. President	_____	___
Miscellaneous Costs	_____	Controller	_____	___
Freight	_____	Division Head	_____	___
Taxes	_____	C.E.O.	_____	___
Total	_____	Bd. of Dir.	_____	___

EXAMPLE 1

Initial investment $8,000
Life   15 years
Cash inflows per year $1,300

$$\text{Depreciation} = \frac{\text{Cost} - \text{Salvage Value}}{\text{Life}} = \frac{\$8,000 - 0}{15} = \$533$$

$$\text{ARR} = \frac{\text{Cash Inflows per Year} - \text{Depreciation}}{\text{Initial Investment}}$$

$$\frac{\$1,300 - \$533}{\$8,000} = \frac{\$767}{\$8,000} = 9.6\%$$

If you use average investment, ARR is:

$$ARR = \frac{\$767}{\$8,000/2} = \frac{\$767}{\$4,000} = 19.2\%$$

Note: When average investment is used rather than the initial investment, ARR is doubled.

Advantages of ARR

- Easy to comprehend and calculate
- Considers profitability
- Numbers relate to financial statement presentation
- Considers full useful life

Disadvantages of ARR

- Ignores time value of money
- Uses income data rather than cash flow data

Note: In an automated environment, the cost of the investment would include engineering, software development, and implementation.

PAYBACK PERIOD

Payback is the number of years it takes to recover your initial investment. Payback assists in evaluating a project's risk and liquidity, faster rate of return, and earlier recoupment of funds. A benefit of payback is that it permits companies that have a cash problem to evaluate the turnover of scarce resources in order to recover earlier those funds invested. In addition, there is likely to be less possibility of loss from changes in economic conditions, obsolescence, and other unavoidable risks when the commitment is short term.

Supporters of the payback period point to its use where preliminary screening is more essential than precise figures, in situations where a poor credit position is a major factor, and when investment funds are exceptionally scarce. Some believe that payback should be used in unstable, uncertain industries subject to rapid technological change because the future is so unpredictable that there is no point in guessing what cash flows will be more than two years from now.

As reported in the July/August 1988 issue of *Financial Executive*, a majority of executives want payback in three years or less.

A company may establish a limit on the payback period beyond which an investment will not be made. Another business may use payback to choose one of several investments, selecting the one with the shortest payback period.

Advantages of Payback

- Easy to use and understand
- Effectively handles investment risk
- Good approach when a weak cash-and-credit position influences the selection of a proposal
- Can be used as a supplement to other more sophisticated techniques since it does indicate risk

Deficiencies of Payback

- Ignores the time value of money
- Does not consider cash flows received after the payback period
- Does not measure profitability
- Does not indicate how long the maximum payback period should be
- Penalizes projects that result in small cash flows in their early years and heavy cash flows in their later years.

Warning: Do not select a proposal simply because the payback method indicates acceptance. You still have to use the discounting methods such as present value and internal rate of return.

EXAMPLE 2

You are considering a new product. It will initially cost $250,000. Expected cash inflows are $80,000 for the next five years. You want your money back in four years.

$$\text{Payback Period} = \frac{\text{Initial Investment}}{\text{Annual Cash Inflow}} = \frac{\$250,000}{\$80,000} = \underline{3.125}$$

Because the payback period (3.125) is less than the cutoff payback period (4), you should accept the proposal.

EXAMPLE 3

You invest $40,000 and receive the following cash inflows:

Year 1 $15,000
Year 2 $20,000
Year 3 $28,000

$$\text{Payback Period} = \frac{\$40,000}{\underbrace{\underset{\$15,000}{\text{Year 1}} + \underset{\$20,000}{\text{Year 2}}}_{\$35,000} + \underset{\begin{array}{c}\$\ 5,000\\ \hline \$28,000\end{array}}{\text{Year 3}}} = \underline{2.18 \text{ years}}$$

$$2 \text{ years} \qquad + \qquad .18$$

If there are unequal cash inflows each year, to determine the payback period just add up the annual cash inflows to come up with the amount of the cash outlay. The answer is how long it takes to recover your investment.

As reported in the November 1987 issue of *Management Accounting* published by the National Association of Accountants, it was found that the majority of manufacturers use an unadjusted payback period of between two and four years when appraising advanced manufacturing equipment.

PAYBACK RECIPROCAL

Payback reciprocal is the reciprocal of the payback time. This often gives a quick, accurate estimate of the *internal rate of return (IRR)* on an investment when the project life is *more than* twice the payback period and the cash inflows are uniform every period.

EXAMPLE 4

ABC Company is contemplating three projects, each of which would require an initial investment of $10,000, and each of which is expected to generate a cash inflow of $2,000 per year. The payback period is five years ($10,000/$2,000), and the payback reciprocal is 1/5, or 20%. The table of the present value of an annuity of $1 shows that the factor of 5.00 applies to the following useful lives and internal rates of return:

Useful Life	IRR
10 years	15%
15	18
20	19

It can be observed that the payback reciprocal is 20% as compared with the IRR of 18% when the life is 15 years, and 20% as compared with the IRR of 19% when the life is 20 years. This shows that the payback reciprocal gives a reasonable approximation of the IRR if the useful life of the project is at least twice the payback period.

DISCOUNTED PAYBACK PERIOD

Before we start looking at discounted cash flow methods, it should be pointed out that less reliability exists with discounted cash flow analysis where there is future uncertainty, the environment is changing, and cash flows themselves are hard to predict.

You can take into account the time value of money by using the discounted payback method. The payback period will be longer using the discounted method because money is worth less over time. **How to Do It:** Discounted payback is computed by adding the present value of each year's cash inflows until they equal the investment.

EXAMPLE 5

Assume the same facts as in Example 3 and a cost of capital of 10%.

$$\text{Discounted Payback} = \frac{\text{Initial Cash Outlay}}{\text{Discounted Annual Cash Inflows}}$$

$40,000

Year 1	Year 2	Year 3
$15,000 +	$20,000 +	$28,000
× .9091 +	× .8264 +	× .7513
$13,637 +	$16,528 +	$21,036

$30,165   + $ 9,835
                       $21,036

2 years   +   .47   =   2.47 years

EXAMPLE 6

Assume a machine purchased for $18,000 yields cash inflows of $4,000, $5,000, $6,000, $6,000, and $8,000. The cost of capital is 10%. Then we have

(Table 3)

Year	Cash flow	PV factor at 10%	PV of cash flow
1	$4,000	.909	$3,636
2	5,000	.826	4,130
3	6,000	.751	4,506
4	6,000	.683	4,098
5	8,000	.621	4,968

The number of years required to recoup the $18,000 investment is:

Year 1 $ 3,636
     2   4,130
     3   4,506
     4   4,098
           $16,370

Balance in year 5: ($18,000 − $16,370) = $1,630

Therefore, the discounted payback period is: 4 years + $1,630/$4,968 = 4.33 years.

The discount payback rule recognizes the time value of money, but still ignores all cash flows after that date.

NET PRESENT VALUE

The present value method compares the present value of future cash flows expected from an investment project to the initial cash outlay for the investment. Net cash flows are the difference between forecasted cash inflow received because of the investment to the expected cash outflow of the investment. You should use as a discount rate the minimum rate of return earned by the company on its money. As reported in the November 1987 issue of *Management Accounting* (page 29), 36% of manufacturers used discount rates between 13% and 17% and more than 30% used discount rates over 19%.

A company should use as the discount rate its cost of capital (see Chapter 39). *Rule of Thumb:* Considering inflation, the cost of debt, and so on, the anticipated return should be about 10-13%. **Note:** The net present value method discounts all cash flows at the cost of capital, thus implicitly assuming that these cash flows can be reinvested at this rate.

Tip: If a proposal is supposed to provide a return, invest in it only if it provides a positive net present value. If two proposals are mutually exclusive (acceptance of one precludes the acceptance of another), accept the proposal with the highest present value. An advantage of net present value is that it considers the time value of money. A disadvantage is the subjectivity in determining expected annual cash inflows and expected period of benefit.

Note: In an advanced automated environment, the terminal value requires managerial accountants to forecast technological, economic, operational, strategic, and market developments over the investment's life so that a reasonable estimate of potential value may be made. **Warning:** Using the return rate earned by the company as the discount rate may be misleading in certain cases. It may be a good idea to also look at the return rate investors earn on similar projects. If the hurdle rates selected are based on the company's return on average projects, an internal company decision will occur that helps to increase the corporate return. Yet if the company is earning a very high rate of return, you will take a lot of good projects and also leave some good ones. What if the project left would really enhance value?

If the corporate return rate is below what investors can earn elsewhere, you delude yourself in believing it's an attractive investment. The project may involve below-normal profitability, lower per-share value, and result in lower creditor and investor ratings of the firm.

The net present value method typically provides more reliable signals than other methods. By employing net present value and using best estimates of reinvestment rates, you can select the most advantageous project.

EXAMPLE 7

You are considering replacing Executive 1 with Executive 2. Executive 2 requires a payment upon contract signing of $200,000. He will receive an annual salary of $300,000. Executive 1's current annual salary is $140,000.

Because Executive 2 is superior in talent, you expect there will be an increase in annual cash flows from operations (ignoring salary) of $350,000 for each of the next ten years. The cost of capital is 12%.

As indicated in the following calculations, since there is a positive net present value, Executive 1 should be replaced with Executive 2.

Year	Explanation	Amount	×	Factor	=	Present Value
0	Contract signing bonus	$-\$200,000$	×	1		$-\$ \ 200,000$
1–10	Increased salary: ($300,000 − $140,000)	$-\$160,000$	×	5.6502*		$-\$ \ 904,032$
1–10	Increase in annual cash flow from operations	$+\$350,000$	×	5.6502*		$\$1,977,570$
	Net present value					$\$ \ 873,538$

*Present value of an ordinary annuity factor for 10 years and an interest rate of 12%.

EXAMPLE 8

You own a business for which you have received a $1,000,000 offer. If you do not sell, you will remain in business for eight years and will invest another $50,000 in your firm. If you stay, you will sell your business in the eighth year for $60,000.

You expect yearly sales to increase by 50% from its present level of $500,000. Direct material is proportional to sales. Direct labor is proportional to sales, but will increase by 30% for all labor. Variable overhead varies with sales, and annual fixed overhead will total $70,000, including depreciation. Straight-line depreciation will increase from $7,000 to $10,000. At the end of eight years, all fixed assets will be fully depreciated. Selling and administrative expenses are assumed to remain constant. The cost of capital is 14%.

Your current year's income statement is:

Sales		$500,000
Less: Cost of Sales		
Direct Material	$100,000	
Direct Labor	120,000	
Variable Overhead	50,000	
Fixed Overhead	65,000	335,000
Gross Margin		$165,000
Less: Selling and Administrative Expenses*		40,000
Net Income		$125,000

*Includes your salary of $20,000

Your forecasted income statement for each of the next eight years follows.

Sales: $500,000 \times 1.5$		$750,000
Less: Cost of Sales		
Direct Material $100,000 \times 1.5$	$150,000	
Direct Labor $120,000 \times 1.5 \times 1.3$	234,000	
Variable Overhead $50,000 \times 1.5$	75,000	
Fixed Overhead	70,000	529,000
Gross Margin		$221,000
Less: Selling and Administrative Expenses		40,000
Net Income		$181,000

Your annual cash flow from operations is

Net Income	$181,000
Add: Depreciation	10,000
Salary	20,000
Annual cash flow from operations	$211,000

A comparison of your alternatives follows.

Sell Business	$+\$1,000,000$

Stay in Business:

Year	Explanation	Amount	$\times$	Factor	$=$	Present Value
0	Investment in assets	$-\$50,000$	$\times$	1		$-\$50,000$
1–8	Annual cash inflow	$+\$211,000$	$\times$	4.6389		$+\$987,808$
8	Sales price of business	$+\$60,000$	$\times$	0.3506		$+\$21,036$
	Net Present Value					$+\$949,844$

Since the net present value is higher to sell the business ($1,000,000) than staying in business ($949,844), you should sell now.

EXAMPLE 9

You are considering replacing an old machine with a new one. The old machine has a book value of $800,000 and a remaining life of 10 years. The expected salvage value of the old machine is $50,000, but if you sold it now you would obtain $700,000. The new machine costs $2,000,000 and has a salvage value of $250,000. The new machine will result in annual savings of $400,000. The tax rate is 50%, tax credit is 10%, and the cost of capital is 14%.

Use straight-line depreciation. You have to determine whether to replace the machine.

The net increase in annual cash flow is

	Net Income	Cash Flow
Annual Savings	$400,000	$400,000

Less: Incremental Depreciation

New Machine $\dfrac{\$2,000,000 - \$250,000}{10} = \$175,000$

Old Machine $\dfrac{\$800,000 - \$50,000}{10} = \$75,000$

	Net Income	Cash Flow
Incremental Depreciation	100,000	
Income before tax	$300,000	
Tax (50%)	150,000	150,000
Income after tax	$150,000	
Net cash inflow		$250,000

The net present value follows:

Year	Explanation	Amount	Factor	Present Value
0	Cost of new machine	$-\$2,000,000 \times 1.000$		$-\$2,000,000$
0	Sale of old machine	$700,000 \times 1.000$		700,000
1	Tax credit	$200,000 \times 0.877$		175,400
1	Tax benefit from loss on sale of old machine	$50,000 \times 0.877$		43,850
1–10	Yearly increase in cash flows	$250,000 \times 5.216$		1,304,000
10	Incremental salvage value	$200,000 \times 0.270$		54,000
				$ 277,500

The replacement of the old machine with a new machine should be made because of the resulting positive net present value.

Deciding whether to lease or purchase involves comparing the leasing and purchasing alternatives.

EXAMPLE 10

You have decided to acquire an asset costing $100,000 with a life of five years and no salvage value. The asset can be purchased with a loan or it can be leased. If leased, the lessor wants a 12% return. Lease payments are made in advance at the end of the year prior to each of the 10 years. The tax rate is 50%, and the cost of capital is 8%.

$$\frac{\text{Annual Lease}}{\text{Payment}} = \frac{\$100,000}{1 + 3.3073} = \frac{\$100,000}{4.3073} = \underline{\$23,216} \text{ (rounded)}$$

Year	Lease Payment	Tax Savings	After-Tax Cash Outflow	Factor	Present Value
0	$23,216		$23,216	1.0000	$23,216
1–4	23,216	$11,608*	11,608	3.3121	38,447
5		11,608	(11,608)	.6806	(7,900)
					$53,763

*23,216 × 50% = 11,608

If you buy the asset, you will take out a 10% loan. Straight line depreciation is used with no salvage value.

$$\text{Depreciation} = \frac{\$100,000}{5} = \$20,000$$

$$\text{Annual Loan Payment} = \frac{\$100,000}{3.7906} = \$26,381$$

The loan amortization schedule follows:

Year	Loan Payment	Beginning of Year Principal	Interest*	Principal**	End of Year Principal
1	26,231	100,000	10,000	16,381	83,619
2	26,231	83,619	8,362	18,019	65,600
3	26,231	65,600	6,560	19,821	45,779
4	26,231	45,779	4,578	21,803	23,976
5	26,231	23,976$^{(a)}$	2,398	23,983$^{(a)}$	

*10% × Beginning of Year Principal
**Loan Payment − Interest
$^{(a)}$Slight difference due to rounding

The computation of the present value of borrowing follows:

(1) Year Loan Payment	(2) Interest	(3) Depreciation	(4) Total Deduction	(5) Tax Savings	(6) Cash Flow	(7) PV Factor at 8%	(8) PV of Cash outflow
1 26,381	10,000	20,000	30,000	15,000	11,381	.9259	10,538
2 26,381	8,362	20,000	28,362	14,181	12,200	.8573	10,459
3 26,381	6,560	20,000	26,560	13,280	13,101	.7938	10,400
4 26,381	4,578	20,000	24,578	12,289	14,092	.7350	10,358
5 26,381	2,398	20,000	22,398	11,199	15,182	.6806	10,333
							52,088

$(4) = (2) + (3)$

$(5) = (4) \times 50\%$

$(6) = (1) - (5)$

$(8) = (6) \times (7)$

The present value of borrowing ($52,088) is less than the present value of leasing ($53,763). Thus, the asset should be bought.

PROFITABILITY INDEX

The profitability (ranking) index (also called excess present value index, cost-benefit ratio) is a net instead of an aggregate index and is employed to differentiate the initial cash investment from later cash inflows. If you have budget constraints, proposals of different dollar magnitude can be ranked on a comparative basis. Use the index as a means of ranking the project in descending order of attractiveness.

$$\text{Profitability index} = \frac{\text{Present value of cash inflows}}{\text{Present value of cash outflows}}$$

Rule of Thumb: Accept a proposal with a profitability index equal to or greater than 1.

Warning: A higher profitability index does not always coincide with the project with the highest net present value.

Tip: The internal rate of return and the net present value approaches may give conflicting signals when competing projects have unequal times. The profitability index gives the correct decision, however, and is superior under these circumstances.

Capital rationing takes place when a business is not able to invest in projects having a net present value greater than or equal to zero. Typically, the firm establishes an upper limit to its capital budget based on budgetary constraints. **Special Note:** With capital rationing, the project with the highest ranking index rather than net present value should be selected for investment.

Figure 1 shows the capital rationing decision process.

Figure 1. Capital Rationing Decision Process

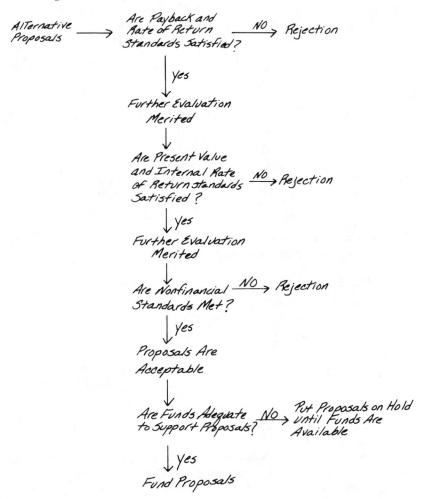

EXAMPLE 11

You have the following information regarding two proposals:

	Proposal A	Proposal B
Initial Investment	$100,000	$10,000
Present Value of Cash Inflows	$500,000	$90,000

The net present value of proposal A is $400,000 and that of proposal B is $80,000. Based on net present value, proposal A is better. However, this is very misleading when a budget constraint exists. In this case, proposal B's profitability index of nine far surpasses proposal A's index of five. Thus, profitability index should be used in evaluating proposals when budget constraints exist. The net result is that proposal B should be selected over proposal A.

EXAMPLE 12

Projects	Investment	Present Value	Profitability Index	Ranking
A	$ 70,000	$112,000	1.6	1
B	100,000	145,000	1.45	2
C	110,000	126,500	1.15	5
D	60,000	79,000	1.32	3
E	40,000	38,000	0.95	6
F	80,000	95,000	1.19	4

The budget constraint is $250,000. You should select projects A, B, and D, as indicated by the following calculations.

Project	Investment	Present Value
A	$ 70,000	$112,000
B	100,000	145,000
D	60,000	79,000
	$230,000	$336,000

where net present value = $336,000 − $230,000 = $106,000

Unfortunately, the profitability index method has some limitations. One of the more serious limitations is that it breaks down whenever more than one resource is rationed.

A more general approach to solving capital rationing problems is the use of mathematical (or zero-one) programming. Here the objective is to select the mix of projects that maximizes the net present value subject to a budget constraint.

EXAMPLE 13

Using the data given in Example 12 we can set up the problem as a mathematical programming one. First we label project A as X_1, B as X_2, and so on; the problem can be stated as follows: Maximize

$$NPV = \$42,000\ X_1 + \$45,000\ X_2 + \$16,500\ X_3 + \$19,000\ X_4 - \$2,000\ X_5 + \$15,000\ X_6$$

subject to

$$\$70,000\ X_1 + \$100,000\ X_2 + \$110,000\ X_3 + \$60,000\ X_4 + \$40,000\ X_5 + \$80,000\ X_6 \leq \$250,000;$$
$$X_i = 0,1\ (i = 1,2, \ldots ,6)$$

Using the mathematical program solution routine, the solution to this problem is:

$$X_1 = 1, X_2 = 1, X_4 = 1$$

and the net present value is $106,000. Thus, projects A, B, and D should be accepted.

CONTINGENT PROPOSALS

A contingent proposal is one that requires acceptance of another related one. Hence, the proposals must be looked at together. You compute a profitability index for the group.

EXAMPLE 14

Proposal	Present Value of Cash Outflow	Present Value of Cash Inflow
A	$160,000	$210,000
B	60,000	40,000
Total	$220,000	$250,000

$$\text{Profitability Index} = \frac{\$250,000}{\$220,000} = 1.14$$

INTERNAL RATE OF RETURN (TIME-ADJUSTED RATE OF RETURN)

The internal rate of return is the return earned on a given proposal. It is the discount rate equating the net present value of cash inflows to the net present value of cash outflows to zero. The internal rate of return assumes cash inflows are reinvested at the internal rate.

This method involves trial and error computations. However, the use of a computer or programmable calculator simplifies the internal rate of return process.

The internal rate of return can be compared with the required rate of return (cutoff or hurdle rate). **Rule of Thumb:** If the internal rate of return equals or exceeds the required rate, the project is accepted. The required rate of return is typically a company's cost of capital, sometimes adjusted for risk.

Advantages of internal rate of return are that it considers the time value of money, and is more realistic and accurate than the accounting rate of return method. Disadvantages are that with internal rate of return it is difficult and time-consuming to compute, particularly when there are uneven cash flows. Also, it does not consider the varying size of investment in competing projects and their respective dollar profitabilities. Further, in limited cases, when there are multiple reversals in the cash flow stream, the project could yield more than one IRR.

To solve for internal rate of return where unequal cash inflows exist, you can use the trial and error method while working through the present value tables. Guidelines in using trial and error follow:

- Compute net present value at the cost of capital, denoted here as r_1
- See if net present value is positive or negative
- If net present value is positive, use a higher rate (r_2) than r_1
- If net present value is negative, use a lower rate (r_2) than r_1. The exact internal rate of return at which net present value equals zero is somewhere between the two rates.
- Compute net present value using r_2
- Perform interpolation for exact rate

EXAMPLE 15

A project costing $100,000 is expected to produce the following cash inflows:

Year	
1	$50,000
2	30,000
3	20,000
4	40,000

Using trial and error, you can calculate the internal rate as follows:

Year	10%	Present Value (PV)	16%	PV	18%	PV
1	0.909	$ 45,450	0.862	$ 43,100	0.847	$ 42,350
2	0.826	24,780	0.743	22,290	0.718	21,540
3	0.751	15,020	0.641	12,820	0.609	12,180
4	0.683	27,320	0.552	22,080	0.516	20,640
		+ $112,570		+ $100,290		+ $ 96,710
Investment		− 100,000		− 100,000		− 100,000
Net PV		+ $ 12,570		+ $ 290		− $ 3,290

The internal rate of return on the project is a little more than 16% because at that rate the net present value of the investment is approximately zero.

If the return on the investment is expected to be in one lump sum after a period of years, you can use the Present Value of $1 table to find the internal rate.

EXAMPLE 16

You are considering two mutually exclusive investment proposals. The cost of capital is 10%. Expected cash flows are as follows:

Project	Investment	Year 1	Year 6
A	$10,000	$12,000	
B	$10,000		$20,000

Internal rates of return are:

$$\text{Project A} \quad \frac{\$10,000}{\$12,000} = 0.8333$$

Looking across one year on the table, 0.8333 corresponds to an internal rate of 20%.

$$\text{Project B} \quad \frac{\$10,000}{\$20,000} = .5000$$

Looking across six years on the table, 0.5000 corresponds to an internal rate of 12%.

Project A should be selected because it has a higher internal rate of return than Project B.

If the cash inflows each year are equal, the internal rate of return is computed first by determining a factor (which happens to be the same as the payback period) and then looking up the rate of return on the present value of an annuity of one table.

EXAMPLE 17

You invest $100,000 in a proposal that will produce annual cash inflows of $15,000 a year for the next 20 years.

$$\text{Internal Rate of Return} = \frac{\$100,000}{\$15,000} = 6.6667$$

Now we go to the Present Value of an Annuity of $1 table. Looking across 20 years, we find that the factor closest to 6.6667 is 6.6231, in the 14% column. Hence the internal rate is about 14%.

EXAMPLE 18

Initial investment $12,950
Estimated Life   10 years
Annual cash inflows $ 3,000
Cost of capital   12%

The internal rate of return (IRR) calculation follows, including interpolation to get the exact rate.

$$\text{PV of Annuity Factor} = \frac{\$12,950}{\$3,000} = \underline{4.317}$$

The value 4.317 is somewhere between 18% and 20% in the 10-year line of the PV of Annuity table. Using interpolation you get:

Present Value of Annuity Factor

18%	4.494	4.494
IRR		4.317
20%	4.192	
Difference	0.302	0.177

$$\text{Therefore, IRR} = 18\% + \frac{0.177}{0.302} \ (20\% - 18\%)$$

$$= 18\% + 0.586(2\%) = 18\% + 1.17\% = \underline{19.17\%}$$

Because the internal rate of return (19.17%) exceeds the cost of capital (12%), the project should be accepted.

NONDISCRETIONARY PROJECTS

Some investments are made out of necessity rather than profitability (e.g., pollution control equipment, safety equipment). Here you will have solely a negative cash flow. Hence, your discretionary projects must earn a return rate in excess of the cost of capital to make up for the losses on nondiscretionary projects.

EXAMPLE 19

A company's cost of capital is 14% and $30 million of capital projects, 25% of which are nondiscretionary projects. It thus has to earn $4.2 million per year (14% × $30 million). The $22.5 million of discretionary projects ($30 million less 25%) must earn 18.7% ($4.2 million/$22.5 million) rather than 14% to achieve the overall corporate earnings goal of $4.2 million.

COMPARISON OF METHODS

In general, the discounting cash flow methods (net present value, internal rate of return, and profitability index) come to the same conclusions for competing proposals. But these methods can give different rankings to mutually exclusive proposals in certain cases. Any one of the following conditions can cause contradictory rankings:

- Project lives differ
- There is a higher cost for one project relative to another
- The trend in cash flow of one project is the reverse of that of another

One of the following characteristics of the company may also produce conflicting rankings:

- Future investment opportunities are expected to be different than at present, and the investor knows whether they will be better or worse.
- There is capital rationing, a maximum level of funding for capital investments.

The major cause for different rankings of alternative projects under present value and internal rate of return methods relates to the varying assumptions regarding the reinvestment rate employed for discounting cash flows. The net present value method assumes cash flows are reinvested at the cost of capital rate. The internal rate of return method assumes cash flows are reinvested at the internal rate. **Tip:** The net present value method typically provides a correct ranking because the cost of capital is a more realistic reinvestment rate. **Recommendations:** Which method is best for a business really depends on which reinvestment rate is nearest the rate the business can earn on future cash flows from a project. **Note:** The Board of Directors typically reviews the company's required rate of return each year, and may increase or decrease it depending on the company's current rate of return and cost of capital.

The minimum rate of return required for a proposal may be waived in a situation where the proposal has significant future benefit (e.g., research and development), applies to a necessity program (e.g., safety requirement), and has qualitative benefit (e.g., product quality).

EXAMPLE 20

Assume the following:

			Cash Flows			
Project	0	1	2	3	4	5
A	$(100)	$120				
B	(100)					$201.14

Computing IRR and NPV at 10% gives the different rankings as follows:

	IRR	NPV
A	20%*	9.09
B	15%	24.90

The general rule is to go by NPV ranking. Thus project B would be chosen over project A.

CAPITAL BUDGETING PROCESS

Questions to Be Asked in the Capital Budgeting Process

- How is risk incorporated into the analysis?
- Is risk versus return considered in choosing projects?
- Prior to making a final decision, are all the results of the capital budgeting techniques considered and integrated?
- In looking at a proposal, are both dollars and time considered?
- Is the proposal consistent with long-term goals?
- Does each project have a cost/benefit analysis?
- Do you know which are your most profitable proposals and products?
- How much business is in each?
- Are there projects of an unusual nature?
- Do you periodically track the performance of current programs in terms of original expectations?
- In the capital budgeting process, are qualitative factors also considered, such as marketing, production, and economic and political variables?
- Has the proposal been considered incorporating the company's financial health?
- What is the quality of the project?
- Given the current environment, are your capital investments adequate?
- Are you risk prone or risk averse?
- Is the discounted payback method being used?
- How are probable cash flows computed?
- How do you come up with the expected life?

To look at the entire picture of the capital budgeting process, a comprehensive example is provided.

EXAMPLE 21

You are deciding whether to buy a business. The initial cash outlay is $35,000. You will receive annual net cash inflows (excluding depreciation) of \$5,000 per year for 10 years. The cost of capital is 10%. The tax rate is 50%. You want to evaluate whether you should buy this business.

The annual cash inflow follows:

	Years 1–10	
	Net Income	Cash Flow
Annual cash savings	\$5,000	+ \$5,000
Depreciation (\$35,000/10)	3,500	
Income before tax	\$1,500	
Tax (50%)	750	− 750
Net income	\$ 750	
Net cash inflow		+ \$4,250

Average Rate of Return on Investment:

$$\frac{\text{Net income}}{\text{Average Investment}} = \frac{\$750}{\$35,000/2} = \frac{\$750}{\$17,500} = \underline{4\%}$$

Payback Period:

$$\frac{\text{Initial Investment}}{\text{Annual Net Cash Inflow}} = \frac{\$35,000}{\$4,250} = \underline{8.2} \text{ years}$$

Net Present Value:

Year	Explanation	Amount	× Factor =	Present Value
0	Initial investment	− \$35,000	× 1	− \$35,000
1–10	Annual net cash inflow	+ 4,250	× 6.1446	26,095
	Net present value			− \$ 8,905

Profitability Index:

$$\frac{\text{Present Value of Cash Inflow}}{\text{Present Value of Cash Outflow}} = \frac{\$26,095}{\$35,000} = \underline{0.74}$$

Internal Rate of Return:

$$\text{Factor} = \frac{\text{Initial Outlay}}{\text{Annual Cash Inflow}} = \frac{\$35,000}{\$4,250} = 8.2$$

Going to the Present Value of Annuity table, we look for the intersection of 10 years and a factor of 8.2. Looking up the column we find 4%, which is the internal rate.

Conclusion: The business should not be bought for the following reasons:

1. An average rate of return of 4% is low.

2. The payback period is long.

3. The net present value is negative.

4. The internal rate of return of 4% is less than the cost of capital of 10%.

CAPITAL BUDGETING AND INFLATION

The accuracy of capital budgeting decisions depends on the accuracy of the data regarding cash inflows and outflows. For example, failure to incorporate price-level changes due to inflation in capital budgeting situations can result in errors in the predicting of cash flows and thus in incorrect decisions. Typically, the managerial accountant has two options dealing with a capital budgeting situation with inflation: Either restate the cash flows in nominal terms and discount them at a nominal cost of capital (*minimum required rate of return*) or restate both the cash flows and cost of capital in constant terms and discount the constant cash flows at a constant cost of capital. The two methods are basically equivalent.

EXAMPLE 22

A company has the following projected cash flows estimated in real terms:

Real Cash Flows (000s)

Period	0	1	2	3
	−100	35	50	30

The nominal cost of capital is 15%. Assume that inflation is projected at 10% a year. Then the first cash flow for year 1, which is $35,000 in current dollars, will be $35,000 \times 1.10 = \$38,500$ in year one dollars. Similarly the cash flow for year two will be $50,000 \times (1.10)^2 = \$60,500$ in year two dollars, and so on. If we discount these nominal cash flows at the 15% nominal cost of capital, we have the following net present value (NPV):

Period	Cash Flows	PVIF	Present Values
0	−100	1.000	−100
1	38.5	.870	33.50
2	60.5	.756	45.74
3	39.9	.658	26.25
		NPV =	5.49 or $5,490

Instead of converting the cash-flow forecasts into nominal terms, we could convert the cost of capital into real terms by using the following formula:

$$\text{Real cost of capital} = \frac{1 + \text{nominal cost of capital}}{1 + \text{inflation rate}} - 1$$

In the example, this gives

Real cost of capital $= (1 + .15)/(1 + .10) = 1.15/1.10 = 0.045$ or 4.5%

We will obtain the same answer except for rounding errors ($5,490 versus $5,580).

Period	Cash Flows	PVIF $= 1/(1 + .045)^n$	Present Values
0	−100	1.000	−100
1	35	$1/(1 + .045) = .957$	33.50
2	50	$1/(1.045)^2 = .916$	45.80
3	30	$1/(1.045)^3 = .876$	26.28
		NPV =	5.58 or $5,580

POSTAUDIT PROJECT REVIEW

The postaudit (postcompletion) project review is a second aspect of reviewing the performance of the project. A comparison is made of the actual cash flow from operations of the project with the estimated cash flow used to justify the project. There are several reasons why the postaudit project review is helpful. First, managers proposing projects will be more careful before recommending a project. Second, it will identify those managers who are repeatedly optimistic or pessimistic regarding cash flow estimates. How reliable are the proposals submitted and approved (perhaps additional investments can be made to result in even greater returns)? Top management will be better able to appraise the bias that may be expected when a certain manager proposes a project.

The postaudit review also gives an opportunity to reinforce successful projects, to strengthen or salvage "problem" projects, to cease unsuccessful projects before excessive losses occur, and to enhance the overall quality of future investment proposals.

In conducting a postaudit, the same technique should be employed as was used in the initial approval process to maintain consistency in evaluation. For example, if a project was approved using present value analysis, the identical procedure should be implemented in the postaudit review.

As per the "management by exception" principle, the managers responsible for the original estimates should be asked to furnish a complete explanation of any significant differences between estimates and actual results.

For control reasons, project performance appraisal should not be conducted by the group that proposed the project. Rather, internal auditors should be given this responsibility to maintain independence. A review report should be issued. Typically, only projects above a specified dollar amount require post-audit and/or periodic evaluation.

CAPITAL BUDGETING AND NONPROFIT ORGANIZATIONS

With regard to nonprofit institutions, the only real problem in using capital budgeting is the selection of an appropriate discount rate. Some nonprofit entities employ the interest rate on special bond issues (e.g., building a school) as the discount rate. Other nonprofit organizations employ the interest rate that could be earned by putting money in an endowment fund instead of spending it on capital improvements. Other nonprofit institutions use discount rates that are arbitrarily established by governing boards.

A pitfall to watch out for is using an excessively low discount rate. This may result in accepting projects that will not be profitable. To guard against this problem, the Office of Management and Budget promulgates a discount rate of at least 10% on all projects to be considered by federal government units (source: Office of Management and Budget Circular No. A-94, March 1972). In the case of nonprofit units such as schools and hospitals, the discount rate should be the average rate of return on private sector investments. The average discount rate will provide more meaningful results than using a specific interest rate on a special bond issue or the interest return on an endowment fund.

RISK AND UNCERTAINTY

Risk analysis is important in making capital investment decisions because of the significant amount of capital involved and the long-term nature of the investments being considered. The higher the risk associated with a proposed project, the greater the return rate that must be earned on the project to compensate for that risk.

You must consider the interrelation of risk among all investments. By properly diversifying, you can obtain the best combination of expected net present value and risk. **Tip:** Do not automatically reject a high-risk project. For example, a new product with much risk may be accepted if there is a chance of a major breakthrough in the market. The business may be able to afford a few unsuccessful new products if one is developed for extraordinary return.

Probabilities can be assigned to expected cash flows based on risk. The probabilities are multiplied by the monetary values to derive the expected monetary value of the investment. A probability distribution function can be generated by computer. **Special Note:** The tighter the probability distribution of expected future returns, the lower the risk associated with a project.

Several methods to incorporate risk into capital budgeting are probability distributions, risk adjusted discount rate, standard deviation and coefficient of variation, certainty equivalent, semi-variance, simulation, sensitivity analysis, and decision (probability) trees. Other means of adjusting for uncertainty are to decrease the expected life of an investment, use pessimistic estimates of cash flow, and compare the results of optimistic, pessimistic, and best-guess estimates of cash flows.

Probability Distributions

Expected values of a probability distribution may be computed. Before any capital budgeting method is applied, compute the expected cash inflows, or in some cases, the expected life of the asset.

EXAMPLE 23

A company is considering a $30,000 investment in equipment that will generate cash savings from operating costs. The following estimates regarding cash savings and useful life, along with their respective probabilities of occurrence, have been made:

Annual Cash Savings		Useful Life	
$ 6,000	0.2	4 years	0.2
$ 8,000	0.5	5 years	0.6
$10,000	0.3	6 years	0.2

Then, the expected annual savings is:

$$
\begin{aligned}
\$ 6{,}000\ (0.2) &= \$1{,}200 \\
\$ 8{,}000\ (0.5) &= 4{,}000 \\
\$10{,}000\ (0.3) &= \underline{3{,}000} \\
&\ \$8{,}200
\end{aligned}
$$

The expected useful life is:

$$
\begin{aligned}
4\ (0.2) &= 0.8 \\
5\ (0.6) &= 3.0 \\
6\ (0.2) &= \underline{1.2} \\
&\ 5\ \text{years}
\end{aligned}
$$

The expected NPV is computed as follows (assuming a 10% cost of capital):

$$
\begin{aligned}
NPV = PV - I &= \$8{,}200\ (PVIFA\ 10\%,\ 5) - \$30{,}000 \\
&= \$8{,}200\ (3.7908) - \$30{,}000 = \$31{,}085 - \$30{,}000 \\
&= \$1{,}085
\end{aligned}
$$

The expected IRR is computed as follows: By definition, at IRR,

$$I = PV$$
$$\$30,000 = \$8,200 \ (PVIFA \ r,5)$$
$$PVIFA \ r,5 = \frac{\$30,000}{\$8,200} = 3.6585$$

which is about halfway between 10% and 12% in Table 4, so that we can estimate the rate to be 11%. Therefore, the equipment should be purchased, since (1) NPV = $1,085, which is positive, and/or (2) IRR = 11%, which is greater than the cost of capital of 10%.

Risk-Adjusted Discount Rate

Risk can be included in capital budgeting by computing probable cash flows on the basis of probabilities and assigning a discount rate based on the riskiness of alternative proposals.

Using this approach, an investment's value is determined by discounting the expected cash flow at a rate allowing for the time value of money and for the risk associated with the cash flow. The cost of capital (discount rate) is adjusted for a project's risk. A profitable investment is indicated by a positive net present value. Using the method, you judge the risk class of the proposed capital investment and the risk-adjusted discount rate appropriate for that class.

Tip: If doubtful of your results, check them by estimating the cost of capital of other companies specializing in the type of investment under consideration.

EXAMPLE 24

You are evaluating whether to accept proposal A or B. Each proposal mandates an initial cash outlay of $12,000 and has a three year life. Annual net cash flows along with expected probabilities are as follows.

Proposal A:

Expected Annual Cash Inflow	Probability
$5,800	.4
6,400	.5
7,000	.1

Proposal B:

Expected Annual Cash Inflow	Probability
$ 3,400	.3
8,000	.5
11,000	.2

The inflation rate and interest rate are estimated at 10%. Proposal A has a lower risk since its cash flows show greater stability than those of

Proposal B. Since Proposal A has less risk, it is assigned a discount rate of 8%, while Proposal B is assigned a 10% discount rate because of the greater risk.

Proposal A:

Cash Flow	Probability	Probable Cash Flow
$5,800	.4	$2,320
6,400	.5	3,200
7,000	.1	700
Expected Annual Cash Inflow		$6,220

Proposal B:

Cash Flow	Probability	Probable Cash Flow
$3,400	.3	$1,020
8,000	.5	4,000
11,000	.2	2,200
Expected Annual Cash Inflow		$7,220

Proposal A:

Year	Explanation	Amount	×	Factor	=	Present Value
0	Initial investment	−$12,000	×	1		−$12,000
1–3	Annual cash flow	+ 6,220	×	2.5771*		+ 16,030
	Net present value					+$ 4,030

*Using an 8% discount rate

Proposal B:

Year	Explanation	Amount	×	Factor	=	Present Value
0	Initial investment	−$12,000	×	1		−$12,000
1–3	Annual cash flow	+ 7,200	×	2.4869**		+ 17,955
	Net present value					+$ 5,955

**Using a 10% discount rate

Even though Project B has more risk, it has a higher risk-adjusted net present value. Project B should thus be selected.

Standard Deviation and Coefficient of Variation

Risk is a measure of dispersion around a probability distribution. It is the variability of cash flow around the expected value. Risk can be measured in either absolute or relative terms. First, the expected value, $\bar{A}$, is

$$\bar{A} = \sum_{i=1}^{n} A_i p_i$$

where A_i = the value of the ith possible outcome

p_i = the probability that the ith outcome will take place

n = the number of possible outcomes

Then, the absolute risk is determined by the standard deviation:

$$\sigma = \sqrt{\sum_{i=1}^{n} (A_i - \bar{A})^2 p_i}$$

The relative risk is expressed by the coefficient of variation:

$$\frac{\sigma}{\bar{A}}$$

EXAMPLE 25

You are considering investing in one of two projects. Depending on the state of the economy, the projects would provide the following cash inflows in each of the next five years:

Economic Condition	Probability	Proposal A	Proposal B
Recession	.3	$1,000	$ 500
Normal	.4	2,000	2,000
Boom	.3	3,000	5,000

We now compute the expected value ($\bar{A}$), the standard deviation (σ), and the coefficient of variation ($\sigma/\bar{A}$).

Proposal A:

A_i	P_i	$A_i P_i$	$(A_i - \bar{A})$	$(A_i - \bar{A})^2$
$1,000	.3	$ 300	-$1,000	$1,000,000
2,000	.4	800	0	0
3,000	.3	900	1,000	1,000,000
	$\bar{A} =$	$2,000	$\sigma^2 =$	$2,000,000

Because $\sigma^2 = \$2,000,000$, $\sigma = \$1,414$. Thus

$$\frac{\sigma}{\bar{A}} = \frac{\$1,414}{\$2,000} = 0.71$$

Proposal B:

A_i	P_i	A_iP_i	$(A_i - \bar{A})$	$(A_i - \bar{A})^2$
$ 500	.3	$ 150	- $1,950	$3,802,500
2,000	.4	800	- 450	202,500
5,000	.3	1,500	2,550	6,502,500
	$\bar{A} =$	$2,450	$\sigma^2 =$	$10,507,500

Since $\sigma^2 = \$10,507,500$, $\sigma = \$3,242$. Thus

$$\frac{\sigma}{\bar{A}} = \frac{\$3,242}{\$2,450} = 1.32$$

Therefore, proposal A is relatively less risky than proposal B, as measured by the coefficient of variation.

Certainty Equivalent

The certainty equivalent approach relates to utility theory. You specify at what point the company is indifferent to the choice between a certain sum of dollars and the expected value of a risky sum. The certainty equivalent is multiplied by the original cash flow to obtain the equivalent certain cash flow. You then use normal capital budgeting. The risk-free rate of return is employed as the discount rate under the net present value method and as the cutoff rate under the internal rate of return method.

EXAMPLE 26

A company's cost of capital is 14% after taxes. Under consideration is a 4-year project that will require an initial investment of $50,000. The following data also exists:

Year	After-Tax Cash Flow	Certainty Equivalent Coefficient
1	$10,000	.95
2	15,000	.80
3	20,000	.70
4	25,000	.60

The risk-free rate of return is 5%.
Equivalent certain cash inflows are:

Year	After-Tax Cash Inflow	Certainty Equivalent Coefficient	Equivalent Certain Cash Inflow		Present Value Factor at 5%		Present Value
1	$10,000	.95	$ 9,500	×	.9524	=	$ 9,048
2	15,000	.80	12,000		.9070		10,884

Year	After-Tax Cash Inflow	Certainty Equivalent Coefficient	Equivalent Certain Cash Inflow	×	Present Value Factor at 5%	=	Present Value
3	20,000	.70	14,000		.8638		12,093
4	25,000	.60	15,000		.8227		12,341
							$44,366

Net Present Value:	
Initial Investment	− $50,000
PV of Cash Inflows	+ 44,366
Net Present Value	− $ 5,634

Using trial and error, an internal rate of 4% is gotten.

The proposal should be rejected because of the negative net present value and an internal rate (4%) less than the risk-free rate (5%).

Semi-variance

Semi-variance is the expected value of the squared negative deviations of the possible outcomes from an arbitrarily chosen point of reference. Semi-variance appraises risks applicable to different distributions by referring to a fixed point designated by you. In computing semi-variance, positive and negative deviations contribute differently to risk, whereas in computing variance, a positive and negative deviation of the same magnitude contribute equally to risk. In effect, since there is an opportunity cost of tying up capital, the risk of an investment is measured principally by the prospect of failure to earn the return.

Simulation

You obtain probability distributions for a number of variables (e.g., investment outlays, unit sales) when doing a simulation. Selecting these variables from the distributions at random results in an estimated net present value. Since a computer is used to generate many results using random numbers, project simulation is expensive.

Sensitivity Analysis

Forecasts of many calculated net present values and internal rates of return under various alternatives are compared to identify how sensitive net present value or internal rate of return is to changing conditions. You see if one or more than one variable significantly affects net present value once that variable is changed. If net present value is materially changed, we are dealing with a much riskier asset than was originally forecast. Sensitivity analysis provides an immediate financial measure of possible errors in forecasts. It focuses on decisions that may be sensitive.

Sensitivity analysis can take various forms. For example, a managerial accountant may want to know how far annual sales will have to decline to break even on the investment. Sensitivity analysis could also be used to test the sensitivity of a decision to estimates of selling price and per-unit variable cost.

Sensitivity analysis provides managers with an idea of the degree to which unfavorable occurrences like lower volumes, shorter useful lives, or higher costs are likely to impact the profitability of a project. It is employed due to the uncertainty in dealing with real-life situations.

Decision Trees

A decision (probability) tree graphically shows the sequence of possible outcomes. The capital budgeting tree shows cash flows and net present value of the project under different possible circumstances. Advantages of this approach are that it shows possible outcomes of the contemplated project, makes you more cognizant of adverse possibilities, and depicts the conditional nature of later years' cash flows. The disadvantage is that many problems are too complex to allow for a year-by-year depiction. For example, a 3-year project with three possible outcomes following each year, has 27 paths. For a 10-year project (with three possible outcomes following each year) there will be about 60,000 paths.

EXAMPLE 27

You want to introduce one of two products. The probabilities and present values of expected cash inflows are

Product	Investment	PV of Cash Inflows	Probability
A	$225,000		
		$450,000	.4
		200,000	.5
		− 100,000	.1
B	80,000		
		320,000	.2
		100,000	.6
		− 150,000	.2

	Initial Investment (1)	Probability (2)	PV of Cash Inflows (3)	PV of Cash Inflows (2) × (3) = (4)
Product A	$225,000	.40 .50 .10	$450,000 200,000 −100,000	$180,000 100,000 −10,000 $270,000
or				
Product B	$ 80,000	.20 .60 .20	$320,000 100,000 −150,000	$ 64,000 60,000 −30,000 $ 94,000

Net present value:

Product A	$270,000	$-$ $225,000	$=$	$45,000
Product B	$ 94,000	$-$ $ 80,000	$=$	$14,000

Product A should be selected.

EXAMPLE 28

A firm has an opportunity to invest in a machine which will last two years, initially cost $125,000, and has the following estimated possible after-tax cash inflow pattern: In year one, there is a 40% chance that the after-tax cash inflow will be $45,000, a 25% chance that it will be $65,000, and a 35% chance that it will be $90,000. In year two, the after-tax cash inflow possibilities depend on the cash inflow that occurs in year one; that is, the year two after-tax cash inflows are conditional probabilities. Assume that the firm's after-tax cost of capital is 12%. The estimated conditional after-tax cash inflows (ATCI) and probabilities are given below.

If ATCI1 = $45,000		If ATCI1 = $65,000		If ATCI1 = $90,000	
ATCI2($)	Probability	ATCI2($)	Probability	ATCI2($)	Probability
30,000	0.3	80,000	0.2	90,000	0.1
60,000	0.4	90,000	0.6	100,000	0.8
90,000	0.3	100,000	0.2	110,000	0.1

Then the decision tree which shows the possible after-tax cash inflow in each year, including the conditional nature of the year two cash inflow and its probabilities, can be depicted as follows:

Time 0	Time 1	Time 2	NPV at 12%	Joint Probability	Expected NPV
		$ 30,000	$-$ $60,905[a]	0.120[b]	$-$ $7,309
	$45,000	$ 60,000	$-$ $36,995	0.160	$-$ 5,919
		$ 90,000	$-$ $13,085	0.120	$-$ 1,570
		$ 80,000	$-$ $ 3,195	0.050	$-$ 160
$-$ $125,000	$65,000	$ 90,000	$ 4,775	0.150	716
		$100,000	$12,745	0.050	637
		$ 90,000	$27,100	0.035	949
	$90,000	$100,000	$35,070	0.280	9,820
		$110,000	$43,040	0.035	1,506
				1.000	$-$ $1,330

$$a) \ NPV = PV - I = \frac{\$45,000}{(1 + 0.12)} + \frac{\$30,000}{(1 + 0.12)^2} - \$125,000$$

$$= \$45,000 \ (PVIF \ 12\%,1) + \$30,000 \ (PVIF \ 12\%, 2) - \$125,000$$
$$= \$45,000 \ (0.893) + \$30,000 \ (0.797) - \$125,000$$
$$= \$40,185 + \$23,910 - \$125,000 = \$60,905$$

b) Joint probability $= (0.4) \ (0.3) = 0.120$

The last column shows the calculation of expected NPV, which is the weighted-average of the individual path NPVs where the weights are the path probabilities. In this example, the expected NPV of the project is $-\$1,330$, and the project should be rejected.

Correlation of Cash Flows Over Time

When cash inflows are independent from period to period, it is fairly easy to measure the overall risk of an investment proposal. In some cases, however, especially with the introduction of a new product, the cash flows experienced in early years affect the size of the cash flows in later years. This is called the *time dependence of cash flows*, and it has the effect of increasing the risk of the project over time.

EXAMPLE 29

Janday Corporation's after-tax cash inflows (ATCI) are time-dependent, so that year one results $(ATCI_1)$ affect the cash flows in year two $(ATCI_2)$ as follows:

If $ATCI_1$ is $8,000 with a 40% probability, the distribution for $ATCI_2$ is:

0.3 $5,000
0.5   10,000
0.2   15,000

If $ATCI_1$ is $15,000 with a 50% probability, the distribution for $ATCI_2$ is:

0.3 $10,000
0.6   20,000
0.1   30,000

If $ATCI_1$ is $20,000 with a 10% chance, the distribution for $ATCI_2$ is:

0.1 $15,000
0.8   40,000
0.1   50,000

The project requires an initial investment of $20,000, and the risk-free rate of capital is 10%.

The company uses the expected NPV from decision tree analysis to determine whether the project should be accepted. The analysis is as follows:

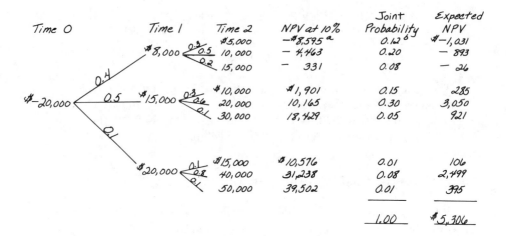

(a) $NPV = PV - I = \$8,000\ PVIF_{10,1}\ \dot{+}\ \$5,000\ PVIF_{10,2} - \$20,000$

$= \$8,000\ (0.9091)\ \dot{+}\ \$5,000\ (0.8264) - \$20,000 = -\$8,595$

(b) Joint probability of the first path = (0.4) (0.3) = 0.12

Since the NPV is positive (5,306), Jandy Corporation should accept the project.

NORMAL DISTRIBUTION AND NPV ANALYSIS: STANDARDIZING THE DISPERSION

With the assumption of independence of cash flows over time, the expected NPV would be

$$NPV = PV - I$$

$$= \sum_{t=1}^{n} \frac{\bar{A}_t}{(1 + r)^t} - I$$

The standard deviation of NPVs is

$$\sigma = \sqrt{\sum_{t=1}^{n} \frac{\sigma_t^2}{(1 + r)^{2t}}}$$

The expected value $(\bar{A})$ and the standard deviation (σ) give a considerable amount of information by which to assess the risk of an investment project. If the probability distribution is normal, some probability statement regarding the project's NPV can be made. For example, the probability of a project's NPV providing an NPV of less or greater than zero can be computed by standardizing the normal variate x as follows:

$$z = \frac{x - NPV}{\sigma}$$

where x = the outcome to be found
NPV = the expected NPV
z = the standardized normal variate whose probability value can be found in Appendix A.

EXAMPLE 30

Assume an investment with the following data:

	Period 1	Period 2	Period 3
Expected cash inflow ($\bar{A}$)	$5,000	$4,000	$3,000
Standard deviation (σ)	1,140	1,140	1,140

Assume that the firm's cost of capital is 8% and the initial investment is $9,000. Then the expected NPV is:

$$NPV = PV - I$$

$$= \frac{\$5,000}{(1 + 0.08)} + \frac{\$4,000}{(1 + 0.08)^2} + \frac{\$3,000}{(1 + 0.08)^3} - \$9,000$$

$$= \$5,000 \, (PVIF_{8,1}) + \$4,000 \, (PVIF_{8,2}) + \$3,000 \, (PVIF_{8,3}) - \$9,000$$
$$= \$5,000 \, (0.9259) + \$4,000 \, (0.8573) + \$3,000 \, (0.7938) - \$9,000$$
$$= \$4,630 + \$3,429 + \$2,381 - \$9,000 = \$1,440$$

The standard deviation about the expected NPV is

$$\sigma = \sqrt{\sum_{t=1}^{n} \frac{\sigma_t^2}{(1+r)^{2t}}}$$

$$= \sqrt{\frac{\$1,140^2}{(1+0.08)^2} + \frac{\$1,140^2}{(1+0.08)^4} + \frac{\$1,140^2}{(1+0.08)^6}}$$

$$= \sqrt{\$2,888,411} = \$1,670$$

The probability that the NPV is less than zero is then:

$$z = \frac{x - NPV}{\sigma} = \frac{0 - \$1,440}{\$1,670} = -0.862$$

The area of normal distribution that is z standard deviations to the left or right of the mean may be found in Appendix A. A value of z equal to -0.862 falls in the area between 0.1977 and 0.1841 in Appendix A. Therefore, there is approximately a 19% chance that the project's NPV will be zero or less. Putting it another way, there is a 19% chance that the internal rate of return of the project will be less than the risk-free rate.

CAPITAL ASSET PRICING MODEL (CAPM) IN CAPITAL BUDGETING

Portfolio considerations play an important role in the overall capital budgeting process. Through diversification, a firm can stabilize earnings, reduce risk, and thereby increase the market price of the firm's stock. The beta coefficient can be used for this purpose.

The capital asset pricing model (CAPM) can be used to determine the appropriate cost of capital. The NPV method uses the cost of capital as the rate to discount future cash flows. The IRR method uses the cost of capital as the cutoff rate. The required rate of return, or cost of capital according to the CAPM, or security market line (SML), is equal to the risk-free rate of return (r_f) plus a risk premium equal to the firms's beta coefficient (b) times the market risk premium

$(r_m - r_f)$:

$$r_j = r_f + b(r_m - r_f)$$

EXAMPLE 31

A project has the following projected cash flows:

Year 0	Year 1	Year 2	Year 3
$(400)	$300	$200	$100

The estimated beta for the project is 1.5. The market return is 12%, and the risk-free rate is 6%. Then the firm's cost of capital, or required rate of return is

$$r_j = r_f + b(r_m - r_f) = 6\% + 1.5(12\% - 6\%) = 15\%$$

The project's NPV can be computed using 15% as the discount rate:

Year	Cash Flow ($)	PV at 15%	PV ($)
0	(400)	1.000	(400)
1	300	0.870	261
2	200	0.756	151
3	100	0.658	66
NPV			78

The project should be accepted since its NPV is positive, that is, $78. Also, the project's IRR can be computed by trial and error. It is almost 30%, which exceeds the cost of capital of 15%. Therefore, by that standard also the project should be accepted.

CONCLUSION

Net present value, internal rate of return, and profitability index are equally effective in selecting economically sound, independent investment proposals. However, the payback method is inadequate since it does not consider the time value of money. For mutually exclusive projects, net present value, internal rate of return, and profitability index methods are not always able to rank projects in the same order; it is possible to come up with different rankings under each method. Risk should be taken into account in the capital budgeting process, such as by using probabilities, simulation, and decision trees.

Appendix A

NORMAL PROBABILITY DISTRIBUTION TABLE

Area of normal distribution that is z standard deviations to the left or right of the mean.

Number of Standard Deviations from Mean (z)	Area to the Left or Right (One tail)	Number of Standard Deviations from Mean (z)	Area to the Left or Right (One tail)
0.00	.5000	1.55	.0606
0.05	.4801	1.60	.0548
0.10	.4602	1.65	.0495
0.15	.4404	1.70	.0446
0.20	.4207	1.75	.0401
0.25	.4013	1.80	.0359
0.30	.3821	1.85	.0322
0.35	.3632	1.90	.0287
0.40	.3446	1.95	.0256
0.45	.3264	2.00	.0228
0.50	.3085	2.05	.0202
0.55	.2912	2.10	.0179
0.60	.2743	2.15	.0158
0.65	.2578	2.20	.0139
0.70	.2420	2.25	.0122
0.75	.2264	2.30	.0107
0.80	.2119	2.35	.0094
0.85	.1977	2.40	.0082

Number of Standard Deviations from Mean (z)	Area to the Left or Right (One tail)	Number of Standard Deviations from Mean (z)	Area to the Left or Right (One tail)
0.90	.1841	2.45	.0071
0.95	.1711	2.50	.0062
1.00	.1577	2.55	.0054
1.05	.1469	2.60	.0047
1.10	.1357	2.65	.0040
1.15	.1251	2.70	.0035
1.20	.1151	2.75	.0030
1.25	.1056	2.80	.0026
1.30	.0968	2.85	.0022
1.35	.0885	2.90	.0019
1.40	.0808	2.95	.0016
1.45	.0735	3.00	.0013
1.50	.0668		

20

Evaluation of Segmental Performance and Transfer Pricing

A segment is a part or activity of an organization from which a manager derives cost or revenue data. Examples of segments are divisions, sales territories, individual stores, service centers, manufacturing plants, sales departments, product lines, geographic areas, and types of customers.

Analysis of segmental performance assists in determining the success or failure of the divisional manager as well as the division. Performance reports should include industry and competitor comparisons. Also, the performance reports should match cycles of major business lines, activities, and geographic areas.

Performance measures look to the contribution of the division to profit and quantity as well as whether the division meets the overall goals of the company. It is difficult to compare profit of different segments of a company, especially when segments are of different sizes or provide different kinds of products or services. Measures of divisional performance for a particular segment should be compared to previous periods, other segments, and predetermined standards.

Profit planning by segments applies to selecting among alternative uses of company resources to accomplish a target profit figure. Segmental profit planning necessitates that the profitability of each segment be measured to see the overall profitability of all feasible combinations or alternatives.

APPRAISING MANAGER PERFORMANCE

In appraising manager performance, you must determine which factors were under the manager's control (e.g., advertising budget) and which factors were not (e.g., economic conditions). Comparison should be made of one division in the company to other divisions as well as of a division in the company to a similar division in a competing company. Appraisal should also be made of the risk and earning potential of a division. Graphic presentation shows comparisons whether of an historical, current, or prognostic nature.

Importance of Measuring Performance of Divisional Manager

- Assists in formulating management incentives and controlling operations to meet corporate goals
- Directs upper management attention to where it would be most productive
- Determines whom to reward for good performance
- Determines who is not doing well so corrective action may be taken
- Provides job satisfaction since the manager receives feedback

In decentralization, profit responsibility is assigned among subunits of the company. The lower the level where decisions are made, the greater is the decentralization. Decentralization is most effective in organizations where cost and profit measurements are necessary and is most successful in organizations where subunits are totally independent and autonomous. Decentralization is in different forms including functional, geographical, and profit.

Advantages of Decentralization

- Top management has more time for strategic planning
- Decisions are made by managers with the most knowledge of local conditions
- There is greater managerial input in decision making
- Managers have more control over results, resulting in motivation

Disadvantages of Decentralization

- Managers become "narrow-sighted" and look solely at the division rather than at the company as a whole
- Duplication of services can result
- There is an increased cost in obtaining additional information

For comparison purposes, replacement cost instead of historical cost should be employed. It furnishes a relative basis of comparison since it represents the comparable necessary investment at the end of a reporting period. Evaluating replacement cost assists in comparing asset valuation to current productivity. If replacement cost cannot be determined, valuation can be based on the present value of future net cash flows.

The major means of analyzing divisional performance are by responsibility center comprising of revenue center, cost center, profit center, and investment center.

RESPONSIBILITY CENTER

Responsibility accounting is the system for collecting and reporting revenue and cost information by areas of responsibility (responsibility centers). It operates on the premise that managers should be held responsible for their performance, the performance of their subordinates, and for all activities within their responsibility centers. It is both a planning and control technique. Responsibility accounting, also called *profitability accounting* and *activity accounting* has the following advantages:

- It facilitates delegation of decision making.
- It helps management promote the concept of management by objective, in which managers agree on a set of goals. The manager's performance is then evaluated based on his or her attainment of these goals.
- It permits effective use of the concept of *management by exception.*

Figure 1 shows responsibility centers within an organization while Figure 2 presents an organization chart of a company.

Figure 1.   Responsibility Centers within a Company

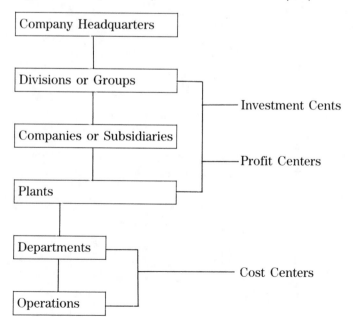

Figure 2. Organization Chart of a Company

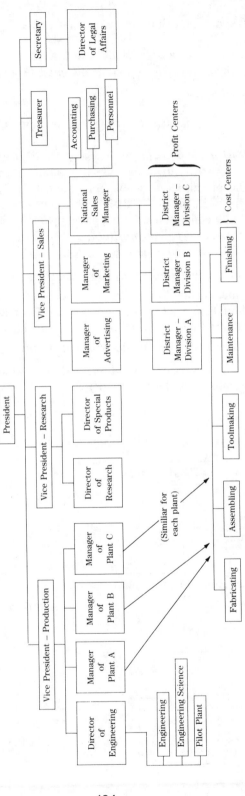

494

A well-designed responsibility accounting system establishes responsibility centers within the organization. A responsibility center is defined as a unit in the organization which has control over costs, revenues, and investment funds. A responsibility center may be responsible for all three functions or for only one function. Responsibility centers can be found in both centralized and decentralized organizations. A profit center is often associated with a decentralized organization while a cost center is usually associated with a centralized one. However, this is not always the case.

There are lines of responsibility within the company. Shell, for example, is organized primarily by business functions: exploitation, refining, and marketing. General Mills, on the other hand, is organized by product lines.

REVENUE CENTER

A revenue center is responsible for obtaining a target level of sales revenue. An example is a district sales office. The performance report for a revenue center should contain the budgeted and actual sales for the center by product including evaluation. Usually, the manager of the revenue center is responsible for marketing a product line. But a revenue center typically has a few costs (e.g., salaries, rent). Hence, a revenue center is responsible mostly for revenues and only incidentally for some costs, typically not product costs.

Sales analysis may involve one or more of the following: prior sales performance, looking at sales trends over the years, and comparing actual sales to budgeted sales.

In a service business, some performance measures include billable time, average billing rate, and cost per hour of employee time.

Accountability for departmental sales revenue assumes the manager has authority to determine product sales prices.

COST CENTER

A cost center is typically the smallest segment of activity or responsibility area for which costs are accumulated. This approach is usually employed by departments rather than divisions. A cost center has no control over sales or marketing activities. Departmental profit is difficult to derive because of problems in allocating revenue and costs.

A cost center is a department head having responsibility and accountability for costs incurred and for the quantity and quality of products or services. For example, the personnel manager is accountable for costs incurred and the quality of services rendered.

Examples of cost centers include a maintenance department and fabricating department in a manufacturing company.

It should be noted, however, that a cost center may be relatively small, such as a single department with a few people. It can also be very large, such as an administrative area of a large company or an entire factory. Some cost centers may consist of a number of smaller cost centers. An example is a factory that is segmented into numerous departments, each of which is a cost center.

A cost center is basically responsible for direct operational costs and in meeting production budgets and quotas. Authority and responsibility for cost centers must be under the control of the department head, usually a foreman.

In the cost center approach, you compare budgeted cost to actual cost. Variances are investigated to determine the reasons for them, necessary corrective action is taken to correct problems, and efficiencies are accorded recognition. This topic is covered in detail in Chapter 18. The cost center approach is useful when a manager possesses control over his costs at a specified operating level. **Recommendation:** Use this approach when problems arise in relating financial measures to output. **Suggestion:** Cost center evaluation is most suitable for the following functions: accounting and financial reporting, legal, computer services, marketing, personnel, and public relations. Here, there is a problem in quantifying the output in financial terms.

Provision should exist for chargebacks, where appropriate. For example, if a quality control department made an error in its evaluation of product quality leading to acceptance by the purchasing department, the quality control department should be charged with the increased costs to improve the purchased goods to meet acceptable standards incurred by the purchasing department.

Note: The cost center approach may be appropriate for nonprofit and governmental units where budgetary appropriations are assigned. Actual expenditures are compared to budgetary amounts. A manager's performance depends on his or her ability to achieve output levels given budgetary constraints.

When looking at a manager's performance, say at bonus time, the relevant costs are those incremental costs he or she has control over. Incremental costs are those expenditures that would not exist if the center were abandoned. Hence, allocated common costs (e.g., general administration) should not be included in appraising manager performance. Such costs should, however, be allocated in determining the profit figure for the entire division. Cost allocation must conform to goal congruence and autonomy and should be applied consistently among divisions.

Cost center evaluation will not be worthwhile unless reliable budget figures exist. If a division's situation significantly changes, an adjustment to the initial budget is necessary. In such a case, actual cost should be compared with the initial budget figure (original goal) and the revised budget. Flexible budgets should be prepared to enable you to look at costs incurred at different levels of capacity. For example, we can have figures budgeted for expected capacity, optimistic capacity, and pessimistic capacity. Better comparisons of budget to actual can thus be made given changing circumstances.

When a transfer occurs between cost centers, the transfer price should be based upon either actual cost, standard cost, or controllable cost. Transfer price is the price charged between divisions for a product or service. **Warning:** Using actual cost has the problem of passing cost inefficiencies onto the next division. There is no incentive for the transferer to control costs. **Solution:** Using standard cost corrects for the problem of transferring cost inefficiencies to the next division. However, it should be noted that standard cost includes allocated fixed cost, which might be subjective.

A good transfer price is a controllable cost. **What to Do:** Charge the cost center with actual controllable cost, and credit it with standard controllable cost for the assembled product or service to other divisions. **Rectifying the Problem:** By just including the controllable cost, the subjectivity of the allocation of fixed noncontrollable cost does not exist.

In evaluating administrative functions, prepare performance reports examining such dollar indicators as executive salaries and service department costs as well as nondollar measures such as number of files handled, phone calls taken, and invoices processed.

In appraising a cost center, look at the ratio of indirect to direct personnel. The ratio equals the number of indirect labor employees to the number of direct labor employees. **Note:** Indirect manpower is not directly involved in production or performing customer services. The ratio of indirect to direct personnel reveals the division manpower planning and control. Manpower needs are based on the individual unit's variable activities and needs. In order to accomplish divisional goals, there should be a proper relationship between indirect labor and direct labor so that services are performed to generate maximum profitability. Indirect personnel should be closely monitored because of their effect on overhead costs. **Warning:** A high ratio of indirect labor may mean the division is top-heavy in administrative and clerical staff because of improper controls on the nature of the division's activities. Perhaps the support activities should be curtailed?

EXAMPLE 1

The indirect personnel to direct personnel ratio averaged about 45% each month over a six-month period. This is favorable because management has maintained a fairly consistent relationship between direct and indirect personnel.

In order to appraise the effectiveness of employee staff in generating divisional revenue, the following ratios may be computed:

- Sales to direct manpower
- Sales to total number of employees
- Sales to total dollar salaries of employees

Higher ratios are desirable because they indicate favorable employee performance in generating sales for the company. For example, an increasing trend in revenue per employee indicates greater productivity. **Caution:** A decline in the ratios may be due to lower sales because of external factors beyond the control of the division manager.

Cost reduction measures may be implemented *without* having a negative long-term effect on the company. Such measures may improve short-term profitability. Short-term cost cutting measures may include:

- Marketing
    1. Paying salespeople on a commission basis instead of a fixed salary
    2. Using distributors rather than direct selling
- Manufacturing
    1. Hiring per diem laborers rather than subcontracting the work
    2. Buying raw materials outside rather than producing them. When the quantity of the product required is relatively low, it is typically better to buy from the outside. Once production exceeds a specified level, the company can increase profitability by doing its own manufacturing
    3. Using parts rather than subassemblies as the raw materials

PROFIT CENTER

A profit center is a responsibility unit that measures the performance of a division, product line, geographic area, or other measurable unit. A profit center has revenue and expenses associated with it. Net income and contribution margin can be computed for a profit center. Profit centers typically do not have significant amounts of invested capital. **Benefits:** The profit center approach enhances decentralization and provides units for decision-making purposes. **When to Use:** Use it when there is a self-contained division (with its own manufacturing and distribution facilities) and when there are a limited number of interdivision transfers. The reason for this is that the profit reported by the division is basically independent of other divisions' operating activities. Each division's profit should be independent of performance efficiency and managerial decisions elsewhere in the company. Further, divisional earnings should not be increased by any action reducing overall corporate profitability. Also use a profit center when divisional managers have decision-making authority in terms of the quantity and mix of goods or services manufactured. Because with a profit center you determine net income as if the division were a separate economic entity, the manager is more cognizant of outside market considerations. There are different ways of expressing profit, such as net income, contribution margin, gross profit, controllable profit, and incremental profit. Some examples of profit centers are an auto repair center in a department store and an appliance department in a retail store.

A profit center has the following characteristics: (1) defined profit objective; (2) managerial authority to make decisions impacting earnings; and (3) use of profit-oriented decision rules. A typical profit center is a division selling a limited number of products or serving a particular geographic area. It includes the means of providing goods and services and the means of marketing them.

In some instances, profit centers are formed when the company's product or service is used solely within the company. For example, the computer department of a company may bill each of the firm's administrative and operating units for computing services. It is not essential that fixed costs be allocated. Hence, contribution margin may be a good indicator of divisional performance. If each division meets its target contribution margin, excess contribution margin will be adequate to cover general corporate expenses. A contribution margin income statement can be prepared to evaluate divisional and managerial performance. It also aids in computing selling price, the price to accept an order given an idle capacity situation, output levels, maximization of resource uses, and break-even analysis. The contribution margin income statement is illustrated in Figure 3. **Note:** Controllable costs are under the division manager's control. They are the incremental costs of operating a division. In effect, they are costs that could have been avoided by the company if the division was shutdown. Noncontrollable costs are common to a group of divisions that are rationally allocated to them.

A difficulty with the profit center idea is that profit is calculated after subtracting noncontrollable costs or costs not directly related to divisional activity that have been arbitrarily allocated. The ensuing profit figure may hence be erroneous. However, cost allocation is required, since divisions must incorporate nondivisional costs that have to be met before the company will show a profit. **Special Note:** Policies optimizing divisional earnings will likewise optimize corporate earnings even before the allocation of nondivisional expenses.

Figure 3. Contribution Margin Income Statement For Divisional Performance Evaluation

Sales

Less variable production cost of sales

Manufacturing contribution margin

Less variable selling and administrative expenses

Contribution margin

Less controllable fixed costs (i.e., salesperson salaries)

Controllable contribution margin by manager (measures performance of the segment manager)

Less uncontrollable fixed costs (i.e., depreciation, property taxes, insurance)

Segment contribution margin (measures performance of the division)

Less unallocated costs to divisions (excessively difficult to allocate objectively or illogical to allocate, such as the president's salary, corporate research)

Income before taxes (measures performance of the company in its entirety)

For details, refer to Chapter 16 on cost allocation.

It is important to recognize that while an uncontrollable income statement item is included in appraising the performance of a profit center, it should *not* be used in evaluating the performance of the manager. An example is the effect of a casualty loss.

A profit center manager should be responsible for not only profit and loss items attributable directly in the division, but also costs incurred outside of the center (e.g., headquarters, other divisions) for which the center will be billed directly. The manager should also be responsible for an expense equal to the company's interest rate times controllable working capital. This charge will take into account tradeoffs between working capital levels and profits. For example, increased inventory balances will mean less losses from stock-outs. The profit center manager is the only person that comprehends these tradeoffs. (For a greater discussion of this topic, see John Dearden, "Measuring Profit Center Managers," *Harvard Business Review*, September–October 1987, pp. 84–88.)

Advantages of the profit center approach are that it creates competition in a decentralized company, provides goal congruence between a division and the company, and aids performance evaluation. A drawback is that profits can be "messaged" since expenses may be shifted among periods. Examples of discretionary costs where management has wide latitude are research and repairs. Also, not considered is the total assets employed in the division to obtain the profit.

EXAMPLE 2

You can sell a product at its intermediate point in Division A for $170 or its final point in Division B at $260. The outlay cost in Division A is $120, while the outlay cost in Division B is $110. Unlimited product demand exists for both the intermediate product and the final product. Capacity is interchangeable. Division performance follows:

	Division A	Division B
Selling Price	$170	$260
Outlay Cost - A	(120)	(120)
Outlay Cost - B		(110)
Profit	$ 50	$ 30

Sell at the intermediate point because of the higher profit.

Other measures in appraising divisional performance that are not of a profit nature that must be considered are:

- Ratios between cost elements and assets to appraise effectiveness and efficiency
- Productivity measures, including input-output relationships. An example

is labor hours in a production run. We have to consider the input in terms of time and money, and the resulting output in terms of quantity and quality. Does the maintenance of equipment ensure future growth? Another example is the utilization rate of facilities.

- Personnel development (e.g., number of promotions, turnover)
- Market measures (e.g., market share, product leadership, growth rate, customer service)
- Product leadership indicators (e.g., patented products, innovative technology, product quality, safety record)
- Human resource relationships (e.g., employee turnover rate, customer relations, including on-time deliveries)
- Social responsibility measures (e.g., consumer medals)

Transfer Pricing

A transfer price has to be formulated so that a realistic and meaningful profit figure can be determined for each division. It should be established only after proper planning. The transfer price is the one credited to the selling division and charged to the buying division for an internal transfer of an assembled product or service. It is the same for each as if an "arms length" transaction had taken place.

The choice of transfer prices not only affects divisional performance, but is also important in decisions involving make or buy, whether to sell or process further, and choosing between alternative production possibilities.

In establishing a transfer price, the following should be noted:

- It should promote the goals of the company, and harmonize divisional goals with organizational goals.
- It should be equitable to all parties involved.
- It should preserve autonomy, so the selling and buying division mangers operate their divisions as decentralized entities.
- There should be minimization of duplication and paperwork.
- It should provide flexibility.
- It should be quick in responding to changing business conditions in various countries.
- It should act as an incentive to keep costs under control.
- It should be developed in such a way as to minimize the conflict between buying and selling divisions.
- It should put profits where you want them. For example, put higher profits in low tax areas and lower profits in high tax areas. It should minimize tariffs in international dealings. Also, put profits where they can best be used such as constructing a new building.

- It should satisfy legal requirements.
- There should be cooperation across divisional and country lines.
- There should exist internal and external reliability.

Recommendation: The best transfer price is the negotiated market value of the assembled product or service, since it is a fair price and treats each profit center as a separate economic entity. It equals the outside service fee or selling price for the item (a quoted price for a product or service is only comparable if the credit terms, grade, quality, delivery, and auxiliary conditions are precisely the same) less internal cost savings that result from dealing internally within the organization (e.g., advertising sales commission, delivery charges, bookkeeping costs for customers' ledgers, credit and collection costs, and bad debts). Even though the selling center does not have a quantity discount policy, a discount may be considered into the transfer price. In many cases, if the buying center were an outside customer, the selling center would provide a volume discount, so a similar discount should be offered as an element of the transfer price. The market value of services performed is based on the going rate for a specific job (e.g., equipment tuneup) and/or the standard hourly rate (e.g., the hourly rate for a plumber). Market price may be determined from price catalogues, obtaining outside bids, and examining published data on completed market transactions. **Warning:** An outside supplier may intentionally quote a low price to obtain the business with the thought of increasing the price at a later date. If two divisions cannot agree on the transfer price, it will be settled by arbitration at a higher level. A temporarily low transfer price (due to oversupply of the item, for example) or high transfer price (due to a strike situation causing a supply shortage, for example), should not be employed. **Solution:** Use the average long-term market price.

A negotiated transfer price works best when outside markets for the intermediate product exist, all parties have access to market information, and one is permitted to deal externally if a negotiated settlement is impossible. If one of these conditions is violated, the negotiated price may break down and cause inefficiencies.

If the outside market price is not ascertainable (e.g., new product, absence of replacement market, or inappropriate, or too costly to be used for transfer pricing), you should use budgeted cost plus profit markup, because this transfer price approximates market value and will spot divisional inefficiencies. Budgeted cost includes the factory cost and any administrative costs applicable to production, such as cost accounting, production planning, industrial engineering, and research and development. Direct material, direct labor, and variable factory overhead are based on standard rates for the budget period. Fixed factory overhead and administrative expenses are unitized at either forecast or normal volume. It is preferred to use normal volume because it levels out the intracompany prices over the years. Profit markup should take into account the particular characteristics of the division rather than the overall corporate profit margin. Profit is often calculated based on a percentage return on capital which is budgeted to be used at the budgeted or normal volume used for unitizing fixed costs. This percentage is established by company policy. It may be the average expected return for the manufacturing unit, purchasing unit, or company. When budgeted cost plus profit is used as the transfer price, a provision typically exists to adjust for changes in raw material prices and wage rates.

There is an incentive to the selling division to control its costs because it will not be credited for an amount in excess of budgeted cost plus a markup. Thus, if the selling division's inefficiencies resulted in actual costs being excessive, it would have to absorb the decline in profit to the extent that actual cost exceeded budgeted cost. Profit markup should be as realistic as possible given the nature of the division and its product.

Note: Even though actual cost plus profit markup is used by some, it has the drawback of passing on cost inefficiencies. In fact, the selling division is encouraged to be cost-inefficient, since the higher its actual cost, the higher its selling price will be (since it shows a greater profit). Some companies employ actual cost as the transfer price because of ease of use, but the problem is that no profit is shown by the selling division, and cost inefficiencies are passed on. Further, the cost-based method treats the divisions as cost centers rather than profit or investment centers. Therefore, measures such as return on investment and residual income cannot be used for evaluation purposes.

The variable-cost-based transfer price has an advantage over the full cost method because, in the short run, it may tend to ensure the best utilization of the overall company's resources. The reason is that, in the short run, fixed costs do not change. Any use of facilities, without incurrence of additional fixed costs, will increase the company's overall profits. In the case where division managers are responsible for costs in their divisions, the cost price approach to transfer pricing is often used.

A transfer price based on cost may be appropriate when there are minimal services provided by one department to another.

A company may have more than one department providing a product or service that is identical or very similar. It may be cost beneficial to centralize that product or service into one department. If more than one department provides an identical or very similar service, a cost basis transfer price may be used since the receiving department will select the services of the department providing the highest quality. Thus, the providing department has an incentive to do a good job.

A company may use a below-cost transfer price to favor a division newly spun off by the parent. This may provide the new firm with a better competitive position, allowing it to get started in an industry other than that of the parent, and compete effectively with established industry leaders.

Incremental cost is another transfer pricing possibility. Incremental costs are the variable costs of making and shipping goods and any costs directly and exclusively traceable to the product. This cost is quite good for use with the company as a whole, but does little for measuring divisional performance. The incremental cost approach assumes the selling division has sufficient capacity to satisfy internal company demands as well as demands of outside customers.

Another way of setting the transfer price is dual pricing. It occurs when the buying division is charged with variable cost ($1) and the selling division is credited with absorption cost and markup ($1.50 plus 60%). Under dual pricing, there is a motivational effect, since each division's performance is enhanced by the transfer. However, profit for the company as a whole will be less than the sum of the divisions' profits.

A last possibility is allocating profit among divisions, say based on input by departments (e.g., time spent, costs incurred).

EXAMPLE 3

Division A manufactures an assembled product that can be sold to outsiders or transferred to Division B. Relevant information for the period follows.

Division A	Units
Production	1,500
Transferred to Division B	1,200
Sold Outside	300
Selling Price $25	
Unit Cost $5	

The units transferred to Division B were processed further at a cost of $7. They were sold outside at $45. Transfers are at market value.

Division profit is

	Division A	Division B	Company
Sales	$ 7,500	$54,000	$61,500
Transfer Price	30,000		
	$37,500	$54,000	$61,500
Product Cost	$ 7,500	$ 8,400	$15,900
Transfer Price		30,000	
	$ 7,500	$38,400	$15,900
Profit	$30,000	$15,600	$45,600

EXAMPLE 4

Zeno Corporation manufactures radios. It has two production divisions (assembly and finishing) and one service division (maintenance). The assembly division both sells assembled radios to other companies and transfers them for further processing to the finishing division. The transfer price used is market value. Relevant data follow.

Assembly Division

Outside sales: 1,000 assembled radios at $30 (included in the price is selling commission fees of $1 per unit and freight costs of $2 per unit). Transferred to finishing division: 10,000 assembled radios.

Direct costs	$80,000
Indirect costs	$45,000

Finishing Division

Outside sales: 10,000 finished radios at $55

Direct costs	$90,000
Indirect costs	$30,000

Maintenance Division

Direct costs (direct labor, parts)	$80,000
Indirect costs	$25,000

9,000 hours rendered for servicing to Assembly Division
12,000 hours rendered for servicing to Finishing Division
Standard hourly rate: $8

A schedule of the gross profit of the separate divisions and the gross profit of Zeno Corporation is shown in Table 1.

Table 1

GROSS PROFIT, ZENO CORPORATION

	Assembly	Finishing	Maintenance	Transfers	Zeno
Revenue					
Sales	$ 30,000	$550,000			$580,000
Transfers	270,000			$270,000	
			$ 72,000	72,000	
			96,000	96,000	
Total	$300,000	$550,000	$168,000	$438,000	$580,000
Costs					
Direct	$ 80,000	$ 90,000	$ 80,000		$250,000
Indirect	45,000	30,000	25,000		100,000
Transfers:					
—Maintenance	72,000	96,000		$168,000	
—Assembly		270,000		270,000	
Total Costs	$197,000	$486,000	$105,000	$438,000	$350,000
Gross Profit	$103,000	$ 64,000	$ 63,000	—	$230,000

Assembly revenue
Sales $30 × 1000
Transfer price $27 × 10,000

EXAMPLE 5

An assembly division wants to charge a finishing division $80 per unit for an internal transfer of 800 units. The variable cost per unit is $50. Total fixed cost in the assembly division is $200,000. Current production is 10,000 units. Idle capacity exists. The finishing division can purchase the item outside for $73 per unit.

The maximum transfer price should be $73, which is the cost to buy it from outside. The finishing division should not have to pay a price greater than the outside market price.

Whether the buying division should be permitted to buy the item outside or be forced to buy inside depends on what is best for overall corporate profitability. Typically, the buying division is required to purchase inside at the maximum transfer price ($73), since the selling division still has to meet its fixed cost when idle capacity exists. The impact on corporate profitability of having the buying division go outside is determined as follows:

Savings to assembly division (Units $\times$ Variable cost per unit):
$$800 \times \$50 \qquad \$40,000$$
Cost to finishing division (units $\times$ outside selling price):
$$800 \times \$73 \qquad \underline{58,400}$$
Stay Inside $\underline{\$18,400}$

The buying division will be asked to purchase inside the company, because if it went outside, corporate profitability would decline by $18,400.

INVESTMENT CENTER

An investment center is a responsibility center within an organization that has control over revenue, cost, and investment funds. It is a profit center whose performance is evaluated on the basis of the return earned on invested capital. Corporate headquarters and product line divisions in a large decentralized organization would be examples of investment centers. Investment centers are widely used in highly diversified companies.

A divisional investment is the amount placed in that division and placed under division management control. Two major divisional performance indicators are return on investment (ROI) and residual income. We should use available total assets in these measures to take into account all assets in the division, whether used or not. By including nonproductive assets in the base, the manager is motivated either to retain or sell them. Assets assigned to a division include direct assets in the division and allocated corporate assets. Assets are reflected at book value. **Suggestion:** Include facilities being constructed in the investment base if the division is committing the funds for the new asset.

You should distinguish between controllable and noncontrollable investment. While the former is helpful in appraising a manager's performance, the latter is used to evaluate the entire division. Controllable investment depends on the degree of a division's autonomy. Thus, an investment center manager accepts responsibility for both the center's assets and its controllable income.

In obtaining divisional investment, there has to be an allocation of general corporate assets to that division. These allocated assets are not considered part of controllable investment. Assets should be allocated to divisions on the basis of measures (e.g., area occupied). **What To Do:** The allocated investment should be part of the division's investment base, but not as an element of controllable investment. Do not allocate general corporate assets attributable to the company as a whole (e.g., security investments). **Advice:** Do not allocate an asset if it requires excessive subjectivity.

The optimal way to assign cash to a division is to agree upon a cash level that meets the minimum needs of the division. If cash is held in excess of this level, there should be an interest income credit using current interest rates. Because the division typically earns a higher return rate on investment than the prevailing interest rate, it will voluntarily return excess cash to the company. This policy maximizes the overall corporate return. Accounts receivable should be assigned to divisions based on sales. Finished goods should be included in the asset base. The division manager has control over it because he determines the production level on the basis of expected sales. Excessive finished goods inventory is partly due to a division's inadequate planning. **Recommendation:** Use the opportunity cost of funds tied up in inventory that could be invested elsewhere for a return in determining divisional profit. Plant and equipment should be allocated on the basis of square footage.

The valuation of assets can be based on book value, gross cost, consumer price index (CPI) adjusted cost, replacement cost, or sales value. Typically, historical cost measures are employed in practice because of availability and consistency with balance sheet valuation. **Warning:** Using book value for asset valuation will artificially increase divisional return on investment as assets become older, since the denominator using book value becomes lower over time. Gross cost corrects for this decline in value, but it still does not consider inflationary cost increases. However, an advantage of using gross book value to value assets is that it is not affected by changes in expansion rates. **Note:** CPI adjusted value takes into account changing price levels. **Recommendation:** Replacement cost is ideal because it truly reflects the current prices of assets. Alternative ways exist to determine replacement cost (e.g., present value of future cash flows, specific price index of item, and current market value). **Tip:** Inventory accounted for using LIFO should be adjusted to the FIFO basis or the replacement value, so that inventory is stated at current prices.

Current liabilities should be subtracted in determining the asset base because division financing policy depends on the decision of upper management.

Return on Investment

Net income determination for return on investment (ROI) purposes requires that divisional earnings measurements comply with the following guidelines:

- Divisional earnings should not be tied to operational efficiency and quality of managerial decisions of other segments.
- Divisional earnings should include all items the divisional manager has control over.
- Divisional earnings should not be increased because of any action that negatively affects current or future profits.

ROI is a superior indicator when the investment employed is outside of the manager's determination. **Caution:** If a manager can significantly determine the capital employed, the return rate is a weakened tool.

$$\text{ROI} = \frac{\text{Net income}}{\text{Available total assets}}$$

Alternative measures are

$$\frac{\text{Operating profit}}{\text{Available total assets}}$$

$$\frac{\text{Controllable operating profit}}{\text{Controllable net investment}}$$
(Controllable assets − Controllable liabilities)

Note: With respect to the last measure, depreciation is a controllable cost since changes in the asset base are controllable by the division manager. **Interesting Point:** Excluded from controllable investment is equipment the manager wants to sell but is unable to because the company is trying to get an alternative use by another division or central headquarters. **Recommendation:** Transfer this asset from the division's controllable investment base. Also, controllable fixed assets allocated to divisions (e.g., research facilities, general administrative offices) should be excluded from controllable investment.

Assets have to be allocated on some rational basis to divisions. Actual cash at each location is known. Home-office cash is typically allocated to plants based on sales or cost of sales. Usually, accounts receivable is segregated by division or plant, but if not they may be allocated based on sales. Inventories and fixed assets are generally identified (e.g., account coding) to a specific plant or division. Other fixed assets (e.g., home-office building, equipment trucking, research facilities) may be allocated to plants and divisions based on services rendered. Building may be allocated based on physical space. Prepaid expenses, deferred charges, and other assets may be allocated based on sales or cost of sales.

Idle facilities should be included in the investment base when the inactivity of the assets is caused by a division not attaining the budgeted share of the actual market or results from insufficient maintenance.

ROI for each division enables management to appraise divisions from the view of efficient utilization of resources allocated to each division. Divisional management effectiveness is assessed and related to salary and/or bonuses. To work effectively, managers should have control over operations and resources.

Advantages of ROI

- Focuses on maximizing a ratio instead of improving absolute profits
- Highlights unprofitable divisions. Perhaps some should be disposed of?
- Can be used as a base against which to evaluate divisions within the company and to compare the division to a comparable division in a competing company
- Assigns profit responsibility
- Aids in appraising divisional manager performance
- When a division maximizes its ROI, the company similarly maximizes its ROI
- Places emphasis on high-return items
- Represents a cumulative audit or appraisal of all capital expenditures incurred during a division's existence
- Serves as a guideline to the division manager in analyzing discounted cash flow internal rates of return for proposed capital expenditures
- Broadest possible measure of financial performance. Because divisions are often geographically disbursed internationally, division managers are given broad authority in using division assets and acquiring and selling assets.
- Help make the goals of the division manager coincide with those of corporate management.

Disadvantages of ROI

- Focuses on maximizing a ratio instead of improving absolute profits
- Alternative profitability measures could be used in the numerator besides net income (e.g., gross profit, contribution margin, segment margin).
- Different assets in the division must earn the same return rate regardless of the assets' riskiness
- Established rate of return may be too high and could discourage incentive.

- To boost profits, needed expenditures may not be incurred (e.g., repairs, research). Here, look at the ratio over time of discretionary costs to sales.
- A division may not want to acquire fixed assets because it will lower its ROI.
- A labor-intensive division generally has a higher ROI than a capital-intensive one.
- ROI is a static indicator; it does not show future flows
- A lack of goal congruence may exist between the company and a division. For instance, if a company's ROI is 12%, a division's ROI is 18%, and a project's ROI is 16%, the division manager will not accept the project because it will lower his ROI, even though the project is best for the entire company.
- It ignores risk.
- ROI emphasizes short-run performance instead of long-term profitability. To protect the current ROI, a manager is motivated to reject other profitable investment opportunities.
- ROI may not be completely controllable by the division manager because of the existence of committed costs. The inability to control ROI may be a problem in distinguishing between the manager's performance and the performance of the division as an investment.
- If the projected ROI at the beginning of the year is set unrealistically high, it could result in discouragement of investment center incentive.

A manager should not be criticized for a disappointing ROI if he does not have significant influence over the factors making up the ROI.

EXAMPLE 6

You are concerned about your company's current return on investment. Your company's income statement for year 19X1 follows.

Sales (100,000 units @$10)	$1,000,000
Cost of Sales	300,000
Gross Margin	$ 700,000
Selling and General Expenses	200,000
Income Before Taxes	$ 500,000
Taxes (40%)	200,000
Net Income	$ 300,000

On December 31, total assets available consist of current assets of $300,000 and fixed assets of $500,000.

You forecast that sales for 19X2 will be 120,000 units at $11 per unit. The cost per unit is estimated at $5. Fixed selling and general expenses are forecasted at $60,000, and variable selling and general expenses are anticipated to be $1.50 per unit. Depreciation for the year is expected to be $30,000.

Forecasted earnings for 19X2 are calculated as follows:

Sales (120,000 @$11)		$1,320,000
Cost of Sales 120,000 @$5		600,000
Gross Margin		$ 720,000
Selling and General Expenses:		
Fixed	$ 60,000	
Variable (120,000 @ $1.50)	180,000	
Total		240,000
Income Before Tax		480,000
Tax (40%)		192,000
Net Income		$ 288,000

The investment expected at December 31, 19X2 is:
Ratio of current assets to sales in 19X1:

$300,000/$1,000,000	30%

Expected current assets at December 31, 19X2:

30% × $1,320,000	$396,000

Expected fixed assets at December 31, 19X2:

Book value on January 1	$500,000	
Less: Depreciation for 19X2	30,000	470,000
Total Investment		$866,000

$$\text{ROI} = \frac{\$288,000}{\$866,000} = 33.3\%$$

Residual Income

The optimal measure of divisional performance is residual income, which equals divisional net income less minimum return times average available total assets.

EXAMPLE 7

Divisional earnings are $250,000, average available total assets are $2,000,000, and the cost of capital is 9%.

Residual income equals	
Divisional net income	$250,000
Less minimum return × Average available total assets	
9% × $2,000,000	$180,000
Residual income	$70,000

The minimum rate of return is based upon the company's overall cost of capital adjusted for divisional risk. The cost of capital should be periodically calculated and used because of shifts in the money rate over time.

Residual income may be projected by division, center, or specific program to assure that the company's rate of return on alternative investments is met or improved upon by each segment of the business.

By looking at residual income, we are assured that segments are not employing corporate credit for less return than could be obtained by owning marketable securities or through investment in a different business segment.

A target residual income may be formulated to act as the division manager's objective. The trend in residual income to total available assets should be examined in appraising divisional performance. (See Figure 4).

A division manager's performance should be appraised on the basis of controllable residual income. A manager should not be penalized for uncontrollable matters. To evaluate a division, we use net residual income after taxes. This is a key figure, because it aids in the decision to make new investments or withdrawals of funds in that division.

Advantages of Residual Income

- The same asset may be required to earn the same return rate throughout the company irrespective of the division the asset is in
- Different return rates may be employed for different types of assets, depending on riskiness
- Different return rates may be assigned to different divisions, depending on the risk associated with those divisions
- Provides an economic income, taking into account the opportunity cost of tying up assets in the division
- Identifies operating problem areas
- Precludes the difficulty that a division with a high ROI would not engage in a project with a lower ROI even though it exceeds the overall corporate ROI rate. This is because residual income maximizes dollars instead of a percentage. It motivates divisional managers to take into account all profitable investments. Unprofitable investments are not included.

Disadvantages of Residual Income

- Assignment of a minimum return involves estimating a risk level that is subjective.
- It may be difficult to determine the valuation basis and means of allocating assets to divisions.
- If book value is used in valuing assets, residual income will artificially increase over time, since the minimum return times total assets becomes lower as the assets become older.

Figure 4. Residual Income Statement for Divisional Evaluation Purposes

Sales	$1,200,000	
Transfers at market value to other divisions	400,000	
Total		$1,600,000
Less		
Variable cost of goods sold and transferred	$ 800,000	
Variable divisional expenses	200,000	
Total		1,000,000
Variable income		$ 600,000
Less		
Controllable divisional overhead	$ 200,000	
Depreciation on controllable plant and equipment	110,000	
Property taxes and insurance on controllable fixed assets	40,000	
Total		$ 350,000
Controllable operating income		$ 250,000
Add		
Nonoperating gains	$ 300,000	
Nonoperating losses	20,000	
Net nonoperating gains		280,000
Total		$ 530,000
Less interest on controllable investment		30,000
Controllable residual income		$ 500,000
Less		
Uncontrollable divisional overhead (e.g., central advertising)	$ 40,000	
Incremental central expenses chargeable to the division	10,000	
Interest on noncontrollable investment	50,000	
Total		100,000
Residual income before taxes		$ 400,000
Less income taxes (40%)		160,000
Net residual income after taxes		$ 240,000

- It cannot be used to compare divisions of different sizes. Residual income tends to favor the larger divisions due to the large amount of dollars involved.

- It does not furnish a direct decision criterion for capital expenditures which have to be based on incremental cash flows, rather than incremental profits.

- Since it is a mixture of controllable and uncontrollable elements, there is no segregation.

Computerized reports should be prepared at critical points for timely managerial action. Such instance may occur when a product's contribution margin percent is below target, or when a product is behind the scheduled days to produce it.

Reports showing excessive age of inventory should be prepared so needed action may be taken such as price reduction, package deals, or other promotions.

Accountants and financial managers aid management in making key decisions involving marketing and general business decisions. Examples are changes in sales mix, pricing, production, product expansion or contraction, territory evaluation, and customer analysis.

CONCLUSION

It is essential to evaluate a segment's performance to identify problem areas. Factors that are controllable or not controllable by the division manager must be considered. The various means of evaluating performance include cost center, profit center, revenue center, and investment center. The calculations for each method along with proper analysis are vital in appraising operating efficiency. You should understand the advantages and disadvantages of each method as well as when each is most appropriate.

The financial manager should be familiar with the profit and loss statements by territory, commodity, method of sale, customer, and salesperson. The profit and loss figures will indicate areas of strength and weakness.

The establishment of a realistic transfer price is essential in order to properly evaluate divisional performance and to arrive at appropriate product costing and profitability.

21

How to Analyze and Improve Management Performance

The ability to measure performance is essential in developing incentives and controlling operations toward the achievement of organizational goals. Perhaps the most widely used single measure of success of an organization and its subunits is the rate of return on investment (ROI). Related is the return to stockholders, known as the return on equity (ROE). This chapter discusses the following:

- What is ROI?
- What is it made up of?
- How can ROI be increased?
- What is the relationship between ROI and ROE?

WHAT IS RETURN ON INVESTMENT (ROI)?

ROI relates net income to invested capital (total assets). It provides a standard for evaluating how efficiently management employs the average dollar invested in a firm's assets, whether that dollar came from owners or creditors. Furthermore, a better ROI can also translate directly into a higher return on the stockholders' equity.

ROI is calculated as:

$$\text{ROI} = \frac{\text{Net profit after taxes}}{\text{Total assets}}$$

EXAMPLE 1

Consider the following financial data:

Total assets $100,000
Net profit after taxes   18,000

$$\text{Then, ROI} = \frac{\text{Net profit after taxes}}{\text{Total assets}} = \frac{\$18,000}{\$100,000} = 18\%$$

The problem with this formula is that it only tells you about how a company did and how well it fared in the industry. Other than that, it has very little value from the standpoint of profit planning.

WHAT IS ROI MADE UP OF—DU PONT FORMULA

In the past, managers have tended to focus only on the margin earned and have ignored the turnover of assets. It is important to realize that excessive funds tied up in assets can be just as much of a drag on profitability as excessive expenses. The Du Pont Corporation was the first major company to recognize the importance of looking at both net profit margin and total asset turnover in assessing the performance of an organization. The ROI breakdown, known as the Du Pont formula, is expressed as a product of these two factors, as shown below.

$$\text{ROI} = \frac{\text{Net profit after taxes}}{\text{Total assets}} = \frac{\text{Net profit after taxes}}{\text{Sales}} \times \frac{\text{Sales}}{\text{Total assets}}$$

$$= \text{Net profit margin} \times \frac{\text{Total asset}}{\text{turnover}}$$

The Du Pont formula combines the income statement and balance sheet into this otherwise static measure of performance. Net profit margin is a measure of profitability or operating efficiency. It is the percentage of profit earned on sales. This percentage shows how many cents attach to each dollar of sales. On the other hand, total asset turnover measures how well a company manages its assets. It is the number of times by which the investment in assets turn over each year to generate sales.

The breakdown of ROI is based on the thesis that the profitability of a firm is directly related to management's ability to manage assets efficiently and to control expenses effectively.

EXAMPLE 2

Assume the same data as in Example 1. Also assume sales of $200,000.

$$\text{Then, ROI} = \frac{\text{Net profit after taxes}}{\text{Total assets}} = \frac{\$18,000}{\$100,000} = 18\%$$

Alternatively,

$$\text{Net profit margin} = \frac{\text{Net profit after taxes}}{\text{Sales}} = \frac{\$18,000}{\$200,000} = 9\%$$

$$\text{Total asset turnover} = \frac{\text{Sales}}{\text{Total assets}} = \frac{\$200,000}{\$100,000} = 2 \text{ times}$$

Therefore,

$$\text{ROI} = \text{Net profit margin} \times \text{Total asset turnover} = 9\% \times 2 \text{ times}$$

The breakdown provides a lot of insights to financial managers on how to improve profitability of the company and investment strategy. (Note that net profit margin and total asset turnover are called hereafter margin and turnover, respectively, for short). Specifically, it has several advantages over the original formula (i.e., net profit after taxes/total assets) for profit planning. They are:

(1) Focusing on the breakdown of ROI provides the basis for integrating many of the management concerns that influence a firm's overall performance. This will help managers gain an advantage in the competitive environment.

(2) The importance of turnover as a key to overall return on investment is emphasized in the breakdown. In fact, turnover is just as important as profit margin in enhancing overall return.

(3) The importance of sales is explicitly recognized, which is not there in the original formula.

(4) The breakdown stresses the possibility of trading one off for the other in an attempt to improve the overall performance of a company. The margin and turnover complement each other. In other words, a low turnover can be made up for by a high margin; and vice versa.

EXAMPLE 3

The breakdown of ROI into its two components shows that a number of combinations of margin and turnover can yield the same rate of return, as shown below:

	Margin	×	Turnover	=	ROI
(1)	9%	×	2 times	=	18%
(2)	6	×	3	=	18
(3)	3	×	6	=	18
(4)	2	×	9	=	18

The turnover-margin relationship and its resulting ROI is depicted in Figure 1.

ROI AND PROFIT OBJECTIVE

Figure 1 can also be looked at as showing six companies that performed equally well (in terms of ROI), but with varying income statements and balance sheets. There is no ROI that is satisfactory for all companies. Manufacturing firms in various industries will have low rates of return. Structure and size of the firm influence the rate considerably. A company with a diversified product line might have only a fair return rate when all products are pooled in the analysis. In such cases, it seems advisable to establish separate objectives for each line as well as for the total company.

Sound and successful operation must point toward the optimum combination of profits, sales, and capital employed. The combination will necessarily vary depending upon the nature of the business and the characteristics of the product. An industry with products tailor-made to customers' specifications will have different margins and turnover ratios, compared with industries that mass produce highly competitive consumer goods. For example, the combination (4) may describe a supermarket operation which inherently works with low margin

Figure 1. The Margin-Turnover Relationship

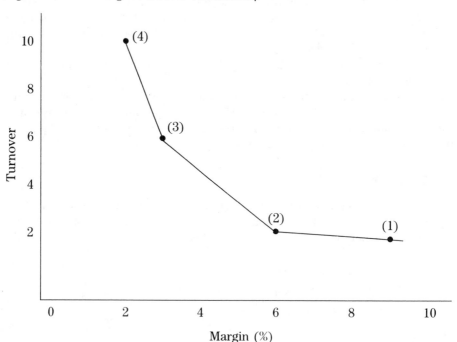

and high turnover, while the combination (1) may be a jewelry store which typically has a low turnover and high margin.

ROI AND PROFIT PLANNING

The breakdown of ROI into margin and turnover gives management insight into planning for profit improvement by revealing where weaknesses exist: margin or turnover, or both. Various actions can be taken to enhance ROI. Generally, management can:

1. Improve margin

2. Improve turnover

3. Improve both

Alternative 1 demonstrates a popular way of improving performance. Margins may be increased by reducing expenses, raising selling prices, or increasing sales faster than expenses. Some of the ways to reduce expenses are:

(a) Use less costly inputs of materials

(b) Automate processes as much as possible to increase labor productivity

(c) Bring the discretionary fixed costs under scrutiny, with various programs either curtailed or eliminated. Discretionary fixed costs arise from annual budgeting decisions by management. Examples include advertising, research and development, and management development programs. The cost-benefit analysis is called for in order to justify the budgeted amount of each discretionary program.

A company with pricing power can raise selling prices and retain profitability without losing business. Pricing power is the ability to raise prices even in poor economic times when unit sales volume may be flat and capacity may not be fully utilized. It is also the ability to pass on cost increases to consumers without attracting domestic and import competition, political opposition, regulation, new entrants, or threats of product substitution. The company with pricing power must have a unique economic position. Companies that offer unique, high-quality goods and services (where the service is more important than the cost) have this economic position.

Alternative 2 may be achieved by increasing sales while holding the investment in assets relatively constant, or by reducing assets. Some of the strategies to reduce assets are:

(a) Dispose of obsolete and redundant inventory. The computer has been extremely helpful in this regard, making perpetual inventory methods more feasible for inventory control.

(b) Devise various methods of speeding up the collection of receivables and also evaluate credit terms and policies

(c) See if there are unused fixed assets

(d) Use the converted assets obtained from the use of the previous methods to repay outstanding debts or repurchase outstanding issues of stock. You may release them elsewhere to get more profit, which will improve margin as well as turnover.

Alternative 3 may be achieved by increasing sales or by any combinations of alternatives 1 and 2.

Figure 2 shows complete details of the relationship of ROI to the underlying ratios—margin and turnover—and their components. This will help identify more detailed strategies to improve margin, turnover, or both.

EXAMPLE 4

Assume that management sets a 20% ROI as a profit target. It is currently making an 18% return on its investment.

Figure 2. Relationships of Factors Influencing ROI

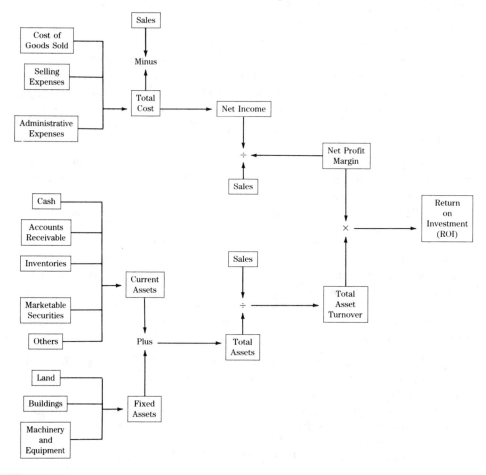

$$\text{ROI} = \frac{\text{Net profit after taxes}}{\text{Total assets}} = \frac{\text{Net profit after taxes}}{\text{Sales}} \times \frac{\text{Sales}}{\text{Total assets}}$$

Present situation:

$$18\% = \frac{18,000}{200,000} \times \frac{200,000}{100,000}$$

The following are illustrative of the strategies which might be used (each strategy is independent of the other).

Alternative 1: Increase the margin while holding turnover constant. Pursuing this strategy would involve leaving selling prices as they are and making every effort to increase efficiency so as to reduce expenses. By doing so, expenses might be reduced by $2,000 without affecting sales and investment to yield a 20% target ROI, as follows:

$$20\% = \frac{20,000}{200,000} \times \frac{200,000}{100,000}$$

Alternative 2: Increase turnover by reducing investment in assets while holding net profit and sales constant. Working capital might be reduced or some land might be sold, reducing investment in assets by $10,000 without affecting sales and net income to yield the 20% target ROI as follows:

$$20\% = \frac{18,000}{200,000} \times \frac{200,000}{90,000}$$

Alternative 3: Increase both margin and turnover by disposing of obsolete and redundant inventories or through an active advertising campaign. For example, trimming down $5,000 worth of investment in inventories would also reduce the inventory holding charge by $1,000. This strategy would increase ROI to 20%.

$$20\% = \frac{19,000}{200,000} \times \frac{200,000}{95,000}$$

Excessive investment in assets is just as much of a drag on profitability as excessive expenses. In this case, cutting unnecessary inventories also helps cut down expenses of carrying those inventories, so that both margin and turnover are improved at the same time. In practice, alternative 3 is much more common than alternative 1 or 2.

ROI AND RETURN ON EQUITY (ROE)

Generally, a better management performance (i.e., a high or above-average ROI) produces a higher return to equity holders. However, even a poorly managed company that suffers from a below-average performance can generate an above-average return on the stockholders' equity, simply called the return on equity (ROE). This is because borrowed funds can magnify the returns a company's profits represent to its stockholders.

Another version of the Du Pont formula, called the modified Du Pont formula reflects this effect. The formula ties together the ROI and the degree of financial leverage (use of borrowed funds). The financial leverage is measured by the equity multiplier, which is the ratio of a company's total asset base to its equity investment, or, stated another way, the ratio of how many dollars of assets held per dollar of stockholders' equity. It is calculated by dividing total assets by stockholders' equity. This measurement gives an indication of how much of a company's assets are financed by stockholders' equity and how much with borrowed funds.

The return on equity (ROE) is calculated as:

$$\text{ROE} = \frac{\text{Net profit after taxes}}{\text{Stockholders' equity}} = \frac{\text{Net profit after taxes}}{\text{Total assets}} \times \frac{\text{Total assets}}{\text{Stockholders' equity}}$$

$$= \quad \text{ROI} \quad \times \quad \text{Equity multiplier}$$

ROE measures the returns earned on the owners' (both preferred and common stockholders') investment. The use of the equity multiplier to convert the ROI to the ROE reflects the impact of the leverage (use of debt) on stockholders' return.

$$\text{The equity multiplier} = \frac{\text{Total assets}}{\text{Stockholders' equity}}$$

$$= \frac{1}{(1 - \text{debt ratio})}$$

Figure 3 shows the relationship among ROI, ROE, and financial leverage.

EXAMPLE 5

In Example 1, assume stockholders' equity of $45,000.

$$\text{Then, equity multiplier} = \frac{\text{Total assets}}{\text{Stockholders' equity}} = \frac{\$100,000}{\$45,000} = 2.22$$

$$= \frac{1}{(1 - \text{debt ratio})} = \frac{1}{(1 - .55)} = \frac{1}{.45} = 2.22$$

Figure 3. ROI, ROE and Financial Leverage

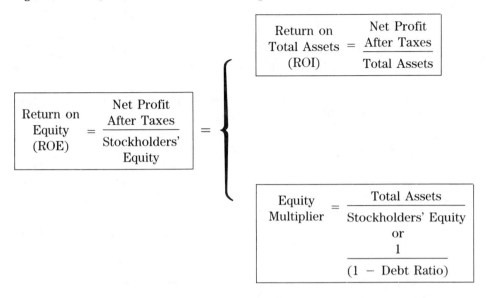

$$ROE = \frac{\text{Net profit after taxes}}{\text{Stockholders' equity}} = \frac{\$18,000}{\$45,000} = 40\%$$

$$ROE = ROI \times \text{equity multiplier} = 18\% \times 2.22 = 40\%$$

If the company used only equity, the 18% ROI would equal ROE. However, 55% of the firm's capital is supplied by creditors ($45,000/$100,000 = 45% is the equity-to-asset ratio; $55,000/$100,000 = 55% is the debt ratio). Since the 18% ROI all goes to stockholders, who put up only 45% of the capital, the ROE is higher than 18%. This example indicates the company was using leverage (debt) favorably.

EXAMPLE 6

To further demonstrate the interrelationship between a firm's financial structure and the return it generates on the stockholders' investments, let us compare two firms that generate $300,000 in operating income. Both firms employ $800,000 in total assets, but they have different capital structures. One firm employs no debt, whereas the other uses $400,000 in borrowed funds. The comparative capital structures are shown as:

	A	B
Total assets	$800,000	$800,000
Total liabilities	–	400,000
Stockholders' equity (a)	800,000	400,000
Total liabilities and stockholders' equity	$800,000	$800,000

Firm B pays 10% interest for borrowed funds. The comparative income statements and ROEs for firms A and B would look as follows:

	A	B
Operating income	$300,000	$300,000
Interest expense	–	(40,000)
Profit before taxes	$300,000	$260,000
Taxes (30% assumed)	(90,000)	(78,000)
Net Profit after taxes (b)	$210,000	$182,000
ROE [(b)/(a)]	26.25%	45.5%

The absence of debt allows firm A to register higher profits after taxes. Yet the owners in firm B enjoy a significantly higher return on their investments. This provides an important view of the positive contribution debt can make to a business, but within a certain limit. Too much debt can increase the firm's financial risk and thus the cost of financing.

If the assets in which the funds are invested are able to earn a return greater than the fixed rate of return required by the creditors, the leverage is positive and the common stockholders benefit. The advantage of this formula is that it enables the company to break its ROE into a profit margin portion (net profit margin), an efficiency-of-asset-utilization portion (total asset turnover), and a use-of-leverage portion (equity multiplier). It shows that the company can raise shareholder return by employing leverage— taking on larger amounts of debt to help finance growth.

Since financial leverage affects net profit margin through the added interest costs, management must look at the various pieces of this ROE equation, within the context of the whole, to earn the highest return for stockholders. Financial managers have the task of determining just what combination of asset return and leverage will work best in its competitive environment. Most companies try to keep at least a level equal to what is considered to be "normal" within the industry.

CONCLUSION

This chapter covered in detail various strategies to increase the return on investment (ROI). The breakdown of ROI into margin and turnover, popularly known as the Du Pont formula, provides lots of insight into: (a) the strengths and weaknesses of a business and its segments, and (b) what needs to be done in order to improve performance. Another version of the Du Pont formula—the modified Du Pont formula—relates ROI to ROE (stockholders' return) through financial leverage. It shows how leverage can work favorably for the shareholders of the company.

22
Activity-Based Costing and Just-in-Time Manufacturing

Many companies are using a traditional cost system such as job-order costing or process costing, or some hybrid of the two. This system would tend to provide distorted product cost information. In fact, companies selling multiple products are making critical decisions about product pricing, making bids, or product mix, based on these inaccurate cost data. In all likelihood the problem is not with assigning the costs of direct labor or direct materials. These prime costs are traceable to individual products, and most conventional cost systems are designed to ensure that this tracing takes place. The assignment of overhead costs to individual products, however, is another matter. Using the traditional methods of assigning overhead costs to products—using a single predetermined overhead rate based on any single activity measure—can produce distorted product costs.

OVERHEAD COSTING: A SINGLE-PRODUCT SITUATION

The accuracy of overhead cost assignment becomes an issue only when multiple products are manufactured in a single facility. If only a single product is produced, all overhead costs are caused by it and traceable to it. The overhead cost per unit is simply total overhead for the year divided by the number of units produced. Accuracy is not an issue. The timing of the computation may be an issue, however; because of this, a predetermined overhead rate is usually required. The cost calculation for a single-product setting is illustrated in Table 1.

There is no question that the cost of manufacturing the product illustrated in Table 1 is $28.00 per unit. All manufacturing costs were incurred specifically

Table 1

UNIT COST COMPUTATION: SINGLE PRODUCT

	Manufacturing Costs	Units Produced	Unit Cost
Direct materials	$ 800,000	50,000	$16.00
Direct labor	200,000	50,000	4.00
Factory overhead	400,000	50,000	8.00
Total	$1,400,000	50,000	$28.00

to make this product. Thus, one way to ensure product-costing accuracy is to focus on producing one product. For this reason, some multiple product firms choose to dedicate plants to the manufacture of a single product.

By focusing on only one or two products, small manufacturers were able to calculate the cost of manufacturing the high-volume products more accurately and price them more effectively.

OVERHEAD COSTING: A MULTIPLE-PRODUCT SITUATION

In a multiple-product situation, manufacturing overhead costs are caused jointly by all products. The problem now becomes one of trying to identify the amount of overhead caused or consumed by each. This is accomplished by searching for cost drivers, or activity measures that causes costs to be incurred.

In a traditional setting, it is normally assumed that overhead consumption is highly correlated with the volume of production activity, measured in terms of direct labor hours, machine hours, or direct labor dollars. These volume-related cost drivers are used to assign overhead to products. Volume-related cost drivers use either plant-wide or departmental rates, which was discussed in detail in the previous chapter.

Case 1

To illustrate the limitation of this traditional approach, assume that ABC has a plant that produces two products: Thingone and Thingtwo. Product costing data are given in Table 2. Because the quantity of Thingtwo produced is five times greater than that of Thingone, Thingone can be labeled a low-volume product and Thingtwo a high-volume product.

For simplicity, only four types of factory overhead costs are assumed: setup, quality control, power, and maintenance. These overhead costs are allocated to the two production departments using the *direct* method.

Table 2

PRODUCT COSTING DATA

	Thingone	Thingtwo	Total
Units produced per year	10,000	50,000	60,000
Production runs	20	30	50
Inspection hours	800	1,200	2,000
Kilowatt hours	5,000	25,000	30,000
Prime costs (direct materials and direct labor)	$ 50,000	$250,000	$300,000

Departmental Data

	Department 1	Department 2	Total
Direct labor hours:			
Thingone	4,000	16,000	20,000
Thingtwo	76,000	24,000	100,000
Total	80,000	40,000	120,000
Machine hours:			
Thingone	4,000	6,000	10,000
Thingtwo	16,000	34,000	50,000
Total	20,000	40,000	60,000
Overhead costs:			
Setup costs	$ 48,000	$ 48,000	$ 96,000
Quality control	37,000	37,000	74,000
Power	14,000	70,000	84,000
Maintenance	13,000	65,000	78,000
Total	$112,000	$220,000	$332,000

Assume that the four service centers do not interact. Setup costs are allocated based on the number of production runs handled by each department. Since the number is identical, each department receives 50% of the total setup costs. Quality control costs are allocated by the number of inspection hours used by each department. Power costs are allocated in proportion to the kilowatt hours used. Maintenance costs are allocated in proportion to the machine hours used.

Plant-Wide Overhead Rate

A common method of assigning overhead to products is to compute a plant-wide rate, using a volume-related cost driver. This approach assumes that all overhead cost variation can be explained by one cost driver. Assume that machine hours is chosen.

Dividing the total overhead by the total machine hours yields the following overhead rate:

$$\text{Plant-wide rate} = \$332,000/60,000$$
$$= \$5.53/\text{machine hour}$$

Using this rate and other information from Table 2, the unit cost for each product can be calculated, as given in Table 3.

Departmental Rates

Based on the distribution of labor hours and machine hours in Table 2, Department 1 is labor intensive and Department 2 machine oriented. Furthermore, the overhead costs of Department 1 are about half those of Department 2. Based on these observations, it is apparent that departmental overhead rates would reflect the consumption of overhead better than a plant-wide rate.

Product costs would be more accurate, using departmental rates. This

Table 3

UNIT COST COMPUTATION: PLANT-WIDE RATE

Thingone	
Prime costs ($50,000/10,000)	$5.00
Overhead costs ($5.53 × 10,000/10,000)	5.53
Unit cost	$10.53

Thingtwo	
Prime costs ($250,000/50,000)	$5.00
Overhead costs ($5.53 × 50,000/50,000)	5.53
Unit cost	$10.53

approach would yield the following departmental rates, using direct labor hours for Department 1 and machine hours for Department 2:

$$\text{Department 1 rate} = \$112,000/80,000$$
$$= \$1.40/\text{labor hour}$$
$$\text{Department 2 rate} = \$220,000/40,000$$
$$= 5.50/\text{machine hour}$$

Using these rates and the data from Table 2, the computation of the unit costs for each product is shown in Table 4.

Problems with Costing Accuracy

The accuracy of the overhead cost assignment can be challenged regardless of whether the plant-wide or departmental rates are used. The main problem with either procedure is the assumption that machine hours or direct labor hours drive or cause all overhead costs.

From Table 2, we know that Thingtwo—with five times the volume of Thingone—uses five times the machine hours and direct labor hours. Thus, if a plant-wide rate is used, Thingtwo will receive five times more overhead cost. But does it make sense? Is all overhead driven by volume? Use of a single driver—especially volume-related—is not proper.

Examination of the data in Table 2 suggests that a significant portion of overhead costs is not driven or caused by volume. For example, setup costs are

Table 4

UNIT COST COMPUTATION: DEPARTMENT RATES

Thingone	
Prime costs ($50,000/10,000)	$5.00
Overhead costs [($1.40 × 4,000) + ($5.50 × 6,000)]/10,000	3.86
Unit cost	$8.86

Thingtwo	
Prime costs ($250,000/50,000)	$5.00
Overhead costs [($1.40 × 76,000) + ($5.50 × 34,000)]/50,000	5.87
Unit cost	$10.87

probably related to the number of setups and quality control costs to the number of hours of inspection. Notice that Thingtwo only has 1.5 times as many setups as the Thingone (30/20) and only 1.5 times as many inspection hours (1,200/800). Use of a volume-related cost driver (machine hours or labor hours) and a plant-wide rate assigns five times more overhead to the Thingtwo than to Thingone. For quality control and setup costs, then, Thingtwo is overcosted, and Thingone is undercosted.

The problems only worsened when departmental rates were used. Thingtwo consumes 19 times as many direct labor hours (76,000/4,000) as Thingone and 5.7 times as many machine hours (34,000/6,000). Thus, Thingtwo receives 19 times more overhead from Department 1 and 5.7 times more overhead from Department 2. As Table 4 shows, with departmental rates the unit cost of the Thingone decreases to $8.86, and the unit cost of Thingtwo increases to $10.87. This change is in the wrong direction, which emphasizes the failure of volume-based cost drivers to reflect accurately each product's consumption of setup and quality control costs.

Why Volume-Related Cost Drivers Fail

At least two major factors impair the ability of a volume-related cost driver to assign overhead costs accurately: (1) the proportion of nonvolume-related overhead costs to total overhead costs; and (2) the degree of product diversity.

Nonvolume-related Overhead Costs. In our example, there are four overhead activities: quality control, setup, maintenance, and power. Two, maintenance and power, are volume related. Quality control and setup are less dependent on volume. As a result, volume-based cost drivers cannot assign these costs accurately to products.

Using volume-based cost drivers to assign nonvolume-related overhead costs creates distorted product costs. The severity of this distortion depends on what proportion of total overhead costs these nonvolume-related costs represent. For our example, setup costs and quality control costs represent a substantial share—50%—of total overhead ($170,000/$332,000). This suggests that some care should be exercised in assigning these costs. If nonvolume-related overhead costs are only a small percentage of total overhead costs, the distortion of product costs would be quite small. In such a case, the use of volume-based cost drivers may be acceptable.

Product Diversity. When products consume overhead activities in different proportions, a firm has product diversity.

To illustrate, the proportion of all overhead activities consumed by both Thingone and Thingtwo is computed and displayed in Table 5. The proportion of each activity consumed by a product is defined as the consumption ratio. As you can see from the table, the consumption ratios for these two products differ from the nonvolume-related categories to the volume-related costs.

Since the nonvolume-related overhead costs are a significant proportion of total overhead and their consumption ratio differs from that of the volume-

Table 5

PRODUCT DIVERSITY: PROPORTION OF CONSUMPTION

Overhead Activity	Thingone	Thingtwo	Consumption Measure
Setups	.40(1)	.60(1)	Production runs
Quality control	.40(2)	.60(2)	Inspection hours
Power	.17(3)	.83(3)	Kilowatt hours
Maintenance	.17(4)	.83(4)	Machine hours

(1) 20/50 (Thingone) and 30/50 (Thingtwo)
(2) 800/2,000 (Thingone) and 1,200/2,000 (Thingtwo)
(3) 5,000/30,000 (Thingone) and 25,000/30,000 (Thingtwo)
(4) 10,000/60,000 (Thingone) and 50,000/60,000 (Thingtwo)

based cost driver, product costs can be distorted if a volume-based cost driver is used. The solution to this costing problem is to use an *activity-based costing* approach.

ACTIVITY-BASED PRODUCT COSTING

An activity-based cost system is one which first traces costs to activities and then to products. Traditional product costing also involves two stages, but in the first stage costs are traced to departments, not to activities. In both traditional and activity-based costing, the second stage consists of tracing costs to the product. The principal difference between the two methods is the number of cost drivers used. Activity-based costing uses a much larger number of cost drivers than the one or two volume-based cost drivers typical in a conventional system. In fact, the approach separates overhead costs into overhead cost pools, where each cost pool is associated with a different cost driver. Then a predetermined overhead rate is computed for each cost pool and each cost driver. In consequence, this method has enhanced accuracy.

First-Stage Procedure

In the first stage of activity-based costing, overhead costs are divided into homogeneous cost pools. A *homogeneous* cost pool is a collection of overhead costs for which cost variations can be explained by a single cost driver. Overhead activities are homogeneous whenever they have the same consumption ratios for all products. Once a cost pool is defined, the cost per unit of the cost driver is computed for that pool. This is referred to as the *pool rate*. Computation of the pool rate completes the first stage. Thus, the first stage produces two outcomes: (1) a set of homogeneous cost pools and (2) a pool rate.

For example, in Table 5, quality control costs and setup costs can be combined into one homogeneous cost pool and maintenance and power costs into a second. For the first cost pool, the number of production runs or inspection hours could be the cost driver. Since the two cost drivers are perfectly correlated, they will assign the same amount of overhead to both products. For the second pool, machine hours or kilowatt hours could be selected as the cost driver.

Assume for purpose of illustration that the number of production runs and machine hours are the cost drivers chosen. Using data from Table 2, the first-stage outcomes are illustrated in Table 6.

Second-Stage Procedure

In the second stage, the costs of each overhead pool are traced to products. This is done using the pool rate computed in the first stage and the measure of the amount of resources consumed by each product. This measure is simply the quantity of the cost driver used by each product. In our example, that would be the number of production runs and machine hours used by each product. Thus, the overhead assigned from each cost pool to each product is computed as follows:

$$\text{Applied overhead} = \text{Pool rate} \times \text{Cost driver units used}$$

To illustrate, consider the assignment of costs from the first overhead pool to Thingone. From Table 6, the rate for this pool is $3,400 per production run.

Table 6

ACTIVITY-BASED COSTING: FIRST-STAGE PROCEDURE

Pool 1:	
Setup costs	$ 96,000
Quality control costs	74,000
Total costs	$170,000
Production runs	50
Pool rate (Cost per run)	$ 3,400
Pool 2:	
Power costs	$ 84,000
Maintenance	78,000
Total costs	$162,000
Machine hours	60,000
Pool rate (Cost per machine hour)	$ 2.70

From Table 2, Thingone uses 20 production runs. Thus, the overhead assigned from the first cost pool is $68,000 ($3,400 × 20 runs). Similar assignments would be made for the other cost pool and for the other product (for both cost pools).

The total overhead cost per unit of product is obtained by first tracing the overhead costs from the pools to the individual products. This total is then divided by the number of units produced. The result is the unit overhead cost. Adding the per-unit overhead cost to the per-unit prime cost yields the manufacturing cost per unit. In Table 7, the manufacturing cost per unit is computed using activity-based costing.

Comparison of Product Costs

In Table 8, the unit cost from activity-based costing is compared with the unit costs produced by conventional costing using either a plant-wide or departmental rate. This comparison clearly illustrates the effects of using only volume-

Table 7

**ACTIVITY-BASED COSTING: SECOND-STAGE PROCEDURE
UNIT COSTS**

Thingone		
Overhead:		
Pool 1: $3,400 × 20	$ 68,000	
Pool 2: $2.70 × 10,000	27,000	
Total overhead costs		$ 95,000
Prime costs		50,000
Total manufacturing costs		$145,000
Units produced		10,000
Unit cost		$ 14.50

Thingtwo		
Overhead:		
Pool 1: $3,400 × 30	$102,000	
Pool 2: $2.70 × 50,000	135,000	
Total overhead costs		$237,000
Prime costs		250,000
Total manufacturing costs		$487,000
Units produced		50,000
Unit cost		$ 9.74

based cost drivers to assign overhead costs. The activity-based cost reflects the correct pattern of overhead consumption and is, therefore, the most accurate of the three costs shown in Table 8. Activity-based product costing reveals that the conventional method undercosts the Thingone significantly—by at least 37.7% = ($14.50 − 10.53)/$10.53) and overcosts the Thingtwo by at least 8.1% = ($10.53 − $9.74)/$9.74).

Using only volume-based cost drivers can lead to one product subsidizing another. This subsidy could create the appearance that one group of products is highly profitable and adversely impact the pricing and competitiveness of another group of products. This seems to be one of the problems facing Sharp Paper. In a highly competitive environment, accurate cost information is critical for sound planning and decision making.

The Choice of Cost Drivers

At least two major factors should be considered in selecting cost drivers: (1) the cost of measurement and (2) the degree of correlation between the cost driver and the actual consumption of overhead.

The Cost of Measurement. In an activity-based cost system, a large number of cost drivers can be selected and used. However, it is preferable to select cost drivers that use information that is readily available. Information that is not available in the existing system must be produced, which will increase the cost of the firm's information system. A homogeneous cost pool could offer a number of possible cost drivers. For this situation, any cost driver that can be used with existing information should be chosen. This choice minimizes the costs of measurement.

In our example, for instance, quality control costs and setup costs were placed in the same cost pool, giving the choice of using either inspection hours or number of production runs as the cost driver. If the quantities of both cost drivers used by the two products are already being produced by the company's information system, then which is chosen is unimportant. Assume, however, that inspection hours by product are not tracked, but data for production runs

Table 8

COMPARISON OF UNIT COSTS

	Thingone	Thingtwo	Source
Conventional:			
Plant-wide rate	10.53	10.53	Table 3
Department rates	8.86	10.87	Table 4
Activity-based cost	$14.50	$9.74	Table 7

are available. In this case, production runs should be chosen as the cost driver, avoiding the need to produce any additional information.

Indirect Measures and the Degree of Correlation. The existing information structure can be exploited in another way to minimize the costs of obtaining cost driver quantities. It is sometimes possible to replace a cost driver that directly measures the consumption of an activity with a cost driver that indirectly measures that consumption. For example, inspection hours could be replaced by the actual number of inspections associated with each product; this number is more likely to be known. This replacement only works, of course, if hours used per inspection are reasonably stable for each product. *Linear regressions* can be utilized to determine the degree of correlation.

A list of potential cost drivers is given in Table 9. Cost drivers that indirectly measure the consumption of an activity usually measure the number of transactions associated with that activity. It is possible to replace a cost driver that directly measures consumption with one that only indirectly measures it without loss of accuracy provided that the quantities of activity consumed per transaction are stable for each product. In such a case, the indirect cost driver has a high correlation and can be used.

Hewlett-Packard Illustration of Multiple Cost Pools

Hewlett-Packard Company's Personal Office Computer Division uses two overhead application rates. One rate is based on direct labor and assigns overhead costs associated with production. The second rate is based on mate-

Table 9

COST DRIVERS

Manufacturing:

Space occupied	
Number of setups	Direct labor hours
Weight of material	Number of vendors
Number of units reworked	Machine hours
Number of orders placed	Number of labor transactions
Number of orders received	Number of units scrapped
Number of inspections	Number of parts
Number of material handling operations	

Nonmanufacturing:

Number of hospital beds occupied
Number of takeoffs and landings for an airline
Number of rooms occupied in a hotel

rial cost and assigns overhead cost associated with procurement. Table 10 illustrates these systems. Overhead costs are initially categorized into three cost pools. Then the overhead costs associated with overall manufacturing support functions are allocated between the production cost pool and the procurement cost pool. This allocation is based on the number of employees and the estimated percentage of time spent on these two types of activities.

Table 10

MULTIPLE OVERHEAD COST POOLS-HEWLETT-PACKARD COMPANY: PERSONAL OFFICE COMPUTER DIVISION

SUPPORT MANUFACTURING OVERHEAD

Includes costs that support the entire manufacturing process but cannot be associated directly with either production or procurement (e.g., production engineering, quality assurance, and central electronic data processing.)

PRODUCTION MANUFACTURING OVERHEAD

Includes such costs as production supervision, indirect labor, depreciation, and operating costs associated with production, assembly, testing, and shipping.

PROCUREMENT MANUFACTURING OVERHEAD

Includes such costs as purchasing, receiving, inspection of raw materials, material handling, production planning and control, and subcontracting.

Applied on the basis of DIRECT LABOR

Applied on the basis of DIRECT MATERIAL

Source: Patell, J. "Cost Accounting, Process Control, and Product Design: A Case Study of the Hewlett-Packard Personal Office Computer Division," *Accounting Review*, October, 1987.

Case 2

Northeastern Metals, Inc. has established the following overhead cost pools and cost drivers for their product:

Overhead Cost Pool	Budgeted Overhead Cost	Cost Driver	Predicted Level for Cost Driver	Predetermined Overhead Rate
Machine set-ups	$100,000	Number of set-ups	100	$1,000 per set-up
Material handling	100,000	Weight of raw material	50,000 pounds	$2 per pound
Waste control	50,000	Weight of hazardous chemicals used	10,000 pounds	$5 per pound
Inspection	75,000	Number of inspections	1,000	$75 per inspection
Other overhead costs	$200,000	Machine hours	20,000	$10 per machine hour
	$525,000			

Job Number 3941 consists of 2,000 special purpose machine tools with the following requirements:

Machine set-ups	2 set-ups
Raw material required	10,000 pounds
Waste materials required	2,000 pounds
Inspections	10 inspections
Machine hours	500 machine hours

The overhead assigned to Job Number 3941 is computed below.

Overhead Cost Pool	Predetermined Overhead Rate	Level of Cost Driver	Assigned Overhead Cost
Machine set-ups	$1,000 per set-up	2 set-ups	$ 2,000
Material handling	$2 per pound	10,000 pounds	20,000
Waste control	$5 per pound	2,000 pounds	10,000
Inspection	$75 per inspection	10 inspections	750
Other overhead costs	$10 per machine hour	500 machine hours	5,000
Total			$37,750

The total overhead cost assigned to Job Number 3941 is $37,750, or $18.88 per tool. Compare this with the overhead cost that is assigned to the job if the firm uses a single predetermined overhead rate based on machine hours:

$$\frac{\text{Total budgeted overhead cost}}{\text{Total predicted machine hours}} = \frac{\$525,000}{20,000}$$

$$= \$26.25 \text{ per machine hour}$$

Under this approach, the total overhead cost assigned to Job Number 3941 is \$13,125 (\$26.25 per machine hour $\times$ 500 machine hours). This is only \$6.56 per tool, which is about one third of the overhead cost per tool computed when multiple cost drivers are used.

The reason for this wide discrepancy is that these special purpose tools require a relatively large number of machine set-ups, a sizable amount of waste materials, and several inspections. Thus, they are relatively costly in terms of driving overhead costs. Use of a single predetermined overhead rate obscures that fact.

Misestimating the overhead cost per drum to the extent illustrated above can have serious adverse consequences for the firm. For example, it can lead to poor decisions about pricing, product mix, or contract bidding. The managerial accountant needs to carefully weigh such considerations in designing a product costing system. A costing system using multiple cost drivers is more costly to implement and use, but it may save millions through improved decisions.

For a more detailed discussion on activity costing, see the following articles:

(1) Shank, John K. and Vijay Govindarajan, "Transaction-Based Costing for the Complex Product Line: A Field Study," *Journal of Cost Management for the Manufacturing Industry*, vol. 2., no. 2 (Summer 1988).

(2) Cooper, Robin and Robert S. Kaplan, "Measuring Costs Right: Make the Right Decisions," *Harvard Business Review*, September/October, 1988.

(3) Cooper, Robin, "The Two-Stage Procedure in Cost Accounting—Part One," *Journal of Cost Management for the Manufacturing Industry*, vol. 1, no. 2, Summer 1987.

(4) Cooper, Robin, "The Two-Stage Procedure in Cost Accounting—Part Two," *Journal of Cost Management for the Manufacturing Industry*, vol. 1, no. 3, Fall 1987.

(5) Cooper, Robin, "The Rise of Activity Costing—Part One," *Journal of Cost Management for the Manufacturing Industry*, vol. 2, no. 2, Summer 1988.

(6) Cooper, Robin, "The Rise of Activity Costing—Part Three," *Journal of Cost Management for the Manufacturing Industry*, vol. 2, no. 4, Winter 1989.

JUST-IN-TIME MANUFACTURING AND COST MANAGEMENT

The inventory control problem occurs in almost every type of organization. It exists whenever products are held to meet some expected future demand. In most industries, cost of inventory represents the largest liquid asset under the control of management. Therefore, it is very important to develop a production and inventory planning system that will minimize both purchasing and carrying costs.

During the 1960s and 1970s, material requirements planning (MRP) was adopted by many U.S. manufacturing companies as the key component of their production and inventory planning systems. While success has not been universal, users typically agreed that the inventory approach inherent in an MRP system generally is more effective than the classical approach to inventory planning. Aside from the manufacturing aspects, the purchasing function also is of major importance to the overall success of the system.

Even though MRP has received a great deal of attention, effective purchasing and management of materials is still a high priority activity in most manufacturing firms. Material cost, as a proportion of total product cost, has continued to rise significantly during the last few years and hence is a primary concern of top management.

Competing on the basis of both price and quality, the Japanese have demonstrated the ability to manage their production systems effectively. Much of their success has been attributed to their "just-in-time" (JIT) approach to production and inventory control, which has generated a great deal of interest among practitioners. The "Kanban" system, as they call it, has been a focal point of interest, with its dramatic impact on the inventory performance and productivity of the Japanese auto industry.

This section provides an overview of the Just-In-Time (JIT) approach and its impact on cost management. We provide some examples of implementation of JIT by U.S. firms.

What Is Just-in-Time (JIT)?

JIT is a demand-pull system. JIT production, in its purest sense, is buying and producing in very small quantities just in time for use. The basic idea has its roots in Japan's densely populated industrial areas and its lack of resources, both of which have produced frugal personal habits among the Japanese people. The idea was developed into a formal management system by Toyota in order to meet the precise demands of customers for various vehicle models and colors with minimum delivery delays. JIT is achieved by techniques such as smoothing production, designing flexible processes, standardizing jobs, and employing the Kanban system for conveying ordering and delivery information within the production system. Furthermore, the little inventory that exists in a JIT system must be of good quality. This requirement has led to JIT purchasing practices uniquely able to deliver high-quality materials. As a philosophy, JIT targets inventory as an evil presence that obscures problems that should be solved, and that by contributing significantly to costs, keeps a company from being as competitive or profitable as it otherwise might be. Practically speaking, JIT has as its principal goal the elimination of waste, and the principal measure of success is how much or how little inventory there is. Virtually anything that achieves this end can be considered a JIT innovation.

JIT systems integrate five functions of the production process—sourcing, storage, transportation, operations, and quality control into one controlled manufacturing process. In manufacturing, JIT means that a company produces only the quantity needed for delivery to dealers or customers. In purchasing, it means suppliers deliver subassemblies just in time to be assembled into finished goods. In delivery, it requires selecting a transportation mode that will deliver purchased components and materials in small-lot sizes at the loading dock of the manufacturing facilities just in time to support the manufacturing process.

JIT Compared with Traditional Manufacturing

JIT manufacturing is a demand-pull, or kanban system, rather than the traditional "push" approach. The philosophy underlying JIT manufacturing is to produce a product when it is needed and only in the quantities demanded by customers. Demand pulls products through the manufacturing process. Each operation produces only what is necessary to satisfy the demand of the succeeding operation. No production takes place until a signal from a succeeding process indicates a need to produce. Parts and materials arrive just in time to be used in production. To illustrate the differences between pull and push systems of material control, the example of a fast food restaurant is used:

> At McDonald's the customer orders a hamburger, the service gets one from the rack, the hamburger maker keeps an eye on the rack and makes new burgers when the number gets too low. The manager orders more ground beef when the maker's inventory gets too low. In effect, the customer purchase triggers the pull of materials through the system. . . . In a push system, the caterer estimates how many steaks are likely to be ordered in any given week. He/she reckons how long it takes to broil a steak: he/she can figure out roughly how many meals are needed in a certain week. . . . (See Reference [3])

Reduced Inventories. The primary goal of JIT is to reduce inventories to insignificant or zero levels. In traditional manufacturing, inventories result whenever production exceeds demand. Inventories are needed as a buffer when production does not meet expected demand.

Manufacturing Cells and Multifunction Labor. In traditional manufacturing, products are moved from one group of identical machines to another. Typically, machines with identical functions are located together in an area referred to as a department or process. Workers who specialize in the operation of a specific machine are located in each department. JIT replaces this traditional pattern with a pattern of manufacturing cells or work centers. Robots supplement people to do many routine operations.

Manufacturing cells contain machines that are grouped in families, usually in a semicircle. The machines are arranged so that they can be used to perform a variety of operations in sequence. Each cell is set up to produce a particular product or product family. Products move from one machine to another from start to finish. Workers are assigned to cells and are trained to operate all machines within the cell. Thus, labor in a JIT environment is multifunction labor, not specialized labor. Each manufacturing cell is basically a minifactory or a factory within a factory. A comparison of the physical layout of JIT with the traditional system is shown in Figure 1.

Total Quality Control. JIT necessarily carries with it a stronger emphasis on quality control. A defective part brings production to a grinding halt. Poor quality simply cannot be tolerated in a stockless manufacturing environment. In other words, JIT cannot be implemented without a commitment to *total quality control (TQC)*. TQC is essentially an endless guest for perfect quality. This approach to quality is opposed to the traditional belief, called *acceptable quality level (AQL)*. AQL allows defects to occur provided they are within a predetermined level.

Decentralization of Services. JIT requires easy and quick access to support services, which means that centralized service departments must be scaled down and their personnel assigned to work directly to support production. For example, with respect to raw materials, JIT calls for multiple stock

Figure 1. Physical Layout: Traditional Versus JIT Manufacturing

<u>Traditional Manufacturing</u>

Department A	Department B	Department C
$P1 >$ X X $> P1 >$	Y Y	$> P1 >$ Z Z
$P2 >$ $> P2 >$		$> P2 >$

Each product passes through departments which specialize in one process. Departments process multiple products.

<u>JIT Manufacturing</u>

Product 1 ($P1$) Manufacturing Cell 1	Product 2 ($P2$) Manufacturing Cell 2
Y	Y
$P1 >$ X Z	$P2 >$ X Z

Notice that each product passes through its own cell. All machines necessary to process each product are placed within the cell. Each cell is dedicated to the production of one product or one subassembly.

Symbols:

X = Machine A $P1$ = Product 1
Y = Machine B $P2$ = Product 2
Z = Machine C

points, each one near where the material will be used. There is no need for a central warehouse location.

Better Cost Management. Cost management differs from cost accounting in that it refers to the management of cost, whether or not the cost has direct impact on inventory or the financial statements. The JIT philosophy simplifies the cost accounting procedure and helps managers manage their costs. JIT recognizes that with simplification comes better management, better quality, better service and better cost. Traditional cost accounting systems have a tendency to be very complex, with many transactions and reporting of data. Simplification of this process will transform a cost "accounting" system into a cost "management" system that can be used to support management's needs for better decisions about product design, pricing, marketing, and mix, and to encourage continual operating movements.

The major differences between JIT manufacturing and traditional manufacturing are summarized in Table 11.

Benefits of JIT

Potential benefits of JIT are numerous. First, JIT practice reduces inventory levels, which means lower investments in inventories. Since the system requires only the small quantity of materials that are needed immediately, it reduces the overall inventory level substantially. In many Japanese companies that use the JIT concept, inventory levels have been reduced to the point that makes the annual working capital turnover ratio much higher than that experienced by U.S. counterparts. For instance, Toyota reported inventory turnover ratios of 41 to 63, while comparable U.S. companies reported inventory turnover ratios of 5 to 8.

Second, since purchasing under JIT requires a significantly shorter delivery lead time, lead time reliability is greatly improved. Reduced lead time and increased reliability also contribute to a significant reduction in the safety stock requirements.

Table 11

COMPARISON OF JIT AND TRADITIONAL MANUFACTURING

JIT	Traditional
1. Pull, or Kanban system	1. Push system
2. Insignificant or zero inventories	2. Significant inventories
3. Manufacturing cells	3. "Process" structure
4. Multifunction labor	4. Specialized labor
5. Total quality control (TQC)	5. Acceptable quality level
6. Decentralized services	6. Centralized services
7. Simple cost accounting	7. Complex cost accounting

Third, reduced lead times and set-up times increase scheduling flexibility. The cumulative lead time, which includes both purchasing and production lead times, is reduced. Thus, the firm schedule within the production planning horizon is reduced. This results in a longer "look-ahead" time that can be used to meet shifts in market demand. The smaller lot size production made possible by reduced set-up time, also adds flexibility.

Fourth, improved quality levels have been reported by many companies. When the order quantity is small, sources of quality problems are quickly identifiable, and can be corrected immediately. In many cases, employee quality consciousness also tends to improve, producing an improvement in quality at the production source.

Fifth, the costs of purchased materials may be reduced through more extensive value analysis and cooperative supplier development activities.

Sixth, other financial benefits reported include:

(1) Lower investments in factory space for inventories and production

(2) Less obsolescence risk in inventories

(3) Reduction in scrap and rework

(4) Decline in paperwork

(5) Reduction in direct material costs through quantity purchases

Examples of JIT Implementation in the U.S.

The following are some of the many implementation experiences of JIT in the U.S.:

(1) The Oldsmobile division of General Motors (GM) has implemented a JIT project which permits immediate electronic communication between Oldsmobile and 70 of its principal suppliers who provide 700 to 800 parts representing around 85% of the parts needed for the new GM-20 cars.

(2) PTC Components, a supplier to GM, has assisted GM in its use of stockless production by sending one truck a week to deliver timing chains to several GM's engine plants rather than accumulate a truckload to ship to each plant.

(3) Ford introduced JIT production at its heavy-duty truck plant in Kentucky, which forced Firestone to switch the tire searching point from Mansfield to Dayton, Ohio. By combining computerized ordering and halving inventory, Firestone has been able to reduce its own finished goods inventory. In addition, its production planning is no longer guesswork.

(4) Each day a truck from Harley-Davidson Motor Co. transports 160 motorcycle seats and assorted accessories 800 miles overnight to Harley's assembly plant in York, PA, as part of their advanced "Materials as Needed" (MAN) program—its version of JIT.

(5) The Hoover Company has used JIT techniques in its two plants at North Canton, Ohio, for a number of years for production scheduling and material flow control of 360 different models and 29,000 part numbers.

(6) Some plants of Du Pont used JIT and had an inventory savings of 30 cents on the dollar for the first year.

(7) The Vancouver division of Hewlett-Packard reported the following benefits two years after the adoption of the JIT method:

Work-in-process inventory dollars	down 82%
Space used	down 40%
Scrap/rework	down 30%
Production time:	
Impact printers	down 7 days to 2 days
Thermal printers	down 7 days to 3 hours
Labor efficiency	up 50%
Shipments	up 20%

JIT Costing and Cost Management

The cost accounting system of a company adopting JIT will be simple compared to job order or processing costing. Under JIT, raw materials and work-in-process (WIP) accounts are typically combined into one account called "resources in process" (RIP) or "raw and in-process." Under JIT, the materials arrive at the receiving area and are whisked immediately to the factory area. Thus, the Stores Control account vanishes. The journal entries that accompany JIT costing are remarkably simple as follows:

Raw and in-process (RIT) inventory	$45,000	
Accounts payable or cash		$45,000
To record purchases		
Finished goods	40,000	
RIP inventory		40,000
To record raw materials in completed units.		

As can be seen, there is no Stores Control and WIP accounts under JIT.

In summary, JIT costing can be characterized as follows:

1. There are less inventory accounts.

2. There are no work orders. Thus, there is no need for detailed tracking of actual raw materials.

3. With JIT, activities can be eliminated on the premise that they do not add value. Prime target for elimination are storage areas for WIP inventory and material handling facilities.

4. The costs of many activities previously classified as indirect costs have

been transferred to the direct cost in the JIT environment. For example, under the JIT system workers on the production line will do plant maintenance and setups, while under traditional systems these activities were done by other workers classified as indirect labor. Table 12 compares the traceability of some manufacturing costs under the traditional system with their traceability in the JIT environment.

We can see that JIT manufacturing increases direct traceability in many manufacturing costs, thus enhancing the accuracy of product costing. Note, however, that JIT does not convert all indirect costs into direct costs. Even with JIT installed, a significant number of overhead activities remain common to the work centers. Nonetheless, JIT, coupled with activity-based accounting, gives rise to a tremendous improvement in product costing accuracy over the traditional approach.

5. Direct labor costs and factory overhead costs are not tracked to specific orders. Direct labor is now regarded as just another part of factory overhead. Furthermore, factory overhead is accounted for as follows. Virtually all of the manufacturing overhead incurred each month, now including direct labor, flows through to cost of goods sold in the same month. Tracking overhead through WIP and finished goods inventory provides no useful information. Therefore, it makes sense to treat manufacturing overhead as an expense charged directly to cost of goods sold. Overhead remaining in work-in-process and finished goods is maintained with end-of-month adjusting entries.

6. Many firms place great emphasis on purchase price variances in traditional purchasing environments. Favorable purchasing price variances can sometimes be achieved by buying larger quantities to take advantage of price

Table 12

TRACEABILITY OF PRODUCT COST
TRADITIONAL VERSUS JIT MANUFACTURING

	Traditional	JIT
Direct labor	Direct	Direct
Direct materials	Direct	Direct
Material handling	Indirect	Direct
Repairs and maintenance	Indirect	Direct
Energy	Indirect	Direct
Operating supplies	Indirect	Direct
Supervision	Indirect	Direct
Insurance and taxes	Indirect	Indirect
Building depreciation	Indirect	Indirect
Equipment depreciation	Indirect	Direct
Building occupancy	Indirect	Indirect
Product support services	Indirect	Indirect
Cafeteria services	Indirect	Indirect

discounts or by buying lower quality materials. In JIT, the emphasis is on the total cost of operations and not just the purchase price. Factors such as quality and availability are given priority, even if they are accompanied by higher purchase prices.

7. In many traditional plants, much of the internal accounting effort is devoted to setting labor and overhead standards and in calculating and reporting variances from these standards. Firms using JIT report reduced emphasis on the use of labor and overhead variances. Firms retaining variance analysis stress that a change in focus is appropriate in a JIT plant. The emphasis is on the analysis at the plant level with focus on trends that may be occurring in the manufacturing process rather than the absolute magnitude of individual variances.

8. Traditional performance measures (such as labor efficiency and machine utilization) that are commonplace in many cost accounting systems are not appropriate within the JIT philosophy of cost management. They are all inappropriate for the following reasons:

(a) They all promote building inventory beyond what is needed in the immediate time frame.

(b) Emphasizing performance to standard gives priority to output, at the expense of quality.

(c) Direct labor in the majority of manufacturers accounts for only 5 to 15% of total product cost.

(d) Using machine utilization is inappropriate because it encourages results in building inventory ahead of needs. Table 13 lists typical performance measures under the traditional and JIT systems.

Table 13

PERFORMANCE MEASURES
TRADITIONAL VS. JIT

Traditional	JIT
Direct labor efficiency	Total head count productivity
Direct labor utilization	Return on assets
Direct labor productivity	Days of inventory
Machine utilization	Group incentives
	Lead time by product
	Response time to customer feedback
	Number of customer complaints
	Cost of quality
	Setup reduction

For more on JIT, see the following articles:

(1) Foster, George and Charles Horngren, "JIT: Cost Accounting and Cost Measurement Issues," *Management Accounting*, June 1987, pp. 19–25.

(2) Hunt, R., L. Garrett, and C. M. Mertz, "Direct Labor Cost Not Always Relevant at H-P," *Management Accounting*, February 1985, p. 61.

(3) Karmarkar, Uday, "Getting Control of Just-In-Time," *Harvard Business Review*, September–October 1989, pp. 122–131.

(4) McIlhattan, Robert D., "How Cost Management Systems Can Support the JIT Philosophy, *Management Accounting*, September 1987, pp. 20–26.

CONCLUSION

The chapter discussed in detail how activity costing provides more accurate product cost figures for product costing and pricing, using multiple overhead cost pools and cost drivers. Conventional cost systems are not able to assign the costs of nonvolume-related overhead activities accurately. For this reason, assigning overhead using only volume-based drivers or a single driver can distort product costs. Two cases were provided to illustrate the use of the activity-based costing system versus the traditional system using a single driver such as machine hours or direct labor hours. Activity-based costing may provide more accurate information about product costs. It helps managers make better decisions about product design, pricing, marketing, and mix, and encourages continual operating improvements.

This chapter also discussed the basic concepts underlying the just-in-time (JIT) system. It does not suggest a quick or across-the-board adaption of this concept. In many companies (particularly U.S. firms), the JIT purchasing concept simply may not be practical or feasible. In others, it may not be applicable to all product lines. However, many progressive companies currently are either investigating or implementing some form of the system. The most important aspects of the JIT purchasing concept focus on (1) new ways of dealing with suppliers, and (2) a clear-cut recognition of the appropriate purchasing role in the development corporate strategy. Suppliers should be viewed as "outside partners" who can contribute to the long-run welfare of the buying firm rather than as outside adversaries. JIT is also impacting product costing. Under JIT manufacturing, many indirect costs are converted to direct costs. This conversion reduces the need to use multiple cost drivers to assign overhead costs to products, thus enhancing product-costing accuracy.

23

Quantitative Applications in Corporate Financial Management

The use of quantitative tools is a common place in financial management. Also, in recent years, much attention has been given to using a variety of quantitative models in financial decision making. With the rapid development of microcomputers, financial officers find it increasingly easy to use quantitative techniques. A knowledge of mathematical and statistical methods will greatly aid the financial managers and accountants in performing their functions. The so-called *Decision Support System (DDS)* is in effect the embodiment of this trend.

The term quantitative models, also known as operations research (OR) and management science, describe sophisticated mathematical and statistical techniques in the solution of planning and decision-making problems. There are numerous tools available under these subject headings. We will explore nine of the most important of these techniques that have been widely applied in finance and accounting. They are:

1. Statistical analysis and evaluation

2. Decision making

3. Optimal Budget and Linear programming

4. Multiple Conflicting Goals and Goal Programming

5. Zero-One Programming and Capital Rationing

6. Beta and Linear Regression

7. Learning curve

8. Inventory planning

9. Program Evaluation and Review Technique (PERT)

STATISTICAL ANALYSIS AND EVALUATION

In many situations, financial managers have a large volume of data that needs to be analyzed. These data could be earnings, cash flows, accounts receivable balances, weights of an incoming shipment, and so on. The most commonly used statistics to describe the characteristics of the data are the mean and the standard deviation. These statistics are also used to measure the return and risk in investment and financial decision making which the financial managers may be asked to participate in by the business entity.

Standard Deviation

The standard deviation measures the tendency of data to be spread out. Accountants can make important inferences from past data with this measure. The standard deviation, denoted with and read as sigma, is defined as follows:

$$\sigma = \sqrt{\frac{\Sigma\,(x - \bar{x})^2}{n - 1}}$$

where $\bar{x}$ is the mean.

More specifically, the standard deviation can be calculated, step-by-step, as follows:

1. Subtract the mean from each value of the data.
2. Square each of the differences obtained in step 1.
3. Add together all the squared differences.
4. Divide the sum of all the squared differences by the number of values minus one.
5. Take the square root of the quotient obtained in step 4.

The standard deviation can be used to measure the variation of such items as the expected contribution margin (CM) or expected variable manufacturing costs. It can also be used to assess the risk associated with investment decisions.

EXAMPLE 1

One and one-half years of quarterly returns are listed below for United Motors stock.

Time period	x	$(x - \bar{x})$	$(x - \bar{x})^2$
1	10%	0	0
2	15	5	25
3	20	10	100
4	5	-5	25
5	-10	-20	400
6	20	10	100
	60		650

From the above table, note that

$$\bar{x} = 60/6 = 10\%$$

$$\sigma = \sqrt{(x - \bar{x})^2/n - 1} = \sqrt{650/(6 - 1)} = \sqrt{130} = 11.40\%$$

The United Motors stock has returned on the average 10% over the last six quarters and the variability about its average return was 11.40%. The high standard deviation (11.40%) relative to the average return of 10% indicates that the stock is very risky.

DECISION MAKING

Decisions are made under certainty or under uncertainty. Decision making under certainty means that for each decision there is only one event and therefore only one outcome for each action. Decision making under uncertainty, which is more common in reality, involves several events for each action with its probability of occurrence.

Decision Making Under Uncertainty

When decisions are made in a world of uncertainty, it is often helpful to make the computations of: (1) expected value, (2) standard deviation, and (3) coefficient of variation.

Decision Matrix

Although statistics such as expected value and standard deviation are essential for choosing the best course of action under uncertainty, the decision problem can best be approached using what is called decision theory. Decision theory is a systematic approach to making decisions especially under uncertainty. Decision theory utilizes an organized approach such as a payoff table (or decision matrix), which is characterized by:

(1) the row representing a set of alternative courses of action available to the decision maker;

(2) the column representing the state of nature or conditions that are likely to occur and the decision maker has no control over; and

(3) the entries in the body of the table representing the outcome of the decision, known as payoffs which may be in the form of costs, revenues, profits, or cash flows. By computing expected value of each action, we will be able to choose the best one.

EXAMPLE 2

Assume the following probability distribution of daily demand for a product:

Daily demand	0	1	2	3
Probability	.2	.3	.3	.2

Also assume that unit cost = $3, selling price = $5 (i.e., profit on sold unit = $2), and salvage value on unsold units = $2 (i.e., loss on unsold unit = $1). We can stock either 0, 1, 2, or 3 units. The question is: How many units should be stocked each day? Assume that units from one day cannot be sold the next day. Then the payoff table can be constructed as follows:

		State of Nature				
	Demand	0	1	2	3	Expected value
	Stock (probability)	(.2)	(.3)	(.3)	(.2)	
	0	$0	0	0	0	$ 0
Actions	1	-1	2	2	2	1.40
	2	-2	1*	4	4	1.90**
	3	-3	0	3	6	1.50

*Profit for (stock 2, demand 1) equals (no. of units sold) (profit per unit) − (no. of units unsold) (loss per unit) = (1) ($5 − 3) − (1) ($3 − 2) = $1
**Expected value for (stock 2) is: $-2(.2) + 1(.3) + 4 (.3) + 4 (.2) = \$1.90$

The optimal stock action is the one with the highest expected monetary value i.e., stock 2 units.

Expected Value of Perfect Information

Suppose the decision maker can obtain a perfect prediction of which event (state of nature) will occur. The expected value with perfect information would be the total expected value of actions selected on the assumption of a perfect forecast. The expected value of perfect information can then be computed as:

Expected value with perfect information minus the expected value with existing information.

EXAMPLE 3

From the payoff table in Example 2, the following analysis yields the expected value with perfect information:

		State of Nature				
	Demand	0	1	2	3	Expected value
	Stock	(.2)	(.3)	(.3)	(.2)	
	0	$0				$0
Actions	1		2			.6
	2			4		1.2
	3				6	1.2
						$3.00

Alternatively,

$$\$0(.2) + 2\,(.3) + 4(.3) + 6(.2) = \$3.00$$

With existing information, the best that the decision maker could obtain was select (stock 2) and obtain $1.90. With perfect information (forecast), the decision maker could make as much as $3. Therefore, the expected value of perfect information is $3.00 − $1.90 = $1.10. This is the maximum price the decision maker is willing to pay for additional information.

Decision Tree

Decision tree is another approach used in discussions of decision making under uncertainty. It is a pictorial representation of a decision situation. As in the case of the decision matrix approach discussed earlier, it shows decision alternatives, states of nature, probabilities attached to the state of nature, and conditional benefits and losses. The decision tree approach is most useful in a sequential decision situation.

EXAMPLE 4

Assume XYZ Corporation wishes to introduce one of two products to the market this year. The probabilities and present values (PV) of projected cash inflows are given below:

Products Probabilities	Initial investment	PV of cash inflows	
A	$225,000		1.00
		$450,000	0.40
		200,000	0.50
		− 100,000	0.10
B	80,000		1.00
		320,000	0.20
		100,000	0.60
		− 150,000	0.20

A decision tree analyzing the two products is given below.

	Initial Investment (1)	Probability (2)	PV of Cash Inflow (3)	PV of Cash Inflow $(2 \times 3) =$ (4)
Product A	$225,000	0.40	$450,000	$180,000
		0.50	$200,000	100,000
		0.10	$-100,000	10,000
		Expected PV of Cash Inflows		$270,000
Choice A or B				
Product B	$80,000	0.20	$320,000	$ 64,000
		0.60	$100,000	$ 60,000
		0.20	$-150,000	$ 30,000
		Expected PV of Cash Inflows		$ 94,000

For Product A:

Expected NPV = Expected PV $-$ I = $270,000 $-$ $225,000 = $45,000

For Product B:

Expected NPV = $94,000 $-$ $80,000 = $14,000

Based on the expected net present value, the company should choose product A over product B.

OPTIMAL BUDGET AND LINEAR PROGRAMMING

Linear programming (LP) is a mathematical technique designed to determine an optimal decision (or an optimal plan) chosen from a large number of possible decisions. The optimal decision is the one that meets the specified objective of the company, subject to various restrictions or constraints. It concerns itself with the problem of allocating scarce resources among competing activities in an optimal manner. The optimal decision yields the highest profit, contribution margin (CM), or revenue, or the lowest cost. A linear programming model consists of two important ingredients:

1. *Objective function.* The company must define the specific objective to be achieved.

2. *Constraints.* Constraints are in the form of restrictions on availability of resources or meeting minimum requirements. As the name linear programming indicates, both the objective function and constraints must be in linear form.

EXAMPLE 5

A firm wishes to find an optimal product mix. The optimal mix would be the one that maximizes its total CM within the allowed budget and production capacity. Or the firm may want to determine a least cost combination of input materials while meeting production requirements, employing production capacities, and using available employees.

Applications of LP

Applications of LP are numerous. They include:

1. Developing an optimal budget
2. Determining an optimal investment portfolio
3. Scheduling jobs to machines
4. Determining a least-cost shipping pattern
5. Scheduling flights
6. Gasoline blending

Formulation of LP

To formulate an LP problem, certain steps are followed. They are:

1. Define decision variables that you are trying to solve for.

2. Express the objective function and constraints in terms of these decision variables. All the expressions must be in linear form. This section shows how optimization techniques such as linear programming or goal programming can help develop an optimal budget. For this purpose, we will illustrate with a simple example.

We will use this technique first to find the optimal product mix and then to develop the budget for the optimal program.

EXAMPLE 6

The Sigma Company produces and sells two products: snowmobiles (A) and outboard motors (B). The sales price of A is $900 per unit and that of B $800 per unit. Production department estimates on the basis of standard cost data are that the capacity required for manufacturing one unit of A is 10 hours while one unit of product B requires 20 hours. The total available capacity for the company is 160 hours. The variable manufacturing costs of A are $300 per unit and they are all paid in cash at the same rate at which the production proceeds. The variable manufacturing costs of B are $600 per unit. These costs are also paid in cash. For simplicity we assume no variable selling costs. Demand forecasts have been developed: the maximum amount of product A that can be sold is 8 units whereas that of B is 12 units. Product A is sold with one period credit while one half of the sales of product B is received in the same period in which the sales are realized.

Additional information:

- The company has existing loans which require $2,100 in payment.
- The company plans to maintain a minimum balance of $500.
- The accounts payable balance of $900 must be paid in cash in this period.
- The balance sheet and the fixed overhead budget are given below:

Balance Sheet

Assets			Liabilities		
Current assets			Current liabilities		
Cash	$1,000		Accounts Payable		900
Accounts Receivable	6,800		Short-term loan	10,000	10,900
Inventory	6,000	13,800	Equity		7,400
Fixed assets		4,500	Total Liabilities		
Total assets		$18,300	& equity		$18,300

Fixed Overhead Budget

Expenses involving cash	$1,900
Accruals	800
Depreciation	500
	$3,200

Formulation of the LP Model

We begin the formulation of the model by setting up the objective function which is to maximize the company's total contribution margin (CM). By definition, CM per unit is the difference between the unit sales price and the variable cost per unit:

	Product	
	A	B
Sales price	$900	$800
Variable cost	300	600
CM per unit	$600	$200

Let us define A = the number of units of product A to be produced
B = the number of units of product B to be produced
Then the total CM is:

$$TCM = 600A + 200B$$

Remember that demand forecasts show that there were upper limits of the demand of each product as follows:

$$A \leqq 6, B \leqq 10$$

The planned use of capacity must not exceed the available capacity. Specifically, we need the restriction:

$$10A + 20B \leqq 160$$

We also need the cash constraint. It is required that the funds tied up in the planned operations will not exceed the available funds. The initial cash balance plus the cash collections of accounts receivable are available for the financing of operations. On the other hand, we need some cash to pay for expenses and maintain a minimum balance. The cash constraint we are developing involves two stages. In the first stage, we observe the cash receipts and disbursements that can be considered fixed regardless of the planned production and sales:

Funds initially available

Beginning cash balance	$1,000	
Accounts receivable	6,800	7,800
Funds to be disbursed		
Accounts payable	$ 900	
Repayment of loans	2,100	
Fixed cash expenses	1,900	4,900
Difference		2,900
Minus: Minimum cash balance		
required		500
Funds available for the financing of operations		$2,400

In the second stage, we observe the cash receipts and disbursements caused by the planned operations.

First, the total sales revenues:

Product A $900A$
B $800B$

The cash collections from:

$$\text{Product A} \quad (0) \; 900A = 0$$
$$B \quad (.5) \; 800B = 400B$$

Secondly, the variable manufacturing costs are:
$$\text{Product A} \quad 300A$$
$$B \quad 600B$$

Therefore, the cash disbursements for:
$$\text{Product A} \quad (1) \; 300A = 300A$$
$$B \quad (1) \; 600B = 600B$$

Then, the cash constraint is formulated by requiring that the cash disbursements for planned operations must not exceed the cash available plus the cash collections resulting from the operations:

$$300A + 600B \leqq 2400 + 0 + 400B$$

This can be simplified to form the following:

$$300A + 200B \leqq 2400$$

Using a widely used LP program known as LINDO (Linear Interactive Discrete Optimization) program, shown below

Exhibit 1

LINDO OUTPUT

```
:  MAX 600A+200B
>  ST
>  A<6
>  B<10
>  10A+20B<160
>  300A+200B<2400
>  END
:  LOOK ALL
```

MAX 600 A + 200 B
SUBJECT TO
$$2) \quad A \leqq 6$$
$$3) \quad B \leqq 10$$
$$4) \quad 10 A + 20 B \leqq 160$$
$$5) \quad 300 A + 200 B \leqq 2400$$
: GO

LP OPTIMUM FOUND AT STEP 2

OBJECTIVE FUNCTION VALUE

1)   4200.00000

Note:

CM = $4,250

VARIABLE	VALUE	REDUCED COST	Note:
A	6.000000	.000000	$A = 6$
B	3.000000	.000000	$B = 3$

ROW	SLACK OR SURPLUS	DUAL PRICES
2)	.000000	300.000000
3)	7.000000	.000000
4)	40.000000	.000000
5)	.000000	1.000000

NO. ITERATIONS =   2

DO RANGE (SENSITIVITY) ANALYSIS? >

4)	40.000000	.000000
5)	.000000	1.000000

NO. ITERATIONS =   2

DO RANGE (SENSITIVITY) ANALYSIS? > YES

RANGES IN WHICH THE BASIS IS UNCHANGED

OBJ COEFFICIENT RANGES

VARIABLE	CURRENT COEF	ALLOWABLE INCREASE	ALLOWABLE DECREASE
A	600.000000	INFINITY	300.000000
B	200.000000	200.000000	200.000000

RIGHTHAND SIDE RANGES

ROW	CURRENT RHS	ALLOWABLE INCREASE	ALLOWABLE DECREASE
2	6.000000	2.000000	2.000000
3	10.000000	INFINITY	7.000000
4	160.000000	INFINITY	40.000000
5	2400.000000	400.000000	600.000000

we obtain the following optimal solution:

$$A = 6, B = 3, \text{ and } CM = \$4{,}200$$

Generation of Budgets on the Basis of Optimal Mix

The sales budget would look like:

Product	Price	Quantity	Revenues
A	$900	6	$5,400
B	800	3	2,400
			$7,800

Similarly, production and cost budgets can be easily developed. We will skip directly to show the cash budget, budgeted balance sheet, and budgeted income statement.

Cash Budget

Beginning cash balance			$1,000
Accounts receivable		6,800	
Cash collections from credit sales			
A: (0) $900A$ = (0)(900)(6)	0		
B: (.5)$800B$ = $400B$ = 400(3)	1,200	1,200	8,000
Total cash available			9,000
Cash disbursements:			
Production:			
A: 300A = 300(6)	1,800		
B: 600B = 600(3)	1,800	3,600	
Fixed cash expenses:			
Accounts payable balance	900		
Repayment of loan	2,100		
Fixed expenses	1,900	4,900	8,500
Ending cash balance			$ 500

Budgeted Income Statement

Sales		$7,800	(1)
Less: Variable costs		3,600	(2)
Contribution margin (CM)		4,200	
Less: Fixed expenses			
Depreciation	500		
Payables in cash	1,900		
Accruals	800	3,200	
Operating income		$1,000	

Supporting calculations:

	A	B	Total
(1)	900(6) = 5,400	800(3) = 2,400	7,800
(2)	300(6) = 1,800	600(3) = 1,800	3,600

Budgeted Balance Sheet

Assets:		
Current assets:		
Cash	$ 500	(1)
Accounts receivable	6,600	(2)
Inventories	6,000	(3)
Total current assets	13,100	

Fixed assets:
Beg. balance 4,500
Less: Accumulated
Depreciation (500) 4,000
Total assets $17,100

Liabilities:
Current liabilities:
Accounts payable 800 (4)
Short-term debt 7,900 (5) 8,700
Equity 8,400 (6)
Total liabilities and equity $17,100

Supporting calculations:

(1) From the cash budget
(2) A: 900(6) = 5,400
B: 400(3) = 1,200
6,600
(3) Production and sales were assumed to be equal. This implies there is no change in inventories.
(4) Accrual of fixed costs
(5) Beginning balance − Repayment = $10,000 − 2,100 = 7,900
(6) Beginning balance + Net income = $7,400 + 1,000 = 8,400

GOAL PROGRAMMING AND MULTIPLE CONFLICTING GOALS

In the previous section, we saw how we can develop an optimal program (or product mix), using LP. LP, however, has one important drawback in that it is limited primarily to solving problems where the objectives of management can be stated in a single goal such as profit maximization or cost minimization. But management must now deal with multiple goals, which are often incompatible and conflicting with each other. Goal programming (GP) gets around this difficulty. In GP, unlike LP, the objective function may consist of multiple, incommensurable, and conflicting goals. Rather than maximizing or minimizing the objective criterion, the deviations from these set goals are minimized, often based on the priority factors assigned to each goal. The fact that management will have multiple goals that are in conflict with each other means that instead of maximize or minimize, management attempts to *satisfice*. In other words, they will look for a satisfactory solution rather than an optimal solution.

Examples of Multiple Conflicting Goals

For example, consider a corporate investor who desires investments that will have a maximum return and minimum risk. These goals are generally incompatible and therefore unachievable. Other examples of multiple conflicting goals can be found in businesses that want to:

(1) Maximize profits and increase wages paid to employees;

(2) Upgrade product quality and reduce product costs;

(3) Pay larger dividends to shareholders and retain earnings for growth;

(4) Increase control of channels of distribution and reduce working-capital requirements; and

(5) Reduce credit losses and increase sales.

To illustrate how we can utilize a GP model in order to develop an optimal—more exactly satisfactory—budget, we will use the same data.

EXAMPLE 7

We will further assume that:

• Fixed cash receipts include (a) new short-term loan amount of $1,200, (b) a dividend payment of $700, and (c) a capital expenditure of $500.

Now the company has two goals, income and working capital. In other words, instead of maximizing net income or contribution margin, the company has a realistic, satisfactory level of income to achieve. On the other hand, the company wants to have a healthy balance sheet with working capital at least at a given level. (For example, a lending institution might want to see that before approving any kind of line of credit).

For illustrative purposes, we will make the following specific assumptions:

• The company wants to achieve a return of 20% on equity. That means 15% of $7,400 = $1,110, which translates into a CM of $1,110 + 3,200 (fixed expenses) = $4,310

• The company wants a working capital balance to be at least $3,000. Currently, it is $2,900 (Current assets of $13,800 − Current liabilities of $10,900 = $2,900).

These two goals are clearly in conflict. The reason is: we can increase the working capital by increasing cash funds or the inventory. However, the funds in the form of idle cash and the goods in the form of unsold inventories will not increase profits. The first goal can be set up as follows:

$$600A + 200B + d^- - d^+ = \$4,310$$

Note that working capital balance = beginning balance + net income + depreciation − dividends − capital expenditures = beginning balance + (sales − variable costs − fixed costs) − dividend − capital expenditure. Using this definition, the second goal can be set up as follows:

$\longleftarrow$ Sales $\longrightarrow$ $\longleftarrow$ Variable costs $\longrightarrow$ Fixed expenses

$2{,}900 + \$900A + 800B - 300A - 600B - 2{,}700 - 700 - 500 \geq 3{,}000$

This can be simplified to form an inequality:

$$600A + 200B \geq 4{,}000$$

Then our GP model is as follows:

$$\text{Min D} = d^- + d^+$$

subject to

$$
\begin{aligned}
A & & & & &\leq 6 \\
& & B & & &\leq 10 \\
10A &+ 20B & & & &\leq 160 \\
300A &+ 200B & & & &\leq 2{,}400 \\
600A &+ 200B & & & &\geq 4{,}000 \\
600A &+ 200B &+ d^- &- d^+ & &= 4{,}310
\end{aligned}
$$

all variables ≥ 0

This particular problem can be easily solved by LINDO.

Exhibit 2

LINDO Output

MAX   D1 + D2   *Note:* D1 = D$^-$

                                        D2 = D$^+$

SUBJECT   TO

       2)   A $\leq$ 6

       3)   B $\leq$ 10

       4)   10 A + 20 B $\leq$ 160

       5)   300 A + 200 B $\leq$ 2400

       6)   600 A + 200 B $\geq$ 4000

       7)   D1 − D2 + 600 A + 200 B = 4310

END

: GO

OBJECTIVE FUNCTION VALUE

1)   310.000000

VARIABLE	VALUE	REDUCED COST	*Note:*
D1	310.000000	.000000	D$^-$ = 310
D2	.000000	−2.000000	D$^+$ = 0
A	6.000000	.000000	A = 6
B	2.000000	.000000	B = 2

ROW	SLACK OR SURPLUS	DUAL PRICES
2)	.000000	.000000
3)	8.000000	.000000
4)	60.000000	.000000
5)	200.000000	.000000
6)	.000000	− 1.000000
7)	.000000	1.000000

NO. ITERATIONS = 3

The GP solution is:

$$A = 6, B = 2, d^- = 310, d^+ = 0,$$

which means that the income target was underachieved by $310. Just in the case of LP, financial executives will be able to develop the budget using this optimal solution in exactly the same manner as presented in the previous section. More sophisticated GP models can be developed with "preemptive" priority factors assigned to multiple goals. For example, the goal can be ranked according to "preemptive" priority factors. Also, the deviational variables at the same priority level may be given different weights in the objective function so that the deviational variables within the same priority have the different cardinal weights. (This topic is not treated here and should be referred to in an advanced operations research text).

Summary

It is not easy, however, to develop an optimization model that incorporates performance variables such as ROI, profits, market share, and cash flow as well as the line items of the income statement, balance sheet, and cash flow statement. Despite the availability of goal programming that handles multiple objectives, the possibility of achieving global optimization is very rare at the corporate level. The usage tends to be limited to submodels and suboptimization within the overall corporate level. Thus, the use of these models in corporate modeling will probably continue to be focused at the operational level. Production planning and scheduling, advertising, resource allocation, and many other problem areas will continue to be solved with huge success by these techniques.

CAPITAL RATIONING AND ZERO-ONE PROGRAMMING

Many firms specify a limit on the overall budget for capital spending. Capital rationing is concerned with the problem of selecting the mix of acceptable projects that provides the highest overall net present value (NPV). The profitability index is used widely in ranking projects competing for limited funds.

EXAMPLE 8

A company with a fixed budget of $250,000 needs to select a mix of acceptable projects from the following:

Projects	I($)	PV($)	NPV($)	Profitability Index	Ranking
A	70,000	112,000	42,000	1.6	1
B	100,000	145,000	45,000	1.45	2
C	110,000	126,500	16,500	1.15	5
D	60,000	79,000	19,000	1.32	3
E	40,000	38,000	−2,000	0.95	6
F	80,000	95,000	15,000	1.19	4

The ranking resulting from the profitability index shows that the company should select projects A, B, and D.

	I	PV
A	$70,000	$112,000
B	100,000	145,000
D	60,000	79,000
	$230,000	$336,000

The overall profitability index for the best combination is

$$\$336,000/\$230,000 = 1.46$$

Therefore,

$$NPV = \$336,000 - \$230,000 = \$106,000$$

Unfortunately, the profitability index method has some limitations. One of the more serious is that it breaks down whenever more than one resource is rationed. In this case, the use of zero-one programming is suggested.

A more general approach to solving capital rationing problems is the use of *zero-one* integer programming. Here the objective is to select the mix of projects that maximizes the net present value (NPV) subject to a budget constraint.

EXAMPLE 9

A company with a fixed budget of $250,000 needs to select a mix of acceptable projects from the following:

Projects	I($)	PV($)	NPV($)
1	70,000	112,000	42,000
2	100,000	145,000	45,000
3	110,000	126,500	16,500
4	60,000	79,000	19,000
5	40,000	38,000	−2,000
6	80,000	95,000	15,000

Using the data given above, we can set up the problem as a zero-one integer programming problem such that

$$x_j = \begin{cases} 1 \text{ if project } j \text{ is selected} \\ 0 \text{ if project } j \text{ is not selected } (j = 1,2,3,4,5,6) \end{cases}$$

The problem then can be formulated as follows:

Maximize:

$$NPV = \$42,000x_1 + \$45,000x_2 + \$16,500x_3 + \$19,000x_4 - \$2,000x_5 + \$15,000x_6$$

subject to

$$\$70,000x_1 + \$100,000x_2 + \$110,000x_3 + \$60,000x_4 + \$40,000x_5 + \$80,000x_6 \leq \$250,000$$
$$x_j = 0,1 \ (j = 1,2, \ldots ,6)$$

Using the zero-one programming solution routine, the solution to the problem is:

$$x_1 = 1, x_2 = 1, x_4 = 1$$

and the NPV is $106,000. Thus, projects 1, 2, and 4 should be accepted.

The strength of the use of zero-one programming is its ability to handle mutually exclusive and interdependent projects.

EXAMPLE 10

Suppose that exactly one project can be selected from the set of projects 1, 3, and 5. Since either 1, 3, or 5 must be selected and only one can be selected, exactly one of the three variables $x_1, x_3,$ or x_5 must be equal to 1 and the rest must be equal to 0. The constraint to be added is:

$$x_1 + x_3 + x_5 = 1$$

Note that, for example, if $x_3 = 1$, then $x_1 = 0$ and $x_5 = 0$ in order for the constraint to hold.

EXAMPLE 11

Suppose that projects 2 and 4 are mutually exclusive, which means neither, either one of both and not both should be selected.

The constraint to be added:

$$x_2 + x_4 \leq 1$$

Note that the following three pairs satisfy this constraint:

$$x_2 = 0 \text{ and } x_4 = 0$$
$$x_2 = 1 \text{ and } x_4 = 0$$
$$x_2 = 0 \text{ and } x_4 = 1$$

But $x_2 = 1$ and $x_4 = 1$ violates this constraint, since $1 + 1 = 2 > 1$

EXAMPLE 12

Suppose if project 3 is selected, then project 4 must be selected. In other words, a mutual dependence exists between projects 3 and 4. An example might be a project such as building a second floor that requires the first floor to precede it. Then the constraint to be added is:

$$x_3 \leq x_4$$

Note that if $x_3 = 1$, then x_4 must be equal to 1. However, x_4 can be equal to 1 and x_3 can be equal to either 1 or 0. That is, the selection of project 4 does not imply that project 3 must be selected.

EXAMPLE 13

Maximize:

$$NPV = \$42,000x_1 + \$45,000x_2 + \$16,500x_3 + \$19,000x_4 - \$2,000x_5 + \$15,000x_6$$

subject to

$$\$70,000x_1 + \$100,000x_2 + \$110,000x_3 + \$60,000x_4 + \$40,000x_5 + \$80,000x_6 \leq \$250,000$$
$$x_1 + x_4 = 1 \text{ (Projects 1 and 4 are mutually exclusive)}$$
$$x_j = 0,1 \ (j = 1,2, \ldots ,6)$$

Using the zero-one programming solution routine, the solution to the problem is, as shown in the LINDO output:

$$x_1 = 1, x_2 = 1, x_6 = 1$$

and the NPV is $102,000. Thus, projects 1, 2, and 6 should be accepted.

Exhibit 3

LINDO's Zero-One Programming Output

: max 42000 x 1 + 45000 x 2 + 16500 x 3 + 19000 x 4 − 2000 x 5 + 1500 x 6
? st

```
? 70000x1 + 100000x2 + 110000x3 + 60000x4 + 40000x5 + 80000x6<250000
? x1 + x4 = 1
? end

: integer 6
: integer  ×1
: integer  ×2
: integer  ×3
: integer  ×4
: integer  ×5
: integer  ×6
: GO
```

OBJECTIVE FUNCTION VALUE

1)   102000.000   NPV = $102,000

VARIABLE	VALUE	REDUCED COST
X1	1.000000	-21500.000000
X2	1.000000	-30000.000000
X3	.000000	.000000
X4	.000000	.000000
X5	.000000	8000.000000
X6	1.000000	$-$ 3000.000000

$X_1 = 1$
$X_2 = 1$
$X_6 = 1$

ROW	SLACK OR SURPLUS	DUAL PRICES
2)	.000000	.150000
3)	.000000	10000.000000

NO. ITERATIONS = 2
BRANCHES = 0 DETERM = 11.000E 4
BOUND ON OPTIMUM: 102000.0
ENUMERATION COMPLETE. BRANCHES = 0 PIVOTS = 2

LAST INTEGER SOLUTION IS THE BEST FOUND
RE-INSTALLING BEST SOLUTION. . .

HOW TO ESTIMATE BETA USING LINEAR REGRESSION

In measuring an asset's systematic risk, beta, an indication is needed of the relationship between the asset's returns and the market returns (such as returns on the Standard & Poor's 500 Stock Composite Index or Dow Jones 30 Industrials). This relationship can be statistically computed by determining the regression coefficient between asset and market returns. The formula is:

$$b = \frac{\text{Cov} (r_j, r_m)}{\sigma_m^2}$$

where Cov (r_j, r_m) is the covariance of the returns of the assets with the market returns, and σ_m^2 is the variance (standard deviation squared) of the market returns.

An easier way to compute beta is to determine the slope of the least-squares regression line

$$r_j = a + b\, r_m$$

where r_j = the return on a stock and r_m = return in the market. The formula for b is:

$$b = \frac{n\Sigma\, r_j r_m - (\Sigma r_j)(\Sigma r_m)}{n\Sigma\, r_m^2 - (\Sigma r_m)^2}$$

where n = number of years

EXAMPLE 14

Given the following data for stock x and the market portfolio:

Historic Rates of Return

Year	$r_j(\%)$	$r_m(\%)$
19X1	-5	10
19X2	4	8
19X3	7	12
19X4	10	20
19X5	12	15

To compute the beta coefficient b, we set up the following spreadsheet and use Lotus 1-2-3 /Data Regression command, as was discussed in detail in Chapter 11.

BETA AND 1-2-3 REGRESSION OUTPUT

Spreadsheet Result for the Model
$$r_j = a + br_m$$

Year	$r_j(\%)$	$r_m(\%)$
19X1	-5	10
19X2	4	8
19X3	7	12
19X4	10	20
19X5	12	15

Regression Output:

Constant (a)	-6.51363
Std Err of Y Est	5.796289
R Squared	0.431202
No. of Observations	5
Degrees of Freedom	3

X Coefficient(s) (b)	0.931818
Std Err of Coef.	0.617886

The equation is: $r_j = -6.51 + .93\ r_m$

Therefore, the beta is 0.93

LEARNING CURVE

The learning curve is based on the proposition that labor hours decrease in a definite pattern as labor operations are repeated. More specifically, it is based on the statistical findings that as the cumulative production doubles, the cumulative average time required per unit will be reduced by some constant percentage, ranging typically from 10% to 20%. By convention, learning curves are referred to in terms of the complements of their improvement rates. For example, an 80% learning curve denotes a 20% decrease in unit time with each doubling of repetitions. As an illustration, a project is known to have an 80% learning curve. It has just taken a laborer 10 hours to produce the first unit. Then each time the cumulative output doubles, the time per unit for that amount should be equal to the previous time multiplied by the learning percentage. Thus:

Unit	Unit time (hours)		
1			10
2	.8(10)	=	8
4	.8(8)	=	6.4
8	.8(6.4)	=	5.12
16	.8(5.12)	=	4.096

An 80% learning curve is shown in Figure 1.

This example, however, raises an interesting question: How do we compute time values for three, five, six, seven, and other units that do not fall into this pattern?

The unit time (i.e., the number of labor hours required) for the nth can be computed using the model:

$$y_n = a\ n^{-b}$$

where y_n = Time for the nth unit
  a = Time for the first unit (in this example, 10 hours)

Figure 1. An 80% Learning Curve

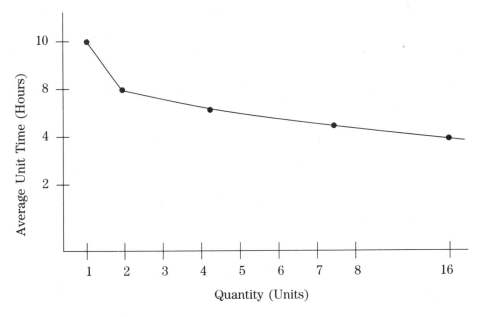

b = The index of the rate of increase in productivity during learning (Log learning rate/log 2)

EXAMPLE 15

For an 80% curve with $a = 10$ hours, the time for the third unit would be computed as:

$$y_3 = 10 \, (3^{-\log \, .8/\log 2}) = 10 \, (3^{(.3219)}) = 7.02$$

Fortunately, it is not necessary to grid through this model each time a learning calculation is made; values (n^{-b}) can be found using Table 1 (Learning Curve Coefficients). The time for the nth unit can be quickly determined by multiplying the table value by the time required for the first unit.

EXAMPLE 16

NBRF Contractors, Inc. is negotiating a contract involving production of 20 jets. The initial jet required 200 labor-days of direct labor. Assuming an 80% learning curve, we will determine the expected number of labor-days for (1) the 20th jet, and (2) all 20 jets as follows:

Using Table 1 with $n = 20$ and an 80% learning rate, we find: Unit = .381 and Total = 10,485. Therefore,

Table 1

LEARNING CURVE COEFFICIENTS

Unit number	70% Unit time	70% Total time	75% Unit time	75% Total time	80% Unit time	80% Total time	85% Unit time	85% Total time	90% Unit time	90% Total time
1	1.000	1.000	1.000	1.000	1.000	1.000	1.000	1.000	1.000	1.000
2	.700	1.700	.750	1.750	.800	1.800	.850	1.850	.900	1.900
3	.568	2.268	.634	2.384	.702	2.502	.773	2.623	.846	2.746
4	.490	2.758	.562	2.946	.640	3.142	.723	3.345	.810	3.556
5	.437	3.195	.513	3.459	.596	3.738	.686	4.031	.783	4.339
6	.398	3.593	.475	3.934	.562	4.299	.657	4.688	.762	5.101
7	.367	3.960	.446	4.380	.534	4.834	.634	5.322	.744	5.845
8	.343	4.303	.422	4.802	.512	5.346	.614	5.936	.729	6.574
9	.323	4.626	.402	5.204	.493	5.839	.597	6.533	.716	7.290
10	.306	4.932	.385	5.589	.477	6.315	.583	7.116	.705	7.994
11	.291	5.223	.370	5.958	.462	6.777	.570	7.686	.695	8.689
12	.278	5.501	.357	6.315	.449	7.227	.558	8.244	.685	9.374
13	.267	5.769	.345	6.660	.438	7.665	.548	8.792	.677	10.052
14	.257	6.026	.334	6.994	.428	8.092	.539	9.331	.670	10.721
15	.248	6.274	.325	7.319	.418	8.511	.530	9.861	.663	11.384
16	.240	6.514	.316	7.635	.410	8.920	.522	10.383	.656	12.040
17	.233	6.747	.309	7.944	.402	9.322	.515	10.898	.650	12.690
18	.226	6.973	.301	8.245	.394	9.716	.508	11.405	.644	13.334
19	.220	7.192	.295	8.540	.338	10.104	.501	11.907	.639	13.974
20	.214	7.407	.288	8.828	.381	10.485	.495	12.402	.634	14.608
21	.209	7.615	.283	9.111	.375	10.860	.490	12.892	.630	15.237
22	.204	7.819	.277	9.388	.370	11.230	.484	13.376	.625	15.862
23	.199	8.018	.272	9.660	.364	11.594	.479	13.856	.621	16.483
24	.195	8.213	.267	9.928	.359	11.954	.475	14.331	.617	17.100
25	.191	8.404	.263	10.191	.355	12.309	.470	14.801	.613	17.713
26	.187	8.591	.259	10.449	.350	12.659	.466	15.267	.609	18.323
27	.183	8.774	.255	10.704	.346	13.005	.462	15.728	.606	18.929
28	.180	8.954	.251	10.955	.342	13.347	.458	16.186	.603	19.531
29	.177	9.131	.247	11.202	.338	13.685	.454	16.640	.599	20.131
30	.174	9.305	.244	11.446	.335	14.020	.450	17.091	.596	20.727
31	.171	9.476	.240	11.686	.331	14.351	.447	17.538	.593	21.320
32	.168	9.644	.237	11.924	.328	14.679	.444	17.981	.590	21.911
33	.165	9.809	.234	12.158	.324	15.003	.441	18.422	.588	22.498
34	.163	9.972	.231	12.389	.321	15.324	.437	18.859	.585	23.084
35	.160	10.133	.229	12.618	.318	15.643	.434	19.294	.583	23.666
36	.158	10.291	.226	12.844	.315	15.958	.432	19.725	.580	24.246
37	.156	10.447	.223	13.067	.313	16.271	.429	20.154	.578	24.824
38	.154	10.601	.221	13.288	.310	16.581	.426	20.580	.575	25.399
39	.152	10.753	.219	13.507	.307	16.888	.424	21.004	.573	25.972
40	.150	10.902	.216	13.723	.305	17.193	.421	21.425	.571	26.543

(1) Expected time for the 20th jet = 200 (.381) = 76.2 labor-days.

(2) Expected total time for all 20 jets = 200 (10.485) = 2,097 labor-days.

The learning curve theory has found useful applications in many areas including:

1. Scheduling labor requirements
2. Setting incentive wage rates
3. Pricing new products
4. Negotiated purchasing
5. Budgeting, purchasing, and inventory planning

Example 17 illustrates the use of the learning curve theory for the pricing of a contract.

EXAMPLE 17

Big Mac Electronics Products, Inc. finds that new product production is affected by an 80% learning effect. The company has just produced 50 units of output at 100 hours per unit. Costs were as follows:

Materials 50 units @$20	$1,000
Labor and labor-related costs:	
Direct labor—100 hours @$8	800
Variable overhead—100 hours @$2	200
	$2,000

The company has just received a contract calling for another 50 units of production. It wants to add a 50% markup to the cost of materials and labor and labor-related costs. To determine the price for this job, the first step is to build up the learning curve table.

Quantity	Total time (hours)	Average time (per unit)
50	100	2 hours
100	160	1.6 (.8 × 2 hours)

Thus, for the new 50-unit job, it takes 60 hours total. The contract price is:

Materials 50 units @$20	$1,000
Labor and labor-related costs:	
Direct labor—60 hours @$8	480
Variable overhead—60 hours @$2	120
	$1,600
50% markup	800
Contract price	$2,400

INVENTORY PLANNING

One of the most common problems which faces financial managers is that of inventory planning. This is understandable since inventory usually represents a sizable portion of a firm's total assets and, more specifically, on the average, more than 30% of total current assets in U.S. industry. Excessive money tied up in inventory is a drag on profitability. The purpose of inventory planning is to develop policies which will achieve an optimal investment in inventory. This objective is achieved by determining the optimal level of inventory necessary to minimize inventory related costs.

Inventory related costs fall into three categories:

(1) Ordering costs, which includes all costs associated with preparing a purchase order.

(2) Carrying (holding) costs, which include storage costs for inventory items plus the cost of money tied up in inventory.

(3) Shortage (stockout) costs, which include those costs incurred when an item is out of stock. These include the lost contribution margin on sales plus lost customer goodwill.

There are many inventory planning models available which try to answer basically the following two questions:

(1) How much to order?

(2) When to order?

They include the so-called economic order quantity (EOQ) model, the reorder point, and the determination of safety stock.

Economic Order Quantity

The economic order quantity (EOQ) determines the order quantity that results in the lowest sum of carrying and ordering costs. The EOQ is computed as:

$$EOQ = \sqrt{\frac{2\,OD}{C}}$$

where C = carrying cost per unit, O = ordering cost per order, D = annual demand (requirements) in units.

If the carrying cost is expressed as a percentage of average inventory value (say, 12% per year to hold inventory), then the denominator value in the EOQ formula would be 12% times the price of an item.

EXAMPLE 18

Assume ABC Store buys sets of steel at $40 per set from an outside vendor. ABC will sell 6,400 sets evenly throughout the year. ABC desires a

16% return on investment (cost of borrowed money) on its inventory investment. In addition, rent, taxes, and so on for each set in inventory is $1.60. The ordering cost if $100 per order. Then the carrying cost per dozen is 16% ($40) + $1.60 = $8.00. Therefore,

$$EOQ = \sqrt{\frac{2(6,400)(\$100)}{8.00}} = \sqrt{160,000} = 400 \text{ sets}$$

$$
\begin{aligned}
\text{Total inventory costs} &= \text{Carrying cost} + \text{Ordering cost} \\
&= C \times (EOQ/2) + O \ (D/EOQ) \\
&= (\$8.00) \ (400/2) + (\$100)(6,400/400) \\
&= \$1,600 + \$1,600 = \$3,200
\end{aligned}
$$

Total number of orders per year = D/EOQ = 6,400/400 = 16 orders

Reorder Point

Reorder point (ROP), which answers when to place a new order, requires a knowledge about the lead time, which is the time interval between placing an order and receiving delivery. Reorder point (ROP) can be calculated as follows:

Reorder point = (Average usage per unit of lead time × lead time)
+ safety stock

First, multiply average daily (or weekly) usage by the lead time in days (or weeks) yielding the lead time demand. Then add safety stock to this to provide for the variation in lead time demand to determine the reorder point. If average usage and lead time are both certain, no safety stock is necessary and should be dropped from the formula.

EXAMPLE 19

Assume in Example 18, lead time is constant at one week, and that there are 50 working weeks in a year.

Then the reorder point is 128 sets = (6,400 sets/50 weeks) × 1 week. Therefore, when the inventory level drops to 128 sets, the new order should be placed. Suppose, however, that the store is faced with variable usage for its steel and requires a safety stock of 150 additional sets to carry. Then the reorder point will be 128 sets plus 150 sets, or 278 sets.

Figure 2 shows this inventory system when the order quantity is 400 sets and the reorder point is 128 sets.

Assumptions and Applications

The EOQ model makes some strong assumptions. They are:

1. Demand is fixed and constant throughout the year.

Figure 2. Basic Inventory System with EOQ and Reorder Point

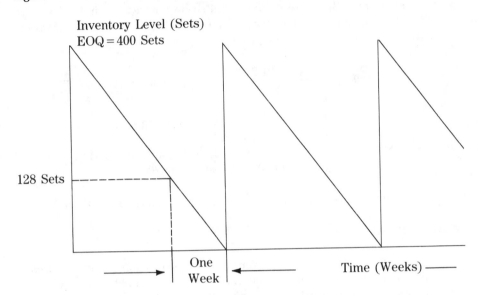

2. Lead time is known with certainty.

3. No quantity discounts are allowed.

4. No shortages are permitted.

The assumptions may be unrealistic. However, the model still proves useful in inventory planning for many firms. In fact, many situations exist where a certain assumption holds or nearly holds. For example, subcontractors who must supply parts on a regular basis to a primary contractor face a constant demand. Even where demand varies, the assumption of uniform usage is not unrealistic. Demand for automobiles, for example, varies from week to week over a season, but the weekly fluctuations tend to cancel out each other so that seasonal demand can be assumed constant.

EOQ with Quantity Discounts

The economic order quantity (EOQ) model does not take into account quantity discounts, which is not realistic in many real world cases. Usually, the more you order, the lower the unit price you pay. Quantity discounts are price reductions for large orders offered to buyers to induce them to buy in large quantities. If quantity discounts are offered, the buyer must weigh the potential benefits of reduced purchase price and fewer orders that will result from buying in large quantities against the increase in carrying costs caused by higher average inventories. Hence, the buyer's goal in this case is to select the order quantity which will minimize total costs, where total cost is the sum of carrying cost, ordering cost, and product cost:

$$\text{Total cost} = \text{Carrying cost} + \text{Ordering cost} + \text{Product cost}$$
$$= C \times (Q/2) + O\ (D/Q) + PD$$

where P = unit price, and Q = order quantity.

A step-by-step approach in computing economic order quantity with quantity discounts is summarized below.

1. Compute the economic order quantity (EOQ) when price discounts are ignored and the corresponding costs using the new cost formula given above. Note $EOQ = \sqrt{20D/C}$.

2. Compute the costs for those quantities greater than the EOQ at which price reductions occur.

3. Select the value of Q which will result in the lowest total cost.

EXAMPLE 20

In Example 18, assume that ABC store was offered the following price discount schedule:

Order quantity (Q)	Unit price (P)
1 to 499	$40.00
500 to 999	39.90
1000 or more	39.80

First, the EOQ with no discounts is computed as follows:

$$EOQ = \sqrt{2(6,400)(100)/8.00} = \sqrt{160,000} = 400 \text{ sets.}$$
$$\text{Total cost} = \$8.00(400/2) + \$100(6,400/400) + \$40.00(6,400)$$
$$= \$1,600 + 1,600 + 256,000 = \$259,200$$

We see that the value which minimized the sum of the carrying cost and the ordering cost but not the purchase cost was EOQ = 400 sets. As can be seen in Figure 3, the further we move from the point 400, the greater will be the sum of the carrying and ordering costs. Thus, 400 is obviously the only candidate for the minimum total cost value within the first price range. Q = 500 is the only candidate within the $39.90 price range and Q = 1,000 is the only candidate within the $39.80 price bracket. These three quantities are evaluated in Table 2 and illustrated in Figure 3. We find that the EOQ with price discounts is 500 sets. Hence, ABC store is justified in going to the first price break but the extra carrying cost of going to the second price break more than outweighs the savings in ordering and in the cost of the product itself.

Figure 3. Inventory Cost and Quantity

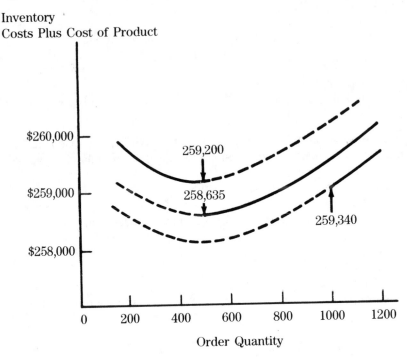

Inventory Costs Plus Cost of Product

$260,000 — 259,200
$259,000 — 258,635
259,340
$258,000 —

0   200   400   600   800   1000   1200

Order Quantity

Advantages and Disadvantages of Quantity Discounts

Buying in large quantities has some favorable and some unfavorable features. The advantages are lower unit costs, lower ordering costs, fewer stockouts, and lower transportation costs. On the other hand, there are disadvantages such as higher inventory carrying costs, greater capital requirement, and higher probability of obsolescence and deterioration.

Determination of Safety Stock

When lead time and demand are not certain, the firm must carry extra units of inventory, called safety stock as protection against possible stockouts. Stockouts can be quite expensive. Lost sales and disgruntled customers are examples of external costs. Idle machine and disrupted production scheduling are examples of internal costs. We will illustrate the probability approach to show how the optimal stock size can be determined in the presence of stockout costs.

Table 2

ANNUAL COSTS WITH VARYING ORDER QUANTITIES

Order Quantity	400	500	1,000
Ordering cost			
$100 × (6,400/order quantity)	$ 1,600	$ 1,280	$ 640
Carrying cost			
$8 × (order quantity/2)	1,600	2,000	4,000
Product cost			
Unit price × 6,400	256,000	255,360	254,720
Total cost	$259,200	$258,640	$259,360

EXAMPLE 21

In Examples 18 and 19, suppose that the total usage over a one-week period is expected to be:

Total usage	Probability
78	.2
128	.4
178	.2
228	.1
278	.1
	1.00

Suppose further that a stockout cost is estimated at $12.00 per set. Recall that the carrying cost is $8.00 per set.

Table 3 shows the computation of safety stock.

The computation shows that the total costs are minimized at $1,200, when a safety stock of 150 sets is maintained. Therefore, the reorder point is: 128 sets + 150 sets = 278 sets.

PROGRAM EVALUATION AND REVIEW TECHNIQUE (PERT)

Program Evaluation and Review Technique (PERT) is a useful management tool for planning, scheduling, costing, coordinating, and controlling complex projects such as

- Formulation of a master budget
- Construction of buildings

Table 3

COMPUTATION OF SAFETY STOCK

Safety stock levels in units	Stock out and probability	Average stockout in units	Average stockout costs	No. of orders	Total annual stockout costs	Carrying costs	Total
0	50 with .2 100 with .1 150 with .1	35*	$420**	16	$6,720***	0	$7,140
50	50 with .1 100 with .1	15	180	16	2,880	400****	3,280
100	50 with .1	5	60	16	960	800	1,760
150	0	0	0	16	0	1,200	1,200

* $50(.2) + 100(.1) + 150 (.1) = 10 + 10 + 15 = 35$ units
** 35 units $\times$ \$12.00 = \$420
*** \$420 $\times$ 16 times = \$6,720
**** 50 units $\times$ \$8.00 = \$400

582

- Installation of computers
- Scheduling the closing of books
- Assembly of a machine
- Research and development activities

Questions to be answered by PERT include:

- When will the project be finished?
- What is the probability that the project will be completed by any given time?

The PERT technique involves the diagrammatic representation of the sequence of activities comprising a project by means of a network. The network (1) visualizes all of the individual tasks (activities) to complete a given job or program; (2) points out interrelationships; and (3) consists of activities (represented by arrows) and events (represented by circles), as shown below.

1. Arrows. Arrows represent "tasks" or "activities," which are distinct segments of the project requiring time and resources.

2. Nodes (circles). Nodes symbolizes "events," or milestone points in the project representing the completion of one or more activities and/or the initiation of one or more subsequent activities. An event is a point in time and does not consume any time in itself as does an activity.

In a real world situation, the estimates of completion times of activities will seldom be certain. To cope with the uncertainty in activity time estimates, the PERT proceeds by estimating three possible duration times for each activity. As shown in Figure 4, the numbers appearing on the arrows represent these three time estimates for activities needed to complete the various events. These time estimates are:

- the most optimistic time, labeled a
- the most likely time, m
- the most pessimistic time, b

For example, the optimistic time for completing activity B is one day, the most likely time is two days, but the pessimistic time is three days. The next step is to calculate an expected time, which is determined as follows:

$$t_e \text{ (expected time)} = (a + 4m + b)/6$$

For example, for activity B, the expected time is

$$t_e = (1 + 4(2) + 3)/6 = 12/6 = 2 \text{ days}$$

As a measure of variation (uncertainty) about the expected time, the standard deviation is calculated as follows:

$$\sigma = (b - a)/6$$

For example, the standard deviation of completion time for activity B is:

$$\sigma = (3 - 1)/6 = 2/6 = .33 \text{ days}$$

Expected activity times and their standard deviations are computed in this manner for all the activities of the network and arranged in the tabular format as shown below.

Activity	Predecessors	a	m	b	t_e	σ
A	None	1	3	5	3.0	.67
B	None	1	2	3	2.0	.33
C	A	1	1	7	2.0	1.00
D	B	7	9	17	10.0	1.67
E	B	2	2	2	2.0	0.00
F	E	2	5	8	5.0	.67
G	C,D,F	3	7	17	8.0	2.33
H	E	2	4	12	5.0	1.67

To answer the first question, we need to determine the network's critical path. A path is a sequence of connected activities. In Figure 4, 1-2-4-6 would be an example of a path. The critical path for a project is the path that takes the longest amount of time. The sum of the estimated times for all activities on the critical path is the total time required to complete the project. These activities are "critical" because any delay in their completion will cause a delay in the project. The critical path is the minimum amount of time needed for the completion of the project. Thus, the activities along this path must be shortened

Figure 4. Network Diagram

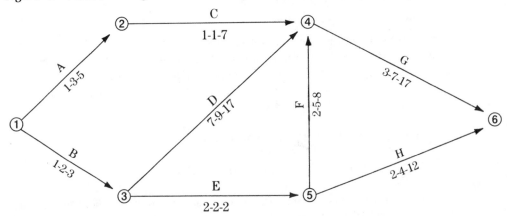

to speed up the project. Activities not on the critical path are not critical, since they will be worked on simultaneously with critical path activities and their completion could be delayed up to a point without delaying the project as a whole.

An easy way to find the critical path involves the following two steps:

1. Identify all possible paths of a project and calculate their completion times.

2. Pick the one with the longest amount of completion time, which is the critical path.

(When the network is large and complex, we need a more systematic and efficient approach, which is reserved for an advanced management science text).

In the example, we have:

Path	Completion time
A-C-G	13 days (3 + 2 + 8)
B-D-G	20 days (2 + 10 + 8)
B-E-F-G	17 days (2 + 2 + 5 + 8)
B-E-H	9 days (2 + 2 + 5)

The critical path is B-D-G, which means it takes 20 days to complete the project.

The next important information we want to obtain is "What is the chance that the project will be completed within a contract time, say, 21 days?" To answer the question, we introduce the standard deviation of total project time around the expected time, which is determined as follows:

$$\text{Standard deviation (project)} = \sqrt{\begin{array}{l}\text{the sum of the squares of the standard}\\\text{deviations of all critical path activities}\end{array}}$$

Using the standard deviation and table of areas under the normal distribution curve (Table 1 of Chapter 14), the probability of completing the project within any given time period can be determined.

Using the formula above, the standard deviation of completion time (the path B-D-G) for the project is as follows:

$$\sqrt{(.33)^2 + (1.67)^2 + (2.33)^2} = \sqrt{.1089 + 2.7889 + 5.4289}$$
$$= \sqrt{8.3267} = 2.885 \text{ days}$$

Assume the expected delivery time is say, 21 days. The first step is to compute z, which is the number of standard deviations from the mean represented by our given time of 21 days. The formula for z is:

$$z = (\text{delivery time} - \text{expected time})/\text{standard deviation}$$

Therefore, $z = (21 \text{ days} - 20 \text{ days})/2.885 \text{ days} = .35$

The next step is to find the probability associated with the calculated value of z by referring to a table of areas under a normal curve.

From Table 1 of Chapter 14 we see the probability is .63683, which means there is close to a 64% chance that the project will be completed in less than 21 days.

To summarize what we have obtained,

1. The expected completion time of the project is 20 days.

2. There is a better than 60% chance of finishing before 21 days. We can also obtain the chances of meeting any other deadline if we wish.

3. Activities B-D-G are on the critical path; they must be watched more closely than the others, for if they fall behind, the whole project falls behind.

4. If extra effort is needed to finish the project on time or before the deadline, we have to borrow resources (such as money and labor) from any activity not on the critical path.

5. It is possible to reduce the completion time of one or more activities, which will require an extra expenditure of cost. The benefit from reducing the total completion time of a project by accelerated efforts on certain activities must be balanced against the extra cost of doing so. A related problem is to determine which activities must be accelerated to reduce the total project completion time. The Critical Path Method (CPM), also known as PERT/COST, is widely used to deal with this subject.

It should be noted that PERT is a technique for project management and control. It is not an optimizing decision model since the decision to undertake a project is initially assumed. It won't evaluate an investment project according to its attractiveness or time specifications.

CONCLUSION

Quantitative applications and modeling in corporate financial management have been on the rise, coupled with the advent of microcomputers and wide availability of software for various quantitative decision-making tools. Financial managers should take advantage of the advances in new technology to analyze and solve a variety of financial problems faced by the business.

IV

INTERNAL AUDITING AND CONTROL

24

The Internal Audit Function and the Internal Control Structure

Internal auditing serves as an independent appraisal activity within an entity for the review of accounting, financial, and other operations as a basis of service to management.

Internal auditing can help improve the efficiency and profitability of the business. Proper review and appraisal of policies is essential. Audit procedures should be periodically performed on a cycle basis so that all individuals will know that the activity may be subject to audit. Where necessary, management may also request special audit reviews.

The purposes of internal auditing are to:

- Understand the nature and scope of the activity/function.

- Check on the administrative efficiency in terms of presently designed policies and procedures. At the same time, determine the extent of actual compliance with those policies and procedures.

- Appraise policies and procedures in terms of possible improvement.

- Increase efficiency (i.e., corporate welfare) by identifying any other means by which the activity/function can be made more effective.

- Ascertain the extent to which company assets are accounted for and safeguarded from losses of all kinds.

- Determine the reliability of management data developed within the organization.

Also relevant is the efficiency in which the various units of the organization are conducting their assigned tasks. Specific audit tasks should be properly communicated to staff by means of formal written documents.

589

Problem areas have to be uncovered, especially vulnerable ones. For example, the internal auditor's examination of sales, receivables and credit activities may point to poor credit policies having a negative affect on profitability.

A vital aspect of internal auditing is the appraisal of the internal control structure. Emphasis should be placed on the prevention rather than on the detection of fraud. The internal auditor should preferably be a planner, eliminating the conditions under which fraudulent activity may cultivate. If there is strong internal control structure, fraud has a higher probability of being detected.

This chapter considers the internal control structure of the company, internal audit techniques and approaches, audit programs, and internal audit reports.

A company's internal control structure consists of management's policies and procedures which are designed to provide reasonable, but not absolute, assurance that specific entity objectives will be achieved.

INTERNAL AUDITING ASPECTS

Internal auditing deals with those procedures and techniques emphasizing adherence to management policies, existence of internal controls, uncovering fraud, existence of proper record keeping, and effective operations of the business. The major elements of the internal auditor's task are to determine the reliability and accuracy of accounting information, determine whether corporate data have been determined in accordance with corporate policies and rules (e.g., manuals), and ascertain the adequacy of the internal control function. Internal auditing is the "eyes and ears of management." It deals not only with financial auditing but also operational auditing. Internal auditing should be carried out in conformity with the *Standards for the Professional Practice of Internal Auditing* and with the *Code of Ethics* of The Institute of Internal Auditors.

Besides looking at the safeguarding and existence of assets, the internal auditor must be assured that resources are used economically and efficiently. Are actual results in conformity with objectives?

The internal auditor plans the audit scope, conducts the audit, appraises the operation, communicates results to the audit manager and auditee, and follows up to ensure that deficiencies have been recognized and steps taken to address them.

The purpose of internal auditing is to assure that there is proper discharge of responsibilities. The internal auditor provides analyses, appraisals, recommendations, and relevant comments regarding the activities.

Internal auditing involves many activities including:

- Reviewing and evaluating the reasonableness, adequacy, and application of accounting, financial, and other operating information and controls. Effective controls should be implemented at reasonable cost. For example, the telephone system should give a reading of numbers called, and should "block out" exchange calls (i.e., "900" calls).

- Determining the degree of compliance with policies.
- Ascertaining the degree to which corporate assets are accounted for and safeguarded.
- Evaluating the quality of performance in conducting responsibilities.
- Determining the reliability of management data.
- Recommending improvements in performance.
- Assisting in ways to improve profit performance.
- Conducting special audits such as developing new procedures as well as the acquisition of subsidiaries and divisions.

In the audit process:

- Determining the audit scope during preaudit through the review of management reports and risk analysis. For example, the audit objective might be to determine if purchase orders are authorized and processed in accordance with policy.
- Identify applicable criteria for evaluation to determine acceptance or nonacceptance. An appropriate standard will have to be developed, such as anything over 10% is considered excessive (depends on materiality and exposure).
- Collect and evaluate information. An example is computing the actual turnover rate.
- Compare information against evaluative criteria. An example is comparing the actual turnover rate of 25% to a standard turnover rate of 10%.
- Form a conclusion, such as the turnover rate is excessive.
- Formulate and provide recommendations to solve the problem at hand.

An audit tool is a means by which the internal auditor achieves his or her objective. It may be either manual or automated. An example of an audit tool is the use of questionnaires in assessing internal control. Common tools in internal auditing include internal control questionnaires, narratives, flowcharts, and audit software. These tools serve to develop an understanding of the area being audited.

The amount of audit evidence required depends on the conclusions to be reached from the preliminary survey and the sufficiency of internal control. The audit evidence typically relates to random pieces of information applying to particular events or transactions. Flowcharting is helpful in presenting a pictorial format.

The workpapers should detail the transactions or accounts examined, the degree of testing, exceptions, and conclusions. The scope of the tests made should be described along with the details of any errors or deficiencies. A record of internal audit operations is especially important when the company does not have standardized procedures.

In a new assignment, the internal auditor will initially examine the organization chart to determine the "key" people involved. For example, in examining procurement, those responsible for purchasing, accounts payable, and treasury functions will be identified. Interviews with these individuals will be made to develop an understanding of the system.

The purpose of testing data for a specific application is to evaluate the appropriateness of current controls, determine compliance with present policies and procedures regarding data reliability, and substantiate processed transactions.

The extent of audit testing necessary depends upon the quality of the internal control structure, the areas tested, and the particular circumstances. If controls seem appropriate, the internal auditor will substantiate whether those controls are indeed operating effectively. If no reliance on the controls exists, the usual substantive testing must be carried out.

In poor internal control situations, detailed verification is required. Here, a large sample is needed. Less field work is necessary when the company has significant self-checking devices to highlight defects and alert management to control breakdowns. Of course, the self-checking devices will still have to be scrutinized by the internal auditor.

In audit testing, the actual results of examining selected transactions or processes are compared to prescribed standards. In so doing, the internal auditor will be able to form an audit opinion. Some or all of the transactions, functions, activities, records, and statements are examined.

The following steps are usually involved in audit testing: (1) determining standards, (2) defining the population, (3) selecting a sample, and (4) examining the sampled items.

Standards may be explicit or implicit. Explicit standards are clearly stated in job instructions, directives, laws, and specifications. An example of an explicit standard is that competitive bids must be received on contracts in excess of $500,000. However, competitive bids may be "rigged" by specification requirements so that only certain suppliers can compete. Implicit standards exist when management formulates objectives and goals but does not establish in particular how they are to be accomplished. In this case, the internal auditor, upon completing a review of the objectives considering the controls in place, will consult with management regarding what is satisfactory performance.

In travel, the policy of upgrading from "coach class" should be spelled out. Is there a separate travel department? Are employees abusing the "frequent flier" privilege? There should be a written policy of who may be entertained and how much may be incurred. What is the policy regarding company vehicles? The personal use of office supplies, copiers, and fax machines must also be controlled.

In proportional analysis, the auditor evaluates certain revenue and expense items by relating them to other revenue and expenses. For instance, the cost of shipping cartons should have a proportional relationship to the number of units sold and shipped.

The population to be tested takes into account audit objectives. If the purpose is to derive an opinion on transactions occurring after last year, all transactions constitute the population. If the objective is to formulate an opinion regarding current controls, the population becomes more restricted. Management wants to know if the system is working properly. If not, ways to improve it must be formulated.

In deriving the population to be tested, a determination must be made of the total transactions (e.g., purchase orders, invoices, billings). These should be serially numbered. If documents are missing, the reasons must be uncovered. The character and location of the inventory must be determined. Are transactions stratified by value or other characteristic?

Whether verifications and analyses are carried out in detail or on a test-check basis depends on the importance of the item and the likelihood of material misstatement. In test-checking, a statistical sample is selected.

The sample should be selected according to the audit objective, whether it be judgmental or statistical. Reliable selection is from lists that are separate from the records themselves. This assures that items which may have been removed from the physical units have not been overlooked.

Statistical sampling used in the internal auditing process include random, discovery, and multistage. Sampling techniques are used to verify such things as recorded amounts in the financial statements and product quality control.

The internal auditor should be assured that there is proper communication within the organization. Needed information should be available when a decision must be made and it must go to the appropriate party. The information must be clearly understood.

To develop an understanding of the structure, the internal auditor must become familiar with the operating unit or area being audited. The stages in this process are preaudit, scope, comprehending the structure, verification, and evaluation.

Preaudit. Information is gathered and the internal auditor becomes thoroughly familiar with the factual content. Departments or operational sections should be separated in the work papers and cross-referenced where there are overlapping data.

Scope. The internal auditor meets with the unit or department manager to start the operational review in his or her area. The scope and objectives should be explained. The information should be filtered down through the organization. The internal auditor should stress that the purpose of an audit is to review internal controls and assess current operations to provide recommendations to improve controls and maximize efficiency to attain the company goal of maximizing profits. A meeting with the manager and supervisory personnel may be in order, depending on the size, and the like. The following should be reviewed with the manager: organization charts, departmental budgets, policy manuals, procedure manuals, flowcharts, activities listings, forms and reports, records, and questions developed in the preaudit.

Comprehending the Structure. Based upon the information furnished by the department manager and other key employees, the internal auditor completes the applicable departmental internal control questionnaire (e.g., purchasing questionnaire). A general summary of the internal auditor's view of the existing situation and activities should be prepared for the functional unit under review. Questionnaires are reviewed and a determination is made of whom is to be interviewed. Sample internal control questionnaires are provided later in the chapter. Questions should be summarized before interviewing to assure a planned approach and to minimize interview time and maximize efficiency of the audit. You should show a desire to understand the person's job, its importance, and difficult tasks. You should review in detail the position analysis questionnaires and discuss matters requiring clarification. In the course of interviewing, a definite effort should be made to put the employee at ease and draw out his or her complaints, criticisms, and improvement suggestions relative to the employee's individual job, the department's operations, and divisional operations. You should summarize the results of the interview, paying particular attention to criticisms, complaints, and constructive suggestions to improve operations.

It is then appropriate to determine specific areas to carry over into the evaluation phase, which may require the preparation of specific worksheets for further clarification. Some worksheets that may be required are: departmental functional activity analysis, forms involved in job function, reports generated or received by department, process worksheets, and paperwork flow analysis.

Verification. During each segment of the verification phase, every situation uncovered and summarized in the scope and understanding phases of this review must be kept in mind. Refer to the summaries throughout this phase, testing each situation to your own satisfaction. Challenge every aspect of significant situations to reveal every opportunity for possible improvement.

Each area requires different techniques and amounts of verification. These will be dictated by the outcome of the scope and understanding phases. Based on departmental files and volume or population information, determine specific documents to be selected for sampling and prepare a listing of such documents to be accumulated by divisional personnel, if possible (selection of sample items), since the audit is limited to a specified time frame. Upon receipt of documents requested for sampling, enter required information and any other pertinent remarks on the sampling worksheet. While performing this step, determine compliance with policies and procedures, effectiveness of internal control, and possible areas for improvement. Before proceeding with this step, reference should be made to specific program segments for the department involved. Where specific report points for improvement in internal control, operation efficiency and so on, affect the operations of other departments or functions, the points in question should be checked and followed up with the responsible operating personnel of such other departments. Notes should be prepared, summarizing the results of the follow-up with each employee contacted. Time devoted to this effort should be charged to this audit segment regardless of the specific segment in which the point in question arose.

Evaluation. When the first four phases have been completed in each area, final evaluation should be initiated. Because of the understanding gained during the course of the review, it is extremely difficult not to form hasty opinions and initiate some preliminary evaluation throughout the review. This should be avoided. The final evaluation is the basis upon which you will determine recommendations and prepare the report, with all the facts being considered in their proper perspective. From the various data, interview notes, and verification summaries, prepare a summary of the major areas of improvement opportunity.

Work out details of report points and recommendations. Review these with other members of the audit team and appropriate divisional personnel. Restudy and verify apparent conflicts of facts or uncertain points. After this review and verification, finalize the report points and review again with other members of the audit team. When report points are finalized and there is agreement on the recommendations, set up a closing meeting with supervisors to coincide with reviews in other areas. Review report points and recommendations with local management.

Internal Audit Reports

The internal audit report should explain the scope of the review and detailed audit findings. In the report, there should be a statement of the general scope of the examination. Further, background information should be given. If limiting factors exist, they should be stated. The body of the audit report contains details of the examination, which is cross-referenced to the summary. Written reports may emphasize:

- Details of verification including reasons for and disposition of exceptions.
- Financial accounting data.
- Information of special executive interest, such as highlighting unusual or defective situations along with corrective action, which will be taken by the auditee.

The internal audit report should include a summary of major findings and recommendations. A conclusion about what was uncovered by the audit will be provided. The internal audit report must be factual, based on hard evidence.

In forming the internal audit opinion, the auditor will typically express opinions on the findings. Contrary opinions by operating management should be noted. Even though opinions may differ, a disagreement as to facts should not exist. The internal auditor's conclusion should be stated clearly with objective support.

To nonaccountants, narrative reports are more meaningful than numerical tabulations. If there is significant numerical information, they should be contained in an exhibit supplementing the report. The body of the report should have a summary of the relevant reference to the exhibit and its importance.

All internal audit reports should contain the same basic structure including:

- *Identification.* The name of the report should identify the unit or operational area reviewed. The auditors involved in the examination should be named. Give the date of the report along with the test period. Determine if the report is a regular one or a follow-up. Indicate the name of the auditor issuing the report.

- *Summary.* Highlighting the major points for management so that it is easier to identify areas requiring action.
- *Scope.* Describe the objectives of the audit work performed.
- *Background.* Provide relevant background information to understand the findings and recommendations of the audit report. Examples are sales volume and number of employees.
- *Findings.* Present findings relating to the factual information uncovered in the review. The audit findings should be given in logical order of importance, or in terms of functions, phases, or account classifications. Prior to report issuance, findings should be discussed with local (auditee) management in a closing meeting to minimize disputes. If the dispute is unresolved, the positions of the auditor and management should be given. Where corrective action has been implemented by management, that should be referred to in the report.
- *Opinion and Recommendations.* Present conclusions regarding the findings. Propose suggestions to solve the problems.
- *Signature.* Have the auditor-in-charge sign the report.
- *Acknowledgement.* Provide a statement recognizing help given the auditor by the manager along with a request for a reply to the report.
- *Appendices* (optional). Appendices should contain information not needed to comprehend the report but valuable if detailed information is desired. Examples are a listing of standards violated, explanations, and statistical information. These data should be after the body of the report.
- *Graphics* (optional). Graphics help explain material in the report including graphs, charts, pictorial representations, and photographs. For instance, a flowchart can explain how a recommendation may be implemented.

The format of the internal audit report depends on the kind of report being issued (e.g., formal versus informal), the readers being addressed, and nature and reasoning of the auditing activity. Different auditing organizations will use different report formats and divide their reports into different subsections. The format should be consistently used. The internal audit report must be accurate, concise, clear, and timely. The internal audit report should be distributed to those who have authority to take corrective action.

Audit Program

The audit program should be tailored to the specific internal audit assignment. Each work step should indicate why the procedure is being performed, the objective, and controls being tested. In-depth analysis and evaluations are required. There should be flexibility in the audit program so that a prescribed procedure may be altered or work extended depending on particular circumstances. Unusual risks should be identified and controls needed to eliminate that risk recommended. Audit findings should be stated along with recommended corrective action.

Compliance Audit

An essential part of internal auditing is substantiating compliance with company and regulatory policies, procedures, and laws. It is essential to review whether employees are conducting their tasks as desired by management. Assurance must be obtained that controls are functioning and responsible parties have been assigned. There should be written compliance directives in such sources as manuals, bulletins, and letters.

In compliance testing, the internal auditor examines evidence to substantiate that the firm's internal control structure elements are performing as intended. **Tip:** It is best to verify that internal controls are working through testing practices of the operations of the control techniques themselves instead of verifying the results of processing.

A key aspect of internal auditing deals with compliance as to accounting procedures. The accounting system must be operating as designed if reliable and consistent accounting data are to be provided. The appropriate forms have to be used in the prescribed manner.

Examples of areas subject to compliance testing are standards for data processing, controller's procedures, procurement, data retention requirements of the company and governmental agencies, security policies, personnel administration, planning, budgeting, payroll, and expense accounts.

Operational Auditing

Operational auditing looks at the effectiveness, efficiency, and economy of operational performance in the business. It examines the reasonableness of recorded financial information. The performance of managers and staff are scrutinized. For example, there should be an examination of operational performance related to payroll, receiving, purchasing, and cost control. Generally, operations should be conducted in such a way that results in profitability.

A determination must be made as to whether corporate policies are being adhered to as well as whether such policies are reasonable in the current environment or if changes are necessary. Areas of inefficiency and uneconomical practice are identified.

Some internal audit departments have engineers to appraise productivity and assist in formulating work standards. Operational performance criteria include the sufficiency of resources acquired, response time to requests, efficient utilization of personnel, proper supervision, up-to-date equipment and technology, and adequacy of storage.

Management Auditing

The management audit is a special type of operational audit. Its ultimate outcome is the same, namely to achieve operating effectiveness and efficiency. But the more immediate concern of the management auditor is more on the effectiveness of the management function than on efficiency. Management audits involve and affect management, typically all the way up to the senior level.

Functional Auditing

A functional audit looks at a process from beginning to end, crossing organizational lines. Functional auditing emphasizes operations and processes rather than administration and people. It looks at how well each department handles the function involved. Are departments cooperating in carrying out the task effectively and efficiently? Examples of functional audits relate to safety practices, uncovering conflicts of interest, changing products, ordering and paying for materials, and deliveries of supplies to user departments.

In performing a functional audit, auditors have to define job parameters, keep the parameters within reasonable range, and cover all major aspects of the function. Functional audits deal with several organizations, some where conflicts of interest exist. The advantages of functional audits are obtaining diverse viewpoints, identifying problem areas, reconciling different objectives, and highlighting duplications.

The internal auditor may be asked to engage in a special review of ongoing programs. A *program* relates to any funded effort for typical ongoing activities of the company. Examples include an employee benefit program, a new contract, an expansion program, a new computerized application, and a training program. The internal auditor provides management with cost data and the results of the program. Possible alternative ways of carrying out the function at less cost are examined.

Financial Auditing

In financial auditing, there is a determination of whether the financial statements present fairly the financial position and operating results of a company in accordance with generally accepted accounting principles. The company must comply with the relevant organizational policies and procedures as well as the laws and regulations governing the business. Work performed in an internal financial audit can be used to reduce fees of the external auditor.

Appraising Internal Control

An entity's internal control structure consists of three elements:

• The control environment

- The accounting system
- Control procedures

The Control Environment

The control environment considers the overall attitude, awareness, and actions of the board of directors, senior management and owners concerning the importance of control and its emphasis in the organization.

The factors to consider in assessing the control environment include:

- Management's philosophy and operating style, including management's approach to taking and monitoring business risks, management's attitude and actions concerning financial statement assertions, and the emphasis management places on meeting budgets, forecasts and other company goals.
- The entity's organizational structure (e.g., the form and nature of organizational units).
- The entity's audit committee and its function in assisting the Board of Directors in discharging its fiduciary responsibilities. The audit committee also should serve as the connecting link between the board of directors and the internal and external auditors.
- Practices pertaining to the delegation of authority and responsibility. Consideration should be given to the entity's policies regarding acceptable business practices, conflicts of interest, and codes of conduct. It is also important to focus on (1) employee job descriptions delineating specific functions, reporting relationships and limitations, (2) computer systems documentation pertaining to the procedures for authorizing transactions and approving changes to computer systems, and (3) assignment of responsibility and delegation of authority.
- Management control methods which include consideration of (1) establishing planning and reporting systems such as budgeting, forecasting, responsibility accounting and profit planning, (2) establishing methods that identify the status of actual performance and exceptions from plans, as well as the means of communication to appropriate managerial levels, (3) methods to identify, investigate, and rectify variances and (4) establishing and maintaining policies for devising and altering accounting systems and control policies and procedures.
- The internal audit function, which is important in monitoring the adequacy and effectiveness of other internal control structure elements.
- Personnel policies and practices, which are essential in enabling the entity to employ sufficient, competent personnel. Emphasis should be placed on policies and procedures involving hiring, training, evaluating, promoting, and compensating employees. Employees should be furnished with the resources necessary to fulfill their assigned responsibilities.
- External influences, such as enforcement of policies established by regulatory agencies such as the Securities and Exchange Commission.

The Accounting System

The accounting system enables the identification, assembly, analysis, classification, recording, and reporting of the entity's transactions as well as the maintenance of accountability for the related assets and liabilities. An effective accounting system should be concerned with:

• Describing transactions in sufficient detail to permit their proper classification for financial reporting.
• Identifying and recording legitimate transactions.
• Properly presenting transactions and related disclosures in the financial statements.
• Measuring the value of transactions so that their proper monetary value may be included in the financial statements.
• Determining the occurrence of the transactions so that they may be entered in the correct accounting period.

Control Procedures

The control procedures represent policies and procedures in addition to the control environment and accounting system that management has adopted in order to provide reasonable assurance that the specific objectives of the entity will be attained. Control procedures should provide for:

• Authorized execution of transactions.
• Safeguards over access to and use of assets and records.
• Independent checks on performance and proper valuation of recorded amounts. Accordingly, consideration should be given to clerical checks, reconciliations, comparison of assets with recorded amounts, computer-programmed controls, and review of computer-generated exception reports.
• Segregation of incompatible functions that would enable an employee to both perpetrate and conceal errors and irregularities in the normal course of his or her assigned duties. Accordingly, custody and recording functions should be segregated.
• Design and use of appropriate documents and records to help ensure that transactions are recorded in a manner that reflects the substance of the transactions; for instance, prenumbered documents that can be accounted for in sequence.

The controls established depend upon the company's size, nature of activities, diversity, organization, processing methods, and regulatory environment.

The Role of the Internal Audit Function

The internal audit function should play an important role in the monitoring of the internal control structure. The internal auditor must obtain a sufficient knowledge of the accounting system, the control environment and the control procedures in order to (1) identify the types of misstatements that could occur in the financial records and (2) ensure that the entity operates in such a way that goals are efficiently and effectively met. Since the entity's external auditors will most likely attempt to utilize the internal control structure to restrict their testing of financial statement assertions, it is important that the internal control structure be properly established and maintained.

The Cycle Approach

In setting up an effective internal control structure, management should utilize the cycle approach which first stratifies the control structure into broad areas of activity and then identifies specific classes of transactions. Accordingly, the following cycles should be considered:

• Revenue Cycle: revenue and accounts receivable (order processing, credit approval, shipping, invoicing, and recording) and cash receipts.
• Expenditure Cycle: purchasing, receiving, accounts payable, payroll, and cash disbursements.
• Production or Conversion Cycle: inventories, cost of sales, and property, plant, and equipment.
• Financing Cycle: notes receivable and investments, notes payable, debt, leases, and other obligations and equity accounts.
• External Reporting: accounting principles and preparation of financial statements.

Identifying Internal Control Structure Deficiencies

The internal control structure should be periodically evaluated in order to identify deficiencies which could adversely affect the (1) operation of the entity and (2) the financial statement presentation.

The internal audit function has the responsibility of testing compliance with the policies and procedures embodied in the internal control structure.

The illustrative internal control structure questionnaire presented in Exhibit 1 should prove useful in monitoring the internal control structure. The questionnaire is reprinted from the *AICPA Audit and Accounting Manual* (with permission). Although normally utilized by an outside independent auditor, the questionnaire is also appropriate for internal use since management objectives are clearly addressed.

The internal auditor must always be aware of the possibility of fraud. Fraud involves the taking of something of value from someone else through deceit. Fraud may involve the following:

• Failing to record sales while simultaneously stealing cash receipts.
• Creating overages in cash funds and cash registers by intentionally under-recording cash receipts.
• The issuance of credit for counterfeit customer claims and returns.

- Recording unwarranted cash discounts.
- Increasing amounts of suppliers' invoices by means of collusion.
- Overstating sales to obtain bonuses.

Possible indicators of management fraud include:

- Lack of compliance with company directives and procedures.
- Payments made to trade creditors which are supported by copies instead of original invoices.
- Consistently late reports.
- Higher commissions which are not based on increased sales.
- Managers who habitually assume the duties of their subordinates.
- Managers who handle matters not within the scope of their authority.

The internal auditor must also be cognizant of embezzlement schemes. Possible indicators of embezzlement include:

- The tendency to cover up inefficiencies or "plugging" figures.
- Excessive criticism of others in order to divert suspicion.
- Displaying annoyance with reasonable questioning.
- The continued willingness to work overtime.
- Reluctance to give custody of assets to others.
- The providing of misinformation or vague answers.

The internal control structure taken as a whole should therefore provide a system of checks and balances. As a result, no one individual should have complete control over a transaction from beginning to end. Furthermore, periodic rotation of job functions is essential. A proper system of internal checks and balances makes it difficult for an employee to steal cash or other assets and concurrently cover up the misappropriation by entering corresponding amounts in the accounts.

Key documents (example, sales invoices) should be prenumbered and used in sequential order. Additionally, custody of and access to these documents should be controlled.

All parties involved in a particular transaction or activity should receive copies of the documents involved (Example: invoice, order, correspondence). This provides an audit trail and aids in coordination among interested parties and assists in detecting errors and irregularities. Accordingly, good internal control requires standard policies regarding the distribution of materials throughout the organization. Access to inventory should be restricted.

Employee responsibilities should be monitored as far down in the company as practical. Employees will act more responsibly if they know that they are accountable and will have to justify deviations from prescribed procedures.

Transactions should only be executed after appropriate authorization is obtained. There are two types of authorization to be considered. General authorization specifies definite limits on what an employee can do without intervention of management. For example, prices to charge, discounts which may be offered and what costs are reimbursable. Specific authorization typically means that supervisory personnel must approve in writing a specific deviation from a company policy. For example, written authorization may be required for corporate expense reimbursement above a prescribed limit.

The Foreign Corrupt Practices Act

According to the Foreign Corrupt Practices Act of 1977 (FCPA), SEC-reporting companies must maintain books, records, and accounts that accurately reflect transactions. In this regard, the company must establish and maintain an effective internal control structure that provides reasonable assurance that:

• Recorded transactions permit the preparation of financial statements in conformity with generally accepted accounting principles.
• Accountability over assets exist.
• Transactions are entered into in conformity with management's general or specific authorization.
• Access to assets is only in accordance with corporate policies.

In addition, there should be periodic reconciliation of assets per books and the physical existence of such assets.

Internal auditors typically have the responsibility that the company's internal control structure is in conformity with the Foreign Corrupt Practices Act.

The FCPA also contains prohibitions against bribery and other corrupt practices.

Fraudulent Financial Reporting

The National Commission on Fraudulent Financial Reporting's Exposure Draft issued in 1987 may well lead to the largest growth in internal auditing. The report, known as the "Treadway Commission Report," defined fraudulent financial reporting as "intentional or reckless conduct, whether act or omission, that results in materially misleading financial statements.

The report identifies opportunities for fraudulent financial reporting arising when there are:

• Weak or nonexistent internal controls that arise from
    • Significant expansion in sales overloading the revenue system
    • Acquisition of new divisions or product lines
    • New business.
• Unusual or complex transactions (Example: closing an operation).
• Significant accounting estimates (Example: reserve for loan losses).
• Ineffective internal audit staffs resulting from inadequate staff size and severely limited audit scope.

A weak corporate ethical climate fosters these situations. Opportunities for fraudulent financial reporting also increase when accounting principles and guidelines for transactions are nonexistent, evolving, or subject to varying interpretations.

The internal auditor will be required to attest to the adequacy of financial reporting and also for the detection and prevention of fraudulent financial reporting.

Exhibit 1

	Yes	No	N/A

I. Control Environment

A. Management Philosophy and Operating Style

Questions—Policies and Procedures

1. Does management have clear objectives in terms of budget, profit, and other financial and operating goals?
2. Are such policies:

   a. Clearly written?
   b. Actively communicated throughout the entity?
   c. Actively monitored?

3. Does management adequately consider the potential effects of taking large or unusual business risks prior to doing so?
4. Are business risks adequately monitored?

B. Organizational Structure

Objective

- Definitions of responsibilities and authority assigned to specific individuals permit identification of whether persons are acting within the scope of their authority.

Questions—Policies and Procedures

1. Is the organization of the entity clearly defined in terms of lines of authority and responsibility?
2. Does the entity have a current organization chart and related materials such as job descriptions and lists of particular individuals which clearly identify:

   a. The responsibilities and authority assigned to senior management personnel?

Source: American Institute of CPAs, "Section 4400: Illustrative Specific Internal Control Structure Objectives and Related Questions—Medium to Large Business," *AICPA Audit and Accounting Manual* (New York, AICPA, 1990).

	Yes	No	N/A

b. Individuals specifically authorized to initiate and execute transactions?

c. Individuals with specific responsibility for custody of various classifications of assets?

d. Individuals with specific responsibility for financial control functions?

3. Are policies and procedures for authorization of transactions established at an adequately high level?

4. Are such policies and procedures adequately adhered to?

C. Audit Committee

Questions—Policies and Procedures

1. Does the Board of Directors have an audit committee?
2. Does the audit committee take an active role in overseeing the entity's accounting and financial reporting policies and practices?
3. Is this evidenced by:

   a. Regularly held meetings?
   b. The appointment of members with adequate qualifications?

4. Does the audit committee:

   a. Adequately assist the Board of Directors in meeting its fiduciary responsibilities?
   b. Adequately assist the board in maintaining a direct line of communication with the entity's internal and external auditors?

D. Methods of Assigning Authority and Responsibility

Questions—Policies and Procedures

1. Does the entity have a written code of conduct and conflict of interest requirements?
2. Are the code and requirements actively enforced?
3. Are authority and responsibility to deal with organizational goals and objectives, operating functions, and regulatory requirements adequately delegated?
4. Are employees given job descriptions which delineate specific duties, reporting relationships, and constraints?
5. Has the entity developed computer systems documentation which indicates the procedures for authorizing transactions and approving systems changes?

Yes   No   N/A

E. Management Control Methods

Questions—Policies and Procedures

1. Are there regular meetings of the Board of Directors (or comparable bodies) to set policies and objectives, review the entity's performance and take appropriate action, and are minutes of such meetings prepared and signed on a timely basis?
2. Has the entity established planning and reporting systems that set forth management's plans and the results of actual performance?
3. Do the planning and reporting systems in place:

    a. Adequately identify variances from planned performance?
    b. Adequately communicate variances to the appropriate management level?

4. Does the appropriate level of management:

    a. Adequately investigate variances?
    b. Take appropriate and timely corrective action:

5. Does the entity have established policies for developing and modifying accounting systems and control procedures?

F. Personnel Policies and Procedures

Questions—Policies and Procedures

1. Does the entity:

    a. Adequately plan for staff needs?
    b. Employ sound hiring practices, including background investigations, where appropriate?

2. Are employees adequately trained to meet their job responsibilities?
3. Does the entity systematically evaluate the performance of employees?
4. Is good performance appropriately rewarded?
5. Does the entity timely dismiss employees for critical violations of control policies?
6. Are employees in positions of trust:

    a. Bonded?
    b. Required to take mandatory vacations?

Yes   No   N/A

II. Accounting System

A. General Accounting

Objectives

- Accounting policies and procedures, including selection among alternative accounting principles, and determined in accordance with management's authorization.
- Access to the accounting and financial records is limited to minimize opportunities for errors and irregularities and to provide reasonable protection from physical hazards.
- Accounting entries are initiated and approved in accordance with management's authorization.
- All accounting entries are appropriately accumulated, classified, and summarized in the accounts.

Questions—Policies and Procedures

1. Does the entity have adequate written statements and explanations of its accounting policies and procedures?

   (Written accounting policies and procedures may include such matters as:

   (i) Chart of accounts accompanied by explanations of the items to be included in the various accounts.
   (ii) Identification and description of the principal accounting records, recurring standard entries, and requirements for supporting documentation. For example, this may include information about the general ledger and journal, and the subsidiary transaction registers, accounts, and detail records for each of the various significant classes of transactions.
   (iii) Expression of the assignment of responsibilities and delegation of authority including identification of the individuals or positions that have authority to approve various types of recurring and non-recurring entries.
   (iv) Explanations of documentation and approval requirements for various types of recurring and non-recurring transactions and journal entries. Documentation requirements, for example, would in-

Yes   No   N/A

clude the basis and supporting computations required for adjustments and write-offs.

(v) Instructions for determining an adequate cutoff and closing of accounts for each reporting period.)

2. Is responsibility assigned for initiation and approval of revisions in the accounting policies and procedures?

3. Are the entity's accounting policies and procedures adequately communicated to appropriate personnel (for example, by distribution of written instructions and manuals to persons who need them)?

4. Does the principal accounting officer of the entity have adequate authority over accounting employees and principal accounting records at all locations?

(Accounting employees of an operating division or subsidiary may report to the operating manager in charge of the division or subsidiary. In these situations it is especially important that those responsible for accounting and reporting at the divisional or subsidiary level be fully advised of tl e accounting and reporting policies they are expected to follow.)

5. Is maintenance of the general ledger performed by persons whose duties do not include:

a. Direct access to assets such as handling cash receipts, custody of marketable securities, receiving of purchased goods, and shipping of finished product?

b. Performance of functions which provide indirect access to assets such as signing checks, approving invoices, approving purchase orders, authorizing production, extending credit, and approving sales orders?

c. Maintenance of subsidiary ledgers and records?

6. Is access to the general ledger and related records restricted to those who are assigned general ledger responsibilities?

7. Are there adequate facilities for custody of the general ledger and related records?

(Examples of such facilities include fire-resistant locked cabinets, vaults, physical barriers, separate rooms, limited access to work areas, alarms, and other detection devices.)

8. Is appropriate insurance coverage maintained in accordance with management's authorization?

Yes   No   N/A

(Such insurance may include loss of records coverage and fidelity bonding of employees in positions of trust.)

9. Are all journal entries reviewed and approved by designated individuals at appropriate levels in the organization?

(The levels at which journal entries are reviewed and approved will usually vary depending on whether the entries are recurring or non-recurring, routine or unusual, accumulations of routine expected transactions or adjustments of balances requiring estimates and judgments.)

10. Are all journal entries adequately explained and supported?

(Explanation and support for an entry should be sufficient to enable the person responsible for its review and approval to reasonably perform this function.)

11. Are the individuals designated to review and approve journal entries independent of initiation of the entries they are authorized to approve?

12. Do all journal entries include indication of approval in accordance with management's general or specific authorization?

13. Are all accounting entries subject to the controls over completeness of processing?

(Examples of controls over completeness of processing include pre-numbering of journal vouchers and accounting for all numbers used, accumulation of control totals of dollar amounts debited and credited, and standard identification numbers for recurring standard accounting entries.)

14. Do all journal entries include adequate identification of the accounts in which they are to be recorded?

15. Are there adequate detailed records to support entries regarding:

   a. Amortization of prepaid expenses, deferred charges, and intangible assets?

   b. Revenue recognition of deferred income?

   c. Liability accruals and provisions relating to such matters as product warranties?

   d. Provisions and liabilities for income taxes and other taxes?

Yes   No   N/A

e. Liability accruals and provisions for such long-term agreements as pension plans and deferred compensation arrangements?   ____ ____ ____

16. Are adequate accounts and records maintained so that adjustments and writeoffs made to account balances do not impair accountability for actual amounts?   ____ ____ ____

(Examples are use of contra (allowance) accounts to accumulate valuation adjustments of asset balances, and use of memorandum accounts to control bad debts which have been written off.)

B. Preparation of Financial Statements

Objectives

- The general ledger and related records permit preparation of financial statements in conformity with generally accepted accounting principles or any other criteria applicable to such statements and reports.
- Individuals at appropriate levels in the organization consider sufficient, reliable information in making the estimates and judgments required for preparation of financial statements including related disclosures and other externally reported financial information.
- Financial statements including related disclosures are prepared and released in accordance with management's authorization.

Questions—Policies and Procedures

1. Are the general ledger accounts arranged in orderly groupings which are conducive to efficient statement preparation?   ____ ____ ____

2. Are financial reports of consolidated divisions, subsidiaries and affiliates prepared in prescribed formats which are conducive to efficient combination and consolidation?   ____ ____ ____

3. Are there adequate instructions and procedures for statement preparation?   ____ ____ ____

(Instructions and procedures, for example, may include the following:

(i) Written financial statement closing schedule with assignment of specific preparation and review responsibilities.

Yes   No   N/A

(ii) Standard forms and accompanying instructions that identify for such entities as branches, divisions, and subsidiaries the data they are to report (for example, consistent groupings and identification of intercompany amounts).

(iii) Accumulation of information on intercompany transactions.

(iv) Accumulation of information for disclosure in notes to financial statements.)

4. Are there adequate detailed records and procedures (for preparation and review) for—

a. Entries to develop consolidated financial statements such as eliminations and recording of goodwill and/ or minority interest?

b. Reclassification entries?

5. Are policies and procedures adequate for informing appropriate levels of management on a timely basis of—

a. Significant, unusual, or nonrecurring transactions or events and considerations concerning their accounting recognition?

b. Requirements of existing and new accounting rules, and of the rules and regulations of appropriate regulatory bodies?

6. Are estimates of net realizable value of assets and related adjustments to provide valuation allowances, and/ or to write down asset balances, reviewed and approved by designated individuals at appropriate levels in the organization who are independent of the persons originating such estimates and adjustments?

7. Are procedures adequate for the review and comparison of financial statement working papers to source data and a comparison of elimination, and reclassification entries to those made in prior periods?

8. Are financial statements subjected to overall review, including comparisons with the prior period and budgeted amounts, by appropriate levels of management before the statements are approved for issuance?

C. Identified Significant Classes of Transactions

1. Revenue Cycle (Revenue, Receivables, and Cash Receipts)?

Yes   No   N/

2. Expenditures Cycle (Purchases, Accounts Payable, Payroll, and Cash Disbursements)?

3. Production (Conversion) Cycle (Production Costs, Inventories, Property, and Equipment)?

4. Financing Cycle (Investments, Borrowings, Equity, Cash Collections, and Disbursements)?

III. Revenue Cycle

A. Revenue and Receivables

Sales Orders

Objectives

- The types of goods and services to be provided, the manner in which they will be provided, and the customers to which they will be provided are in accordance with management's authorization.
- The prices and other terms of sale of goods and services are established in accordance with management's authorization.

Questions—Control Policies and Procedures

1. Do policies and procedures for acceptance and approval of sales orders appear clearly defined and adequately communicated for:

   a. Standard goods and services?
   b. Nonstandard goods and services?
   c. Unusual delivery arrangements?
   d. Export sales?
   e. Sales to related parties?

2. Is responsibility clearly assigned for approval of sales orders (customer acceptance, credit clearance, and other terms of sale) before shipment or performance?

3. Are sales orders approved in accordance with management's general or specific authorization before shipment or other performance concerning:

   a. Customer?
   b. Description and quantities?
   c. Price?
   d. Other terms of sale (for example, discounts, warranties, time commitments)?
   e. Credit (account balance limits)?

Yes No N/A

(In some instances, these matters may be recorded in computer stored master files. In these instances, consideration should be given to controls over the integrity and timely updating of the files.)

4. Are all approved sales orders recorded on appropriate forms (shipping orders, work orders, and so on) which include indication of proper approval and are subject to:

    a. Pre-numbering?
    b. Accounting for all forms used?
    c. Recording in detail?

    (For example, listing in a register or log, or retention of copies of all sales orders issued in a file.)

    d. Timely communication to persons who perform the shipping or service function?

5. Are there appropriate procedures for approval of "No charge" services and services performed under a warranty?

6. Are unfilled sales commitments periodically reviewed?

7. Is current information on prices, and policies on such matters as discounts, sales taxes, freight, service, warranties, and returned goods clearly communicated to sales and billing personnel?

    (For example, such information may be communicated through approved sales catalogs; sales manuals, or authorized price lists.)

8. Is there timely communication of salesmen's commission rates to persons performing the sales and accounting functions?

    (For example, approved commission schedules.)

Credit

Objective

• Credit terms and limits are established in accordance with management's authorization.

Questions—Control Policies and Procedures

1. Do policies on acceptance of credit risk appear clearly defined and adequately communicated?

2. Is the credit of prospective customers investigated before it is extended to them?

Yes   No   N/A

3. Is there periodic review of credit limits?

4. Are persons who perform the credit function independent of sales, billing, collection, and accounting functions?

5. Do persons who perform the credit function receive timely information about past due accounts?

6. Is there timely communication of credit limits and changes of credit limits to persons responsible for approving sales orders?

Shipments

Objectives

- Goods delivered and services provided are based on orders which have been approved in accordance with management's authorization.
- Deliveries of goods and rendering of services result in preparation of accurate and timely billings.

Questions—Control Policies and Procedures

1. Are goods shipped or services rendered based on documented sales or work orders which include indication of approval in accordance with management's authorization?

2. Are shipping documents prepared for all shipments?

3. Are shipping documents subjected to:

   a. Pre-numbering?

   b. Accounting for all shipping documents issued?

   c. Recording in detail?

     (For example, listing in a register or log, or retention of copies of all shipping documents issued in a file.)

   d. Timely communication to persons who physically perform the shipping function?

   e. Timely communication to persons who perform the billing function?

   f. Timely communication to persons who perform the inventory control function?

     (In some systems, copies of the sales order may serve as shipping documents.)

4. Do shipping documents provide indication of:

   a. Adequate cross-reference to the applicable properly approved sales order?

	Yes	No	N/A

b. Customer identity?

c. Location to which shipment is made?

d. Description and quantities of goods shipped?

e. Date of shipment?

f. Means of shipment (carrier, and so on)?

g. Indication of receipt?

5. Are persons who perform the shipping function independent of the sales, billing, cash, and accounting functions?

6. Is access to finished goods and merchandise restricted so that withdrawals of inventory are based only on properly approved sales orders?

7. Are quantities of goods shipped verified, for example, by double counting or comparison with independent counts by common carriers?

8. Are shipping and performance documents reviewed and compared with billings on a timely basis to determine that all goods shipped or services rendered are billed and accounted for?

Billings and Records

Objectives

- Sales and such related transactions as commissions and sales taxes are based on deliveries of goods or rendering of services and recorded at the correct amounts and in the appropriate period and are properly classified in the accounts.
- Sales related deductions and adjustments are made in accordance with management's authorization.

Questions—Control Policies and Procedures

1. Are sales invoices prepared for all shipments of goods or services rendered (including purchases which are shipped directly to customers)?

    (In some situations, it is practical to have posting of sales orders include simultaneous preparation of such related forms as shipping orders, billings, and if applicable, salesmen's commission advices.)

2. Are billing and invoice preparation functions performed by persons who are independent of the selling (soliciting and receiving orders from customers), credit, and cash functions?

3. Are all sales invoices:

    a. Pre-numbered?

Yes   No   N/A

b. Accounted for to determine all invoices are recorded?

c. Matched with properly approved sales orders?

d. Matched with shipping documents?

e. Traced to authorized current source information on
prices and terms (for example, price lists, schedules,
catalogues, or computer stored master files)?

f. Checked for clerical accuracy by recomputation of
extensions and footings?

g. Recorded promptly?

4. Are sales invoices listed in detail?

(For example, the listing may be a sales journal, file of
invoice copies, or computer prepared transaction file.)

5. Are there suitable chart of accounts, standard journal
entries, control accounts and subsidiary records for recording, classifying and summarizing revenues, receivables, collections and such related items as commissions, and provision of allowances for doubtful accounts
and product warranties?

6. Is there a proper cutoff of sales and sales adjustments at
month end?

(For example, adjustments for shipments not invoiced to
customers, sales invoices not recorded, and sales returns
or credit adjustments not recorded.)

7. Are all credit memos (for example, adjustments, allowances and returns):

a. Pre-numbered and all numbers accounted for?

b. Matched when applicable and receiving reports for
returns?

c. Approved by a responsible employee other than the
person initiating preparation of the credit memo?

d. Recorded promptly?

8. Are commissions based on rates which are in accordance with management's general or specific authorization?

9. Is the accounts receivable subsidiary ledger reconciled
monthly to the general ledger control account?

10. Are monthly statements and specific billings sent for
trade receivables:

a. Reviewed by a responsible employee who is independent of the accounts receivable and cash functions?

Yes   No   N/A

b. Mailed by a responsible employee who is independent of the accounts receivable and cash functions?

11. Is an aging schedule or schedule of past due accounts prepared monthly by someone independent of the billing and cash receipts functions?

12. Does the credit manager review monthly aging schedules or listings of past due customer accounts and investigate delinquent accounts and unusual items on a timely basis?

13. Is there documentation of review and analysis of accounts receivable balances to determine valuation allowances (for doubtful accounts) and any specific balances to be written-off?

14. Are valuation allowances and write-offs approved by a responsible employee?

15. Are written-off accounts receivable subject to memorandum control and follow-up by an employee independent of the cash receipts function?

16. Are written-off accounts receivable turned over to lawyers or collection agencies?

B. Cash Receipts

Processing Collections

Objectives

- Access to cash receipts and cash receipts records, accounts receivable records, and billing and shipping records is controlled to prevent or detect, on a timely basis, the taking of unrecorded cash receipts or the abstraction of recorded cash receipts.
- Detail transaction and account balance records are reconciled, at reasonable intervals, with applicable control accounts and bank statements for timely detection and correction of errors.

Questions—Control Policies and Procedures

1. Is the mail opened by a person(s) whose duties do not involve any shipping, billing, accounts receivable detail, general ledger, invoice processing, payroll, and cash disbursement functions?

2. Does the person(s) who opens the mail:

a. Place restrictive endorsements on all checks as received so they are for deposit only to the bank accounts of the company?

	Yes	No	N/A

b. List or otherwise obtain control (for example, by photocopying) over all remittances and prepare totals at least daily?

c. Forward all remittances to the person who prepares and makes the daily bank deposit?

d. Forward the total of remittances to persons independent of physical handling of remittances and accounts receivable detail functions for subsequent comparison with the authenticated duplicate deposit slip and control over postings to subsidiary records?

(In lock box arrangements, customers would mail their remittances to a post office box controlled by the company's bank which would have responsibility for functions 2a–2d.)

3. Are receipts of currency controlled by cash registers and/or pre-numbered cash receipt forms?

a. If cash registers are used, is a copy of the tape given to the customer as a receipt, and:

(1) Is the key to the cash register tape compartment in the custody at all times of a responsible employee other than the cash register operator(s)?

(2) Are readings of the register periodically taken and compared with the cashier's records of receipts by a responsible employee other than the cash register operators?

b. If pre-numbered receipts are used for currency collections:

(1) Is a copy given to the payor as a receipt?

(2) Are all pre-numbered receipts accounted for by a person(s) other than the person(s) handling cash received and balanced with the daily cash received?

c. If cash collections are for payments on account, is adequate information given for accurate posting to accounts receivable detail?

d. If significant cash sales are made (as in a retail store) are spot checks made to determine that cashiers are following prescribed procedures?

Yes   No   N/A

4. Are currency receipts forwarded daily to the person who prepares the daily bank deposit?

5. Is a summary listing of daily currency receipts forwarded to a person(s) independent of physical handling of remittances and accounts receivable detail functions?

6. Do areas involving physical handling of cash appear reasonably safeguarded?

   (For example, protective windows, vaults, cashier cages, and so on.)

7. Are each day's receipts (by mail and over the counter) except for post-dated items deposited intact daily?

8. Are post-dated items segregated on daily detail listings of remittances to aid in control of total items received?

9. Are all employees who handle receipts adequately bonded?

10. Are banks instructed not to cash checks and other instruments (for example, drafts, money orders, and so on) drawn to the order of the company?

11. Does company policy prohibit the cashing of any accommodation checks (for example, personal and payroll checks) out of collections?

12. Are local bank accounts used for branch office collections subject to withdrawal only by the home office?

13. Are banks instructed to deliver charged back deposit items (such as checks returned because of insufficient funds) directly to an employee independent of physical handling of cash receipts and posting of accounts receivable detail?

14. Are bank chargebacks received directly from the bank and investigated by a person independent of:

    a. Physical handling of collections?
    b. Posting accounts receivable subsidiary detail?

15. Are entries to the cash receipts journal compared with:

    a. Duplicate deposit slips authenticated by the bank?
    b. Deposits per the bank statements?
    c. Listings prepared (initial control) when mail is opened?

16. Are the comparisons described in item 15 above made by a person(s) whose duties do not include cash receipts and accounts receivable functions?

Yes   No   N/A

Recording Collections

Objective

- All cash receipts are recorded at the correct amounts in the period in which received, and are properly classified and summarized.

Questions—Control Policies and Procedures

1. Is information captured from remittances (by mail and over the counter) adequate for accurate posting of credits to individual accounts receivable subsidiary records or to classifications concerning such other sources as investment income, rents, sales of property or scrap, and proceeds of financing?   ____ ____ ____

   (This information, for example, may be included on the listing prepared when the mail is opened, remittance advices which accompany customers' checks, detachable stubs from billings, photocopies of checks, copies of pre-numbered receipts issued for currency collections, and so on.)

2. Are details of daily collections balanced with the total credits to be distributed to appropriate general ledger accounts and to the total collections for the day before posting to the subsidiary records?   ____ ____ ____

3. Do postings of the general ledger control accounts and subsidiary records include the data on which the remittance was received?   ____ ____ ____

4. Are postings to the general ledger control accounts made by a person(s) independent of:

   a. Physical handling of collections?   ____ ____ ____
   b. Posting accounts receivable subsidiary detail?   ____ ____ ____

5. Are details of collections posted to subsidiary accounts receivable records by a person(s) independent of:

   a. General ledger functions?   ____ ____ ____
   b. Physical handling of collections?   ____ ____ ____
   c. Receipt and investigation of bank chargebacks?   ____ ____ ____

IV. Expenditures Cycle

A. Purchases and Accounts Payable

Purchases

Objectives

- The types of goods, other assets, and services to be obtained, the manner in which they are obtained, the

Yes No N/A

vendors from which they are obtained, the quantities to be obtained and the prices and other terms are initiated and executed in accordance with management's general or specific authorization.
• Adjustments to vendor accounts and account distributions are made in accordance with management's general or specific authorization.

Questions—Control Policies and Procedures

1. Are all purchases based on requisitions which have been approved in accordance with management's authorization?

   (For example, management's authorization may be general in that requisitions for certain types of purchases may be based on automatic reorder points which were previously approved. Management's authorization may be specific in that only specific employees may be authorized to approve requisitions for certain types of purchases.)

2. Are purchases made in accordance with management's prescribed guidelines for vendor acceptability?

   (For example, guidelines for vendor acceptability may be based on such considerations as past performance, reputation, and credit standing; ability to meet delivery, quality, and service specifications; price competitiveness; legal restrictions; and policies on related party transactions. Lists of approved vendors may be developed based on such acceptability guidelines. Competitive bids may be required for items over predetermined dollar amounts from a list of several designated major vendors.)

3. Are written purchase orders used for all commitments and do those orders include the vendor description, quantity, quality, price, terms, and delivery requirements for the goods or services ordered?

4. Are all purchase orders, before issuance, approved by specific individuals or classes of individuals designated by management?

5. Are all purchase orders pre-numbered?

6. Are all purchase orders routinely accounted for?

7. Are all purchase orders listed in detail?

   (Examples include a register, log, computer tabulation, or file of copies of issued order forms.)

Yes   No   N/A

8. Is there a record of open purchase commitments?

(Examples include periodic routine listings of open items prepared from a register, a file of open order copies, a computer master file of open orders.)

9. Is the purchasing function independent of receiving, shipping, invoice processing, and cash functions?

10. Is custody of unissued purchase order forms adequate to prevent their misuse?

11. Are open purchase orders periodically reviewed and investigated?

Receiving

Objectives

- All goods, other assets and services received are accurately accounted for on a timely basis.
- Only authorized goods, other assets, and services are accepted and/or paid for.

Questions—Control Policies and Procedures

1. Are all goods received inspected for condition and independently counted, weighed or measured to provide for comparison with the applicable purchase order?

2. Is there evidence that all services received are evaluated for quality and completeness?

3. Are procedures adequate for timely communication concerning shortages or damaged goods?

4. Are receiving reports prepared promptly for all goods received?

(For example, copies of purchase orders with the quantities blanked out may serve this purpose. Receiving reports may also be used to record such matters as receipt of pieces of leased equipment.)

5. Do receiving reports provide for recording of:

   a. Description, quantity, and acceptability of goods or services received?
   b. Date on which the goods or services are received?
   c. Signature of the individual approving the receipt?

6. Are receiving reports subjected to the following:

   a. Pre-numbering?
   b. Listing in detail?

Yes   No   N/A

(For example, a complete set of file copies in numerical or chronological sequence, a receiving log, and so on)

c. Accounting for all receiving reports used?

d. Distribution of copies for timely matching with purchase orders and vendor's invoices and, if applicable, timely maintenance of perpetual inventory records?

7. Are receiving functions performed by designated employees who are independent of the purchasing, shipping, invoice processing, and cash functions?

8. Is there a separate inspection function?

Invoice Processing

Objectives

- Only authorized goods, other assets and services received are paid for.
- Amounts payable for goods and services received are accurately recorded at the correct amounts in the appropriate period and are classified in the accounts to:

  (1) Permit preparation of reports and statements in conformity with generally accepted accounting principles or other criteria

  (2) Maintain accountability for costs incurred

- Access to purchasing, receiving, and accounts payable records is suitably controlled to prevent or detect within a timely period duplicate or improper payments

Questions—Control Policies and Procedures

1. Are vendors' invoices processed by designated employees who are independent of the purchasing, receiving, shipping, and cash functions?

2. Are all vendors' invoices received directly by the designated employees (accounts payable department) who perform the invoice processing function?

3. Is control established over all invoices received?

(For example, control may be established over invoices received by prompt matching with a pre-numbered internally prepared document such as a purchase order and assignment of that number to the invoice. Another approach may consist of assignment of a voucher number and entry into a register.)

Yes　No　N/A

4. Are duplicate invoices conspicuously stamped or destroyed as a precaution against duplicate payment? _____ _____ _____

5. Are there a suitable chart of accounts and established guidelines for assigning account distributions to processed invoices? _____ _____ _____

6. Are vendors' invoices, prior to payment, compared in detail to:

   a. Purchase orders? _____ _____ _____
   b. Receiving reports? _____ _____ _____
   c. Evidence of direct shipment to customers? _____ _____ _____

      (For example, copy of vendor's shipping document or acknowledgment of receipt by the customer.)

   d. Debit memoranda? _____ _____ _____
   e. Evaluation reports on services rendered? _____ _____ _____

7. Are vendors' invoices prior to payment, reviewed for correctness of:

   a. Clerical accuracy (extensions and footings)? _____ _____ _____
   b. Freight charges? _____ _____ _____
   c. Account distribution? _____ _____ _____

8. Is there documented evidence that invoices have been subjected to prescribed processing routines, assigned specific account distributions and approved before payment? _____ _____ _____

   (Examples include use of a block stamp which has been initialed or signed, attachment of a completed voucher form, attachment of copies of the purchase order and receiving report, and routine annotations on the invoice.)

9. Are all available discounts taken? _____ _____ _____

10. Are processed invoices and supporting documents approved by designated employees before payment? _____ _____ _____

11. Are there procedures for periodic review and investigation of unprocessed invoices, unmatched purchase orders, and unmatched receiving reports which provide for appropriate follow-up and appropriate financial statement accruals? _____ _____ _____

12. Are approved debit memos used to notify vendors of goods returned and other adjustments of their accounts? _____ _____ _____

13. Are processed invoices listed in detail to facilitate timely determination of accounts payable and related account distribution of filled purchase commitments? _____ _____ _____

Yes   No   N/A

(For example, entries in a voucher register and periodic preparation of unpaid voucher listings, computer prepared listings of transaction detail and master files for vendor accounts, files of unpaid processed invoices, and so on.)

14. Are accumulation of processed invoices and follow-up of unmatched purchase orders and receiving reports adequate to result in a proper cutoff for financial reporting purposes?

15. Is accounts payable detail periodically reconciled with the control accounts at reasonable intervals?

16. Are vendors' statements reviewed for overdue items and reconciled with accounts payable detail?

17. Is there independent follow-up of such matters as overdue items on vendors' statements, payment requests, and complaints?

18. Are employee expense accounts

    a. Prepared in accordance with criteria set by management?

    b. Submitted promptly?

    c. Adequately supported?

    d. Approved before payment?

B. Payroll

Authorization of Wages, Salaries, Withholdings, and Deductions Objectives

Objectives

- Employees are hired and retained only at rates, benefits, and perquisites determined in accordance with management's (Board of Directors, if appropriate) general or specific authorization.
- Payroll withholdings and deductions are based on evidence of appropriate authorization.

Questions—Control Policies and Procedures

1. Are all new hires, rates of pay and changes thereto, changes in position, and separations based on written authorizations in accordance with management's criteria?

(Management's criteria, for example, may include—

(i) support for such authorizations by written person-

Yes   No   N/A

nel requisitions which have been initiated and approved at designated levels of management,

(ii) conformity of pay rates with previously approved wage and salary schedules, and

(iii) appropriate investigation of the job candidate's background.)

2. Are methods for determining premium pay rates for such matters as overtime, night shift work, and production in excess of certain quotas based on written authorization in accordance with management's criteria?

(Such written authorization may, for example, consist of a schedule based on a labor agreement and/or management policy statements.)

3. Are all employee benefits and perquisites granted in accordance with management's authorization?

(Employee benefits may be generally authorized as, for example, under a pension plan applicable to a number of employees or specifically authorized as in a deferred compensation agreement with a particular individual authorized by the board of directors.)

4. Are appropriate written authorizations obtained from employees for all payroll deductions and withholding exemptions?

5. Are personnel files maintained on individual employees which include appropriate written authorizations for rates of pay, payroll deductions, and withholding exemptions?

6. Are the following reported promptly to employees who perform the payroll processing function:

   a. Wage and salary rates resulting from new hires, rate changes, changes in position, and separations?

   b. Changes in authorized deductions and withholding exemptions?

Preparation and Recording

Objectives

- Compensation is made only to company employees at authorized rates and for services rendered (hours worked, piecework, commissions on sales, and so on) in accordance with management's authorization.

Yes   No   N/A

- Gross pay, withholdings, deductions, and net pay are correctly computed based on authorized rates and services rendered and properly authorized withholding exemptions and deductions.
- Payroll costs and related liabilities are correctly accumulated, classified, and summarized in the accounts in the appropriate period.
- Comparisons are made of personnel, payroll, and work records at reasonable intervals for timely detection and correction of errors.

Questions—Control Policies and Procedures

1. Do employees who perform the payroll processing function receive timely notification of:

   a. Wage and salary rates resulting from new hires, rate changes, changes in position, and separations?

   b. Changes in authorized deductions and withholding exemptions?

2. Is gross pay determined using authorized rates and:

   a. Time or attendance records for employees paid by the hour or by salary?

   b. Piecework records for employees whose wages are based on production?

   c. Adequate detail records of sales for commission salesmen?

3. Is there a suitable chart of accounts and established guidelines for determining account distributions for wages and salaries and controlling liabilities for payroll deductions and taxes withheld?

4. Do records of individual employee time, piecework, and/ or commissions on sales—

   a. Permit computation of gross pay in accordance with management's criteria?

   b. Include adequate information for distribution of payroll costs or reconciliation with payroll costs charged to particular cost centers in accordance with management's criteria?

   c. Receive written approval of applicable supervisors or foremen before submission to persons who prepare the payroll?

Yes   No   N/A

(Management criteria for determination of gross pay may include such additional considerations as formulas for overtime premium, shift differential premiums, and incentive bonuses. In some situations, records of employee time or production may involve charges to several job order or departmental cost centers. Management criteria may also include additional approvals of time or production increments which result in pay over and above certain base amounts.)

5. Are total production hours used for determination of gross pay reconciled with production statistics used for cost accounting purposes?

6. Are piece rate records reconciled with production records, or are counts spot checked?

7. Are salesmen's commission records reconciled with recorded sales?

8. Are clerical operations in the preparation of payrolls verified by reperformance or reconciliation with independent controls (such as predetermined totals for gross pay and/or net pay) over source data?

9. Is a reconciliation prepared of:

   a. Payroll cost distributions to gross pay?
   b. Net pay, deductions, and withholding to gross pay?

10. Are comparisons made at reasonable intervals of pay rates per the payroll with rates per the written authorizations in the personnel files by responsible persons whose duties are independent of the personnel, payroll processing, disbursement, and general ledger functions?

11. Are such data as hours worked, piecework, and commission sales used to determine gross pay compared at reasonable intervals with applicable production and sales records by responsible persons whose duties are independent of personnel, timekeeping, payroll processing, disbursement, and general ledger functions?

12. Are the results of comparisons made per items 10 and 11 above reviewed by a responsible official and appropriate action taken?

Disbursements (Payroll)

Objective

- Net pay and related withholdings and deductions are remitted to the appropriate employees and entities respectively, when due.

Yes No N/A

Questions—Control Policies and Procedures

1. Are payrolls approved in writing by responsible employees before issuance of payroll checks or distribution of cash for net pay? _____ _____ _____

2. Is net pay distributed by persons who are independent of personnel, payroll preparation, time-keeping, and check preparation functions? _____ _____ _____

3. For payrolls paid by check:

   a. Are checks drawn on a separate imprest account? _____ _____ _____
   b. Are deposits equal to the amount of net pay? _____ _____ _____

4. For payrolls paid in cash:

   a. Are adequate security precautions taken? _____ _____ _____
   b. Does the cash requisition equal the amount of net pay to be distributed as cash? _____ _____ _____
   c. Is distribution made by persons independent of payroll preparation functions? _____ _____ _____
   d. Are receipts obtained from employees? _____ _____ _____

5. Is responsibility for custody and follow-up of unclaimed wages assigned to a responsible person independent of personnel, payroll processing, and cash disbursements functions? _____ _____ _____

6. Are procedures adequate to result in timely and accurate preparation and filing of payroll tax returns and payment of accumulated withholdings and related accrued taxes? _____ _____ _____

(Examples of procedures include use of a tax calendar or tickler file, instructions and tables for tax return preparation, use of competent tax information services, and appropriate account classifications, and subsidiary records to accumulate required information.)

7. Are procedures adequate to result in timely and accurate remittance of accumulated payroll deductions for fringe benefits? _____ _____ _____

(Examples include timely availability of information on benefit plans and amendments, use of a payment calendar or tickler file, appropriate account classifications and subsidiary records to accumulate required information.)

Segregation of Functions and Physical Safeguards

Objectives

• Functions are assigned so that no single individual is in a

Yes   No   N/A

position to both perpetrate and conceal errors or irregularities in the normal course of his duties.
- Access to personnel and payroll records is limited to
minimize opportunities for errors and irregularities.

Questions—Control Policies and Procedures

1. Is there adequate separation of duties among employees
who perform the following functions:

   a. Written authorization of new hires, pay rates and
   changes thereto, benefits, changes in position, and
   separations?   ____ ____ ____
   b. Maintenance of personnel records?   ____ ____ ____
   c. Timekeeping and accumulation of piecework and/or
   commission information?   ____ ____ ____
   d. Preparation of payrolls?   ____ ____ ____
   e. Approval of payrolls?   ____ ____ ____
   f. Cash disbursements?   ____ ____ ____
   g. General ledger?   ____ ____ ____

2. Do the personnel and payroll records appear reasonably
safeguarded?   ____ ____ ____

   (Examples include locked file cabinets, work areas with
   limited access.)

C. Cash Disbursements
Assignment of Functions

Objective

- Functions are assigned so that no single individual is in a
position to both perpetrate and conceal errors or irregularities in the normal course of his duties.

Questions—Control Policies and Procedures

1. Is the cash disbursements function performed by persons who are independent of the following functions:

   a. Purchasing?   ____ ____ ____
   b. Receiving?   ____ ____ ____
   c. Invoice processing?   ____ ____ ____
   d. Payroll preparation and approval?   ____ ____ ____
   e. Shipping?   ____ ____ ____
   f. Accounts receivable?   ____ ____ ____
   g. Cash receipts?   ____ ____ ____
   h. General ledger?   ____ ____ ____

Yes   No   N/A

2. Is there adequate separation of duties within the cash disbursement function among persons who perform the following:

   a. Control access to unissued checks?
   b. Prepare checks?
   c. Sign checks and inspect support?
   d. Mail checks?
   e. Maintain custody of petty cash?
   f. Maintain the cash disbursement journal?
   g. Reconcile the bank accounts?

Processing Disbursements

Objectives

- Disbursements are made only for expenditures incurred in accordance with management's authorization.
- Adjustments to cash accounts are made only in accordance with management's authorization.
- Disbursements are recorded at correct amounts in the appropriate period and are properly classified in the accounts.
- Access to cash and cash disbursements records is restricted to minimize opportunities for irregular or erroneous disbursements.

Questions—Control Policies and Procedures

1. Are all bank accounts authorized by the Board of Directors?
2. Are all check signers authorized by the Board of Directors?
3. Are banks promptly notified of any changes in authorized check signers?
4. Are banks instructed not to cash checks and other instruments (for example, drafts, money orders, and so on) drawn to the order of the company?
5. Are all bank accounts and cash funds subjected to general ledger control?
6. Are all disbursements and bank transfers based on vouchers and check requests which have been approved by responsible employees designated by management?
7. Are all disbursements except from petty cash made by check?
8. Are properly approved supporting documents (processed invoices, purchase orders, receiving reports, and

Yes   No   N/A

so on) presented with the checks and reviewed by the check signer(s) before signing the checks?

9. Is a mechanical check protector used to inscribe amounts on checks as a precaution against alteration?

10. Are supporting documents for checks properly cancelled to avoid duplicate payment?

11. Are signed checks independently mailed directly after signing without being returned to persons involved in the invoice processing and check preparation functions?

12. Is access to unissued checks limited to designated responsible employees who are independent of the check signing function, including operation of mechanical check signing machines?

13. Are checks pre-numbered and all numbers accounted for?

14. Are all voided checks retained and mutilated?

15. Are all checks promptly recorded when issued and listed in detail (cash disbursements journal, check register, and so on)?

16. Are details of individual disbursements balanced with the totals to be posted to appropriate general ledger account distributions and to total disbursements to be posted to the general ledger control accounts for cash?

17. Is there a written policy which prohibits:

     a. Drawing checks payable to cash or bearer?

     b. Signing or countersigning of blank checks?

18. If dual signatures are required:

     a. Are the two signers independent of one another?

     b. Does each signer determine that the disbursement is supported by approved documentation?

19. If a check signing machine is used:

     a. Are checks approved before mechanical signing by designated responsible employees who are subject to the same segregation of duties as if they were authorized check signers?

     (Use of a check signing machine allows an entity to delegate authority for approving checks to a greater number of persons than those registered with the bank as authorized signers. However, approval procedures should be sufficient to assure the official

Yes No N/A

whose name is on the signature plate that all mechanically signed checks would have met his approval if he had reviewed and manually signed them himself.)

b. Are the keys, signature plate, and operation of the signing machine under control at all times of the official whose signature is on the plate?

c. Are the employees who have custody of the keys, plate, and operate the check signing machine independent of voucher and check preparation functions and denied access to blank checks?

d. Are the checks issued to the machine operator(s) counted in advance and reconciled with the totals of the counting device on the check signing machine by someone other than the machine operator?

(Control may be strengthened by having a locked compartment on the machine which receives the signed checks and can be opened only by someone independent of the machine operator.)

20. Are cash funds on an imprest basis and:

a. Kept in a safe place?

b. Reasonable in amount?

c. Controlled by one custodian who is independent of invoice processing, check signing, general accounting, and cash receipts functions?

d. Periodically counted by someone other than the custodian?

21. Are all disbursements from cash funds:

a. Supported by vouchers which are prepared in ink?

b. Approved in accordance with management's authorization?

c. Canceled to prevent reuse?

d. Subject to a predetermined maximum dollar limit for any individual disbursement?

22. Are reimbursements of cash funds:

a. Subject to the same review and approval as processed invoices?

b. Remitted by checks drawn payable to the order of the custodian of the cash fund?

Yes   No   N/A

Bank Reconciliations

Objective

- Comparison of detail records, control accounts, and bank statements are made at reasonable intervals for detection and appropriate disposition of errors or irregularities.

Questions—Control Policies and Procedures

1. Are the bank accounts reconciled monthly by an employee(s) who is independent of invoice processing, cash disbursements, cash receipts, petty cash, and general ledger functions?

2. Are bank statements, related paid checks, debit and credit memos received directly from the bank by the employee(s) performing the reconciliations?

3. Does the bank reconciliation procedure include:

   a. Reconciliation of the balance per bank to balance per the general ledger control account and subsidiary detail records?

   b. Comparison in detail of deposits per the bank statement with deposits per cash receipts detail records?

   c. Comparisons in detail of disbursements per bank with the cash disbursements journal (check register) as to date drawn, payee, and amount?

   d. Comparison of payees with endorsements?

   e. Follow up of reconciling items and initiation of entries to record such transactions as checks returned for insufficient funds and bank charges?

4. Are old outstanding checks investigated and subjected to proper disposition (in compliance with applicable escheat laws if present)?

V. Production (Conversion) Cycle

A. Production Costs and Inventories

Authorization of Production Activities, Planned Inventory Levels, and Service Capabilities

Objective

- All production activity (including planned inventory levels and service capabilities) and accounting therefore is

Yes   No   N/A

determined in accordance with management's general or specific authorization.

Questions—Control Policies and Procedures

1. Are the types and quantities of goods to be manufactured and/or services to be provided determined in accordance with management's authorization?

   (Some examples of how management may record and communicate its authorization include approval of:

   (i) Production goals and schedules based on accompanying sales forecasts
   (ii) Overall production and inventory control plans
   (iii) Establishment of a production control function
   (iv) Definitions and policy statements on services to be provided)

2. Are the methods and materials to be used determined in accordance with management's authorization?

   (Some examples of how management may evidence its authorization include approval of:

   (i) Product engineering plans and specifications
   (ii) Acquisitions and use of property and equipment
   (iii) Procedural instructions for services to be provided)

3. Are planned inventory levels or service capabilities to be maintained determined in accordance with management's authorization?

   (Some examples of how management may evidence its authorization include approval of:

   (i) Budgeted inventory levels
   (ii) Policies on whether to produce for specific customer orders, for stock, or a combination of both
   (iii) Predetermined reorder points
   (iv) Policies on identification and disposition of excess or obsolete inventory
   (v) Planned personnel rosters of individuals with specific knowledge, experience, and skills relating to services to be provided.)

4. Is the scheduling of goods to be produced and/or services to be provided determined in accordance with management's authorization?

Yes   No   N/A

(Some examples of how management may evidence its authorization include approval of:

(i) Production schedules and forecasts

(ii) Forecasts of time requirements

(iii) Policies and procedures for budgeting individual job or project orders)

5. Are all adjustments to inventory and cost of sales made in accordance with management's authorization?

6. Are all dispositions of obsolete or excess inventory or scrap made in accordance with management's authorization?

Recording Resources Used in Production and Completed Results

Objective

- Resources obtained and used in the production process and completed results are accurately recorded on a timely basis.

Questions—Control Policies and Procedures

1. Are receiving reports prepared which include adequate information for posting detailed inventory records and allow for summarization into a source for posting inventory control accounts?

2. Are all releases from storage of raw materials, supplies, and purchased parts inventory based on approved requisition documents which:

   a. Include adequate information to be used as a reliable and consistent source for posting detailed inventory records?

   (For example, descriptions, quantities, and inventory cost.)

   b. Allow for summarization into a source for maintaining inventory control accounts?

   c. Provide a means (such as pre-numbering or batching) of accounting for all requisitions issued?

3. Is authority to approve inventory requisitions assigned to responsible employees whose duties do not include the following:

   a. Physical custody of raw materials, supplies, and purchased parts inventories?

Yes   No   N/A

b. Maintenance of detailed inventory records?

c. Maintenance of inventory control accounts?

4. Is labor effort (time, cost, or both) reported promptly and recorded in sufficient detail to be identified with applicable classifications such as job orders or allocation to units in process, and to provide for:

a. Accumulation into reliable and consistent sources for maintaining detail production control and cost accounting records?

b. Summarization into a source for posting inventory control accounts?

c. Reconciliation with payroll costs charged to the production process?

d. A means (such as pre-numbering or batching) of accounting for all labor reports issued?

5. Are transfers of completed units from production to custody of finished goods inventory based on approved completion reports which authorize such transfer and:

a. Include adequate information to be used for reliable and consistent maintenance of detailed finished goods inventory and reconciliation with applicable materials and labor put into the production process?

b. Allow for summarization into a reliable and consistent source for maintaining general ledger control accounts?

c. Provide a means (such as pre-numbering or batching) of accounting for all completion reports issued?

6. Do completion reports include indication of approval by designated individuals in accordance with management's criteria?

(Such criteria may concern completion of prescribed production steps and conformity with prescribed quality standards.)

7. Are there adequate procedures for reporting defective units and scrap resulting from the production process?

8. Are perpetual inventory records maintained of both quantities and dollar amounts for:

a. Raw materials?

b. Supplies?

c. Work in process?

d. Finished goods?

	Yes	No	N/A

e. Scrap?

f. Inventory held by outside parties?

(For example, bonded warehouses, consignees, subcontractors, suppliers.)

g. Inventory held for outside parties?

(For example, goods billed but not yet shipped, goods held on consignment, materials being processed as a subcontractor, and so on.)

9. Are the perpetual records of inventory detail:

a. Controlled by general ledger accounts?

b. Based on documentation of inventory movement and adjustments which have been approved in accordance with management's authorization?

c. Adjusted to periodic physical inventories taken annually or on a cycle basis at least once a year?

d. Reconciled with the inventory control accounts at reasonable intervals?

e. Kept by persons whose duties do not include the following:

(1) Custody of the physical stock

(2) Maintenance of the general ledger control accounts

(3) Authority to requisition withdrawals or other movement of inventory.

10. Is documentation of inventory movement accounted for to determine complete and adequate recording thereof?

11. Are there adequate procedures for identifying and reporting excess, slow-moving, and obsolete inventories?

12. Do the duties of the persons engaged in production, inventory planning, and inventory custody exclude the following functions:

a. Maintenance of detail inventory records?

b. Cost accounting?

c. General accounting?

Recording Transfers to Customers and Other Inventory Dispositions

Objective

• Transfer of finished production to customers and other

Yes   No   N/A

dispositions such as sales of scrap are accurately recorded on a timely basis.

Questions—Control Policies and Procedures

1. Are releases of finished goods inventory for delivery to customers based on shipping documents which have been approved in accordance with management's authorization?

2. Are releases of excess, obsolete, defective, or scrap inventory for disposition based on documented instructions which have been approved in accordance with management's authorization?

3. Is authority to approve instructions for the release of inventory assigned to responsible employees whose duties do not include the following:

   a. Physical custody and handling of inventories including preparation of goods for shipment?
   b. Maintenance of detailed inventory records?
   c. Maintenance of general ledger control accounts?

4. Do shipping documents and release documents for such other dispositions as sales of scrap—

   a. Include adequate information for recording reductions in the detailed inventory records, charges to cost of sales, and cross-reference or connection with source documents used to recognize revenue and the related receivable?

      (If practicable, the same document may serve as the source for recognition of revenue and the related receivable and of cost of sales and the related reduction of inventory.)

   b. Allow for summarization into a source for maintaining the inventory control accounts?
   c. Provide a means (such as pre-numbering or batching) of accounting for all shipping documents and other release documents issued?

Accumulation and Classification of Production and Inventory Costs and Costs of Sales

Objective

- Inventory, production costs, and costs of sales are accumulated and classified in the accounts to—

Yes　No　N/A

(1) permit preparation of statements in conformity with generally accepted accounting principles or any other criteria applicable to such statements.

(2) maintain accountability for costs incurred.

Questions—Control Policies and Procedures

1. Do the chart of accounts and standard journal entries provide adequate general ledger control accounts and subsidiary detail for the following:

   a. Accumulation and classification of costs of materials, direct labor, and overhead (including indirect labor)?

   b. Accumulation of information such as the following in sufficient detail and with proper cutoff to provide for adequate determination of inventory costs and cost of goods sold:

      (1) Quantities of raw materials and supplies used in production?

      (2) Labor hours and/or machine hours expended?

      (3) Quantities or units of product produced?

      (4) Quantities or units of product transferred to customers?

   (Accounts and records vary extensively among companies because of such variables as industry, company size, and nature of the production or service process. Examples of techniques to consider in addressing a company's needs include:

      (i) Identification and allocation of costs directly to units or jobs produced and to overhead; application of overhead to units or jobs using a burden rate, and a factor such as direct labor hours incurred or units produced.

      (ii) Use of a job order or process cost system or combination of both, or an allocation of costs incurred to units produced based on units sold, and the units in the physical inventories as of the closing and opening of a period.

      (iii) Identification of costs incurred with departments or cost centers responsible for incurring the particular costs.

      (iv) Use of departmental or cost center burden rates to apply overhead to production.

Yes   No   N/A

(v) Use of a standard cost system with investigation of variances.

(vi) Account classifications which provide for preparation of reports and statements in conformity with generally accepted accounting principles and, if appropriate, such other criteria as direct costing practices selected by management for internal purposes and statutory accounting practices required by regulatory bodies.)

2. If a cost accounting system is used, is it reconciled at reasonable intervals with the general ledger?

3. If perpetual records are maintained, are they reconciled at reasonable intervals with the:

  a. General ledger?

  b. Cost accounting system?

4. Are requisitions for materials, supplies, finished goods, and physical transfers of inventory subjected to the following:

  a. Review to determine that requisitions are completed and approved in accordance with management's authorization?

  b. Accounting for all requisitions used?

  (For example, by accounting for all numbers preassigned to particular types of requisition forms.)

  c. Summarization of requisitions at reasonable intervals for consistent and timely maintenance of control accounts?

  d. Accurate and timely recording in the subsidiary detail records?

5. Are reports of direct and indirect labor effort (for example: job tickets, time cards, and so on) subjected to the following:

  a. Review to determine that the reports are completed and approved in accordance with criteria authorized by management?

  b. Accounting for all reports issued?

  (For example, by accounting for all numbers preassigned to particular types of reporting forms.)

  c. Reconciliation with account distribution of payroll

Yes   No   N/A

for consistent and timely maintenance of the control accounts?

d. Accurate and timely recording in the subsidiary detail records?

6. Are the detailed inventory records and control accounts adjusted for reports of excess, slow-moving, and obsolete inventories in accordance with management's general or specific authorization?

7. Are burden rates and amounts of overhead applied to production compared at reasonable intervals with actual overhead costs incurred and updated in accordance with management's authorization?

8. For standard cost systems:

a. Are standard rates and volume compared at reasonable intervals with actual costs and activity and revised accordingly for changes in underlying conditions?

(For example, comparison of raw material costs with vendors' invoices, standard labor rates with actual rates, standard materials usage and machine hours with product engineering changes, standard labor hours with time studies, and so on.)

b. Are significant variances investigated and the resulting explanation brought to management's attention on a timely basis?

9. Do the duties of persons who maintain the detailed inventory and cost accounting records exclude the following functions:

a. Physical custody and handling of inventories?

b. Maintenance of the general ledger control accounts?

10. Is access to the detailed inventory records and control accounts limited to persons responsible for their maintenance, oversight, and internal audit?

11. Are the inventory detail records and control accounts adjusted to physical counts at least annually?

Inventory Safeguarding

Objectives

- Inventory is protected from unauthorized use or removal.
- Access to inventory, property, cost, and production re-

Yes   No   N/A

cords is limited to designated individuals in accordance with management authority so that unauthorized dispositions may be prevented or detected within a timely period.

Questions—Control Policies and Procedures

1. Do physical safeguards of inventory appear reasonably adequate in relation to the materiality of the inventory and its susceptibility to theft?

(Examples include:

- Fenced areas,
- Restricted-access storerooms or vaults,
- Guards,
- Detection and scanning devices (for example, alarms, television cameras),
- Inspection of personnel,
- Independent storeroom clerks,
- Maximum visibility by supervisors and security personnel of work and storage areas.)

2. Does inventory appear reasonably protected from physical deterioration?

(Examples include:

- Shelters and buildings,
- Maintenance of environment at appropriate temperature and humidity,
- Containers and storage facilities.)

3. Are persons responsible for custody of inventory independent of inventory recording, cost accounting, and general accounting functions?

4. Is insurance coverage of the inventory maintained and reviewed in accordance with management's authorization?

Physical Counts of Inventory

Objective

- Recorded balances of inventory are substantiated and evaluated at reasonable intervals by comparison with and evaluation of actual quantities on hand. (For example, physical counts and review for excess, slow-moving, and obsolete stock.)

Yes   No   N/A

Questions—Control Policies and Procedures

1. Is inventory subjected to physical count at least annually?

2. If the complete physical count is made at other than the fiscal year end are the controls over physical movement (receipts, internal transfers, and shipments) of inventory, accuracy of recording cutoffs and segregation of duties satisfactory for such timing?

3. If counts are made on a cycle basis rather than as complete counts, are all of the following conditions present for classes of inventory subjected to cycle counts?

   a. Complete and accurate perpetual records which are maintained on a timely basis?

   b. The nature of the inventory items allows for practicable comparison with perpetual records?

   c. Adequate control over physical movement of inventories (receipts, internal transfers, and shipments) and accurate recording of cutoffs to provide timely and accurate source data for maintaining the perpetual records and clear identification of classes or groups of items to be counted?

   d. Sufficient segregation of duties so that errors of omission or commission are prevented or detected promptly?

4. Do detailed written inventory procedures and instructions exist which have been approved in accordance with management's authorization before issuance and use?

5. Do the inventory procedures adequately address the following matters:

   a. Location and orderly physical arrangement of inventories?

   b. Identification and description of the inventories by persons familiar with it?

   c. Segregation and proper identification of goods that are not property of the client, such as customers' goods and goods held on consignment?

   d. Method of determining quantities such as weight, count, or measure?

   e. Recording of items on count sheets or tickets including complete descriptions, identifying codes (serial numbers, model numbers), as well as quantities counted?

	Yes	No	N/A

f. Special considerations for work in process such as identifying stage of completion?

g. Identification of stock counted to determine whether all items are counted and to preclude duplicate counting?

h. Cutoff of receipts, internal transfers, and shipments?

i. Control of physical inventory records, such as pre-numbering of all count sheets, count tickets, and accounting for all numbered records issued and used?

j. Identification of slow-moving, obsolete, and damaged items?

k. Substantiation of inventories held by others?

l. Pricing, extension, and summarization of the physical counts?

m. Investigation and disposition of differences between physical counts and detailed inventory records?

6. Are physical count procedures supervised by a responsible official whose duties do not include physical custody of inventories and performance of purchasing, receiving, and shipping functions?

7. Are inventory instructions adequately communicated to and understood by persons who perform the physical counts?

8. Are physical counts performed by persons whose duties do not include the following:

a. Physical custody of inventories?

b. Detailed inventory record keeping (maintaining perpetual records)?

c. Maintenance of inventory control account(s)?

9. Is inventory movement adequately controlled during the count so that items are not missed or double-counted because of:

a. Receiving activity?

b. Internal inventory movement?

c. Shipping activity?

10. Are controls over purchases and receiving activity sufficient to result in recording of liabilities for any items included in inventory which have not been paid for?

11. Are controls over sales and shipping activity sufficient to result in exclusion from the physical inventory of any items which have been sold and billed but not yet shipped?

Yes   No   N/A

12. Are inventory counts subject to adequate verification such as recounts by persons other than those who made the initial counts or spot checks by others, such as internal auditors?

13. Are pricing, extension, and summarization of the physical counts performed by persons whose duties do not include the following:

    a. Physical custody of inventories?
    b. Detailed inventory record keeping?
    c. Maintenance of the inventory control accounts?

14. Are pricing, extension, and summarization of the physical counts subject to adequate verification such as reperformance by persons other than those who initially performed the tasks on a complete or test basis?

15. Are differences between physical counts and detailed inventory records investigated in accordance with management's authorization before the records are adjusted?

16. Is there documentation of review and analysis of the physical inventory to:

    a. Conform with the lower of cost or market principle,
    b. Identify items which are excessive, slow-moving, defective or obsolete,
    c. Determine the need for adjustments or valuation allowances?

17. Are adjustments of the inventory detail records and control accounts given prior approval in accordance with management's authorization?

18. Are dispositions of obsolete or excess inventories and scrap made in accordance with criteria authorized by management?

B. Property and Equipment

Initiation and Execution of Property and Equipment Transactions

Objective

- Additions and related accumulation of depreciation or amortization, retirements, and dispositions of property and equipment (owned and leased) are made in accordance with management's authorization.

Yes   No   N/A

Questions—Control Policies and Procedures

1. Is advance approval in accordance with management's criteria required for all property and equipment transactions?

   (For significant additions (purchases or leases) approval authority may be kept at such levels as the Board of Directors. In some closely held entities, authority for such approval may be reserved by the stockholders or partners. Some entities, however, may have a framework of policies and procedures within which general authority for property and equipment transactions within certain dollar limits may be delegated to management levels below the Board of Directors. It is desirable that such policies be clearly expressed and documented.)

2. Are requests for additions, transfers, major maintenance and repair, retirement and disposition of property and equipment—

   a. Initiated by designated individuals in accordance with management's authorization?

      (These individuals generally are responsible employees or officials in the department which would use the asset.)

   b. Formally documented, including an adequate description of the proposal, its reasons, and the estimated amount of the transaction?

      (Some entities may use standardized forms to document requests for property and equipment transactions including signatures of employees who initiated and approved the request.)

   c. Reviewed for key considerations in accordance with management's criteria?

      (Key considerations may include such issues as:

      (i) Whether to make or buy the asset.
      (ii) Selection of vendors, prices, and terms including consideration of soliciting competitive bids.
      (iii) Selection among financing alternatives such as use of internally generated funds, entering debt or lease agreements, and issuing preferred or common stock.

Yes   No   N/

(iv) Accounting matters, such as whether the transaction should be capitalized or expensed, classification of leases, determination of estimated
useful life, salvage value, and methods of depreciation or amortization.)

d. Approval at a higher level than the department or
official who initiated the request?   ____ ____ ____

3. Are authorizations to execute property and equipment
transactions adequately documented?   ____ ____ ____

(Following are some examples of such documentation:

(i) Decisions recorded in meetings of the Board of
Directors or finance committee accompanied by
relevant detailed proposals and cost-benefit analyses which may be part of the minutes by reference.

(ii) Work order forms approved by designated individuals in accordance with clearly stated management
criteria.

(iii) Contracts and agreements signed by individuals in
accordance with appropriately documented designation by the Board of Directors.)

4. Are procedures adequate for determining that components and services for property and equipment are re-
ceived or performed?   ____ ____ ____

(Examples include status or completion reports prepared by architects and engineers and approved in accordance with management's authorization; or transactions processed through the company's normal
purchasing procedures.)

5. Are procedures adequate for determining that all dispositions of property and equipment have been executed
and proceeds, if any, received in accordance with man-
agement's authorization?   ____ ____ ____

Recording Property and Equipment and Related Depreciation and Amortization

Objective

• Transactions involving property and equipment and related depreciation and/or amortization are accurately
recorded, accumulated, and classified in detail and in
control accounts to—

Yes   No   N/A

(1) permit preparation of statements in conformity with generally accepted accounting principles or other criteria applicable to such statements, and

(2) maintain accountability for assets.

Questions—Control Policies and Procedure

1. Are detailed records maintained for the classes of property and equipment (owned and leased) which present:

   a. Description of specific assets, their location, and if applicable, such specific identification as serial or other control numbers?

   b. Cost, acquisition date, and date placed in service (if different from acquisition date)?

   c. Depreciable or amortizable life and method of depreciation or amortization?

      (1) For financial reporting purposes?

      (2) For tax purposes if different from financial reporting?

   d. Estimated salvage value and amount subject to depreciation or amortization?

   e. Amount of related accumulated depreciation or amortization?

2. Are general ledger control accounts maintained for the appropriate classes of owned and leased property and equipment and related depreciation and amortization?

3. Are responsibilities for maintaining the detailed property records segregated from those of—

   a. Maintaining the general ledger control accounts?

   b. Custody of property and equipment?

4. Do persons who maintain the detail records and control accounts receive timely and adequate information about—

   a. Additions, transfers, retirement from service, and dispositions of property and equipment?

   b. Depreciable (or amortizable) lives and methods of depreciation or amortization as prescribed in accordance with management's authorization?

5. Are the detailed property and equipment records reconciled at reasonable intervals with the control accounts and differences, if any, investigated and resolved in accordance with management's authorization?

Yes   No   N/

6. Are depreciable and amortizable lives reviewed at reasonable intervals for adequacy in relation to use or obsolescence based on actual experience?

Safeguarding Property and Equipment

Objective

- Property and equipment is reasonably safeguarded from loss.

Questions—Control Policies and Procedures

1. Is property and equipment insured in accordance with management's authorization based on appraisals made at reasonable intervals?
2. Are items of property and equipment (owned and leased) subject to reasonably adequate physical protection techniques?

   (Examples of such techniques include fire alarms and extinguishers, fences, security guards, burglar alarms, limited access, and requisitioning procedures for use of portable equipment, and so on.)

3. Is responsibility for physical custody of property and equipment assigned to employees whose duties are independent of:

   a. Maintaining detailed property records?
   b. General ledger functions?

4. Are items of property and equipment (owned and leased) physically inspected at reasonable intervals and compared with the detailed property records?

   (This may be done in coordination with appraisals made to determine insurable values.)

5. Are documents of title and property rights, such as deeds and leases, in the custody of a responsible employee whose duties do not include maintenance of the detailed property records or physical custody of the assets?
6. Are documents of title and property rights compared with the detailed property records at reasonable intervals by persons whose duties do not include the following:

   a. Custody of such documents?
   b. Maintenance of the detailed property and equipment records?

Yes No N/A

VI. Financing (Treasury) Cycle

A. Investments
Authorization of Investment Transactions

Objective

- The nature and terms of investment transactions (marketable securities, notes receivable, and long-term debt or equity investments) are made in accordance with management's authorization.

Questions—Control Policies and Procedures

1. Are investment transactions initiated and approved in accordance with management authorization?

   (If investments are infrequent and significant, management may deal with each purchase or sale on a case by case basis with approval exercised by the board of directors or a finance committee. If investment transactions are relatively frequent, management may establish standard policies and procedures for initiation and approval of investment transactions.)

2. Are investment transactions approved before execution by responsible officials other than those who proposed the transactions?

   (For example, a transaction may be proposed by the chief executive officer and executed after authorization and approval by the Board of Directors. Another example would be purchases of treasury bills by the chief financial officer pursuant to authorization by the Board of Directors.)

3. Are investment transactions initiated and approved by persons whose duties do not include:

   a. Accounting for investment transactions?
   b. Custody of investment securities?

4. Are initiation and approval of investment transactions adequately documented?

5. Are brokers advices and other evidence of execution of transactions promptly compared with documented authorizations and differences brought to the timely attention of management?

Yes   No   N/

Recording and Classifying Investment Transactions

Objective

- Investment transactions, including accrual and collection of related income, are recorded at the correct amounts in the accounting periods in which they were executed or earned, and properly classified in the accounts.

Questions—Control Policies and Procedures

1. Are adequate general ledger control accounts maintained for various investment classifications and related income?

2. Are adequate detailed investment records maintained currently including control of related income?

3. Are procedures adequate to determine that investment income (interest, dividends) is properly accrued and promptly collected?

   (Examples of these procedures include comparison of interest accrued with terms of the securities or loan agreements and interest income received, or comparison of dividend income with published dividend records or reports by the investee.)

4. Are the detailed investment records reconciled with the general ledger control accounts, including related income, by persons whose duties do not include:

   a. Maintenance of the detailed investment records?
   b. Maintenance of the general ledger?
   c. Physical custody of the investment securities?

5. Are investments and related collateral reviewed and appraised or valued at market at reasonable intervals for comparison with cost valuations and—

   a. Reporting of the findings to management?
   b. Determination of need for any valuation allowances?

Physical Safeguards and Custodial Accountability

Objective

- Documents evidencing ownership of investments and related collateral, and other investment records are subjected to reasonably adequate physical safeguards and effective custodial accountability procedures.

Yes   No   N/A

Questions—Control Policies and Procedures

1. Are investment securities and related collateral subject to reasonably adequate physical safeguards?

   (Examples include use of safe deposit boxes and/or vaults which require two individuals to gain access; custodial accounts with banks and trust companies, and accounts with brokers.)

2. Are investment securities, except for bearer securities, registered in the name of the company or nominees designated in accordance with management's authorization?

3. If an independent custodian is used, has the custodian been approved by the Board of Directors?

4. Is custody of investment securities held by the company assigned to designated bonded employees whose duties do not include:

   a. Maintenance of detailed investment records?
   b. Maintenance of general ledger control accounts?
   c. Cash receipts and disbursement functions?

5. Is authority to withdraw investment securities from custody limited to written authorization and joint signatures of responsible officials whose duties do not include:

   a. Custody of investment securities?
   b. Maintenance of detailed investment records?

6. Are investment securities examined at reasonable intervals and compared with detailed investment records by responsible persons whose duties do not include:

   a. Custody of the investment securities?
   b. Maintenance of the detailed investment records?
   c. Maintenance of the general ledger control accounts?
   d. Cash functions?

B. Borrowing (Debt and Leases)

Authorization of Debt and Other Borrowing Arrangements

Objective

• All debt and other borrowing arrangements (such as leases) are initiated and executed in accordance with management's authorization.

Yes   No   N/A

Questions—Control Policies and Procedures

1. Are debt and other borrowing arrangements initiated and approved in accordance with management authorization?

2. Are authorizations for specific debt and other borrowings recorded?

   (Authorizations may be recorded, for example, as decisions in the minutes of Board of Directors' meetings, finance committee meetings, or partners' meetings.)

3. Do the authorizations specify:

   a. The officials authorized to negotiate debt and leases?
   b. The maximum commitments such officials can make?
   c. Property which may be pledged to collateralize debt?
   d. Covenants which may be made to obtain the loan or lease?

      (Some entities may require that all loan and other borrowing agreements be reviewed by legal counsel before signing.)

4. Are the signatures of two authorized officials required to execute debt instruments or leases?

5. Do procedures appear adequate for initiating proposed debt and lease transactions?

   (In some entities, debt and lease transactions may be infrequent and of such significance that management participates directly in the proposal and approval process on a case by case basis using specialized assistance where appropriate. In other entities, there may be regular procedures concerning matters such as:

   (i) Study of alternatives such as debt, lease or equity financing.
   (ii) Review of corporate charter, bylaws, and covenants of existing debt and lease agreements and obtaining appropriate advice from legal counsel.
   (iii) Review of financial forecasts, tax and financial reporting considerations and obtaining appropriate professional advice.)

6. If an agent (generally a bank or trust company) is used for the interest disbursing and redemption functions, have the agent and arrangements been authorized by the Board of Directors?

Yes   No   N/A

Recording and Classifying Debt and Other Borrowings

Objective

- Transactions and obligations concerning debt and other borrowing arrangements are promptly and accurately recorded and classified in detail records and control accounts to—

  (a) permit preparation of financial statements including required disclosures in conformity with generally accepted accounting principles or other criteria applicable to such statements, and

  (b) provide timely and accurate information as a basis for conforming with payment obligations and other covenants in the applicable agreements.

Questions—Control Policies and Procedures

1. Are detailed, timely records maintained of such debt and other borrowings as notes payable, long-term debt, and capitalized leases that include such information as:

   a. Date of inception?
   b. Type of obligation?
   c. Face amount?
   d. Interest rate?
   e. Maturity?
   f. Timing and amount of payments?
   g. Proceeds initially received?
   h. Payments of principal?
   i. Outstanding principal balance?
   j. Accrued interest expense?
   k. Payments of interest?
   l. Outstanding balance of accrued interest payable?
   m. Premium or discount at inception?
   n. Amortization of premium or discount?
   o. Balance of unamortized premium or discount?
   p. Summarized information or collateral and/or restrictive covenants connected with the obligation (such as minimum current ratios and/or debt to equity ratios; restrictions on paying dividends, purchasing property and equipment, and/or entering lease agreements?

2. Does the chart of accounts provide adequate control accounts for principal amounts and related interest expenses of debt and other borrowings?

Yes   No   N/A

3. Are the detailed records maintained by responsible person(s) whose duties do not include:

   a. Maintenance of the general ledger control accounts?   ____ ____ ____
   b. Physical custody of agreements connected with borrowings and unissued debt instruments?   ____ ____ ____
   c. Cash functions?   ____ ____ ____

4. Do persons who maintain the detail records and control accounts receive timely and adequate information about debt and other borrowing obligations (for example, copies or abstracts of the debt and lease agreements)?   ____ ____ ____

5. Are detailed records reconciled with the control accounts at reasonable intervals by persons whose duties do not include:

   a. Maintenance of the detailed records on debt and other borrowings?   ____ ____ ____
   b. Custody of agreements connected with borrowings and unissued debt instruments?   ____ ____ ____

6. Are adequate reports developed from the detailed records and actual debt and lease agreements which provide timely and accurate information as a basis for:

   a. Payments of principal and interest in conformity with the agreements?   ____ ____ ____
   b. Monitoring compliance with terms and covenants in the agreements?   ____ ____ ____

7. Are detailed records compared with debt and lease agreements at reasonable intervals by responsible persons whose duties do not include:

   a. Maintenance of the detailed records?   ____ ____ ____
   b. Custody of the debt and lease agreements?   ____ ____ ____
   c. Maintenance of the general ledger control accounts?   ____ ____ ____
   d. Cash functions?   ____ ____ ____

8. If independent agents are retained for the interest paying and redemption functions, are the agents' reports promptly reconciled with the control accounts and subsidiary records?   ____ ____ ____

Safeguarding Records, Documents, and Unissued Debt Instruments

Objective

• Access to records, documents, and instruments concern-

Yes   No   N/A

ing debt and other borrowing arrangements is permitted only in accordance with management's authorization.

Questions—Control Policies and Procedures

1. Does a responsible individual maintain adequate files of copies of notes payable, long-term debt mortgage agreements, and leases?

2. Are unissued debt instruments such as notes and bonds adequately safeguarded and in the custody of a responsible employee whose duties do not include—

   a. Maintenance of detailed records on borrowings and other term obligations?
   b. Maintenance of general ledger control accounts?
   c. Cash functions?

3. Are unissued debt instruments subject to pre-assigned numerical control and are all such instruments accounted for at reasonable intervals?

4. Are paid bonds and notes effectively canceled to preclude their further use?

C. Equity Capital
Authorization of Equity Capital Transactions

Objective

- Equity capital transactions are—

   (a) appropriately authorized and approved in conformity with the entity's governing document (corporate charter, partnership agreement, and so on).
   (b) initiated and executed in accordance with management's authorization.

Questions—Control Policies and Procedures

1. Are capital transactions (issuance, reacquisition, and redemption of stock, dividends, granting of options, rights, conversion privileges, and so on) authorized and approved in conformity with the entity's governing document?

   (The entity's governing document (corporate charter, partnership agreement, etc.) may clearly specify the groups or designated officials who have authority concerning the initiation and approval of specific types of capital transactions.)

Yes　No　N/A

2. Are authorizations and approvals for specific capital transactions appropriately recorded?

(For example, if the corporate charter provides that capital transactions be initiated by the Board of Directors subject to approval of the stockholders, such authorizations and approvals would be recorded in the respective minutes of Board of Directors' meetings and stockholders' meetings.)

3. Are two officials specifically authorized by the Board of Directors required to sign and countersign stock certificates?

4. Are all stock certificates prepared and approved before issuance in accordance with management's authorization?

(Prescribed procedures would include, for example, compliance with tax and other statutory requirements before signing and issuing certificates. For transfers and retirements of certificates, prescribed procedures would include cancellation and disposition of the certificates received.)

5. If a registrar, transfer agent and/or dividend paying agent is retained, have they been authorized by the Board of Directors?

Recording and Classifying Equity Capital Transactions

Objective

- Transactions and obligations concerning equity capital are promptly and accurately recorded and classified in detailed records and control accounts.

Questions—Control Policies and Procedures

1. Does the general ledger include appropriate control accounts for equity capital?

2. Are appropriate control records maintained for each class of stock on such information as number of shares authorized, issued and outstanding, and number of shares subject to options, warrants, and conversion privileges?

3. Are timely detailed records maintained on the specific stock certificates issued and outstanding for each class

Yes   No   N/A

of capital stock and the identity of holders of record and number of shares for each certificate?

(In a closely held corporation with a limited number of shareholders and outstanding certificates, properly completed stubs in capital stock certificate books may serve this purpose. Retired certificates would normally be cancelled and reattached to the related stubs. Other situations may require a data base that permits timely rendering of listings of each certificate by number and/or of each shareholder and number of shares held.)

4. Are detailed stock certificate records reconciled at reasonable intervals with the control records and the general ledger?

(If the corporation retains independent agents for the registrar and transfer functions, for example, the agents' periodic reports would be promptly reconciled with the general ledger.)

5. Are reconciliations of detailed records with the control records and general ledger performed by persons whose duties do not include:

   a. Custody of unissued stock certificates?
   b. Maintenance of the detailed records?
   c. Cash functions?

Physical Safeguards and Custodial Procedures

Objectives

- Access to records, agreements, and such negotiable documents as stock certificates concerning equity capital is permitted only in accordance with management's authorization.
- Records, agreements, and negotiable documents are subjected to reasonably adequate physical safeguards and custodial procedures.

Questions—Control Policies and Procedures

1. Are unissued stock certificates, reacquired certificates and detailed stockholder records subject to reasonable physical safeguards?

(Examples include fire-resistant files, vaults, and use of safe deposit boxes.)

Yes   No   N/A

2. Are stock certificates subject to controls such as pre-numbering which provides that all certificates (unissued, issued, and retired) may be accounted for?

3. Are unissued and retired stock certificates examined and all certificate numbers accounted for at reasonable intervals by a person(s) whose duties do not include:

   a. Physical custody of unissued stock certificates?
   b. Maintenance of stockholder detail records?
   c. Cash functions?
   d. General ledger functions?

4. Are retired stock certificates—

   a. Examined for proper endorsement and effectively canceled by a person(s) whose duties do not include maintenance of the detailed stockholder records?
   b. Matched and recorded promptly in the detailed records of certificates (reattached to related stubs in the certificate book)?

5. Are treasury stock certificates registered in the name of the company and recorded to be readily distinguished from other outstanding shares?

Dividends Disbursements

Objective

- Dividends are disbursed accurately and in conformity with decisions of the Board of Directors.

Questions—Control Policies and Procedures

1. Are dividends declared recorded in the minutes of the Board of Directors meetings regarding class of stock, amount per share, total amount, record date, and payment date?

2. Do procedures result in an accurate cutoff and accurate listing of stockholders as of the record date?

3. Are dividend checks prepared based on appropriate stockholder listings and subjected to the following:

   a. Approval and signature in accordance with management's authorization?
   b. Mailing by a person(s) whose duties do not include maintenance of detailed records of stockholders, custody of unissued and retired stock certificates, and check preparation functions?

Yes   No   N/A

4. Are total dividends disbursed reconciled to total outstanding shares as of the record date?

D. Cash

Processing Collections

Objectives

- Access to cash receipts and cash receipts records, accounts receivable records, and billing and shipping records is controlled to prevent or detect, on a timely basis, the taking of unrecorded cash receipts or the abstraction of recorded cash receipts.
- Detail transaction and account balance records are reconciled, at reasonable intervals, with applicable control accounts and bank statements for timely detection and corrections of errors.

Questions—Control Policies and Procedures

1. Is the mail opened by a person(s) whose duties do not involve any shipping, billing, accounts receivable detail, general ledger, invoice processing, payroll, and cash disbursement functions?

2. Does the person(s) who opens the mail:

   a. Place restrictive endorsements on all checks when received so they are for deposit only to the bank accounts of the company?

   b. List or otherwise obtain control (for example, by photocopying) over all remittances and prepare totals at least daily?

   c. Forward all remittances to the person who prepares and makes the daily bank deposit?

   d. Forward the total of remittances to persons, who are independent of physical handling of remittances and accounts receivable detail functions, for subsequent comparison with the authenticated duplicate deposit slip and with control total over postings to subsidiary records?

   (In lock box arrangements, customers would mail their remittances to a post office box controlled by the company's bank which would have responsibility for functions 2a–2d.)

3. Are receipts of currency controlled by cash registers and/or pre-numbered cash receipt forms?

Yes   No   N/A

a. If cash registers are used, is a copy of the tape given to the customer as a receipt, and:

   (1) Is the key to the cash register tape compartment in the custody at all times of a responsible employee other than the cash register operator(s)?

   (2) Are readings of the register periodically taken and compared with the cashier's records of receipts by a responsible employee other than the cash register operator(s)?

b. If pre-numbered receipts are used for currency collections:

   (1) Is a copy given to the payor as a receipt?

   (2) Are all prenumbered receipts accounted for by a person(s) other than the person(s) handling cash received and balanced with the daily cash received?

c. If cash collections are for payments on account, is adequate information given for accurate posting to accounts receivable detail?

d. If significant cash sales are made (as in a retail store) are spot checks made to determine that cashiers are following prescribed procedures?

4. Are currency receipts forwarded daily to the person who prepares the daily bank deposit?

5. Is a summary listing of daily currency receipts forwarded to a person(s) independent of physical handling of remittances and accounts receivable detail functions?

6. Do areas involving physical handling of cash appear reasonably safeguarded? (For example, protective windows, vaults, cashier cages, and so on.)

7. Are each day's receipts (by mail, and over the counter) except for postdated items deposited intact daily?

8. Are postdated items segregated on daily detail listings of remittances to aid in control of total items received?

9. Are all employees who handle receipts adequately bonded?

10. Are banks instructed not to cash checks and other instruments (for example, drafts, money orders, and so on) drawn to the order of the company?

11. Does company policy prohibit the cashing of any accommodation checks (for example, personal and payroll checks) out of collections?

	Yes	No	N/A

12. Are local bank accounts used for branch office collections subject to withdrawal only by the home office?

13. Are banks instructed to deliver charged back deposit items (such as checks returned because of insufficient funds) directly to an employee independent of physical handling of cash receipts and posting of accounts receivable detail?

14. Are bank chargebacks received directly from the bank and investigated by a person independent of:

   a. Physical handling of collections?
   b. Posting accounts receivable subsidiary detail?

15. Are entries to the cash receipts journal compared with:

   a. Duplicate deposit slips authenticated by the bank?
   b. Deposits per the bank statements?
   c. Listings prepared (initial control) when mail is opened?

16. Are the comparisons described in item 15 above made by a person(s) whose duties do not include cash receipts and accounts receivable functions?

Recording Collections

Objective

- All cash receipts are recorded at the correct amounts in the period in which received, and are properly classified and summarized.

Questions—Control Policies and Procedures

1. Is information captured from remittances (by mail and over the counter) adequate for accurate posting of credits to individual accounts receivable subsidiary records or to classifications concerning such other sources as investment income, rents, sales of property or scrap, and proceeds of financing?

   (This information, for example, may be included on the listing prepared when the mail is opened, remittance advices which accompany customers' checks, detachable stubs from billings, photocopies of checks, copies of pre-numbered receipts issued for currency collections, and so on.)

2. Are details of daily collections balanced with the total credits to be distributed to appropriate general ledger

Yes   No   N/A

accounts and to the total collections for the day before posting to the subsidiary records?

3. Do postings of the general ledger control accounts and subsidiary records include the date on which the remittance was received?

4. Are postings to the general ledger control accounts made by a person(s) independent of:

   a. Physical handling of collections?
   b. Posting accounts receivable subsidiary detail?

5. Are details of collections posted to subsidiary accounts receivable records by a person(s) independent of:

   a. General ledger functions?
   b. Physical handling of collections?
   c. Receipt and investigation of bank chargebacks?

Assignment of Disbursement Functions

Objective

- Functions are assigned so that no single individual is in a position to both perpetrate and conceal errors or irregularities in the normal course of his duties.

Questions—Control Policies and Procedures

1. Is the cash disbursements function performed by persons who are independent of the following functions?

   a. Purchasing?
   b. Receiving?
   c. Invoice processing?
   d. Payroll preparation and approval?
   e. Shipping?
   f. Accounts receivable?
   g. Cash receipts?
   h. General ledger?

2. Is there adequate separation of duties within the cash disbursement function among persons who perform the following:

   a. Control access to unissued checks?
   b. Prepare checks?
   c. Sign checks and inspect support?
   d. Mail checks?
   e. Maintain custody of petty cash?

Yes   No   N/A

f. Maintain the cash disbursement journal?   ____ ____ ____
g. Reconcile the bank accounts?   ____ ____ ____

Processing Disbursements

Objectives

- Disbursements are made only for expenditures incurred in accordance with management's authorization.
- Adjustments to cash accounts are made only in accordance with management's authorization.
- Disbursements are recorded at correct amounts in the appropriate period and are properly classified in the accounts.
- Access to cash and cash disbursements records is restricted to minimize opportunities for irregular or erroneous disbursements.

Questions—Control Policies and Procedures

1. Are all bank accounts authorized by the Board of Directors?   ____ ____ ____
2. Are all check signers authorized by the Board of Directors?   ____ ____ ____
3. Are banks promptly notified of any changes in authorized check signers?   ____ ____ ____
4. Are banks instructed not to cash checks and other instruments (for example, drafts, money orders, etc.) drawn to the order of the company?   ____ ____ ____
5. Are all bank accounts and cash funds subjected to general ledger control?   ____ ____ ____
6. Are all disbursements and bank transfers based on vouchers and check requests which have been approved by responsible employees designated by management?   ____ ____ ____
7. Are all disbursements except from petty cash made by check?   ____ ____ ____
8. Are properly approved supporting documents (processed invoices, purchase orders, receiving reports, and so on) presented with the checks and reviewed by the check signer(s) before signing the checks?   ____ ____ ____
9. Is a mechanical check protector used to inscribe amounts on checks as a precaution against alteration?   ____ ____ ____
10. Are supporting documents for checks properly cancelled to avoid duplicate payment?   ____ ____ ____
11. Are signed checks independently mailed directly after signing without being returned to persons involved in the invoice processing and check preparation functions?   ____ ____ ____

Yes   No   N/A

12. Is access to unissued checks limited to designated responsible employees who are independent of the check signing function, including operation of mechanical check signing machines?

13. Are checks pre-numbered and all numbers accounted for?

14. Are all voided checks retained and mutilated?

15. Are all checks promptly recorded when issued and listed in detail (cash disbursements journal, check register, etc.)?

16. Are details of individual disbursements balanced with the totals to be posted to appropriate general ledger account distributions and to total disbursements to be posted to the general ledger control accounts for cash?

17. Is there a written policy which prohibits:

   a. Drawing checks payable to cash or bearer?
   b. Signing or countersigning of blank checks?

18. If dual signatures are required:

   a. Are the two signers independent of one another?
   b. Does each signer determine that the disbursement is supported by approved documentation?

19. If a check signing machine is used:

   a. Are checks approved before mechanical signing by designated responsible employees who are subject to the same segregation of duties as if they were authorized check signers?

      (Use of a check signing machine allows an entity to delegate authority for approving checks to a greater number of persons than those registered with the bank as authorized signers. However, approval procedures should be sufficient to assure the official whose name is on the signature plate that all mechanically signed checks would have met his approval if he had reviewed and manually signed them himself.)

   b. Are the keys, signature plate, and operation of the signing machine under control at all times of the official whose signature is on the plate?

   c. Are the employees who have custody of the keys, plate, and operate the check signing machine inde-

Yes   No   N/A

pendent of voucher and check preparation functions and denied access to blank checks?

d. Are the checks issued to the machine operator(s) counted in advance and reconciled with the totals of the counting device on the check signing machine by someone other than the machine operator?

(Control may be strengthened by having a locked compartment on the machine which receives the signed checks and can be opened only by someone independent of the machine operator.)

20. Are cash funds on an imprest basis and:

a. Kept in a safe place?

b. Reasonable in amount?

c. Controlled by one custodian who is independent of invoice processing, check signing, general accounting, and cash receipts functions?

d. Periodically counted by someone other than the custodian?

21. Are all disbursements from cash funds:

a. Supported by vouchers which are prepared in ink?

b. Approved in accordance with management's authorization?

c. Canceled to prevent reuse?

d. Subject to a predetermined maximum dollar limit for any individual disbursement?

22. Are reimbursements of cash funds:

a. Subject to the same review and approval as processed invoices?

b. Remitted by checks drawn payable to the order of the custodian of the cash fund?

Bank Reconciliations

Objective

• Comparison of detail records, control accounts, and bank statements are made at reasonable intervals for detection and appropriate disposition of errors or irregularities.

Questions—Control Policies and Procedures

1. Are the bank accounts reconciled monthly by an employee(s) who is independent of invoice processing, cash

Yes   No   N/A

disbursements, cash receipts, petty cash, and general ledger functions?

2. Are bank statements, related paid checks, debit and credit memos received directly from the bank by the employee(s) performing the reconciliations?

3. Does the bank reconciliation procedure include:

   a. Reconciliation of the balance per bank to balance per the general ledger control account and subsidiary detail records?

   b. Comparison in detail of deposits per the bank statement with deposits per cash receipts detail records?

   c. Comparisons in detail of disbursements per bank with the cash disbursements journal (check register) as to date drawn, payee, and amount?

   d. Comparison of payees with endorsements?

   e. Follow up of reconciling items and initiation of entries to record such transactions as checks returned for insufficient funds and bank charges?

4. Are old outstanding checks investigated and subjected to proper disposition (in compliance with applicable escheat laws if present)?

25

Internal Audit of Financial Statement Accounts

An important function of the internal audit staff is to ensure that the financial statements prepared by management are presented fairly, in all material respects, in conformity with generally accepted accounting principles. This will facilitate the annual audit performed by the independent certified public accountant.

Financial statements, in general, consist of assertions which are representations of the management of the company.

Specific financial statement assertions include:

- *Existence or occurrence*—Assertions about existence or occurrence are concerned with whether assets or liabilities of the entity exist at a particular date and whether recorded transactions have truly occurred during a specified time period.

- *Completeness*—Assertions pertaining to completeness apply to whether all transactions and accounts that should be included in the financial statements are actually included.

- *Rights and obligations*—Assertions relating to rights and obligations deal with whether the entity has legal title to assets and whether the recorded liabilities are in fact obligations of the entity.

- *Valuation or allocation*—Assertions about valuation or allocation are concerned with whether asset, liability, revenue, and expense components have been included in the financial statements at appropriate amounts.

- *Presentation and disclosure*—Assertions about presentation and disclosure deal with whether particular components of the financial statements are properly described, disclosed and classified.

After financial statement assertions are identified, the internal auditor should then develop audit objectives, which are often restatements of the broad assertions but fine tuned for the specific accounts being examined.

In developing an internal audit work program, the auditor must also establish the procedures to be used.

Some of the more common auditing procedures include:

- *Inquiry,* often defined as the seeking of information, is based on interviewing appropriate personnel at all organizational levels. The responses derived from inquiry may be written or oral but should be corroborated by more additional evidence.
- *Observation* involves watching employees perform their assigned functions.
- *Inspection* entails careful examination of pertinent documents and records as well as the physical examination of assets.
- *Tracing* involves tracking source documents from their creation to the recorded amounts in the books of original entry.
- *Reperformance* means repeating an activity.
- *Vouching* involves selecting amounts recorded in the books and examining documents that support those recorded amounts.
- *Scrutinizing* is a careful visual review of records, reports and schedules in order to identify unusual items.
- *Confirmation* is a process whereby the auditor can obtain corroborating evidential matter from an independent party which is outside the organization.
- *Analytical procedures* involving the study and comparison of the plausible relationships that exist among financial and non-financial data. Analytical procedures include ratio analysis and comparisons of current period financial information to (1) prior period financial information, (2) anticipated results, (3) predictable patterns, (4) similar information within the same industry, and (5) nonfinancial data.

It should be understood that in addition to the procedures reviewed above, there are other basic procedures which may be used. Accordingly, the following should also be considered:

- Reading and reviewing pertinent documents
- Analyzing details of account balances
- Verifying the validity of statements or representations

Since an audit procedure may enable satisfaction of more than one audit objective, it is practical to establish the audit objectives and then select audit procedures which avoid duplication of work.

SAMPLE AUDIT PROGRAM FOR CASH IN BANK

I. Audit Objectives:
   A. Determine that cash recorded in books exists and is owned by the company (Existence).
   B. Determine that cash transactions are recorded in the correct accounting period, i.e., that there is a proper cutoff of cash receipts and disbursements (Completeness).
   C. Determine that balance sheet amounts include items in transit as well as cash on deposit with third parties (Completeness).
   D. Determine that cash is properly classified in the balance sheet and that relevant disclosures are presented in the financial statement notes (Presentation and Disclosure).

II. Procedures:
   A. With respect to the bank reconciliations prepared by accounting personnel:
      • Trace book balances to general ledger control totals.
      • Compare ending balances per the bank statements to the ending balances on the bank reconciliation.
      • Verify the mathematical and clerical accuracy including checking extensions.
      • Identify unusual reconciling items and obtain documentation to corroborate the validity of such items.
      • Trace deposits in transit and outstanding checks to subsequent months' bank statements which are intercepted before accounting personnel have access to them.
      • Inspect canceled checks for dates of cancellation in order to identify checks which were not recorded in the proper accounting period.
      • Ascertain that checks listed as outstanding are in fact (1) recorded in the proper time period, and (2) checks that have not cleared. Scrutinize data when outstanding checks have cleared to see if the books have been held open to improve ratios.
      • Identify and investigate checks that are (1) above limits prescribed by management, (2) drawn to "bearer," and (3) drawn payable to cash.
      • Inquire about checks which have been outstanding for a more than reasonable time period.
      • If balances have been confirmed with banks, compare confirmed balances with bank balances per the year-end bank statements.
   B. With respect to listings of cash investments:
      • Trace book balances to general ledger control accounts.
      • Verify the accuracy of all extensions and footings.
      • Consider confirming balances directly with bank personnel.

- Obtain and inspect passbooks and certificates of deposit.
- Recalculate income derived from cash investments and trace the income amounts to the books of original entry. Also, reconcile interest revenue amounts to the amount of cash investments for reasonableness.
- Consider using a custodian to maintain physical custody for safekeeping and to guard against forgeries.

C. Prepare a bank transfer schedule which identifies:
  - Name of disbursing bank
  - Check number
  - Dollar amount
  - Date disbursement is recorded in books
  - Name of receiving bank
  - Date receipt is recorded in books
  - Date receipt is recorded by bank

D. Perform cutoff test wherein transactions for the last few days of the year and the first few days of the next year are scrutinized.

E. Inspect bank statements in order to identify obvious erasures or alterations.

F. Inspect debit and credit memos and trace them to the bank statements.

G. Read financial statements and investment certificates for appropriate classification of cash balances.

H. With respect to cash on hand (i.e., petty cash funds):
  - Determine the identity of all funds
  - Select funds to be counted and
    - List currency and coins by denomination
    - Account for vouchers, stamps, and checks
    - Trace fund balances to general ledger control accounts.

I. Investigate the reasons for delays in deposits.

J. Note unusual activity in inactive accounts since it may be indicative of cash being hidden.

K. In a cash-basis entity, reconcile sales with cash receipts.

L. List unusual cash receipts (e.g., currency receipts).

M. Examine third party endorsements by reviewing canceled checks.

SAMPLE AUDIT PROGRAM FOR TRADE ACCOUNTS AND NOTES RECEIVABLE

I. Audit Objectives:
  A. Determine that the trade accounts and notes receivable represent bona fide receivables and are valued properly (Existence and Valuation).
  B. Determine that the allowances for doubtful accounts are adequate and reasonable (Valuation).
  C. Determine the propriety of disclosures pertaining to pledging, assigning, and discounting of receivables (Presentation and Disclosure).

D. Determine the correctness of the recorded interest income that is attributable to accounts and notes receivable (Completeness).

E. Determine that receivables are properly classified in the balance sheet (Presentation and Disclosure).

II. Audit Procedures:

A. Scan general ledger accounts in order to identify significant and unusual transactions.

B. Compare opening general ledger balances with closing general ledger balances of the prior period.

C. Perform analytical procedures by evaluating the relationships between (1) receivables and sales and (2) notes receivable and interest income attributable thereon.

D. With respect to the aged trial balance prepared by accounting personnel:
  • Verify extensions and footings
  • Trace the total of the aged trial balance to the general ledger control total
  • Trace selected entries on the aging schedule to respective accounts in the subsidiary ledger
  • Trace selected subsidiary ledger balances to the aging schedule
  • Verify extensions and footings in subsidiary ledger accounts
  • Investigate negative (i.e., credit) balances.

E. Consider confirmation of account balances with customers:
  • Select accounts for positive confirmation
  • Select accounts for negative confirmation
  • Control confirmation requests by mailing in internal audit department envelopes and with the return address of the internal audit department. Consider using a post office box to ensure that unauthorized individuals cannot tamper with responses.
  • After 14 days, mail second requests to all those not replying to a positive request
  • Investigate all accounts for which envelopes are returned as undeliverable
  • Reconcile differences reported by customers
  • Review accounts of significant customers not replying to a second request by examining subsequent receipts and supporting documentation (i.e., remittance advices, invoices, and/or shipping documents) in order to corroborate that the amounts represent bona fide receivables for goods or services
  • Prepare a schedule summarizing the receivable confirmations as follows:

	No.	%	Dollar Amount	%
Total at Confirm Date Requested				
Total Positive Type				

<u>No.</u>   %   <u>Dollar Amount</u>   %

Total at Confirm
        Date
Requested

    Total Negative Type
    Total Requested

Results

    Positive Exceptions
    Positive Clean
    Positive Non-replies

Total Positive Type
    Exceptions
Total Negative Type
    Exceptions

F. Examine cash receipts in subsequent periods in order to identify receivables which have not been recorded previously.
G. With respect to trade notes receivable, prepare or verify schedules and analyses which detail the following:
   • Makers of the notes
   • Dates the notes were made
   • Due dates of the notes
   • Original terms of repayment
   • Any collateral
   • Applicable interest rates
   • Balances at the end of the prior accounting period
   • Additions and repayments of principal.
H. Inspect notes and confirm notes receivable discounted with banks.
 I. Identify collateral and verify that such amounts are not recorded as assets.
 J. Verify the accuracy of interest income, accrued interest, and unearned discount by recalculating such amounts.
K. Read pertinent documents, including the minutes of board meetings, in order to identify situations in which receivables have been pledged as collateral, assigned, or discounted, verify that such situations are disclosed in the financial statements.
L. Obtain evidence pertaining to related party transactions which need to be disclosed in the financial statements.
M. With respect to the analysis of the allowance for doubtful accounts prepared by accounting personnel:
   • Ascertain that write-offs have in fact been authorized
   • Ascertain the reasonableness of the allowance
   • Perform analytical procedures by comparing:

- Accounts receivable to credit sales
- Allowance for doubtful accounts to accounts receivable totals
- Sales to sales returns and allowances
- Doubtful accounts expense to net credit sales
- Accounts receivable to total assets
- Notes receivable totals to accounts receivable totals
- Consider differences between the book and tax basis for doubtful accounts expense.

SAMPLE AUDIT PROGRAM FOR INVENTORY

I. Audit Objectives:
  A. Determine that inventory quantities properly include products, materials, and supplies on hand, in-transit, in storage and out on consignment to others (Existence, Completeness, and Valuation or Allocation).
  B. Determine that inventory items are priced consistently in accordance with GAAP (Valuation or Allocation).
  C. Determine that inventory listings are accurately compiled, extended, footed, and summarized and determine that the totals are properly reflected in the accounts (Existence, Completeness, and Valuation or Allocation).
  D. Determine that excess, slow-moving, obsolete, and defective items are reduced to their net realizable value (Valuation or Allocation).
  E. Determine that the financial statements include disclosure of any liens resulting from the pledging or assignment of inventories (Presentation and Disclosure).

II. Audit Procedures:
  A. Review management's instructions pertaining to inventory counts and arrange to have sufficient internal audit personnel present to observe the physical count at major corporate locations. Keep in mind that all locations should be counted simultaneously in order to prevent substitution of items.
  B. At each location where inventory is counted:
    - Observe the physical inventory count, record test counts, and write an overall observation memo
    - Determine that prenumbered inventory tags are utilized
    - Test the control of inventory tags
    - Test shipping and receiving cutoffs
    - Discuss obsolescence and overstock with operating personnel
    - Verify that employees are indicating on inventory tags obsolete items
    - Note the condition of inventory
    - Note pledged or consigned inventory
    - Determine if any inventory is at other locations and consider confirmation or observation, if material
    - Determine that inventory marked for destruction is actually destroyed and is destroyed by authorized personnel.

C. Follow up all points that might result in a material adjustment.

D. Trace recorded test counts to the listings obtained from management, list all exceptions, and value the total effect.

E. Trace the receiving and shipping cutoffs obtained during the observation to the inventory records, accounts receivable records, and accounts payable records. Also trace inventory to production and sales.

F. Obtain a cutoff of purchases and sales subsequent to the audit date and trace to accounts receivable, accounts payable, and inventory records.

G. Note any sharp drop in market value relative to book value.

H. "Red flag" excessive product returns which might be indicative of quality problems. Returned merchandise should be warehoused apart from finished goods until quality control has tested the items. Are returns due to the salesperson overstocking the customer? Returns should be controlled as to actual physical receipt, and the reasons for the returns should be noted for analytical purposes.

I. Trace for possible obsolete merchandise that is continually carried on the books. For example, the author had a situation in which a company continued to carry obsolete goods on the books even though it wrote-off only a small portion.

J. With respect to price tests of raw materials:
   • Ascertain management's inventory pricing procedures
   • Schedule, for a test of pricing, all inventory items in excess of a prescribed limit and sample additional items
   • Inspect purchase invoices and trace to journal entries
   • Inquire and investigate whether trade discounts, special rebates, and similar price reductions have been reflected in inventory prices
   • Determine and test treatment of freight and duty costs.
   • If standard costs are utilized:
      • Determine whether such costs differ materially from actual costs on a first-in, first-out basis
      • Investigate variance accounts and compute the effect of the balances in such accounts on inventory prices
      • Ascertain the policy and practice as to changes in standards
      • With respect to changes during the period, investigate the effect on inventory pricing
      • If process costs are used, trace selected quantities per the physical inventory to the departmental cost of production reports and determine that quantities have been adjusted to the physical inventory as of the date of the physical counts.

K. With respect to work-in-process and finished goods:
   • Ascertain the procedures used in pricing inventory and determine the basis of pricing
   • Review tax returns to determine that the valuation methods conform to those methods used for financial statement purposes
   • On a test basis, trace unit costs per the physical inventory to the cost accounting records and perform the following:

- Obtain, review, and compare the current period and prior period's trial balances or tabulations of detailed components of production costs for the year; note explanations for apparent inconsistencies in classifications and significant fluctuations in amounts; ascertain that the cost classifications accumulated as production costs and absorbed in inventory are in conformity with GAAP.
- Review computations of unit costs and costs credited against inventory and charged to cost of sales.
- Review activity in the general ledger control accounts for raw materials, supplies, work-in-process and finished goods inventories and investigate any significant and unusual entries or fluctuations.
- Review labor and overhead allocations to inventory and cost of sales; compare to actual labor and overhead costs incurred, and ascertain that variances appear reasonable in amount and have been properly accounted for.
- Trace who obtains the funds received from the sale of scrap.

SAMPLE AUDIT PROGRAM FOR FIXED ASSETS

I. Audit Objectives:
   A. Determine that fixed assets exist (Existence or Occurrence).
   B. Determine that fixed assets are owned by the entity (Rights and Obligations).
   C. Determine that fixed asset accounts are recorded at historical cost (Valuation or Allocation).
   D. Determine that depreciation is calculated and recorded in conformity with generally accepted accounting principles (Valuation or Allocation).
   E. Determine that relevant disclosures are made in the financial statements (Presentation and Disclosure).
II. Audit Procedures:
   A. With respect to the schedule of fixed assets prepared by accounting personnel:
   - Trace beginning balances to prior-year schedules
   - Trace ending balances to general ledger control accounts
   - Verify that additions are recorded at historical cost
   - Examine supporting documentation for asset additions, retirements, and dispositions:
     - Purchase contracts
     - Canceled checks
     - Invoices
     - Purchase orders
     - Receiving reports
     - Retirement work orders
     - Sale contracts
     - Bills of sale

- Bills of lading
- Trade-in agreements
- Verify that depreciation methods, estimated useful lives, and estimated salvage values are in accordance with generally accepted accounting principles (GAAP)
- Recalculate gains and losses on dispositions of fixed assets in accordance with methods that are in conformity with GAAP.

B. Determine that additions, retirements, and dispositions have been authorized by management.

C. Analyze repairs and maintenance accounts to ascertain the propriety of classification of transactions.

D. Tour facilities in order to physically inspect fixed assets. A lack of cleanliness and orderliness infer the possible existence of internal control problems.

E. To verify ownership, examine:
- Personal property tax returns
- Title certificates
- Insurance policies
- Invoices
- Purchase contracts.

F. Read lease agreements and ascertain that the accounting treatment is in conformity with GAAP.

G. Ascertain that obsolete assets are given proper accounting recognition. Trace salvage receipts to source.

H. Perform analytical procedures by comparing:
- Dispositions of fixed assets to replacements
- Depreciation and amortization expenses to the cost of fixed assets
- Accumulated depreciation to the cost of fixed assets.

I. Read (1) minutes of board meetings, (2) note agreements, and (3) purchase contracts to identify situations in which assets have been pledged as collateral.

SAMPLE AUDIT PROGRAM FOR PREPAID EXPENSES AND DEFERRED CHARGES

I. Audit Objectives:

A. Determine that balances represent proper charges against future operations and can reasonably be realized through future operations or are otherwise in conformity with GAAP (Valuation or Allocation).

B. Determine that additions during the audit period are proper charges to these accounts and represent actual cost (Existence or Occurrence and Valuation or Allocation).

C. Determine that amortization or write-offs against revenues in the current period and to date have been determined in a rational and consistent manner (Valuation or Allocation).

D. Determine that material items have been properly classified and disclosed in the financial statements (Presentation and Disclosure)

II. Audit Procedures:

A. Obtain or prepare a schedule of the prepaid and deferred items.

B. Perform analytical procedures by comparing current-period amounts to those of the prior period; investigate significant fluctuations.

C. With respect to prepaid insurance:
- Obtain a schedule of insurance policies, coverage, total premiums, prepaid premiums, and expense as of the audit date; note that some companies maintain an insurance register
- Verify the clerical and mathematical accuracy of schedules or insurance registers
- Trace schedule or register totals to trial balances and general ledger control accounts
- Inspect policies on hand and check details to schedules or registers
- Vouch significant premiums paid during the audit period
- Obtain confirmation directly from insurance brokers of premiums and other significant and relevant data
- Verify that proper accounting treatment is applied to advance or deposit premiums, as well as dividend or premium credits
- Test check calculations of prepaid premiums and investigate and determine the disposition of major differences.

D. With respect to prepaid taxes:
- Obtain or prepare an analysis of prepaid taxes, including taxes charged directly to expense accounts
- Verify the mathematical and clerical accuracy of the analysis
- Trace amounts on the analysis to the trial balance and pertinent general ledger control accounts
- Examine tax bills and receipts or other data which corroborates prepaid taxes
- Ascertain that prepaid tax accounts have been accounted for consistently in conformity with GAAP.

E. With respect to other major items:
- Review deferred expenses such as moving costs and determine:
  - What procedures are used to evaluate the future usefulness of the asset
  - How these assets will benefit the future
- Test the amortization of material prepaid or deferred items and trace to the income statement and general ledger accounts
- Inspect relevant documents.

SAMPLE AUDIT PROGRAM FOR ACCOUNTS PAYABLE

I. Audit Objectives:

A. Determine that accounts payable in fact exist (Existence or Occurrence).

B. Determine that accounts payable represent authorized obligations of the entity (Existence or Occurrence).

C. Determine that accounts payable are properly classified in the financial statements (Presentation and Disclosure).

D. Determine that recorded accounts payable are complete (Completeness).

E. Determine that appropriate disclosures are included in the financial statements (Presentation and Disclosure).

II. Audit Procedures:

A. With respect to the schedule of accounts payable prepared by accounting personnel:
- Verify mathematical accuracy of extensions and footings
- Trace totals to general ledger control accounts
- Trace selected individual accounts to the accounts payable subsidiary ledger
- Trace individual account balances in the subsidiary ledger to the accounts payable schedule
- Investigate accounts payable which are in dispute
- Investigate any debit balances
- Read minutes of board meetings to ascertain the existence of pledging agreements.

B. Consider confirming accounts payable if there is (1) poor internal control structure, or (2) suspicion of misstatement.

C. Search for unrecorded liabilities by
- Examining receiving reports and matching them with invoices
- Inspecting unprocessed invoices
- Inspecting vendor's statements for unrecorded invoiced amounts
- Examine cash disbursements made in the period subsequent to year-end and examine supporting documentation in order to ascertain the appropriate cutoff for recording purposes.

D. With respect to obligations for payroll tax liabilities:
- Examine payroll tax deposit receipts
- Examine cash disbursements in the period subsequent to year-end to identify deposits that relate to prior period
- Reconcile general ledger control totals to payroll tax forms
- Trace liabilities for amounts withheld from employee checks to payroll registers, journals, and summaries
- Perform analytical procedures by comparing:
  - Payroll tax expense to liabilities for payroll taxes
  - Liability to accrued payroll taxes
- Reconcile calendar year payroll returns to fiscal year financial statements for payroll amounts.

E. Reconcile vendor statements with accounts payable accounts.

F. Compare vendor invoices with purchase requisitions, purchase orders, and receiving reports for price and quantity.

G. Investigate unusually large purchases.

H. With respect to accrued expenses:
- Consider the existence of unasserted claims
- Obtain schedule of accrued expenses from accounting personnel
- Recalculate accruals after verifying the validity of assumptions utilized
- Perform analytical procedures by comparing current and prior period accrued expenses
- Ascertain that accrued expenses are paid within a reasonable time after year-end
- Inquire of management and indicate all details of contingent or known liabilities arising from product warranties, guarantees, contests, advertising promotions, and dealer "arrangements or promises"
- Determine liability for expenses in connection with pending litigation:
  - Inquire of management
  - Confirm in writing with outside legal counsel.

SAMPLE AUDIT PROGRAM FOR STOCKHOLDERS' EQUITY

I. Audit Objectives:
   A. Determine that all stock transactions (including transactions involving warrants, options, and rights) have been authorized in accordance with management's plans (All Assertions Are Addressed).
   B. Determine that equity transactions are properly classified in the financial statements (Presentation and Disclosure).
   C. Determine that equity transactions have been recorded in the proper time period at the correct amounts (Existence or Occurrence, Completeness, and Presentation and Disclosure).
   D. Determine that equity transactions are reflected in the financial statements in accordance with generally accepted accounting principles (Presentation and Disclosure).
II. Audit Procedures:
   A. With respect to each class of stock, identify the:
   - Number of shares authorized
   - Number of shares issued
   - Number of shares outstanding
   - Par or stated value
   - Privileges
   - Restrictions.
   B. With respect to the schedule of equity transactions prepared by accounting personnel:
   - Trace opening balances of the current year to the balance sheet and ledger accounts as of the prior year's balance sheet date
   - Account for all proceeds from stock issues by recomputing sales prices and relevant proceeds
   - Verify the validity of the classification of proceeds between capital stock and additional paid-in capital

- Reconcile ending schedule balances with general ledger control totals
- Verify that equity transactions are not in conflict with the requirements of the corporate charter (or articles of incorporation), or with the applicable statutes of the state of incorporation.

C. Account for all stock certificates that remain unissued at the end of the accounting period.

D. Examine stock certificate books or confirm stock register.

E. With respect to schedules of stock options and related stock option plans prepared by accounting personnel, verify:
- The date of the plan
- Class and number of shares reserved for the plan
- The accounting method used for determining option prices
- The names of individuals entitled to receive stock options
- The names of individuals to which options have been granted
- The terms relevant to options which have been granted
- That measurement of stock options granted is in accordance with generally accepted accounting principles.

F. With respect to stock subscriptions receivable:
- Ascertain that execution of such transactions is approved by appropriate personnel
- Verify that stock subscriptions receivable are properly classified in the financial statements.

G. With respect to treasury stock:
- Verify the validity of treasury stock acquisitions by examining canceled checks and other corroborating documentation
- Inspect treasury stock certificates in order to ascertain their existence
- Obtain assurance that treasury stock certificates have been endorsed to the company or are in the company's name by physically inspecting the certificates
- Reconcile treasury stock totals to general ledger control accounts.

H. With respect to retained earnings:
- Trace the opening balance in the general ledger to the ending balance in the general ledger of the prior period
- Analyze current year transactions and obtain corroborating documentation for all or selected transactions
- Verify that current year net income or loss has been reflected as a current-year transaction
- With respect to dividends declared and or paid:
  - Ascertain the authorization of such dividends by reading the minutes of board meetings
  - Examine canceled checks in support of dividend payments
  - Verify the accuracy of dividend declarations and payments by recalculating such dividends
  - Ascertain that prior period adjustments have been given proper accounting recognition in accordance with generally accepted accounting principles

- Apply other appropriate procedures to determine the existence of restrictions on or appropriations of retained earnings.

I. Ascertain that the financial statements include adequate disclosure of:
  - Restrictions on stock
  - Stock subscription rights
  - Stock reservations
  - Stock options and warrants
  - Stock repurchase plans or obligations
  - Preferred dividends in arrears
  - Voting rights in the event of preferred dividend arrearages
  - Liquidation preferences
  - Other relevant items.

SAMPLE AUDIT PROGRAM FOR SALES AND OTHER TYPES OF INCOME

I. Audit Objectives:
  A. Determine that proper income recognition is afforded ordinary sales transactions (Existence or Occurrence, Rights and Obligations, Valuation or Allocation, and Presentation and Disclosure).
  B. Determine that sales transactions have been recorded in the proper time period (Existence or Occurrence, Completeness, and Presentation and Disclosure).
  C. Determine that all types of revenues are properly classified and disclosed in the financial statements (Valuation or Allocation and Presentation and Disclosure).

II. Audit Procedures:
  A. Trace sales and cash receipts journal totals to relevant general ledger control accounts.
  B. Trace sales and cash receipts journal entries to applicable subsidiary ledger accounts.
  C. Verify the mathematical accuracy of footings and extensions in sales and cash receipts journals.
  D. Perform analytical procedures by:
    - Comparing current and prior period sales, returns and allowances, discounts, and gross profit percentages
    - Comparing the current period items referred to above to anticipated results (i.e., budgeted amounts)
    - Compare company statistics (e.g., gross profit percentage) to industry standards
    - Investigate any significant or unexplained fluctuations.
  E. With respect to consignment shipments to others:
    - Examine applicable consignment agreements
    - Verify that consignment transactions are afforded proper accounting treatment in accordance with generally accepted accounting principles

F. Ascertain that sales to related parties are accounted for at arm's-length terms.

G. Perform sales and inventory cutoff tests at the end of the fiscal year.

H. Verify by recalculation that the following have been properly recorded and disclosed:
- Dividend income
- Interest income
- Gains on dispositions of marketable securities
- Gains on dispositions of fixed assets
- Increases in investment accounts reflecting the equity method of accounting
- Other or miscellaneous income accounts.

SAMPLE AUDIT PROGRAM FOR EXPENSE ITEMS

I. Audit Objectives:

A. Determine that expenses are recorded in the proper time period (Existence or Occurrence and Completeness).

B. Determine that expenses have been properly classified and disclosed in the financial statements (Presentation and Disclosure).

C. Determine that expense items are recognized in accordance with generally accepted accounting principles (Valuation or Allocation).

II. Audit Procedures:

A. Trace cash disbursements journal totals to relevant general ledger control accounts.

B. Trace cash disbursements journal items to relevant subsidiary ledgers (e.g., payroll subledger).

C. Verify the mathematical accuracy of footings and extensions of relevant journals.

D. Perform analytical procedures by:
- Comparing current and prior-period expense items
- Comparing the current period expense items to anticipated results (i.e., budgeted amounts)
- Compare the current period expense items to industry standards
- Relate various expense items to gross sales or revenue by means of percentages
- Investigate any significant or unexplained fluctuations
- Vouch bills on a sampling basis.

E. Consider analyzing the following accounts which are often subject to intentional or unintentional misstatement:
- Depreciation and amortization
- Taxes
  - Real estate
  - Personal property
  - Income

- Payroll
- Rent
- Insurance
- Bad debts
- Interest
- Professional fees
- Officers' salaries
- Directors' fees
- Travel and entertainment
- Research and development
- Charitable contributions
- Repairs and maintenance.

F. With respect to payroll:
- Search for fictitious employees
- Determine improper alterations of amounts
- Verify that proper tax deductions are taken
- Examine time cards and trace to payroll records in order to verify the proper recording of employee hours
- Verify the accuracy of pay rates by obtaining a list of authorized pay rates from the personnel department
- Review the adequacy of internal controls relating to hiring, overtime, and retirement
- Determine if proper payroll forms exist such as W-4s and I-9s.

CONCLUSION

This chapter has addressed the objectives and procedures to consider in auditing major financial statement accounts. It is obvious that the results of audit testing should be clearly documented. Discrepancies between the audit results and the books and records should clearly be investigated. The exceptions could be indicative of widespread problems which could have an overall adverse effect on the entity.

26

Statistical Sampling in Internal Auditing

There are a number of statistical sampling methods that will aid internal auditors in conducting their examinations. They include attribute sampling, classical variables sampling, discovery sampling, multistage sampling, and stratified sampling. Of course, nonstatistical sampling may also be undertaken.

METHODS OF CHOOSING A RANDOM SAMPLE

A random sample may be chosen through a random sampling table or systematic sampling.

Random Number Sampling Technique (Using A Random Number Table)

In random sampling, there is an equal probability of each sampling unit being chosen. Further, every possible combination of sampling units has the same chance of being in the sample. The internal auditor has to be sure that the sample being selected is representative of the population from which it is drawn.

Random sampling typically involves the following steps:

- Relating identifying numbers (or letters) to sampling units in the population

- Deriving a random sample from the population with the aid of a random number table or a random number generator computer program

The sampling unit may be in physical terms. Examples of physical identifiers are check number, invoice number, page number, and warehouse row and bin number.

Random sampling may be used for nonstatistical and statistical applications.

Systematic Sampling Technique

Systematic sampling consists of sequencing all items of the population. Sampling units are put in order (e.g., numerical). Audit software exist having routines for systematic sampling. The auditor then divides the population into n intervals of equal size based on the number of sampling units that must be chosen for the sample (n). He or she then chooses a sampling unit from each of the derived intervals. The selection interval can be determined by dividing the population size (N) by the required sample size (n).

EXAMPLE 1

The auditor is examining 1,000 sales invoices from a population of 20,000 invoices. One random starting point is employed. Each 20th invoice is chosen. In order that 1,000 invoices are selected, the auditor moves up or down from the random starting point. If a random starting point of invoice number 100 is selected, invoice number 80 ($100 - 20$) and 60 ($100 - 40$) are included in the sample, as well as every 20th invoice number after 100 (i.e., 120, 140, 160, and so on). If the auditor selected 10 random starting points, 100 invoices (1000/10) would be selected for audit. Thus, the auditor would select every 200th invoice number (20,000/100) before and after each random beginning point.

EXAMPLE 2

The population is 10,000 units and the sample size is 1,000 units. The auditor selects a random starting point between one and the sampling interval of 10 (10,000/1,000). This forces the auditor to choose the first sampling unit from the first interval. After including the random start unit as part of the sample, the accountant then sequentially selects every 10th item of the population. Typically, this approach results in a true random sample. Note that if a cyclical pattern in the population exists that coincides with the selection interval, a bias may result i.e., if every 10th sampling unit or multiple of 10 happens to be a departmental manager, then based on the random start, the sample derived may yield either all departmental managers or none. However, the possibility of introducing a bias into the sample as a result of a cyclical pattern in the population would be minimized by picking multiple starting points in the selection process. But

if multiple starting points are chosen, then the sampling interval that was previously selected must be multiplied by the number of random starts so that the required sample size is unchanged.

When there is no numerical sequence to a population, the auditor will find it easier to use a systematic random sample rather than a pure random sample. If documents, records, or transactions are unnumbered, there is no need with systematic sampling to number them physically. If random number table selection was involved, the drawback would be to require numbering. With systematic sampling, the auditor uses the sampling interval as the basis to select the document to examine.

Systematic sampling may be employed for both statistical and non-statistical sampling.

ATTRIBUTE SAMPLING

An attribute is defined as a characteristic that a component of the population has or does not have. For instance, a customer's account is either past due or not. Authorization to pay a vendor has either been given or not.

In attribute sampling, an estimate is made of the proportion of the population that contains a particular characteristic. It can apply to a random sample of physical units or to a systematic sample that approximates a random sample. A sample item possesses or does not possess the specific characteristic. No consideration is given to the magnitude of the characteristic. Based on the sample result, it is found if the true occurrence rate in the population is not greater than a specified percentage expressed at a given reliability level. The auditor may test for several different attributes in a sample.

Attribute sampling is based on a binomial distribution. An estimation may be made of the probable occurrence rates of particular characteristics in a population where each characteristic has two mutually exclusive outcomes. Software for attribute sampling purposes are available from time sharing vendors.

An application of attribute sampling is the auditor's substantiation of breakdown of control procedures. Examples are the measurement of the degree of breakdown of control procedures related to cash disbursements, cash receipts, sales, payroll, and the extent of incorrect entries and incorrect postings.

Attribute sampling of physical units cannot be employed to estimate the total of a variable characteristic (e.g., values).

In determining sample size, the auditor should select an acceptable risk level. In practical terms, auditors select either a 5% or 10% risk because these levels will furnish the auditor with a 95% or 90% confidence, respectively, that the sample is representative of the population. The lower the risk the auditor selects, the greater will be the sample size.

A tolerable deviation rate will have to be selected. It is the maximum rate of deviation the auditor is willing to tolerate and still be able to rely on the control. The tolerable rate depends on professional judgment and the extent of reliance placed on the control or procedure. The following guidelines exist:

Degree of Reliance	Tolerable Rate
Little	11–20%
Moderate	6–12%
Substantial	2–7%

An evaluation should be made of the anticipated deviation rate which may be based on deviations in prior years taking into account corrective changes in the current year.

The actual deviation rate in the sample equals:

$$\frac{\text{Number of Deviations}}{\text{Sample Size}}$$

The auditor should ascertain whether the deviations are due to errors (unintentional) or irregularities (intentional). When the sample deviation is in excess of the tolerable rate, no reliance may be placed on the control.

In examining the population, the population should be complete so that representative testing is possible. For instance, in testing purchase transactions, unpaid as well as paid invoices should be included.

The auditor should define the period covered by the examination. If interim testing is involved, the period after testing to the end of the year should be reviewed. Consideration should be given to the nature and amount of transactions and balances, and the length of the remaining period. The working papers should contain definitions of attributes and occurrences.

Attribute sampling is helpful in tests of controls. An example is evaluating the appropriateness of accounting controls through transaction testing.

Tables are referred to in determining sample size given the risk of overreliance, tolerable occurrence rate, and anticipated occurrence rate.

EXAMPLE 3

In ascertaining if the credit department is performing well, the internal auditor uses attribute sampling in examining sales orders through tests of controls. The internal auditor determines that (1) the deviation condition is the lack of the credit manager's initials on a sales order, (2) the population is comprised of the duplicate sales orders for the whole year, (3) the sampling unit is the sales order, (4) random number selection is used, (5) a 5% risk of overreliance on internal control will be used, (6) the tolerable rate of deviation is 6%, and (7) the anticipated population deviation rate is 2%.

Using Table 1, 127 is the sample size. The internal auditor uses a random number table (Table 5) to select the sample. Because the population is comprised of sales orders numbered 1 to 500, the internal auditor decides to use the first three digits of items selected from the random

Table 1

5 PERCENT RISK OF OVERRELIANCE

Statistical Sample Sizes for Tests of Controls
(For Large Populations)

Expected Population Deviation Rate	Tolerable Occurrence Rate								
	2%	3%	4%	5%	6%	7%	8%	9%	10%
0.00%	129	99	74	59	49	42	36	32	29
.50	*	157	117	93	78	66	58	51	46
1.00	*	*	156	93	78	66	58	51	46
1.50	*	*	192	124	103	66	58	51	46
2.00	*	*	*	181	127	88	77	68	46
2.50	*	*	*	*	150	109	77	68	61
3.00	*	*	*	*	195	129	95	84	61
4.00	*	*	*	*	*	*	146	100	89
5.00	*	*	*	*	*	*	*	158	116
6.00	*	*	*	*	*	*	*	*	179

Table 2

10 PERCENT RISK OF OVERRELIANCE

Expected Population Deviation Rate	Tolerable Occurrence Rate								
	2%	3%	4%	5%	6%	7%	8%	9%	10%
0.00%	114	76	57	45	38	32	28	25	22
.50	194	129	96	77	64	55	48	42	38
1.00	*	176	96	77	64	55	48	42	38
1.50	*	*	132	105	64	55	48	42	38
2.00	*	*	198	132	88	75	48	42	38
2.50	*	*	*	158	110	75	65	58	38
3.00	*	*	*	*	132	94	65	58	52
4.00	*	*	*	*	*	149	98	73	65
5.00	*	*	*	*	*	*	160	115	78
6.00	*	*	*	*	*	*	*	182	116

*Sample size is too large to be cost/effective for most audit applications.

691

Table 3

5 PERCENT RISK OF OVERRELIANCE

Statistical Sample Results Evaluation Table for Test of Controls
Upper Occurrence Limit (for large populations)

Sample Size	Actual Number of Occurrences Found								
	0	1	2	3	4	5	6	7	8
25	11.3	17.6	*	*	*	*	*	*	*
30	9.5	14.9	19.5	*	*	*	*	*	*
35	8.2	12.9	16.9	*	*	*	*	*	*
40	7.2	11.3	14.9	18.3	*	*	*	*	*
45	6.4	10.1	13.3	16.3	19.2	*	*	*	*
50	5.8	9.1	12.1	14.8	17.4	19.9	*	*	*
55	5.3	8.3	11.0	13.5	15.9	18.1	*	*	*
60	4.9	7.7	10.1	12.4	14.6	16.7	18.8	*	*
65	4.5	7.1	9.4	11.5	13.5	15.5	17.4	19.3	*
70	4.2	6.6	8.7	10.7	12.6	14.4	16.2	18.0	19.7
75	3.9	6.2	8.2	10.0	11.8	13.5	15.2	16.9	18.4
80	3.7	5.8	7.7	9.4	11.1	12.7	14.3	15.8	17.3
90	3.3	5.2	6.8	8.4	9.9	11.3	12.7	14.1	15.5
100	3.0	4.7	6.2	7.6	8.9	10.2	11.5	12.7	14.0
125	2.4	3.7	4.9	6.1	7.2	8.2	9.3	10.3	11.3
150	2.0	3.1	4.1	5.1	6.0	6.9	7.7	8.6	9.4
200	1.5	2.3	3.1	3.8	4.5	5.2	5.8	6.5	7.1

number table. With a blind start at column 5, row 6, the auditor selects the following sales orders: 277, 188, 174, 496, 482, 312, and so on.

After carrying out the sampling plan, the auditor discovers that four sales orders are missing the credit manager's signature (apparently an error on the part of the credit manager). The sample deviation rate is thus 4/127 or 3.1%. The upper occurrence limits, determined by referring to Table 3 is 7.2. In evaluating the results 127 is used for the sample size for conservative reasons. Because the upper occurrence limit exceeds the tolerable rate of 7%, the auditor rejects the control and attempts to identify a compensating control for further tests of compliance.

DISCOVERY SAMPLING

Discovery sampling is used in a search for critical deviations such as for fraud and irregularities. This sampling technique may be employed when the auditor wants to determine if an acceptable irregularity rate in the population has been exceeded. If the rate is not excessive, no additional audit testing is required. If it is exceeded, alternative audit procedures are necessary. An

Table 4

10 PERCENT RISK OF OVERRELIANCE

Sample Size	Actual Number of Occurrences Found								
	0	1	2	3	4	5	6	7	8
20	10.9	18.1	*	*	*	*	*	*	*
25	8.8	14.7	19.9	*	*	*	*	*	*
30	7.4	12.4	16.8	*	*	*	*	*	*
35	6.4	10.7	14.5	18.1	*	*	*	*	*
40	5.6	9.4	12.8	15.9	19.0	*	*	*	*
45	5.0	8.4	11.4	14.2	17.0	19.6	*	*	*
50	4.5	7.6	10.3	12.9	15.4	17.8	*	*	*
55	4.1	6.9	9.4	11.7	14.0	16.2	18.4	*	*
60	3.8	6.3	8.6	10.8	12.9	14.9	15.9	18.8	*
70	3.2	5.4	7.4	9.3	11.1	12.8	14.6	16.2	17.9
80	2.8	4.8	6.5	8.3	9.7	11.3	12.8	14.3	15.7
90	2.5	4.3	5.8	7.3	8.7	10.1	11.4	12.7	14.0
100	2.3	3.8	5.2	6.6	7.8	9.1	10.3	11.5	12.7
120	1.9	3.2	4.4	5.5	6.6	7.6	8.6	9.6	10.6
160	1.4	2.4	3.3	4.1	4.9	5.7	6.5	7.2	8.0
200	1.1	1.9	2.6	3.3	4.0	4.6	5.2	5.8	6.4

*over 20%

attribute estimate may also be required. In discovery sampling, there is a minimum sample size that would include at least one irregularity if the population errors are greater than a given rate. Hence, if one irregularity is found in the sample, the test is resolved. Because discovery sampling is based on a minimum sample size to uncover only one irregularity, the sample size has to be increased in the event a useful attribute estimate is needed, such as the real irregularity rate in the population.

In using discovery sampling, a determination has to be made regarding population size, minimum unacceptable error rate, and confidence level. Sample size is determined from a sampling table. In the event that none of the random samples show an irregularity, it is concluded that the actual irregularity rate is less than the minimum unacceptable irregularity rate at the desired confidence level. Typically, the technique is used to spot groups of documents needing thorough testing.

EXAMPLE 4

The auditor suspects fraud and wants to determine if any such fraud exists. The auditor is examining vouchers for proper authorization. Cost/benefit makes it not practical for the internal auditor to look at all vouch-

Table 5

RANDOM NUMBER TABLE

Column

Line	(1)	(2)	(3)	(4)	(5)	(6)	(7)	(8)	(9)	(10)	(11)	(12)	(13)	(14)
1	10480	15011	01536	02011	81647	91646	69179	14194	62590	36207	20969	99570	91291	90700
2	22368	46573	25595	85393	30995	89198	27982	53402	93965	34095	52666	19174	39615	99505
3	24130	48360	22527	97265	76393	64809	15179	24830	49340	32081	30680	19655	63348	58629
4	42167	93093	06243	61650	07856	16376	39440	53537	71341	57004	00849	74917	97758	16379
5	37570	39975	81837	16656	06121	91782	60468	81305	49684	60672	14110	06927	01263	54613
6	77921	06907	11008	42751	27756	53498	18602	70659	90655	15053	21916	81825	44394	42880
7	99562	72905	56420	69994	98872	31016	71194	18738	44013	48840	63213	21069	10634	12952
8	96301	91977	05463	07972	18876	20922	94595	56869	69014	60045	18425	84903	42508	32307
9	89579	14342	63661	10281	17453	18103	57740	84378	25331	12566	58678	44947	05585	56941
10	85475	36857	53342	53988	53060	59533	38867	62300	08158	17983	16439	11458	18593	64952
11	28918	69578	88231	33276	70997	79936	56865	05859	90106	31595	01547	85590	91610	78188
12	63553	40961	48235	03427	49626	69445	18663	72695	52180	20847	12234	90511	33703	90332
13	09429	93969	52636	92737	88974	33488	36320	17617	30015	08272	84115	27156	30613	74952
14	10365	61129	87529	85689	48237	52267	67689	93394	01511	26358	85104	20285	29975	89868
15	07119	97336	71048	08178	77233	13916	47564	81056	97735	85977	29372	74461	28551	90707
16	51085	12765	51821	51259	77452	16308	60756	92144	49442	53900	70960	63990	75601	40719
17	02368	21382	52404	60268	89368	19885	55322	44819	01188	63255	64835	44919	05944	55157
18	01011	54092	33362	94904	31273	04146	18594	29852	71585	85030	51132	01915	92747	64951
19	52162	53916	46369	58586	23216	14513	83149	98736	23495	64350	94738	17752	35156	35749
20	07056	97628	33787	09998	42698	06691	76988	13602	51851	46104	88916	19509	25625	58104
21	48663	91245	85828	14346	09172	30168	90229	04734	59193	22178	30421	61666	99904	32812
22	54164	58492	22421	74103	47070	25306	76468	26384	58151	06646	21524	15227	96909	44592

694

23	32639	32363	05597	24200	13363	38005	94342	28728	35806	06912	17012	64161	18296	22851
24	29334	27001	87637	87308	58731	00256	45834	15398	46557	41135	10367	07684	36188	18510
25	02488	33062	28834	07351	19731	92420	60952	61280	50001	67658	32586	86679	50720	94953
26	81525	72295	04839	96423	24878	82651	66566	14778	76797	14780	13300	87074	79666	95725
27	29676	20591	68085	26432	46901	20849	89768	81536	86645	12659	92259	57102	80428	25280
28	00742	57392	39064	66432	84673	40027	32832	61362	98947	96067	64760	64584	96096	98253
29	05366	04213	25669	26422	44407	44048	37937	63904	45766	66134	75470	66520	34693	90449
30	91921	26418	64117	94305	26766	25940	39972	22209	71500	64568	91402	42416	07844	69618
31	00582	04711	87917	77341	42206	35126	74087	99547	81817	42607	43808	76655	62028	76630
32	00725	69884	62797	56170	86324	88072	76222	36086	84637	93161	76038	65855	77919	88006
33	69011	65795	95876	55293	18988	27354	26575	08625	40801	59920	29841	80150	12777	48501
34	25976	57948	29888	80604	67917	48708	18912	82271	65424	69774	33611	54262	85963	03547
35	09763	83473	73577	12908	30883	18317	28290	35797	05998	41688	34952	37888	38917	80050
36	91567	42595	29758	30134	04024	86385	29880	99730	55536	84855	29080	09250	79656	73211
37	17955	56349	90999	49127	20044	59931	06115	20542	18059	02008	73708	83517	36103	42791
38	46503	18584	18845	49618	02304	51038	20655	58727	28168	15475	56942	53389	20562	87338
39	92157	89634	94824	78171	84610	82834	09922	25417	44137	48413	25555	21246	35509	20468
40	14577	62765	35605	81263	39667	47358	56873	56307	61607	49518	89656	20103	77490	18062
41	98427	07523	33362	64270	01638	92477	66969	98420	04880	45585	46565	04102	46880	45709
42	34914	63976	88720	82765	34476	17032	87589	40836	32427	70002	70663	88863	77775	69348
43	70060	28277	39475	46473	23219	53416	94970	25832	69975	94884	19661	72828	00102	66794
44	53976	54914	06990	67245	68350	82948	11398	42878	80287	98267	47363	46634	06541	97809
45	76072	29515	40980	07391	58745	25774	22987	80059	39911	96189	41151	14322	60697	59583
46	90725	52210	83974	29992	65831	38857	50490	83765	55657	14361	31720	57375	56228	41546
47	64364	67412	33339	31926	14883	24413	59744	92351	97473	89286	38931	04110	23726	51900
48	08962	00358	31662	25388	61642	34072	81249	35648	56891	69352	48373	45578	78547	81788
49	95012	68379	93526	70765	10592	04542	76463	54328	02349	17247	28865	14777	62730	92277
50	15664	10493	20492	38391	91132	21999	59516	81652	27195	48223	46751	22923	32261	85653

ers. Discovery sampling can be used to obtain a 90% confidence level that the absence of proper authorization is less than 1%. According to the table, for 2,000 voucher items, a random sample size of 220 is needed. If fraud does not exist in the sample, we can conclude that the population contains less than 1% fraud. In the event a single fraudulent situation if found, the internal auditor stops sampling and examines all vouchers.

MULTISTAGE SAMPLING

Multistage sampling consists of sampling at multilevels where an estimate of the total dollars of the population that is in groups over a wide area is required. For example, if an estimate of the total dollar value of inventory of a chain store or supermarket with widely distributed outlets is required, the multistage techniques would be appropriate. Selections at any level may be accomplished using alternative sampling methods (e.g., random, stratified, systematic).

Multistage sampling will necessitate a larger sample size and more sophisticated evaluation formulas than is the case with simple or stratified sampling methods.

CLASSICAL VARIABLES SAMPLING

Classical variables sampling is comprised of a family of three statistical techniques (mean per unit approach, difference sampling, and ratio sampling) which use normal distribution theory and are concerned with ascertaining whether the total dollar value of account balances are properly stated. The method estimates the statistical range within which the true account balance being tested falls. It requires an estimate of population variability (population standard deviation) and necessitates the use of a computer.

It is an approach to predict what the value of a particular variable in the population will be. Audit-related variables are usually the total population or the arithmetic mean. For example, an internal auditor may estimate the cost of a group of inventory components. The per item cost is determined. Finally, there is a statistical derivation of the plus or minus range of the total inventory value under audit. Variables sampling may also be used to estimate the dollar amount of error (misstatement) in a population.

STRATIFIED SAMPLING

When using stratified sampling, the internal auditor segregates the population into homogeneous subgroups (strata) according to a common characteristic (such as the stratification of total credit sales into open account sales and credit card sales). The auditor then samples each strata. The sample results should be separately appraised and combined to provide an estimate of the population characteristics. Homogeneity is enhanced when very high or low value items are segregated into individual strata. Homogeneity in the population improves the efficiency of the sample. Thus, usually fewer items have to be examined to appraise several strata separately then to evaluate the whole population. Stratification benefits the sampling process and enhances auditor ability to relate sample selection to the materiality and turnover of items. The type of audit procedures applied to each stratum may vary based on individual circumstances and the nature of the environment. An application of stratified sampling is when total inventory (population) is broken down into major groups based on dollar balances for testing purposes. An illustration follows:

Stratum	Method of Selection Used
1. All inventory items of $50,000 or more	100% tested
2. All other inventory items under $50,000	Random number table selection

NONSTATISTICAL SAMPLING

Nonstatistical sampling is when an auditor uses his or her prior experience and knowledge to compute the number of sampling units and specific items to be studied from the population. The sample takes into account the nature of the business and unique characteristics that may exist. The internal auditor must be objective in carrying out the sample and perform detailed analysis to assure the sampled units are correct. This approach may be advisable when a particular area of the population is being carefully examined or immediate results and feedback are needed. This technique is used primarily when the audit population consists of either a small number of high dollar-value items or items with an immaterial aggregate cost. For example, this approach may be used in selecting twenty additions to property and equipment, worth $200,000, for vouching when total additions consist of forty items aggregating $250,000.

Note: A nonstatistical sample does *not* involve random selection. There is no computation made of sampling error, precision, or confidence level. Thus, there is an absence of statistical techniques and conclusions.

The auditor in using nonstatistical sampling considers the same factors in determining sample size and in evaluating sample results as in statistical sampling. The difference is that in nonstatistical sampling, the auditor does not quantify or explicitly enumerate values for these factors. In statistical sampling, however, they are explicitly quantified. That is, in nonstatistical sampling, the auditor determines the sample size, selects a sample, and evaluates the sample results entirely on the basis of subjective criteria and his own experience, i.e., judgment. In addition, it is important to note that a properly designed nonstatistical sample may be just as effective as a statistical sample.

V

FINANCIAL ANALYSIS

27

Financial Statement Analysis*

Financial statement analysis is an appraisal of a company's previous financial performance and its future potential. It looks at the overall health and operating performance of the business. This chapter covers analytical tools to be followed in appraising the balance sheet, analyzing the income statement, and evaluating financial structure. Financial management analyzes the financial statements to see how the company looks to the financial community and what corrective steps and policies can be initiated to minimize and solve financial problems. Areas of risk are identified. Means to efficiently utilize assets and earn greater returns are concentrated on. Financial statement analysis aids in determining the appropriateness of mergers and acquisitions.

A company's financial health has a bearing upon its price-earnings ratio, bond rating, cost of financing, and availability of financing.

To obtain worthwhile conclusions from financial ratios, the financial manager has to make two comparisons:

- *Industry Comparison.* The financial executive should compare the company's ratios to those of competing companies in the industry or with industry standards. Industry norms can be obtained from such services as Dun and Bradstreet, Robert Morris Associates, Standard and Poor's, and Value Line.

    Examples: Dun and Bradstreet computes 14 ratios for each of 125 lines of business. They are published annually in *Dun's Review and Key Business Ratios.* Robert Morris Associates publishes *Annual Statement Studies.* Sixteen ratios are computed for more than 300 lines of business, as is a percentage distribution of items on the balance sheet and income statement (common size financial statements).

*We express our appreciation to Stan Chu, MS, CPA, of the City University of New York, for his coauthoring of this chapter.

In analyzing a company, you should appraise the trends in its industry. What is the pattern of growth or decline in the industry? The profit dollar is worth more if earned in a healthy, expanding industry than in a declining one.

You have to make certain that the financial data of competitors are comparable to yours. For example, you can not compare profitability when your company uses FIFO while a competitor uses LIFO for inventory valuation. In this case, you must restate the earnings of both companies on a comparative basis.

- *Trend Analysis.* A company's ratio may be compared over several years to identify direction of financial health or operational performance. An attempt should be made to uncover the reasons for the change.

The optimum value for any given ratio usually varies across industry lines, through time, and within different companies in the same industry. In other words, a ratio deemed optimum for one company may be inadequate for another. A particular ratio is typically deemed optimum within a given range of values. An increase or decrease beyond this range points to weakness or inefficiency.

Example: While a low current ratio may indicate poor liquidity, a very high current ratio may reflect inefficient utilization of assets (e.g., excessive inventory) or inability to use short-term credit to the firm's advantage.

For a seasonal business, you may find that year-end financial data are not representative. Thus, averages based on quarterly or monthly information may be used to level out seasonality effects.

When computing ratios for *analytical* purposes, you may also want to use the realistic values for balance sheet accounts rather than reported amounts. For example, marketable securities are shown at the lower of cost or market applied on a total portfolio basis. Thus, if cost is $100,000 and market is $180,000, the portfolio would be shown at $100,000. But realistically the securities are worth $180,000 in today's market.

A distorted trend signals a possible problem requiring management attention. However, a lack of change does not always mean normalcy. For example, manpower growth may be up but production/sales may be static or down. Hence, manpower costs may be disproportionate to operational activity.

AUDIT ATTENTION

Financial statement analysis indicates areas requiring audit attention. You should look at the percentage change in an account over the years or relative to some base year to identify inconsistencies. **Example**: If promotion and entertainment expense to sales was 3% last year and shot up to 15% this year, the internal auditor would want to know the reasons. This would be particularly disturbing if other competing companies still had a percentage relationship of 3%. The internal auditor might suspect that the promotion and entertainment expense account contained some personal rather than business charges. Supporting documentation for the charges would be requested and carefully reviewed by the internal auditor.

HORIZONTAL AND VERTICAL ANALYSIS

Horizontal analysis looks at the trend in accounts over the years and aids in identifying areas of wide divergence mandating further attention. Horizontal analysis may also be presented by showing trends relative to a base year.

EXAMPLE 1

X Company's revenue in 19X1 was $200,000 and in 19X2 was $250,000. The percentage increase equals:

$$\frac{\text{Change}}{\text{Prior Year}} = \frac{\$\ 50,000}{\$200,000} = 25\%$$

In vertical analysis, a significant item on a financial statement is used as a base value, and all other items on the financial statement are compared to it. In performing vertical analysis for the balance sheet, total assets is assigned 100%. Each asset is expressed as a percentage of total assets. Total liabilities and stockholders' equity is also assigned 100%. Each liability and stockholders' equity account is then expressed as a percentage of total liabilities and stockholders' equity. In the income statement, net sales are given the value of 100% and all other accounts are appraised in comparison to net sales. The resulting figures are then given in a common size statement.

Vertical analysis is helpful in disclosing the internal structure of the business and possible problem areas. It shows the relationship between each income statement account and revenue. It indicates the mix of assets that produces the income and the mix of the sources of capital, whether by current or long-term liabilities or by equity funding. Besides making internal evaluation possible, the results of vertical analysis are also employed to appraise the company's relative position in the industry. Horizontal and vertical analysis point to possible problem areas to be evaluated by the financial manager.

EXAMPLE 2

X Company
Common-Size Income
Statement
For the Year Ended 12/31/19X5

Sales	$40,000	100%
Less: Cost of Sales	10,000	25%
Gross Profit	$30,000	75%
Less: Expenses	4,000	10%
Net Income	$26,000	65%

BALANCE SHEET ANALYSIS

As a financial manager, you have to be able to analyze asset and liability accounts, evaluate corporate liquidity, appraise business solvency, and look to signs of possible business failure. You are concerned with the realizability of assets, turnover, and earning potential. Besides analyzing your company's financial health, you will want to make recommendations for improvement so that financial problems are rectified. Also, you can identify corporate strength which may further be taken advantage of. The evaluation of liabilities considers their possible overstatement or understatement.

Appraising Asset Quality

Asset quality applies to the certainty associated with the amount and timing of the realization of the assets in cash. Therefore, assets should be categorized by risk category. **What to Do:** Calculate the following ratios: (1) high-risk assets to total assets, and (2) high-risk assets to sales. If high risk exists in assets, future write-offs may occur. For instance, the realization of goodwill is more doubtful than machinery. Also evaluate the risk of each major asset category. For example, receivables from an economically unstable government (e.g., Mexico) has greater risk than a receivable from ITT. **Special Note:** Single-purpose assets have greater risk than multipurpose ones. **What to Watch Out for:** Assets with no separable value that cannot be sold easily, such as intangibles and work-in-process. On the contrary, marketable securities are readily salable.

In appraising realization risk in assets, the effect of changing government policies on the entity has to be taken into account. Risk may exist with chemicals and other products deemed hazardous to health. Huge inventory losses may have to be taken.

EXAMPLE 3

Company A presents total assets of $6 million and sales of $10 million. Included in total assets are the following high risk assets:

Deferred moving costs	$300,000
Deferred plant rearrangement costs	100,000
Receivables for claims under a government contract	200,000
Goodwill	150,000

Applicable ratios are:

$$\frac{\text{High-risk Assets}}{\text{Total Assets}} = \frac{\$\ 750,000}{\$6,000,000} = \underline{12.5\%}$$

$$\frac{\text{High-risk Assets}}{\text{Sales}} = \frac{\$\ 750,000}{\$10,000,000} = \underline{7.5\%}$$

Cash

How much of the cash balance is unavailable for use or restricted? Examples are a compensating balance and cash held in a foreign country where remission restrictions exist. Note that foreign currency holdings are generally stated at year-end exchange rates but may change rapidly.

You should determine the ratio of sales to cash. A high turnover rate may indicate a deficient cash position. This may lead to financial problems if additional financing is not available at reasonable interest rates. A low turnover ratio indicates excessive cash being held.

EXAMPLE 4

	19X1	19X2
Cash	$ 500,000	$ 400,000
Sales	8,000,000	9,000,000
Industry norm for cash turnover rate	15.8 times	16.2 times

The turnover of cash is 16 ($8,000,000/$500,000) in 19X1 and 22.5 ($9,000,000/$400,000) in 19X2. It is clear that the company has a cash deficiency in 19X2, which implies a possible liquidity problem.

You should distinguish between two types of cash: cash needed for operating purposes and cash required for capital expenditures. While the former must be paid, the latter is postponable.

Accounts Receivable

Realization risk in receivables can be appraised by studying the nature of the receivable balance. Examples of high risk receivables include amounts from economically unstable foreign countries, receivables subject to offset provisions, and receivables due from a company experiencing severe financial problems. Further, companies dependent on a few customers have greater risk than those with a large number of important accounts. Receivables due from industry are typically safer than receivables arising from consumers. Fair trade laws are more protective of consumers.

Accounts receivable ratios include the accounts receivable turnover and the average collection period. The accounts receivable turnover ratio reveals the number of times accounts receivable is collected during the period. It equals net sales divided by average accounts receivable. Average accounts receivable for the period is the beginning accounts receivable balance plus the ending accounts receivable balance divided by 2. (However, in a seasonal business where sales vary greatly during the year, this ratio can become distorted unless proper averaging takes place. In such a case, monthly or quarterly sales figures should be used). A higher turnover rate is generally desirable because it indicates faster collections. However, an excessively high ratio may point to too tight a credit policy, with the company not tapping the potential for profit through sales to customers in higher risk classes. But in changing its credit policy, the company must weigh the profit potential against the risk inherent in selling to more marginal customers.

The *average collection period* (days sales in receivables) is the number of days it takes to collect receivables.

$$\text{Average collection period} = \frac{365}{\text{accounts receivable turnover}}$$

Separate collection periods may be calculated by type of customer, major product line, and market territory.

A significant increase in collection days may indicate a danger that customer balances may become uncollectible. However, reference should be made to the collection period common in the industry. One reason for an increase may be that the company is now selling to highly marginal customers. The financial manager should compare the company's credit terms with the degree to which customer accounts are delinquent. An *aging schedule* is helpful.

The quality of receivables may also be appraised by referring to customer ratings given by credit agencies.

Also look for a buildup over time in the ratios of (1) accounts receivable to total assets and (2) accounts receivable to sales as indicative of a receivable collection problem. Receivables outstanding in excess of the expected payment date and relative to industry norm implies a higher probability of uncollectibility.

The financial manager should appraise the trends in bad debts to accounts receivable and bad debts to sales. An unwarranted decrease in bad debts lowers the quality of earnings. This may happen when there is a decline in bad debts even though the company is selling to less credit worthy customers and/or actual bad debt losses are increasing.

EXAMPLE 5

A company reports the following information:

	19X1	19X2
Sales	$100,000	$130,000
Accounts receivable	30,000	40,000
Bad debts	2,000	2,200

You conclude that the company is selling to more risky customers in 19X2 relative to 19X1.

Relevant ratios follow:

	19X1	19X2
Bad debts to sales	2.0%	1.7%
Bad debts to accounts receivable	6.7%	5.5%

Because the company is selling to more marginal customers, its bad debt provision should increase in 19X2. However, the ratios of bad debts to sales and bad debts to accounts receivable actually decreased. The impact of understating bad debts is to overstate net income and accounts receivable. Thus, net income should be lowered for the incremental profit arising from the unwarranted lowering of bad debts. If you decide that a realistic bad debt percentage to accounts receivable is 6.5%, then the bad debt expense should be $2,600 ($40,000 × 6.5%). Net income should thus be reduced by $400 ($2,600 less $2,200).

Receivables are of low quality if they arose from loading customers up with unneeded merchandise by giving generous credit terms. "Red flags" as to this happening include:

- A significant increase in sales in the final quarter of the year
- A substantial amount of sales returns in the first quarter of the next year
- A material decrease in sales for the first quarter of the next year

The trend in sales returns and allowances is often a good reflection of the quality of merchandise sold to customers. A significant decrease in a firm's sales allowance account as a percentage of sales is not in conformity with reality when a greater liability for dealer returns exist. This will result in lower earnings quality.

EXAMPLE 6

Company X's sales and sales returns for the period 19X3 to 19X5 follow:

	19X5	19X4	19X3
Balance in sales returns account at year-end	$2,000	$3,800	$ 1,550
Sales	$240,000	$215,000	$100,000
Percentage of sales returns to sales	.0083	.0177	.0155

The reduction in the ratio of sales returns to sales from 19X4 to 19X5 indicates that less of a provision for returns is being made by the company. This would appear unrealistic if there is a greater liability for dealer returns and credits on an expanded sales base.

Inventory

An inventory buildup may mean realization problems. The buildup may be at the plant, wholesaler, or retailer. A sign of a buildup is when inventory increases at a much faster rate than the increase in sales. **What to Watch Out for:** A decline in raw materials coupled with a rise in work-in-process and finished goods pointing to a future production slowdown.

If the company is holding excess inventory, there is an opportunity cost of tying up money in inventory. Further, there is a high carrying cost for storing merchandise. Why aren't certain types of merchandise selling well? Calculate turnover rates for each inventory category and by department. Possible reasons for a low turnover rate are overstocking, obsolescence, product line deficiencies, or poor marketing efforts. There are cases where a low inventory rate is appropriate. **Examples:** A higher inventory level may arise because of expected future increases in price or when a new product has been introduced for which the advertising efforts have not been felt yet.

Note: The turnover rate may be unrepresentatively high when the business uses a "natural year-end" because at that time the inventory balance will be exceptionally low. **What to Do:** Compute the number of days inventory is held and compare it to the industry norm and previous years.

$$\text{Inventory turnover} = \frac{\text{Cost of Goods Sold}}{\text{Average Inventory}}$$

$$\text{Age of inventory} = \frac{365}{\text{Turnover}}$$

Also look at the trend in inventory to sales.

The effect of changing government policies on the entity has to be taken into account. Risk may exist, for example, with chemicals and other products deemed hazardous to health. Huge inventory losses may have to be taken.

A high turnover rate may point to inadequate inventory, possibly leading to a loss in business.

What to Watch Out for: Merchandise that is susceptible to price variability, "fad," specialized, perishable, technological, and luxurious goods. On the contrary, low realization risk is with standardized, staple, and necessity items.

Note: Raw material inventory is safer than finished goods or work-in-process since raw material has more universal and varied uses.

Questions to be asked:

- Is inventory collateralized against a loan? If so, creditors can retain it in the event of nonpayment of the obligation.
- Is there adequate insurance in case of loss? There is a particular problem when insurance cannot be obtained for the item because of high risk (e.g.,

geographic location of inventory is in a high crime area or there is susceptibility to floods).

- Is it subject to political risk (e.g., big cars and an oil crisis)?

Look for inventory that is overstated due to mistakes in quantities, costing, pricing, and valuation.

Warning: The more technical a product and the more dependent the valuation on internally developed cost records, the more susceptible are cost estimates to misstatement. Also, sudden inventory write-offs raise questions about the overall salability of inventory.

Is the change in inventory method appropriate (e.g., *new* FASB pronouncement, SEC Release, or IRS ruling)?

In gauging manufacturing efficiency, you should look at the relationship between indirect labor and direct labor since a constant level of both are needed to efficiently run the organization.

EXAMPLE 7

A company presents the following makeup of inventory:

	19X1	19X2
Raw materials	$89,000	$78,000
Work-in-process	67,000	120,000
Finished goods	16,000	31,000

Your analysis of the inventory shows there was a material divergence in the inventory components between 19X1 and 19X2. There was a reduction in raw material by 12.4% ($11,000/$89,000), while work-in-process rose by 79.1% ($53,000/$67,000) and finished goods rose by 93.8% ($15,000/$16,000). The lack of consistency in the trend between raw materials relative to work-in-process and finished goods may imply a forthcoming cutback in production. An obsolescence problem may also exist applicable to work-in-process and finished goods due to the sizable buildup.

The company's operating cycle should be determined which equals the average collection period plus the average age of inventory. A short operating cycle is desired so that cash flow is expedited.

Investments

An indication of the fair value of investments may be the revenue (dividend income, interest income) obtained from them. Have decreases in portfolio market values been recognized in the accounts? Higher realization risk exists where there is a declining trend in the percentage of earnings derived from investments to their carrying value. Also check for unrealized losses in the portfolio occurring after year-end.

EXAMPLE 8

Company X presents the following information:

	19X1	19X2
Investments	$50,000	$60,000
Investment Income	$ 7,000	$ 5,000

The percent of investment income to total investments decreased from 14% in 19X1 to 8.3% in 19X2, pointing to higher realization risk in the portfolio.

If a company is buying securities in other companies for diversification purposes, this will reduce overall risk. Risk in an investment portfolio can be ascertained by computing the standard deviation of its rate of return.

When an investment portfolio has a market value above cost, it constitutes an undervalued asset.

An investment portfolio of securities fluctuating widely in price is of higher realization risk than a portfolio that is diversified by industry and economic sector. However, the former portfolio will show greater profitability in a bull market. **Recommendations:** Appraise the extent of diversification and stability of the investment portfolio. There is less risk when securities are negatively correlated (price goes in opposite directions) or not correlated compared to a portfolio of positively correlated securities (price goes in same direction). Is the portfolio of poor quality securities, such as "junk" bonds?

Note cases where debt securities have a cost in excess of market value.

Fixed Assets

Is there sufficient maintenance of productive assets to ensure current and future earning power? Lessened operational efficiency and breakdowns occur when obsolete assets have not been replaced and/or required repairs made. **What to Do:** Determine the age and condition of each major asset category, as well as the cost to replace old assets. Determine output levels, downtime, and temporary discontinuances. Inactive and unproductive assets are a drain on the firm. Are the fixed assets specialized or risky, making them susceptible to obsolescence?

Note: Pollution-causing equipment may necessitate replacement or modification to meet governmental ecology requirements.

Ratio trends to be calculated are:

• Fixed asset acquisitions to total assets. The trend is particularly revealing for a technological company that has to keep up-to-date. A decrease in the trend points to the failure to replace older assets on a timely basis.

• Repairs and maintenance to fixed assets

• Repairs and maintenance to sales

- Sales to fixed assets
- Net income to fixed assets

The fixed asset turnover ratio (net sales to average fixed assets) aids in appraising a company's ability to use its asset base efficiently to obtain revenue. A low ratio may mean that investment in fixed assets is excessive relative to the output generated.

A high ratio of sales to floor space indicates the efficient utilization of space.

A company having specialized or risky fixed assets has greater vulnerability to asset obsolescence. Examples include machinery used to manufacture specialized products and "fad" items.

When a company's rate of return on assets (e.g., net income to fixed assets) is poor, the firm may be justified in not maintaining fixed assets. If the industry is declining, fixed asset replacement and repairs may have been restricted.

It is better for a company when assets are mobile and/or can easily be modified since it affords the firm greater flexibility. If the assets are easily accessible, it will also be easier to repair them. The location of the assets is also important since that may affect their condition and security. The location will also affect property taxes, so a company may be able to save on taxes by having the plant located in a low tax area.

EXAMPLE 9

The following information applies to X Company:

	19X1	19X2
Depreciation expense to fixed assets	5.3%	4.4%
Depreciation expense to sales	4.0%	3.3%

The above declining ratios indicate improper provision for the deterioration of assets.

Recommendation: Use a depreciation method that best approximates the decline in usefulness of the fixed asset. Compare the depreciation rate to the industry norm. **What to Do:** Calculate the trend in depreciation expense to fixed assets and depreciation expense to sales. If there are decreasing trends, inadequate depreciation charges may exist. Compare the book depreciation rate to the tax depreciation rate.

A vacillating depreciation policy will distort continuity in earnings.

What to Watch Out for: A material decline in sales coupled with a significant increase in capital expenditures may be inconsistent. It could point to overexpansion and later write-offs.

EXAMPLE 10

Company T presents the following information regarding its fixed assets:

	19X1	19X2
Fixed Assets	$120,000	$105,000
Repairs and Maintenance	6,000	4,500
Replacement Cost	205,000	250,000

The company has inadequately maintained its assets as indicated by:

- The reduction in the ratio of repairs and maintenance to fixed assets from 5% in 19X1 to 4.3% in 19X2
- The material variation between replacement cost and historical cost
- The reduction in fixed assets over the year

Management of Fixed Assets

Fixed assets should meet the operational needs of the business with maximum productivity at minimum cost. These long-term expenditures are significant in amount, and can result in great loss to the company if fixed assets are improperly managed. Capital investments result in a higher break-even point due to the resulting costs associated with them including depreciation, insurance, and property taxes.

A new company requires greater capital expansion for growth. There is less of a need for additional capital facilities by an established, mature company with strong market share.

For control purposes, unique control numbers should be securely affixed to fixed assets. There should be periodic appraisals to assess the adequacy of insurance coverage.

You should not buy elaborate manufacturing facilities for a new product until it has shown success. In the initial stages, it is recommended that production be subcontracted. With an established product, productivity is achieved through internal capital expansion. In evaluating production facilities, consideration should be given to scrap, rejects, cost per unit, and malfunctioning time.

The financial manager is concerned with the following in managing fixed assets:

- Purchasing the "right" equipment for the firm's needs
- Proper timing of capital expenditures
- Keeping capital expenditures within the financial capabilities of the firm
- Optimally financing capital expenditures
- Physical care and security of property
- Correlating capital expenditures to fully use "tax breaks"

Intangible Assets

Realization risk is indicated when there is a high ratio of intangible assets to total assets. The amounts recorded for intangibles may be overstated relative to their market value or to their future income-generating capacity. For instance, in a recessionary environment, goodwill on the books may be worthless. Since APB Opinion 17 provides for a 40-year amortization period for intangibles, your company should not ignore economic reality by making only minimum amortization provisions. Further, intangibles acquired before the effective date of the opinion are not even subject to such minimum amortization.

What to Do: Calculate trends in the following ratios:

- Intangible assets to total assets
- Intangible assets to stockholders' equity
- Intangible assets to sales
- Intangible assets to net income
- Specific, questionable intangible assets (e.g., goodwill) to total assets
- Change in intangible assets to change in net income

EXAMPLE 11

A company shows the following data:

	19X1	19X2
Intangible assets	$ 58,000	$187,000
Total assets	512,000	530,000
Sales	640,000	655,000
Net income	120,000	140,000

Relevant ratios can now be computed as follows:

	19X1	19X2
Intangible assets to total assets	11.3%	35.3%
Intangible assets to sales	9.1%	28.5%

Higher realization risk in intangibles is indicated by the higher ratios of intangible assets to total assets and intangible assets to sales. Also, the 222.4% increase in intangibles along with the 16.7% increase in net income imply that earnings have been overstated as a result of the failure to incorporate items that have been expensed rather than capitalized.

What to Watch Out for: Leasehold improvements because they have no cash realizability.

Note: In some instances, intangible assets may be undervalued, such as a highly successful patented product. However, can the patent product be infringed upon by minor alteration? Is it a high-technological item? What is the financial strength of the company to defend itself against those infringing upon its patented product? What are the expiration dates of patents, and are new ones coming on stream?

A company's goodwill account should be appraised to ascertain whether the firm acquired has superior earning potential to justify the excess of cost over fair market value of net assets paid for it. If the acquired company does not have superior profit potential, the goodwill has no value because excess earnings do not exist relative to other companies in the industry. However, internally developed goodwill is expensed and not capitalized. It represents an undervalued asset, such as the good reputation of McDonald's.

Deferred Charges

Deferred charges depend on estimates of future probabilities and developments to a greater extent than do other assets. These estimates are often overly optimistic. Is the business deferring an item that has no future economic benefit only to defer costs so as not to burden reported results? Further, deferred charges do not constitute cash-realizable assets, and thus cannot meet creditor claims. Examples of questionable deferred costs are start up costs, rearrangement costs, and promotional costs.

What to Do: Calculate trends in the ratios of (1) deferred charges to sales, (2) deferred charges to net income, and (3) deferred charges (e.g., advertising) to total expenditures (e.g., total advertising). Watch out for increasing trends.

A high ratio of intangible assets and deferred charges to total assets points to an asset structure of greater realization risk. Overstated assets in terms of realizability may necessitate later write-offs.

EXAMPLE 12

A company presents the following information:

	19X1	19X2
Deferred charges	$47,000	$121,000
Total assets	580,000	650,000
Sales	680,000	720,000
Net income	190,000	205,000

Relevant ratios are now calculated as follows:

	19X1	19X2
Deferred charges to total assets	8.1%	18.6%
Deferred charges to sales	6.9%	16.8%
Deferred charges to net income	24.7%	59.0%

Greater realization risk is indicated from the higher ratios. The net income for 19X2 is most likely overstated, since items that should have been expensed are probably included in the deferred charge balance.

Asset Utilization

Asset utilization may be measured by the total asset turnover. It is useful in appraising an entity's ability to use its asset base efficiently to obtain revenue. A low ratio may be caused from numerous factors, and it is essential to identify the causes. For instance, it must be determined if the investment in assets is excessive relative to the value of the output being produced. If so, the business may wish to consolidate its present operation, perhaps by selling some of its assets and investing the funds for a higher return or using them to expand into a more profitable area.

$$\text{Total asset turnover} = \frac{\text{net sales}}{\text{average total assets}}$$

The operating assets ratio (total operating assets to total assets) concentrates on those assets *actively employed in current operations*. Such assets exclude (1) past-oriented assets and (2) future-oriented assets. Past-oriented assets arise from prior errors, inefficiencies, or losses because of competitive factors or changes in business plans. These assets have not yet been formerly recognized in the accounts. Examples are obsolete goods, idle plants, receivables under litigation, delinquent receivables, and nonperforming loans (no interest being recognized). Future-oriented assets are acquired for corporate growth or generating future sales. Examples are land held for speculation and factories under construction. Nonoperating assets reduce profits and return on investment because no benefit to current operations occurs. They neither generate sales nor reduce costs. Rather, they are a "drain" on the company and may require financing.

Asset Profile

Are any of the current assets used to secure long-term debt or contingent liabilities as pledges or guarantees?

Even though current assets are about the same or slightly above current liabilities, the company may still experience liquidity difficulties if the maturity schedule of the liabilities is ahead of the expected cash realization of the assets. For example, the payment schedule of the debts may be concentrated towards the beginning of the year but the cash realization of the assets may be evenly disbursed throughout the year. If this occurs, the company may be forced to discount its receivables or quickly liquidate inventory at lower prices. Although this will generate immediate cash, it dilutes the realizable value of the current assets. In effect, the actual value of the assets becomes less than the fair value of the liabilities.

Assets that are interdependent create a financial disadvantage for the company. For example, the sale of equipment on the assembly line may adversely affect the remaining equipment. On the other hand, you can sell one marketable security without affecting another.

Sharp vacillation in the price of assets is a negative sign, because the company may be forced to sell an asset at a time of financial need at great loss (i.e., market value is significantly less than book value).

Greater liquidity risk exists with noncurrent assets than with current assets because of the greater disposition difficulty.

You must also determine whether off-balance-sheet assets (unrecorded resources) exist. Examples are a tax loss carry/forward benefit, expected rebates, and a purchase commitment to acquire an item at a price lower than the prevailing price. You should also review for assets that are reflected on the balance sheet at an amount substantially less than their real value. Examples are patents recorded at cost, even though the present value of future benefits substantially exceeds it, and land that does not reflect its appreciated value.

FASB 87 on pension plans does not allow the recognition of a minimum asset for the excess of the fair value of pension plan assets less the accumulated benefit obligation. For analytical purposes, such minimum asset should be considered as an unrecorded asset for the excess of fair value of plan assets over the projected benefit obligation.

Recommendation: Note the existence of unrecorded assets representing resources of the business or items expected to have future economic benefit.

Liabilities

If liabilities are understated, net income is overstated because it does not include necessary charges to reflect the proper valuation of liabilities.

The provision for estimated liabilities for future costs and losses (e.g., lawsuits, warranties) may impair the significance of net income. In evaluating the adequacy of estimated liability accounts, you should carefully examine footnote disclosures and familiarize yourself with the financial and accounting characteristics of the industry. **What to Do:** Eliminate arbitrary adjustments of estimated liabilities in arriving at corporate earning power. Estimated liability provisions should be realistic given the nature of the circumstances. **Example:** Profits derived from a recoupment of prior year reserves may necessitate elimination.

What to Watch Out For: An unrealistically low provision for future costs. For example, it is inconsistent for a firm to decrease its warranty provision when previous experience indicates a poor quality product.

An overprovision in estimated liabilities is sometimes made. In effect, the company is providing a reserve for a "rainy day." **Example:** Profits are too high and management wants to bring them down.

Note: Poor earnings quality is indicated when more operating expenses and losses are being charged to reserve accounts compared to prior years.

EXAMPLE 13

A company reports the following data:

	19X1	19X2	19X3
Estimated liability for warranties	$ 30,000	$ 33,000	$ 40,000
Sales	100,000	130,000	190,000

From 19X1 to 19X3, the company reports that there has been a higher rate of defective merchandise that has to be repaired. Relevant ratios follow.

	19X1–19X2	19X2–19X3
Percentage increase in the estimated liability account	10.0%	21.2%
Percentage increase in sales	30.0%	46.2%

The percentage increase in the estimated liability account is materially less than the percentage increase in sales. Since the firm is experiencing quality problems, it is clear that the estimated liability account is understated.

Calculate the trends in the ratios of

- Current liabilities to total liabilities
- Current liabilities to stockholders' equity
- Current liabilities to sales

Increasing trends point to liquidity difficulty. **Caution:** Stretching short-term payables is not a good sign.

Determine the trend in "patient" (e.g., supplier) to "pressing" (e.g., bank, IRS) liabilities. When liquidity problems exist, you are better off with patient creditors who will work with you. Thus, a high ratio of pressing liabilities to total liabilities is disadvantageous.

Useful disclosures of long-term obligations is mandated by FASB 47. The financial manager may want to review commitments applicable to unconditional purchase obligations and future payments on long-term debt and redeemable stock.

FASB Interpretation 34 requires disclosure of indirect guarantees of indebtedness. Included are contracts in which a company promises to advance funds to another if financial problems occur, as when sales drop below a stipulated level.

EXAMPLE 14

A company presents the following information:

	19X1	19X2
Current Liabilities		
Trade payables	$ 33,000	$ 28,000
Bank loans	51,000	78,000
Commercial paper	35,000	62,000
Taxes payable	8,000	12,000
Total current liabilities	$ 127,000	$ 180,000
Total noncurrent liabilities	$ 310,000	$ 315,000
Total liabilities	$ 437,000	$ 495,000
Total revenue	$1,100,000	$1,150,000

Relevant ratios are

	19X1	19X2
Current liabilities to total revenue	11.5%	15.7%
Current liabilities to total liabilities	29.1%	36.4%
Pressing current liabilities to patient current liabilities	2.85	5.43

There is more liquidity risk in 19X2, as reflected by the higher ratios. In fact, pressing liabilities have significantly risen in terms of percentage.

Overstated Liabilities

Certain liabilities shown in the balance sheet should not be considered obligations for analytical purposes because they may not require future payment. Examples are

- The deferred tax credit account if it applies to a temporary difference that will keep recurring (e.g., depreciation as long as capital expansion occurs)
- Unearned revenue related to passive income sources, such as rents
- Convertible bonds with an attractive conversion feature

Undervalued or Unrecorded Liabilities

Corporate obligations that are not recorded in the balance sheet must be considered when evaluating the entity's going-concern potential. Examples are lawsuits, dispute under a government contract, operating leases, commitments for future loans to a troubled company, guarantees of future performance, and bonus payment obligations.

The minimum liability for the pension plan equals the accumulated benefit obligation less the fair value of pension plan assets. However, the projected benefit obligation (based on anticipated future salaries) is a better measure of the plan's obligation than the accumulated benefit obligation (based on current salaries). Therefore, we should consider as an unrecorded liability the excess of the projected benefit obligation over the accumulated benefit obligation.

EXAMPLE

Accumulated Benefit Obligation	$50,000,000
Less: Fair Value of Plan Assets	40,000,000
Minimum (Booked) Liability	$10,000,000

If the projected benefit obligation is $58 million, the unrecorded liability is $8 million ($58 million less $50 million).

An equity account may be in essence a liability, such as preferred stock with a maturity date or subject to sinking fund requirements.

Avenues of Financing

The company's ability to obtain financing at reasonable rates is affected by external considerations (e.g., Federal Reserve policy) and internal considerations (e.g., degree of existing debt).

The extent of loan restrictions on the company should be examined. How close is the company to violating a given restriction, which may in turn call the loan?

Can the company issue commercial paper and short-term bank debt? If there is a loan, has the collateral value of the loan diminished relative to the balance of the loan? If so, additional security may be required. Also examine the trend in the effective interest rate and compensating balance requirement relative to competition. Does the weighted-average debt significantly exceed the year-end debt balance?

Management of Liabilities

In managing liabilities, a prime purpose is to assure that the business has sufficient funds to meet maturing debt. Otherwise, the company will be in financial difficulty. The debt structure affects both the short-term and long-term financial position of the company.

The financial manager must be assured that all financial obligations are properly presented and disclosed in the financial statements. Also, the liability position and related financial ratios must satisfy any restrictions in loan agreements. The financial manager must borrow money when needed on a timely basis and at a reasonable interest rate.

Liability management involves the proper planning of all types of obligations. The financial manager must know current balances of accounts payable and accrued expenses, and how far they may be stretched. Are liabilities within acceptable industry norms? Can the firm withstand periods of adversity? How does the overall economic picture look, and what effect does it have on the company?

The controller should prepare a number of reports to analyze the actual status of liabilities and to properly plan the debt structure. Some useful reports include:

- Periodic reports (e.g., quarterly, monthly) on the status of material liabilities, such as pensions, leases, and health care
- Periodic reports comparing actual liabilities with amounts by category to allowable amounts in credit agreements
- Comparisons of budgeted liabilities to actual liabilities
- Listing and status of contingent liabilities and their values
- Aging of accounts payable

Stockholders' Equity

If a company cuts back on its dividends or omits them, it may mean it is having financial problems. It is better when a company varies its dividends rather than paying constant dividends so it can more easily reduce them in troubled times. If stockholders are used to receiving constant dividends each time, it will be more difficult for the company to adjust such dividends without materially upsetting stockholders.

If a loan agreement places restrictions on the company, such as its ability to pay dividends, this inhibits management's freedom of action and is a negative sign.

If treasury stock is acquired, the market price of the company's stock will rise because less shares will be on the market. If a company had previously purchased treasury stock at a cost which is significantly below the current market price, it is "sitting on" a significant potential increase in cash flow and paid-in-capital.

If a company issues preferred stock for the first time or if it substantially issues preferred stock in the current year, it may mean the company had problems with issuing its common stock. This is a negative sign since the investing public may be viewing its common stock as too risky.

If convertible bonds or convertible preferred stock are converted to common stock that means that bondholders or preferred stockholders are optimistic about the company. However, this will result in a drop in the market price of common stock as more shares are issued. On the plus side, the company will be able to omit the interest payment on bonds and the dividend payment on preferred stock.

Foreign translation gains and losses are reported as a separate item in the stockholders' equity section. However, for analytical purposes it should be reclassified as an income statement item and includable in the net income figure because such gains and losses are a reflection of management's operating performance. For example, if the company did poorly in foreign exchange markets, that should affect its bottom-line.

While unrealized losses on long-term investments are reported as a separate item in the stockholders' equity section, they should be reclassified for analytical purposes in the income statement. These unrealized losses on noncurrent investments shows that management's investment performance has been poor and the company is losing money. This holding loss adversely affects operating performance and more appropriately belongs as a charge against earnings.

A high ratio of retained earnings to stockholders' equity is a good sign because it indicates that capital financing is being achieved internally.

Stockholders are interested in dividends and prefer high ratios for dividend yield (dividends per share/market price per share) and dividend payout (dividends per share/earnings per share). A decline in these ratios may cause concern among stockholders.

Liquidity Analysis

Liquidity is the company's ability to convert noncash assets into cash or to obtain cash to meet impending obligations. You have to look at the stock and flow of liquid resources. Also, what is the timing of the cash inflows and outflows?

Liquidity is important in carrying out business activity, especially in times of adversity, such as is the case when a business is shut down by a strike or when operating losses result from a recession or a significant rise in the price of a raw material. If liquidity is inadequate to cushion such losses, serious financial problems may ensue. Poor liquidity is analogous to a person having a fever—it is a symptom of a fundamental problem.

Liquidity is affected by the company's ability to obtain financing (e.g., lines of credit) and to postpone cash payments. Also considered is the mixture of current assets and current liabilities. How "close to cash" are the assets and liabilities? If a company's liquidity position is poor, it may be unable to make timely interest and principal payments on debt.

Liquidity ratios are static in nature as of year-end. Thus, it is essential for the financial manager to examine expected future cash flows. If future cash outflows are significantly more than inflows, a deteriorating liquidity position will occur.

What to Watch Out for: If you are a seasonal business, year-end financial data are not representative. Instead, use averages based on quarterly or monthly information to level out seasonal effects.

A seasonal business that is a net borrower should use more long-term financing as a precautionary measure. Also, a company with financial troubles should have debts mature during the peak rather than the trough.

Can you adjust to unexpected difficulties by changing the amount and timing of future cash flows? Consideration should be given to the closeness to cash of assets, ability to obtain further financing, degree of nonoperating assets that can be sold, ability to change operating and investing activities, and short payback periods on projects.

Funds Flow Ratios

- Current Ratio $= \dfrac{\text{Current Assets}}{\text{Current Liabilities}}$

Seasonal fluctuations will have an impact on this ratio. The current ratio is used to appraise the ability of the company to satisfy its current debt out of current assets. A high ratio is required if the company has a problem borrowing quickly, and if there are turbulent business conditions, among other reasons. A limitation of this ratio is that it may increase just prior to financial distress because of a company's attempt to improve its cash position by selling property and equipment. Such dispositions have a negative effect upon productive capacity. Another limitation of the ratio is that it will be higher when inventory is carried on a LIFO basis. **Note:** Current assets that are pledged to secure long-term liabilities are not available to meet current debt. If these current assets are included in the calculation of the ratio, a distortion results.

- Quick Ratio $= \dfrac{\text{Cash} + \text{Marketable Securities} + \text{Accounts Receivable}}{\text{Current Liabilities}}$

This is a more stringent test of liquidity than the current ratio because it excludes inventories and prepaid expenses.

- Working Capital = Current Assets − Current Liabilities

A high working capital is needed when the company may have difficulty borrowing on short notice. However, an excess working capital may be bad because funds could be invested in noncurrent assets for a greater return. Working capital should be compared to other financial statement items such as sales and total assets. For example, working capital to sales indicates if the company is optimally employing its liquid balance. To identify changes in the composition of working capital, the financial manager should ascertain the trend in the percentage of each current asset to total current assets. A movement from cash to inventory, for instance, points to less liquidity.

- $\dfrac{\text{Working Capital}}{\text{Long-term Debt}}$

This ratio reveals whether sufficient working capital exists to satisfy long-term debt obligations.

- $\dfrac{\text{Working Capital}}{\text{Current Liabilities}}$

A low ratio indicates poor liquidity because liquid funds are insufficient to meet current debt.

- $$\frac{\text{A Specific Current Asset}}{\text{Total Current Assets}}$$

For example, a shift of cash to inventory indicates less liquidity.

- $$\frac{\text{Sales}}{\text{Current Assets}}$$

A high ratio infers deficient working capital. Current liabilities may be due prior to inventories and receivables turning over to cash.

- $$\frac{\text{Working Capital Provided from Operations}}{\text{Net Income}}$$

A high ratio is desirable because it indicates the profits are backed up by liquid funds.

- $$\frac{\text{Working Capital Provided from Operations}}{\text{Total Liabilities}}$$

This shows the extent to which internally generated working capital can meet obligations.

- $$\frac{\text{Cash} + \text{Marketable Securities}}{\text{Current Liabilities}}$$

This reflects the cash available to meet short-term debt.

- $$\frac{\text{Cost of Sales, Operating Expenses, and Taxes}}{\text{Average Total Current Assets}}$$

This ratio indicates the adequacy of current assets in meeting ongoing business-related expenses.

- $$\frac{\text{Quick Assets}}{\text{Year's Cash Expenses}}$$

This tells how many days of expenses the highly liquid assets could meet.

- $$\frac{\text{Sales}}{\text{Short-term Trade Liabilities}}$$

This indicates whether the business could partly finance its operations with cost-free funds. If the firm can readily get trade credit, this is a positive sign. A decline in trade credit means creditors have less faith in the financial strength of the business.

- $$\frac{\text{Net Income}}{\text{Sales}}$$

This indicates the profitability generated from revenue and hence is an important measure of operating performance. It also provides clues to a company' pricing, cost structure, and production efficiency. If the ratio drops, loan repayment difficulty may be indicated because a lack in profitability spells financial distress.

- $$\dfrac{\text{Fixed Assets}}{\text{Short-term Debt}}$$

If you finance long-term assets with current debt, there may be a problem in meeting the debt when due because the return and proceeds from the fixed asset will not be realized before the maturity dates of the current debt.

- $$\dfrac{\text{Short-term Debt}}{\text{Long-term Debt}}$$

A high ratio indicates greater liquidity risk. The entity has vulnerability in a money-market squeeze.

- $$\dfrac{\text{Accounts Payable}}{\text{Average Daily Purchases}}$$

This indicates the number of days required for the firm to pay creditors. Is the company meeting its payables commitment?

- Accounts payable payment period (in days) equal to:

$$\dfrac{365}{\text{Accounts Payable Turnover}}$$

(The accounts payable turnover equals purchases divided by accounts payable).

A decline in the payment period may indicate the company is taking advantage of prompt payment discounts, or has used the shorter purchase terms as leverage in negotiating with suppliers in order to lower the purchase price. However, an extension of the payment terms may infer the company is having financial problems. Perhaps that is why the firm is stretching its payables. Alternatively, the lengthening of the payment terms may mean the business is properly managing its payables. By delaying payments to creditors, it is taking greater advantage of interest-free financing.

- $$\dfrac{\text{Current Liabilities}}{\text{Total Liabilities}}$$

A high ratio means less corporate liquidity since there is a greater proportion of current debt.

(Accounts Receivable + Inventory) − (Accounts Payable + Accrued Expenses Payable)

Some banks look at this figure as a major indicator of a company's liquid position since it deals with major current accounts.

- Liquidity Index. This applies to the number of days current assets are removed from cash. A shorter period is preferred.

EXAMPLE 15

	Amount	Days Removed From Cash	Total
Cash	$ 10,000 ×	−	−
Accounts receivable	40,000 ×	25	$1,000,000
Inventory	60,000 ×	40	2,400,000
	$110,000		$3,400,000

$$\text{Index} = \frac{\$3,400,000}{\$110,000} = \underline{30.9} \text{ days}$$

EXAMPLE 16

Company B provides the following financial information:

Current assets	$ 400,000
Fixed assets	800,000
Current liabilities	500,000
Noncurrent liabilities	600,000
Sales	5,000,000
Working capital provided from operations	100,000
Industry norms are:	
Fixed assets to current liabilities	4.0 times
Current liabilities to noncurrent liabilities	45.0%
Sales to current assets	8.3 times
Working capital provided from operations to total liabilities	30.5%
Company B's ratios are:	
Fixed assets to current liabilities	1.6 times
Current liabilities to noncurrent liabilities	83.3%
Sales to current assets	12.5 times
Working capital provided from operations to total liabilities	9.1%

Company B's liquidity ratios are all unfavorable compared to industry standards. There is a high level of short-term debt as well as deficiency in current assets. Also, working capital provided from operations to satisfy total debt is inadequate.

A company's failure to take cash discounts raises a question as to management's financial astuteness because a high opportunity cost is involved.

EXAMPLE 17

Company C bought goods for $300,000 on terms of 2/10, net/60. It failed to take advantage of the discount. The opportunity cost is:

$$\frac{\text{Discount foregone}}{\text{Proceeds Use Of}} \times \frac{360}{\text{Days Delayed}}$$

$$\frac{\$6,000}{\$294,000} \times \frac{360}{50} = \underline{14.7\%}$$

The firm would have been better-off financially paying within the discount period by taking out a loan since the prime interest rate is below 14.7%.

There is a tradeoff between liquidity risk and return. Liquidity risk is minimized by holding greater current assets than noncurrent assets. However, the return rate will drop because the return on current assets (e.g., marketable securities) is usually less than the rate earned on productive fixed assets. Further, excessively high liquidity may mean that management has not aggressively searched for desirable capital investment opportunities. Having a proper balance between liquidity and return is essential to the overall financial health of the business.

Appraisal of Solvency

Solvency is the ability of a company to meet its long-term debt payments (principal and interest). Long-term creditors (e.g., suppliers, loan officers) are interested in whether the company will have adequate funds to satisfy obligations when they mature. Consideration is given to the long-term financial and operating structure of the business. An analysis is made of the magnitude of noncurrent liabilities and the realization risk in noncurrent assets. There should be a high ratio of long-term assets to long-term liabilities. Corporate solvency also depends on earning power since a company will not be able to satisfy its obligations unless it is profitable.

When it is practical to do so, the financial manager should use market value of assets instead of book value in ratio computations since it is more representative of current value.

Stability in earnings and cash flow from operations enhances confidence in the firm's ability to meet debt. Long-term debt-related ratios to be examined include:

- *Total Liabilities to Total Assets.* This ratio reveals the percentage of total funds obtained from creditors. Creditors would prefer to see a low ratio since there is a better cushion for creditor losses if the company goes bankrupt. At the optimum debt/assets ratio the weighted-average cost of capital is less than at any other debt to asset level.

- *Long-term Debt to Stockholders' Equity.* High leverage indicates risk because it may be difficult for the company to meet interest and principal payments as well as obtain further reasonable financing. The problem is particularly acute when a company has cash problems. Excessive debt means less financial flexibility because the entity will have more of a problem in obtaining funds during a tight money market. A desirable debt/equity ratio depends on numerous factors, including the rates of other firms in the industry, the access to debt financing, and earnings stability.

- *Cash Flow From Operations to Long-term Debt.* This ratio shows whether internally generated cash funds are adequate to meet noncurrent liabilities.

- *Interest Coverage (Net Income + Interest + Taxes/Interest).* This reveals the adequacy of earnings to meet interest charges. A high ratio is desired. It is a safety margin indicator that shows the degree of decline in income the company can tolerate.

- *Cash Flow Generated From Operations Plus Interest to Interest.* This ratio indicates available cash to meet interest charges. Cash not profit pays interest. A higher ratio is needed for a cyclical business.

- *Net Income Before Taxes and Fixed Charges to Fixed Charges.* This ratio helps in appraising a firm's ability to meet fixed costs. A low ratio points to risk since when corporate activity falls, the company is unable to meet its fixed charges.

- *Cash Flow From Operations Plus Fixed Charges to Fixed Charges.* A high ratio indicates the ability of the company to meet its fixed charges. Further, a company with stability in operations is better able to meet fixed costs.

- *Noncurrent Assets to Noncurrent Liabilities.* Long-term debt is ultimately paid from long-term assets. Thus, a high ratio affords more protection for long-term creditors.

- *Retained Earnings to Total Assets.* The trend in this ratio reflects the firm's profitability over the years.

- *Total Liabilities to Sales.* This ratio reflects the amount of sales financed by creditors.

- *Stockholders' Equity to Sales.* This ratio indicates the proportion of sales financed by stockholders' equity. It is generally safer for sales to be financed through equity capital than debt funds. An examination of the ratio will reveal if the owners are investing too much or too little for the sales volume involved. Is owners' equity being employed effectively?

EXAMPLE 18

The following partial balance sheet and income statement data are provided for Company D:

Long-term assets	$700,000
Long-term liabilities	500,000
Stockholders' equity	300,000
Net income before tax	80,000
Cash flow provided from operations	100,000
Interest expense	20,000
Average norms taken from competitors:	
Long-term assets to long-term liabilities	2.0
Long-term debt to stockholders' equity	.8
Cash flow to long-term liabilities	.3
Net income before tax plus interest to interest	7.0

Company D's ratios are:

Long-term assets to long-term liabilities	1.4
Long-term debt to stockholders' equity	1.67
Cash flow to long-term liabilities	.2
Net income before tax plus interest to interest	5.0

After comparing the company's ratios with the industry norms, it is evident that the firm's solvency is worse than its competitor's due to the greater degree of long-term liabilities in the capital structure and lower interest coverage.

POTENTIAL FOR BUSINESS FAILURE

Will your company go bankrupt? Will your major customers or suppliers go bankrupt? What warning signs exist and what can be done to avoid failure?

Bankruptcy occurs when the company is unable to meet maturing financial obligations. We are thus particularly interested in predicting cash flow. Financial difficulties affect the P/E ratio, bond ratings, and the effective interest rate.

A comprehensive quantitative indicator used to predict failure is Altman's "Z-score."

The Z-score is known to be about 90% accurate in forecasting business failure one year in the future and about 80% accurate in forecasting it two years in the future. For a more detailed discussion of "Z-Score," see Altman, Edward I., "Financial Ratios, Discriminant Analysis, and the Prediction of Corporate Bankrupcy," *Journal of Finance*, September 1968.

The "Z-Score" equals:

$$\frac{\text{Working Capital}}{\text{Total Assets}} \times 1.2 + \frac{\text{Retained Earnings}}{\text{Total Assets}} \times 1.4 +$$

$$\frac{\text{Operating Income}}{\text{Total Assets}} \times 3.3 + \frac{\text{Market Value of Common and Preferred Stock} \times 0.6}{\text{Total Liabilities}} +$$

$$\frac{\text{Sales}}{\text{Total Assets}} \times 1$$

The scores and the probability of short-term illiquidity follow.

Score	Probability of Illiquidity
1.80 or less	Very high
1.81 – 2.7	High
2.8 – 2.9	Possible
3.0 or greater	Not likely

EXAMPLE 19

A company presents the following information:

Working capital	$280,000
Total assets	875,000
Total liabilities	320,000
Retained earnings	215,000
Sales	950,000
Operating income	130,000
Common stock	
Book vale	220,000
Market value	310,000
Preferred stock	
Book value	115,000
Market value	170,000

The "Z-score" equals:

$$\frac{\$280,000}{\$875,000} \times 1.2 + \frac{\$215,000}{\$875,000} \times 1.4 + \frac{\$130,000}{\$875,000} \times 3.3 +$$

$$\frac{\$480,000}{\$320,000} \times 0.6 + \frac{\$950,000}{\$875,000} \times 1$$

$$= 0.384 + 0.344 + 0.490 + 0.9 + 1.0857 = \underline{\underline{3.2037}}$$

The probability of failure is not likely.

Incidently, there are more updated versions of Altman's model. Interested readers should refer to Altman's *Corporate Financial Distress* (John Wiley & Sons, 1983). For an excellent step-by-step discussion on how to develop a spreadsheet and graphing for the Z-score model, refer to Charles W. Kyd, "Forecasting Bankrupcy with Z-Scores," *Lotus*, September 1985, pp. 43–47.

The liquidation value of a company may be estimated by using J. Wilcox's gambler's ruin prediction formula:

Cash + (Marketable securities at market value) + (70% of inventory, accounts receivable, and prepaid expenses) + (50% of other assets) − (Current liabilities + long-term liabilities).

Quantitative Factors in Predicting Corporate Failure

- Low cash flow to total liabilities
- High debt-to-equity ratio and high debt to total assets
- Low return on investment
- Low profit margin
- Low retained earnings to total assets
- Low working capital to total assets and low working capital to sales
- Low fixed assets to noncurrent liabilities
- Inadequate interest-coverage ratio
- Instability in earnings
- Small-size company measured in sales and/or total assets
- Sharp decline in price of stock, bond price, and earnings
- A significant increase in Beta. Beta is the variability in the price of the company's stock relative to a market index
- Market price per share is significantly less than book value per share
- Reduction in dividend payments
- A significant rise in the company's weighted-average cost of capital
- High fixed cost to total cost structure (high operating leverage)
- Failure to maintain capital assets. An example is a decline in the ratio of repairs to fixed assets.

Qualitative Factors in Predicting Failure

- Poor financial reporting system and inability to control costs
- New company
- Declining industry
- High degree of competition
- Inability to obtain adequate financing, and when obtained there are significant loan restrictions
- Inability to meet past-due obligations

- A lack in management quality
- Moving into new areas in which management lacks expertise
- Failure of the company to keep up to date, especially in a technologically oriented business
- High business risk (e.g., positive correlation in the product line; susceptibility to strikes)
- Inadequate insurance coverage
- Fraudulent actions (e.g., misstating inventories to stave off impending bankruptcy)
- Cyclicality in business operations
- Inability to adjust production to meet consumption needs
- Susceptibility of the business to stringent governmental regulation (e.g., companies in the real estate industry)
- Susceptibility to energy shortages
- Susceptibility to unreliable suppliers
- Renegotiation of debt and/or lease agreements
- Deficient accounting and financial reporting systems

If you can predict with reasonable accuracy that the company is developing financial distress, you can better protect yourself and recommend means for corrective action.

Financial/Quantitative Factors to Minimize the Potential for Failure

- Avoid heavy debt. If liabilities are excessive, finance with equity
- Dispose of losing divisions and product lines
- Manage assets for maximum return and minimum risk
- Stagger and extend the maturity dates of debt
- Use quantitative techniques such as multiple regression analysis to compute the correlation between given variables and the likelihood of business failure
- Assure that there is a "safety buffer" between actual status and compliance requirements (e.g., working capital) in connection with loan agreements.
- Have a negative correlation in product line and in investments held.
- Lower dividend payouts.

Nonfinancial Factors That Minimize the Potential for Failure

- Vertically and horizontally diversify the product line and operations.
- Finance assets with liabilities of similar maturity (hedging).

- Diversify geographically.
- Have adequate insurance.
- Enhance the marketing effort (e.g., advertise in the right place).
- Engage in cost reduction programs.
- Improve productivity (e.g., use timely and detailed variance analysis).
- Implement computer technology (e.g., microcomputers).
- Minimize the adverse effect of inflation and recession on the entity (e.g., price on a next-in, first-out basis).
- Invest in multi-purpose, rather than single-purpose, assets, because of their lower risks.
- Reconsider entering new industries that have a predicted high rate of past failure.
- Have many projects, rather than only a few, that significantly affect operations.
- Consider introducing product lines that are the least affected by the business cycle and that possess stable demand.
- Avoid going from a labor-intensive to a capital-intensive business, since the latter has a high degree of operating leverage.
- Avoid long-term fixed-fee contracts to customers. Rather, incorporate inflation adjustment and energy-cost indices in contracts.
- Avoid entering markets that are on the downturn or that are already highly competitive.
- Adjust to changes in technology.

INCOME STATEMENT ANALYSIS

The analysis of the income statement indicates a company's earning power, quality of earnings, and operating performance. The financial manager should be familiar with the important factors in appraising the income statement. Net income backed-up by cash is essential for corporate liquidity. The accounting policies should be realistic in reflecting the substance of the transactions. Accounting changes should only be made for proper reasons. Further, a high degree of estimation in the income measurement process results in uncertainty in reported figures. Earnings stability enhances the predictability of future results based on currently reported profits.

In analyzing the income statement, you should look at quantitative (e.g., ratio analysis) and qualitative factors (e.g., pending litigation). Reported earnings can be adjusted to make them relevant to suit your needs for analytical purposes. Data in the footnotes will assist in the restatement process.

Your company's earnings quality relates to the degree net income is overstated or understated, as well as to the stability of income statement elements.

Earnings quality affects the price-earnings ratio, bond rating, effective interest rate, compensating balance requirement, availability of financing, and desirability of the firm as either an acquirer or acquiree. Earnings quality attributes exist in different proportions and intensities in the earnings profiles of different companies. The favorable and unfavorable characteristics of your company's earnings are carefully examined by investors, creditors, and suppliers.

Analyzing Discretionary Costs

Discretionary costs can be changed at management's will. They may be decreased when a company is having problems or wants to show a stable earnings trend. **What to Do:** Examine current discretionary costs relative to previous years and to future requirements. An index number may be used to compare the current-year discretionary cost to the base amount. A reduction in discretionary costs is undesirable if their absence will have a detrimental effect on the future (e.g., advertising, research, repairs) by starving the company of needed expenses. **Recommendation:** Analyze the trend in the following ratios: (1) discretionary costs to sales, and (2) discretionary costs to assets. If, in connection with a cost-reduction program, material cuts are made in discretionary costs, future profitability will suffer. However, cost control is warranted when (1) in prior years discretionary expenditures were excessive because of deficient and ill-conceived corporate strategy, or (2) competition has decreased. A material increase in discretionary costs in a given year may have a significant positive impact on corporate earning power and future growth.

EXAMPLE 20

The following data are supplied:

	19X1	19X2	19X3
Sales	$95,000	$125,000	$84,000
Research	9,000	14,000	3,000

The most representative year (base year) is 19X1. After 19X4, you believe that research is essential for the company's success because of technological factors in the industry.

	19X1	19X2	19X3
Research to sales	9.5%	11.2%	3.6%

Looking in base dollars, 19X1 represents 100. 19X2 is 156 ($14,000/ $9,000). 19X3 has an index of 33 ($3,000/$9,000).

A red flag is posted for 19X3. Research is lower than in previous periods. There should have been a boost in research in light of the technological updating needed for 19X4.

EXAMPLE 21

The following information applies for a company with respect to its plant assets.

	19X1	19X2
Equipment	$ 4,500	$ 4,800
Less: Accumulated depreciation	3,000	3,200
Book value	$ 1,500	$ 1,600
Repairs	400	320
Replacement cost of equipment	6,800	7,700
CPI value of equipment	7,400	8,500
Revenue	48,000	53,000
Working capital	2,900	2,600
Cash	1,100	970
Debt-to-equity ratio	42%	71%
Downtime of equipment	2%	5%

Finance company loans have increased relative to bank loans over the year.

You want to analyze equipment and repairs.

Repairs to gross equipment decreased from 8.9% in 19X1 ($400/$4,500) to 6.7% in 19X2 ($320/$4,800). In a similar vein, repairs to revenue went from 0.83% in 19X1 ($400/$48,000) to 0.6% in 19X2 ($320/$53,000).

Over the year there was a greater variation between replacement cost and book value and CPI value and book value, indicating equipment is aging.

As indicated by the greater amount of downtime, more equipment malfunction is taking place.

Equipment purchased over the year was minimal, 6.7% ($300/$4,500).

The company's capital maintenance is deficient. Repairs to fixed assets and repairs to revenue are down, and insufficient replacements are being made. Perhaps these are the causes for the greater downtime.

It may be a problem for the company to purchase fixed assets when required because of the deterioration in its liquidity position. Financial leverage has significantly increased over the year. It is more difficult for the company to obtain adequate financing at reasonable interest rates, as evidenced by the need to borrow to a greater extent from finance companies than from banks.

Cash Flow from Operations

Cash flow from operations equals net income plus noncash expenses less noncash revenue. You should evaluate the trend in the ratio of cash flow from operations to net income. A higher ratio is desirable because it means that earnings are backed-up by cash.

The closer a transaction is to cash, the more objective is the evidence supporting revenue and expense recognition. As the proximity to cash becomes less, the less objective is the transaction and the more subjective are the interpretations. Higher earnings quality relates to recording transactions close to cash realization.

In appraising the cash adequacy of a company, compute the following:

- Cash flow generated from operations before interest expense
- Cash flow generated from operations less cash payments to meet debt principal, dividends, and capital expenditures

EXAMPLE 22

The following condensed income statement appears for a company:

Sales		$1,300,000
Less: Cost of sales		400,000
		$ 900,000
Gross margin		
Less: Operating expenses		
Wages	$150,000	
Rent	80,000	
Electricity	50,000	
Depreciation expense	90,000	
Amortization expense	70,000	
Total operating expenses		440,000
Income before other items		$ 460,000
Other revenue and expenses:		
Interest	$ 60,000	
Amortization of deferred revenue	20,000	
Total other items		40,000
Net income		$ 420,000

The ratio of cash flow from operations to net income is:

Net income		$ 420,000
Add: Noncash expenses		
Depreciation expense	$ 90,000	
Amortization expense	70,000	160,000
Less: Noncash revenue		
Amortization of deferred revenue		(20,000)
Cash flow from operations		$ 560,000

$$\frac{\text{Cash flow from operations}}{\text{Net income}} = \frac{\$560,000}{\$420,000} = \underline{1.33}$$

The Role of Taxable Income

If a company reports significant stockholder earnings and a substantial tax loss, evaluate the quality of reported results.

A company having a significant deferred income tax credit account will have book profits in excess of taxable earnings. An increase in the deferred tax credit account may indicate the company is moving toward more liberal accounting policies. This is because a widening gap in the deferred tax credit account indicates a greater disparity between book earnings and taxable earnings.

You should determine the effective tax rate, which equals tax expense divided by income before tax. A low effective tax rate for the current year due to a one-time source (e.g., tax credit for a one-time major item, a loss carryforward that will shortly expire) will not repeat to benefit later years. However, the effective tax rate may be stable when it results from a recurring source (e.g., foreign tax credit, interest on municipal bonds).

Earnings are not really available if there is a high percentage of foreign profits that will not be repatriated to the U.S. for a long time.

It is better if your company's earnings and growth do not rely on a lowered tax rate that is vulnerable to a future change in the tax law or that places material restrictions on the firm.

Residual Income

Residual income represents an economic income, taking into account the opportunity cost of putting money in the business. An increasing trend in residual income to net income points to a strong degree of corporate profitability because the company is earning enough to meet its imputed cost of capital.

Residual income equals:

Net income

Less: Minimum return (cost of capital) × Total Assets

Residual income

EXAMPLE 23

A company's net income is $800,000, total assets are $4,600,000, and cost of capital is 13.40%.

Residual income equals:

Net income $800,000

Less: Minimum return $\times$ total assets

13.40% $\times$ \$4,600,000   616,400

Residual income   \$183,600

The ratio of residual income to net income is 23% (\$183,600/\$800,000).

(Residual income is discussed in more detail in Chapter 20).

Accounting Policies

Conservatively determined net income is of higher quality than liberally determined net income. Conservatism relates to the accounting methods and estimates employed. A comparison should be made between the company's accounting policies and the prevailing accounting policies in the industry. If the firm's policies are more liberal, earnings quality may be lower. The financial manager should consider the firm's timing of revenue recognition and the deferral of costs compared to usual industry practices.

The accounting policies should be realistic in reflecting the economic substance of the company's transactions. The underlying business and financial realities of the company and industry have to be taken into account. For example, the depreciation method should approximately measure the decline in usefulness of the asset. Examples of realistic accounting policies are cited in AICPA Industry Audit Guides and in accounting policy guides published by various CPA firms. If the use of realistic policies would have resulted in substantially lower earnings than the policies used, earnings quality is lower.

Accounting changes made to conform with new FASB Statements, AICPA Industry Audit Guides, and IRS Regulations are justifiable. However, an unjustified accounting change causes an earnings increment of low quality. Unwarranted changes may be made in accounting principles and estimates. If there are numerous accounting changes, it will be more difficult to use current profits as a predictor of future earnings.

Accounting Estimates

The greater the degree of subjective accounting estimates in the income measurement process, the more uncertainty associated with net income. **What to Do:** Examine the difference between actual experience and the estimates employed. The wider the difference, the more uncertain is profitability. Look at the variation over time between a loss provision and the actual loss. A continually understated loss provision means inaccurate estimates. Sizable gains and losses on the sale of assets may infer inaccurate depreciation estimates.

Examine the trend in the following ratios:

- High estimation assets (e.g., fixed assets) to total assets
- Cash expenses to revenue
- Estimated expenses to revenue

- Cash revenue to revenue
- Estimated revenue to revenue
- Estimated expenses to net income
- Estimated revenue to net income

Higher estimation is indicated by long-term construction work using the percentage-of-completion contract method, and a material amount of estimated liability provisions. Also, a higher percentage of assets subject to accounting estimates (e.g., intangibles) to total assets means uncertain earnings.

EXAMPLE 24

The following information applies to a company:

	19X1	19X2
Cash and near-cash revenue	$ 98,000	$107,000
Noncash revenue items	143,000	195,000
Total revenue	$241,000	$302,000
Cash and near-cash expenses	$ 37,000	$ 58,000
Noncash expenses	67,000	112,000
Total expenses	$104,000	$170,000
Net income	$137,000	$132,000

Estimation-related ratios can now be calculated.

	19X1	19X2
Estimated revenue to total revenue	59%	65%
Estimated revenue to net income	104%	148%
Estimated expenses to total expenses	64%	66%
Estimated expenses to total revenue	28%	37%
Estimated expenses to net income	49%	85%

In every case, there was greater estimation involved in the income measurement process in 19X2 relative to 19X1. The higher degree of estimation resulted in uncertain earnings.

Discontinued Operations

Income from discontinued operations is usually of a one-time nature and should be ignored when forecasting future earnings. Further, a discontinued operation implies a company is in a state of decline or that a poor management decision is the cause for the firm's entering the discontinued line of business in the first place.

Profitability Measures

A sign of good financial health and how effectively the firm is managed is its ability to generate a satisfactory profit and return on investment. Investors will refrain from investing in the business if it has poor earning potential because of the adverse effect on market price of stock and dividends. Creditors will be reluctant to get involved with a company having poor profitability because of collection risk. Absolute dollar profit by itself has minimal significance unless it is compared to its source.

A company's profit margin (net income to sales) indicates how well it is being managed and provides clues to a company's pricing, cost structure, and production efficiency. A high gross profit percent (gross profit to sales) is favorable since it indicates the company is able to control its manufacturing costs.

Return on investment points to the degree to which profit is achieved on the investment. Two key ratios of return on investment are *return on total assets* and *return on owners' equity.*

The return on total assets (net income/average total assets) points to the efficiency with which management has employed its resources to obtain income. Further, a decline in the ratio may result from a productivity problem.

The return on common equity (earnings available to common stock/average stockholders' equity) measures the rate of return on the common stockholders' investment.

(Return on investment is fully discussed in Chapter 20).

An increase in the gross profit margin (gross profit to sales) may mean the company was able to increase its sales volume or selling price, or to reduce its cost of sales. In general, manufacturers have higher gross profit rates than merchandisers.

The net operating profit ratio (net operating profit to sales) reveals what is left over for interest, nonrecurring charges, taxes and profit for the stockholders. It may be used as a basis to evaluate operating managers. The analysis is before considering interest expense since financing is typically arranged by the finance managers.

A high ratio of sales to working capital indicates efficient utilization of liquid funds. The sales backlog should be used to monitor sales status and planning. Compute the days of sales in backlog equal to:

$$\frac{\text{Backlog Balance}}{\text{Sales Volume divided by Days in Period}}$$

Is the backlog for long range delivery (e.g., five years from now) or on a recurring basis to maintain continuing stability?

Some other ratios reflective of operations are:

• Revenue to number of employees as well as revenue to employee salaries. Higher ratios are reflective of better employee productivity.

- Average yearly wage per employee and average hourly wage rate. These ratios examine the ability to control labor costs.
- Average fixed assets per employee. This shows the productivity of using fixed assets by employees.
- Indirect labor to direct labor. A low ratio is reflective of controlling the labor component of overhead.
- Purchase discounts to purchases. A high ratio indicates effective management of purchases.
- General and administrative expenses to selling expense. This ratio indicates the degree of control and surveillance over G&A expense relative to sales activities. G&A expenses relative to selling expenses should decline with increased sales volume. If the ratio is increasing, inadequate controls over administrative activities may exist.

Growth Rate

A company's growth rate should be compared to that of competitors and industry norms.

Measures of Growth Rate:

- $$\frac{\text{Change in retained earnings}}{\text{Stockholders' equity at beginning of year}}$$

- $$\frac{\text{EPS (end of year)} - \text{EPS (beginning of year)}}{\text{EPS (beginning of year)}}$$

The growth rate in sales, dividends, total assets, and the like may be computed in a similar fashion.

Internal Control and Management Honesty

Deficient internal control casts doubt upon the integrity of the earnings stream. Look at the trend in audit fees and in audit time over the years. Increasing trends may point to internal control and audit problems. Examine disclosure of previous accounting errors. Are there any indicators of a dishonest management, such as corporate bribes, payoffs, or hiding of defective merchandise?

Market Value Measures

Market value ratios apply to a comparison of the company's stock price to its earnings (or book value) per share. Also involved are dividend-related ratios. Included are:

- Earnings per share
- Price-Earnings ratio
- Book value per share. This equals:

$$\frac{\text{Total stockholders' equity } - \text{ (Liquidation value of preferred stock} + \text{ Preferred dividends in arrears)}}{\text{Common stock outstanding}}$$

By comparing book value per share to market price per share, the financial manager can see how investors feel about the business.

- Dividend yield. This equals dividends per share divided by market price per share.

- Dividend payout. This equals dividends per share divided by earnings per share. The investing public looks unfavorably upon lower dividends since dividend payout is a sign of the financial health of the entity.

HOW TO ANALYZE THE FINANCIAL STRUCTURE OF THE FIRM

Various quantitative measurements can be used to analyze a firm's stability over time. Comparisons can then be made to prior years of the firm, competing companies, and industry norms.

Types of Stability Measurements

- *Trend in average reported earnings.* Average earnings over a relatively long period (such as five years) will level out abnormal and erratic income statement components as well as cyclical effects upon the business.

- *Average pessimistic earnings.* This represents the average earnings based on the worst possible scenario for the company's operational activities. The average minimum earnings is useful in appraising a risky company.

- *One-time gains or losses to net income and/or sales.* A high percentage of nonrecurring items to reported earnings indicates instability in income statement components, pointing to uncertainty and unrepresentativeness of what is typical. An example is the gain on the sale of low-cost basis land.

- *Standard Deviation.* $S.D. = \sqrt{\dfrac{\Sigma (y - \bar{y})^2}{n}}$

  where y = net income for period t

  $\bar{y}$ = average net income

  n = number of periods

  The higher the standard deviation, the greater is the instability.

- *Coefficient of Variation.* $C.V. = \dfrac{S.D.}{\bar{y}}$

The coefficient of variation is a relative measure of instability to facilitate a comparison between competing companies. The higher the coefficient, the greater the risk.

- *Instability Index of Earnings.* $I = \sqrt{\dfrac{\Sigma (y - y^T)^2}{n}}$

  where y^T = trend earnings for period t, and is determined as follows:

  $$y^T = a + bt$$

  where a = dollar intercept
          b = slope of trend line
          t = time period

Trend income is computed using a simple trend equation solved by computer. The index reflects the deviation between actual income and trend income. A higher index is reflective of greater instability.

- *Beta.* Beta is calculated by a computer run based on the following equation:

  $$r_{jt} = a_j + B_j r_{Mt} + E_{jt}$$

  where r_{jt} = return of security j for period t
          a_j = constant
          B_j = Beta for security j
          r_{Mt} = return on a market index such as the New York Stock Exchange Index
          E_{jt} = error term

Beta measures the systematic risk of a stock. A Beta greater than one indicates the company's market price of stock vacillates more than the change in the market index, pointing to a risky security. Fluctuation in stock price implies greater business risk and instability with the firm. For example, a Beta of 1.3 means the company's stock price rises or falls 30% faster than the market. A Beta of one means the company's stock price moves the same as the market index. A Beta of less than one indicates the company's stock price vacillates less than the stock market index, pointing to lower corporate risk. Of course, a company's Beta may change over time. Betas for individual companies may be gotten from various sources, such as Standard and Poor's.

EXAMPLE 25

A company shows the following trend in reported earnings:

19X0	$100,000
19X1	110,000
19X2	80,000
19X3	120,000
19X4	140,000

Standard Deviation $= \sqrt{\dfrac{\Sigma (y - \bar{y})^2}{n}}$

$$\bar{y} = \Sigma \frac{y}{n} = \frac{\begin{array}{c} 100{,}000 + 110{,}000 + 80{,}000 \\ + 120{,}000 + 140{,}000 \end{array}}{5} = \frac{550{,}000}{5} = 110{,}000$$

Year	$(y - \bar{y})$	$(y - \bar{y})^2$
19X0	$-10{,}000$	$100{,}000{,}000$
19X1	0	0
19X2	$-30{,}000$	$900{,}000{,}000$
19X3	$+10{,}000$	$100{,}000{,}000$
19X4	$+30{,}000$	$900{,}000{,}000$
		$2{,}000{,}000{,}000$

$$\text{Standard Deviation} = \sqrt{\frac{2{,}000{,}000{,}000}{5}} = \sqrt{400{,}000{,}000} = 20{,}000$$

$$\text{Coefficient of Variation} = \frac{\text{Standard Deviation}}{\bar{y}}$$

$$= \frac{20{,}000}{110{,}000} = 18.2\%$$

Operating Leverage

Operating leverage is the degree to which fixed charges exist in a company's cost structure. Measures of operating leverage are:

- Fixed costs to total costs
- Percentage change in operating income to the percentage change in sales volume
- Net income to fixed costs

Notes: An increase in (1) and (2) or decrease in (3) may point to lower earnings quality because higher fixed charges may result in greater earnings instability.

A high percentage of variable costs to total costs indicates greater earnings stability. Variable costs can be adjusted more easily than fixed costs in meeting a decline in product demand.

A high break-even company is very susceptible to economic declines.

Stability Elements

In looking at earnings stability, it should be noted that the trend in income is more important than its absolute size. Stable revenue sources include the following.

- Nonoperating income that is recurring and serves as a cushion to total income. Examples are royalty income under long-term contracts with financially secure parties and rental income under long-term leases. Increased trends in the percentage of stable revenue sources to gross income and to net income are positive indicators.

- Obtaining further revenue from original sales. An example is maintenance services and replacement parts derived from selling an item. You should calculate the trend in replacement and maintenance revenue as a percentage of (1) new sales, (2) total revenue, and (3) net income.

- Sales to diversified industries (industries affected in different ways by cyclical factors).

Abnormal and erratic income statement items (e.g., gain on the sale of land) distort the current year's net income as a predictor of future earnings. **Warning:** Watch out for a company that starts selling off part of its fixed assets, since it may be in a state of contraction.

Examples of unstable revenue sources are listed below.

- Export sales to a major foreign market that will disappear as that country develops a domestic capacity to manufacture the item. An opportunist market (e.g., electronic calculators) is a nonrepetitive source of earnings, since the saturation of a company's market will reduce its potential to derive continued earnings.

- Short-term schemes (e.g., a single government contract) increase earnings temporarily. You should determine the percentage of short-lived income to total revenue and to net income.

- The loss of a unique advantage in the near future that will hurt future years' revenues, such as the exhaustion of mineral rights.

Product Line Characteristics

A company's product line deeply affects its overall business stability and profitability. Where possible, product risk should be minimized, such as by moving toward negative correlation among products.

Product Line Measures

- The degree of correlation between products is evident from a correlation matrix determined by a computer run.

- Product demand elasticity is determined as follows:

Percentage change in quantity
$\overline{\text{Percentage change in price}}$

If > 1 Elastic demand
If $= 1$ Unitary demand
If < 1 Inelastic demand

Red Flag: Products that are positively correlated and have elastic demands are of high risk. On the other hand, companies with product lines having negative correlations and inelastic demand (e.g., health-care products) are stable. Further, products with different seasonal peaks should be added to stabilize production and marketing operations.

EXAMPLE 26

The correlation matrix of a product line follows:

Product	A	B	C	D	E	F
A	1.0	.13	−.02	−.01	−.07	.22
B	.13	1.0	−.02	−.07	.00	.00
C	−.02	−.02	1.0	.01	.48	.13
D	−.01	−.07	.01	1.0	.01	−.02
E	−.07	.00	.48	.01	1.0	.45
F	.22	.00	.13	−.02	.45	1.0

Obviously, perfect correlation exists with the same product. For instance, the correlation between product F and product F is 1.0.

High positive correlation exists between products E and C (.48) and products E and F (.45). Because these products are tightly interwoven, risk exists.

Low negative correlation exists between products A and D (−.01) and products A and C (−.02).

No correlation is present between products B and E (.00) and products B and F (.00).

It would be better if some products had significant negative correlations (e.g., −.7) but such is not the case.

EXAMPLE 27

Data for products X and Y follow:

	X	Y
Selling price	$10	$8
Unit sales	10,000	13,000

If the selling price of product X is increased to $11, it is predicted that sales volume will decrease by 500 units. If the selling price of product Y is raised to $9.50, sales volume is anticipated to fall by 4,000 units.

Product demand elasticity equals:

$$\frac{\text{Percentage change in quantity}}{\text{Percentage change in price}}$$

Inelastic demand exists with product X:

$$\frac{\dfrac{500}{10,000}}{\dfrac{\$1}{\$10}} = \frac{.05}{.10} = .5$$

Elastic demand occurs with product Y:

$$\frac{\dfrac{4,000}{13,000}}{\dfrac{\$1.50}{\$8.00}} = \frac{.307}{.188} = 1.63$$

Variances in the product line may exist for volume, price, and cost. The greater the fluctuation in each, the wider is the variability in earnings. You should examine variability for each major product by:

- Charting via graphs to uncover trends
- Determine the standard deviation
- Compute variances

Product Lines Promoting Stability

- Necessity items
- Retail trade (mostly low-priced items appealing to a wide market)
- Growth and mature products
- Low unit-cost items. These have a greater chance of succeeding in periods of economic health and also have greater resistance to declining demand in recessionary periods. If a firm with low-priced goods also provides a substitute for more expensive items (e.g., cereal for meat), it has a built-in hedge in inflationary and recessionary periods.
- "Piggy-back" product base where similar products are associated with the company's basic business
- Ability to introduce new products. What is the number of patented products that come on stream annually?

Product Lines Causing Instability

- Novelty and nonessential goods
- High-priced items (e.g., expensive jewelry) that add to variable demand during recessionary times. An exception is high-priced quality goods

serving a select market, such as Mercedes Benz, because the wealthy are not materially impacted by a temporary decline in economic conditions.

- Heavy goods and raw materials, because reduction in buying is magnified as it goes from the consumer to the source of production. For raw materials, there is price fluctuation in commodity markets as well as instability in demand for end products. With capital good sales, industry can postpone purchases of durable equipment.

- A single-product company since it has less stability and more obsolescence risk than a multi-product one. **Recommendation:** Have a diversified product line to guard against adverse effects resulting from differing economic conditions. It is best to have negatively correlated items (e.g., winter clothing and summer clothing) to promote stability, as revenue obtained from one product increases while revenue obtained from the other decreases. At a minimum, there should be no correlation (e.g., food and office furniture). **Danger:** If a positive correlation exists between products (e.g., autos and steel) there is significant risk, since product demand moves in the same direction for both.

- Those that are susceptible to rapid changes in consumer tastes, such as novelty goods that depend on fads.

- Those closely tied to changes in real gross national product. You should try to move toward stable demand items.

- Those for which demand is obtained from a very few large industrial users. The loss of one customer can have a significant negative effect.

- Those with unusual demand coupled with skyrocketing prices (e.g., copper).

- High percentage of developmental products.

- Low profit margin products.

Ways to Measure Marketing Effectiveness

- Evaluate product warranty complaints and their dispositions.

- Calculate revenue, cost, and profit by product line, customer, industry segment, geographic area, distribution channel, type of marketing effort, and average order size.

- Evaluate new products in terms of risk and profitability.

- Appraise strengths and weaknesses of competition as well as their reactions to your promotion efforts.

- Determine revenue, marketing costs, and profits prior to, during, and subsequent to promotion programs.

- Appraise sales generated by different types of selling efforts (e.g., direct mail, television, newspaper).

- Analyze sales force effectiveness by determining the profit generated by salespeople, call frequency, sales incentives, sales personnel costs (e.g., auto), and dollar value of orders obtained per hour spent.
- Determine revenue and/or net income per employee.
- Examine the trend in the ratio of marketing costs to sales.
- Determine marketing share.
- Evaluate the trend in inventory at wholesalers and retailers, including order processing, packaging, warehousing, carrier, and customer services.

Consider Raw Materials

In analyzing raw materials, we should determine variability in cost. **Recommendation:** Review trade publications for price instability. A problem exists if there is a lack of alternative raw material sources, especially if the current source of supply is unreliable. **Special Note:** Vertical integration reduces price and supply risk.

Management Quality

The success of a business depends greatly on the quality of executive decisions. Deficient competence in management holds in question the viability of the enterprise.

Signs of Poor Management Quality

- Instability and lack of experience of leadership
- Previous incidents of mismanagement
- Past occurrence of corporate bankruptcy
- Prior inaccurate management projections (e.g., overexaggerated predictions in the president's letter in the annual report)
- Inability to adjust to changing times (e.g., nature of the business)

Employees

Labor tranquility can be appraised by determining the number and duration of prior strikes, degree of union militancy, and employee turnover. However, consideration should be given to the ratio of fringe benefits to total labor dollars. Fringe benefits include retirement, insurance, sick leave, vacation, and so on. The trend in this ratio with comparisons to other companies will reveal whether fringe benefits are proportionately higher than they should be.

A constant relationship should typically exist between indirect labor and direct labor since both are needed to efficiently run the organization.

Risk

In evaluating risk, you should compare the company's risk exposure to the competition and to past trends of the firm. Uncertainty about the business makes it difficult to reliably predict future performance.

The following list covers some of the main risks you should consider:

- Corporate risk, such as overdependence on a few key executives or the underinsurance of assets (e.g., declining trend in insurance expense to fixed assets, unusual casualty losses). One means of minimizing corporate risk is to diversify operations.

- Social risk, such as a company experiencing customer boycotts or bias suits. One way of reducing social risk is to have some degree of community involvement with the firm.

- Environmental risk, such as a product line or service susceptible to changes in the weather. A way to lower this risk is to have counterseasonal products.

- Industry risk, such as an industry under public and governmental scrutiny (e.g., real estate tax shelters). An approach to diminish industry risk is to move toward a variable-cost-oriented business.

- Economic risk, such as the effect of a depression on product demand.

- Curtail this risk by having a low-priced product substitute for a high-priced item (i.e., cereal for meat).

- Political risk, such as the need for lobbying efforts. Avoid operations in strictly regulated areas.

Industry Characteristics

Corporate earnings are worth more if earned in a healthy, expanding industry than in an unhealthy, declining one. For example, an expanding and mature industry in which a restricted number of companies control a high percentage of the market and whose selling prices can be upwardly adjusted for rising costs, is in a strong position.

Labor-intensive businesses typically have greater stability than capital-intensive ones, since the former have a higher percentage of variable costs whereas the latter has a higher percentage of fixed costs. Capital-intensive industries have a higher susceptibility to cyclical performance. Companies in a staple industry have greater stability because of inelastic product demand.

A company may have variability because of an industry cycle. An example is the steel industry, which has a 5- to 10-year cycle because of the refurbishing of steel furnaces.

Industry Characteristics Indicative of Greater Risk

- High degree of competition. What is the ease of entry, price wars, and cheaper imports?

- Highly technological (e.g., computers), causing obsolescence risk and difficulty in keeping up to date
- Overly dependent on energy, making it prone to energy shortages and price rises
- Subject to tight governmental regulation, such as by a utility regulatory commission
- Susceptibility to cyclical effects
- High-risk product line without sufficient insurance coverage. If you have difficulty obtaining insurance in your industry, try to pool risks by setting up mutual insurance companies.

Political Factors

Political risk refers to foreign operations and governmental regulation. Multinational companies with significant foreign activities have uncertainties with respect to repatriation of funds, currency fluctuations, and local customs and regulations. Operations in politically and economically unstable foreign regions means instability.

Ratios to Be Examined

- Questionable foreign revenue to total revenue
- Questionable foreign earnings to net income
- Total export revenue to total revenue
- Total export earnings to net income
- Total assets in "questionable" foreign countries to total assets
- Total assets in foreign countries to total assets

Considerations in Foreign Operations

- Foreign exchange rates. **Red Flag:** Vacillating foreign exchange rates, which can be measured by the percentage change over time and/or its standard deviation. Also look at the trend in the ratio of foreign translation gains and losses (reported in the stockholders' equity section). When foreign assets are appropriately balanced against foreign liabilities, you are better insulated from changes in exchange rates, thus stabilizing earnings. Evaluate your exposed position for each foreign country in which there is a major operation. When the dollar is devalued, net foreign assets and income in countries with strong currencies are worth more dollars. Forward exchange contracts should be viewed positively, since the company is trying to minimize its foreign currency exposure by hedging against exchange risks emanating from foreign currency transactions.
- Foreign country's tax rate and duties.
- Varying year-ends of foreign subsidiaries.

• Degree of intercountry transactions.

Companies dependent on government contracts and subsidies have more instability, since government spending is vulnerable to changing political whims of legislators and war-threatening situations. **Suggestion:** Determine the percentage of earnings obtained from government contract work and subsidies, and the extent to which such work and subsidies are recurring.

Look at the degree of government regulation over the company since it affects the bottom line (e.g., utility rate increases are less than that which has been asked for). **Recommendation:** Examine present and prospective effects of governmental interference on the company by reviewing current and proposed laws and regulations of governmental bodies. Possible sources of such information are legislative hearings, trade journals, and newspapers. Stringent environmental and safety regulations may eat into profits.

Analyze the effect on the company of present and proposed tax legislation. What are the areas of IRS scrutiny?

CONCLUSION

An analysis of a company's financial position and funds flow is essential in ascertaining its ability to continue and prosper. Areas of deficiency and potential ramifications can be highlighted so that corrective action may be taken. Managers closely scrutinize segmental operations to identify areas of risk and poor profit potential.

Quality of earnings involves those factors that would influence investors or creditors considering investing or giving credit to your company. The key in evaluating your company's earnings quality is to compare its earnings profile (the mixture and degree of favorable and unfavorable characteristics associated with reported results) with the earnings profile of other companies in the same industry. You assess earnings quality in order to render earnings comparable among competing companies, and to determine what valuation should be placed upon them.

Quality of earnings can be looked at only in terms of accounting and financial characteristics that have an effect on the earning power of a firm, as shown in its net income figure. These characteristics are complex and interrelated, and are subject to wide varieties of interpretation depending upon your own analytical objective. Further, measurements of some of the characteristics may be very difficult. Nevertheless, you cannot avoid sorting through the characteristics to determine which of them are favorable in terms of earnings quality and which are unfavorable, and to determine the degree to which they exist. You are then in a position to rank the relative quality of earnings of your company to those of others.

An analysis and evaluation of the company's financial structure and stability is needed to ascertain profit potential, degree of risk, and viability. Areas of analysis include sources of earnings, economic and inflationary effects, political aspects, industry characteristics, and marketing effectiveness. Quantitative measurements can be looked at over time to gauge performance.

After completing his or her financial statement analysis, the financial manager will consult with top management to discuss their plans and prospects, any problem areas surfaced in the analysis, and possible solutions.

28

Analysis, Evaluation, and Control of Revenue and Costs

A company can improve its bottom-line and overall operations by analyzing, planning, monitoring, and controlling revenue and costs. Control reports will help in this process. This chapter provides some benchmarks in this evaluation and control process.

CONTROL REPORTS

Control reports are issued in order to highlight poor performance so that timely corrective action may be taken. The reports should be frequent, detailed, and look at each important operational level.

Summary reports should also be prepared presenting performance over a long time period (e.g., monthly) and providing an overview of performance.

The form and content of the control report should vary depending upon the functions and responsibilities of the executives receiving it. The reports may take the form of narrative, tabular, or graphic. A lower level manager is more concerned with details. A higher level manager is more interested with departmental summaries, trends, and relationships. The reports may be in both financial and nonfinancial terms.

CONTROL OF REVENUE

Important questions needing answering in sales analysis are: What was sold? Where was it sold? Who sold it? What was the profit?

753

Sales and profitability analysis involves the following:

- *Customer*—industry or retail, corporate or governmental, domestic or foreign
- *Product*—type of commodity, size, price, quality, and color
- *Distribution channel*—wholesaler, retailer, agent, broker
- *Sales effort*—personal visit, direct mail, coupon, ad (e.g., newspaper, magazine), media (television, radio)
- *Territory*—country, state, city, suburb
- *Order size*—individual purchase
- *Organization*—department, branch
- *Salesperson*—group, individual
- *Terms of sale*—cash purchase, cash on delivery, charge account, installment purchase

Profitability may be determined by territory, product, customer, channel of distribution, salesmen, method of sale, organization, and operating division. In deciding upon a product line, economies of production have to be taken into account.

The financial manager should watch out for significant changes in sales trends in terms of profit margin and distribution channels. How do actual sales conform to sales goals and budgets? In analyzing the trend in sales, the financial manager may see the need to redirect sales effort and/or change the product. The types and sizes of desirable accounts and orders should be determined. Volume selling price breaks may be given for different order sizes.

In appraising sales volume and prices, the manager should not ignore the possibility that unfavorable variances have arisen from salespeople having excessive authority in establishing selling prices.

Pricing should be periodically reviewed after considering relevant factors such as increasing costs. All types of cost must be considered including total cost, marginal cost, and out-of-pocket costs.

The financial manager should compare the profit margins on alternative products in deciding which ones to emphasize. He or she should also consider the probable effect of volume on the profit margin. Consideration should also be given to the importance of changes in composition, manufacturing processes, and quality on the costs to produce and distribute the product.

The financial manager should determine the following:

- The least cost geographic location for warehouses
- The minimum acceptable order
- How best to serve particular accounts, such as by mail order, telephone, jobber and so on.

The financial manager may find that most sales are concentrated in a few products. In fact, a few customers may represent a significant portion of company sales. This involves a small amount of the sales effort. The financial manager may be able to reduce selling costs by concentrating sales effort on the major customers and products. Perhaps salesperson assignments should be modified, such as concentrating on only a few territories. Perhaps a simplification of the product line is needed.

The controller should provide the alternative costs for the varying methods of sale. For example, how should samples be distributed to result in the best effect on sales at minimum cost.

In evaluating sales effort, we should consider the success of business development expense (e.g., promotion and entertainment) by customer, territory, or salesperson.

Customer analysis should indicate the number of accounts and dollar sales by customer volume bracket and average order size. A small order size may result in unprofitable sales because of such factors as high distribution costs and high order costs. In this case, the controller should analyze distribution costs by size of order in order to bring the problem under control and take appropriate corrective action.

It may cost more to sell to certain types of customers than others among different classes as well as within a particular class. For example, a particular customer may require greater services than typical, such as delivery and warehousing. A particular customer may demand a different price, such as for volume purchases. Profitability analysis by customer should be made so as to see where to place salespeople time, what selling price to establish, where to control distribution costs, and what customer classes to discontinue. A determination should also be made as to which customers have increasing or decreasing sales volume. Sales effort may be curtailed on: (1) large volume accounts that only buy low profit margin items, and (2) low volume accounts that are at best marginally profitable.

It may not pay to carry all varieties, sizes, and colors from a sales and profitability perspective. The company should emphasize the profitable products which may not be the odd items (e.g., unusual colors, odd sizes).

Sales which have not been realized should be listed and analyzed, particularly with regard to any problems that may have been experienced. Such analysis involves the following:

- Orders received
- Unfilled orders
- Lost sales
- Cancellations

Note: The analysis of orders is particularly crucial when goods are made to order.

Sales deductions should be analyzed to indicate problems possibly leading to deficient profits. Problems may be indicated when excessive discounts, allowances, and freight costs exist. What is the extent and reasons for returns, price adjustments, freight allowances, and so on. A determination should be made of whom is responsible. A defective product is the responsibility of manufacturing. An excessive freight cost or wrong delay is the responsibility of traffic.

In conclusion, sales should be analyzed in terms of both price and volume to identify unfavorable trends, weaknesses, and positive directions.

CONTROL OF COSTS

Cost control must be exercised over manufacturing and nonmanufacturing costs. Costs should only be incurred for necessary business expenditures that will provide revenue benefit to the firm.

Manufacturing Costs

The purpose of cost control is to obtain an optimum product consistent with quality standards from the various input factors including material, labor, and facilities. The input-output relationship is crucial. In other words, the best result should be forthcoming at the least cost. The office should be shut down when the factory is not in operation. Since most costs are controllable by someone within the organization, responsibility should be assigned.

Changes in standard prices for material, labor, and overhead should be noted along with their effects upon the unit standard cost of the product. Perhaps there is a need for material substitutions or modifications in specifications or processes.

Labor control should be jointly developed between staff and management. Line supervisors have prime responsibility to control labor costs. Actual performance of labor should be compared against a realistic yardstick. Unfavorable discrepancies should be followed up.

The controller may assist in controlling labor costs in the following ways:

- Prepare an analysis of overtime hours and cost. Make sure overtime is approved in advance.
- Prepare a report on labor turnover, training cost, and years of service.
- Determine the standard man-hours for the production program.
- Establish procedures to limit the number of employees placed on the payroll to that called for by the production plan.
- Make sure that an employee is performing services per his/her job description. Are high-paid employees doing menial work?
- Consider overtime hours and cost, turnover rate, output per worker, and relationship between indirect labor and direct labor.
- Working conditions should be improved to enhance productivity.
- Analyze machinery to assure they are up-to-date.

Because most overhead items are small in amount, proper control may be neglected. Of course, in the aggregate overhead may be substantial. Areas to look at include the personal use of supplies and xeroxing, and use of customized forms where standardized ones would suffice.

In order to control overhead, standards must be established and compared against actual performance. Periodic reports of budget and actual overhead costs should be prepared to identify problem areas. Preplanning of overhead costs may be done such as planning indirect labor staff (e.g., maintenance) to avoid excessive hours. The preplanning approach may be beneficial when significant dollar cost is involved, such as in the purchase of repair material and supplies. A record of purchases by responsibility unit may be helpful. Purchase requirements should be properly approved.

The cost of idle equipment should be determined to gauge whether facilities are being utilized properly. What is the degree of plant utilization relative to what is normal?

Nonmanufacturing Costs

The control of distribution costs is a much more difficult problem than the control of manufacturing costs. In distribution, we have to consider the varying nature of the personality of seller and buyer. Competitive factors must be taken into account. On the contrary, in production the worker is the only human element. In marketing, there are more methods and greater flexibility relative to production. Several distribution channels may be used. Because of the greater possibility for variability, distribution processes are more difficult to standardize than production activities. If distribution costs are excessive, who and where does the responsibility lie? Is it a problem territory? Is the salesperson doing a poor job?

Distribution costs and effort must be planned, controlled, and monitored. Distribution costs may be analyzed by functional operation, nature of expense, and application of distribution effort.

In functional operation, distribution costs are analyzed in terms of individual responsibility. This is a particularly useful approach in large companies. Functional operations requiring measurement are identified. Examples of such operations might be circular mailing, warehouse shipments, and salespeople calls on customers.

In looking at the nature of the expense, costs are segregated by month and trends in distribution costs are examined. The ratio of distribution costs to sales over time should be enlightening. A comparison to industry norms is recommended.

In looking at the manner of application, distribution costs must be segregated into direct costs, indirect costs, and semidirect costs.

Direct costs are specifically identifiable to a particular segment. Examples of direct costs assignable to a salesperson are salary, commission, and travel and entertainment expense. But these same costs may be indirect or semidirect if attributable to product analysis. An expense that is direct in one application may not be in another.

Indirect costs are general corporate costs and must be allocated to segments (e.g., territory, product) on a rational basis. Examples are corporate advertising and salaries of general sales executives. Advertising may be allocated based on sales. General sales executives' salaries may be allocated based on time spent by territory or product. Here, a time log may be kept.

Semidirect costs are related in some measurable way to particular segments. Such costs may be distributed in accordance with the services required. For example, the variable factor for warehousing may be weight handled. Order handling costs may be in terms of the number of orders. The allocation base is considerably less arbitrary than with indirect costs.

A comparison should be made between actual and budgeted figures for salesperson salaries, bonuses, and expenses. The salary structure in the industry may serve as a good reference point.

An examination should be made as to the effect of advertising on sales. Perhaps a change in media is needed.

Telephone expense may be controlled in the following ways:

- Prior approval for long-distance calls
- Controls to restrict personal use of the telephone, such as a key lock
- Discarding or returning unnecessary equipment

The trend in warehouse expense to sales should be analyzed. Increasing trends may have to be investigated.

To control dues and subscription expenses, a control is necessary such as having a card record of each publication by subscribed to, by whom, and why. If another employee must use that publication, he or she knows where to go.

There should be centralized control over contributions such as in the hands of a committee of senior management. A general policy must be established as to amount and for what purposes.

29

Insurance and Legal Considerations

The financial manager should have some familiarity with insurance and law in performing his or her functions. Governmental and private insurance coverage can be used to protect against such things as inconvertibility of assets and contract repudiation. Federal and state laws affect the relationship between employer and employee.

INSURANCE COVERAGE

In a large company, a risk manager may be held responsible for insurance matters. He or she will report directly to the treasurer or controller. In a smaller company, this function may be one of the duties of the controller, treasurer, or other corporate officer.

One of the functions of the financial manager's job may be to provide insurance coverage for the company so as to control the risks the firm is susceptible to. Some insurance coverage is required by law such as worker's compensation. Some coverage is required by contract such as fire insurance in order to abide by the terms of a loan agreement. Other coverage is to protect against the general risk inherent in the business. The financial manager must comprehend insurance requirements and procedures and furnish needed information and advice. The financial manager should attempt to find ways to monitor and control costs while maintaining adequate insurance protection. Consideration has to be given to the limits for risk assumption or retention, self-insurance, and uninsurable risks. Further, there should be proper documentation of insurance procedures.

The financial manager has many duties in insurance protection including identifying and evaluating risks, maintaining records of insurance administration, keeping up-to-date with new developments in insurance, monitoring changes in the corporate environment as it affects insurance, estimating the probability of loss, and assuring compliance with federal and local regulatory requirements.

The financial manager in appraising insurable hazards should analyze in detail properties and locations along with related contractual obligations (e.g., mortgages, leases). Each structure should be listed along with its location, condition, safety, and replacement cost.

In the case of insignificant risk areas, deductibles should be established to meet company needs and result in premium savings. **Tip:** A new business should have higher deductibles until experience can be gotten of the number of incidences of losses and their magnitude.

At periodic times, insurance coverage should be reviewed to avoid uninsured losses. As the company changes in size, products, geographic areas, and so on, it may have to alter the type and amount of insurance coverage. Policy limits and deductibles may have to be revised given the company's current setting. The higher the deductible of a policy, the lower the premium. Some considerations in the insurance review process are new risks (e.g., AIDS), trends in legal cases, sale or purchase of fixed assets, changes in inventory policy, switch in distribution channels, and fair market value of property.

Note: Not everything needs to be insured. In some nonessential areas, self insurance may be sufficient. In deciding whether to insure against a risk, the financial manager must weigh the probability of loss and amount against the insurance premium cost. If the difference is marginal, it may not be financially advantageous to insure. **General Rule:** Insure potential catastrophes that would significantly impair the ongoing operations of the business and result in financial hardship.

Insurance Records

There are many insurance records that should be kept including:

- Expense distribution records including information about payments, refunds, accruals, write-offs, and allocation amounts and bases to segments
- Records of premiums, losses, and settlements. A ratio of premiums to losses should be determined.
- Records of the approved values of insured items
- Claim records including the names of claim representatives, claim procedures, documentation, claim information (e.g., date), and status of the claim
- Location records describing the physical location of the insured items among the various plant facilities
- Transportation logs for corporate vehicles including delivery trucks and automobiles. Information includes miles driven and to be driven, condition, and location.

- Binder records of pending insurance coverage
- Other files including dates premiums are due, notice of hearings, and inspections

An insurance manual should be kept detailing the procedures to be followed on all aspects of insurance coverage by type including obtaining insurance, filing claims, financial reporting and presentation, allocation bases to allocate premiums to reporting units, and settlement issues.

All insurable losses must be immediately reported and documented. The financial manager must know what types of losses have occurred, where, and magnitude. Damaged items must be segregated until the adjuster has made a review. The appropriate claims representative should be contacted. The financial manager should evaluate the cause of the loss and suggest necessary remedial measures.

An insurance report should be prepared at the end of the year. Information contained therein should include a description of the types of insurance and related coverage, premiums paid, self-insured items, and the adequacy of established reserves.

An illustrative insurance record appears in Exhibit 1.

The insurance record lists all insurance policies, policy dates, annual premium, and what is covered under the policies.

The controller keeps records related to the history of acquisition, use, and sale of fixed assets. Information about insurance claims for cash, securities, and inventory are also kept. Internal auditors should check the track record, support, and documentation for all claims.

Deciding on an Insurance Broker

In selecting an insurance broker, the following should be taken into account:

- Financial strength of the insurer
- Types of coverage
- Insurance rates
- Services provided and expertise of staff
- Timely resolution of insurance claims
- Up-to-date with latest insurance products

The types of business insurance include product liability, commercial property, umbrella excess liability, marine, contingent business interruption, automobile, and aircraft.

Product Liability

Insurance protection is needed for loss arising from damages suffered by other parties due to defects in the company's products, services, operations, or

Exhibit 1

INSURANCE RECORD

Insurance Company	Name of Broker	Identifying Number of Policy	Amount of Policy	Term	Expiration Date	Annual Premium	Coverage	Exclusions

acts of employees. Here, an analysis should be made of contracts, leases, and sales orders. It is essential to consider federal and state statutes applying to the company's product liability requirements. What is the probability of loss, the degree, and the frequency?

Commercial Property Policy

The commercial property policy is an "all-risk" policy in insuring inventory on the premises, warehouses, and in-transit. It also covers personal injuries, property damage, product liability, advertising liability, fire damage on rental premises, loss of valuable records, and flood and earthquake losses. Excluded are coverage for cash and securities, property sold under installments, imports or exports, precious metals, and aircraft. These are covered under other policies mentioned herein. Everything is covered except the specific excluded items.

The commercial property policy is the prime "all-risk" policy of the company. Losses exceeding the policy limits may be recovered under the umbrella policy.

Casualty Insurance Computations

Casualty insurance covers such items as fire loss and water damage. The premiums are usually paid in advance and debited to Prepaid Insurance which is then amortized over the policy period. Casualty insurance reimburses the holder for the fair market value of property lost. Insurance companies typically have a coinsurance clause so that the insured bears part of the loss. The insurance reimbursement formula follows (assumes an 80% coinsurance clause):

$$\frac{\text{Face of Policy}}{.8 \times \text{Fair Market Value of Insured Property}} \times \begin{array}{c}\text{Fair Market}\\\text{Value of}\\\text{Loss}\end{array} = \begin{array}{c}\text{Possible}\\\text{Reimbursement}\end{array}$$

Insurance reimbursement is based on the lower of the face of the policy, fair market value of loss, or possible reimbursement.

EXAMPLE 1

Case	Face of Policy	Fair Market Value of Property	Fair Market Value of Loss
A	$ 4,000	$10,000	$ 6,000
B	6,000	10,000	10,000
C	10,000	10,000	4,000

Insurance reimbursement follows:

Case A:

$$\frac{\$4,000}{.8 \times \$10,000} \times \$6,000 = \$3,000$$

Case B:

$$\frac{\$6,000}{.8 \times \$10,000} \times \$10,000 = \$7,500$$

Case C:

$$\frac{\$10,000}{.8 \times \$10,000} \times \$4,000 = \$5,000$$

A blanket policy covers several items of property. The face of the policy is allocated based upon the fair market values of the insured assets.

EXAMPLE 2

A blanket policy of $15,000 applies to equipment I and equipment II. The fair value of equipment I and II are $30,000 and $15,000, respectively. Equipment II is partially destroyed resulting in a fire loss of $3,000.

The policy allocation to equipment II is computed below:

	Fair Market Value	Policy
Equipment I	$30,000	$10,000
Equipment II	15,000	5,000
	$45,000	$15,000

The insurance reimbursement is:

$$\frac{\$5,000}{.8 \times \$15,000} \times \$3,000 = \$1,500$$

When a fire loss occurs, the asset destroyed has to be removed from the accounts with the resulting fire loss recorded based on book value. The insurance reimbursement reduces the fire loss. The fire loss is an extraordinary item (net of tax).

EXAMPLE 3

The following fire loss information exists for ABC Company. Merchandise costing $5,000 is fully destroyed. There is no insurance for it. Furniture costing $10,000 with accumulated depreciation of $1,000 and having a fair market value of $7,000 is entirely destroyed. The policy is for $10,000.

Building costing $30,000 with accumulated depreciation of $3,000 and having a fair market value of $20,000 is 50% destroyed. The face of the policy is $15,000. The journal entries to record the book loss follow:

Fire Loss	5,000	
Inventory		5,000
Fire Loss	9,000	
Accumulated Depreciation	1,000	
Furniture		10,000
Fire Loss	13,500	
Accumulated Depreciation	1,500	
Building		15,000

Insurance reimbursement totals $16,375 computed as follows:

Furniture:

$$\frac{\$10,000}{.8 \times \$7,000} \times \$7,000 = \$12,500$$

Building:

$$\frac{\$15,000}{.8 \times \$20,000} \times \$10,000 = \$9,375$$

The journal entry for the insurance reimbursement is:

Cash	16,375	
Fire Loss		16,375

The net fire loss if $11,125 ($27,500 − $16,375) which will typically be shown as an extraordinary item.

Boiler Explosion Insurance

This insurance covers losses to the property insured and to others caused from the explosion.

Umbrella Excess Liability Policy (Blanket Policy)

The umbrella policy insures against all risk not covered under another policy. For example, if the commercial property policy covers up to $10 million, the umbrella policy would provide coverage in excess of $10 million but not to exceed $25 million. It is an "excess coverage" policy coming into being only after another policy has reached its limit. The umbrella policy is a must in a complete insurance program.

Marine Open Cargo Policy

This policy is suggested when the company imports goods on terms of FOB shipping point. The policy covers goods in transit. Because the company obtains title when the goods are shipped, insurance coverage is needed. Each shipment is covered separately and the premium is directly tied to the value of that shipment. Coverage should be to the receiving warehouse dock, where the commercial property policy will pick up the coverage. **Note:** Also take out a General Term Bond for Entry of Merchandise which covers landed merchandise while it passes through customs and brokers' hands.

Contingent Business Interruption Coverage

This provides insurance coverage if business operations are interrupted or ceased because of an unpredictable or infrequent event, such as fire, earthquake, flood, tornado, and vandalism. This policy reimburses for the loss of net income during the shutdown, continuing fixed costs, incremental costs to replace equipment, overtime, or cost of having the goods manufactured elsewhere. The policy may also cover losses because of a supplier's inability to deliver because of an unexpected, unusual, and infrequent event.

Automobile and Aircraft Insurance

Adequate insurance is needed for company-owned vehicles. Insurance for corporate planes includes normal property damage and liability insurance to insured parties.

Insurance Bonds

There are several types of insurance bonds that may be needed including comprehensive bond and miscellaneous bid and performance bond. A comprehensive bond is fidelity coverage for employees due to theft of cash or property. If the company sells to a municipality, it may be required to have miscellaneous bid and performance bonds. The bid bond is typically in lieu of a certified check which has to accompany government bonds. The performance bond insures against the company's inability to perform under the government contract.

Medical and Catastrophe Coverage

Many employers provide medical and catastrophe insurance for current and retired employees.

Worker's Compensation

This policy covers the employer for liability due to occupational health hazards which fall under state law. It typically also covers the employer's liability for employee suits charging personal injuries. The premium is based on the total dollar payroll.

Disability Coverage

Some states require the employee to take out coverage for accidents and disabilities occurring off the job. The premium is set by state statute and paid for by the employee. Sometimes, the employer elects to pay the entire premium as a fringe benefit. If a state does not have a disability law, private insurance may be taken out.

Life Insurance

Life insurance may be taken out on "key" executives. The insurance may also provide cash to buy the deceased's shares. **Note:** If the company is the beneficiary, the premiums are not deductible for tax purposes although they are an expense for financial reporting purposes. The proceeds received upon death are not taxable income.

Cash surrender value of life insurance is the sum payable upon cancellation of the policy by the insured; the insured will of course receive less than the premiums paid in. Cash surrender value is classified under long-term investments. It applies to ordinary life and limited payment policies. It is not usually applicable to term insurance. The insurance premium payment consists of two elements—expense and cash surrender value.

EXAMPLE 4

A premium of $6,000 is paid that increases the cash surrender value by $2,000. The appropriate entry is

Life Insurance Expense	4,000	
Cash Surrender Value of Life Insurance	2,000	
Cash		6,000

The gain on a life insurance policy is not typically considered an extraordinary item since it is in the ordinary course of business.

BUSINESS LAW

What follows is a brief discussion about business law. Obviously, the financial manager must consult with legal counsel regarding all legal matters.

Legal considerations regarding the employer-employee relationship follows.

- *Federal Insurance Contribution Act (FICA)*, commonly known as social security, requires a FICA tax to be withheld from employee's salary with an equal matching by the employer.
- *Fair Labor Standards Act (FLSA)* is concerned with wages and hours. A minimum wage is specified. Employees must be paid equal pay for equal

work. Thus, wage discrimination is prohibited (e.g., race, sex). Certain employees must be paid time and one half for overtime. An employer can not hire a child below a certain age, typically 16.

- *Occupational Safety and Health Act (OSHA)* requires that employers provide a safe and healthy working environment.
- *Employee Retirement Income Security Act (ERISA)* mandates that pension plans be in conformity with certain requirements including funding, vesting, participation, and disclosure.
- *Worker's Compensation* relates to employee injuries on the job. The employer pays a specified amount into an insurance fund.
- *Employment Discrimination* prohibits employer discrimination against employees on the basis of race, color, religion, national origin, or sex. Persons between the ages of 40 and 65 may not be discriminated against unless a legitimate reason exists because of the type of job.

Antitrust laws also exist to prevent restraints of trade and monopoly. The following agreements are illegal:

- Group boycott of a customer
- Price-fixing
- Division of markets
- Sale of product to retailer only if the retailer agrees not to resell the product below a certain price
- Forcing the buyer to purchase a second product if he or she orders a first one

30
What You Should Know About Economics

Financial management is a type of applied economics significantly based on economic theory. In effect, the parent discipline of finance is economics. Financial managers require familiarity with some selected concepts, terms and tools utilized in economics to better understand the effect of the economy on the company as well as to comprehend the financial setting in order to make proper financial and investment decisions.

The two general divisions of economics are microeconomics and macroeconomics. The dividing line between them may sometimes overlap.

MICROECONOMICS

Microeconomics is the study of the individual units of the economy—individuals, households, firms, and industries. Microeconomics zeros in on such economic variables as the prices and outputs of specific firms and industries, the expenditures of consumers, wage rates, competition, and markets. The focus is on the trees, not the forest!

Microeconomics examines corporate policies and activities. Examples of relevant microeconomics as it affects the company are supply-demand relationships, and profit maximization strategies. Microeconomics affects product pricing, productive inputs, and so on.

Questions answered by microeconomics include:

- What determines the price and output of individual goods and services in your department?

769

- What are the factors that determine supply and demand of a particular good you are manufacturing?
- How government policies such as price controls, subsidies, and excise taxes affect the price and output levels of your individual product markets?

Demand, Supply, and Market Equilibrium

There exists a relationship between the market price of a good (such as wheat) and the quantity demanded. This relationship between price and quantity is called the *demand function*. On the other hand, the relationship between the market price of the good and the amount of that good the producers are willing to supply is the *supply function*.

Market equilibrium can take place as shown in Figure 1 only at a price where the quantities supplied and demanded are equal. At any price higher than the equilibrium price, the quantity producers will want to go on supplying will exceed the quantity that consumers will want to go on demanding. Downward pressure on price will then result as some of the excess sellers undermine the going price. Similarly, a price lower than the equilibrium price will tend to generate shortages and to meet upward pressure from bids of excess buyers.

EXAMPLE 1

The interest rate, which is the price of money, is determined in the market based on the demand for a supply of capital, as shown in Figure 2.

Figure 1. Market Equilibrium

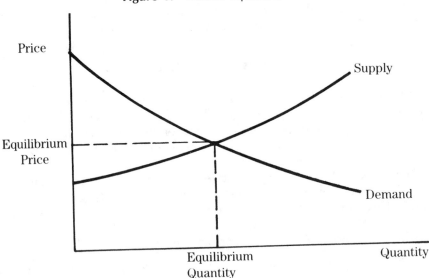

Figure 2. Interest Rate Determination

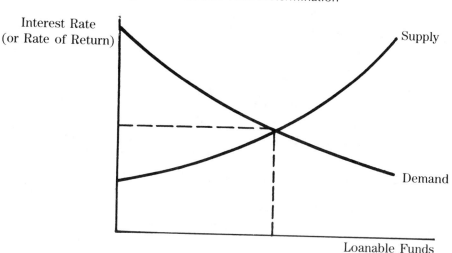

Profit Maximization

Your company will find its maximum profit position where the last unit it sells brings in extra revenue just equal to its extra cost. That is, marginal revenue (MR) = marginal cost (MC). The reasoning is that as long as MR exceeds MC, the supplier expands output, adding more to total revenue than to total cost, and so total profits rise. On the other hand, it does not pay for the manufacturer to produce when MR is smaller than MC because it would be adding more to total costs than to total revenue, and the total profit could fall. This leaves the output at which MR = MC as the profit maximization or best level of output for the manufacturer. In summary, corporate actions should be taken as long as marginal profitability results (MR > MC).

MACROECONOMICS

Macroeconomics is the study of the national economy as a whole, or of its major sectors. It looks at the general institutional and international environment the company operates in. It deals with national output, employment levels, inflation, budgetary condition, tax policies, and international trade. It looks at the forest, not the trees. Note there is an intermingling between economics and politics.

Macroeconomics looks at governmental policies and regulations as well as those of private institutions that influence economic activities. Macroeconomics examines the structure of the federal treasury, financial intermediaries, banking system, and governmental economic policies. The objectives of macroeconomics are to have the free flow of funds, reduce unemployment, and generate a stable economic environment.

Typical macroeconomics questions include:

- What determines national income and employment levels and how does that affect your department's activities?
- What determines the general price level or rate of inflation and what impact does it have on your pricing of products?
- What are the fiscal and monetary policies that combat typical economic problems such as inflation, unemployment, and recession? How does the economic environment impact upon your department's operations?

You should be familiar with the macroeconomic setting since your company operates in this environment. The effect of a change in the economic situation (e.g., inflation, recession) on your company must be understood so needed adjustments to cope may be made. What would happen to the company's financial condition if credit is tightened or eased? For example, the tightening of credit may cause problems in obtaining funds. An understanding of financial institutions is needed so that a careful appraisal may be made of prospective financing and investment possibilities.

Let us now look at specific macroeconomic areas.

Gross National Product. Gross national product (GNP) measures total spending in terms of market value of all economic units (e.g., households, companies, government, non-profit entities) or final products and services for a given time period. Excluded from GNP are products moving through intermediate manufacturing steps. Also excluded are services performed but not sold in the market (e.g., housewife, self-repair). Also excluded are sources of illegally nonreported income (e.g., unreported cash income of a business person, monies received for stolen goods). Thus, the reported GNP may significantly be less than the actual economic output.

Inflation. Inflation is the rise in a general price level commonly measured by the consumer price index (CPI) or some comparable price index. As prices increase, lenders and investors want to guard against the decline in purchasing power and as a result will want higher returns. Companies may cut back on borrowings because of the high interest rates and thus reduce their expenditures on property, plant and equipment. In consequence, there may be decreased output resulting in layoffs.

During inflation, your salary may go up to keep pace with inflation but your real earnings are still the same. You still lose out, since your tax liability will increase.

Employment. A high level of employment provides a healthy economy because recipients have money to consume creating additional sales of products and services thus stimulating the economy.

Interest Rates. Interest is the price a borrower pays to use money for a period of time. Interest comes in many guises. There are long-term and short-term interest rates, depending on the length of the loan; there are fixed interest rate loans and variable interest rate loans; there are interest rates on super-safe bonds (like U.S. T-bills) and there are interest rates on "junk bonds" of companies that have low credit ratings; there are nominal (coupon) interest rates, real (inflation-adjusted) or risk adjusted interest rates, and effective interest rates (or yield).

In inflation, lenders demand the basic interest rate plus a premium to neutralize the effect of the decline in the purchasing power of the dollar as it affects principal. Thus, during inflation, you must use real interest rates to calculate the yield on investments, not nominal rates. The real interest rate is the nominal rate less the inflation rate.

EXAMPLE 2

The basic interest rate is 5% and the inflation rate is 4%. A lender will want a 9% interest rate.

Interest rates are also affected by the maturity period of the security. The relationship is called the "term structure" of interest rates.

Monetary Policy. Monetary policy is the policy of the Federal Reserve System (FRS) in exercising its control over money supply, thereby affecting interest rates, price levels, and credit conditions. The "narrowly defined" money supply (M1) consists of coins, paper currency, plus all demand or checking deposits; this is narrow, or transactions, money. The "broadly defined" money supply (M2) includes all items in M1 plus "time deposits"—savings deposits, money funds, and the like, against which checks may not be drawn. The instruments of monetary policy are primarily open-market operations involving sale and purchase of government securities, reserve requirements, and the discount rate.

When the money supply increases more than the normal increase in activity (usually about 4%), the economy is heating up and therefore inflationary. This is when FRS usually steps in and tries to reduce the money supply, for example, by raising the discount rate. The increased interest rates, however, tend to dampen the loan demand and bring recession.

Some economists believe that as money supply expands there will be greater economic activity resulting in more employment. They favor FRS to increase the money supply so that interest rates will drop causing an increase in corporate capital spending.

FRS may use a forementioned tool to control money supply and affect interest rates. Tight-money policy restrains or reduces the money supply and raises interest rates. These steps are taken to hold down or reduce the level of real GNP, reduce inflation, or strengthen the balance of international payments by attracting capital inflows. Easy-money policy, on the other hand, is designed to increase the money supply to reduce interest rates. The intent of such a policy is to increase aggregate demand and thereby raise real GNP.

Fiscal Policy. Fiscal policy are governmental policies regarding tax law, federal budgets, and financing the deficit to increase aggregate demand. A lowering in taxes for a particular industry (e.g., oil and natural gas) stimulates more activity in it because the additional earnings can be reinvested. As an example, the job tax credit results in greater employment.

The federal budget significantly affects economic activity. Governmental expenditures positively affect economic activity and employment. But if governmental revenues are not obtained to offset increased expenditures, a budget deficit will result. However, additional revenues come from taxes resulting in less consumer spending thus slowing economic activity.

In the short run, a federal budget deficit generates demand. Some economists believe this action results in increased inflation having a long-term negative effect on the economy. Furthermore, the financing of the federal deficit by the issuance of debt will compete for funds to be raised by companies and will detract from economic expansion. This is called the "crowding-out effect." The payment of debt by the government has the effect of redistributing income from taxpayers to the holders of debt obligations.

Government Regulation. The government can regulate corporate policies, such as those related to products, services, output, and employment. Restrictive governmental actions can adversely affect economic activities and may raise company prices for goods and services.

Supply-Side Economics. In contrast with Keynesian economics which focuses on increasing aggregate demand, supply side-economics concentrates on increasing supply. It is a view emphasizing policy measures to affect aggregate supply or potential output. In this approach, it is believed that high marginal tax rates on labor and capital incomes reduce work effort and saving; a cut in marginal tax rates will thereby increase factor supplies and total output. An extreme view, sometimes put forth by Professor Laffer, is that a tax cut will actually raise total tax revenues. The reasoning goes that the improved output through tax cuts lowers the inflation rate, increases employment, and enhances overall economic activity.

In addition to lower tax rates, in the view of supply-side economists, other governmental measures to achieve price stability and economic growth are increased depreciation allowances and reduction in regulatory requirements.

Budget Deficits. Economics generally believe that larger federal deficits result in higher interest rates. There are two reasons for this belief. First, increased budget deficits raise the demand for loanable funds, shifting the demand curve upward from D_1 to D_2 (see Fig. 3) and raising interest rates (I_1 to I_2). Second, financial market participants may believe that larger deficits are likely to lead to higher inflation. This may be true either because the sources of the increased deficits—larger government spending and/or lower taxes—result directly in greater pressure for loan demand and hence inflation, or because the deficits will induce FRS to expand the money supply to help finance the deficits, thus causing inflation. In any event, if the increased deficits elevate the public's expectation of inflation, it will tend to raise the level of interest rates.

Figure 3. Demand for Loanable Funds and Interest Rates

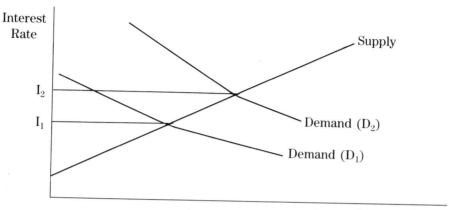

CONCLUSION

The financial manager should have some familiarity with the impact of economic factors on the firm. In this way, the manager will understand the overall financial setting he or she is operating in so that sound financial and investment decisions may be made. Economic forces consist of microeconomics and macroeconomics.

VI

MANAGEMENT OF ASSETS

31
Working Capital and Cash Management

The ability to manage working capital will improve return and minimize the risk of running short of cash. There are various ways of managing working capital and cash to achieve success including using quantitative techniques to find optimal asset levels. The amount invested in any current asset may change daily and requires close appraisal. Improper asset management occurs when funds tied up in the asset can be used more productively elsewhere.

EVALUATING WORKING CAPITAL

Working capital equals current assets less current liabilities. Management of working capital involves regulating the various types of current assets and current liabilities. Involved are decisions on how assets should be financed (e.g., short-term debt, long-term debt, or equity). Managing working capital involves a tradeoff between return and risk. If funds go from fixed assets to current assets, there is a reduction in liquidity risk, greater ability to obtain short-term financing, and greater flexibility, because the company can more readily adjust current assets to changes in sales volume. But less of a return is earned because the yield on fixed assets is more than that of current assets. Financing with noncurrent debt has less liquidity risk than financing with current debt. However, long-term debt often has a higher cost than short-term debt because of the greater uncertainty, which detracts from the company's overall return.

What to Do: Use the hedging approach of financing where assets are financed by liabilities of similar maturity. In this way, there are adequate funds

779

to meet debt when due. For instance, permanent assets should be financed with long-term debt instead of short-term debt.

Rule of Thumb: The longer it takes to purchase or manufacture goods, the more working capital required. Working capital also applies to the volume of purchases and the cost per unit. For example, if the company can receive a raw material in two weeks, it needs less of an inventory level than if two months lead time is involved. **Tip:** Purchase material early if materially lower prices are available and if the material's cost savings exceed inventory carrying costs.

CASH MANAGEMENT

In a small company, the controller may be responsible for cash management. In a large company, cash management is typically the responsibility of the treasurer.

A centralized cash management system minimizes idle cash in the system and maximizes cash available for use. The cash management system should integrate all cash flows of the firm (e.g., domestic and international divisions and subsidiaries). A centralized system will identify situations where one subsidiary is borrowing at high interest rates while another subsidiary has excess, idle cash. The cash processes should be coordinated, such as investment, disbursement, and collection.

Cash should be made available to cash-using divisions from cash-generating ones of the company so as to keep borrowing at a minimum and to have sufficient funds available for investment. For example, foreign currency payments should be netted among divisions to eliminate currency conversion and reduce float time between operations. There should be an integration of foreign currency requirements between the parent and subsidiaries. An international company must use a bank known for *quality* international services including networking, cash concentration, and clearing. The financial manager should determine the average number of competitive quotations received before making a disbursement in a foreign country.

The purpose of cash management is to invest excess cash for a return and at the same time have adequate liquidity to meet future needs. A proper cash balance should exist, neither excessive nor deficient. For example, companies with many bank accounts may be accumulating excessive balances. Do you know how much cash you need, how much you have, where the cash is, what the sources of cash are, and where the cash will be used? This is particularly crucial in recession. Proper cash forecasting is required to determine (1) the optimal time to incur and pay back debt and (2) the amount to transfer daily between accounts. A daily computerized listing of cash balances and transaction reporting should be prepared. This lets the financial officer know the up-to-date cash balance so a decision can be made where it is best to put the funds into use. A listing of daily transactions enables one to find out if any problems exist so immediate rectification may be made. **Recommendation:** The financial manager should establish, control, and report bank accounts, services, and activities. Are banking services cost-effective? Analyze each bank account as to type, balance, and cost. What is the processing cost for checks, bank transfers, and direct debits? The adequacy of controls for intercompany transactions and transfers should be reviewed. When cash receipts and cash payments are highly synchronized and predictable, the company may keep a smaller cash balance. If quick liquidity is needed, invest in marketable securities. **General Rule:** Additional cash should be invested in income-producing securities with maturities structured to provide the necessary liquidity.

Companies that are strong financially and able to borrow at favorable rates even in problem financial markets can afford a lower level of cash and cash equivalents than companies that are highly leveraged or considered poor credit risks.

A high tech company may want to have more cash on hand to weather unforeseen occurrences or problems in the financial markets. A company in a mature industry could have minimal cash on hand with short-term cash requirements met through short-term borrowing.

The minimum cash to hold is the greater of (1) compensating balances (a deposit held by a bank to compensate it for providing services) or (2) precautionary balances (money held for emergency purposes) plus transaction balances (money to cover checks outstanding). The firm must hold enough cash to meet its daily requirements.

Factors in Determining the Amount of Cash to Be Held

- Use of effective cash management
- Asset size
- Financial philosophy and strength
- Utility preferences regarding liquidity and business risks
- Expected future cash flows, considering the probabilities of different cash flows under alternative circumstances. Since cash forecasting may result in errors, there should be some excess cash on hand or short-term debt capacity to cover such eventuality.
- Maturity period of debt
- Ability to borrow on short notice and on favorable terms
- Return rates
- Possibility of unexpected problems (e.g., customer defaults)

Less cash needs to be kept on hand when a company can borrow quickly from a bank, such as under a line of credit agreement, which permits a firm to borrow instantly up to a specified maximum amount. However, make sure the line of credit is not excessive because of the associated commitment fee on the unused line (if any).

Watch the amount of the compensating balance, since the portion of a loan that serves as collateral is restricted and unavailable for corporate use. Are compensating balances too costly? Often, keeping compensating balances is more costly than paying fees for banking services provided. Is cash unnecessarily tied up in other accounts (e.g., loans to employees, insurance deposits)? **Warning:** Liquid asset holdings are required during a downturn in a company's cycle, when funds from operations decline.

Excess cash should be invested in marketable securities for a return. Automatic short-term money market investments means that excess cash is immediately deposited in money market securities so a return is earned on the funds. Holding marketable securities serves as protection against cash shortages. Companies with seasonal operations may purchase marketable securities when they have excess funds and then sell the securities when cash deficits occur. A firm may also invest in marketable securities when funds are being held temporarily in expectation of short-term capital expansion. In selecting an investment portfolio, consideration should be given to return, default risk, marketability, and maturity date.

Coupon and security collection is needed to assure that any interest the company is entitled to is gotten and that securities maturing or sold are properly collected and deposited.

Recommendation: Do not seek to fund peak seasonal cash requirements internally. Rather, borrow on a short-term basis to enable internal funds to be used more profitably throughout the year, such as by investing in plant and equipment.

The thrust of cash management is to accelerate cash receipts and delay cash payments.

Acceleration of Cash Inflow

You should evaluate the causes and take corrective action for delays in having cash receipts deposited. **What To Do:** Ascertain how and where cash receipts come, how cash is transferred from outlying accounts to the main corporate account, banking policy regarding availability of funds, and time lag between receiving a check and depositing it.

Types of Delays in Processing Checks

- Mail float–the time required for a check to move from debtor to creditor
- Processing float–the time needed for the creditor to enter the payment
- Deposit collection float–the time for a check to clear

Figure 1 depicts the total float of a check.

Means of Accelerating Cash Receipts

- Lockbox arrangement where the optimum collection point is placed near customers. Customer payments are mailed to strategic post office boxes

Figure 1. Float Due to a Check Issued and Mailed by Payer to Payee

Check issued and mailed by payer company to payee company

Check received by payee company

Journal entries prepared and check deposited by payee company

Check clears the bank and monies are available to payee company

Mail float (3 days)

Processing float (2 days)

Transit float (4 days)

Total float (9 days)

Time (days)

0

geographically situated to hasten mailing and depositing time. Banks collect from these boxes several times a day and make deposits to the corporate account. A computer listing is prepared of payments received by account and a daily total. **Recommendation:** Undertake a cost-benefit analysis to ensure that instituting a lockbox arrangement will result in net savings. Determine the average face value of checks received, cost of operations eliminated, reducible processing overhead, and reduction in "mail float" days. Because per-item processing cost is typically significant, it is most advantageous to use a lockbox when low-volume, high-dollar collections are involved. But the system is becoming increasingly more available to firms with high-volume, low-dollar receipts as technological advances (such as machine-readable documents) lower the per-item cost of lockboxes. **Tip:** Compare the return earned on freed cash to the cost of the lockbox arrangement. A wholesale lockbox is used for checks received from other companies. The average cash receipts is large and the number of cash receipts is small. The bank prepares an electronic list of payments received and transmits the information to the company. A wholesale lockbox system aids in internal control because there is a separation between billing and receivables processing. Many wholesale lockboxes only result in mail time reductions of no more than one business day, and check clearing time reductions of only a few tenths of one day. Wholesale lockboxes are beneficial for companies with gross revenues of several million dollars or more. It is best when large checks are received from distant customers. A retail lockbox is best if the company is dealing with the public (retail consumers as distinguished from companies). Retail lockboxes typically have many transactions of a nominal amount. The lockbox reduces float and transfers workload from the company to the bank. The net effect should be improved cash flow and a reduction in expenses. In general, remittances are processed in an automated environment.

- Concentration banking, where funds are collected in local banks and transferred to a main concentration account.

- Identify and monitor changes in collection patterns. Determine the reasons for any delays.

- On the return envelope for customer remission, use bar codes, nine-digit code numbers, and post office box numbers. **Note:** Accelerated Reply Mail (ARM) is the assignment of a unique "truncating" ZIP code to payments, such as lockbox receivables. The coded remittances are removed from the postal system and processed by banks or third parties.

- Send customers preaddressed, stamped envelopes.

- Obtain approval from a customer to have a pre-authorized debit (PAD) charged to the customer's bank account automatically for repetitive charges. An example is an insurance company that has PADs charged to its policyholders for insurance premiums. These debits may take the form of paper pre-authorized checks (PACs) or paperless automatic clearing house entries. PADs are cost-effective because they avoid the process of billing a customer, receiving and processing a payment, and depositing a check. **Note:** Variable payments are not as efficient as fixed payments because the amount of the PAD must be changed each period and typically the customer must be advised by mail of the amount of the debit. PADs are best for constant, relatively nominal periodic (e.g., monthly, semi-weekly) payments.

• Transfer funds between banks by wire transfers or depository transfer checks (DTCs). Wire transfers may be used for intracompany transactions. Wire transfers may be made by computer terminal and telephone. A wire transfer allows for the same day transfer of funds. It should only be made for significant dollar amounts because of the cost since per wire transfer fees are assessed by both the originating bank and the receiving bank. Wire transfers are best for intraorganization transfers. Examples include making transfers to and from investments, placing funds in an account the day checks are expected to clear, and putting funds in any other account that requires immediate availability of funds. Two types of wire transfers are preformatted (recurring) and free-form (nonrepetitive). With preformatted wire transfers, there is not extensive authorization. This type is suitable for typical transfers such as for investments and other company accounts. The company specifies an issuing bank and a receiving bank along with the account number. There is greater control for nonrecurring transfers. The control includes written confirmation instead of confirmation only from telephone or computer terminal. Wire transfers may also be used to fund other types of checking accounts, such as payroll accounts. In order to control balances in the account, the account may be funded on a staggered basis. However, to prevent an overdraft, make sure balances are maintained in another account at the bank.

Paper or paperless depository transfer checks may be used to transfer funds between the company's bank accounts. No signature is required on depository transfer checks but of course the check is payable to the bank for credit to the company's account. However, control must exist to assure that an employee does not use depository transfer checks to transfer funds from an account on which he or she does not have signature authorization to an account in which he or she does. Depository transfer checks typically clear in one day. If manual depository transfer checks are used, pre-printed checks include all information except the amount and date. Manual preparation is advisable if there are only a few checks prepared daily. If there is automated depository transfer checks, they are printed as needed. **Tip:** Usually it is best to use the bank's printer since it is not cost-effective for the company to purchase the printer. Automatic check preparation is only advisable when there are a large number of transfer checks to be prepared daily.

- Accelerate billing
- Require deposits on large or custom orders or progress billings as the work progresses
- Charge interest on accounts receivable after a certain amount of time
- Use personal collection efforts
- Offer discounts for early payment
- Have postdated checks for customers
- Have cash-on-delivery terms
- Deposit checks immediately
- Make repeated collection calls and visits

EXAMPLE 1

The financial officer is determining whether to initiate a lockbox arrangement that will cost $150,000 annually. The daily average collections are $700,000. The system will reduce mailing and processing time by two days. The rate of return is 14%.

Return on freed cash (14% × 2 × $700,000)	$196,000
Annual cost	150,000
Net advantage of lockbox system	$ 46,000

EXAMPLE 2

You presently have a lockbox arrangement with Bank A in which it handles $5 million a day in return for an $800,000 compensating balance. You are thinking of canceling this arrangement and further dividing your western region by entering into contracts with two other banks. Bank B will handle $3 million a day in collections with a compensating balance of $600,000. Collections will be half a day quicker than the current situation. Your return rate is 12%.

Accelerated cash receipts ($5 million per day × 0.5 day)	$2,500,000
Increased compensating balance	500,000
Improved cash flow	$2,000,000
Rate of return	× 0.12
Net annual savings	$ 240,000

Delay of Cash Outlay

The company should delay cash payments to earn a greater return. Evaluate who the payees are and to what extent one can reasonably stretch time limits.

Ways of Delaying Cash Payments

- Centralize the payables operation so that debt may be paid at the most profitable time and so that the amount of disbursement float in the system may be ascertained.

- Have zero balance accounts where zero balances are established for all of the company's disbursing units. These accounts are in the same concentration bank. Checks are drawn against these accounts, with the balance in each account never exceeding $0. Divisional disbursing authority is thus maintained at the local level of management. The advantages of zero balance accounts are better control over cash payments, reduction in excess cash balances held in regional banks, and a possible increase in disbursing float. Under the zero balance account concept the company only puts funds into its payroll and payables checking accounts when it expects checks to clear. This is an aggressive strategy. **Caution:** Watch out for overdrafts and service charges. In a zero balance account (ZBA) system, the bank automatically transfers funds from a master (concentration) account as checks are presented against the payroll and payables accounts. Therefore, payroll and payable accounts are retained at zero balances. Under ZBA, the financial manager does not have to anticipate clearing times on each account.

- Make partial payments.

- Request additional information about an invoice before approving it for payment.

- Use payment drafts, where payment is not made on demand. Instead, the draft is presented for collection to the bank, which in turn goes to the issuer for acceptance. A draft may be used to provide for inspection before payment. When approved, the company deposits the funds. **Net Result:** Less of a required checking balance. **Note:** The use of drafts may require bank charges (e.g., fixed monthly fee) and the inconveniences of always having to formerly approve the draft before payment.

- Draw checks on remote banks (e.g., a New York company using a Texas bank).

- Mail from post offices with limited service or where mail has to go through numerous handling points. **Tip:** If you utilize float properly you can maintain higher bank balances than the actual lower book balances. For instance, if you write checks averaging $200,000 per day and three days are necessary for them to clear, you will have a $600,000 checking balance less than the bank's records.

- Use probability analysis to determine the expected date for checks to clear. **Suggestion:** Have separate checking accounts (e.g., payroll, dividends) and monitor check clearing dates. For example, payroll checks are not all cashed on the payroll date, so funds can be deposited later to earn a return.

- Use a computer terminal to transfer funds between various bank accounts at opportune times.
- Use a charge account to lengthen the time between buying goods and paying for them.
- Stretch payments provided there is no associated finance charge or impairment in credit rating.
- Do not pay bills before the due date.
- Utilize noncash compensation and remuneration methods (e.g., stock).
- Delay the frequency of payments to employees (e.g., expense account reimbursements, payrolls).
- Disburse commissions on sales when the receivables are collected rather than when they are made.

A cash management system is shown in Table 1.

EXAMPLE 3

Every two weeks the company disburses checks that average $500,000 and take three days to clear. The financial manager wants to find out how much money can be saved annually if the transfer of funds are delayed from an interest-bearing account that pays 0.0384% per day (annual rate of 14%) for those three days.

$$\$500,000 \times (0.000384 \times 3) = \underline{\$576}$$

The savings per year is $576 × 26 (yearly payrolls) = $14,976

Cash Models

William Baumol developed a model to determine the optimum amount of transaction cash under conditions of certainty. The objective is to

Table 1

CASH MANAGEMENT SYSTEM

Acceleration of Cash Receipts	Delay of Cash Payments
Lockbox System	Pay By Draft
Concentration Banking	Requisition More Frequently
Pre-Authorized Checks	Disbursing Float
Pre-Addressed Stamp Envelopes	Make Partial Payments
Obtain Deposits on Large Orders	Use Charge Accounts
Charge Interest on Overdue Receivables	Delay Frequency of Paying Employees

minimize the sum of the fixed costs of transactions and the opportunity cost of holding cash balances. These costs are expressed as

$$F \cdot \frac{(T)}{C} + i \frac{(C)}{2}$$

where F = the fixed cost of a transaction
T = the total cash needed for the time period involved
i = the interest rate on marketable securities
C = cash balance

The optimal level of cash is determined using the following formula:

$$C^* \sqrt{\frac{2FT}{i}}$$

A helpful graph follows:

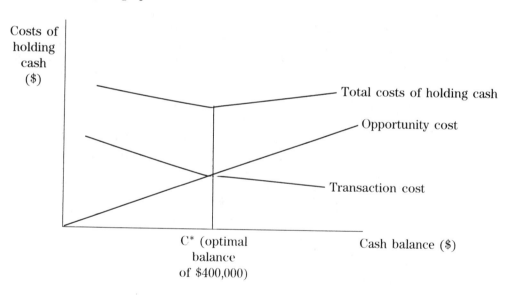

EXAMPLE 4

You estimate a cash need for $4,000,000 over a one-month period where the cash account is expected to be disbursed at a constant rate. The opportunity interest rate is 6% per annum, or 0.5% for a one-month period. The transaction cost each time you borrow or withdraw is $100.

The optimal transaction size (the optimal borrowing or withdrawal lot size) and the number of transactions you should make during the month follow:

$$C^* = \sqrt{\frac{2FT}{i}} = \sqrt{\frac{2(100)(4,000,000)}{0.005}} = \underline{\$400,000}$$

The optimal transaction size is $400,000.
The average cash balance is

$$\frac{C^*}{2} = \frac{\$400,000}{2} = \underline{\$200,000}$$

The number of transactions required are

$$\frac{\$4,000,000}{\$400,000} = 10 \text{ transactions during the month.}$$

You can use a stochastic model for cash management where major uncertainty exists regarding cash payments. The Miller-Orr model places an upper and lower limit for cash balances. When the upper limit is reached, a transfer of cash to marketable securities is made. When the lower limit is reached, a transfer from securities to cash takes place. A transaction will not occur as long as the cash balance falls within the limits.

Factors taken into account in the Miller-Orr model are the fixed costs of a securities transaction (F), assumed to be the same for buying as well as selling, the daily interest rate on marketable securities (i), and the variance of daily net cash flows (σ^2). The objective is to meet cash requirements at the lowest possible cost. A major assumption is the randomness of cash flows. The two control limits in the Miller-Orr model may be specified as d dollars as an upper limit and zero dollars at the lower limit. When the cash balance reaches the upper level, d less z dollars of securities are bought and the new balance becomes z dollars. When the cash balance equals zero, z dollars of securities are sold and the new balance again reaches z. Of course, practically speaking you should note that the minimum cash balance is established at an amount greater than zero due to delays in transfer as well as to having a safety buffer.

The optimal cash balance z is computed as follows:

$$z = \sqrt[3]{\frac{3F\sigma^2}{4i}}$$

The optimal value for d is computed as $3z$.

The average cash balance will approximate $\dfrac{(z+d)}{3}$.

EXAMPLE 5

You wish to use the Miller-Orr model. The following information is supplied:

Fixed cost of a securities transaction	$10
Variance of daily net cash flows	$50
Daily interest rate on securities (10%/360)	0.0003

The optimal cash balance, the upper limit of cash needed, and the average cash balance follow:

$$z = \sqrt[3]{\frac{3(10)(50)}{4(0.0003)}} = \sqrt[3]{\frac{3(10)(50)}{.0012}} = \sqrt[3]{\frac{1,500}{0.0012}} =$$

$$\sqrt[3]{1,250,000}$$

$$\underline{\$102}$$

The optimal cash balance is $102.

The upper limit is $306 (3 × $102).

The average cash balance is $136 $\dfrac{(\$102 + \$306)}{3}$

A brief elaboration on these findings is needed for clarification. When the upper limit of $306 is reached, $204 of securities ($306 − $102) will be purchased to bring you to the optimal cash balance of $102. When the lower limit of zero dollars is reached, $102 of securities will be sold to again bring you to the optimal cash balance of $102.

An informative graph follows:

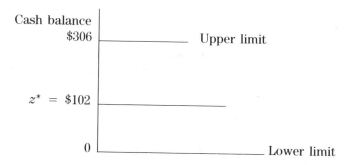

BANKING RELATIONSHIPS

The company may want to restrict the maximum total deposits at particular banks having financial problems to no more than the insurance provided by the Federal Deposit Insurance Corporation for commercial banks or the Federal Savings and Loan Insurance Corporation for savings and loan institutions. **Note:** With a checking account, the maximum deposit may be exceeded on the bank's records but not on the company's books due to the clearing time required for checks and concentration entries.

A maximum deposit should be determined to keep at specific banks that exceeds the insurance limit. Deposits of unlimited amounts should be authorized at given financial institutions.

Different banks can be used for different services depending on what is best for the company. In selecting a bank, the following should be considered:

- Location (affects lockboxes and disbursement points)
- Type of cost of services
- Availability of funds

An appraisal should be made of the financial soundness of the bank. Here, reference may be made to ratings provided by services tracking banks.

Undertake a bank account analysis by comparing the value of the company balance maintained at the bank to the service charges. Banks will provide such analysis, if you wish, but the bank's analysis must be closely scrutinized.

A balance reporting system may be used where the lead bank gathers relevant and essential information for all other banks. The information may then be transferred to the company via telecommunications. The cost-effectiveness of the system should be periodically evaluated.

Most checks clear in one business day. Clearing time of three or more business days is rare. Try to arrange for the financial institution to give same-day credit on a deposit received prior to a specified cutoff time. However, if the deposit is made over-the-counter with a letter, immediate availability of those funds may not be received. However, if the deposit is made early enough, especially through a lockbox, immediate availability of those funds may be received.

It is usually financially better to pay a higher deposited item charge in return for accelerated availability of funds.

In doing an account reconciliation, the bank sorts checks into serial number order, lists all checks cleared, and matches issued checks provided by the company to paid checks so as to list outstanding checks and exception items. One purpose is to reconcile the cash balances on deposit at various banks for control purposes. If voluminous checks are issued, the services are cost-effective.

A bank reconciliation is prepared by the company of each bank account to ensure the balance per books equals the balance per bank after adjusting for reconciling items. The bank reconciliation is done as an internal control of cash.

32

Management of Accounts Receivable

Credit management falls under the responsibility of the controller or treasurer. Accounts receivable management directly impacts the profitability of the firm. It considers discount policy, whether to extend credit to marginal customers, ways of speeding up collections and reducing bad debts, and setting terms.

The financial manager should appraise order entry, billing, and accounts receivable activities to assure proper procedures and controls from the time an order is received until ultimate collection. What is the average time lag between completing the sales transaction and invoicing the customer?

Accounts receivable management involves two types of float—invoicing and mail. Invoicing float is the days between the time goods are shipped to the customer and the time the invoice is rendered. The company should mail invoices out on a timely basis. Mail float is the time between the preparation of an invoice and the time it is received by the customer. This mail float may be reduced by the following:

- Decentralizing invoicing and mailing
- Coordinating outgoing mail with post office schedules
- Using express mail services for large invoices
- Enforcing due dates
- Offering discounts

In managing accounts receivable, the financial manager should consider that there is an opportunity cost associated with holding receivables. The opportunity cost is tying up money in accounts receivable resulting in losing the

793

the return that could be earned on having those funds invested elsewhere. Therefore, means to analyze and expedite collections should be undertaken.

A key concern is the amount and credit terms given to customers since this will affect sales volume and collections. For example, a longer credit term will probably result in increased sales. The credit terms have a direct bearing on the costs and revenue generated from receivables. If credit terms are tight, there will be less investment in accounts receivable and less bad debt losses, but there will also be lower sales, reduced profits, and adverse customer reaction. On the other hand, if credit terms are lax, there will be higher sales and gross profit but greater bad debts and a higher opportunity cost of carrying the investment in accounts receivable because marginal customers take longer to pay. Receivable terms should be liberalized when you want to get rid of excessive inventory or items near obsolescence. Longer receivable terms are appropriate for industries in which products are sold in advance of retail seasons (e.g., swimsuits). If products are perishable, short receivable terms or even payment on delivery is recommended.

In evaluating a potential customer's ability to pay, consider the customer's integrity, financial soundness, and collateral to be pledged. A customer's credit soundness may be appraised through quantitative techniques such as regression analysis. Such techniques are most useful when a large number of small customers are involved. Bad debt losses can be estimated reliably when a company sells to many customers and when its credit policies have not changed for a long time.

The financial manager has to consider the costs of giving credit including administrative costs of the credit department, computer services, fees to rating agencies, and periodic field investigations.

CREDIT REFERENCES

Reference may be made to retail credit bureaus and professional credit reference services in appraising a customer's ability to pay. One service is Dun and Bradstreet (D&B), which rates companies. D&B reports contain information about a company's nature of business, product line, management, financial statement information, number of employees, previous payment history as reported by suppliers, amounts currently owed and past due, terms of sale, audit opinion, lawsuits, insurance coverage, leases, criminal proceedings, banking relationships and account information (e.g., current bank loans), location of business, and seasonality aspects.

SETTING ACCOUNTS RECEIVABLE STANDARDS

To monitor and improve accounts receivable functional activities, we can establish unit credit standards to be accomplished. For invoice preparation, unit cost standards might be based on cost per invoice, order, or item. For credit investigation and approval, unit cost standards may include cost per account, sales order, or credit sales transaction. In looking at credit correspondence records, we may use cost per sales order, account sold, or letter. In terms of preparing customer statements, unit cost standards may be in terms of cost per statement, or account sold. The standard for the computation of commissions on cash collections may be based on cost per remittance.

MONITORING RECEIVABLES

There are many ways to optimize profitability from accounts receivable and keep losses to a minimum. These include:

- "Cycle bill" to produce greater uniformity in the billing process
- Mail customer statements within 24 hours of the close of the accounting period
- Send an invoice to customers when the order is processed at the warehouse instead of when merchandise is shipped.
- Bill for services periodically when work is performed or charge a retainer. **Tip:** Bill large sales immediately.
- Use seasonal datings. **Recommendation:** When business is slow, sell to customers with delayed payment terms to stimulate demand for customers who are unable to pay until later in the season. **What to Do:** Compare profitability on incremental sales plus the reduction in inventory carrying costs, which have to exceed the opportunity cost on the additional investment in average accounts receivable.
- Carefully analyze customer financial statements before giving credit. Also, obtain ratings from financial advisory sources.
- Avoid typically high-risk receivables (e.g., customers in a financially troubled industry or region). Be careful of accounts in business less than one year (about 50% of businesses fail within the first two years).
- Modify credit limits based on changes in customer's financial health.
- Ask for collateral in support of questionable accounts. **Tip:** The collateral value should equal or exceed the account balance.
- Factor accounts receivable when net savings ensue. However, beware that confidential information may be disclosed.
- Use outside collection agencies where warranted.
- Consider marketing factors, since a stringent credit policy might result in a loss of business.
- Note that consumer receivables have greater risk of default than corporate receivables.
- Age accounts receivable to spot delinquent customers. Interest should be charged on such accounts. Aged receivables can be compared to prior years, industry norms, and competition. Bad Debt Loss Reports should be

prepared showing cumulative bad debt losses detailed by customer, terms of sale, size of account, and summarized by department, product line, and type of customer (e.g., industry). **Note:** Bad debt losses are typically higher for smaller companies than for larger ones. Of course, the company should charge back to the salesperson the commission already paid on an uncollectible account.

- Accelerate collections from customers currently having financial problems. Also, withhold products or services until payment is made.
- Have credit insurance to guard against unusual bad debt losses. **What to Consider:** In deciding whether to get this insurance, take into account expected average bad debt losses, financial capability of the firm to withstand the losses, and the cost of insurance.
- Keep track of customer complaints about order item and invoice errors and orders not filled on time.
- Look at the relationship of credit department costs to credit sales.

The collection period for accounts receivable partly depends on corporate policy and conditions. In granting trade credit, competition and economic conditions have to be taken into account. In recession, the financial manager may relax the credit policy because additional business is needed. For example, the company may not rebill customers who take a cash discount even after the discount period has elapsed. On the contrary, in times of short supply, credit policy may be tightened because the seller is at an advantage.

Attributes of a Good Credit System

- Clear, quick, and uniform in application
- Does not intrude on customer's privacy
- Inexpensive (e.g., centralization of credit decisions by experienced staff)
- Based upon past experience, considering characteristics of good, questionable, and bad accounts. **Tip:** Determine the correlation between customer characteristics and future uncollectibility.

WHAT'S THE INVESTMENT IN ACCOUNTS RECEIVABLE?

The financial executive often has to determine the dollar investment tied up in accounts receivable.

EXAMPLE 1

A company sells on terms of net/30. The accounts are on average 20 days past due. Annual credit sales are $600,000. The investment in accounts receivable is:

$$\frac{50}{360} \times \$600,000 = \underline{\$83,333.28}$$

EXAMPLE 2

The cost of a product is 30% of selling price, and the cost of capital is 10% of selling price. On average, accounts are paid four months after sale. Average sales are $70,000 per month.

The investment in accounts receivable from this product is

Accounts receivable (4 months $\times$ $70,000)	$280,000
Investment in accounts receivable [$280,000 $\times$ (0.30 + 0.10)]	112,000

EXAMPLE 3

You have accounts receivable of $700,000. The average manufacturing cost is 40% of the sales price. The before-tax profit margin is 10%. The carrying cost of inventory is 3% of selling price. The sales commission is 8% of sales. The investment in accounts receivable is:

$$\$700,000 \, (0.40 + 0.03 + 0.08) = \$700,000 \, (0.51) = \$357,000$$

DISCOUNT POLICY

Should customers be offered a discount for the early payment of account balances? The financial manager has to compare the return on freed cash resulting from customer's paying sooner to the cost of the discount.

EXAMPLE 4

The following data are provided:

Current annual credit sales	$14,000,000
Collection period	3 months
Terms	net/30
Minimum rate of return	15%

The company is considering offering a 3/10, net/30 discount. We expect 25% of the customers to take advantage of it. The collection period will decline to two months.

The discount should be offered, as indicated in the following calculations:

Advantage

Increased profitability:

Average accounts receivable balance before a change in policy

$$\frac{\text{Credit sales}}{\text{Accounts receivable turnover}} \quad \frac{\$14,000,000}{4} \qquad \$3,500,000$$

Average accounts receivable balance after change in policy

$$\frac{\text{Credit sales}}{\text{Accounts receivable turnover}} \quad \frac{\$14,000,000}{6} \qquad \underline{\$2,333,333}$$

Reduction in average accounts receivable balance	$1,116,667
Rate of return	× .15
Return	$ 175,000

Disadvantage

Cost of the discount 0.30 × 0.25 × $14,000,000	$ 105,000
Net advantage of discount	$ 70,000

SHOULD CREDIT POLICY BE CHANGED?

Should the company give credit to marginal customers? We have to compare the earnings on sales obtained to the added cost of the receivables. **Note:** If the company has idle capacity, the additional earnings is the contribution margin on the incremental sales because fixed costs are constant. The additional cost on the additional receivables results from the greater number of bad debts and the opportunity cost of tying up funds in receivables for a longer time period.

EXAMPLE 5

Sales price per unit	$120
Variable cost per unit	80
Fixed cost per unit	15
Annual credit sales	$600,000
Collection period	1 month
Minimum return	16%

If you liberalize the credit policy, you project that

- Sales will increase by 40%
- The collection period on total accounts will be two months
- Bad debts on the increased sales will be 5%

Preliminary calculations:

Current units ($600,000/$120)   5,000
Additional units (5,000 × 0.4)   2,000

The new average unit cost is now calculated:

	Units	×	Unit Cost	=	Total Cost
Current units	5,000	×	$95		$475,000
Additional units	2,000	×	$80		160,000
Total	7,000				$635,000

$$\text{New average unit cost} = \frac{\text{Total cost}}{\text{Units}} = \frac{\$635,000}{7,000} = \underline{\$90.71}$$

Note that at idle capacity, fixed cost remains constant. Thus, the incremental cost is only the variable cost of $80 per unit. This will cause the new average unit cost to drop.

Advantage

Additional profitability:

Incremental sales volume   2,000 units
× Contribution margin per unit (Selling price −
   variable cost) $120 − $80   × $40
Incremental profitability $80,000

Disadvantage

Incremental bad debts:

Incremental units × Selling price 2,000 × $120 $240,000
Bad debt percentage   × 0.05
Additional bad debts $12,000

Opportunity cost of funds tied up in accounts receivable:
Average investment in accounts receivable after change in policy:

$$\frac{\text{Credit sales}}{\text{Accounts receivable turnover}} \times \frac{\text{Unit cost}}{\text{Selling price}}$$

$$\frac{\$840,000@}{6} \times \frac{\$90.71}{\$120} \qquad \$105,828$$

@ 7,000 units × $120 = $840,000

Current average investment in accounts receivable:

$$\frac{\$600,000}{12} \times \frac{\$95}{\$120} \qquad \underline{39,583}$$

Additional investment in accounts receivable	$ 66,245
Minimum return	× 0.16
Opportunity cost of funds tied up	$ 10,599

Net advantage of relaxation in credit standards:

Additional earnings		$80,000
Less:		
Additional bad debt losses	$12,000	
Opportunity cost	10,599	22,599
Net savings		$ 57,401

The company may have to decide whether to extend full credit to presently limited credit customers or no-credit customers. Full credit should be given only if net profitability occurs.

EXAMPLE 6

Category	Bad Debt Percentage	Collection Period	Credit Policy	Increase in Annual Sales if Credit Restrictions are Relaxed
X	2%	30 days	Unlimited	$80,000
Y	5%	40 days	Restricted	600,000
Z	30%	80 days	No Credit	850,000

Gross profit is 25% of sales. The minimum return on investment is 12%.

	Category Y	Category Z
Gross profit		
$600,000 × .25	$150,000	
$850,000 × .25		$212,500
Less bad debts		
$600,000 × .05	− 30,000	
$850,000 × .30		−255,000
Incremental average investment in accounts receivable		
$\frac{40}{360}$ × (0.75 × $600,000)	$ 50,000	
$\frac{80}{360}$ × (0.75 × $850,000)		$141,667
Opportunity cost of incremental investment in accounts receivable	× 0.12 −6,000	× 0.12 −17,000
Net earnings	$114,000	$(59,500)

Credit should be extended to category Y.

EXAMPLE 7

You are considering liberalizing the credit policy to encourage more customers to purchase on credit. Currently, 80% of sales are on credit and there is a gross margin of 30%. Other relevant data are:

	Currently	Proposal
Sales	$300,000	$450,000
Credit sales	240,000	360,000
Collection expenses	4% of credit sales	5% of credit sales
Accounts receivable turnover	4.5	3

An analysis of the proposal yields the following results:

Average accounts receivable balance (credit sales/ accounts receivable turnover)

Expected average accounts receivable $360,000/3		$120,000
Current average accounts receivable $240,000/4.5		53,333
Increase		$ 66,667

Gross profit:

Expected increase in credit sales ($360,000 − $240,000)		$120,000
Gross profit rate		× 0.30
Increase		$ 36,000

Collection expenses:

Expected collection expenses 0.05 × $360,000		$ 18,000
Current collection expenses 0.04 × $240,000		9,600
Increase		$ 8,400

You would benefit from a more liberal credit policy.

EXAMPLE 8

The company is planning a sales campaign in which it will offer credit terms of 3/10, net/45. We expect the collection period to increase from 60 days to 80 days. Relevant data for the contemplated campaign follows.

	Percent of Sales Before Campaign	Percent of Sales During Campaign
Cash sales	40%	30%
Payment from		
1–10	25	55
11–100	35	15

The proposed sales strategy will probably increase sales from $8 million to $10 million. There is a gross margin rate of 30%. The rate of return is 14%. Sales discounts are given on cash sales.

	Without Sales Campaign		With Sales Campaign	
Gross margin (0.3 x $8,000,000)	$2,400,000	0.3 x $10,000,000	$3,000,000	
Sales subject to discount				
0.65 x $8,000,000	$5,200,000			
0.85 x $10,000,000			$8,500,000	
Sales discount	x 0.03 – 156,000		x 0.03	– 255,000
Investment in average accounts receivable				
$\frac{60}{360}$ x $8,000,000 x 0.7	$933,333			
$\frac{80}{360}$ x $10,000,000 x 0.7			$1,555,555	
Return rate	x 0.14 – 130,667		x 0.14	– 217,778
Net profit	$2,113,333		$2,527,222	

The company should undertake the sales campaign, because earnings will increase by $413,889 ($2,527,222 – $2,113,333).

OTHER THAN SALES

A significant amount of receivable transactions other than regular sales may result in losses. Examples include insurance claims and freight claims. The financial manager should develop a plan to handle these transactions. Unfortunately, some companies lack formalized record keeping in this area. In fact, some firms only retain pieces of correspondence.

CONCLUSION

Your major decisions regarding accounts receivable is the determination of whether to give credit, to whom, the amount, and terms. A useful ratio is sales to cash collections which may be looked at over a three month period as an indicator of overall collections on sales.

33

Inventory Management

The purpose of inventory management is to develop policies that will achieve an optimal inventory investment. The optimal level of inventory varies among industries and among companies in a particular industry. Successful inventory management minimizes inventory at all stages of manufacturing while retaining cost-effective production volume. This improves profitability and cash flow. By operating with minimum inventory levels and with short production lead times, the company increases its flexibility. This flexibility is needed to immediately respond to changing market conditions.

Inventory files should contain inventory location, quantity on hand, and quantity committed. Adequate inventory must be maintained to meet customer orders, properly utilize machines, keep production schedules, and assure smooth production activity. By maintaining a functional inventory supply, a company will be able to protect itself against unplanned changes in supply. Some inventory must be held at the different manufacturing stages as hedges against the variabilities of supply and demand as well hedging in the event problems surface in the manufacturing process itself. A sales forecast is the starting point for effective inventory management since expected sales determines how much inventory is needed.

Inventory records should provide needed information to satisfy the needs of the financial, sales, purchasing, and production managers. Inventory information may include the following by major type: unit cost, historical usage, quantity on order, minimum-maximum quantities, quantities in transit, delivery times, scheduling dates, and quantities set aside for specific contracts, production orders and customers. With regard to minimum-maximum quantities, such a procedure is practical when *stability* exists in the rate of sale or the use of the product and where the order time is short. The minimum is a "cushion" to be used only in an emergency. The maximum is the "ceiling" of the desirable inventory. The reorder point is between the minimum and maximum.

There should be a master item file containing identification, description, and specifications of the item's raw material, component parts, and assembly relationship. An item specification should include up-to-date data about the part, the production process, the uses of the item, possible substitutions, demand information, competitive factors, and the overall supply. Information may also be furnished about suppliers and relevant information that may affect the availability and price of the item.

The inventory balance is affected by many factors including the production cycle, product perishability and obsolescence, sales flexibility, cyclicality of business, liquidity, inventory financing available, and markdowns in the industry. The goal is to maximize sales with minimum inventory. Thus, inventory levels should be closely correlated to the selling cycle. A poor inventory management system may be revealed by failure to meet production plans, expediting of parts, slow-moving or obsolete goods, poor customer service, "rush" jobs in the factory, production bottlenecks, downtime, poor forecasts and deficient performance reporting, and internal conflicts between members of the organization such as production and marketing.

An advantage of a "bloated" inventory is the resulting reduction in production costs from larger production runs. It also provides a safety buffer if there is a nondelivery of raw materials or the prior department's manufacturing process breaks down.

Sales forecasting is crucial because an inaccurately high sales forecast can result in high inventory levels, markdowns, obsolescence, and inventory write-offs. An inaccurately low forecast will result in low inventory and lost sales. See Chapter 17 which covers sales forecasting.

Suppliers should be evaluated in terms of fairness in pricing, meeting delivery times, quality of goods shipped (e.g., in accordance with product specifications), and ability to meet "rush " jobs.

There are many benefits to be obtained from proper inventory management including:

- Reduces waste and cost arising from excess storage, handling, and obsolescence.
- Reduces the risk of inventory theft
- Reduces production delays because needed raw materials are maintained. This results in lower production costs and longer runs.
- Improves customer service because needed materials are available

Inventory Management Policies

- Appraise the adequacy of the raw materials level, which depends on expected production, condition of equipment, supplier reliability, and seasonal considerations. Raw material requirements may be forecast using such techniques as statistical analysis of historical trends and cycles, econometric models, and Delphi methods. **Recommendation:** Have sound material management guidelines to specify what and how much should be stored. Manufacturing requires an appropriate balance of parts to produce an end item. **What to Watch Out For:** A situation in which you have four of five needed components, because this results in having four excess inventories when a stockout of the fifth occurs.

- Forecast future movements in raw materials prices, so that if prices are expected to increase, additional materials are bought at lower prices.

- Discard slow-moving products to reduce inventory carrying costs and improve cash flow.

- Stock higher profit margin items for quick sale.

- Guard against inventory buildup, since it is associated with substantial carrying and opportunity costs.

- Minimize inventory levels when liquidity and/or inventory financing problems exist.

- Plan for a stock balance that will guard against and cushion the possible loss of business from a shortage in materials. The timing of an order also depends on seasonability factors.

- Ensure that inventory is received when needed so that production runs smoothly. **What To Do:** Compare vendor and production receipts to promised delivery due dates.

- A long sales order entry process requires the stocking of additional inventory.

- Try to convince customers to keep higher stock levels to reduce the company's inventory of finished goods.

- Examine the quality of merchandise received. The ratio of purchase returns to purchases should be enlightening. A sharp increase in the ratio indicates that a new supplier may be warranted. A performance measurement and evaluation system should exist to appraise vendor quality and reliability (e.g., meeting promised delivery dates). If there is a problem with the vendor, problems will arise in production scheduling, imbalances in work-in-process, and "rush" purchase orders.

- Keep a careful record of back orders. A high back order level indicates that less inventory balances are needed. This is because back orders may be used as indicators of the production required, resulting in improved production planning and procurement. The trend in the ratio of the dollar amount of back orders to the average per-day sales will prove useful.

- Appraise the acquisition and inventory control functions. Any problems must be identified and rectified. In areas where control is weak, inventory balances should be restricted.

- Accuracy is needed for the bills of materials to indicate the parts and quantities received to produce an end product. **What To Do:** Conduct audits on the production floor when the parts are assembled.

- Have accurate inventory records and assign inventory responsibilities to managers. For example, assign to the engineering manager responsibility for the bills of material. Do you have the necessary inventory measurement tools (e.g., scales)?

- Closely supervise warehouse and materials handling staff to guard against theft and to maximize efficiency.

- Frequently review stock lines for poor earnings.

- Minimize the lead time in the acquisition, manufacturing, and distribution functions. The lead time is how long it takes to receive merchandise from suppliers after an order is placed. Depending upon lead times, an increase in inventory stocking may be required or the purchasing pattern may have to be altered. **What To Do:** Calculate the ratio of the value of outstanding orders to average daily purchases to indicate the lead time for receiving orders from suppliers. The ratio indicates whether you should increase the inventory balance or change your buying pattern. Are vendors keeping their delivery date promises?

- Examine the time between raw materials input and the completion of production to see if production and engineering techniques can be implemented to hasten the production operation.

- Examine the degree of spoilage and take steps to reduce it.

- Prepare an inventory analysis report presenting the number of months of insurance coverage. The report should highlight items with excess inventory coverage resulting from such cause as changes in customer demand or poor inventory practices.

- Maintain proper inventory control, such as through the application of computer techniques. For example, a point-of-sale computerized electronic register may be used by a retail business. The register continually updates inventory for sales and purchases. This data facilitates the computation of reorder points and quantity per order.

- Look at the trend in the unit cost of manufactured items. Reasons for variations should be analyzed to see if they are due to factors within or beyond company control (i.e., increase in oil prices, managerial inefficiencies).

- Have economies in production run size to reduce setup costs and idle time.

- Have vendors consign inventory to you and invoice as used.

- Utilize computer techniques and operations research to properly control inventory. For example, statistical forecasting methods can be used to determine inventory levels related to a pre-set acceptability level of outage probability.

The purchasing department can assist in inventory management in the following ways:

- Have blanket orders for operating supplies
- Have tight control over subcontracted operations
- Determine a price for raw materials that will protect the company in volatile markets
- Gradually increase purchase size as you get to know the supplier better
- Schedule delivery of raw materials using statistical and just-in-time techniques

Symptoms of Problems in Inventory Management

- Periodic extension of back orders
- Material shortages
- Material inventory writedowns at the end of the accounting period
- Uneven production and downtime
- Order cancellations
- Periodic lack of storage space
- Frequent layoffs and rehirings
- Differing rates of turnover among inventory items within the same inventory category
- Significant differences between book inventory and physical inventory

Good internal control over inventory is necessary to guard against theft or other irregularities. A surprise inventory count should periodically occur to assure agreement between the book inventory and physical inventory. Have controlled audit groups of work-in-process moving through the manufacturing process to see the accuracy with which work-in-process is documented.

Major shortages may take place and be unnoticed for a long time if satisfactory control is lacking. Inventory is vulnerable to theft. Good control is needed in the acquisition and handling phases. Segregation should exist in purchasing, receiving, storing, and shipping of inventories.

An inventory control system should accomplish the following objectives: (1) proper record keeping, (2) implementing inventory decision models, (3) reporting exceptions, (4) aiding in forecasting usage and needs, and (5) maintaining proper safeguards to prevent misuse. If there is a lack of internal control, inventory balances should be restricted.

INVENTORY ANALYSIS

Inventory analysis should include consideration of the following:

- Customer order backlog as a percent of the inventory balance
- Inventory carrying cost by month and by year

- Inventory months' supply on hand by period for the major product lines
- Customer order backlog in weeks as a percent of the production process cycle (lead time)
- Safety stock and slow-moving (obsolete) inventory as a percent of cost of sales and of the inventory balance

Try to have work-in-process processed into finished goods as soon as possible. Work-in-process should arise only from manageable variability in the production process.

In inflationary and tight money periods, flexibility in inventory management is needed. For example, the quantity to be ordered may have to be adjusted to reflect increased costs.

The financial manager must consider the obsolescence and spoilage risk of inventory. For example, technological, perishable, fashionable, flammable, and specialized goods usually have high salability risk. The nature of the risks should be taken into account in computing desired inventory levels. The marketing department should be held accountable for obsolete and slow-moving items that they originally recommended. Before a product design is changed at the insistence of marketing, it should be carefully reviewed.

Different inventory items vary in profitability and the amount of space they occupy. Inventory management involves a tradeoff between the costs of keeping inventory versus the benefits of holding it. Higher inventory levels result in increased costs from storage, casualty and theft insurance, spoilage, higher property taxes for larger facilities, increased manpower requirements, and interest on borrowed funds to finance inventory acquisition. However, an increase in inventory lowers the possibility of lost sales from stockouts and the incidence of production slowdowns from inadequate inventory. Additionally, large volume purchases will result in greater purchase discounts. Inventory levels are also affected by short-term interest rates. For instance, as short-term interest rates increase, the optimum level of holding inventory will be reduced.

To reduce costs of handling inventory:

- Use several assembly lines and move crews to the next line which has already been setup.
- Hasten routing reproduction by using standardized forms.
- Keep materials at subassemblies, not final assemblies.
- Minimize seasonal stocking of material.
- Consolidate the number of inventory storage locations and/or warehouses.
- Simplify and standardize the product.
- Avoid shutting down the plant, such as having varying vacations.
- Decrease the time between filling an order and replacing the stock sold.
- Stop supplying "old" service parts but rather give customers the blueprint so they may internally manufacture them.

The inventory balance to be held depends upon:

- Vertical integration of the product line as indicated by manufactured versus purchased parts.
- Accuracy of manufacturing documents (e.g., route sheets, bill of materials).
- Accuracy of inventory records considering the deviation between the books and physical amounts.
- Reliability in estimating customer needs. Here, consideration should be given to the forecasting error.

Inventory of raw materials depends upon:

- Expected level and seasonability of production
- Reliability of supply sources

Inventory of work-in-process typically varies the most. Inventory of work-in-process depends upon:

- Length and time of the production run
- Number of stages in the production cycle, lot-sizing, quality problems, lead time, line balancing, and manufacturing scheduling

Work-in-process inventory may be viewed as a "liability" to inventory managers. Work-in-process takes away essential production capacity and cash while increasing the risk of obsolescence and shrinkage. While high machine utilization is good, an associated buildup of work-in-process is bad.

The financial manager may have to decide whether it is more profitable to sell inventory as is, or sell it after further processing. For example, inventory can be sold as is for $40,000, or sold for $80,000 if it is put into further processing costing $20,000. The latter should be selected because further processing yields a $60,000 profit relative to $40,000 for the current sale.

Inventory should be counted at regular, cyclic intervals because this provides the ability to check inventory on an ongoing basis as well as to reconcile the book and physical amounts. **Recommendation:** To lessen the time needed for counting, use standardized labeling procedures and quantity markings as well as orderly warehouse stocking. **Tip:** Take the count during nonworking hours to guard against duplicate counting. Alternatively, warehouse pickers could carefully enter daily movement when the cycle count takes place. Cyclic counting has the following advantages.

- Permits the efficient use of a few full-time experienced counters throughout the year
- Enables the timely detection and correction of the causes of inventory error
- Does not require a plant shutdown, as does a year-end count
- Facilitates the modifications of computer inventory programs, if needed

MATERIALS REQUIREMENTS PLANNING

The manager can use materials requirements planning, which is a technique using bills of material, inventory information, and the production schedule to compute material requirements. It indicates when material should be replenished and how much to order. **Tip:** Determine raw materials needed per item at each level. **Note:** A particular component may be needed for a number of assemblies at different levels. It is a good approach to formulate and maintain appropriate due dates on orders. If the production schedule changes, the timing and amount of materials needed will also change. The production quantities (how much) are based on specific identifiable customer orders. **Note:** Consider replacement (service) parts needs of customers. The amount ordered is based on periodic forecasts. There must be immediate feedback of changes in the production schedule (e.g., due to changes in priority) in order to adjust and control the planning and scheduling system. There should exist a master assembly schedule.

The computerized system should answer "what-if" questions. There is operational planning in units and financial planning in dollars.

There is a linkage of production planning, business planning, materials requirements planning, capacity requirements planning, and the support systems for material and capacity. The output generated by these systems should be linked with the financial reports. Financial reports include inventory forecasts, shipping budget, purchase commitment analysis, and the overall business plan. Materials requirement planning will aid in planning manufacturing resources.

Materials requirements planning requires information about bills of material, routing of parts through the production stages, lead times, and availability of material information and status.

In materials requirements planning, ascertain material requirements at what level and when to order to produce the needed finished goods. Materials requirements planning is involved with having sufficient materials when needed to manufacture quality products in a timely and efficient manner.

A production and inventory management system involves:

- A product structure, such as the materials needed and when to produce
- The necessary sequence of production steps
- The work centers involved in production and their functions
- Managing product configuration and available parts

The production schedule depends on the organization of the work centers, time-phased material requirements, production constraints (e.g., bottlenecks), and routing sequences.

In scheduling production, all constraints should be looked at simultaneously. Of course, the production schedule will influence the lead time needed. **Note:** High machine utilization does not necessarily mean good production performance.

MANUFACTURING PROCESS DESIGN

Poor manufacturing process design may be indicated by:

- A high ratio of actual in-process time to standard process time
- The scheduling of long production runs under lot-sizing systems

A long setup time means a longer run and the resulting higher inventory balances. Long production runs may indicate poor quality output because machine settings often go out of place in long runs. Significant rework may be required to solve the problem.

The engineering department must work closely with the production and inventory management centers, otherwise design problems may occur resulting in production difficulties and unsuitable products. A change in product design should carefully be reviewed and approved because it may affect product quality, demand, and safety.

There should be good facilities design to avoid excess inventory or excess labor to move inventories around. Every move wastes time and increases the risk of damage. The longer the distance between sequential operations, the more inspection needed and the loss of automated transfer to the next production point. A multidimension matrix model should be used in looking at the facilities design. An optimum layout should be formulated for the facility and product mix. Analysis of facilities is needed to identify and correct for flow problems, reduce inventory balances, and minimize move times with their related costs.

The cause of rejections occurring during the production process must be carefully analyzed.

DETERMINING CARRYING AND ORDERING COSTS

Inventory carrying costs include warehousing, handling, insurance, and property taxes. Further, the opportunity cost of holding inventory should be taken into account. A provisional cost for spoilage and obsolescence should also be included in the analysis. The more the inventory held, the greater is the carrying cost. Carrying cost equals:

$$\text{Carrying Cost} = \frac{Q}{2} \times C$$

where $\frac{Q}{2}$ represents average quantity and C is the carrying cost per unit.

Inventory ordering costs are the costs of placing an order and receiving the merchandise. They include freight and the clerical costs to place the order. To

Figure 1. EOQ Point

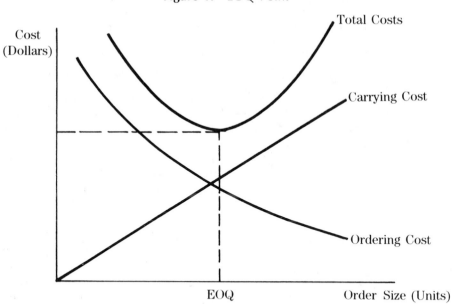

minimize ordering costs, enter the fewest number of orders possible. In the case of produced items, ordering cost includes scheduling cost. Ordering cost equals:

$$\text{Ordering Cost} = \frac{S}{Q} \times P$$

where S = total usage, Q = quantity per order, and P = cost of placing an order

The total inventory cost is therefore:

$$\frac{QC}{2} + \frac{SP}{C}$$

A tradeoff exists between ordering and carrying costs. A greater order quantity will increase carrying costs but lower ordering costs.

WHAT IS THE ECONOMIC ORDER QUANTITY (EOQ)?

The economic order quantity (EOQ) is the optimum amount of goods to order each time so that total inventory costs are minimized. EOQ analysis should be applied to every product that represents a significant proportion of sales.

$$EOQ = \sqrt{\frac{2SP}{C}}$$

There are some basic assumptions underlying the EOQ model. They are:

- Demand is constant and known with certainty
- Depletion of stock is linear and constant
- No discount is allowed for quantity purchases
- Lead time, which is the time interval between placing an order and receiving delivery, is a constant, i.e., stockout is not possible

The number of orders for a period is the usage (S) divided by the EOQ. Figure 1 graphically shows the EOQ point.

EXAMPLE 1

The manager wants to know how frequenty to place orders. The following information is provided:

S = 500 units per month
P = \$40 per order
C = \$4 per unit

$$EOQ = \sqrt{\frac{2SP}{C}} = \sqrt{\frac{2(500)(40)}{4}} = \sqrt{10,000} = 100 \text{ units}$$

The number of orders each month is:

$S/EOQ = 500/100 = 5$

Therefore, an order should be placed about every six days (31/5).

EXAMPLE 2

A company is determining its frequency of orders for product X. Each product X costs \$15. The annual carrying cost is \$200. The ordering cost is \$10. The company anticipates selling 50 product Xs each month. Its desired average inventory level is 40.

$S = 50 \times 12 = 600$
$P = \$10$
$C = \dfrac{\text{Purchase price} \times \text{carrying cost}}{\text{Average investment}} = \dfrac{\$15 \times \$200}{40 \times \$15} = \$5$

$$EOQ = \sqrt{\frac{2SP}{C}} = \sqrt{\frac{2(600)(10)}{5}} = \sqrt{\frac{12,000}{5}}$$

$$= \sqrt{2,400} = 49 \text{ (rounded)}$$

The number of orders per year is:

$$\frac{S}{EOQ} = \frac{600}{49} = 12 \text{ orders (rounded)}$$

The company should place an order about every 30 days (365/12).

For a detailed discussion of the EOQ model, see Chapter 23.

HOW ARE STOCKOUTS AVOIDED?

Stockout of raw materials or work-in-process can cause a slowdown in production. To avoid a stockout situation, a safety stock should be kept. Safety stock is the minimum inventory for an item, based on expected usage (demand) and delivery (lead) time of materials. This cushion guards against unusual product demand or unexpected delivery problems. The variability in demand of the item can be measured by the standard deviation or mean absolute deviation. The standard deviation measures the degree to which the actual level at the end of the cycle differs from the normal level. The trend period used in computing standard deviation should take into account market characteristics, demand volatility, and product maturity. A large standard deviation indicates that each period the inventory levels vary significantly. Therefore, the probability of being significantly out of stock at various times during the year is high if no safety stock exists. Safety stock helps to prevent the potential damage to customer relations and to future sales that can occur when there is a lack of inventory to fill an order immediately. The need for a safety stock increases the total inventory required. In effect, safety stock requires a balancing of expected costs of stockouts against the costs of carrying the additional inventory. **Rule of Thumb:** A typical inventory management system uses a 5% stockout factor.

EXAMPLE 3

An order is placed when the inventory level reaches 210 units rather than 180 units. Thus, the safety stock is 30 units. In other words, one expects to be stocked with 30 units when the new order is received.

The optimum safety stock is the point where the increased carrying cost equals the opportunity cost of a potential stockout. The increased carrying cost equals the carrying cost per unit multiplied by the safety stock.

$$\text{Stockout cost} = \text{number of orders} \left(\frac{\text{usage}}{\text{order quantity}} \right) \times \text{stockout units}$$

$$\times \text{ unit stockout cost} \times \text{ probability of a stockout}$$

EXAMPLE 4

A company uses 100,000 units annually. Each order is for 10,000 units. Stockout is 1,000 units; this amount is the difference between the maximum daily usage during the lead time less the reorder point, ignoring a safety stock factor. The stockout probability the manager wishes to take is 30%. The per unit stockout cost is $2.30. The carrying cost per unit is $5.

The stockout cost is:

$$\frac{100,000}{10,000} \times 1,000 \times \$2.30 \times .3 = \$6,900$$

The amount of safety stock needed is computed below:

Let X = safety stock

Stockout cost = carrying cost of safety stock
$6,900   = $5X
1,380 units = X

EXAMPLE 5

A company uses 250,000 units per year. Each order is for 25,000 units. Stockout is 4,000 units. The tolerable stockout probability is 25%. The per unit stockout cost is $4. The carrying cost per unit is $8.

$$\text{Stockout cost} = \frac{250,000}{25,000} \times 4,000 \times \$4 \times 0.25 = \$40,000$$

$$\text{Amount of safety stock needed} = \frac{\text{Stockout cost}}{\text{Carrying cost per unit}}$$

$$= \frac{\$40,000}{\$8} = 5,000 \text{ units}$$

WHAT IS THE REORDER POINT?

The reorder point (ROP) signals when to place an order. However, the reorder point requires a knowledge of the lead time from placing to receiving an order. The reorder point may be influenced by the months of supply or total dollar ceilings on inventory to be held or inventory to be ordered.

Reorder point is computed as follows:

ROP = Lead time × Average usage per unit of time

This reveals the inventory level at which a new order should be placed. If a safety stock is needed, then add this amount to the ROP.

The more the vendor's backlog, the greater will be the ensuing work-in-process. This results in a longer and more inaccurate lead time. If a product is made to a customer's order, the lead time is the run time, queue time, move time, setup time, and procurement time for raw material.

EXAMPLE 6

A company needs 6,400 units evenly throughout the year. There is a lead time of one week. There are 50 working weeks in the year. The reorder point is:

$$1 \text{ week} \times \frac{6,400}{50 \text{ weeks}} = 1 \times 128 = 128 \text{ units}$$

When the inventory level drops to 128 units, a new order should be placed.

An optimal inventory level can be based on consideration of the incremental profitability resulting from having more merchandise to the opportunity cost of carrying the higher inventory balances.

EXAMPLE 7

The current inventory turnover is 12 times. Variable costs are 60% of sales. An increase in inventory balances is expected to prevent stockouts, thus increasing sales. Minimum rate of return is 18%. Relevant data follow.

Sales	Turnover
$800,000	12
890,000	10
940,000	8
980,000	7

(1) Sales	(2) Turnover	(3) [(1)/(2)] Average Inventory Balance	(4) Opportunity Cost of Carrying Incremental Inventory[a]	(5) Increased Profitability[b]	(6) [(5)–(4)] Net Savings
$800,000	12	$ 66,667	—	—	—
890,000	10	89,000	$4,020	$36,000	$31,980
940,000	8	117,500	5,130	20,000	14,870
980,000	7	140,000	4,050	16,000	11,950

[a] Increased inventory × 0.18.
[b] Increased sales × 0.40.

The optimal inventory level is $89,000, because it results in the highest net savings.

SERVICE LEVEL

Service level can be defined as the probability that demand will not exceed supply during lead time. Thus, a service level of 90% implies a probability of 90% that demand will not exceed supply during lead time. To determine the optimal level of safety stock size, you might want to measure costs of not having enough inventory (stockout costs). Here are three cases for computing the safety stock. The first two do not recognize stockout costs; the third case does.

Case 1: Variable usage rate, constant lead time

$$ROP = \text{Expected usage during lead time} + \text{Safety stock}$$
$$= \bar{\mu}LT + z \, LOT \, (\sigma_\mu)$$

where $\bar{\mu}$ = average usage rate

LT = lead time

σ_μ = standard deviation of usage rate

z = standard normal variable as defined in Table 1.

For a normal distribution, a given service level amounts to the shaded area under the curve to the left of ROP in Figure 2.

EXAMPLE 8

A company uses large cases of a product at an average rate of 50 units per day. Usage can be approximated by a normal distribution with a standard deviation of five units per day. Lead time is four days. Thus:

$$\bar{\mu} = 50 \text{ units per day}$$
$$\sigma_\mu = 5 \text{ units}$$
$$LT = 4 \text{ days}$$

For a service level of 99%, $z = 2.33$ (from Table 1)

Thus:

Safety stock $= 2.33 \sqrt{4} \, (5) = 23.3$ cans

$ROP = 50(4) + 23.3 = 223.3$ cans

Case 2: Constant usage rate, variable lead time

For constant usage with variable lead time, the reorder point is computed as follows:

$$ROP = \text{expected usage during lead time} + \text{safety stock}$$
$$= \bar{\mu} \, \overline{LT} + z_\mu \, \sigma_{LT}$$

Table 1

VALUES OF Z_P FOR SPECIFIED PROBABILITIES P

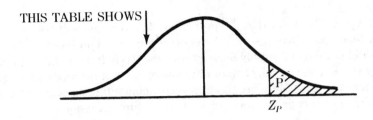

THIS TABLE SHOWS

P	z_P	P	z_P	P	z_P
0.0005	3.29053	0.005	2.57583	0.11	1.22653
0.0010	3.09023	0.010	2.32635	0.12	1.17499
0.0015	2.96774	0.015	2.17009	0.13	1.12639
0.0020	2.87816	0.020	2.05375	0.14	1.08032
0.0025	2.80703	0.025	1.95996	0.15	1.03643
0.0030	2.74778	0.030	1.88079	0.16	0.99446
0.0035	2.69684	0.035	1.81191	0.17	0.95417
0.0040	2.65207	0.040	1.75069	0.18	0.91537
0.0045	2.61205	0.045	1.69540	0.19	0.87790
0.0050	2.57583	0.050	1.64485	0.20	0.84162
0.006	2.51214	0.06	1.55477	0.25	0.67449
0.007	2.45726	0.07	1.47579	0.30	0.52440
0.008	2.40892	0.08	1.40507	0.35	0.38532
0.009	2.36562	0.09	1.34076	0.40	0.25335
0.010	2.32635	0.10	1.28155	0.45	0.12566

z_P is the value of the standardized normal (mean = 0, standard deviation = 1) random variable z such that the probability of obtaining a sample z value at least as large as z_P is P. The value of P must be doubled if two sided statements are made using the same z_P value.

Source: Croxton/Cowden/Bolch, *Practical Business Statistics*, 4th Ed., © 1969, p. 393. Reprinted by permission of Prentice-Hall, Inc., Englewood Cliffs, N.J.

Figure 2. Service Level

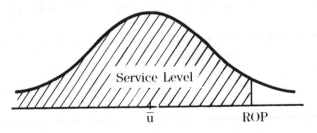

Figure 3. Service Level = 99%

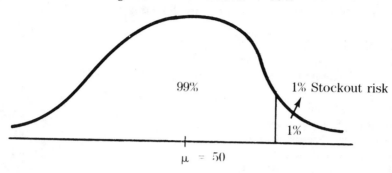

where μ = constant usage rate

$\overline{LT}$ = average lead time

σ_{LT} = standard deviation of lead time

EXAMPLE 9

A company uses 10 gallons of product X per day. Lead time is normally distributed with a mean of six days and a standard deviation of two days. Thus,

μ = 10 gallons per day

$\overline{LT}$ = 6 days

σ_{LT} = 2 days

Safety stock = 2.33 (10)(2) = 46.6 gallons

ROP = 10 (6) + 46.6 = 106.6 gallons

Exhibit 1 shows the changes in level of inventory over time.

Exhibit 1

CHANGES IN LEVEL OF INVENTORY OVER TIME

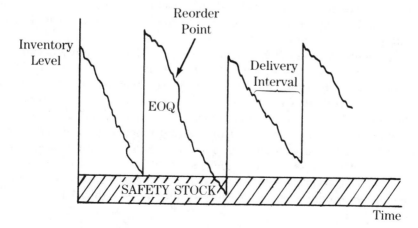

The product that results in the highest contribution margin per square foot should typically have the most priority in allocating space.

EXAMPLE 10

The following information pertains to product X:

Sales price	$ 15
Variable cost per unit	5
Contribution margin per unit	$ 10
Contribution margin per dozen	$120
Storage space per dozen	2 cubic feet
Contribution margin per cubic foot	$ 60
Number of units sold per period	4
Expected contribution margin per cubic foot	$240

STOCHASTIC INVENTORY MODELS

Stochastic inventory models are models which treat demands or lead times or both as random variables with specific probability distributions. A classic model is the single-period model with probabilistic demand whereby a single stocking decision is made for one time period for an item which is either perishable or salvageable. Examples are stocking of newspapers, magazines, food, and so on. Multi-period periodic review models with stochastic demand represent another important class of models. Different approaches to solving stochastic inventory models are Markov process, dynamic programming, simulation, and classical methods such as statistics and calculus. Quantitative methods are discussed in Chapter 23.

How to Use the ABC Inventory Control Method

ABC analysis focuses on the most critical items looking at gross profitability, sensitive price or demand patterns, and supply excesses or shortages. The ABC method requires the classification of inventory into one of four groups, A, B, C, or D. The classification is according to the potential savings associated with a proper level of such control.

Perpetual inventory records should be maintained for "A" items because of the required accuracy and frequent attention, often daily. "A" items typically refer to one out of every ten items in inventory usually consisting of 70% of the dollar value of inventory. Group "B" items are less expensive than group "A" items but are still important and require intermediate level control. The group "B" items usually account for 20% of the inventory items and also 20% of the dollar value of the inventory. Group "C" items is for most of the inventory items. Since they are usually less expensive and less used, there is less attention given to them. There is typically a high safety stock level for group "C" items. Blanket purchase orders should exist for "A" items and only "spot buys" for "Bs" and

"Cs". Group "D" items are the losers. There has been no usage of "D" items for an extended time period (e.g., six months). "D" items should not be reordered unless special authorization is given. The ABC classification assigned should not be changed for at least six months. Items may be reclassified as need be. For instance, a "fragile" item or one being stolen can be reclassified from "C" to "A."

The higher the value of the inventory items, the more control that is needed. For example, in looking at "A" items, carefully examine records, bills of material, customer orders, open purchase orders, and open manufacturing orders. The steps under the ABC method are:

1. A segregation is made of merchandise into components (e.g., varying models) based on dollar value.

2. Annual dollar usage is computed by inventory type (anticipated annual usage times unit cost).

3. There is a ranking given to inventory in terms of dollar usage ranging from high to low (e.g., "As" in top 30%, "Bs" in next 50%, and "Cs" in last 20%.

4. Inventory is tagged with the appropriate classification so proper emphasis may be placed on them. A recording is made in the inventory records of the classifications.

EXAMPLE 11

An actual distribution in a manufacturing operation that the authors are familiar with shows that the top 15% of the line items in terms of annual dollar usage represents 80% of the total annual dollar usage. These items were classified as "A" items. The next 15% of the line items in terms of the annual dollar usage represent an additional 15% of the annual dollar usage and were classified as "B" items. The remaining 70% of the items in inventory account for only 5% of the total annual dollar usage. These were classified as "C" items.

Figure 4 depicts an ABC inventory control system.

Table 2 illustrates an ABC distribution.

INVENTORY IN A SERVICE BUSINESS

In a service business, inventories are less tangible than durable goods and they are perishable by nature. Examples of inventory in a service business are an empty hotel room, empty seat in an airplane, and empty table in a restaurant. In these cases, inventory is lost as time passes by and the "empty" condition persists. Inventory also includes service parts.

Inventory in a service business consists of the following levels:

1. *Primary Level.* This level represents the capacity of the facility or equipment to provide the service.

Figure 4. ABC Inventory Control System

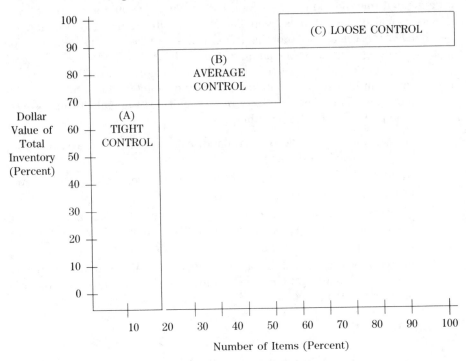

Number of Items (Percent)

2. *Secondary Level.* This level is the variable capacity employed at different time periods to deliver the service.

Marginal pricing may be used to obtain income from otherwise lost opportunities. Examples are hotels offering "weekend specials" and airlines offering "off-peak" fares. The goal is to divert minimal income from the normal service customer by attracting lower margin business. The profit of the service business may depend on the perishability of the service inventory.

The labor force should be such that labor costs are matched with the ability to sell the product.

Table 2

ABC INVENTORY DISTRIBUTION

Classification	Population (Percent)	Dollar Usage (Percent)
A	20	80
B	30	15
C	50	5

CONCLUSION

It is not an easy task to find the proper amount of investment in inventory. The amount may change daily and require close evaluation. Improper inventory management occurs when funds tied up in inventory can be used more productively elsewhere. A buildup may imply risk, such as obsolete inventory. On the other hand, an excessively low inventory may result in less profit such as inadequate stocking of inventory resulting in lost sales.

VII

INVESTMENTS

34

Corporate Investments in Securities

This chapter covers how to manage a company's surplus liquidity funds. A firm's surplus funds or idle cash are usually considered only of a temporary nature. The funds should be made available to cover a shortfall in cash flow or working capital or to serve as a reservoir for capital spending and acquisition. Most corporate financial officers are conservative (not speculative) when considering investing idle cash in financial securities since the money should be on hand without loss in value of the funds when needed.

Securities covers a broad range of investment instruments, including common stocks, preferred stocks, bonds, and options. There are two broad categories of securities available to corporate investors: equity securities, which represent ownership of a company, and debt (or fixed income) securities, which represent a loan from the investor to a company or government. Fixed income securities generally stress current fixed income and offer little or no opportunity for appreciation in value. They are usually liquid and bear less market risk than other types of investments. This type of investment performs well during stable economic conditions and lower inflation. Examples of fixed income securities include:

- Corporate bonds
- Government securities
- Mortgage-backed securities
- Preferred stocks
- Short-term debt securities

Each type of security has not only distinct characteristics, but also advantages and disadvantages which vary by a corporate investor. This chapter focuses on investing in fixed income (debt) securities—with especially short- and intermediate-term maturity—normally utilized by corporate investors.

FACTORS TO BE CONSIDERED IN INVESTMENT DECISIONS

Consideration should be given to safety of principal, yield and risk, stability of income, and marketability and liquidity.

Security of principal. It is the degree of risk involved in a particular investment. The company will not want to lose part or all of the initial investment.

Yield and risk. The primary purpose of investing is to earn a return on invested money in the form of: interest, dividends, rental income, and capital appreciation. However, increasing total returns would entail greater investment risks. Thus, yield and degree of risk are directly related. Greater risk also means sacrificing security of principal. A corporate investment officer (CIO) has to choose the priority that fits the corporation's financial circumstances and objectives.

Stability of income. When steady income is the most important consideration, bond interest or preferred stock dividends should be emphasized. This might be the situation if the company needs to supplement its earned income on a regular basis with income from its outside investments.

Marketability and liquidity. It is the ability to find a ready market to dispose of the investment at the right price.

Tax Factors. Corporate investors in high tax brackets will have different investment objectives than those in lower brackets. If the company is in a high tax bracket, it may prefer municipal bonds (interest is not taxable) or investments that provide tax credits or tax shelters, such as those in oil and gas.

In addition, there are many other factors to be considered, including:

- Current and future income needs
- Hedging against inflation
- Ability to withstand financial losses
- Ease of management
- Amount of investment
- Diversification
- Long-term versus short-term potential

Questions to Be Asked

In developing the corporation's investment strategy, it will be advisable to ask the following questions:

Table 1

SHORT- AND LONG-TERM INVESTMENT VEHICLE CATEGORIES

Short-Term Vehicles

- U.S. Treasury bills
- Certificates of deposit (CDs)
- Banker's acceptances (BAs)
- Commercial paper
- Repurchase agreements (Repos)
- Money market funds
- Eurodollar time deposits

Long-Term Vehicles

- U.S. Treasury notes and bonds
- Corporate bonds
- Mortgage-backed securities
- Municipal bonds
- Preferred stock, fixed or adjustable
- Bond funds
- Unit investment trusts

- What proportions of funds does the company want safe and liquid?
- Is the company willing to invest for higher return but greater risk?
- How long of a maturity period is the company willing to take on its investment?
- What should be the mix of its investments for diversification?
- Does the company need to invest in tax-free securities?

Types of Investment Instruments

There are many fixed income securities a CIO can choose from. They can be categorized into short-term and long-term investments, as indicated in Table 1.

CORPORATE BONDS

A bond is a certificate or security showing the corporate investor loaned funds to an issuing company or to a government in return for fixed future interest and repayment of principal. Bonds have the following advantages:

- There is fixed interest income each year.
- Bonds are safer than equity securities such as common stock. This is because bondholders come before common stockholders in the event of corporate bankruptcy.

Bonds suffer from the following disadvantages:

- They do not participate in incremental profitability.
- There are no voting rights.

Terms and Features of Bonds

There are certain terms and features of bonds a corporate investment officer should be familiar with, including:

1. *Par value*. The par value of a bond is the face value, usually $1,000.
2. *Coupon rate*. The coupon rate is the nominal interest rate that determines the actual interest to be received on a bond. It is an annual interest per par value. For example, if a corporate investor owns a $1,000,000 bond having a coupon rate of 10%, the annual interest to be received will be $100,000.
3. *Maturity date*. It is the final date on which repayment of the bond principal is due.
4. *Indenture*. The bond indenture is the lengthy, legal agreement detailing the issuer's obligations pertaining to a bond issue. It contains the terms and conditions of the bond issue as well as any restrictive provisions placed on the firm, known as restrictive covenants. The indenture is administered by an independent trustee. A restrictive covenant includes maintenance of (a) required levels of working capital, (b) a particular current ratio, and (c) a specified debt ratio.
5. *Trustee*. The trustee is the third party with whom the indenture is made. The trustee's job is to see that the terms of the indenture are actually carried out.
6. *Yield*. The yield is different than the coupon interest rate. It is the effective interest rate the corporate investor earns on the bond investment. If a bond is bought below its face value (i.e., purchased at a discount), the yield is higher than the coupon rate. If a bond is acquired above its face value (i.e., bought at a premium), the yield is below the coupon rate.
7. *Call provision*. A call provision entitles the issuing corporation to repurchase, or "call" the bond from their holders at stated prices over specified periods.
8. *Sinking fund*. In a sinking fund bond, money is put aside by the issuing company periodically for the repayment of debt, thus reducing the total amount of debt outstanding. This particular provision may be included in the bond indenture to protect investors.

Types of Bonds

There are many types of bonds according to different criteria including:

1. *Mortgage bonds*. Mortgage bonds are secured by physical property. In case of default, the bondholders may foreclose on the secured property and sell it to satisfy their claims.

2. *Debentures*. Debentures are unsecured bonds. They are protected by the general credit of the issuing corporation. Credit ratings are very important for this type of bond. Federal, state, and municipal government issues are debentures. Subordinated debentures are junior issues ranking after other unsecured debt as a result of explicit provisions in the indenture. Finance companies have made extensive use of these types of bonds.

3. *Convertible bonds*. These bonds are subordinated debentures which may be converted, at the investor's option, into a specified amount of other securities (usually common stock) at a fixed price. They are hybrid securities having characteristics of both bonds and common stock in that they provide fixed interest income and potential appreciation through participation in future price increases of the underlying common stock.

4. *Income bonds*. In income bonds, interest is paid only if earned. They are often called reorganization bonds.

5. *Tax-exempt bonds*. Tax-exempt bonds are usually municipal bonds where interest income is not subject to federal tax, although the Tax Reform Act (TRA) of 1986 imposed restrictions on the issuance of tax-exempt municipal bonds. Municipal bonds may carry a lower interest than taxable bonds of similar quality and safety. However, after-tax yield from these bonds are usually more than a bond with a higher rate of taxable interest. Note that municipal bonds are subject to two principal risks—interest rate and default.

6. *U.S. government and agency securities*. They include Treasury bills, notes, bonds, and mortgage-backed securities such as "Ginnie Maes." Treasury bills represent short-term government financing and mature in 12 months or less. U.S. Treasury notes have a maturity of one to ten years whereas U.S. Treasury bonds have a maturity of 10 to 25 years and can be purchased in denominations as low as $1,000. All these types of U.S. government securities are subject to federal income taxes, but not subject to state and local income taxes. "Ginnie Maes" represent pools of 25- to 30-year Federal Housing Administration (FHA) or Veterans Administration (VA) mortgages purchased by the Government National Mortgage Association.

7. *Zero-coupon bonds*. With zero coupon bonds, the interest instead of being paid out directly is added to the principal semiannually and both the principal and accumulated interest are paid at maturity. **Tip:** This compounding factor results in the investor receiving higher returns on the original investment at maturity. Zero-coupon bonds are not fixed income securities in the historical sense, because they provide no periodic income. The interest on the bond is paid at maturity. However, accrued interest, though not received, is taxable

yearly as ordinary income. Zero coupon bonds have two basic advantages over regular coupon-bearing bonds: (1) A relatively small investment is required to buy these bonds; and (2) The investor is assured of a specific yield throughout the term of the investment.

8. *Junk bonds.* Junk bonds, or high-yield bonds, are bonds with a speculative credit rating of Baa or lower by Moody's and BBB or lower by Standard and Poor's rating systems. Coupon rates on junk bonds are considerably higher than those of better quality issues. Note that junk bonds are issued by companies without track records of sales and earnings and therefore are subject to high default risk. Today, many non-mortgage-backed bonds issued by corporations are junk. Very recently, a large number of junk bonds have been issued as part of corporate mergers or takeovers. Since junk bonds are known for their high yields and high risk, many risk-oriented corporate investors including banks specialize in trading them. However, the bonds may be defaulted on. During the periods of recession and high interest rates where servicing debts is very difficult, junk bonds can pose a serious default risk to investors.

How to Select a Bond

When selecting a bond, corporate investors should take into consideration basically four factors:

1. Investment quality - Rating of bonds
2. Length of maturity - Short term (0-5 years)
   Medium (6-15 years)
   Long-term (over 15 years)
3. Features of bonds - call or conversion features
4. Tax status
5. Yield to maturity

Bond ratings. The investment quality of a bond is measured by its bond rating which reflects the probability that a bond issue will go into default. The rating should influence the investor's perception of risk and therefore have an impact on the interest rate the investor is willing to accept, the price the investor is willing to pay, and the maturity period of the bond the investor is willing to accept.

Bond investors tend to place more emphasis on independent analysis of quality than do common stock investors. Bond analysis and ratings are done, among others, by Standard & Poor's and Moody's. Below is an actual listing of the designations used by these well-known independent agencies. Descriptions on ratings are summarized. For original versions of descriptions, see Moody's *Bond Record* and Standard & Poor's *Bond Guide.*

DESCRIPTION OF BOND RATINGS

Moody's	Standard & Poor's	Quality Indication
Aaa	AAA	Highest quality
Aa	AA	High quality
A	A	Upper medium grade
Baa	BBB	Medium grade
Ba	BB	Contains speculative elements
B	B	Outright speculative
Caa	CCC & CC	Default definitely possible
Ca	C	Default, only partial recovery likely
C	D	Default, little recovery likely

*Ratings may also have + or − signs to show relative standings in each class.

Corporate investors should pay careful attention to ratings since they can affect not only potential market behavior but relative yields as well. Specifically, the higher the rating, the lower the yield of a bond, other things being equal. It should be noted that the ratings do change over time and the rating agencies have "credit watch lists" of various types. Corporate investment policy should specify this point: for example, the company is allowed to invest in only those bonds rated Baa or above by Moody's or BBB or above by Standard & Poor's, even though doing so means giving up about 3/4 of a percentage point in yield.

Maturity. In addition to the ratings, an investment officer can control the risk element through the maturities to be selected. The maturity indicates how much the company stands to lose if interest rates rise. The longer a bond's maturity, the more volatile its price. There is a tradeoff: Shorter maturities usually mean lower yields. A conservative corporate investor, which is typical, may select bonds with shorter maturities.

Features. Check to see whether a bond has a call provision, which allows the issuing company to redeem its bonds after a certain date if it chooses to, rather than at maturity. The investor is generally paid a small premium over par if an issue is called but not as much as the investor would have received if the bond was held until maturity. That is because bonds are usually called only if their interest rates are higher than the going market rate. Try to avoid bonds of companies that have a call provision and may be involved in "event risk" (mergers and acquisitions, leveraged buyouts, and so on.)

Also check to see if a bond has a convertible feature. Convertible bonds can be converted into common stock at a later date. They provide fixed income in the form of interest. The corporate investor also can benefit from the appreciation value of common stock.

Tax status. If the investing company is in a high tax bracket, it may want to consider tax-exempt bonds. Most municipal bonds are rated A or above, making them a good grade risk. They can also be bought in mutual funds.

Yield to maturity. Yield has a lot to do with the rating of a bond. How to calculate various yield measures is taken up later.

How to Read a Bond Quotation

To see how bond quotations are presented in the newspaper, let us look at the data for an IBM bond.

Bonds	Cur Yld	Vol	High	Low	Close	Net Chg
IBM 9 3/8 04	11.	169	84 5/8	84	84	− 1 1/8

The column numbers immediately following the company name gives the bond coupon rate and maturity date. This particular bond carries a 9.375% interest rate and matures in 2004. The next column, labeled "cur yld," provides the current yield calculated by dividing the annual interest income (9 3/8%) by the current market price of the bond (a closing price of 84). Thus, the current yield for the IBM bond is 11% (9 3/8 divided by 84). This figure represents the effective, or real rate of return on the current market price represented by the bond's interest earnings. The "vol" column indicates the number of bonds traded on the given day. (i.e., 169 bonds).

The market price of a bond is usually expressed as a percent of its par (face) value, which is customarily $1,000. Corporate bonds are quoted to the nearest one-eighth of a percent, and a quote of 84 5/8 in the above indicates a price of $846.25 or 84 5/8% of $1,000.

U.S. government bonds are highly marketable and deal in keenly competitive markets so they are quoted in thirty-seconds or sixty-fourths rather than eighths.

Moreover, decimals are used, rather than fractions, in quoting prices. For example, a quotation of 106.17 for a treasury bond indicates a price of $1,065.31 [$1,060 + (17/32 × $10)]. When a plus sign follows the quotation, the treasury bond is being quoted in sixty-fourth. We must double the number following the decimal point and add one to determine the fraction of $10 represented in the quote. For example, a quote of 95.16+ indicates a price of $955.16 [$950 + (33/64 × $10)].

How to Calculate Yield (Effective Rate of Return) on a Bond

Bonds are evaluated on many different types of returns including current yield, yield to maturity, yield to call, and realized yield.

1. *Current yield.* The current yield is the annual interest payment divided by the current price of the bond, which was discussed in the previous section

("Bond Quotation.") This is reported in the *Wall Street Journal*, among others. The current yield is:

$$\frac{\text{Annual interest payment}}{\text{Current price}}$$

EXAMPLE 1

Assume a 12% coupon rate $1,000 par value bond selling for $960. The current yield = $120/$960 = 12.5%

The problem with this measure of return is that it does not take into account the maturity date of the bond. A bond with one year to run and another with 15 years to run would have the same current yield quote if interest payments were $120 and the price were $960. Clearly, the one year bond would be preferable under this circumstance because you would not only get $120 in interest, but also a gain of $40 ($1000 − $960) with a one-year time period, and this amount could be reinvested.

2. *Yield to maturity (YTM)*. The yield to maturity takes into account the maturity date of the bond. It is the real return the investor would receive from interest income plus capital gain assuming the bond is held to maturity. The exact way of calculating this measure is a little complicated and not presented here. But the approximate method is:

$$\text{Yield} = \frac{I + (\$1{,}000 - V)/n}{(\$1{,}000 + V)/2}$$

where V = the market value of the bond
I = dollars of interest paid per year
n = number of years to maturity

EXAMPLE 2

An investor bought a 10-year, 8% coupon, $1,000 par value bond at a price of $877.60. The rate of return (yield) on the bond if held to maturity is

$$\text{Yield} = \frac{\$80 + (\$1{,}000 - \$877.60)/10}{(\$1{,}000 + \$877.60)/2} = \frac{\$80 + \$12.24}{\$938.80} = \frac{\$92.24}{\$938.80} = 9.8\%$$

As can be seen, since the bond was bought at a discount, the yield (9.8%) came out greater than the coupon rate of 8%.

3. *Yield to call*. Not all bonds are held to maturity. If the bond may be called prior to maturity, the yield to maturity formula will have the call price in place of the par value of $1,000.

EXAMPLE 3

Assume a 20-year bond was initially bought at a 13.5% coupon rate, and after two years, rates have dropped. Assume further that the bond is currently selling for $1,180, the yield to maturity on the bond is 11.15%, and the bond can be called in five years after issue at $1,090. Thus if the investor buys the bond two years after issue, the bond may be called back after three more years at $1,090. The yield to call can be calculated as follows:

$$\frac{\$135 + (\$1,090 - \$1,180)/3}{(\$1,090 + \$1,180)/2} = \frac{\$135 + (-\$90/3)}{\$1,135} = \frac{\$105}{\$1,135} = 9.25\%$$

Note: The yield to call figure of 9.25% is 190 basis points less than the yield to maturity of 11.15%. Clearly, you need to be aware of the differential because a lower return is earned.

4. *Realized yield.* The investor may trade in and out of a bond long before it matures. The investor obviously needs a measure of return to evaluate the investment appeal of any bonds that are intended to be bought and quickly sold. Realized yield is used for this purpose. This measure is simply a variation of yield to maturity, as only two variables are changed in the yield to maturity formula. Future price is used in place of par value ($1,000), and the length of the holding period is substituted for the number of years to maturity.

EXAMPLE 4

In Example 2, assume that the investor anticipates holding the bond only three years and that the investor has estimated interest rates will change in the future so that the price of the bond will move to about $925 from its present level of $877.70. Thus, the investor will buy the bond today at a market price of $877.70 and sell the issue three years later at a price of $925. Given these assumptions, the realized yield of this bond would be

$$\text{Realized yield} = \frac{\$80 + (\$925 - \$877.70)/3}{(\$925 + \$877.70)/2} = \frac{\$80 + \$15.77}{\$901.35} = \frac{\$95.77}{\$901.35}$$

$$= 10.63\%$$

Note: Use a bond table to find the value for various yield measures. A source is *Thorndike Encyclopedia of Banking and Financial Tables* by Warren, Gorham & Lamont, Boston.

5. *Equivalent before-tax yield.* Yield on a municipal bond needs to be looked at on an equivalent before-tax yield basis, because the interest received is not subject to federal income taxes. The formula used to equate interest on municipals to other investments is:

$$\text{Tax equivalent yield} = \text{Tax-exempt yield}/ (1 - \text{tax rate})$$

EXAMPLE 5

If a company has a marginal tax rate of 34% and is evaluating a municipal bond paying 10% interest, the equivalent before-tax yield on a taxable investment would be:

$$10\%/(1 - .34) = 15.15\%$$

Thus, the company could choose between a taxable investment paying 15.15% and a tax-exempt bond paying 10% and be indifferent between the two.

Determining Interest-Rate Risk

Interest-rate risk can be determined in two ways. One way is to look at the term structure of a debt security by measuring its average term to maturity—a duration. The other way is to measure the sensitivity of changes in a debt security's price associated with changes in its yield to maturity. We will discuss two measurement approaches: Macaulay's duration coefficient and the interest elasticity.

Macaulay's Duration Coefficient. Macaulay's duration (D) is an attempt to measure risk in a bond. It is defined as the weighted-average number of years required to recover principal and all interest payments. A simple example below illustrates the duration calculations.

EXAMPLE 6

A bond pays a 7% coupon rate annually on its $1,000 face value if it has three years until its maturity and has a YTM of 6%. The computation of Macaulay's duration coefficient involves the following three steps:

Step 1: Calculate the present value of the bond for each year.

Step 2: Express present values as proportions of the price of the bond.

Step 3: Multiply proportions by years' digits to obtain the weighted-average time.

(1)	(2)	(3)	(Step 1) (4)	(Step 2) (5)	(Step 3) (6)
Year	Cash flow	PV factor @ 6%	PV of Cashflow	PV as proportion of price of bond	Column (1) × Column (5)
1	$ 70	.9434	$ 66.04	.0643	.0643
2	70	.8900	62.30	.0607	.1214
3	1,070	.8396	898.39	.8750	2.6250
			$1,026.73	1.0000	2.8107

This 3-year bond's duration is a little over 2.8 years. In all cases, a bond's duration is less than or equal to its term to maturity. Only a pure discount bond—that is, one with no coupon or sinking-fund payments—has duration equal to the maturity.

The higher the D value, the greater the interest rate risk, since it implies a longer recovery period.

Interest Rate Elasticity

A bond's interest rate elasticity (E) is defined as

$$E = \frac{\text{Percentage change in bond price}}{\text{Percentage change in YTM}}$$

Since bond prices and YTMs always move inversely, the elasticity will always be a negative number. Any bond's elasticity can be determined directly with the above formula. Knowing the duration coefficient (D), we can calculate the E using the following simple formula:

$$(-1)\, E = D\, \frac{\text{YTM}}{(1+\text{YTM})}$$

EXAMPLE 7

Using the same data in Example 6, the elasticity is calculated as follows:

$$(-1)\, E = 2.8107\ [0.6/(1.06)] = .1586$$

INVESTING IN A BOND FUND

It is possible that a corporate investor may decide to invest in a bond fund. There are the following three key facts about the bonds in any portfolio.

• *Quality.* Check the credit rating of the typical bond in the fund. Ratings by Standard & Poor's and Moody's show the relative danger that an issuer will default on interest or principal payments. AAA is the best grade. A rating of BB or lower signifies a junk bond.

• *Maturity.* The average maturity of your fund's bonds indicates how much a corporate investor stands to lose if interest rates rise. The longer the term of the bonds, the more volatile the price. For example, a 20-year bond may fluctuate in price four times as much as a four-year issue.

• *Premium or discount.* Some funds with high current yields hold bonds that trade for more than their face value, or at a premium. Such funds are less vulnerable to losses if rates go up. Funds that hold bonds trading at a discount to face value can lose most.

Corporate investors must keep in mind the following guidelines:

• Rising interest rates drive down the value of all bond funds. For this reason, rather than focusing only on current yield, the investor should look primarily at total return (yield plus capital gains from falling interest rates or minus capital losses if rates climb).

• All bond funds do not benefit equally from tumbling interest rates. If a corporate investment officer thinks interest rates will decline and he/she wants to increase total return, he/she should buy funds that invest in U.S. Treasuries or top-rated corporate bonds. The investment officer should consider high-yield corporate bonds (junk bonds) if he/she believes interest rates are stabilizing.

• Unlike bonds, bond funds do not allow the corporate investor to lock in a yield. A mutual fund with a constantly changing portfolio is not like an individual bond, which can be kept to maturity. If the investor wants steady, secure income over several years or more, he/she should consider, as alternatives to funds, buying individual top-quality bonds or investing in a municipal bond *unit trust*, which maintains a fixed portfolio.

CONSIDERING UNIT INVESTMENT TRUSTS

Like a mutual fund, a unit investment trust offers to investors the advantages of a large, professional selected and diversified portfolio. Unlike a mutual fund, however, its portfolio is fixed; once structured, it is not actively managed. Unit investment trusts are available of tax-exempt bonds, money market securities, corporate bonds of different grades; mortgage-backed securities; preferred stocks; utility common stocks; and other investments. Unit trusts are most suitable for corporate investors who need a fixed income and a guaranteed return of capital. They disband and pay off investors after the majority of their investments have been redeemed.

INVESTING IN MORTGAGE-BACKED SECURITIES

A mortgage-backed security is a share in an organized pool of residential mortgages. Some are pass-through securities where the principal and interest payments on them are passed through to shareholders, usually monthly. There are several kinds of mortgage-backed securities. They include:

(a) *Government National Mortgage Association (GNMA—Ginnie Mae)* securities. GNMA primarily issues pass-through securities. These securities pass through all payments of interest and principal received on a pool of federally insured mortgage loans. GNMA guarantees that all payments of principal and interest will be made on the mortgages on a timely basis. Since many mortgages are repaid before maturity, corporate investors in GNMA pools usually recover most of their principal investment well ahead of schedule. Ginnie Mae is considered an excellent investment. The higher yields, coupled with the U.S. government guarantee, provide a competitive edge over the intermediate-term to long-term securities issued by the U.S. government and other agencies.

(b) *Federal Home Loan Mortgage Corporation (FHLMC—Freddie Mac)* securities. Freddie Mac was established to provide a secondary market for conventional mortgages. It can purchase conventional mortgages for its own portfolio. Freddie Mac also issues pass-through securities—called participation certificates (PCs)—and guaranteed mortgage certificates (GMCs) that resemble bonds. Freddie Mac securities do not carry direct government guarantees and are subject to state and federal income tax.

(c) *Federal National Mortgage Association (FNMA—Fannie Mae)* securities. The FNMA is a publicly held corporation whose goal is to provide a secondary market for government-guaranteed mortgages. It does so by financing its purchase by selling debentures with maturities of several years and short-term discount notes from 30 to 360 days to private investors. The FNMA securities are not government guaranteed and are an unsecured obligation of the issuer. For this reason, they often provide considerably higher yields than Treasury securities.

(d) *Collaterized mortgage obligations* (CMOs). CMOs are mortgage-backed securities that separate mortgage pools into short-, medium-, and long-term portions. Corporate investors can choose between short-term pools (such as 5-year pools) and long-term pools (such as 20-year pools).

Mortgage-backed securities enjoy liquidity and a high degree of safety since they are either government-sponsored or otherwise insured.

OTHER SHORT-TERM FIXED INCOME SECURITIES

Besides bonds and mortgage-backed securities, there are other significant forms of debt instruments from which corporate investors may choose, and they are primarily short-term in nature.

• *Certificates of deposit (CDs).* These safe instruments are issued by commercial banks and thrift institutions and have traditionally been in amounts of $10,000 or $100,000 (jumbo CDs). CDs have a fixed maturity period varying from several months to many years. There is a penalty for cashing in the certificate prior to the maturity date, however.

• *Repurchase agreements (repos).* Repurchase agreements are a form of loan in which the borrower sells securities (such as government securities and other marketable securities) to the lender, but simultaneously contracts to repurchase the same securities either on call or on a specified date at a price that will produce an agreed yield. For example, a corporate investment officer agrees to buy a 90-day Treasury bill from a bank at a price to yield 7% with a contract to buy the bills back one day later. Repos are attractive to corporate investors because, unlike demand deposits, repos pay explicit interest and it may be difficult to locate a one-day-maturity government security. Although repos can be a sound investment, it will cost to buy them (such as bank safekeeping fees, legal fees, and paperwork).

• *Banker's acceptances (BAs).* A banker's acceptance is a draft drawn on a bank by a corporation to pay for merchandise. The draft promises payment of a certain sum of money to its holder at some future date. What makes BAs unique is that by prearrangement a bank accepts them, thereby guaranteeing their payment at the stated time. Most BAs arise in foreign trade transactions. The most common maturity for BAs is three months, although they can have maturities of up to 270 days. Their typical denominations are $500,000 and $1 million. BAs offer the following advantages as a corporate investment vehicle:

- Safety
- Negotiability
- Liquidity since an active secondary market for instruments of $1 million or more exists
- BAs offer several basis points higher yield spread than those of T-bills.
- Smaller investment amount producing a yield similar to that of a CD with a comparable face value.

- *Commercial paper.* Commercial paper is issued by large corporations to the public. It usually comes in minimum denominations of $25,000. It represents an unsecured promissory note. It usually carries a higher yield than small CDs. The maturity is usually 30, 60, and 90 days. The degree of risk depends on the company's credit rating.

- *Treasury bills.* Treasury bills have a maximum maturity of one year and common maturities of 91 and 182 days. They trade in minimum units of $10,000. They do not pay interest in the traditional sense; they are sold at a discount, and redeemed when the maturity date comes around, at face value. T-bills are extremely liquid in that there is an active secondary or resale market for these securities. T-bills have an extremely low risk because they are backed by the U.S. government.

Yields on discount securities such as T-bills are calculated using the formula:

$$\frac{P_1 - P_0}{P_0} \times \frac{52}{n}$$

where P_1 = redemption price, P_0 = purchase price, and n = maturity in weeks.

EXAMPLE 8

Assume that P_1 = $10,000, P_0 = $9,800, and n = 13 weeks. Then the T-bill yield is

$$\frac{\$10,000 - \$9,800}{\$9,800} \times \frac{52}{13} = \frac{\$200}{\$9,800}$$

$$\times 4 = .0816 = 8.16\%$$

- *Eurodollar time deposits and CDs.* Eurodollar time deposits are essentially nonnegotiable, full liability, U.S. dollar-denominated time deposits in an offshore branch of an American or foreign bank. Hence, these time deposits are not liquid or marketable. Eurodollar CDs, on the other hand, are negotiable and typically offer a higher return than domestic CDs because its exposure to sovereign risk.

• *Student Loan Marketing Association (Sallie Mae)* securities. Sallie Mae purchases loans made by financial institutions under a variety of federal and state loan programs. Sallie Mae securities are not guaranteed, but generally insured by the federal government and its agencies. These securities include floating rate and fixed rate obligations with maturities of five years or more as well as discount notes with maturities from a few days to 360 days.

INVESTING IN MONEY MARKET FUNDS

Money market funds are a special form of mutual funds. The investor can own a portfolio of high-yielding CDs, T-bills, and other similar securities of short-term nature, with a small amount to invest. There is a great deal of liquidity and flexibility in withdrawing funds through check-writing privileges. Money market funds are considered very conservative, because most of the securities purchased by the funds are quite safe.

Money market mutual funds invest in short-term government securities, commercial paper, and certificates of deposits. They provide more safety of principal than other mutual funds since net asset value never fluctuates. Each share has a net asset value of $1. The yield, however, fluctuates daily. The advantages are:

• Money market funds are no-load.
• There may be a low deposit in these funds.
• The fund is a form of checking account, allowing a firm to write checks against its balance in the account.

Disadvantage: The deposit in these funds is not insured as it is in a money market account or other federally insured deposit in banks.

Table 2

DEFAULT RISK AMONG SHORT-TERM INVESTMENT VEHICLES

	Higher
	Eurodollar time deposits and CDs
	Commercial paper (top quality)
Degree	Bank CDs (uninsured)
of	Bankers' acceptances (BAs)
Risk	U.S. Treasury repos
	U.S. government agency obligations
	U.S. Treasury obligations
	Lower

Table 2 ranks various short-term investment vehicles in terms of their default risk.

PREFERRED STOCK—A HYBRID SECURITY

Preferred stock carries a fixed dividend that is paid quarterly. The dividend is stated in dollar terms per share, or as a percentage of par (stated) value of the stock. Preferred stock is considered a hybrid security because it possesses features of both common stock and a corporate bond. It is like common stock in that:

• It represents equity ownership and is issued without stated maturity dates;
• It pays dividends.

Preferred stock is also like a corporate bond in that:

• It provides for prior claims on earnings and assets;
• Its dividend is fixed for the life of the issue;
• It can carry call and convertible features and sinking fund provisions.

Since preferred stocks are traded on the basis of the yield offered to investors, they are in effect viewed as fixed income securities and, as a result, are in competition with bonds in the marketplace. **Note:** Corporate bonds, however, occupy a position senior to preferred stocks.

Advantages of owning preferred stocks include:

• Their high current income, which is highly predictable

• Safety

• Lower unit cost ($10 to $25 per share)

Disadvantages are:

• Their susceptibility to inflation and high interest rates

• They lack substantial capital gains potential

Preferred Stock Ratings

Like bond ratings, Standard & Poor's and Moody's have long rated the investment quality of preferred stocks. S&P uses basically the same rating system as they do with bonds, except that triple A ratings are not given to preferred stocks. Moody's uses a slightly different system, which is given below. These ratings are intended to provide an indication of the quality of the issue and are based largely on an assessment of the firm's ability to pay preferred dividends in a prompt and timely fashion. **Note:** Preferred stock ratings should not be compared with bond ratings as they are not equivalent; preferred stocks occupy a position junior to bonds.

Moody's Preferred Stock Rating System

Rating Symbol	Definition
aaa	Top quality
aa	High grade
a	Upper medium grade
baa	Lower medium grade
ba	Speculative type
b	Little assurance of future dividends
caa	Likely to be already in arrears

HOW TO CALCULATE EXPECTED RETURN FROM PREFERRED STOCK

The expected return from preferred stock is calculated in a manner similar to the expected return on bonds. The calculations depend upon whether the preferred stock is issued in perpetuity or if it has a call that is likely to be exercised.

A Perpetuity. Since preferred stock usually has no maturity date when the company must redeem it, you cannot calculate a yield to maturity. You can calculate a current yield as follows:

$$\text{Current yield} = D/P$$

where D = annual dividend, and P = the market price of the preferred stock.

EXAMPLE 9

A preferred stock paying $4.00 a year in dividends and having a market price of $25 would have a current yield of 16% ($4/$25).

Yield to Call. If a call is likely, a more appropriate return measure is yield to call (YTC). Theoretically, YTC is the rate that equates the present value of the future dividends and the call price with the current market price of the preferred stock. Two examples are given below.

EXAMPLE 10

Consider the following two preferreds:

Preferreds	Market Price	Call Price	Dividends	Term to call	YTC
A	$8/share	$9	$1/year	3 years	16.06%
B	10	9	$1	3	6.89

Comparison to Bond Yields. The example shows that yields on straight preferreds are closely correlated to bond yields, since both are fixed income securities. However, yields on preferreds are often below bond yields, which seems unusual because preferreds have a position junior to bonds. The reason is that corporate investors favor preferreds over bonds because of a dividend exclusion allowed in determining corporate taxable income, which will be explained below.

ADJUSTABLE RATE PREFERRED STOCK (ARPS)

Corporate treasurers with excess funds can make short-term investments in long-term securities such as long-term bonds and common and preferred stocks. They may be naturally adverse to the price volatility of long-term bonds, especially when they put money aside for a specific payment such as income taxes. Perhaps for a similar reason, common and preferred stocks would be equally unattractive for short-term investments. But this is not quite true, since these securities provide an interesting tax advantage for corporations. For example, if the company invests its surplus funds in a short or long-term debt, it must pay tax on the interest received. Thus, for $1 of interest, a corporation in a 46% marginal tax bracket ends up with only $0.54. However, companies pay tax on only 20% of dividends received from investments in stocks. (Under current tax laws, corporations are allowed to exclude 80% of the dividends they receive from a stock (either common or preferred) from their taxable income. Thus, for $1 of dividends received, the firm winds up with $1 - (.20 \times .46) = $0.91. The effective tax rate is only 9.1%.

The problem with preferred stocks is that since preferred dividends are fixed, the prices of preferred shares change when long-term interest rates change. Many corporate money managers are reluctant to buy straight preferred because of its interest risk. To encourage corporate investments in preferred shares, a new type of preferred stock was introduced in May 1982 by Chemical New York Corporation. These securities—the so-called *adjustable rate (floating rate) preferreds*—pay dividends that go up and down with the general level of interest rates. The prices of these securities are therefore less volatile than fixed-dividend preferreds, and they are a safer haven for the corporation's excess cash. Yields obtained from preferreds may be lower than the debt issue. The corporations buying the preferreds would still be happy with the lower yield because 80% of the dividends they receive escape tax.

Preferred Stock Quotation

If preferred stocks are listed on the organized exchanges, they are reported in the same sections as common stocks in newspapers. The symbol "pf" appears after the name of the corporation, designating the issue as preferred. Preferred stocks are read the same way as common stock quotations. Two companies are illustrated below.

Stock	Div.	Yld %	P/E Ratio	Sales 100s	High	Low	Close	Net Chg.
(1) A can pf	13.75	11.8	—	5	117	117	117	$-7/8$
(2) Aetna pf	4.97e	9.3	—	10	$53\frac{1}{4}$	$43\frac{1}{8}$	$43\frac{1}{4}$	$-1/8$

In stock (2), the e symbol after the dividend indicates a varying dividend payment; this issue is probably adjustable preferred.

INVESTING IN MONEY MARKET PREFERRED STOCK

The money market preferred stock (MMPS), also known as auction-rate preferred stock, is the newest and most popular member of the preferred stock group attractive to corporate investors since it offers the following advantages:

- Low market risk in the event of price decline
- Competitive yield
- Liquidity

MMPS pays dividends and adjusts rates up or down, depending on the current market, every seven weeks. Unlike other adjustable preferreds, the market, not the issuer, sets the rate at the auction. If no bids are placed for a stock, MMPS' dividend rate is automatically set at the 60-day AA commercial paper rate quoted by the Federal Reserve Bank. There is a possibility, however, of a failed auction if no buyers show up at the auction. Corporate investors must take into account the credit quality of a money market preferred stock. Money market preferreds include:

- Short-term Auction-Rate Stock (STARS)
- Dutch-Auction-Rate Transferable Securities (DARTS)
- Market-Auction Preferred Stock (MAPS)
- Auction-Market Preferred Stock (AMPS)
- Cumulative Auction-Market Preferred Stock (CAMPS)

CONCLUSION

Fixed income securities such as bonds and preferred stocks have a twofold appeal to corporate investors: They are usually safer than equity securities such as common stocks and they generate typically a higher current return. It is important to realize that yields on bonds and their prices can be just as volatile as common stock prices and almost as risky. Bonds are subject to risks such as default risk, interest rate risk, and inflation risk. Preferred stock is a hybrid security since it has features of both common stock and bonds. In investing in fixed income securities, corporate investors should have an understanding of quality ratings, yields, safety, and risks associated with the securities.

VIII

FINANCING THE BUSINESS

35

Short-Term Financing

This chapter provides the financial manager with a "broad picture" of short-term financing sources including their advantages and disadvantages. "Short term" refers to financing that will be repaid in one year or less. Short-term financing may be used to meet seasonal and temporary fluctuations in funds position as well as to meet permanent needs. For instance, short-term financing may be used to provide additional working capital, finance current assets (such as receivables and inventory), or provide interim financing for a long-term project (such as the acquisition of plant and equipment) until long-term financing may be issued. Long-term financing may not be appropriate at the present time because of say perceived long-term credit risk or excessively high cost.

When compared to long-term financing (Chapter 37), short-term financing has several advantages including easier to arrange, less expensive, and more flexibility. The drawbacks of short-term financing are that interest rates fluctuate more often (also resulting in greater earnings sensitivity), refinancing is frequently required, there is greater risk of not being able to pay,. and delinquent repayment may be detrimental to the company's credit rating. The financial manager can *hedge* interest rate risk by selling and later buying back interest rate futures contracts to offset an increase in interest expense with the corresponding profit from the futures transaction.

What sources of short-term financing may you tap? They include trade credit, bank loans, bankers' acceptances, finance company loans, commercial paper, receivable financing, and inventory financing. A particular source may be more appropriate in a given circumstance. Some are more desirable than others because of interest rates or collateral requirements.

You should consider the merits of the different alternative sources of short-

851

term financing. The factors bearing upon the selection of a particular source include:

- Cost.
- Effect on financial ratios.
- Effect on credit rating. Some sources of short-term financing may negatively impact the company's credit rating, such as factoring accounts receivable.
- Risk. Consider the reliability of the source of funds for future borrowing. If the company is materially affected by outside forces, it will need more stability and reliability in financing.
- Restrictions. Certain lenders may impose restrictions, such as requiring a minimum level of working capital.
- Flexibility. Certain lenders are more willing to work with the company, for example, to periodically adjust the amount of funds needed.
- Expected money market conditions (e.g., future interest rates) and availability of future financing.
- Inflation rate.
- Profitability and liquidity positions. A company must be liquid to pay its near-term obligations.
- Stability and maturity of operations.
- Tax rate.

If the company will be short of cash during certain times, the financial manager should arrange for financing (such as a line of credit) in advance instead of waiting for an emergency.

HOW TO USE TRADE CREDIT

Trade credit (accounts payable) are balances owed suppliers. It is a spontaneous (recurring) financing source since it comes from normal operations. Trade credit is the least expensive form of financing inventory. The benefits of trade credit are: it is readily available, since suppliers want business; collateral is not required; interest is typically not demanded or, if so, the rate is minimal; it is convenient; and trade creditors are frequently lenient if the company gets into financial trouble. If the company has liquidity difficulties, it may be able to stretch (extend) accounts payable; however, among the disadvantages of doing so are the giving up of any cash discount offered and the probability of lowering the company's credit rating. A report should be prepared analyzing accounts payable in terms of lost discounts, aged debit balances, aged unpaid invoices, and days to pay.

EXAMPLE 1

The company purchases $500 worth of merchandise per day from suppliers. The terms of purchase are net/60, and the company pays on time. The accounts payable balance is:

$500 per day $\times$ 60 days $=$ $30,000

The company should typically take advantage of a cash discount offered on the early payment of accounts payable because the failure to do so results in a high opportunity cost. The cost of not taking a discount equals:

$$\left(\frac{\text{Discount Lost}}{\begin{array}{c}\text{Dollar Proceeds You}\\\text{Have Use of by Not}\\\text{Taking the Discount}\end{array}}\right) \times \left(\frac{360}{\begin{array}{c}\text{Number of Days You Have}\\\text{Use of the Money by}\\\text{Not Taking the Discount}\end{array}}\right)$$

EXAMPLE 2

The company buys $1,000 in merchandise on terms of 2/10, net/30. The company fails to take the discount and pays the bill on the 30th day. The cost of the discount is:

$$\frac{\$20}{\$980} \times \frac{360}{20} = 36.7\%$$

The company would be better off taking the discount since the opportunity cost is 36.7%, even if it needed to borrow the money from the bank. The interest rate on a bank loan would be far less than 36.7%.

WHEN ARE BANK LOANS ADVISABLE?

Even though other institutions (e.g., savings and loan associations, credit unions) provide banking services, most banking activities are conducted by commercial banks. Commercial banks give the company the ability to operate with minimal cash and still be confident of planning activities even in light of uncertainty.

Commercial banks favor short-term loans since they like to see their money back within one year. However, loans in excess of one year may be given (See Chapter 36). There is an intimacy between the company and the bank that is the case with typical supplier relationships. If the company is large, a group of banks may form a consortium to furnish the desired level of capital.

Bank loans are not spontaneous financing as is trade credit. One example is a self-liquidating (seasonal) loan used to pay for a temporary increase in accounts receivable or inventory. As soon as the assets realize cash, the loan is repaid.

The prime interest rate is the lowest interest rate applied to short-term loans from a bank charged the most creditworthy companies. The company's interest rate may be higher depending upon its risk.

Bank financing may take the following forms:

- Unsecured loans
- Secured loans
- Lines of credit
- Installment loans

Unsecured Loan

Most short-term unsecured (no collateral) loans are self-liquidating. This kind of loan is recommended if the company has an excellent credit rating. It is usually used to finance projects having quick cash flows. It is appropriate if the company has immediate cash and can either repay the loan in the near future or quickly obtain longer-term financing. Seasonal cash shortfalls and desired inventory buildups are reasons to use an unsecured loan. The disadvantages of this kind of loan are that, because it is made for the short term, it carries a higher interest rate than a secured loan and payment in a lump sum is required.

Secured Loan

If the company's credit rating is deficient, the bank may lend money only on a secured basis. Collateral may take many forms including inventory, marketable securities, or fixed assets. **Tip:** Even though the company is able to obtain an unsecured loan, it may still give collateral to get a lower interest rate.

How Much Line of Credit Can the Company Get?

Under a line of credit, the bank agrees to lend money on a recurring basis up to a specified amount. Credit lines are typically established for a 1-year period and may be renewed annually. Determine if the line of credit is adequate for present and immediate future needs.

The advantages of a line of credit are the easy and immediate access to funds during tight money market conditions and the ability to borrow only as much as needed and repay immediately when cash is available. **Recommendation:** Use a line of credit if the company is working on large individual projects for a long time period and obtain minimal or no payments until the job is completed. The disadvantages relate to the collateral requirements and the additional financial information that must be presented to the bank. Also, the bank may place restrictions upon the company, such as a ceiling on capital expenditures or the maintenance of a minimum level of working capital. Further, the bank typically charges a commitment fee on the amount of the unused credit line.

When the company borrows under a line of credit, it may be required to maintain a compensating balance (deposit with the bank that does not earn interest). The compensating balance is stated as a percentage of the loan and effectively increases the cost of the loan. A compensating balance may also be placed on the unused portion of a line of credit, in which case the interest rate would be reduced.

EXAMPLE 3

The company borrows $200,000 and is required to keep a 12% compensating balance. It also has an unused line of credit of $100,000, for which a 10% compensating balance is required. The minimum balance that must be maintained is:

$$(\$200,000 \times .12) + (\$100,000 \times .10) = \$24,000 + \$10,000$$
$$= \$34,000$$

A line of credit is typically decided upon prior to the actual borrowing. In the days between the arrangement for the loan and the actual borrowing, interest rates will change. Therefore, the agreement will stipulate the loan is at the prime interest rate prevailing when the loan is extended plus a risk premium. **Note:** The prime interest rate is not known until you actually borrow the money.

The bank may test the company's financial capability by requiring it to "clean up," that is, repay the loan for a brief time during the year (e.g., for one month). If the company is unable to repay a short-term loan, it should probably finance with long-term funds. The payment shows the bank that the loan is actually seasonal rather than permanent.

Letter of Credit

A letter of credit is a conditional bank commitment on behalf of the company to pay a third party in accordance with specified terms and commitments. Payment may be made on submission of proof of shipment or other performance. The advantages are that the company does not have to pay cash in advance of shipment and funds could be used elsewhere in the business. Banks charge a fee and a rate for bankers' acceptances arising after shipment which approximates the prime interest rate.

Revolving Credit

With revolving credit, notes are short term (typically 90 days). The financial officer may renew the loan or borrow additional funds up to a maximum amount. Advantages are readily available credit and fewer restrictions relative to the line-of-credit agreement. A disadvantage is the bank restrictions.

Installment Loan

An installment loan requires monthly payments. When the principal on the loan decreases sufficiently, refinancing can take place at lower interest rates. The advantage of this kind of loan is that it may be tailored to satisfy seasonal financing needs.

Interest

Interest on a loan may be paid either at maturity (ordinary interest) or in advance (discounting the loan). When interest is paid in advance, the loan proceeds are reduced and the effective (true) interest cost is increased.

EXAMPLE 4

The company borrows $30,000 at 16% interest per annum and repays the loan one year later. The interest is $30,000 \times .16 = $4,800$. The effective interest rate is 16% ($4,800/$30,000).

EXAMPLE 5

Assume the same facts as in the prior example, except the note is discounted. The effective interest rate increases as follows:

$$\text{Proceeds} = \text{principal} - \text{interest} = \$30,000 - \$4,800 = \$25,200$$

$$\text{Effective interest rate} = \frac{\text{Interest}}{\text{Proceeds}} = \frac{\$4,800}{\$25,000} = 19\%$$

A compensating balance will increase the effective interest rate.

EXAMPLE 6

The effective interest rate for a 1-year, $600,000 loan that has a nominal interest rate of 19%, with interest due at maturity and requiring a 15% compensating balance follows.

Effective interest rate (with compensating balance) equals:

$$\frac{\text{Interest rate} \times \text{principal}}{\text{Proceeds, \%} \times \text{principal}} = \frac{.19 \times \$600,000}{(1.00 - .15) \times \$600,000}$$

$$= \frac{\$114,000}{\$510,000} = 22.4\%$$

EXAMPLE 7

Assume the same facts as in the prior example, except that the loan is discounted. The effective interest rate is:

Effective interest rate (with discount) equals:

$$\frac{\text{Interest rate} \times \text{pricipal}}{(\text{Proceeds, } \% \times \text{principal}) - \text{interest}}$$

$$\frac{0.19 \times \$600,000}{(0.85 \times \$600,000) - \$114,000} = \frac{\$114,000}{\$396,000} = 28.8\%$$

EXAMPLE 8

The company has a credit line of $400,000, but it must maintain a compensating balance of 13% on outstanding loans and a compensating balance of 10% on the unused credit. The interest rate on the loan is 18%. The company borrows $275,000. The effective interest rate on the loan is calculated below.

The required compensating balance is:

$$
\begin{array}{lll}
.13 \times \$275,000 & \$35,750 \\
.10 \times 125,000 & \underline{12,500} \\
& \$48,250
\end{array}
$$

Effective interest rate (with line of credit) equals:

$$\frac{\text{Interest rate (on loan)} \times \text{principal}}{\text{Principal} - \text{compensating balance}}$$

$$\frac{0.18 \times \$275,000}{\$275,000 - \$48,250} = \frac{\$49,500}{\$226,750} = 21.8\%$$

On an installment loan, the effective interest rate computation is illustrated below. Assuming a 1-year loan payable in equal monthly install-ments, the effective rate is based on the average amount outstanding for the year. The interest is computed on the face amount of the loan.

EXAMPLE 9

The company borrows $40,000 at an interest rate of 10% to be paid in 12 monthly installments. The average loan balance is $40,000/2 = $20,000. The effective interest rate is $4,000/$20,000 = 20%.

EXAMPLE 10

Assume the same facts as in the prior example, except that the loan is discounted. The interest of $4,000 is deducted in advance so the proceeds received are $40,000 − $4,000 = $36,000. The average loan balance is $36,000/2 = $18,000. The effective interest rate is $4,000/$18,000 = 22.2%.

The effective interest cost computation may be more complicated when installment payments differ. The true interest cost of an installment loan is the internal rate of return of the applicable cash flows converted on an annual basis (if desired).

EXAMPLE 11

The company borrows $100,000 and will repay it in three monthly installments of $25,000, $25,000, and $50,000. The interest rate is 12%.

Amount of Borrowing equals:	
Installment loan	$100,000
Less: Interest on first installment	
($100,000 × .25 × .12)	3,000
Balance	$ 97,000

Effective interest cost of installment loan equals:

$$0 = -\$97,000 + \$25,000/(1 + \text{Cost}) + \$25,000/(1 + \text{Cost})2$$
$$+ \$50,000/(1 + \text{Cost})3$$
$$= 1.37\% \text{ on monthly basis}$$
$$= 1.37\% \times 12 = 16.44\% \text{ on annual basis}$$

Bankers' Acceptances

A banker's acceptance is a short-term noninterest bearing draft (age to six months), drawn by the company and accepted by a bank, that orders payment to a third party at a later date. It is typically issued up to $1 million on a discount basis. The creditworthiness of the draft is of good quality because it has the backing of the bank, not the drawer. It is, in essence, a debt instrument created out of a self-liquidating business transaction. Bankers' acceptances are often used to finance the shipment and handling of both domestic and foreign merchandise. Acceptances are classed as short-term financing because they typically have maturities of less than 180 days.

Dealing with the Banker

Banks are anxious to lend money to meet self-liquidating, cyclical business needs. A short-term bank loan is an inexpensive way to obtain funds to satisfy working capital requirements during the business cycle. However, the financial officer must be able to explain what the company's needs are in an intelligent manner.

IS THE COMPANY FORCED TO TAKE OUT A COMMERCIAL FINANCE LOAN?

When credit is unavailable from a bank, the company may have to go to a commercial finance company. The finance company loan has a higher interest rate than a bank, and generally is secured. Typically, the amount of collateral placed will be greater than the balance of the loan. Collateral includes accounts receivable, inventories, and fixed assets. Commercial finance companies also finance the installment purchases of industrial equipment by firms. A portion of their financing is sometimes obtained through commercial bank borrowing at wholesale rates.

IS THE COMPANY FINANCIALLY STRONG ENOUGH TO ISSUE COMMERCIAL PAPER?

Commercial paper can be issued only if the company possesses a very high credit rating. Therefore, the interest rate is less than that of a bank loan, typically 1/2% below the prime interest rate. Commercial paper is unsecured and sold at a discount (below face value). The maturity date is usually less than 270 days, otherwise Securities and Exchange Commission (SEC) registration is needed. Since the note is sold at a discount, the interest is immediately deducted from the face of the note by the creditor, but the company will pay the full face value. Commercial paper may be issued through a dealer or directly placed to an institutional investor.

The benefits of commercial paper are that no security is required, the interest rate is typically less than through bank or finance company borrowing, and the commercial paper dealer often offers financial advice. The drawbacks are that commercial paper can be issued only by large, financially sound companies, and commercial paper dealings relative to bank dealings are impersonal.

EXAMPLE 12

A company's balance sheet appears below.

ASSETS

Current assets	$ 540,000
Fixed assets	800,000
Total assets	$1,340,000

LIABILITIES AND STOCKHOLDERS' EQUITY

Current Liabilities:	
Notes payable to banks	$ 100,000
Commercial paper	650,000
Total current liabilities	$ 750,000
Long-term liabilities	260,000
Total liabilities	$1,010,000
Stockholders' equity	330,000
Total liabilities and stockholders' equity	$1,340,000

The amount of commercial paper issued by the company is a high percentage of both its current liabilities, 86.7% ($650,000/$750,000), and its total liabilities, 64.4% ($650,000/$1,010,000). Probably the company should do more bank borrowing because in the event of a money market squeeze, the company would find it advantageous to have a working relationship with a bank.

EXAMPLE 13

The company issues $500,000 of commercial paper every two months at a 13% rate. There is a $1,000 placement cost each time. The percentage cost of the commercial paper is:

Interest ($500,000 $\times$ .13)	$ 65,000
Placement cost ($1,000 $\times$ 6)	6,000
Cost	$ 71,000

$$\text{Percentage cost of commercial paper} = \frac{\$71,000}{\$500,000} = 14.2\%$$

EXAMPLE 14

The company needs $300,000 for the month of November. Its options are:

1. A 1-year line of credit for $300,000 with a bank. The commitment fee is 0.5%, and the interest charge on the used funds is 12%.

2. Issue 2-month commercial paper at 10% interest. Because the funds are only needed for one month, the excess funds ($300,000) can be invested in 8% marketable securities for December. The total transaction fee for the marketable securities is 0.3%.

The line of credit costs:

Commitment fee for unused period (0.005)(300,000)(11/12)	$1,375

Interest for one month (0.12)(300,000)(1/12)	3,000
Total cost	$4,375

The commercial paper costs:

Interest charge (0.10)(300,000)(2/12)	$5,000
Transaction fee (0.003)(300,000)	900
Less interest earned on marketable securities (0.08)(300,000)(1/12)	(2,000)
Total cost	$3,900

The commercial paper arrangement is less costly.

Should Receivables Be Used for Financing

In accounts receivable financing, the accounts receivable are the security for the loan as well as the source of repayment.

When may the financing of accounts receivable generally take place?

- Receivables are a minimum of $25,000
- Sales are a minimum of $250,000
- Individual receivables are at a minimum of $100
- Receivables apply to selling merchandise rather than rendering services
- Customers are financially strong
- Sales returns are not great
- Title to the goods is received by the buyer at shipment

Receivable financing has several advantages, including avoiding the need for long-term financing and obtaining a recurring cash flow. Accounts receivable financing has the drawback of high administrative costs when there are many small accounts.

Accounts receivable may be financed under either a factoring or assignment (pledging) arrangement. Factoring is the outright sale of accounts receivable to a bank or finance company without recourse. The purchaser takes all credit and collection risks. The proceeds received are equal to the face value of the receivables less the commission charge, which is usually 2% to 4% higher than the prime interest rate. The cost of the factoring arrangement is the factor's commission for credit investigation, interest on the unpaid balance of advanced funds, and a discount from the face value of the receivables where high credit risk exist. Remissions by customers are made directly to the factor.

The advantages of factoring are immediate availability of cash, reduction in overhead because the credit examination function is no longer needed, obtaining financial advice, receipt of advances as required on a seasonal basis, and strengthening of the balance sheet position.

The disadvantages of factoring include both the high cost and the negative impression left with customers due to the change in ownership of the receivables. Also, factors may antagonize customers by their demanding methods of collecting delinquent accounts.

In an assignment (pledging), there is no transfer of the ownership of the accounts receivable. Receivables are given to a finance company with recourse. The finance company usually advances between 50% and 85% of the face value of the receivables in cash. You are responsible for a service charge, interest on the advance, and any resulting bad debt losses. Customer remissions continue to be made directly to the company.

The assignment of accounts receivable has the advantage of immediate availability of cash, cash advances available on a seasonal basis, and avoidance of negative customer feelings. The disadvantages include the high cost, the continuance of the clerical function associated with accounts receivable, and the bearing of all credit risk.

The financial manager has to be aware of the impact of a change in accounts receivable policy on the cost of financing receivables. When accounts receivable are financed, the cost of financing may rise or fall under different conditions. For example, (1) when credit standards are relaxed, costs rise; (2) when recourse for defaults is given to the finance company, costs decrease; and (3) when the minimum invoice amount of a credit sale is increased, costs decline.

The financial officer should compute the costs of accounts receivable financing and select the least expensive alternative.

EXAMPLE 15

A factor will purchase the company's $120,000 per month accounts receivable. The factor will advance up to 80% of the receivables for an annual charge of 14%, and a 1.5% fee on receivables purchased. The cost of this factoring arrangement is:

Factor fee $[0.015 \times (\$120,000 \times 12)]$	$21,600
Cost of borrowing $[0.14 \times (\$120,000 \times 0.8)]$	13,440
Total cost	$35,040

EXAMPLE 16

A factor charges a 3% fee per month. The factor lends the company up to 75% of receivables purchased for an additional 1% per month. Credit sales are $400,000 per month. As a result of the factoring arrangement, the company saves $6,500 per month in credit costs and a bad debt expense of 2% of credit sales.

XYZ Bank has offered an arrangement to lend the company up to 75% of the receivables. The bank will charge 2% per month interest plus a 4% processing charge on receivable lending.

The collection period is 30 days. If the company borrows the maximum per month, should it stay with the factor or switch to XYZ Bank?

Cost of factor:

Purchase receivables (0.03 × $400,000)	$12,000
Lending fee (0.01 × $300,000)	3,000
Total cost	$15,000

Cost of bank financing:

Interest (0.02 × $300,000)	$ 6,000
Processing charge (0.04 × $300,000)	12,000
Additional Cost of not using the factor:	
Credit costs	6,500
Bad debts (0.02 × $400,000)	8,000
Total cost	$32,500

The company should stay with the factor.

EXAMPLE 17

A company needs $250,000 and is weighing the alternatives of arranging a bank loan or going to a factor. The bank loan terms are 18% interest, discounted, with a compensating balance of 20%. The factor will charge a 4% commission on invoices purchased monthly, and the interest rate on the purchased invoices is 12%, deducted in advance. By using a factor, the company will save $1,000 monthly credit department costs, and uncollectible accounts estimated at 3% of the factored accounts receivable will not occur. Which is the better alternative for the company?

The bank loan which will net the company its desired $250,000 in proceeds is:

$$\frac{\text{Proceeds}}{(100\% - \text{proceeds deducted})} = \frac{\$250,000}{100\% - (18\% + 20\%)}$$

$$\frac{\$250,000}{1.0 - 0.38} = \frac{\$250,000}{0.62} = \$403,226$$

The effective interest rate associated with the bank loan is:

$$\text{Effective interest rate} = \frac{\text{interest rate}}{\text{proceeds, \%}} = \frac{.18}{.62} = 29.0\%$$

The amount of accounts receivable that should be factored to net the firm $250,000 is:

$$\frac{\$250,000}{1.0 - 0.16} = \frac{\$250,000}{0.84} = \$297,619$$

The total annual cost of the bank arrangement is:

Interest ($250,000 × 0.29)	$72,500

Additional cost of not using a factor:

Credit costs ($1,000 × 12)	12,000
Uncollectible accounts ($297,619 × 0.03)	8,929
Total cost	$93,429

The effective interest rate associated with factoring accounts receivable is:

$$\text{Effective interest rate} = \frac{\text{interest rate}}{\text{proceeds, \%}} = \frac{12\%}{100\% - (12\% + 4\%)}$$

$$= \frac{0.12}{0.84} = 14.3\%$$

The total annual cost of the factoring alternative is:

Interest ($250,000 × 0.143)	$35,750
Factoring ($297,619 × 0.04)	11,905
Total cost	$47,655

Factoring should be used since it will cost almost half as much as the bank loan.

EXAMPLE 18

A company is considering a factoring arrangement. The company's sales are $2,700,000, accounts receivable turnover is nine times, and a 17% reserve on accounts receivable is required. The factor's commission charge on average accounts receivable payable at the point of receivable purchase is 2.0%. The factor's interest charge is 16% of receivables after subtracting the commission charge and reserve. The interest charge reduces the advance. The annual effective cost under the factoring arrangement is computed below.

$$\text{Average accounts receivable} = \frac{\text{credit sales}}{\text{turnover}} = \frac{\$2,700,000}{9}$$

$$= \$300,000$$

The company will receive the following amount by factoring its accounts receivable:

Average accounts receivable	$300,000
Less: Reserve ($300,000 × 0.17)	−51,000
Commission ($300,000 × 0.02)	− 6,000
Net prior to interest	$243,000
Less: Interest ($243,000 × (16%/9)	4,320
Proceeds received	$238,680

The annual cost of the factoring arrangement is:

Commission ($300,000 $\times$ 0.02)	$ 6,000
Interest ($243,000 $\times$ (16%/9)	4,320
Cost each 40 days (360/9)	$ 10,320
Turnover	$\times$ 9
Total annual cost	$ 92,880

The annual effective cost under the factoring arrangement based on the amount received is:

$$\frac{\text{Annual Cost}}{\text{Average amount received}} = \frac{\$92,880}{\$238,680} = 38.9\%$$

SHOULD INVENTORIES BE USED FOR FINANCING?

Financing inventory typically takes place when the company has completely used its borrowing capacity on receivables. Inventory financing requires the existence of marketable, nonperishable, and standardized goods that have quick turnover. The merchandise should not be subject to rapid obsolescence. Good collateral inventory can be marketed apart from the company's marketing organization. Inventory financing should consider the price stability of the merchandise and the costs of selling it.

The advance is high when there is marketable inventory. In general, the financing of raw materials and finished goods is about 75% of their value. The interest rate approximates 3 to 5 points over the prime interest rate.

The drawbacks to inventory financing include the high interest rate and the restrictions placed on inventory.

The types of inventory financing include a floating (blanket) lien, warehouse receipt, and trust receipt. With a *floating lien*, the creditor's security lies in the aggregate inventory rather than in its components. Even though the company sells and restocks, the lender's security interest continues. With a *warehouse receipt*, the lender receives an interest in the inventory stored at a public warehouse; however, the fixed costs of this arrangement are high. There may be a field warehouse arrangement where the warehouser sets up a secured area directly at the company's location. The company has access to the goods but must continually account for them. With a *trust receipt* loan, the creditor has title to the goods but releases them to the company to sell on the creditor's behalf. As goods are sold, the company remits the funds to the lender. A good example of trust receipt use is in automobile dealer financing. The drawback of the trust receipt arrangement is that a trust receipt must be given for specific items.

A collateral certificate may be issued by a third party to the lender guaranteeing the existence of pledged inventory. The advantage of a collateral certificate is flexibility because merchandise does not have to be segregated or possessed by the lender.

EXAMPLE 19

The company wants to finance $500,000 of inventory. Funds are required for three months. A warehouse receipt loan may be taken at 16% with a 90% advance against the inventory's value. The warehousing cost is $4,000 for the 3-month period. The cost of financing the inventory is:

Interest [0.16 × 0.90 × $500,000 × (3/12)]	$18,000
Warehousing cost	4,000
Total cost	$22,000

EXAMPLE 20

The company shows growth in operations but is experiencing liquidity difficulties. Six large financially sound companies are customers, being responsible for 75% of sales. On the basis of the below financial information for 19X1, should the financial manager borrow on receivables or inventory?

Balance sheet data follow:

Balance Sheet

ASSETS

Current Assets

Cash	$27,000	
Receivables	380,000	
Inventory (consisting of 55% of work-in-process)	320,000	
Total Current Assets		$727,000
Fixed Assets		250,000
Total Assets		$977,000

LIABILITIES AND STOCKHOLDERS' EQUITY

Current Liabilities

Accounts Payable	$260,000	
Loans Payable	200,000	
Accrued Expenses	35,000	
Total Current Liabilities		$495,000
Noncurrent Liabilities		
Bonds Payable		110,000
Total Liabilities		$605,000
Stockholders' Equity		
Common Stock	$250,000	
Retained Earnings	122,000	
Total Stockholders' Equity		372,000
Total Liabilities and Stockholders' Equity		$977,000

Selected income statement information follows:

Sales	$1,800,000
Net income	130,000

Receivable financing can be expected since a high percentage of sales are made to only six large financially strong companies. Receivables thus show collectibility. It is also easier to control a few large customer accounts.

Inventory financing is not likely, due to the high percentage of partially completed items. Lenders are reluctant to finance inventory when a large work-in-process balance exists since the goods will be difficult to process and sell by lenders.

WHAT OTHER ASSETS MAY BE USED FOR FINANCING?

Assets other than inventory and receivables may be used as security for short-term bank loans such as real estate, plant and equipment, cash surrender value of life insurance policies, and securities. Also, lenders are typically willing to advance a high percentage of the market value of bonds. Further, loans may be made based on a guaranty of a third party.

Table 1 presents a summary of the major features of short-term financing coverage.

COMPARING SHORT-TERM TO LONG-TERM FINANCING

Short-term financing is easier to arrange, has lower cost, and is more flexible than long-term financing. However, short-term financing makes the borrower subject to interest rate swings, requires refinancing more quickly, and is more difficult to repay. **Recommendation:** Use short-term financing as additional working capital, finance short-lived assets, or as interim financing on long-term projects. Long-term financing is more appropriate to finance long-term assets or construction projects.

CONCLUSION

In short-term financing, the best financing tool should be used to meet the company's objectives. The financing instrument depends upon the company's particular circumstances. Consideration is given to such factors as cost, risk, restrictions, stability of operations, and tax rate. Sources of short-term financing include trade credit, bank loans, bankers' acceptances, finance company loans, commercial paper, receivable financing, and inventory financing.

Table 1

SUMMARY OF MAJOR SHORT-TERM FINANCING SOURCES

Type of Financing	Source	Cost or Terms	Features
A. Spontaneous sources Accounts payable	Suppliers	No explicit cost but there is an opportunity cost if a cash discount for early payment is not taken. Companies should take advantage of the discount offered.	The main source of short-term financing typically on terms of 0 to 120 days.
Accrued expenses	Employees and tax agencies	None	Expenses incurred but not yet paid (e.g., accrued wages payable, accrued taxes payable)
B. Unsecured sources Bank loans 1. Single-payment note	Commercial banks	Prime interest rate plus risk premium. The interest rate may be fixed or variable. Unsecured loans are less costly than secured loans.	A single-payment loan to satisfy a funds shortage to last a short time period.
2. Lines of credit	Commercial Banks	Prime interest rate plus risk premium. The interest rate may be fixed or variable. A compensating balance is typically required. The line of credit must be "cleaned up" periodically.	An agreed upon borrowing limit for funds to satisfy seasonal needs.
Commercial paper	Commercial banks, insurance companies, other financial institutions, and other companies	A little less than the prime interest rate.	Unsecured, short-term note of financially strong companies

C. Secured sources
Accounts receivable as collateral

1. Pledging	Commercial banks and finance companies	2% to 5% above prime plus fees (usually 2%–3%). Low administrative costs. Advances typically ranging from 60% to 85%.	Qualified accounts receivable accounts serve as collateral. Upon collection of the account, the borrower remits to the lender. Customers are not notified of the arrangement. With recourse meaning that the risk of nonpayment is borne by the company.
2. Factoring	Factors, commercial banks, and commercial finance companies	Typically a 2%–3% discount from the face value of factored receivables. Interest on advances of almost 3% over prime. Interest on surplus balances held by factor of about $\frac{1}{2}$% per month. Costs with factoring are higher than with pledging.	Certain accounts receivable are sold on a discount basis without recourse. Customers are notified of the arrangement. The factor provides more services than is the case with pledging.

Inventory Collateral

1. Floating liens	Commercial banks and commercial finance companies	About 4% above prime. Advance is about 40% of collateral value.	Collateral is all the inventory. There should be a stable inventory with many inexpensive items.
2. Trust receipts (floor planning)	Commercial banks and commercial finance companies	About 3% above prime. Advances ranging from 80% to 100% of collateral value.	Collateral is specific inventory that is typically expensive. Borrower retains collateral. Borrower remits proceeds to lender upon sale of the inventory.
3. Warehouse receipts	Commercial banks and commercial finance companies	About 4% above prime plus about a 2% warehouse fee. Advance of about 80% of collateral value.	Collateralized inventory is controlled by lender. A warehousing company issues a warehouse receipt held by the lender. The warehousing company acts as the lender's agent.

869

36

Term Loans and Leasing

This chapter considers intermediate-term loans primarily from banks and leasing arrangements to meet corporate financing needs. Intermediate-term loans include bank loans such as revolving credit, insurance company term loans, and equipment financing.

SHOULD YOU TAKE OUT AN INTERMEDIATE-TERM BANK LOAN?

Intermediate-term loans are loans with a maturity of more than one year. They are appropriate when short-term unsecured loans are not, such as when a business is acquired, new fixed assets are purchased, and long-term debt is retired. If a company wants to float long-term debt or issue common stock but conditions are unfavorable in the market, it may seek an intermediate loan to bridge the gap until long-term financing can be undertaken on favorable terms. A company may use extendible debt when there is a continuing financing need. This reduces the time and cost of many debt issuances.

The interest rate on an intermediate-term loan is typically more than on a short-term loan due to the longer maturity period. The interest rate may be either fixed or variable (according to, for instance, changes in the prime interest rate). The cost of an intermediate-term loan changes with the amount of the loan and the company's financial strength.

Ordinary intermediate-term loans are payable in periodic equal installments except for the last payment, which may be higher (referred to as a balloon payment). The schedule of loan payments should be based on the company's cash flow position to satisfy the debt. The periodic payment in a term loan equals:

$$\text{Periodic Payment} = \frac{\text{Amount of loan}}{\text{Present value factor}}$$

EXAMPLE 1

The company contracts to repay a term loan in five equal year-end installments. The amount of the loan is $150,000 and the interest rate is 10%. The payment each year is:

$$\frac{\$150,000}{3.7908(a)} = \$39,569.48$$

(a) Present value of annuity for five years at 10%.

The total interest on the loan is:

Total payments (5 × $39,569.48)	$197,847.40
Principal	150,000.00
Interest	$47,847.40

EXAMPLE 2

The company takes out a term loan in 20 year-end annual installments of $2,000 each. The interest rate is 12%. The amount of the loan is:

$$\$2,000 = \frac{\text{Amount of loan}}{7.4694(a)}$$

Amount of loan = $2,000 × 7.4694 = $14,939.80

(a) Present value of annuity for 20 years at 12%.

The amortization schedule for the first two years is:

Year	Payment	Interest(a)	Principal	Balance
0				$14,938.80
1	$2,000	$1,792.66	$207.34	14,731.46
2	2,000	1,767.78	232.22	14,499.24

(a) 12% times the balance of the loan at the beginning of the year.

What restrictions does the company face? Restrictive provisions to protect the lender in an intermediate-term loan agreement may be:

• General provisions used in most agreements which vary depending upon the company's situation. Examples are working capital and cash dividend requirements.

• Routine (uniform) provisions that are employed universally in most agreements. Examples are the payment of taxes and the maintenance of proper insurance to assure maximum lender protection.

• Specific provisions tailored to a particular situation. Examples are the placing of limits on future loans and the carrying of adequate life insurance for executives.

Advantages of Intermediate-Term Loans

• Flexibility in that the terms may be altered as the company's financing requirements change

• Financial information is kept confidential, since no public issuance is involved

• The loan may be arranged quickly, relative to a public offering

• Avoids the possible nonrenewal of a short-term loan

• Public flotation costs are not involved

Disadvantages of Intermediate-Term Loans

• Collateral and possible restrictive covenants are required, as opposed to none for commercial paper and unsecured short-term bank loans.

• Budgets and financial statements may have to be submitted periodically to the lender.

• "Kickers," or "sweeteners," such as stock warrants or a share of the profits are sometimes requested by the bank.

REVOLVING CREDIT

Revolving credit, usually used for seasonal financing, may have a 3-year maturity, but the notes evidencing the revolving credit are short-term, usually 90 days. The advantages of revolving credit are flexibility and ready availability. Within the time period of the revolving credit agreement, the company may renew a loan or enter into additional financing up to a specified maximum amount. Relative to a line of credit, there are typically fewer restrictions on revolving credit but at the cost of a slightly higher interest rate.

INSURANCE COMPANY TERM LOAN

Insurance companies and other institutional lenders may extend intermediate-term loans. Insurance companies typically accept loan maturity dates exceeding 10 years, but their rate of interest is often higher than that of bank loans. Insurance companies do not require compensating balances, but usually there is a prepayment penalty, which is typically not the case with a bank loan. A company may take out an insurance company loan when it desires a longer maturity range.

FINANCING WITH EQUIPMENT

Equipment may serve as collateral for a loan. An advance is made against the market value of the equipment. The more marketable the equipment is, the higher the advance will be. Also considered is the cost of selling the equipment. The repayment schedule is designed so that the market value of the equipment at any given time is in excess of the unpaid loan principal.

Equipment financing may be obtained from banks, finance companies, and manufacturers of equipment. Equipment loans may be secured by a chattel mortgage or a conditional sales contract. A chattel mortgage serves as a lien on property except for real estate. In a conditional sales contract, the seller of the equipment keeps title to it until the buyer has satisfied the terms; otherwise the seller will repossess the equipment. The buyer makes periodic payments to the seller over a specified time period. A conditional sales contract is generally used by a small company with a low credit rating.

Equipment trust certificates may be issued to finance the purchase of readily salable equipment. Preferably, the equipment should be general purpose and movable. A trust is formed to buy the equipment and lease it to the user. The trust issues the certificates to finance 75% to 85% of the purchase price and holds title to the equipment until *all* the certificates have been fully repaid at which time the title passes to the lessee.

ARE YOU BETTER OFF LEASING?

The parties in a lease are the lessor, who legally owns the property, and the lessee, who uses it in exchange for making rental payments. Of course, your company is the lessee.

The following types of leases exist:

1. *Operating (service) lease.* This type of lease includes both financing and maintenance services. The company leases property that is owned by the lessor. The lessor may be the manufacturer of the asset or it may be a leasing company that buys assets from the manufacturer to lease to others. The lease payments under the contract are typically not adequate to recover the full cost of the property. Maintenance and service are provided by the lessor and related costs are included in the lease payments. There usually exists a cancellation clause that provides the lessee with the right to cancel the contract and return the property prior to the expiration date of the agreement. The life of the contract is less than the economic life of the property.

2. *Financial lease.* This type of lease does not typically provide for maintenance services, is noncancelable, and the rental payments equal the full price of the leased property. The life of the contract approximates the life of the property.

3. *Sale and leaseback.* With this lease arrangement, the company sells an asset to another (usually a financial institution) and then leases it back. This allows the company to obtain cash from the sale and still have the property for use.

4. *Leveraged lease.* In a leveraged lease, there is a third party who serves as the lender. Here, the lessor borrows a significant portion of the purchase price (usually up to 80%) to buy the asset and provides the balance of the purchase price as his equity investment. The property is then leased to the lessee. As security for the loan, the lessor grants the long-term lender a mortgage on the asset and assigns the lease contract to the lender. Leverage leasing is a cost-effective alternative to debt financing when the lessee cannot use the full tax benefits of asset ownership.

Advantages of Leasing

- Immediate cash outlay is not required.
- Provides for temporary equipment need and flexibility in operations.
- Typically, a purchase option exists, allowing the company to obtain the property at a bargain price at the expiration of the lease. This provides the flexibility to make the purchase decision based on the value of the property at the termination date.
- Lessor's expert service is available.
- Typically, fewer financing restrictions (e.g., limitations on dividends) are placed by the lessor than are imposed when obtaining a loan to purchase the asset.
- Obligation for future rental payment does not have to be reported on the balance sheet if the lease is considered an operating lease.
- Leasing allows the company, in effect, to depreciate land, which is not allowed if land is purchased.
- In bankruptcy or reorganization, the maximum claim of lessors is three years of lease payments. With debt, creditors have a claim for the total amount of the unpaid financing.
- Eliminates equipment disposal.

Leasing may be more attractive than buying when a business cannot use all of the tax deductions and tax credits associated with the assets in a timely fashion.

Drawbacks to Leasing

- Higher cost in the long run than if the asset is bought. The lessee is not building equity.
- Interest cost of leasing is typically higher than the interest cost on debt.

• If the property reverts to the lessor at termination of the lease, the lessee must either sign a new lease or buy the property at higher current prices. Also, the salvage value of the property is realized by the lessor.
• May have to retain property no longer needed (i.e., obsolete equipment).
• Unable to make improvements to the leased property without the permission of the lessor.

EXAMPLE 3

The company enters into a lease for a $100,000 machine. It is to make 10 equal annual payments at year-end. The interest rate on the lease is 14%. The periodic payment equals:

$$\frac{\$100,000}{5.2161(a)} = \$19,171$$

(a) The present value of an ordinary annuity factor for $n = 10, i = 14\%$ is 5.2161.

EXAMPLE 4

Assume the same facts as Example 3, except that now the annual payments are to be made at the beginning of each year. The periodic payment equals:

Year	Factor
0	1.0
1–9	4.9464
	5.9464

$$\frac{\$100,000}{5.9464} = \$16,817$$

The interest rate associated with a lease agreement can also be computed. Divide the value of the leased property by the annual payment to obtain the factor, which is then used to find the interest rate with the help of an annuity table.

EXAMPLE 5

The company leased $300,000 of property and is to make equal annual payments at year-end of $40,000 for 11 years. The interest rate associated with the lease agreement is:

$$\frac{\$300,000}{\$40,000} = 7.5$$

Going to the present value of annuity table and looking across 11 years to a factor nearest to 7.5, we find 7.4987 at a 7% interest rate. Thus, the interest rate in the lease agreement is 7%.

The capitalized value of a lease can be found by dividing the annual lease payment by an appropriate present value of annuity factor.

EXAMPLE 6

Property is to be leased for eight years at an annual rental payment of $140,000 payable at the beginning of each year. The capitalization rate is 12%. The capitalized value of the lease is:

$$\frac{\text{Annual lease payment}}{\text{Present value factor}} = \frac{\$140,000}{1 + 4.5638} = \$25,163$$

Lease-Purchase Decision

Often, a decision must be made as to whether it is better to buy an asset or lease it. Present value analysis may be used to determine the cheapest alternative (see Chapter 19).

37

Deciding on Long-Term Financing

Long-term financing generally refers to financing for more than five years. This chapter discusses the what, why, and how to of equity and long-term debt financing. Equity financing consists of issuing preferred stock and common stock while long-term debt financing consists primarily of issuing bonds. Long-term financing is often used to finance long-lived assets (e.g., land, plant) or construction projects. The more capital intensive the business, the greater should be the reliance on long-term debt and equity. First, the role of the investment banker is mentioned. Also, a comparison of public versus private placement of securities is given. The advantages and disadvantages of issuing long-term debt, preferred stock, and common stock are presented. We will discuss what financing strategy is most appropriate under a given set of circumstances that your company is experiencing. The financing policies should be in response to the overall strategic direction of the company.

A company's mix of long-term funds is referred to as the *capital structure.* The ideal capital structure maximizes the total value of the company and minimizes the overall cost of capital. The formulation of an appropriate capital structure should take into account the nature of the business and industry, strategic business plan of the company, current and historical capital structure, and planned growth rate.

INVESTMENT BANKING

Investment banking involves the sale of a security issue. Investment bankers conduct the following activities:

879

- *Underwriting.* The investment banker buys a new security issue, pays the issuer, and markets the securities. The underwriter's compensation is the difference between the price at which the securities are sold to the public, and the price paid to the issuing company.
- *Distributing.* The investment banker markets the company's security issue.
- *Advice.* The investment banker gives advice to the company regarding the optimal way to obtain funds. The investment banker is knowledgeable with the alternative sources of long-term funds, debt and equity markets, and Securities and Exchange Commission (SEC) regulations.
- *Providing Funds.* The investment banker provides funds to the company during the distribution period.

When several investment bankers form a group because a particular issue is large and/or risky, they are termed a *syndicate.* A syndicate is a temporary association of investment bankers brought together for the purpose of selling new securities. One investment banker among the group will be selected to manage the syndicate (originating house) and underwrite the major amount of the issue. One bid price for the issue is made on behalf of the group, but the terms and features of the issue are set by the company.

The distribution channels for a new security issue appear in Figure 1.

In another approach to investment banking, the investment banker agrees to sell the company's securities on a best-efforts basis, or as an agent. Here, the investment banker does not act as underwriter but instead sells the stock and receives a sales commission. An investment banker may insist on this type of arrangement when he or she has reservations about the success of the security offering.

In selecting an investment banker for a new issue of securities, the following are positive signs:

- Low spread
- Good references

Figure 1. Distribution Channels for a New Security Issue

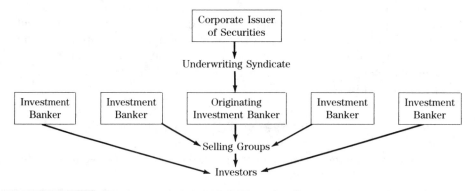

- Able to float many shares at a good price
- Institutional and retail support
- Good after market performance
- Wide geographic distribution
- Attractive secondary markets
- Knowledge of market, regulations, industry, and company

SHOULD SECURITIES BE PUBLICLY OR PRIVATELY PLACED?

Equity and debt securities may be issued either publicly or privately. A consideration in determining whether to issue securities to the public or privately is the type and amount of required financing.

In a public issuance, the shares are bought by the general public. In a private placement, the company issues securities directly to either one or a few large investors. The large investors are financial institutions such as insurance companies, pension plans, and commercial banks.

Private placement has the following advantages relative to a public issuance:

- The flotation cost is less. Flotation cost is the expense of registering and selling the stock issue. Examples are brokerage commissions and underwriting fees. The flotation cost for common stock exceeds that for preferred stock. Flotation cost expressed as a percentage of gross proceeds is higher for smaller issues than for larger ones.
- It avoids SEC filing requirements.
- It avoids the disclosure of information to the public.
- There is less time involved in obtaining funds.
- There is greater flexibility.
- It may not be practical to issue securities in the public market if the company is so small that an investment banker would not find it profitable.
- The company's credit rating may be low, and as a result investors may not be interested in purchasing securities when the money supply is limited.

Private placement has the following drawbacks relative to a public issuance:

- There is a higher interest rate due to less liquidity of a debt issue relative to public issuance.
- There is typically a shorter maturity period than for a public issue.
- It is more difficult to obtain significant amounts of money privately than publicly.
- Large investors typically use stringent credit standards requiring the company to be in strong financial condition. In addition, there are more restrictive terms.
- Large institutional investors may watch more closely the company's activities than smaller investors in a public issue.

• Large institutional investors are more capable of obtaining voting control of the company.

Most private placements involve debt securities. In fact, only about 2% of common stock is placed privately. The private market is more receptive to smaller issues (e.g., several million dollars). Small and medium size companies typically find it cheaper to place debt privately than publicly, especially when the issue is $5 million or less.

TYPES OF LONG-TERM DEBT AND WHEN EACH SHOULD BE USED

We now discuss the characteristics, advantages, and disadvantages of long-term debt financing. In addition to the various types of debt instruments, the circumstances in which a particular type of debt is most appropriate are mentioned. Sources of long-term debt include mortgages and bonds. The amount of debt a company may have depends largely on its available collateral. Bond refunding is also highlighted.

What You Should Know About Mortgages

Mortgages are notes payable that have as collateral real assets and require periodic payments. Mortgages can be issued to finance the purchase of assets, construction of plant, and modernization of facilities. The bank will require that the value of the property exceed the mortgage on that property. Most mortgage loans are between 70% and 90% of the value of the collateral. Mortgages may be obtained from a bank, life insurance company, or other financial institution. It is easier to obtain mortgage loans for multiple-use real assets than for single-use real assets.

There are two types of mortgages: a senior mortgage, which has first claim on assets and earnings, and a junior mortgage, which has a subordinate lien.

A mortgage may have a closed-end provision that prevents the company from issuing additional debt of the same priority against the specific property. If the mortgage is open-ended, the company can issue additional first-mortgage bonds against the property.

Mortgages have a number of advantages, including favorable interest rates, less financing restrictions, extended maturity date for loan repayment, and relatively easy availability. A drawback is the collateral requirement.

When to Use Bonds

Long-term debt principally takes the form of bonds payable and loans payable. A *bond* is a certificate indicating that the company has borrowed a given sum of money and agrees to repay it. A written agreement, called an *indenture,* describes the features of the bond issue (e.g., payment dates, call and conversion privileges (if any), and restrictions). The indenture is a contract between the company, the bondholder, and the trustee. The trustee makes sure that the company meets the terms of the bond contract. In many instances, the trustee is the trust department of a commercial bank. Although the trustee is an agent for the bondholder, it is selected by the company prior to the issuance of the bonds. The indenture provides for certain restrictions on the company such as a limitation on dividends and minimum working capital requirements. If a provision of the indenture is violated, the bonds are in default. **Note:** Covenants should be flexible because of the quick changes in the financial world. The indenture may also have a negative pledge clause, which precludes the issuance of new debt taking priority over existing debt in the event of liquidation. The clause can apply to assets currently held as well as to assets that may be purchased in the future.

Tip: Try to avoid issuing a bond where there is a large Treasury financing because that can temporarily depress the private debt market. The price of a bond depends on several factors such as its maturity date, interest rate, and collateral. In selecting a maturity period for long-term debt, consider the debt repayment schedule which should not be overloaded at one time. Also, if a company's credit rating is expected to get better in the near term, short-term debt should be issued because the company will be able to refinance at a lower interest rate.

Bond prices and market interest rates are inversely related. For example, as market interest rates increase, the price of the existing bond falls because investors can invest in new bonds paying higher interest rates.

Types of Bonds

The various types of bonds that may be issued by a company are:

• *Debentures.* Because debentures are unsecured (no collateral) debt, they can be issued only by large, financially strong companies with excellent credit ratings.

• *Subordinated Debentures.* The claims of the holders of these bonds are subordinated to those of senior creditors. Debt having a prior claim over the subordinated debentures is set forth in the bond indenture. Typically, in liquidation, subordinated debentures come after short-term debt.

• *Mortgage Bonds.* These are bonds secured by real assets. The first-mortgage claim must be met before a distribution is made to a second-mortgage claim. There may be several mortgages for the same property (e.g., building).

• *Collateral Trust Bonds.* The collateral for these bonds is the company's security investments in other companies (bonds or stocks), which are given to a trustee for safekeeping.

• *Convertible Bonds.* These may be converted to stock at a later date based on a specified conversion ratio. The conversion ratio equals the par value of the convertible security divided by the conversion price. Convertible bonds are typically issued in the form of subordinated debentures. Convertible bonds are more marketable and are typically issued at a lower interest rate than are regular bonds because they offer the conversion right to common stock. Of course, if bonds are converted to stock, debt repayment is not involved. A convertible bond is a quasi-equity security because its market value is tied to its value if converted rather than as a bond. The degree of importance of the reasons to issue convertible bonds appears in Exhibit 1. Convertible bonds are discussed in detail in Chapter 38.

• *Income Bonds.* These bonds pay interest only if there is a profit. The interest may be cumulative or noncumulative. If cumulative, the interest accumulates regardless of earnings, and if bypassed, must be paid in a later year when adequate earnings exist. Income bonds are appropriate for companies with large fixed capital investments and large fluctuations in earnings, or for emerging companies with the expectation of low earnings in the early years.

• *Guaranteed Bonds.* These are debt issued by one party with payment guaranteed by another.

• *Serial Bonds.* A portion of these bonds comes due each year. At the time serial bonds are issued, a schedule shows the yields, interest rates, and prices for each maturity. The interest rate on the shorter maturities is lower than the interest rate on the longer maturities because less uncertainty exists regarding the future.

• *Deep Discount Bonds.* These bonds have very low interest rates and thus are issued at substantial discounts from face value. The return to the holder comes primarily from appreciation in price rather than from interest payments. The bonds are volatile in price. Since these bonds are typically callable at par, this reduces the refunding flexibility of the issuer.

• *Zero Coupon Bonds.* These bonds do not provide for interest. The return to the holder is in the form of appreciation in price. **Note:** Lower interest rates may be available for zero coupon bonds (and deep discount bonds) because of the lack of callability and possible foreign tax laws.

• *Variable-Rate Bonds.* The interest rates on the bonds are adjusted periodically to changes in money market conditions (e.g., prime interest rate). These bonds are popular when there is uncertainty of future interest rates and inflation.

• *Deferred Interest Bonds.* The periodic interest payments are fully or partially deferred in the first few years. The deferred period allows the issuer to improve financial performance, sell under-performing assets, and refinance loan agreements.

• *Industrial Revenue Bonds.* The company offers tax-free interest to lenders. These bonds can be issued at a lower cost because of the resulting tax-exemption. However, there are many conditions imposed upon the company issuing these bonds by the government. For example, the types of facilities that may be funded are restricted, usually these are public service facilities. For a more detailed discussion on this type of bond, see John Hennessy, Handbook of Long-term Financing, Prentice-Hall, 1986, Chapter 6.

• *Eurobonds.* Eurobonds are issued outside the country in whose currency the bonds are denominated. Eurobonds cannot be issued to U.S. investors but only to foreign investors. The reason is that Eurobonds are not registered with

Exhibit 1

DEGREE OF IMPORTANCE OF REASONS TO ISSUE CONVERTIBLE BONDS

Reason	Not Important (1.0)	Slightly Important (2.0)	Important (3.0)	Very Important (4.0)	Average For All Responses*
1. To reduce the *issuing* cost of the debt issue.					1.64
2. To reduce the *interest* cost of the debt issue.					3.31
3. To provide a means for selling common stock at a price above the existing market (i.e., delayed equity financing).					2.81
4. To enhance the salability or marketability of the issue.					3.13
5. Advice and counsel of an investment banking firm.					2.68
6. Institutional investors restricted from purchasing common stock.					1.42
7. To avoid immediate dilution of earnings per share.					2.08
8. High interest cost of debt at time of issue.					2.37
9. Depressed common stock price at time of issue.					1.87
10. High debt to equity or low interest coverage levels.					1.71

Source: Ronald W. Melicher and J. Ronald Hoffmeister, "The Issue is Convertible Bonds," *Financial Executive* (November, 1977), pp. 46–50.

the S.E.C. The bonds are typically in bearer form. **Tip:** Check to see if at the present time the Eurodollar market will give the company a lower cost option than the U.S. market. These bonds typically can only be issued by high quality borrowers.

A summary of the characteristics and priority claims associated with bonds appears in Table 1.

If the company is small and emerging with an unproven track record, it may have to issue what is commonly referred to as "junk bonds" (high-yielding risky bonds rated by Standard and Poor's as B+ or below or Moody's Investors Service as B 1 or below). These are considered "non-investment grade" bonds.

How Are Bonds Rated?

Financial advisory services (e.g., Standard and Poor's, Moody's) rate publicly traded bonds according to risk in terms of the receipt of principal and interest. An inverse relationship exists between the quality of a bond issue and its yield. That is, low-quality bonds will have a higher yield than high-quality bonds. Hence, a risk-return tradeoff exists for the bondholder. Bond ratings are important because they influence marketability and the cost associated with the bond issue. Bond ratings are fully discussed in Chapter 34.

What Are the Advantages and Disadvantages to Debt Financing?

The advantage of issuing long-term debt include:

- Interest is tax-deductible, while dividends are not.
- Bondholders do not participate in superior earnings of the company.
- The repayment of debt is in cheaper dollars during inflation.
- There is no dilution of company control.
- Financing flexibility can be achieved by including a call provision in the bond indenture. A call provision allows the company to pay the debt before the expiration date of the bond.
- It may safeguard the company's future financial stability, for instance, in times of tight money markets when short-term loans are not available.

The disadvantages of issuing long-term debt include:

- Interest charges must be met regardless of the company's earnings.
- Debt must be repaid at maturity.
- Higher debt infers greater financial risk, which may increase the cost of financing.
- Indenture provisions may place stringent restrictions on the company.
- Overcommitments may arise due to forecasting errors.

How does issuing debt stack up against issuing equity securities? The advantages of issuing debt rather than equity securities are that interest is tax deductible whereas dividends are not, during inflation the payback will be in

Table 1

SUMMARY OF CHARACTERISTICS AND PRIORITY CLAIMS OF BONDS

Bond Type	Characteristics	Priority of Lender's Claims
Debentures	Available only to financially strong companies. Convertible bonds are typically debentures	General creditor
Subordinated Debentures	Comes after senior debt holders	General creditor
Mortgage Bonds	Collateral is real property or buildings	Paid from the proceeds from the sale of the mortgaged assets. If any deficiency exists, general creditor status applies
Collateral Trust Bonds	Secured by stock and (or) bonds owned by the issuer. Collateral value is usually 30% more than bond value	Paid from the proceeds of stock and (or) bond that is collateralized. If there is a deficiency, general creditor status applies.
Income Bonds	Interest is only paid if there is net income. Often issued when a company is in reorganization because of financial problems.	General creditor
Deep Discount (and Zero Coupon) Bonds	Issued at very low or no (zero) coupon rates. Issued at prices significantly below face value. Usually callable at par value.	Unsecured or secured status may apply depending on the features of the issue
Variable-rate Bonds	Coupon rate changes within limits based on changes in money or capital market rates. Appropriate when uncertainty exists regarding inflation and future interest rates. Because of the automatic adjustment to changing market conditions, the bonds sell near face value	Unsecured or secured status may apply depending on the features of the issue

887

cheaper dollars, no dilution of voting control occurs, and flexibility in financing can be achieved by including a call provision in the bond indenture. The disadvantages of debt incurrence relative to issuing equity securities are that fixed interest charges and principal repayment must be met irrespective of the firm's cash flow position, and stringent indenture restrictions often exist.

The proper mixture of long-term debt to equity depends on company organization, credit availability, and after-tax cost of financing. Where a high degree of debt already exists, the company should take steps to minimize other corporate risks.

When should long-term debt be issued? Debt financing is more appropriate when:

• The interest rate on debt is less than the rate of return earned on the money borrowed. By using other people's money (OPM), the after-tax profit of the company will increase. Stockholders have made an extra profit with no extra investment!

• Stability in revenue and earnings exist so that the company will be able to meet interest and principal payments in both good and bad years. However, cyclical factors should not scare a company away from having any debt. The important thing is to accumulate no more interest and principal repayment obligations than can reasonably be satisfied in bad times as well as good.

• There is a satisfactory profit margin so that earnings exist to meet debt obligations.

• There is a good liquidity and cash flow position.

• The debt/equity ratio is low so the company can handle additional obligations.

• The risk level of the firm is low.

• Stock prices are currently depressed so that it does not pay to issue common stock at the present time.

• Control considerations are a primary factor so if common stock was issued greater control might fall in the wrong hands.

• The firm is mature.

• Inflation is expected so that debt can be paid back in cheaper dollars.

• There is a lack of competition (e.g., barriers of entry in the industry exist).

• The markets for the company's products are expanding and the company is growing.

• The tax rate is high so there is a benefit from the tax deductibility of interest.

• Bond indenture restrictions are not burdensome.

• Money market trends and availability of financing are favorable.

Project financing is tied to particular projects and may be suitable for large, self-contained undertakings perhaps involving joint ventures.

Tip: If your company is experiencing financial difficulties, it may wish to refinance short-term debt on a long-term basis such as by extending the maturity dates of existing loans. This may alleviate current liquidity and cash flow problems.

As the default risk of your company becomes higher, so will the interest rate to compensate for the greater risk.

Recommendation: When a high degree of debt (financial leverage) exists, try to reduce other risks (e.g., product risk) so that total corporate risk is controlled. The amount of leverage in the capital structure depends upon the company's propensity for risk and the debt levels at competing companies.

The threat of financial distress or even bankruptcy is the ultimate limitation on leverage. Beyond a debt limit, the tax savings on interest expense will be offset by an increased interest rate demanded by creditors for the increased risk. Excessive debt will lower the market price of stock because greater risk is associated with the company.

Note: Smaller companies with thinly traded stocks often issue debt and equity securities together in the form of units. A company may elect to issue units instead of convertible debt if it desires to increase its common equity immediately.

Long-term financing may be from unexpected sources. Is governmental financing available in terms of grants, low interest rate loans, and tax relief? Is export financing available in foreign countries? Can the company use current and/or interest rate swaps? Will the supplier or customer provide the company with financing?

EXAMPLE 1

Your company has $10 million of 12% mortgage bonds outstanding. The indenture permits additional bonds to be issued provided all of the following conditions are met:

1. The pretax times-interest-earned ratio exceeds 5.
2. Book value of the mortgaged assets are at least 1.5 times the amount of debt.
3. The debt/equity ratio is below 0.6.

The following additional information is provided:

1. Income before tax is $9 million.
2. Equity is $30 million.
3. Book value of assets is $34 million.
4. There are no sinking fund payments for the current year. (A sinking fund is money set aside to be used to retire a bond issue.)
5. Half the proceeds of a new issue would be added to the base of mortgaged assets.

Only $7 million more of 12% debt can be issued based on the following calculations:

1. The before-tax times-interest-earned ratio is:

$$\frac{\text{Income before tax and interest}}{\text{Interest}} = \frac{\$9,000,000 + \$1,200,000''}{\$1,200,000 + 0.12X} = 5$$

$$\frac{\$10,200,000}{\$1,200,000 + 0.12X} = 5$$

$$\$10,200,000 = \$6,000,000 + 0.60X$$

$$X = \$7,000,000$$

"Interest is:

$$\$10,000,000 \times 0.12 = \$1,200,000$$

2. $$\frac{\text{Book value of mortgaged assets}}{\text{Debt}} = \frac{\$34,000,000 + 0.5X}{\$10,000,000 + X} = 1.5$$

$$\$34,000,000 + 0.5X = \$15,000,000 + 1.5X$$
$$X = \$19,000,000$$

3. $$\frac{\text{Debt}}{\text{Equity}} = \frac{\$10,000,000 + X}{\$30,000,000} = 0.6$$
$$\$10,000,000 + X = \$18,000,000$$
$$X = \$8,000,000$$

The first condition is controlling and hence limits the amount of new debt to $7 million.

Should Bond Refunding Take Place?

Bonds may be refunded before maturity through either the issuance of a serial bond or exercising a call privilege on a straight bond. The issuance of serial bonds allows the company to refund the debt over the life of the issue. A call feature in a bond enables the company to retire it before the expiration date. The call feature is included in many corporate bond issues.

When future interest rates are expected to drop, a call provision is recommended. Such a provision enables the firm to buy back the higher-interest bond and issue a lower-interest one. The timing for the refunding depends on expected future interest rates. A call price is typically set in excess of the face value of the bond. The resulting call premium equals the difference between the call price and the maturity value. The company pays the premium to the bondholder in order to acquire the outstanding bonds prior to the maturity date. The call premium is usually equal to one year's interest if the bond is called in the first year, and it declines at a constant rate each year thereafter. Also involved in selling a new issue are flotation costs (e.g., brokerage commissions, printing costs).

A bond with a call provision typically will have a lower offering price, and will be issued at an interest rate higher than one without the call provision. The investor prefers not to have a situation where the company can buy back the bond at its option prior to maturity. The investor would obviously desire to hold onto a high-interest bond when prevailing interest rates are low.

EXAMPLE 2

A $100,000, 8%, 10-year bond is issued at 94%. The call price is 103%. Three years after the issue the bond is called. The call premium is equal to:

Call price	$103,000
Face value of bond	100,000
Call premium	$3,000

The desirability of refunding a bond requires present value analysis, which was discussed in Chapter 19.

EXAMPLE 3

Your company has a $20 million, 10% bond issue outstanding that has 10 years to maturity. The call premium is 7% of face value. New 10-year bonds in the amount of $20 million can be issued at an 8% interest rate. Flotation costs of the new issue are $600,000.

Refunding of the original bond issue should occur as shown below.

Old interest payments ($20,000,000 × 0.10)	$2,000,000
New interest payments ($20,000,000 × 0.08)	1,600,000
Annual Savings	$ 400,000
Call premium ($20,000,000 × 0.07)	$1,400,000
Flotation cost	600,000
Total cost	$2,000,000

Year	Calculation	Present Value
0	− $2,000,000 × 1	− $2,000,000
1–10	$ 400,000 × 6.71(a)	2,684,000
Net Present value		$ 684,000

(a) Present value of annuity factor for $i = 8\%$, $n = 10$

EXAMPLE 4

Your company is considering calling a $10 million, 20-year bond that was issued five years ago at a nominal interest rate of 10%. The call price on the bonds is 105. The bonds were initially sold at 90. The discount on bonds payable at the time of sale was, therefore, $1 million and the net proceeds received were $9 million. The initial flotation cost was $100,000. The firm is considering issuing $10 million, 8%, 15-year bonds and using the net proceeds to retire the old bonds. The new bonds will be issued at face value. The flotation cost for the new issue is $150,000. The company's tax rate is 46%. The after-tax cost of new debt ignoring flotation costs, is 4.32% (8% × 54%). With the flotation cost, the after-tax cost of new debt is estimated at 5%. There is an overlap period of three months in which interest must be paid on the old and new bonds.

The initial cash outlay is:

Cost to call old bonds	
($10,000,000 × 105%)	$10,500,00
Cost to issue new bond	150,000
Interest on old bonds for overlap period	
($10,000,000 × 10% × 3/12)	250,000
Initial cash outlay	$10,900,000

The initial cash inflow is:

Proceeds from selling new bond		$10,000,000
Tax-deductible items		
Call premium	$ 500,000	
Unamortized discount		
($1,000,000 × 15/20)	750,000	
Overlap in interest		
($10,000,000 × 10% × 3/12)	250,000	
Unamortized issue cost of old bond		
($100,000 × 15/20)	75,000	
Total tax-deductible items	$1,575,000	
Tax rate	× 0.46	
Tax savings		724,500
Initial cash inflow		$10,724,500

The *net* initial cash outlay is therefore:

Initial cash outlay	$10,900,000
Initial cash inflow	10,724,500
Net initial cash outlay	$ 175,500

The annual cash flow for the old bond is:

Interest (10% × $10,000,000		$1,000,000
Less: Tax-deductible items		
Interest	$1,000,000	
Amortization of discount		
($1,000,000/20 years)	50,000	

Amortization of issue cost ($100,000/20 years)	5,000	
Total tax-deductible items	$1,055,000	
Tax rate	×0.46	
Tax savings		485,300
Annual cash outflow with old bond		$ 514,700

The annual cash flow for the new bond is:

Interest		$800,000
Less: Tax-deductible items		
Interest	$800,000	
Amortization of issue cost ($150,000/15 years)	10,000	
Total tax-deductible items	$810,000	
Tax rate	×0.46	
Tax savings		372,600
Annual cash outflow with new bond		$427,400

The net annual cash savings with the new bond compared to the old bond is:

Annual cash outflow with old bond	$514,700
Annual cash outflow with new bond	427,400
Net annual cash savings	$ 87,300

The net present value associated with the refunding is:

	Calculation	Present Value
Year 0	− $175,500 × 1	− $175,500
Year 1–15	$87,300 × 10.38ª	+ 906,174
Net present value		$730,674

Present value of annuity factor for $i = 5\%$, $n = 15$.

Since a positive net present value exists, the refunding of the old bond should be made.

Sinking fund requirements may exist in a bond issue. With a sinking fund, the company puts aside money to buy and retire part of a bond issue each year. Usually, there is a mandatory fixed amount that must be retired, but occasionally the retirement may relate to the company's sales or profit for the current year. If a sinking fund payment is not made, the bond issue may be in default.

In many instances, the company can handle the sinking fund in one of the following two ways:

1. It can call a given percentage of the bonds at a specified price each year, for instance, 10% of the original amount at a price of $1,070.
2. It can buy its own bonds on the open market.

The least costly alternative should be selected. If interest rates have increased, the price of the bonds will have decreased, and the open market option should be employed. If interest rates have decreased, the bond prices will have increased, and thus calling the bonds is preferred.

EXAMPLE 5

Your company has to reduce bonds payable by $300,000. The call price is 104. The market price of the bonds is 103. The company will opt to buy back the bonds on the open market because it is less expensive, as indicated below:

Call price ($300,000 × 104%)	$312,000
Purchase on open market ($300,000 × 103%)	309,000
Advantage of purchasing bonds on the open market	$ 3,000

VARIABLE COUPON RENEWABLE NOTES

Variable coupon renewable notes are long-term financing vehicles with the prospect of significant cost savings to the issuing company. They are generally for 50 years and contain a put feature permitting note holders to accept a reduced coupon spread for the last three payments. The coupon is changed weekly based on a spread over the rates for 3-month treasury bills. Interest is paid quarterly. The issuing company may use this as a long-term financing source while paying short-term interest rates.

FEDERAL LOAN PROGRAMS

The company may elect to take advantage of federal loan programs, where appropriate. The three major loan agencies are:

• *Small Business Association* (SBA). The SBA will lend money only for a feasible project and where the security is adequate. Bond financing at a reasonable interest rate must not be available. The bank must confirm that it will not participate without an SBA guarantee.

• *Economic Development Administration.* This agency provides financial assistance if the company is upgrading an area economically by providing well-paying jobs for local residents. The company must expand or locate new facilities in areas of high unemployment or low family income.

• *Farmers Home Administration.* This agency encourages the creation and maintenance of employment in rural communities.

THE ISSUANCE OF EQUITY SECURITIES

The sources of equity financing consist of preferred stock and common stock. The advantages and disadvantages of issuing preferred and common are addressed, along with the various circumstances in which either financing source is most suited. Stock rights are also described.

When to Use Preferred Stock

Preferred stock is a hybrid between bonds and common stock. Preferred stock comes after debt but before common stock in liquidation and in the distribution of earnings. Preferred stock may be issued when the cost of common stock is high. The optimal time to issue preferred stock is when the company has excessive debt and an issue of common stock might result in control problems. Preferred stock is a more expensive way to raise capital than a bond issue because the dividend payment is not tax-deductible. Many utilities offer preferred stock.

Preferred stock may be cumulative or noncumulative. Cumulative preferred stock means that if any prior year's dividend payments have been missed, they must be paid before dividends can be paid to common stockholders. If preferred dividends are in arrears for a long time, the company may find it difficult to resume its dividend payments to common stockholders. With noncumulative preferred stock, the company need not pay missed preferred dividends. Preferred stock dividends are limited to the rate specified, which is based on the total par value of the outstanding shares. Most preferred stock is cumulative.

Participating preferred stock means that if declared dividends exceed the amount typically given to preferred stockholders and common stockholders, the preferred and common stockholders will participate in the excess dividends. Unless stated otherwise, the distribution of the excess dividends will be based on the relative total par values. Nonparticipating preferred stock does not participate with common stock in excess dividends. Most preferred stock is nonparticipating.

Dividend concepts are discussed in Chapter 40.

Preferred stock may be callable, which means that the company can purchase it back at a subsequent date at a specified call price. The call provision is advantageous when interest rates decline, since the company has the option of discontinuing payments of dividends at a rate that has become excessive by buying back preferred stock that was issued when bond interest rates were high. Unlike bonds, preferred stock rarely has a maturity date. However, if preferred stock has a sinking fund associated with it, this, in effect, establishes a maturity date for repayment.

There are possible variations to preferred stock issues. Limited life preferred stock has a specified maturity date or can be redeemed at the holder's option. Perpetual preferred stock automatically converts to common stock at a given date. There are also preferred stock with "floating rate" dividends so as to keep the preferred stock at par by altering the dividend rate.

In bankruptcy, preferred stockholders are paid after creditors and before common stockholders. In such a case, preferred stockholders receive the par value of their shares, dividends in arrears, and the current year's dividend. Any asset balance then goes to the common stockholders.

The cost of preferred stock usually follows changes in interest rates. Hence, the cost of preferred stock will most likely be low when interest rates are low. When the cost of common stock is high, preferred stock issuance may be achieved at a lower cost.

A preferred stock issue has the following advantages:

• Preferred dividends do not have to be paid (important during periods of financial distress), whereas interest on debt must be paid.

• Preferred stockholders cannot force the company into bankruptcy.

• Preferred shareholders do not share in unusually high profits because the common stockholders are the real owners of the business.

• If the company is a growth one, it can generate better earnings for its original owners by issuing preferred stock having a fixed dividend rate than by issuing common stock.

• Preferred stock issuance does not dilute the ownership interest of common stockholders in terms of earnings participation and voting rights.

• The company does not have to collateralize its assets as it may have to do if bonds are issued.

• The debt to equity ratio is improved.

A preferred stock issue has the following disadvantages:

• Preferred stock requires a higher yield than bonds because of greater risk.

• Preferred dividends are not tax-deductible.

• There are higher flotation costs than with bonds.

The advantages of preferred stock over bonds is that the company can omit a dividend readily, no maturity date exists, and no sinking fund is required. Preferred stock also has a number of advantages over common stock. It avoids dilution of control and the equal participation in profits that are afforded to common stockholders. Disadvantages of preferred stock issuance compared to bonds are that it requires a higher yield than debt because it is more risky to the holder. Also, dividends are not tax deductible.

The Issuance of Common Stock

Common stock is the residual equity ownership in the business. Common stockholders have voting power but come after preferred stockholders in receiving dividends and in liquidation. Common stock does not involve fixed charges, maturity dates, or sinking fund requirements.

In a few cases, a company may issue different classes of common stock. Class A is stock issued to the public and typically has no dividends. However, it usually has voting rights. Class B stock is typically kept by the company's organizers. Dividends are usually not paid on it until the company has generated adequate earnings. Voting rights are provided in order for control to be maintained.

The price of common stock moves in the opposite direction as market interest rates. For example, if market interest rates increase, stock prices fall because investors will transfer funds out of stock into higher yielding money market instruments and bank accounts. Further, higher interest rates make it costly for a company to borrow resulting in lower profits and the resulting decline in stock price.

Common stock may basically be issued in one of the following ways:

- *Broad syndication.* This is the most common method because it gives the issuer the greatest control over distribution and thus probably achieves the highest net price. It also provides the most public exposure. The drawbacks are that it may take longer and there are high transaction costs.
- *Limited distribution.* There are a limited number of underwriters involved in the issuance.
- *Sole distribution.* Only one underwriter is used which may result in unsold shares. The company has less control in the distribution process. This will lower transaction costs and is fast.
- *Dribble out.* The company periodically issues stock over time resulting in an average price. This approach is not recommended because of the high associated costs, and it may depress stock price because of the constant issuance of shares.

In timing a public issuance of common stock, the following should be noted:

- Do not offer shares near the expiration date for options on the company's shares since the option related transaction may affect share price.
- Offer higher yielding common stock just before the ex-dividend date so investors will be attracted to it.
- Issue common stock when there is little competition of share issuance by other companies in the industry.
- Issue shares in bull markets and refrain from issuing them in bear markets.

A number of options exist for equity financing in the case of small businesses, including:

- Venture capital (investor) groups who invest in typically high risk ventures
- Issuances directly to institutional investors (e.g., insurance companies, banks)
- Issuances to relatives or friends
- Issuances to major customers and suppliers

A determination of the number of shares that must be issued to raise adequate funds to satisfy a capital budget may be needed.

EXAMPLE 7

Your company currently has 650,000 shares of common stock outstanding. The capital budget for the upcoming year is $1.8 million.

Assuming new stock may be issued for $16 a share, the number of shares that must be issued to provide the necessary funds to meet the capital budget is:

$$\frac{\text{Funds Needed}}{\text{Market Price Per Share}} = \frac{\$1,800,000}{\$16} = 112,500 \text{ shares}$$

EXAMPLE 8

Your company wants to raise $3 million in its first public issue of common stock. After its issuance, the total market value of stock is expected to be $7 million. Currently, there are 140,000 outstanding shares that are closely held.

We want to compute the number of new shares that must be issued to raise the $3 million.

The new shares will have 3/7 ($3 million/$7 million) of the outstanding shares after the stock issuance. Thus, current stockholders will be holding 4/7 of the shares.

140,000 shares = 4/7 of the total shares
Total shares = 245,000
New shares = 3/7 × 245,000 = 105,000 shares

After the stock issuance, the expected price per share is:

$$\text{Price per share} = \frac{\text{Market Value}}{\text{Shares Outstanding}} = \frac{\$7,000,000}{245,000} = \$28.57$$

A company that initially issues its common stock publicly is referred to as "going public." The estimated price per share to sell the securities is equal to:

$$\frac{\text{Anticipated market value of the company}}{\text{Total outstanding shares}}$$

For an established company, the market price per share can be determined as follows:

$$\frac{\text{Expected dividend}}{\text{Cost of capital} - \text{Growth rate in dividends}}$$

EXAMPLE 9

Your company expected the dividend for the year to be $10 a share. The cost of capital is 13%. The growth rate in dividends is expected to be constant at 8%. The price per share is:

$$\frac{\text{Price per}}{\text{Share}} = \frac{\text{Expected dividend}}{\substack{\text{Cost of capital} - \\ \text{growth rate in dividends}}}$$

$$= \frac{\$10}{0.13 - 0.08} = \frac{\$10}{0.05} = \$200$$

Another approach to pricing the share of stock for an existing company is through the use of the price/earnings (P/E) ratio, which is equal to:

$$\frac{\text{Market price per share}}{\text{Earnings per share}}$$

EXAMPLE 10

Your company's earnings per share is $7. It is expected that the company's stock should sell at eight times its earnings. The market price per share is therefore:

$$\text{P/E} = \frac{\text{Market Price per Share}}{\text{Earnings per Share}}$$

$$\text{Market price per share} = \text{P/E multiple} \times \text{earnings per share}$$
$$= 8 \times \$7 = \$56$$

You may want to determine the market value of your company's stock. There are a number of different ways to accomplish this.

EXAMPLE 11

Assuming an indefinite stream of future dividends of $300,000 and a required return rate of 14%, the market value of the stock equals:

$$\text{Market value} = \frac{\text{Expected dividends}}{\text{Rate of return}} = \frac{\$300,000}{0.14} = \$2,142,857$$

If there are 200,000 shares, the market price per share is:

$$\text{Market value} = \frac{\$2,142,857}{200,000} = \underline{\$10.71}$$

EXAMPLE 12

Your company is considering a public issue of its securities. The average price/earnings multiple in the industry is 15. The company's earnings are $400,000. There will be 100,000 shares outstanding after the issuance of the stock. The expected price per share is:

$$\text{Total market value} = \text{Net income} \times \text{Price/earnings multiple}$$
$$= \$400,000 \times 15 = \$6,000,000$$

$$\text{Price per Share} = \frac{\text{Market value}}{\text{Shares}} = \frac{\$6,000,000}{100,000} = \$60$$

EXAMPLE 13

Your company issues 400,000 new shares of common stock to current stockholders at a $25 price per share. The price per share before the new issue was $29. Currently, there are 500,000 outstanding shares. The expected price per share after the new issue is:

Value of outstanding shares (500,000 × $29)	$14,500,000
Value of newly issued shares (400,000 × $25)	10,000,000
Value of entire issue	$24,500,000

$$\text{Value per share} = \frac{\text{Value of entire shares}}{\text{Total number of shares}} = \frac{\$24,500,000}{900,000} = \$27.22$$

EXAMPLE 14

Your company is considering constructing a new plant. The firm has usually distributed all its earnings in dividends. Capital expansion has been financed through the issue of common stock. The firm has no preferred stock or debt.

The following expectations exist:

Net income	$23,000,000
Shares outstanding	5,000,000
Construction cost of new plant	$16,000,000

Incremental annual earnings expected because of the new plant is $2 million. The rate of return expected by stockholders is 12% per annum. The total market value of the firm if the plant is financed through the issuance of common stock is:

$$\frac{\text{Total net income}}{\text{Rate of return}} = \frac{\$25,000,000}{0.12} = \$208,330,000$$

The financial manager may want to compute the company's price-earnings ratio and required rate of return.

EXAMPLE 15

Your company has experienced an 8% growth rate in profits and dividends. Next year, it expects earnings per share of $4 and dividends per share of $2.50. The company will be having its first public issue of common stock. The stock will be issued at $50 per share.

The price-earnings ratio is:

$$\frac{\text{Market price per share}}{\text{Earnings per share}} = \frac{\$50}{\$4} = 12.5 \text{ times}$$

The required rate of return on the stock is:

$$\frac{\text{Dividends per share}}{\text{Market price per share}} + \text{Growth rate in dividends}$$

$$\frac{\$2.50}{\$50.00} + 0.08 = 0.13$$

If your company has significant debt, it would be better off financing with an equity issue to lower overall financial risk.

Financing with common stock has the following advantages:

- There is no requirement to pay fixed charges such as interest or dividends.
- There is no repayment date or sinking fund requirement.
- A common stock issue improves the company's credit rating relative to the issuance of debt. For example, the debt-equity ratio is improved.

Financing with common stock has the following disadvantages:

- Dividends are not tax-deductible.
- Ownership interest is diluted. The additional voting rights could vote to take control away from the current ownership group.
- Earnings and dividends are spread over more shares outstanding.
- The flotation costs of a common stock issue are higher than with preferred stock and debt financing.

It is always cheaper to finance operations from internally generated funds because financing out of retained earnings involves no flotation costs. Retained earnings may be used as equity funding if the company believes its stock price is lower than the true value of its assets. Retained earnings are also preferred if transaction costs are high for external financing.

The company may make use of dividend reinvestment plans and employee stock option plans to raise financing and thus avoid issuance costs and the market impact of a public offering.

Stockholders are typically better off when a company cuts back on its dividends instead of issuing common stock as a source of additional funds. When earnings are retained rather than new stock issued, the market price per share of existing stock will rise, as indicated by higher earnings per share. Also, a company typically earns a higher rate of return than stockholders, so by retaining funds market price of stock should appreciate. One caution, however: Lower dividend payments may be looked at negatively in the market and may cause a reduction in the market price of stock due to psychological factors.

A summary comparison of bonds and common stock is presented in Exhibit 2.

Exhibit 2

SUMMARY COMPARISON OF BONDS AND COMMON STOCK

Bonds	Common Stock
Bondholders are creditors	Stockholders are owners
No voting rights exist	Voting rights exist
There is a maturity date	There is no maturity date
Bondholders have prior claims on profits and assets in bankruptcy	Stockholders have residual claims on profits and assets in bankruptcy
Interest payments represent fixed charges	Dividend payments do not constitute fixed charges
Interest payments are deductible on the tax return	There is no tax deductibility for dividend payments
The rate of return required by bondholders is typically lower than that by stockholders	The required rate of return by stockholders is typically greater than that by bondholders

STOCK RIGHTS

Stock rights are options to buy securities at a specified price at a later date. They are a good source of common stock financing. The preemptive right provides that existing stockholders have the first option to buy additional shares. Exercising this right permits investors to maintain voting control and protects against dilution in ownership and earnings.

Financial management decides on the life of the right (typically about two months), its price (typically below the current market price), and the number of rights needed to buy a share.

EXAMPLE 16

Your company has 500,000 shares of common stock outstanding and is planning to issue another 100,000 shares through stock rights. Each current stockholder will receive one right per share. Each right permits the stockholder to buy 1/5 of a share of new common stock (100,000 shares/500,000 shares). Hence, 5 rights are needed to buy one share of stock. Thus, a shareholder holding 10,000 shares would be able to buy 2,000 new shares (10,000 $\times$ 1/5). By exercising his or her right, the stockholder would now have a total of 12,000 shares, representing a 2% interest (12,000/600,000) in the total shares outstanding. This is the same 2% ownership (10,000/500,000) the stockholder held prior to the rights offering.

In a rights offering, there is a date of record, which states the last day that the receiver of the right must be the legal owner as reflected in the company's stock ledger. Because of a lag in bookkeeping, stocks are often sold *ex rights* (without rights) four business days before the record date. Before this point, the stock is sold rights on, which means the purchasers receive the rights.

The recipient of the rights can exercise them, sell them, or let them expire. Since stock rights are transferable, many are traded on the stock exchange and over-the-counter markets. They may be exercised for a given period of time at a subscription price, which is set somewhat below the prevailing market price.

After the subscription price has been determined, management must ascertain the number of rights necessary to purchase a share of stock. The total number of shares that must be sold equals:

$$\text{Shares to be sold} = \frac{\text{Amount of funds to be obtained}}{\text{Subscription price}}$$

The number of rights needed to acquire one share equals:

$$\text{Rights per share} = \frac{\text{Total shares outstanding}}{\text{Shares to be sold}}$$

EXAMPLE 17

Your company wants to obtain $800,000 by a rights offering. There are presently 100,000 shares outstanding. The subscription price is $40 a share. The shares to be sold equal:

$$\text{Shares to be sold} = \frac{\text{Amount of funds to be obtained}}{\text{Subscription price}} = \frac{\$800,000}{\$40}$$
$$= 20,000 \text{ shares}$$

The number of rights needed to acquire one share equals:

$$\text{Rights per share} = \frac{\text{Total shares outstanding}}{\text{Shares to be sold}} = \frac{100,000}{20,000} = 5$$

Thus, five rights will be required to buy each new share at $40. Each right enables the holder to buy 1/5 of a share of stock.

Value of a Right

The value of a right should, theoretically, be the same whether the stock is selling with rights on or with ex rights.

When stock is selling with rights on, the value of a right equals:

$$\frac{\text{Market value of stock with rights on} - \text{subscription price}}{\text{Number of rights needed to buy one share} + 1}$$

EXAMPLE 18

Your company's common stock sells for $55 a share with rights on. Each stockholder is given the right to buy one new share at $35 for every four shares held. The value of each right is:

$$\frac{\$55 - \$35}{4+1} = \frac{\$20}{5} = \$4$$

When stock is traded ex rights, the market price is expected to decline by the value of the right. The market value of stock trading ex rights should theoretically equal:

Market value of stock with rights on – Value of a right when stock is selling rights on.

The value of a right when stock is selling ex rights equals:

$$\frac{\text{Market value of stock trading ex rights} - \text{Subscription price}}{\text{Number of rights needed to buy one new share}}$$

EXAMPLE 19

Assuming the same information as in Example 18, the value of the company's stock trading ex rights should equal:

Market value of stock with rights on – Value of a right when stock is selling rights on

$$\$55 - \$4 = \$51$$

The value of a right when stock is selling ex rights is therefore:

$$\frac{\text{Market value of stock trading ex rights} - \text{Subscription price}}{\text{Number of rights needed to buy one new share}}$$

$$\frac{\$51 - \$35}{4} = \frac{\$16}{4} = \$4$$

Note: The theoretical value of the right is identical when the stock is selling rights on or ex rights.

GOVERNMENTAL REGULATION

When securities are issued publicly, they must conform to federal and state regulations. State rules are referred to as blue sky laws. The major federal laws are the Securities Act of 1933 and the Securities Exchange Act of 1934. The 1934 act applies to existing security transactions, while the 1933 act deals with regulation of new security issues. The acts require full disclosure to investors concerning the company's affairs. Prior to the issuance of a new security the company must prepare a prospectus for investors which contains a condensed version of the registration statement filed with the SEC. For a more detailed discussion of financial reporting to the SEC, please see Chapter 2.

HOW SHOULD THE COMPANY FINANCE?

Some companies obtain most of their funds from issuing stock and from earnings retained in the business. Other companies borrow as much as possible and raise additional money from stockholders only when they can no longer borrow. Most companies are somewhere in the middle.

The financial manager is concerned with selecting the best possible source of financing based on the facts of the situation. He or she has to look at the various circumstances to determine the mix of financing required.

In formulating a financing strategy in terms of source and amount, the company should consider the following:

- The cost and risk of alternative financing strategies
- The future trend in market conditions and how they will impact upon future fund availability and interest rates. For example, if interest rates are expected to go up, the company would be better off financing with long-term debt at the currently lower interest rates. If stock prices are high, equity issuance may be preferred over debt.
- The current debt to equity ratio. A very high ratio, for example, indicates financial risk so additional funds should come from equity sources.
- The maturity dates of present debt instruments. For example, the company should avoid having all debt come due at the same time because in an economic downturn the company may not have adequate funds to meet all that debt.
- The restrictions in loan agreements. For instance, a restriction may exist placing a cap on the allowable debt-equity ratio.
- The type and amount of collateral required by long-term creditors.
- The ability to change financing strategy to adjust to changing economic conditions. For example, a company subject to large cyclical variations should have less debt because the company may not be able to meet principal and interest at the low point of the cycle. If earnings are unstable and/or there is a highly competitive environment, more emphasis should be given to equity financing.
- The amount, nature, and stability of internally generated funds. If stability exists in earnings generation, the company is better able to meet debt obligations.
- The adequacy of present lines of credit for current and future needs
- The inflation rate, since with debt the repayment is in cheaper dollars
- The earning power and liquidity position of the firm. For example, a liquid company is better able to meet debt payments.
- The nature and risk of assets. High quality assets allow for greater debt.
- The nature of the product line. A company, for example, that has techno-

logical obsolescence risk in its product line (e.g., computers) should refrain from overuse of debt.

• The uncertainty of large expenditures. If huge cash outlays may be required (e.g., lawsuit, acquisition of another company), there should be unused debt capacity available.

• The tax rate. For example, a higher tax rate makes debt more attractive because there is a greater tax savings from interest expense.

• Foreign operations. If operations are in questionable foreign areas and foreign competition is keen, or the exchange rate fluctuates widely, the debt position should be conservative.

What financing situations does the company face? What is it doing about it? You have to select the best possible source of financing based on the facts.

EXAMPLE 21

Your company is considering issuing either debt or preferred stock to finance the purchase of a plant costing $1.3 million. The interest rate on the debt is 15%. The dividend rate on the preferred stock is 10%. The tax rate is 34%.

The annual interest payment on the debt is:

$15\% \times \$1,300,000 = \$195,000$

The annual dividend on the preferred stock is:

$10\% \times \$1,300,000 = \$130,000$

The required earnings before interest and taxes to meet the dividend payment is:

$$\frac{\$130,000}{(1 - 0.34)} = \$196,970$$

If your company anticipates earning $196,970 without a problem, it should issue the preferred stock.

EXAMPLE 22

Your company has sales of $30 million a year. It needs $6 million in financing for capital expansion. The debt/equity ratio is 68%. Your company is in a risky industry, and net income is not stable. The common stock is selling at a high P/E ratio compared to competition. Under consideration is either the issuance of common stock or debt.

Because your company is in a high-risk industry and has a high debt/equity ratio and unstable earnings, issuing debt would be costly, restrictive, and potentially dangerous to future financial health. The issuance of common stock is recommended.

EXAMPLE 23

Your company is a mature one in its industry. There is limited ownership. The company has vacillating sales and earnings. Your firm's debt/equity ratio is 70% relative to the industry standard of 55%. The after-tax rate of return is 16%. Since your company is a seasonal business, there are certain times during the year when its liquidity position is inadequate. Your company is unsure on the best way to finance.

Preferred stock is one possible means of financing. Debt financing is not recommended due to the already high debt/equity ratio, the fluctuation in profit, seasonal nature of the business, and the deficient liquidity posture. Because of the limited ownership, common stock financing may not be appropriate because this would dilute the ownership.

EXAMPLE 24

A new company is established and it plans to raise $15 million in funds. The company expects that it will obtain contracts that will provide $1,200,000 a year in before-tax profits. The firm is considering whether to issue bonds only or an equal amount of bonds and preferred stock. The interest rate on AA corporate bonds is 12%. The tax rate is 50%.

The company will probably have difficulty issuing $15 million of AA bonds because the interest cost of $1,800,000 ($12\% \times \$15,000,000$) associated with these bonds is greater than the estimated earnings before interest and taxes. The issuance of debt by a new company is a risky alternative.

Financing with $7.5 million in debt and $7.5 million in preferred stock is also not recommended. While some debt may be issued, it is not practical to finance the balance with preferred stock. In the case that $7.5 million of AA bonds were issued at the 12% rate, the company would be required to pay $900,000 in interest. In this event, a forecasted income statement would look as follows:

Earnings before interest and taxes	$1,200,000
Interest	900,000
Taxable income	$ 300,000
Taxes	150,000
Net income	$ 150,000

The amount available for the payment of preferred dividends is only $150,000. Hence, the maximum rate of return that could be paid on $7.5 million of preferred stock is .02 ($150,000/$7,500,000).

Stockholders would not invest in preferred stock that offers only a 2% rate of return.

The company should consider financing with common stock.

EXAMPLE 25

Your company wants to construct a plant that will take about $1\frac{1}{2}$ years to construct. The plant will be used to produce a new product line, for which your company expects a high demand. The new plant will materially increase corporate size. The following costs are expected:
1. The cost to build the plant, $800,000
2. Funds needed for contingencies, $100,000
3. Annual operating costs, $175,000

The asset, debt, and equity positions of your company are similar to industry standards. The market price of the company's stock is less than it should be, taking into account the future earning power of the new product line. What would be an appropriate means to finance the construction?

Since the market price of stock is less than it should be and considering the potential of the product line, convertible bonds and installment bank loans might be appropriate means of financing, since interest expense is tax-deductible. Additionally, the issuance of convertible bonds might not require repayment, since the bonds are likely to be converted to common stock because of the company's profitability. Installment bank loans can be gradually paid off as the new product generates cash inflow. Funds needed for contingencies can be in the form of open bank lines of credit.

If the market price of the stock was not at a depressed level, financing through equity would be an alternative financing strategy.

EXAMPLE 26

Your company wants to acquire another business but has not determined an optimal means to finance the acquisition. The current debt/equity position is within the industry guideline. In prior years, financing has been achieved through the issuance of short-term debt.

Profit has shown vacillation and as a result the market price of the stock has fluctuated. Currently, however, the market price of stock is strong.

Your company's tax bracket is low.

The purchase should be financed through the issuance of equity securities for the following reasons:

• The market price of stock is currently at a high level.

• The issuance of long-term debt will cause greater instability in earnings because of the high fixed interest charges. In consequence, there will be more instability in stock price.

• The issuance of debt will result in a higher debt/equity ratio relative to the industry norm. This will negatively impact the company's cost of capital and availability of financing.

• Because it will take a long-time to derive the funds needed for the purchase price, short-term debt should not be issued. If short-term debt is issued, the debt would have to be paid before the receipt of the return from the acquired business.

EXAMPLE 27

Breakstone Corporation wants to undertake a capital expansion program and must, therefore, obtain $7 million in financing. The company has a good credit rating. The current market price of its common stock is $60. The interest rate for long-term debt is 18%. The dividend rate associated with preferred stock is 16%, and Breakstone's tax rate is 46%.

Relevant ratios for the industry and the company are:

	Industry	Breakstone
Net income to total assets	13%	22%
Long-term debt to total assets	31%	29%
Total liabilities to total assets	47%	45%
Preferred stock to total assets	3%	0
Current ratio	2.6	3.2
Net income plus interest to interest	8	17

Dividends per share are $8, the dividend growth rate is 7%, no sinking fund provisions exist, the trend in earnings shows stability, and the present ownership group wishes to retain control. The cost of common stock is:

$$\frac{\text{Dividends per share}}{\text{Market price per share}} + \text{dividend growth rate}$$

$$\frac{\$8}{\$60} + 0.07 = 20.3\%$$

The after-tax cost of long-term debt is 9.7% (18% × 54%). The cost of preferred stock is 16%. How should Breakstone finance its expansion?

The issuance of long-term debt is more appropriate for the following reasons:

1. Its after-tax cost is the lowest.

2. The company's ratios of long-term debt to total assets and total liabilities to total assets are less than the industry average, pointing to the company's ability to issue additional debt.

3. Corporate liquidity is satisfactory based on the favorable current ratio relative to the industry standard.

4. Fixed interest charges can be met, taking into account the stability in earnings, the earning power of the firm, and the very favorable times-interest-earned ratio. Additional interest charges should be met without difficulty.

5. The firm's credit rating is satisfactory.

6. There are no required sinking fund provisions.

7. The leveraging effect can take place to further improve earnings.

In the case that the firm does not want to finance through further debt, preferred stock would be the next best financing alternative, since its cost is lower than that associated with common stock and no dilution in the ownership interest will take place.

EXAMPLE 28

Harris Corporation has experienced growth in sales and net income but is in a weak liquidity position. The inflation rate is high. At the end of 19X5, the company needs $600,000 for the following reasons:

New equipment	$175,000
Research and development	95,000
Paying overdue accounts payable	215,000
Paying accrued liabilities	60,000
Desired increase in cash balance	55,000
	$600,000

Presented below are the financial statements for 19X5.

Harris Corporation
Balance Sheet
Dec. 31, 19X5

ASSETS

Current assets		
Cash	$ 12,000	
Accounts receivable	140,000	
Notes receivable	25,000	
Inventory	165,000	
Office supplies	20,000	
Total current assets		$362,000
Fixed assets		468,000
Total assets		$830,000

LIABILITIES AND STOCKHOLDERS' EQUITY

Current liabilities		
Loans payable	$ 74,000	
Accounts payable	360,000	
Accrued liabilities	55,000	

Total current liabilities		$489,000
Long-term debt		61,000
Total liabilities		$550,000
Stockholders' equity		
Common stock	$200,000	
Retained earnings	80,000	
Total stockholders' equity		280,000
Total liabilities and stockholders' equity		$830,000

Harris Corporation
Income Statement
For the Year Ended Dec. 31, 19X5

Sales	$1,400,000
Cost of sales	750,000
Gross margin	$ 650,000
Operating expenses	480,000
Income before tax	$ 170,000
Tax	68,000
Net income	$ 102,000

It is anticipated that sales will increase on a yearly basis by 22% and that net income will increase by 17%. What type of financing is best suited for Harris Corporation?

The most suitable source of financing is long-term. A company in a growth stage needs a large investment in equipment, and research and development expenditure. With regard to 19X5, $270,000 of the $600,000 is required for this purpose. A growth company also needs funds to satisfy working capital requirements. Here, 45.8% of financing is necessary to pay overdue accounts payable and accrued liabilities. The firm also needs sufficient cash to capitalize on lucrative opportunities. The present cash balance to total assets is at a low 1.4%.

Long-term debt financing is recommended for the following reasons:

1. The ratio of long-term debt to stockholders' equity is a low 21.8%. The additional issuance of long-term debt will not impair the overall capital structure.

2. The company has been profitable and there is an expectation of future growth in earnings. Internally generated funds should therefore ensue, enabling the payment of fixed interest charges.

3. During inflation, the issuance of long-term debt generates purchasing power gains because the firm will be repaying creditors in cheaper dollars.

4. Interest expense is tax-deductible.

EXAMPLE 29

On average over the past 10 years, Tektronix's return on equity has not been sufficient to finance growth of the business, thus an infusion of new capital from outside sources has been required. Most of the additional capital has been in the form of long-term debt, which represented 13% of total capital in fiscal 1977 and 21% of total capital in fiscal 1981.

With expansion of the business expected to accelerate in the next few years after the current lull, but, with return on equity likely to remain somewhat depressed because of competitive factors and costs associated with "preparing for the 1980s," a need for additional capital is developing. Also, of the $146 million of long-term debt outstanding at the fiscal 1981 year-end, nearly $65 million matures in the fiscal 1982 to fiscal 1984 period. Thus, it is possible that as much as $100 million of capital may have to be raised to meet all requirements.

In anticipation of capital needs, Tektronix in fiscal 1981 borrowed funds in the commercial paper market, and the company intends to replace these commercial paper borrowings at some future time with long-term financing.

Given the foregoing circumstances, and also given that Tektronix common stock currently is quoted on the New York Stock Exchange at 160% of book value and that the current interest rate on newly issued triple-A industrial bonds of long maturity is 14%, evaluate on an immediate and longer term basis each of the following options. Include in your answers economic and capital market assumptions. (*a*) Tektronix is selling two million shares of common stock at $50 per share, (*b*) Tektronix is selling a $100 million straight debenture issue maturing in 20 years, and (*c*) Tektronix is selling a $100 million bond issue convertible into common stock and maturing in 20 years. (CFA, adapted.)

Solution

(*a*) From the timing viewpoint, selling equity is attractive considering price-to-book rates (160%) and comparatively modest dilution (two million shares represents 11% of currently outstanding shares, less impact of after-tax cost of borrowing to be retired). However, price soon could move higher given a better economic environment, earnings recovery, and resultant stronger general stock market. Long-term, selling equity is expensive, as continuing dividend service is with after-tax dollars. Also, immediate return on equity capital will diminish with reduced leverage as debt matures.

(*b*) Increasing debt, net of maturities, to a larger part of total capital is tolerable by most standards. According to the data provided, debt of about $146 million would increase to around $181 million ($146 + $100 − $65), and by 1984 this sum presumably would not represent much more than the current 21% subject to earnings retention during the interim. However, this would be an appealing option only if interest rate assumptions indicate other than a rather meaningful decline over the next year or two, and if pro forma interest charge coverage and/or the current lull in the business do not seriously impact the rating and issue price of the bonds. The after-tax cost of debt service will be comparatively low, and so would be the net cost of capital. Another consideration will be sinking fund requirements and call restrictions and price.

(c) A convertible bond issue has certain disadvantages but it also has advantages; (1) it can be sold at a lower interest cost than a straight debt, and (2) the potential dilution is less than an issue of common reflecting the premium over the common market.

CONCLUSION

Your company may finance long-term with debt or equity (preferred stock and common stock) funds. Each has its own advantages and disadvantages. The facts of a situation have to be examined to determine which type is best under the circumstances. For example, a rapid growing company needs flexibility in its capital structure. While to sustain growth, a high debt position may be needed, it is important that periodic additions to equity are made.

38

Warrants and Convertibles

Warrants and convertibles are unique relative to other kinds of securities because they may be converted into common stock. This chapter discusses warrants and convertibles along with their valuation, presents their advantages and disadvantages, and discusses when their issuance is most appropriate.

WARRANTS

A warrant is the option given holders to purchase a given number of shares of stock at a specified price. Warrants can be either detachable or nondetachable. A detachable warrant may be sold separately from the bond with which it is associated. Thus, the holder may exercise the warrant but not redeem the bond if he or she wishes. A company may issue bonds with detachable warrants to purchase additional bonds if it wants to hedge the risk of adverse future interest rate movements since the warrant is convertible into a bond at a fixed interest rate. If interest rates rise, the warrant will be worthless, and the issue price of the warrant will partially offset the higher interest cost of the future debt issue. A nondetachable warrant is sold with its bond to be exercised by the bond owner simultaneously with the convertible bond.

A company may sell warrants separately (e.g., American Express) or in combination with other securities (e.g., MGM/UA).

To obtain common stock the warrant must be given up along with the payment of cash called the exercise price. Although warrants typically expire on a given date, some are perpetual. A holder of a warrant may exercise it by buying the stock, sell it on the market to other investors, or continue to hold it. The company cannot force the exercise of a warrant.

If desired, the company may have the exercise price associated with a warrant vary over time (e.g., increase each year).

If there is a stock split or stock dividend before the warrant is exercised, the option price of the warrant is usually adjusted for it.

Through warrants additional funds are received by the issuer. When a bond is issued with a warrant, the warrant price is typically set between 10% and 20% above the stock's market price. If the company's stock price goes above the option price, the warrants will, of course, be exercised at the option price. The closer the warrants are to their expiration date, the greater the chance is that they will be exercised.

Valuation of a Warrant

The theoretical value of a warrant may be computed by a formula. The formula value is usually less than the market price of the warrant. This is because the speculative appeal of a warrant allows the investor to obtain a good degree of personal leverage.

Value of a Warrant = (Market price per share − Exercise price)
                       × Number of shares that may be bought

EXAMPLE 1

A warrant for XYZ company's stock gives the owner the right to buy one share of common stock at $25 a share. The market price of the common stock is $53. The formula price of the warrant is $28 (($53 − $25) × 1).

If the owner had the right to buy three shares of common stock with one warrant, the theoretical value of the warrant would be $84 ($53 − $25) × 3).

If the stock is selling for an amount below the option price, there will be a negative value. Since this is illogical, we use a formula value of zero.

EXAMPLE 2

Assume the same facts as in Example 1, except that the stock is selling at $21 a share. The formula amount is: $4 (($21 − $25) × 1). However, zero will be assigned.

Warrants do not have an investment value because there is no interest or dividends paid on them nor voting rights given. Hence, the market value of a warrant is solely attributable to its convertibility value into common stock. However, the market price of a warrant is usually more than its theoretical value, which is referred to as the premium on the warrant. The lowest amount that a warrant will sell for is its theoretical value.

The value of a warrant depends on the remaining life of the option, dividend payments on the common stock, the variability in price of the common stock, whether the warrant is listed on the exchange, and the opportunity cost of funds for the investor. A high value is associated with a warrant when its life is long, the dividend payment on common stock is small, the stock price is volatile, it is listed on the exchange, and the value of funds to the investor is great (because the warrant requires a lesser investment).

EXAMPLE 3

ABC stock currently has a market value of $50. The exercise price of the warrant is also $50. Therefore, the theoretical value of the warrant is $0. However, the warrant will sell at a premium (positive price) provided there is the possibility that the market price of the common stock will exceed $50 before the expiration date of the warrant. The further into the future the expiration date is, the greater will be the premium, since there is a longer period for possible price appreciation.

Of course, the lower the market price compared to the exercise price, the less the premium is.

EXAMPLE 4

Assume the same facts as in Example 3, except that the current market price of the stock is $35. The warrant's premium in this instance will be much lower, since it would take a long time for the stock's price to increase above $50 a share. If investors anticipated that the stock price would not increase above $50 at a subsequent date, the value of the warrant would be $0.

If the market price of ABC stock rises above $50, the market price of the warrant will increase and the premium will decrease. In other words, when the stock price exceeds the exercise price, the market price of the warrant approximately equals the theoretical value causing the premium to disappear. The reduction in the premium arises because of the lessening of the advantage of owning the warrant relative to exercising it.

Advantages and Disadvantages of Warrants

The advantages of issuing warrants include the following:

1. They allow for balanced financing between debt and equity.
2. They permit the issuance of debt at a low interest rate.
3. They serve as a "sweetener" for an issue of debt or preferred stock.
4. Additional cash is received when the warrants are exercised.

The disadvantages of issuing warrants include the following:

1. When exercised they will result in a dilution of common stock. This may result in a decline in the market price of stock.
2. They may be exercised at a time when the business has no need for additional capital.

CONVERTIBLE SECURITIES

A convertible security is one that may be exchanged for common stock by the holder, and in some cases the issuer, according to agreed upon terms. Examples are convertible bonds and convertible preferred stock. A specified number of shares of stock are received by the holder of the convertible security when he or she makes the exchange. This is referred to as the conversion ratio, which equals:

$$\text{Conversion ratio} = \frac{\text{Par value of convertible security}}{\text{Conversion price}}$$

The conversion price applies to the effective price the holder pays for the common stock when the conversion is effected. The conversion price and the conversion ratio are set when the convertible security is issued. The conversion price should be tied to the growth potential of the company. The greater the potential, the greater the conversion price should be.

A convertible bond is a quasi-equity security because its market value is tied to its value if converted rather than as a bond. The convertible bond may be considered a delayed issue of common stock at a price above the current level.

EXAMPLE 5

A $1,000 bond is convertible into 30 shares of stock. The conversion price is $33.33 ($1,000/30 shares).

EXAMPLE 6

A share of convertible preferred stock with a par value of $50 is convertible into four shares of common stock. The conversion price is $12.50 ($50/4).

EXAMPLE 7

A $1,000 convertible bond is issued that entitles the holder to convert the bond into 10 shares of common stock. Hence, the conversion ratio is 10 shares for one bond. Since the face value of the bond is $1,000 the holder is tendering this amount upon conversion. The conversion price equals $100 per share ($1,000/10 shares).

EXAMPLE 8

Y Company issued a $1,000 convertible bond at par. The conversion price is $40. The conversion ratio is:

$$\text{Conversion ratio} = \frac{\text{Par value of convertible security}}{\text{Conversion price}}$$

$$= \frac{\$1,000}{\$40} = 25$$

The conversion value of a security is computed as follows:

Conversion value = common stock price × conversion ratio

When a convertible security is issued, it is priced higher than its conversion value. The difference is referred to as the conversion premium. The percentage conversion premium is computed in the following manner:

$$\frac{\text{Percentage}}{\text{conversion premium}} = \frac{\text{Market value} - \text{Conversion value}}{\text{Conversion value}}$$

EXAMPLE 9

LA Corporation issued a $1,000 convertible bond at par. The market price of the common stock at the date of issue was $48. The conversion price is $55.

$$\text{Conversion ratio} = \frac{\text{Par value of convertible security}}{\text{Conversion price}}$$

$$= \frac{\$1,000}{\$55} = 18.18$$

Conversion value of the bond equals:

Common stock price × Conversion ratio = $48 × 18.18 = $872

The difference between the conversion value of $872 and the issue price of $1000 constitutes the conversion premium of $128. The conversion premium may also be expressed as a percentage of the conversion value. The percent in this case is:

Percentage conversion premium equals:

$$\frac{\text{Market value} - \text{Conversion value}}{\text{Conversion value}} = \frac{\$1,000 - \$872}{\$872} = \frac{\$128}{\$872} = 14.7\%$$

The conversion terms may not be static but may increase in steps over specified time periods. Hence, as time passes fewer common shares are exchanged for the bond. In some instances, after a certain time period the conversion option may expire.

Typically, the convertible security contains a clause that protects it from dilution caused by stock dividends, stock splits, and stock rights. The clause usually prevents the issuance of common stock at a price lower than the conversion price. Also, the conversion price is reduced by the percentage amount of any stock split or stock dividend. This enables the shareholder of common stock to maintain his or her proportionate interest.

EXAMPLE 10

A 3-for-1 stock split occurs, which requires a tripling of the conversion ratio. A 20% stock dividend requires a 20% increase in the conversion ratio.

The voluntary conversion of a security by the holder depends on the relationship of the interest on the bond relative to the dividend on the stock, the risk preference of the holder (stock has a greater risk than a bond), and the current and expected market price of the stock.

Valuation of Convertibles

A convertible security is a hybrid security, because it has attributes that are similar to common stock and bonds. The expectation is that the holder will ultimately receive both interest yield and a capital gain. Interest yield relates to the coupon interest relative to the market price of the bond when purchased. The capital gain yield applies to the difference between the conversion price and the stock price at the issuance date and the expected growth rate in stock price.

The investment value of a convertible security is the value of the security, assuming it was not convertible but had all other attributes. For a convertible bond, its investment value equals the present value of future interest payments plus the present value of the maturity amount. For preferred stock the investment value equals the present value of future dividend payments plus the present value of expected selling price.

Conversion value refers to the value of stock received upon converting the bond. As the price of the stock increases so will its conversion value.

EXAMPLE 11

A $1,000 bond is convertible into 18 shares of common stock with a market value of $52 per share. The conversion value of the bond equals:

$52 $\times$ 18 shares = $936

EXAMPLE 12

At the date a $100,000 convertible bond is issued, the market price of the stock is $18 a share. Each $1,000 bond is convertible into 50 shares of stock. The conversion ratio is thus 50. The number of shares the bond is convertible into is:

100 bonds ($100,000/$1,000) $\times$ 50 shares = 5,000 shares

The conversion value is $90,000 ($18 $\times$ 5,000 shares).

If the stock price is expected to grow at 6% per year, the conversion value at the end of the first year is:

Shares	5,000
Stock price ($18 $\times$ 1.06)	$19.08
Conversion value	$95,400

A convertible security will not sell at less than its value as straight debt (nonconvertible security). This is because the conversion privilege has to have some value in terms of its potential convertibility to common stock and in terms of reducing the holder's risk exposure to a declining bond price (convertible bonds fall off less in price than straight debt issues). Market value will equal investment value only when the conversion privilege is worthless due to a low market price of the common stock compared to the conversion price.

When convertible bonds are issued, the business expects that the value of common stock will appreciate and that the bonds will ultimately be converted. If conversion does occur, the company could then issue another convertible bond. Such a financial policy is termed "leapfrog financing."

If the market price of common stock drops instead of rising, the holder will not convert the debt into equity. In this instance, the convertible security continues as debt and is termed a "hung" convertible.

A convertible security holder may prefer to hold the security instead of converting it even though the conversion value exceeds the price paid for it. First, as the price of the common stock increases so will the price of the convertible security. Second, the holder receives regular interest payments or preferred dividends. To force conversion, companies issuing convertibles often have a call price. The call price is above the face value of the bond (about 10% to 20% higher). This forces the conversion of stock as long as the stock price exceeds the conversion price. The holder would prefer a higher-value common stock than a lower call price for the bond.

The issuing company may force conversion of its convertible bond to common stock when financially advantageous such as when the market price of the stock has dropped, or when the interest rate on the convertible debt is currently higher than the prevailing market interest rates. An example of a company that has in the past had a conversion of its convertible bond when the market price of its stock was low was United Technologies.

EXAMPLE 13

The conversion price on a $1,000 debenture is $40 and the call price is $1,100. In order for the conversion value of the bond to equal the call price, the market price of the stock would have to be $44 ($1,100/25). If the conversion value of a bond is 15% higher than the call price, the approximate market price of common stock would be $51 (1.15 × $44). At a $51 price, conversion is virtually guaranteed, since if the investor did not convert he or she would incur a material opportunity loss.

EXAMPLE 14

ABC Company's convertible bond has a conversion price of $80. The conversion ratio is 10. The market price of the stock is $140. The call price is $1,100. The bondholder would rather convert to common stock with a market value of $1,400 ($140 × 10) than have his or her convertible bond redeemed at $1,100. In this instance, the call provision forces the conversion when the bondholder might be tempted to wait longer.

Advantages and Disadvantages of Convertibles

The advantages of issuing convertible securities are:

1. It is a "sweetener" in a debt offering by giving the investor a chance to take part in the price appreciation of common stock.
2. The issuance of convertible debt allows for a lower interest rate on the financing relative to issuing straight debt.
3. A convertible security may be issued in a tight money market, when it is difficult for a creditworthy firm to issue a straight bond or preferred stock.
4. There are fewer financing restrictions involved with a convertible security issuance.
5. Convertibles provide a means of issuing equity at prices higher than current market prices.
6. The call provision enables the company to force conversion whenever the market price of the stock exceeds the conversion price.
7. In the case the company issued straight debt now and common stock later to meet the debt, they would incur flotation costs twice, whereas with convertible debt, flotation costs would occur only once, with the initial issuance of the convertible bonds.

The disadvantages of issuing convertible securities are:

1. If the company's stock price appreciably increases in value, it would have been better off financing through a regular issuance of common stock by waiting to issue it at the higher price instead of allowing conversion at the lower price.
2. The company is obligated to pay the convertible debt if the stock price does not rise.

Corporate Financing Strategy

When a firm's stock price is currently depressed, convertible debt instead of common stock issuance may be called for if the price of stock is anticipated to increase. Establishing a conversion price above the present market price of stock will involve the issuance of fewer shares when the bonds are converted compared to selling the shares at a current lower price. Also, less share dilution will be involved. Of course, the conversion will occur only if the price of the stock rises above the conversion price. The drawback is that if the stock price does not increase and conversion does not take place, an additional debt burden is placed upon the company.

The issuance of convertible debt is suggested when the company wants to leverage itself in the short run but desires not to incur interest cost and pay principal on the convertible debt in the long run (due to its conversion).

A convertible issue is often a good financing tool for a growth company with a low dividend yield on stock. The quicker the growth rate, the earlier the conversion. For instance, a convertible bond may act as a temporary source of funds in a construction period. It is a relatively inexpensive source for financing growth. A convertible issuance is not recommended for a company with a modest growth rate, since it would take a long time to force conversion. During such a time the company will not be able to easily issue additional financing. A long conversion interval may imply to the investing public that the firm is a prime consideration in determining whether convertibles are the best method of financing.

A company may also issue bonds exchangeable for the common stock of other companies. The issuer may do this if it owns a sizable stake in another company's stock and it wants to raise cash currently and intends to sell the shares at a later date because it expects the share price to rise.

In conclusion, a convertible bond is a delayed common equity financing. The issuer expects stock price to rise in the future (e.g., 2–4 years) to stimulate conversion. Convertible bonds may be suitable for smaller, rapidly growing companies.

Note: A company that has an uncertain future tax position can issue convertible preferred stock exchangeable at the option of the company (i.e., when it becomes a taxpayer) into convertible debt of the company.

CONVERTIBLES VERSUS WARRANTS

The differences between convertibles and warrants are as follows:

1. Exercising convertibles does not typically provide additional funds to the company, while the exercise of warrants does.

2. When conversion occurs the debt ratio is reduced. However, the exercise of warrants adds to the equity position with debt still remaining.

3. Because of the call feature, the company has more control over the timing of the capital structure with convertibles than with warrants.

39

Cost of Capital
and Capital Structure Decisions

Cost of capital is defined as the rate of return that is necessary to maintain the market value of the firm (or price of the firm's stock). Financial managers must know the cost of capital (the minimum required rate of return) in (1) making capital budgeting decisions, (2) helping to establish the optimal capital structure, and (3) making decisions such as leasing, bond refunding, and working capital management. The cost of capital is computed as a weighted average of the various capital components, which are items on the right-hand side of the balance sheet such as debt, preferred stock, common stock, and retained earnings. This chapter covers the following topics:

- How to compute costs of capital
- EBIT-EPS approach to financial leverage
- Capital structure decisions in practice

COMPUTING INDIVIDUAL COSTS OF CAPITAL

Each element of capital has a component cost that is identified by the following:

k_i = before-tax cost of debt
k_d = $k_i (1 - t)$ = after-tax cost of debt, where t = tax rate
k_p = cost of preferred stock
k_s = cost of retained earnings (or internal equity)
k_e = cost of external equity, or cost of issuing new common stock
k_o = firm's overall cost of capital, or a weighted average cost of capital

925

Cost of Debt

The before-tax cost of debt can be found by determining the internal rate of return (or yield to maturity) on the bond cash flows.

However, the following short-cut formula may be used for approximating the yield to maturity on a bond:

$$k_i = \frac{I + (M - V)/n}{(M + V)/2}$$

where I = annual interest payments in dollars
M = par value, usually $1,000 per bond
V = value or net proceeds from the sale of a bond
n = term of the bond in years

Since the interest payments are tax-deductible, the cost of debt must be stated on an after-tax basis. The after-tax cost of debt is:

$$k_d = k_i (1 - t)$$

where t is the tax rate.

EXAMPLE 1

Assume that the Carter Company issues a $1,000, 8%, 20-year bond whose net proceeds are $940. The tax rate is 40%. Then, the before-tax cost of debt, k_i, is:

$$k_i = \frac{I + (M - V)/n}{(M + V)/2}$$

$$= \frac{\$80 + (\$1,000 - \$940)/20}{(\$1,000 + \$940)/2} = \frac{\$83}{\$970} = 8.56\%$$

Therefore, the after-tax cost of debt is:

$$k_d = k_i (1 - t)$$
$$= 8.56\% (1 - 0.4) = 5.14\%$$

Cost of Preferred Stock

The cost of preferred stock k_p, is found by dividing the annual preferred stock dividend d_p, by the net proceeds from the sale of the preferred stock p, as follows:

$$k_p = \frac{d_p}{p}$$

Since preferred stock dividends are not a tax-deductible expense, these dividends are paid out after taxes. Consequently, no tax adjustment is required.

EXAMPLE 2

Suppose that the Carter Company has preferred stock that pays a $13 dividend per share and sells for $100 per share in the market. The flotation (or underwriting) cost is 3%, or $3 per share. Then the cost of preferred stock is:

$$k_p = \frac{d_p}{p}$$

$$= \frac{\$13}{\$97} = 13.4\%$$

Cost of Equity Capital

The cost of common stock k_c, is generally viewed as the rate of return investors require on a firm's common stock. Three techniques for measuring the cost of common stock equity capital are available: (1) the Gordon's growth model, (2) the capital asset pricing model (CAPM) approach, and (3) the bond plus approach.

The Gordon's Growth Model. The Gordon's model is:

$$P_o = \frac{D_1}{r - g}$$

where P_o = value of common stock
D_1 = dividend to be received in one year
r = investor's required rate of return
g = rate of growth (assumed to be constant over time)

Solving the model for r results in the formula for the cost of common stock:

$$r = \frac{D_1}{P_o} + g \quad \text{or} \quad k_e = \frac{D_1}{P_o} + g$$

Note that the symbol r is changed to k_e to show that it is used for the computation of cost of capital.

EXAMPLE 3

Assume that the market price of the Carter Company's stock is $40. The dividend to be paid at the end of the coming year is $4 per share and is expected to grow at a constant annual rate of 6%. Then the cost of this common stock is:

$$k_e = \frac{D_1}{P_o} + g = \frac{\$4}{\$40} + 6\% = 16\%$$

The cost of new common stock, or external equity capital, is higher than the cost of existing common stock because of the flotation costs involved in selling the new common stock.

If f is flotation cost in percent, the formula for the cost of new common stock is:

$$k_e = \frac{D_1}{P_o \, (1 - f)} + g$$

EXAMPLE 4

Assume the same data as in Example 3, except the firm is trying to sell new issues of Stock A and its flotation cost is 10%. Then:

$$k_e = \frac{D_1}{P_o \, (1 - f)} + g$$

$$= \frac{\$4}{\$40(1 - 0.1)} + 6\% = \frac{\$4}{\$36} + 6\% = 11.11\% + 6\% = 17.11\%$$

The CAPM Approach. An alternative approach to measuring the cost of common stock is to use the CAPM, which involves the following steps:

1. Estimate the risk-free rate r, generally taken to be the United States Treasury bill rate.

2. Estimate the stock's beta coefficient b, which is an index of systematic (or nondiversifiable market) risk.

3. Estimate the rate of return on the market portfolio such as the Standard & Poor's 500 Stock Composite Index or Dow Jones 30 Industrials.

4. Estimate the required rate of return on the firm's stock, using the CAPM (or SML) equation:

$$k_e = r_f + b(r_m - r_f)$$

Again, note that the symbol r_j is changed to k_e.

EXAMPLE 5

Assuming that r_f is 7%, b is 1.5, and r_m is 13%, then:

$$k_e = r_f + b \, (r_m - r_f) = 7\% + 1.5(13\% - 7\%) = 16\%.$$

This 16% cost of common stock can be viewed as consisting of a 7% risk-free rate plus a 9% risk premium, which reflects that the firm's stock price is 1.5 times more volatile than the market portfolio to the factors affecting nondiversifiable, or systematic, risk.

The Bond Plus Approach. Still another simple but useful approach to determining the cost of common stock is to add a risk premium to the firm's own cost of long-term debt, as follows:

$$k_e = \text{long-term bond rate} + \text{risk premium}$$
$$= k_i (1 - t) + \text{risk premium}$$

A risk premium of about 4% is commonly used with this approach.

EXAMPLE 6

Using the data found in Example 1, the cost of common stock using the bond plus approach is:

$$k_e = \text{long-term bond rate} + \text{risk premium}$$
$$= k_i (1 - t) + \text{risk premium}$$
$$= 5.14\% + 4\% = 9.14\%$$

Cost of Retained Earnings

The cost of retained earnings k_s, is closely related to the cost of existing common stock, since the cost of equity obtained by retained earnings is the same as the rate of return investors require on the firm's common stock. Therefore,

$$k_e = k_s$$

Measuring the Overall Cost of Capital

The firm's overall cost of capital is the weighted-average of the individual capital costs, with the weights being the proportions of each type of capital used. Let k_o be the overall cost of capital.

$$k_o = \Sigma \left(\begin{array}{c} \% \text{ of total capital} \\ \text{structure supplied by} \\ \text{each type of} \\ \text{capital} \end{array} \times \begin{array}{c} \text{Cost of} \\ \text{capital for} \\ \text{each source} \\ \text{of capital} \end{array} \right)$$

$$= w_d \cdot k_d + w_p \cdot k_p + w_e \cdot k_e + w_s \cdot k_s$$

where w_d = % of total capital supplied by debt
w_p = % of total capital supplied by preferred stock

w_e = % of total capital supplied by external equity
w_s = % of total capital supplied by retained earnings (or internal equity)

The weights can be historical, target, or marginal.

Historical Weights

Historical weights are based on a firm's existing capital structure. The use of these weights is based on the assumption that the firm's existing capital structure is optimal and therefore should be maintained in the future. Two types of historical weights can be used—book value weights and market value weights.

Book Value Weights. The use of book value weights in calculating the firm's weighted cost of capital assumes that new financing will be raised using the same method the firm used for its present capital structure. The weights are determined by dividing the book value of each capital component by the sum of the book values of all the long-term capital sources. The computation of overall cost of capital is illustrated in the following example.

EXAMPLE 7

Assume the following capital structure for the Carter Company:

Mortgage bonds ($1,000 par)	$20,000,000
Preferred stock ($100 par)	5,000,000
Common stock ($40 par)	20,000,000
Retained earnings	5,000,000
Total	$50,000,000

The book value weights and the overall cost of capital are computed as follows:

Source	Book Value	Weights	Cost	Weighted Cost
Debt	$20,000,000	40%	5.14%	2.06%
Preferred stock	5,000,000	10	13.40%	1.34
Common stock	20,000,000	40	17.11%	6.84
Retained earnings	5,000,000	10	16.00%	1.60
	$50,000,000	100%		11.84%

Overall cost of capital = k_o = 11.84%

Market Value Weights. Market value weights are determined by dividing the market value of each source by the sum of the market values of all sources. The use of market value weights for computing a firm's weighted-average cost of capital is theoretically more appealing than the use of book value weights because the market values of the securities closely approximate the actual dollars to be received from their sale.

EXAMPLE 8

In addition to the data from Example 7, assume that the security market prices are as follows:

Mortgage bonds = $1,100 per bond
Preferred stock = $90 per share
Common stock = $80 per share

The firm's number of securities in each category is:

$$\text{Mortgage bonds} = \frac{\$20,000,000}{\$1,000} = 20,000$$

$$\text{Preferred stock} = \frac{\$5,000,000}{\$100} = 50,000$$

$$\text{Common stock} = \frac{\$20,000,000}{\$40} = 500,000$$

Therefore, the market value weights are:

Source	Number of Securities	Price	Market Value
Debt	20,000	$1,100	$22,000,000
Preferred stock	50,000	$90	4,500,000
Common stock	500,000	$80	40,000,000
			$66,500,000

The $40 million common stock value must be split in the ratio of 4 to 1 (the $20 million common stock versus the $5 million retained earnings in the original capital structure), since the market value of the retained earnings has been impounded into the common stock.

The firm's cost of capital is as follows:

Source	Market Value	Weights	Cost	Weighted Average
Debt	$22,000,000	33.08%	5.14%	1.70%
Preferred stock	4,500,000	6.77	13.40%	0.91
Common stock	32,000,000	48.12	17.11%	8.23
Retained earnings	8,000,000	12.03	16.00%	1.92
	$66,500,000	100.00%		12.76%

Overall cost of capital = k_o = 12.76%

Target Weights

If the firm has determined that the capital structure is consistent with its goals, the use of that capital structure and associated weights is appropriate.

Marginal Weights

The use of marginal weights involves weighing the specific costs of various types of financing by the percentage of the total financing expected to be raised using each method. In using target weights, the firm is concerned with what it believes to be the optimal capital structure or target percentage. In using marginal weights, the firm is concerned with the actual dollar amounts of each type of financing to be needed for a given investment project.

EXAMPLE 9

The Carter Company is considering raising $8 million for plant expansion. Management estimates using the following mix for financing this project:

Debt	$4,000,000	50%
Common stock	2,000,000	25%
Retained earnings	2,000,000	25%
	$8,000,000	100%

The company's cost of capital is computed as follows:

Source	Marginal Weights	Cost	Weighted Cost
Debt	50%	5.14%	2.57%
Common stock	25	17.11%	4.28
Retained Earnings	25	16.00%	4.00
	100%		10.85%

Overall cost of capital = k_o = 10.85%

Level of Financing and the Marginal Cost of Capital (MCC)

Because external equity capital has a higher cost than retained earnings due to flotation costs, the weighted cost of capital increases for each dollar of new financing. Therefore, the lower-cost capital sources are used first. In fact, the firm's cost of capital is a function of the size of its total investment. A schedule or graph relating the firm's cost of capital to the level of new financing is called the weighted marginal cost of capital (MCC). Such a schedule is used to determine the discount rate to be used in the firm's capital budgeting process. The steps to be followed in calculating the firm's marginal cost of capital are summarized below.

1. Determine the cost and the percentage of financing to be used for each source of capital (debt, preferred stock, common stock equity).

2. Compute the break points on the MCC curve where the weighted cost will increase. The formula for computing the break points is:

$$\text{Break point} = \frac{\text{Maximum amount of the lower-cost source of capital}}{\text{Percentage financing provided by the source}}$$

3. Calculate the weighted cost of capital over the range of total financing between break points.

4. Construct a MCC schedule or graph that shows the weighted cost of capital for each level of total new financing. This schedule will be used in conjunction with the firm's available investment opportunities schedule (IOS) in order to select the investments. As long as a project's IRR is greater than the marginal cost of new financing, the project should be accepted. Also, the point at which the IRR intersects the MCC gives the optimal capital budget.

EXAMPLE 10

A firm is contemplating three investment projects, A, B, and C, whose initial cash outlays and expected IRR are shown below. IOS for these projects is:

Project	Cash Outlay	IRR
A	$2,000,000	13%
B	$2,000,000	15%
C	$1,000,000	10%

If these projects are accepted, the financing will consist of 50% debt and 50% common stock. The firm should have $1.8 million in earnings available for reinvestment (internal common). This firm will consider only the effects of increases in the cost of common stock on its marginal cost of capital.

1. The costs of capital for each source of financing have been computed and are given below:

Source	Cost
Debt	5%
Common stock ($1.8 million)	15%
New common stock	19%

If the firm uses only internally generated common stock, the weighted cost of capital is:

$k_o = \Sigma$ Percentage of the total capital structure supplied by each source $\times$ Cost of capital for each source

In this case, the capital structure is composed of 50% debt and 50% internally generated common stock. Thus,

$k_o = (0.5)5\% + (0.5)15\% = 10\%$

If the firm uses only new common stock, the weighted cost of capital is

$$k_o = (0.5)5\% + (0.5)19\% = 12\%$$

Range of Total New Financing (In Millions of Dollars)	Type of Capital	Proportion	Cost	Weighted Cost
$0 – $3.6	Debt	0.5	5%	2.5%
	Internal common	0.5	15%	7.5
				10.0%
$3.6 and up	Debt	0.5	5%	2.5%
	New common	0.5	19%	9.5
				12.0%

2. Next compute the break point, which is the level of financing at which the weighted cost of capital increases.

Break point =

$$\frac{\text{Maximum amount of source of the lower-cost source of capital}}{\text{Percentage financing provided by the source}}$$

$$= \frac{\$1,800,000}{0.5} = \$3,600,000$$

3. That is, the firm may be able to finance $3.6 million in new investments with internal common stock and debt without having to change the current mix of 50% debt and 50% common stock. Therefore, if the total financing is $3.6 million or less, the firm's cost of capital is 10%.

4. Construct the MCC schedule on the IOS graph to determine the discount rate to be used in order to decide in which project to invest and to show the firm's optimal capital budget. See Figure 1.

The firm should continue to invest up to the point where the IRR equals the MCC. From the graph in Figure 1, note that the firm should invest in projects B and A, since each IRR exceeds the marginal cost of capital. The firm should reject project C since its cost of capital is greater than the IRR. The optimal capital budget is $4 million, since this is the sum of the cash outlay required for projects A and B.

EBIT-EPS APPROACH TO CAPITAL STRUCTURE

The EBIT-EPS approach to capital structure is a practical tool for use by financial managers in order to evaluate alternative financing plans. This is a practical effort to move towards achieving an optimal capital structure which results in the lowest overall cost of capital.

Figure 1. MCC Schedule and IOS Graph

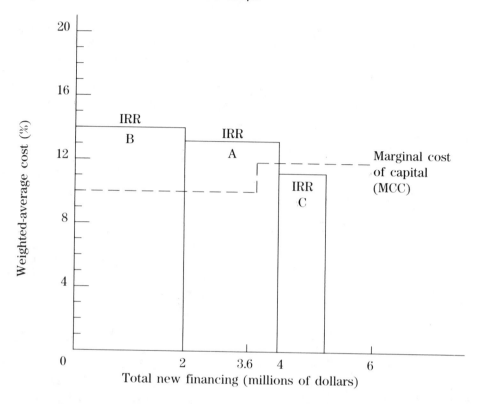

The use of financial leverage has two effects on the earnings that go to the firm's common stockholders: (1) an increased risk in earnings per share (EPS) due to the use of fixed financial obligations, and (2) a change in the level of EPS at a given EBIT associated with a specific capital structure.

The first effect is measured by the degree of financial leverage. The second effect is analyzed by means of EBIT-EPS analysis. This analysis is a practical approach that enables the financial manager to evaluate alternative financing plans by investigating their effect on EPS over a range of EBIT levels. Its primary objective is to determine the EBIT break-even, or indifference, points between the various alternative financing plans. The indifference points between any two methods of financing can be determined by solving for EBIT in the following equality:

$$\frac{(EBIT - I)(1 - t) - PD}{S_1} = \frac{(EBIT - I)(1 - t) - PD}{S_2}$$

where
$$t = \text{tax rate}$$
$$PD = \text{preferred stock dividends}$$
$$S_1 \text{ and } S_2 = \text{number of shares of common stock outstanding after financing for plan 1 and plan 2, respectively.}$$

EXAMPLE 11

Assume that ABC Company, with long-term capitalization consisting entirely of $5 million in stock, wants to raise $2 million for the acquisition of special equipment by (1) selling 40,000 shares of common stock at $50 each, (2) selling bonds, at 10% interest, or (3) issuing preferred stock with an 8% dividend. The present EBIT is $8 million, the income tax rate is 50%, and 100,000 shares of common stock are now outstanding. In order to compute the indifference points, we begin by calculating EPS at a projected level of $1 million.

	All Common	All Debt	All Preferred
EBIT	$1,000,000	$1,000,000	$1,000,000
Interest		200,000	
Earnings before taxes (EBT)	$1,000,000	$ 800,000	$1,000,000
Taxes	500,000	400,000	500,000
Earnings after taxes (EAT)	$ 500,000	$ 400,000	$ 500,000
Preferred stock dividend			160,000
EAC	$ 500,000	$ 400,000	$ 340,000
Number of shares	140,000	100,000	100,000
EPS	$ 3.57	$ 4.00	$ 3.40

Now connect the EPSs at the level of EBIT of $1 million with the EBITs for each financing alternative on the horizontal axis to obtain the EPS-EBIT graphs. We plot the EBIT necessary to cover all fixed financial costs for each financing alternative on the horizontal axis. For the common stock plan, there are no fixed costs, so the intercept on the horizontal axis is zero. For the debt plan, there must be an EBIT of $200,000 to cover interest charges. For the preferred stock plan, there must be an EBIT of $320,000 [$160,000/(1 − 0.5)] to cover $160,000 in preferred stock dividends at a 50% income tax rate; or $320,000 becomes the horizontal axis intercept. See Figure 2.

In this example, the indifference point between all common and all debt is:

$$\frac{(EBIT - I)(1 - t) - PD}{S_1} = \frac{(EBIT - I)(1 - t - PD}{S_2}$$

$$\frac{(EBIT - 0)(1 - 0.5) - 0}{140,000} = \frac{(EBIT - 200,000)(1 - 0.5) - 0}{100,000}$$

Rearranging yields:

$$0.5(EBIT)(100,000) = 0.5(EBIT)(140,000) - 0.5(200,000)(140,000)$$
$$20,000\ EBIT = 14,000,000,000$$
$$EBIT = \$700,000$$

Similarly, the indifference point between all common and all preferred would be:

$$\frac{(EBIT - I)(1 - t) - PD}{S_1} = \frac{(EBIT - I)(1 - t) - PD}{S_2}$$

$$\frac{(EBIT - 0)(1 - 0.5) - 0}{140,000} = \frac{(EBIT - 0)(1 - 0.5) - 160,000}{100,000}$$

Rearranging yields:

$$0.5(EBIT)(100,000) = 0.5(EBIT)(140,000) - 160,000(140,000)$$
$$20,000 \text{ EBIT} = 22,400,000,000$$
$$\text{EBIT} = \$1,120,000$$

Based on the above computations, we can draw the following conclusions:

1. At any level of EBIT, debt is better than preferred stock.
2. At a level of EBIT above $700,000, debt is better than common stock. If EBIT is below $700,000, the reverse is true.
3. At a level of EBIT above $1,120,000, preferred stock is better than common. At or below that point, the reverse is true.

Financial leverage is a two-edge sword. It can magnify profits but it can also increase losses. The EBIT-EPS approach helps financial managers

Figure 2. EPS-EBIT Graph

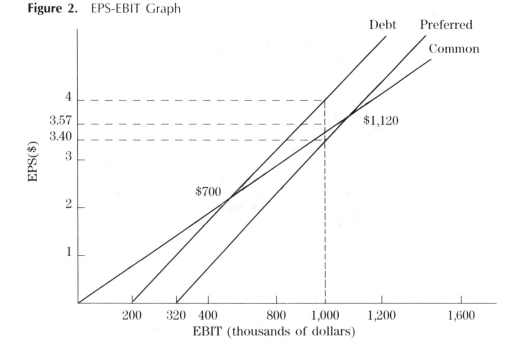

examine the impact of financial leverage as a financing method. It is important to realize that investment performance is crucial to the successful application of any leveraging strategy.

CAPITAL STRUCTURE DECISIONS IN PRACTICE

Many financial officers believe that there is an optimum capital structure for the corporation. How do companies decide which financing source to use? It is a complex decision, related to a company's balance sheet, market conditions, outstanding obligations and a host of other factors. Surveys consistently point out that (1) financial officers set target debt ratios for their companies, and (2) the values of those ratios are affected by a prudent evaluation of the basic business risk to which the firm is exposed. The most frequently mentioned influence on the target debt ratio is the firm's cash-flow ability to service fixed charges. The greater the dollar amount of senior securities the firm issues and the shorter their maturity, the greater the fixed charges of the firm. These charges include principal and interest payments on debt, lease payments, and preferred stock dividends. Before assuming additional fixed charges, the firm should analyze its expected future cash flows, for fixed charges must be met with cash. The inability to meet these charges, with the exception of preferred stock dividends, may result in insolvency. The greater and more stable the expected future cash flows of the firm, the greater the debt capacity of the company.

Other factors identified as affecting the target debt ratio are:

(1) Providing adequate borrowing reserve
(2) Maintaining a desired bond rating
(3) Business risk to which the firm is exposed
(4) Exploiting the advantages of positive financial leverage (or trading on equity)
(5) Restrictive debt covenants
(6) Industry standard
(7) Voting control of the firm

Coverage Ratios

Among the ways we can gain insight into the debt capacity of a firm is through the use of coverage ratios. In the computation of these ratios, a corporate financial officer typically uses earnings before interest and taxes (EBIT) as a rough measure of the cash flow available to cover debt-servicing obligations. Perhaps the most widely used coverage ratio is times interest earned, which is simply:

$$\text{Times interest earned} = \frac{\text{EBIT}}{\text{Interest on debt}}$$

Assume that the most recent annual EBIT for a company were $4 million, and that interest payments on all debt obligations were $1 million. Therefore, times interest earned would be four times. This tells us that EBIT can drop by as much as 75% and the firm still will be able to cover its interest payments out of earnings.

However, a coverage ratio of only one indicates that earnings are just sufficient to satisfy the interest burden. While it is difficult to generalize as to what is an appropriate interest coverage ratio, a corporate financial officer usually is concerned when the ratio gets much below $3:1$. However, it all depends. In a highly stable industry, a relatively low times-interest-earned ratio may be appropriate, whereas it is not appropriate in a highly cyclical one.

Unfortunately, the times-interest-earned ratio tells us nothing about the ability of the firm to meet principal payments on its debt. The inability to meet a principal payment constitutes the same legal default as failure to meet an interest payment. Therefore it is useful to compute the coverage ratio for the full debt-service burden. This ratio is

$$\text{Debt-service coverage} = \frac{\text{EBIT}}{\text{Interest} + \dfrac{\text{Principal payments}}{1 - \text{Tax rate}}}$$

Here principal payments are adjusted upward for the tax effect. The reason is that EBIT represents earnings before taxes. Because principal payments are not tax deductible, they must be paid out of after-tax earnings. Therefore, we must adjust principal payments so that they are consistent with EBIT. If principal payments in our previous example were $1.5 million per annum and the tax rate was 34%, the debt-service coverage ratio would be

$$\text{Debt-service coverage} = \frac{\$4 \text{ million}}{\$1 \text{ million} + \dfrac{\$1.5 \text{ million}}{1 - .34}} = 1.22$$

A coverage ratio of 1.22 means that EBIT can fall by only 22% before earnings coverage is insufficient to service the debt. Obviously, the closer the ratio is to 1.0, the worse things are, all other things being equal. However, even with a coverage ratio of less than 1.0, a company may still meet its obligations if it can renew some of its debt when it comes due.

The financial risk associated with leverage should be analyzed on the basis of the firm's ability to service total fixed charges. While lease financing is not debt per se, its impact on cash flows is exactly the same as the payment of interest and principal on a debt obligation. Therefore, annual lease payments should be added to the denominator of the formula in order to properly reflect the total cash-flow burden associated with financing.

Trend Analysis and Industry Comparisons

Two types of comparison should be undertaken with coverage ratios. First, it should be compared with past and expected future ratios of the same company. The purpose is to determine if there has been an improvement or a deterioration in coverage over time. Another method of analyzing the appropriate capital structure for a company is to evaluate the capital structure of other companies having similar business risk. Companies used in this comparison may be those in the same industry. If the firm is contemplating a capital structure significantly out of line with that of similar companies, it is conspicuous to the marketplace. This is not to say, however, that the firm is wrong; other companies in the industry may be too conservative with respect to the use of debt. The optimal capital structure for all companies in the industry might call for a higher proportion of debt to equity than the industry average. As a result, the firm may well be able to justify more debt than the industry average. Because investment analysts and creditors tend to evaluate companies by industry, however, the firm should be able to justify its position if its capital structure is noticeably out of line in either direction.

Ultimately, a financial officer wants to make generalizations about the appropriate amount of debt (and leases) for a firm to have in its capital structure. It is clear that over the long run the source to service debt for the going concern is earnings. Therefore, coverage ratios are an important tool of analysis. However, they are but one tool by which a financial manager is able to reach conclusions with respect to the appropriate capital structure for the firm. Coverage ratios are subject to certain limitations and, consequently, cannot be used as a sole means for determining a capital structure. For one thing, the fact that EBIT falls below the debt-service burden does not spell immediate doom for the company. Often alternative sources of funds, including renewal of the loan, are available, and these sources must be considered.

CONCLUSION

The chapter discussed how to calculate the cost of capital. The use of the cost of capital for a company or division as an acceptance criterion has been widespread. Financial officers should be thoroughly familiar with the ways to compute the costs of various sources of financing for financial, capital budgeting, and capital structure decisions.

In deciding upon an appropriate capital structure, the financial manager should take into account a number of factors. One important method of gaining insight into the question of the optimal capital structure involves analyzing the relationship between earnings before interest and taxes (EBIT) and earnings per share (EPS) for alternative methods of financing. In addition, the financial manager can learn much from a comparison of capital structure ratios and coverage ratios (such as times interest earned and debt-service coverage) for similar companies and over time.

40

Dividend Policy

A company's dividend policy is important for the following reasons:

• It influences investor attitudes. For instance, stockholders look negatively upon the company when dividends are cut, since they associate the cutback with corporate financial difficulties. Further, in establishing a dividend policy, management must determine and fulfill the owners' objectives. Otherwise, the stockholders may sell their shares, which in turn may lower the market price of the stock. Stockholder dissatisfaction raises the possibility that control of the company may be seized by an outside group.

• It impacts the financing program and capital budget of the firm.

• It affects the company's cash flow. A company with a poor liquidity position may be forced to restrict its dividend payments.

• It lowers stockholders' equity, since dividends are paid from retained earnings, and so results in a higher debt to equity ratio.

If a company's cash flows and investment requirements are volatile, the company should not establish a high regular dividend. It would be better to establish a low regular dividend that can be met even in bad years.

COMPANY POLICY

A financial manager's objectives for the company's dividend policy is to maximize owner wealth while providing adequate financing for the firm. When a company's earnings increase, management does not automatically raise the dividend. Generally, there is a time lag between increased earnings and the payment of a higher dividend. Only when management is optimistic that the increased earnings will be sustained should they increase the dividend. Once

941

dividends are increased, they should continue to be paid at the higher rate. There are different types of dividend policies that may be established including:

1. *Stable dividend-per-share policy.* Many companies use a stable dividend-per-share policy since it is looked upon positively by investors. Dividend stability implies a low-risk company. Even in a year that the company shows a loss instead of a profit the dividend should be maintained to avoid negative connotations to current and prospective investors. By continuing to pay the dividend, the shareholders are more apt to consider the loss as temporary. Some stockholders rely on the receipt of stable dividends for income. A stable dividend policy is also necessary for a company to be placed on a list of securities in which financial institutions (pension funds, insurance companies) invest. Being on such a list provides greater marketability for corporate shares.

2. *Constant dividend-payout ratio (dividends per share/earnings per share).* With this policy a constant percentage of earnings is paid out in dividends. Because net income fluctuates, dividends paid will also vary using this approach. The problem this policy causes is that if the company's earnings fall drastically or there is a loss, the dividends paid will be significantly reduced or nonexistent. This policy will not maximize market price per share since most stockholders do not want variability in their dividend receipts.

3. *A compromise policy.* A compromise between the policies of a stable dollar amount and a percentage amount of dividends is for a company to pay a lower dollar amount per share plus a percentage increment in good years. While this policy gives flexibility, it also results in uncertainty in the minds of investors as to the amount of dividends they are likely to receive. Stockholders typically do not like such uncertainty. However, this policy may be appropriate when earnings vary considerably over the years. The percentage, or extra, portion of the dividend should not be paid regularly, otherwise it becomes meaningless.

4. *Residual-dividend policy.* When a company's investment opportunities are not stable, management may wish to consider a vacillating dividend policy. With this type of policy the amount of earnings retained depends upon the availability of investment opportunities in a given year. Dividends constitute the residual amount from earnings after the company's investment needs are met.

EXAMPLE 1

Company A and Company B are identical in every respect except for their dividend policies. Company A pays out a constant percentage of its net income (60% dividends), while company B pays out a constant dollar dividend. Company B's market price per share is higher than that of company A because the stock market looks favorably upon stable dollar dividends. They reflect less uncertainty about the firm.

EXAMPLE 2

Most Corporation had a net income of $800,000 in 19X1. Earnings have grown at an 8% annual rate. Dividends in 19X1 were $300,000. In 19X2, the net income was $1,100,000. This was much higher than the typical 8% annual growth rate. It is expected that profits will be back to the 8% rate in future years. The investment in 19X2 was $700,000.

Assuming a stable dividend payout ratio of 25%, the dividends to be paid in 19X2 will be $275,000 ($1,100,000 × 25%).

If a stable dollar dividend policy is maintained, the 19X2 dividend payment will be $324,000 ($300,000 × 1.08).

Assuming a residual dividend policy is maintained and 40% of the 19X2 investment is financed with debt, the 19X2 dividend will be:

Equity needed = $700,000 × 60% = $420,000

Because net income exceeds the equity needed, all of the $420,000 of equity investment will be derived from net income.

Dividend = $1,100,000 − $420,000 = $680,000

If the investment for 19X2 is to be financed with 80% debt and 20% retained earnings, and any net income not invested is paid out in dividends, then the dividends will be:

Earnings retained = $700,000 × 20% = $140,000

Dividend = net income − Earnings retained

$960,000 = $1,100,000 − $140,000

Theoretical Position

Theoretically, a company should retain earnings rather than distribute them when the corporate return exceeds the return investors can obtain on their money elsewhere. Further, if the company obtains a return on its profits that exceeds the cost of capital, the market price of its stock will be maximized. On the other hand, a company should not, theoretically, keep funds for investment if it earns less of a return than what the investors can earn elsewhere. If the owners have better investment opportunities outside the company, the firm should pay a high dividend.

Although theoretical considerations from a financial perspective should be taken into account when establishing dividend policy, the *practicality* of the situation is that investors expect to be paid dividends. Psychological factors come into play which may adversely impact the market price of the stock of a company that does not pay dividends.

FACTORS THAT INFLUENCE DIVIDEND POLICY

A company's dividend policy depends on many variables, some of which have been already mentioned. Other factors to be considered are:

• *Company growth rate.* A rapidly growing business, even if profitable, may have to restrict dividends to keep needed funds within the company for growth.

- *Restrictive covenants.* Sometimes there is a restriction in a credit agreement that will limit the dividends that may be paid.
- *Profitability.* Dividend distribution is keyed to the profitability of the company.
- *Earnings stability.* A company with stable earnings is more apt to distribute a higher percentage of its earnings than one with unstable earnings.
- *Maintenance of control.* Management that is reluctant to issue additional common stock because it does not want to dilute control of the firm will retain a higher percentage of its earnings. Internal financing enables control to be kept within.
- *Degree of financial leverage.* A company with a high debt-to-equity ratio is more likely to retain profits so that it will have the required funds to pay interest and principal on debt.
- *Ability to finance externally.* A company that is capable of entering the capital markets easily can afford to have a higher dividend payout ratio. Where there is a limitation to external sources of funds, more earnings will be retained for planned financial needs.
- *Uncertainty.* Payment of dividends reduces the chance of uncertainty in stockholders' minds about the firm's financial health.
- *Age and size.* The age and size of the company bear upon its ease of access to capital markets.
- *Tax penalties.* Possible tax penalties for excess accumulation of retained earnings may result in high dividend payouts.

Controversy

The dividend policy controversy can best be described by presenting the approaches put forth by various authors:

1. Gordon et al. believe that cash flows of a company having a low dividend payout will be capitalized at a higher rate because investors will consider capital gains resulting from earnings retention to be more risky than dividends.

2. Miller and Modigliani argue that a change in dividends impacts the price of the stock since investors will consider such a change as being a statement about expected future profits. They believe that investors are generally indifferent as to dividends or capital gains.

3. Weston and Brigham et. al. believe that the best dividend policy varies with the particular characteristics of the company and its owners, depending on such factors as the tax bracket and income needs of stockholders, and corporate investment opportunities.

STOCK REPURCHASES

The purchase of treasury stock is an alternative to paying dividends. Since outstanding shares will be fewer after stock has been repurchased, earnings per share will increase (assuming net income is held constant). The increase in earnings per share may result in a higher market price per share.

EXAMPLE 3

A company earned \$2.5 million in 19X1. Of this amount, it decided that 20% would be used to buy treasury stock. Currently, there are 400,000 shares outstanding. Market price per share is \$18. The company can use \$500,000 (20% $\times$ \$2.5 million) to buy back 25,000 shares through a tender offer of \$20 per share.

Current earnings per share is:

$$\text{EPS} = \frac{\text{Net income}}{\text{Outstanding shares}} = \frac{\$2,500,000}{\$400,000} = \$6.25$$

The current P/E multiple is:

$$\frac{\text{Market price per share}}{\text{Earnings per share}} = \frac{\$18}{\$6.25} = 2.88 \text{ times}$$

Earnings per share after treasury stock is acquired becomes:

$$\frac{\$2,500,000}{375,000} = \$6.67$$

The expected market price, assuming the P/E ratio remains the same, is:

P/E multiple $\times$ New earnings per share = Expected market price
$$2.88 \times \$6.67 = \$19.21$$

The benefits from a stock repurchase include the following:

1. If there is excess cash flow that is deemed temporary, management may prefer to repurchase stock than to pay a higher dividend that they feel cannot be maintained.

2. Treasury stock can be used for future acquisitions or used as a basis for stock options.

3. If management is holding stock, they would favor a stock repurchase rather than a dividend because of the favorable tax treatment.

4. Treasury stock can be resold in the market if additional funds are needed.

The disadvantages of treasury stock acquisition include:

1. If investors believe that the company is engaging in a repurchase plan because its management does not have alternative good investment opportunities, a drop in the market price of stock may ensue. However, there are cases where this has not happened, such as when General Electric

announced in 1989 its plan of periodic reacquisitions of stock because of a lack of more attractive investment opportunities.

2. If the reacquisition of stock appears that the company is manipulating its stock price, the company will have problems with the Securities and Exchange Commission (SEC). Further, if the Internal Revenue Service (IRS) concludes that the repurchase is designed to avoid the payment of tax on dividends, tax penalties may be imposed because of the improper accumulation of earnings as specified in the tax code.

41

International Finance

Many companies are multinational corporations (MNCs) that have significant foreign operations deriving a high percentage of their sales overseas. Financial managers of MNCs require an understanding of the complexities of international finance to make sound decisions. Important international developments include import prices, cost of labor, and cost of raw materials.

International finance involves consideration of managing cash, financing the business, foreign operations, and monetary position. Most importantly, the financial manager has to consider the value of the U.S. dollar relative to the value of the currency of the foreign country in which business activities are being conducted. Currency exchange rates may materially affect imports and exports of the U.S. company in its multinational operations. The effect is more pronounced with increasing activities abroad.

CASH MANAGEMENT

International cash management deals with minimizing the exposure of foreign located funds to exchange rate risks and minimizing governmental restrictions on the movement of funds among countries. For example, Spain, Brazil, and India have restrictions on cash remissions back to the United States. Cash held in a politically unstable foreign country is subject to risk. The financial manager must analyze the political and economic trends in the foreign countries.

Cash may be accelerated by having bank accounts in each country. In many countries, customers pay their bills by requesting their bank to deduct the amount owed from their account and to transfer the funds to another firm's account.

FINANCING

A company may finance its activities abroad, especially in countries it is operating in. A successful company in domestic markets is more likely to be able to attract financing for international expansion.

A type of commercial bank financing is the use of overdrafts. An overdraft agreement allows a customer to draw checks up to a given ceiling amount above the checking account base.

In Europe, commercial banks conduct many investment banking operations.

Eurobonds are long-term debt in the Eurocurrency market. They are offered for sale in more than one country through international syndicates of underwriters, usually denominated in a strong currency, such as the British pound. If a Eurobond is not issued to U.S. residents, the issue need not be registered.

Eurobonds may be of different types such as straight, convertible, and with warrants. While most Eurobonds are fixed rate, variable rate bonds also exist. Maturities vary but 10-12 years is typical.

Although Eurobonds are issued in many currencies, you wish to select a stable, fully convertible, and actively traded currency. In some cases, if a Eurobond is denominated in a weak currency the holder has the option of requesting payment in another currency. In some cases, the Eurobond involves repayment in a mix of currencies, such as the European Unit of Account (EUA).

The U.S. dollar is the major transaction currency, Eurobonds are sometimes denominated for repayment in multiple currencies. The creditor can demand payment of the interest and principal in any of the predetermined currencies at previously established parity.

Convertible Eurobonds have relatively low interest rates plus the potential of capital gain.

Wholly owned offshore finance subsidiaries are established by large companies. These subsidiaries issue Eurobond debt and the proceeds are given to the parent or to overseas operating subsidiaries. Debt service goes back to bondholders through the finance subsidiaries.

If the Eurobond was issued by the parent directly, the U.S. would require a withholding tax on interest. There may also be an estate tax when the bondholder dies. These tax problems do not arise when a bond is issued by a finance subsidiary incorporated in a tax haven. Hence, the subsidiary may borrow at less cost than the parent.

FOREIGN OPERATIONS

If a subsidiary is operating in a high-tax country with a double-tax agreement, dividend payments are not subject to further U.S. taxes. One way to transfer income from high tax areas to low tax areas is to levy royalties or management fees on the subsidiaries.

When strong competition exists in the U.S., a company may look to enter or expand its foreign base. However, if a company is unsuccessful in the domestic market, it is likely to have problems overseas as well. Further, the financial manager must be cognizant of local customs and risks in the international markets.

A large, well-established company with much international experience may eventually have wholly-owned subsidiaries. However, a small company with limited foreign experience operating in "risky areas" may be restricted to export and import activity.

If the company's sales force has minimal experience in export sales, it is advisable to use foreign brokers when specialized knowledge of foreign markets is needed. When sufficient volume exists, the company may establish a foreign branch sales office including sales people and technical service staff. As the operation matures, production facilities may be located in the foreign market. However, some foreign countries require licensing before foreign sales and production can take place. In this case, a *foreign licensee* sells and produces the product. A problem with this is that confidential information and knowledge are passed on to the licensees who can then become a competitor at the expiration of the agreement.

A joint venture with a foreign company is another way to proceed internationally and share the risk. Some foreign governments require this to be the path to follow to operate in their countries. The foreign company may have local goodwill to assure success. A drawback is less control over activities and a conflict of interest.

In evaluating the impact that foreign operations have on the entity's financial health, the financial manager should consider the extent of intercountry transactions, foreign restrictions and laws, tax structure of the foreign country, and the economic and political stability of the country.

MONETARY POSITION

Monetary balance is avoiding either a net receivable or a net payable position. Monetary assets and liabilities do not change in value with devaluation or revaluation in foreign currencies.

A company with a long position in a foreign currency will be receiving more funds in the foreign currency. It will have a net monetary asset position (monetary assets exceed monetary liabilities) in that currency.

A company with net receipts is a net monetary creditor. Its foreign exchange rate risk exposure has a net receipts position in a foreign currency that is susceptible to a drop in value.

A company with a future net obligation in foreign currency has a net monetary debtor position. It faces a foreign exchange risk of the possibility of an increase in the value of the foreign currency.

FOREIGN CURRENCY EXCHANGE

An exchange rate is the ratio of one unit of currency to another. The conversion rate between currencies depends on the demand/supply relationship. Exchange rates may be in terms of dollars per foreign currency unit or units of foreign currency per dollar. An exchange rate is established between the different currencies. Because of the change in exchange rates, companies are susceptible to exchange rate fluctuation risks because of a net asset or net liability position in a foreign currency. A rate of $.40/German Deutschemark (DM) means each DM costs the U.S. company $.40. In other words, the U.S. company gets $1/.4 = 2.5$ DM for each dollar.

Except in a few European centers, there is no central marketplace for the foreign exchange market. Rather, business is carried out over telephone or telex. The major dealers are large banks. A company that wants to buy or sell currency typically uses a commercial bank.

International transactions and investments involve more than one currency. For example, when a U.S. company sells merchandise to an Italian firm, the former wants to be paid in dollars but the Italian company typically expects to receive lira. Due to the foreign exchange market, the buyer may pay in one currency while the seller can receive payment in another currency.

EXAMPLE 1

An American company that imports merchandise from France buys francs in order to pay for the purchase. An American company exporting to France receives francs which it sells in exchange for dollars. Both companies use the foreign exchange market.

Spot Rates and Forward Rates

The spot rate is the exchange rate for immediate delivery of currencies exchanged, while the forward rate is the exchange rate for later delivery of currencies exchanged. For example, there may be a 90-day exchange rate. The forward exchange rate of a currency will be slightly different from the spot rate at the current date because of future expectations and uncertainties. Forward rates may be greater than the current spot rate (premium) or less than the current spot rate (discount).

EXAMPLE 2

On February 1, 19X5, forward rates on the British pound were at a premium in relation to the spot rate, while the forward rates for the Italian lira were at a discount from the spot rate. This means that participants in the foreign exchange market anticipated that the British pound would appreciate relative to the U.S. dollar in the future but the Italian lira would depreciate against the dollar.

The percentage discount or premium is computed as follows. Forward premium (or discount) equals:

$$\frac{\text{Forward rate } - \text{ spot rate}}{\text{Spot rate}} \times \frac{12}{\text{Length of forward contract in months}} \times 100$$

EXAMPLE 3

On March 8, 19X3, a 60-day forward contract in French francs was selling at a 11.9834% discount:

$$\frac{.1423 - .1452}{.1452} \times \frac{12}{2} \times 100 = 11.9834\%$$

On the same date, a 90-day forward contract in British pounds was selling at a 2.3859% premium:

$$\frac{1.6528 - 1.6430}{1.6430} \times \frac{12}{3} \times 100 = 2.3859\%$$

Long versus Short Position

When there is a devaluation of the dollar, foreign assets and income in strong currency countries are worth more dollars as long as foreign liabilities do not offset this beneficial effect.

Foreign exchange risk may be analyzed by examining expected receipts or obligations in foreign currency units. A company expecting receipts in foreign currency units ("long" position in the foreign currency units) has the risk that the value of the foreign currency units will drop. This results in devaluing the foreign currency relative to the dollar. If a company is expecting to have obligations in foreign currency units ("short" position in the foreign currency units), there is risk that the value of the foreign currency will rise and it will need to buy the currency at a higher price.

If net claims are greater than liabilities in a foreign currency, the company has a "long" position since it will benefit if the value of the foreign currency rises. If net liabilities exceed claims with respect to foreign currencies, the company is in a "short" position because it will gain if the foreign currency drops in value.

Stability of Exchange Rate

If the exchange rate is stable, there will be no exchange problem. Because the exchange rates of some countries are more unstable than that of others, the financial manager should determine in which countries the company is operating. The financial manager should also determine whether the instability in exchange rates is a short-term or long-term problem.

An erratic foreign exchange rate leads to instability. The degree of vacillation of the foreign exchange rate may be measured by its percentage change over time and/or its standard deviation.

Rapid exchange shifts detract from earnings stability. The trend in the ratio of (1) foreign exchange gains and losses to net income and (2) foreign exchange gains and losses to total revenue should be examined. To what extent do foreign currency gains and losses contribute to variability in the earnings stream?

Foreign Exchange Risk

A company that properly balances its foreign assets and liabilities protects the parent from exchange rates and its resulting variability effect upon consolidated profit. The financial manager should consider the exposed position of the firm by each foreign country in which there exists a major operation.

If a foreign currency is rising in value, the U.S. company has risk exposure if it has a short position in the foreign currency. In other words, if the company must make payments in foreign currency units or has liabilities expressed in such units, an increase in the value of the foreign currency unit will mandate more dollars to be used to buy it after it has increased in value. In other words, a company with future obligations expressed in foreign currency units has risk exposure from the potential risk in the value of those units.

Certain overseas investments have practically no exchange risk. For instance, since oil prices are fixed in dollars, Texaco's investment in the British North Sea is basically immune to a devaluation of sterling. Texaco's least-risky strategy is therefore to finance its North Sea investment with dollars instead of pounds. On the other hand, other companies may be exposed to exchange risk even though all of their activities are conducted in the United States. For instance, because a devaluation of the yen will probably reduce the dollar price of Japanese cars, a General Motors dealer may be susceptible to changes in the Japanese exchange rate and could be protected from exchange risk by financing partly with yen.

A company may take an aggressive posture by being a net monetary debtor in a country in which exchange rates are expected to drop and a net monetary creditor in a country in which exchange rates are likely to increase.

Foreign exchange risk exposure may be reduced through hedging in the forward market or borrowing and lending through the money markets.

A forward exchange contract is an agreement to purchase or sell identifiable foreign currency where the actual delivery of the foreign currency is at a later date. It is used to protect or hedge against exchange risks emanating from foreign currency transactions. The contract guards against unexpected fluctuations in foreign exchange rates. The cost of forward hedging is like an insurance premium to avoid larger exchange losses. The financial manager should look upon such a contract favorably since the company is minimizing its potential foreign currency exposure. Typically, forward contracts are for 30, 60, or 90 days.

A forward exchange contract can also be used to speculate in the foreign exchange market. The financial manager must be careful when engaging in speculative contracts because of the high risk.

A hedge can still occur even if a forward exchange contract does not exist. A foreign currency transaction can serve as an economic hedge offsetting a parent's net investment in a foreign entity when the transaction is entered into for hedging purposes.

EXAMPLE 4

A U.S. parent completely owns a French subsidiary having net assets of $3 million in francs. The U.S. parent can borrow $3 million francs to hedge its investment in the French subsidiary. Also assume the French franc is the functional currency, and the $3 million obligation is denominated in francs. Variability in the exchange rate for francs does not have a net impact on the parent's consolidated balance sheet, since increases in the translation adjustments balance arising from translation of the net investment will be netted against decreases in this balance emanating from the adjustment of the obligation denominated in francs.

Financial Strategies

In countries where currency values are likely to drop, financial management of the subsidiaries should:

• Avoid paying advances on purchase orders unless the seller pays interest on the advances sufficient to cover the loss of purchasing power.

• Not have excess idle cash. Excess cash can be used to buy inventory or other real assets.

• Buy materials and supplies on credit in the country in which the foreign subsidiary is operating, extending the final payment date as long as possible.

• Avoid giving excessive trade credit. If accounts receivable balances are outstanding for an extended time period, interest should be charged to absorb the loss in purchasing power.

• Borrow local currency funds when the interest rate charged does not exceed U.S. rates after taking into account expected devaluation in the foreign country.

The Translation Process

A major purpose of translation is to provide data of expected impacts of rate changes on cash flow and equity. In the translation of the foreign subsidiaries' financial statements into the U.S. parent's financial statements, the following steps are involved:

1. The foreign financial statements are put into United States' generally accepted accounting principles.

2. The foreign currency is translated into U.S. dollars.

Balance sheet accounts are translated using the current exchange rate at the balance sheet date. If a current exchange rate is not available at the balance sheet date, use the first exchange rate available after that date.

Income statement accounts are translated using the weighted-average exchange rate for the period.

The current exchange rate is used to translate the statement of cash flows, except for those items found in the income statement which are translated using the weighted-average rate.

Translation gains and losses are reported as a separate item in the stockholders' equity section of the balance sheet. Translation gains and losses are only included in net income when there is a sale or liquidation of the entire investment in a foreign entity.

Also see the section on "Foreign Currency Translation and Transactions" in Chapter 9.

Foreign Currency Transactions

Foreign currency transactions may result in receivables or payables fixed in terms of the amount of foreign currency to be received or paid. Transaction gains and losses are reported in the income statement.

Foreign currency transactions are those transactions whose terms are denominated in a currency other than the entity's functional currency. Foreign currency transactions take place when a business:

• Buys or sells on credit goods or services the prices of which are denominated in foreign currency.

• Borrows or lends funds, and the amounts payable or receivable are denominated in foreign currency.

• Is a party to an unperformed forward exchange contract.

• Acquires or disposes of assets, or incurs or settles liabilities denominated in foreign currency.

An exchange gain or loss occurs when the exchange rate changes between the purchase date and sale date.

Also see the section on "Foreign Currency Translation and Transactions" in Chapter 9.

CONCLUSION

When a company penetrates a foreign market it may use foreign brokers, foreign licensees, or joint ventures. Financial instruments to support foreign operations may be issued such as Eurobonds. The tax structure in foreign countries also has to be considered. An unstable foreign exchange rate may lead to earnings fluctuations unless hedging activities are undertaken. Foreign currency translations and transactions have to be determined along with their financial effects.

IX

TAX PREPARATION AND PLANNING

42

How Taxes Affect Business Decisions

The objective of companies is to maximize profits while simultaneously minimizing income taxes. Tax planning strategies are essential in satisfying this basic objective. The controller must (1) be familiar with certain basic federal income tax rules, and (2) be aware of the complex tax implications of business combinations.

The company and the shareholders must be considered when planning and implementing tax strategies. The determination of whether a business should operate as a C corporation or an S corporation involves consideration of tax rates at both the entity and owner's levels. Further consideration should be given to Internal Revenue Code restrictions. Long-term considerations, including liquidation possibilities are crucial. The selection of the cash or accrual basis of accounting must be based on a variety of factors including regulatory agency requirements, federal income tax provisions, and basic timing factors in accounting recognition. Where alternatives exist, the controller is called upon for analysis and recommendations.

TAX ACCOUNTING METHODS

The cash method of accounting results in the recognition of income when collected and expenses when paid. Under this method, constructive receipt of income results in recognition. The apparent advantage to the cash method of accounting is that careful planning can result in the deferral of income from the current period to the next. Billing and collection should therefore be timed carefully. Under Internal Revenue Code (IRC) §408, however, the cash method of accounting may be elected only by (1) corporations with average annual gross receipts of $5 million or less, (2) qualified personal service corporations, and (3) farming and timber businesses. Taxpayers failing to qualify for the cash method of accounting must use the accrual method of accounting, whereby income is recognized when earned and expenses are recognized when incurred.

INSTALLMENT SALES

Pursuant to IRC Sec. 453, the installment sale provisions prorate the gross profit on a sale over the years in which payments are to be received. Depending on current and potential tax rate changes, the installment sale provisions might be advantageous. The installment sale provisions are automatic; i.e., a taxpayer must elect not to be covered by the statutory provisions. The installment sale provisions are applicable to sales of real property and casual sales of personal property at a gain. Sales by dealers of personal or real property are generally not eligible for the installment sale provisions, nor are revolving credit sales and sales of publicly traded securities. The character of gain recognized will not be altered under the installment sale provisions; accordingly, the disposition of a capital asset will result in capital gain. Caution must be exercised in case of depreciable property since any depreciation that must be recaptured under IRC Sec 1245 and IRC Sec 1250 must be recaptured in the year of sale, regardless of the installment sale provisions.

DIVIDENDS-RECEIVED DEDUCTION

Corporations that receive dividends from unaffiliated domestic taxable corporations are generally entitled to a 70% dividends-received deduction. The deduction, however, is limited to 70% of the corporation's tentative taxable income, which is the taxable income of the corporation before consideration of the dividend-received deduction and any applicable net operating loss deduction. The 70% of tentative taxable income limitation is not applicable when the corporation sustains a net operating loss before or after the dividends-received deduction. Additionally, the deduction is increased to 80% in cases where the dividends are received from a 20%-or-more owned corporation.

A corporation whose stock is included in a debt-financed portfolio will partially or totally lose the dividends-received deduction. The beneficial provisions will also not be applicable in cases involving the receipt of dividends from mutual savings banks, since such receipts in essence represent interest income.

It should be noted that dividends received from affiliated corporations are generally entitled to a 100% dividends-received deduction.

CHARITABLE CONTRIBUTIONS

The deduction for charitable contributions is limited annually to 10% of taxable income, computed without regard to the deduction for charitable contributions, and with taking into account (1) the dividends-received deduction, (2) any net operating loss carryback and (3) any net capital loss carryback. Furthermore, the charitable contribution deduction may not increase an existing net operating loss. Any charitable contributions which may not be deducted in the current year by virtue of the 10% limitation may be carried forward up to five years. Corporations using the accrual method of accounting may deduct charitable contributions authorized by the Board of Directors but paid after year end as long as payment is made within 2½ months after year end. Otherwise, cash basis accounting is applicable.

With respect to contributions of property, the deduction is generally measured by the corporation's basis in the property. In the case of contributions of inventory and other ordinary income producing property for the care of the ill, the needy or infants, the deduction is equal to the corporation's basis in the property increased by 50% of the property's appreciation. In no event, however, may the deduction exceed twice the property's basis.

NET OPERATING LOSS DEDUCTIONS

Net operating losses of corporations may be carried back up to three years and carried forward up to 15 years. An election may be made, however, to forego the carryback. This may be advisable when tax rates in future years render the loss deduction more valuable. IRS attention is drawn to the tax return for the year to which the carry back is claimed. Accordingly, it might be judicious to relinquish the right to a carryback claim since the prior year's tax return may be subject to IRS scrutiny. When calculating the net operating loss deduction, no deduction is allowed for net operating loss carrybacks or carryovers. The dividends-received deduction, however, is allowable.

AMORTIZATION OF ORGANIZATION COSTS

Costs incurred in connection with organizing a corporation may be amortized over a minimum 60-month period. Amortizable expenses include legal and accounting fees as well as filing fees and payments to temporary directors. Costs incurred in connection with the printing and issuance of stock certificates represent nondeductible expenses which are not eligible for amortization.

DEPRECIATION

With respect to tangible depreciable property placed into service after 1986, the modified accelerated cost recovery system (MACRS) of depreciation is applicable.

Under MACRS, assets are placed into recovery periods based on estimated economic lives specified in the Code.

The table below represents the recovery periods applicable to tangible personal property subject to depreciation recapture under IRC Sec 1245.

Recovery Period	Qualifying Property
3 years	Assets with a life of 4 years or less
5 years	Assets with a life of at least 4 years and less than 10 years
7 years	Assets with a life of at least 10 years and less than 16 years
10 years	Assets with a life of at least 16 years and less than 20 years
15 years	Assets with a life of at least 20 years and less than 25 years
20 years	Assets with a life of at least 25 years

Examples of tangible personal property classified by recovery period are presented in the following table:

Recovery Period	Examples of Eligible Property
3 years	Special tools
5 years	Light duty trucks, automobiles, and computers
7 years	Office furniture and fixtures, and other equipment
10 years	Railroad tank cars
15 years	Industrial generation systems
20 years	Sewer pipes

Real Property is classified into two recovery periods. Residential real property is 27.5-year recovery property while nonresidential real property is 31.5-year recovery property.

Personal property in the 3-year, 5-year, 7-year, and 10-year recovery period categories is to be depreciated using the 200% declining balance method with a switch to the straight line method at the point in time when deductions will be maximized (i.e., generally in the middle of the recovery period). The 150% declining balance method is applicable to 15-year and 20-year recovery property. The provision regarding the switch to straight line is also applicable. An election may be made to calculate the cost recovery deduction utilizing the straight-line method. The election must be made for all assets placed into service in a particular class in each year.

Real property must be depreciated utilizing the straight-line method. Classification into residential and nonresidential categories is irrelevant.

Whether the accelerated method or the straight line method is used for personal property, a half-year convention is applicable in the year the asset is placed into service and in the year the property is disposed of, if prior to the expiration of the recovery period.

The timing of asset purchases must be planned because the "mid-quarter convention" may be triggered. Under the "mid-quarter convention," if more than 40% of the aggregate value of personal property is placed into service during the last quarter of the year, the half-year convention must be replaced by the mid-quarter convention. With respect to real property, a mid-month convention is to be applied when the asset is placed into service and when the asset is disposed of prior to the expiration of the recovery period.

The *Alternative Depreciation System* (ADS) must be used for certain types of property including personal property used outside of the United States and property leased to tax-exempt entities. ADS, however, may be elected for any class of property placed into service. The recovery deduction will be based on the straight-line method and longer recovery periods. Personal property with no class life will be recovered over 12 years, while real property will be recovered over 40 years. All other property will be recovered over the applicable class life.

Automobiles are included in a special category of property referred to as "listed property." The annual deduction for autos placed into service after 1988 is limited as follows:

Year	Allowable Deduction
1	$2,660
2	4,200
3	2,550
Each Year Thereafter	1,475

The deductible amounts are periodically adjusted for inflation. Listed property not used more than 50% of the time for business must use the alternative depreciation system.

The Section 179 election allows the expensing of certain depreciable assets. Under the statute, in lieu of capitalizing the asset and depreciating it, the assets may be expensed in the year they are placed into service. There is, however, a $10,000 annual limitation, which must be reduced dollar for dollar by the amount by which the cost of Section 179 property placed into service during the year exceeds $200,000. Additionally, the deduction cannot be used to create or increase a net operating loss. Furthermore, the deduction must be considered for depreciation recapture purposes.

CAPITAL GAINS AND LOSSES

Corporations cannot deduct capital losses against ordinary income. Capital losses can only be offset against capital gains. Capital losses that cannot be utilized in the year sustained may be carried back up to three years and then carried forward for up to five years. The net capital loss, if carried forward, is treated as a short-term loss. Capital gains are taxed at the corporation's ordinary tax rates.

FEDERAL TAX RATES

IRC §63 specifies the regular income tax rates as follows:

Taxable Income	Tax Rate
First $50,000	15%
$50,001 − $75,000	25%
In excess of $75,000	34%

Personal Service Corporations, however, may not avail themselves of the preferential brackets. In such cases, a flat 34% rate is applicable.

When a corporation's taxable income is in excess of $100,000, they are liable for an additional tax in the amount of the lesser of (1) 5% of such excess, or (2) $11,750.

Generally, a corporation must make quarterly estimated tax payments if it expects its estimated tax to be $500 or more. In the case of a calendar year corporation, these estimated tax payments are generally due on April 15, June 15, September 15 and December 15.

FOREIGN TAX CREDIT

If a corporation pays income taxes to a foreign country, it may be entitled to a U.S. foreign tax credit. This credit, however, cannot be used to reduce the U.S. tax liability on income from U.S. sources. The tentative U.S. foreign tax credit is calculated using the following formula:

$$\text{Foreign tax credit} = \frac{\text{Foreign source income}}{\text{Total worldwide income}} \times \text{U.S. tax liability}$$

THE ALTERNATIVE MINIMUM TAX

The alternative minimum tax (AMT) calculation represents perhaps the most difficult provision of the IRC. The AMT is designed to prevent taxpayers from minimizing their tax liability through the deduction of preferential items.

The AMT is based on the following formula:

Regular Taxable Income (Before Net Operating Loss Deductions)

+ Tax Preference Items and Adjustments

= Pre-Net Operating Loss Alternative Minimum Taxable Income

− Up to 90% of Alternative Minimum Tax Net Operating Loss Deductions

= Alternative Minimum Taxable Income

− Exemption Amount

= Balance

× 20%

= Alternative Minimum Tax

− Applicable Credits

− Regular Current Year Tax Liability

= Alternative Minimum Tax Liability

Some of the more common tax preference items are:

(1) Excess accelerated depreciation on real property

(2) Excess percentage depletion for coal and iron ore

(3) With respect to tangible depreciable personal property placed into service after December 31, 1986, the excess of accelerated depreciation over the amount calculated using the 150% declining balance method with the appropriate switch to straight line

(4) Excess amortization of pollution control facilities

(5) The untaxed appreciation on property donated to charitable organizations

The main adjustment to be considered in the calculation of the AMT relates to depreciation. The depreciation adjustment is essentially equal to the depreciation of the assets placed into service after 1986 using the alternative depreciation system (discussed earlier) reduced by the company's regular depreciation expense.

Beginning in 1990, a new adjustment must be considered. Called the adjusted current earnings adjustment, it is equal to the company's regular taxable income plus adjustments used to calculate the company's earnings and profits.

The calculation of the AMT is extremely complex. It is suggested that a tax advisor be consulted.

THE PERSONAL HOLDING COMPANY TAX

The intent of the personal holding company tax is to compel corporations to annually distribute earnings derived from investments. Corporations subject to the personal holding company tax must pay a 28% tax on undistributed personal holding company income. The tax is in the nature of a penalty tax and is in addition to the company's regular income tax liability.

In order to be classified as a personal holding company, two tests must be satisfied. Generally, the income test requires that at least 60% of the corporation's adjusted ordinary gross income be derived from interest, dividends, certain royalties, certain types of rental income, as well as certain types of annuities and pass-through items from estates and trusts. The stock ownership test is essentially met if during the last half of the tax year more than 50% of the entity's stock is owned by five or fewer shareholders.

The personal holding company tax is self-imposed; i.e., corporations must determine their status as a personal holding company and then file a Form 1120-PH along with their regular tax return.

Corporations may plan to mitigate the personal holding company tax by paying sufficient dividends to their shareholders.

ACCUMULATED EARNINGS TAX

The accumulated earnings tax, like the personal holding company tax, is in the nature of a penalty tax. Also imposed at the rate of 28%, this tax is in addition to the corporation's regular income tax liability. The imposition of the accumulated earnings tax forces corporations to distribute earnings and profits in the form of dividends. If not for the provisions of the accumulated earnings tax, the tax at the shareholder level (which is in addition to the corporate tax imposed on the entity's regular taxable income) could be avoided.

The accumulated earnings tax is imposed on the year's "accumulated taxable income," which is regular taxable income reduced by (1) dividends paid to shareholders, (2) federal income taxes, (3) charitable contributions in excess of the 10% limitation discussed earlier, (4) net capital losses not deductible in calculating ordinary taxable income, (5) net capital gain for the year (reduced by the taxes attributed thereto), and (6) the accumulated earnings credit. The taxable base must be increased by the dividends-received deduction. The accumulated earnings credit is equal to the earnings retained for the reasonable needs of the business. The minimum accumulated earnings credit is $250,000 except for a personal service corporation, in which case the credit is reduced to $150,000.

As in the case of the personal holding company tax, careful tax planning can mitigate the imposition of the penalty tax. The payment of sufficient dividends to the shareholders can mitigate the tax. Dividends paid after year end but on or before the fifteenth day of the third month of the new year may be considered in reducing the base subject to the accumulated earnings tax.

Unlike the personal holding company tax, the accumulated earnings tax is not self-imposed. Rather, the Internal Revenue Service must determine that a liability exists for the accumulated earnings tax.

CORPORATE REORGANIZATIONS

Generally, corporate reorganizations do not result in the imposition of income tax. IRC Sec. 368 defines the seven types of corporate reorganizations.

A Type A reorganization may be a statutory merger or consolidation. A merger is effected when there is a union between two or more corporations. Pursuant to the union, one corporation retains its existence while the other parties to the reorganization are absorbed. A consolidation, on the other hand, is effected when a new corporation is created and the other parties are absorbed.

A Type B reorganization involves the acquisition by one corporation, in exchange solely for all or part of its voting stock (or in exchange solely for all of the voting stock of a corporation which is in control of the acquiring corporation), of stock of another corporation if, immediately after the acquisition, the acquiring corporation has control (i.e., 80%) of such other corporation (whether or not such acquiring corporation had control immediately before the acquisition).

A Type C reorganization results in the acquisition by one corporation, in exchange solely for all or part of its voting stock (or in exchange for all or a part of the voting stock of a corporation which is in control of the acquiring corporation), of substantially all of the properties of another corporation, but in determining whether the exchange is solely for stock the assumption by the acquiring corporation of a liability of the other, or the fact that property acquired is subject to a liability, shall be disregarded.

A Type D reorganization is predicated on a transfer by a corporation of all or a part of its assets to another corporation if immediately after the transfer the transferer, or one or more of its shareholders (including persons who were shareholders immediately before the transfer), or any combination thereof, is in control of the corporation to which the assets were transferred; but only if, in pursuance of the plan, stock or securities of the corporation to which the assets are transferred are distributed to the shareholders in a tax free or partially tax free transaction.

A Type E reorganization, called a recapitalization, involves changes in the amount and/or character of the corporation's stock or paid-in capital. An exchange of stock for stock, for example, qualifies as a Type E reorganization.

A Type F reorganization entails a mere change in identity, form, or place of organization of one corporation, however effected.

A Type G reorganization results in a transfer by a corporation of all or a part of its assets to another corporation (under title 11 of the Bankruptcy Code) but only if, in pursuance of the plan, stock or securities of the corporation to which the assets are transferred are distributed to the shareholders in a tax free or partially tax free transaction.

In general, no tax gain arises in corporate reorganizations unless "boot" is involved. "Boot" is generally property in addition to the stock of the parties involved. For example, when cash in received in a statutory merger, it is treated as boot.

CORPORATE LIQUIDATIONS

The tax consequences of complete liquidations are relatively straightforward. A shareholder will generally recognize capital gain or loss upon receipt of cash or other property in complete liquidation of the corporation. The gain or loss is measured by the difference between the cash and fair market value of property received reduced by the adjusted basis of the stock surrendered. The liquidating corporation must recognize gain or loss on its normal business transactions during the liquidation period. Additionally, gain must be recognized by the distributing corporation to the extent that the fair market value of any property distributed exceeds the adjusted basis of that property. In calculating the gain, assets subject to liabilities cannot have a fair market value less than the amount of the liability.

Liquidation of corporate subsidiaries can be effected tax free if (1) the parent corporation owns at least 80% of the subsidiary, and (2) the basis of the assets in the hands of the parent corporation is the same as the basis to the subsidiary. It should be noted that cancellation of debt in exchange for assets will not result in a taxable transaction.

Partial liquidations are extremely complex and should be consummated only after consulting a tax advisor.

S CORPORATIONS

An S corporation is a corporation that has elected to be treated essentially like a partnership. Accordingly, an S corporation will generally not pay tax.

ELECTION

To elect status as an S corporation, a Form 2553 must be filed on or before the fifteenth day of the third month of the corporation's tax year. An election which is filed late becomes effective the first day of the following tax year. All shareholders must consent to the election. In addition, the following conditions must be satisfied:

(1) The corporation is a domestic corporation; i.e., organized or incorporated in the United States.

(2) The corporation has no more than 35 shareholders who are individuals, estates or certain types of trusts. Other corporations, partnerships, nonqualifying trusts and nonresident aliens may not be shareholders.

(3) The corporation may not be an active member of an affiliated group.

(4) The corporation may have only one class of stock. Different voting rights associated with different shares of common stock will not be construed as a violation of the one class of stock rule.

The decision to elect S corporation status should be based on the following:

(1) An extremely profitable C corporation will generally pay more income tax than the tax levied on the shareholders of an S corporation.

(2) Corporations that become S corporations at inception are not subject to corporate tax upon liquidation.

(3) S corporations are not liable for the alternative minimum tax.

(4) Small C corporations, which generally strip their profits by paying additional salaries to their owner-employees, may derive no additional benefit by electing S corporation status.

(5) Many states do not recognize S corporation status. Accordingly, there may be no savings of tax at the state level.

(6) Certain states that do recognize S corporation status, require nonresident shareholders to report their respective pass-through items. Accordingly, nonresident tax returns may be required.

COMPUTING TAXABLE INCOME

With certain exceptions, the computation of an S corporation's taxable income is similar to the computation of the taxable income of a C corporation. Since an S corporation is a flow-though entity, any items of income, deduction, gain, loss or credit which would receive special handling or treatment on the returns of the shareholders are passed through and accounted for separately. All other items are considered in the computation of the corporation's taxable income. Some of the more common items which are passed through and accounted for separately are:

(1) Capital gains and losses

(2) Ordinary gains and losses properly reported on Form 4797

(3) Gains and losses on the disposition of tangible depreciable property used in the trade or business activity of the corporation

(4) Donations to charitable organizations

(5) Interest income derived from tax-exempt securities

(6) Portfolio income such as interest and dividend income

(7) Income and deductions attributable to passive activity

Shareholders must report on their tax returns a pro rata portion of the items which are separately stated in addition to a pro rata portion of the corporation's taxable income which is not separately computed. Whether or not the shareholders received distributions is irrelevant.

S Corporations may not deduct net operating losses since they pass through to the shareholders on a pro rata basis. Ownership of stock at the end of the year is not necessary in order to deduct a portion of the corporation's net operating loss, because the proration of the loss is based on the days of ownership. Losses, however, may only be deducted to the extent of the shareholder's basis in (1) the corporate stock held during the year and (2) any indebtedness owed to the shareholder by the corporation. In the event that a net operating loss is not deductible because basis does not exceed zero. The shareholder may carry forward the losses indefinitely until basis does exist.

DISTRIBUTIONS TO SHAREHOLDERS

With respect to distributions by S corporations that have accumulated earnings and profits from its days as a C Corporation, a four-level system is to be followed:

- *Level one distributions* are treated as nontaxable returns of capital since these distributions are derived from the accumulated adjustments account (AAA). AAA is essentially the post-1982 taxable income of the S Corporation reported by the shareholders, reduced by certain nondeductible expenses of the corporation.

- *Level two distributions* are taxed as dividends since they are traced to the corporation's accumulated earnings and profits earned from operating as a C corporation.

- *Level three distributions* reduce the basis of the shareholder's stock and accordingly represent tax-free distributions.

• *Level four distributions* result in the recognition of capital gain.

Corporations that have elected S status from inception obviously need not be concerned with level two distributions.

BASIS OF S CORPORATION STOCK

In determining the basis of S corporation stock, the starting point is either the price paid in a stock purchase or the initial contribution to capital in exchange for the stock. The shareholder's basis is then increased by his or her ratable share of separately stated and non separately stated items of income. The shareholder's basis is reduced by (1) his or her ratable share of corporate loss and deductions, whether or not separately stated, (2) distributions representing a return of capital (i.e., level one and level three distributions), and (3) all expenses not deducted in computing taxable income and not properly charged to the capital account. The fair market value of property distributions, it should be noted, reduces the shareholder's basis in stock. In no event may the basis in stock go below zero. Since the shareholder's deduction of net operating losses of S corporations is affected by the shareholder's basis in his or her stock, planning is crucial. If the shareholder's basis in stock is insufficient, loans to the corporation should be considered. Caution must be exercised because the payback of the loan might result in a taxable situation.

SHAREHOLDER/EMPLOYEE BENEFITS

A problem arises in the case of fringe benefits paid to shareholders possessing more than 2% of the corporations outstanding stock. If a shareholder, at any time during the year, actually or by virtue of the attribution rules of IRC §318, owned more than 2% of the corporation's outstanding stock (or more than 2% of the total voting power), then the following fringe benefits, while normally tax-free, will be taxable:

(1) The $5,000 death benefit exclusion under IRC §101(b)

(2) The exclusion under IRC §105(b)–(d) of amounts paid pursuant to certain accident and health plans

(3) The exclusion under IRC §106 of employer-paid accident and health insurance plans

(4) The $50,000 group-term life insurance premium exclusion under IRC §79

The Internal Revenue Service has great latitude in defining fringe benefits. Accordingly, the above list of fringe benefits should not be construed as all inclusive.

TAX YEAR

An S Corporation, in general, must adopt a calendar year. A fiscal year is available if it can be demonstrated that there is a bona fide business purpose for the fiscal year. Additionally, under IRC Sec. 444, an S corporation may adopt a fiscal year if the deferral period for the year is not more than three months. If a fiscal year is adopted, liability may exist for an annual "required payment" which essentially represents the prepayment of tax on the income attributable to the deferral period.

PITFALLS IN CONVERTING FROM A C CORPORATION TO AN S CORPORATION

The conversion from C corporation status to S corporation status may result in certain problems as discussed below.

Passive Investment Income Tax

The possibility of the passive investment income tax is only applicable to an S corporation that was previously a C corporation. Tax liability arises when the S corporation (1) has Subchapter C earnings and profits, and (2) more than 25% of its income is in the form of passive investment income (which includes rents, royalties, interest, dividends, annuities and capital gains resulting from the disposition of stock and securities). The tax is imposed at the highest rate of corporate tax. The base subject to tax is the lesser of (1) excess net passive income, or (2) current taxable income, computed as if the corporation were a C corporation. Excess net passive income is equal to the entity's net passive investment income multiplied by a fraction (the numerator of which is the excess of passive investment income over 25% of gross income, the denominator of which is the passive investment income). It becomes obvious that in order to avoid the imposition of this tax, dividend distributions should be considered.

Built-In Gains Tax

The built-in gains tax is a corporate-level tax imposed under IRC §1374. The tax is imposed on the built-in gains attributable to assets disposed within 10 years after converting to S corporation status. An asset's built-in gain is its appreciation in value while held by the C corporation. The tax is imposed at the highest corporate rate multiplied by the lesser of the current year (1) the recognized built-in gain or (2) taxable income computed as if the corporation were a C corporation.

Termination and Revocation

Three situations may result in revocation or termination of the S corporation election:

(1) Revocation by shareholders owning more than 50% of the outstanding stock of the corporation.

(2) The corporation ceases to qualify as an S corporation.

(3) The corporation has passive investment income in excess of 25% of its gross income for three consecutive years. Termination will result, however, only if the corporation has accumulated earnings and profits (from its days as a C corporation) at the end of each of these three years.

In the case of a revocation by shareholders owning more than 50% of the outstanding stock, the effective date is the first day of the year if the election is made on or before the fifteenth day of the third month of the tax year. Otherwise, the revocation becomes effective on the first day of the following tax year.

In the case of an election that is terminated because the corporation ceases to qualify as an S corporation, the effective date is the date of cessation of operations as an S corporation. This will require that the tax year be split into two short years, with a proration of tax due on the income attributable to the days as a C corporation.

The effective date of a termination due to the passive investment income limitation is the first day of the fourth year (i.e., after the three consecutive year rule is met).

CONCLUSION

When making business decisions, a controller must consider both tax and non-tax factors. The controller should possess a basic understanding of pertinent tax laws. When the need arises, it is prudent to consult a detailed tax information service. Prentice Hall, Commerce Clearing House, Research Institute of America, and Matthew Bender publish such outstanding tax reporters.

43

Payroll Taxes

Payroll usually represents the largest operating expense of a company. It is obvious then that the related payroll taxes become a significant consideration for the controller. The controller must be familiar with federal, state, and local payroll tax payment and filing requirements. In addition, attention must be given to worker's compensation and disability insurance.

SOCIAL SECURITY AND MEDICARE TAXES

Social security and medicare taxes are burdens to both employees and their employers. Employers must match the amount withheld from their employees' payroll checks and remit to the Internal Revenue Service both the employer and employee portions of the taxes. For 1991, social security must be withheld from the first $53,400 of employee wages. The maximum wage base is subject to a tax rate of 6.2%. Accordingly, the maximum amount that can be withheld from an employee's wages during 1991 is $3310.80. For 1991, the maximum wage base for the medicare tax is $125,000. The medicare tax is imposed at the rate of 1.45%. Accordingly, the maximum amount that can be withheld from an employee's wages during 1991 is $1,812.50. Prior to 1991, the social security tax and the medicare tax were not separately stated. Future increases in the social security and medicare taxes are inevitable.

Since cost reduction is an important function of the controller, he or she should attempt to minimize the social security and medicare tax burdens by considering (1) independent contractor status of workers, and (2) the common paymaster provisions of the Internal Revenue Code.

INDEPENDENT CONTRACTOR STATUS

The definition of an employee in IRC §3121 leaves much to be desired. The statute refers to common law provisions, which have been subject to interpretation throughout the years. The overriding consideration seems to be whether the person rendering the services is under the control of the so-called "employer." If the worker can be supervised, guided, and told where the work is to be performed, control is presumed and employee status is generally mandated. Furthermore, employee status is usually presumed when work hours are fixed and when the individual is forbidden by contract to perform services for others. Similarly, participation in profit sharing plans is a good indication that employee status is present.

Clearly, from a company's point of view, the independent contractor status of an individual results in a savings of social security and medicare taxes, since the independent contractor is responsible for the payment of his or her own taxes. An independent contractor is also responsible for his or her own worker's compensation and disability insurance.

To ensure that the taxing authorities do not successfully contest independent contractor status of a worker, an indemnification agreement should be drafted. In the agreement, the independent contractor should acknowledge his or her responsibility for social security, medicare, federal, and state (and local, if applicable) income taxes as well as worker's compensation and disability insurance. It would be prudent to obtain a copy of the independent contractor's worker's compensation policy. This one document is often useful in sustaining independent status upon challenge by unemployment insurance agencies.

THE COMMON PAYMASTER PROVISION

If an individual performs services for two or more related companies, one of the corporations may serve as a common paymaster. In such instances, the common paymaster is responsible for the payment of all wages and payroll taxes. Failure, on the part of the common paymaster, to withhold and pay the appropriate taxes could prove to be costly, since all of the corporations involved would then become liable for the deficiencies.

For a particular calendar quarter, to be included in the group of corporations treated as a common paymaster for a particular quarter, at least one of the following tests must be satisfied:

(1) The company is a member of either a brother-sister or parent-subsidiary controlled group, except that the 80%-ownership requirement of IRC §1563 is replaced with a 50%-ownership requirement.

(2) At least 50% of one corporation's officers are officers of the other corporation(s) that is (are) included in the group.

(3) At least 30% of the employees of one corporation are employed by one of the other corporations included in the group.

FEDERAL WITHHOLDING TAXES

Every employer is required to withhold federal withholding taxes from employee wage payments in accordance with the allowances claimed by the employee on Form W-2.

TAX DEPOSITS

The amount of taxes owed by the company determines the frequency of required deposits. The liability for payment of federal withholding, social security and medicare taxes arises when the wages are paid, not when the payroll period ends. Tax deposits are generally made payable to an authorized financial institution or a Federal Reserve bank or branch, and should be accompanied by Form 8109, Federal Tax Deposit Coupon. Form 8109 should clearly indicate the kind of tax being deposited, as well as the applicable quarter. A company's tax liability and deposits are reported quarterly on Form 941. To determine when payroll tax deposits are due, the following guidelines should be utilized:

(1) Less than $500 at the end of a calendar quarter: If at the end of the quarter the total undeposited taxes for the quarter are less than $500, the taxes do not have to (although they may) be deposited. Rather, the taxes may be paid to the Internal Revenue Service with Form 941.

(2) Less than $500 at the end of any month: If at the end of any month the total undeposited taxes are less than $500, the taxes do not have to be deposited. The undeposited taxes may be carried forward to the following month within the calendar quarter.

(3) $500 or more but less than $3,000 at the end of any month: If at the end of any month the total undeposited taxes are $500 or more but less than $3,000, the taxes must be deposited within 15 days after the end of the month. However, if a deposit of $3,000 or more must be made during the month under rule 4 below, carry over any balance of less than $3,000 at the end of the first or second month of the quarter to the next month. Rules 3 and 4 should then be followed in determining when the next deposit must be made. If a deposit of $3,000 or more is required during the third month of the quarter, a deposit must be made for any balance of $500 or more but less than $3,000 by the end of the next month. A balance due of less than $500 may be paid with the return, as under rule 1.

(4) $3,000 or more at the end of any eighth-monthly period: If at the end of any eighth-monthly period the total undeposited taxes are $3,000 or more, then the taxes must be deposited within three banking days after the end of that eighth-monthly period. Banking days, for tax purposes do not include Saturdays, Sundays, legal holidays, or local holidays observed by authorized financial institutions. The deposit periods, referred to as the eighth-monthly periods, end on the 3rd, 7th, 11th, 15th,

19th, 22nd, 25th, and last day of each month. It should be noted that deposits of $20,000 or more that are made by taxpayers required to deposit taxes more than once a month must be received by the due date to be timely.

Rule 4 will be deemed to be satisfied if (1) a deposit is made for at least 95% of the tax liability for that eighth-monthly period within three banking days after the end of that period, and (2) any underpayment is deposited as follows:

(a) If an eighth-monthly period is in the first or second month of the quarter, the underpayment is deposited with the first deposit that is required to be made after the 15th of the following month.

(b) If an eighth-monthly period is in the last month of the quarter, any underpayment of $500 or more is deposited by the due date of the return (i.e., Form 941). Any underpayment less than $500 may be paid with the return, as discussed in rule 1.

An exception to rule 4 exists, under which a deposit may be made by the 15th day of the next month (instead of within three banking days after the end of the eighth-monthly period). The exception provision is only available the first time that you are normally required to make a deposit within three banking days after the end of an eighth-monthly period. To qualify for the exception, (1) you cannot have been required to deposit taxes for any eighth-monthly period during the four quarters preceding the current quarter, (2) no requirement may have existed during earlier months of the quarter for a deposit of taxes for any eighth-monthly period, and (3) the total undeposited taxes at the end of any eighth-monthly period during the month are less than $10,000.

It should be noted that employers must make a deposit of taxes by the close of the next banking day if the undeposited tax liability (i.e., generally federal income tax withheld plus both the employee and employer social security and medicare taxes) is $100,000 or more.

Form 941, Employer's Quarterly Federal Tax Return (Exhibit 2), must be filed as follows:

Calendar Quarter Ending	Due Date
March 31	April 30
June 30	July 31
September 30	October 31
December 31	January 31

WORKER'S COMPENSATION AND DISABILITY INSURANCE

Worker's compensation insurance is intended to cover the cost of medical expenses incurred by employees who sustain injuries during the course of their employment. In addition, worker's compensation insurance reimburses an employee for the loss of income during the employee's convalescing period.

A company's premiums for worker's compensation insurance are dependent upon (1) the nature of the employer's business, (2) the classification of the company's employees, (3) the wages paid to the employees, and (4) the volume of company claims filed by the company in the past.

Rules and regulations pertaining to premium calculations are normally dependent upon state statutes. However, to minimize premiums, an employer should exercise caution when classifying employees. For instance, employees who work with heavy-duty machinery are subject to higher premiums than those who are classified as clerical workers. Furthermore, employers should be careful not to overstate the payroll base subject to the premiums. Officers' salaries are usually capped at a maximum amount and overtime for other employees is often excluded.

Adequate and accurate records should be maintained by the controller in order to ensure that (1) premiums are minimized, and (2) the company will not be liable for additional premiums upon audit by the insurance carrier.

Disability insurance is designed to compensate an employee for lost wages resulting from a "disabling" injury or illness which is not work related. Unlike the calculation of premiums for worker's compensation insurance, disability insurance premiums are not based on employee classification. Quite often, a uniform rate is applicable to a maximum wage base which is established by the insurer. Other times, the premium is set at a given dollar amount per employee in a given month. Many disability insurers establish premiums based on the gender of the employee. Depending upon the insurer, premiums could be due quarterly, semi-annually or annually.

UNEMPLOYMENT INSURANCE

State unemployment insurance coverage varies from state to state. Each year an employer is assigned an experience rating which determines the rate of tax to be imposed upon the employer. The maximum wage base also varies from state to state.

Rules pertaining to federal unemployment insurance tax, on the other hand, are uniform throughout the United States.

An employer must generally file either an annual Form 940 or 940-EZ by January 31, which covers the payroll of the prior year. If the amount of tax for the year is not more than $100, the tax may be paid with the return. If an entity's annual liability is in excess of $100, the tax must be deposited on a timely basis at an authorized financial institution or a Federal Reserve Bank or branch. An employer must calculate the liability for federal unemployment taxes on a quarterly basis (based on a calendar year). Deposits must be made by the last day of the month following the close of the quarter when the liability is in excess of $100. The deposit must be accompanied by Form 8109, Federal Tax Deposit Coupon, which should clearly indicate the kind of tax being deposited, as well as the applicable quarter. At present, the tax is imposed on the first $7,000 of wages paid to each employee during the calendar year. The rate of tax is dependent upon whether the employer has paid all required contributions to the state unemployment funds by the due date of Form 940 or Form 940-EZ. If state unemployment insurance contributions are made timely, the federal rate will normally be 0.8%.

Form 940-EZ can be used in lieu of the longer Form 940 if (1) the employer paid unemployment insurance contributions to only one state, (2) all the state contributions were paid by the due date of Form 940-EZ, and (3) all wages that are taxable for federal unemployment insurance purposes are also taxable for state unemployment purposes.

CONCLUSION

The controller plays an important role in the payroll tax function. The controller is responsible for (1) making timely tax deposits and (2) filing tax reports when due. It is also important to establish whether a worker is an employee or an independent contractor since the former is subject to a variety of payroll taxes. Classification of workers as independent contractors may reduce the company's tax liability.

Tax forms referred to in this chapter are available from various governmental offices and have not been reproduced herein since they are constantly subject to change.

X

MERGERS, DIVESTITURES, AND FAILURE

44

Mergers and Acquisitions

This chapter discusses all facets of mergers and acquisitions including deciding on terms, key factors to consider, pros and cons of mergers, types of arrangements, evaluative criteria, valuation methods, financial effects of the merger, holding companies, takeover bids, SEC filing requirements, accounting and reporting requirements for business combinations, and financial analysis of combinations.

External growth occurs when a business purchases the existing assets of another entity through a merger. You are often required to appraise the suitability of a potential merger as well as participate in negotiations. Besides the growth aspect, a merger may reduce risk through diversification. The three common ways of joining two or more companies are a merger, consolidation, or a holding company.

In a merger, two or more companies are combined into one, where only the acquiring company retains its identity. Generally, the larger of the two companies is the acquirer.

With a consolidation, two or more companies combine to create a new company. None of the consolidation firms legally survive. For example, companies A and B give all their assets, liabilities, and stock to the new company, C, in return for C's stock, bonds, or cash.

A holding company possesses voting control of one or more other companies. The holding company comprises a group of businesses, each operating as a separate entity. By possessing more than 50% of the voting rights through common stock, the holding company has effective control of another company with a smaller percent of ownership.

Depending on the intent of the combination, there are three common ways in which businesses get together so as to obtain advantages in their markets. They are:

- *Vertical merger.* This occurs when a company combines with a supplier or customer. An example is when a wholesaler combines with retailers.

- *Horizontal merger.* This occurs when two companies in a similar business combine. An example is the combining of two airlines.

- *Conglomerate merger.* This occurs when two companies in unrelated industries combine, such as where an electronics company joins with an insurance company.

MERGERS

A merger may be accomplished in one of two ways. The acquirer may negotiate with the management of the prospective acquired company, which is preferred. If negotiations fail, the acquirer may make a tender offer directly to the stockholders of the targeted company. A tender offer represents a cash offering (but can be a stock offering) for the common shares held by stockholders. A good takeover candidate includes a cash-rich business, a company with significant growth potential, and a company with a low debt-to-equity ratio.

In discussions with management, the acquirer typically makes a stock offer at a specified exchange ratio. The merger may take place if the acquired company receives an offer at an acceptable premium over the current market price of stock. Sometimes contingent payments are also given, such as stock warrants.

There are several financing packages that buyers may use for mergers, such as common stock, preferred stock, convertible bonds, debt, cash, and warrants. A key factor in selecting the final package is its impact on current earnings per share (EPS).

If common stock is exchanged, the seller's stock is given in exchange for the buyer's stock, resulting in a tax-free exchange. The drawback is that the stock issuance lowers earnings per share because the buyer's outstanding shares are increased. When there is an exchange of cash for common stock, the selling company's stockholders receive cash, resulting in a taxable transaction. This type of exchange may increase EPS since the buying company is obtaining new earnings without increasing outstanding shares.

There are many reasons why your company may prefer external growth through mergers instead of internal growth.

Advantages of a Merger

- Increases corporate power and improves market share and product lines

- Aids in diversification, such as reducing cyclical and operational effects

- Helps the company's ability to raise financing when it merges with another entity having significant liquid assets and low debt

- Provides a good return on investment when the market value of the acquired business is significantly less than its replacement cost

- Improves the market price of stock in some cases, resulting in a higher P/E ratio. For example, the stock of a larger company may be viewed as more marketable, secure, and stable.

- Provides a missed attribute; that is, a company gains something it lacked. For instance, superior management quality or research capability may be obtained.

- Aids the company in financing an acquisition that would not otherwise be possible to obtain, such as where acquiring a company by exchanging stock is less costly than building new capital facilities, which would require an enormous cash outlay. For instance, a company may be unable to finance significant internal expansion but can achieve it by purchasing a business already possessing such capital facilities.

- Achieves a synergistic effect, which means that the results of the combination are greater than the sum of the parts. For instance, greater profit may result from the combined entity than would occur from each individual company due to increased efficiency (e.g., economies of scale) and cost savings (e.g., eliminating overlapping administrative functions, volume discounts on purchases). There is better use of people and resources. A greater probability of synergy exists with a horizontal merger since duplicate facilities are eliminated.

- Obtains a tax loss carryforward benefit if the acquired company has been losing money. The acquirer may utilize the tax loss carryforward benefit to offset its own profitability, thus reducing its taxes. The tax loss may be carried forward 15 years to reduce the acquiring company's future earnings. In effect, the government is financing part of the acquisition.

EXAMPLE 1

H Company is deciding whether to buy S Company. S has a tax loss of $500,000. H Company anticipates pretax earnings of $400,000 and $300,000 for the next two years. The tax rate is 34%. The taxes to be paid by H Company follow.

Year 1: $400,000 - $400,000 = 0
Year 2: $300,000 - $100,000 = $200,000 \times 34\% = $68,000

Disadvantages of a Merger

- Reverse synergies which reduce the net value of the combined entity (e.g., adjustments of pay scales, costs of servicing acquisition debt, defections of key acquired company staff)

- Adverse financial effects because the anticipated benefits did not materialize; for example, expected cost reductions were not forthcoming

- Antitrust action delaying or preventing the proposed merger

- Problems caused by dissenting minority stockholders

In evaluating a potential merger, you have to consider its possible effect upon the financial performance of the company, including:

- *Earnings per share.* The merger should result in higher earnings or improve its stability.
- *Dividends per share.* The dividends before and after the merger should be maintained to stabilize the market price of stock.
- *Market price of stock.* The market price of the stock should be higher or at least the same after the merger.
- *Risk.* The merged business should have less financial and operating risk than before.

DECIDING ON ACQUISITION TERMS

In deciding on acquisition terms, consideration should be given to the following:

- Earnings in terms of absolute dollars and percentage change
- Dividends
- Market price of stock
- Book value per share
- Net working capital per share

The weight assigned to each of the above varies with the circumstances involved.

Earnings

In determining the value of earnings in a merger, you should take into account anticipated future earnings and projected P/E ratio. A rapidly growing company is expected to have a higher P/E multiple.

Dividends

Dividends are attractive to stockholders. However, the more a company's growth rate and earnings, the less is the impact of dividends on market price of stock. On the other hand, if earnings are falling, the greater is the effect of dividends on per share price.

Market Price of Stock

The price of a security considers projected earnings and dividends. The value assigned to the company in the acquisition will most likely be greater than the present market price in the following instances:

- The business is in a depressed industry.
- The acquired company is of greater value to the acquirer than to the stock market in general.
- A higher market price than the current one is offered to induce existing stockholders to give up their shares.

Book Value per Share

Since book value is based on historical cost rather than current value, it is not a key factor to consider. However, when book value exceeds market value, there may be an expectation that market price will increase subsequent to the merger due to improved circumstances (e.g., superior management).

Net Working Capital per Share

If the acquired company has very low debt or very liquid assets, the acquirer may borrow the funds for the acquisition by using the acquired company's strong liquidity position.

FACTORS IN DETERMINING A PRICE

There are many factors to be considered in determining the price to be paid for a business including:

- Financial health of the acquired company (e.g., quality of earnings, growth rate, realizability of assets)
- Type and stability of operations
- Maturity of business
- Degree of competition
- Tax consequences, such as unused tax credits
- Expected return on assets and sales
- Employee relations, such as the absence of unionization
- Risk level, such as having adequate insurance
- Corporate characteristics, including having negatively correlated product lines, and favorable lease terms
- Management quality, such as experienced executives
- Marketing position, such as quality product line, market share, distribution channels, and customer base
- Economic environment, including recession-resistant business
- Political environment, such as the absence of strict governmental regulation and operations in politically unstable areas

- Structure of the arrangement, including debt or equity, cash or stock, costs of the transaction, and time period
- Improvement in diversification and/or integration
- Ease of transferability of ownership
- Exchange rate fluctuations
- Legal issues, such as the possibility of stockholder liability suits
- Industry characteristics, such as being in a growing industry instead of a declining one. For example, in 1981, Sohio's acquisition of Kennecott Copper for $1.77 billion resulted in financial disaster due to downside trends in the industry.
- Impact of the acquisition on the acquiring company's financial strength and operating performance. For instance, Baldwin United's acquisition of Mortgage Guaranty Insurance ultimately forced both companies into bankruptcy. There was an evident failure to appropriately appraise the effect of the acquisition on financial posture.
- Possible violation of antitrust laws. These laws are administered by the Department of Justice's Antitrust Division and the Federal Trade Commission.

When looking at the targeted company, see what the positive and negative effects of the acquisition would be on you. By examining what the overall picture after the merger would be, you can properly assess what to pay for the candidate. If your analysis includes many uncertain factors, sensitivity analysis may be used to look at the effect of changes in outcome.

Be Careful: Detailed financial planning and analysis are required in the acquisition process. An example of an acquisition that did not work out well is the 1980 acquisition by Pan American of National Airlines for $400 million. A major reason of the acquisition was to enable Pan Am to use National's routes to feed its overseas routes. However, management did not make progress in rescheduling for almost two years.

Warning: If an acquiring company overpays for a target company, this negatively affects its financial position. For example, was it worth it to J. Ray McDermott to fight off United Technologies to obtain control of Babcock and Wilcox, even though it pushed the stock price up from about $35 to $65?

GRADING CRITERIA

In acquisition strategy, you document what you want to accomplish by the acquisition and how the acquisition will complement your overall strategy. Industries and companies are then screened by employing various quantitative measures and considering qualitative factors. The broad industry sectors should be narrowed down by comparing each industry to your specified industry criteria. The industry best satisfying your goals is then selected. After you have identified the target industry, companies in that industry are then screened. Make sure to compare the target's trend to industry averages to determine the company's relative position.

In identifying an acquisition target, clearly-defined criteria should be established for acceptable candidates, all companies within the category should be reviewed, suitable companies should be listed in priority order, and a short list of targets (generally no more than 10) coming closest to the ideal profile should be prepared. This short list can either consist of the highest scoring companies regardless of score or all companies. The profile criteria includes what is important to you, such as industry classification, size, profitability, leverage, market share, and geographic area. You may not be able to get your first choice, so flexibility is needed.

Different criteria should have different weights depending upon importance to you. For example, the weight may go from 1 (least important) to 10 (most important). For example, you may decide to assign a 1 to dividend history and a 10 to industry. Most criteria will fall between 1 to 10 (e.g., leverage may be assigned a weight of 2 because all candidates have already been screened to have a debt to equity ratio below 25%). Intermediate attributes within a range may also be scored. For example, revenues under $100 million or above $300 million may be given a score of 4. An illustrative grading guide follows.

Illustrative Grading Guide

Industry Classification

 1 = specialty shops, diversified companies in which food products retailing is only minor

10 = convenience store chain

Size

 1 = revenues under $10 million or over $40 million

10 = revenues of $30 million

Fixed Assets (book value)

 1 = $2 million

10 = over $5 million

Net Income

 1 = profit margin below 2%

 5 = profit margin above 10%

Leverage

 1 = over 40% debt to equity ratio

10 = below 5% debt to equity ratio

Geographics

1 = West

5 = South

10 = Northeast

You can save time by using a computer database to find possible target companies. The database enables you to select ranges for size, profitability, leverage, and so on and then screen out candidates fulfilling your requirements. Information on publicly-held companies is much more available than closely-held businesses.

ACQUISITION STRATEGY AND PROCESS

A brochure should be prepared by the buyer of itself so the target company may be acquainted with the buyer's objectives, philosophy, and background. A proposal should also be prepared explaining to the target company the financial and operating benefits to it of a merger.

Planning to integrate the acquired company into the buyer should take place early in the acquisition process. Areas requiring planning include policies and procedures, data processing, organizational and management structure, personnel, operations, financial reporting, customer base, and supplier relationships.

After discussions become serious, the investigation of the target company should involve reviewing available financial information and audit work papers, tax returns, visiting the target's facilities, and interviewing management (e.g., research and development programs, manufacturing and distribution methods). There should be a purchase audit, particularly to "key" accounts and exposure areas to uncover problems and issues not fully disclosed in the financial statements. For example, inventory should be observed and counted as well as determining whether their valuation in the financial records is appropriate. The purchase audit must consider financial, accounting and operating matters. Outside consultants may need to be retained in specialized areas (e.g., technology, product capability).

The areas of investigation include:

- Industry (e.g., competition, growth rate, governmental regulation, barriers to entry).
- Target company background and history (e.g., nature of business, locations and facilities, lawsuits, environmental considerations).
- Financial and accounting information (e.g., ratios by major business segment, effect of inflation or recession on company, current values). The financial statements for the last three years should be reviewed.
- Taxes (e.g., tax attributes of target, tax planning strategies). Tax returns should be reviewed and analyzed for the last three years. Financial

income and taxable income should be reconciled. Does the state penalize multistate enterprises? Will foreign countries impose significant tax burdens? What tax benefits will the purchase accomplish (e.g., available tax credits)? Are there any questionable items or limitations that may be challenged by the tax authorities?

- Management quality (particularly important when moving into an unrelated industry).
- Pension and health care obligations.
- Marketing (e.g., backlog, new product developments, obsolescence problems).
- Manufacturing (e.g., production facilities, manufacturing processes and efficiencies).
- Distribution network, facilities, and methods.
- R&D experience.

Watch out for litigation matters, tax contingencies, regulatory problems, reliance on a few contracts and/or customers, "window-dressing" management honesty, and poor financial and operating controls.

FINANCING OF THE MERGER

The range of possible transaction structures is infinite, but below are some of the basic alternatives:

- All cash transaction, financed from existing cash resources
- All cash transaction, financed by issuing stock
- Stock transaction, merger through exchange of stock
- Mixed stock/cash
- Leveraged cash transaction, financed through debt issue
- Leveraged buyout, majority of equity replaced by debt
- Debt transaction, debt offered to selling company shareholders
- Mixed cash/debt

Should stock or assets (generally cash) be given in the acquisition?

Advantages of Giving Stock

- No cash or financing requirement for acquirer.
- Quick and simple in terms of document preparation. There is a transfer of stock certificates in exchange for immediate or deferred payment.
- In certain cases, stock transactions can be exempt from taxation to shareholders, thus potentially raising the value of the transaction.

- A stock acquisition can maintain the equity to assets ratio, and even provide additional capital for further growth strategies.
- Target shareholders share risk of acquisition.
- Minority stockholders may not have appraisal rights.
- Typically, stockholder votes authorizing the purchase or sale are not required.
- May take advantage of acquirer's high stock price.
- Target management has incentive to maintain commitment.

Disadvantages of Giving Stock

- Can be less attractive to target shareholders
- The acquirer in buying stock of the target company assumes its liabilities, whether disclosed or not
- Dilution of acquirer shareholder earnings
- Dilution of ownership/control
- Risk of conflict after merger
- If the target is liquidated subsequent to acquisition, much work is needed in conveying the target company's assets as part of the liquidation

Advantages of Giving Assets

- Acquirer has complete control over the assets it buys and the liabilities it assumes
- Attractive to shareholders because they receive value immediately and have no risk
- Typically, no acquiring company stockholder vote is needed
- Easier to understand

Disadvantages of Giving Assets

- Dilution of earnings
- Difficult to determine the fair value of each asset
- Current target management may have little incentive to facilitate transaction or maintain commitment after transaction
- Target company's stockholders must approve
- State transfer taxes must be paid
- A cash acquisition can materially lower the equity to assets ratio of the surviving company
- Creation of goodwill which is amortized to expense but not tax deductible. Further, income depressed by significant amortization costs may

result in a lower stock price, potentially making the buyer in turn vulnerable to takeover.

- Creditor agreement may be needed for certain transfers and assignments
- Must conform to bulk sales laws

If the decision is made to give cash to the targeted company shareholders, some form of equity and/or debt will have to be issued because it is usual for the acquiring company to have sufficient cash or liquid assets to finance the entire transaction. Debt financing may range from an intermediate-term loan for part of the purchase price, to structural debt financing of 90% or more of the price (leveraged buyout). There are many considerations in deciding whether to use leverage, and in determining the appropriate amount of leverage.

Advantages of Leverage

- Interest expense is tax deductible
- Increased return to shareholders
- Since shareholders' ownership is maintained, there is a lack of dilution

Disadvantages of Leverage

- Creditors have priority claim on merged company
- The greater financing risk may lower the company's stock and bond prices as well as result in increasing costs of financing
- Possible lowering in credit standing and bond ratings
- A cash problem may result in default
- Interest payments lower earnings
- Interest and principal payments reduce cash flow

Leveraged buyouts are quite popular. A leveraged buyout occurs when an entity primarily borrows money (sometimes 90% or more) in order to buy another company. Typically, the acquiring company uses as collateral the assets of the acquired business. Generally, repayment of the debt will be made from the yearly operating funds flow of the acquired company. A leveraged buyout may also be made when the acquiring company uses its own assets as security for the loan. It may also be used if a firm wishes to go private. In most cases, the stockholders of the acquired company will receive an amount greater than the current price of the stock. A leveraged buyout involves more risk than an acquisition done through the issuance of equity securities.

The high debt service requirement drains cash flow during the period that the debt is outstanding. However, once debt is retired, shareholders enjoy ownership of the remaining enterprise. The debt may be reduced rapidly by selling off some assets or divisions of the acquired company, if warranted.

The characteristics conducive to a leveraged buyout are:

- The earnings and cash flow of the company must be predictable so they may cover interest and principal payments on the debt financing.
- The growth rate of the firm should exceed the inflation rate.
- There must be a good market share and product line otherwise the firm is vulnerable to an economic decline or competitive actions.
- There should be a good asset base to serve as collateral.
- The assets should not be presently encumbered and the debt/equity ratio should be currently low.
- There is minimal capital expenditure requirements.
- The company should be liquid so that it has enough cash to meet its debt obligations.
- There is future salability of the company, if desired.
- Technological change is not a problem.
- Management is highly qualified, and is given a significant equity stake.
- The business is selling at a low P/E ratio.

THE USE OF CAPITAL BUDGETING TECHNIQUES IN APPRAISING THE ACQUISITION

In deciding whether to buy another business, capital budgeting may be used. Also, the effect of the new capital structure on the firm's overall cost of capital has to be projected.

EXAMPLE 2

W Company is contemplating purchasing P Company for $95,000. W's current cost of capital is 12%. P's estimated overall cost of capital after the acquisition is 10%. Projected cash inflows from years one through eight are $13,000. (Assume no residual value).

The net present value is:

Year	Present Value
0 ($-95,000 \times 1$)	$-\$95,000$
1–8 ($13,000 \times 5.334926$)	$+\ 69,354^{*}$
Net present value	$-\$25,646$

*Using 10% as the discount rate.

The acquisition is not feasible since there is a negative net present value.

EXAMPLE 3

C Company wants to buy some fixed assets of B Company. However, the latter wants to sell out its business. The balance sheet of B Company follows:

Assets

Cash	$ 4,000
Accounts receivable	8,000
Inventory	10,000
Equipment 1	16,000
Equipment 2	28,000
Equipment 3	42,000
Building	110,000
Total assets	$218,000

Liabilities and Stockholders' Equity

Total liabilities	$ 80,000
Total equity	138,000
Total liabilities and equity	$218,000

C wants only equipment 1 and 2 and the building. The other assets excluding cash, can be sold for $24,000. The total cash received is thus $28,000 ($24,000 + $4,000 initial cash balance). B desires $50,000 for the whole business. C will thus have to pay a total of $130,000, which is $80,000 in total liabilities and $50,000 for its owners. The actual net cash outlay is therefore $102,000 ($130,000 − $28,000). It is expected that the after-tax cash inflows from the new equipment will be $27,000 per year for the next five years. The cost of capital is 8%. (Assume no residual value).

The net present value of the acquisition is:

Year	Present Value
0 (−$102,000 × 1)	− $102,000
1–5 (27,000 × 3.992710)	107,803
Net present value	$ 5,803

Since there is a positive net present value the acquisition should be made.

EXCHANGE RATIO

T Company buys B Company. T Company's stock sells for $75 per share while B's stock sells for $45. As per the merger terms, T offers $50 per share. The exchange ratio is 0.667 ($50/$75). Thus, T exchanges 0.667 shares of its stock for one share of B.

EFFECT OF MERGER ON EARNINGS PER SHARE
AND MARKET PRICE PER SHARE

A merger can have a positive or negative impact on net income and market price per share of common stock.

EXAMPLE 4

Relevant information follows:

	Company A	Company B
Net income	$50,000	$84,000
Outstanding shares	5,000	12,000
EPS	$ 10	$ 7
P/E ratio	7	10
Market price	$ 70	$ 70

Company B acquires Company A and exchanges its shares for A's shares on a one-for-one basis. The effect on EPS follows:

	B Shares Owned After Merger	EPS Before Merger	EPS After Merger
A stockholders	5,000	$10	$7.88*
B stockholders	12,000	7	7.88*
Total	17,000		

*Total net income is determined as:

5,000 shares × $10	$50,000
12,000 shares × $7	84,000
	$134,000

$$\text{EPS} = \frac{\text{Net income}}{\text{Total shares}} = \frac{\$134,000}{17,000} = \$7.88$$

EPS decreases by $2.12 for A stockholders and increases by $0.88 for B stockholders.

The effect on market price is not clear. Assuming the combined entity has the same P/E ratio as Company B, the market price per share will be $78.80 (10 × $7.88). The stockholders experience a higher market value per share. The increased market value occurs because net income of the combined entity is valued at a P/E ratio of 10, the same as Company B, while before the merger Company A had a lower P/E multiplier of 7. However, if the combined entity is valued at Company A's multiplier of 7, the market value would be $55.16 (7 × $7.88). In this case, the stockholders in each firm experience a reduction in market value of $14.84 ($70.00 − $55.16). Since the effect of the merger on market value per share is not clear, the crucial consideration is EPS.

EXAMPLE 5

The following situation exists:

Market price per share of acquiring company = $100
Market price per share of acquired company = $ 20
Price per share offered = $ 24
The exchange ratio equals:

Shares $24/$100 = 0.24
Market price $24/$20 = 1.20

EXAMPLE 6

M Company wants to buy J Company by issuing its shares. Relevant information follows:

	M Company	J Company
Net income	$40,000	$26,000
Outstanding shares	20,000	8,000

The exchange ratio is 2 to 1. The EPS based on the original shares of each company follows:

$$\text{EPS of combined entity} = \frac{\text{Combined net income}}{\text{Total shares}}$$

$$\frac{\$66,000}{20,000 + (8,000 \times 2)} = \frac{\$66,000}{36,000 \text{ shares}} = \frac{\$1.83}{}$$

EPS of Mart = $1.83
EPS of James = $1.83 × 2 = $3.66

EXAMPLE 7

O Company wants to buy P Company by exchanging 1.8 shares of its stock for each share of P. O expects to have the same P/E ratio after the merger as before. Applicable data follow.

	O Company	P Company
Net income	$500,000	$150,000
Shares	225,000	30,000
Market price per share	$ 50	$ 60

The exchange ratio of market price equals:

$$\frac{\text{Offer price}}{\text{Market price of P}} = \frac{\$50 \times 1.8}{\$60} = \frac{\$90}{\$60} = 1.5$$

EPS and P/E ratios for each company follow.

O Company	P Company
EPS $500,000/225,000 = \$2.22$	$\$150,000/30,000 = \$5$
P/E ratio $\$50/\$2.22 = 22.5$	$\$60/\$5 = 12$

The P/E ratio used in obtaining P is:

$$\frac{1.8 \times \$50}{\$5} = \frac{\$90}{\$5} = 18 \text{ times}$$

The EPS of O after the acquisition is:

$$\frac{\$650,000}{225,000 + (30,000 \times 1.8)} = \frac{\$650,000}{279,000 \text{ shares}} = \$2.33$$

The expected market price per share of the combined entity is:

$$\$2.33 \times 22.5 \text{ times} = \$52.43$$

RISK OF THE ACQUISITION

In appraising the risk associated with an acquisition, a scenario analysis may be used, looking at best case, worst case, and most likely case. Operating scenarios consider assumptions as to variables, including sales, volume, cost, competitive reaction, governmental interference, and customer perception. You derive the probability for each scenario on the basis of experience. Sensitivity analysis may be used to indicate how sensitive the project's returns are to variances from expected values of essential variables. (Sensitivity analysis is discussed in Chapter 23). For example, you may undertake a sensitivity analysis on selling prices assuming they are, for example, 10% to 15% higher or lower than expected. The theory behind sensitivity analysis is to adjust key variables from their expected values in the most likely case. The analysis can be performed assuming one purchase price or all possible purchase prices. What is the effect, for example, of a 4% change in the gross profit rate on projected returns?

Based on sensitivity analysis, you should pay an amount for a target company resulting in a cutoff return given the most likely operating scenario.

Warning: It is difficult to accomplish successful unrelated diversification. An example is General Electric's acquisition of Utah International. The firm eventually divested of its acquisition. **Recommendation:** Acquisition of companies operating in related fields usually have a higher success rate.

HOLDING COMPANY

A holding company is one whose sole purpose is to own the stock of other companies. To obtain voting control of a business, the holding company may make a direct market purchase or tender offer. A company may elect to become a holding company if its basic business is declining and it decides to liquidate its assets and uses the funds to invest in growth companies.

Since the operating companies owned by the holding company are separate legal entities, the obligations of one are isolated from the others. **Recommendation:** A loan officer lending to one company should attempt to obtain a guarantee by the other companies.

Advantages of a Holding Company

- Risk protection, in that the failure of one company does not cause the failure of another or of the holding company. If the owned company fails, the loss of the holding company is restricted to its investment in it.

- Ability to obtain a significant amount of assets with a small investment. The holding company can control more assets than it could acquire through a merger.

- Ease of obtaining control of another company; all that is needed is to purchase enough stock in the marketplace. Unlike a merger which requires stockholder or management approval, no approval is needed for a holding company.

Disadvantages of a Holding Company

- More costly to administer than a single company resulting from a merger because economies of scale are not achieved

- Incurrence of increased debt because the acquisition may magnify variability in earnings, thus subjecting the holding company to more risk

- The chance that the U.S. Department of Justice will deem the holding company a monopoly and force dissolution of some of the owned companies

- Multiple tax because the income the holding company receives is in the form of cash. Before paying dividends, the subsidiary must pay taxes on the earnings. When profit is distributed to the holding company as dividends, it must pay tax on the dividends received less an 80% dividend exclusion. However, if the holding company owns 80% or more of the subsidiary's shares, a 100% dividend exemption exists. No multiple tax exists for a subsidiary that is part of a merged company.

EXAMPLE 8

A holding company owns 70% of another firm. Dividends received are $20,000. The tax rate is 34%. The tax paid on the dividends follows:

Dividend	$20,000
Dividend exclusion (80%)	16,000
Dividend subject to tax	$ 4,000
Tax rate	× 34%
Tax	$ 1,360

The effective tax rate is 6.8% ($1,360/$20,000).

HOSTILE TAKEOVER BIDS

If a negotiated takeover of another company is impossible, a hostile bid may be needed. In a hostile bid management of the targeted company is bypassed, and the stockholders are directly approached. The acquirer argues that management are not maximizing the potential of the company, and are not protecting the interests of shareholders.

In a tender offer, the buyer goes directly to the stockholders of the target business to tender (sell) their shares, typically for cash. The tender in some cases may be shares in the acquiring company rather than cash. If the buyer obtains enough stock, it can gain control of the target company and force the merger. Cash is usually used rather than securities because a stock offering requires a prospectus thereby losing the advantages of timeliness and surprise. Stockholders are induced to sell when the tender price substantially exceeds the current market price of the target company stock. Typically, there is an expiration date to the tender.

Hostile takeovers are typically quite costly because they usually involve a significant price incentive, and anti-takeover measures. They can be disruptive to both buyer and seller because of "slur" campaigns. It is rare that smooth transitions of management take place.

The typical features of a hostile takeover candidate may include:

1. A multi-divisional organization having diverse business activities

2. Asset values of component divisions are not reflected in the market price of the company's stock

3. Financial performance of the individual business lines could be better

4. Existing management who are unable to realize the true value of the company

The usual initial step in launching a hostile bid is to buy stock of the target company in the open market. The SEC requires that any investor who buys more than a 5% interest in a public company should register his holding and provide the intent (e.g., passive or to gain eventual control) through a Schedule 13-D filing. Beyond 5% ownership, it becomes difficult to make open-market purchases of stock without revealing the intention to acquire control—except acquirers may accumulate a greater holding within the five days allowed for the 13-D filing, or they may elect to make a passive investment for a limited period before reassessing the intention to acquire control. The acquiring business must furnish to the management of the potential acquired company and to the SEC, 30 days notice of its intent to acquire. Once the intention to acquire control is made public, the stock price of the target company generally rises in expectation of a tender offer at a higher price.

The direct appeal to shareholders which often follows is frequently made through a public tender offer. Management of the target company will typically recommend shareholders to reject the offer, and possibly propose an alternative restructuring arrangement.

The management of a targeted company can fight the takeover attempt in the following ways:

1. Purchase treasury stock to make fewer shares available for tendering
2. Initiate legal action to prevent the takeover, such as by applying antitrust laws
3. Postpone the tender offer (some states have laws to delay the tender offer)
4. Declare an attractive dividend to keep stockholders happy

Advantages of a Hostile Bid

- Communicate directly with stockholders to bypass management intransigency
- Flexibility to alter terms
- Increase value of existing stake
- Improve the target's profitability

Disadvantages of a Hostile Bid

- Price: hostile bidders may pay a high premium especially if competition arises in the takeover attempt
- Cost: high transaction and advisory costs
- Risk: hostile bids often fail
- Creation of ill-will and problems with integrating the target after merger
- Possible adverse litigation or regulatory action
- Possible retaliatory action by target (see PAC-MAN below)

SEC FILING REQUIREMENTS

When an acquisition of a significant business will occur, the buyer, and where appropriate, the target company must file a Form 8-K (filing for important events), a proxy or information statement (if shareholders must vote), and a registration statement (if securities are to be issued). Significant means the acquirer's investment in the target exceeds 10% of its consolidated assets. In addition, certain information on the acquisition must be presented in Form 10-Q (quarterly filing).

If a significant business has been acquired, a Form 8-K must be filed within 15 days containing information about the acquisition and including historical financial statements and pro forma data.

If the combination must be voted upon by shareholders of any of the companies, a Form S-4 must be filed. In other cases, one of the other "S" forms (e.g., S-1, S-2, or S-3) must be filed.

If Form S-4 is filed, there is a 20 business day waiting period between the date the prospectus is sent to stockholders and the date of the stockholder meeting. Also, if the acquisition must be voted upon by shareholders of one or both of the companies, a proxy or information statement must be furnished to shareholders and filed with the SEC.

Regulation S-X requires audited historical financial statements of a business to be acquired. The financial statements must be for the last three years and any interim period. In a purchase combination, there must be a pro forma statement of income for the most recent year and interim period. In a pooling, the financial statements are typically restated.

TAX CONSIDERATIONS

The tax effect of a transaction may require an adjustment in selling price. It may be desirable to have an "open-end" arrangement, whereby with the attainment of a given sales volume or profit, additional stock will be issued by the purchaser to the selling company or its stockholders—so handled to be nontaxable.

The acquiring company should prefer a taxable transaction. In a taxable transaction, the acquiring company must allocate its purchase cost among the assets acquired based on the present values of those assets. Any residual balance is goodwill. The acquired company's net assets will typically have a book value far below their fair market value. A taxable transaction allows the acquiring company to step up the tax basis of these assets, sometimes to a level even higher than original cost, and to start the depreciation cycle all over again. When the acquired company's assets are sold, this stepped-up basis will reduce the taxable gain on the sale.

Also see Chapter 42 on taxation.

DEFENSIVE MEASURES BY TARGETED COMPANY

The targeted company may have in place preventive measures against being taken over including:

1. *Golden Parachute.* Management compensation arrangements that are triggered when there is a purchase of the business such as lump-sum

benefits, employment agreements, and stock options. Recent examples are Greyhound and Hughes Tool.

2. *Poison Pill.* When a hostile bid is eminent, the targeted company takes out significant debt (or issues preferred stock) that makes the company unattractive to the hostile acquirer because of the high debt position. Recent examples are Union Carbide and CBS Inc.

3. *Self Tender.* After a hostile bid, the target company itself makes a counter-offer for its own shares. A recent example is Newmont Mining.

4. *Greenmail.* The target company buys back the stock accumulated by the raider, at a premium. Recent examples are Texaco, Walt Disney, and Goodyear.

5. *PAC-MAN.* The defending company makes a counter-offer for the stock of the raiding company. Recent examples are American Brands and Bendix Corporation.

6. *White Knight.* The defending company finds a third party who is willing to pay a higher premium, typically with more "friendlier" intentions than the raider. Recent examples are Gulf Oil Corp. (Chevron) and Sterling Drugs (Eastman Kodak).

7. *Asset Spin Off.* The defending party identifies the assets most desirable to the raider. It then spins off the assets to one of its separate companies or sells them to a third party. Recent examples are Union Carbide and Marathon Oil.

THE VALUATION OF A TARGETED COMPANY

In a merger, we have to value the targeted company. As a starting point in valuation, the key financial data must be accumulated and analyzed including historical financial statements, forecasted financial statements, and tax returns. The assumptions of the valuation must be clearly spelled out.

The valuation approaches may be profit or asset-oriented. Adjusted earnings may be capitalized at an appropriate multiple. Future adjusted cash earnings may be discounted by the rate of return that may be earned. Assets may be valued at fair market value, such as through appraisal. Comparative values of similar companies may serve as excellent benchmarks. Commercial software programs are available to do merger analysis.

Comparison with Industry Averages

Valid comparisons can be made between the entity being valued and others in the same industry. Industry norms should be noted. General sources of comparative industry data found in financial advisory services include Standard and Poor's, Moody's, Value Line, Dun and Bradstreet, and Robert Morris Associates. Trade publications may also be consulted. Reference may be made to the

Almanac of Business and Industrial Financial Ratios (based on corporate tax returns to the Internal Revenue Service) written by Leo Troy and published by Prentice Hall. If a small company is being acquired, reference may be made to *Financial Studies of the Small Business* published annually by Financial Research Associates (Washington, D.C.: Financial Research Associates, 1984).

Publicly available information on the targeted company include the annual report, SEC Forms 10-K, 10-Q, and 8-K, interim shareholder reports, proxy statements, press releases, and offering prospectuses.

We now look at the various approaches to business valuation comprising of capitalization of earnings, capitalization of excess earnings, capitalization of cash flow, present value (discounted) of future cash flows, book value of net assets, tangible net worth, economic net worth, fair market value of net assets, gross revenue multiplier, profit margin/capitalization rate, price-earnings factor, comparative value of similar going concerns, and recent sales of stock. A combination of approaches may be used to obtain a representative value.

Capitalization of Earnings

Primary consideration should be given to earnings when valuing a company. Historical earnings is typically the beginning point in applying a capitalization method to most business valuations. In general, historical earnings are a reliable predictor of future earnings. According to IRS Revenue Ruling 59-60, 1959-1, C.B. 237, the greatest emphasis should be placed on profitability when looking at a "going concern."

The value of the business may be based on its adjusted earnings times a multiplier for what the business sells for in the industry.

Net income should be adjusted for unusual and nonrecurring revenue and expense items. In adjusting net income of the business, we should add back the portion of the following items if personal rather than business-related: auto expense, travel expense, and promotion and entertainment expense. Interest expense should also be added back to net income because it is the cost to borrow funds to buy assets or obtain working capital, and as such, is not relevant in determining the operating profit of the business. In the event lease payments arise from a low-cost lease, earnings should be adjusted to arrive at a fair rental charge. Extraordinary items (e.g., gain on the sale of land) should be removed from earnings to obtain typical earnings. If business assets are being depreciated at an accelerated rate, you should adjust net income upward.[1] Therefore, the difference between the straight-line method and an accelerated depreciation method should be added back.

We should add back expenses for a closely-held business solely for fringe benefits, health plan, pension plan, and life insurance. In addition, we should add back excessive salary representing the difference between the owner's

---

[1] Irving Blackman, The Valuation of Privately-Held Businesses (Illinois: Probus Publishing, 1986), p. 23.

salary and what a reasonable salary would be if we hired someone to do the job. All compensation should be considered including perks.[2] Thus, if the owner gets a salary of $300,000 and a competent worker would get $80,000, the add back to net income is $220,000.

A tax provision (if none exists) should be made in arriving at the adjusted net income. The tax provision should be based on the current rates for each of the years.

If the company has a significant amount of investment income (e.g., dividend income, interest income, rental income from nonoperating property), net income may be reduced for the investment income with taxes being adjusted accordingly. We are primarily concerned with the income from operations.

The adjusted (restated) earnings results in a quality of earnings figure. The restated earnings is then multiplied by a multiplier to determine the value of a business. The multiplier should be higher for a low risk business but generally not more than 10. The multiplier should be lower for a high risk business, often only one or two. Of course, an average multiplier would be used when average risk exists, such as five. The P/E ratio for a comparable company would be a good benchmark.

Some investment bankers use in valuation a multiple of the latest year's earnings, or the annual rate of earnings of a current interim period (if representative). An example follows based on a multiplier of one-year profits.

EXAMPLE 9

Adjusted Net Income for the Current Year	$400,000*
$\times$ Multiplier	$\times$ 4*
Valuation	$1,600,000

*The adjusted net income is computed below:

Reported Net Income	$325,000
Adjustments:	
Personal expenses (e.g., promotion and entertainment)	50,000
Extraordinary or nonrecurring gain	(60,000)
Owner's fringe benefits (e.g., pension plan)	40,000
Excessive owner's salary relative to a reasonable salary	30,000
Interest expense	20,000
Dividend revenue	(10,000)
Low cost rental payments relative to a fair rental charge	(5,000)
Excess depreciation from using an accelerated method	10,000
Restated Net Income	$400,000

---

[2] Shannon Pratt, Valuing Small Businesses and Professional Practices (Illinois: Dow-Jones-Irwin, 1986), p. 59.

Typically, a 5-year average adjusted historical earnings figure is used. The five years' earnings up to the valuation date demonstrates past earning power. Note that for SEC registration and reporting purposes a 5-year period is used. Assuming a simple average is used, the computation follows:

Simple Average Adjusted Earnings over 5 years × Multiplier
(Capitalization Factor, P/E Ratio) of 5 (based on industry standard)

Value of Business

EXAMPLE 10

Assume the following net incomes:

19X9 $120,000
19X8 $100,000
19X7 $110,000
19X6 $ 90,000
19X5 $115,000
The multiplier is 4.

$$\text{Simple Average Earnings} = \frac{\$120,000 + \$100,000 + \$110,000 + \$90,000 + \$115.000}{5}$$

$$= \frac{\$535,000}{5} = \$107,000$$

Simple Average Adjusted Earnings over 5 years	$107,000
× Multiplier	× 4
Value of Business	$428,000

Instead of a simple average, a weighted-average adjusted historical earnings figure is recommended. This gives more weight to the most recent years[3] which reflects higher current prices and recent business performance. If a 5-year weighted-average is used, the current year is given a weight of five while the first year is assigned a weight of one. The multiplier is then applied to the weighted-average 5-year adjusted earnings to get the value of the business.

EXAMPLE 11

Year	Net Income	×	Weight	=	Total
19X9	$120,000	×	5	=	$ 600,000
19X8	100,000	×	4	=	400,000

³American Institute of CPAs, Valuation of a Closely-Held Business, Small Business Consulting Practice Aid No. 8, Management Advisory Services Practice Aids, New York, 1987, p. 13.

Year	Net Income	×	Weight	=	Total
19X7	110,000	×	3	=	330,000
19X6	90,000	×	2	=	180,000
19X5	115,000	×	1	=	115,000
			15		$1,625,000

Weighted-Average 5-year earnings:

$1,625,000/15 = $108,333

Weighted-Average 5-year earnings	$108,333
× Capitalization Factor	× 4*
Capitalization-of-Earnings Valuation	$433,332

*The capitalization factor should be based on such factors as risk, stability of earnings, expected future earnings, liquidity, etc.

If the company's financial statements are not audited, you should insist on an audit to assure accurate reporting.

Has the owner of a closely-held company failed to record cash sales to hide income? One way of determining this is to take purchases and add a typical profit markup in the industry. To verify reported profit, you can multiply the sales by the profit margin in the industry. If reported earnings are significantly below what the earnings should be based on the industry standard, there may be some hidden income.

Capitalization of Excess Earnings

The best method is to capitalize excess earnings. The normal rate of return on the weighted-average net tangible assets is subtracted from the weighted-average adjusted earnings to determine excess earnings. It is suggested that the weighting be based on a 5-year period. The excess earnings are then capitalized to determine the value of the intangibles (primarily goodwill). The addition of the value of the intangibles and the fair market value of the net tangible assets equals the total valuation. As per IRS Revenue Ruling 68-609, 1968-2 C.B. 327, the IRS recommends this method to value a business for tax purposes. The Revenue Ruling states that the return on average net tangible assets should be the percentage prevailing in the industry. If an industry percentage is not available, an 8% to 10% rate may be used. An 8% return rate is used for a business with a small risk factor and stable earnings while a 10% rate of return is used for a business having a high risk factor and unstable earnings. The capitalization rate for excess earnings should be 15% (multiple of 6.67) for a business with a small risk factor and stable earnings and a 20% capitalization rate (multiple of five) should be used for a business having a high risk factor and unstable earnings. Thus, the suggested return rate range is between 8% to 10%. The range for the capitalization rate may be between 15% to 20%.

EXAMPLE 12

Weighted-average net tangible assets are computed below:

Year	Amount	×	Weight	=	Total
19X1	$950,000	×	1	=	$ 950,000
19X2	1,000,000	×	2	=	2,000,000
19X3	1,200,000	×	3	=	3,600,000
19X4	1,400,000	×	4	=	5,600,000
19X5	1,500,000	×	5	=	7,500,000
			15		$19,650,000

Weighted-Average Net Tangible Assets:

$19,650,000/15 = $1,310,000

Weighted-Average Adjusted Net Income (5 years) – assumed	$ 600,000
Reasonable Rate of Return on Weighted-Average Tangible Net Assets ($1,310,000 × 10%)	131,000
Excess Earnings	$ 469,000
Capitalization Rate (20%)	× 5
Value of Intangibles	$2,345,000
Fair Market Value of Net Tangible Assets	3,000,000
Capitalization-of-Excess-Earnings Valuation	$5,345,000

Capitalization of Cash Flow

The adjusted cash earnings may be capitalized in arriving at a value for the firm. This method may be suitable for a service business.

EXAMPLE 13

Adjusted Cash Earnings	$100,000
× Capitalization Factor (25%)	× 4
Capitalization of Cash Flow	$400,000
Less Liabilities Assumed	50,000
Capitalization-of-Cash-Flow Earnings	$350,000

Present Value (Discounting) of Future Cash Flows

A business is worth the discounted value of future cash earnings plus the discounted value of the expected selling price. Cash flow may be a more valid criterion of value than book profits because cash flow can be used for reinvestment. The growth rate in earnings may be based on past growth, future expectations, and the inflation rate. This approach is suggested in a third-party sale situation. We also have more confidence in it when the company is strong in the industry and has solid earnings growth. The problem with the method is the many estimates required of future events. It probably should not be used when there has been an inconsistent trend in earnings.

Step 1: Present Value of Cash Earnings. The earnings should be estimated over future years using an estimated growth rate. A common time frame for a cash flow valuation is 10 years. Once the future earnings are determined, they should be discounted. Future earnings may be based on the prior years' earnings and the current profit margin applied to sales. Cash earnings equals net income plus noncash expense adjustments such as depreciation.

Step 2: Present Value of Sales Price. The present value of the expected selling price of the business at the date of sale should be determined. This residual value may be based on a multiple of earnings or cash flow, expected market value, and so on.

You may use as the discount rate the minimum acceptable return to the buyer for investing in the target company. The discount rate may take into account the usual return rate for money, inflation rate, a risk premium (based on such factors as local market conditions, earnings instability, and level of debt), and maybe a premium for the illiquidity of the investment. If the risk-free interest rate is 7% (on government bonds), the risk premium is 8%, and the illiquidity premium is 7%, the capitalization (discount) rate will be 22%. The risk premium may range from 5% to 10% while the illiquidity premium may range from 5% to 15%.[1] Some evaluators simply use as the discount rate the market interest rate of a low risk asset investment.

Assuming you expect to hold the business for 14 years, and anticipate a 12% rate of return, and a constant earnings each year, the value of the business is based on:

For cash earnings. Present value of an ordinary annuity for $n = 14$, $i = 12\%$

For selling price. Present value of $1 for $n = 14$, $i = 12\%$
Total Present Value

If earnings grow at an 8% rate, a present value of $1 table would be used to discount the annual earnings which would change each year.

EXAMPLE 14

In 19X1, the net income is $200,000. Earnings are expected to grow at 8% per year. The discount rate is 10%. You estimate that the business is worth the discounted value of future earnings. The valuation equals:

[1]Charles Hays and Lawrence Finley, "Valuation of the Closely-Held Business," National Public Accountant, March 1989, p. 31.

Year	Net Income (based on an 8% growth rate)		PV of $1 Factor (at 10% interest)	Present Value
19X1	$200,000	×	.909	$181,800
19X2	208,000	×	.826	171,808
19X3	224,600	×	.751	168,675
19X4	242,568	×	.683	165,674
19X5	261,973	×	.621	162,685
Present Value of Future Earnings				$850,642

If the expected selling price at the end of year 19X5 is $600,000, the valuation of the business equals:

Present value of earnings	$850,642
Selling price in 19X5 $600,000 × .621	372,600
Valuation	$1,223,242

Operating Cash Flow

Some businesses may be valued at a multiple of operating cash flow. For example, radio and TV stations often sell for between 8 to 12 times operating cash flow.

Book Value (Net Worth)

The business may be valued based on the book value of the net assets (assets less liabilities) at the most recent balance sheet date. This method is unrealistic because it does not take into account current values. It may only be appropriate when it is impossible to determine fair value of net assets and/or goodwill. However, book value may be adjusted for obvious understatements such as excess depreciation, LIFO reserve, favorable leases, and for low debt (e.g., low rental payments or unfunded pension and postretirement benefits). Unfortunately, it may be difficult for a buying company to have access to information regarding these adjustments.

Tangible Net Worth

The valuation of the company is its tangible net worth for the current year equal to:

Stockholders' Equity
Less: Intangible Assets
Tangible Net Worth

Economic Net Worth (Adjusted Book Value)

Economic net worth equals:

Fair market value of net assets

Plus: Goodwill (as per agreement)

Economic Net Worth

Fair Market Value of Net Assets

The fair market value of the net tangible assets of the business may be determined through independent appraisal. To it, we add the value of the goodwill (if any). Note that goodwill applies to such aspects as reputation of the company, customer base, and high quality merchandise. IRS Appeals and Review Memorandums (ARM) 34 and 38 present formula methods to value goodwill. In case of a small business, a business broker may be retained to do the appraisal of property, plant and equipment. A business broker is experienced because he or she puts together the purchase of small businesses. According to Equitable Business Brokers, about 25% of businesses changing hands are sold through business brokers. Typically, the fair value of the net tangible assets (assets less liabilities) is higher than book value.

The general practice is to value inventory at a maximum value of cost.[5] IRS Revenue Procedure 77-12 provides acceptable ways to allocate a lump-sum purchase price to inventories.

Unrecognized and unrecorded liabilities should be considered when determining the fair market value of net assets. For example, one company the author consulted had both an unrecorded liability for liquidated damages for non-union contracts of $3,100,000 and an unrecorded liability for $4,900,000 related to the estimated employer final withdrawal liability. Obviously, as a result of unrecorded liabilities the value of a business will be reduced further.

A tax liability may also exist that has not been recognized in the accounts. For example, the company's tax position may be adjusted by the IRS which is currently auditing the tax return. This contingent liability should be considered in valuing the business.

In a similar vein, unrecorded and undervalued assets should be considered because they increase the value of the business such as customer lists, patents, and licensing agreements.

(Note: IRS Revenue Ruling 65-193 approves only those approaches where valuations can be determined separately for tangible and intangible assets.)

Liquidation Value

Liquidation value is a conservative figure of value because it does not take into account the earning power of the business. Liquidation value is a "floor" price in negotiations. Liquidation value is the estimated value of the company's

---

[5] Charles Hays and Lawrence Finley, *op.cit.*, p. 32.

assets and assuming their conversion into cash in a short time period. All liabilities and the costs of liquidating the business (e.g., appraisal fees, real estate fees, legal and accounting fees, recapture taxes) are subtracted from the total cash to obtain net liquidation value.

Liquidation value may be computed based on an orderly liquidation or a forced (rapid) liquidation. In the case of the latter, there will obviously be a lower value.

Replacement Cost

Replacement cost ("new") is the cost of duplicating from scratch the business's assets on an "as-if-new" basis. It will typically result in a higher figure than book value or fair market value of existing assets. Replacement cost provides a meaningful basis of comparison with other methods but should not be used as the acquisition value. A more accurate indicator of value is when replacement cost is adjusted for relevant depreciation and obsolescence.

Secured-Loan Value

The secured loan-value reflects the borrowing power of the seller's assets. Typically, banks will lend up to 90% of accounts receivable and 10%–60% of the value of inventory depending on how much represents finished goods, work-in-process, and raw materials. The least percentage amount will be work-in-process because of its greater realization risk and difficulty of sale. Also considered are turnover rates.

Gross Revenue Multiplier

The value of the business may be determined by multiplying the revenue by the gross revenue multiplier common in the industry. The industry standard gross revenue multiplier is based on the average ratio of market price to sales prevalent in the industry. This approach may be used when earnings are questionable.

EXAMPLE 15

If revenue is $14,000,000 and the multiplier is .2, the valuation is: $14,000,000 \times .2 = \$2,800,000$.

In a similar fashion, insurance agencies often sell for about 150% of annual commissions.

Profit Margin/Capitalization Rate

The profit margin divided by the capitalization rate provides a multiplier which is then applied to revenue. A multiplier of revenue that a company would sell at is the company's profit margin. The profit margin may be based on the industry average. The formula is:

$$\frac{\text{Profit Margin}}{\text{Capitalization Rate}} = \frac{\text{Net Income/Sales}}{\text{Capitalization Rate}} = \text{Multiplier}$$

The capitalization rate in earnings is the return demanded by investors. In arriving at a capitalization rate, the prime interest rate may be taken into account. The multiplier is what the buyer is willing to pay.

EXAMPLE 16

Assume sales of $14,000,000, a profit margin of 5%, and a capitalization rate of 20%. The multiplier is 25% (5%/20%). The valuation is:

Sales × 25%
$14,000,000 × 25% = $3,500,000

The IRS and the courts have considered recent sales as an important factor.[6]

Price-Earnings Factor

The value of a business may be based on the price-earnings factor applied to current (or expected) earnings per share (EPS). For publicly traded companies, the P/E ratio is known. Valuation for a privately-held company is more difficult. Historical earnings must be adjusted for a closely-held company to be consistent with the reported earnings of a public company. After suitable adjustments have been made, the average P/E ratio for the industry or for several comparable public companies is used to arrive at a value. Typically, a premium is added to the value estimate to incorporate uncertainty and additional risk and lack of marketability associated with private companies. A variation of the P/E method may also be used. Assuming an expected earnings growth rate of the seller and a desired ROI, the acquirer determines an earnings multiple he would pay to achieve the ROI goal. Under this approach, the buyer determines the price he would be willing to pay instead of using a stock-market related price.

---

[6]American Institute of CPAs, *op.cit.*, p. 16.

EXAMPLE 17

Net Income	$ 800,000
Outstanding Shares	/100,000
EPS	$ 8
P/E Multiple	× 10
Market Price per Share	$ 80
× Number of Shares Outstanding	× 100,000
Price-Earnings Valuation	$8,000,000

Comparative Values of Similar Going Concerns

What would someone pay for this business? Reference may be made to the market price of similar publicly traded companies. Under this approach, you obtain the market prices of companies in the industry similar in nature to the one being examined. Recent sales prices of similar businesses may be used, and an average taken. Upward or downward adjustments to this average will be made depending on the particular circumstances of the company being valued. There are two ways of arriving at an adjusted average value for a company based on comparable transactions. Under the equivalency adjustment method, you make an adjustment to each transaction before averaging based on such factors as size, profitability, earnings stability, and transaction structure. Transactions are adjusted downward if you deem a higher price was paid than would be appropriate for the target company, and vice versa. The average of the adjusted comparables approximates the estimated value of the target company. With the simple averaging method, you determine a simple average of the comparable transactions, after excluding noncomparable cases, and adjust the target company's price in so far as it differs from the average features of the companies purchased in comparable transactions. The former approach is suggested where extensive data is available on the comparable transactions, and where they differ substantially in their features. The latter approach is preferable where the comparable transactions are broadly similar, or where many comparable transactions have occurred.

While a perfect match is not possible, the companies should be reasonably similar (e.g., size, product, structure, geographic locations, diversity). The comparable transactions value will often be higher than the market value of the target's stock price. Several sources of industry information are Standard & Poor's, Dow Jones-Irwin, on-line information services (e.g., Compustat, Media General), and trade association reports. Extensive databases exist to assist in the analysis of merger-market history.

EXAMPLE 18

A competing company has just been sold for $6,000,000. We believe the company is worth 90% of the competing business. Therefore, the valuation is $5,400,000.

Sales of Stock

The value of the business may be based on the outstanding shares times the market price of the stock. For an actively traded stock, the stock price provides an important benchmark. For a thinly traded stock, the stock price may not reflect an informed market consensus. Typically, the market price of the stock should be based on a discounted amount from the current market price since if all the shares are being sold the market price per share may drop somewhat based on the demand/supply relationship. Further, market value of stock is of use only in planning the actual strategy of acquiring a target company since the stock may be overvalued or undervalued relative to the worth of the target company to the acquirer.

Combination of Methods

The value of the business may be approximated by determining the average value of two or more methods.

EXAMPLE 19

Assume that the fair market value of net assets approach gives a value of $2,100,000 while the capitalization of excess earnings method provides a value of $2,500,000. The value of the business would then be the average of these two methods, or $2,300,000 ($2,100,000 + $2,500,000/2).

Some courts have found a combination of methods supportable as long as greater weight is given to the earnings methods. S. Pratt writes that the most weight should be placed on the earnings approaches and less on the asset approaches.[7]

EXAMPLE 20

Using the same information as the prior example, if a two weight was assigned to the earnings approach and a one weight was assigned to the fair market value of net assets method, the valuation would be:

Method	Amount	×	Weight	=	Total
Fair Market Value of Net Assets	$2,100,000	×	1		$2,100,000
Capitalization-of-Excess					
Earnings	2,500,000	×	2		5,000,000
			3		$7,100,000
					/3
Valuation					$2,366,667

---

[7]Shannon Pratt, *op.cit.*, p. 196.

Accounting Adjustments

Material accounting adjustments should be made to the acquired company's figures to place them on a comparable basis to those of the acquirer. Adjustments should be made, where practical, for savings in administrative, technical, sales, plant, and clerical personnel costs resulting from the combination. These savings arise from the elimination of duplicate personnel, plant, office, and warehouse facilities. Savings in freight may result from the combination by shifting production to plants closer to markets.

Conclusion

The price to be paid for a business depends upon many factors including the seller's strengths, weaknesses, and prospects. The buyer's objectives and requirements are also relevant. A total cash transaction justifies a lower price than an installment sale because with an installment sale there are the uncertainties of cash collection and the time value of money.

When valuing a company, the most weight should be placed on the earnings approaches and less on the asset approaches. Valuation may be based on a combined approach of methods including earnings and asset valuation. In deriving a value, industry standards may be quite helpful. Consideration should be given to adjusted cash earnings, gross revenue, fair value of net assets, and recent sales of similar businesses. A proper valuation is needed so as to come up with a realistic price that is fair to all concerned parties. IRS Revenue Procedure 66-49 discusses how the IRS comes up at its valuations. Some of the contents of what should be in a valuation report are mentioned.

ACCOUNTING, REPORTING AND DISCLOSURES
FOR BUSINESS COMBINATIONS

A business combination occurs before a consolidation. Business combinations may be accounted for under the pooling-of-interests method and the purchase method. Criteria for pooling and purchase, accounting and reporting requirements, and disclosures are dealt with.

The purchase method is used when cash or other assets are given or liabilities incurred to effect the combination. An acquisition of a minority interest is always a purchase at a later date even if the original acquisition was accounted for as a pooling.

The pooling-of-interests method is used when there is an exchange of voting common stock and *all* 12 criteria for a pooling are satisfied. In a pooling, it is assumed for accounting purposes that both companies were always combined. No purchase or sale is assumed to have taken place. A pooling is a union of the ownership interests of the two previously separated groups of stockholders.

Pooling-of-Interests Method

The criteria for a pooling-of-interests deal with independence of the combining companies, time period for consummation of the combination, voting rights, consideration given in the exchange, purchase of treasury stock, ownership interests, and absence of planned transactions. The accounting for a pooling is based on recognizing net assets at book value with earnings recognized for the entire year. Footnote disclosure describes the terms of the agreement and accounting adjustments made.

Criteria for a Pooling. The 12 criteria for a pooling are indicated below. When more than one company is acquired in a combination plan, each pooling consideration must be met by each company.

1. The combining companies are autonomous, meaning that a combining company must not have been a subsidiary or division of any other combining company within two years before the initiation date. **Note:** A new company incorporated within two years qualifies unless it is in any respect a successor to a company not considered autonomous.

2. The combining companies are independent, meaning that a combining company does not own 10% or more of another combining company's voting common stock at the initiation or consummation dates or at any time in between. **Note:** A change in the exchange ratio results in a new initiation date. The consummation date is the one when the net assets are transferred to the acquiring company. However, temporary assets (e.g., cash, marketable securities) may be held to settle liabilities and contingent items.

3. The combining companies come together in a single transaction or within one year after the initiation date. A delay is allowed for litigation or governmental action. For instance, if the combination took 15 months but four months involved a delay because of antitrust litigation, this criteria is still satisfied.

4. The acquiring company issues voting common stock in exchange for 90% or more of the voting common stock of the acquired company. The following shares of the combiners are excluded from the 90% minimum.

   • Shares owned by the issuing company or its subsidiaries prior to the initiation date.

   • Shares acquired by the initiating company other than by issuing its own common stock.

   • Shares outstanding subsequent to the consummation date.

   • In determining if 90% of the stock of the combiner has been transferred to the issuing corporation, the number of shares transferred must be reduced by the equivalent number of shares of the issuing corporation owned by the combiner before combination. This reduced number of shares is then compared to 90% of the total outstanding shares of the combiner company, to determine if the requirement is satisfied.

An acquiring company may give cash or common stock for debt or preferred stock of an acquired business and qualify as a pooling, but only if the debt securities and preferred stock were not issued in an exchange for voting common stock of the acquired business within two years before the initiation date.

A combination plan may not provide for a pro rata cash distribution but may within certain restrictions have a cash distribution for fractional shares. Cash may also be used in a combination plan to retire or redeem callable debt and equity securities.

5. None of the combining companies alters the equity interest of voting common stock within two years before the combination in contemplation of it. The voting interest is deemed changed for abnormal dividends based on taking into account profits and prior dividends.

6. Treasury stock is acquired by a combining company for reasons other than the business combination between the initiation and consummation dates. Treasury stock may be acquired for purposes of a stock option plan, compensation plan, and similar recurring transactions.

7. The relative ownership percentage of each stockholder in the combined entity remains the same as before. For example, if Mr. A and Mr. B owned 2% of XYZ Company they should still own the same percentage in the newly formed entity (e.g., 1.5%).

8. There is no restriction in voting rights among stockholders by the combined entity (e.g., delayed voting rights).

9. The combination is finalized at the consummation date with no pending provisions of any kind related to the combination. For instance, no contingently issuable shares or distribution of assets to the former stockholders of the combining companies are allowed.

10-12. There is an absence of planned or subsequent transactions related to the combination as follows:

10. Repurchase of stock issued to effect the combination.

11. Financial arrangements benefiting former stockholders of the combining companies. An example is guarantying loans secured by stock issued in the combination which in substance negates the exchange of equity securities.

12. Sale of a significant part of the combined entity's assets within two years subsequent to the combination, such as the disposal of a division. However, the disposal of a duplicate warehouse would be in the ordinary course of business.

Accounting Under Pooling-of-Interests. The accounting under the pooling method follows:

- Net assets of the acquired company are brought forth at book value.
- Retained earnings and paid-in-capital of the acquired company are brought forth at book value. There is no change in total stockholders' equity but the equity components do change. Any necessary adjustments are made to paid-in-capital. In the event that paid-in-capital is insufficient to absorb the difference, retained earnings would next be reduced. However, retained earnings could never be increased. If there is a deficit in retained earnings for a combining entity, it is continued in the combined entity.
- Net income of the acquired company is brought forth for the entire year irrespective of the date of acquisition.
- Expenses of the pooling are charged against earnings as incurred. Examples are registration fees, finders' fees, and consultants' fees.
- A gain or loss from the sale of a major part of the assets of the acquired business within two years subsequent to combination is considered an extraordinary item.

EXAMPLE 21

The mechanics of a pooling follow:

	Company X	Company Y	Combined
Assets	$300	$100	$200
Liabilities	50	20	30
Equity	250	80	*

*Addition of:

- Capital stock of Company X before.
- Capital stock issued in the pooling.
- Retained earnings of both.
- Paid-in-capital absorbs the difference.

Note: There can be no new assets from a pooling. In the year of pooling, recurring intercompany transactions should be eliminated to the degree possible from the beginning of the period. However, nonrecurring intercompany transactions relating to long-term assets and liabilities do not have to be eliminated.

Where one combining company employs a different GAAP than another (e.g., straight-line vs. double declining balance depreciation), the company is permitted to change to the GAAP used by the other combiner(s) and to record the cumulative effect of a change in accounting principle. Prior year financial statements, when issued on a pooled basis should be restated for accounting principle changes.

An issuing company may effect a pooling by distributing treasury stock (acquired prior to two years before combination). The transfer of this stock is accounted for as if the stock had been retired and then reissued to effect the combination. The reissuance of this stock is accounted the same as the issuance of new shares.

Combining companies may hold investments in the common stock of each other. The accounting treatment follows:

- Investment of a combiner in the common stock of the issuing corporation—The stock is in effect returned to the resulting combined entity and hence should be accounted for as treasury stock.

- Investments in the common stock of the other combining companies—This is an investment in the type of stock which is exchanged for the new shares issued. It should be accounted for as retired stock.

Disclosures Under Pooling. Footnote disclosure of a pooling follows:

- Name and description of combined companies

- A statement that it is a pooling

- Description and number of shares issued to effect the pooling

- Net income of the previously separate companies

- Accounting method used for intercompany transactions

- Adjustments required to net assets so the combining companies are employing the same accounting methods and the related effects on earnings

- Particulars of changes in retained earnings due to a change in fiscal year of a combining company

- Reconciliation of profits previously reported by the issuing company

Advantages and Disadvantages of Pooling. An advantage of pooling is the retention of historical cost. A disadvantage from a financial reader's perspective is the possible overstated earnings (e.g., picking up net income for the whole year regardless of acquisition date, lower depreciation charges related to purchase method, and sale of low-cost basis assets at a gain.

Purchase Method

If any one of the 12 criteria is not satisfied for a pooling, the business combination is accounted for as a purchase. A purchase typically involves either the payment of assets or incurrence of liabilities for the other business. To effect a purchase, more than 50% of voting common stock has to be acquired.

Accounting Under Purchase Method. The accounting followed for a purchase is indicated below:

- Net assets of the acquired company are brought forth at fair market value. Guidelines in assigning values to individual assets acquired and liabilities assumed (except goodwill) follow:

  - *Marketable securities*—Current net realizable values
  - *Receivables*—Present value of net receivables using present interest rates
  - *Inventories*—Finished goods at estimated net realizable value less a reasonable profit allowance (lower limit). Work-in-process at estimated net realizable value of finished goods less costs to complete and profit allowance. Raw materials at current replacement cost.
  - *Plant and equipment*—If to be employed in operations, show at replacement cost. If to be sold, reflect at net realizable value. If to be used temporarily, show at net realizable value recognizing depreciation for the period.
  - *Identifiable intangibles*—At appraisal value
  - *Other assets* (including land and noncurrent securities)—At appraised values
  - *Payables*—At estimated present value
  - *Liabilities and accruals*—At estimated present value
  - *Other liabilities and commitments*—At estimated present value. However, a deferred income tax credit account of the acquired company is not brought forth.

- The excess of cost paid over book value of assets acquired is attributed to the identifiable net assets. The remaining balance not attributable to specific assets is of an unidentifiable nature and is assigned to goodwill. The identifiable assets are depreciated. Goodwill is amortized over the period benefited not exceeding 40 years. Note that adjustments for fair value and amortization of goodwill are factors just in preparing consolidated financial statements.

- Goodwill of the acquired company is not brought forth

- None of the equity accounts of the acquired business (e.g., retained earnings) appear on the acquirer's books. Ownership interests of the acquired company stockholders are not continued subsequent to the merger.

- Net income of the acquired company is brought forth from the date of acquisition to year-end

- Direct costs of the purchase are a deduction from the fair value of the securities issued while indirect costs are expensed as incurred.

When stock is issued in a purchase transaction, quoted market price of stock is typically a clear indication of asset cost. Consideration should be given to price fluctuations, volume, and issue price of stock.

If liabilities are assumed in a purchase, the difference between the fixed rate of the debt securities and the present yield rate for comparable securities is reflected as a premium or discount.

There is the following step-by-step acquisition procedure:

- If control is not accomplished on the initial purchase, the subsidiary is not includable in consolidation until control has been accomplished.

- Once the parent owns in excess of 50% of the subsidiary, a retroactive restatement should be made including all of the subsidiary's earnings in consolidated retained earnings in a step-by-step fashion commencing with the initial investment.

- The subsidiary's earnings are included for the ownership years at the appropriate ownership percentage.

- After control is accomplished, fair value and adjustments for goodwill will be applied retroactively on a step-by-step basis. Each acquisition is separately determined.

The acquiring company can not generally record a net operating loss carryforward of the acquired company since there is no assurance of realization. However, if realized in a later year recognition will be a retroactive adjustment of the purchase transaction allocation thus causing the residual purchase cost to be reallocated to the other assets acquired. In effect, there will be a reduction of goodwill or the other assets.

FASB 38 provides guidelines for recording "preacquisition contingencies" during the "allocation period" as a part of allocating the cost of an investment in an enterprise acquired under the purchase method. A preacquisition contingency is a contingency of a business that is acquired with the purchase method and that exists prior to the consummation date. Examples of preacquisition contingencies are a contingent asset, a contingent liability, or a contingent impairment of an asset. The allocation period is the one required to identify and quantify the acquired assets and liabilities assumed. The allocation period ceases when the acquiring company no longer needs information it has arranged to obtain and that is known to be available. Hence, the existence of a preacquisition contingency for which an asset, a liability, or an impairment of an asset cannot be estimated does not, of itself, extend the allocation period. Although the time required depends on the circumstances, the allocation period typically is not greater than one year from the consummation date.

Preacquisition contingencies (except for tax benefits of NOL carryforwards) must be included in the allocation of purchase cost. The allocation basis is determined in the following manner:

- The fair value of the preacquisition contingency, assuming a fair value can be determined during the "allocation period."

- If fair value is not determinable, the following criteria is used:
  - Information available before the termination of the allocation period indicates that it is probable that an asset existed, a liability had been incurred, or an asset had been impaired at the consummation date. It must be probable that one or more future events will occur confirming the existence of the asset, liability, or impairment.
  - The amount of the asset or liability can be reasonably estimated.

Adjustments necessitated from a preacquisition contingency occurring after the end of the "allocation period" must be included in income in the year the adjustment is made.

Disclosures Under Purchase. Footnote disclosures under the purchase method include:

- Name and description of companies combined
- A statement that the purchase method is being used
- The period in which earnings of the acquired company is included
- Cost of the acquired company including the number and value of shares issued, if any
- Amortization period of goodwill
- Contingencies arising under the acquisition agreement
- Earnings for the current and prior periods as if the companies were combined at the beginning of the period. This "pro forma" disclosure is to make the purchase method comparable to that of pooling.

Advantages and Disadvantages of Purchase Method. An advantage of the purchase method is that fair value is used to recognize the acquired company's assets just as in the case of acquiring a separate asset. Disadvantages are the difficulty in determining fair value, the amortization period to use, and mixing fair value of acquired company's assets and historical cost for the acquiring company's assets.

FINANCIAL STATEMENT ANALYSIS OF BUSINESS COMBINATIONS

Acquisitions must be analyzed, especially by examining footnote disclosures, because they can create an appearance of earnings and growth when they are not really present.

As previously mentioned, the pooling of interest method requires a company to pick up earnings of the acquired business for the whole year even though the acquisition took place during the year. This can result in artificial earnings growth through merely acquiring other companies.

In a pooling, as previously mentioned, the assets of the acquired company are reported at book value instead of market value. Because of inflation, book value is typically lower than market value. The understatement of assets (inventory, fixed assets, and intangible assets) results in the understatement of expenses (cost of sales, depreciation, and amortization) with the concurrent overstatement in net income. The analyst should adjust the net assets of the acquired company from book value to fair market value. In this way, the omitted value arising from the pooling will be reflected. He should then depreciate and amortize this difference against net income to arrive at a more realistic earnings figure that is comparable to what net income would be if the purchase method (which uses fair market value) were used to account for the business combination.

For analytical purposes, net income should be downwardly adjusted for the difference between reported gain and what the gain would have been if the assets were valued at fair market value.

The analyst must recognize that pooling can result in meaningless ratios, as in the overstatement of ROI due to the overstatement of net income and understatement of total assets.

EXAMPLE 22

Company A reports that it acquired company X on December 1, 19X1 in a business combination accounted for under the pooling method.

The following data are available:

	19X1	19X2
Company A's net income without including the acquired company's earnings	$ 800,000	$ 810,000
Inclusion of company X's net income for the entire year	200,000	210,000
Reported earnings	$1,000,000	$1,020,000

The net income for company X from December 1, 19X1 to December 31, 19X1 is $15,000.

In 19X2, company A had sold assets, picked up from acquiring company X, for $65,000 which were originally recorded at $40,000 book value (market value is approximated at $60,000).

The restatement of earnings for 19X1 and 19X2 follows:

	19X1	19X2
Reported earnings	$1,000,000	$1,020,000
Less:		
Company X's net income prior to the acquisition date (Jan. 1 – Nov. 30) $200,000 – $15,000	(185,000)	
Low quality gain from the sale of company X's undervalued assets:		

		19X1	19X2
Reported gain	$25,000		
Gain if assets were recorded at fair market value	5,000		
Overstated gain	$20,000		(20,000)
Restated earnings		$ 815,000	$1,000,000

The purchase method is more realistic than the pooling method because it uses fair market value to reflect the net assets acquired rather than the outdated original cost.

The analyst must carefully scrutinize disclosures relating to deriving fair market values of the assets and liabilities of the acquired company. He must ascertain the reasonableness of such valuations.

If equity securities are involved in the purchase transaction, the analyst should determine whether the market prices of the securities were unusually high at the transaction date. If so, net assets will be inflated due to the temporary ceiling market prices. In this case, the analyst may wish to use the average market price of the securities for his own valuation of the acquired assets.

The analyst must be alert to the possible overstatement of estimated liabilities for future costs and losses that may increase postacquisition earnings.

CONCLUSION

Generally, do not acquire another business unless you are a growth, successful company. Do not try to make a "bargain" purchase. You get what you pay for!

In analyzing a potential merger and acquisition, many considerations must be taken into account, such as the market price of stock, earnings per share, dividends, book value of assets, risk, and tax considerations. A detailed analysis of the target company is required to ensure that a realistic price is paid based on the particular circumstances. Two methods to account for a business combination are the pooling-of-interests and purchase. The former involves an exchange of voting common stock while the latter requires cash payment or the incurrence of a liability.

45

Divestiture

The divestiture of business segments by corporations has become an accepted strategy for growth rather than diversification. Divestiture involves the partial or complete conversion, disposition and reallocation of people, money, inventories, plants, equipment and products. It is the process of eliminating a portion of the enterprise for subsequent use of the freed resources for some other purpose. A divestment may involve a manufacturing, marketing, research or other business function. A parent may sell a segment because it needs funds to pay off debt.

A business segment may be subject to divestiture if they:

(1) Do not produce an acceptable return on invested capital;

(2) Do not generate sufficient cash flow;

(3) Fit in with the overall corporate strategy;

(4) The worth of the pieces is greater than that of the whole.

During the 1960s, many corporations were acquiring other firms, often in different industries to form large conglomerates. In the 1970s a general economic downturn made many companies reduce the pace of the acquisition process. Divestiture first appeared in the early stages of the downturn as corporations needed cash. Many dynamic, fast-growing companies were combining with slower growing, mature companies to produce a more diversified corporate portfolio. However, during this time many companies found that if you have too many businesses it spreads the cash too thin. Also, this random mixture of businesses under one corporate umbrella caused a great deal of concern among the financial industry. This mix made it difficult to measure actual segment performance.

In 1976, the Securities and Exchange Commission persuaded the Financial

Accounting Standards Board (FASB) that publicly held companies should report the assets held and income generated by disaggregated corporate segments of similar products and services. Thus, for the first time the public found out that many of a company's business segments were unprofitable! This disclosure forced management to explain to the shareholders why certain segments of the corporation were producing such low returns on the stockholder's invested capital. For the first time, corporate executives were forced into developing divestiture strategies to eliminate the unprofitable section of the business.

Resource allocation becomes an important consideration in a diversified business. These resources are not only capital but also include management talent. If management finds itself spending an excessive amount of time and energy on one segment of the corporation, that segment may be a candidate for divestiture. Then those resources can be redirected to the growing segments of the business. However, this operation also requires the attention of management.

OBJECTIVES AND TYPES OF DIVESTITURES

Sooner or later a corporation will find itself in the position of needing to divest some of its assets. This may be for a variety of reasons. The usual objectives behind divestiture are to reposition the company in a market, raise cash, and to reduce losses. The other alternatives to divestiture are liquidation and bankruptcy, however, in this time of acquisitions and buyouts usually a buyer can be found for the other guy's dog. There are four primary types of divestitures:

(a) Sale of an operating unit to another firm;
(b) Sale of the managers of the unit being divested;
(c) Setting up the business to be divested as a separate corporation and then giving (or "spinning off") its stock to the divesting firm's stockholders on a pro rata basis;
(d) Outright liquidation of assets.

When the divestiture is in the form of a sale to another firm, it usually involves an entire division or unit and is generally for cash but sometimes for stock of the acquiring firm. In a managerial buyout, the division managers themselves purchase the division, often through a leverage buyout (LBO), and reorganize it as a closely held firm. In a spin off, the firm's existing stockholders are given new stock representing separate ownership in the company that was divested. The new company establishes its own board of directors and officers and operates as a separate entity. In a liquidation, the assets of the divested unit are sold off separately instead of as a whole.

REASONS FOR DIVESTITURE

Prior to formulating a divestiture strategy and determining which segments should be divested, the reasons for divestiture need to be listed. Table 1

Table 1

REASONS MANAGERS CITE FOR DIVESTING SEGMENTS OF THEIR BUSINESS

	Frequency Given
Poor Performance	26%
Changes in Plans	23%
Excessive Resource Needs	19%
Constraints in Operation	15%
Source of Funds	10%
Anti-trust	7%
	100%

Source: L. Vignola, Jr. *Strategic Divestment* (New York: Amacon, 1974), p. 52.

summarizes the reasons given by management for divesting segments of their business.

As a result of the FASB decision in FASB No. 14 (see Chapter 10) regarding the reporting of each business segment's operating costs and whether a profit is made or not, corporate management has been less reluctant to hold on to poorly performing business segments. However, there may be a logical reason to keep a poorly performing segment, such as a turn around is expected or the unit provides components or a service to another unit within the company.

A diversified decision may result after the corporation has reviewed its operational philosophy and overall business strategy (whether this reevaluation was voluntary or forced by environment changes), and found business segments that no longer fit into the corporate image or are a business the company does not want to be involved in any more. An example of this is Schering-Plough's attempt to sell its Maybelline Cosmetics Division so they can concentrate their resources and time on their more profitable prescription and consumer drug businesses. This restructuring will allow Schering-Plough to earn more on its invested capital. Operating margins for drugs are near 24% which is more than twice that of the Maybelline Division.

The need to raise cash to pay off debt resulting from operations or acquisition/diversification is another frequent reason for selling off a segment of the corporation. In this case, though many times the segment being sold is a winner. By selling a winning segment the company may hope to put itself on firmer financial ground by reducing debt. In this case where the company is trying to raise cash, the best segment to sell is the one that would require the least work to sell and bring in the greatest amount of cash over book value. For example, if a company had two divisions, a retail operation and the other which builds and leases railcars, and the sale of either would make a significant dent in the company's debt load, which division should be sold? In this case, the retail should be sold because the market for that type of operation is much better than for railcars.

There are other less common reasons such as personality conflicts among division management and that of the parent company, government decree or public outcry, as in the case of many companies that had dealings in South Africa. On a rare occasion, the company may actually be approached and asked if they would be willing to sell the business.

DETERMINING WHAT AREAS/UNITS SHOULD BE SOLD

When trying to determine which areas or units of the company could be sold off, there are some simple guidelines that management should follow:

- The sum of a division's parts may be greater in value than the whole division;
- Simple components of a division may be sold more easily than the whole division itself;
- The disposal of a corporate division is a major marketing operation;
- Planning should include an evaluation from the viewpoint of the potential buyer;
- A spin off should be considered if the division is large enough and may be potentially publicly traded.

In addition, management must review existing operations and identify those divisions that don't relate to the primary focus of the company or don't meet internal financial and performance standards. Special strength of each division must also be considered. Does a division provide a unique service, have a special marketing, distribution system or production facilities that may be of more value to another company? Also, the financial aspects must be considered. The historical and projected return on investment need to be calculated and tabulated for each division.

Using these guidelines and the information determined above, management can focus on three topics. First, the attractiveness and value to others versus the arguments for keeping the division. Secondly, what corrective action would need to be taken to make the division a keeper. Thirdly, the current value of the division to the company. Only after considering all of these factors can a divestiture decision be made for a division.

EMPLOYEE CONSIDERATIONS

Once the decision to divest a division has been made, there are two approaches to dealing with employees. The first, and least often done, is to be up front and tell them that the division is for sale. This can result in a variety of negative responses. The employees' morale may further deteriorate (usually the morale is already poor because the division is not doing well). Or worse, the employees may engage in a job action. The employees can also be a potential source of a buy-out of the company so unless the upper management is very aware of the employees' attitude the decision to tell or not is a difficult one. Another tactic is for management to tell the employees that the division is being sold and offer incentive bonuses to all employees who stay on through the divestiture and following acquisition.

Typically though, the parent company will form a senior management team whose sole function is to divest the division, occasionally even the top management of the division being divested doesn't know it is being sold. There are some reasons behind choosing an upper management team to do the divestiture. First, companies tend to divest in secret. Any leak of the news could cause any of the employee problems mentioned above. This is especially true in the case where finding a buyer may take a long time. (A longer time means more likelihood for a leak.) Secondly, the head of a division is never the right person to sell the division. No matter how the decision to divest is sugar coated it is still an admission of failure. This makes it difficult for the managers to take an objective view of the business. It also impedes the decision on who is a suitable and qualified buyer of the company. Having the management team doing the divestiture also avoids or minimizes any conflict between those who may be responsible for the failure and those who were not. The third reason to appoint a top management team to do the divestiture is that it is simply not a job that would be welcomed by lower level managers. It is a thankless task that brings little reward for a hard job well done and has no future. It is a dead-end job!

Because the job falls on senior management, this also creates a problem. Their time is limited, particularly during a period where the company is trying to recover. If the team has little time nor the inclination to do this divestiture, the job performed may be sloppy. The decision analysis could be approximate rather than one based on actual numbers as may be the selling price. Also, if pressed for time the team may be restricted to dealing with only one buyer instead of negotiating with many suitors, which will improve the selling price and the return for the parent. This time pressure may be caused by the division's cash requirements rather than the divestiture team time constraints. If the parent can only support the cash drain of the division for a certain time period after the decision to divest, this puts a definite time constraint on the timing of the sale.

MEANS OF DIVESTITURE

After the initial planning of the divestiture comes the tricky part of approaching potential buyers. The trick involved is to present enough information to peak the interest but also present the need for confidentiality (if required by the situation). The usual technique is to sound out a few potential buyers at a time, to see if they would be interested in acquiring a business in your industry with sales potential of X dollars.

This is done by sending out a short letter or a phone call to the CEO of the possibly interested firms. This communication again should just wet their appetite for information. If they express a desire for further dialogue, a prospectus should be sent. However, if after reviewing the prospectus and no further interest exists, this potential acquirer should be crossed off the list.

The other option depending on the skills and time demands of the members of the divestiture team is to use a third party (broker) to find suitable buyers and enter into negotiations. The use of the third party will in many cases provide a needed veil of secrecy, if needed. The third party is also useful in trying to market the division on a world wide scale. This can get exposure for the division. This is particularly important where the parent or division had no previous exposure.

VALUATION AND APPRAISAL IN DIVESTITURE

When the time comes to sell a division, an asking price needs to be determined. Valuation of a division is not an exact science, and in the final analysis the value of a division is in the eye of the purchaser. While the expertise of an investment banker or business broker can and should be enlisted in setting the price of the division there are some standard accounting methods that can be used to estimate a division's value. A business broker will usually be very willing to help in the initial estimate phase in hopes that they will get the opportunity to act as your agent in selling the division. These valuation methods will be broken down into asset valuation methods, those based on sales and income, and those based on market comparisons. Although these methods vary in their applicability and depend on certain facts and circumstances they can be used to determine a range of values for a division.

There are basically four groups of methods of valuation or appraisal: (1) asset valuation methods, (2) sales and income methods, (3) market comparison methods, and (4) discounted cash flow methods.

Asset Valuation Methods

Asset valuation methods are based on the asset value of a business segment. Four popular methods are described below.

Adjusted Net Book Value. One of the most conservative methods of valuation is the adjusted net book value, because it determines the value based on historical (book) value and not on market value. This can be adjusted to compensate for this shortage by adding in such items as favorable lease arrangements, and other intangible items such as customer lists, patents, and goodwill.

Replacement Cost. Another method is the replacement cost technique. It asks "What would it cost to purchase the division's assets new?" This method will give a higher division value than the adjusted net book value method and is therefore good for adjusting the book value to account for new costs. This figure can also be used as a basis for determining the liquidation value of the division's assets. The most reasonable value comes from adjusting the replacement value for depreciation and obsolescence of equipment.

Liquidation Value. The liquidation value is also a conservative estimate of a division's value since it does not consider the division's ongoing earning power. The liquidation value does provide the seller with a bottom line figure as to how low the price can be. The liquidation value is determined by estimating the cash value of assets assuming that they are to be sold in a short period of time. All the liabilities, real and estimated, are then deducted from the cash that was raised to determine the net liquidation value. Liquidation value can be determined based on fire sale prices or on a longer term sales price. Obviously, the fire sale value would be lower.

Secured Loan Value. The secured loan value technique is based on the borrowing power of the division's assets. Banks will usually lend up to 90% of the value of accounts receivable and anywhere from 10–60% on the value of inventory depending on the quantity of the inventory in the conversion process.

Sales and Income Factors

Using sales and/or income figures as the basis for valuation can be made in two different ways.

Price-Earnings (P-E) Ratios. The P-E ratio for publicly held companies is known and therefore valuation is made easy. The division's value can be determined by multiplying the P-E ratio by the expected earnings for the division. This will give a derived price that all suitors can readily understand. The earnings can be estimated from quarterly or annual reports published by the company.

For privately held companies, however, it is difficult to determine a P-E ratio as the stock of the company is not traded and the earnings are rarely disclosed. However, the earnings can be estimated and an industry average P-E ratio can be used in the calculation to estimate the private company's sales value.

Sales or Earnings Multiples. There are many rules of thumb that can be used when estimating a division's value based on a multiple of sales or earnings. For example, insurance agencies sell for 200% of annual commissions or liquor stores sell for 10 times monthly sales. Another example would be radio stations selling for eight times earnings or cash flow. These rules are fast and dirty and may result in a completely erroneous estimate of a division's value. Most business brokers will know these rule of thumb values to assist management in estimating the value of a division.

Market Based Comparisons

Every day that a public company is traded on the stock market a new value is assigned to it by the traders. Thus, the stock price can be compared to equivalent companies, in terms of products, size of operations, and average P-E ratios. From these P-E ratios, an estimated sales price can be estimated as described earlier.

In the case of private companies, it is difficult for the buyer to determine the earnings of the company. However, they can compare the company to other companies that are publicly traded. Comparison to publicly traded companies is necessary as the sales price is typically disclosed in the sale or acquisition announcement.

Discounted Cash Flow Analysis

Another method of determining value of a business segment is to use discounted cash flow (DCF) analysis. This bases the value of the segment on the current value of its projected cash flow. In theory, this method should result in a division's value being equal to that determined by one of the P-E ratio calculations, since both reflect the current worth of the company's earnings. In actuality, discounted cash flow is basing the value of the company on actual forecasted cash flows whereas the stock market is basing the stock price on other things including the markets perception of the company and its potential cash flow.

The DCF method requires information on

- Forecasted actual cash flows
- Assumed terminal (residual) value of the division at the end of the forecast period (book value, zero, or a multiple of earnings are frequently used)
- Discount rate

Choosing the right discount rate is the key to the successful use of the DCF technique. It must take into account the following factors:

- Purchaser's expected return on investment (ROI)
- Purchaser's assessment of risk
- Cost of capital
- Projected inflation rates
- Current interest rates

In general, whichever method of evaluation is chosen it is wise to check that resulting value with at least one other method to see if it is a reasonable figure. We have to be careful of excessively high or low figures. It is also a good idea to determine the liquidation value of the company or division as this will set a floor for negotiations.

AN ILLUSTRATION: DISCOUNTED CASH FLOW ANALYSIS

Management will choose to divest a segment of their business if they perceive that the action will increase the wealth of the stockholders, as reflected in the price of the firm's stock. It can be further said that the price of the firm's stock will react favorably to a divestiture if the new present value of the transaction is perceived by the market to be positive.

Should a profitable business segment be retained and not divested, it would generate annual cash inflows for a particular or infinite number of years. Discounted cash flow analysis involves a comparison of initial incoming cash flows resulting from the sale of a business unit with the present value of the foregone future cash inflows given up by the firm. Foregone future cash flows refer to the cash flows that the business unit is anticipated to generate and will do so for the acquiring firm. The divesting firm gives up these cash inflows in exchange for the selling price of the business segment. For divestiture analysis to be of any value, the foregone future cash flow must be accurately estimated. The present value of these future inflows are found by discounting them at the firm's weighted-average cost of capital k_o.

EXAMPLE 1

Table 2 shows estimated cash inflows and outflows for a fictitious divestment candidate (FDC) over the next five years. The cash flows represent the best estimates by the managers of FDC's parent company and they further believe that FDC will be able to be sold at its residual value of $58.7 million in five years. The firm's cost of capital is assumed to be known and is 15%.

The net present value of the future cash inflows of FDC is $47.3 million. If FDC were to be divested, the managers of its parent company should only

Table 2

FDC's CASH FLOW PROJECTIONS (IN MILLIONS)

Cash Inflows	1	2	3	4	5
Net Operating Profit	$ 3.1	$3.6	$4.0	$5.1	$ 6.0
Depreciation	2.1	2.4	1.8	2.3	2.1
Residual Value					58.7
Total	$ 5.2	$6.0	$5.8	$7.4	$66.8
Cash Outflows					
Capital Expenditure	$ 1.7	$1.3	$0.8	$2.1	$ 1.7
Increase (Decrease)					
in working Capital	(6.3)	1.3	2.6	(0.5)	2.2
Total	$ (4.6)	$2.6	$3.4	$1.6	$ 3.9
Net Cash Inflow (NCF)	$ 9.8	$3.4	$2.4	$5.8	$62.9
PVIF*	0.8696	0.7561	0.6575	0.5718	0.4972
Net Present Value	$ 8.5	$2.6	$1.6	$3.3	$31.3
Total NPV:	$ 47.3				

*Note: PVIF = Present value interest factor for the cost of capital of 15%.

consider selling prices greater than this amount. This logic also assumes that the \$47.3 million can be reinvested at a 15% rate of return.

Another way of looking at this valuing task makes use of the following equation for divestiture net present value (DNPV):

$$DNPV = P - \Sigma \frac{NCF_t}{(1 + k)^t} \qquad (1)$$

where P = the selling price of the business unit and NCF_t = net cash flow in period t. If a \$50 million offer was made by a firm for FDC, the DNPV from Equation 1 will equal \$2.7 million, as shown below.

$$DNPV = 50 - \frac{9.8}{1.15 +} + \frac{.4}{(1.15)^2} + \frac{2.4}{(1.15)^3} + \frac{5.8}{(1.15)^4} + \frac{62.9}{(1.15)^5}$$

$$DNPV = 50 - 47.3 = \$ 2.7 \text{ million}$$

From a financial point of view, this divestment is acceptable. If the divestment candidate has an unlimited life, such as a division in a healthy industry, then cash flows must be forecasted to infinity. This task is made simple by treating the cash flows similarly to a constant growth stock and value accordingly. If the cash inflows are expected to remain constant (zero growth) to infinity, then the present value of the NCF can be determined in the same manner as for a preferred stock, or perpetuity. In this case, the DNPV will be

$$DNPV = P - \frac{NCF}{k} \qquad (2)$$

For future cash flows that are expected to grow at an after tax rate of g, the present value of those flows can be found using the constant growth valuation model. In this case, the DNPV will be

$$DNPV = P - \frac{NCF_1}{k - g} \qquad (3)$$

where NCF_1 = the expected NCF in the next period.

A final situation encountered often when evaluating divestiture candidates is the case where the NCF's are expected to be uneven for a number of years followed by even growth. In this case, the DNPV can be found as

$$DNPV = R - \frac{NCF_1}{(1 + k)} + \frac{NCF_2}{(1 + k)^2} + \ldots + \frac{NCF_{c-1}}{(k - g)} * \frac{1}{(1 + k)}$$

where NCF_1 and NCF_2 represent foregone cash flows in periods 1 and 2 and c = the first year in which constant growth applies.

Firms should only divest of assets with positive DNPV's. To do so will increase the value of the firm and subsequently, the price of its stock. If two different candidates are mutually exclusive, the one with the highest DNPV should be chosen since this will increase the value of the firm the most. If divestiture is forced by the government, for example, and the firm finds it has a choice of candidates, all with negative DNPV's, it should divest the one whose DNPV is closest to zero, since this will reduce the value of the firm the least.

Divestiture with Uncertainty

Due to the difficulty in predicting the NCF's and also in knowing what kinds of prices will be offered for the divestment candidate, the divestment's net present value is normally uncertain.

For situations involving an unknown selling price (due to a lack of offers) the parent firm can either elect not to divest of the candidate or set its asking price such that the DNPV will equal zero. This should be the minimum they are willing to accept. They can also look for other divestment candidates that offer promising DNPV's.

Adjusting for uncertain NCF's is much more difficult and while there is no generally accepted method for accounting for this risk, there are a number of useful techniques that are borrowed from capital budgeting and can be used here.

Risk Adjusted Discount Rate. Employing a risk adjusted discount rate is one technique that can be used to account for the uncertainty of the expected NCF's. In the previous examples, the firm's weighted-average cost of capital was used to discount the NCF's to their present value. This is an appropriate choice when the divestiture candidate is as risky as the firm itself. When it is more risky, the use of a higher discount rate can be used for adjustment. This will reduce the present values of the cash flows and increase the DNPV. This is logical since a relatively risky divestment candidate with uncertain cash flows will be of less value to the firm, in present dollars. The added benefit of divesting such a candidate will be reflected in the increased DNPV. On the other hand, when the NCF's are more certain than those of the rest of the firm, the discount rate should be lowered. This lowers the DNPV and makes the divestiture less attractive. Equation 1 can be rewritten as shown below:

$$\text{DNPV} = P - \Sigma \frac{NCF_t}{(1 + k')^t} \qquad (4)$$

where all terms are the same except for k' which now is the adjusted rate to be used for discounting the cash flows. Using data from Table 2 and assuming that the divestment candidate is less risky than the firm as a whole (lowering k from .15 to .14) shows:

$$\text{DNPV} = 50 - \frac{9.8}{1.14} + \frac{3.4}{(1.14)^2} + \frac{2.4}{(1.14)^3} + \frac{5.8}{(1.14)^4} + \frac{62.9}{(1.14)^5}$$

$$\text{DNPV} = 50 - 48.9 = \$ 1.1 \text{ million}$$

Using a lower discount rate lessened the DNPV by $1.6 million ($2.7 million − $1.1 million). This is reasonable in that the attractiveness of a divestment candidate at a certain selling price will be lessened as the candidate is found to be less risky.

Sensitivity Analysis. Sensitivity analysis is another technique which can be used in making divestiture decisions. In sensitivity analysis, the parent company evaluates the effect that certain factors have on the NCF's. For example, a divestment candidate's NCF's might be largely influenced by the price of copper, the US Navy Defense budget, and upcoming union contract talks. For these three influencing factors, a number of different scenarios or forecasts, can be projected, each with their expected NCF's. For instance, the expected NCF's would be highest in the scenario where all three influencing factors are favorable. Having evaluated the NCF's and DNPV's for different scenarios, the parent firm has a better understanding of the range that the NCF's might fall in and also what factors influence them the most. Further, if the probability of the scenarios can be forecasted, statistical techniques can be used to give the probability of realizing a negative DNPV, the expected DNPV and the standard deviation, and coefficient of variation of DNPV's. This information would be very useful in making divestment decisions. It should be noted that the NCF's using sensitivity analysis are discounted at the firm's weighted-average cost of capital.

Simulation. Simulation is a third technique used to account for the uncertainty of future cash flows. It is similar to but more sophisticated than the sensitivity analysis previously discussed. In simulation, the parent firm's managers first identify key factors which they believe are likely to influence the NCF's of a divestment candidate. Next they create a probability distribution describing the future outcome of each key factor. The managers finally must specify the impact of each key variable on the NCF's and ultimately the DNPV's. The firm's cost of capital is again used to discount the NCF's. Computer programs are available to assist managers in the simulation analysis. After the data has been input and the program run, the computer will estimate NCF's and corresponding DNPV's over the whole range of probabilities. From this distribution, the analyst can determine the expected DNPV and the probability that the actual DNPV will be above or below some critical value. The uncertainty associated with the DNPV can also be determined, as measured by the dispersion of possible DNPV value. It is important to note that this technique is only as good as the input it receives from managers, and even then, it cannot make a firm's divestment decision. It does, however, provide a comprehensive evaluation of the divestiture proposal.

LIQUIDATION PROCESS

Divestment of a company or division is nearly always preferred to liquidation even though liquidation may provide the greatest potential for monetary gain. The reason why it is not the method of choice is that it usually takes longer to liquidate a business than it does to sell one outright. However should the case exist where the value of the business is zero or less and no buyer can be found liquidation becomes the obvious alternative. Liquidation may be so expensive that it is not feasible. This would be the result of the cost of getting out of leases, contracts and possible salary continuation requirements that it may be cheaper to pay the existing management or an entrepreneur to take over the business. The other option is bankruptcy which is covered in Chapter 46.

The liquidation can be accomplished by contacting a liquidation company and having them perform all of the work involved in the liquidation process such as asset valuation, advertising the sale, negotiating the sale prices, and collecting the money for the goods. From this they will take a pre-negotiated sum of money for their services. Another technique involves doing all the work in-house that the liquidation company would do and contacting competitors and the various vendor representatives in the area and alert them to the fact that you will be having a going out of business sale. They will typically already know you are about to go out of business since word has probably already spread in these circles.

CONCLUSION

The present business environment has made both divestiture and diversification an acceptable strategy for business to pursue. The requirement for public disclosure of business segment operating results has forced management to take action when a segment is not performing to company standards. Their action has been divestiture of the undesirable divisions. However, there are other alternatives for underperforming divisions. Divestiture has become an accepted method of dealing with problem business segments.

When developing the strategies involved with divestiture, management must consider the interrelationships between that division and the rest of the company and the costs of discontinuing that operation. The carrying out of a divestiture has an affect across the whole company, including the production, distribution, and marketing areas. Divestiture may also greatly affect the public's image of the company.

When considering divestiture as an alternative, all of these factors must be evaluated. The divestiture decision must be closely thought out.

46

Failure and Reorganization

When a company fails it can be either reorganized or dissolved depending on the circumstances. A number of ways exist for business failure to occur, including a poor rate of return, technical insolvency, and bankruptcy.

Deficient Rate of Return. A company may fail if its rate of return is negative or poor. If there are operating losses, the company may not be able to satisfy its debt. A negative rate of return will result in a drop in the market price of its stock. When a company does not earn a return greater than its cost of capital, it may fail. If corrective action is not forthcoming, perhaps the company should liquidate. A poor return, however, does not constitute legal evidence of failure.

Technical Insolvency. Technical insolvency means that the company cannot meet current obligations when due even if total assets exceed total liabilities.

Bankruptcy. In bankruptcy, liabilities are greater than the fair market value of assets. There exists a negative real net worth.

According to law, failure of a company can be either technical insolvency or bankruptcy. When creditor claims against a business are in question, the law gives creditors recourse against the company.

Some causes of business failure include poor management, an economic downturn affecting the company and/or industry, overexpansion, the end of the life cycle of the firm, lawsuit, and catastrophe.

VOLUNTARY SETTLEMENT

A voluntary settlement with creditors allows the company to save many of the costs that would occur in bankruptcy. Such a settlement is reached out of court. The voluntary settlement permits the company to either continue or be liquidated and is initiated to enable the debtor firm to recover some of its investment.

A creditor committee may elect to permit the company to operate if it is anticipated that the firm will recover. Creditors may also keep doing business with the company. In sustaining the company's existence, there may be:

- An extension
- A composition
- Creditor control
- Integration of each of the above

Extension

In an extension, creditors will receive the balances due but over an extended time period. Current purchases are made with cash. It is also possible that the creditors may agree not only to extend the maturity date for payment but also to subordinate their claims to current debt for suppliers providing credit in the extension period. The creditors expect the debtor will be able to work out its problems.

The creditor committee may mandate certain controls, including legal control over the firm's assets or common stock, obtaining a security interest in assets, and approval of all cash payments.

If there are creditors dissenting to the extension agreement, they may be paid immediately to prevent them from having the firm declared bankrupt.

Composition

In a composition, there is a voluntary reduction of the amount the debtor owes the creditor. The creditor obtains from the debtor a specified percent of the obligation in full satisfaction of the debt irrespective of how low the percent is. The agreement permits the debtor to continue to operate. The creditor may attempt to work with the debtor in handling the company's financial difficulties, since a stable customer may result. The benefits of a composition are that court costs are eliminated as well as the stigma of a bankrupt company.

If dissenting stockholders exist, they may be paid in full or they may be allowed to recover a higher percentage so that they do not force the business to close.

For an extension or composition to be practical, there should be an expectation that the debtor will recover, and that present business conditions must be conducive to that recovery.

Creditor Committee Takes Control

A committee of creditors may take control of the firm if they are not pleased with current management. They will operate the business so as to satisfy their claims. Once paid, the creditors may recommend new management replace the old before further credit may be given.

Integration

The company and creditors negotiate a plan involving a combination of extension, composition, and creditor control. For example, the agreement may provide for a 10% cash payment of the balance owed plus five future payments of 15%, usually in notes. The total payment is thus 85%.

The benefits of a negotiated settlement are:

- They cost less, particularly in legal fees.
- They are easier to implement than bankruptcy proceedings.
- They are less formal than bankruptcy.

The following drawbacks exist to a negotiated settlement:

- If the troubled debtor still has control over its business affairs, there may occur further decline in asset values. However, creditor control can provide some protection.
- Unrealistic small creditors may drain the negotiating process.

BANKRUPTCY REORGANIZATION

If no voluntary settlement is agreed upon, the company may be put into bankruptcy by its creditors. The bankruptcy proceeding may either reorganize or liquidate the company.

Bankruptcy occurs when the company cannot pay its bills or when liabilities exceed the fair market value of the assets. Here, legal bankruptcy may be declared. A company may file for reorganization under which it will formulate a plan for continued life.

Chapter 7 of the Bankruptcy Reform Act of 1978 outlines the procedures to be followed for liquidation. This chapter applies when reorganization is not practical. Chapter 11 goes into the steps of reorganizing a failed business.

The two kinds of reorganization petitions are:

1. *Voluntary.* The company petitions for its own reorganization. The firm does not have to be insolvent to file for voluntary reorganization.

2. *Involuntary.* Creditors file for an involuntary reorganization of the company. An involuntary petition must establish either that the debtor firm is not meeting its debts when due or that a creditor or another party has taken control over the debtor's assets. In general, most of the creditors or claims must support the petition.

The five steps in a reorganization are:

1. A reorganization petition is filed under Chapter 11 in court.

2. A judge approves the petition and either appoints a trustee or allows the creditors to elect one to handle the disposition of the assets.

3. The trustee provides a fair plan of reorganization to the court.

4. The plan is given to the creditors and stockholders of the company for approval.

5. The debtor pays the expenses of the parties performing services in the reorganization proceedings.

The trustee in a reorganization plan is required to:

• Value the company

• Recapitalize the company

• Exchange outstanding debts for new securities

Valuation

In valuing the company, the trustee must estimate its liquidation value versus its value as a going concern. Liquidation is called for when the liquidation value exceeds the continuity value. If the company is more valuable when operating, reorganization is the answer. Future earnings must be predicted when arriving at the value of the reorganized company. The going concern value represents the present value of future earnings.

EXAMPLE 1

A petition for reorganization of a company was filed under Chapter 11. The trustee computed the firm's liquidation value after deducting expenses as $4.5 million. The trustee estimates that the reorganized business will generate $530,000 in annual earnings. The cost of capital is 10%. Assuming the earnings continue indefinitely, the value of the business as a going concern is:

$$\$530,000/.10 = \$5,300,000$$

Since the company's value as a going concern ($5.3 million) exceeds its liquidation value ($4.5 million), reorganization is called for.

Recapitalization

If the trustee recommends reorganization, a plan must be formulated. The obligations may be extended or equity securities may be issued in place of the debt. Income bonds may be given for the debentures. As noted in a prior chapter, with an income bond, interest is paid only when there are earnings. This process of exchanging liabilities for other types of liabilities or equity securities is referred to as recapitalization. In recapitalizing the company, the objective is to have a mixture of debt and equity that will allow the company to meet its debts and furnish a reasonable profit for the owners.

EXAMPLE 2

The current capital structure of Y Corporation is presented below.

Debentures	$1,500,000
Collateral bonds	3,000,000
Preferred stock	800,000
Common stock	2,500,000
Total	$7,800,000

There exists high financial leverage:

$$\frac{\text{Debt}}{\text{Equity}} = \frac{\$4,500,000}{\$3,300,000} = 1.36$$

Assuming the company is deemed to be worth $5 million as a going concern, the trustee can develop a less leveraged capital structure having a total capital of $5 million as follows:

Debentures	$1,000,000
Collateral bonds	1,000,000
Income bonds	1,500,000
Preferred stock	500,000
Common stock	1,000,000
Total	$5,000,000

The income bond of $1.5 million is similar to equity in appraising financial leverage, since interest is not paid unless there is income. The new debt/equity ratio is safer:

$$\frac{\text{Debt} + \text{collateral bonds}}{\text{Income bonds} + \text{preferred stock} + \text{common stock}} = \frac{\$2,000,000}{\$3,000,000} = 0.67$$

Exchange of Obligations

In exchanging obligations to arrive at the optimal capital structure, priorities must be followed. Senior claims are paid before junior ones. Senior debt holders receive a claim on new capital equal to their prior claims. The last priority goes to common stockholders in receiving new securities. A debt holder typically receives a combination of different securities. Preferred and common stockholders may receive nothing. Typically, however, they retain some small ownership. After the exchange, the debt holders may become the company's new owners.

LIQUIDATION DUE TO BANKRUPTCY

When a company becomes bankrupt it may be liquidated under Chapter 7 of the Bankruptcy Reform Act of 1978. The major elements of liquidation are legal considerations, claim priority, and dissolution.

Legal Considerations

When a firm is declared bankrupt, creditors have to meet between 10 and 30 days after that declaration. A judge or referee takes charge of the meeting in which the creditors provide their claims. A trustee is appointed by the creditors. The trustee handles the property of the defaulted firm, liquidates the business, maintains records, appraises the creditors' claims, makes payments, and provides relevant information of the liquidation process.

Claim Priority

Some claims against the company take precedence over others in bankruptcy. The following rank order exists in meeting claims:

1. *Secured claims.* Secured creditors receive the value of the secured assets in support of their claims. If the value of the secured assets is inadequate to meet their claims in full, the balance reverts to general creditor status.

2. *Bankruptcy administrative costs.* These costs include any expenses of handling bankruptcy such as legal and trustee expenses.

3. *Unsecured salaries and commissions.* These claims are limited to a maximum specified amount per individual and must have been incurred within 90 days of the bankruptcy petition.

4. *Unsecured customer deposit claims.* These claims are limited to a nominal amount each.

5. *Taxes.* Tax claims apply to unpaid taxes due the government.

6. *General creditor claims.* General creditors loaned the company money without specific collateral. Included are debentures and accounts payable.

7. *Preferred stockholders.*

8. *Common stockholders.*

Dissolution

After claims have been met in priority order and an accounting made of the proceedings, there may then be instituted an application to discharge the bankrupt business. A discharge occurs when the court releases the company from legitimate debts in bankruptcy, with the exception of debts that are immune to discharge. As long as a debtor has not been discharged within the previous six years and was not bankrupt due to fraud, the debtor may then start a new business.

EXAMPLE 3

The balance sheet of Ace Corporation for the year ended December 31, 19X4, follows:

Balance Sheet

Current assets	$400,000	Current liabilities	$475,000
Fixed assets	410,000	Long-term liabilities	250,000
		Common stock	175,000
		Retained earnings	(90,000)
Total assets	$810,000	Total liabilities and stockholders' equity	$810,000

The company's liquidation value is $625,000. Rather than liquidate, there could be a reorganization with an investment of an additional $320,000. The reorganization is expected to generate earnings of $115,000 per year. A multiplier of 7.5 is appropriate. If the $320,000 is obtained, long-term debt holders will receive 40% of the common stock in the reorganized business in substitution for their current claims.

If $320,000 of further investment is made, the firm's going-concern value is $862,500 ($7.5 \times \$115,000$). The liquidation value is given at $625,000. Since the reorganization value exceeds the liquidation value, reorganization is called for.

EXAMPLE 4

Fixed assets with a book value of $1.5 million were sold for $1.3 million. There are mortgage bonds on the fixed assets amounting to $1.8 million. The proceeds from the collateral sale are inadequate to meet the secured claim. Therefore, the unsatisfied portion of $500,000 ($1,800,000 − $1,300,000) of the claim becomes a general creditor claim.

EXAMPLE 5

Land having a book value of $1.2 million was sold for $800,000. Mortgage bonds on the land are $600,000. The excess of $200,000 will be returned to the trustee to pay other creditors.

EXAMPLE 6

Charles Company is bankrupt. The book and liquidation values follow:

	Book Value	Liquidation Value
Cash	$ 600,000	$ 600,000
Accounts receivable	1,900,000	1,500,000
Inventory	3,700,000	2,100,000
Land	5,000,000	3,200,000
Building	7,800,000	5,300,000
Equipment	6,700,000	2,800,000
Total assets	$25,700,000	$15,500,000

The liabilities and stockholders' equity at the date of liquidation are:

Current liabilities		
Accounts payable	$ 1,800,000	
Notes payable	900,000	
Accrued taxes	650,000	
Accrued salaries	450,000[a]	
Total current liabilities		$ 3,800,000
Long-term liabilities		
Mortgage on land	$ 3,200,000	
First mortgage—building	2,800,000	
Second mortgage—building	2,500,000	
Subordinated debentures	4,800,000	
Total long-term liabilities		13,300,000
Total liabilities		$17,100,000
Stockholders' equity		
Preferred stock	$ 4,700,000	
Common stock	6,800,000	
Retained earnings	(2,900,000)	
Total stockholders' equity		8,600,000
Total liabilities and stockholders' equity		$25,700,000

[a]The salary owed each worker is below the specified amount and was incurred within 90 days of the bankruptcy petition.

Expenses of the liquidation including legal costs were 15% of the proceeds. The debentures are subordinated only with regard to the two first-mortgage bonds.

The distribution of the proceeds follows:

Proceeds		$15,500,000
Mortgage on land	$3,200,000	

First mortgage—building	2,800,000	
Second mortgage—building	2,500,000	
Liquidation expenses		
(15% × $15,500,000)	2,325,000	
Accrued salaries	450,000	
Accrued taxes	650,000	
Total		11,925,000
Balance		$ 3,575,000

The percent to be paid to general creditors is:

$$\frac{\text{Proceeds balance}}{\text{Total owed}} = \frac{\$3,575,000}{\$7,500,000} = 47.66667\%$$

The balance due general creditors follows:

General Creditors	Owed	Paid
Accounts payable	$1,800,000	$ 858,000
Notes payable	900,000	429,000
Subordinated debentures	4,800,000	2,288,000
Total	$7,500,000	$3,575,000

EXAMPLE 7

The balance sheet of the Oakhurst Company is presented below.

Assets

Current assets		
Cash	$ 9,000	
Marketable securities	6,000	
Receivables	1,100,000	
Inventory	3,000,000	
Prepaid expenses	4,000	
Total current assets		$4,119,000
Noncurrent assets		
Land	$1,800,000	
Fixed assets	2,000,000	
Total noncurrent assets		3,800,000
Total assets		$7,919,000

Liabilities and Stockholders' Equity

Current liabilities		
Accounts payable	$ 180,000	

Bank loan payable	900,000	
Accrued salaries	300,000[a]	
Employee benefits payable	70,000[b]	
Customer claims—unsecured	80,000[c]	
Taxes payable	350,000	
Total current liabilities		$1,880,000
Noncurrent liabilities		
First mortgage payable	$1,600,000	
Second mortgage payable	1,100,000	
Subordinated debentures	700,000	
Total noncurrent liabilities		3,400,000
Total liabilities		$5,280,000
Stockholders' equity		
Preferred stock (3,500 shares)	$ 350,000	
Common stock (8,000 shares)	480,000	
Paid-in capital	1,600,000	
Retained earnings	209,000	
Total stockholders' equity		2,639,000
Total liabilities and stockholders' equity		$7,919,000

[a]The salary owed to each worker is below the specified amount and was incurred within 90 days of the bankruptcy petition.

[b]Employee benefits payable have the same limitations as unsecured wages and satisfy for eligibility in bankruptcy distribution.

[c]No customer claim is greater than the nominal amount.

Additional data are as follows:

1. The mortgages apply to the company's total noncurrent assets.

2. The subordinated debentures are subordinated to the bank loan payable. Therefore, they come after the bank loan payable in liquidation.

3. The trustee has sold the company's current assets for $2.1 million and the noncurrent assets for $1.9 million. Therefore, a total of $4 million was received.

4. The business is bankrupt, since the total liabilities of $5.28 million are greater than the $4 million of the fair value of the assets.

Assume that the administration expense for handling the bankrupt company is $900,000. This liability is not reflected in the above balance sheet.

The allocation of the $4 million to the creditors follows.

Proceeds		$4,000,000
Available to secured creditors		
First mortgage—payable from $1,900,000		
proceeds of noncurrent assets	$1,600,000	

Second mortgage—payable from balance of proceeds of noncurrent assets	300,000	1,900,000
Balance after secured creditors		$2,100,000
Next priority		
Administrative expenses	$ 900,000	
Accrued salaries	300,000	
Employee benefits payable	70,000	
Customer claims—unsecured	80,000	
Taxes payable	350,000	1,700,000
Proceeds available to general creditors		$ 400,000

Now that the claims on the proceeds from liquidation have been met, general creditors receive the balance on a pro rata basis. The distribution of the $400,000 follows:

General Creditor	Amount	Pro Rata Allocation for Balance to Be Paid
Second-mortgage balance ($1,100,000 − $300,000)	$ 800,000	$124,031
Accounts payable	180,000	27,907
Bank loan payable	900,000	248,062[a]
Subordinated debentures	700,000	0
Total	$2,580,000	$400,000

[a]Since the debentures are subordinated, the bank loan payable must be satisfied in full before any amount can go to the subordinated debentures. The subordinated debenture holders therefore receive nothing.

EXAMPLE 8

Nolan Company is having severe financial problems. Jefferson Bank holds a first mortgage on the plant and has an $800,000 unsecured loan that is already delinquent. The Alto Insurance Company holds $4.7 million of the company's subordinated debentures to the notes payable. Nolan is deciding whether to reorganize the business or declare bankruptcy.

Another company is considering acquiring Nolan Company by offering to take over the mortgage of $7.5 million, pay the past due taxes, and pay $4.38 million for the firm.

Nolan's balance sheet follows:

Assets

Current assets	$ 2,800,000
Plant assets	11,700,000
Other assets	3,000,000
Total assets	$17,500,000

Liabilities and Stockholders' Equity

Current liabilities		
Accounts payable	$ 1,800,000	
Taxes payable	170,000	
Bank note payable	260,000	
Other current liabilities	1,400,000	
Total current liabilities		$ 3,630,000
Noncurrent liabilities		
Mortgage payable	$ 7,500,000	
Subordinated debentures	5,300,000	
Total noncurrent liabilities		12,800,000
Total liabilities		$16,430,000
Stockholders' equity		
Common stock	$ 1,000,000	
Premium on common stock	2,300,000	
Retained earnings	(2,230,000)	
Total stockholders' equity		1,070,000
Total liabilities and stockholders' equity		$17,500,000

The impact of the proposed reorganization on creditor claims is indicated below.

Outstanding obligations		$16,430,000
Claims met through the reorganization		
Mortgage payable	$7,500,000	
Taxes payable	170,000	
Total		7,670,000
Balance of claims		$ 8,760,000

The cash arising from reorganization is given as $4.38 million, which is 50% ($4,380,000/$8,760,000) of the unsatisfied claims.

The distribution to general creditors follows:

General Creditor	Liability Due	50%	Adjusted for Subordination
Bank note payable	$ 260,000	$ 130,000	$ 260,000"
Subordinated debenture	5,300,000	2,650,000	2,520,000
Other creditors (accounts payable + other current liabilities)	3,200,000	1,600,000	1,600,000
Total	$8,760,000	$4,380,000	$4,380,000

"The bank note payable is paid in full before the subordinated debenture.

47
Business Strategies and Shareholder Value Analysis

Critics of large corporations allege that corporate financial managers have too much power and that they act in ways that benefit themselves at the expense of shareholders. Many managers view corporate growth, survival or personal ambition as taking precedence over shareholder interests. These misguided policies may be one of the reasons for the recent surge in takeover activity. Corporate raiders like T. Boone Pickens and Carl Icahn are constantly searching for poorly managed companies, where aggressive changes in strategic direction and/or the redeployment of underutilized assets can dramatically improve the value of a stock.

There is, however, a growing number of business leaders who are realizing that the interests of the shareholder are of primary concern to the corporation, and are beginning to employ strategies designed to create shareholder value. They believe that value is not created by the manipulation of accounting statements, but by managing the real economic value of the firm. These financial executives feel that a stock's value is tied to the perceived present value of the firm's future cash flows and that value is added when they are able to invest at rates that exceed the firm's cost of capital.

To achieve rates of return above the cost of capital, management must select and implement strategies that will position the firm in such a manner as to give it the greatest sustainable competitive advantage. The value of a strategy can be determined by discounting the anticipated cash flows generated by the strategy by the firm's cost of capital. The technique known as Shareholder Value Analysis (SVA) is an offshoot of the Discounted Cash Flow (DCF) method used in capital budgeting. With a few modifications DCF can be adopted to evaluate strategies as well. SVA enables a firm to measure how alternative strategies will affect the firm's value. SVA also enables a firm to identify the specific operating factors that drive the value of a business. This chapter will explore SVA by first examining the shortcomings of traditional accounting measures, then introduce SVA through the use of a simplified example, then go on to address some of the limitations of SVA and finally discuss its benefits to management.

SHORTCOMINGS OF ACCOUNTING MEASURES

Eventually most strategic and long-term plans are translated into pro forma financial statements. Many financial managers use these statements to measure the financial implications of their strategies. Unfortunately, accrual-based accounting measures do not provide an accurate picture of the current or future economic performance of an organization. For example, earnings per share can grow as a company invests above its cost of capital. This happens because accrual-based accounting uses alternative methods to attempt to match costs with revenues. Arbitrary methods such as FIFO versus LIFO and straight line versus accelerated depreciation do not affect pretax cash flows, vary between companies and change over time. These methods are arbitrary because there is no sound basis for choosing one method over another. Conventional earnings determination by the matching process does not nor do accountants purport it to, measure changes in the value of a firm.

In addition to differing methods, accrual-based accounting does not assess changes in risk, dividend policies, time value of money and additional investment in working capital and fixed capital investment necessary to ensure growth. Further discussion of these factors follows.

Risk is of primary concern when establishing the economic value of any asset. The level of risk is determined by the nature of a firm's operations (business risk) and by the capital structure of the firm (financial risk). The higher the risk the greater the return an investor will expect.

Dividends are not included in earnings calculations. If a firm's objective was to increase earnings, then it could be argued that dividends should not be paid. However, the return to shareholders is a function of stock appreciation and dividends paid, therefore dividends are a very important factor in calculating economic value.

Earnings measures also fail to take into consideration the time value of money. The economic value of an investment is determined by discounting anticipated cash flows. The discount rate used to determine the economic value of an investment not only determines the time value of money but inflation expectations as well.

Finally, accounting earnings fail to consider the additional investment in working capital and fixed capital investment needed for growth. As a business grows, its working capital increases because inventory swells to meet anticipated demand and receivables increase as sales outpace cash collections. Fixed investment also rises as firms increase capacity and invest in the latest technologies.

SHAREHOLDER VALUE APPROACH

The shareholder value approach estimates the economic value of an investment by discounting forecasted cash flows by the cost of capital. These cash flows, in turn, serve as the foundation for shareholder returns from dividends and share-price appreciation. Basic valuation parameters or value drivers are used in the shareholder value calculation. These drivers are: forecast duration, sales growth rate, operating profit margin, cash income tax rate, incremental working capital investment, incremental fixed capital investment, and cost of capital.

Estimating Shareholder Value

The total value of a company is the sum of the values of its debt and its equity. The debt portion is called "corporate value" and the equity portion is called "shareholder value." The debt portion of corporate value includes the market value of debt, unfunded pension liabilities and other claims such as preferred stock. Therefore:

$$\text{Shareholder Value} = \text{Corporate Value} - \text{Debt}$$

Before shareholder value can be determined, corporate value must be calculated. Corporate value consists of the present value of forecasted cash flows from operations plus residual value plus marketable securities and investments. Residual value represents the present value of cash flows beyond the forecast period.

Corporate Value = Present value of forecasted cash flows from operations
+ Present value of the residual value
+ Marketable securities

To show how Shareholder Value Analysis can be applied, a simple example will be used to explain the components of the calculation.

The management of Amercom, Inc., a manufacturing firm, have finished their long-term plan for the next five years. This plan was translated into the financial statements presented in Exhibit 1. Management feels that their strategy will increase earnings per share nearly 14% a year. The plan's impact on shareholder value will be assessed.

Cash Flows from Operations

The present value of forecasted cash flows from operations consist of cash operating inflows and outflows discounted back at the company's cost of capital. Each year the cash flow is calculated as follows:

Exhibit 1

AMERCOM, INC.
LONG TERM BUSINESS PLAN

$ Thousands

	1989	1990	1991	1992	1993	1994
				Forecast		
Income Statement						
Sales	100,000	110,000	121,000	133,100	146,410	161,051
Cost of Sales	75,000	82,500	90,750	99,825	109,807	120,788
Gross Profit	25,000	27,500	30,250	33,275	36,602	40,263
SG&A Expenses	18,000	19,800	21,780	23,958	26,354	28,989
Other Income/(Expense)	2,000	2,200	2,420	2,662	2,928	3,221
Interest Expense	2,302	2,280	2,457	2,657	2,874	3,111
Income before Taxes	6,698	7,620	8,433	9,322	10,303	11,384
Income Taxes	2,679	3,048	3,373	3,729	4,121	4,553
Net Income	4,019	4,572	5,060	5,593	6,182	6,830
Balance Sheet—Assets						
Marketable Securities	7,000	7,000	7,000	7,000	7,000	7,000
Accounts Receivable	20,000	22,000	24,200	26,620	29,282	32,210
Inventories	15,000	16,500	18,150	19,965	21,961	24,158
Total Current Assets	42,000	45,500	49,350	53,585	58,243	63,368
Property, Plant & Equip.	52,000	57,200	62,920	69,212	76,133	83,746

Accumulated Depreciation	27,000	29,700	32,670	35,937	39,531	43,484
Net PP&E	25,000	27,500	30,250	33,275	36,602	40,263
Total Assets	67,000	73,000	79,600	86,860	94,846	103,631
Balance Sheets—Liabilities & Equity						
Accounts Payable	5,000	5,500	6,050	6,655	7,320	8,053
Short Term Debt	0	2,476	5,139	7,951	10,925	14,075
Accrued Liabilities	7,000	7,700	8,470	9,317	10,249	11,274
Total Current Liabilities	12,000	15,676	19,659	23,923	28,494	33,401
Deferred Income Taxes	7,943	8,705	9,548	10,480	11,510	12,649
Long Term Debt	19,000	18,000	17,000	16,000	15,000	14,000
Total Liabilities	38,943	42,380	46,207	50,403	55,004	60,049
Capital Stock	9,000	9,000	9,000	9,000	9,000	9,000
Retained Earnings	19,057	21,619	24,393	27,457	30,842	34,581
Total Equity	28,057	30,619	33,393	36,457	39,842	43,581
Total Liabilities & Equity	67,000	73,000	79,600	86,860	94,846	103,631
Sales growth rate		10.0%	10.0%	10.0%	10.0%	10.0%
Operating profit margin		9.0%	9.0%	9.0%	9.0%	9.0%
Cash income tax rate		30.0%	30.0%	30.0%	30.0%	30.0%
Incremental fixed capital investment		25.0%	25.0%	25.0%	25.0%	25.0%
Incremental working capital investment		23.0%	23.0%	23.0%	23.0%	23.0%
Debt to Equity	67.7%	66.9%	66.3%	65.7%	65.1%	64.4%
Current Ratio	3.5	2.9	2.5	2.2	2.0	1.9

Cash flow = [(Sales in prior year)(1 + Sales growth rate)
              (Operating profit margin)(1 − Cash income tax rate)]
              − (Incremental fixed capital investment
              + incremental working capital investment)

The sales growth rate is simply the year to year increase in sales as a percent of the prior period's sales. In our example the sales growth rate is 10% a year.

The operating profit margin is the ratio of pre-interest, pre-tax operating income to sales. It is calculated:

Operating profit margin = (Sales − Cost of goods sold − SG&A expense
                            + Other operating income) ÷ Sales

Amercom's operating profit margin equals 9% of sales each forecasted year.

The cash income tax rate represents taxes on operating profit for a fiscal year that are either paid during the year or are a liability (income taxes payable) at the end of the year. Cash income taxes are often less than the book income tax expense. This occurs because of deferred taxes which arise from temporary differences in the recognition of some revenue and expense items for book and tax purposes. Amercom's cash income tax rate was determined by subtracting the change in deferred taxes from the provision for income taxes and then dividing the difference by the pretax income resulting in a rate of 30%.

Incremental fixed capital investment is defined as capital expenditures in excess of depreciation expense, where the depreciation is assumed to approximate the cost of replacing equipment to maintain existing plant without adding capacity. Note that depreciation was not added back when calculating the operating profit margin. Depreciation, a noncash expense is eliminated from the analysis by taking the capital expenditures over total depreciation. Therefore, the incremental fixed capital investment represents the portion of total expenditures for the capacity expansion necessary to support increased sales.

Incremental fixed capital investment ratio = (Capital expenditures
                                              − Depreciation expense)
                                              ÷ Change in sales

Incremental working capital investment required for operations is defined as the increase in total current assets (excluding marketable securities) minus the increase in total current liabilities (excluding debt). It too is expressed as a percentage of sales and is calculated as follows:

Incremental working capital = (Increase in current assets − Increase in
investment ratio   marketable securities − Increase in
                                current liabilities + Increase in current
                                portion of long term debt + Increase in
                                notes payable) ÷ Change in sales

Amercom's incremental fixed capital and working capital investment ratios are 25% and 23% respectively.

Cost of Capital

In order to calculate the present value of the forecasted cash flows from operations, one needs the firm's cost of capital. The cost of capital is equal to the weighted-average of the costs of debt and equity. The cost of debt is measured as the long-term rate or yield to maturity which reflects the rate currently demanded by debtholders. It is important that the cost of new debt rather than existing debt be incorporated because the economic desirability of a perspective investment depends upon future costs and not past or sunk costs.

The cost of equity is the minimum expected return that will induce investors to buy a company's shares. The assumption is made that investors will demand the risk-free rate as reflected in the current yields available on U.S. Treasury securities, plus an additional equity risk premium for investing in the company's more risky shares. The equity risk premium, in turn, is a function of the expected variability of the future yields of the stock.

In pricing common stocks the equity risk premium would depend on the market risk premium, adjusted by the stock's beta coefficient. The market risk premium can be estimated by taking the expected rate of return on a market index such as the S&P 500 and then subtracting the risk-free rate. A number of investment banking firms publish their estimates of the expected rate of return on the stock market using discounted cash flow models.

The beta coefficient reflects the volatility of a stock's price, relative to that of the market as a whole. If its beta is greater than one, a stock is more volatile and therefore riskier than the market. A beta less than one is below average in risk, while a beta of zero would imply a risk-free security. The beta coefficient of a stock is calculated by performing a linear regression analysis between past returns for the stock and past returns on a market index such as the S&P 500. Services like Value Line regularly publish betas for publicly traded stocks.

In summary, the cost of capital is the weighted-average cost of future debt and equity. The cost of equity is calculated as follows:

Cost of equity = Risk-free rate + [Beta(Expected return on Market
                    − Risk-free rate)]

When estimating the cost of capital it is important that the relative weights attached to debt and equity are based upon the firm's long-term targeted capital structure and not that of past levels of debt and equity. Amercom's management want to maintain a debt to equity ratio of approximately 65%, therefore their cost of capital is estimated to be 20%.

Residual Value

The residual value is the amount of total corporate value that is attributable to the period after the forecast period. In most cases the residual value is the largest portion of the value of the firm. Its size is directly dependent upon the assumptions made for the forecast period. Unfortunately there are no unique formulas for calculating residual value. There are however several methods for estimating residual value that can be applied in different circumstances. For example, a liquidation value might be used if the strategy is to "harvest" the business. Most strategies assume a going concern and therefore require an appropriate estimating method. One such method is known as the perpetuity method. The expected earnings from a business are assumed to behave like a perpetual annuity, so they can be capitalized. The assumption is made that any business able to generate returns greater than the minimum return required by its owners will eventually attract competitors whose entry into the industry will drive the returns of the company down to the owners' minimum rate of return.

Once the rate of return has been driven down to the minimum acceptable, period-by-period differences in future cash flows do not alter the value of the business. Therefore these future cash flows can be treated as if they were a "perpetuity" or an infinite stream of identical cash flows.

The present value of any perpetuity is simply the value of the expected annual cash flows divided by the rate of return. Using the perpetuity method, the present value of the residual value is therefore calculated by dividing the after-tax perpetuity operating profit by the cost of capital. The perpetuity calculation is based on operating profit rather than cash flow because there is no need to take into account the additional investment in fixed and working capital during the post-forecast period. Although investments in expansion projects in the post-forecast period may help increase the future cash inflows, as long as the investment is earning only the cost of capital rate of return, any increase in cash inflows will be offset by the investment cash outflows required to expand capacity.

$$\text{Residual value} = \text{Perpetuity cash flow} \div \text{Cost of capital}$$

The perpetuity method for estimating residual value is not based on the assumption that all future cash flows will actually be identical. It simply reflects the fact that the cash flows resulting from future investments will not affect the value of the firm because the overall rate of return earned on those investments is equal to the cost of capital.

Shareholder Value Creation

From the financial statements prepared for the management of Amercom, Inc. the ratios explained above were calculated and presented in Exhibit 2.

Exhibit 3 takes the ratios and calculates the shareholder value created by the strategy. For the sake of argument, it is assumed that the market value of Amercom's debt is equal to its current balance of $19 million. Marketable securities equals $7 million. Total economic value resulting from the strategy (shareholder value) is estimated to be $15.9 million. The value lost by the five-year strategy is $3.6 million. Clearly, the strategy proposed by management, while increasing earnings per share, will decrease shareholder value.

Exhibit 2

SHAREHOLDER VALUE ASSUMPTIONS

$ Millions

Number of periods in forecast	5
Sales (last historical period)	$100
Sales growth rate	10%
Operating profit margin	9%
Cash income tax rate	30%
Incremental fixed capital investment	25%
Incremental working capital investment	23%
Cost of capital	20%
Marketable securities & investments	$ 7
Market value of debt & other obligations	$ 19

The year-by-year decrease in value is calculated by the annual change in the cumulative present value of the cash flows plus the present value of the residual value. For example, the decrease in year 3 of $0.714 million is equal to $29.157 million less $29.871 million. In other words, the value created or lost is the difference between shareholder value and prestrategy value.

Prestrategy value represents the value of the business today assuming no additional value created. In other words, it does not anticipate any value creation potential associated with the firm's prospective investments. Pre-strategy value is calculated by applying the appropriate residual value method to the most recent period of historical data. Returning to the example, sales for the most recent year were $100 million. With an operating profit margin of 9% and a cash income tax rate of 30%, cash flow before new investment amounts to $6.3 million. Assuming the perpetuity method for estimating residual value, the pre-strategy shareholder value is calculated as follows:

$$
\begin{aligned}
\text{Prestrategy value} &= \text{(After tax operating profit cash flow} \div \text{Cost of} \\
&\quad \text{capital)} + \text{Marketable securities} - \text{Debt} \\
&= (6.3 \div 20\%) + 7 - 19 \\
&= 31.5 + 7 - 19 \\
&= 19.5
\end{aligned}
$$

The value lost by the strategy of $3.598 million is the difference between the $15.9 million shareholder value and the $19.5 million prestrategy value.

Impact of Value Drivers

The management of Amercom, Inc. can also measure the impact on share-holder value from changes in the value drivers (sales growth rate, operating profit margin, cost of capital, and so on). Exhibit 4 shows the impact on

Exhibit 3

SHAREHOLDER VALUE CALCULATION

Cost of Capital = 20.0%
$ Millions

Year	Sales	Operating Profit Cash Flow	Incremental Fixed Capital Investment	Incremental Working Capital Investment	Total Cash Flow	Present Value of Cash Flow	Cumulative PV of Cash Flow	Future Value of Residual Value	Present Value of Residual Value	Cumulative PV CF + PV RV	Increase Value
0	100	6.300						31.500	31.500	31.500	
1	110	6.930	2.500	2.300	2.130	1.775	1.775	34.650	28.875	30.650	−0.850
2	121	7.623	2.750	2.530	2.343	1.627	3.402	38.115	26.469	29.871	−0.779
3	133	8.385	3.025	2.783	2.577	1.491	4.894	41.926	24.263	29.157	−0.714
4	146	9.224	3.328	3.061	2.835	1.367	6.261	46.119	22.241	28.502	−0.655
5	161	10.146	3.660	3.367	3.119	1.253	7.514	50.731	20.388	27.902	−0.600
											−3.598

Present Value of Cash Flows	7.514
Present Value of Residual Value	20.388
Marketable Securities & Investments	7.000
CORPORATE VALUE	34.902
Less: Market Value of Debt & Other	19.000
SHAREHOLDER VALUE	15.902

Exhibit 4

RELATIVE IMPACT OF VALUE DRIVERS

$ Millions

A One Percentage Point Increase In:	$	%
Sales growth rate	-0.4	-2.7%
Operating profit margin	5.0	31.3%
Cash income tax rate	-0.6	-4.0%
Incremental fixed capital investment	-0.4	-2.2%
Incremental working capital investment	-0.4	-2.2%
Cost of capital	-1.9	-12.2%

shareholder value of a one percentage point increase in each of the value drivers. If you compare the sales growth rate and operating profit margin, you can see that a 1 percentage point increase in sales growth (10% to 11%) will decrease Amercom's value by about $400,000, where as a percentage point improvement in the operating profit margin will increase value $5.0 million. In other words, for this business, value is affected by improvements in margins not sales growth. Therefore managements' preoccupation with sales growth will reduce the firm's overall value.

Limitations

Shareholder Value Analysis has a long list of limitations. At the top of the list is complexity and difficulty of use. SVA often frustrates business managers because accounting systems fail to provide the balance sheet and cost information the analysis requires. Another limitation is that managers seldom agree on the value drivers that influence the results, like the cost of capital and the duration of the forecast period. Still another limitation lies in the measure of residual value. This projection is the furthest in the future and therefore the least certain.

Many critics of SVA complain that using the method can lead to a preoccupation with calculating values and relative impacts at the expense of creative strategic thinking. Finally, how well SVA will estimate the value of a strategy designed to open markets whose possibilities are not known yet is questionable.

CONCLUSION

Proponents of SVA claim it is superior to any other method of analyzing the economic implications of strategies. Companies like Westinghouse, Dexter, Signode, and Trinova have the greatest success with it, financial theorists endorse it, and a consulting industry has been built on it.

Shareholder value analysis has several important benefits for financial management. First, it provides a consistent basis for systematically evaluating and measuring internal and external capital allocation decisions and management performance. Second, it overcomes shortcomings of accounting measures that never were designed to evaluate future investment opportunities. Third, it reduces the corporate gamesmanship in submitting divisional plans and budgets. Fourth, it can provide a standard for investor communications that reflects how the market actually behaves. By using SVA for evaluating strategic plans and measuring business performance, management can anticipate the probable market reaction to its strategies and understand which components of its business drive value and why.

For more on share value analysis, see:

(1) Blyth, Michael L., Elizabeth A. Friskey and Alfred Rappaport. "Implementing The Shareholder Value Approach." *The Journal of Business Strategy*, 1989, 48–58.

(2) Day, George S. and Liam Fahey. "Putting Strategy into Shareholder Value Analysis." *Harvard Business Review* (March–April 1990): 156–162.

(3) Gale, Bradley T. and Donald J. Swire. "Business Strategies That Create Wealth." *Planning Review* (March–April 1988): 6–47.

(4) Moskowitz, Jerald I. "What's Your Business Worth?" *Management Accounting* (March 1988): 30–34.

(5) Reimann, Bernard C. "Managing For The Shareholders: An Overview of Value-Based Planning." *Planning Review* (January–February 1988): 10–22.

(6) Seed III, Allen H. "Winning Strategies For Shareholder Value Creation." *The Journal of Business Strategy*, 1989, 44–51.

(7) Wenner, David L. and Richard W. LeBer. "Managing for Shareholder Value - From Top To Bottom." *Harvard Business Review* (November–December 1989): 52–65.

APPENDIX

TABLE 1
Future Value of $1

Number of Years	Interest Rate																			
	1%	2%	3%	4%	5%	6%	7%	8%	9%	10%	12%	14%	15%	16%	18%	20%	24%	28%	32%	36%
1	1.0100	1.0200	1.0300	1.0400	1.0500	1.0600	1.0700	1.0800	1.0900	1.1000	1.1200	1.1400	1.1500	1.1600	1.1800	1.2000	1.2400	1.2800	1.3200	1.3600
2	1.0201	1.0404	1.0609	1.0816	1.1025	1.1236	1.1449	1.1664	1.1881	1.2100	1.2544	1.2996	1.3225	1.3456	1.3924	1.4400	1.5376	1.6384	1.7424	1.8496
3	1.0303	1.0612	1.0927	1.1249	1.1576	1.1910	1.2250	1.2597	1.2950	1.3310	1.4049	1.4815	1.5209	1.5609	1.6430	1.7280	1.9066	2.0972	2.3000	2.5155
4	1.0406	1.0824	1.1255	1.1699	1.2155	1.2625	1.3108	1.3605	1.4116	1.4641	1.5735	1.6890	1.7490	1.8106	1.9388	2.0736	2.3642	2.6844	3.0360	3.4210
5	1.0510	1.1041	1.1593	1.2167	1.2763	1.3382	1.4026	1.4693	1.5386	1.6105	1.7623	1.9254	2.0144	2.1003	2.2878	2.4883	2.9316	3.4360	4.0075	4.6526
6	1.0615	1.1262	1.1941	1.2653	1.3401	1.4185	1.5007	1.5869	1.6771	1.7716	1.9738	2.1950	2.3131	2.4364	2.6996	2.9860	3.6352	4.3980	5.2899	6.3275
7	1.0721	1.1487	1.2299	1.3159	1.4071	1.5036	1.6058	1.7138	1.8280	1.9487	2.2107	2.5023	2.6600	2.8262	3.1855	3.5832	4.5077	5.6295	6.9826	8.6054
8	1.0829	1.1717	1.2668	1.3686	1.4775	1.5938	1.7182	1.8509	1.9926	2.1436	2.4760	2.8526	3.0590	3.2784	3.7589	4.2998	5.5895	7.2058	9.2170	11.703
9	1.0937	1.1951	1.3048	1.4233	1.5513	1.6895	1.8385	1.9990	2.1719	2.3579	2.7731	3.2519	3.5179	3.8030	4.4355	5.1598	6.9310	9.2234	12.166	15.916
10	1.1046	1.2190	1.3439	1.4802	1.6289	1.7908	1.9672	2.1589	2.3674	2.5937	3.1058	3.7072	4.0456	4.4114	5.2338	6.1917	8.5944	11.805	16.059	21.646
11	1.1157	1.2434	1.3842	1.5395	1.7103	1.8983	2.1049	2.3316	2.5804	2.8531	3.4785	4.2262	4.6524	5.1173	6.1759	7.4301	10.657	15.111	21.198	29.439
12	1.1268	1.2682	1.4258	1.6010	1.7959	2.0122	2.2522	2.5182	2.8127	3.1384	3.8960	4.8179	5.3502	5.9360	7.2876	8.9161	13.214	19.342	27.982	40.037
13	1.1381	1.2936	1.4685	1.6651	1.8856	2.1329	2.4098	2.7196	3.0658	3.4523	4.3635	5.4924	6.1528	6.8858	8.5994	10.699	16.386	24.748	36.937	54.451
14	1.1495	1.3195	1.5126	1.7317	1.9799	2.2609	2.5785	2.9372	3.3417	3.7975	4.8871	6.2613	7.0757	7.9875	10.147	12.839	20.319	31.691	48.756	74.053
15	1.1610	1.3459	1.5580	1.8009	2.0789	2.3966	2.7590	3.1722	3.6425	4.1772	5.4736	7.1379	8.1371	9.2655	11.973	15.407	25.195	40.564	53.358	100.71
16	1.1726	1.3728	1.6047	1.8730	2.1829	2.5404	2.9522	3.4259	3.9703	4.5950	6.1304	8.1372	9.3576	10.748	14.129	18.488	31.242	51.923	84.953	136.96
17	1.1834	1.4002	1.6528	1.9479	2.2920	2.6928	3.1588	3.7000	4.3276	5.0545	6.8660	9.2765	10.761	12.467	16.672	22.186	38.740	66.461	112.13	186.27
18	1.1961	1.4282	1.7024	2.0258	2.4066	2.8543	3.3799	3.9960	4.7171	5.5599	7.6900	10.575	12.375	14.462	19.673	26.623	48.038	85.070	148.02	253.33
19	1.2081	1.4568	1.7535	2.1068	2.5270	3.0256	3.6165	4.3157	5.1417	6.1159	8.6129	12.055	14.231	16.776	23.214	31.948	59.567	108.89	195.39	344.53
20	1.2202	1.4859	1.8061	2.1911	2.6533	3.2071	3.8697	4.6610	5.6044	6.7275	9.6463	13.743	16.366	19.460	27.393	38.337	73.864	139.37	257.91	468.57
21	1.2324	1.5157	1.8603	2.2788	2.7860	3.3996	4.1406	5.0338	6.1088	7.4002	10.803	15.667	18.821	22.574	32.323	46.005	91.591	178.40	340.44	637.26
22	1.2447	1.5460	1.9161	2.3699	2.9253	3.6035	4.4304	5.4365	6.6586	8.1403	12.100	17.861	21.644	26.186	38.142	55.206	113.57	228.35	449.39	866.67
23	1.2572	1.5769	1.9736	2.4647	3.0715	3.1897	4.7405	5.8715	7.2579	8.9543	13.552	20.361	24.891	30.376	45.007	66.247	140.83	292.30	593.19	1178.6
24	1.2697	1.6084	2.0328	2.5633	3.2251	4.0489	5.0724	6.3412	7.9111	9.8497	15.178	23.212	28.625	35.236	53.108	79.496	174.63	374.14	783.02	1602.9
25	1.2824	1.6406	2.0938	2.6658	3.3864	4.2919	5.2474	6.8485	8.6231	10.834	17.000	26.461	32.918	40.874	62.668	95.396	216.54	478.90	1033.5	2180.0
26	1.2953	1.6734	2.1566	2.7725	3.5557	4.5497	5.8074	7.3964	9.3992	11.918	19.040	30.166	37.856	47.414	73.948	114.47	268.51	612.99	1364.3	2964.9
27	1.3082	1.7069	2.2213	2.8834	3.7335	4.8223	6.2139	7.9881	10.245	13.110	21.324	34.389	43.535	55.000	87.259	137.37	332.95	784.63	1800.9	4032.2
28	1.3213	1.7410	2.2879	2.9987	3.9201	5.1117	6.6488	8.6271	11.167	14.421	23.883	39.204	50.065	63.800	102.96	164.84	412.86	1004.3	2377.2	5483.8
29	1.3345	1.7758	2.3566	3.1187	4.1161	5.4184	7.1143	9.3173	12.172	15.863	26.749	44.693	57.575	74.008	121.50	197.81	511.95	128.5	3137.9	7458.0
30	1.3478	1.8114	2.4273	3.2434	4.3219	5.7435	7.6123	10.062	13.267	17.449	29.959	50.950	66.211	85.849	143.37	237.37	634.81	1645.5	4142.0	10143.
40	1.4889	2.2080	3.2620	4.8010	7.0400	10.285	14.974	21.724	31.409	45.259	93.050	188.88	267.86	378.72	750.37	1469.7	5455.9	19426.	66520	*
50	1.6446	2.6916	4.3839	7.1067	11.467	18.420	29.457	46.901	74.357	117.39	289.00	700.23	1083.6	1670.7	3927.3	9100.4	46890.	*	*	*
60	1.8167	3.2810	5.8916	10.519	18.679	32.987	57.946	101.25	176.03	304.48	897.59	2595.9	4383.9	7370.1	20555	56347	*	*	*	*

1065

TABLE 2
Future Value of an Annuity of $1

Number of Years	1%	2%	3%	4%	5%	6%	7%	8%	9%	10%	12%	14%	15%	16%	18%	20%	24%	28%	32%	36%
													Interest Rate							
1	1.0000	1.0000	1.0000	1.0000	1.0000	1.0000	1.0000	1.0000	1.0000	1.0000	1.0000	1.0000	1.0000	1.0000	1.0000	1.0000	1.0000	1.0000	1.0000	1.0000
2	2.0100	2.0200	2.0300	2.0400	2.0500	2.0600	2.0700	2.0800	2.0900	2.1000	2.1200	2.1400	2.1500	2.1600	2.1800	2.2000	2.2400	2.2800	2.3200	2.3600
3	3.0301	3.0604	3.0909	3.1216	3.1525	3.1836	3.2149	3.2464	3.2781	3.3100	3.3744	3.4396	3.4725	3.5056	3.5724	3.6400	3.7776	3.9184	4.0624	4.2096
4	4.0604	4.1216	4.1836	4.2465	4.3101	4.3746	4.4399	4.5061	4.5731	4.6410	4.7793	4.9211	4.9934	5.0665	5.2154	5.3680	5.6842	6.0156	6.3624	6.7251
5	5.1010	5.2040	5.3091	5.4163	5.5256	5.6371	5.7507	5.8666	5.9847	6.1051	6.3528	6.6101	6.7424	6.8771	7.1542	7.4416	8.0484	8.6999	9.3983	10.146
6	6.1520	6.3081	6.4684	6.6330	6.8019	6.9753	7.1533	7.3359	7.5233	7.7156	8.1152	8.5355	8.7537	8.9775	9.4420	9.9299	10.980	12.135	13.405	14.798
7	7.2135	7.4343	7.6625	7.8983	8.1420	8.3938	8.6540	8.9228	9.2004	9.4872	10.089	10.730	11.066	11.413	12.141	12.915	14.615	16.533	18.695	21.126
8	8.2857	8.5830	8.8923	9.2142	9.5491	9.8975	10.259	10.636	11.028	11.435	12.299	13.232	13.726	14.240	15.327	16.499	19.122	22.163	25.678	29.731
9	9.3685	9.7546	10.159	10.582	11.026	11.491	11.978	12.487	13.021	13.579	14.775	16.085	16.785	17.518	19.085	20.798	24.712	29.369	34.895	41.435
10	10.462	10.949	11.463	12.006	12.577	13.180	13.816	14.486	15.192	15.937	17.548	19.337	20.303	21.321	23.521	25.958	31.643	38.592	47.061	57.351
11	11.566	12.168	12.807	13.486	14.206	14.971	15.783	16.645	17.560	18.531	20.654	23.044	24.349	25.732	28.755	32.150	40.237	50.398	63.121	78.998
12	12.682	13.412	14.192	15.025	15.917	16.869	17.888	18.977	20.140	21.384	24.133	27.270	29.001	30.850	34.931	39.580	50.894	65.510	84.320	108.43
13	13.809	14.680	15.617	16.626	17.713	18.882	20.140	21.495	22.953	24.522	28.029	32.088	34.351	36.786	42.218	48.496	64.109	84.852	112.30	148.47
14	14.947	15.973	17.086	18.291	19.598	21.015	22.550	24.214	26.019	27.975	32.392	37.581	40.504	43.672	50.818	59.195	80.496	109.61	149.23	202.92
15	16.096	17.293	18.598	20.023	21.578	23.276	25.129	27.152	29.360	31.772	37.279	43.842	47.580	51.659	60.965	72.035	100.81	141.30	197.99	276.97
16	17.257	18.639	20.156	21.824	23.657	25.672	27.888	30.324	33.003	35.949	42.753	50.980	55.717	60.925	72.939	87.442	126.01	181.86	262.35	377.69
17	18.430	20.012	21.761	23.697	25.840	28.212	30.840	33.750	36.973	40.544	48.883	59.117	65.075	71.673	87.068	105.93	157.25	233.79	347.30	514.66
18	19.614	21.412	23.414	25.645	28.132	30.905	33.99	37.450	41.301	45.599	55.749	68.394	75.836	84.140	103.74	128.11	195.99	300.25	459.44	700.93
19	20.810	22.840	25.116	27.671	30.539	33.760	37.379	41.446	46.018	51.159	63.439	78.969	88.211	98.603	123.41	154.74	244.03	385.32	607.47	954.27
20	22.019	24.297	26.870	29.778	33.066	36.785	40.995	45.762	51.160	57.275	72.052	91.024	102.44	115.37	146.62	186.68	303.60	494.21	802.86	1298.8
21	23.239	25.783	28.676	31.969	35.719	39.992	44.865	50.442	56.764	64.002	81.698	104.76	118.81	134.84	174.02	225.02	377.46	633.59	1060.7	1767.3
22	24.471	27.299	30.536	34.248	38.505	43.392	49.005	55.456	62.873	71.402	92.502	120.43	137.63	157.41	206.34	271.03	469.05	811.99	1401.2	2404.6
23	25.716	28.845	32.452	36.617	41.430	46.995	53.436	60.893	69.531	79.543	104.60	138.29	159.27	183.60	244.48	326.23	582.62	1040.3	1850.6	3271.3
24	26.973	30.421	34.426	39.082	44.502	50.815	58.176	66.764	76.789	88.497	118.15	158.65	184.16	213.97	289.49	392.48	723.46	1332.6	2443.8	4449.9
25	28.243	32.030	36.459	41.645	47.727	54.864	63.249	73.105	84.700	98.347	133.33	181.87	212.79	249.21	342.60	471.98	898.09	1706.8	3226.8	6052.9
26	29.525	33.670	38.553	44.311	51.113	59.156	68.676	79.954	93.323	109.18	150.33	208.33	245.71	290.08	405.27	567.37	1114.6	2185.7	4260.4	8233.0
27	30.820	35.344	40.709	47.084	54.669	63.705	74.483	87.350	102.72	121.09	169.37	238.49	283.56	337.50	479.22	681.85	1383.1	2798.7	5624.7	11197.9
28	32.129	37.051	42.930	49.967	58.402	68.528	80.697	95.338	112.96	134.20	190.69	272.88	327.10	392.50	566.48	819.22	1716.0	3583.3	7425.6	15230.2
29	32.450	38.792	45.218	52.966	62.322	73.689	87.346	103.96	124.13	148.63	214.58	312.09	377.16	456.30	669.44	984.06	2128.9	4587.6	9802.9	20714.1
30	34.784	40.568	47.576	56.084	66.438	79.058	94.460	113.28	136.30	164.49	241.33	356.78	434.74	530.31	790.94	1181.8	2640.9	5873.2	12940	28172.2
40	48.886	60.402	75.401	95.025	120.79	154.76	199.63	259.05	337.88	442.59	767.09	1342.0	1779.0	2360.7	4163.2	7343.8	22728	63977	.	.
50	64.473	84.579	112.79	152.66	209.34	290.33	406.52	573.76	815.08	1163.9	2400.0	4994.5	7217.7	10435	21813	45497	.	.	.	.
60	81.669	114.05	163.05	237.90	353.58	533.12	813.52	1253.2	1944.7	3034.8	7471.6	18535	29219	46057	.	.	.	.	.	.

TABLE 3
Present Value of $1

Number of Years	Interest Rate																			
	1%	2%	3%	4%	5%	6%	7%	8%	9%	10%	12%	14%	15%	16%	18%	20%	24%	28%	32%	36%
1	0.9901	0.9804	0.9709	0.9615	0.9524	0.9434	0.9346	0.9259	0.9174	0.9091	0.8929	0.8772	0.8696	0.8621	0.8475	0.8333	0.8065	0.7813	0.7576	0.7353
2	0.9803	0.9612	0.9426	0.9246	0.9070	0.8900	0.8734	0.8573	0.8417	0.8264	0.7972	0.7695	0.7561	0.7432	0.7182	0.6944	0.6504	0.6104	0.5739	0.5407
3	0.9706	0.9423	0.9151	0.8890	0.8638	0.8396	0.8163	0.7938	0.7722	0.7513	0.7118	0.6750	0.6575	0.6407	0.6086	0.5787	0.5245	0.4768	0.4348	0.3975
4	0.9610	0.9238	0.8885	0.8548	0.8227	0.7921	0.7629	0.7350	0.7084	0.6830	0.6355	0.5921	0.5718	0.5523	0.5158	0.4823	0.4230	0.3725	0.3294	0.2923
5	0.9515	0.9057	0.8626	0.8219	0.7835	0.7473	0.7130	0.6806	0.6499	0.6209	0.5674	0.5194	0.4972	0.4761	0.4371	0.4019	0.3411	0.2910	0.2495	0.2149
6	0.9420	0.8880	0.8375	0.7903	0.7462	0.7050	0.6663	0.6302	0.5963	0.5645	0.5066	0.4556	0.4323	0.4104	0.3704	0.3349	0.2751	0.2274	0.1890	0.1580
7	0.9327	0.8706	0.8131	0.7599	0.7107	0.6651	0.6227	0.5835	0.5470	0.5132	0.4523	0.3996	0.3759	0.3538	0.3139	0.2791	0.2218	0.1776	0.1432	0.1162
8	0.9235	0.8535	0.7894	0.7307	0.6768	0.6274	0.5820	0.5403	0.5019	0.4665	0.4039	0.3506	0.3269	0.3050	0.2660	0.2326	0.1789	0.1388	0.1085	0.0854
9	0.9143	0.8368	0.7664	0.7026	0.6446	0.5919	0.5439	0.5002	0.4604	0.4241	0.3606	0.3075	0.2843	0.2630	0.2255	0.1938	0.1443	0.1084	0.0822	0.0628
10	0.9053	0.8203	0.7441	0.6756	0.6139	0.5584	0.5083	0.4632	0.4224	0.3855	0.3220	0.2697	0.2472	0.2267	0.1911	0.1615	0.1164	0.0847	0.0623	0.0462
11	0.8963	0.8043	0.7224	0.6496	0.5847	0.5268	0.4751	0.4289	0.3875	0.3505	0.2875	0.2366	0.2149	0.1954	0.1619	0.1346	0.0938	0.0662	0.0472	0.0340
12	0.8874	0.7885	0.7014	0.6246	0.5568	0.4970	0.4440	0.3971	0.3555	0.3186	0.2567	0.2076	0.1869	0.1685	0.1372	0.1122	0.0757	0.0517	0.0357	0.0250
13	0.8787	0.7730	0.6810	0.6006	0.5303	0.4688	0.4150	0.3677	0.3262	0.2897	0.2292	0.1821	0.1625	0.1452	0.1163	0.0935	0.0610	0.0404	0.0271	0.0184
14	0.8700	0.7579	0.6611	0.5775	0.5051	0.4423	0.3878	0.3405	0.2992	0.2633	0.2046	0.1597	0.1413	0.1252	0.0985	0.0779	0.0492	0.0316	0.0205	0.0135
15	0.8613	0.7430	0.6419	0.5553	0.4810	0.4173	0.3624	0.3152	0.2745	0.2394	0.1827	0.1401	0.1229	0.1079	0.0835	0.0649	0.0397	0.0247	0.0155	0.0099
16	0.8528	0.7284	0.6232	0.5339	0.4581	0.3936	0.3387	0.2919	0.2519	0.2176	0.1631	0.1229	0.1069	0.0930	0.0708	0.0541	0.0320	0.0193	0.0118	0.0073
17	0.8444	0.7142	0.6050	0.5134	0.4363	0.3714	0.3166	0.2703	0.2311	0.1978	0.1456	0.1078	0.0929	0.0802	0.0600	0.0451	0.0258	0.0150	0.0089	0.0054
18	0.8360	0.7002	0.5874	0.4936	0.4155	0.3503	0.2959	0.2502	0.2120	0.1799	0.1300	0.0946	0.0808	0.0691	0.0508	0.0376	0.0208	0.0118	0.0068	0.0038
19	0.8277	0.6864	0.5703	0.4746	0.3957	0.3305	0.2765	0.2317	0.1945	0.1635	0.1161	0.0829	0.0703	0.0596	0.0431	0.0313	0.0168	0.0092	0.0051	0.0029
20	0.8195	0.6730	0.5537	0.4564	0.3769	0.3118	0.2584	0.2145	0.1784	0.1486	0.1037	0.0728	0.0611	0.0514	0.0365	0.0261	0.0135	0.0072	0.0039	0.0021
25	0.7798	0.6095	0.4776	0.3751	0.2953	0.2330	0.1842	0.1460	0.1160	0.0923	0.0588	0.0378	0.0304	0.0245	0.0160	0.0105	0.0046	0.0021	0.0010	0.0005
30	0.7419	0.5521	0.4120	0.3083	0.2314	0.1741	0.1314	0.0994	0.0754	0.0573	0.0334	0.0196	0.0151	0.0116	0.0070	0.0042	0.0016	0.0006	0.0002	0.0001
40	0.6717	0.4529	0.3066	0.2083	0.1420	0.0972	0.0668	0.0460	0.0318	0.0221	0.0107	0.0053	0.0037	0.0026	0.0013	0.0007	0.0002	0.0001	·	·
50	0.6080	0.3715	0.2281	0.1407	0.0872	0.0543	0.0339	0.0213	0.0132	0.0085	0.0035	0.0014	0.0009	0.0006	0.0003	0.0001	·	·	·	·
60	0.5504	0.3048	0.1697	0.0951	0.0535	0.0303	0.0173	0.0099	0.0057	0.0033	0.0011	0.0004	0.0002	0.0001			·	·	·	·

TABLE 4
Present Value of an Annuity of $1

Number of Years	Interest Rate																		
	1%	2%	3%	4%	5%	6%	7%	8%	9%	10%	12%	14%	15%	16%	18%	20%	24%	28%	32%
1	0.9901	0.9804	0.9709	0.9615	0.9524	0.9434	0.9346	0.9259	0.9174	0.9091	0.8929	0.8772	0.8696	0.8621	0.8475	0.8333	0.8065	0.7813	0.7576
2	1.9704	1.9415	1.9135	1.8861	1.8594	1.8334	1.8080	1.7833	1.7591	1.7355	1.6901	1.6467	1.6257	1.6052	1.5656	1.5278	1.4568	1.3916	1.3315
3	2.9410	2.8839	2.8286	2.7751	2.7232	2.6730	2.6243	2.5771	2.5313	2.4869	2.4018	2.3216	2.2832	2.2459	2.1743	2.1065	1.9813	1.8684	1.7663
4	3.9020	3.8077	3.7171	3.6299	3.5460	3.4651	3.3872	3.3121	3.2397	3.1699	3.0373	2.9137	2.8550	2.7982	2.6901	2.5887	2.4043	2.2410	2.0957
5	4.8534	4.7135	4.5797	4.4518	4.3295	4.2124	4.1002	3.9927	3.8897	3.7908	3.6048	3.4331	3.3522	3.2743	3.1272	2.9906	2.7454	2.5320	2.3452
6	5.7955	5.6014	5.4172	5.2421	5.0757	4.9173	4.7665	4.6229	4.4859	4.3553	4.1114	3.8887	3.7845	3.6847	3.4976	3.3255	3.0205	2.7594	2.5342
7	6.7282	6.4720	6.2303	6.0021	5.7864	5.5824	5.3893	5.2064	5.0330	4.8684	4.5638	4.2883	4.1604	4.0386	3.8115	3.6046	3.2423	2.9370	2.6775
8	7.6517	7.3255	7.0197	6.7327	6.4632	6.2098	5.9713	5.7466	5.5348	5.3349	4.9676	4.6389	4.4873	4.3436	4.0776	3.8372	3.4212	3.0758	2.7860
9	8.5660	8.1622	7.7861	7.4353	7.1078	6.8017	6.5152	6.2469	5.9952	5.7590	5.3282	4.9464	4.7716	4.6065	4.3030	4.0310	3.5655	3.1842	2.8681
10	9.4713	8.9826	8.5302	8.1109	7.7217	7.3601	7.0236	6.7101	6.4177	6.1446	5.6502	5.2161	5.0188	4.8332	4.4941	4.1925	3.6819	3.2689	2.9304
11	10.3676	9.7858	9.2526	8.7605	8.3064	7.8869	7.4987	7.1390	6.8052	6.4951	5.9377	5.4527	5.2337	5.0286	4.6560	4.3271	3.7757	3.3351	2.9776
12	11.2551	10.5753	9.9540	9.3851	8.8633	8.3838	7.9427	7.5361	7.1607	6.8137	6.1944	5.6603	5.4206	5.1971	4.7932	4.4392	3.8514	3.3868	3.0133
13	12.1337	11.3484	10.6350	9.9856	9.3936	8.8527	8.3577	7.9038	7.1889	7.1034	6.4235	5.8424	5.5831	5.3423	4.9095	4.5327	3.9124	3.4272	3.0404
14	13.0037	12.1062	11.2961	10.5631	9.8986	9.2950	8.7455	8.2442	7.7862	7.3667	6.6282	6.0021	5.7245	5.4675	5.0081	4.6106	3.9616	3.4587	3.0609
15	13.8651	12.8493	11.9379	11.1184	10.3797	9.7122	9.1079	8.5595	8.0607	7.6061	6.8109	6.1422	5.8474	5.5755	5.0916	4.6755	4.0013	3.4834	3.0764
16	14.7179	13.5777	12.5611	11.6523	10.8378	10.1059	9.4466	8.8514	8.3126	7.8237	6.9740	6.2651	5.9542	5.6685	5.1724	4.7296	4.0333	3.5026	3.0882
17	15.5623	14.2919	13.1661	12.1657	11.2741	10.4773	9.7632	9.1216	8.5436	8.0216	7.1196	6.3729	6.0472	5.7487	5.2223	4.7746	4.0591	3.5177	3.0971
18	16.3983	14.9920	13.7535	12.6593	11.6896	10.8276	10.0591	9.3719	8.7556	8.2014	7.2497	6.4674	6.1280	5.8178	5.2732	4.8122	4.0799	3.5294	3.1039
19	17.2260	15.6785	14.3238	13.1339	12.0853	11.1581	10.3356	9.6036	8.9501	8.3649	7.3658	6.5504	6.1982	5.8775	5.3162	4.8435	4.0967	3.5386	3.1090
20	18.0456	16.3514	14.8775	13.5903	12.4622	11.4699	10.5940	9.8181	9.1285	8.5436	7.4694	6.6231	6.2593	5.9288	5.3527	4.8696	4.1103	3.5458	3.1129
25	22.0232	19.5235	17.4131	15.6221	14.0939	12.7834	11.6536	10.6748	9.8226	9.0770	7.8431	6.8729	6.4641	6.0971	5.4669	4.9476	4.1474	3.5640	3.1220
30	25.8077	22.3965	19.6004	17.2920	15.3725	13.7648	12.4090	11.2578	10.2737	9.4269	8.0552	7.0072	6.5660	6.1772	5.5168	4.9789	4.1601	3.5693	3.1242
40	32.8347	27.3555	23.1148	19.7928	17.1591	15.0463	13.3317	11.9246	10.7574	9.7791	8.2438	7.1050	6.6418	6.2335	5.5482	4.9966	4.1659	3.5712	3.1250
50	39.1961	31.4236	25.7298	21.4822	18.2559	15.7619	13.8007	12.2335	10.9617	9.9148	8.3045	7.1327	6.6605	6.2463	5.5541	4.9995	4.1666	3.5714	3.1250
60	44.9550	34.7609	27.8656	22.6235	18.9293	16.1614	14.0392	12.3766	11.0480	9.9672	8.3240	7.1401	6.6651	6.2492	5.5553	4.9999	4.1667	3.5714	3.1250

1068

Index

Y

Yield
of bonds, 93, 830, 834–37
of preferred stock, 844–45
and variance analysis, 409–18

Z

Zero base budgeting (ZBB), 374–78
Zero coupon bonds, 831–32, 884
Zero-one programming, 567–70